VOLUME

7

E—Eye
pages 1-392

Compton's Encyclopedia

and Fact-Index

Compton's Learning Company, a division of
Encyclopædia Britannica, Inc.
Chicago · Auckland · Geneva · London · Madrid · Manila
Paris · Rome · Seoul · Sydney · Tokyo · Toronto

1991 EDITION COMPTON'S ENCYCLOPEDIA

Library of Congress Catalog Card Number: 89-81651
International Standard Book Number: 0-85229-530-8
Printed in U.S.A.

THE UNIVERSITY OF CHICAGO
COMPTON'S ENCYCLOPEDIA IS PUBLISHED WITH THE EDITORIAL ADVICE
OF THE FACULTIES OF THE UNIVERSITY OF CHICAGO

"Let knowledge grow from more to more and thus be human life enriched"

PHOTOS: Row 1: (far left) Cameramann International; (center) American Airlines. Row 2: (right) © Leon Oboler–Kulicke & Soffa Industries, Inc./Phototake. Row 3: (left) © David Hurn–Magnum. Row 4: (right) NASA. Row 5: (far left) Peter Slater; (center) Africapix.

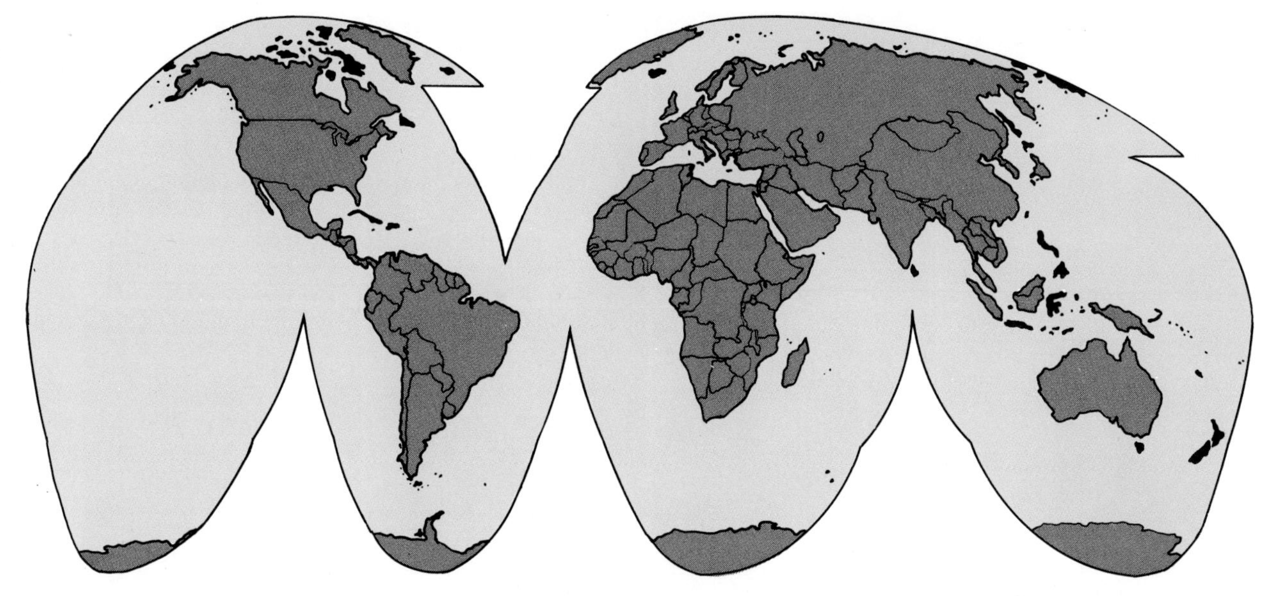

HERE AND THERE IN VOLUME 7

From the A-1 satellite to the zygote cell, thousands of subjects are gathered together in Compton's Encyclopedia and Fact-Index. Organized alphabetically, they are drawn from every field of knowledge. Readers who want to explore their favorite fields in this volume can use this subject-area outline. While it may serve as a study guide, a specialized learning experience, or simply a key for browsing, it is not a complete table of contents.

Arts

Physical Science

Living Things

Medicine

Technology and Business

Geography

History

Social and Political Science

Potpourri

EXPLORING VOLUME 7

Ernest Manewal—Shostal Associates

How could the stone statues on Easter Island have been moved from a quarry to their present sites? 42.

Canadian Government Travel Bureau

What is the meaning of the name Eskimo and why is it considered a misnomer? 299.

Which king of ancient Egypt is portrayed on the head of the Great Sphinx, which rises from the sand near the pyramid in which he is entombed? 125.

© Luis Villota

In what ways does a volcano cause sudden changes in the earth's surface features? 33. Iceland Tourist Bureau

Old English was the language used in this 8th-century gospel. How does it differ from Middle English and Modern English? 262.

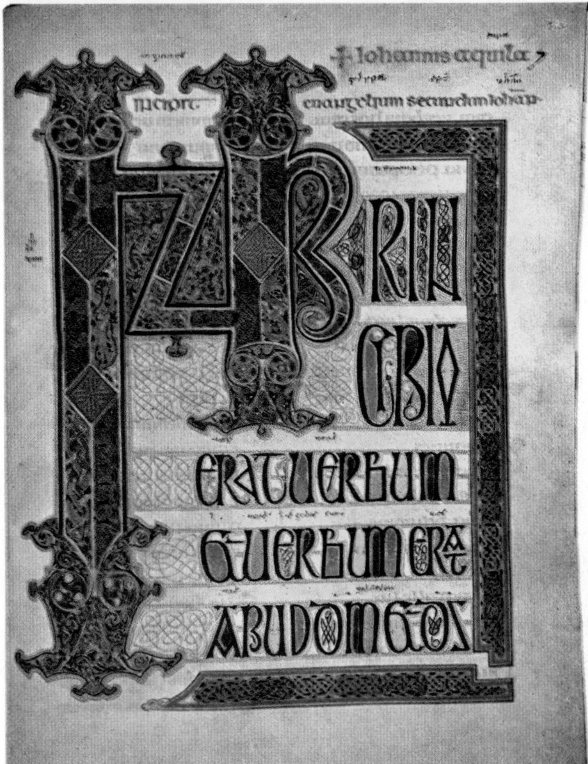

By courtesy of the trustees of the British Museum

Why were the portrait busts created by Jacob Epstein accepted while his large sculptures aroused protests? 293.

A. C. Cooper Ltd.

Robert Harding Picture Library

What is the largest medieval church in England? 232 illustration.

Why do some people's glasses have concave lenses and others have convex lenses? 390.

What kind of eye problem is being treated by using video games? 174.

How was Sir Isaac Newton able to measure the speed of sound? 48.

Why are the oceans salty? 13.

How long did the famous Pony Express remain in existence? 384.

What did Thor Heyerdahl do to prove that the Polynesians could have come from South America? 377.

Using the base-2 system, how do you write the number 40? 175.

What late-19th-century musical composition consists of variations on an unknown melody? 188.

How have scientists recently been able to measure the earth more accurately? 10.

Why did England have three different kings in 1936? 256.

What are the names of the three small republics called the "Baltic states?" 308.

What kinds of houses do Eskimos use when their igloos melt? 300.

What observations provide striking evidence in favor of the Continental Drift theory? 35.

How big is a newborn elephant? 182.

What are the earliest and latest dates Easter can occur? 41.

Why did Erasmus, himself a reformer, oppose the Reformation? 296.

Where is the world's longest working escalator located? 187.

What is primogeniture and what purpose was it intended to serve? 307.

In what ways do Eskimos differ from American Indians? 299.

What was Ikhnaton's original name? 126.

What is photoresist and how is it used? 177.

What three kinds of writing are inscribed on the Rosetta Stone? 131.

What was the name of the first archbishop of Canterbury? 238.

Who was called the Virgin Queen? 190.

What famous warship was given the nickname "cheesebox on a raft?" 297.

Who was president when the 49th and 50th states of the United States were admitted to the Union? 141.

What bird that existed in vast numbers in the 1800s became extinct in 1914? 210.

What five nations are known as the Norden countries? 333.

What tree disease changed the appearance of many towns and cities in the United States? 194.

What is Wallace's Line? 46.

Name the location of the first major nuclear power station in the world. 234.

What name did the Romans who built it give to the Colosseum? 347 illustration.

Where are the best fossils apt to be found? 366.

What Swedish inventor devised a way of making nitroglycerin less sensitive so that it could be safely used as an explosive? 380.

In what Texas city do two college football teams meet each year for the Sun Bowl game? 194.

Promising young British poets lost their lives in World War I. Name two of them. 280.

In the famous equation that expresses the special theory of relativity, $E = mc^2$, what do the E, the m, and the c stand for? 133.

In 1982 Great Britain succeeded in regaining control of islands in the South Atlantic that had been invaded by Argentina. What is the British name for those islands? 259.

T.S. Eliot wrote a play called 'Murder in the Cathedral'. Who was the person whose death is alluded to in the title? 189.

What is a "blind" rivet? 381.

How can a candidate for the United States presidency get the most votes and still lose the election? 148.

How can an African elephant be distinguished from an Asian elephant? 181 illustration.

Abraham Lincoln completed the Emancipation Proclamation in July 1862. Why did he wait until September to issue it? 197.

What two names are given to the kinds of energy that can travel across empty space? 215.

What was the world's first travel agency? 236.

What is the longitude of the prime meridian? 293.

What did Margaretha Zelle do that caused her to be executed? 303.

What invention by Elijah Otis made the use of passenger elevators practical? 186.

What were the first words Edison recorded on his newly invented phonograph? 75.

In 1788 King Louis XVI of France assembled the Estates-General for the first time in 174 years. What problem was he facing that caused him to do this? 307.

What is visual purple and what does it do? 388.

What English poet and painter founded the Kelmscott Press? 276.

How can cats help a farmer grow more red clover? 50.

Name the British prime minister who met with Hitler in Munich in 1938 and came away feeling that he had achieved "peace in our time." 257.

The letter E

may have started as a picture sign of a man with arms upraised, as in Egyptian hieroglyphic writing (1) and in a very early Semitic writing used about 1500 B.C. on the Sinai Peninsula (2). The sign meant "joy" or "rejoice" to the Egyptians. About 1000 B.C., in Byblos and in other Phoenician and Canaanite centers, the sign was given a linear form (3), the source of all later forms. The sign was called *he* in the Semitic languages and stood for the sound "h" in English.

The Greeks reversed the sign for greater ease in writing from left to right (4). They rejected the Semitic value "h" and gave it the value of the vowel "e." They called the sign *epsilon,* which means "short e."

The Romans adopted this sign for the Latin capital E. From Latin this form came unchanged into English. The handwriting of Graeco-Roman times changed the letter to a more quickly written form (5). From this is derived the English handwritten and printed small "e."

EADS, James B. (1820–87). The best-known achievement of James B. Eads was the construction of the steel triple-arch bridge in Saint Louis, Mo. The Eads Bridge was the largest bridge of any type built up to that time, and it was considered a landmark in engineering. Eads pioneered the use of structural steel, planted the foundations of the bridge at record depths, and used a cantilevering technique of his own design to raise the arches. (*See also* Bridge, "Modern Arch Bridges.")

James Buchanan Eads was born in Lawrenceburg, Ind., on May 23, 1820. He was named for a cousin of his mother, the Pennsylvania Congressman who later became the 15th president of the United States. Eads had little formal education. He taught himself through reading books. At 18 he went to work on a Mississippi riverboat. His interest in the river led him to devise a means of salvaging cargoes from riverboat disasters. From age 22 he worked at this task and made a fortune. He left the river 12 years later and started a glass factory. This enterprise eventually failed, and Eads went back into the salvage business.

When the Civil War began, he built for the North a fleet of steam-powered ironclad ships that could navigate in the shallow waters of the Mississippi River. These significantly aided the North in keeping control of the river. After the war Eads was given the contract to build the St. Louis bridge. Work began on Aug. 20, 1867. The bridge was to be in three spans, 502, 520, and 502 feet (153, 158, and 153 meters) long. Steel, subject to his rigorous standards, was bought from Andrew Carnegie's steel company. The bridge was officially opened on July 4, 1874.

Eads's other major project was to provide a year-round shipping channel in the Mississippi at New Orleans. He finished it in 1879. He also proposed building a railway across the isthmus of Tehuantepec in Mexico as an alternative to the Panama Canal. This project was rejected, however. While at Nassau in the Bahamas, Eads died on March 8, 1887.

EAGLE. Because of the eagle's majestic appearance and power of flight, it has been called the "king of birds." Since ancient times it has been a symbol of strength and courage. The Sumerians chose the "spread eagle" as their emblem of power 5,000 years ago. So did imperial Rome many centuries later.

The American bald eagle was chosen by Congress in 1782 as the emblem of the United States. On the national seal the bird is shown with its wings spread, holding an olive branch in one claw and arrows in the other. On coins, military insignia, and other devices, the eagle appears in a variety of postures.

Only two species of eagles are found in North America—the bald and the golden. The more common bald eagle has white tail feathers and white plumes on the head and neck. Early colonists, used to the gray sea eagle of Europe, called these birds "bald-headed." (Bald originally meant "white.") The female is fiercer than the male and is several inches larger. A sea eagle, the bald eagle migrates only if the body of water that it normally fishes freezes. It returns each year to the same nest, called an aerie, with the same mate. The golden eagle, a magnificent bird, is more common in the Old World than in the New, but it is found in the western part of North America from Mexico to Alaska. It is somewhat larger than the bald eagle, and its plumage is darker except for tawny feathers on its head and neck that shimmer like gold. The bald eagle has bare "ankles," whereas the legs of the golden eagle are feathered to the toes. The golden eagle builds its huge nest on a high mountain crag.

(Top) Alexander Sprunt IV; (bottom) J.R. Simon—Ostman Agency

The bald eagle (top) serves as a United States symbol and is protected in all states. The golden eagle (bottom) is the national bird of Mexico.

Eagles are birds of prey, related to vultures, hawks, and falcons (*see* Birds of Prey). The scientific name of the bald eagle is *Haliaetus leucocephalus;* the golden eagle, *Aquila chrysaetos.* The common eagle of Europe is the white-tailed sea eagle, *Haliaetus albicilla.*

EAKINS, Thomas (1844–1916). As has been true for so many great artists, the work of Thomas Eakins was not appreciated in his lifetime. No museum bought one of his paintings until 1916, the year he died. Nor was there a major exhibition of his work until a year later. Today he is considered one of the masters of American realism.

Thomas Eakins was born on July 25, 1844, in Philadelphia, the city where he would spend most of his life. He studied at the Pennsylvania Academy of Fine Arts, and, because of his special interest in painting the human figure, he attended lectures in anatomy at Jefferson Medical College. From 1866 to 1869 he studied in Paris at the École des Beaux-Arts (School of Fine Arts), where he gained a solid background in traditional art. He ignored all of the experimental, avant-garde work of the French impressionists and pursued his own interest in realism. After a brief visit to Spain, he returned to Philadelphia in 1870.

Eakins was a man of varied interests: painting, sculpture, anatomy, music, photography, and the study of locomotion. In the 1880s he experimented with multiple-image photography of moving animals and athletes. His interest in motion also led him to paint an impressive series of boxing scenes.

Nearly all of his work was portraiture—depictions of people he knew. His paintings demonstrated his technical expertise with external and anatomical details, combined with representations of inner character and situation. His first subjects were members of his family and an assortment of friends. Among his outdoor scenes were 'Max Schmitt in a Single Scull' and 'The Swimming Hole'.

Eakins was invited to provide a painting for the Philadelphia Centennial Exposition of 1876. He painted a work entitled 'The Gross Clinic', showing the physician Samuel Gross performing surgery before a class of medical students. Now generally considered Eakins' masterpiece, it was rejected for the exposition.

From the late 1870s until 1886 he taught at the Pennsylvania Academy of Fine Arts. Eventually he was forced to resign, mostly over the notoriety caused by his insistence on using live, nude models in classes of both men and women. He continued to teach from time to time at the new Art Students League and at the National Academy of Design in New York City. He died on June 25, 1916.

'The Gross Clinic', painted by Thomas Eakins for the Philadelphia Centennial Exposition of 1876, is considered his masterpiece. It measures 2 by 2.5 meters.

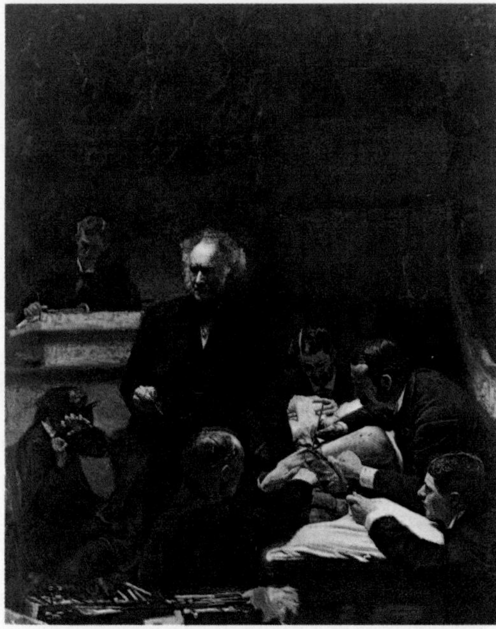

The Jefferson Medical College, Thomas Jefferson University, Philadelphia

EAR. Vibrations of air molecules moving through the air are received and translated into messages that the brain recognizes as sound by a complex organ—the ear. The ear has two important, but different, functions: hearing and sensing the body's equilibrium, or balance. The mechanisms for these processes are located within a hollow space in the skull's temporal bone (*see* Skeleton; Sound).

Parts of the Ear and Hearing

The ear has three separate sections—the outer ear, the middle ear, and the inner ear. Each section performs a specific function, related to either hearing or balance. The three parts of the outer ear are the auricle (also called the pinna), the external auditory meatus (or ear canal), and the tympanic membrane (or eardrum).

The pinna collects sound waves from the air. It funnels them into a channellike tube, the external auditory meatus. This is a curved corridor that leads to the tympanic membrane.

The eardrum separates the external ear from the middle ear. The middle ear is an irregular-shaped, air-filled space, about 0.75 inch (1.9 centimeters) high and 0.2 inch (0.5 centimeter) wide. A chainlike link of three tiny bones, the ossicles, spans the middle ear.

When sound waves strike the outer surface of the eardrum, it vibrates. These vibrations are mechanically transmitted through the middle ear by the ossicles. The malleus, or hammer, is the first ossicle to receive vibrations from the eardrum. It passes them to the second ossicle—the incus, or anvil. The third ossicle—the stapes, or stirrup—relays the vibrations to a membrane that covers the opening into the inner ear. This opening is the round window.

Like the eardrum, the round window's membrane transmits vibrations. It directs vibrations into the inner ear, where they enter a fluid that fills a structure called the cochlea. This is a coiled tube that resembles a snail's shell. If the cochlea were straightened out, it would measure slightly more than 1 inch (2.54 centimeters).

Within the cochlea is the true mechanism of hearing—the organ of Corti. It contains tiny hairlike nerve endings anchored in a basilar membrane, which extends throughout the cochlea. The unattached tips of these nerve endings are in contact with an overhanging "roof membrane," the tectorial membrane.

When vibrations pass into the inner ear, they cause waves to form in the cochlear fluid. Receptor nerve cells in the organ of Corti are highly sensitive to these waves. Other specialized nerve cells send the electrochemical impulses produced by the wave motion into the cochlear branch of the acoustic nerve. This nerve carries the impulses to the brain, where sound is identified.

Equilibrium and the Inner Ear

The inner ear also functions, independently of hearing, as the organ of equilibrium. In addition to the cochlea, the inner ear contains special structures

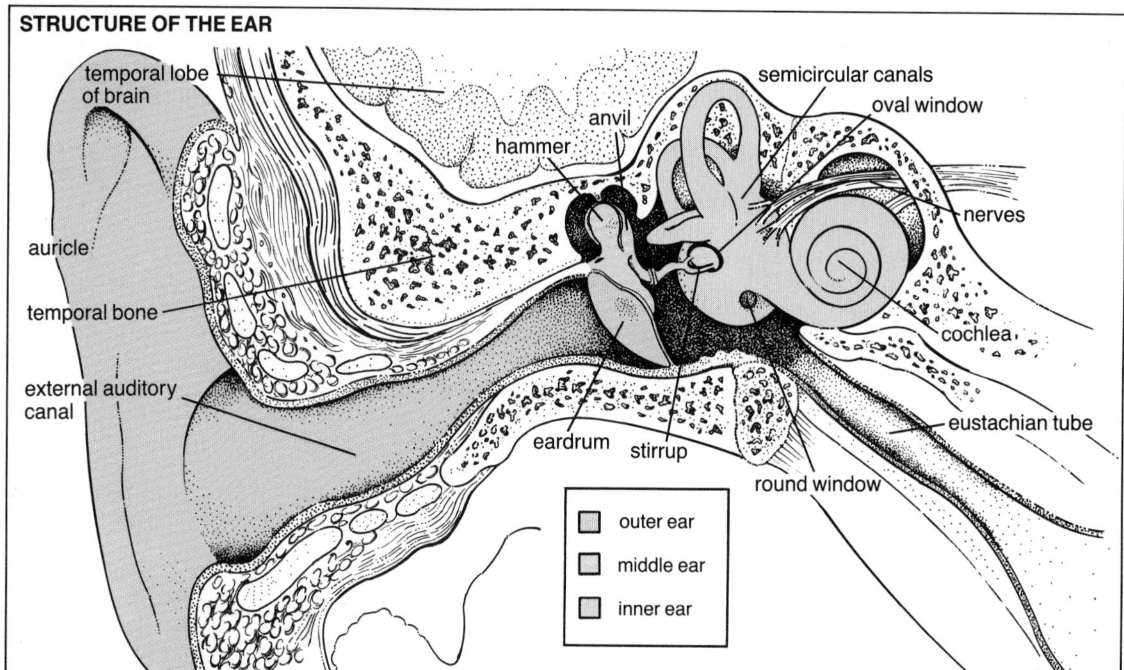

that sense equilibrium. These are the utricle, the saccule, and the three semicircular canals.

The saclike utricle and saccule sense the body's relationship to gravity, or its static equilibrium. A person knows that the body is right side up because these structures relay messages about the body's position to the brain.

Both sacs are hollow. Hairlike nerve endings are anchored into the inner surface of each structure. The free ends of the nerve endings project into the hollow space. Tiny particles of limestone, known as otoliths, rest against the bottom of each sac. If the head moves, the otoliths change position. In shifting, they pass over sensitive nerve endings. These send immediate impulses to the brain. Notified of a change in body position, the brain triggers the reflex mechanisms to correct the position of the body (*see* Reflexes).

Each of the three semicircular canals of the inner ear forms about two thirds of a circular loop. This loop begins and ends in the utricle. The canals are positioned at right angles to each other, similar to the way that the front wall, side wall, and floor of a room are at right angles to each other. The semicircular canals are fluid-filled tubes. If straightened out, each tube would be from about 0.4 inch (1 centimeter) to 0.8 inch (2 centimeters) long. Each canal is also lined with hairlike nerve endings. When the head turns, the fluid flows through these canals. As it passes over the nerve endings, impulses are triggered to the brain. At this time, appropriate reflex action immediately occurs.

Examination

At the beginning of an ear examination, a physician first checks the cerumen, or earwax, that is in the external auditory meatus. Cerumen is secreted by glands lining the passage to the eardrum. The sticky, waxy substance protects the eardrum from damage by attracting such substances as dust and dirt before they can pass through the meatus to damage the eardrum.

The eardrum is examined with an instrument called an otoscope. As viewed through the otoscope, the eardrum appears as a pearly-gray, oval-shaped membrane. Its longest diameter is about 0.5 inch (1.3 centimeters). A cross section of the eardrum looks like a shallow funnel.

The drum is divided into four separate parts, or quadrants. One of these is called the cone of light. Through it can be seen the handle of the malleus, the hammerlike ossicle. If its position is normal, the ear is probably capable of hearing. If the cone of light appears cloudy or blurred, it may be a sign of a common infection of the middle ear known as acute otitis media. Bacteria causing such an infection may enter the middle ear by way of the eustachian tube, a duct that connects the middle ear to the throat.

The eustachian tube helps to insure that there is equal air pressure on both sides of the eardrum. Going down too rapidly in an elevator, for example, often causes an uncomfortable feeling of fullness in the ear. The same thing happens to passengers in a descending aircraft. This occurs because air pressure pushing in on the ear is greatly increased as the elevator descends. The pressure bends the eardrum inward, causing discomfort. When swallowing occurs, the throat muscles open the eustachian tube's outlet into the throat. Air is able to pass upward into the middle ear. Pressure inside the middle ear pushes the eardrum back to normal.

Diseases

Each of the ear's three sections can be affected by diseases that relate to the structure, tissues, and function of that particular part of the ear. Diseases of the outer ear affect the skin, cartilage, and the glands and hair follicles in the outer ear canal. The sound-transmitting function of the outer ear is damaged when the ear canal becomes filled with a tumor, earwax, or infected material. When these conditions occur, sound cannot reach the eardrum.

There are several common diseases of the outer ear. Frostbite is a condition in which the exposed part of the ear becomes frozen and numb, resulting in a temporary loss of skin sensation. An injury that causes bleeding between the cartilage and the skin may produce a hematoma, which is a smooth, rounded, non-tender, purplish swelling. External otitis is an infection of the outer ear canal caused by molds or microorganisms. It occurs most often in warm humid climates and among swimmers. A greenish or brownish, musty, foul-smelling discharge develops in the outer ear canal, and the outer ear becomes tender, red, and much thicker than usual.

A common middle ear infection is secretory otitis media, in which the middle-ear cavity becomes filled with a clear, pale-yellowish, noninfected fluid. This develops when not enough air comes into the cavity from the eustachian tube. A painless impairment of hearing results. Head colds, allergic reactions of the membranes of the eustachian tube, and an enlarged adenoid are common causes of this condition.

A common inner-ear disease is congenital nerve deafness, which is caused by a defect of the hearing nerves in the cochlea. This may be present at birth or develop during or soon after birth. Usually both inner ears are affected to a similar degree. A severe impairment of hearing generally occurs but not always (*see* Deafness).

Ototoxic, or ear-poisoning, drugs can cause temporary and even permanent damage to the hearing-nerve function. Large doses of such salicylates as aspirin may cause ringing in the ears of some persons, followed by a temporary decrease in hearing. When a person stops taking the drug, hearing returns to normal. Certain antibiotics may cause permanent damage to the hearing-nerve function.

Exposure to various degrees of noise may cause temporary or permanent hearing damage. A single exposure to such an extremely intense sound as an explosion may produce a severe and permanent loss of hearing. Repeated exposures to sounds that reach more than 80 to 90 decibels may cause gradual loss of hearing. This happens because the hair cells of the inner ear, and sometimes even the nerve fibers, may be destroyed. The levels of noise produced by rock music bands is frequently more than 110 decibels. In the United States there are laws that require workers who are exposed to sound levels higher than 90 decibels to wear some form of protection. Earplugs or earmuffs are often used. (*See also* Sound.)

EARHART, Amelia (1897–1937). One of the most intriguing mysteries of the 20th century is: What happened to Amelia Earhart? In June 1937 she and her copilot, Lieutenant Commander Fred J. Noonan, left Miami, Fla., on an around-the-world flight attempt in a twin-engine Lockheed aircraft. On July 2 the plane vanished near Howland Island in the South Pacific. The world waited with fascination as search teams from the United States Army and Navy, along with the Japanese Navy, converged on the scene. But not she, Noonan, or the plane was ever found.

As time went on, questions were raised about the flight. Was it simply an around-the-world adventure, or was she perhaps sent to spy on Japanese war preparations for the United States government? Historians have claimed that she was almost certainly forced down and killed by the Japanese.

Amelia Earhart was born on July 24, 1897, in Atchison, Kan. During World War I she worked as a military nurse in Canada, and for several years she was a social worker in Boston. She first gained fame in 1928 when she was the first woman to fly across the Atlantic Ocean—even though only as a passenger. Four years later, in May 1932, she made a solo flight across the Atlantic, followed by several solo long-distance flights in the United States. She was greatly interested in the development of commercial aviation and took an active role in opening the field to women. For a time Earhart served as an officer of the Luddington line, which operated one of the first regular passenger services between New York City and Washington, D.C. In January 1935 she made a solo flight from Hawaii to California.

In 1931 Earhart had married publisher George P. Putnam. After her disappearance he wrote her biography, 'Soaring Wings', which was published in 1939.

EARP, Wyatt (1848–1929). He was one of many frontier lawmen whose exploits have been transformed by television and movies into heroic and legendary episodes. The reality, however, is considerably less than noble.

Wyatt Berry Stapp Earp was born in Monmouth, Ill., on March 19, 1848. By 1864 his family was living in California. He held a variety of jobs—buffalo hunter, stagecoach driver, minor peace officer—before settling temporarily in Dodge City, Kan., as assistant marshal in 1876. There he associated with Bat Masterson, a gambler, and Doc Holliday, a former dentist who was an alcoholic. Earp was also a card dealer for the game of faro at the famous Long Branch Saloon.

In the late 1870s Earp and some of his associates moved to Tombstone, Ariz. His brother Virgil became the town marshal. It was here that three Earp brothers—Wyatt, Virgil, and Morgan—and Doc Holliday fought the Ike Clanton gang in what is known as the gunfight at the O.K. Corral on Oct. 26, 1881. The Clanton gang lost, ending what was really a bitter feud, not a triumph of justice. Wyatt spent his last years in California, living off real estate and mining income. He died in Los Angeles on Jan. 13, 1929.

EARTH

EARTH. The earth, man's home, is a planet. It moves around the sun in a regular orbit, as do the eight other planets in the *solar system.* Each of the solar planets has special characteristics, some of which are well known. Saturn, for example, is surrounded by a set of rings, and Jupiter is famous as the largest planet. The earth also has special characteristics, and these are important to man. It is the only planet known to have the right temperature and the right atmosphere to support the kind of life man knows. *(See also* Planets.)

The earth's special characteristics make possible the kinds of environments and natural resources in which plants and man and other animals can survive. This fact is so important to man that he has developed a special science called *ecology,* which deals with the dependence of all living things upon one another and upon their environments. Ecologists try to find out how the earth's environments can be preserved so that living things will continue to survive on the planet.

Some scientists believe that millions of planets in the Milky Way, the galaxy that contains the earth, may be able to support life. But no one can predict the forms that such life might take. An indication of just how difficult such a prediction might be is illustrated by the vast variety of life forms on earth.

Many millions of kinds of plants and animals have developed on the earth. They range in size from microscopic plants and animals to giant trees and mammoth whales. Distinct types of plants or animals may be common in many parts of the world or may be limited to a small area. Some kinds thrive under conditions that are deadly for others. So some persons suggest that forms of life quite different from those known on earth might possibly survive on planets with conditions that are far different from conditions on earth.

Many persons believe that the earth is the only planet in the solar system that can support any kind of life. Scientists have theorized that some primitive forms of life may exist on the surface of Mars, but evidence gathered in 1976 by unmanned probes sent to the Martian surface seems to indicate that this is unlikely.

Scientists at one time also believed that Venus might support life. Clouds always hide the surface of Venus, so it was thought possible that the temperature and atmosphere on the planet's surface might be suitable for living things. But it is now known that the surface of Venus is too hot—an average of 800° F (425° C)—for liquid water to exist there. The life forms man is familiar with could not possibly live on Venus.

The earth has excellent conditions for the kinds of life man knows. The temperature is cool enough so that liquid water can remain on the earth's surface. In fact, oceans cover more than two thirds of the surface. But the temperature is also warm enough so that only a small fraction of this water is permanently frozen—near the North and South Poles and on some mountaintops.

The earth's atmosphere is dense enough for animals to breathe easily and for plants to take up the carbon dioxide they need for growth. But the atmosphere is not so dense that it blocks out sunlight. Although clouds often appear in the sky, on the average enough sunlight reaches the surface of the earth so that plants flourish. Growing plants convert the energy of sunlight into the chemical energy of their own bodies. This interaction between plants and the sun is the basic source of energy for virtually all forms of life on earth. (*See also* Energy; Plants; Sun.)

Preview

The article Earth is divided into the following sections:

This article was contributed by Albert R. Hibbs, Senior Staff Scientist, Jet Propulsion Laboratory, California Institute of Technology, and by Donald Wolberg, Graduate Assistant in Geology, University of Minnesota.

Facts About the Earth

Size: The radius at the equator is 3,963 miles (6,378 kilometers); radius at the poles is 3,950 miles (6,357 kilometers).

Mean Density: 344.7 pounds per cubic foot (5.522 grams per cubic centimeter).

Mass: 6.595×10^{21} tons (5.983×10^{24} kilograms).

Average Distance from the Sun: 92,900,000 miles (149,500,000 kilometers).

Average Distance from the Moon: 238,854 miles (384,393 kilometers).

Average Speed of the Earth in Orbit: 18.5 miles (29.78 kilometers) per second.

Average Speed of Rotation at the Equator: 0.289 miles (0.465 kilometers) per second.

Mean Surface Density of the Continents: 166.7 pounds per cubic foot (2.67 grams per cubic centimeter).

Land Area: 57.470×10^6 square miles (148.847×10^6 square kilometers).

Ocean Area: 139.480×10^6 square miles (361.254×10^6 square kilometers).

Highest Mountain: Mount Everest, 29,028 feet (8,848 meters).

Greatest Ocean Depth: Mariana Trench (explored depth), 35,800 feet (10,912 meters) below sea level.

Extensive exploration of the seafloor since 1977, however, has uncovered the existence of biological communities that are not based on solar energy. Active areas of seafloor spreading, such as the centers in the eastern Pacific that lie far below the limit of light penetration, have chimneylike structures known as smokers that spew mineral-laden water at temperatures of approximately 660° F (350° C).

Observations and studies of these active and inactive hydrothermal vents have radically altered many views of biological, geological, and geochemical processes that exist in the deep sea. One of the most significant discoveries is that the vents and associated chemical constituents provide the energy source for chemosynthetic bacteria. These bacteria form, in turn, the bottom of the food chain, sustaining the lush biological communities at the hydrothermal vent sites. Chemosynthetic bacteria are those that use energy obtained from the chemical oxidation of inorganic compounds, such as hydrogen sulfide, for the fixation of carbon dioxide into organic matter (*see* Deep-Sea Life).

Although the atmosphere allows sunlight to reach the earth's surface, it blocks out certain portions of solar radiation, especially X rays and ultraviolet light. Such radiation is very harmful, and, if the atmosphere did not filter it out, probably none of the life forms on earth could ever have developed. So, the necessary conditions for these life forms—water, the right kind of atmosphere, and the right amount and kind of sunlight—exist on the surface of the earth. The earth is the only planet in the solar system known to have all of these "right" conditions.

The earth looked so tiny in the heavens that there were times during the Apollo 8 mission when I had trouble finding it. If you can imagine yourself in a darkened room with only one clearly visible object, a small blue-green sphere about the size of a Christmas-tree ornament, then you can begin to grasp what the earth looks like from space. I think that all of us subconsciously think that the earth is flat or at least almost infinite. Let me assure you that, rather than a massive giant, it should be thought of as a fragile Christmas-tree ball which we should handle with considerable care.

Astronaut William A. Anders

By courtesy of (left) NASA; (background photograph) Hale Observatory—California Institute of Technology

The Earth's Place in Space

DESPITE ITS OWN special conditions, the earth is in some ways similar to the other inner planets—the group of planets nearer to the sun. Of these planets, Mercury is the closest to the sun; Venus is second; the earth is third; and Mars is fourth. All of these planets, including the earth, are basically balls of rock. Mercury is the smallest in size. Its diameter is about two thirds the greatest width of the Atlantic Ocean. Mars is larger than Mercury, but its diameter is only a little more than half that of the earth. Venus, with a diameter of roughly 7,600 miles (12,000 km.), is almost as large as the earth.

Four of the five outer planets are much bigger than any of the inner planets. The largest, Jupiter, has a diameter more than 11 times as great as that of the earth. These four outer planets are also much less dense than the inner planets. They seem to be balls of substances that are gases on earth but chiefly solids at the low temperatures and high pressures that exist on the outer planets.

The exact size or mass of Pluto, the most distant planet, is not known. Its composition is also a mystery. All that is known for sure about Pluto is its orbit. Pluto's average distance from the sun is almost 40 times that of the earth.

At the outer reaches of the solar system are the comets. A comet consists of a nucleus of frozen gases called ices, water and mineral particles; and a coma of gases and dust particles. Some comets also have tails. A comet's tail consists of gases and particles of dust from the coma. As the comet approaches the sun, light from the sun and the solar wind cause tails to form. For this reason the tails point generally away from the sun.

Movements of the Planets

Each planet, including the earth, travels around the sun in a regular orbit. Ancient astronomers thought that the orbits of the planets were circular. It is now known that the orbits are elliptical, though the orbits of most planets are almost circular. The

SOME FACTS ABOUT SPACE

Largest Planet: *Jupiter,* with an equatorial diameter of 88,670 miles (142,700 kilometers).

Smallest Planet: *Mercury,* with an equatorial diameter of 3,000 miles (4,840 kilometers).

Densest Planet: *Earth,* with an average density about $5\frac{1}{2}$ times that of water.

Lightest Planet: *Saturn,* with an average density about 0.68 times that of water.

Closest Star: *Proxima Centauri,* about 4.25 light-years (2.50×10^{13} miles, or 4.02×10^{13} kilometers) from the earth.

Most Luminous Star: *Zeta*[1] *Scorpii,* about 170,000 times as bright as the sun.

Largest Asteroid: *Ceres,* located between Mars and Jupiter, with a diameter of about 480 miles (772 kilometers).

Farthest Object Visible to the Naked Eye: *Andromeda galaxy,* 2.2 million light-years (1.29×10^{19} miles, or 2.08×10^{19} kilometers) from the earth.

earth's orbital eccentricity—the extent to which it departs from a perfectly circular path—is very slight. The orbits of Mercury and Mars are more eccentric. But Pluto is the only planet that has a markedly elliptical orbit.

The planets nearest to the sun move faster than do those farther away. Mercury, the closest, orbits the sun in about three months. Pluto, the most distant, takes 248 years to make one trip around the sun.

To man, the earth seems steady and immovable. It gives no sensation of motion, so it is hard to realize how rapidly the earth moves through space in its orbit around the sun. It takes a whole year to make one round trip, which seems rather slow. But on the average, the earth moves in its orbit at 18.5 miles (29.78 km.) per second, or 66,600 miles per hour.

Size and Movement of the Milky Way

While the earth and the other planets move around the sun, the sun itself moves through a *galaxy*, or large group of stars, called the Milky Way. The Milky Way is a collection of about a hundred billion stars. They are arranged in a disklike shape with a bulge at the center. This central bulge contains about three quarters of all the stars in the galaxy.

No one has made exact measurements of the Milky Way. Clouds of dust block much of it from view, and many stars between the earth and the center of the galaxy obscure the center from sight. Scientists, however, can see other galaxies in the sky. By comparing what they see with what they know about the Milky Way, they can make rough guesses about its size and shape and the number of stars it contains.

The Milky Way is almost 100,000 light-years in diameter, and its central bulge is about 10,000 light-years across. A *light-year* is an astronomer's measurement. It is a unit of length equal to the distance light travels in one year. Light travels 186,300 miles (299,800 km.) per second. So one light-year equals almost 5,880 billion miles (9,460 billion km.).

The Milky Way contains millions of stars similar to the sun. Among all stars, the sun rates as average in size and temperature. But the sun is much larger than any of the planets in the solar system. It has a diameter of 865,000 miles, and a volume more than a million times as great as that of the earth. The two stars closest to the solar system are Proxima Centauri, 4.25 light-years away, and Alpha Centauri, 4.3 light-years away. The two nearest stars that resemble the sun in size and brilliance are 11 light-years away.

The whole Milky Way seems to be slowly rotating. The stars near the center probably move around the hub faster than those near the edge, just as the planets nearest to the sun move faster in their orbits than do those farther away. The sun is 30,000 light-years, or about two thirds of the way out, from the center of the galaxy. Astronomers estimate that the sun with its planets will take about 200 million years to make one trip around the Milky Way.

The Milky Way galaxy is part of a cluster of galaxies known as the *Local Group*. This group consists of 17 galaxies. All are within 2.5 million light-years of the Milky Way.

Other Planetary Systems

No one has ever seen planets around other stars. However, indirect measurements taken by astronomers indicate that some nearby stars have large planets moving around them. For this reason, it seems possible that many stars besides the sun may have families of planets in orbit around them.

It also seems possible that among the planets rotating around other stars, some, like the earth, may have the right conditions of temperature and atmosphere to support life. So, though the earth is unique in the solar system, the Milky Way may hold many other star systems, and planets much like the earth may be circling around their central sun.

This diagram shows the relative sizes of the planets and their order from the sun. It does not portray the distances between the planets or their distance from the sun.

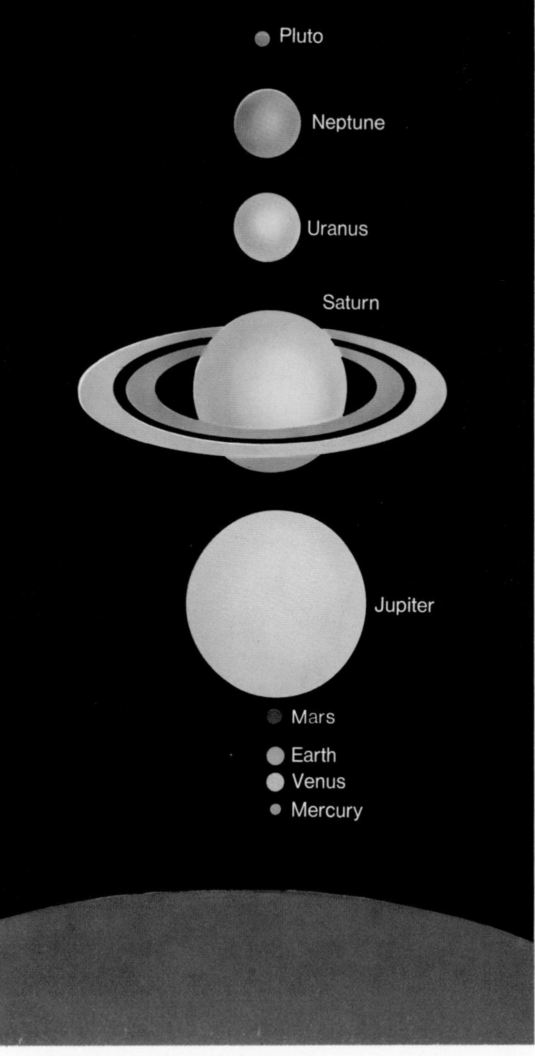

The Planet Earth

FOR SEVERAL HUNDRED years almost everyone has accepted the fact that the world is round. Most persons think of it as a sphere, somewhat like a solid ball. Actually, the earth is nearly, but not exactly, spherical. It has a slight bulge around the equator. Measured at sea level, the diameter of the earth around the equator is 7,926.7 miles (12,756.8 km.).

The distance from the North to the South Pole, also measured at sea level, is 7,900.0 miles (12,713.8 km.). Compared to overall diameter, the difference seems small—only 26.7 miles (43 km.). But compared to the height of the earth's surface features, it is large. For example, the tallest mountain, Mount Everest, juts less than 6 miles (9 km.) above sea level.

The earth's shape has another slight distortion. It seems slightly fatter around the southern hemisphere than around the northern hemisphere. This difference is, at most, about 100 ft. (30 m.).

The shape of the earth was originally calculated from measurements made by surveyors who worked their way mile by mile across the continents. Today, artificial satellites provide a much more accurate and complete measuring tool. Mathematicians carefully measure the orbits of artificial satellites, then calculate the gravitational force that the earth exerts on the satellites. From these calculations, they can deduce the shape of the earth. The slight bulge around the southern hemisphere was discovered from calculations made in this way.

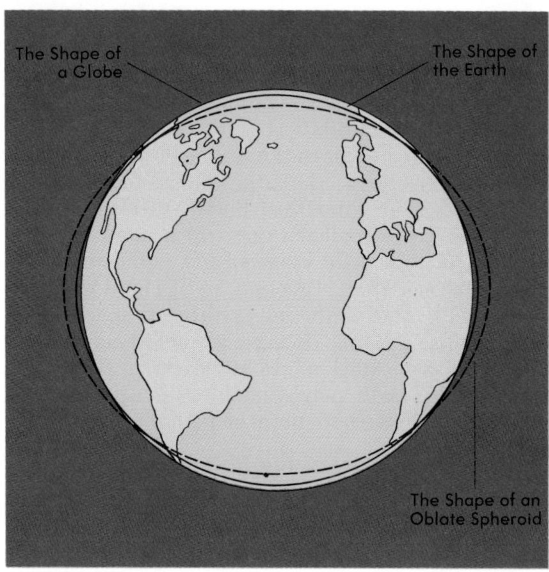

The earth is neither a true globe nor a true oblate spheroid. It bulges slightly in the southern hemisphere.

The Earth's Mass, Volume, and Density

The mass of the earth has been found to be 6.595×10^{21} tons (5.983×10^{24} kg.). In numerals this would read 6 sextillion, 595 quintillion tons. Scientists measure the earth's mass by means of a very delicate laboratory experiment. They place heavy lead weights of carefully measured mass near each other in an apparatus that measures the force of the gravitational attraction between them.

According to Newton's law of gravitation, the force of gravity is proportional to the products of the two masses involved. The force of the earth's gravity on the experimental mass is easily measured. It is simply the weight of the mass itself. The force of gravity between two known masses in the laboratory can be measured in the experiment. The only missing factor is the mass of the earth, which can be determined by comparison.

Scientists can calculate the earth's volume because they know the shape of the earth. They divide the mass of the earth by the volume, which gives the average density of the material in the earth as 3.2 ounces per cubic inch (5.5 g. per cc).

The highest point on the earth is Mount Everest, which juts about 5½ miles above sea level. The deepest known point on the earth is the Mariana Trench. No one has yet explored the bottom of this ocean deep.

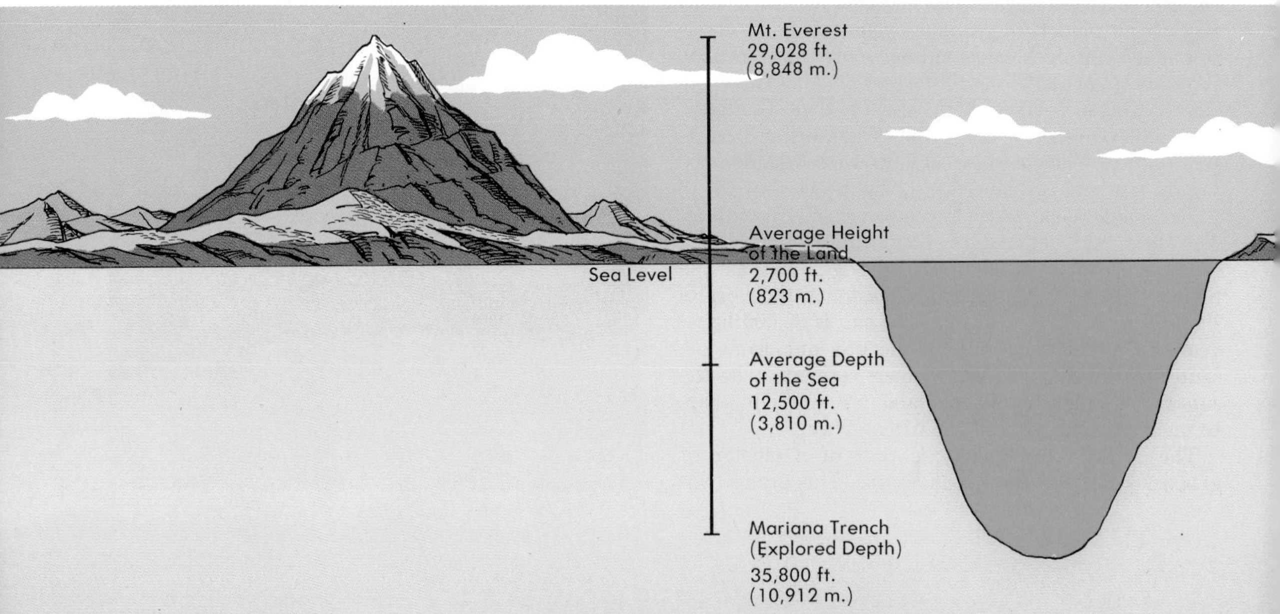

This average value includes all the material from the surface down to the center of the earth. But not all of the material in the earth has the same density. Most of the material on the continents is only about half as dense as this average value. The density of the material at the center of the earth is still somewhat uncertain, but the best evidence available shows that it is about three times the average density of the earth.

The Earth's Layers

The difference in density is not the only difference between the earth's surface and its center. The kinds of materials at these two locations also seem to be quite different. In fact, the earth appears to be built up in a series of layers.

The earth's structure comprises three basic layers. The outermost layer, which covers the earth like a thin skin, is called the *crust*. Beneath that is a thick layer called the *mantle*. Occupying the central region is the *core*. Each layer is subdivided into other, more complex, structures.

The crust varies in thickness from place to place. The average thickness of the crust under the oceans is 3 miles (5 km.), but under the continents the average thickness is 19 miles (31 km.). This difference in thickness under the continents and under the oceans is an important characteristic of the crust.

These two parts of the crust differ in other ways. Each has different kinds of rocks. Continental rocks, such as granite, are less dense than rocks in ocean basins, such as basalt. Each part also has a different structure. The basaltic type of rock that covers most of the ocean floors also lies underneath the continents. It appears almost as though the lighter rocks of the continent were floating on the heavier rocks beneath. Modern theories about the earth's structure suggest that this is exactly what is happening. But to understand this theory of floating rocks, called *isostasy*, it is necessary to know something about the earth's next deeper layer, the mantle.

The mantle has never been seen. Men have drilled deep holes, such as those for oil wells, into the crust of the earth both in the continents and in the ocean floor. But no hole has ever been drilled all the way

Elements in the Earth's Crust

Element	% by Weight
Oxygen	46.60
Silicon	27.72
Aluminum	8.13
Iron	5.00
Magnesium	2.09
Calcium	3.63
Sodium	2.83
Potassium	2.59

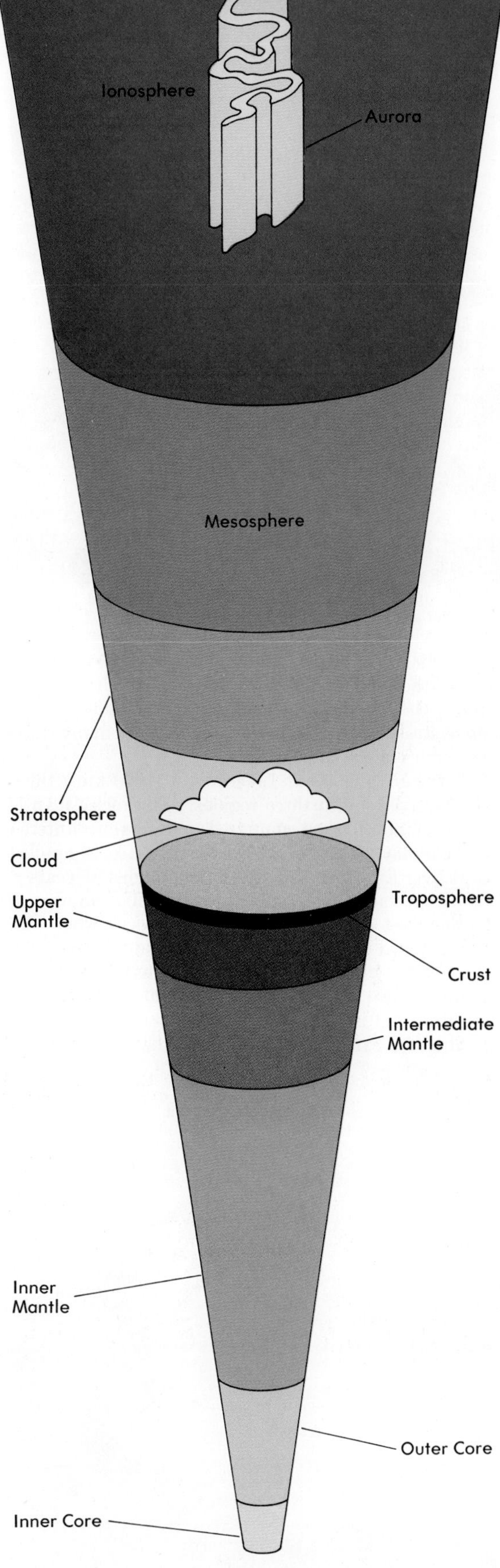

This diagram shows the layers of the planet earth and some of the layers of the atmosphere that envelops it. It does not portray the relative sizes of the layers.

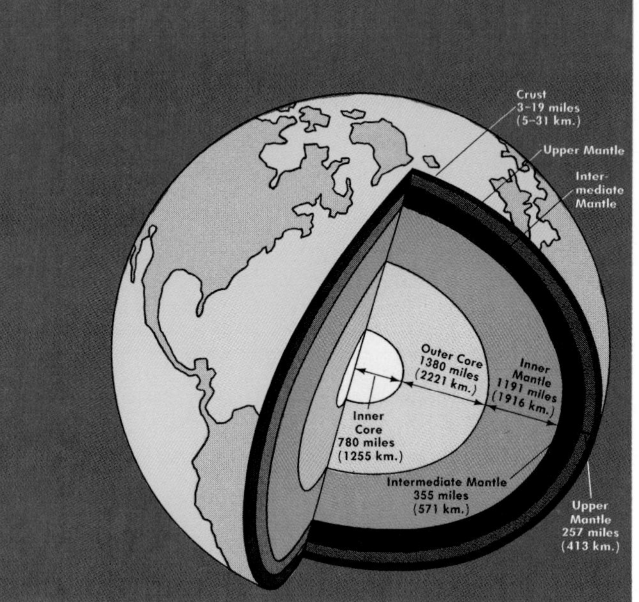

In this globe drawing of the earth, a wedge-shaped piece has been cut away to show the earth's interior layers.

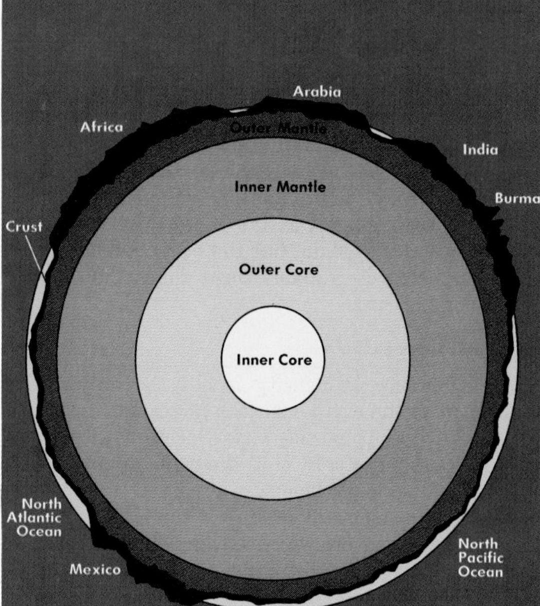

A cut through the earth shows the northern hemisphere. The continents and oceans ride on the thin crustal layer.

through the crust into the mantle. All information about the mantle has come from measuring *seismic waves*, the vibrations caused by earthquakes. From these measurements, scientists can deduce many characteristics of the mantle.

The mantle is about 1,800 miles (2,900 km.) thick and is divided into three regions. The rocky mantle material is quite rigid compared to things encountered in everyday experience. But if pressure is applied to it over a long period—perhaps millions of years—it will give a little bit. So, if the distribution of rock in the crust changes gradually, as it does when material eroded off mountains is deposited in the ocean, the mantle will slowly give way to make up for the change in the weight of the rock above it. This is the theory of isostasy.

The core extends outward from the earth's center to a radius of about 2,160 miles (3,480 km.). Obtaining information about the earth's interior is so difficult that many ideas about its structure remain uncertain. Some evidence indicates that the core is divided into zones. The inner core, which has a radius of about 780 miles (1,255 km.), is quite rigid, but the outer core surrounding it is almost liquid.

Scientists disagree about this description of the core because it is based on incomplete seismic wave data. The theory suggests that the density of the inner core material is about 9 to 12 ounces per cubic inch (16 to 20 g. per cc). The density of the outer core material is about 6 to 7 ounces per cubic inch (11 to 12 g. per cc).

The Earth's Surface Areas

Much scientific study has been devoted to the thin crustal area on which man lives, and most of the

The continents seem almost to float on a layer of basaltic rock, their weight pressing the rock down into the mantle.

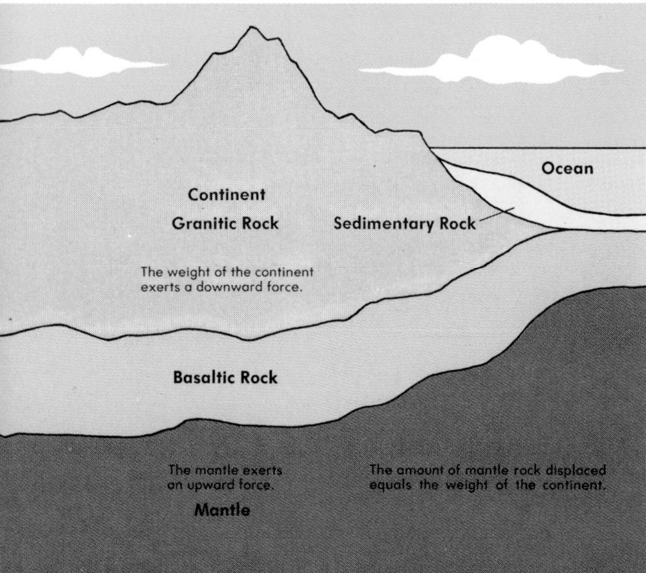

A simple experiment with wood, tar, and mud illustrates the theory of isostasy, also shown in diagram at left.

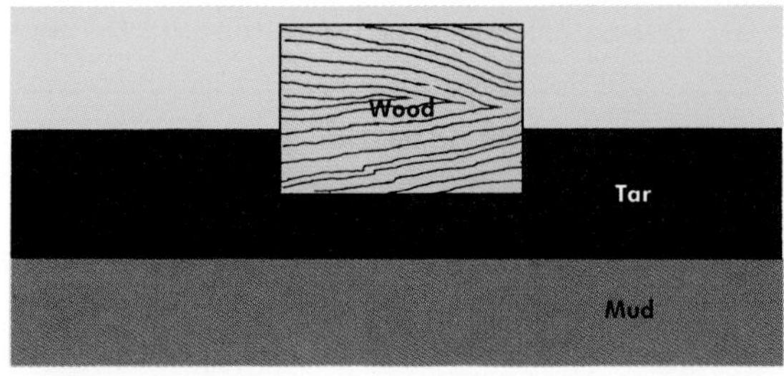

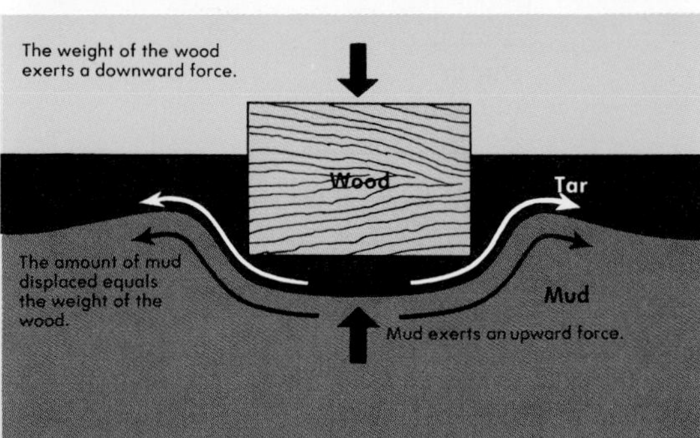

earth's surface features are well known. The oceans occupy 70.8 percent of the surface area of the earth, leaving less than a third of the earth's surface for the continents.

Of course, not all of the earth's land area is dry. A fraction of it is covered by lakes, streams, and ice. Actually, the dry land portion totals less than a quarter of the earth's total surface area.

The Salty Oceans

The oceans are salty. Salt is a rather common mineral on the earth and dissolves easily in water. Small amounts of salt from land areas dissolve in the waters of streams and rivers and are carried to the sea. This salt has steadily accumulated in the oceans for billions of years.

When water evaporates from the oceans into the atmosphere, the salt is left behind. The amount of salt dissolved in the oceans is, on the average, 34.5 percent by weight. About the same percentage can be obtained if three quarters of a teaspoonful of salt is dissolved in eight ounces of water.

The Balance of Moisture and Temperature

The movement of water in a cycle, from the oceans to the atmosphere to the land and then back to the oceans, is called the *hydrologic cycle*. The oceans have a strong balancing force on this cycle. They interact with the atmosphere to maintain an almost constant average value of water vapor in the atmosphere. Without the balancing effect of the oceans, whole continents could be totally dry at some times and completely flooded at others.

The oceans also act as a reservoir of heat. When the atmosphere above an ocean is cold, heat from the ocean warms it. When the atmosphere is warmer than the ocean, the ocean cools it. Again, the effect is one of balance. Without it, the differences between winter and summer temperatures, and even between those of day and night, probably would be greater.

Surface Features of the Ocean Floor

There are mountains, canyons, and plains on the floor of the oceans just as there are on the surface

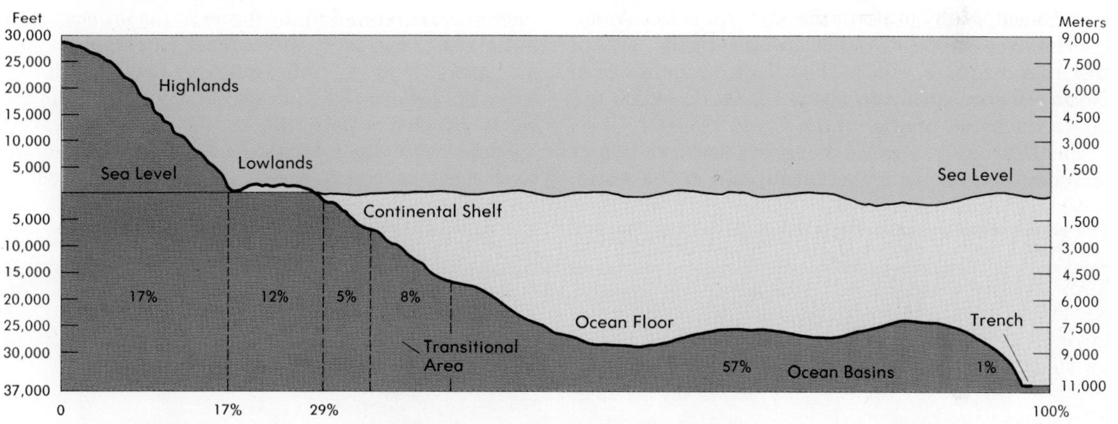

This graph shows what proportions of various kinds of land and water features—from mountain heights to ocean depths—make up the surface of the earth. Not all of the land or water areas shown can be productively employed by man.

of the continents. Changes take place in the features of the ocean floor as well as in those of the continents.

On the continents, many forces of erosion are constantly at work. They wear away the mountains and carry the dirt down to the lower valleys and plains. Some of the dirt is carried all the way to the ocean by rivers. Other forces, such as winds and temperature changes, also help wear away the high mountains.

In the oceans, there are no rainstorms and only very slight temperature changes. But there are forces that act somewhat like winds. These are the deep ocean currents, called *turbidity currents*. They carry mud and silt from the higher slopes of the ocean floor down to the depths. They also cause some erosion of the surface features of the ocean floor.

Many of the continents have broad, flat plains that cover hundreds of thousands of square miles. Among these are the prairies of North America, the steppes of central Russia, and the Amazon Basin in South

Water Supply for the Earth

Water that evaporates from the surface of the oceans into the atmosphere provides most of the rain that falls on the continents. Steadily moving air currents in the earth's atmosphere carry the moist air inland. When the air cools, the vapor condenses to form water droplets. These are seen most commonly as clouds. Often the droplets come together to form raindrops. If the atmosphere is cold enough, snowflakes form instead of raindrops. In either case, water that has traveled from an ocean hundreds or even thousands of miles away falls to the earth's surface. There it gathers into streams or soaks into the ground and begins its journey back to the sea.

Much of the earth's water moves underground, supplying trees and other plants with the moisture they need to live. Most groundwater, like surface water, moves toward the sea, but it moves more slowly.

America. The deep oceans also have broad plains, called *abyssal plains.* The abyssal plain in the North Atlantic Ocean is 20,000 ft. (6,000 m.) below the ocean surface. Most of it is almost completely level, but a few submarine mountains jut up here and there.

Just as there are mountain ranges on the continents, so there are mountain ridges across the ocean floor. These ridges, which seem to be organized in definite patterns, are generally near the center of the ocean basin. For this reason they are called *mid-ocean ridges.*

Mid-ocean ridges jut high above the ocean floor. For example, on both sides of the Mid-Atlantic Ridge the ocean floor is about 16,000 ft. (5,000 m.) below the ocean surface. The mountains that make up the ridge rise 10,000 to 13,000 ft. (3,000 to 4,000 m.) above the ocean floor. Some peaks may be so high that they extend above the ocean surface. The Azores and Ascension island are peaks of the Mid-Atlantic Ridge.

The Continental Mountains

The mountain ranges on the continents, like the mid-ocean ridges, rise high above the plains that surround them. Many peaks of the Andes of South America rise over 20,000 ft. (6,000 m.) above the level of the Amazon River valley. The Rocky Mountains of North America jut up to about 13,000 ft. (4,000 m.) above the broad prairies of the Great Plains.

The Himalayas, a range along the northern border of India, contain the highest mountain in the world, Mount Everest, with an altitude of 29,028 ft. (8,848 m.). Many mountains in the Himalayas are almost as high, rising more than 24,000 ft. (7,000 m.) above the plain of the Ganges River.

Many persons feel that mountains are the earth's most spectacular surface feature. Mountains usually connect to form long ranges that stretch hundreds or thousands of miles across the earth's surface. The Alps in Europe, the Himalayas in Asia, and the Rockies in North America are mountain ranges.

Geologists recognize even larger groupings of mountains, groupings which comprise a number of ranges. Such a grouping is called a *mountain system.* Mountain systems are often found at the edges of continents, particularly in North and South America. Scientists believe that because mountain ranges form systems and because they have special locations on the continents, they must have something to do with the deep structure of the earth. No one knows exactly what relationship exists between the mountain systems and the earth's interior. But the relationship is believed to be connected with the way mountains form.

Mountains seem to be formed by rising blocks of rock that are pushed up by forces in the lower portion of the crust or in the mantle. Since mountain systems are arrayed in a comparatively regular pattern, scientists believe this indicates that forces within the earth also have a pattern.

Some mountain systems, such as those along the west coast of North America and the east coast of

The earth's water is constantly recycled. It falls on the land as rain and snow, is carried by rivers or underground to the oceans, rises as water vapor, and travels inland again. This process is called the hydrologic cycle.

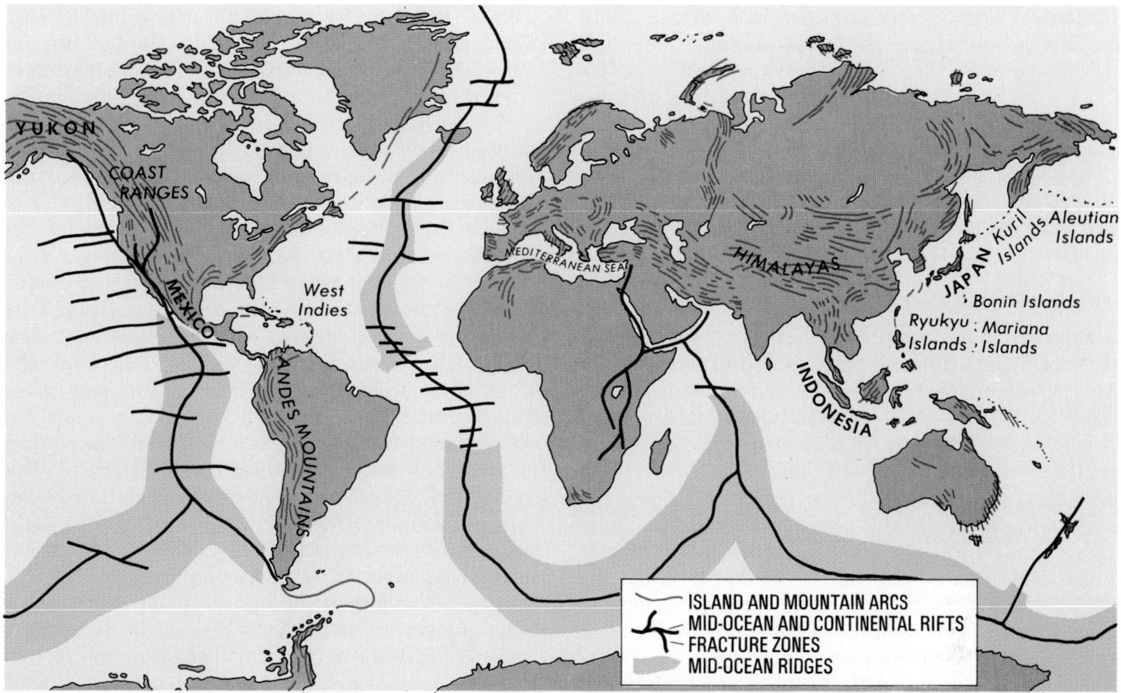

This map-diagram of the world shows the locations of the major mountain ranges, systems, and belts. Viewed on a worldwide basis, the relationships that exist among the various mountain groups are easier to recognize.

Asia, are still rising. Other mountain systems, such as the Appalachia group in the eastern United States, are being eroded away.

Although no one has conclusive information about the forces that build mountains, it is clear that earthquakes and volcanic action are closely related to mountain building. Scientists know that earthquakes and volcanic eruptions generally take place within young mountain systems. But no one knows exactly what forces deep within the earth cause them to occur.

Mountains form in three general ways. Certain features of each make it possible to trace out on the earth's surface the movements that result in mountain building. Most mountain systems are formed over many years by a combination of these three ways.

In one kind of mountain building, molten rock is either pushed up violently or seeps out from beneath the earth's surface. Hardened deposits of such rock build up to form mountains. Most submarine mountains form in this way.

In another kind of mountain building, a portion of the crust is cracked and tilted up on one side. The side on which the crack occurs is quite steep and rugged. The opposite side slopes gently down to the level of the remaining crust. The Sierra Nevadas in California seem to have been formed in this way.

The third type of mountain building takes place when two slabs of the earth's crust begin to move closer to each other. The portion of the crust between the slabs is compressed and folded. This is similar to what happens if you put your hands on two sides of a tablecloth and push them toward each other. The part of the tablecloth between your hands folds and crumples. The Appalachian Highlands in the eastern United States are an example of this type of mountain building.

The Valleys and Plains

Valleys separate mountain ranges. In some instances, the formation of a valley seems to be directly connected with the formation of the mountains that flank it. In Death Valley, in the United States Southwest, this effect is quite pronounced.

Death Valley is bordered on the east and west by two small mountain ranges that are young and still growing. As these ranges grow in height, they also move farther apart. The broad expanse of rock between them is steadily dropping into the slot left by the separating ranges. As a result, Death Valley, already the lowest spot in the United States, century by century is getting lower.

Death Valley is a very special case, the result of an unusual pattern of movement in the surrounding mountains. A more common type of valley is the *syncline*. This type of valley is especially noticeable where mountains have been formed by compression and folding. As with the folded tablecloth, some of the folds are up and some are down. The up folds, called *anticlines*, are the tops of the mountain ridges, and the synclines are the valleys between the ridges.

The surface of the earth between the large mountain systems is comparatively level. These broad areas are called *plains*. The Great Plains region of central North America is an example. Hundreds of millions of years ago, mountain ranges covered many of the plains areas. But the mountain-building process stopped long ago. Forces of erosion gradually wore away the tops of the mountains and deposited the dirt in the valleys, until finally the whole area was nearly level.

In some areas, there is evidence that such plains were once below the surface of the sea. Fossils of sea creatures have been found in rocks that are now far above sea level.

The Rivers and Streams

Broad river systems run through most plains. These rivers are quite different from those in the mountain ranges. Mountain streams and rivers move rapidly downhill. They tumble almost straight down, moving pebbles and rocks out of their way and sometimes creating waterfalls that pitch down over cliffs. These streams carry a large volume of water.

Rapidly moving water seems clear and sparkling. But every stream and river, whether in the mountains or in the plains, carries sediment from the higher places along the way. Mountain streams seem clear because they have so much water compared to the amount of sediment they are carrying.

Streams and rivers of the plains often look brown and muddy. They carry a much greater concentration of sediment and move much more slowly than do those in the mountains. In addition, they *meander;* that is, they curve back and forth in large loops.

It takes a very long time for a meander to develop in a stream bed. Imagine a slow-moving river stretching across a prairie. A section of it moves in a straight line. Slowly but steadily the water wears away the stream bed, and eventually it exposes a rock formation or a group of boulders. Since the river does not have enough force to erode the rocks or to push away the boulders, it must go around them. In this way, a slight curve gradually develops.

High mountains can be built by movements of the earth's crust. A huge block of the crust may be thrust straight up above the surrounding area, or one edge of the block may be forced higher than the others so that the block tilts.

Water at the outer edge of the curve moves more rapidly than water at the inner edge, just as the rim of a wheel moves more rapidly than the part nearest to the hub. The rapidly moving water erodes dirt more quickly and tends to make the curve more pronounced. As the curve becomes more pronounced, the effect of the water gets stronger. Eventually, the water cuts a wide arc around the obstruction.

The effect progresses downstream. When the water comes out of the curve, its momentum carries it up against the far bank. Gradually, this bank wears away, and the water begins to cut a curve on that side of the original stream bed. The effect continues downstream: a cut first on one side, then on the other. Over millions of years a meandering river channel forms.

The curving loops are sometimes so pronounced that the riverbank forms an almost complete circle. The narrow neck of land left between the beginning of the loop and its end may eventually wear away. The main stream will flow through the cut. Then the long loop is left with almost no water flowing through it.

As the river moves through its main channel, deposits of sediment build up. The sediment forms a barrier between the main channel and the open ends of the loop. Eventually, the loop is completely cut off from the river and only the curving link, called an *oxbow lake,* remains.

Rivers continually wear away the areas through which they flow, gradually making the valleys deeper. In some cases the wear has created remarkable land features. The Colorado River in the western United States has carved gigantic canyons out of the high tableland through which it flows. One of these, the Grand Canyon of the Colorado, is among the most spectacular sights in the world.

The Food and Water Supply

All of man's food comes from the earth. Very little comes from the sea. Almost all of it comes from farms on the continents. But man can use only a small portion of the continents for farming. About 7 percent of the earth's land is considered *arable,* or suitable for farming. The rest is taken up by the swamps and jungles near the equator, the millions of square miles of desert, the rugged mountain ranges, and—mostly in the Far North—the frozen tundra.

Man has been searching for ways to produce more food to supply the demands of the earth's continually increasing population. Many persons have suggested that the oceans might supply more food. They point out that the oceans cover more than 70 percent of the earth's surface and absorb about 70 percent of the sunlight. Since sunlight is a basic requirement for agriculture, it seems reasonable that the oceans could supply a great deal of food. But what seems reasonable is not always so.

Almost all the plants that live in the oceans and absorb sunlight as they grow are algae. Algae do not make a very tasty dish for man, but they are an important part of the food pyramid of the oceans. In this pyramid the algae are eaten by small sea creatures. These, in turn, are eaten by larger and larger ones.

Man now enters the pyramid when he catches fish, but the fish he catches are near the top of the pyramid. All the steps between are very inefficient. It takes about a thousand pounds of algae to produce a pound of codfish, less than a day's supply of food for a man. To feed the growing population of the world, man must find an efficient way to farm the sea. He cannot depend simply on catching fish.

Much of the earth's land area is unusable for agriculture because of the lack of adequate water. Millions of acres of land have been converted into farmland by damming rivers to obtain water for irrigation. Some scientists have estimated that if all the rivers of the world were used efficiently, the amount of land suitable for farming might increase by about 10 percent.

Another way to increase the water supply would be to convert ocean water into fresh water. Man has known how to do this for more than 2,000 years. But the process has been slow, and even with modern equipment it is costly. The distillation plant for the United States naval base at Guantánamo, Cuba, produces more than 2 million gallons of water a day, but at a cost of $1.25 for every thousand gallons. In New York City, where fresh water is available, the cost is about 20 cents per thousand gallons.

Scientists have investigated the use of nuclear-powered distillation plants. One plant would produce 150 million gallons of water daily at a cost of 35 to 40 cents per thousand gallons. It also would provide nearly 2 million kilowatts of electricity.

The Atmosphere

The earth's structure consists of the crust, the mantle, and the core. Another way of defining the

Rock layers fill a geosyncline (a troughlike depression in the crust) and form huge folds when squeezed by pressure from both sides. The mountains that result are called fold mountains. The Appalachians were formed in this way.

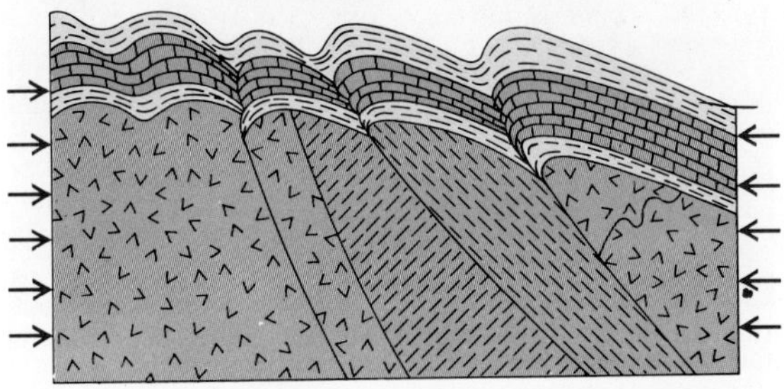

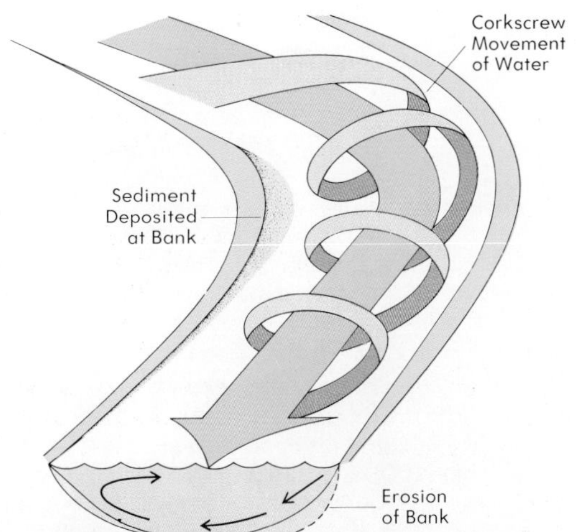

The corkscrew movement of water erodes one bank and deposits eroded material downstream on the other bank. Such deposits may close off a loop in the stream. The loop, cut off from the main stream, becomes a curving oxbow lake.

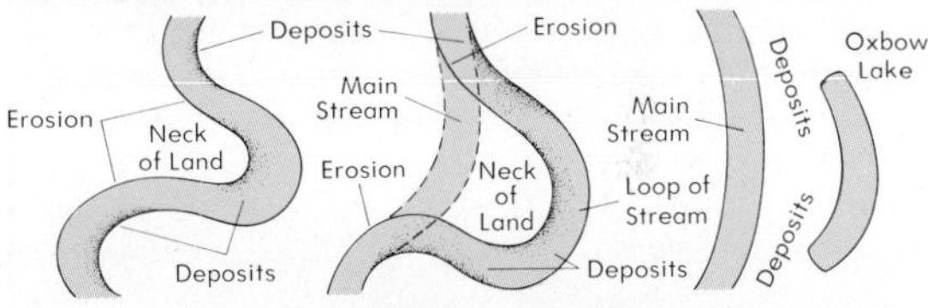

earth's regions, especially those near the surface, makes it easier to understand important interactions that take place. In this definition, the regions are called the lithosphere, the hydrosphere, and the atmosphere. The major part of this article has dealt with the lithosphere and the hydrosphere, though these terms were not used.

The *lithosphere* includes all the solid material of the earth. *Litho* refers to stone, and the lithosphere is made up of all the stone, soil, rock, and the whole interior of the planet earth.

The *hydrosphere* includes all the water on the earth's surface. *Hydro* means water, and the hydrosphere is made up of all the liquid water in the crust—the oceans, streams, lakes, and groundwater—as well as the frozen water in glaciers, on mountains, and in the Arctic and Antarctic ice sheets.

The *atmosphere* includes all the gases above the earth to the beginning of interplanetary space. *Atmo* means gas or vapor. The atmosphere extends to a few hundred miles above the surface, but it has no sharp boundary. At high altitudes it simply gets thinner and thinner until it becomes impossible to tell where the gas of the earth ends and where the gas of interplanetary space begins.

The atmosphere contains water vapor and a number of other gases. Near the surface of the earth, 78 percent of the atmosphere is nitrogen. Oxygen, vital for all animal species, including man, makes up 21 percent. The remaining one percent is composed of a number of different gases, such as argon, carbon dioxide, helium, and neon. One of these—carbon dioxide—is as vital to plant life as oxygen is to animal

Bob Glaze—Artstreet

The erosion of Niagara Falls takes place from underneath. The falls plunge over the hard limestone at the top, eroding the softer stones beneath. Chunks of the undermined limestone break off and plunge into the pool at the base.

Bob Glaze—Artstreet

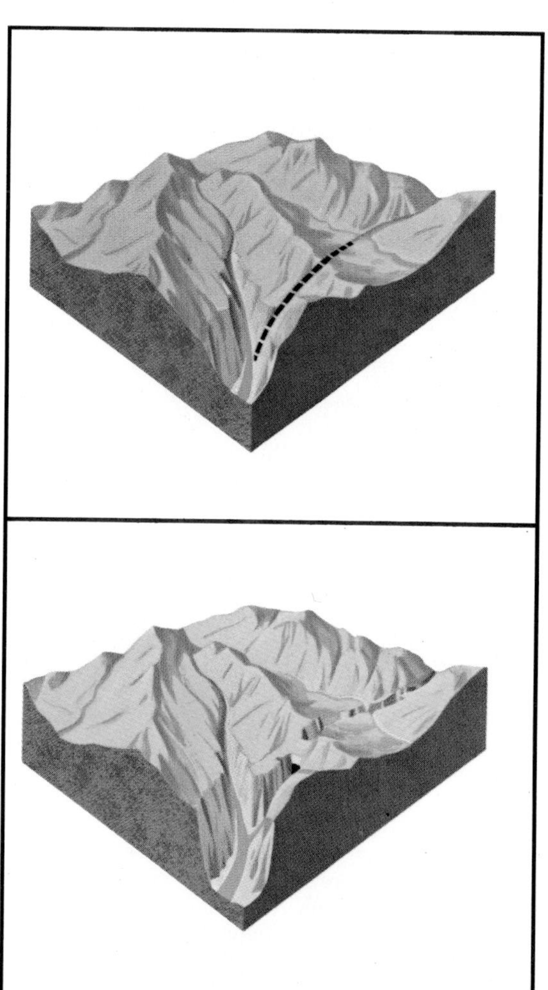

The Natural Bridge of Virginia (right) was formed by a creek which tunneled through hills instead of going around them (top diagram). As the tunnel became larger, both ends of the roof caved in, leaving a narrow arch (bottom diagram).

life. But carbon dioxide makes up only about 0.03 percent of the atmosphere.

The weight of the atmosphere as it presses on the earth's surface is great enough to exert an average force of about 14.7 lb. per sq. in. (1.03 kg. per sq. cm.) at sea level. The pressure changes slightly from place to place and develops the high- and low-pressure regions associated with weather patterns. The pressure is less at higher altitudes, because there is less atmosphere pressing down from above. Atmospheric pressure at 36,000 ft. (11,000 m.)—a typical cruising altitude for commercial jet planes—is only about one fifth as great as atmospheric pressure at sea level.

The temperature of the atmosphere also falls at high altitudes. At 36,000 ft. (11,000 m.), the temperature averages −56° C. The average temperature remains steady at −56° C up to an altitude of 82,000 ft. (25,000 m.). Above this altitude, the temperature rises.

The atmosphere has been divided into regions. The one nearest the earth—below 6 miles (10 km.)—is called the *troposphere.* The next higher region, where the temperature remains steady, is called the *stratosphere.* Above that is the *mesosphere,* and still higher, starting about 50 miles (80 km.) above the surface, is the *ionosphere.*

In this uppermost region many of the molecules and atoms of the earth's atmosphere are ionized. That is, they carry either a positive or negative electrical charge.

The composition of the upper atmosphere is different from that of the atmosphere near the earth's surface. High in the stratosphere and upward into the mesosphere, chemical reactions take place among the various molecules. Ozone, a molecule that contains three atoms of oxygen, is formed. (A molecule of the oxygen animals breathe has two atoms.) Other molecules have various combinations of nitrogen and oxygen. In higher regions the atmosphere is made up almost completely of nitrogen, and higher still almost completely of oxygen. At the outermost reaches of the atmosphere, the light gases, helium and hydrogen, predominate. (*See also* Atmosphere.)

The Earth's Magnetic Field

Another boundary besides the atmosphere seems to separate the environment of the earth from the environment of space. This boundary is known as the *magnetopause.* It is the boundary between that region of space dominated by the earth's magnetic field, called the *magnetosphere,* and interplanetary space, where magnetic fields are dominated primarily by the sun.

The earth has a strong magnetic field. It is as if the earth were a huge bar magnet. The magnetic compass used to find directions on the earth's surface works because of this magnetic field. This same magnetic field extends far out into space.

The earth's magnetic field exerts a force on any electrically charged particle that moves through it. There appears to be a steady "wind" of charged particles moving outward from the sun. This *solar wind* is deflected near the earth by the earth's magnetic field. In this interaction, the earth's magnetic field is slightly squeezed in on the side that faces the sun, and pulled out into a long tail on the side away from the sun.

In the magnetosphere, orbiting swarms of charged particles move in huge broad belts around the earth. Their movement is regular because they are dominated by the comparatively constant magnetic field of the earth. The discovery of these radiation belts by the first American satellite, Explorer 1, was one of the earliest accomplishments of the space age.

The charged particles within the radiation belts actually travel in a complex corkscrew pattern. They move back and forth from north to south while the whole group slowly drifts around the earth.

When the magnetic field of the sun is especially strong, the magnetosphere is squeezed. The belts of trapped particles are pushed nearer to the earth. Scientists are not certain what causes the famous *aurora borealis,* or northern lights, and the *aurora australis,* or southern lights. According to one explanation, when the trapped particles are forced down into the earth's atmosphere, they collide with particles there and a great deal of energy is exchanged. This energy is changed into light, and the spectacular auroras result. (*See also* the subhead of this article "The Earth's Motion and the Magnetic Field.")

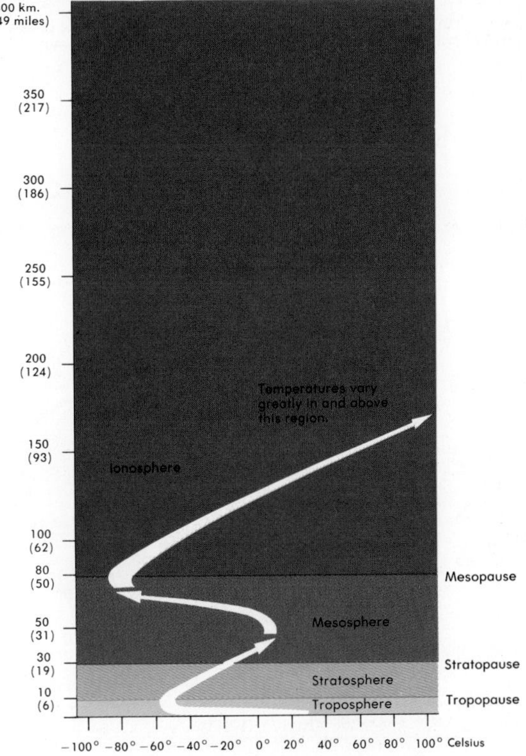

The relative positions of some layers of the atmosphere are shown in this diagram. The arrow indicates temperature.

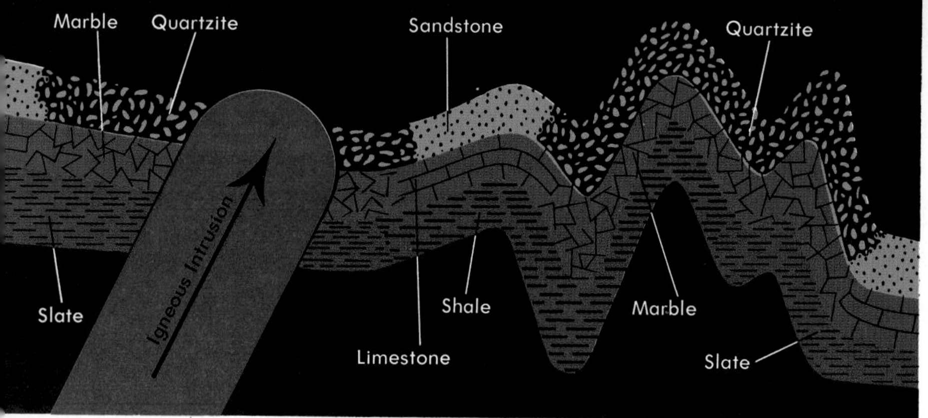

Metamorphic rocks form when the powerful forces of heat or pressure cause the composition of rocks to change. At the left of the diagram, heat has changed limestone to marble, sandstone to quartzite, and shale to slate. At the right, the same changes have been produced by pressure. Subjected to further heat or pressure, shale could undergo a series of changes and become a type of granite.

ROCKS AND MINERALS

The earth is often called a ball of rock. Rocks form on and beneath the earth's surface under a wide range of physical and chemical conditions.

All rocks are made up of minerals. The minerals in some rocks are single chemical elements such as gold or copper. But the minerals in most rocks are compounds, combinations of elements with a definite chemical composition and a precisely patterned structure. Most minerals form crystals. Each crystal has a characteristic shape and structure that is determined by the type and arrangement of its atoms. (*See also* Rock; Minerals; Crystals.)

Igneous Rock

Igneous rock is the primary rock of the earth's crust. Most other kinds of rock form from it. Igneous rock is rock that solidifies from a molten state. The molten rock material under the earth's surface is called magma. Magma that is forced out onto the earth's surface, as in volcanic action, is called lava (*see* Lava and Magma).

Magma deep beneath the surface may cool slowly. When this happens the minerals grow slowly and may reach a relatively large size. This slow-cooling process produces coarse-grained rocks such as granite or gabbro. The type of rock produced depends on the chemicals in the magma. Each type can be distinguished by its characteristic mineral composition.

Magma closer to the surface cools more quickly, giving the minerals little chance to grow. As a result, fine-grained rocks similar in composition to the coarse-grained ones are produced. The fine-grained rhyolite is the equivalent of the coarse-grained granite and the fine-grained basalt, of gabbro (*see* Basalt).

Some materials ejected from volcanoes cool so quickly that they solidify before they strike the

Soil forms a relatively thin cover over the earth's rock crust. Only a small portion of the surface is arable soil. Soil contains particles of rock that have been broken down by erosion.

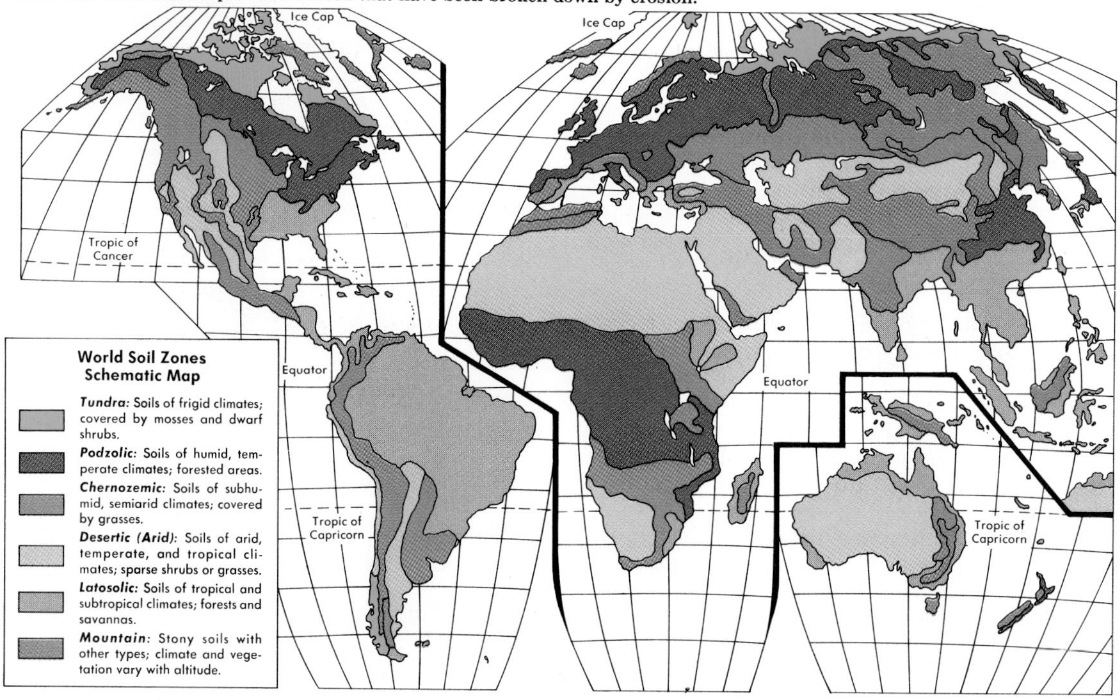

Ice Cap
Ice Cap
Tropic of Cancer
Equator
Equator
Tropic of Capricorn
Tropic of Capricorn

World Soil Zones Schematic Map

- ***Tundra:*** Soils of frigid climates; covered by mosses and dwarf shrubs.
- ***Podzolic:*** Soils of humid, temperate climates; forested areas.
- ***Chernozemic:*** Soils of subhumid, semiarid climates; covered by grasses.
- ***Desertic (Arid):*** Soils of arid, temperate, and tropical climates; sparse shrubs or grasses.
- ***Latosolic:*** Soils of tropical and subtropical climates; forests and savannas.
- ***Mountain:*** Stony soils with other types; climate and vegetation vary with altitude.

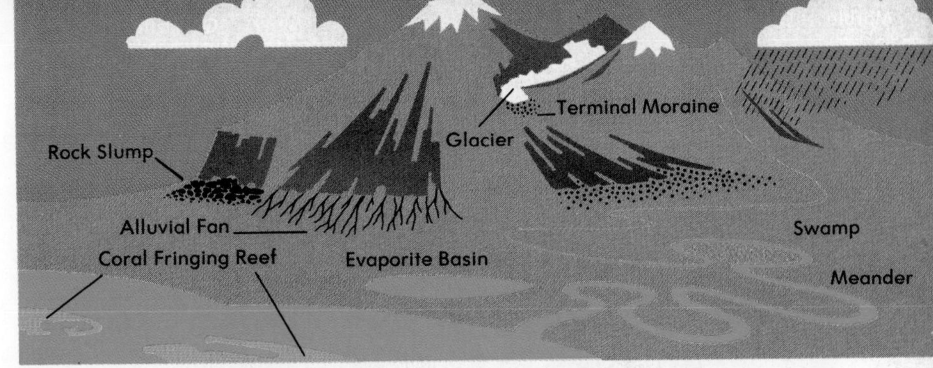

Sedimentary rocks are formed from the debris that results from the processes of erosion on land or in the sea. Glaciers carry rock fragments to their terminal moraines, rock slumps form, streams deposit materials in an alluvial fan, and rivers carry particles to the sea.

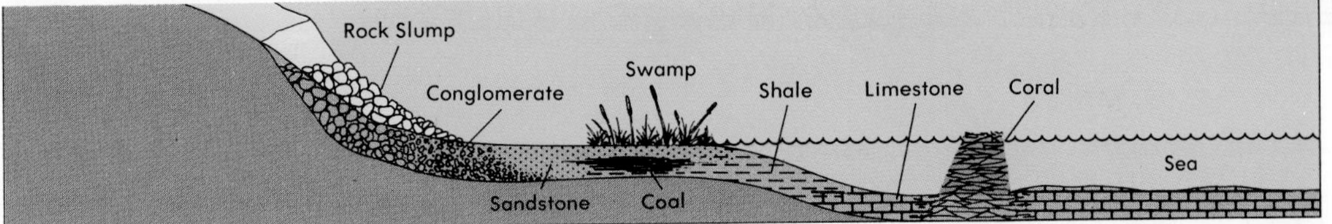

ground. Lava cools very rapidly. Often gas bubbles are trapped within it. When such lava hardens, it is light and porous. Pumice is formed in this way. The natural glass obsidian is also formed from lava.

Metamorphic Rock

Metamorphic rock results when heat and pressure change the original composition and structure of rock. Deep in the earth's crust the heat is much greater than it is near the surface. There the hot rock is subjected to pressures from the weight of the crust above and from lateral movements of the crust. Sometimes fluids and gases also act on the rock. These forces cause the rock's composition and structure to change.

Limestone, a sedimentary rock, changes to marble as a result of such forces. Under stress the mineral grains in shale grow in new directions to form slate, a metamorphic rock. Continued stress changes the slate to phyllite and then to schist, a rock that is very different in appearance, composition, and structure from the original shale. Quartzite, one of the hardest and most compact rocks, is the metamorphic form of the relatively soft, grainy sandstone.

Sedimentary Rock

Sedimentary rocks cover much of the earth's surface, but they are often hidden by a thin veneer of soil. For convenience sedimentary rocks are divided into two major groups: clastic rocks and crystalline rocks. Clastic rocks are composed of particles of varying sizes. Crystalline rocks are composed of minerals that have been precipitated out of solutions.

Particles of rock, eroded from exposed areas such as mountains, are transported by streams and rivers to the sea. The smallest particles are carried far out into the sea. There they slowly settle as fine silts or clays. Coarser particles, such as sands, are deposited nearer the shore, and the largest particles, such as pebbles and cobbles, settle at the shoreline. As these materials slowly accumulate over long periods of time, water is squeezed out from between the particles. Cementing agents carried in solution in the water—for example, calcium carbonate, silica, and iron oxide—may bind the particles together.

The pebbles close to shore are cemented together into a conglomerate. A little farther out shales form. In the open oceans limestones form from calcium carbonate and the shells of dead sea animals.

Crystalline rocks can form in shallow inland seas where access to open water has been restricted or cut off. In such places the seas may evaporate slowly, leaving behind compounds that form sedimentary rocks such as gypsum and rock salt.

Geologists can reconstruct the ancient geography and environment of a region by studying the distribution of its sedimentary rocks. Fossils are found almost exclusively in sedimentary rocks. They record the history of life on earth. Mineral resources such as coal occur in sedimentary rocks.

THE EARTH THROUGH TIME

The earth's crust formed about 4.5 billion years ago. Since then the surface features of the land have been shaped, destroyed, and reshaped, and even

Igneous rock comes from lava or magma. Magma seeps through layers of rock and hardens to form huge batholiths and smaller laccoliths. These may stretch for hundreds of miles. Magma forced upward into a fissure may harden to form a dike. Magma may find a conduit—a natural vertical passageway—and burst through the crust as a volcano, spewing pumice or tuff into the air.

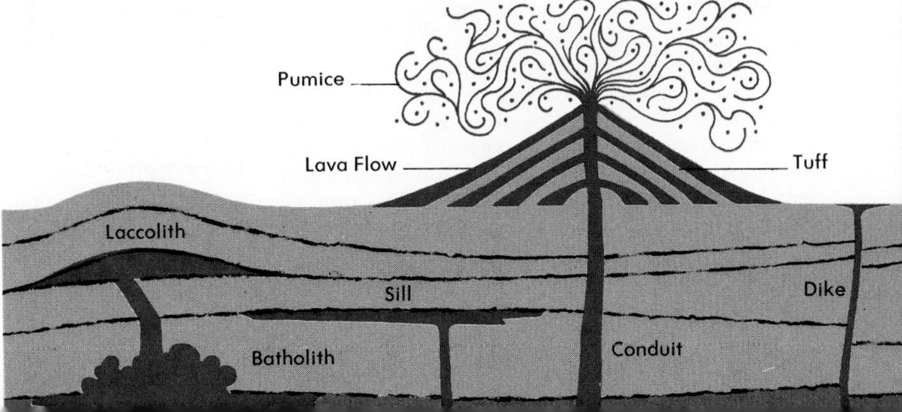

Reptiles such as the dinosaur dominated the earth during the Mesozoic. Scientists at Dinosaur National Monument in Colorado carefully dig the fossil bones of one of these ancient creatures from the rocky face of a quarry wall.

By courtesy of National Park Service

the positions of the continents have changed. Over the years, various kinds of plants and animals have developed. Some thrived for a time and then died off: others adapted to new conditions and survived.

All these events are recorded in the earth's rocks, but the record is not continuous in any one region. Geologists can sometimes fill in the gaps by studying sequences of rocks in various regions of the earth.

The Stratigraphic Record and Fossils

Stratigraphy is the study of the earth's strata, or rock layers. Stratigraphers attempt to reconstruct the history of the earth by studying the sequences of rock layers. Correlating the sequences of rock layers in different areas enables them to trace a particular geologic event to a particular period.

Fossils, the remains of organisms that once lived on earth, are usually found in sedimentary rocks. The remains often consist of the shell, skeleton, or teeth of animals or the woody structure of plants. In unusual circumstances, the flesh and soft tissues of animals have been preserved. The frozen remains of mammoths, for example, have been found in Siberia and Alaska. In one instance, even the undigested contents of the mammoth's stomach were preserved. The mammoth fell into a crevasse more than 38,000 years ago.

Fossils with hard parts are usually petrified, or turned to stone. Ancient insects have been preserved in amber, the hardened resin of certain types of trees. (*See also* Fossils.)

Radiometric Dating

Geologists assign dates to many rock masses by means of radiometric dating. This technique is based on the atomic structure of the elements.

Elements are made up of protons, neutrons, and electrons. An atom of any element has a small nucleus which contains one or more protons and which may contain one or more neutrons. The protons carry a positive electrical charge; the neutrons have no charge. Circulating around the nucleus are one or more electrons. These carry a negative electrical charge.

All the atoms of an element have the same number of protons. The number, unique for each element, is called the atomic number. Hydrogen, for example, has only one proton, so its atomic number is 1. Uranium, with 92 protons, has the atomic number 92.

The atomic weight, or mass, of an element is the sum of all its protons and neutrons. Hydrogen, with one proton and no neutrons, has an atomic weight of 1. Uranium, with 92 protons and 146 neutrons, has an atomic weight of 238.

Many elements occur in forms that have different numbers of neutrons and therefore have different atomic weights. These varieties are called *isotopes.* For example, one isotope of uranium (U^{235}) has 143 neutrons, while another (U^{238}) has 146 neutrons.

The atomic structure of some isotopes is unstable. Changes occur in the atoms of these isotopes that bring them to a stable state. During these changes, particles from the nucleus are discharged with high energy in a phenomenon called *radioactivity.*

The discharge of high-energy particles takes place at a relatively constant rate. The time in which half the quantity of an isotope loses its radioactivity is called its half-life. Half-life is important because it always is the same amount of time for a particular isotope. This means that a sample having a million atoms will lose half a million atoms in the same amount of time that a sample having a thousand atoms will lose five hundred atoms.

Half-life is the basis for radiometric dating. The uranium isotope U^{238} decays to form the element lead. Since it takes 4.51 billion years for half of a quantity of U^{238} to change into lead, its half-life is 4.51 billion years. (*See also* Radioactivity.)

The Precambrian

Geologists have divided the earth's history into very long spans of time called eras and into shorter, but still very long, spans called periods, epochs, and ages. Frequently, all of geologic time is divided into only two periods. The earlier period is called the Cryptozoic eon (the eon of hidden life). It coincides with the Precambrian. The later period, from the end of the Precambrian to the present, is called the Phanerozoic eon (the eon of visible life).

The Precambrian is by far the greatest span of geologic time. It includes all of the time from the formation of the earth's crust, about 4.5 billion years ago, to the beginning of the Paleozoic era, about 570 million years ago. Thus, the Precambrian encompasses all but an eighth of the earth's history.

The most extensive exposures of Precambrian rocks occur in regions known as continental shields. These are stable, low-lying core areas of the continents that are relatively uncovered by younger rocks. Each continent has at least one shield.

North America's Canadian Shield has the largest exposures of Precambrian rocks in the world. The shield covers more than 1,800,000 sq. miles (4,660,000 sq. km.). It is a rich source of many minerals, including gold, silver, and platinum, and it supplies more than half of the world's nickel. (*See also* Laurentian Plateau.) There are two other important Precambrian exposures in North America. These are in the Grand Canyon region and in the Rockies.

The first living organisms appeared on earth during the Precambrian. Efforts are being made to find out how they developed. The oldest known microorganisms resembled blue-green algae. Fossils of such organisms found in rocks from South Africa are about 3.2 billion years old. Fossils of similar organisms found in Precambrian rocks in Australia and North America are 1.9 to 1.0 billion years old.

The Paleozoic Era

The Paleozoic era, which began about 570 million years ago, lasted about 345 million years. Geologists generally divide the era into seven periods. From the earliest to the latest, these are the Cambrian, the Ordovician, the Silurian, the Devonian, the Mississippian, the Pennsylvanian, and the Permian.

Most of the major groups of plants and animals evolved during the Paleozoic era. Mild climates and gradually encroaching seas characterized the early Paleozoic. The seas of the Cambrian and Ordovician periods teemed with life. Dominating the seas were such creatures as the arthropods called trilobites, predecessors of spiders and lobster; the cephalopods, ancestors of nautiluses and squid; the brachiopods, bivalve shelled animals that still exist; and the graptolites, floating colonial animals that some scientists believe may have been chordates.

The great predators of the Silurian period were the scorpionlike eurypterids, some of which were more than three feet long. The first land animals, also scorpionlike, and the first land plants, much like lichens, may have developed during the Silurian.

Fish dominated the seas in the late Paleozoic, and the Devonian period is often called the Age of Fishes. But during this period the first vertebrates—primitive amphibians—also appeared, and forests of giant, treelike ferns grew on the land.

In the Mississippian period, a shallow inland sea covered much of the interior of North America and widespread limestones formed. The seas of the Mississippian period contained crinoids (called sea lilies), tentacled animals in the same group as starfish.

Mildred Adams Fenton

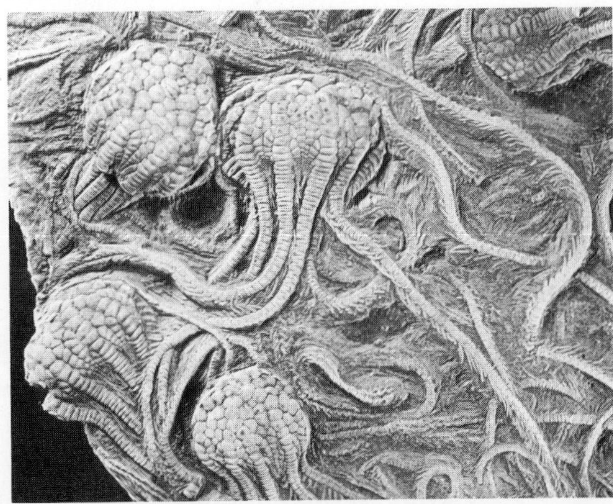

These crinoid fossils, found in Kansas, date back to the Cretaceous, when a shallow sea covered the inland plains.

A dragonfly fossil from Bavaria (right) dates from the Jurassic. Body imprints of these creatures are rare. These dinosaur eggs (below), found in Mongolia, date from the Cretaceous. They were probably buried in warm sand and left to hatch.

American Museum of Natural History, New York

Frank M. Carpenter

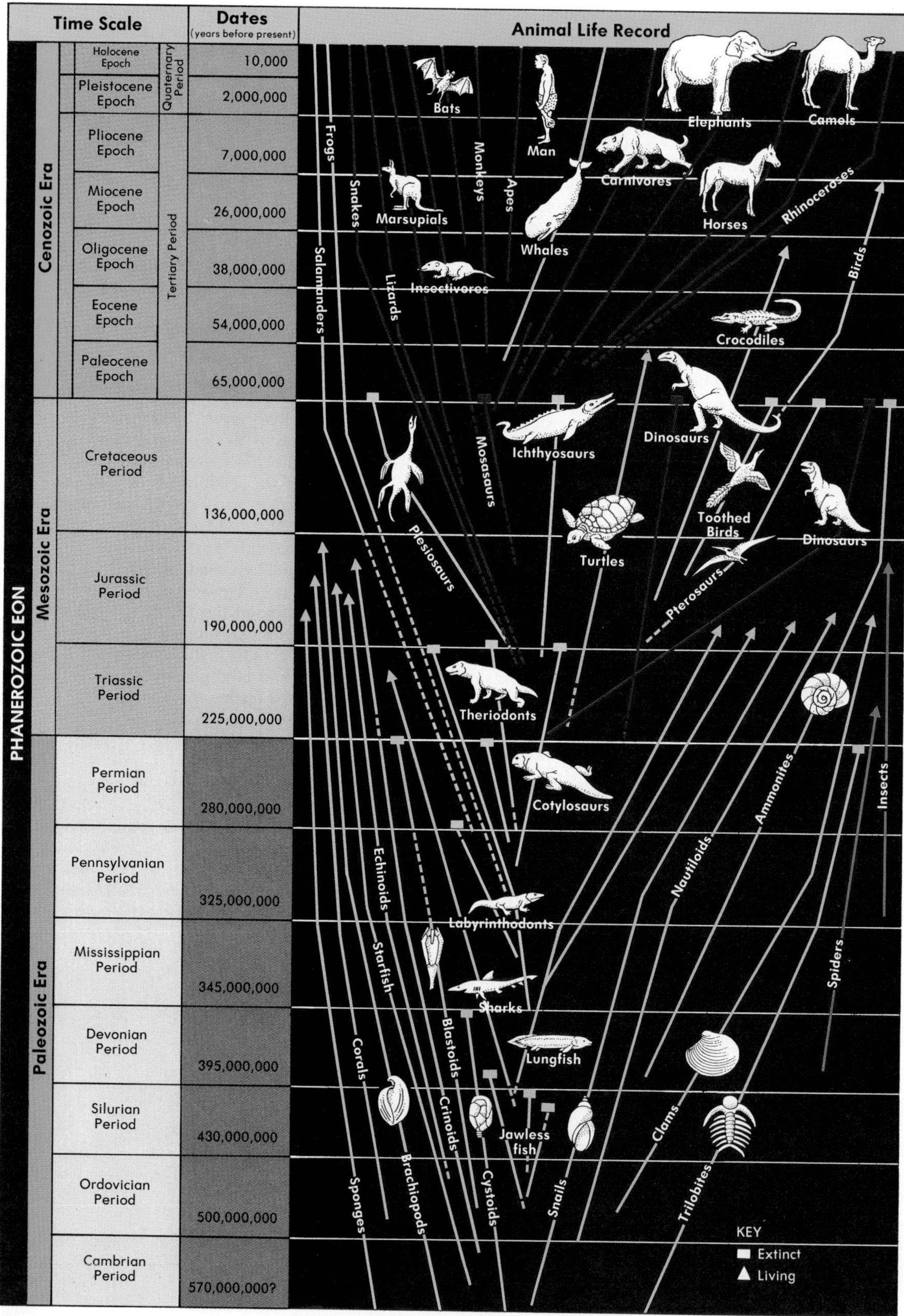
Time Scale
Dates
(years before present)
Animal Life Record
PHANEROZOIC EON
Cenozoic Era
Mesozoic Era
Paleozoic Era
Quaternary Period
Tertiary Period
Holocene Epoch
10,000
Pleistocene Epoch
2,000,000
Pliocene Epoch
7,000,000
Miocene Epoch
26,000,000
Oligocene Epoch
38,000,000
Eocene Epoch
54,000,000
Paleocene Epoch
65,000,000
Cretaceous Period
136,000,000
Jurassic Period
190,000,000
Triassic Period
225,000,000
Permian Period
280,000,000
Pennsylvanian Period
325,000,000
Mississippian Period
345,000,000
Devonian Period
395,000,000
Silurian Period
430,000,000
Ordovician Period
500,000,000
Cambrian Period
570,000,000?
Bats
Man
Elephants
Camels
Frogs
Monkeys
Apes
Carnivores
Snakes
Marsupials
Horses
Rhinoceroses
Whales
Salamanders
Lizards
Insectivores
Birds
Crocodiles
Dinosaurs
Ichthyosaurs
Mosasaurs
Plesiosaurs
Turtles
Toothed Birds
Dinosaurs
Pterosaurs
Theriodonts
Cotylosaurs
Ammonites
Insects
Echinoids
Nautiloids
Labyrinthodonts
Starfish
Spiders
Sharks
Blastoids
Lungfish
Corals
Crinoids
Jawless fish
Clams
Sponges
Brachiopods
Cystoids
Snails
Trilobites
KEY
Extinct
Living

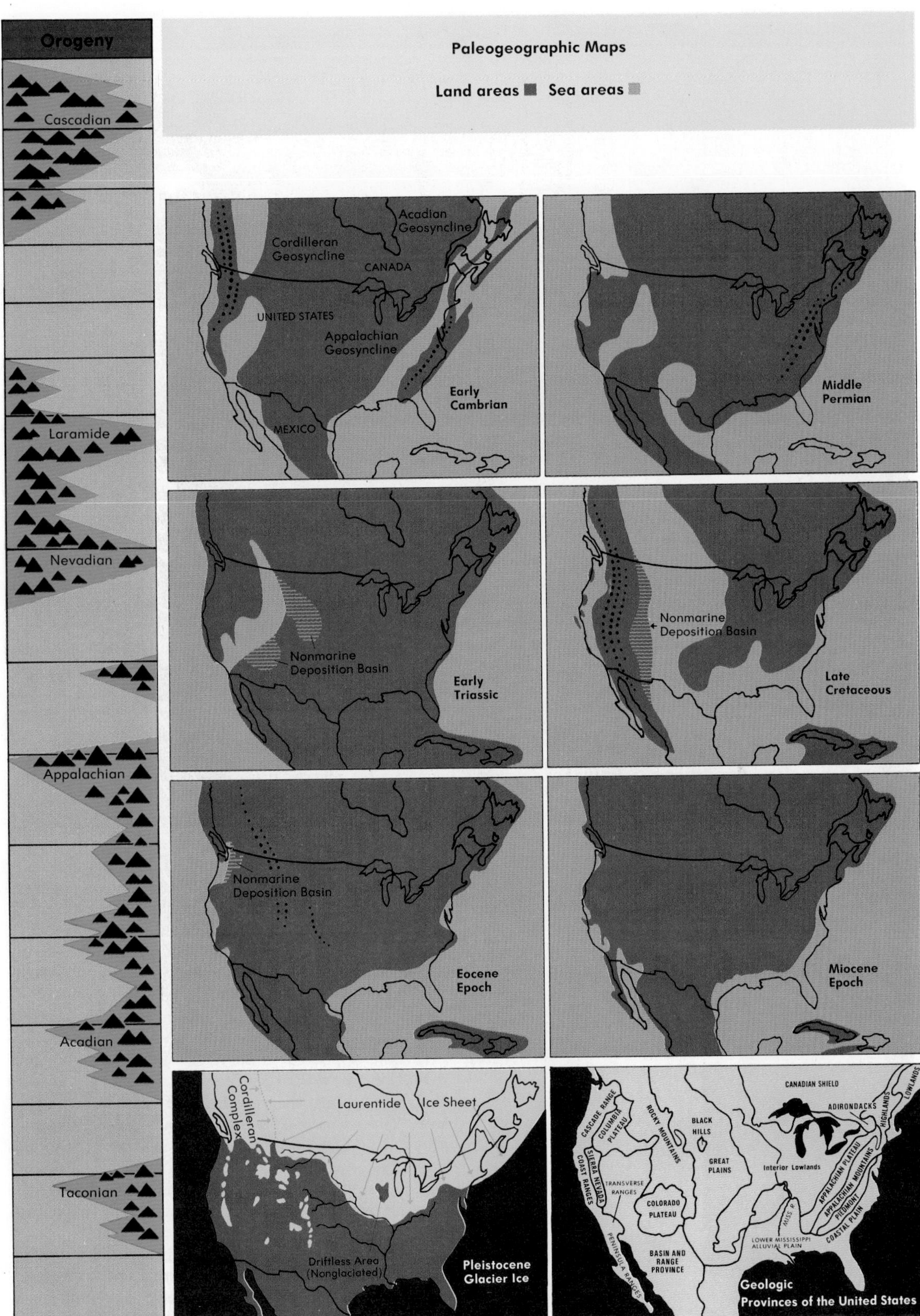
Orogeny
Cascadian
Laramide
Nevadian
Appalachian
Acadian
Taconian
Paleogeographic Maps
Land areas
Sea areas
Acadian Geosyncline
Cordilleran Geosyncline
CANADA
UNITED STATES
Appalachian Geosyncline
MEXICO
Early Cambrian
Middle Permian
Nonmarine Deposition Basin
Early Triassic
Nonmarine Deposition Basin
Late Cretaceous
Nonmarine Deposition Basin
Eocene Epoch
Miocene Epoch
Cordilleran Complex
Laurentide Ice Sheet
Driftless Area (Nonglaciated)
Pleistocene Glacier Ice
CANADIAN SHIELD
ADIRONDACKS
HIGHLANDS
LOWLANDS
CASCADE RANGE
COLUMBIA PLATEAU
ROCKY MOUNTAINS
BLACK HILLS
GREAT PLAINS
Interior Lowlands
SIERRA NEVADA
COAST RANGES
TRANSVERSE RANGES
COLORADO PLATEAU
APPALACHIAN PLATEAU
APPALACHIAN MOUNTAINS
PIEDMONT
COASTAL PLAIN
MISS R.
LOWER MISSISSIPPI ALLUVIAL PLAIN
BASIN AND RANGE PROVINCE
PENINSULA RANGES
Geologic Provinces of the United States

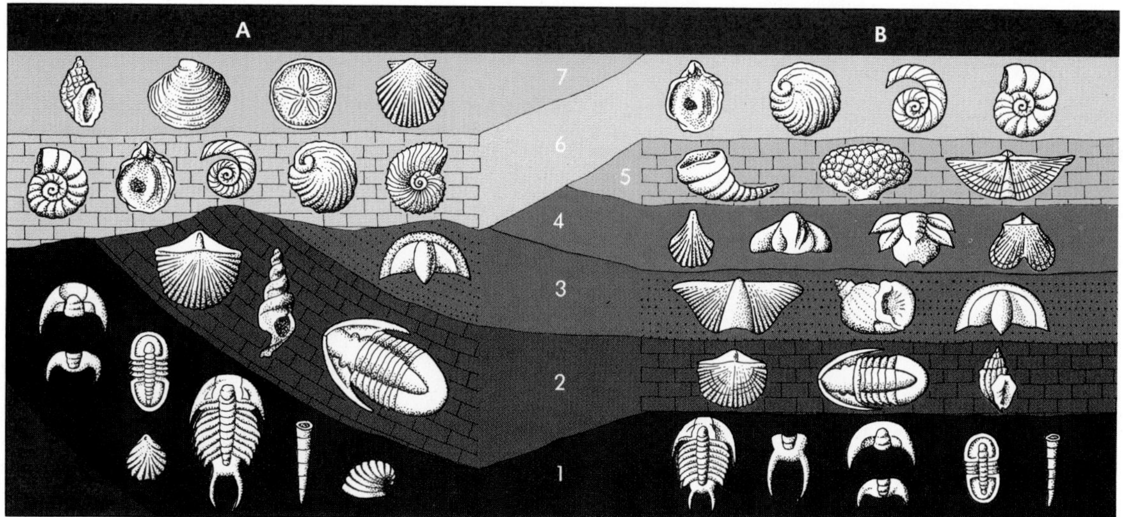

Fossils help geologists establish the relative geologic ages of layers of rock. In this diagram, sections A and B represent rock layers 200 miles apart. Their respective ages can be established by means of the fossils in each layer.

Huge swamps developed in many areas during the Pennsylvanian period, and the great coal deposits of the eastern United States formed in such areas. The climate was warm and humid. The first reptiles appeared, and insects grew to an enormous size.

During the Permian period, deserts became widespread. The climate of the northern continents was dry and warm, but ice sheets covered most of the southern continents. The number and kinds of reptiles began to increase at the close of the Paleozoic era.

At left are photographs of brachiopod (top) and trilobite (bottom) fossils as they appear in rocks. Drawings of these animals (top and bottom right) show details of their form and structure.

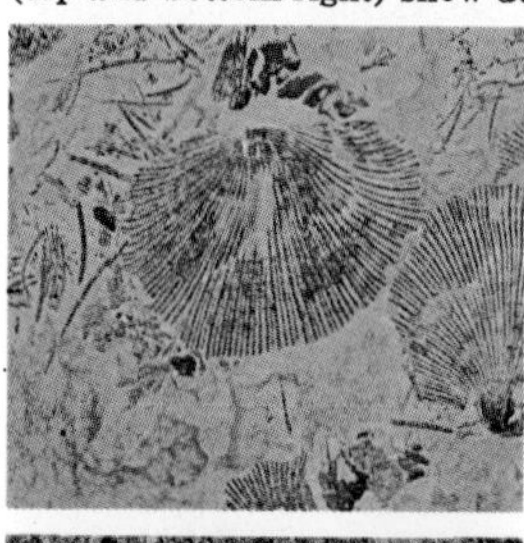

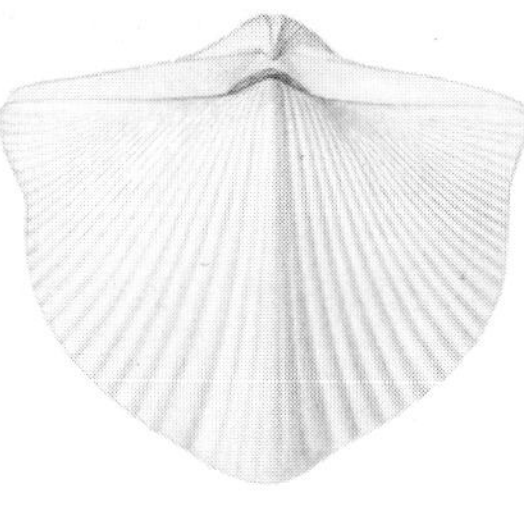

Bill Ratcliffe

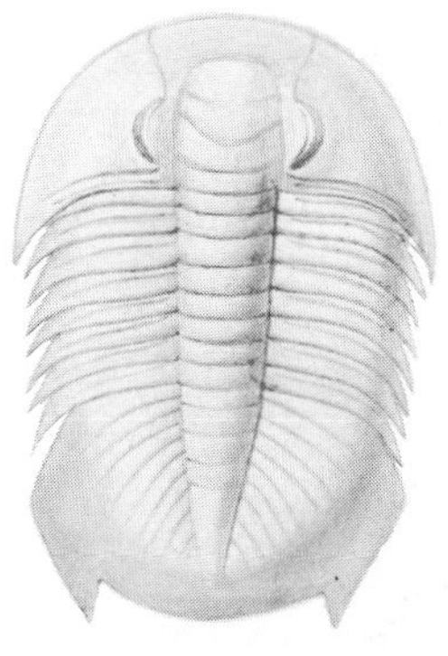

'Historical Geology', 3d Edition, by Dunbar and Waage

The Mesozoic Era

The Mesozoic era consists of three periods. From the earliest to the most recent, these are the Triassic, the Jurassic, and the Cretaceous. The Mesozoic era, which lasted about 160 million years, ended about 65 million years ago.

Many scientists believe that during the Mesozoic continents were formed from a supercontinent called Pangaea that existed during the Paleozoic. This view is a part of the continental drift theory, which suggests that the supercontinent began to break up during the Mesozoic. According to one version, the continental masses were sheared apart by the outward flow of mantle material from the mid-ocean ridges and moved somewhat like great plates.

Late in the Triassic period, which began about 225 million years ago, Pangaea broke up into two masses. The northern mass was called Laurasia; the southern mass, Gondwana. By the end of the Mesozoic, South America and Madagascar separated from Africa. Australia remained attached to Antarctica, and North America, Greenland, and Eurasia were connected. (*See also* subhead "The Continental Drift Theory.")

The Mesozoic is sometimes called the Age of Reptiles. Reptiles dominated the land, and the earliest dinosaurs appeared in the Triassic period. In their evolution, some reptiles invaded the seas or took to the air. Among the reptiles that remained on land were *Tyrannosaurus*, the most fearsome carnivore of all time, and *Brontosaurus*, one of the largest land animals that ever lived. (*See also* Reptiles.) *Archaeopteryx*, the first known bird, appeared during the Jurassic period, and the earliest mammals may have appeared late in the Triassic.

With the end of the Mesozoic era reptilian domination also came to an end. Many kinds of reptiles, including the dinosaurs, became extinct. Some kinds survived. The survivors included snakes, turtles, crocodiles, and lizards. No one knows exactly why these reptiles survived or why others disappeared. (*See also* Animals, Prehistoric.)

The Cenozoic Era

The Cenozoic era, which followed the Mesozoic, has continued into the present. It comprises the Tertiary and Quaternary periods, which began about 65 million and 2 million years ago, respectively. The Tertiary is further divided into the Paleocene, Eocene, Oligocene, Miocene, and Pliocene epochs; and the Quaternary into the Pleistocene and Holocene epochs. The names of epochs all end in the suffix "-cene," from the Greek *kainos,* meaning "recent." The Pleistocene epoch began about 2 million years ago and the Holocene about 10,000 years ago.

If the Mesozoic era was the Age of Reptiles, the Cenozoic was the Age of Mammals. Mammals that were similar to rhinoceroses and horses, called titanotheres, grew to great size. One genus, *Baluchitherium,* was the largest known land mammal. Remains found in Asia indicate that it stood 18 feet high at the shoulder and was more than 25 feet long. The earliest known horses, whales, and apes appeared in the Tertiary.

In the Quaternary much of the earth's surface—about a third of the land surface according to geologists' estimates—was covered by vast continental ice sheets. During four successive periods continental glaciers advanced over the Northern Hemisphere. These periods were separated by long warm periods called interglacials. In the Southern Hemisphere there were rainy periods called pluvials. These may have occurred at the same time as did glaciation in the North.

The glaciers had a profound effect on both the seas and the land. They lowered the sea level by about 300 feet, exposing large areas of shallow sea bottom. They affected the world's climates and shaped the earth's modern landscape. They formed lakes, including the Great Lakes, and built up thick deposits of till, or mixed clay, sand, gravel, and boulders.

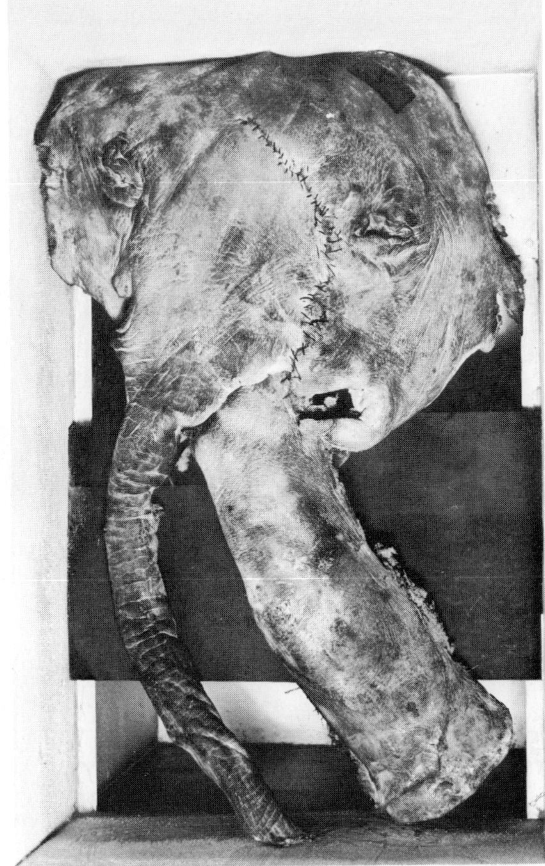

American Museum of Natural History, New York

The frozen remains of a baby woolly mammoth were dug out of the ground in Alaska. It may have been born more than 20,000 years ago when mammoths roamed the Arctic tundra.

Mankind's earliest appearance has been traced to the Quaternary. Archaeologists have found human skulls and other bones as well as stone implements and other artifacts dating from the period.

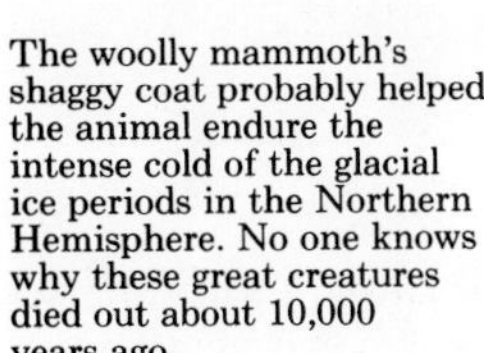

The woolly mammoth's shaggy coat probably helped the animal endure the intense cold of the glacial ice periods in the Northern Hemisphere. No one knows why these great creatures died out about 10,000 years ago.

Field Museum of Natural History, Chicago

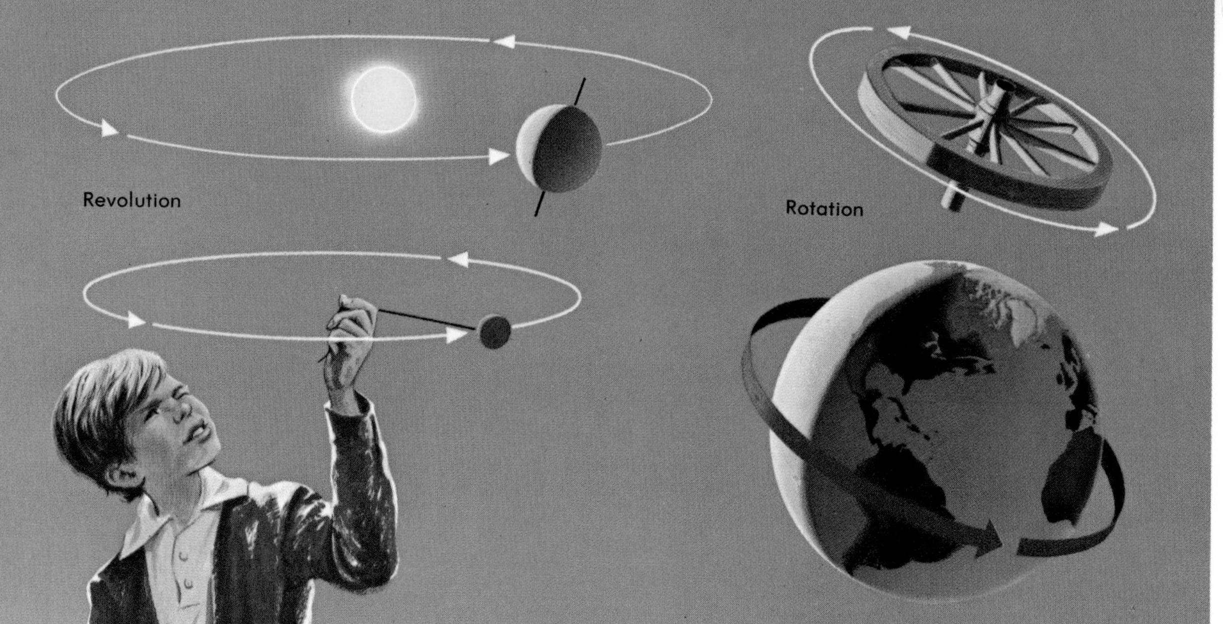

The earth's revolution—its yearly journey around the sun—is similar to the movement of a ball that is being whirled at the end of a string. The earth's rotation is like the motion of a wheel turning on its axle. The rotation of the earth makes the sun seem to rise in the east and set in the west.

The Moving Earth

THE WORDS rotation and revolution mean nearly the same thing. But in describing the earth's movements, each word is used for a different kind of motion. *Revolution* refers to the motion of the earth in its yearly orbit around the sun. *Rotation* refers to the spinning of the earth around its own axis each day.

In its revolution around the sun, the earth moves in a slightly elliptical orbit. At its closest point, called *perihelion,* the earth is 2 percent closer to the sun than its average distance from the sun. At its farthest point, called *aphelion,* it is 2 percent farther away than its average distance from the sun.

The Earth's Motion and the Seasons

The earth's revolution around the sun accounts for the changes of the seasons. The seasons have nothing to do with the earth's distance from the sun. Instead, they result from the fact that the earth's axis of rotation is slightly tipped compared to the plane of its orbit. The earth's axis is not perpendicular to the plane of its orbit—not "straight up and down"—but tilts away from this perpendicular plane by 23.45 degrees.

Although the earth moves almost in a circle around the sun, the North Pole always points in the same direction in space. As a result, at one time of the year (winter in the northern hemisphere), the North Pole is tilted away from the sun. Six months later (summer in the northern hemisphere), the North Pole is tilted toward the sun. The reason that the earth's axis of rotation remains constant is that the earth is actually a huge gyroscope (*see* Gyroscope).

The Earth's Motion and Time

The earth makes one rotation on its axis every 24 hours with reference to the sun. It is 24 hours from high noon on one day to high noon on the next. It takes 365.26 days—one year—for the earth to travel once around the sun. Calendars mark 365 days for most years, but every fourth year—leap year—has 366 days.

When observed from over the North Pole, the earth rotates and revolves in a counterclockwise direction. When observed from over the South Pole, the earth rotates and revolves in a clockwise direction.

The Earth's Motion and Weather

The earth's rotation is responsible for weather patterns. The atmosphere receives energy from the sun for its constant movement. Warm air near the equator expands and rises, and the air near the poles cools and sinks. If the earth were not rotating, the circulation might be rather simple. There would be a steady wind from the north in the northern hemisphere and a steady south wind in the southern hemisphere.

These generally prevailing wind currents are also disturbed by *cyclones*—large, swirling masses of air that rotate like huge eddies in the atmosphere. Concentrated cyclones in the Atlantic Ocean are called

The tilt of the earth's axis, which always remains at the same angle, causes the seasons by varying the amounts of heat and light that can reach each hemisphere.

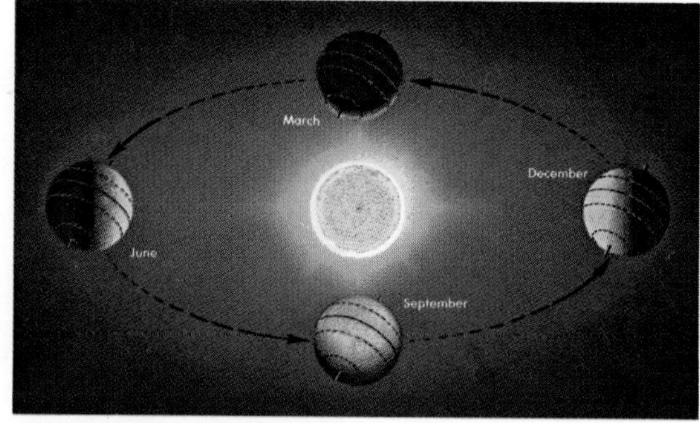

hurricanes. Those that occur in the Pacific Ocean, are called *typhoons*.

The rotation of the earth affects cyclones by means of an apparent process called the *coriolis effect*. The coriolis effect causes a deflection in the motion of any object moving on or near the earth's surface.

In the Northern Hemisphere, in the earth's lower latitudes, about 30 degrees from the equator, the air near the earth's surface starts its journey by moving down from high altitudes and heading for the equator. The coriolis effect bends the motion of this southward-moving wind to the *west* to create the winds that move *from the east*—the trade winds.

In the Northern Hemisphere, in the higher latitudes, between about 40 degrees and 65 degrees from the equator, the air near the earth's surface also starts its journey by moving down from high altitudes and heading for the pole. The coriolis effect bends the motion of this northward-moving wind to the *east* to create the winds that move *from the west*—the prevailing westerlies. In the Southern Hemisphere, the same phenomena occur, but in the opposite directions.

Low-pressure areas may develop. They act like huge vacuum cleaners, sucking air in from all directions. Sometimes the low-pressure effect and the coriolis effect combine and the swirling motion can become so violent that a great storm, such as a hurricane, develops.

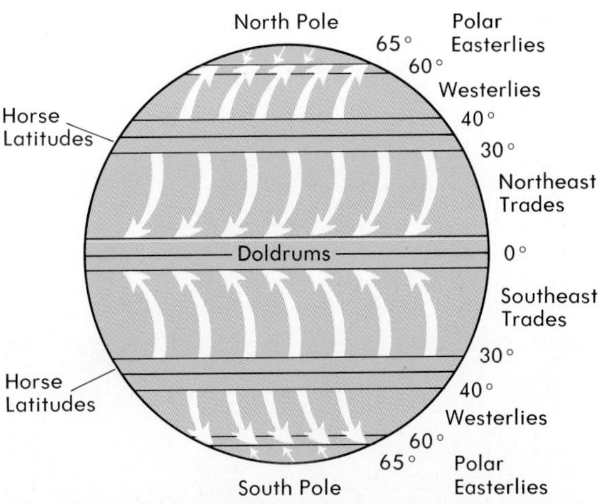

The arrows show the usual direction of surface winds. Winds in the northern hemisphere move clockwise. Those in the southern hemisphere move counterclockwise.

The Earth's Motion and the Magnetic Field

Many scientists believe that the rotation of the earth may be a factor in creating the earth's magnetic field. From the study of seismic waves, scientists have deduced that the earth's core is molten. They also reason that it must be made of a heavy substance, such as iron. It also seems possible that large, slow-moving eddies of molten iron are swirling in the core. This characteristic of the core could result from a combination of the heat being generated in the earth's interior by radioactive elements and the rotation of the earth.

If this theory is correct, it could account for the earth's magnetic field. The swirling eddies of molten iron in the core would act somewhat like an electromagnet and could create the magnetic field.

The Earth's Motion and Gravity

Gravity is the most important force that governs the motion of the earth through space. It also keeps the moon in orbit around the earth, and the earth and all of the other planets in orbit around the sun. Scientists have learned that gravity also governs the motion of the sun in the Milky Way. They believe that it is probably the major factor in explaining the origin of the galaxies, the stars, and the planets.

The force of gravity is a two-way affair. The sun exerts a gravitational force upon the earth to keep it in orbit. The earth exerts an equal—but opposite—force upon the sun. Gravitational forces between the earth and the moon interact in much the same way.

The moon's gravity affects the whole planet earth. Just as the moon swings around the earth because of the earth's gravity, so the earth—to a smaller extent—swings around the moon because of the moon's gravity. The difference in the extent of the swing results from differences in the mass and distance. The earth's mass is 81 times as great as that of the moon. So as the moon swings one way in its orbit around the earth,

Hurricanes begin over warm ocean water. Air flowing over the ocean picks up heat and moisture and begins to rise. The apparent coriolis effect caused by the earth's rotation twists the rising air into a counterclockwise motion. The air may reach high altitudes before beginning to descend. In the center of the moving air is the eye, an area of calm.

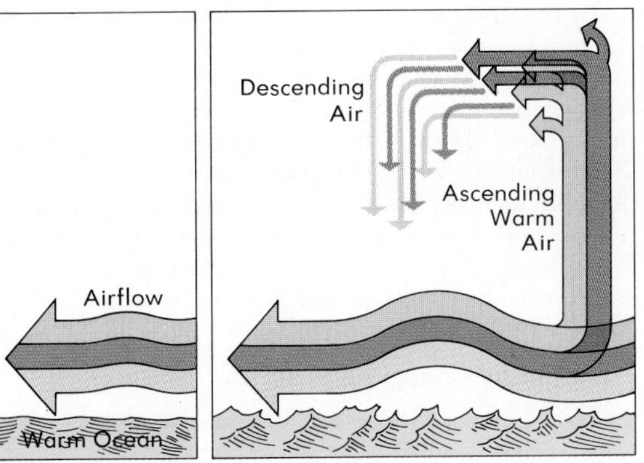

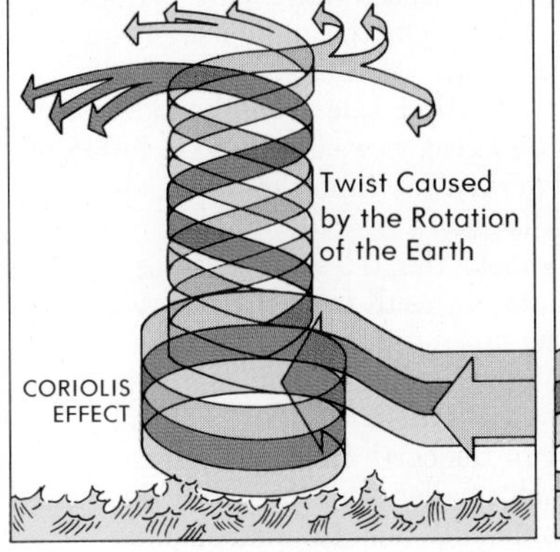

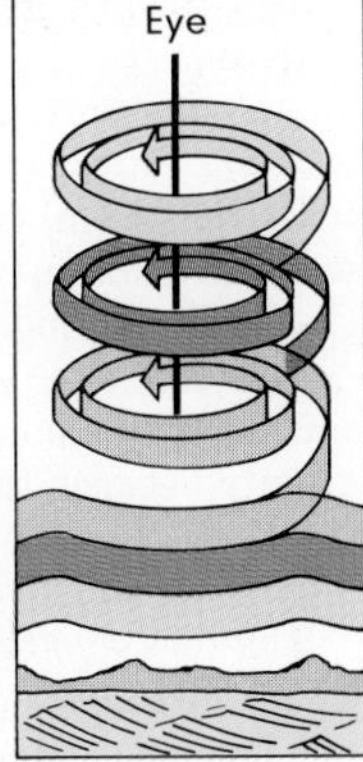

Dan Morrill—EB Inc.

Materials eroded from the Calico Mountains formed an alluvial fan in California's Mojave Desert.

the earth swings 1/81 as far in an answering orbit around the moon.

The actual center of rotation for the earth-moon system is about 500 miles (800 km.) below the earth's surface. Imagine a gigantic pin stuck through the earth, about parallel with the earth's true axis but about 3,500 miles (5,600 km.) from it—just barely through the edge of the earth. The earth and the moon rotate about this pin. The *center of the earth* is in balance with the gravitational attraction of the moon. The moon's effect complicates the earth's motion so that the earth does not move in a smooth path around the sun but has a monthly "wobble" as it moves in its joint orbit with the moon. (*See also* Gravitation.)

The moon's gravity causes daily ocean tides on both sides of the earth. On the side nearer to the moon, the gravity effect is stronger, so a bulge of water is pulled out on that side. On the side away from the moon, the effect is weaker, and a bulge of water extends outward, away from the moon. (*See also* Ocean Waves and Tides.)

The sun also affects the tides. Sun tides, much smaller than moon tides, result from the interaction of gravity between the sun and the earth. Twice a month the tidal effects of the sun and moon are combined. The earth's highest and lowest tides occur then.

The rocky body of the earth itself has tides. These earth tides are much smaller than the ocean tides and can be measured only with delicate instruments.

The Changing Earth

THE GREAT FEATURES of the earth seem permanent and unchanging. The giant mountain ranges, the long river valleys, and the broad plains have been known throughout recorded history. All appear changeless, but changes occur steadily. Small ones can be seen almost any day. The rivulets of mud that form on the side of a hill during a rainstorm move soil from one place to another. Sudden gusts of wind blow dust and sand around, redistributing these materials.

Occasionally, spectacular changes take place. A volcano erupts and spreads lava over the surrounding landscape, burying it under a thick layer of fresh rock. Earthquakes break the earth's crust, causing portions of it to slide and move into new positions.

In the lifetime of one man, or even in the generations of recorded history, these changes have been small compared to the changes that created mountains or the vast expanse of the prairie. But the recorded history of man covers only a short period of the earth's history. Scientists believe that the earth has existed for about 4.5 billion years. Man's recorded history extends back only about 6,000 years, or 0.0000013 percent of the earth's age. There is ample evidence that the earth's surface has changed greatly since its original formation. Even now it is continuing to change.

Weathering Changes the Earth

Weathering is the breakdown of large masses of rock into smaller and smaller pieces, and eventually into soil. One kind of weathering is mechanical. It occurs when some sort of force actually causes the rock to break apart.

Mechanical weathering may depend upon slight imperfections, usually fine cracks, that exist in the rock mass. Sometimes the fine roots of a tree, a bush, or almost any kind of plant reach into these tiny cracks. As the roots grow, they act as wedges that finally split the rock. Sometimes water seeps into the fine cracks of a rock and is held there. If the water freezes, it expands. The volume of water increases when it freezes, and in a confined space freezing water exerts much pressure. Even the small amount of water that a fine crack holds can exert enough pressure to crack a rock.

Temperature changes can help crack a rock. Exposed rocks are subjected to the heat of the sun during the day and to cool air at night. Seasonal changes, such as the heat of the summer and the cold of winter, also affect them. The outer surface of a rock expands and contracts as it heats and cools. The inside, which is protected, does not. Stresses between the changing outer layer and the stable inner layer can be strong enough to break the rock apart.

Chemical weathering occurs when chemicals in a rock react with water or with elements in the atmosphere. Most rocks contain some form of iron. Oxygen, one of the atmospheric gases, reacts readily with iron and causes it to rust. The oxidation of the iron in an exposed rock helps break it down.

Carbon dioxide, another gas in the air, combines with water seeping through a rock formation to form carbonic acid. This acid is able to dissolve and carry away the carbonates that are formed when carbon dioxide combines with various minerals. This process weakens the rock so that the whole structure eventually crumbles.

Water also weathers rock by *hydration*. In this process molecules of certain minerals absorb molecules of water and form a new mineral. Often, the resulting mineral is softer than the original, and again the structure of the rock is destroyed.

Even the wind can cause weathering. In the deserts, the wind blows sand particles against the rock faces of nearby mountains. This sandblasting action wears away the mountain rocks.

Geologic evidence shows that all the rocks on earth were originally igneous; that is, they were originally in a molten state. Some of the molten rock remained below the surface. But some was thrown out over the surface and exposed to weathering, which broke down the original rock into finer particles.

Erosion Changes the Earth

Erosion is a process of change that takes over after weathering. In erosion, material from a high place is moved to a lower one. The movement of water is the most common cause of erosion. Mountain streams carry weathered rock and dirt, called *sediment*, into the valleys. Much of this sediment is carried all the way to the sea.

Wide World Photos

From a hill denuded of vegetation, a mudslide—an aftermath of rainstorms—covers part of a California highway.

Examples of erosion are easy to find. During a rainstorm, soil washes out of a garden; mud puddles form at the bottom of a hill; sand is carried along the gutter at the side of a street. These are all instances of erosion. Streams and rivers are discolored by the eroded particles they carry. All give evidence of the movement of solid particles from one place to another.

Rain is a forceful agent of erosion. A single raindrop has a maximum speed of 25 miles per hour as it strikes the earth. The earth's average annual rainfall is about 33 inches, and it exerts a pressure of about a pound per square inch. Under extreme conditions, a hard rainfall may dislodge and move as much as 100 tons of earth per acre.

A river collects water from a broad area around it called a *watershed*. For example, the watershed of the Missouri and Mississippi River system comprises almost all of the central plains of the United States. Rain that falls in the plains area collects in this river system and eventually is deposited in the Gulf of Mexico.

Some rainwater evaporates back into the atmosphere. Some sinks into the ground and travels underground to a river. But a large proportion of the rainwater flows over the earth's surface. All moving water, the garden rivulet as well as the mighty river, carries sand and soil that it picks up from the land through which it moves. In this way, land is gradually worn away and carried out to sea.

Water that moves rapidly erodes the land much more quickly than does water that moves slowly. The swift mountain streams are much more efficient in moving the soil than are the slow-moving rivers in flatlands. Except where rainfall is slight, as in the southwestern United States, mountains and hills are generally being eroded at a much faster rate than are the plains.

Sometimes erosion is quick and spectacular. Tons of material may suddenly slide downhill in mud slides and avalanches. Usually these occur because water has weakened part of the basic structure. Mud slides generally take place after a heavy rainfall. Some avalanches result from the freezing and thawing of water, which cracks and loosens the rocky structure of part of the mountainside.

An enormous amount of material eroded from the land is carried out to sea by the rivers. This material is in the form of very fine particles called *silt*. The silt is kept in suspension in the water by the river's *turbulence*, a steady stirring motion. Even the slowest-moving river has some turbulence and carries silt.

When the river reaches the sea, the turbulence stops and the silt gradually sinks to the bottom as sediment. In some places this happens near the edge of the ocean, where the river meets the sea. Then a *delta* forms. Two famous deltas are those at the mouths of the Mississippi River and the Nile River.

The Amazon River also carries a large quantity of silt, but no delta has formed at its mouth. The reason for this is that the Amazon empties into the Atlantic Ocean, which has rather high tides. The Mississippi empties into the Gulf of Mexico, the Nile into the Mediterranean Sea. These two rather small portions of the oceans have almost no tidal motion. Tidal motion creates turbulence and keeps silt suspended until it is carried far out to sea. There it slowly sinks to the bottom.

Rivers carry many tons of silt to the sea each day. This means that the mass of material on the earth's surface is steadily being redistributed. Over millions of years, the weight of the portion of the crust bearing the mountains has been decreasing. The weight of the material near the mouths of major rivers has been increasing. The parts of the crust near the mouths of rivers tend to sink into the yielding mantle beneath, and the mantle tends to push up under the lightening mountain ranges. The weighty edges of the continental shelf will continue to sink and the mountain areas will continue to rise, as predicted by the theory of isostasy.

In spite of the theory, however, such changes do not always occur. The Appalachian Highlands, for example, are no longer growing though they are being steadily eroded. This means that other forces within the earth's interior bring about changes, and the mass movement resulting from erosion is only one of many effects that shape the details of the crust.

Glaciers also contribute to erosion. Glaciers are bodies of ice. They are formed on high mountains when blankets of snow that never melt away completely accumulate year after year. The weight of the top layers compresses the lower portion into ice. The force of gravity on the layers of snow and ice increases as the mass increases. Eventually, primarily as a result of the gravitational force, the mass may slowly begin to slide down the mountainside. Additional snows on the mountain continue to feed the glacier.

These bodies of ice, sometimes called rivers of ice, move much more slowly than do rivers of liquid water. Some slip downward only a fraction of an inch a day. Others, however, during the summer, may move up to fifty feet a day. But whether they move slowly or quickly, they are powerful erosive agents. They scrape

Movements of the earth's crust along the San Andreas Fault in California cause earthquakes along the West coast.

By courtesy of the U. S. Geological Survey

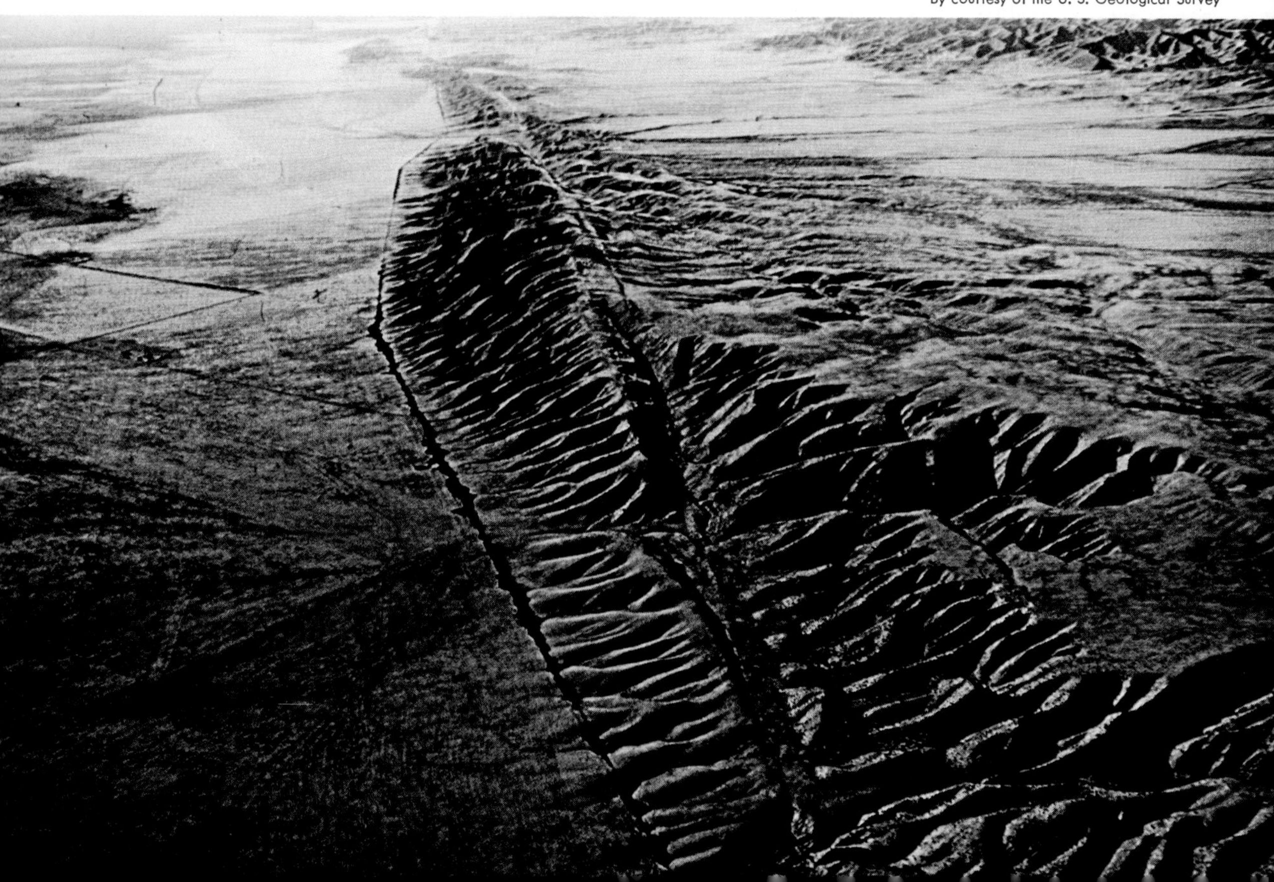

These pictures show the birth of Surtsey Island off the coast of the Vestmann Islands in the North Atlantic Ocean. The island rose from the sea on Nov. 14, 1963, with explosive eruptions of ash and steam. Thin streams of basaltic lava created towering steam clouds. By the end of 1964, the island was 568 feet high and covered an area a mile square.
Solarfilma

away the sides of the valleys through which they move, carrying huge rocks and boulders. Boulders caught under the ice and pushed along by glaciers are usually smooth and rounded and often look polished. Some of the debris caught underneath glaciers is ground into a fine powder which is sometimes called glacial flour.

Glaciers in the Far North and Far South move all the way to the sea. Like the rivers of the earth, they carry all the eroded material down to the ocean and dump it on the ocean floor.

Earthquakes Change the Earth

Erosion changes the details of the earth's surface in a slow, steady process, but earthquakes and volcanoes bring about rapid changes. Geologists attach great importance to the fact that earthquakes and volcanoes are concentrated in rather narrow zones across the surface of the earth. The same zones contain the young and growing mountain systems.

An earthquake occurs when two neighboring slabs in the earth's crust suddenly slip, one in one direction, the other in the opposite direction. The crack along which they slip is called the earthquake *fault*. It can be straight up and down or tilted over at an angle.

Several kinds of motion may take place in the slip. One is *vertical displacement*, in which one side moves up and the other side down. A second is a *sideways movement*. The San Andreas Fault in California is an example of this. A huge slab of the earth on the western side of the fault is moving northward compared to the slab on the other side of the fault. A third way is a *squeezing action*, when two slabs on both sides of a broad fault zone move closer together. The area between them folds and crumples, and a complicated system of cracks develops. Still another possible kind of motion is a separation. In this case the two slabs of the crust move apart, like those under the two mountain ranges that border Death Valley. Although earthquakes seem to occur suddenly, the force that causes them builds up over many years. The rock layers accumulate stress, which may cause them to bend. When the stress limit is reached, the layers crack. (*See also* Earthquake.)

Volcanoes Change the Earth

Like earthquakes, volcanoes cause sudden changes in the earth's surface features. When a volcano erupts, hot molten rock and ashes are pushed out from the interior of the earth through a hole or crack in the surface. The molten rock pours out of the crack and flows across the earth's surface, covering everything in its path. Ashes blown out of the volcano settle in deep layers nearby. But some of the fine ash is blown out with such force that it goes into the upper atmosphere. Winds may carry it for hundreds of miles. (*See also* Volcanoes.)

When lava from a volcano solidifies, it is called *igneous rock*, which means rock formed by heat. Much of the earth's crust is igneous rock, but only a small part of the rock came from volcanoes. Most of it formed when molten rock was pushed up from the interior of the earth and cooled beneath the surface.

Sedimentary rock is another type of rock that is found on and near the earth's surface. Sedimentary rock is the result of erosion. It usually forms from igneous rock that has been weathered and eroded away from the mountains and hills. (*See also* Rock.)

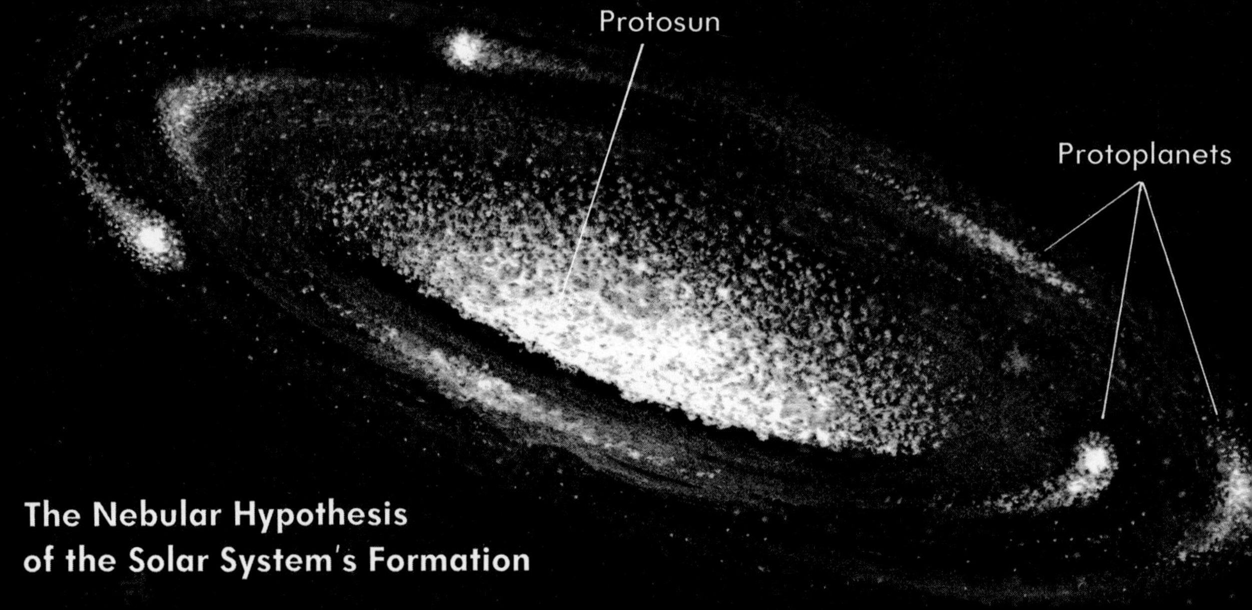

According to the nebular hypothesis of the solar system's formation, swirling clouds of dust and gas were drawn together by gravity. The largest mass of swirling material became the sun, and other masses eventually became planets.

The Forming Earth

MAN IS DEEPLY interested in knowing when and how the earth was formed. No one has yet found a completely satisfactory scientific explanation, but several theories have been advanced.

The Two-Star Theory

The two-star theory suggests that the earth might have been formed when two stars passed quite close to each other. Their gravitational attraction would cause huge tides on the surface of each, and great masses of material might be pulled from the surface. These would be left circling each star and would eventually solidify into planets.

Scientists used computers to test this theory. They concluded that after the stars had passed each other most of the material pulled out would fall back into them. Very little, if any, would remain to circle outside.

The Cloud Theory

Most scientific work has centered on the theory that the sun and planets were formed by the slow condensation of a gigantic cloud of dust and gas. Such clouds exist in the Milky Way and other galaxies. It seems reasonable that the gravitational attraction among the cloud's particles would gradually pull them together. Thus, the observation of dust and gas clouds serves as a starting point for the *nebular hypothesis* of the solar system's formation.

As the cloud of gas and dust became more concentrated because of its own gravity, the particles would move closer to each other. They would also start swirling faster and faster around the center.

At first, all the particles would have their own direction and speed, although one direction would be favored. Through constant collisions they would slow down and change direction until a swirling disk slowly would be formed.

Each collision would cause the particles to lose a little of their energy of motion and become heated. As a particle lost energy, it would move closer to the center of the disk. At the same time, its speed around the center would increase. The idea is similar to the movement of water going down a drain. Water far from the drain does not seem to swirl, but near the center of the drain it moves in a small whirlpool. In the forming solar system, this central whirlpool became the sun. It was surrounded by a rotating disk of gas and dust, somewhat like the rings around Saturn.

The theory suggests that a second and a third stage then took place. Other centers of concentration began to develop. Some of these became the planets, others the moons that circle the planets. Several theories have been suggested to explain planetary formation, but none is completely satisfactory.

Most scientists believe that the nebular hypothesis is basically correct. But many details have not yet been explained in terms of this theory.

The Age Theories

Age is an important factor in any theory about the earth's formation. If modern theories are correct, all parts of the solar system would be about the same in age. All would have formed within a few hundred million years of one another.

Scientists estimate the earth's age by measuring the ratios of various radioactive elements in rocks. The oldest earth rocks tested thus far are about $3\frac{1}{3}$ billion years old. But no one knows whether these are the oldest rocks on earth. Tests on rocks from the moon and on meteorites show that these are about 4.5 billion years old. Scientists believe that this is the true age of the solar system and probably the true age of the earth.

The Continental Drift Theory

One of the most important theories is the theory of continental drift. The most widely held version of this theory suggests that the continents originally formed one huge plate. This plate broke up about 200 million years ago. Various sections slowly drifted away, floating on top of the supporting mantle. The most striking evidence for the theory is the close "fit" between the eastern edges of the continents of North and South America and the western edges of the continents of Europe and Africa.

Oceanographers measuring the floor of the Atlantic Ocean have found evidence to support the continental drift theory. They have discovered small magnetic fields connected with veins of iron ore on the ocean floor (*see* Magnets and Magnetism). Such magnetic fields have also been found in rocks on the continents. They were "locked in" when the minerals solidified.

Originally, the magnetic fields lined up with the earth's magnetic field. After the rocks solidified, they were moved about in the crust. They carried their original magnetic field with them but were no longer affected by the general magnetic field of the earth. Maps of the locked-in magnetism make it possible to determine the position of a huge mass of rocks when it first solidified.

Measurements taken on the ocean floor show that it is spreading on both sides from the center. This is extremely important evidence in support of the theory that the continents have been moving apart.

The continental drift theory has also been used to explain earthquakes, volcanoes, and mountain building. The western edge of the United States and the eastern edge of Asia seem to mark the boundaries of moving blocks in the earth's crust. The theory is that as these blocks slowly move across the earth's surface they tend to crack and crumble along the edges. This could account for the concentration of earthquakes in these regions and perhaps for the fact that young mountains are being built nearby.

It might also account for the presence of volcanoes in such regions. Friction between the moving blocks generates heat. The heat could melt underlying strata of rock, turning them into magma. The magma could then be forced up through the surface and flow out of the volcanoes as lava.

Scientists Study the Earth

EARTH SCIENCE comprises many specialized fields. These fields of study overlap, and the findings of one field are often applied to the problems of other fields.

The Development of Earth Studies

Geology, the broadest of all the fields of earth science, has a very ancient history. The Greek philosophers proposed many theories to account for the form and origin of the earth. Eratosthenes, a scientist of ancient Greece, made the first accurate measurement of the earth's diameter.

The ancient philosophers were impressed by volcanoes and earthquakes. Some of their attempts to explain these phenomena sound very strange today. Aristotle, for example, speculated that earthquakes resulted from winds within the earth caused by the earth's own heat and heat from the sun. Volcanoes, he thought, marked the points at which these winds finally escaped from inside the earth into the atmosphere.

Careful observation of the earth's details and their implications began with the Renaissance. Leonardo da Vinci, the great Renaissance artist, made many such observations.

René Descartes, a French philosopher and mathematician of the 1600's, advanced the first modern theory to account for the formation of the solar system. He suggested that the planets had condensed from hot balls of rock and gas that were originally somewhat like the sun.

These maps—reconstructed from computerized information—show how the present-day continents may have originated in a giant landmass. The theory of the drifting apart of continents is only one of many about how the earth has changed.

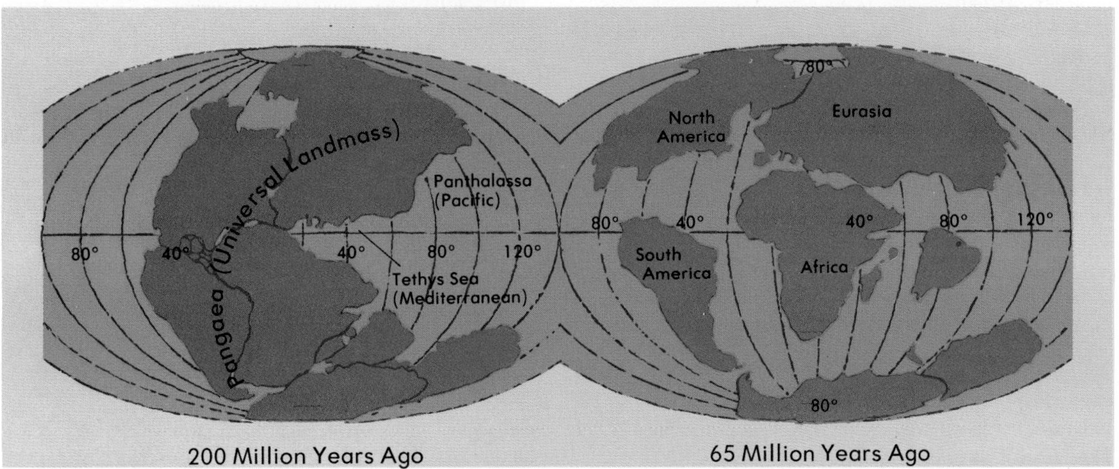

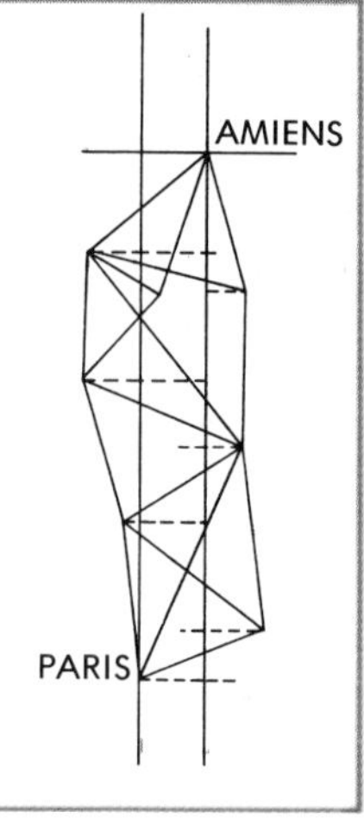

The 17th-century French astronomer Jean Picard made the first accurate measurement of the distance between two French cities by means of triangulation. The drawing shows the instrument he used, and the diagram shows the method of triangulation. In a book on earth measurement, published in 1671, Picard gave the figure for a degree of longitude.

In the 1800's, geologists began to specialize. Paleontologists concentrated on the story told by fossils. Mineralogists analyzed the details of rocks.

Among the intellectual giants of this time was William Smith, a British engineer. Almost as a hobby, he made a complete geologic map of England. His work and his methods made an enormous contribution to the science of geology.

Charles Darwin, one of the most famous scientists of all time, combined geology and biology in his career. Darwin began his professional work as a geologist but is remembered as a biologist—the creator of the theory of evolution.

Some Major Fields of Earth Study

During the 1900's, further specialization took place within the science of geology, mainly because of the increase in knowledge. In addition, the development of special instruments made possible detailed studies in many areas.

Geophysicists study the physical processes that occur within the earth, especially those that occur deep inside the earth.

Mineralogists study the nature of rocks in detail. They try to find out how minerals form and what clues might help locate them.

Geochemists study the chemistry of rocks and try to explain concentrations of minerals, such as those that occur in veins of gold or silver.

Stratigraphers map out the strata, or layers, of the different kinds of rock that make up various rock formations.

Seismologists and *volcanologists* study the dramatic aspects of crustal motion—earthquakes and volcanoes.

Oceanographers study the sea. They are concerned with the ocean waters and with the ocean basins.

Meteorologists study the earth's atmosphere and the weather and their effects on the land.

Paleontologists study the fossil remains of ancient plants and animals. Their findings are the basis for a calendar of the earth's history stretching back over the last 600 million years. (*See also* Geology.)

BIBLIOGRAPHY FOR EARTH

Books for Children

Asimov, Isaac. How Did We Find Out the Earth Is Round? (Walker, 1972).
Attenborough, David. Discovering Life on Earth (Little, 1982).
Jennings, Gary. The Earth Book (Harper, 1974).
Jennings, Gary. Killer Storms (Harper, 1970).
Lambert, David. The Active Earth (Lothrop, 1982).
Lampton, Christopher. Planet Earth (Watts, 1982).
Marks, Graham. The World Is Round (Michael Joseph, 1984).
Scarry, Huck. Our Earth (Wanderer, 1984).
Selden, Paul. The Face of the Earth (Children's, 1982).
Watson, Nancy and others. Our Violent Earth (National Geographic, 1982).

Land Formations

Bains, Rae. Forests and Jungles (Troll, 1985).
Brandt, Keith. Deserts (Troll, 1985).
Lauber, Patricia. Earthquakes (Random, 1972).
Marcus, Elizabeth. All About Mountains and Volcanoes (Troll, 1984).
Naden, C.J. I Can Read About Caves (Troll, 1979).
Rydell, Wendy. All About Islands (Troll, 1984).
Sabin, Francene. Arctic and Antarctic Regions (Troll, 1985).
White, A.T. All About Rocks and Minerals (Random, 1963).

Rivers and Oceans

Bains, Rae. The Wonders of Rivers (Troll, 1981).
Bramwell, Martin. Oceans (Watts, 1984).
Lauber, Patricia. Junior Science Book of Icebergs and Glaciers (Garrard, 1961).
Nixon, H.H. and J.L. Land Under the Sea (Dodd, 1985).
Updegraffe, Imelda and Robert. Seas and Oceans (Penguin, 1983).

Books for Young Adults and Teachers

Branley, F.M. The Earth (Crowell, 1966).
Cattermole, Peter and Moore, Patrick. The Story of the Earth (Cambridge Univ. Press, 1984).
Jeffreys, Harold. The Earth: Its Origins, History, and Physical Constitution, 6th ed. (Cambridge Univ. Press, 1976).
Lyttleton, R.A. The Earth and Its Mountains (Wiley, 1982).
O'Donnell, J.J. Earthly Matters (Messner, 1982).
Pough, F.H. A Field Guide to Rocks and Minerals, 4th ed. (Houghton, 1976).
Selby, M.J. Earth's Changing Surface (Oxford, 1985).
Stanley, S.M. Earth and Life Through Time (W.H. Freeman, 1985).
Tuttle, S.D. Landforms and Landscapes, 3rd ed. (W.C. Brown, 1980).
Walker, J.C. History of the Earth (Jones and Bartlett, 1985).
Wegener, Alfred. The Origin of Continents and Oceans (Dover, 1966).
York, D. Planet Earth (McGraw, 1975).
Zim, H.S. Caves and Life (Morrow, 1978).

(*See also* bibliographies for **Geography** and **Geology.**)

EARTHQUAKE. The sudden shaking of the ground that occurs when masses of rock change position below the Earth's surface is called an earthquake. The shifting masses send out shock waves that may be powerful enough to alter the surface of the Earth, thrusting up cliffs and opening great cracks in the ground.

Earthquakes, called temblors by scientists, occur almost continuously. Fortunately, most of them can be detected only by sensitive instruments called seismographs. Others are felt as small tremors. Some of the rest, however, cause major catastrophes. They produce such tragic and dramatic effects as destroyed cities, broken dams, earth slides, giant sea waves called tsunamis, and volcanic eruptions. A very great earthquake usually occurs at least once a year in some part of the world.

On the average about 10,000 people die each year from earthquakes. According to a study carried out by the United Nations and covering the years 1926 to 1950, there were 350,000 deaths, and property damage losses exceeded 10 billion dollars. As cities expand to shelter a rapidly increasing world population, it is likely that there will be even greater losses of life and property in spite of improved methods of detection and better warning systems. Mankind has long been concerned about earthquake hazards. The oldest chronicle comes from the Chinese as early as the Shang Dynasty more than 3,000 years ago.

Although it is certain that violent Earth tremors in themselves are destructive, there are often other kinds of Earth movements that are triggered by earthquake shock waves. Thus, the violent shaking that accompanies many earthquakes often causes rockslides, snow avalanches, and landslides. In some areas these events are frequently more devastating than the Earth tremor itself.

Floods and fires are also caused by earthquakes. Floods arise from tsunamis along coast lines, from large-scale seiches in enclosed bodies of water such as lakes and canals, and from the failure of dams. Fire produced the greatest property loss following the 1906 San Francisco earthquake, when 521 blocks in the city center burned uncontrollably for three days. Fire also followed the 1923 Tokyo earthquake, causing much damage and hardship for the citizens.

Causes

Most of the worst earthquakes are associated with changes in the shape of the Earth's outermost shell, particularly the crust. These so-called tectonic earthquakes are generated by the rapid release of strain energy that is stored within the rocks of the crust, which on continents is about 22 miles (35 kilometers) thick (*see* Continent). A small proportion of earthquakes are associated with human activity. Dynamite or atomic explosions, for example, can sometimes cause mild quakes. The injection of liquid wastes deep into the Earth and the pressures resulting from holding vast amounts of water in reservoirs behind large dams can also trigger minor earthquakes.

The strongest and most destructive quakes, however, are associated with ruptures of the Earth's crust, which are known as faults. Although faults are present in most regions of the world, earthquakes are not associated with all of them. Pressures from within the Earth strain the great rock masses beneath the Earth's surface. The strain builds until suddenly the masses move along faults, thereby releasing energy. The masses slip and slide in opposite directions along this fracture in the rock, shaking the ground above. The masses may move up and down, sideways, or vertically and horizontally. On the Earth's surface displacement of the ground may vary from several centimeters to many meters (1 centimeter = about 0.4 inch; 1 meter = about 3.3 feet). Some fault lines appear on the surface of the Earth (*see* Earth).

Shock Waves

The shifting rock in an earthquake causes shock waves—called seismic waves—to spread through the rock in all directions. In a great earthquake shocks may be felt by people thousands of kilometers away from the center (1 kilometer = about 0.6 mile). Detection and recording devices called seismographs can pick up the waves on the other side of the world.

There are two broad classes of seismic waves: interior and surface. In addition, there are three basic types of seismic waves. The primary waves, known as P waves, spread in the crust from the point of rupture, which is called the focus of the earthquake. The point on the Earth's surface immediately above the focus is termed the epicenter of an earthquake. P waves alternately compress and expand the rock through which they pass and vibrate in the same direction in which the waves travel. Secondary waves, known as S waves, vibrate at right angles to the direction of wave travel. These secondary waves are the "shake" waves that move particles up and down or from side to side. The speed of S waves is always less than that of P waves. By comparing the arrival times of both P waves and S waves at seismological observatories, scientists can determine the location of an earthquake many thousands of kilometers away. Finally, after both P and S waves have moved through the body of the Earth, they are followed by two types of surface waves known as L (I) and L (II) waves. Because of their larger amplitude, these L waves are responsible for much of the destructive shaking that occurs far from the epicenter. These surface waves, which travel more slowly than the interior waves, are the most powerful shock waves.

The focus of an earthquake may occur from quite close to the surface down to a maximum depth of about 435 miles (700 kilometers). More than 75 percent of the seismic energy produced each year, however, is

This article was contributed by Charles W. Finkl, Jr., Professor of Geology, Florida Atlantic University, Boca Raton, and Executive Director, Coastal Education and Research Foundation, Fort Lauderdale, Fla.

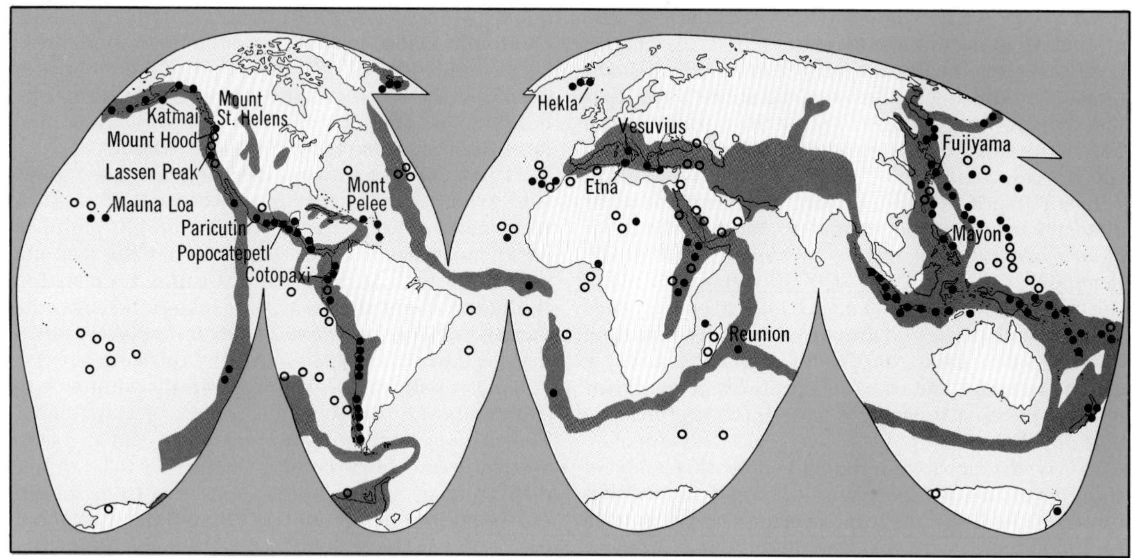

Earthquake zones are marked in red. Black dots indicate active volcanoes and open dots dead ones.

released by earthquakes with foci less than about 37 miles (60 kilometers) deep. These are the dangerous earthquakes that pose a significant hazard to populated regions. They are known as shallow-focus earthquakes.

Measurement

A seismograph records the pattern of shock waves on a revolving drum of paper. These wavy lines show the strength of the various seismic waves and the times at which they occur. The tracing is called a seismogram. The study of earthquakes is seismology.

The seismograph is basically a heavy pendulum with a stylus, or needle, suspended above or in front of a revolving drum. A damping mechanism, either mechanical or electromagnetic, helps keep the pendulum steady. During an earthquake the pendulum and needle remain stable while the drum on the base moves, recording the wave patterns. In some seismographs a ray of light traces the pattern on photographic paper.

Some instruments, such as the electromagnetic pendulum seismometer, record induced tension that passes through an electronic amplifier to a recording galvanometer. A photographic seismic recorder scans a rapidly moving film, making sensitive time-movement registrations. Refraction and reflection waves are usually recorded on magnetic tapes, which are readily adapted to computer analysis. Strain seismographs, employing electronic measurement of the change in distance between two concrete pylons about 30 meters (100 feet) apart, can detect compressional and extensional movement in the ground during seismic vibrations. The Benioff linear strain seismograph detects strains related to tectonic processes, those associated with propagating seismic waves, and tidal yielding of the solid Earth. Still more recent inventions include rotation seismographs; tiltmeters; wide-frequency-band, long-period seismographs; and ocean-bottom seismographs.

Seismographs of exactly the same character are deployed at stations around the world to record signals from earthquakes and underground nuclear explosions. The World Wide Standard Seismograph Network incorporates some 125 stations.

The strength of an earthquake may be measured either by the amount of damage done or by instrument readings. The Modified Mercalli Intensity Scale is commonly used by seismologists to determine the amount of destruction caused by an earthquake. It defines 12 levels of earthquake strength. The Richter Magnitude Scale grades earthquakes on a 1 to 10 scale. It is based upon the amount of energy released by the rock movements rather than upon surface damage.

The definition of magnitude in the Richter scale is "the logarithm, to the base 10, of the maximum seismic wave amplitude [in thousandths of a millimeter] recorded on a special seismograph called the Wood-Anderson, at a distance of 100 kilometers [62 miles] from the epicenter." The definition has been extended to permit the use of any calibrated seismograph at any distance. An increase of one magnitude step corresponds roughly to an increase of 30 times the amount of energy released as seismic waves. Thus, the energy of the 1964 Alaska earthquake, which had a magnitude of 8.6, is not twice as large as that in a shock of 4.3 magnitude, but rather the magnitude 8.6 earthquake releases more than 800,000 times as much energy as one of magnitude 4.3

It is estimated that 9.0 is the upper limit that can be produced by tectonic means in the Earth. At the other end of the scale, magnitude 2 is about the smallest earthquake that can be felt by humans without instrumental assistance. Each year there are between 18,000 and 22,000 shallow-focus earthquakes of magnitude 2.5 or greater.

Active Regions

Most earthquakes take place on one of two great earthquake belts that girdle the world. The belts coincide with the more recently formed mountain ranges and with belts of volcanic activity. One earthquake belt circles the Pacific Ocean along the mountainous west coasts of North and South America and runs through the island areas of Asia. A second, less active belt is between Europe and North Africa in the Mediterranean region and includes portions of Asia.

The world's major earthquakes occur within well defined, long, narrow zones between which lie large areas of little seismic activity. These areas of little activity are known as aseismic zones. The long, narrow seismic zones correspond generally to the location of mid-oceanic ridges and the so-called circumpacific ring of fire. The recently developed concept of plate tectonics in modern geology leaves little doubt that there is a causal relationship between the geometry of the world's tectonic plates and the geographical distribution of earthquakes.

Plate Tectonics

The Earth's crust is broken up into a number of separate plates, the edges of which rarely coincide with continental shorelines. These plate margins are extremely significant in earthquake studies. Major earthquakes located along active plate margins are associated with geophysical processes known as extrusion, subduction, and transcursion.

When a current of molten material from the upper mantle rises along the juncture of two adjoining plates, the plates move apart from the spreading center, which creates a rift valley filled with the molten material. This type of tectonic movement is known as extrusion; the rift is generally associated with the formation of a volcanic zone. One of the best examples of such a plate boundary is that which forms the Mid-Atlantic Ridge. It marks the zone where Africa was formerly joined to South America and where Europe split from North America some 200 million years ago. Mid-oceanic ridges are sites of numerous earthquakes, most of which take place below the seabed.

Although some plates are moving apart, some are moving toward each other. Accommodation of such movements involves the principle of overriding in which one plate passes above another in collision. When one plate is consumed into the deeper parts of the mantle, it is said to be subducted. Many submarine junctions are marked by an oceanic trench beneath which is a gigantic zone of thrusting. This is known as the Benioff zone. On the landward side of the oceanic trenches lie island arcs, as exemplified by the Aleutians and the Kuril Isles. These island chains are associated with the Earth's most active seismic zones.

A third type of tectonic movement known as transcursion occurs when two adjoining plates slide past one another along a series of tear or transcurrent faults. The best example of this type of junction is where the Pacific Plate is grinding transversely past the North American Plate, largely along the well-known San Andreas Fault of California. The San Andreas Fault of California is visible for many miles. It is a nearly continuous fracture extending 650 miles (1,050 kilometers) from southern California to Point Arena on the northern California coast. Beyond Point Arena it continues under the Pacific Ocean. The great San Francisco earthquake of 1906 occurred on this fault.

Even though scientists are in general agreement that the regions of greatest tectonic instability coincide with the marginal zones of slowly moving plates, it must not be assumed that major earthquakes occur only along plate margins. Severe earthquakes occur on

The cracked street (right) was the result of a series of earthquakes in southern Italy on Nov. 23-24, 1980, which jolted 179 communities and killed about 3,000 people. Building destruction (far right) was extensive in the severe earthquakes that shook Mexico City on Sept. 19-20, 1985. More than 20,000 persons were killed and 40,000 injured.

(Right) Ginies—Sipa/Special Features; (far right) © Xavier Garza—Picture Group

SOME NOTABLE EARTHQUAKES*

365—Knossos, Crete; 50,000 deaths.
526—Antioch, Syria; 250,000 deaths.
844—Damascus; 50,000 deaths.
847—Damascus; 70,000 deaths.
847—Mosul, Iraq; 50,000 deaths.
856—Qumis, Damghan, Iran; 200,000 deaths.
856—Corinth, Greece; 45,000 deaths.
893—Daipur, India; 180,000 deaths.
893—Ardabil, Iran; 150,000 deaths.
893—Caucasus, Russia; 82,000 deaths.
1042—Palmyra, Baalbek, Syria; 50,000 deaths.
1138—Ganzah, Aleppo, Syria; 230,000 deaths.
1201—Upper Egypt or Syria; 1,000,000 deaths.
1268—Cilicia, Anatolia; 60,000 deaths.
1290—China; 100,000 deaths; magnitude estimated at 6.75.
1293—Kamakura, Japan; 30,000 deaths.
1456—Naples, Italy; 60,000 deaths.
1531—Lisbon, Portugal; 30,000 deaths.
1556—Shaanxi Province, China; 830,000 deaths.
1667—Shemakha, Azerbaijan; 80,000 deaths; magnitude estimated at 6.9.
1668—Shantung Province, China; 50,000 deaths.
1693—Sicily, Catania, Italy; 100,000 deaths.
1703—Jeddo, Japan; 200,000 deaths.
1727—Tabriz, Iran; 77,000 deaths.
1730—Hokkaido, Japan; 137,000 deaths.
1731—Peking; 100,000 deaths.
1737—Calcutta, India; 300,000 deaths.
1755—Lisbon, Portugal; Spain; Morocco; 62,000 deaths.
1780—Tabriz, Iran; 100,000 deaths.
1783—Calabria, Italy; 50,000 deaths.
1811-12 —New Madrid, Mo.; 3 quakes; few deaths; magnitudes estimated at 8.4 to 8.7.
1828—Echigo (Honshu), Japan; 30,000 deaths.
1836—Northern Japan; 28,300 deaths; magnitude 7.6.
1847—Zenkoji, Japan; 34,000 deaths.
1857—Tejon Pass (Palmdale), Calif.; unknown number of deaths; magnitude estimated at 8.3.
1868—Ecuador; 70,000 deaths.
1883—Java; 100,000 deaths.
1905—India; 19,000 deaths; magnitude 8.6.
1906—San Francisco, Calif.; 700 deaths; magnitude 8.3.
1906—Valparaiso, Chile; 1,500 deaths; magnitude 8.6.
1908—Calabria, Messina, Italy; 58,000 deaths; magnitude 7.5.
1915—Abruzzi, Italy; 32,600 deaths; magnitude 7.5.
1920—Gansu Province, China; 200,000 deaths; magnitude 8.5.
1923—Tokyo; Yokohama; 99,000 deaths; magnitude 8.3.
1932—Gansu Province, China; 70,000 deaths; magnitude 7.6.
1935—India; 25,000 deaths; magnitude 7.5.
1939—Erzincan, Turkey; 32,000 deaths; magnitude 8.0.
1939—Chillan, Chile; 28,000 deaths; magnitude 8.3.
1948—Ashkhabad, Turkmen Soviet Socialist Republic; 19,-800 deaths; magnitude 7.3.
1949—Ecuador; 6,000 deaths.
1960—Agadir, Morocco; 12,000 deaths; magnitude 5.9.
1960—Puerto Montt, Valdivia, Chile; 2,200 deaths; magnitude 8.5.
1962—Northwestern Iran; 12,000 deaths.
1964—Prince William Sound, Alaska; 130 deaths; magnitude 8.3.
1970—Northern Peru; 66,800 deaths; magnitude 7.8.
1971—San Fernando, Calif.; 60 deaths; magnitude 6.4.
1972—Nicaragua; 5,000 deaths; magnitude 6.2.
1976—Northeastern Italy; 900 deaths; magnitude 6.5.
1976—Tangshan, China; 240,000 deaths; magnitude 7.8.
1977—Bucharest, Romania; 1,500 deaths; magnitude 7.2.
1979—Colombia; Ecuador; 600 deaths; magnitude 7.9.
1980—El Asnam, Algeria; 4,000 deaths; magnitude 7.7.
1980—Southern Italy; 4,800 deaths; magnitude 7.2.
1983—Eastern Turkey; 1,400 deaths; magnitude 7.1.
1985—Mexico City; 20,000 deaths; magnitude 8.1.
1986—San Salvador, El Salvador; 1,000 deaths; magnitude 5.4.
1988—Armenian Soviet Socialist Republic; 25,000 deaths; magnitude 6.9.
1989—San Francisco and Oakland, Calif.; 60 deaths; magnitude 6.9.
1990—Northwestern Iran; 40,000 deaths; magnitude 7.3.
1990—Northern Philippines; 1,000 deaths; magnitude 7.7.

*Numbers of deaths are approximate.

rare occasions with equally destructive force in zones of weakness within the plates. In the United States three earthquakes having magnitudes of 8.4 or higher occurred in the Mississippi River valley during the winter of 1811–12. No earthquakes larger than these have ever occurred within the coterminous United States during historic time. The magnitudes of the quakes were comparable to the largest California quakes and were felt over much larger areas. Strong quakes have also occurred within stable landmasses.

Forecasting

Of the many attempts to find clues for the prediction of the location, time, and size of an impending earthquake, best results seem to be associated with seismicity studies using earthquake observatories. Chinese researchers have achieved some success using, in part, animal restlessness for forewarning. Other methods, particularly those deployed in the United States, are based on detecting gaps in the seismic record of a region. Segments along a fault where displacement has not taken place for a long time, so-called temporal seismic gaps, are more likely to release built-up stresses in the future than are segments that have recently released internal pressures.

Application of this theory, however, depends on accurately determining a zero epoch with which to compare the average background occurrence rate. Another problem is that from short-term records it is impossible to predict with any accuracy the likely occurrence of major quakes in future years. Yet risk maps can be prepared for some earthquake-prone regions, as in California, where surface faults can be monitored. Although useful in transcursion zones, such as along the San Andreas Fault, the method is not applicable to subduction zones where seismic activity, generated deep in the Benioff zone, is only vaguely correlated with surface structures.

EARTH SCIENCES. The studies of the solid Earth and the water on and within it and the air around it are called Earth sciences. Included in the Earth sciences are the geological, the hydrological, and the atmospheric sciences, which are concerned respectively with the nature and behavior of the Earth itself, the water, and the air (*see* Earth; Geology; Ocean; Atmosphere).

The Earth sciences are basically physical sciences that utilize advances in mathematics, physics, chemistry, and, to a smaller extent, biology. Most of the Earth sciences make use of observations on a global scale, and for this reason many problems in the Earth sciences could be undertaken only when exploration of the Earth's surface was well advanced. In this connection great use has been made of satellite observations. Closely related fields of study include: geography and topography, which are concerned with description and interpretation of the Earth's physical features, and the economic and social interactions of mankind with the environment; and geodesy, the science of measuring the Earth (*see* Geography; Maps and Globes; Surveying).

Geology embraces a number of sciences. Among these is geomorphology, the study of the nature, origin, and processes of change of landforms such as the rising and subsiding of continents and mountains (*see* Continent; Mountain). Geophysics is concerned with the study of the physical phenomena of the Earth such as its magnetic field, the flow of heat from the interior, and the study of gravity, including tides. Seismology is the science of earthquakes (*see* Earthquake). Geochemistry studies the chemical composition of the Earth and the laws governing the distribution of elements within the Earth (*see* Minerals; Mines and Mining; Rock).

Meteorology, the study of the atmosphere, particularly for forecasting weather, can be considered as the branch of atmospheric physics concerned with the behavior and properties of the Earth's atmosphere. Satellite observations have proved of great use in gathering meteorological data, and powerful computers are employed to analyze the great quantities of data so gathered (*see* Weather; Wind; Cloud). Climatology, the study of past and present climates, is concerned with longer variations than those investigated by meteorologists and is now proving of practical importance in indicating the possible future growth of deserts and glaciated areas (*see* Climate; Desert).

Hydrology (derived from the Greek word for water, *hydor*) is concerned with the circulation of water in the atmosphere and the outer parts of the Earth (*see* Water). Groundwater is the term applied to water contained within the soil and bedrock, which together with lakes and rivers forms the principal store of fresh water available to mankind; glaciers comprise the remainder (*see* Lake; River; Glacier). Oceanography, the study of seas and oceans, began as an aid to navigation and fishing (*see* Oceanography).

EARTHWORM *see* WORM.

EASTER. The greatest festival of the Christian church commemorates the resurrection of Jesus Christ. It is a movable feast; that is, it is not always held on the same date. In AD 325 the church council of Nicaea decided that it should be celebrated on the first Sunday after the first full moon on or after the vernal equinox of March 21. Easter can come as early as March 22 or as late as April 25.

In many churches Easter is preceded by a season of prayer, abstinence, and fasting called Lent. This is observed in memory of the 40 days' fast of Christ in the desert. In Eastern Orthodox churches Lent is 50 days. In Western Christendom Lent is observed for six weeks and four days.

Ash Wednesday, the first day of Lent, gets its name from the practice, mainly in the Roman Catholic church, of putting ashes on the foreheads of the faithful to remind them that "man is but dust." Palm Sunday, one week before Easter, celebrates the entry of Jesus into Jerusalem. Holy Week begins on this day. Holy Thursday, or Maundy Thursday, is in memory of the Last Supper of Christ with his disciples. Good Friday commemorates the crucifixion.

Many Easter customs come from the Old World. The white lily, the symbol of the resurrection, is the special Easter flower. Rabbits and colored eggs have come from pagan antiquity as symbols of new life. Easter Monday egg rolling, a custom of European origin, has become a tradition on the lawn of the White House in Washington, D.C.

Lent may be preceded by a carnival season. The origin of the word carnival is probably from the Latin *carne vale,* meaning "flesh (meat), farewell." Elaborate pageants often close this season on Shrove Tuesday, the day before the beginning of Lent. This day is also called by its French name, *Mardi Gras* (Fat Tuesday).

The name Easter comes from *Eostre,* an ancient Anglo-Saxon goddess, originally of the dawn. In pagan times an annual spring festival was held in her honor. Some Easter customs have come from this and other pre-Christian spring festivals. Others come from the Passover feast of the Jews, observed in memory of their deliverance from Egypt (*see* Passover).

The word paschal comes from a Latin word that means "belonging to Passover or to Easter." Formerly, Easter and the Passover were closely associated. The resurrection of Jesus took place during the Passover. Christians of the Eastern church initially celebrated both holidays together. But the Passover can fall on any day of the week, and Christians of the Western church preferred to celebrate Easter on Sunday—the day of the resurrection.

	Ash Wed.		Easter			Ash Wed.		Easter	
1987	March	4	April	19	1992	March	4	April	19
1988	Feb.	17	April	3	1993	Feb.	24	April	11
1989	Feb.	8	March	26	1994	Feb.	16	April	3
1990	Feb.	28	April	15	1995	March	1	April	16
1991	Feb.	13	March	31	1996	Feb.	21	April	7

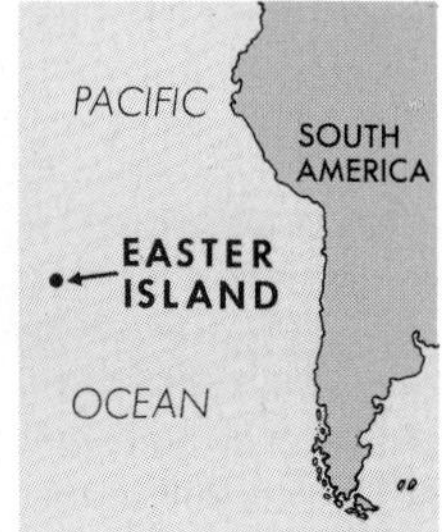

EASTER ISLAND. Far out in the South Pacific Ocean, about 2,350 miles (3,780 kilometers) west of Chile, lies Easter Island, one of the loneliest islands in the world. Its nearest inhabited neighbor is Pitcairn Island, 1,300 miles (2,100 kilometers) away. The inhabitants are survivors of a people who were once skilled workers in stone and wood and had a form of writing differing from any other known.

Scattered over this volcanic island of about 46 square miles (120 square kilometers) are many gigantic statues, each carved out of a single block of soft stone. Some are more than 30 feet (9 meters) high. Many have been transported several miles from the quarry in which they were carved and set up on great stone foundations. No one knows why these huge figures were carved, and for many years no one knew how they were moved. In 1957 the Norwegian scientist Thor Heyerdahl led an expedition to the island. The islanders showed Heyerdahl's party how such statues could be raised from the quarry using logs for levers and many small stones. Alternately jacking up the left and the right side of a statue while piling stones under it, they raised it to the top of the quarry. The pile of stones was removed when the statue was hauled upright. The statues were probably pulled to their sites on wooden sleds. Log levers and stones were again used to raise the statues onto their permanent platforms.

The island, called Rapa Nui by the inhabitants, was named Easter Island by a Dutch navigator, Jacob Roggeveen, who discovered it on Easter Day, 1722. Chile annexed it in 1888 and made it into a national park in 1935. Population (1985 estimate), 1,928.

The statues of Easter Island have survived a culture that existed centuries ago.

Life © Time Inc.

EASTERN ORTHODOX CHURCHES. In the year 1054 a major split occurred in Christianity. The churches in Western Europe, under the authority of the pope at Rome, separated from the churches in the Eastern Roman (or Byzantine) Empire, under the authority of the patriarch (bishop) of Constantinople. The churches of the Eastern Empire have come to be known by the collective term Eastern Orthodoxy. The word orthodoxy simply means "correct teaching," or "right belief." The official designation is actually Orthodox Catholic Church to set it off from the Roman Catholic church (*see* Eastern Rite Churches).

Organization

Eastern Orthodoxy is a fellowship of autonomous, or independent self-governing, churches, each of which is under the rule of a bishop. The patriarch of Constantinople (now Istanbul) is considered the first among equals, but he has no authority comparable to that of the Roman pope.

The number of independent churches has varied throughout history. Today there are the Church of Constantinople, the Church of Alexandria (Egypt), the Church of Antioch (headquartered at Damascus, Syria), the Church of Jerusalem, the Russian Orthodox Church, the Church of Georgia, the Church of Serbia, the Church of Romania, the Church of Bulgaria, the Church of Cyprus, the Church of Greece, the Church of Albania, the Polish Orthodox Church, and the Church of Czechoslovakia. There are also smaller autonomous churches in Finland, Crete, and Japan and many in the United States.

As can be noted from the names of the churches, many of them today exist in hostile surroundings. The Russian Orthodox Church has suffered severe persecution in the past, and it must now cooperate with the authorities of the Soviet Union in order to function. The church in Albania has been outlawed altogether. The churches in Turkey, Egypt, and the Middle East live as minorities amid large Muslim majorities. Eastern Orthodoxy in the United States is represented by almost every national Orthodox body, each having been brought to America by immigrants.

The Orthodox understanding of the church is based on the principle that each local community of Christians, gathered around its bishop and celebrating the Lord's Supper, or Eucharist, is a local realization of the whole church on Earth. This concept of wholeness is called catholicity. This may seem an abstract concept, but what it means essentially is that everything necessary to be a church is found in the local congregation. The idea of catholicity may be compared to a loaf of bread. Each single slice is not the whole loaf, but each slice has all the ingredients necessary to be bread. Hence, wherever a bishop and congregation are gathered together, there is the church.

This continuity of the church is demonstrated by the fact that the consecration of a bishop requires the presence of several other bishops. This testifies to the continuity of the whole church in the present and to its unbroken heritage from the time of the Apostles.

Besides bishops, there are two other orders of clergy—priests and deacons. These may be married men, though bishops are always chosen from among unmarried or widowed clergy.

Eastern Orthodoxy also has a strong tradition of monasticism, dating back to the 3rd and 4th centuries. It has been primarily a contemplative movement, seeking to experience God through a life of prayer. There has not been the development of religious orders with missionary or educational goals as in Western Christianity (*see* Monks and Monasticism).

Belief and Worship

Eastern Orthodoxy considers itself the bearer of an unbroken living tradition of Christian faith and worship inherited from the earliest believers. Its beliefs are based on consistency with the Bible and tradition as expressed in the ancient councils—the seven ecumenical church councils that took place between 325 and 787. The churches also accept the decrees of some later councils as reflecting the same faith (*see* Christianity; Church Councils).

The churches accept seven sacraments, or holy acts: baptism, chrismation (similar to confirmation), the Lord's Supper, ordination, penance, anointing of the sick (called extreme unction in the West), and marriage. This number of sacraments was never defined in the early church. It was only in response to the Protestant Reformers of the 16th century, who accepted only two sacraments, that the number seven was determined.

The sacrament of chrismation is peculiar to the Eastern churches. In it newly baptized infants are anointed with oil and immediately admitted to the Lord's Supper. In Western churches children must wait until they are older before receiving their first communion. In admitting infants the Orthodox churches maintain that baptism is the beginning of a new life that must be sustained by the Eucharist. When given communion, the bread is dipped in the wine—a procedure called intinction—and administered to, or placed on the tongue of, the recipient.

Liturgies. Forms of worship are called liturgies. The two chief eucharistic liturgies in the Orthodox churches are those of Saint John Chrysostom and of St. Basil the Great. Both acquired their present form in the 9th century. There is also a liturgy of St. James, often used in Jerusalem. All of the liturgies are elaborate, festive occasions.

The liturgies are divided into three segments. The first is a rite of preparation, during which the priest puts on a plate particles of bread symbolizing the gathering of the saints, both living and dead, around the living Christ. This is followed by the liturgy of the catechumens, or learners. This segment includes the reading of the lessons and the sermon. Finally comes the liturgy of the faithful, or baptized Christians, which includes the recitation of the creed and the administering of communion.

The Orthodox churches follow the traditional church calendar, the church year beginning with Advent, four Sundays before Christmas. The greatest festival is Easter. The date of Easter normally varies from its celebration in the West because the Eastern churches still use the Julian calendar to compute the date (*see* Calendar).

Courtesy of the Greek Orthodox Cathedral, London; photo A.C. Cooper Ltd.

The iconostasis in an Eastern Orthodox church separates the sanctuary, or altar area, from the congregation.

The Orthodox churches have a rich tradition of musical composition for hymns and liturgies. Since the tradition bans the use of musical instruments or accompaniment (with the exception of some American congregations), all singing is done without them.

Architecture. Some of the most beautiful and highly decorated church buildings in the world have been built by Christians of the Orthodox tradition. The first major house of worship, and still one of the great buildings of the world, was built during the reign of Emperor Justinian I in the 6th century at Constantinople (*see* Justinian). It is the Hagia Sophia, or Holy Wisdom. It consists of a huge round dome set atop a classical basilica-style building. Most Orthodox churches today have one or more domes. (For a picture of Hagia Sophia, *see* Architecture.) The Hagia Sophia was turned into a mosque by the Ottoman Turks, and later it became a museum.

The interior of an Orthodox church is somewhat different from other churches. In most Western churches the altar is readily visible from the entryway. But in Orthodox churches there is a screen, or wall, called an iconostasis, with one or more doors in it, largely concealing the altar area from the worshipers. It is called an iconostasis because it is richly decorated with icons in the form of pictures of Christ and the saints. Orthodox churches have no statues or other three-dimensional images. The purpose of the iconostasis is to suggest a contrast between the visible manifestation of God in Christ as a man and his more perfect and invisible presence in the communion.

It is largely because of its emphasis on the gathered community in worship that the Orthodox churches have survived in often hostile surroundings. For this reason it is impossible to overestimate the significance of the liturgy in the life of the Eastern churches.

EASTERN RITE CHURCHES. There are several Eastern rite churches, most of whose members live in the Middle East, North Africa, or Eastern Europe. They are also called Eastern Catholics because they are part of the Roman Catholic church under the authority of the pope. These churches trace their origins to various ancient national or ethnic Christian groups, some of which have a history dating back to the 1st century AD. Some of the groups, in fact, claim as founders one or more apostles of Jesus Christ (*see* Apostle).

The historical origin of the relationship with the church of Rome dates from the Council of Ferrara–Florence in 1439, which failed to unite the Christians of the East and West. Those in the East were mostly Eastern Orthodox and remain so today. The Eastern rite churches, however, chose to affiliate with Rome, and they did so, singly, over a period of centuries.

These churches are divided into five distinct Eastern rite traditions: Byzantine, Alexandrian, Antiochene, Chaldean, and Armenian. In this context the word rite suggests more than a worship form; it also means a specific religious discipline and way of life. Some of the Eastern traditions are quite different from those in the Western Catholic churches. The Eastern rites permit a married clergy, in marked contrast to the Western rite. They also permit newly baptized infants admission to communion, or the Lord's Supper. These and other practices are more comparable to the traditions of the Eastern Orthodox churches (*see* Eastern Orthodox Churches).

The most significant of the rites is the Byzantine. It affects more people and is more widely distributed than the others. From the original Byzantine rite there have emerged 13 subrites: Albanian, Belorussian, Bulgarian, Greek, Hungarian, Italo-Albanian, Melkite (Syrian background), Romanian, Russian, Ruthenian, Slovakian, Ukrainian, and Yugoslavian. Many of these have been persecuted or suppressed in their native lands by communist authorities. Some of the suppressed groups have members in other countries, especially in the United States. With the exception of the Maronites of Lebanon, all Eastern rite groups are minorities among the Christians in their homelands, which are either communist or Muslim.

The Alexandrian rite is composed of two major groups: Egyptian Catholics and Ethiopian Catholics. The Egyptian Catholics are Coptic Christians in communion with Rome, and they are a minority among the other Coptics. Their strength is among the poorest and least privileged of Egypt's citizens.

The Antiochene rite consists of the Maronites, the Syrian Catholics, and the Malankars. The Maronites live mainly in Lebanon, the Syrians in west Syria, and the Malankars in southwestern India along the Malankar, or Malabar, coast. The Chaldean rite is an east Syrian group, but it also includes some Syrian Catholics on the Malankar coast. The Armenian rite, or the Armenian Catholic church, has a population distributed among the nations of Turkey, Syria, Iraq, Lebanon, Egypt, Romania, Greece, and France. The church's headquarters are in Beirut.

EAST INDIA COMPANY. The term East Indies refers loosely to the Dutch East Indies (now Indonesia), the islands of the Malay archipelago, Southeast Asia, and India. During the 17th and 18th centuries, merchant companies were established by England, the Dutch Republic, France, Scotland, Denmark, Spain, Austria, and Sweden to dominate—and if possible to monopolize—trade with these areas. The most powerful and significant of these associations was the English East India Company.

In September 1599 a group of London merchants formed an association for direct trade with the Indies in order to compete with the Dutch and combat Portuguese attempts to monopolize the spice trade. On Dec. 31, 1600, Queen Elizabeth I granted the company a charter, giving it a monopoly of trade and a limited authority to govern the territories of the Indies.

The goal of breaking the Dutch predominance in the islands of the Indies was not attained, but the East India Company gained a strong foothold on the Indian subcontinent. Here its control led eventually to the colonization of India by England. In 1623, after a conflict with the Dutch, the company decided to concentrate its efforts on India. It inaugurated a lucrative trade in calicoes, indigo, raw cotton and silk, and spices.

In 1661 King Charles II granted the company a new charter, giving it extensive rights to govern its territories. New and profitable trade sources were opened, notably with China. Gradually, as the Mughal Empire of India disintegrated, it became necessary for the company to see to the fortification and defense of its territories there. From the 1680s the history of the company became the history of British rule in India.

By 1691 rival factions had formed a competing trading company, but the old company continued to dominate trade. In 1709 the two companies were merged into the United Company of Merchants trading to the East Indies. The charter was continually renewed until 1783. (*See also* India, "History.")

Robert Clive's military exploits in India in the service of the East India Company made the company the ruler of rich and extensive territories. Clive became governor of Bengal in 1765 and is generally considered the founder of Britain's Indian Empire (*see* Clive). Warren Hastings succeeded Clive and was made the first governor-general (*see* Hastings). Hastings undertook a reform of the colonial administration, but back in England there was no agency to keep track of Indian affairs. Enemies of the company accused it of misgovernment, and a campaign against Hastings began in London, led by Edmund Burke (*see* Burke).

To resolve this situation, William Pitt offered the India bill of 1784 to Parliament. A government department, the board of control for India, was set up to oversee the colony. In 1813 an act was passed ending the East India Company's monopoly in India, and in 1833 an act was passed that left the company without administrative or commercial functions. By 1858 the company had transferred its possessions to the British government.

Shostal Associates

A traditional house of the Batak tribe in northern Sumatra is built up off the ground for protection from water.

EAST INDIES. Once fabled as the Spice Islands, the East Indies (also known as the Malay Archipelago) extends in a great arc of islands astride the equator between mainland Southeast Asia and Australia. It connects the Indian and Pacific oceans. The world's largest island group, it has more than 4,000 islands in an area that extends more than 3,300 miles (5,300 kilometers) from east to west and more than 1,400 miles (2,250 kilometers) from north to south. Geographically the Philippine islands are part of the archipelago, but for historical reasons the name East Indies usually refers to the islands to their south.

The vast number of islands is dominated by a few huge ones and one very populous one. The islands of Borneo and New Guinea are larger than Texas; Java is about the size of North Carolina; Celebes—also known by its Indonesian name Sulawesi—is about the size of North Dakota; and Sumatra is larger than California. On these islands live more than 160 million people, about 60 percent of them on the island of Java. Except for the Melanesian peoples of New Guinea, the inhabitants are descendants of Malay peoples and speak Malayo-Polynesian languages.

The East Indies today is divided among several independent countries. The nation of Singapore occupies the first island lying off the Malay peninsula. The northern side of the island of Borneo contains two states—Sabah and Sarawak—which are part of the Federation of Malaysia. Also on northern Borneo is the nation of Brunei, which gained independence in 1984. These three states were formerly known as British Borneo. The remainder of Borneo is known by its Indonesian name, Kalimantan, and was formerly ruled by the Dutch. The former Dutch East Indies, extending from Sumatra in the west to western New Guinea—Irian Jaya in Indonesian—in the east, to-

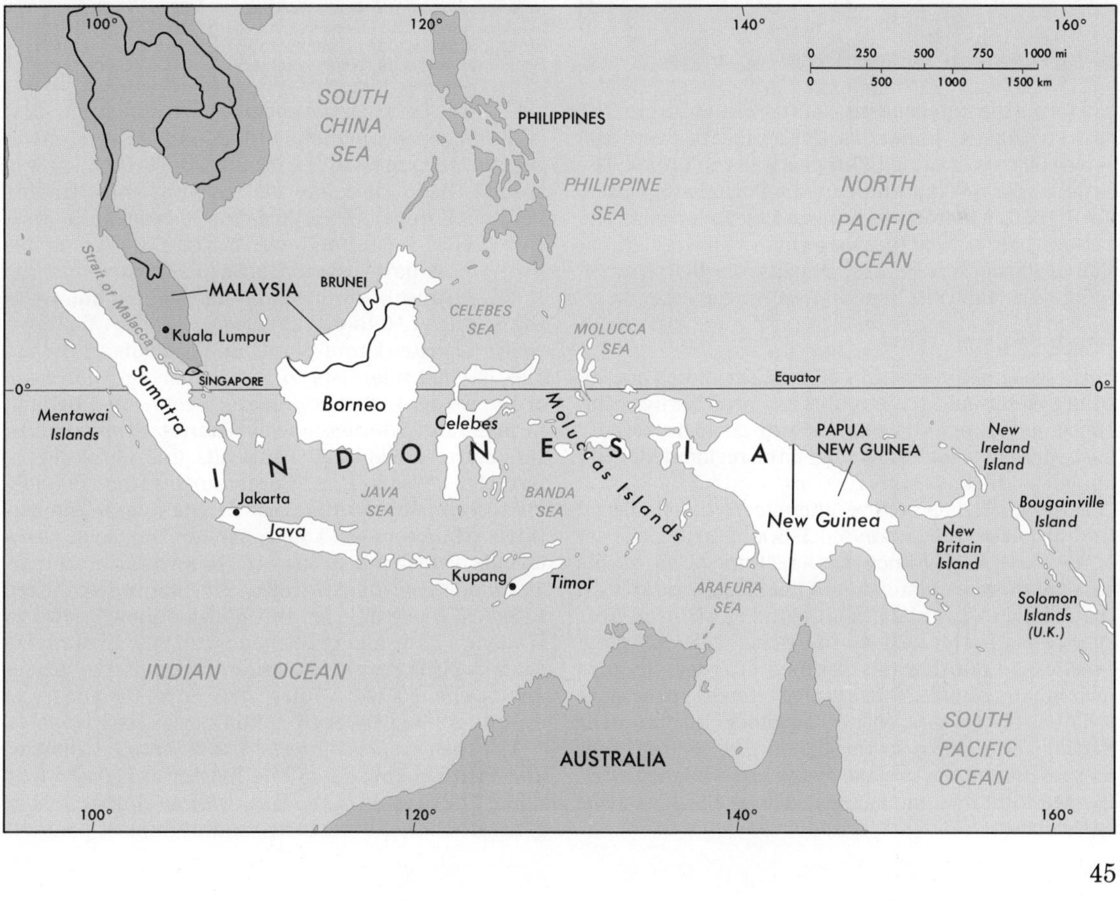

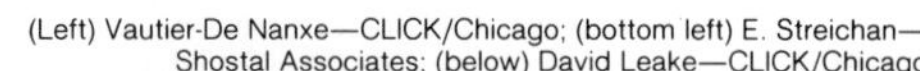

(Left) Vautier-De Nanxe—CLICK/Chicago; (bottom left) E. Streichan—Shostal Associates; (below) David Leake—CLICK/Chicago

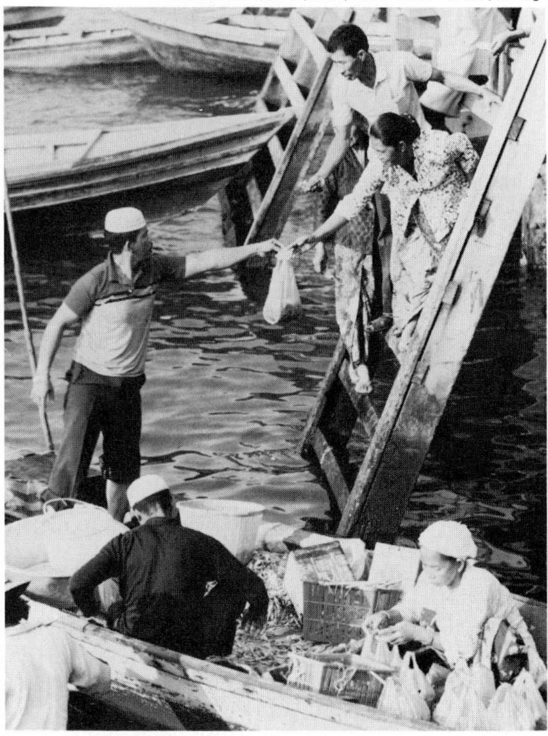

Salt is harvested (top left) along the coast of Java, Indonesia. Singapore (left) has one of the most prosperous economies in Southeast Asia. The tall building right of center is the headquarters of the Overseas-Chinese Banking Corporation. Singapore is also one of the world's largest ports. A family in Brunei (above) sells freshly caught prawns at dockside.

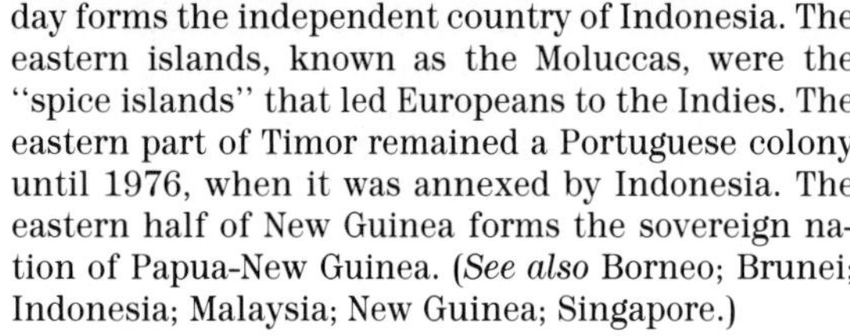

day forms the independent country of Indonesia. The eastern islands, known as the Moluccas, were the "spice islands" that led Europeans to the Indies. The eastern part of Timor remained a Portuguese colony until 1976, when it was annexed by Indonesia. The eastern half of New Guinea forms the sovereign nation of Papua-New Guinea. (*See also* Borneo; Brunei; Indonesia; Malaysia; New Guinea; Singapore.)

Land, Sea, and Wind

The geographic position of the East Indies astride wind systems and trade routes has profoundly influenced its history. Its climate and geologic activity have formed its land and created the regional identity known as the East Indies.

Once, geologists believe, there were no islands in the ancient sea that separated Asia and Australia. Part of the Earth's crust known as a tectonic plate, in this case an undersea plate, moved northeastward toward the Pacific Ocean plate. As it collided with the next crustal plate, the heat and movement of one plate overriding the other raised ridges of crust, the tops forming the islands. These geologic forces are evident today in the geysers, active volcanoes, and frequent earthquakes that occur throughout the Indies. Other movements of the crustal plates are evident in the twisted form of some islands such as the four arms of Celebes.

The seas between the islands are very shallow, and currents are strong. It is difficult for large ships to pass between most of the islands, and it is a long way around them. Therefore for centuries ships trading between Europe, Africa, Arabia, and India in the west and China, Japan, and the Western United States in the east have passed between Sumatra and the Malay peninsula through the deep water known as the Straits of Malacca.

The distribution of plants and animals in the Indies has led scientists to the conclusion that some of the western islands were once connected by land to mainland Southeast Asia. The relatively shallow seas between the Malay peninsula and the islands of Sumatra, Java, Bali, and Borneo are less than 300 feet (90 meters) deep. Animals of the mainland—such as tigers, rhinoceroses, and apes—are found on these islands. On islands to the east, however, the animals are like those of Australia. The naturalist Alfred Russel Wallace mapped this division, now known as Wallace's Line, and published it in 1869. In studying the way birds were spreading and changing in species among the islands, Wallace arrived at the theory of evolution independently from Charles Darwin.

The lush tropical forests, palms, ferns, bamboos, and brilliant flowers of the Indies form part of its fable. They result from an equatorial climate that is generally hot and wet. The rainfall in most places is between 100 and 150 inches (250 and 380 centimeters) a year. At sea level the temperature in most places is between 80° and 90° F (26° and 32° C) all year long. The islands are mountainous, however, and many places lie within the rain shadow of a mountain and get little or only seasonal rain. On the higher mountains and plateaus the climate is subtropical, and the peaks above 10,000 feet (3,050 meters) have a cool climate and even snow. The more northerly islands are strongly influenced by the monsoon winds in their rainfall patterns.

The shifting winds were very important for trade and navigation until the steamship was developed in the 19th century. Merchants sailed from China to Sumatra on the northeast monsoon, stored their goods in warehouses, and took on cargo from India or the Muslim-dominated lands. Then on the southwestern monsoon they sailed back to China while merchants arrived from India, unloaded their cargoes, took aboard the Chinese goods in the warehouses, and returned to India with the next northeastern monsoon. In this way cities and empires flourished in the Indies.

European Possession and Independence

When Arab traders who controlled the flow of spices from the Moluccas across the Indian Ocean and overland to the Mediterranean charged ever higher prices, Europeans set out to find a sea route to the islands themselves. In 1488 Bartholomew Diaz returned to Portugal from the first voyage around Africa to India. Christopher Columbus sailed to the west only four years later, hoping to find a shorter route for Spain. He believed that the Caribbean islands he found were the Indies and that the people living there were Indians. After Europeans realized his mistake, the Caribbean islands were named the West Indies. At first the term East Indies was applied to India and Farther India (most of Southeast Asia). After the British developed India as a colony, the term came to apply only to the islands of the Malay Archipelago.

For centuries European powers fought over the riches of the Indies. Local rulers were set against each other. Spices and other goods were burned and destroyed until the Europeans had a monopoly of trade and production. First the Portuguese arrived and later struggled with the Spanish. Later the British struggled with the Dutch. Finally the Dutch ruled the Dutch East Indies, Britain ruled Malaya and northern Borneo, the Portuguese ruled Timor, and the Spanish were left in the Philippines until the United States defeated them in the Spanish-American War of 1898.

In most of the East Indies the Japanese were first welcomed as liberators in World War II but later hated as oppressors. After the war, however, the indigenous peoples resisted the return of European powers. The Indonesians especially fought hard for their independence. Indonesia became independent in 1949, though it did not annex western New Guinea until 1969. British Borneo became part of the Federation of Malaysia in 1963 except for Brunei, which remained a colony until independence in 1984. Singapore was also joined to Malaysia in 1963, but it seceded in 1965 to become an independent country. No colonies remain in the East Indies today.

EASTMAN, George (1854–1932). The man who transformed photography from a complicated and expensive chore into an inexpensive hobby for millions of people was George Eastman. He was the founder of the Eastman Kodak Company and a philanthropist who gave about $75 million to educational institutions and other causes. (*See also* Photography.)

Eastman was born at Waterville, N.Y., on July 12, 1854. The family moved to Rochester, N.Y., six years later. There he attended school and held his first jobs—for an insurance company and in a bank. He had become interested in photography, and by 1880 he had developed a process for making what were called dry plates. With a partner he formed the Eastman Dry Plate and Film Company. In 1884 he came up with a breakthrough that forever changed modern photography—paper-backed film. Eastman began marketing it the following year. In 1888 he introduced the simple box camera, named Kodak. This, one of the world's best-known trademarks, is a coined word of no known meaning. It, along with the familiar yellow and black packaging, has come virtually to mean photography.

When the camera was introduced, it came already loaded with film. The buyer had only to take the pictures and send the whole camera back to the factory for developing the film. The camera was reloaded and returned to the customer. The cumbersome process was eliminated in 1892, when daylight-loading film was perfected. By 1900 the firm, which had been renamed the Eastman Kodak Company in 1892, was relocated to new surroundings—it had become the major industry in Rochester. By 1927 Eastman Kodak had a near monopoly on the photography business in the United States, and it is still one of the largest producers of photographic equipment in the world.

Among his many bequests were the Eastman School of Music and the Eastman School of Medicine and Dentistry at the University of Rochester. Eastman died on March 14, 1932, at Rochester.

EBBINGHAUS, Hermann (1850–1909). Rote learning is the process of memorizing by repetition, much as many young children learn the alphabet or the multiplication tables. It was German psychologist Hermann Ebbinghaus who demonstrated that scientific methods could be applied to the study and measurement of the mental processes involved in rote learning. Denying the long-held belief that these processes could not be subject to experimentation, his work proved a major advance in psychology, one that helped separate psychology from philosophy.

Ebbinghaus was born in Barmen, Germany, on Jan. 24, 1850. After schooling in his hometown, he went on to study at the universities of Bonn, Berlin, and Halle. He served in the army during the Franco-

Prussian War, leaving the army in the spring of 1871. He returned to school, where he received his doctor's degree in 1873.

To study the learning process, Ebbinghaus worked independently and used himself as a subject for observation. He devised 2,300 three-letter nonsense syllables for measuring the formation of mental associations. This invention, along with his strict experimentation controls and careful use of data, convinced him that memory is an orderly process. He also concluded that there is a "forgetting curve" that relates forgetting to the passage of time. These findings were published in a book entitled 'Memory', published in 1885. In 1897 Ebbinghaus created a type of word-completion test used in intelligence testing. He taught at the universities of Berlin, Breslau, and Halle successively. He died at Halle on Feb. 26, 1909.

EBONY. The expression "black as ebony" suggests one reason why this wood is used for piano keys, inlaying, cabinetwork, and knife handles. Craftsmen value ebony for its jet-black color and ability to take a high polish.

Ebony wood is obtained from about 15 species of tropical and semitropical trees, which grow in the East Indies, India, and Africa. Sri Lanka and southern India are the leading producers of the true ebony of jet-black color. Only the heartwood of the true ebony is used, because the sapwood is white. Some species yield a brown rather than black wood. One species, the persimmon, grows in the United States from Connecticut to eastern Texas (*see* Persimmon).

Most of the commercially important ebony trees belong to the genus *Diospyros* of the family Ebenaceae. Chief among them is *D. ebenum* of southern India and Sri Lanka.

ECHINODERM *see* STARFISH AND SEA URCHIN.

ECHO. According to Greek myth, a beautiful nymph named Echo fell hopelessly in love with Narcissus, who loved only his own image. She faded away until her voice had only strength enough to whisper the last word of any call she heard.

This was the poetical Greek explanation of an echo. The scientific explanation is that sound waves are reflected from flat surfaces. An irregular surface breaks up the waves, just as a rocky shore breaks water waves into spray. A smooth surface, such as the side of a cliff, reflects sound waves, and the reflection is heard as an echo.

Because the reflected waves have lost strength, they cannot be heard until the original sound has ceased. A person standing about a hundred feet from the reflecting surface can hear only the final syllable of what is called. If the person stands farther back, more and more syllables can be heard.

Sir Isaac Newton used the echo in a corridor at Trinity College, Cambridge, to measure the speed at which sound travels. Standing at one end of the corridor, he started a group of sound waves by stamping his foot. These waves were thrown back by the wall at the far end of the corridor. He knew the distance to the wall and back, and he timed the interval between stamping his foot and hearing the echo. From these factors he calculated a speed for sound that was within a few feet a second of the speed that modern science has determined (*see* Sound).

ECLIPSE. When three celestial objects become aligned, an eclipse is said to occur. The many eclipse events known to astronomers are of two different types. In the first, the eclipsing body comes between an observer and the eclipsed object. The eclipsed object appears to the observer to be totally or partially covered by the eclipsing object. Eclipses of the second type affect only planets or natural satellites. In this case, the eclipsing body comes between the sun and the eclipsed object. The eclipsed object remains in view of the observer, but the sun's light no longer shines on any of it or part of it, and it becomes darkened by entering into the shadow of the eclipsing object. Examples of this kind of eclipse event are eclipses of the moon and eclipses of the satellites of Jupiter.

Solar and lunar eclipses have long been of interest because they are easily seen without a telescope and offer an impressive spectacle. Primitive peoples were struck with fear by the falling darkness during a total solar eclipse or by the strange sight of the eclipsed moon. Accounts of such eclipses are found among the oldest records of history (*see* Astronomy).

Solar Eclipses

A solar eclipse occurs when the moon, revolving in its orbit around the Earth, moves across the disk of the sun so that the moon's shadow sweeps over the face of the Earth. No sunlight penetrates the inner part of the shadow, or umbra. To observers on the Earth within the umbra, the disk of the sun appears completely covered by that of the moon. Such a solar eclipse is said to be total. Because the umbra is narrow at its intersection with the Earth, a total eclipse can be observed only within a very narrow area called the zone of totality. Because of the relative motion of the Earth and moon, the shadow moves rapidly over the Earth's surface. A total solar eclipse thus lasts only a short time—less than eight minutes at any one place on Earth. To observers located within the outer part of the moon's shadow, or penumbra, the disk of the moon appears to overlap the sun's disk in part. This event is called a partial solar eclipse.

Because the Earth revolves around the sun in an elliptical orbit, the distance between Earth and sun changes slightly during the course of a year. Similarly, the apparent size of the lunar disk changes to some degree during a month because of the elliptical shape of the moon's orbit. If a solar eclipse occurs when the sun is closest to the Earth and the moon is farthest away, the moon does not completely cover the sun; the rim of the sun is visible around the edge, or limb, of the moon. This type of solar eclipse is known as

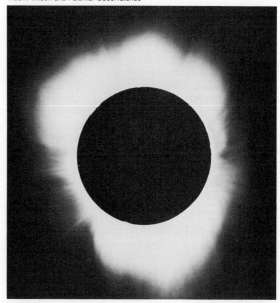

Mount Wilson and Palomar Observatories

The total solar eclipse on June 8, 1918, was photographed at Green River, Wyo.

an annular eclipse. Eclipses of the sun occur two to four times a year. In rare instances more may occur, as in 1935, when five solar eclipses took place.

Partial solar eclipses are of little scientific interest. Total eclipses, however, have contributed much knowledge about the nature of the sun's chromosphere and corona, the thin external layers of the sun that are usually lost in the brilliant glare from the shining solar surface, or photosphere. During a total solar eclipse the moon acts as a screen outside the Earth's atmosphere, cutting off the direct rays from the photosphere. The brilliance of the sky is decreased greatly, and the fainter parts of the sun become visible. The scientific value of observing eclipses has decreased in recent years, largely as a result of the invention of the coronagraph. This instrument blocks the photosphere artificially, making it possible for investigators to conduct studies of the solar chromosphere and corona without waiting for eclipses to occur.

Lunar Eclipses

When the moon travels through the shadow of the Earth and loses its bright illumination by the sun, a lunar eclipse takes place. It can occur only at the time of the full moon—that is, when the moon is directly opposite the sun—because the Earth's shadow is directed away from the sun. A lunar eclipse can be seen from any place on the Earth where the moon is above the horizon. Such an eclipse can be total, partial, or penumbral, depending on the moon's position. If the moon passes through the center of the Earth's umbra, a total lunar eclipse occurs. Totality may extend up to 100 minutes, with the entire eclipse lasting about 3½ hours. A partial lunar eclipse is observable when only a part of the moon passes through the umbra. The penumbral type occurs when the moon moves only through the outer part of the shadow. Lunar eclipses generally occur twice a year. In some years, however, there may be none, while in others, one or possibly three may take place.

Other Types of Eclipses

From the Earth, the moon appears against a background of distant stars. As the moon moves eastward across the constellations, it occasionally passes in front of a star or a planet, causing an occultation. Accurately timed observations of occultations are used to study the orbital motion of the moon. Measurements of the time required for a star to disappear also provide information about the diameters of the stars.

The two planets Mercury and Venus, which are closer to the sun than is the Earth, occasionally pass between the Earth and the sun. At such a time either of these planets appears as a small, dark, circular disk projected on the brilliant disk of the sun, crossing it slowly as the planet makes a transit.

Eclipsing binaries are double-star systems consisting of two stellar bodies that revolve around one another. One star passes periodically in front of or behind the other as seen from the Earth, and two eclipses take place during each revolution. From the way in which the light from the binary system varies, it is possible to calculate the orbit and relative sizes of the two bodies (*see* Star).

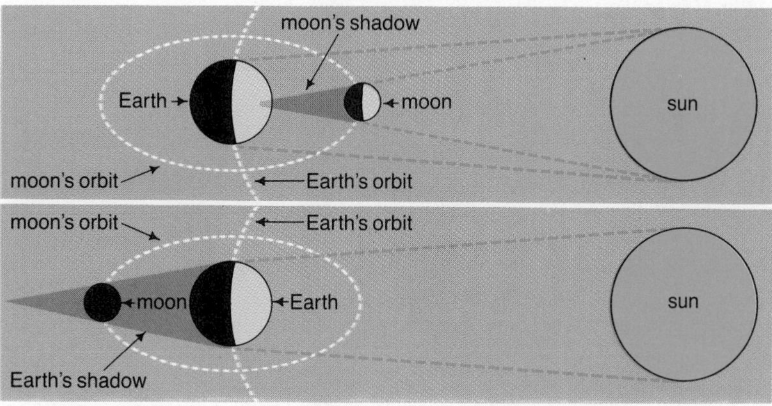

In a solar eclipse, top, the moon is between the sun and the Earth. The moon blots out the view of the sun from an area on Earth, and the moon's shadow falls on that area. During a lunar eclipse, bottom, the Earth is between the sun and the moon. Earth blots out the light of the sun from the moon as Earth's shadow falls on the moon.

ECOLOGY

ECOLOGY. The science that deals with the ways in which plants and animals depend upon one another and upon the physical settings in which they live is called ecology. Ecologists investigate the interactions of organisms in various kinds of environments. In this way they learn how nature establishes orderly patterns among a great variety of living things. The word "ecology" was coined in 1869. It comes from the Greek *oikos*, which means "household." Economics is derived from the same word. However, economics deals with human "housekeeping," while ecology concerns the "housekeeping" of nature.

Interdependence in Nature

Ecology emphasizes the dependence of every form of life on other living things and on the natural resources in its environment, such as air, soil, and water. Before there was a science of ecology, the great English biologist Charles Darwin noted this interdependence when he wrote: "It is interesting to contemplate a tangled bank, clothed with plants of many kinds, with birds singing on the bushes, with various insects flitting about, and with worms crawling through the damp earth, and to reflect that these elaborately constructed forms, so different from each other, and so dependent upon each other in so complex a manner, have all been produced by laws acting around us."

Ecology shows that man cannot regard nature as separate and detached—something to look at on a visit to a forest preserve or a drive through the country. Any change man makes in his environment affects all the organisms in it. When his vehicles and factories hurl pollutants into the air, animals and plants as well as man himself are harmed. The water he fouls with wastes and silt threatens remote streams and lakes. Even ocean fisheries may experience reduced catches because of pollution. (*See also* Conservation; Pollution, Environmental.)

The Balance of Nature

Each kind of life is suited to the physical conditions of its habitat—the type of soil, the amount of moisture and light, the quality of air, the annual variations in temperature. Each survives because it can hold its own with its neighbors. However, the continued existence of the whole group, or *life community*, involves a shifting balance among its members, a "dynamic equilibrium."

Natural balances are disrupted when crops are planted, since ordinarily the crops are not native to the areas in which they are grown. Such disturbances of natural balances make it necessary for man to impose artificial balances that will maintain or increase crop production. For the effective manipulation of these new equilibriums, information on nature's checks and balances is absolutely essential, and often only a specialist is able to provide it. For example, if a farmer were told that he could increase the red clover in his pasture with the help of domestic cats, he might ridicule the suggestion. Yet the relationship between cats and red clover has been clearly

This article was contributed by E. J. Dyksterhuis, professor of range ecology, Texas A & M University.

Light penetrates the treetops of the tropical deciduous forest, thus permitting dense plant life at the surface. Vegetation is especially lush during the hot, rainy seasons.

Grasslands are found in varying middle-latitude climates. Some grasses are adapted to moist settings, others to dry ones. Grazing animals and other herbivores thrive in grasslands.

established. Cats kill field mice, thus preventing them from destroying the nests and larvae of bumblebees. As a result, more bumblebees are available to pollinate clover blossoms—a task for which they are especially adapted. The more thoroughly the blossoms are pollinated, the more seed will be produced and the richer the clover crop will be. This cat-mouse-bee-clover relationship is typical of the cause-and-effect chains that ecologists study.

The Wide Scope of Ecology

Long before a separate science of ecology arose, men in all sorts of occupations were guided by what are now regarded as ecological considerations. The primitive hunter who knew that deer had to stop at a salt lick for salt was a practical ecologist. So too was the early fisherman who realized that gulls hovering over the water marked the position of a school of fish. In the absence of calendars, men used ecological facts to guide their seasonal endeavors. They planted corn when oak leaves were the size of a squirrel's ear. They regarded the noise of geese flying south as a warning to prepare for winter.

Until about 1850, the scientific study of such phenomena was called natural history, and the student of the great outdoors was called a naturalist. Afterward, natural history became subdivided into special fields, such as geology, zoology, and botany, and the naturalist moved indoors. There he performed laboratory work with the aid of scientific equipment.

While the scientists were at work in their laboratories, other men were continuing to cope with living things in their natural settings—on timberlands, on rangelands, on croplands, in streams and seas. Although these men often needed help, many of their problems could not be solved in the laboratory.

The forester, for example, wanted to know why trees do not thrive on the prairie, the desert, and the mountaintop. The rancher wanted to know how to manage his pastures so that his cattle would flourish, and how such creatures as coyotes, hawks, rabbits, gophers, and grasshoppers would affect his efforts.

As for the farmer, almost every part of his work posed problems for which scientific answers were needed. The game manager came to realize that his duties entailed much more than the regulation of hunting. To preserve the animals for which he was responsible, he had to make sure they had the right kinds of food in all seasons, suitable places to live and raise their young, and appropriate cover.

The fisherman learned that most aquatic life fares poorly in muddy and polluted waters. He became interested in land management and waste disposal when he discovered that the silt he found so troublesome came from rural areas where timber, rangeland, and cropland were mishandled and that the waters he fished were polluted by urban wastes. The ocean fisherman wanted to know why fish were abundant in one place and scarce in another. He needed information on the breeding habits of his catches and of the tiny animals and plants upon which they fed.

These are all ecological problems. To solve them the ecologist must draw upon many sciences. He must understand biology—the science of living things—including botany and zoology. He must also understand the sciences that deal with weather, climate, rocks, earth, soil, and water.

An ecologist is concerned with both the past and the future. The present and potential condition of a field, stream, or forest cannot be understood without knowing its earlier history. For example, great stretches of light-green aspen trees may grow in parts

Many of the deciduous forests that once flourished in the middle latitudes were cleared for crops. Some famous civilizations have flourished in these warm, moist regions.

Even the parched desert can support life. Since water is scarce in arid regions, desert plants store it in their tissues. Desert animals are specially adapted to conserve water.

of the Rocky Mountains while nearby slopes are covered with dark-green fir and spruce trees. This indicates that a forest fire once destroyed stands of evergreens. Aspens are the first trees capable of growing on the fire-scarred land. After about 40 years spruce and fir seeds begin to germinate in the shade of the aspens. In the course of time the evergreens can be expected to regain their lost territory. Thus, by means of ecology it is possible to look both backward and forward in time.

SOME PRINCIPLES OF ECOLOGY

Ecology is a relatively young science. Its laws are still being developed. Nevertheless, some of its principles have already won wide acceptance.

The Special Environmental Needs of Living Things

One of these principles can be stated as follows: life patterns reflect the patterns of the physical environment. In land communities vegetation patterns are influenced by climate and soil (*see* Climate; Soil). Climate has a marked effect on the height of dominant native plants. For instance, the humid climate of the Eastern United States supports tall forest trees. Westward from Minnesota and Texas the climate changes from subhumid to semiarid. At first the land has squatty, scattered trees and tall grasses or thickets. As the climate becomes drier, tall-grass prairies dominate (*see* Grasslands). Finally, on the dry plains at the eastern base of the Rockies, short-grass steppe appears. (*See also* Plants, Distribution of.)

Climates and plant varieties change quickly at the various elevations of mountain range. At very high altitudes in the Rockies, alpine rangelands exist above the timberline. Here, the climatic factor of cold outweighs that of moisture, and tundra vegetation similar to that of the Arctic regions is nurtured. West of the Rockies, however, in basins between other mountains, the desert scrub vegetation of arid climates prevails. Near the northern Pacific coast may be found lush rain forests typical of extremely humid temperature climates.

Though moisture and temperature determine the overall pattern of a region's vegetation, unusual soil conditions may promote the growth of untypical plant species. Thus, even in arid climates cattails grow near ponds and forests rise along streams or from rocky outcrops where runoff water collects in cracks.

In short, every kind of plant and animal flourishes only when certain physical conditions are present. In the absence of such conditions, plants and animals cannot survive without artificial help. Domestic plants and animals ordinarily die out within a few generations without the continued protection of man. Of all the forms of life, man seems least bound by environmental limitations. He can create livable conditions nearly everywhere on the planet by means of fire, shelters, clothing, and tools. Without these aids, man would be as restricted in his choice of habitat as are, for example, such species as the polar bear, the camel, and the beech tree. However, given his capacity to develop artificial environments, man is able to range not only over the entire earth but also in the heights of outer space and the depths of the ocean bottom.

Communities of Plants and Animals

Closely related to the life patterns principle is the principle of biotic communities. According to this principle, the plants and animals of a given area—its biota—tend to group themselves into loosely organized units known as *communities*. The com-

The primary succession of plants illustrated below begins in a pond and ends in either a grassland or a forest. Many plants play a part in succession; those diagramed are merely typical examples. At the submerged stage, such plants as eelgrass and elodea are rooted in the muddy bottom. As humus accumulates, the water becomes shallower. Floating plants such as water lilies take hold. At the water's edge, the soil supports cattails and reeds. Away from the pond, rushes begin to form a meadow. In the drier soil, even further from the pond, dogwoods and cottonwoods develop. This mixed forest is finally succeeded by a climax forest of oaks and hickories or of the more dominant beeches and maples.

munity is the natural home of each member-species.

This means that certain types of plants and animals live together in readily identified communities. Pronghorn antelope are associated with dry steppe grasslands; moose inhabit northern spruce forests; and such trees as oak and hickory or beech and maple are found together in forests. By contrast, certain living things—cattail and cactus, for example—never share the same natural environment.

Large communities contain smaller ones, each with its characteristic biota. Bison, coyotes, and jackrabbits are part of the grasslands community. Fox squirrels, wood pigeons, and black bears are part of the forest community. By means of computers, ecologists have simulated communities containing various plants and animals. In this way they have been able to determine optimum populations for each of the species in a community.

Competition in Communities

Competition is a characteristic of all communities. Plant roots in dry rangelands compete for water. The trees of a rain forest compete for light. Crops compete for both of these as well as for nutrients. Competition is usually keen in areas where one type of community seems to overlap another. For example, a continuum between a shrub community and a marsh contains some aspects of both communities. Animals and plants trying to establish a foothold in such an overlap must cope with difficulties often nonexistent in a stable community. Shrubs moving toward the marshy area must compete with other pioneer shrubs and reeds for light and nutrients. Similarly, reeds attempting to invade the shrubby area must compete with shrubs and other reeds. This shows that competition may often be greatest among living things that have the same needs. For the same reason, competition may be extremely harsh within a species—among wolves for meat or among cattle for grass, for example.

On the other hand, competition is sometimes modified through behavioral adjustments—even *cooperation*—among the members of a community. Shrubs are spaced widely on deserts. Birds nest in patterns that prevent overcrowding. Bees live together in a hive. Man can make similar adjustments, and unlike other species he can achieve cooperation by rational means. Yet human competition sometimes ends in wars, and wars frequently destroy the very things which the belligerents are striving to take away from one another.

Should it become necessary to control an undesirable species in a community, this can best be done by modifying the community. A rancher, for example, may discover that weedy annual plants are invading his native perennial pastures. His initial reaction might be to attack the weeds with chemical herbicides. This approach would be self-defeating since nature would provide the resultant bare soil with an unlimited supply of weed seed. To solve the problem ecologically, the rancher should manage the degree

Photographs, Soil Conservation Service

The West once had millions of acres of prairie where bison ranged. Cattlemen discovered that, covered with hardy natural grass, the land was ideal for cattle grazing.

The range eventually became overstocked. The grass was cropped by cattle and sheep, and the underlying sod dried up.

Settlers were mistakenly encouraged to farm this land. When the plow broke the sod, wind and water eroded good topsoil.

Ecology helped reclaim the desert. Furrows were cut across slopes to hold water. Oats, sorghum, and Sudan grass, with a scattering of shrubs and trees, were planted to hold soil.

In less than a year, the desert had been reclaimed. Later, the land was seeded to grass again and restocked with cattle.

Man can modify the environment of some species for his own needs without unduly upsetting natural balances. Young pines (left) are bunched so closely that they cannot grow into tall marketable trees. When a portion of the stand is removed, the remaining trees (right) flourish because competition for water, light, and nutrients is greatly eased.

and time of cattle grazing to permit normal growth of the native plant community, which would then crowd out the undesirable weeds.

Succession in Communities

A third major principle of ecology is that an orderly, predictable sequence of development takes place in any area. This sequence is called *ecological succession.* The successive changes produce increasingly mature communities from a barren or nearly barren start. Succession usually culminates in a *climax,* a fairly stable community in equilibrium with, and limited by, climate and soil.

At one time or another virtually all land surfaces have undergone basic climatic changes and been occupied by types of plants and animals which they may no longer be able to sustain. This, however, is not what is meant by ecological succession. It is known as biotic history, extends over the vast scale of geologic time, and is deduced from fossil remains. The future communities of an area cannot be predicted from its biotic history. Such prediction can be based only on a knowledge of ecological succession.

As soon as the first patches of soil are formed in barren areas, a series of events takes place that eventually terminates in the establishment of a climax community. This process is called *primary succession.* Because soil formation requires the slow weathering of rock, primary succession ordinarily spans hundreds of years. Once it begins, however, the sequence of events rarely alters. As soil formation proceeds, a succession of plants and animals appear. The last stage in this progression is the climax community.

A disturbance at any point during primary succession or even at the climax can destroy the vegetation of a primary succession in whole or in part. The vegetation that follows a disturbance of this kind is called a *disclimax.* The disturbance can be caused by plowing, logging, or overgrazing. When such a disturbance takes place, climate and soil are no longer the principal determinants of vegetation. The further natural growth of plants at the site of a disclimax, as contrasted with the raising of crops, is called *secondary succession.* This can be completed in a few years or, at most, in decades because soil has already been formed. After secondary succession restores a balance between eroded soil and vegetation, the further development of both again becomes dependent on primary succession. Wise landowners use secondary succession to restore overgrazed rangelands, cutover timberlands, and abandoned croplands. They need only protect the land from further disturbances while secondary succession heals the scars of abuse.

Changes in the community during secondary succession are rapid, because every living thing contributes to its alteration. For instance, the weeds that grow on a vacant lot produce shade and increase the soil's ability to absorb and store water. They also attract insects and birds and enrich the soil when they die and decay. The bare ground of the vacant lot is the best possible place for the pioneer sun-loving weeds to grow. Later the weeds are replaced by tree seedlings if the lot is in a forest climate, by native grasses if it is in a grasslands climate. Such changes occur until plants and animals that can make maximum use of the soil and climate are established.

The Ecosystem

A fourth key principle of ecology asserts that a community and its environment—the living and the nonliving—constitute an ecological system, or *ecosystem.* Every natural community draws vital materials from its surroundings and transfers materials to it. Raw materials and decay products are exchanged continuously. Thus, in an undisturbed area basic resources are sustained, never exhausted.

Ecosystems exist on many kinds of lands, in lakes, in streams, and in oceans. They are found wherever soil, air, and water support communities. The combined ecosystems of the earth constitute the *biosphere.*

Ecosystems generally contain many kinds of life. A cornfield, for example, contains more than just corn. Also present are smaller plant species, insects, earthworms, and a host of soil microbes. Each of these organisms fills a specific *niche*—each performs an essential function in the ecosystem.

The inhabitants of an ecosystem are classified as *producers*, *consumers*, and *decomposers*. Green plants of any kind, whether stately oaks or tiny algae, are producers because they make their own food through photosynthesis (*see* Plants, Physiology of). Animals, including man, feed on plants or on other animals and are therefore classed as consumers. Organisms that cause decay—bacteria and fungi—are decomposers.

The sequences in which the organisms within an ecosystem feed on one another are called *food chains*. Usually organisms of higher biological rank feed on those of lower rank. Ecologists group the members of any food chain into a *pyramid of numbers*. At the base of such a pyramid are the green plants, which are the most numerous organisms in the chain. The next level might contain first-order consumers, such as the sheep that eat the green plants. At the peak of the pyramid might be second-order consumers, such as the herdsmen who feed on the sheep. When the producers and consumers of an ecosystem die, their bodies are broken down by the decomposers into nutrients used by new plants for growth. In this manner, the food chain is perpetuated.

The biosphere seems capable of sustaining life even in the absence of consumers. Without consumers, the rate of plant growth would eventually strike a balance with the rate of decay caused by the decomposers. Hence, even if all herbivores, or plant-eaters, were absent from the biosphere, plant growth could be expected to stabilize at certain levels.

Through plant growth and decay, water and carbon, nitrogen, and other elements are circulated in endless cycles. The driving force behind these cycles is the sun. Solar energy becomes converted into food through the photosynthesis of green plants and into heat through the respiration of plants and animals. (*See also* Carbon; Nitrogen; Water.)

APPLICATIONS OF ECOLOGY

Ecologists are often employed to solve serious environmental problems. Early in this century, for example, southern Ohio was ravaged by a terrible flood. The inhabitants of the area, determined to prevent a repetition of the disaster, constructed large earthen dams across the valleys north of Dayton to contain future floodwaters. Since the slopes of these dams consisted of gravel with an admixture of clay, they washed away easily. It was necessary to stabilize the steep slopes quickly with plant cover. Knowing which plants would grow best in such places, an ecologist recommended the scattering of alfalfa and clover seed, followed by bromegrass and Japanese honeysuckle. His recommendations were followed, and dam slopes were soon covered with a fine cohesive turf. Many of the hills on neighboring farms lacked such cover and were quickly eroded.

The alligator (left) fills an important niche in the Florida Everglades. Females build their nests by ponds commonly called 'gator holes (right, top). Succeeding generations of female alligators improve the holes, making them wider and deeper. Other kinds of Everglades wildlife feed and take water at the holes (right, bottom), particularly during dry weather.

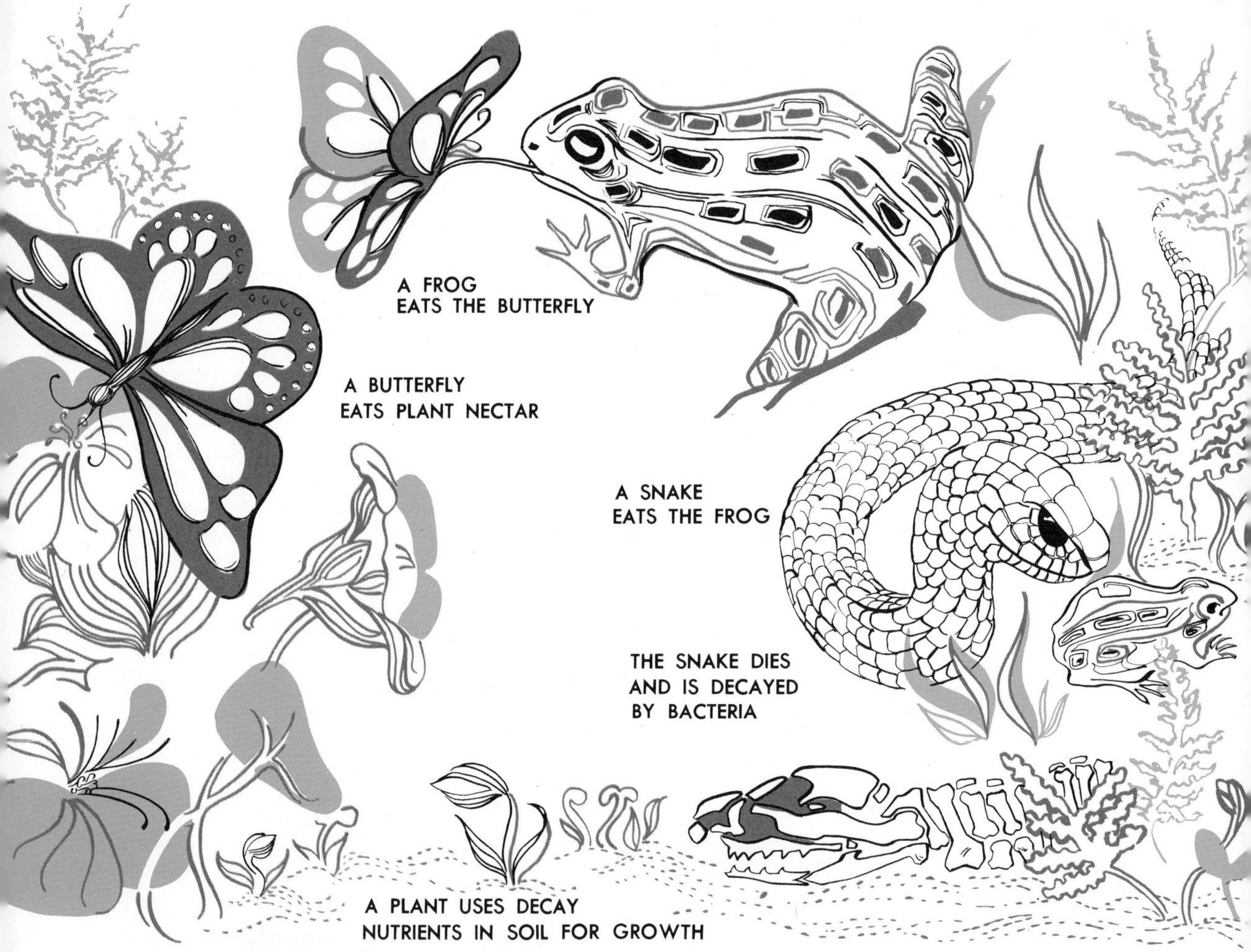

A FROG
EATS THE BUTTERFLY

A BUTTERFLY
EATS PLANT NECTAR

A SNAKE
EATS THE FROG

THE SNAKE DIES
AND IS DECAYED
BY BACTERIA

A PLANT USES DECAY
NUTRIENTS IN SOIL FOR GROWTH

Plants are the producers in a food chain. They make their own food. Animals in the chain are the consumers. They derive energy from plant matter, whether they eat plants or plant-eating animals. When members of the food chain die, decomposers—microorganisms—chemically break down their bodies into nutrients, minerals used by plants for growth.

In the Dust Bowl region of Texas, sandy soil in dry areas blew into great dunes after the land was plowed for wheat. Bulldozing these dunes was thought too expensive. However, an ecologist recommended that certain plants be raised near the shifting dunes. The plants in front of the dunes caught and held the soil, while those behind them kept the rear from blowing deeper. In a remarkably short time, wind had leveled off the high dune tops and vegetation had anchored the soil in place.

Ecology and Wildlife Conservation

Measures for the preservation of ducks and other migratory wild fowl are examples of ecological work with animals. When these birds grew scarce, state and federal agencies sought ways to protect them and help them reproduce. At first, laws were recommended that forbade shooting the birds in the spring when they were flying north to nest. Every female killed in the spring could mean one brood less returning in the fall. Further studies showed that many of the birds' breeding places were being destroyed when the land was drained for other uses. Some of these sites were not well-suited for the sustained growth of crops; others, where marshes and potholes once released stored water slowly, now contributed to downstream floods. Draining thus had a doubly harmful effect. Ecologists captured the endangered birds and put aluminum bands on their legs to trace their breeding places and movements. In this way it was discovered that the problem was international. As a result, the United States began to work in close cooperation with Canada and Mexico for the protection of migratory birds.

Ecologists also investigated the food habits of birds. They recognized that if proper food was unavailable, the birds would disappear even if hunting was regulated.

Experts examined the stomach contents of thousands of birds from many different areas. This work led to the finding that bird food consists mainly of plant materials that thrive under natural conditions. To ensure the availability of these materials, man had to cease altering many natural communities and to stop polluting them with his wastes.

By the 1970's ecologists had accumulated considerable evidence demonstrating that the widely used pesticide DDT and its metabolites, principally DDE, altered the calcium metabolism of certain birds. The birds laid eggs with such thin shells that they were crushed during incubation. This discovery was one of many that led to the imposition of legal restraints on the use of some agricultural pesticides. (*See also* Birds; Pollution, Environmental.)

Ecologists know that the well-being of a biotic community may require the preservation of a key member-species. For example, the alligator performs a valuable service in the Florida Everglades by digging "'gator holes." These are ponds created by female alligators when they dig up grass and mud for their nests. During extremely dry spells, these holes often retain enough water to meet the needs of such animals as the bobcat and the raccoon. They also provide a haven for fish until the arrival of rainy weather. Many birds use the holes for watering. Willow seeds take root along the edges, and fallen willow leaves later add substance to the soil. Thus, many forms of life are sustained by 'gator holes. But poachers have been hunting the alligators almost to extinction for their valuable hides. As a result, the number of 'gator holes can be expected to dwindle, and various forms of Everglades wildlife may be deprived of these refuges. Such ecological findings strengthen the case for the protection of alligators. (*See also* Conservation, subhead "Wildlife Conservation.")

Another ecological threat to the Everglades arose in the late 1960's, when plans were made to build a jet airport near the northern end of the national park. The airport would have wiped out part of a large swamp that furnishes the Everglades with much of its surface water. Ecologists and conservationists opposed the project, arguing that it would hamper the flow of surface water through the park and thus endanger the biota of the unique Everglades ecosystem. Their arguments aroused public concern, and in 1970 plans for the airport were dropped.

An ecosystem contains interdependent plants and animals and their environment. In an aquatic ecosystem, producers (phytoplankton) supply energy to consumers (zooplankton and fish). Oxygen and carbon dioxide are exchanged between phytoplankton (which need carbon dioxide for photosynthesis) and aquatic animals (which need oxygen for respiration).

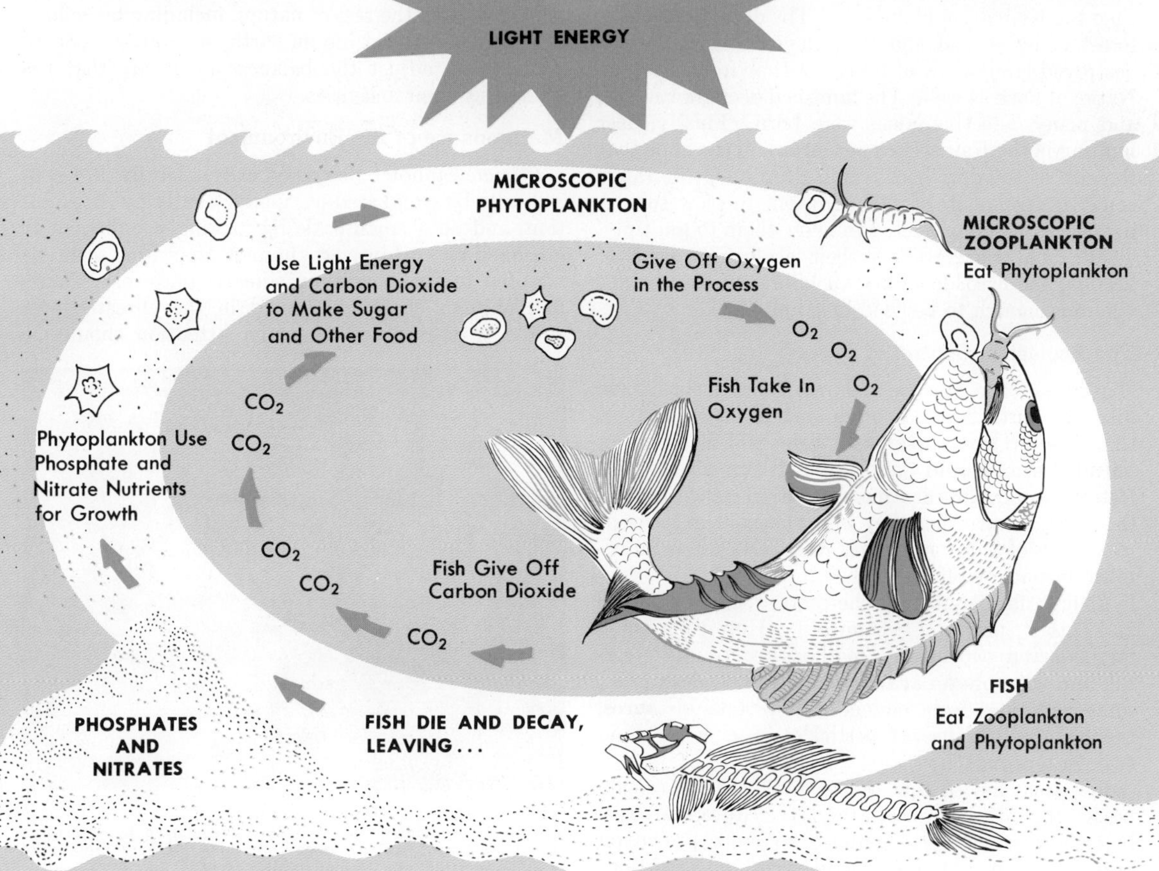

HOW DDT KILLED THE ROBINS

Dutch elm disease threatened to destroy most of the majestic elms that once flourished along residential streets. To eliminate the beetles that carry this fungus disease, many communities sprayed their elms with massive doses of DDT. The pesticide stuck to the leaves even after they fell in the autumn. Earthworms then fed on the leaves and accumulated DDT in their bodies. When spring came, robins returned to the communities to nest. They ate the earthworms and began to die in alarming numbers. Of the females that survived, some took in enough DDT to hamper the production or hatching of eggs. Robin populations were so seriously affected by DDT poisoning that the very survival of the songbird seemed in jeopardy. This experience was a vivid example of the far-ranging effects that flow from upsets in the delicate balances of nature. Ironically, the DDT did little to prevent the spread of Dutch elm disease.

An Ecological Mistake

At times, seemingly practical conservation efforts turn out to be mistakes. Cougars, or mountain lions, and deer were once abundant in Grand Canyon National Park and Kaibab National Forest. Because the cougars preyed on the deer, hunters were allowed to shoot the cougars until only a few were left.

With their chief enemy gone, the deer of the area increased so rapidly that they consumed more forage than the Kaibab could produce. The deer stripped the forest of every leaf and twig they could reach and destroyed large areas of forage in the Grand Canyon National Park as well. The famished deer grew feeble, and many defective fawns were born. Finally, deer hunting in the Kaibab was permitted, in the hope that the size of the deer herd would drop until the range could accommodate it. In addition, the few surviving cougars were protected to allow them to multiply. They could then resume their ecological niche of keeping the herd down and of killing those deer not vigorous enough to be good breeding stock.

The Ecological Control of Pests

Many of the insects and other pests that have plagued North America originated in other parts of the world. There these pests were held in check by natural enemies, and the plants and animals they infested had developed a measure of tolerance toward them. However, when they were placed in an environment free of these restraints, the pests often multiplied uncontrollably.

At first, farmers fought the pests with toxic sprays and other powerful chemicals. However, these methods were expensive, sometimes proved unsuccessful, and were often dangerous. After decades of use, some pesticides were banned. In certain instances, the ill-conceived use of pesticides gave way to an ecological approach.

Research showed that severe damage from certain pests—the Mexican beetle and the European corn borer, for example—is confined to crops grown on particular types of soil or under certain conditions of moisture. Changes in land use helped control some pests. Others were controlled biologically by importing parasites or predators from their native lands. This important form of pest control proved successful in limiting damage by scale insects (*see* Scale Insects).

By destroying the breeding places of birds and other animals, man loses valuable allies in his constant war with insects. Once, when the sportsmen of Ohio supported a proposal to permit quail hunting, the farmers of the state objected. They knew that a single quail killed enough insects to make it worth at least as much to them as a dozen chickens.

In some 3,000 locally organized Resource Conservation Districts ecological principles are being used to guide land use and community maintenance practices. These districts encompass the federal lands of the United States and more than 95 percent of its privately owned farmlands.

GOALS OF ECOLOGY

Throughout the world man-made communities have been replacing the communities of nature. However, the principles that govern the life of natural communities must be observed if these man-made communities are to thrive. Man must think less about "conquering nature" and more about learning to work with nature.

In addition, each person must realize his interdependence with the rest of nature, including his fellowmen. To safeguard life on earth, men must learn to control and adjust the balances in nature that are altered by their activities.

Maintenance of the Environment

Climate cannot be changed except locally and sporadically by cloud seeding, inadvertently by air pollution, and on a small scale by making windbreaks or greenhouses. However, human activities can be adapted to the prevailing climatic patterns. Plants and animals should be raised in the climates best suited to them, and particular attention should be

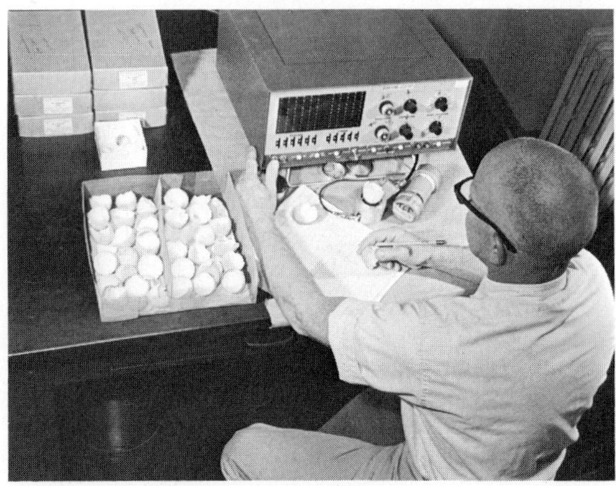

A research biologist uses a radioactive source to determine the thickness of mallard eggs containing DDE, a metabolite of DDT that reduces the hatchability of eggs.

paid to the cold and dry years rather than to average years or exceptionally productive years. In the United States the serious dust storms of the 1930s occurred because land that was plowed in wet years to grow wheat blew away in dry years. Much of that land should have been kept as rangeland.

Soil is a measure of an environment's capacity to support life. It forms very slowly but can be lost quickly—as much as an inch in a rainstorm (*see* Soil). Wise land use ensures its retention and improvement.

For agricultural purposes, land is used principally as timberland, rangeland, or cropland. Timberland and rangeland are natural communities. Cropland is formed when what was originally timberland or rangeland is cultivated. To ensure the best possible use of land, it is classified according to its ability to sustain the production of timber, pasture, or crops. (For information on land classifications, *see* Conservation, "Soil Conservation"; Land Use.)

Water, like soil, is a measure of the abundance of life. Usable water depends on the amount and retention of rainfall. An excessive runoff of rainwater, however, may result from human activities—for example, the building of roads and drainage ditches; the construction of extensive parking areas and shopping centers; the unwise harvesting of timber; year-round grazing of ranges; and the cultivation of easily eroded lands. Excessive runoff may cause floods. It may also lead to drought, which can occur when too little water is stored underground. Moreover, runoff strips soil from the land. This is deposited in reservoirs, ship channels, and other bodies of water. These silt-laden bodies must then be either dredged or abandoned. Water movements in and out of the soil must be controlled in such a way as to minimize damage and maximize benefits. (*See also* Flood; Flood Control.)

The Conservation of Natural Communities

The communities of plants and animals established by humans usually consist of only a few varieties, often managed in a way that harms the environment. By contrast, natural communities usually enhance the environment and still yield many products and sources of pleasure to people.

Land once cultivated but now lying idle should be restored to the natural communities that formerly occupied it. In addition, people should use the findings of ecology to improve their artificial communities such as fields, gardens, orchards, and pastures. For example, few man-made agents for the control of pests can outperform the insect-eating birds that breed in uncut patches of trees or bushes on a farm.

The Curtailment of Waste

Modern machines and weapons and the harmful wastes of technology can be used to destroy the environment. At the same time, the wise use of machinery can also enable humans to conserve their surroundings. Just as negotiation rather than warfare can be employed to resolve international disputes, no doubt the means can be devised to curtail the destructive wastes of factories and vehicles. True, ever-growing demands for goods and services, nurtured by increasing human populations and rising expectations, are placing more and more pressure on the environment. An understanding of the causes and consequences of environmental deterioration, however, may bring about a change in the goals that people pursue and the means they use to achieve these goals. (*See also* Pollution, Environmental.)

Increases in human material possessions have been accompanied by a potentially dangerous worsening of the natural environment. A central function of ecology is to study human interactions with the natural environment in order to modify them favorably.

BIBLIOGRAPHY FOR ECOLOGY

Books for Children

Jaspersohn, William. How the Forest Grew (Greenwillow, 1980).
Pringle, Laurence. City and Suburb: Exploring an Ecosystem (Macmillan, 1975).
Sabin, Francene. Ecosystems and Food Chains (Troll, 1985).
Selsam, M.E. How Animals Live Together, rev. ed. (Morrow, 1979).

Books for Young Adults and Teachers

Billington, E.T. Understanding Ecology, rev. ed. (Warne, 1971).
Pringle, Laurence. Lives at Stake: the Science and Politics of Environmental Health (Macmillan, 1980).
Sharpe, G.W. Interpreting the Environment, 2nd ed. (Wiley, 1982).
Sharpe, G.W. and others. Introduction to Forestry, 4th ed. (McGraw, 1976).

Eggs of green lacewings, insects that prey on destructive worms, are being spread among tomato plants. When the eggs hatch, the larvae begin to destroy the tomato pests.

Ryan Marty

Photos, CLICK/Chicago; (top) Peter Fronk; (above) Harold L. Barnett

Productive labor in agriculture and manufacturing are the primary wealth-creating processes in any society. The farms and factories make the goods to satisfy the needs and desires of a country's population, and the surpluses can be exported.

ECONOMICS

ECONOMICS. The 19th-century British writer Thomas Carlyle called economics the "pig philosophy." He held this unfavorable view because he regarded the businessman's quest for profits as mere greed. He also called economics the "dismal science" because the matters it deals with at such length are so ordinary. Carlyle lived at the time when the Industrial Revolution was still new and the modern economic system was in process of formation. His attitudes represented the way people for centuries past had thought about economic functions.

More recent writers have taken a much more realistic view of economics. The management consultant Earl Bunting stated that: "The goals of business are inseparable from the goals of the whole community." And the noted economist John Kenneth Galbraith made much the same point: "Economics deals with matters which men consider very close to their lives."

Bunting and Galbraith are more realistic because, no matter where people in the civilized world live, they are part of an economic system. To speak of a developed society is to speak of a society that has been built through vigorous economic functioning. Without economies there is no prosperity. Since the ancient world, civilization itself has been built upon economic growth. When the growth stopped, as it did at the end of the Roman Empire, civilization went into a long decline. What brought it back was the painstakingly slow emergence of workable economies. (*See also* Civilization, "Economics and Civilization.")

The word economy originally referred to household management—from the Greek *oikos,* meaning "household," and *nomos,* meaning "rule," or "governance." Economics is the social science that studies how economies operate. There have been economies since the dawn of civilization, but economics is a recently developed field of study. It originated as a discipline during the 18th century.

What an Economy Is

An economy is the wealth-producing segment of society. Wealth is defined as the total produce of agriculture and manufacturing. Without products there can be no wealth. This means, of course, that money is not wealth. Money is a means of exchange and may be called the economic equivalent of wealth.

Economies exist because all human beings have needs and desires. All human physical needs are the same: food, clothing, and shelter. Desires, on the other hand, are virtually infinite. No one actually needs a television set, automobile, stereo set, or microwave oven. But such commodities have become so common in modern industrialized societies that few people would be without them.

The needs of society are satisfied by the production of goods—society's wealth. The desires are satisfied in the same way. Societies that cannot feed, shelter, and clothe themselves are poor. They have few products to satisfy basic needs and cannot even think of desires. In the United States, by contrast, there is a great abundance of products for most people. Needs and desires can both be satisfied.

Wealth—all products taken together—is produced by labor. This type of labor can therefore be called productive labor. Much of society's labor does not create wealth. It is thus called nonproductive labor. To say that it is nonproductive is not to say something negative about it. Most forms of nonproductive labor are necessary in civilized societies. The labor of those who work in government, education, religion, athletics, some of the arts, and the military does not produce products. Therefore it does not create wealth to add to the prosperity of a nation. But these services are needed because no society is entirely economic in its nature, though most modern societies are basically economic units or collections of such units.

The products that are wealth serve to create money. Without products there would be no need for money. If every family grew its own food, built its own housing, and made its own clothing, it would have no need for money—unless, of course, it had desires that it could not satisfy within the household. Money emerges as a product substitute, a means by which unlike products can be exchanged for each other. It is much easier to use money to buy a pair of shoes than to trade a cow for 20 pairs of shoes that are not needed. (*See also* Coins; Money.)

Money facilitates the movement of goods. It becomes a standard that people in a society use in exchange for what they need and want. It also helps keep production going. The person who produces shoes and sells them obtains money to buy more leather and make more shoes.

The laborer who produces wealth receives payment in return. With this payment it is possible to buy what is needed and wanted as well as to produce more goods. From where, then, does nonproductive labor receive payment? It comes from the producers of wealth, mostly in the form of taxes to support programs of government—national, state, and local. It also comes from productive laborers who willingly give it to see spectator sports, movies, theatrical events, or hear concerts of music. Much of it is also given to support religious enterprises and charitable organizations. A good deal of support goes to the service enterprises: physicians, dentists, barbers, hospitals, veterinarians, house painters, and many more.

The many nonproductive forms of labor, though they do not create wealth, purchase much of it. So their payments go back into the productive sector to help create more wealth. House painters need paints, brushes, and ladders. Hospitals need a vast array of equipment, medicines, and other goods.

Management of Economies

As noted, economy originally had to do with household management. Whether they are single households or whole societies, economies are always managed to some extent. Management is necessary because, no matter how extensive the needs or unlimited the desires, the resources required to satisfy them are limited. There is never an infinite amount of anything—no matter how much is produced.

People in a society of abundance may not notice the limits on resources until a crisis occurs. The petroleum price increases of the 1970s, for instance, alerted the whole world to the fact that petroleum is a nonrenewable resource. If its allocation is not carefully managed, severe economic hardships can result.

There are primarily three types of management in economies. An economy may be almost totally planned, as it is in the Soviet Union. An economy may be almost totally unplanned, as it is in the United States. Or there may be a combination of planning and freedom of operation, as is the case in Japan, South Korea, and Singapore.

In a planned economy the government decides what goods are to be produced and how they are to be marketed. Government sets all the priorities, and the producers follow the directives handed to them.

In a partially planned economy, such as Japan's, the government frequently takes the lead in encouraging manufactures and industry and helps with subsidies from taxation. Government can also promote investment and regulate trade policies so that they favor domestic manufactures.

The United States is the foremost example of an unplanned economy. This does not mean, however, that there is no government involvement in economic functions. There is a great deal. As the economy of the United States grew, and as government and its scope of responsibility increased, it was inevitable that government policy at every level would affect economic functions.

Nevertheless, the economy of the United States can be considered unplanned because the government does not mandate what will be produced or how it will be marketed. These decisions are left largely to the private sector. Even the enormous amount of government regulation that has emerged since the Great Depression has not turned the United States into a planned economy.

If an economy is not planned, how can it be managed? No one seems to be in control. There are, in fact, many controls; but the prime control is what is called the marketplace.

The name of the American economic system is capitalism. Another name for it is the free market economy (*see* Capitalism). Although markets are not nearly so free as they were a century ago, capitalism is a self-regulating economy. This self-regulation occurs through the operation of markets.

A market is composed of two factors: supply and demand. Which one predominates has never been decided by economists. In reality they probably alternate like the swings of a pendulum. Sometimes a popular demand calls forth a product; at other times a supply creates a demand.

In the 1950s, for instance, someone decided that a toy called the hula hoop might become a popular fad. Many hula hoops were made, they became a craze, and millions were sold. Eventually the craze died, no more were sold, and manufacture stopped.

An even more interesting case of market forces occurred in 1985. The Coca-Cola Company stopped producing and selling its decades-old formula for Coke and replaced it with a new formula in April. By July the new formula had proved sufficiently unpopular that the old formula was again being produced and marketed—now under the name "Classic Coca-Cola." The new formula continued to be sold as well.

In the late 20th century the great economic issue is the planned versus unplanned economy. The planned one is generally called socialist or communist. The unplanned and partially planned are considered capitalist because most of the actual production of wealth takes place in the private sector. Historically, after decades of competition between planned and unplanned economies, the latter have proved themselves far more adept at creating wealth. A chief reason for this success is that unplanned economies depend on individual initiative, personal ambition and ingenuity, and the openness of opportunities in an arena of political freedom.

Against unplanned economies, it may be said that wealth is unevenly distributed. A significant minority is very rich, a more significant minority lives in relative poverty, and the great bulk of the population—the middle class—lives in fair abundance. It is primarily this uneven distribution of wealth that planned economies hoped to solve.

The debate between planned and unplanned economies, however, is uneven. It is really a clash between an assortment of political systems and one economic system. To understand this, it is necessary to learn what an economic system is.

The Economic System

From the earliest days of civilization until the end of the Middle Ages—about 5,550 years—all societies had economic arrangements to satisfy the needs and desires of their populations. But the societies themselves were political, religious, and military units made up of the rulers and the ruled. It was the ruled who produced the wealth. They were slaves, peasants, or craftsmen, and most of their wealth went to enrich the ruling classes. In other words, nonproductive labor lived off productive labor.

Late in the Middle Ages a number of factors slowly came together to create the modern economic system called capitalism. Among these factors were the emergence of international banking, the creation of overseas colonial empires, expanded international trade, the growing independence of working people from their overlords, and the gradually lessened control by governments over economic functions. To these was added in the 18th century the start of the Industrial Revolution. This was the most potent agent of economic change (*see* Industrial Revolution). It was a real revolution in that it transformed societies completely and, for the first time, into primarily economic units or collections of economic units.

Everyone in a society, from the ruler down to the lowliest worker, became involved in the economy. What had been a matter of convenient and random economic arrangements was changed into an economic system. Nearly everything in society became a commodity to be bought or sold. Labor itself was uprooted from its fixed place on land or in guilds and became a commodity. People offered their services to employers, who paid them instead of taking their wealth by force. Now they worked for entrepreneurs, or businessmen, instead of for rulers. Societies had become economies.

There were still political, military, and other institutional arrangements, but the real well-being of a society depended on its economic function. Societies were rapidly expanding marketplaces that existed primarily for the creation of wealth.

For the first time in history it was possible to think of improving everyone's material status in life. People could see themselves as having a stake in society—a chance to raise their status and to obtain some wealth for themselves.

Capitalism is the only real economic system that has emerged in the world. It can be called a system because it embraces all of society and because it operates on its own terms. It does not need government or any other traditional institutional framework to make it operate.

Competing Political Systems

Capitalism is not without serious flaws. The uneven distribution of wealth has been noted. The growing pains of capitalism and the Industrial Revolution caused massive social dislocations, the growth of robust but filth-laden factory towns, classes of workers who were virtual wage slaves, appalling child labor exploitation, and many more problems.

These flaws called forth vigorous protests. By chance, popular democracy was emerging as a social force at the same time capitalism was in its early stages. The call for political democracy merged with demands for economic democracy. Socialism, which is one type of political democracy, was born at the same time as the object of its criticism—the free market economy—was taking shape.

But neither socialism, nor one of the developments from it called communism, are economic systems. They are political arrangements that attempt to do away with what are perceived as the worst features of capitalism. They do this in much the same way governments did before the advent of capitalism—by managing the economy. The erratic nature of the marketplace is removed and replaced by economic planners who are essentially political figures. Systems of production and consumption become government-operated, much as in ancient Egypt or Rome.

Fiction of National Economies

The nation-state and capitalism emerged together toward the end of the Middle Ages. This coincidence has led traditional economists to assume that economies were national features. There was, and still is, talk of the American, British, Japanese, or West German economies.

Large nations are actually collections of many economies. In the United States, for example, the economies of Detroit, New York City, Chicago, Los Angeles, and other cities all have their own characteristics. Wealth is created locally, though it may depend on resources obtained elsewhere.

Economies are primarily city-based and city-originated operations. This fact is easily camouflaged by a government when it issues reports on Gross National Product (GNP), the total of all goods and services produced by all segments of a nation's economies.

But the goods are produced and the services rendered in specific localities—in cities and the regions around them. At any given time one city and region may be prosperous, while another may be in decline and have high unemployment. One of the few nations in the world that can be said to have an economy instead of economies is Singapore. It is a small island nation that is really a city-state—a city and its surrounding region. Prosperous Hong Kong, though not independent, also qualifies as an economy.

Imperfection and Complexity

The larger a machine and the more numerous its parts, the greater likelihood of a breakdown and the more expensive to repair. What has been said about market forces and management was necessarily oversimplified. The economies of modern industrial nations are large and very complex. To be sure, there is management, and there are market forces at work, but there are also many other factors that help or hinder economic function.

In modern industrial societies governments play a large role. There is a great amount of regulation, most of it meant for the protection of the public. All regulations affect the way businesses operate, often increasing their costs and reducing their profits. Lower profits, in turn, reduce the amount of money—which is known as working capital—that a company can use for expansion. Auto emission standards, for instance, have had a significant impact on the manufacture and pricing of automobiles. Other government policies—such as taxation, budget deficits, and regulation of the money supply—have an effect on how much money is available for people to spend on goods and services.

International crises and other conditions also affect the working of an economy. A severe frost in Brazil can ruin a coffee crop and raise the price of that commodity. War can cut off the supply of such resources as petroleum, chromium, or copper.

In the United States environmental protests have slowed the development of nuclear energy capacity and the mining of vast tracts of protected land. Weather affects agriculture: a hot, dry summer can damage the wheat crop; floods can destroy thousands of acres of crops suddenly; and insect pests can devastate cropland with a rapid onslaught.

People's attitudes also have an impact on the marketing of goods. Health-conscious individuals, for example, may stop smoking, curtail their intake of alcohol, and eat less of certain kinds of food. Advertising affects what people buy, and it can create a market where none existed. Style and fashion are significant for many consumers.

There are other economic problems that are more difficult to understand. For centuries economies have been subject to periods of prosperity followed by periods of decline. These alternations are commonly called times of "boom and bust" (*see* Business Cycle). Although periods of prosperity can be explained rather easily, the reasons for panics, recessions, and depressions are complex. So many factors contributed to the Great Depression of the 1930s, for example, that no economist has ever been able to account for all of them.

Because the causes of decline are uncertain, the remedies are equally uncertain. In the late 20th century all industrialized societies through their governments have tried to stabilize economies, keep them prosperous, and reduce unemployment. None of the remedies has worked to the extent that was hoped. How economies work and what remedies can be found to keep them operating efficiently are the tasks of economists, who must work together with businessmen and politicians.

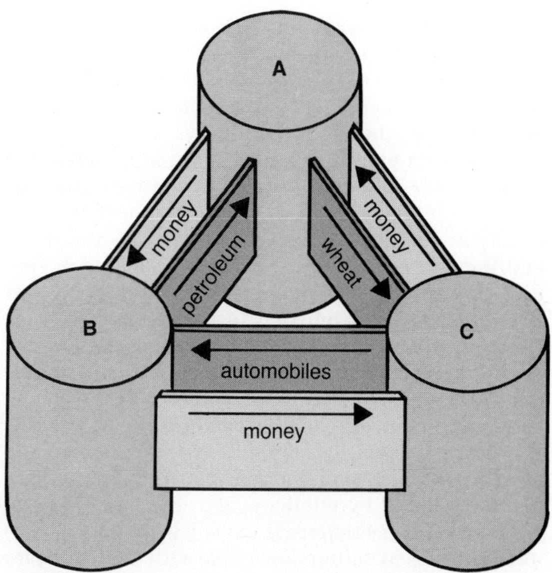

The real wealth of a society consists of what it produces. When sold or sent abroad in trade, goods become circulating capital and are exchanged for money. The money then becomes circulating capital, which finds its way back to the producing nations to pay for what they import.

The Discipline of Economics

The English economist Alfred Marshall defined his work as "a study of mankind in the ordinary business of life." For Marshall and his 19th-century predecessors, economics was a social science that had its birth in 1776, when the Scottish moral philosopher Adam Smith published his classic 'Inquiry into the Nature and Causes of the Wealth of Nations'. This book, still one of the most readable in the whole field, was the first to recognize the nature of the economic system that was developing in Great Britain and continental Europe. It laid the foundations for all future study of the subject and provided the basic definitions of wealth and labor used in this article.

In the 20th century, economics has become a far more complex and diverse study than either Smith or Marshall (a century later) could have envisioned. There are first of all three approaches to thinking about economics: microeconomics, macroeconomics, and development economics. (The prefixes *micro* and *macro* mean "small" and "large" respectively.) There are also several specialized fields of study that deal with different facets of economic functioning. Among them are public finance, monetary (or money) economics, international economics, labor economics, industrial organization, agricultural economics, growth economics, mathematical economics, and econometrics. Beyond these there are even more specialized areas such as the economics of banking, the investment markets, insurance, corporate management, and marketing, to name a few.

Microeconomics focuses on individual economic units. It is the study of the economic behavior of individual consumers, firms, and industries and the distribution of total production and income among them. It considers individuals both as the suppliers of labor and as consumers of final products, and it analyzes firms both as suppliers of products and as consumers of labor and capital.

Macroeconomics, by contrast, is the study of the whole economy in all of its interrelationships: the total amount of goods and services produced, total income earned, the level of use of productive resources, and the general behavior of prices. This area of economics owes its development to the work of John Maynard Keynes, who tried to point out ways that governments could use fiscal policy and the control of the money supply to achieve prosperity and full employment (*see* Keynes).

Development economics is concerned with all the factors responsible for self-sustaining economic growth and with the extent that these factors can be manipulated by public, or government, policies. Development economics is especially applicable to underdeveloped nations and those with low per capita incomes. It seeks means of increased production and effective use of resources.

Public finance in the 19th century was mostly concerned with determining the operation of tax systems—who really pays taxes. Did corporations pay taxes, or were they passed on to consumers? If passed on to consumers, did the rise in price tend to lower demand, thereby leading to unemployment? In the 20th century, especially under the influence of Keynes, public finance has broadened considerably to deal with the relation of the public budget and its uses in the economy. In the 1960s the technique called cost-benefit analysis came into prominence. This technique tries to appraise all costs and benefits of a particular expenditure to determine how public funds should be most sensibly distributed.

Monetary economics deals primarily with two issues: government control over the money supply and fiscal, or budgetary, policy to see how government can best influence the operation of the economy by its decisions. Related to government policy in this area are, of course, such matters as employment, inflation, investment decisions, and interest rates.

International economics deals with the distribution of the gains from trade among all countries, the balance of payments problem, the workings of foreign exchange markets, and the relation between balance of payments and levels of economic development. It tries to explain patterns of international trade in terms of the land, capital, and labor resources of a nation. It also analyzes the effects of a change in trade on the industrial structures of economies. (*See also* International Trade.)

Labor economics, as its name suggests, is concerned with the supply of and demand for labor. It also pays attention to the makeup of the labor market, the increasing tendency of women to work outside the home, the problem of minimum wages in keeping young people out of the labor market, and the economics of training people for the labor force. It also seeks to explain the factors that determine wage

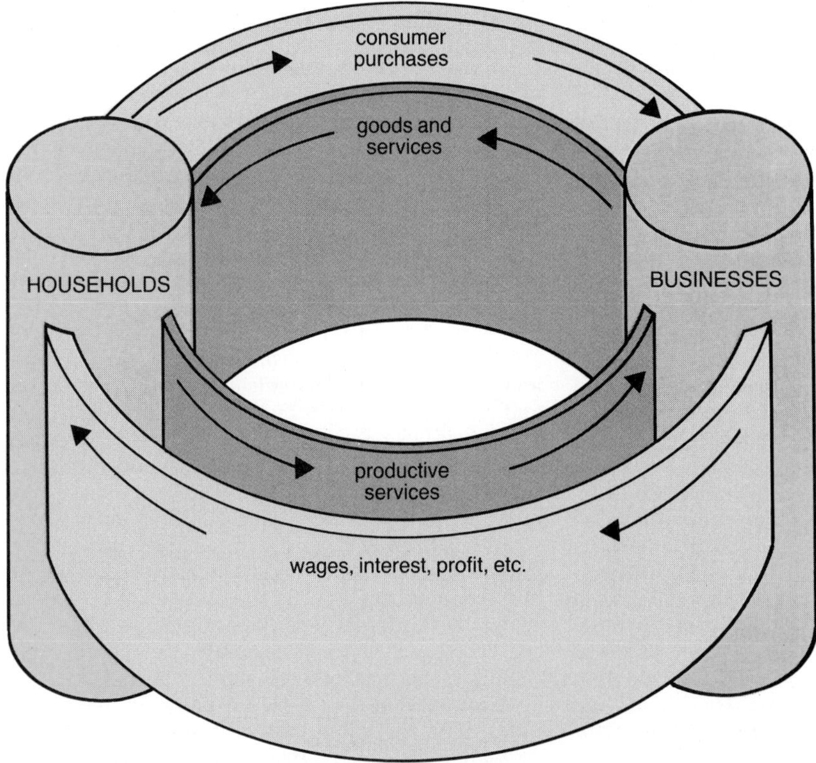

A modern industrial economy consists of a circular flow of goods, services, and money. Labor flows through businesses to produce goods or services. Money flows from businesses to individuals as wages, interest, and profits. Much of that money finds its way back to the businesses through the purchase of products or services. The gross national product of an economy measures the total value of all goods and services.

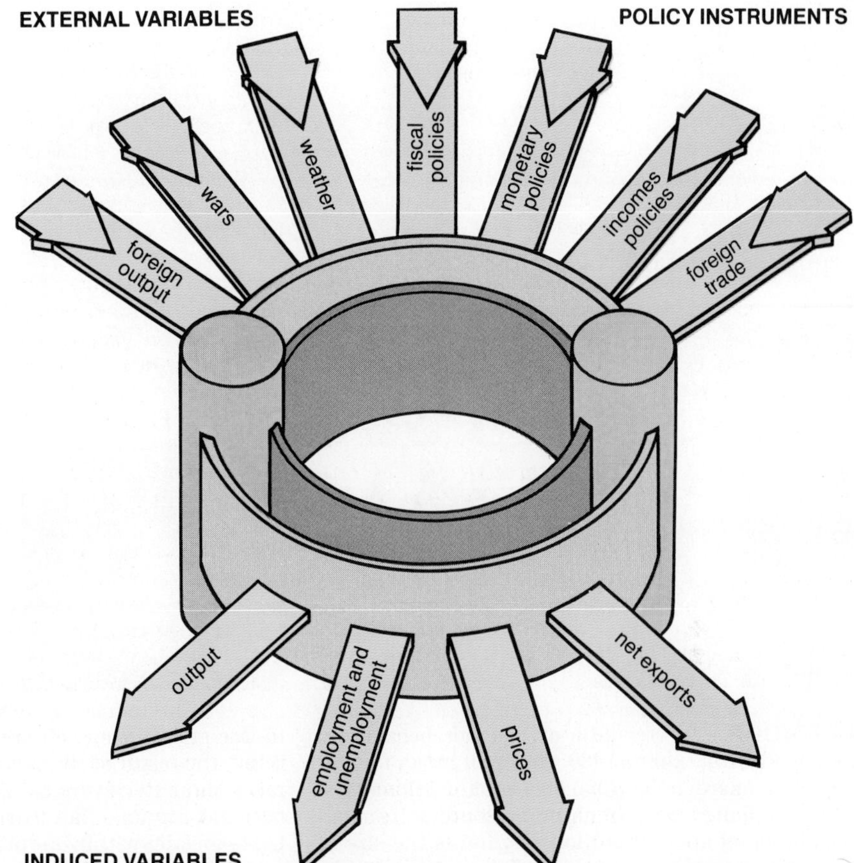

Macroeconomics is the study of the interrelationship of all components of economic functioning, both nationally and internationally. All economies are affected by variables. Some variables are external—such as weather or foreign wars. Others are induced—the outcome of the operation of the economic processes in the microeconomy. Still others are policy variables, which may be established by governments and changed from time to time to promote prosperity by slowing inflation and increasing employment.

levels and the effect of wages on prices, especially on inflation. (*See also* Labor.)

Industrial economics deals with the structure of markets, public policy toward monopolies, the regulation of public utilities, and the influence of technology on the economy.

Agricultural economics has for a long time focused its attention on farming as the perfectly competitive segment of the economy. But changes in government policy in this century have changed the farming picture a great deal. Now there are price controls, income supports, output ceilings, and marketing cartels or monopolies. Much attention in recent decades has centered on agricultural policies of the underdeveloped societies, where there is still much subsistence farming and little commercial agriculture.

Growth economics, mathematical economics, and econometrics are very complex areas of study, using a great deal of mathematics, differential calculus, and statistics to do their work. Growth economics is considered one of the most demanding fields with its use of complicated models to forecast the way an economy should act under certain circumstances. Mathematical economics considers the purely theoretical aspects of economic analysis, while econometrics tries to prove or disprove economic theories that are expressed in explicit mathematical terms.

BIBLIOGRAPHY FOR ECONOMICS

*Classical Works**

Keynes, J.M. The General Theory of Employment, Interest, and Money (1936).
Malthus, Thomas. Essay on Population (1798).
Marshall, Alfred. Principles of Economics (1890).
Marx, Karl. Capital (Vol. 1, 1867).
Mill, John. Principles of Political Economy (1848).
Ricardo, David. Principles of Political Economy and Taxation (1817).
Smith, Adam. The Wealth of Nations (1776).

Recent Works

Barber, W.J. A History of Economic Thought (Praeger, 1968).
Friedman, M. and R. Free to Choose (Harcourt, 1980).
Galbraith, J.K. The Affluent Society, 4th ed. (Houghton, 1984).
Heilbroner, R.L. The Making of Economic Society (Prentice, 1985).
Heilbroner, R.L. The Nature and Logic of Capitalism (W.W. Norton, 1985).
Jacobs, Jane. Cities and the Wealth of Nations (Random, 1984).
Polanyi, Karl. The Great Transformation (Holt, 1944).
Reich, Robert. The Next American Frontier (Times, 1983).
Rosenberg, N. and Birdzell, L. How the West Grew Rich (Basic Books, 1985).
Samuelson, P.A. and Nordhaus, W. Economics, 12th ed. (McGraw, 1985).
Schumpeter, Joseph. Capitalism, Socialism, and Democracy (Harper, 1946).
Strachey, John. Contemporary Capitalism (Random, 1956).
Warsh, David. The Idea of Economic Complexity (Viking Press, 1984).

*Published in a variety of modern editions.

Quito, Ecuador, with its large Government Palace, sits on the lower slopes of the dormant Pichincha volcano.

David Forbert—Shostal Associates

ECUADOR. The republic of Ecuador became an independent nation in 1830. Its small area of about 108,000 square miles (280,000 square kilometers) gives it a limited range of natural resources. Its small population of about 9 million also limits the size of the domestic market. It is bounded on the north by Colombia and surrounded on the east and south by Peru, with which it has had frequent border disputes. Since 1973 it has benefited from petroleum exports that have stimulated both industrialization and increasing urban migration.

Regions

Ecuador can be divided into three ecological regions: the coastal lowlands, the Andean highlands, and the eastern forested plains—known respectively as costa, sierra, and oriente. The Andean highlands run like a wide backbone north-southward through the center of the country, and it is their altitude that dramatically diversifies the equatorial climate and vegetation of the whole country. Two parallel ranges containing high volcanic peaks—such as Cotopaxi at 19,347 feet (5,897 meters) and Chimborazo at 20,577 feet (6,272 meters)—mark the edges of these highlands. The ranges are separated by a wide trough composed of ten basins averaging more than 7,000 feet (2,100 meters) in height. Though each basin varies in size and altitude, all are characterized by rugged relief, the result of rivers cutting through glacial terraces and extensive fans of volcanic ash. Quito, the national capital—like Ibarra, Cuenca, Ambato, and Loja—nestles within one of these basins. In the sierra region the principal resources are a fertile but easily eroded soil and a climate that has been compared to an eternal spring.

The plains that descend abruptly eastward from the flanks of the highlands toward the Amazon River are predominantly shrouded in thick tropical rain forest. The resources of hardwoods and petroleum and other minerals have hardly begun to be explored, let alone exploited.

The characteristics of the western coastal region perhaps explain the relative neglect of the east of Ecuador. Here, at elevations of normally less than 1,000 feet (300 meters), there is relatively flat land that is easily accessible from the historic highland core. It is firmly connected to the outside world by international commerce. On the coast one can pass within a few degrees of latitude from tropical rain forest in the north to absolute desert conditions in the south. This is the region that for generations has produced Ecuador's best-known export—bananas. It is now not only the agricultural breadbasket of the country but also the focus of industrial development. Guayaquil and Esmeraldas are the two dominant cities of the costa, the former exceeding the population of Quito since 1910.

People and Culture

Ecuador has four ethnic groups: Indians, mestizos, blacks, and whites. The historic homeland of the Indi-

This article was contributed by David J. Robinson, Dellplain Professor of Latin American Geography, Syracuse University, N.Y.; Director of USAID Technical Assistance to the Integrated Regional Development Project, Peru (1981–84); and author of 'Studying Latin America' (1981) and 'Social Fabric and Spatial Structure of Colonial Latin America' (1979).

ans—some 40 percent of the total population—is the sierra. It was here that a relatively advanced culture was encountered in the 16th century by the invading Spaniards. For the last 400 years this Indian population, after recovering from near destruction caused by the introduced European diseases, has struggled to maintain some of the symbols and functions of its cultural identity: the *quichua* language, traditional dress (especially the ruana shawl), foodstuffs, the strength of local community organization, and a suspicion of non-Indian ways. Yet modernization has encouraged change that has normally meant migration out of the sierra and the adoption of modern technology in agriculture. Indians are the least significant population element of Ecuador in terms of economic and political power as well as social status.

The mestizos—called *cholos* in the highlands—are the product of the rapid racial intermixture of whites with Indians. The majority of this group—some 40 percent of the total population—live in the coastal region and are employed on the rice, banana, and cacao plantations. Many have gained economic benefits, but relatively few have political power.

The 10 percent of blacks and mulattoes reflects the colonial past of Ecuador when black African slaves were imported to work coastal plantations. They are now mostly concentrated in the northern section of the coast.

The whites of Spanish descent, who make up the remaining 10 percent of the population, are the elite of Ecuadorian society. Since they form the majority of the industrialists, large agricultural estate owners, politicians, and businessmen, they usually decide what other Ecuadorians will have and what they can do. This group is typically urban-based, concentrated in the largest cities.

Economy

Each of Ecuador's ecological regions has a distinctive economic base and has experienced a distinctive economic history. The sierra economy continues to be directly or indirectly based on agriculture, primarily subsistence production for domestic use. Typical crops are corn, potatoes, wheat, and barley. On the high grassy pastures sheep and cattle are also raised to supply the urban markets with meat. The most significant problem in agriculture is that of the uneven distribution of land. Farms are either too large or too small. In spite of agrarian reform laws that were passed in 1964 and 1974, 10 percent of the land area still accommodates 75 percent of the total number of farm units. Almost 2 million peasant farmers have less than 4 acres (1.6 hectares) each on which to make a living, and fragmentation continues at a rapid rate. The only manufacturing industy in the sierra is the remnant of the so-called Panama hat industry in the city of Cuenca. It uses palms brought from the southern coast. The textile industry of Quito and other towns of the highlands was destroyed by competition from British imports in the 19th century. For this reason persons who abandon farming in the sierra have few alternative employment opportunities. They thus tend to migrate directly out of the central region to seek their fortune on the coast.

The coast has experienced what is best described as a series of "boom" economic cycles, each of which has further strengthened the coast's dominant role in Ecuadorian development. From 1870 to 1924 cacao cultivation triggered an economic boom that quickly boosted national revenues, financed the construction of the railway from Guayaquil to Quito, and stimulated agricultural colonization in the Guayas River basin. Cacao production was badly affected, however, by the effects of witchbroom disease after 1922. In the 1930s first rice and then coffee were cultivated, but it was not until around 1945 that Ecuador's principal export crop—bananas—spread rapidly throughout the coastal zone. Ecuador's coast has almost optimum conditions for the cultivation of this crop that rapidly achieved popularity in Western Europe and the United States. Before the export of petroleum, bananas accounted for some 60 percent of total export revenues, and by 1953 Ecuador had become the world's leading supplier. The two centers of production and export have been Esmeraldas and Guayaquil. Since the construction of a specialized port near Guayaquil, there has been a significant shift southward of areas under cultivation. Access to foreign markets is the key to success in banana production. The activity in and relative prosperity of the costa have attracted *serranos*, or natives of the sierra, in very large numbers. Many work as sharecroppers on the commercial estates.

The oriente, long an isolated and undeveloped region except for scattered logging camps, quickly reoriented the entire national economy following the major petroleum strikes in 1967 near Lake Agrio in the northeast. With the rapid construction of a pipeline from the oil fields to Quito and then to Esmeraldas on

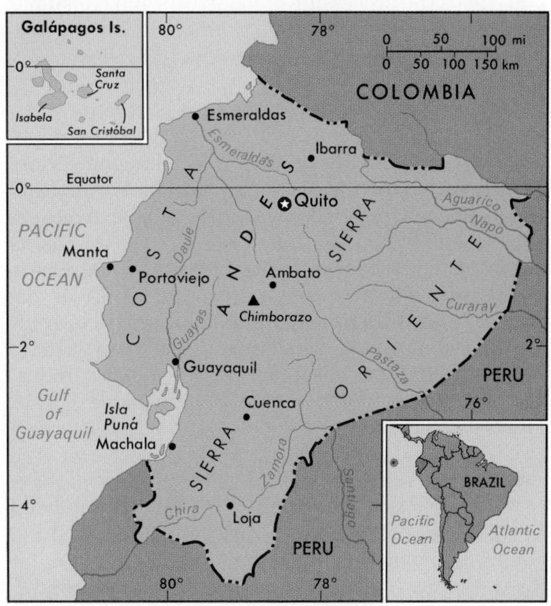

Elizabeth Harris—CLICK/Chicago

Elizabeth Harris—CLICK/Chicago

Bananas (left), Ecuador's largest export crop, are harvested at a plantation in the western lowland of the Pacific coast. This area is ideally suited for growing bananas and has made Ecuador the world's leading supplier. A farmer (right) at Otavalo teaches his grandson to use the plow.

the coast, Ecuador began to export petroleum in 1971 and joined the OPEC group in 1974. The rapid rise in world prices for oil after 1973 meant huge gains in foreign currency for Ecuador. Export earnings rose fivefold between 1971 and 1975, and Ecuador came to be seen as a creditworthy nation by the international financial market.

Income from the new export earnings and loans began to be invested in major planned projects. The national road network, for example, was extended from 6,200 to 17,400 miles (10,000 to 28,000 kilometers) between 1970 and 1985. The government also invested money in industrial enterprises such as steel, petrochemicals, shipbuilding, and fishing after 1973. In spite of such attempts to diversify the basis of the economy, and as a result of the disadvantageous competitive position of Ecuador in world trade, in the mid-1980s the processing of foodstuffs and consumer goods still accounted for two thirds of industrial production, three quarters of which is located in Quito and Guayaquil.

The changing regional basis of resource development in Ecuador has had a dramatic effect on population distribution. By 1974 the coastal region's share exceeded that of the sierra for the first time, and cities everywhere acted as magnets to poor migrants who saw little hope in agriculture. New settlements began to appear in the forests of the eastern region, as did vast shantytowns around almost all of the coastal towns. Thousands of Ecuadorians were literally on the move to a better future. As many were to find to their bitter disappointment, modern industrial technology did not require their eager hands. Thus, thousands were forced to enter the so-called "informal" industrial sector, working part-time in a variety of menial jobs such as shoe shining, garbage collecting, or street vending. For those who did not speak Spanish, had little formal education, and did not have personal contacts who could find jobs for them, the rosy future became a desperate present.

History and Government

In 1533 Sebastián de Benalcazar was sent northward from Peru by Francisco Pizarro to conquer the local Indians. Present-day Ecuador was occupied by a culture that had only recently been absorbed within the Inca empire. The sierra became rapidly colonized by the Spaniards, who established a chain of townships through the length of the mountains to connect settlement areas in Peru with those of New Granada (now Colombia).

From 1563 the province of Quito became part of the Viceroyalty of Peru, but it was later transferred to become a subdivision of the Viceroyalty of New Granada. This closer relationship with the north, rather than the south, was strengthened after political independence from Spain in 1822. Ecuador became one of three regional units in the Federation of Greater Colombia—together with Venezuela and Colombia. This grand idea of Simón Bolívar, however, did not endure the strains of nationalistic feelings.

Ecuador separated in 1830 to become an independent nation-state. Since that date Ecuador insists that it has unjustly lost vast territories to its several neighboring states, especially Peru. As recently as 1981 armed conflict broke out in a disputed sector of the Condor Mountains on Ecuador's southern border. Ecuador controls the Galápagos Islands and insists on its rights to a 200-mile limit for its territorial waters in the Pacific.

Based on the Constitution of 1978, Ecuador is a republic with a one-house legislature known as the National Congress. The president, elected to a single five-year term, is both head of state and head of the government. The judicial system is headed by the Supreme Court of Justice, which is elected by the National Congress.

During the first century of political independence, Ecuador experienced a rapid sequence of presidents, dictators, and ruling juntas. Between 1922 and 1948, for example, some 22 chiefs of state began, but did not finish, their terms of office. Political power in Ecuador has been fought over by two rival groups. The first is a combination of Roman Catholic conservatives whose power base is in the landholding elite of the sierra and the extensive national bureaucracy of Quito. The second is a group of more liberal progressives of Guayaquil and the coast who challenged the longstanding authority of the traditional elite of the sierra. For this second group commerce and wealth were avenues to power and prestige.

Great inequalities of wealth are still evident in almost every sector of Ecuador, and some argue that they are increasing rather than diminishing. The most wealthy 20 percent of the nation still receives almost 80 percent of the national income. The country is divided into two classes: the one rich, powerful, and bent on modernization; the other poor, powerless, neglected, and questioning the alleged benefits of modern life.

BIBLIOGRAPHY FOR ECUADOR

Hurtado, O. Political Power in Ecuador (Westview, 1985).

Linke, L. Ecuador: Country of Contrasts (Oxford, 1964).

Luzuriaga, C. Income Distribution and Poverty in Rural Ecuador (Arizona State Univ. Press, 1983).

Redclift, M.R. Agrarian Reform and Peasant Organization in Coastal Ecuador (London Univ. Press, 1978).

Schodt, D.W. Ecuador (Westview, 1986).

Whitten, N.E., ed. Cultural Transformations and Ethnicity in Modern Ecuador (Univ. of Ill. Press, 1981).

FACTS ABOUT ECUADOR

Offical Name: Republic of Ecuador.

Capital: Quito.

Area: 108,624 square miles (281,335 square kilometers).

Population (1985 census): 8,604,000; 79 persons per square mile (31 persons per square kilometer); 49 percent urban, 51 percent rural.

Major Language: Spanish (official).

Major Religion: Roman Catholicism.

Literacy: 85 percent.

Highest Peak: Chimborazo.

Major Rivers: Aguarico, Curaray, Esmeraldas, Guayas, Napo, Pastaza, Zamora.

Form of Government: Republic.

Head of State and Government: President.

Legislature: National Congress.

Voting Qualifications: Voting is compulsory for citizens over age 18 who are literate.

Political Divisions: 20 provinces.

Major Cities (1982 census): Guayaquil (1,204,532), Quito (890,355), Cuenca (157,213), Ambato (112,775), Machala (105,283).

Chief Manufactured and Mined Products: Cement, copper, processed foods, gold, natural gas, petrochemicals, petroleum, silver, steel.

Chief Agricultural and Food Products: *Crops*—bananas, barley, cacao, cassavas, coffee, corn (maize), potatoes, rice, sugarcane, wheat. *Livestock and fish*—cattle, pigs, seafood, sheep.

Flag: *Colors*—yellow, blue, and red. The state flag also has the national coat of arms at the center (*see* Flags of the World).

Monetary Unit: 1 sucre = 100 centavos.

ECUMENISM. There is a Greek word *oikos*, meaning "household"; and closely related to it is *oikoumene*, meaning "the inhabited world." From the latter is derived the relatively modern term ecumenism, which is used by Christian denominations to suggest the whole "household of God."

In the early centuries of its existence, the Christian church was undivided, but as the centuries passed separations occurred. These were mostly the result of strong differences in beliefs: The Eastern churches broke with those in the West in 1054; the Protestant Reformation began in 1517 (*see* Christianity; Reformation). There have been other splits, even within denominations, over the years. Ecumenism, or the ecumenical movement, of the 20th century is a recognition that the church is not united; and it is, as well, a strong attempt to seek and express the unity that Christianity once had.

Prior to the 20th century there were few attempts to heal the breaches between denominations. One major exception was the persistent overtures made by the Eastern Orthodox churches, specifically the Church of Constantinople, to make common cause with other denominations. These attempts did not come to fruition until the 20th century.

Since 1900, and especially since 1950, there have been several successful undertakings that have brought most Christian denominations closer together. These endeavors have operated at several levels: intra-denominational mergers; interdenominational mergers or discussions; national interdenominational agencies; and international agencies.

Much of the drive behind the modern ecumenical movement came from the International Missionary Conference at Edinburgh, Scotland, in 1910. This was followed by the International Missionary Council of 1921, the founding of the Life and Work Conferences in 1925, and the founding of the Faith and Order Conferences in 1927. These movements were incorporated into the World Council of Churches, founded in 1948.

The World Council is today the chief agency of Christian international cooperation. Among those who inspired this cooperation were John R. Mott of the United States; Nathan Söderblom, primate of Sweden; William Temple, archbishop of Canterbury, and G.K.A. Bell, bishop of Chichester, England; Germanos, bishop of Thyateira (Greek Orthodox church); and W.A. Visser t'Hooft of The Netherlands.

The Roman Catholic church is not a member of the World Council, though it sends observers to its meetings. But the Roman church has done a great deal to promote ecumenism through the work of the Second Vatican Council, held from 1962 to 1965, that was convened by Pope John XXIII. His successors Paul VI and John Paul II have continued to support the movement toward unity. The efforts by the Roman church are carried out through the Secretariat for the Promotion of Christian Unity, organized by Augustin Cardinal Bea of Germany. The secretariat accepts the idea of unity within diversity and works for dialogue to bring churches closer together.

EDDY, Mary Baker (1821–1910). The founder of the religious denomination known as Christian Science was Mary Baker Eddy. Born Mary Baker on July, 16, 1821, on a farm near Concord, N.H., she was a child who had little formal education because of persistent ill health. In 1843 she married George W. Glover. He died about six months later, and she returned to her parents' home. Ten years later she married a dentist named Daniel Patterson. This marriage ended in divorce in 1873.

For many years her health was bad, and she turned to the Bible for consolation. In the early 1860s she met and was healed by Phineas P. Quimby, who performed remarkable cures without medication. In 1866, following his death, she suffered a severe fall. On the third day after her injury, when she lay apparently near death, she called for her Bible and read the account in Matthew 9 of how Jesus healed the palsied man. She recovered in a seemingly miraculous manner. This experience led her to the discovery of the principle of Christian Science. There followed years of thought and study of the Bible, resulting in 1875 in her book 'Science and Health with Key to the Scriptures', the textbook of Christian Science (*see* Christian Science).

Among the students who gathered around her was Asa Gilbert Eddy, whom she married in 1877. In 1879 Mrs. Eddy organized the church in Boston, which came to be called the Mother Church, the First Church of Christ, Scientist. From this, branches spread to all parts of the United States and abroad. Mrs. Eddy remained the active leader of the Christian Science movement until she died on Dec. 3, 1910.

EDEN, Anthony (1897–1977). He served as Great Britain's prime minister for less than two years, but during his long career in politics Anthony Eden was regarded as a highly competent statesman and a brilliant diplomat.

Robert Anthony Eden was born on June 12, 1897, at Windlestone Hall in Durham. After attending Eton College he served as an infantry officer in World War I. After the war he attended Oxford University, where he earned an honors degree in Oriental languages. He entered Parliament in 1923 and remained there until his resignation in 1957. From 1926 until 1929 Eden was private secretary for the foreign secretary, Sir Austen Chamberlain. After serving in other posts, he became foreign secretary in December 1935 under Prime Minister Neville Chamberlain. It was at this time that Nazi Germany began its military buildup, and Eden was in favor of Britain's rapid rearmament. Chamberlain's overly optimistic dealings with Adolf Hitler angered Eden, and he resigned on Feb. 20, 1938 (*see* Chamberlain, Neville).

At the outbreak of World War II, Eden re-entered the Chamberlain government, and, when Churchill became prime minister in May 1940, he served as foreign secretary once again. The Conservatives were out of office from 1945 until 1951, but when Churchill returned as prime minister Eden was again foreign

Anthony Eden, Earl of Avon

secretary. He served with distinction trying to settle the Indochina War and in setting up the European Defense Community in 1954. In April 1955 he succeeded Churchill as prime minister and led the Conservatives through a successful election a few weeks later.

Eden had been seriously ill in 1953 and underwent three separate operations. He never totally regained his health, and this was a factor in his short service as prime minister. The Suez crisis of 1956 occupied much of his time. Dealing with this complicated affair, during which Egypt nationalized the canal and Israel attacked Egypt, broke Eden's health. He resigned from office on Jan. 9, 1957. In retirement he published his memoirs in three volumes and a book of essays, 'Toward Peace in Indochina', published in 1966. He received the title Earl of Avon in July 1961. He died at Alvediston in Wiltshire on Jan. 14, 1977.

EDERLE, Gertrude (born 1906). They told her to quit. She answered, "What for?" Nineteen-year-old Gertrude Ederle was on her way to becoming the first woman to swim the English Channel, and neither the pleas of her coach nor a storm that closed the channel to normal shipping would stop her. She completed the crossing in record time.

Gertrude Caroline Ederle was born in New York City on Oct. 23, 1906. She began swimming competitively at an early age and by 1922 was expert enough to break seven records in one afternoon at a Brighton Beach, N.Y., meet. At the 1924 Olympics Ederle won two individual bronze medals and a gold as a member of the freestyle relay team. Before she turned professional in 1925, she had broken a total of 29 different national and world amateur records.

In 1925 she made her first, unsuccessful, attempt to swim the English Channel. Her successful effort on Aug. 6, 1926, took only 14 hours, 31 minutes, which broke the men's record by 1 hour, 59 minutes, despite the fact that rough seas forced her to swim 35 miles (56 kilometers) to cover the 21-mile (34-kilometer) distance. She was an overnight celebrity and toured for some time giving swimming exhibitions. A spinal injury in 1933 made it necessary for her to wear body casts for nearly four years, but she recovered and again swam for the public.

EDINBURGH, Scotland. One of the loveliest cities of Europe, historic Edinburgh is the capital of Scotland. It is built on a series of ridges, separated by ravines, and its buildings harmonize with its unusual setting. Edinburgh was affectionately nicknamed "Auld Reekie" because of the smoke (reek) from its thousands of chimneys.

Edinburgh lies on the southern shores of the Firth of Forth, a long arm of the North Sea. The Old Town, which was the original burgh, or village, grew up on a mile- (1.6-kilometer-) long rocky spine that rises at its western end to massive Castle Rock. Its easily defended position high on a rock was the result of fears of attack in medieval times. Beyond a deep ravine to the north spreads the spacious New Town, which dates back to the 18th century. Modern suburbs stretch southward into the beautiful Pentland Hills and northward to the shores of the Firth of Forth. Leith, Edinburgh's port, was added to the city in 1920.

On the summit of Castle Rock stands Edinburgh Castle, ancient home of Scottish kings, now a museum of old armor and weapons. It has been a fortress from at least the 6th century. The oldest surviving building dates back to the 11th century. On either side of the valley are important east-west thoroughfares. One is the Royal Mile, and the other is Princes Street. To the east the Royal Mile runs along the ridged backbone of the picturesque Old Town. The Royal Mile, once jammed with sellers' booths and where people both lived and worked, was the center of city life. It is now quiet and clean and runs along other historic sections, including Lawnmarket, which was once the center for linen sellers. Lawnmarket turns into High Street with Parliament Square and the church of Saint Giles, where John Knox, leader of the Protestant Reformation in Scotland, often preached.

Dominating the city of Edinburgh is Castle Rock, the site of Edinburgh Castle, ancient home of Scottish kings.

Central Press—Pictorial Parade

For hundreds of years the Old Town was crowded within protecting walls and had to grow upward rather than outward. Its old stone houses—now tenements of the poor—are 10 and 12 stories high. The side streets, called wynds, are steep and narrow. These winding stone lanes are sometimes not much more than long staircases, some with a left-handed spiral that worked to the advantage of right-handed defending swordsmen in earlier centuries.

On the southern slope is the University of Edinburgh, which was founded in 1583. The Royal Mile ends at Holyrood Palace, where the rooms of Mary, Queen of Scots, are still preserved. It is also the official Edinburgh residence of the British monarch. Behind the palace is Holyrood Abbey. South of the palace spreads the treeless King's Park, from which rises Arthur's Seat, a mass of rock more than 5 miles (8 kilometers) around.

The New Town is connected with the old by bridges and by the Mound, an artificial causeway. On the Mound are Scotland's two most famous art centers—the National Gallery and the Royal Scottish Academy. Princes Street is the city's main thoroughfare with hotels, clubs, banks, and shops.

To the south are the Princes Street Gardens. The world's first floral clock was built there in 1903. In East Princes Street Gardens stands an ornate monument to Sir Walter Scott. Behind Princes Street run the higher George Street and then Queen Street, lined with stately houses of business.

There are many recreational facilities. There are 9 miles (14 kilometers) of coastline for boating, along with several beaches, numerous golf courses, and many bowling greens, public football and hockey fields, cricket pitches, and tennis courts. The Meadowbank Sports Center just east of the city was built for the 1970 Commonwealth Games.

Edinburgh is Scotland's center of medicine, law, banking, insurance, and tourism. Its three main manufacturing groups are food, beverages, and tobacco; engineering, electrical goods, and electronics; and paper, printing, and publishing.

Edinburgh's name comes from the Gaelic word *Duneideann*, meaning "fortress on a hill." It is also associated with Edwin, the 7th-century king of Northumbria. In 1436 Edinburgh became the capital of Scotland. The union of Scotland and England in 1707 reduced Edinburgh's importance, but it remained the legal and cultural center of Scotland. In the 18th and 19th centuries it was the center of a brilliant literary and philosophical circle that included David Hume, Adam Smith, Robert Burns, and Sir Walter Scott. Since 1947 Edinburgh has held an annual three-week international festival of music and drama. (*See also* Scotland; United Kingdom.) Population (1981 census), 419,187.

Thomas Edison's first successful incandescent light bulb had a carbonized cotton thread for a filament. Edison is shown here making a similar filament on the 50th anniversary of the bulb's invention.

EDISON

EDISON, Thomas Alva (1847–1931). When he was 21 years old, Thomas Edison took out his first patent. It was for an electric vote counter to be used in the United States House of Representatives. The machine worked perfectly, but the congressmen would not buy it. They did not want vote counting to be done quickly. Often the roll call was used for purposes of delay (filibustering).

This experience taught the young inventor a lesson. He decided to follow a simple rule: "First, be sure a thing is wanted or needed, then go ahead." When he died at 84, Edison had patented 1,093 inventions. They included the motion-picture projector, phonograph, electric-light bulb, and hundreds of others. Many were among the most useful and helpful inventions ever developed. (*See also* Electric Light; Inventions; Motion Pictures; Phonograph.)

Mother His Teacher

The man who was often to be called the greatest inventor who ever lived was born at Milan, Ohio, Feb. 11, 1847. His father, Samuel Edison, was a shingle maker. His mother, Nancy Elliott Edison, was a schoolteacher. When young Edison was seven, the family moved to Port Huron, Mich. There he went to school for three months—the only formal schooling he ever had.

Because of his very large but well-shaped head, the doctors thought young Edison might have brain trouble. His teachers thought him stupid because he questioned every answer given him. His mother, however, understood that her son asked so many questions because he wanted to know exactly how things worked. She encouraged him in his eagerness to learn. By the time he was 12, with his mother's help, he had read Gibbon's 'Decline and Fall of the Roman Empire', Hume's 'History of England', Sears's 'History of the World', Burton's 'Anatomy of Melancholy', and the 'Dictionary of Sciences'. He had also begun to do chemistry experiments and had his own laboratory in his father's basement.

By this time Edison's father was a successful grain and feed dealer in Port Huron. The young inventor did not really have to go to work, but he wanted his own money. He wanted to buy chemicals and equipment for his experiments. When he was 13, Edison became a newsboy on the Grand Trunk railroad between Port Huron and Detroit. Between trips he spent his free time reading science and reference books in the library.

In order to continue his chemistry experiments Edison set up a laboratory in a baggage car on the train. He also began publishing his own newspaper there on a press that had been used for printing handbills. He was typesetter, press operator, editor, publisher, and newsboy for this paper, which he called *The Herald.* He published not only local news but also national and international events. He got this news from telegraphers at stations along the way. He printed many reports of the Civil War battles, and these helped to make his newspaper a success. The *London Times* carried a story about Edison's paper, pointing out that it was the first newspaper in the world to be printed on a moving train.

Accident Caused Deafness

An accident at about this time started the deafness which Edison had for the rest of his life. One day he was trying to climb into a freight car with both arms full of newspapers. The conductor took him by both ears to lift him into the car. Edison felt something snap in his head, and his deafness began then. He always said he did not mind being deaf. It kept him from being bothered by outside noises and he could give full thought to the work at hand.

One day Edison was making an experiment in his baggage-car laboratory when a stick of phosphorus accidentally set the car on fire. The conductor threw out the boy and his equipment. Edison's railroading days came to an end.

Experiences as Boy Telegrapher

When Edison was 15, he saved the life of the baby son of a station agent at Mount Clemens, Mich. Edison was standing on the station platform when he saw that a freight car was about to run over a child who was playing on the tracks. He dashed to the rescue. The child's grateful father, John Mackenzie, offered to teach young Edison how to be a telegraph operator. He soon learned the Morse code and became skilled in sending and taking messages. At 16 he became a telegrapher at Stratford Junction, Canada. In his spare time Edison experimented with an old telegraph set, taking it apart and putting it together again. Finally he understood exactly how it worked.

One of Edison's first inventions was a telegraph repeater which automatically relayed a message to a second line. The second instrument was made to work at a slower rate of speed than the first. When a message came in too fast over the first receiver for Edison to copy easily, he could slow down the message by relaying it over the second machine. This device was the germ from which some of his later important inventions were developed. However, all it earned for him at the time was a reprimand from the manager of the telegraph office. The manager thought young Edison was wasting the telegraph company's time using such "toys."

As a young telegraph operator Edison dressed poorly. He spent all he earned on books and equipment. His employers were impatient with his habit of forgetting about his work as a telegrapher while he worked on his own experiments. Even so, he became a skilled operator. Soon he began to wander about the country, getting jobs as a "tramp telegrapher" whenever he had to have money. He continued to work hard on his ideas for inventions. After five years of this wandering life Edison went to Boston and then to New York City.

Perfects Stock Ticker

In Boston in 1869 at the age of 21 Edison patented his commercially unsuccessful vote counter. He brought with him to New York an idea for a stock quotation printing device. In New York he met a Dr. Samuel Laws, who already had a "stock ticker" in operation. When this primitive machine broke down, Edison repaired it. He was then hired by Laws and out of this association grew the development of a stock ticker that worked perfectly. For this and other inventions useful in stockbrokers' offices Edison expected to be paid only a few hundred dollars. He was sure he was being made the victim of a practical joke when Laws handed him a check for $40,000.

The only interest Edison ever had in money was to use it to buy more scientific equipment to work on new inventions. He used this $40,000 to start a laboratory and factory at Newark, N. J. He soon had 300 employees and began turning out a number of money-making inventions. He had as many as 50 inventions at various stages of development and manufacture at one time. Most of these had to do with various kinds of multiplex systems of telegraphy. But before he was 30 Edison's health failed, and he gave up his Newark factory.

"The Wizard of Menlo Park"

When he regained his health, Edison opened a laboratory at Menlo Park, N. J. There, from 1876 to 1886, he devoted his time entirely to invention. He soon became world-famous as "the wizard of Menlo Park." In one year alone (1882) Edison applied for 141 patents, 75 of which were granted. His major inventions were the incandescent electric light bulb, the phonograph, the motion-picture projector, automatic and multiplex telegraph, the carbon telephone trans-

HERALD.

Pubished on the Mixed Train. June

THE WEEKLY HERALD

PUBLISHED BY THE NEWSBOY ON THE MIXED TRAIN.

TERMS

Our Paper will be delivered to subecribers of the line of the Grand Trunk for eight cents per month in advance.

To Grand Trunk Aagents—We would feel obliged to the several Agents along the line of the Grand Trunk Railway if they would be kind enough to send their orders for the Herald to the Newsboy (T. Edison) Mixed Train Detroit Secion. Inclose eight cents per month strictly in advance. N, B, Aall items gladly received.

ITEMS.

The Norfolk Navy Yard is not to be rebuilt.

The ship builders of Philadelpha never enjoyed more prosperous times than at present.

Gen Sickles left Washington on Tuesday to resume command of the Excleior Brigade.

A vessel will sail from Baltimore for Liberia on the 15th of June by which emigrants can go.

In Toronto a crusade has been commenced by the authorities against the unlicenced grog-shops,

Col Corcoran is hourly expected at Norfolk under a flag of truce.

England.

Tom Sayers starts for Australia in September

The newspapers published in Great Britain number 1, 165,

John C, Heenan is showing in the south of Wales.

It is officially notified that Queen Victoria will this year hold no levee or drawing-room.

The celebrated English ratter Jacko recently finished 1558 rats in the marvellously quick time of 5min & 28 sc.

It is stated that the Duc'd A mle on visiting the French court at the Great Exhibition was dogged from spot to spot by a French detective, who took down the name of every exhibitor at whose stall the royal guest lingered

We understand that a memo al is about to be presented to her Mejesty to allow the State apartments at Windsor Castle to be thrown open to the public, in anticipation of Windsor being visited by numerous foriguers during the Exhibition.

Thus far the Great Exhibition in London has been perfectly successful in a pecuniary sence The amount received for season tickets to the 9th inst was 459, 649, Crowds of delighted and wondering daily congregate about the American sewing machienes watching the operators,

France.

Murphy the famous Irish giant has just died of small-pox at Marseilles,

The Emperor Napoleon is attending the Paris spring races,

The *Moniteur* announced the departure of Prince Napoleon to Naples adds he has no political misson,

It is reported in Paris that the Emperor of China intends sending an embassy extraordinary to France and England,

The Emperor and Empress and the Queen of Holland honered the Gymnase Theatre. Paris, with their presence to see Mr. Sarnou's new peice of La Perle Noire,

Local Intellegence,

There is great excitement in Montreal over an attempt to reduce the current value of the British shilling to 24c. The newspapers are reaping a good harvest from the advertisements of long lists of tetailers who will, and those who wont agree to the resolution.

Information wanted—Mr W. McSweeney while in Port Huron or Fort Gartiot a few days ago met in with a few of his old cronys, and very kindly invited them to partake of a Little John' Barley Corn, they did so, and were "unco happy" which however termenated in a little fuss that ended. Billy went to bed, and on getting up in the morning, his repeater, and all the loose Bank notes were gone, much to Billys discomfiture any information respecting either, will be gladly received by him,

We would say to Mr. McSweeney, the only cure for the above is to use one quart la a of John Barley Corn, each time you and friends meet and in the course of a few weeks, the nett gain will more than remunerate for the loss, Ed H

Oil—We learn that a combination is being entered into by the Canada Oil well diggers, with a view of raising the price of the crude Oil, to a remuneritive figure, a very necessary move, as the difference between the prices of crude and re-

Continued on 24 page.

In his early teens, Edison (left) was newsboy, editor, and publisher of *The Herald* (right). He printed and sold his weekly newspaper on one of the trains of the Grand Trunk railroad which ran between Port Huron and Detroit, Mich.

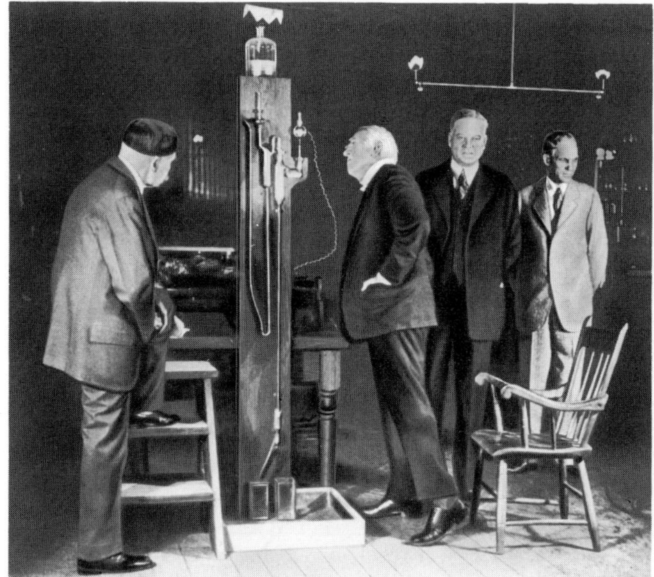

Edison's assistant Francis Jehl, Edison, Herbert Hoover, and Henry Ford are shown (left) at the re-enactment of electric light's invention. At right are Edison and his second wife. The pictures were taken in 1929 during Light's Golden Jubilee.

mitter, a stock ticker, and the alkaline storage battery. Not all his inventions were made easily. He worked on some for years and spent thousands of dollars in perfecting them.

First Used "Hello!" as Telephone Greeting

The first Bell telephone was both a transmitter and a receiver. One spoke through it and then put it to one's ear to hear the reply. The instrument was also weak in reproducing the voice and picked up much static. Edison invented a carbon transmitter that gave the voice unlimited power. He also invented a receiver that contained a button-sized chalk diaphragm. This chalk receiver was widely used for many years, particularly in England. (*See also* Bell, Alexander Graham.)

In using the early telephones people rang a bell by hand and then said into the instrument, "Are you ready to talk?" or asked some similar question. One day Edison was working in his laboratory to perfect the telephone. According to one story, he picked up the instrument during a test and said into the transmitter, "Hello!" This greeting soon became a standard way to start a telephone conversation.

Family Life

Edison married his first wife, Mary G. Stillwell, in 1871. She had worked in his laboratory. They had three children—Marion, Thomas, and William. Edison nicknamed his first two children "Dot" and "Dash." Mrs. Edison died in 1884, and the inventor married Mina Miller in 1886. They also had three children—Madeline, Charles, and Theodore. Charles later became governor of New Jersey.

A big workshop and a small house suited Edison. He went about in shabby work clothes and with acid-stained hands. Most of the time his wife and children dined alone, for Edison ate when he was hungry and rested when he was tired. He worked 18 and 19 hours a day as a rule and was so absorbed in his work that he seldom knew if it was night or day. "I owe my success," he often said, "to the fact that I never had a clock in my workroom." Another secret of Edison's success was his unlimited patience. "Genius," he said, "is two per cent inspiration and ninety-eight per cent perspiration." His powerful imagination, his firm optimism, and his complete self-confidence were

This camera, or kinetograph, invented by Edison in 1891, was an important step in the development of motion pictures.

other traits that helped to distinguish him from ordinary men.

Invention of the Phonograph

When he was about 30, Edison invented the phonograph. He called it a "talking machine." It worked much like the dictating machines that were later adapted from it. Edison's phonograph consisted of a revolving cylinder wrapped in tinfoil. A sharp point was pressed against the foil-wrapped cylinder. Attached to the point were a diaphragm and a large mouthpiece. The cylinder was rotated by hand.

When Edison spoke into the mouthpiece, his voice made the diaphragm vibrate. This caused the sharp point to cut a trace in the tinfoil. When a needle replaced the cutting point, the talking machine reproduced Edison's original words. When Edison first demonstrated the machine to his laboratory assistants, they were startled to hear coming from it the words, "Mary had a little lamb." For a time they would not believe that the device actually worked as Edison said it did. They thought he was playing some kind of trick on them. Later, when everyone had become convinced of the reality of Edison's latest invention, he continued to work on improvements for it. He spent more than 3 million dollars perfecting the phonograph. (*See also* Phonograph.)

The Motion-Picture Camera and Projector

While perfecting the phonograph, Edison was also developing a motion-picture camera and projector. The camera, called a kinetograph, and the projector, called a kinetoscope, used roll film developed by George Eastman (*see* Eastman). Previously single-plate film had been used in an effort to produce motion pictures.

Edison's kinetograph was the first practical motion-picture camera; the kinetoscope was the first workable projector. The kinetoscope was a small "peep-show" type of box inside which the motion picture was projected. The picture was viewed through an eyehole in the top of the box. A disadvantage was that only one person at a time could view the show.

It was Thomas Armat who invented a projector that would show pictures on a screen in a room where many people could watch them. Edison later marketed this forerunner of the modern motion-picture projector under the name Vitascope.

Among his many other "firsts," Edison developed the first motion-picture studio. This was a tar-paper shack at West Orange, N.J. It was called "the black Maria" and was built on rails so that it could be moved about to take advantage of the sun as a scene was being filmed. (*See also* Motion Pictures.)

The Electric-Light Bulb

In an effort to produce electric light, Edison studied the entire history of lighting. He filled 200 notebooks containing more than 40,000 pages with his notes on gas illumination alone. His aim was to invent a lamp that would become incandescent, or luminous, as a result of heat passing through it. He made threads of many heat-resistant materials. He put these filaments into glass globes. The heat crumbled the filaments into ashes. Later he pumped air out of the bulbs. Using platinum filaments in these vacuum bulbs, he had some success. But he needed an inexpensive substance to use for filaments. He continued his research for many months, spending thousands of dollars.

On Oct. 21, 1879, Edison introduced the modern age of light. In his laboratory at Menlo Park, the young man tensely watched a charred cotton thread

Edison's success was due in part to his work habits. The picture at the left was taken of the inventor at the close of five days and five nights of continuous work in perfecting the early wax-cylinder type of phonograph. At the right the wizard of electricity stands beside an early automobile powered by the improved Edison lightweight storage battery.

glow for 40 hours in a glass vacuum bulb. He knew then that he had invented the first commercially practical incandescent electric light. In his continuing search for a filament that would work better than the cotton thread, carbonized bamboo seemed most successful. He sent men into tropical jungles for samples of bamboo, and for nine years millions of Edison lamp bulbs were made with bamboo filaments. In time, however, the modern filament of drawn tungsten wire was developed.

Edison also devoted his energies to improving the dynamo to furnish the necessary power for electric lighting systems. In addition, he developed a complete system of distributing the current and built a central power station.

"Invention Factory" at West Orange

In 1887 Edison opened a new laboratory at West Orange, N.J. He called it his "invention factory." In 1914 the plant burned to the ground. Edison took the loss calmly. "All of our mistakes have been destroyed," he said. "In a new factory we can start our experiments with a clean slate."

During World War I Edison headed the Naval Consulting Board for the government and directed research into torpedo mechanisms and antisubmarine devices. In 1920, largely at his instigation, Congress established the Naval Research Laboratory, the first institution for military research.

In October 1929, 50 years after Edison had invented the electric-light bulb, America paid tribute to him on Light's Golden Jubilee. The setting for the event was the "permanent birthplace of light," created by Henry Ford at Dearborn, Mich., in the Edison Institute. Here Ford moved the Menlo Park laboratory and the railroad station where the newsboy Edison was "dumped" after he set fire to a car with his chemicals. Honors came to Edison until he could "count his medals by the quart," as he often jokingly said.

Edison died on Oct. 18, 1931, and was buried at Orange, N.J. His West Orange laboratory and his 23-room home, Glenmont, were designated a national historic site in 1955. The laboratory, in which Edison worked for a large part of his life, is exactly as he left it. It includes his library, papers, and early models of many of his inventions.

Thomas Edison used the dictating machine, one of his hundreds of inventions, in answering letters.

Henry Ford Museum

EDMONTON, Alta. The capital city of the Canadian province of Alberta, Edmonton lies on the North Saskatchewan River. It has been a distribution center for northwestern Canada since it was founded in 1795 as a Hudson's Bay Company fur-trading post.

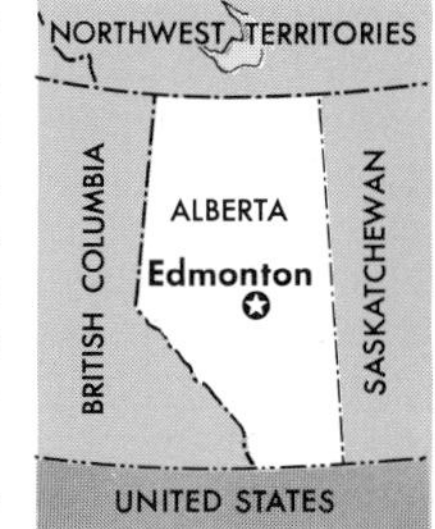

Agriculture and petroleum refining are the basis of Edmonton's most important industries. Other major industries include lumbering, flour milling, meat-packing, tanning, dairying, and the production of plastics. Oil and gas pipelines radiate from the city. The discovery of petroleum after 1947 within a 75-mile (120-kilometer) radius greatly helped the city's urban and industrial development. Three major railroad lines and Edmonton's international airport have kept the city the wholesaling, retailing, and distribution center of western Canada.

Edmonton is the headquarters of Athabasca University and the site of the University of Alberta and the Northern Alberta Institute of Technology. The Provincial Museum of Alberta, the Queen Elizabeth Planetarium, and the Valley Zoo are also in Edmonton. Each year the city hosts the Agricultural and Industrial Exhibition, the Muk-Luk Mardi Gras, which is a winter sports carnival, and the Klondike Days, a July celebration of the 1890s gold rush. Fort Edmonton Historical Park has a replica of the original fort. The province's main government building has 305 bells in its dome. Overlooking the North Saskatchewan, it is on the site of old Fort Edmonton.

Edmonton's origins date back to 1795 when the Fort Edmonton fur-trading post was built on one bank of the North Saskatchewan River, and Fort Augustus, a North West Company post, was built on the opposite bank. Both posts were abandoned in 1810, and five other forts were later built along the river. A trading settlement developed after 1864 and survived the Cree Indian Rebellion of 1885. After the arrival of the Canadian Pacific Railway in 1891, Edmonton was a successful agricultural distributing and processing center. It became Alberta's capital when the province was formed in 1905. In 1912 Strathcona, on the river's south bank, became part of Edmonton. The city has a mayor-council form of government. Population (1981 census), 532,246; metropolitan area, 595,557.

EDUCATION

EDUCATION. The American educator Horace Mann once said: "As an apple is not in any proper sense an apple until it is ripe, so a human being is not in any proper sense a human being until he is educated." Education is the process through which people endeavor to pass along to their children their hard-won wisdom and their aspirations for a better world. This process begins shortly after birth, as parents seek to train the infant to behave as their culture demands. They soon, for instance, teach the child how to turn babbling sounds into language and, through example and precept, they try to instill in the child the attitudes, values, skills, and knowledge that will govern their offspring's behavior throughout later life. Schooling, or formal education, consists of experiences that are deliberately planned and utilized to help young people learn what adults consider important for them to know and to help teach them how they should respond to choices.

Carl Purcell

A student concentrates on improving his handwriting. Penmanship has always been practiced in the classroom, but for generations of pupils it was taught as a skill rather than as a form of communication.

WHAT IS "GOOD" EDUCATION?

While almost everyone accepts the goal of developing skill in the three "R's"—reading, writing, and arithmetic—it often seems impossible to reach agreement on any goal beyond that. In the broadest terms the conflict about educational goals can be viewed as a conflict between conservatives and liberals, or, as they are sometimes called, essentialists and progressives.

The conservatives, or essentialists, tend to identify a desirable education with the transmission of the cultural heritage, a no-nonsense curriculum featuring the three R's at the elementary-school level and academic studies or strong vocational or business courses in the secondary school. They stress training of the mind and cultivation of the intellect.

The liberals, or progressives, tend to be interested in the development of the whole child, not merely in training the child's mind or in preparing the child for adult life in a remote future. They emphasize rich, meaningful school living in the present, and they view subject matter as a resource for total human development rather than as a goal in itself. They do not downgrade content but believe it should be acquired not for its own sake but as a means of fostering thought and inquiry.

The chart on pages 80 and 81 indicates how the conservatives and the liberals view man and how they answer such basic questions about education as these: (1) Why teach? (2) What should be taught? (3) What teaching methods should be used? (4) Who should teach? (5) What is the best setting for learning? (6) How long should schooling continue? To fully understand present conservative and liberal theories and practices, something must be known about the history of education.

FACT FINDER FOR EDUCATION

The subject of education is a broad one. Readers will obtain additional information in the related articles listed here. (*See also* related references in the Fact-Index.)

- Academy
- Adult Education
- Alternative School
- Apprenticeship
- Bilingual Education
- Child Development
- Communication Skills
- Guidance
- Health Education and Physical Education
- Intelligence Tests
- Kindergarten and Nursery School
- Learning
- Library
- Literacy and Illiteracy
- Military Education
- Parent-Teacher Association
- Reading
- Reference Books
- Religious Education
- Report Writing
- School Systems
- Special Education
- Study
- Universities and Colleges
- Vocational Training

This article was contributed by Harold G. Shane, University Professor Emeritus and former Dean, School of Education, Indiana University.

Preview

The article Education is divided into the following sections and subsections:

THE EDUCATIONAL PAST

In the absence of written records, no one can be sure what education man first provided for his children. Most anthropologists believe, though, that the educational practices of prehistoric times were probably like those of primitive tribes in the 20th century, such as the Australian aborigines and the Aleuts. Formal instruction was probably given just before the child's initiation into adulthood—the puberty rite—and involved tribal customs and beliefs too complicated to be learned by direct experience. Children learned most of the skills, duties, customs, and beliefs of the tribe through an informal apprenticeship—by taking part in such adult activities as hunting, fishing, farming, toolmaking, and cooking. In such simple tribal societies, school was not a special place—it was life itself.

Early Civilizations

With the gradual rise of more complex civilizations in the river valleys of Egypt and Babylonia, knowledge, customs, and beliefs became too complicated to transmit directly from person to person and from generation to generation. To be able to function in complex societies, man needed some way of accumulating, recording, and preserving his cultural heritage. So with the rise of trade, government, and formal religion came the invention of writing, by about 3100 B.C.

Because firsthand experience in everyday living could not teach such skills as writing and reading, a place devoted exclusively to learning—the school—appeared. And with the school appeared a group of adults specially designated as teachers—the scribes of the court and the priests of the temple. The children also fell into two different classes—the vast majority who continued to learn exclusively by an informal apprenticeship and the tiny minority who received formal schooling.

The method of learning was memorization, and the motivation was the fear of harsh physical discipline. On an ancient Egyptian clay tablet discovered by archaeologists, a child had written: "Thou didst beat me and knowledge entered my head." (*See also* Babylonia and Assyria; Egypt, Ancient.)

Of the ancient peoples of the Middle East, the Jews were the most insistent that all children—regardless of class—be educated. In the 1st century A.D., the historian Flavius Josephus wrote: "We take most pains of all with the instruction of the children and esteem the observance of the laws and the piety corresponding with them the most important affair of our whole life." The Jews established elementary schools where boys from about 6 to 13 years of age probably learned rudimentary mathematics and certainly learned reading and writing. The main concern of these schools was the study of the first five books of the Old Testament—the Pentateuch—and the precepts of the oral tradition that had grown up around them. At age 13, brighter boys could continue their studies as disciples of a rabbi, the "master" or "teacher." So vital was the concept of instruction for the Jews that the synagogues existed at least as much for education as for worship.

Ancient Greece

The Greek gods were much more down-to-earth and much less awesome than the remote gods of the East. Because they were endowed with human qualities and often represented aspects of the physical world—such as the sun, the moon, and the sea—they were closer to man and to the world he lived in. The Greeks, therefore, could find spiritual satisfaction in the ordinary, everyday world. They could develop a secular life free from the domination of a priesthood that exacted homage to gods remote from everyday life.

The goal of education in the Greek city-states was to prepare the child for adult activities as a citizen. The nature of the city-states varied greatly, and this was also true of the education they considered appropriate. The goal of education in Sparta, an authoritarian, military city-state, was to produce soldier-citizens. On the other hand, the goal of education in Athens, a democratic city-state, was to produce citizens trained in the arts of both peace and war. (*See also* Greece, Ancient.)

Sparta. The boys of Sparta were obliged to leave home at the age of seven to join sternly disciplined groups under the supervision of a hierarchy of officers. From age 7 to 18, they underwent an increasingly severe course of training. They walked barefoot, slept on hard beds, and worked at gymnastics and other physical activities such as running, jumping, javelin and discus throwing, swimming, and hunting. They were subjected to strict discipline and harsh physical punishment; indeed, they were taught to take pride in the amount of pain they could endure.

At 18, Spartan boys became military cadets and

A school scene painted on a Greek vase shows a seated teacher and pupil during a music lesson. To the left, another student, accompanied by a slave, arrives with his lyre, while, to the right, a third prepares to leave and a fourth awaits his turn.

learned the arts of war. At 20, they joined the state militia—a standing reserve force available for duty in time of emergency—in which they served until they were 60 years old.

The typical Spartan may or may not have been able to read. But reading, writing, literature, and the arts were considered unsuitable for the soldier-citizen and were therefore not part of his education. Music and dancing were a part of that education, but only because they served military ends. (*See also* Sparta.)

Unlike the other Greek city-states, Sparta provided training for girls that went beyond the domestic arts. The girls were not forced to leave home, but otherwise their training was similar to that of the boys. They too learned to run, jump, throw the javelin and discus, and wrestle. The Athenians apparently made sport of the physique prized in Spartan women, for in a comedy by the Athenian playwright Aristophanes a character says to a Spartan girl:

> How lovely thou art, how blooming thy skin,
> how rounded thy flesh! What a prize! Thou
> mightest strangle a bull.

Athens. In Athens the ideal citizen was a person educated in the arts of both peace and war, and this made both schools and exercise fields necessary. Other than requiring two years of military training that began at age 18, the state left parents to educate their sons as they saw fit. The schools were private, but the tuition was low enough so that even the poorest citizens could afford to send their children for at least a few years.

Boys attended elementary school from the time they were about age six or seven until they were 13 or 14. Part of their training was gymnastics. The younger boys learned to move gracefully, do calisthenics, and play ball and other games. The older boys learned running, jumping, boxing, wrestling, and discus and javelin throwing. The boys also learned to play the lyre and sing, to count, and to read and write. But it was literature that was at the heart of their schooling. The national epic poems of the Greeks—Homer's 'Odyssey' and 'Iliad'—were a vital part of the life of the Athenian people. As soon as their pupils could write, the teachers dictated passages from Homer for them to take down, memorize, and later act out. Teachers and pupils also discussed the feats of the Greek heroes described by Homer. The education of mind, body, and aesthetic sense was, according to Plato, so that the boys "may learn to be more gentle, and harmonious, and rhythmical, and so more fitted for speech and action; for the life of man in every part has need of harmony and rhythm."

At 13 or 14, the formal education of the poorer boys probably ended and was followed by apprenticeship at a trade. The wealthier boys continued their education under the tutelage of philosopher-teachers. Until about 390 B.C. there were no permanent schools and no formal courses for such higher education. Socrates, for example, wandered around Athens, stopping here or there to hold discussions with the people about all sorts of things pertaining to the conduct of man's life. But gradually, as groups of students attached themselves to one teacher or another, permanent schools were established. It was in such schools that Plato, Isocrates, and Aristotle taught.

WHAT SHOULD EDUCATION BE?		
	The "Conservative" Position	**The "Liberal" Position**
Premises on Which the Educational Positions Are Based	The mind is purely intellectual and cognitive, separate from the physical and emotional self.	Mind, body, and emotions are a unity, each affecting the others.
	The mind—reason—is developed by application to purely intellectual and cognitive subject matter—especially to books written and ideas generated by the greatest minds that the human race has produced. Learning "activity" should be purely mental.	Mind—thinking or intelligence—is not born ready-made but is *created* through firsthand experiences. The initial stages of learning must involve the "whole child" in the physical, emotional, and social experience of carrying out an activity that has immediate meaning and purpose for him.
	One's ability to think can be developed by systematic exposure to examples of disciplined thinking.	Formulated, abstract bodies of knowledge that represent the result of adult mental processes stifle the development of thinking in the beginning learner.
	Subject matter is used to train the mind and cultivate the faculty of reason.	Subject matter acquires its value as a means of fostering thought and inquiry that are aroused by firsthand experience. Subject matter is used to extend and enrich immediate firsthand experience, and firsthand experience makes the subject matter vivid and meaningful to the learner.
	Emphasis is on the quantitative mastery of certain basic content.	Emphasis is on the quality of the learner's mental processes.
	Curriculum is subject-centered.	Curriculum is child- and society-centered.
	The student applies his mind to subject matter because he accepts on faith the word of adults that it will be valuable to him in his adult life.	The student himself decides what subject matter is important to solve some problem that absorbs his interest in the present. He seeks knowledge not because he "should" but because he *wants* to.
	Discipline, not interest, is of primary importance in learning. Discipline is a part of training the mind. Students must exert effort even when they are not interested.	Self-discipline cannot be separated from interest. External discipline from the teacher is not necessary when interest is present.
Why Teach?	To train the mind and cultivate man's highest faculty—reason. To transmit the classical-traditional heritage of Western culture to all who are capable of absorbing it. For those with little or no ability to absorb it, to transmit practical skills such as reading, writing, arithmetic and craft and vocational techniques as needed to make a living.	To develop human potential; to serve the needs, purposes, and interests of the "whole child" and every child. To bring about desirable, observable changes in the individual's social, intellectual, and emotional behavior. To develop individuals who will bring about desirable changes necessary in a healthy society.
	Emphasis on social stability through preservation of values of the past.	Emphasis on social change through active inquiry.
What Should Be Taught?	For the less intellectually able, a thorough grounding in the three R's and vocational training. For the most intellectually able, the content of man's intellectual heritage, which includes the great works of literature, art, philosophy, history, science, politics, mathematics, and economics.	Content is determined by the needs and interests of the developing child. A general curriculum may be followed, but in some instances content is determined through the process of working with the children. Relevance of the subject matter to the child's immediate needs and purposes and to current social problems is stressed.
	Content is usually presented in terms of logically organized "subjects." This increases the likelihood that children will attain an orderly, comprehensive overview of the cultural heritage.	Content is usually psychologically organized (in terms of the child), not marked off as separate "subjects." This increases the likelihood that content will have meaning for the individual child and for particular groups of children belonging to various subcultures.

WHAT SHOULD EDUCATION BE?		
	The "Conservative" Position	**The "Liberal" Position**
What Teaching Methods Should Be Used?	Methods are designed to encourage the mastery of formulated bodies of knowledge.	Methods are intended to develop the potentialities of the ''whole child.''
	Emphasis is on answer-giving based on lecture, drill, memorization, and recitation. Daily lesson plan determines scope and sequence of material to be learned by all pupils.	Emphasis is on answer-seeking. Activities carefully chosen to stimulate individual development through processes of inquiry and discovery.
	Amount of knowledge acquired is evaluated by examinations.	Child is evaluated in terms of the ripening of his own potentialities rather than examinations alone.
	Motivation for learning is supplied by inspiration from the teacher and rewards and punishments such as grades.	Motivation comes from within the child as he engages in purposeful learning activity; comparative grades replaced by progress reports.
	The teacher is a figure of authority—the source of knowledge and of discipline.	The teacher is a guide.
	Physical activity and expression of feelings are considered an interference to learning and are discouraged.	Physical activity and expression of emotion are encouraged as indispensable parts of education of the ''whole child'' and as contributing factors in development of his ability to inquire and think.
	Heavy emphasis is on books and programmed instructional materials designed to facilitate academic performance.	Heavy emphasis is on varied firsthand experience and, increasingly, on varied teaching aids such as films and recordings.
Who Should Teach?	Professionally educated teachers who are thoroughly familiar with the subject matter and the best methods of organizing and presenting it. Those who know how to inspire interest in learning and maintain discipline.	Professionally educated teachers thoroughly familiar with the subject matter, human development, and educational theory and methods. Paraprofessionals, interested adults, unlicensed personnel with special skills, and other pupils are also considered qualified to contribute to the process of education.
What Is the Best Setting for Learning?	Schools built to house graded groups and equipped for instruction in special fields such as science. The setting should be conducive to lecture and recitation: desks formally arranged in rows facing teacher's desk and chalkboard.	Schools built for flexible use of space to encourage large group, small group, and individual instruction. Carrels for individual study; areas designed for team teaching and for use of teaching aids. *OR* Schools with even more flexible use of space —open schools—and provision for more advanced teaching aids such as computers. The community itself (parks, civic buildings, and factories) may also be a setting for learning.
How Long Should Schooling Continue?	Should be determined predominantly by the learner's tested and proven ability to master academic subject matter and meet established standards of intellectual excellence.	Should be determined by the individual's desire to extend and enrich his learning experience. University enrollment should be ''open'' to permit persons whose academic records do not meet the highest standards of intellectual excellence to begin post-secondary education. Possibility has been suggested for publicly supported lifelong schooling conceived as a ''seamless curriculum'' from which, and back into which, the learner can move as his needs and desires to learn carry him.

The boys who attended these schools fell more or less into two groups. Those who wanted learning for its own sake studied with philosophers like Plato who taught such subjects as geometry, astronomy, harmonics (the mathematical theory of music), and arithmetic. Those who wanted training for public life studied with philosophers like Isocrates who primarily taught oratory and rhetoric. In democratic Athens such training was appropriate and necessary because power rested with the men who had the ability to persuade their fellow senators to act.

Most Athenian girls had a primarily domestic education. The most highly educated women were the hetaerae, or courtesans, who attended special schools where they learned to be interesting companions for the men who could afford to maintain them. (*See also* Athens.)

Ancient Rome

The military conquest of Greece by Rome in 146 B.C. resulted in the cultural conquest of Rome by Greece. As the Roman poet Horace said, "Captive Greece took captive her rude conqueror and brought the arts to Latium." Actually, Greek influence on Roman education had begun about a century before the conquest. Originally, most if not all of the Roman boy's education took place at home. If the father himself were educated, the boy would learn to read and would learn Roman law, history, and customs. The father also saw to his son's physical training. When the boy was older, he sometimes prepared himself for public life by a kind of apprenticeship to one of the orators of the time. He thus learned the arts of oratory first-hand by listening to the debates in the Senate and in the public forum. The element introduced into Roman education by the Greeks was book learning.

When they were six or seven years old, boys (and sometimes girls) of all classes could be sent by their parents to the *ludus publicus*, the elementary school, where they studied reading, writing, and counting. At age 12 or 13, the boys of the upper classes attended a "grammar" school where they learned Latin or Greek or both and studied grammar and literature. Grammar consisted of the study of declensions and conjugations and the analysis of verbal forms. Both Greek and Latin literature were studied (the latter written after Greek models). The teacher would read the work and then lecture on it, while the students took notes that they later memorized. At age 16, the boys who wanted training for public service went on to study public speaking at the rhetoric schools, where most of the teachers were Greek.

The graded arrangement of schools established in Rome by the middle of the 1st century B.C. ultimately spread throughout the Roman Empire. It continued until the fall of the empire in the 5th century A.D.

Although deeply influenced by Greek education, Roman education was nonetheless quite different. For most Greeks, the end of education was to produce a

A fresco uncovered at the ancient Italian city of Herculaneum (buried by mud and volcanic matter in A.D. 79) shows a Roman schoolmaster punishing a wayward student with a whip made of leather thongs.

good citizen, and a good citizen meant a well-rounded individual. The goal of Roman education was the same, but for the Romans a good citizen meant an effective speaker. The result was that they disregarded such nonutilitarian Greek studies as science, philosophy, music, dancing, and gymnastics, basing their education instead on literature and oratory. Even their study of literature, with its overemphasis on the technicalities of grammar and its underemphasis on content, had the purpose of producing good orators.

When the Roman Republic became an empire, in 31 B.C., the school studies lost even their practical value. For then it was not the orator in the Senate but the emperor who had the power.

Because of the emphasis on the technical study of language and literature and because the language and literature studied represented the culture of a foreign people, Roman education was remote from the real world and the interests of the schoolboys. Vigorous discipline was therefore necessary to motivate them to study. And the Roman boys were not the last to suffer in this situation. When the empire fell, the education that was originally intended to train orators for the Roman Senate became the model for European education and dominated it until the 20th century.

The Romans also left the legacy of their language. For nearly a thousand years after the fall of the empire, Latin continued to be the language spoken in commerce, public service, education, and the Roman Catholic church. Most books written in Europe until about the year 1200 were written in Latin. (*See also* Roman History.)

The Middle Ages

The invading Germanic tribes that moved into the civilized world of the West and all but destroyed ancient culture provided virtually no formal education for their young. In the early Middle Ages the elaborate Roman school system had disappeared. Mankind in 5th-century Europe might well have reverted almost to the level of primitive education had it not been for the medieval church, which preserved what little Western learning had survived the collapse of the Roman Empire. In the drafty, inhospitable corridors of church schools, the lamp of learning continued to burn low, though it flickered badly.

Cathedral, monastic, and palace schools were operated by the clergy in parts of Western Europe. Most students were future or present members of the clergy, though a few lay students were trained to be clerks. Unlike the Greek and Roman schools, which sought to prepare men for this life, the church schools sought to prepare men for life beyond the grave through the contemplation of God during their life on earth. The schools taught students to read Latin so that they could copy and thereby preserve and perpetuate the writings of the Church Fathers. Students learned the rudiments of mathematics so that they could calculate the dates of religious festivals, and they practiced singing so that they could take part in church services.

A teacher in the typical medieval school towered over his students on a thronelike chair and wielded authority with a ferule, or rod.

Unlike the Greeks, who considered physical health and vigor a part of the education of the whole man, the church considered the human body a part of the profane world and therefore something to be ignored or harshly disciplined. The students attended schools that were dreary and cold, and physical activity was severely repressed.

Schools were ungraded—a six-year-old and a 16-year-old (or an adult for that matter) sometimes sharing the same bench. Medieval education can be understood better if one realizes that for thousands of years childhood as it is known today literally did not exist. No psychological distinction was made between child and adult. The medieval school was not really intended for children. Rather, it was a kind of vocational school for clerks and clergymen. A seven-year-old in the Middle Ages became an integral part of the adult world, absorbing adult knowledge and doing a man's work as best he could during what today would be the middle years of elementary education. It was not until the 18th century that childhood was recognized; not until the 20th that it began to be understood.

The 12th and 13th centuries, toward the end of the Middle Ages, saw the rise of the universities. The university curriculum in about 1200 consisted of what were then called the seven liberal arts. These were grouped into two divisions. The first was the preparatory *trivium:* grammar, rhetoric, and logic. The second, more advanced division was the *quadrivium:* arithmetic, geometry, music, and astronomy.

Like the Romans, the scholars of the Middle Ages took over the content of Greek education and adapted it to their own culture. The traditional subjects were clouded with religious assumptions. Astronomy, for example, was permeated by astrology, and arithmetic was full of mystical meaning:

> There are 22 sextarii in a bushel because God in the beginning made 22 works; there are 22 generations from Adam to Jacob; and 22 books of the Old Testament as far as Esther and 22 letters of the alphabet out of which the divine law is composed.

For the Middle Ages knowledge was an authoritative body of revealed truth. It was not for the scholar to observe nature and to test, question, and discover truth for himself but to interpret and expound accepted doctrines. Thus the medieval scholar might debate about how many angels could stand on the head of a pin, but he did not question the existence of angels.

To the credit of medieval education, by the 12th century the education of women was no longer ignored, though only a small percentage of girls actually attended schools. Most convents educated women, as is shown by the famous letters of the French nun Héloïse, who received a classical education at the nunnery of Argenteuil before becoming its abbess. Early in the 12th century, girls from noble families were enrolled at Notre Dame de Paris in the classes of the French theologian and philosopher Peter Abelard (*see* Abelard).

Like education in the 20th century, medieval education had its problems. There were many dropouts; the influence of the church sometimes drugged rather than enlivened the mind; and scholars were often expected to accept the unreasoned and the unproved. Materials were few and poor. Many university libraries had fewer than a hundred volumes. Because books were so scarce, lessons had to be dictated and then memorized. Nevertheless, medieval schooling ended the long era of barbarism, launched the careers of able men, and sharpened the minds and tongues of the thoughtful and ambitious students.

For youngsters of the aristocracy in the Middle Ages of the 13th century, there was chivalric education. This was a kind of secondary education that young men received while living in the homes of nobles or at court. It included some poetry, national history, heraldry, manners and customs, physical training, dancing, a little music, and battle skills. Chivalric, secular education was governed by a code rather than a curriculum. Boys of the lower classes could learn a trade through apprenticeship in a craftsman's shop. (*See also* Middle Ages.)

The Renaissance

The essence of the Renaissance, which began in Italy in the 14th century and spread to northern European countries in the 15th and 16th centuries, was a revolt against the narrowness and otherworldliness of the Middle Ages. For inspiration the early Renaissance humanists turned to the ideals expressed in the literature of ancient Greece. Like the Greeks, they wanted education to develop man's intellectual, spiritual, and physical powers for the enrichment and enjoyment of life in this world.

The actual content of the humanists' "liberal education" was not much different from that of medieval education. To the seven liberal arts, the humanists added history and physical games and exercises. Humanist education was primarily enlivened by the addition of Greek to the curriculum and an emphasis on the content of Greek and Roman literature. After nearly a thousand years grammar at last was studied not as an end in itself but because it gave access to the vital content of literature. In keeping with their renewed interest in and respect for nature, the humanists also gradually purged astronomy of many of the distortions of astrology.

Along with the changed attitudes toward the goals and the content of education, in a few innovative schools, came the first signs of a change in attitude toward educational methods. Rather than bitter medicine to be forced down the students' throats, education was to be exciting, pleasant, and fun.

The school that most closely embodied these early Renaissance ideals was founded in Mantua, Italy, in 1423 by Vittorino da Feltre. Even the name of his school, Casa Giocosa (Happy House), broke with the medieval tradition of cheerless institutions in which grammar—along with Holy Writ—was flogged into the learner's memory. The school served children beginning at age six and extended upward to include youths in their mid-twenties. The pupils studied history, philosophy, arithmetic, geometry, music, and astronomy, but the basis of the curriculum was the study of Greek and Roman literature. Physical development was encouraged through exercise and games.

The humanist ideal did not affect the lower classes, who remained as ignorant as they had been in the Middle Ages. Its impact was appreciable, however, on the secondary education that was provided for the upper classes. This is not to say that there was a proliferation of Happy Houses. Unlike Vittorino's school, the other Latin grammar schools that introduced Greek and Roman literature into the curriculum soon shifted the emphasis—as the Romans had done—from the study of the content of the literature to the form of the language. The physical development so important to the early humanist ideal of the well-rounded man found no place in the curriculum. Instead of the joy of learning, there was harsh, repressive discipline. (*See also* Renaissance.)

The Reformation

The degeneration in practice of the early humanists' educational goals and methods continued during the 16th-century Reformation and its aftermath. The religious conflict that dominated men's thoughts also dominated the "humanistic" curriculum of the Protestant secondary schools. The Protestants' need to defend their new religion resulted in the further sacrifice of "pagan" content and more emphasis on drill in the mechanics of the Greek and Latin languages. In actual practice, then, the humanistic ideal deteriorated into the narrowness and other-worldliness that the original humanists had opposed.

From 'The Orbis Pictus of John Amos Comenius'; reproduced by permission of C. W. Bardeen, Publisher

The Chanels and Bones. XLI. Canales & Ossa.

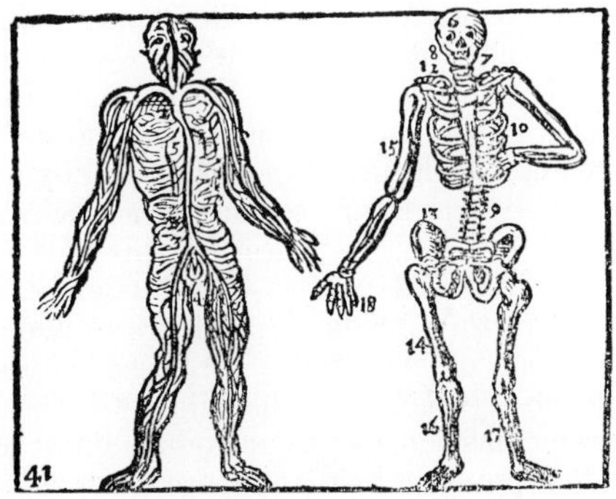

The Chanels of the Body are the *Veins*, carrying the Blood from the Liver;	Canales Corporis sunt *Venæ* deferentes Sanguinem ex Hepate;
The *Arteries* (carrying) *Heart* and *Life* from the *Heat;*	*Arteriæ*, *Calorem* & *Vitam* è *Corde;*
The *Nerves* (carrying) Sense and Motion throughout the Body from the *Brain.*	*Nervi*, Sensum et Motum, per Corpus a *Cerebro.*
You shall find these three, 1. everywhere joined together.	Invenies hæc tria, 1. ubique sociata.
Besides, from the Mouth into the Stomach is the *Gullet*, 2. the way of the meat and drink; and by it to the Lights, the *Wezand*, 5. for breathing; from the Stomach to the Anus is a great *Intestine*, 3. to purge out the *Ordure;*	Porrò, ab Ore in Ventriculum *Gula*, 2. via cibi ac potus; & juxta hanc, ad Pulmonem *Guttur*, 5. pro respiratione; à ventriculo ad Anum *Colon*, 3. ad excernendum *Stercus;*

This facsimile is from the 1658 English edition of 'Orbis Pictus', the first illustrated textbook. Popular in European and American schools, it had columns of text in Latin and in the vernacular to explain the numbered parts of the drawings.

The Protestants emphasized the need for universal education and established elementary vernacular schools in Germany where the children of the poor could learn reading, writing, and religion. This innovation was to have far-reaching effects on education in the Western world. (*See also* Reformation.)

17th- and 18th-Century Europe

The vast majority of schools remained in a state of stagnation during the 17th and 18th centuries. By and large, the teachers were incompetent and the discipline cruel. The learning methods were drill and memorization of words, sentences, and facts that the children often did not understand. Most members of the lower classes got no schooling whatsoever, and what some did get was at the hands of teachers who often were themselves barely educated.

In the secondary Latin grammar schools and the universities the linguistic narrowness and otherworldliness of classical studies persisted. By the 17th century the study of Latin removed students even farther from real life than it had in the 16th, because Latin had ceased to be the language of commerce or the exclusive language of religion. In the 17th century it also slowly ceased to be even the exclusive language of scholarly discourse. Yet most humanist schools made no provision for studying the vernacular and clung to Latin because it was thought to "train" the mind. The scientific movement—with its skeptical, inquiring spirit—that began to permeate the Western world in the 17th century was successfully barred from both the Catholic and Protestant schools, which continued to emphasize classical linguistic studies.

Although the general state of education was retrogressive, there were some advanced educators and philosophers. Their ideas about learning pointed toward the educational revolution of the 20th century.

The 17th Century. One of the educational pioneers of great stature was John (Johann) Amos Comenius (1592–1670). Effective education, Comenius insisted, must take into account the nature of the child. His own observations of children led him to the conclusion that they were not miniature adults. He characterized the schools, which treated them as if they were, as "the slaughterhouses of minds" and "places where minds are fed on words." Comenius believed that understanding comes "not in the mere learning the names of things, but in the actual perception of the things themselves." Education should begin, therefore, with the child's observation of actual objects or, if not the objects themselves, models or pictures of them. The practical result of this theory was Comenius' 'Orbis Pictus' (The World in Pictures), the first—and for a long time the only—textbook in the Western world that had illustrations for children to look at. Although the ideas on which it was based were at first ridiculed by educators, Comenius' book was widely used by schoolchildren for about 200 years.

In the 17th century philosophers, too, were beginning to develop theories of learning that reflected the new scientific reliance on firsthand observation. One of the men whose theories had the greatest impact on educational thought and practice was the English philosopher John Locke (1632–1704). According to Locke (who did not originate the idea but gave impetus to it), the mind at birth is a blank tablet (*tabula rasa*). That is, it has no innate, God-given knowledge. But it does have a number of powers or faculties, such as perceiving, discriminating, comparing, thinking, and recalling. Locke believed that knowledge comes when these faculties are exercised upon the raw material of sense impressions received from objects in the external world. Once the mind has passively received such sense impressions, its faculties go to work—discriminating among and comparing them, sifting and sorting them until they take shape as "knowledge."

One aspect of Locke's theory—the notion that the mind is made up of "faculties"—was interpreted to mean that the function of schooling was to "train" the various mental faculties. Latin and mathematics, for example, were thought to be especially good for strengthening reason and memory. This idea clung to educational practice well into the 20th century—long after "faculty" psychology had been proved invalid.

The more significant aspect of the theory, in terms of educational reform, was the insistence upon firsthand experience with its implicit protest against the mere book learning of the Middle Ages and the humanists. If the raw material of knowledge comes from the impressions made upon the mind by natural objects, then education cannot function without objects. Eventually, the effect of this part of the theory was reflected in the introduction into the schools of pictures, models, field trips, and other manifestations of education's increased respect for firsthand observation. By the mid-19th century it had become fashionable to introduce into schools objects that provided firsthand sense impressions and that filled out, supplemented, and gave interest to abstract book learning. The materials and the methods of traditional book learning were not radically revised, however, for another 75 years. (*See also* Learning; Locke, John.)

The 18th Century. It was the delayed shock waves of the ideas of an 18th-century Frenchman that were to crack the foundations of education in the 20th century and cause their virtual upheaval in the United States. The man was Jean Jacques Rousseau (1712–78). The child, as Rousseau saw him, unfolds or develops—intellectually, physically, and emotionally—much like a plant. He believed, moreover, that the child is innately good but that all social institutions, including schools, are evil, distorting the child into their own image. He doubted, therefore, that there should be formal schools at all. Whether there were or not, however, he believed that the aim of education should be the natural development of the learner.

Rousseau's observations and their educational ramifications were a complete reversal of the educational theories and practices of the 1700's. The prevailing theory was that the child differs from the adult in the *quantity* of his mind. The child, presumably, is born with the same, but weaker, mental faculties as the adult. To bring his faculties up to an adult level, education must cultivate them through exercise—that is, through drill and memorization. Rousseau, however, believed that the child differs from the adult in the *quality* of his mind, which successively unfolds in different stages of growth. "We are always looking for the man in the child," he said, "without thinking what he is before he becomes a man."

"Children," observed Rousseau, "are always in motion: a sedentary life is injurious." From age 2 to 12, therefore, Rousseau envisioned the cultivation of the body and the senses, not the intellect. When the youngster's intellect begins to develop, at about 12 to 15, he can begin the study of such things as science and geography. The study, however, should begin not with an organized body of abstract knowledge but with the things that interest the child in the world around him. He must learn not by memorizing but by firsthand experience. "He is not to learn science: he is to find it out for himself," Rousseau said. Only when he is 15 should book learning begin. So much for the entire Latin school if one accepted Rousseau.

Rousseau also attacked the teaching methods of his time. The theory of mental faculties recognized no innate differences among children. It was thought that children are born with the same faculties, and

The cruel discipline in this 18th-century German classroom is similar to that which prevailed in most European schools at the time. Two boys are being severely beaten, two forced to stand with their legs tied together, and two made to wear dunce caps. The boy hanging from the ceiling is probably the safest.

that the differences among them depend on their education—on the amount of "exercise" their faculties receive. For Rousseau such exercise stunts "the true gifts of nature. . . . We indiscriminately employ children of different bents on the same exercises; their education destroys the special bent and leaves a dull uniformity."

Since Rousseau believed that the child is innately good and that the aim of education should be his natural development, there was little for the teacher to do except stand aside and watch. Rousseau's overemphasis of the individuality and freedom of the child and his underemphasis of the needs of the child as a social being represent a reaction against the repressive social, political, and educational practices of the time. Those who were influenced by Rousseau tried to create schools that would provide a controlled environment in which natural growth could take place and at the same time be guided by society in the person of the teacher.

Ironically, shortly after Rousseau's death Prussia became the first modern state to create a centrally controlled school system. For more than a century it operated on principles almost diametrically opposed to those of the great French thinker. (*See also* Rousseau, Jean Jacques.)

Colonial America

While the schools that the colonists established in the 17th century in the New England, Southern, and Middle colonies differed from one another, each reflected a concept of schooling that had been left behind in Europe. Most poor children learned through apprenticeship and had no formal schooling at all. Those who did go to elementary school were taught reading, writing, arithmetic, and religion. Learning consisted of memorizing, which was stimulated by whipping. The secondary school, attended by the wealthier children, was, as in most of Europe, the Latin grammar school. The teachers were no better prepared, and perhaps less so, than the teachers in Europe.

Harvard College, which traces its history to 1636, had as its primary purpose the training of Latin school graduates for the ministry. Like most of the colleges in Europe, its curriculum was humanist.

Most of the books used in the elementary and secondary schools were also used in Europe: Bibles, psalters, Latin and Greek texts, Comenius' 'Orbis Pictus', and the hornbook, which was widely used in England at the end of the 16th century. Not really a book at all, the hornbook was a paddle-shaped board. A piece of parchment (and, later, paper) with the lesson written on it was attached to the board and covered with a transparent sheet of horn to keep it clean.

The first "basic textbook"—'The New England Primer'—was America's own contribution to education. Used from 1690 until the beginning of the 19th century, its purpose was to teach both religion and reading. The child learning the letter *a*, for example, also learned that "In Adam's fall, We sinned all."

As in Europe, then, the schools in the colonies were strongly influenced by religion. This was particularly true of the schools in the New England area, which had been settled by Puritans and other English religious dissenters. Like the Protestants of the Reformation, who established vernacular elementary schools in Germany in the 16th century, the Puritans sought to make education universal. They took the first steps toward government-supported universal education in the colonies. In 1642 Puritan Massachusetts passed a law requiring that every child be taught to read. And in 1647 it passed the "Old Deluder Satan Act," so named because its purpose was to defeat Satan's attempts to keep men, through an inability to read, from the knowledge of the Scriptures. The law required every town of 50 or more families to establish an elementary school and every town of 100 or more families to maintain a grammar school as well.

In colonial America, religion was central to learning. A beginner studied the alphabet and the Lord's Prayer from his hornbook (left) and learned rhymes about Biblical characters from his basic textbook—'The New England Primer' (right).

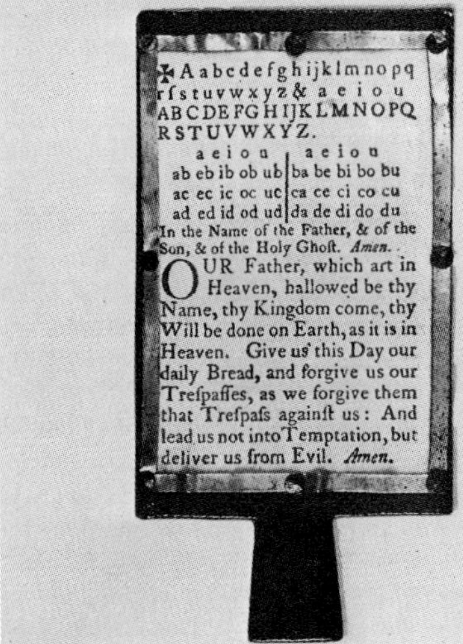

Frank Rowland

The Bettmann Archive

The early American schoolroom was ungraded, with students ranging from small children to adolescents. Here, one group of pupils stands to recite while others study, figure on their slates, or—despite the master's stick—whisper.

Puritan or not, virtually all of the colonial schools had clear-cut moral purposes. Skills and knowledge were considered important to the degree that they served religious ends and, of course, "trained" the mind.

18th-Century United States

As the spirit of science, commercialism, secularism, and individualism quickened in the Western world, education in the colonies was called upon to satisfy the practical needs of seamen, merchants, artisans, and frontiersmen. The effect of these new developments on the curriculum in American schools was more immediate and widespread than its effect in European schools. Practical content was soon competing vigorously with religious concerns.

The academy that Benjamin Franklin helped found in 1751 was the first of a growing number of secondary schools that sprang up in competition with the Latin schools. Franklin's academy continued to offer the humanist-religious curriculum, but it also brought education closer to the needs of everyday life by teaching such courses as history, geography, merchant accounts, geometry, algebra, surveying, modern languages, navigation, and astronomy. By the mid-19th century this new diversification in the curriculum characterized virtually all American secondary education.

After the Revolutionary War new textbooks—mostly American histories and geographies—began to appear. Often they were written with a strong nationalistic flavor. Also, beginning in 1783 'The New England Primer' began to share its supremacy with what was to become an even more popular schoolbook, Noah Webster's 'American Spelling Book'. This work standardized American spelling and emancipated it from English spelling. It also exposed American schoolchildren to more than a century of grueling drill. The speller was used until the end of the 19th century, but the stress on spelling accuracy and the spelling-bee craze continued to grip the schools into the early years of the 20th century.

19th-Century Europe

In the 19th century the spirit of nationalism grew strong in Europe and, with it, the belief in the power of education to shape the future of nations as well as individuals. Other European countries followed Prussia's example and established national school systems. France had one by the 1880's, and by the 1890's the primary schools in England were free and compulsory.

The attitude toward women, too, was slowly changing. By the last half of the 19th century both France and Germany had established secondary schools for women. Only the most liberal educators, however, entertained the notion of coeducation.

By and large, European elementary schools in the 19th century were much like those of the 16th, 17th, and 18th centuries. They were attended by children of the lower classes until, at the latest, age 10 or 11, when schooling terminated for all but a few of the "brightest" among them. The usual subjects were reading, writing, religion, and, if the teacher had mastered it himself, arithmetic. The teacher was often poorly informed; frequently, he taught because he was unable to get any other kind of work. School might still be held in apprentice shops, industrial plants, living rooms, kitchens, or outdoor areas, though regular classrooms were becoming the rule. If the teacher could maintain order at all, it was by bullying, beating, and ridiculing the children. Perhaps the best description of the children who attended such schools is by the English novelist Charles Dickens:

> Pale and haggard faced, lank and bony figures, children with the countenances of old men. . . . There was childhood with the light of its eyes quenched, its beauty gone, and its helplessness alone remaining.

It is no wonder then that Johann Heinrich Pestalozzi's (1746–1827) school at Yverdon, Switzerland, created international attention and attracted thousands of European and American visitors. What they saw was a school for children—for real children, not miniature adults. They saw physically active children—running, jumping, and playing. They saw small children learning the names of numbers by counting real objects and preparing to learn reading by playing with letter blocks. They saw older children engaged in object lessons—progressing in their study of geography from observing the area around the school, to measuring it, making their own relief maps of it, and finally seeing a professionally executed map of it.

This was the school and these were the methods developed by Pestalozzi in accordance with his belief that the goal of education should be the natural development of the individual child, and that educators should focus on the development of the child rather than on memorization of subject matter that he was unable to understand. Pestalozzi's school also mirrored the idea that learning begins with firsthand observation of an object and moves gradually toward the remote and abstract realm of words and ideas. The teacher's job was to guide—not distort—the natural growth of the child by selecting his experiences and then directing those experiences toward the realm of ideas.

The German educator Friedrich Wilhelm Froebel (1782–1852) is the father of the *Kleinkinderbeschäftigungsanstalt* (institution where small children are occupied). The name, too long even for the Germans, quickly shrank to *Kindergarten* (garden for children).

Froebel wanted his school to be a garden where children unfolded as naturally as flowers. Like Pestalozzi, with whom he had studied, he felt that natural development took place through self-activity, activity springing from and sustained by the interests of the child himself. The kindergarten provided the free environment in which such self-activity could take place.

It also provided the materials for self-activity. For example, blocks in different shapes and sizes led the child to observe, compare and contrast, measure, and count. Materials for handwork—such as drawing, coloring, modeling, and sewing—helped develop motor coordination and encourage self-expression. (*See also* Froebel; Kindergarten and Nursery School.)

For another of Pestalozzi's admirers, the German philosopher and psychologist Johann Friedrich Herbart (1776–1841), education was neither the training of faculties that exist ready-made in the mind nor a natural unfolding from within. Education was instruction—literally a *building into* the mind from the outside. The building blocks were the materials of instruction—the subject matter. The builder was the teacher. The job of the teacher was to form the child's mind by building into it the knowledge of man's cultural heritage through the teaching of such subjects as literature, history, science, and mathematics. Since the individual mind was presumably formed by building into it the products of the collective mind, methods of instruction were concerned wholly with *how* this was to be done. Herbart's interest lay in determining how knowledge could be presented so that it would be understood and therefore retained. He insisted that education must be based on psychological knowledge of the child so that he could be instructed effectively.

The psychology on which Herbart based his teaching methods was later proved incorrect. His systematized lesson plans, however, guiding the teacher in

For a period of five months during the Napoleonic era, Pestalozzi established and ran an orphanage and school at the small village of Stans, Switzerland. Although Pestalozzi was successful from his and the children's viewpoints, some inspectors and other local visitors objected to the seeming disorder. Beneath the nonregimented surface confusion, however, the children were busy learning and developing, and Pestalozzi was working out and testing his ideas on education. Later, in 1805, he opened a school at Yverdon, Switzerland, that became an international showplace and influenced education throughout the world.

what he considered the proper manner and sequence of presenting subject matter to pupils, were a real innovation in education. By denying that the mind consists of inborn faculties that can be exercised on any kind of material, Herbart drew the attention of educators to the subject matter itself, to the content of the material. He took the emphasis off memorizing—at least in theory—and put it on understanding. He also transformed the image of the teacher. No longer an ignorant bully beating knowledge into children, the teacher became a person trained in effective methods of imparting knowledge. He controlled the learning situation through psychological insight, not physical force. The teacher inspired the child's "interest" in the material because he knew how to present it.

Before arriving at his own educational theory, Herbart had visited—and been impressed by—Pestalozzi's school in Switzerland. The teaching methods Herbart evolved represented an attempt to create in the German schools the same joy of learning that animated Pestalozzi's school. That is why he insisted on the need to study the child to determine his interests.

Herbart's educational goal was different from Pestalozzi's, however, and his teaching methods created a different kind of school. Herbart was working within the framework of a state-controlled school system. For him the goal of education was to create individuals who were part of the sociopolitical community. While Pestalozzi emphasized the individuality that makes men distinct from one another, Herbart emphasized their common cultural heritage. Herbart's school created an intellectual environment, conducive to the child's absorption of formulated, authoritative bodies of knowledge, while Pestalozzi's school created a physical environment, conducive to the child's physical activity and firsthand learning experiences. While "interest" resided in the physical activity that Pestalozzi's child engaged in and was to be encouraged for the sake of his natural development, "interest" for Herbart's child was stimulated by the teacher for the purpose of instruction. While Pestalozzi's teacher unobtrusively guided the natural development of the individual child's innate powers, Herbart's teacher built knowledge into the child's mind through a systematic method of instruction that was uniform for all pupils. Thus, the instruction in Europe and the United States that was influenced by Herbart's theories was teacher- and curriculum-centered; that influenced by Pestalozzi, child-centered.

The concern of some educators in the late 19th century for the welfare and development of the individual eventually began to encompass children previously considered ineducable. One of the first to become interested in educating the mentally retarded, who were then called "idiot children," was the Italian physician Maria Montessori (1870–1952). The techniques and materials she devised for educating mentally retarded children were so effective that many learned to read and write almost as well as normal children. While Italian educators wondered at the progress of her pupils, Montessori wondered at the lack of progress of the normal children who attended schools for the poor. She concluded that the educational techniques used in these schools stifled development, whereas those that she had developed encouraged it.

In the early 1900's Montessori was put in charge of the *Case dei Bambini* (Children's Houses), schools for three- to seven-year-olds established in newly built tenement buildings in Rome. In these schools she emphasized freedom and individual development. Her idea of freedom, however, was a very special one. To be free, children must be as independent of other people as possible. So they learned to perform everyday, practical tasks, such as dressing themselves and keeping their schoolroom clean. They were also free to choose the materials they wanted to work with and the places where they wanted to work. To make them as independent of the teacher as possible, the children were given materials that allowed them to see and correct their own mistakes—such as variously shaped pegs to be fitted into matching holes.

Like Froebel, Montessori believed in the value of self-activity, sense training through the handling of physical objects, and the importance of the child's growth as an individual. For Montessori, however, growth was primarily cognitive rather than emotional. In her schoolroom, self-activity manifested itself mostly in contemplative self-absorption. In Froebel's schoolroom, it manifested itself mostly in the robust physical and social activity of songs and games.

Because the development of cognition was a more specific goal for Montessori than for Froebel, many of the physical objects she designed for the children led directly to such cognitive ends as reading and writing. If a child wanted to learn to write, for example, he could begin by literally getting the feel of the letters—running his hand over letters made of sandpaper. In this way, four- and five-year-olds learned to write, read, and count. (*See also* Montessori.)

19th-Century United States

America came into its own educationally with the movement toward state-supported, secular free schools for all children, which began in the 1820's with the common (elementary) school. The movement gained impetus in 1837 when Massachusetts established a state board of education and appointed the lawyer and politician Horace Mann (1796–1859) as its secretary. One of Mann's many reforms was the improvement of the quality of teaching by the establishment of the first public normal (teacher-training) schools in the United States. State after state followed Massachusetts' example until by the end of the 19th century the common-school system was firmly established. It was the first rung of what was to develop into the American educational ladder.

After the common school had been accepted, people began to urge that higher education, too, be tax supported. As early as 1821 the Boston School Committee established the English Classical School (later

BENCHMARKS IN CONTEMPORARY AMERICAN EDUCATION

1896 The University of Chicago Laboratory School opens under the direction of John Dewey and begins to experiment with what becomes the activity, or project, method of teaching.

1897 J.M. Rice's article "The Futility of the Spelling Grind," in *Forum* magazine, provides the first modern research report in the field of education.

1901 The Francis W. Parker School opens in Chicago, Ill. It emphasizes the importance of children's motivation, needs, and growth and uses the activity method proposed by Dewey.

1905 Alfred Binet publishes the first of his scales for the measurement of intelligence, which become important scientific tools in education.

1909 The first White House Conference on Children and Youth is held, an event that leads to the formation of the Children's Bureau in the Department of Labor.

1919 The Progressive Education Association is founded. It emphasizes respect for the uniqueness and dignity of the individual, the recognition of children's varied needs and purposes, and the importance of a warm, humane classroom.

1924 Franklin Bobbitt's 'How to Make a Curriculum' stresses the importance of applying scientific procedures to curriculum building.

1926 One of the first works to suggest that socioeconomic change requires concomitant changes in American education is William H. Kilpatrick's 'Education for a Changing Civilization'.

Jean Piaget, a pioneer inquirer into the development of children's concepts and reasoning, publishes his influential 'The Language and Thought of the Child'.

1932 George S. Counts writes 'Dare the Schools Build a New Social Order?' This provocative work asserts that schools have an obligation to exert leadership in social change rather than to play a merely passive role.

1935 The dynamics of interaction and development are presented by Kurt Lewin in 'A Dynamic Theory of Personality'. He also gives leadership to the group dynamics movement.

1935 The Eight Year Study is begun by the Progressive Education Association to assess the effects of progressive practices in 30 high schools. W.M. Aiken reports the generally favorable results in 'The Story of the Eight Year Study' (1942).

1938 The Educational Policies Commission publishes its widely cited objectives of education in 'The Purposes of Education in American Democracy'.

1940 Allison Davis and John Dollard's 'Children of Bondage' (1940), James H.S. Bossard's 'The Sociology of Child Development' (1948), and Davis' research on cultural bias as it works to the detriment of the black child anticipates the need to modify schools for the culturally deprived.

1943 Contributions to the field of child development are made by Arnold Gesell, Frances Ilg, and their associates. 'Infant and Child in the Culture of Today' (1943) and 'The Child from Five to Ten' (1946) are among the series of reports made by Gesell and his co-workers.

1950 'Developmental Tasks and Education' by Robert Havighurst indicates how cultural pressures and expectations require that the individual learn to master certain tasks at various stages of life.

In 'Childhood and Society', Erik Erikson presents his "eight ages of man," a "developmental timetable" of personality growth.

1953 Arthur E. Bestor's 'Educational Wastelands' makes a critical evaluation of American schools that gives him national prominence as an opponent of "educationists" and especially of "progressive" educators.

Robert M. Hutchins' analysis of educational practices in 'The Conflict in Education' identifies what he considers educational errors of the decade.

1955 Rudolph Flesch's 'Why Johnny Can't Read' becomes a conversation piece. It attacks existing practices in the teaching of reading and triggers many rebuttals from reading specialists.

1959 'The American High School Today', by James B. Conant, assesses education more than criticizes it. Many unmet educational needs are highlighted in Conant's proposals for change.

1960 Under the title 'The Process of Education' Jerome S. Bruner publishes his "sense of the meeting" report on the Woods Hole Conference. In 1962, his 'On Knowing' presents ten essays that stimulate thought on new approaches to teaching and learning.

1964 A new wave of educational critics begins to appear. They urge improved in-school and out-of-school learning experiences for children. Representative of their views are John Holt's 'How Children Fail' (1964), 'How Children Learn' (1967), and 'The Underachieving School' (1969).

1966 Jean Piaget is rediscovered as a result of fresh interest in cognitive development in early childhood.

Studies by James Coleman, published under the title 'Equality of Educational Opportunity', develop a strong case for compensatory education for the culturally deprived.

1967 Education for the poor, the black American, and other minority groups gains wide attention.

1970 'Crisis in the Classroom', a Carnegie-funded report by Charles E. Silberman, summarizes the "multiple crises" from which education suffers.

1983 'A Nation at Risk: the Imperative for Educational Reform', a report by the National Commission on Excellence in Education, warns of "a rising tide of mediocrity" in public schools.

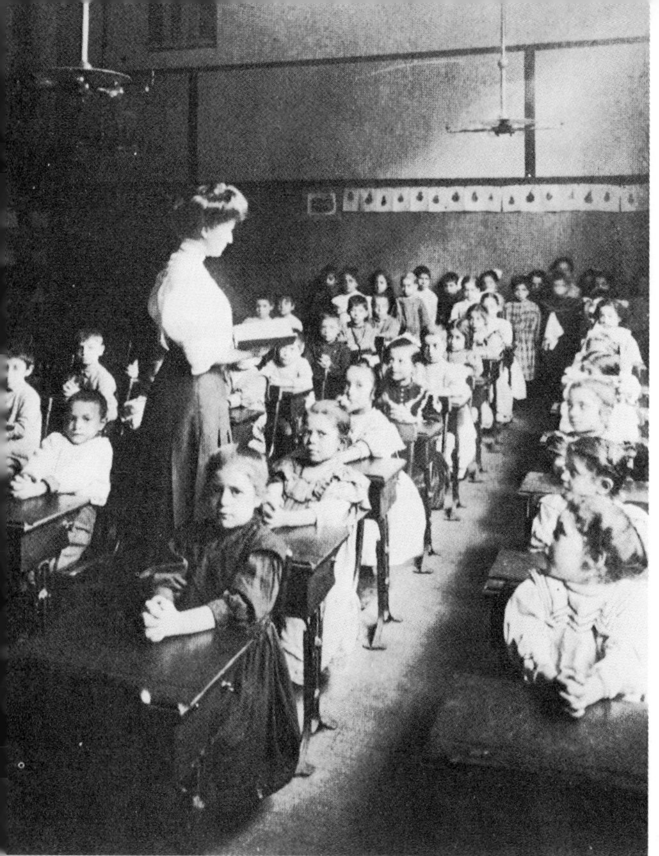

Historical Pictures Service, Chicago

In the often cheerless19th-century American schoolroom, learning was no laughing matter. The children (usually grouped by age) sat, prim and sober, in bolted-down rows of desks.

the English High School), which was the first public secondary school in the United States. By the end of the century, such secondary schools had begun to outnumber the private academies.

The original purpose of the American high school was to allow all children to extend and enrich their common-school education. With the establishment of the land-grant colleges after 1862, the high school also became a preparation for college—the step by which students who had begun at the lowest rung of the educational ladder might reach the highest. In 1873, when the kindergarten became part of the St. Louis, Mo., school system, there was a hint that in time a lower rung might be added.

America's educational ladder was unique. Where public school systems existed in European countries such as France and Germany, they were dual systems. When a child of the lower and middle classes finished his elementary schooling, he could go on to a vocational or technical school. The upper-class child often did not attend the elementary school but was instead tutored until he was about 9 years old and could enter a secondary school, generally a Latin grammar school. The purpose of this school was to prepare him for the university, from which he might well emerge as one of the potential leaders of his country. Instead of two separate and distinct educational systems for separate and distinct classes, the United States provided one system open to everyone.

As in mid-19th-century Europe, women were slowly gaining educational ground in the United States. "Female academies" established by such pioneers as Emma Willard (1787–1870) and Catharine Beecher (1800–78) prepared the way for secondary education for women. In 1861 Vassar—the first real college for women—was founded. Even earlier—in 1833—Oberlin College was founded as a coeducational college, and in 1837 four women began to study there.

In the mid-19th century there was yet another change in education. The secondary-school curriculum that had been slowly expanding since the founding of the academies in the mid-18th century virtually exploded in the mid-19th. A new society, complicated by the latest discoveries in the physical and biological sciences and the rise of industrialism and capitalism, called for more and newer kinds of knowledge. By 1861 as many as 73 subjects or branches thereof were being offered by the Massachusetts secondary schools. People still believed that the mind could be "trained," but they now thought that science could do a better job than could the classics. The result was a curriculum that was top-heavy with scientific instruction.

The mid-19th-century knowledge explosion also modestly affected some of the common schools, which expanded their curricula to include such courses as science and nature study. The content of instruction in the common school, beyond which few students went, consisted of the material in a relatively small number of books: assorted arithmetic, history, and geography texts, Webster's 'American Spelling Book', and two new books that appeared in 1836—the 'First' and 'Second' in the series of 'McGuffey's Eclectic Readers'. Whereas 'The New England Primer' admonished children against sin, the stories and poems in the readers pressed for the moral virtues. Countless children were required to memorize such admonitions as "Work while you work, play while you play. One thing each time, that is the way." (*See also* McGuffey.)

In the early days the common schools, like those in Europe, consisted of one room where one teacher taught pupils ranging in age from 6 to about 13—and sometimes older. The teacher instructed the children separately, not as a group. The good teacher had a strong right arm and an unshakable determination to cram information into his pupils.

Once the fight to provide free education for all children had been substantially won, educators turned their attention to the quality of that education. To find out more about learning and the learning process, American normal schools looked to Europe. In the 1860's they discovered—and for about 20 years were influenced by—Pestalozzi. The general effect on the common schools was to shift the emphasis from memorization of abstract facts to the firsthand observation of real objects.

Pestalozzi's diminishing influence roughly coincided with the rapid expansion of the cities. By the 1880's the United States was absorbing several million immigrants a year, a human flood that created new problems for the common school. The question confronting educators was how to impart the largest amount of information to the greatest number of children in the shortest possible time. The goal of educators and the means through which they attained it were reflected in the new schools they built and in the new teaching practices they adopted.

Expediency dictated, particularly in the cities, that the one-room common school be replaced by larger schools. To make it easier and faster for one teacher to instruct many students, there had to be as few differences between the children as possible. Since the most conspicuous difference was age, children were grouped on this basis, and each group had a separate room. To discourage physical activity that might disrupt discipline and interrupt the teaching process, to encourage close attention to and absorption of the teacher's words, and to increase eye contact, the seats were arranged in formal rows. For good measure, they frequently were bolted to the floor.

It is not surprising, at about this time, when the goal of education was to expedite the transfer of information to a large number of students, that the normal schools began to fall under the influence of Herbart. The essence of his influence probably lay not so much in his carefully evolved five-step lesson plan but in the basic idea of a lesson plan. Such a plan suggested the possibility of evolving a systematic method of instruction that was the same for all pupils. Perhaps Herbart's emphasis on the importance of motivating pupils to learn—whether through presentation of the material or, failing that, through rewards and punishments—also influenced the new teaching methods of the 1880's and 1890's.

The new methods, combined with the physical organization of the school, represented the antithesis of Pestalozzi's belief that the child's innate powers should be allowed to unfold naturally. Rather, the child must be lopped off or stretched to fit the procrustean curriculum bed. Subjects were graded according to difficulty, assigned to certain years, and taught by a rigid daily timetable. The amount of information that the child had absorbed through drill and memorization was determined by how much could be extracted from him by examinations. Reward or punishment came in the form of grades.

At the end of the 19th century the methods of presenting information had thus been streamlined. The curriculum had been enlarged and brought closer to the concerns of everyday life. Book learning had been supplemented somewhat by direct observation. And psychological flogging in the form of grades had perhaps diminished the amount of physical flogging. In one respect, however, the schools of the late 19th century were no different from those, say, of the Middle Ages: they were still based on what adults thought children were or should be, not what they really were.

20th-Century Changes in Education

Concepts of teaching and learning—and school practice—have changed more since 1900 than in all preceding human history. And they are still changing.

1900–1930. Before the 20th century the ideas of such men as Rousseau, Pestalozzi, Froebel, and, in the United States, Francis W. Parker (1837–1902) had caused little more than rumblings beneath the floor of the traditional schoolhouse. Because of John Dewey (1859–1952) they gathered force, and in the 1920's and 1930's new and old ideas collided right in the middle of the classroom.

Some of the schools where neat rows of subdued children had sat immobilized in their bolted-down seats—listening to a teacher armed with textbook, lesson plan, grade book, and disciplinary ruler—became buzzing places where virtually everything

HASTE THEE, SCHOOL-BOY

Haste thee, school-boy, haste away,
Far too long has been thy stay;
Often you have tardy been,
Many a lesson you've not seen;
Haste thee, school-boy, haste away,
Far too long has been thy stay.

Haste thee, school-boy, haste away,
Join no more the idler's play;
Quickly speed your steps to school,
And there mind your teacher's rule;
Haste thee, school-boy, haste away,
Join no more the idler's play.

Haste thee, school-boy, haste away,
Learn thy lessons well to-day;
Love the truth, and shun the wrong,
Then no day will seem too long.

The seven McGuffey readers quickly became best sellers. Between 1836 and 1920, many editions and about 122 million copies were printed. This illustration is from the 'New Third Eclectic Reader' of 1857.

Historical Pictures Service, Chicago

The Francis W. Parker School, which opened in Chicago, Ill., in 1901, was one of the earliest progressive schools in the United States. Using the activity method proposed by John Dewey, its students learned by doing.

By courtesy of Francis W. Parker School (1938 photograph)

moved, including the chairs. The children were occupied in groups or worked by themselves, depending on what they were doing. Above all, they were always *doing:* reading a favorite book, writing, painting, or learning botany by tending, observing, and discussing the plants they were growing. The teacher moved around the room, asking and answering questions, giving a child the spelling of a word he wanted to write or the pronunciation of a word he wanted to read, and in general acting as a helpful guide for the children's chosen activities. The chattering and noise and activity were signs that the children were excited about and absorbed by what they were doing. They were, in fact, learning by *doing.*

Dewey maintained that the child is not born with a ready-made faculty called thinking, which needs the exercise of repeated drill to make it as strong as the adult faculty. Nor, he said, is the mind a blank tablet on which knowledge is impressed. Mind—thinking or intelligence—is, according to Dewey, a developing, growing thing. And the early stages of growth and of knowledge are different from the later stages.

The development of the mind begins with the child's perception of things and facts as they are related to himself, to his personal, immediate world. A dog is *his* dog or his neighbor's dog; it is something furry and warm, something to hug, feed, and play with. The child may recognize the fact that though his neighbor's dog looks different from his, they are both dogs. When he sees a wolf at the zoo, he may decide that his dog is a nicer and friendlier animal. The child's zoological knowledge is thus organized around his own experiences with particular animals and his perceptions of similarities and differences between those experiences; it is psychologically organized knowledge.

The last step in the growth of intelligence is the ability to organize facts logically—that is, in terms of their relationship to one another. The formulated, logically organized knowledge of the zoologist is that both the wolf and the domesticated dogs belong to the family *Canidae,* order *Carnivora;* that the dogs belong to the genus *Canis* and species *familiaris;* and that one dog belongs to the sporting breed spaniel, the other to the working breed collie.

Presented to the child in this form, however, the study of zoology has no relation to the animals he plays with, feeds, and observes. His own experience outside of school does not bring the information to life, and the information does not enrich and extend his own experience. It represents another world entirely—a world of empty words. All he can do, therefore, is memorize what he reads and is told. He is not developing the power to think.

To stimulate the growth of intelligence rather than stifle it, as Dewey saw it, education must begin not at the end but at the beginning of the growth process; that is, with activity that engages the whole child—mentally, socially, physically, and emotionally. In the school, as in his spontaneous activities outside of school, it is the process of doing something that has meaning for the child—handling, making, growing, observing. The purpose of the school, however, is not to re-create an environment of relatively random activity but to create an environment where activities are carefully chosen to promote the development of intelligence. Carefully selected and guided, they become nets for gathering and retaining knowledge.

Instead of presenting children with an already packaged study of elementary science, Dewey might well have recommended that they study life in an aquarium. The child's natural curiosity should lead to such questions as "Why does the fish move his mouth like that? Is he always drinking?" His search for the answer will lead his intelligence in the same direction as that taken by the scientist—the direction of formulated conclusions based on observation of the phenomenon. He will be learning the *method* as well as the subject matter of science—learning to think as a scientist does. Moreover, the inquiry process need not be confined to one narrow area of knowledge but can be guided naturally by the teacher into investigations of fishing and then, conceivably (depending on the maturity of the young learner), of the role of the sea in the life of man. The barriers between "subjects" thus break down as the child's curiosity impels him to draw upon information from all areas of human knowledge. Books, films, recordings, and other such tools serve this end.

Learning the skills—reading, writing, spelling, and arithmetic—can be made meaningful to the child more easily if he is not forced through purposeless mechanical exercises, which, he is told, are important as a preparation for activities in later life. He should be led to discover that in order to do something he recognizes to be important right now, he needs certain skills. If he wants to write a letter, he must know how to spell; if he wants to make a belt, he must know how to measure the leather correctly.

Of course, Dewey was not suggesting that in order to learn an individual must recapitulate the whole history of the human race through personal inquiry. While the need for a background of direct experiences is great in elementary school, as children get older they should become increasingly able to carry out intellectual investigations without having to depend upon direct experiences. The principle of experiencing does apply, however, to the elementary phase of all subjects—even when the learner is a high-school or college student or an adult. The purpose is to encourage in the learner a habitual attitude of establishing connections between the everyday life of human beings and the materials of formal instruction in a way that has meaning and application.

The measuring and comparative grading of a student's assumed abilities, processes that reflect the educator's desire to assess the "results" of schooling, are incompatible with Dewey's thinking. The *quantity* of what is acquired does not in itself have anything to do with the development of mind. The "quality of mental process, not the production of correct answers," he wrote, "is the measure of educative growth." Because it is a process, learning is cumulative, and cannot be forced or rushed.

For Dewey, the educative growth of the individual assures the healthy growth of a society. A society grows only by changes brought about by free individuals with independent intelligence and resourcefulness. The beginning of a better society, then, lies in the creation of better schools. (*See also* Dewey, John.)

At about the same time that a few pioneering schools of the 1920's were trying to put Dewey's theories into practice, the "testing" movement, which started in about 1910, was working up steam. The child had first become the object of methodical-scientific research in 1897, when experiments conducted by Joseph M. Rice suggested that drill in spelling did not produce effective results. By 1913 Edward L. Thorndike had concluded that learning was the establishment of connections between a stimulus and a response and that the theory of mental faculties was nonsense. Alfred Binet, in 1905, published the first scale for measuring intelligence.

Jane said, "Down, down.
Down it comes.
Run, Dick.
We can find it."

"See me run," said Sally.
"See Spot run.
Oh, oh!
This is fun."

Between 1931 and 1970, about 50 million Americans were taught to read from the Dick and Jane series of reading texts. Unlike the dour earlier primers, these had an element of fun.

During the 1920's, children began to be given IQ (intelligence quotient) and achievement tests on a wide scale and sometimes were carefully grouped by ability and intelligence. Many of the spelling and reading books they used, foreshadowing the 1931 Dick and Jane readers, were based on "controlled" vocabularies.

So while Dewey's "progressive" educators were trying to develop the child's ability to think, the conservatives, or essentialists, were testing his memory. While the progressives were concerned with the child's awareness of the scientific method, the conservatives were measuring his knowledge of various forms of subject matter. While the progressives were trying to create an individualized classroom where the child's total personality could grow, the conservatives were hoping to improve instruction by grouping children according to mental ability. While the progressives saw in the child-centered classroom the hope for social change, the conservatives saw in uniform curriculum content the hope for social stability. Begun in the

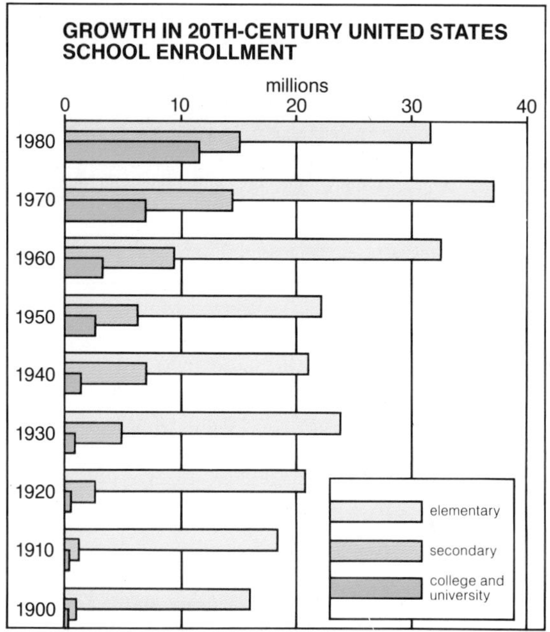

1920's, the dispute as to which educational policies lead to the "good life" was still going on in the 1980's

1930–60. Progressive theories seem to have been in the ascendancy during the 1930's, though only a handful of schools had genuinely liberal programs. One of the widespread—if modest—changes in the traditional schools was the attempt to relax the rigid categorization of subjects in the curriculum. Each body of knowledge was still organized according to its own internal logic, but it was taught in relation to other subjects. History, for example, was enriched by material from geography, sociology, and anthropology. This correlation of subjects led in the late 1930's to the development on the high-school level of what is sometimes called a core curriculum. Here the related subjects were merged into a whole, organized by a unifying theme—or core—that drew on the content of all of them. Some of the more liberal core curriculums focused on such topics as housing or problems of democracy as part of an effort to draw the students' attention to the problems and possible ways of reforming a society threatened by economic depression and the international problems that led to World War II.

Conservative criticism of modern school practices died down somewhat in the 1930's but was revived in the early 1940's because of low scores made on military intelligence and ability tests. Especially bitter criticism was leveled in the early 1950's at "soft" or "cream puff" pedagogy; critics alleged that progressives had created a low quality of instruction, weakened discipline, and led to the decline of both moral values and traditional content in school programs.

After the shock Americans felt when the Russians launched the first space satellite (Sputnik) in 1957, criticism of the schools swelled into loud demands for renewed emphasis on content mastery. The insistence on cognitive "performance" and "excellence" accomplished four things. It increased competitive academic pressures on students at all levels. It stimulated serious and sustained interest in preschool education, which manifested itself in various ways—from the revival of the "Montessori method" in the 1960's to the preschool television series Sesame Street in 1969. It created a new interest in testing, this time in such forms as national assessments of student performance, experiments with programmed materials, and attempts to gauge when children could begin to read. And it stimulated interest in the application of technology and instructional systems to education as a means of improving instruction.

Perhaps the most conspicuous result of the emphasis on cognitive performance was the large number of curriculum reform studies undertaken not by professional educators only but also by specialists in such fields as mathematics, science, and linguistics. This trend had begun in the pre-Sputnik days but was greatly accelerated by the Russians' successful spaceflight and American fears of losing technological preeminence. Curriculum changes led to the "new math" and the "new science" in the 1950's and early 1960's. Changes in English and social studies instruction followed in the middle and late 1960's.

From the 18th century onward, as knowledge of the world increased, new subjects had been added and old ones split up into branches. Later, new combinations of courses resulted from the attempt to put the scattered pieces of knowledge back together again. The curriculum change represented by, say, the new math, however, involved a major restructuring of subject content. The purpose was to make knowledge more rational and meaningful so that it could be understood instead of mechanically memorized. It also encouraged young learners to begin to think and inquire as scholars do. In other words, many of the new programs developed for use in the schools, particularly in the 1960's, stressed the inquiry approach as a means of mastering a body of knowledge and of creating a desire for more knowledge. To further vitalize instruction, the new programs often used films, programmed materials, and laboratory experiments.

Recent Developments. Resistance to the 1954 United States Supreme Court decision terminating segregation placed the schools in the middle of a bitter and sometimes violent dispute over which children were going to attend what schools. By 1965, when a measure of genuine integration had become a reality in many school districts, the schools again found themselves in the eye of a stormy controversy. This time the question was not which children were going to what schools but what kind of education society should provide for the students. The goal of high academic performance, which had been revived by criticisms and reforms of the 1950's and early 1960's, began to be challenged by demands for more "humane," "relevant," and "pressure-free" schooling.

By courtesy of Thomas Vreeland, Chairman, School of Architecture, University of California at Los Angeles

Among Thomas Vreeland's innovative proposals to revitalize city education is the electronically equipped and programmed bus that would take education into the neighborhoods.

Many university and some high-school students from all ethnic groups and classes had been growing more and more frustrated—some of them desperately so—over what they felt was a cruel and senseless war in Vietnam and a cruel, discriminatory, competitive, loveless society at home. They demanded curriculum reform, improved teaching methods, and greater stress and action on such problems as overpopulation, pollution, international strife, deadly weaponry, and discrimination. Pressure for reform came not only from students but also from many educators. While students and educators alike spoke of the need for greater "relevance" in what was taught, opinions as to what *was* relevant varied greatly.

The blacks wanted new textbooks in which their people were recognized and fairly represented, and some of them wanted courses in black studies. They, and many white educators, also objected to culturally biased intelligence and aptitude tests and to academic college entrance standards and examinations. Such tests, they said, did not take into account the diverse backgrounds of students who belonged to ethnic minorities and whose culture was therefore different from that of the white middle-class student. Whites and blacks alike also wanted a curriculum that touched more closely on contemporary social problems and teaching methods that recognized their existence as individual human beings rather than as faceless robots competing for grades.

Alarmed by the helplessness and hopelessness of the urban ghetto schools, educators began to insist on curricula and teaching methods flexible enough to provide for differences in students' social and ethnic backgrounds. Moreover, for educational reformers the urban ghetto school became a symbol of a general failure of American education to accomplish the goal of individual development. Both the liberal educators—the "new humanists"—and the students seemed to mean by *relevance* very much what the progressives of the 1920's and 1930's meant when they said that education should contribute to the development of the student by leading him to establish living, human links between the subject matter and his personal and social experiences. Also reminiscent of those decades were the child-centered "open" schools that sprang up in the later 1960's as alternatives to and examples for the traditional schools. The clash between the academically and the humanistically oriented schools of thought, therefore, was in many ways one more encounter in the continuing battle between conservatives and liberals. (*See also* Psychology.)

EDUCATION TODAY

Compared to pre-20th-century schools, all schools of the 1980's in the United States are liberal. Latin and Greek have given way to the modern, spoken languages. Literature and philosophy have lost ground to such "practical" studies as science and the social sciences and to skills such as driver training. Emphasis on intellectual brilliance has given way to social accomplishments that are more group-oriented. Teachers are less austere, better informed, and more considerate of the total growth and well-being of the young.

Compared, however, to Dewey's totally child-centered elementary school, his ideas about how knowl-

By courtesy of Charles Colbert, Architect, New Orleans

Charles Colbert's proposed shoulder carrel could provide individual instruction by means of such media as tapes, computer connections, telephone, projectors, records, radio, and television. It would weigh about 20 pounds, be air conditioned, and run by either electricity or battery.

edge should be taught on the upper levels, and the priority he gives to personal development over academic excellence, most American schools of the 1980's are conservative. There may be less emphasis on textbooks and more on instructional systems and educational media such as films, but the medium of instruction is still predominantly teaching by telling, rather than by stimulating independent inquiry. Subjects such as science that were originally excluded from the curriculum may have fought their way in, but once in they are often taught in a compartmentalized way. Furthermore, they have become as much a part of the authoritative knowledge that the student must master—and as remote from his everyday life—as Latin in the 19th century was remote from the life of an American farm boy. Laboratories have been introduced into many schools, but they are often used to supplement the ready-made knowledge of textbooks, not as a means toward *discovery* of knowledge and mastery of the scientific method.

Early Childhood Education. In the early 1970's, neither nursery schools (for two- to four-year-olds) nor kindergartens (for four- and five-year-olds) had become a universal feature of public education in the United States. Educators, however—convinced that many of the child's basic potentialities are determined by his experiences even before he enters first grade—are urging that top priority be given to early childhood education, beginning no later than age two or three.

Elementary Schools. Four basic subject areas are included in virtually all elementary schools in the United States: language arts (reading, writing, spelling, and related language skills), mathematics, science, and social science (usually history, geography, and relevant material from the social and behavioral sciences). In the fourth, fifth, and sixth grades, subject matter generally assumes a more distinct form and in some schools becomes quite sharply delineated.

Although some progressive "open" schools appeared in the late 1960's and early 1970's, most elementary schools are still relatively traditional—particularly in the middle and upper years. Most of the time, the child is expected to remain seated and quiet, and he must adjust himself to a teacher's plans that sometimes are uniform for the entire class. The learner is not appraised on the basis of total personality growth but is graded on the basis of his mastery of content. The teacher remains the figure of authority who frequently teaches "subjects," rather than serving as an unobtrusive guide of human development.

Secondary Schools. In most high schools the basic courses that are offered are English, science, mathematics, foreign languages, and history. Large, comprehensive high schools may offer more than 100 courses, including art, music, vocational, business, and technical subjects.

The experiments with alternative methods of drawing together isolated subjects, which began in the 1950's and continued into the 1980's, have brought about striking changes in some high schools. The traditional academic and vocational programs offered by a plurality, if not a majority, of schools, however, have changed but little. There are still classes that meet at prescribed times, and set time intervals govern their length. Compartmentalized subjects remain the rule, and graduation requirements generally are based on a specified number of units of content.

Colleges and Universities. Although the admissions policies of some colleges and universities have been somewhat modified to allow for students who cannot qualify on a strictly academic basis, most maintain their traditional emphasis on "excellence." Despite numerous limited innovations, higher education in the 1980's is not radically different from what it was about 30 years before. There are refinements rather than fundamental changes on the typical campus. Pressures from students and the increasing open-mindedness of teachers at all levels from early childhood to the doctoral level suggest, however, the likelihood of massive change within the next decade or two.

Private Schools. Most private schools fall into three broad categories: parochial schools operated by religious groups; private schools (such as the Choate School and the Francis W. Parker School) supported by patrons; and private colleges and universities.

A 1971 Supreme Court decision, which held unconstitutional direct state aid to nonpublic elementary and secondary schools, aggravated the problems of the public school system, which had to absorb millions of new students. However, the annual rate of Roman Catholic school shutdowns stabilized by the early 1980's. In 1984 Congress rejected a plan to give tuition tax credits to the parents of children in private schools.

Education and Architecture

School buildings themselves can reflect liberal or conservative views about what should go on in a classroom. The earliest schools built to accommodate large numbers of children had separate classrooms for graded groups. The rooms were laid out formally, with pupils' desks bolted to the floor in straight rows facing the teacher's desk. Clearly, the school itself reflected a teacher- and subject-centered view of education. (For illustration, *see* page 92.)

Schools of the next generation, built after 1940, were lighter and airier and had more open space, and most had movable desks. They also often provided special rooms or areas for science, art, music, and physical education. There were still separate rooms for different grade levels, however, and the desks still were likely to be formally arranged in straight rows. That is, the schoolroom was still largely designed to implement the old school program, which involved grade levels, uniform time blocks, uniformity of instruction, and absorption of subject matter. Newer subjects, not newer teaching methods, accounted for most of what was new in school design.

The first school buildings constructed specifically to facilitate liberal teaching methods began to appear in the mid-1950's. Folding interior walls—or no walls at all—permitted the flexible use of space to encourage large-group, small-group, or individual instruction. Some provided carrels for individual study, areas designed for team teaching, centers for programmed instruction, and a language laboratory.

In the newest buildings—called open schools—the use of space is even more flexible. Since so much of the space is undifferentiated, areas within the buildings can be readily expanded, converted to accommodate program changes, and used for many kinds of functions.

A DECADE OF AMERICAN EDUCATION

	1970–71*	1980–81*
Students		
Elementary		
Public	32,577,000	27,674,000
Nonpublic	4,052,000	3,623,000
Secondary		
Public	13,332,000	13,313,000
Nonpublic	1,311,000	1,339,000
Colleges and universities		
Public	6,427,000	9,460,000
Nonpublic	2,154,000	2,637,000
Total	59,853,000	58,046,000
Teachers		
Elementary		
Public	1,128,000	1,177,000
Nonpublic	153,000	188,000
Secondary		
Public	927,000	985,000
Nonpublic	80,000	89,000
Colleges and universities		
Public	314,000	502,000
Nonpublic	160,000	193,000
Total	2,762,000	3,134,000
Administrators and Supervisors		
Superintendents of schools	12,849	13,269
Principals and supervisors	125,432	143,430
College and university presidents	2,556	3,056
Total	140,837	159,755
Schools†		
Elementary		
Public	65,800	61,069
Nonpublic	14,372	16,792
Secondary		
Public	25,352	24,362
Nonpublic	3,770	5,678
Colleges and universities		
Public	1,089	1,334
Nonpublic	1,467	1,722
Total	111,850	110,957

*Some figures are estimates.
†Schools with both elementary and secondary programs are included under elementary schools and also under secondary schools.

Sources: U.S. Department of Education, National Center for Education Statistics; Higher Education General Information Survey

As a reflection of a conservative or liberal attitude toward education, the physical layout of a school can either facilitate or hinder conservative or liberal teaching practices. But it cannot determine what those practices will be. It may be difficult for a conservative teacher to operate in a physically open classroom or for a liberal teacher to operate in a formal classroom, but it is not impossible. What determines

Perkins & Will, Eliel & Eero Saarinen, Architects; Hedrich-Blessing Photo

By courtesy of Perkins & Will, Robert Nowell Ward Photo

whether the classroom is liberal or conservative is the spirit and attitude of the teacher.

Education and Technology

The educational media, or instructional systems and technology, field had become increasingly prominent in the 1970's. It has spread far beyond the casual use of films and slides to encompass such innovations as programmed learning through teaching machines, computer-based or computer-assisted instruction, learning systems approaches, and education on closed-circuit television.

It is probable that one day the rapidly developing techniques of holography will make possible classroom replication of three-dimensional objects that appear to be completely solid and genuine. (For color pictures, *see* Color.) Other interesting innovations are Charles Colbert's shoulder carrel and Thomas Vreeland's electronically programmed and equipped bus, which suggests that part of tomorrow's education may move from school to street.

Europe Today

The rapid changes that took place in United States schools during the first part of the 20th century can ultimately be traced back to theories born in 18th- and 19th-century Europe. Yet as late as the 1940's most European countries had not been fundamentally changed by the liberal ideas of such men as Rousseau, Pestalozzi, and Froebel or by the liberal American ideal of a general elementary and secondary education for all. They retained, with relatively few changes, the school system they had established in the 19th century—a dual system based on the concept of an academic education for the elite and basic literacy plus some vocational training for the masses. The minority, destined to become potential leaders, attended the elite secondary schools: the English "public" schools (such as Harrow, Eton, and Rugby), the French *lycées*, or the German *Gymnasien*. The majority, destined to become followers, either went from elementary schooling to vocational training or dropped out of school to go to work.

After World War II rigid class stratification began to give way, and Europe moved toward a one-track system of education. This system was based on the recognition that all citizens are entitled to equal opportunities for schooling.

Changes in Great Britain illustrate the shift from class to mass education that has been taking place in Europe since the mid-1940's. The number of years of compulsory education was raised, and new secondary schools were established to meet a variety of student needs. These new public schools at first offered three different kinds of programs: the college preparatory program of the grammar schools, the general education provided by the "modern schools" for students who were not likely to go on to the university, and the specialized training given by secondary technical schools. By the late 1960's, steps were being taken to integrate these three programs—and the students enrolled in them—into one "comprehensive" all-purpose secondary school. By the 1970's the comprehensive school had begun to replace the three specialized schools. In all European countries the elite private secondary schools still exist—as they do in the United States—but they are no longer the only means of entrance to the universities.

The distinguished universities of continental Europe still accept students on a purely academic basis, as do England's traditional universities—such as Oxford and Cambridge. But by 1971 England had made a university degree attainable without resident study on a conventional university campus. For the first time in history it was possible for some 40,000 students to enroll in degree-granting university programs (about five years in length) in which credit was earned not by attending classes but by learning through specially designed television programs.

When Europe began to switch from the two- to the one-track public school system, the liberal educational theories born in Europe at last began to be implemented there. Although most European public schools remain more conservative than United States schools, many of them have become at least as much concerned with the student's all-around growth as they are with the acquisition of subject matter. The schools have moved away from the traditional academic subject matter toward more general, practical, socially oriented curricula. To overcome rigid compartmentalization of subjects, the schools have experimented with programs of study, some of which have

School architecture has tended to reflect changing educational practices. The Crow Island School in Winnetka, Ill. (far left), was lighter and airier than earlier school buildings. The Carlton W. Washburne School in Winnetka (left) was built specifically to facilitate contemporary teaching methods. The folding interior walls permit flexible use of space; this room is arranged for group instruction. The James Howard Monroe Junior High School in Wheaton, Ill. (right), is one of the newest, "open" schools. In sharp contrast to 19th-century classrooms, the huge expanses of undifferentiated space in the rooms can be converted to facilitate the most varied activities.

By courtesy of Orlando Cabanban, Photography; Orput-Orput, Architects

been similar to the American core program. Perhaps the most liberal practices in the 1960's and 1970's occurred in England's "open" primary schools, which in many ways closely follow the ideas of Dewey and his adherents.

The Soviet Union Today

In the 1920's and 1930's virtually the whole world was aware of the ideas of progressive educators. China and Turkey, for example, invited Dewey to help with their school reforms. For a brief period in the late 1920's and early 1930's, the Soviet Union's government encouraged the use of liberal teaching methods. But this was while the government was still struggling to set up the educational machinery to combat widespread illiteracy.

When the Soviets came to power in 1917, no more than 30 percent of the population could read. One of the first decrees signed by the Soviet leader Lenin established universal, coeducational, free education. Implementing such a decree was especially difficult, however. Among the problems the government had to face were the huge size of the country and the existence of at least 100 languages (some even without alphabets) spoken by the peoples of what are now republics of the Soviet Union. Again, in some sections, such as the Central Asian areas, schools had never existed. Therefore, there was no broad educational base of equipment and buildings.

In the face of such difficulties, the progress that was made before the 1980's is remarkable. Soviet preschools enroll about 14 million of the country's children—more than twice the number served by day-care centers in the United States. Ten years of education are compulsory where available (five years of elementary and three of lower and two of higher secondary). Statistics from the Soviet Union suggest that approximately 97 percent of the youth will obtain some secondary education. Higher education, too, has expanded. More than 860 institutions exist, as compared with 105 in 1917. They enroll about 4 million students, including those doing work in correspondence schools and at night. They graduated 817,300 students in 1980. Specialized secondary schools, with programs comparable to those of junior colleges, enroll another 4.6 million students.

Figures such as these, however, give no idea of the quality of Soviet education. Not long after taking power, the Soviet Union's communist rulers discovered that liberal curricula and teaching methods, designed to promote the growth of the individual and desirable change in society, were incompatible with the goal of communist education. Countries such as the Soviet Union, East Germany, and China expect their schools to produce citizens loyal to the party and capable of contributing to the material growth of the state.

Beginning in about 1931, then, the Soviet government began to exercise rigid control over textbooks, curricula, and teaching methods. Above all, the schools were to stress obedience, industriousness, and loyalty, and they were to teach facts. Soon schools throughout the country were teaching exactly the same things in exactly the same way.

From the lower schools through the upper, emphasis is now placed on such practical studies as mathematics, science, and technology, and work experience frequently accompanies classroom studies. A Soviet approach that stresses the practical aspect of education is called polytechnical education. It has no exact parallel in the United States. When chemistry, for example, is "polytechnized," students study not only the subject itself, but they also study the roles and relationships of chemistry to the Soviet economy and to trends and research in the Soviet chemical industry.

Beyond the Borders of Western Europe

Many of the countries of Asia, the Middle East, and other non-European areas retain the dual pattern of education imported from Great Britain, France, or Germany about 50 years ago when these countries ruled or at least administered many areas of the world. In the developing countries, educational systems that were originally designed to train a small native bureaucracy no longer serve the purpose for which they were intended. As a result, one of the tasks that developing nations continue to face for the 1980's and 1990's is to create educational systems that more adequately serve their cultural, social, political, and economic needs (*see* sections on education in individual country articles).

TEACHERS AND TEACHING IN THE UNITED STATES

A teacher is someone who communicates information or skill so that someone else may learn. Parents are the first teachers. Just by living with their child and sharing their everyday activities with him, they teach him their language, their values and mores, and their manners. Information and skills difficult to teach through family living are taught in a school by a person whose special occupation is teaching.

Before 1900 it was widely assumed that a man was qualified to teach if he could read and write—and well qualified if he knew arithmetic. With modest qualifications like these, it is no wonder that teachers had low salaries and little prestige. Literature and history frequently portray teachers as fools, sadists, and ignoramuses. In the 1700's, for example, William Cowper noted that conjugated verbs and nouns declined were "all the mental food purveyed/By public hackneys in the schooling trade." Washington Irving made Ichabod Crane a fool in 'The Legend of Sleepy Hollow'; Mr. Brocklehurst was a sadistic schoolmaster in Charlotte Brontë's 'Jane Eyre'; and Thomas Hughes described the savage temper of the master in 'Tom Brown's School Days'. In the mid-19th century Thomas B. Macaulay, speaking in the British Parliament, derided teachers as "the refuse of all other callings, discarded footmen, ruined pedlars, men . . . who [do] not know whether the earth is a sphere or a cube."

By the late 19th century, there were signs that the status of teachers was slowly improving. Great educators such as Pestalozzi and Herbart, distinguished leaders such as Mann and Henry Barnard, and innovative thinkers such as Dewey and Parker began to command a respect that in a few decades had to some degree permeated classrooms in the United States. Progress was more glacial than meteoric, however, until the last half of the century.

In the 20th century the status of teachers rose as the standards for their education rose. By 1950 the average teacher had an education that greatly exceeded that of the average citizen.

Oddly enough, during the 19th century and well into the first third of the 20th, public disdain for teachers went right along with the idea that they must be models of moral integrity. In many small towns, there were often "conduct codes" that forbade the teacher those activities in which many parents and other citizens engaged—such as card playing, moderate drinking, smoking, and divorce. It is a commentary on changing times that the conduct codes that formerly set teachers apart have disappeared almost completely.

The changing attitudes toward the role of women also had an effect on the teaching profession. Before 1830, nearly all teachers were men. A century later, there were many women in teaching, and the elementary school had become a woman's world. The original shift in the ratio between men and women occurred partly because educational leaders urged that, in the interest of simple justice, qualified women be employed. Another reason for the shift was the grouping of children by age in the graded schools that replaced the ungraded common school. In the ungraded school, where the students ranged from small children to adolescents, a female teacher was often faced with the problem of disciplining unruly boys who were bigger and stronger than she. In the new schools, which were graded by age, women could teach classes made up only of younger children. In later years, shifts in the male-female ratio occurred when women moved into schools to fill manpower shortages caused by war or periods of widespread male employment.

The Education of Teachers

In the 1830's, when the states began to take responsibility for supporting the schools, they also began to realize that they must provide trained teachers. The first public normal school opened in 1839 in Massachusetts. Normal schools originally offered only one year of training. This consisted of a review of "common subjects" (arithmetic and grammar); "advanced subjects" (algebra, geometry, moral philosophy, and natural history); child development; and rudimentary teaching methods. Practice teaching took place in the model schools sometimes attached to the normal schools. (*Normal*, from the Latin *norma*, means "model.")

By the 1930's the old normal school was beginning to give way to training in four-year, degree-granting colleges. The expansion of knowledge—both in substantive fields and in educational methods—had made more extensive teacher training imperative. Furthermore, state certification requirements had increased to the point where teachers without a bachelor's degree found it hard to obtain licenses. After 1940 a master's degree was required of most secondary and many elementary-school teachers.

Modern teacher education programs at the undergraduate level usually require four years of study consisting of content courses such as English and history; methods courses; and practice teaching. Content courses prepare students for general teaching or for teaching in specialized academic fields or in specialized nonacademic fields such as art, physical education, educational media, music, or home economics.

Teaching "methods" are procedures used to help the learner. College methods courses acquaint the teacher with instructional theory and materials, the preparation of lesson plans, the use of educational media such as projectors and teaching machines, and similar "how-to-do-it" activities.

The elementary-school teacher education program usually includes a total of one year of methods courses, the secondary program less. Content courses in the secondary program generally are more numerous and more concentrated in academic fields such as language arts and biological sciences.

For high-school teachers, graduate schools usually offer courses in specialized academic fields; for elementary teachers, advanced courses in such specialties as reading, curriculum, and child development. At some universities a person with a bachelor's degree from a college of arts and sciences can earn a master of arts degree in teaching by taking methods courses and practice teaching.

Certification

State laws and regulations determine the qualifications for teaching. Licenses are usually issued by a subdivision of the state department of education.

Certification has done much to protect pupils from substandard teachers, but some critics feel that many such laws are arbitrary, that too often they license teachers merely because they have accumulated college credits. By the 1970's, attempts were underway to find additional means of determining who is best qualified to teach.

Conditions of Employment

In 1936 an educational historian compared the teacher to an "indentured servant." Since the depression years of the 1930's, however, working conditions of teachers have improved at least as much as those of other Americans.

Salaries. In 1938 the average lifetime income of a public school teacher was $29,700. By 1983 the average annual salary for classroom teachers in the United States was about $20,700.

Contracts, Tenure, and Leave. In the 1930's, many teachers lacked the security of tenure and, if fired, could not get another job. Today the beginning teacher usually signs a one-year contract or salary agreement and remains on a limited contract until going on tenure. Tenure, or a continuing contract, is usually attained in three to five years, depending on the policy of the local board of education and state laws.

Most school boards have leave policies, which provide for illness, maternity, and, with increasing frequency, either study or sabbatical leaves with full or partial salary payments. Both the study leave and the salary schedule, which usually provides pay increments for advanced degrees, serve as incentives to further the teacher's professional preparation.

The Range of Teaching Opportunities

As products of or students in United States schools, most people are familiar with the work of classroom teachers and teachers of music, art, and physical education. There are, however, many special teaching fields that are less well known:

Special Services. Among special teaching personnel are those who work in educational media (also called instructional systems and technology), library science, guidance, various forms of special education for the handicapped, school psychology, and evaluation of performance (or psychometry). Others work with culturally different and disadvantaged children. Bilingual education, or instruction in both a native language and in English, has been officially encouraged by the federal government since passage of legislation in 1965.

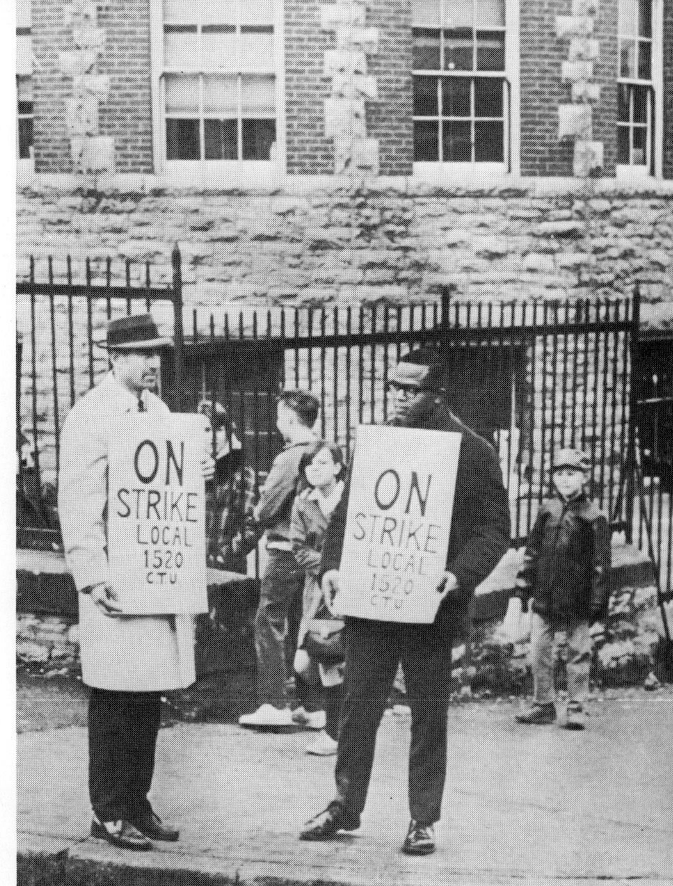

Wide World

The teacher strikes that became common after the late 1960's suggest how much conditions have changed since the 1930's, when teachers were still bound by low salaries, lack of job security, and unreasonable conduct codes.

Paraprofessional Posts. Teacher aids, or paraprofessionals, have helped out in schools at least since the early 19th century, but their participation on teaching teams and in new diversified staffing plans in open schools is recent. Teacher aids fall into four groups: (1) unskilled aids, who do such things as dress younger children and clean up after classes; (2) clerical aids, who type and duplicate materials; (3) subprofessional aids, who read to the children and supervise rest periods, and (4) co-professional aids, or junior teachers, who grade themes, supervise tests, and help on the playground.

In the early 1980's questions of wages, hours, duties, necessary training, and licensing had not been entirely clarified. Despite the uncertainties, the paraprofessional had established his worth and seemed likely to have a permanent place in the classroom.

College and University Instruction. As a rule, a doctoral degree is a prerequisite for a permanent university appointment. While pursuing the degree, the student often serves a form of subsidized internship or apprenticeship as a graduate assistant, research assistant, or teaching associate in a chosen field

FEDERAL MILESTONES IN EDUCATION

The **Ordinance of 1785,** which established the pattern for land survey in the American West with its provisions for the survey of the Northwest Territory, set aside the 16th section of every township for the support of education.

The **Morrill Act of 1862** provided every state 30,000 acres of land per congressman, thus launching the land-grant colleges of which there are now 70. Military training of students, along with agricultural and mechanical studies, was required for qualification. The second Morrill Act, in 1890, provided annual funding.

The **Office of Education** was established in 1867. In 1869 it became a part of the Department of the Interior, and in 1939 it was transferred to the Federal Security Agency. It became a constituent agency of the Department of Health, Education, and Welfare, which was established in 1953.

The **Smith-Lever Act of 1914** began extension services in homemaking and agriculture through the land-grant colleges. It continued the principle of matching federal and states funds, begun under the Marine Schools Act of 1911. The provisions of the Smith-Lever Act were extended by the **Capper-Ketcham Act of 1928** and the **Bankhead-Jones Act of 1935.**

The **Smith-Hughes Act of 1917** provided federal aid for vocational education programs below the college level. It involved the principle of matching funds.

The **National Defense Act, 1920,** extended federal participation in military training at the secondary and college levels. The ROTC programs are an outgrowth of the legislation. Instructors, equipment, and facilities are provided. The armed forces design the course of study and supervise the program. Private as well as public institutions have participated.

The **Civilian Conservation Corps (CCC)** and the **National Youth Administration (NYA)** were financed by the federal government during the depression that began in 1929. The NYA provided funds so that students could continue their education. The money was earned, usually by working in the institution attended. Classes, mainly for adults, were operated under the **Federal Emergency Relief Administration** and the **Works Progress** (later, **Work Projects) Administration.** This emergency education program was staffed, for the most part, by unemployed teachers. The government also made some direct grants to school districts in especially depressed areas to keep schools open.

Under the **Lanham Act, 1941–45,** care for the children of working mothers was provided during World War II. Nursery schools were established throughout the United States. Federal and local control were involved in the implementation.

The **"GI Bill," 1944,** had broad provisions for financing the education of veterans of World War II. Later it was extended to include veterans subsequently discharged.

The **Supreme Court Decision on Segregation, 1954** (Brown *vs.* Board of Education), legally terminated racial segregation in United States schools, and the abolition of dual (separate black and white) school systems began.

The **National Defense Education Act, 1958,** provided assistance, for four years, to all levels of education from elementary through graduate school in science, mathematics, foreign language, counseling and guidance, graduate fellowships, research and experimentation in instructional aids such as television, and improvement in informational and statistical services. It was extended in 1961 for two years.

The **Educational Television Act, 1962,** authorized grants to educational institutions or non-profit groups to build educational television stations.

The **Civil Rights Act, 1964,** provided for technical and financial aid to local public school districts to help with desegregation. Discrimination was barred under federally assisted programs.

The **Economic Opportunity Act, 1964,** stimulated the cooperation of local, state, and federal governments in establishing programs to aid public schools. Youth programs, work experience programs, volunteer services in America, urban and rural community action programs, and special programs for the poor in rural areas were included.

The **Elementary and Secondary Education Act, 1965,** strengthened secondary and elementary education programs for educationally deprived children in low-income areas and provided for additional school library resources, textbooks, and other instructional materials, supplementary educational centers and services, and the improvement of educational research and state departments of education. Students in nonpublic schools were also included as beneficiaries of the act.

The **Higher Education Act, 1965,** provided undergraduate scholarships and fellowships for experienced or prospective teachers. A Teacher Corps was authorized to serve in urban and rural poverty areas.

The **Education Professions Development Act, 1967,** was designed to help school systems, state education agencies, and colleges and universities develop more effective ways to recruit, train, and utilize educational personnel.

The **Supreme Court Decision on Bussing, 1971** (Swann *vs.* Charlotte-Mecklenburg Board of Education), ruled that bussing to "dismantle the dual school systems" of the South was constitutional.

The **Supreme Court Decision on Financial Assistance to Nonpublic Schools, 1971** (Earley *vs.* DiCenso and other cases), ruled that direct state support for nonpublic elementary and secondary schools was unconstitutional.

The **Supreme Court Decision on Racial Quotas, 1978** (Regents of the University of California *vs.* Bakke), ruled that, although universities may consider race as a factor in admitting students, admission quotas based on race alone are unconstitutional.

The **Department of Education** was established at the Cabinet level in 1980. It absorbed several federal agencies, including offices of the Education Division that had been created in the Department of Health, Education, and Welfare by the **Education Amendments of 1972.**

of study. Entry rank is normally as an instructor, which is sometimes possible before the final granting of a doctorate. The next ranks are then progressively assistant professor, associate professor, and finally full professor. Some universities have distinguished professor chairs, usually held by someone eminent in a special field. The conventional activities of the teacher in higher education are instruction, research and publication, and campus service activities such as membership on faculty committees. Advancement in some institutions is heavily dependent on the publishing of works in the field. The granting of tenure was once associated with promotion to associate professor, but this practice is no longer as prevalent as before.

Administration, Supervision, and Business Management. University graduate study, teaching experience, and suitable personal characteristics are among the usual prerequisites for administrative or supervisory positions. In many school systems the chief administrator is the superintendent of schools. This office handles such matters as budgeting, hiring, purchasing supplies, planning and building new schools, developing the curriculum, and serving as liaison between local and state or federal agencies. The superintendent's staff may range from two or three people in rural areas to many hundreds in large districts such as those in New York City, Chicago, and Los Angeles. Principals are the largest group of administrators in most school districts and perform a wide variety of tasks related to their faculties and the operation of their buildings.

Universities and colleges are usually headed by a president. The president is expected to be both an academic and a financial manager, though academic responsibilities may be delegated to an assistant sometimes called a provost. The provost may in turn supervise academic deans. Smaller institutions sometimes have a single dean with complete academic responsibility; large universities may have a dean for each college and such officers as dean of students, dean of faculties, and so on.

Unusual Opportunities. Particularly since the late 1940's new opportunities have opened for teachers. Among them are industry-related positions, a variety of overseas assignments, and ACTION, an agency formed in 1971 by merging the former Peace Corps, Teacher Corps, VISTA, and several smaller government volunteer-service groups.

Positions in industry range from teaching in nursery schools operated by corporations to providing on-the-job technical or vocational education for adults. Overseas assignments include teaching in schools for the children of members of the United States armed forces, of employees of corporations with overseas operations, and of United States citizens performing nonmilitary governmental functions. ACTION, which functions at home as well as abroad, is not limited to teachers, but teachers are needed not only as instructors but also to serve in early-childhood education programs, to tutor, and to direct recreational activities. (*See also* ACTION.)

Teachers' Associations

Teachers' associations range from local and county groups through state, national, and international organizations. The largest of the professional organizations in the United States is the National Education Association, which was formed in 1870 in a merger of three earlier organizations. Such groups have a variety of purposes: to improve teaching, to define and protect teacher rights, to disseminate professional information and news, and to influence educational legislation. Many groups also publish educational journals, newsletters, and books.

The American Federation of Teachers (AFT), organized in 1916 and now part of the AFL–CIO, is representative of the vocational associations of teachers. The AFT has been vigorous in its opposition to child labor and to what it considered undemocratic controls of education. It has also sought to improve salaries, tenure laws, and working conditions. Individual chapters are often involved in teacher strikes in order to achieve their goals.

BIBLIOGRAPHY FOR EDUCATION

Books for Children

Benson, Christopher. Careers in Education (Lerner Publications, 1974).
Carruth, E.K. She Wanted to Read: the Story of Mary McLeod Bethune (Abingdon, 1966).
Forte, Imogene and others. Pumpkins, Pinwheels, and Peppermint Packages (Incentive, 1974).
Galbraith, Judy. The Gifted Kids Survival Guide (Free Spirit, 1984).
Loeper, John. Going to School in 1776 (Atheneum, 1973).
Loeper, John. Going to School in 1876 (Atheneum, 1984).

Books for Young Adults and Teachers

Adler, M.J. The Paideia Proposal (Macmillan, 1982).
Botkin, J.W. and others. No Limits to Learning (Pergamon Press, 1979).
Boyd, William and King, E.J. The History of Western Education, 11th ed. (Barnes, 1980).
Bruner, J.S. The Process of Education (Harvard Univ. Press, 1960).
Carter, B. and Dapper, G. School Volunteers: What They Do and How They Do It (Scholastic, 1972).
Conant, J.B. Education in a Divided World: the Function of the Public Schools in Our Unique Society (Greenwood, 1970).
Cremin, L.A. Public Education (Basic Books, 1979).
Dewey, John. Democracy and Education (Free Press, 1966).
Ehlers, Henry. Crucial Issues in Education, 7th ed. (Holt, 1981).
Gardner, J.W. Excellence, rev. ed. (W.W. Norton, 1984).
Gillett, Margaret and Laska, J.A. Foundation Studies in Education: Justifications and New Directions (Scarecrow, 1973).
Highet, Gilbert. The Art of Teaching (Random, 1954).
Holt, John. How Children Fail, rev. ed. (Dell, 1982).
Holt, John. How Children Learn, rev. ed. (Dell, 1983).
Hutchins, R.M. and others. What's a College For? (Public Affairs Press, 1961).
Mayer, Frederick. Creative Universities (New College Univ. Press, 1961).
Montessori, Maria. The Montessori Method, rev. ed. (Schocken, 1964).
Pierce, E.G. Horace Mann: Our Nation's First Educator (Lerner Publications, 1972).
Powell, A.G. and others. The Shopping Mall High School (Houghton, 1985).
Shane, H.G., ed. United States and International Education (Univ. of Chicago Press, 1969).
Silberman, C.E. Crisis in the Classroom (Random, 1970).
Westmeyer, Paul. A History of American Higher Education (C.C. Thomas, 1985).

(*See also* bibliography for **Guidance**.)

Edward the Confessor—so called because of his piety—died a few days after Westminster Abbey, which he built, was consecrated. He was reared in France and at heart was more like a French monk than an English king.

Edward VI, the son of King Henry VIII by his third queen, Jane Seymour, succeeded his father at the age of ten. He lived to be only 16, however, and during his short reign, others maneuvered for power.

EDWARD, Kings of England. Three Anglo-Saxon kings bore the name of Edward before the Norman Conquest in 1066. Eight Edwards have reigned since then. As the numbering of English rulers of the same name began after the Conquest, the three earlier Edwards have only distinguishing nicknames.

Edward the Elder (ruled 899–924) was the son of Alfred the Great (*see* Alfred). He conquered a large part of central England, which at Alfred's death still remained in the hands of the Danes.

Edward the Martyr (ruled 975–978) obtained his nickname because of a miracle supposed to have been performed at his tomb in Shaftesbury. He had been buried there after being murdered by the supporters of his half brother, Ethelred the Unready, who then gained the throne.

Edward the Confessor (ruled 1042–1066) was the elder son of Ethelred the Unready. His election to the throne after the death of the Danish king Harthacanute marked the end of Danish rule in England. Edward was noted alike for his weakness as a ruler and his piety as a man. His great legacy to England was Westminster Abbey.

Edward I (born 1239, ruled 1272–1307) was one of England's greatest kings. He was a handsome man, with fair hair and ruddy cheeks, and so tall that he was nicknamed Longshanks. He delighted in tournaments and hunting, but he was also practical and hardworking. For seven years before he came to the throne, he was the real ruler for his weak father, Henry III (*see* Henry, Kings of England; Montfort). He was in the Holy Land involved in the crusades when his father died, but there was no question that he would take the throne.

Edward has been called the "English Justinian" because, like the Roman emperor Justinian, he organized the laws. His laws were not restatements of existing customs but statutes in the modern sense. Many of them, particularly the land laws, had a long-lasting influence. A statute of 1285 limited church courts to strictly church matters—a change that Edward's great-grandfather, Henry II, had been unable to make because of the murder of Thomas à Becket (*see* Becket; Henry, Kings of England). Edward also stopped paying a feudal tribute to the pope.

Parliament grew in strength during Edward's reign because he continued the policy of Simon de Montfort in summoning to it representatives of the towns and lesser knights. His parliament of 1295 is known as the Model Parliament (*see* Parliament, British). In 1297 he reaffirmed the Magna Carta in the famous confirmation of the charters. All of Edward's moves were not fair and admirable ones, however; he forced Jews out of England in 1290.

Soon after coming to the throne, Edward conquered Wales and gave to his infant son, Edward, the title Prince of Wales (*see* Wales). Until 1289 the care of his French possessions, principally Aquitaine, in

Southern France, absorbed much of his attention. For the rest of his life, his main concern was Scotland. He conquered the country in 1296; but in 1297 all Scotland rose in revolt against him under the popular leader, William Wallace. Edward defeated Wallace at Falkirk the next year, but the Scots still resisted. Near the end of Edward's reign Scotland found a new leader in Robert Bruce. In 1307 King Edward, then 70 years old, led an army toward Scotland but died before he reached the border.

Edward II (born 1284, ruled 1307–1327), the son of Edward I, was the first English prince of Wales (*see* Wales). He was tall and handsome like his father, but he was a coward in battle; and in spite of his father's careful training he had no aptitude for government. His reign was one of disorder and disaster. He continued the war with Scotland that his father had begun. The Scottish leader, Bruce, defeated the English forces in the famous battle of Bannockburn (1314) and compelled Edward to recognize the independence of Scotland.

In 1326 the king's enemies planned a widespread revolt. They easily captured the king, and in January 1327 Parliament declared him deposed and set in his place his young son Edward III. Eight months later the deposed king was brutally murdered.

Edward III (born 1312, ruled 1327–1377) became king at the age of 15 when his father, Edward II, was overthrown. He proved himself a chivalrous knight rather than a great ruler. He loved warfare, like so many of his line, and tried to give it the glamour of the "good old days" by setting up a Round Table at Windsor Castle in imitation of King Arthur. He also organized the most famous of the English chivalric orders of knighthood, the Order of the Garter. He gained temporary glory but no lasting profit through prolonged fighting in Scotland and in France, where he began the Hundred Years' War (*see* Hundred Years' War).

During Edward's reign a terrible plague, called the Black Death, wiped out from one third to one half of the country's population and caused great social and economic changes (*see* Bubonic Plague).

Edward IV (born 1442, ruled 1461–1483) was the first of the Yorkist kings. He grew up in the midst of the struggle between two great families, York and Lancaster, that is known as the Wars of the Roses. (The Yorkists took a white rose as their badge and the Lancastrians a red one. *See* Roses, Wars of the.) Edward became the leader of the Yorkist party through the death of his father, Richard, duke of York, at the battle of Wakefield (1460). He secured the throne the next year largely through the support of his powerful cousin, the earl of Warwick, later called the "Kingmaker."

Edward soon offended Warwick by marrying, against his wishes, Elizabeth Woodville, and placing his wife's relatives in positions of influence at court. Warwick finally went over to the Lancastrians and forced Edward to leave England and take refuge in Flanders (1470). Edward, however, proved more than a match for his enemies. He returned to England in 1471, defeated and killed Warwick in battle at Barnet, in Herts, and re-established himself on the throne. Immediately he caused the insane Henry VI to be killed; and some years later he brought about the death of his own brother, the duke of Clarence.

A popular and able ruler, Edward encouraged trade and helped restore the country to a settled condition. By relying on the growing merchant class rather than on the feudal nobility, he won back for the kingship much of the power that had been lost to Parliament by the Lancastrian kings. Soon after Edward's death, his young sons were murdered (*see* Edward V).

Edward V (born 1470, ruled 1483), the elder son of Edward IV, was nominally king from April to June 1483, at the age of 12. His uncle Richard, duke of Gloucester, was appointed Protector and soon placed Edward and his brother Richard, duke of York, in the Tower of London. Edward V's right to the throne was then challenged, and his uncle was crowned king as Richard III. The boys were not seen alive again; Richard III was suspected of having had them killed. In 1674 the bones of two children of about the boys'

Edward VII, who had been a worldly prince of Wales, earned the title of Edward the Peacemaker because of his prolonged efforts to maintain peace in Europe.

British Information Services

ages were found in a wooden chest when part of the tower was being altered. Careful examination indicated that the bones were the remains of the two princes. (*See also* Richard, Kings of England; Tower of London.)

Edward VI (born 1537, ruled 1547–1553) belonged to the House of Tudor, which came to the throne on the fall of Richard III in 1485. The son of King Henry VIII by his third queen, Jane Seymour, he became king at the age of 10. Great things were expected of the young ruler, but he was never strong and died of tuberculosis at the age of 16. During his short reign the government was controlled first by his mother's brother, the duke of Somerset, and then by the duke of Northumberland. Edward VI was followed to the throne by his half-sister, Mary.

Edward VII (born 1841, ruled 1901–1910) was nearly 60 years old when he took the throne from his mother, Queen Victoria. He had married Princess Alexandra of Denmark in 1863. Before taking the throne he was the most active member of the royal family, since Queen Victoria remained in seclusion after his father's death in 1861.

After the death of Albert, the Prince Consort, Victoria excluded Edward from any role in the conduct of government. Until he was 50 he was forbidden to read the reports of Cabinet meetings. During the decades before he became king, he traveled widely and cemented contacts with the other royal houses of Europe—most of whom were relatives of him or his wife. He was also a familiar figure in the worlds of racing, yachting, and grouse shooting.

The man who was crowned on Aug. 9, 1901, was an individual of unusual social gifts and worldly experience, and as king his course was marked by tact and judgment. He set out first to restore to the Crown some of the traditional splendor that had lapsed during the years of his mother's seclusion. In 1902 he set out to revisit European capitals in order to strengthen the British position on the Continent. Already aware of the war clouds that were looming over Europe, he strove to avoid armed conflict. (By the time World War I erupted in 1914, Edward was dead.) He played an influential part in bringing Great Britain, France, and Russia together in 1907 into the Triple Entente. Unfortunately, his nephew Kaiser Wilhelm II regarded Edward's diplomatic triumphs as an attempt to encircle Germany with a ring of enemies.

At home Edward strongly supported the military reforms of the secretary of state for war, Richard Burdon Haldane. Finding himself in declining health and concerned about the likelihood of war, he considered abdicating before he became ill and died on May 6, 1910.

Edward VIII (born 1894, ruled 1936) was nearly 42 years old when he became king on the death of his father, George V, on Jan. 20, 1936. Toward the end of that year he expressed the desire to marry an American woman, Wallis Warfield Simpson, whom he had met in 1931. Simpson had already been married twice, and her second divorce was not yet final.

Cecil Beaton—Camera Press/Photo Trends

Edward VIII abdicated in 1936 to marry Wallis Simpson. They became the duke and duchess of Windsor.

The British and Commonwealth governments strongly opposed this marriage as not in keeping with the dignity of the Crown. Edward, however, had made up his mind; and on Dec. 11, 1936, he abdicated, or gave up the throne. His younger brother, George VI, took the throne. The first act of the new king was to name his brother duke of Windsor. The duke married Simpson in France on June 3, 1937.

From 1937 to 1939 and after 1945 they made their home in Paris. During World War II he served as governor of the Bahamas. He died in Paris on May 28, 1972. She died there on April 24, 1986.

EDWARDS, Jonathan (1703–58). New England Puritanism never had a more able or eloquent spokesman, nor conservative Christianity in America a more articulate defender, than Jonathan Edwards. He is still considered one of the most brilliant theological minds ever produced in North America, and he was a man of broader interests as well. He was fascinated by natural science, of which he was a careful observer and writer. He might have pursued it intently had not his religious responsibilities occupied his time so fully.

Edwards was born on Oct. 5, 1703, at East Windsor, Conn., the only son among 11 children. He was graduated from Yale College in 1720 and remained there for two more years studying theology. After a short time as a pastor in New York, Edwards returned to Yale as a tutor before accepting a position as an associate pastor in Northampton, Mass., with his mother's father, Solomon Stoddard. After Stoddard's death in 1729, Edwards stayed on there until 1750. From 1751 until 1757 he served a congregation at Stockbridge, Mass., and then moved on to become president of the College of New Jersey (now Princeton University). He had just taken up his duties there when he caught smallpox and died on March 22, 1758.

The Puritanism of Edwards' day had become an easygoing affair that stressed moral self-sufficiency, the good life, and free will while tending to ignore the darker aspects of human nature. It was against this that Edwards directed his attacks and emphasized the goodness of God and faith in Him as the only means of salvation. In his most famous work, 'Freedom of Will', published in 1754, he said that people are free to do as they please and are therefore held morally responsible for their actions. His book 'The Nature of True Virtue' (1765) was an important treatise on ethics. His sermons and writings were a major element in the last years of the religious revival known as the Great Awakening, which lasted from about 1720 into the 1740s. These paved the way for the more far-reaching revival of the early 19th century.

EEL. There are more than 500 species of eels, long, snakelike fishes that live in major oceans, freshwater lakes, and rivers. Eels belong to about 20 different families, most of which are relatively unknown. They live in tropical seas or deep in the ocean. Freshwater eels are members of the family Anguillidae. They live in the waters of almost every continent. Commonly known saltwater species are the conger eels, members of the family Congridae, and the moray eels that belong to the family Muraenidae.

The freshwater eel is a slender fish that has a gracefully waving fin running in a continuous line along the length of its back and around and under its tail. It has a small, conical head, a pair of pectoral fins directly behind the head, and a wide mouth with strong teeth. The scales of all eels are so tiny and deeply set in the skin that they appear to be scaleless. The freshwater eel has a slick, velvety appearance. It has an olive brown back, greenish yellow sides, and gray or white underparts.

North American freshwater eels are born in the ocean. Adult males and females swim from the Atlantic coast to an area in the Sargasso Sea, which is south of Bermuda. When they arrive there, the females spawn—that is, they lay their eggs. After mating, both the male and female adults die. Several days after the eggs are deposited, glasslike baby eels, called leptocephalus larvae, hatch. Each larva carries a tiny drop of oil, which allows it to float upward. The larvae drift with the ocean currents, feeding on the microscopic life at the surface of the ocean.

As they begin to grow, the leptocephalus larvae either swim or slowly drift toward land. A year later, when they are near the eastern Atlantic or Gulf coasts, the eel larvae are about 3 inches (8 centimeters) long. As a leptocephalus larva develops into an elver, or young eel, its thin body becomes shorter, round, and turns pink. At this stage the elver looks like a miniature adult eel.

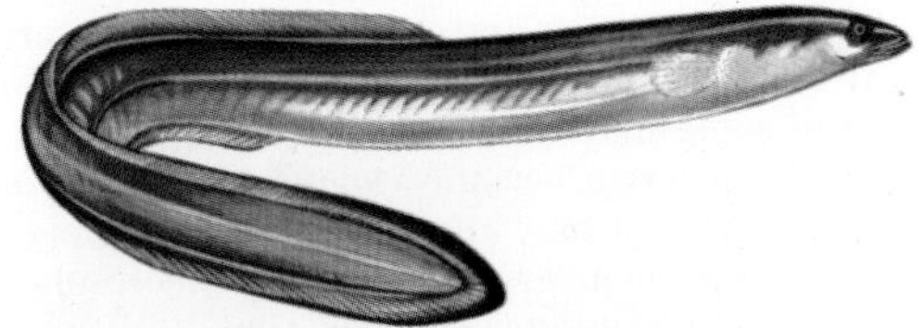

American freshwater eel (*Anguilla rostrata*)

American conger eel (*Conger oceanicus*)

Millions of elvers swim into the rivers of eastern North America during the spring. The males stay in the salty tidewater waiting for the return of the females. The females swim upstream, usually making their homes in fresh waters, sometimes far away from the ocean. They live in creeks, lakes, and reservoirs until they return to the sea for breeding. At maturity the females may grow to about 47 inches (1.2 meters) long and weigh about 15.4 pounds (7 kilograms). The males are about two thirds as big as the females.

The freshwater eels of western Europe also breed in the depths of the Sargasso Sea. However, they travel about 4,350 miles (7,000 kilometers) to reach their breeding spots. It takes the larvae about three years to return to western Europe. Similar central breeding places exist for eels that are native to other continents. But there are no freshwater eels of this type living in South America or on the west coast of North America. This is probably because the ocean currents in these areas make it too difficult for the larvae to travel.

Conger eels are strictly marine fishes. They live mostly along the Atlantic coasts of both Europe and North America. These eels grow to about 6.6 feet (2 meters) long and weigh more than 110 pounds (50 kilograms). They are thicker than freshwater eels. Some congers breed in the Sargasso Sea; others breed near the Azores or in the Mediterranean Sea.

Moray populations are the most widespread of all the eels. They live in all the tropical seas. They have

Electric eel (*Electrophorus electricus*)

large mouths and teeth, and some are brightly colored or patterned. Morays grow to about 3.3 feet (1 meter) long, and some may even grow to about 10 feet (3 meters). Morays can become vicious when they are disturbed, and they may attack underwater divers.

Electric eels, members of the family Electrophoridae, belong to a group of fishes that is different from the other eels. They live in the fresh waters of South America. They are known for their capacity to generate an electric charge.

The scientific name of the American freshwater eel is *Anguilla rostrata;* of the European species, *A. anguilla;* of the American conger, *Conger oceanicus;* of the European conger, *C. conger;* of electric eel, *Electrophorus electricus.*

EGG. All animals and plants, except for the most primitive types, begin their journey toward independent life when an egg is fertilized. An egg is a single female germ cell, or reproductive cell. It eventually develops into a new organism after it has been fertilized by a male germ cell (*see* Biology; Genetics). The egg cells of plants, when fertilized, develop into seeds (*see* Flower; Seeds).

The development of a mammal begins when the female egg cell, or ovum, is fertilized by a male cell, or sperm. Very soon after fertilization the egg begins to divide. This process is called cleavage. The earliest stages of a mammal's development occur in its mother's body, from the time of fertilization until birth. In the early stages of development, a mammal is called an embryo. After specific external features are clearly formed, the unborn animal is referred to as a fetus. The developing human is called an embryo for the seven weeks following fertilization. Beginning in the eighth week it is called a fetus (*see* Embryology). The duckbill platypus and the spiny anteater are the only mammals that lay shelled eggs. All other mammals develop from shell-less eggs and remain inside their mothers' bodies until they are born.

A true egg, as distinguished from a shell-less egg cell, consists of the germ cell and materials that nourish the embryo, enclosed in a protective covering. These coverings may be a rigid shell made mostly of calcium carbonate, as in the eggs of birds, or they may be tough, elastic membranes, like those found on the eggs of most reptiles.

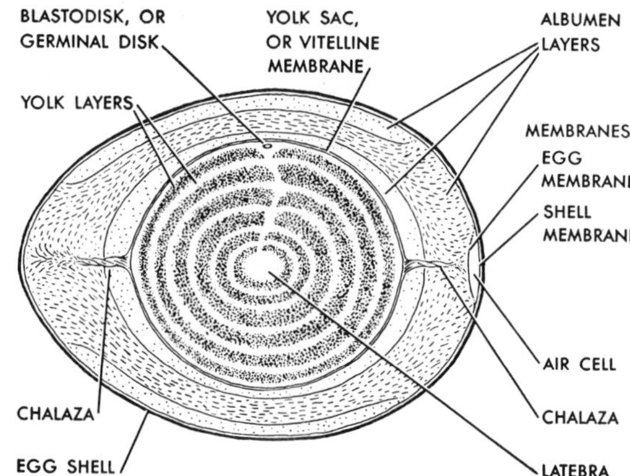

The yolk of a hen's egg cradles the germinal disk (blastodisk) from which the embryo chick develops, and it provides the embryo with the food materials necessary for its development. Outside the yolk are the albumen, or egg white, and finally the shell. Each part is built in a series of concentric layers, and each is enclosed in protective sheaths. The chalazas are twisted strands of fiber that help to hold the yolk in the center of the egg. They are attached to the albumen at one end and to the yolk at the other.

All birds lay their eggs before the eggs are ready to hatch. Some snakes, lizards, fishes, and insects keep their eggs inside their bodies until the moment of hatching. The egg-laying habits of animals seem to be related to the dangers to which their eggs may be exposed. Hence, some birds that nest in remote places lay only one egg each season. But certain fishes, whose eggs become food for hundreds of enemies, lay millions of eggs at a time.

Many birds build elaborate nests in which they shelter their eggs (*see* Birds). The ways in which some insects protect their eggs are equally complicated. Bees and wasps lay eggs in specially constructed wax cells; ichneumon flies plant them in the bodies of

Hatching larvae (far left) will become woolly bear caterpillars, then nocturnal moths. The king snake (below) coils around its eggs to keep them warm. Masses of frog eggs (right), laid in the water, may cling to plants or sink to the bottom.

(Far left) E.S. Ross; (below) H.A. Thornhill—National Audubon Society Collection/Photo Researchers; (right) C.G. Maxwell—National Audubon Society Collection/Photo Researchers

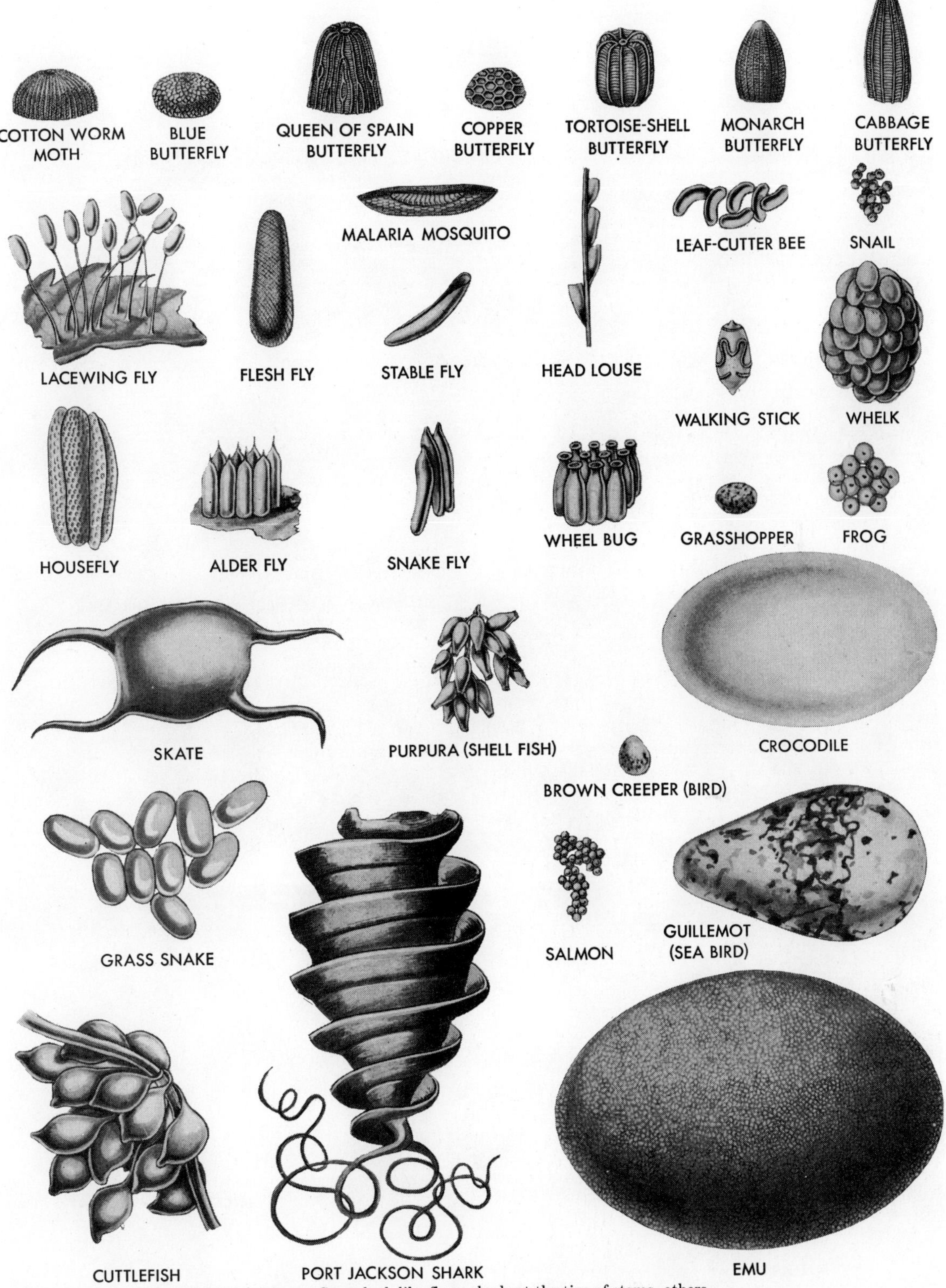

There is great variety in the shape of eggs. Some look like flower buds at the tips of stems, others like bunches of grapes or clusters of strange fruit. Eggs may be laid singly or in sticky masses held together by a gelatinlike material. In addition to the great variety in form, there is also a much greater difference in size than appears above. The egg of the emu, for instance, is about six inches long and weighs nearly three pounds, while most of the insect eggs are no bigger than a pencil point, and some can be seen only under a microscope.

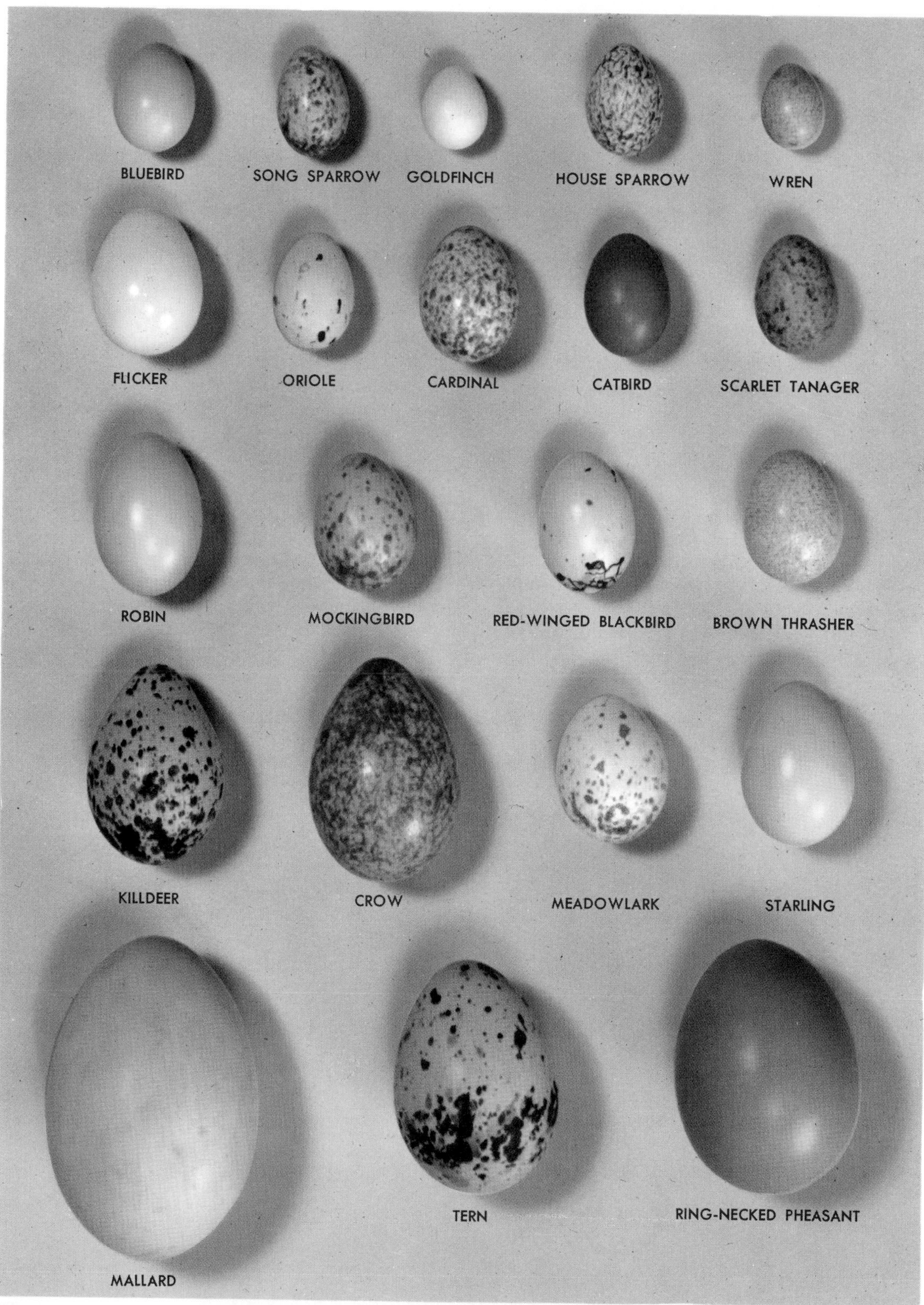

Eggs of some of the common birds effectively illustrate the great variety of egg size, color, and markings. Egg collecting is now forbidden by federal laws that protect songbirds. They should never be taken from the nest. As a rule, eggs that are laid in holes or in hollow trees are white. Those that are laid in exposed places have the "protective coloration" of spots and streaks that blend into the background and make them almost invisible to the predators that might eat them.

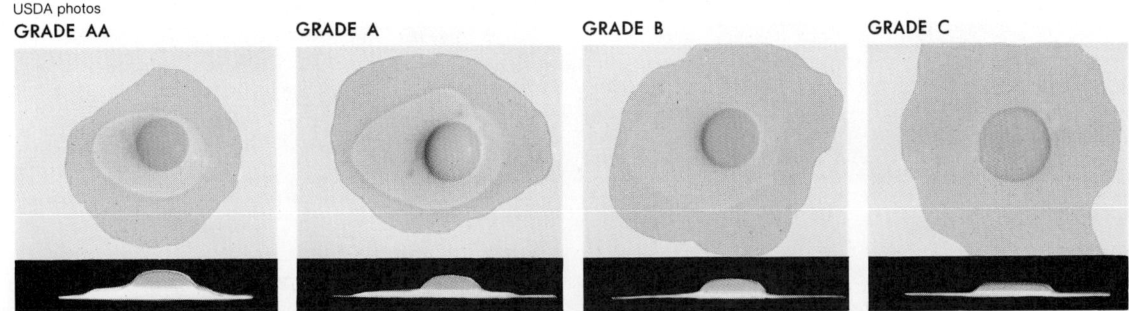

Standards for egg quality have been established by the United States Department of Agriculture. These are based on the average eggs in each of four classes, graded from AA to C. The standards are as follows: a broken grade AA egg covers a small area, the white is thick and stands high, and the yolk is firm and high; a grade A egg covers a moderate area, the white is reasonably thick and stands fairly high, and the yolk is firm and high; a grade B egg covers a wide area, has small amounts of thick white, and the yolk is somewhat flattened and enlarged; a grade C egg covers a very wide area, the white is thin and watery, and the yolk is flat and enlarged and breaks easily.

other insects; the gall flies bury them in plant tissues; and buffalo gnats glue their eggs to submerged rocks (*see* Insect). Reptiles usually leave their eggs to be hatched by the heat of the sun.

Nearly all birds warm their eggs with their own bodies. But a group of Australian birds, the megapodes, hatch their eggs like reptiles. For example, the Australian brush turkey and the mallee bird simply dig up mounds of dirt and leaves into which they lay their eggs. The heat generated by the sun and the decaying vegetation do the rest of the work.

The Hen's Egg

The bird's egg, of which that of the female chicken, or hen, is typical, has been called "the most perfect thing in the universe." On the outside is the shell, which is covered with a thin skin called the cuticle. The shell surrounds the soft inner parts. Inside the shell are two membranes. One membrane clings to the shell and the other clings to the albumen. The albumen is a transparent watery jelly. When an egg is cooked the albumen becomes firm and turns white, so the albumen is known as the white. In the center of the egg is the yolk. The yolk is especially important because the embryo chick and the food it needs to develop are contained within it. The yolk is enclosed in a thin yolk sac which is called the vitelline membrane. There are twelve alternating layers of yellow and white yolk.

In the core of the yolk is a mass of white material that is called the latebra. A part of the latebra is connected to the germinal disk, or blastodisk, which is located on the outer surface of the yolk. The embryo chick develops from the blastodisk. Twisted strands of fiber, the chalazas, are located on the long axis of the egg. When the egg is turned, the chalazas tighten and hold the yolk in the center.

The yolk is formed in the hen's ovary. In the oviduct, the passage down which the egg moves, the yolk receives the albumen, the two shell membranes, and the shell. The shell contains pores or openings, through which air enters. This allows the embryo to breathe. It is in the lower part of the oviduct that the shell takes on any color. Usually, but not always, the egg is laid with the small end emerging first. After the egg is laid, the two membranes lining the shell separate at the larger end to form an air pocket. This gives the chick its first breath of air as it pecks its way out of the shell.

Because warmth, as well as food, is necessary for the embryo to develop fully, hens sit on their eggs. The shell is strong enough to protect the ovum from the hen's weight. The developing embryo feeds on the material that makes up the yolk. As the embryo grows larger, the albumen disappears.

Some chicks, like those of the blackbird, are hatched blind and helpless with naked bodies. Others, like ducklings, come out of their eggs covered with feathers and with their eyes open. A large bird lays a bigger egg than a small bird. The smallest bird's egg, that of the hummingbird, is the size of a big pea. In contrast, the egg laid by the ostrich measures up to about 6.7 inches (17 centimeters) in length and weighs up to about 4 pounds (1.8 kilograms).

The Egg as Food

Most of the eggs used for food in the United States and Europe are produced by hens. In several parts of the world, however, duck eggs are more popular. In the United States eggs are graded on size and quality. There are four general weight classes of eggs, ranging from extra large to small. Eggs are served as individual food, or they can be used in the preparation of many other kinds of foods.

About 74 percent of the weight of an egg is water. Most of the food materials are in the yolk. A 2-ounce (57-gram) egg provides 6 grams of complete protein, which is about 15 percent of an adult's daily requirement, and 12 grams of fat. An egg has about 80 calories. It also has about 0.0097 ounce (275 milligrams) of cholesterol, almost the maximum amount that is currently recommended for consumption in a day. Many health professionals advise limiting cholesterol intake to about 0.011 ounce (300 milligrams) per day. An egg contains significant amounts of iron, vitamins A and D, thiamine, and riboflavin.

Robert Frerck—Odyssey Productions

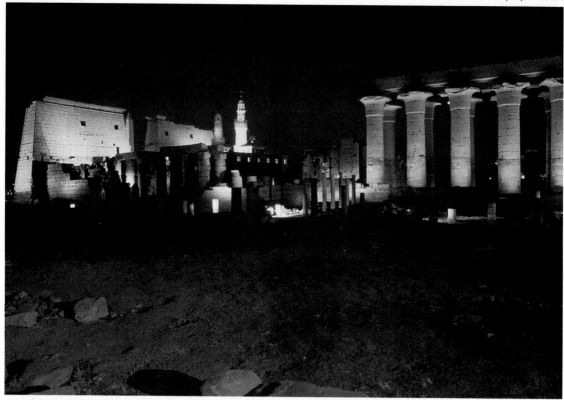

The Temple of Luxor, on the east bank of the Nile in Upper Egypt, was built during the reign of Amenhotep III (ruled 1417–1379 BC) and expanded by Ramses II (ruled 1304–1237 BC).

EGYPT. The Arab Republic of Egypt occupies the northeastern corner of the African continent and the Sinai Peninsula. It has an area of about 390,540 square miles (1,011,500 square kilometers), including the 23,440 square miles (60,710 square kilometers) of the Sinai. Ninety-nine percent of the Egyptian population lives on only 3.5 percent of the land. Most of them are in the Nile River valley and large delta. The Egyptian people refer to their country as Misr.

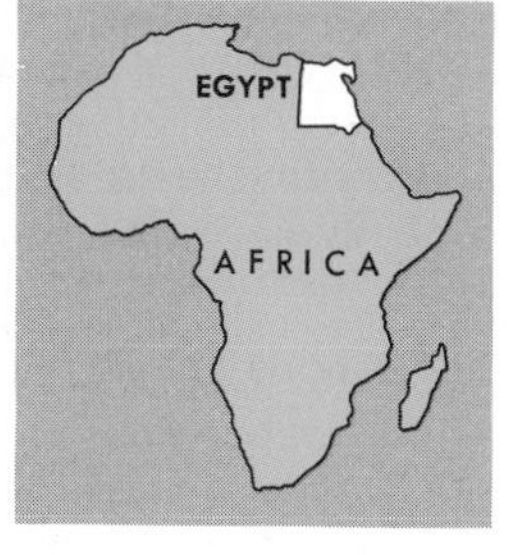

Egypt is bordered on the south by the Sudan and on the west by Libya. Its northern coast is on the Mediterranean Sea, and its eastern coasts are on the Red Sea and the Gulf of Aqaba, between Sinai and Saudi Arabia. The Gulf of Suez and the Suez Canal separate African Egypt from Sinai. In northern Sinai Egypt's border with Israel was fixed in 1979 by a peace treaty.

This article was contributed by Gary L. Fowler, Associate Professor of Geography and Department Head, University of Illinois at Chicago.

The Land and Climate

The headwaters of the Nile River are in the highlands of East Africa. The Nile flows northward across the Sudan and enters Egypt near Wadi Halfa. It is 4,130 miles (6,650 kilometers) long, with 960 miles (1,545 kilometers) in Egypt. Annual flooding is a natural feature of the Nile. Fed by summer rains in the highlands, the flood travels northward, reaching Egypt in August.

The Upper Nile is confined to a narrow valley that is no more than 2 miles (3 kilometers) wide. Outcrops of resistant granite rock form stretches of cascades and rapids called cataracts. The First Cataract is at Aswan, the only one in Egypt. A dam was built here in 1902 to help control the floodwaters for irrigation. Four other cataracts are located upstream of Aswan in the Sudan. (*See also* Nile River.)

The Aswan High Dam is located upstream of the original dam. Construction began in January 1960 and was completed in July 1970. The high dam created Lake Nasser, the largest artificial lake in the world. It extends for 350 miles (560 kilometers) southward to the Third Cataract and averages 6 miles (10 kilometers) wide. The high dam makes possible the large-scale storage and use of Nile water independent of natural floods, and it provides Egypt with low-cost hydroelectric power. (*See also* Aswan High Dam.)

Between Aswan and Cairo the Nile Valley widens into a plain ranging in width from 6 to 9 miles (10 to 15 kilometers). The delta of the Nile begins near Cairo, where the river separates into the Damietta branch on the west and the Rosetta on the east. The delta, which contains about 8,500 square miles (22,000 square kilometers), has numerous small waterways and canals. At its northern edge several large shallow lakes have formed as the delta continues to expand into the Mediterranean. The largest of these is El Manzala, which is between Damietta and Port Said.

West of the Nile the Western Desert is one of the world's driest areas. It is a low-lying plateau that gradually rises from a narrow coastal plain to an elevation of more than 3,300 feet (1,000 meters) in the southwest. In the Libyan Desert large areas are covered by shifting sand dunes. Several large depressions have been hollowed out of the limestone and sandstone by wind erosion. The oases of Bahariya, Dakhla, Farafra, El Faiyum, and Siwa and the great oasis of Kharga have underground water supplies that support permanent agriculture. A branch of the Nile, the Bahr Yusef, flows through a gap in the Nile's western cliffs to water El Faiyum. In Wadi Natrun northwest of Cairo and the Qattara Depression, the water is salty. Located near Siwa on the edge of the Libyan Plateau, the Qattara is 437 feet (133 meters) below sea level.

The area between the Nile River and Red Sea is the Arabian, or Eastern, Desert. It is a rugged, heavily dissected plateau with elevations of more than 3,300 feet (1,000 meters). Along the Red Sea coast, Jebel, or Mount, Shayib is 7,178 feet (2,188 meters) above sea level. The highest point in Egypt is in the Musa Mountains of southern Sinai, where Jebel Katherina reaches 8,655 feet (2,638 meters). In the north is the Sinai Desert, which extends to the coast between the Suez Canal and Israel.

Egypt has an arid climate. Alexandria has the highest rainfall, with a mean of 7.4 inches (18.8 centimeters) annually. Other parts of the Mediterranean coast receive even less rainfall, with only 2.5 inches (6.4 centimeters) annually at Port Said. Most rain falls in the winter, none in the summer. The mean annual temperature is 69° F (20° C), reaching a high of 80° F (27° C) in the summer.

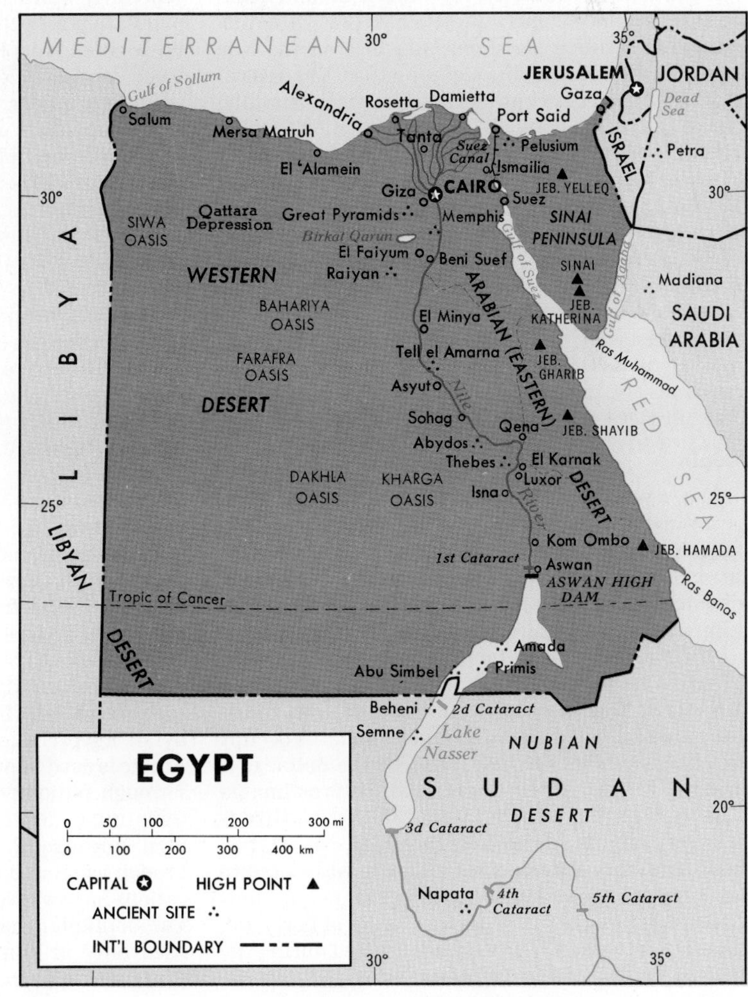

Irrigation is used in the fields near the Aswan High Dam in Upper Egypt. The region's farming thus does not depend on the flooding of the Nile River for its water supply.

Donald Smetzer—CLICK/Chicago

Cairo is a desert capital. It receives slightly less than 1 inch (2.5 centimeters) of rainfall annually, and the mean annual temperature is 71° F (22° C). In the spring and summer early morning fogs on the Nile Delta provide some additional moisture. The rest of Egypt has only a few centimeters of rainfall annually. Most of the year is hot and dry, and periodic droughts extending over several years are common. Aswan, for example, has a mean annual rainfall of 0.2 inches (0.5 centimeters) and a temperature of 80° F (27° C) with a high of 94° F (34° C) in the summer.

During the spring, hot dry khamsin winds blow northward from the Sahara across Egypt to the Mediterranean coast. The khamsin, which often produces sandstorms, can last for several days, destroying crops. Egypt has no forests and only a few permanent grasslands for pasture. At best the deserts support sparse drought-resistant scrub vegetation.

People

Egypt's population is about 48.5 million. The average annual rate of growth is 1.7 percent. In the delta and valley of the Nile, densities reach 3,243 persons per square mile (1,252 per square kilometer). About 49 percent of the population live in cities. The majority of Egyptians live in rural agricultural villages, some of which have 20,000 or more people.

Egypt's largest cities are Cairo, the capital, and Alexandria. Together they contain about two thirds of the urban population. Cairo and its suburbs occupy both banks of the Nile just south of the delta. It is the largest city in Africa. Greater Cairo was estimated to have 10 million people in the mid-1980s. Giza is its largest suburb. Alexandria, the chief seaport, had about 3 million. Fifteen other cities, most located in the delta and the valley of the Nile, had populations of 100,000 or more. The Suez Canal cities of Port Said, Ismailia, and Suez, which were abandoned during the 1967 war with Israel, have been rebuilt.

Large-scale migration from rural areas to cities, especially Cairo and Alexandria, has caused urban population growth at twice the average national rate. Both cities have severe housing shortages and lack basic services. Extensive urban redevelopment programs are under way, and new towns are planned near Damietta, Cairo, and Aswan. Land reclamation in the Nile and planned agricultural settlements in the Western Desert are designed to help relieve population pressures. (*See also* Cairo; Alexandria.)

Most Egyptians are Hamitic Arabs. They are descendants of the Hamites of ancient Egypt and Arabs who migrated to Egypt after the Muslim conquests of the 7th century. The Nubians, who are related to the Berber tribes of North Africa, are located south of Aswan. They were resettled in new villages near Kom Ombo when Lake Nasser flooded their homeland. A few Europeans, primarily Armenians and Greeks, live in cities. Most are in Alexandria.

About 86 percent of the Egyptians, including Nubians, are Sunni Muslims. Islam is the state religion and the basis for Egyptian law. The largest minority is made up of members of the Coptic church, one of the oldest Christian churches. The Copts, who are also descended from the Hamites, number about 6 million, or 13.5 percent of the total population. Egypt also has about 250,000 other Christians, and a small Jewish community remains in Cairo.

Arabic is the official language. Although it is spoken by all Egyptians, there are many dialects. Classical Arabic is used in printed materials and in the schools. Through radio and television the government is attempting to develop a vernacular Arabic as the common language. Educated Egyptians use English and French as second languages. French-language publications have wide circulation in Cairo and Alexandria. The Coptic language, related to ancient Egyptian, is used only in church services. The Nubian dialect, while still spoken, is no longer written.

Operation of the Economy

Major segments of Egypt's economy are controlled by the government. Most commercial and industrial companies are either state-owned or are run under government supervision. Only agricultural land and urban real estate are relatively free of government control. President Gamal Abdel Nasser instituted a centrally planned socialist economy. His successor, Anwar el-Sadat, encouraged foreign investment and private enterprise. Increased aid came from petroleum-rich Arab states, primarily the Gulf Organization for the Development of Egypt.

After the 1979 peace treaty with Israel, most Arab countries withdrew economic and political support from Egypt. President Hosni Mubarak reestablished ties with Arab countries and instituted policies to increase exports, particularly of petroleum, and private investment.

From 1970 to 1980 Egypt's gross domestic product (GDP) grew at an average annual rate of 8.1 percent. Agriculture contributed 19 percent, mining 17 percent, and manufacturing, wholesale and retail trade, and services 12 to 13 percent each. Because of limited opportunities in Egypt, many professionals and skilled workers took jobs in other Arab countries, primarily the Gulf States and Libya.

Agriculture

Agriculture in Egypt depends almost entirely on irrigation from the Nile. Barrages and dams on the Nile, especially the Aswan High Dam, allow water to be stored for use when the river level is low. Canals distribute it where it is needed throughout the year. Under perennial irrigation, a field may yield several crops each year. Cotton, rice, corn (maize), and sorghum are grown in summer. Barley, wheat, and beans are winter crops. Citrus fruits and vegetables are grown on the Mediterranean coast. Although enough fruits and vegetables are grown for the Egyptian people, only 38 percent of the demand for wheat is met. Egypt imports about half of its food supplies, primarily wheat and flour.

Three quarters of Egypt's agricultural income is from cotton and rice. Cotton and cotton products account for 23 percent of its export trade. Egypt produces about one third of the world's long-staple cotton. The area planted in cotton, however, has declined by half since 1968, and exports have been limited. Rice, fruits, and vegetables are also export crops. Sugarcane is grown to produce sugar for Egypt. Most cattle are used as draft animals, and sheep and goats are raised for wool and hair. Despite recent attempts to improve livestock husbandry, Egypt is a net importer of meat.

Egypt faces growing food shortages. Rapid population growth, rapid urbanization, and an increased production of commercial export crops have intensified the pressure on a limited supply of agricultural land. Farms are limited to a maximum of 50 feddans, or 52 acres (21 hectares). Cooperatives aid farmers by renting implements and distributing seeds, fertilizers, and pesticides. Programs to increase the cultivated area through land reclamation, however, have not had significant results. The Aswan High Dam's potential to add 30 percent to the cultivated area has not been realized. In fact, large areas have gone out of cultivation because of poor drainage and salinization, urban

A shadoof (left) is a hand-held device for lifting water to fields that are higher than the water level. In use since ancient times, it is a rope with a bucket raised by a counterweight. To raise water several levels, a series of shadoofs is mounted one above the other. Villagers harvest sugarcane (below) in western Thebes.

Photos, Diana Rasche

Robert Frerck—Odyssey Productions

© Index Stock Inc.

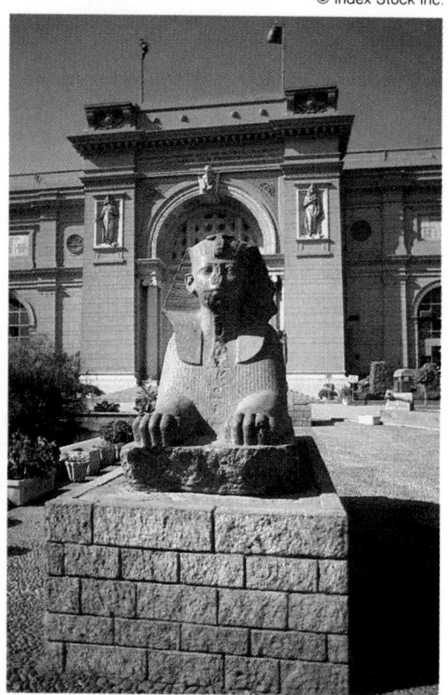

El Azhar University and Mosque (above) in Cairo, which were completed in about 970, make up one of the world's oldest centers of education. The Egyptian Antiquities Museum (right) in Cairo has an outstanding collection of the nation's antiquities, including the treasures of King Tutankhamen.

expansion, and industrial growth—especially in the Nile Delta. The government has plans to reclaim 3 million acres (1.2 million hectares). The largest projects are at West Nuberiya, which is near Alexandria, and in the northern Tahriv region. Projects are also planned for the "new territories" in the oases of the Western Desert.

Industry

Textiles and food processing are the most important industries. Textiles, primarily cotton, account for one third of the total output. Food processing, including the refining of sugarcane and preparation of fruits, is the second largest industry. Iron and steel plants are located at Helwan and El Dikheila, near Alexandria. An aluminum plant at Nag Hammadi processes imported bauxite. Cement is produced for the construction industry, but Egypt imports half of the cement used. Ten new cement plants are under construction. Fertilizer plants that use Egyptian natural gas are located at Takla and El Dikheila, and plants are planned or under construction at Alexandria, Mansura, and Asyut.

A food stand in Luxor is typical of the many outdoor markets found in small towns as well as in large cities.

Diana Rasche

Energy

Egypt depends on fossil fuels and hydroelectric power for its energy supplies. In the late 1970s petroleum supplied the majority of the energy and hydroelectric power, 20 percent. Other renewable resources—such as crop residues, animal wastes, and wood—supplied 14 percent of the total energy consumed. Industry used 48 percent of the energy; residential, commercial, and municipal, 32 percent; and transportation, 14 percent. Only 6 percent was for agriculture and irrigation.

Egypt has the capacity to generate 5,610 million kilowatt hours. Two thirds is generated by hydroelectric plants, most at the Aswan High Dam. Power plants that burn petroleum produce most of the rest. These facilities are near Cairo and Alexandria and on the Nile Delta. High-voltage transmission lines link the Aswan hydroelectric plants with Cairo.

Industrialization and a national program of rural electrification have demanded additional generating capacity. A large coal-burning power plant under construction near Cairo in the mid-1980s will supply three quarters of the city's electricity. Eight nuclear reactors, which will generate 8,000 megawatts, are also planned. The first two units were being built at El Dabaa, about 100 miles (160 kilometers) west of Alexandria. Plans to generate hydroelectricity by flooding the Qattara Depression with water from the Mediterranean are also under way.

Petroleum, Natural Gas, and Minerals

Crude oil provided about 60 percent of Egypt's export revenues in the early 1980s, helping the nation to remain financially independent of its Arab neighbors. Petroleum exports have increased since 1976, with crude oil production reaching 860,000 million barrels per day in 1984. The main fields are in the southern Gulf of Suez and adjacent coastal areas of the Arabian Desert and Sinai. The offshore fields of El Morgan, Ramadan, July, October, and Belayim accounted for about 90 percent of the total crude oil production. In the Western Desert are the major fields of El ʿAlamein, Razzak, and Abu Gharadiq. Large new reserves were found as the Egyptian government encouraged exploration and made concessions.

Egypt has six petroleum refineries with a total capacity of 369,000 barrels per day. Two are located near Alexandria (47 percent of the total), two are at Suez, and the others are at Tanta and Mostarud near Cairo. They are linked by pipeline to the main producing fields. The largest and most important is the Suez-Mediterranean (Sumed) pipeline, which extends from Ain Sukhna on the Gulf of Suez to Sidi Krer west of Alexandria. It is being expanded. A new refinery planned for Asyut will be linked by pipeline to the Ras Gharib and Ras Shuqair fields in the Arabian Desert.

Natural gas is produced from five fields. Located at the edge of the delta, the Abu Madi field supplies gas to Tanta and Abu Qir, to Alexandria. Cairo (Helwan) is supplied by Abu Gharadiq, which is 124 miles (200 kilometers) to the west. In addition, two offshore fields provide a quarter of total production. Egypt uses all of the natural gas it produces, and demand is growing rapidly.

Manganese, phosphates, iron ore, and coal are in the western Sinai. Iron ore is also mined near Aswan, and large deposits have been found in Bahariya. Phosphates are mined in the Nile Valley and near Safaga in the Arabian Desert. Chromium, lead, asbestos, gypsum, and talc are also mined. Granite is quarried near Aswan, and limestone comes from the cliffs along the Nile.

Transportation, Communication, and Education

Water transportation is of primary importance in Egypt. It has about 1,925 miles (3,100 kilometers) of navigable waterways, half on the Nile and the other half on canals, mostly in the delta. The main canals are the Nubariya on the delta and the Bahr el Yusef, which links El Faiyum with Asyut on the Nile.

The Suez Canal is an international shipping link between the Mediterranean Sea and the Red Sea. The canal extends 121 miles (195 kilometers) from Port Said to Suez, on the Gulf of Suez. It has a 624-foot (190-meter) channel and a maximum draft of 54 feet (16.5 meters). Since 1975 the canal has been expanded and facilities improved to accommodate supertankers.

Cairo (below) straddles the Nile River. In the upper right is Roda Island, with the Meridien Hotel at the tip. The Nile is quite wide as it passes through the city, allowing for a great amount of traffic. The Khan Khalili bazaar (right), founded in 1400, is Cairo's oldest shopping quarter.

(Below) © Berlitz—CLICK/Chicago; (right) Robert Frerck—Odyssey Productions

Frank Folwell—CLICK/Chicago

Egyptian men work at a power plant developed as an Egyptian-American effort of the Bechtel Corporation.

Alexandria, Port Said, and Suez are Egypt's major ports. Alexandria's port is being expanded, and new ports are planned or are under construction at Dakheila, Damietta, and Safaga.

Egypt has 4,130 miles (6,650 kilometers) of railways. From Cairo lines extend along the Nile to Aswan, across the north coast to Salum, and to Alexandria, Port Said, and Suez. A railroad parallels the west bank of the Suez Canal between Suez and Ismailia. A railway also connects the iron ore mines at Bahariya with Helwan. A 26-mile (42-kilometer) subway transit system for Cairo began operation in 1988. Egypt also has 7,640 miles (12,300 kilometers) of paved roads and 10,380 miles (16,700 kilometers) of graveled or improved roads that connect the main cities and towns. The 1-mile (1.6-kilometer) Ahmad Hamdi tunnel under the Suez Canal opened in 1980. Egyptair operates a full schedule of domestic and international flights. Service to Tel Aviv began in March 1980. The Nuzbah International Airport near Cairo opened in 1983.

Cairo is the major publishing center in the Middle East. It has four major companies. *Al Ahram,* which was founded in 1875, is the most authoritative daily newspaper. Cairo is also a center for radio and television. Egyptian radio and television broadcast in several African and Asian languages. Egyptians have 12 million radios—more per capita than any other Middle Eastern or North African country—and nearly 4 million television sets.

Illiteracy is one of Egypt's most severe problems. Although elementary schooling is compulsory, an estimated 62 percent of the population is illiterate.

Secondary-school graduates may take examinations for entrance to universities, or they may attend technical institutes specializing in agriculture, commerce, and industry. Egypt has 13 independent universities. The six major state universities are coeducational. The largest of these is the University of Cairo at Giza, founded as the Egyptian University in 1908. Universities were opened at Alexandria in 1942 and at Asyut in 1957. Ain Shams University, incorporating several other schools near Cairo, was established in 1950. There are also state universities at Helwan, Mansura, and Tanta.

One of the world's oldest centers of Islamic education is El Azhar University in Cairo. Shortly after El Azhar Mosque was built in 972, it had one of the leading academies in the Muslim world. Since 1961 it has also provided secular education. The American University in Cairo was founded in 1919, and the Suez Canal University was established in Ismailia in 1976.

Government

The Arab Republic of Egypt is governed under the 1971 constitution. Islam is the state religion, and Islamic jurisprudence is the basis of Egyptian law. Arabic is the official language. The constitution provides for a strong presidency and a unicameral, or one-house, legislature—the People's Assembly. About half of the members of the assembly must be farmers and workers. Members are elected for five-year terms by direct universal suffrage. The president has extensive executive powers. He is nominated by at least one third of the members of the People's Assembly, approved by at least two thirds of them, and elected by popular referendum.

From 1962 to 1977 the Arab Socialist Union was the only legal political organization in Egypt. Political parties had been abolished in 1953. In 1976, however, groups within the union were allowed to support candidates. Political parties were legalized in 1977. The National Democratic party replaced the Arab Socialist party as the majority, and the Socialist Labor party formed the official opposition.

In 1979 the People's Assembly was expanded from 350 to 392 members, ten of whom the president appointed. In the 1984 elections new laws required parties to receive at least 8 percent of the vote in order to be represented. The number of seats was increased from 392 to 458. Members are elected from 48 constituencies. From three to 12 members are elected from each, and an extra member, who must be a woman, is added to the elected members of the majority party in 31 constituencies.

The National Democratic party continued to dominate Egyptian politics. Its strongest opposition since Egypt became a republic came from the New Wafd party. The other independent parties were forced to form a coalition in order to gain more than 8 percent of the vote.

History

After the death of the prophet Muhammad in 632, Arabs conquered Egypt in 639 to 641. Most Egyptians, who were Christians, converted to Islam. Those who resisted despite persecution were called Copts, from an Arabic word meaning "Egyptian." Arabic replaced the Egyptian language, which was restricted to use in the Coptic church. In 973 Cairo was founded, replacing the old capital of Al Fustat. Egypt became part of the Ottoman Empire in 1517. Napoleon I invaded Egypt in 1798, defeating the Turks in the battle of the Pyramids, but his fleet was destroyed by Britain's Admiral Horatio Nelson in the battle of the Nile. The British left Egypt by 1803.

Mehemet Ali, an Albanian officer in the Ottoman forces, became pasha, or governor, of Egypt in 1805. He defeated the British at Alexandria in 1807 and conquered most of the northern Sudan between 1820 and 1822. In 1856 Saʿid Pasha, Mehemet Ali's son, granted Ferdinand de Lesseps the right to build the Suez Canal (*see* Suez Canal). It was opened in 1869 during the reign of Ismail Pasha. To repay his debts to British and French bankers, Ismail Pasha sold Egypt's shares of Suez stock to Britain, giving it control of the canal. In 1876, again in debt, he allowed British and French officials strict control of Egypt's finances. In 1883 British forces occupied Egypt to support the monarchy in the face of a growing nationalist movement. In 1899 the Anglo-Egyptian Sudan was established under joint British and Egyptian rule.

In World War I Turkey sided with Germany, but Egypt supported the British. Britain proclaimed Egypt a protectorate in November 1914 and assumed responsibility for defending the Suez Canal. The Wafd, or nationalist, movement gained strength in wartime. After failing to reach a settlement with the Wafd, Britain abolished the protectorate and recognized Egyptian independence on Feb. 28, 1922. Britain retained responsibility for the security of the Suez Canal and the defense of Egypt.

Farm workers near Sakha in the Nile Delta pick boll weevils off young cotton plants.

Philip Gendreau—The Bettmann Archive

In 1923 a constitutional monarchy was established with Sultan Fuad as king. He was succeeded in 1936 by his son Farouk. A treaty that year ended the British occupation of Egypt but confirmed its control of the canal zone and joint rule of the Sudan. When the British left Palestine in 1948, Egypt and its Arab allies invaded the area proclaimed as the state of Israel. Although defeated, Egypt kept the Gaza Strip.

Farouk was overthrown by a military junta on July 23, 1952. The Revolutionary Command Council, which was led by Major General Mohammed Naguib and Colonel Gamal Abdel Nasser, controlled the government. The constitution was abolished, and political parties were dissolved. Egypt was declared a republic on June 18, 1953, and Nasser became prime minister (*see* Nasser). An Anglo-Egyptian agreement in the same year ended the union of Egypt and the Sudan, resulting in independence for Sudan.

After a new Egyptian constitution was approved in June 1956, Nasser was elected president. The British forces left Egypt in July. Nasser declared the internationally owned Suez Canal Egyptian property. The United States and Britain had withdrawn financial aid for the Aswan High Dam, and Nasser planned to use revenues from the canal to finance Egypt's share of the project. Israel invaded Sinai in October, and British and French forces landed in the canal zone in November. Nasser sank some 40 ships in the canal to block it. United Nations (UN) pressure brought a cease-fire and withdrawal of forces, and the canal reopened in March 1957 under Egyptian control, with guarantees of international use.

Egypt and Syria merged as the United Arab Republic in 1958 and, with Yemen, formed the United Arab States. Syria withdrew from the union in 1961 after a military coup, and Egypt ousted Yemen. A 1963 agreement between Egypt, Syria, and Iraq to form another United Arab Republic failed, though steps were taken in 1965 to join Egypt and Iraq.

Because of tensions between Israel and Syria, Nasser forced UN troops to withdraw from Egypt and blockaded the Gulf of Aqaba against Israeli shipping. Israel attacked on June 5, 1967, defeating the allied Arab forces in a six-day war and occupying the Gaza Strip and the Sinai. The Suez Canal was again blocked by damaged ships. A UN-negotiated cease-fire failed to result in a peace settlement. After the war Egypt faced severe financial crises and widespread discontent among students and workers. As efforts to reach a settlement continued through 1970, Egyptian and Israeli forces dueled across the canal.

Nasser died in September 1970 and was succeeded by Anwar el-Sadat (*see* Sadat). In April 1971 Egypt, Libya, and Syria agreed to form the Confederation of Arab Republics. Full union was prevented by worsening relations between Egypt and Libya. On Oct. 6, 1973, Egypt and Syria launched surprise coordinated attacks on Israeli-held Arab lands. A UN-sponsored cease-fire took effect, and in January 1974 Egypt and Israel signed a disengagement agreement that returned to Egypt a strip of land east of the Suez Canal. The canal was reopened in 1975.

Egypt reestablished diplomatic relations with the United States after the 1973 war with Israel. In 1976 Sadat canceled a 1971 mutual friendship treaty with the Soviet Union. In 1977 he became the first Arab head of state to visit Israel. As a result of the 1979 Camp David agreements, moderated by United States President Jimmy Carter, Egypt and Israel signed a peace treaty that provided for a phased withdrawal of Israeli forces from the Sinai. As Palestinian autonomy talks continued, the two countries established diplomatic relations, and Egypt took control of parts of the Sinai. Egypt was suspended from the Arab League, which it had once dominated, and most member countries withdrew economic aid from Egypt.

Sadat was assassinated by Muslim extremists in October 1981. Vice-President Hosni Mubarak became president (*see* Mubarak). Although most of the Sinai was returned to Egypt in April 1982, relations with Israel worsened because of Israel's invasion of Lebanon.

In October 1984 Egypt withdrew from its 1971 confederation with Syria and Libya. Despite economic difficulties, Mubarak remained in control of the government as a result of the 1984 legislative elections. A five-day mutiny in Cairo by security police in 1986 raised questions about Mubarak's ability to cope with forces that were steadily eroding the nation's stability.

In October 1987 Mubarak began a second six-year term after receiving 97 percent of the vote in a popular referendum. As a result of his moderate policies Egypt gradually improved its relationships with other Arab states. After an Arab League summit in Jordan that November many of the members reestablished diplomatic relations with Egypt. In 1989, Egypt rejoined the Arab League, and Mubarak was elected chairman of the Organization of African Unity. Relations with Libya remained strained, however.

BIBLIOGRAPHY FOR EGYPT

Bendick, Jeanne. Egyptian Tombs (Watts, 1989).
Fodor's Egypt (McKay, 1987).
Hoving, Thomas. Tutankhamen: the Untold Story (Simon & Schuster, 1984).
Lye, Keith. Take a Trip to Egypt (Watts, 1983).
Romer, John. Ancient Lives (Holt, 1984).
Stead, Miriam. Ancient Egypt (Watts, 1985).
Stead, Miriam. Egyptian Life (Harvard Univ. Press, 1986).

Egypt Fact Summary

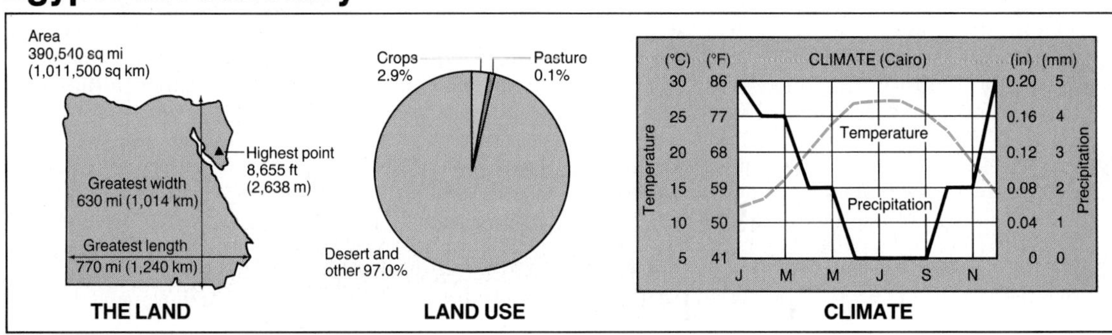

Official Name: Arab Republic of Egypt.
Capital: Cairo.

NATURAL FEATURES

Prominent Features: Nile Valley, Qattara Depression, the First Cataract, Western Desert, Eastern (Arabian) Desert.
Highest Peak: Jebel Katherina, 8,655 feet (2,638 meters).
Major River: Nile.
Largest Lake: Nasser.

PEOPLE

Population (1989 estimate): 51,748,000; 132.5 persons per square mile (51.2 persons per square kilometer); 43.9 percent urban, 56.1 percent rural.
Major Cities (1986 estimate): Cairo (6,053,000), Alexandria (2,917,000), Giza (1,670,800), Shubra El Kheima (533,300), Port Said (399,000), El Mahalla El Kubra (385,300).
Major Religion: Islam (official).
Major Language: Arabic (official).
Literacy: 45 percent.
Leading Universities: Ain Shams University (Cairo), Alexandria University, Asyut University, Cairo University, El Azhar University (Cairo), University of Helman, Zagazig University.

GOVERNMENT

Form of Government: Republic.
Chief of State: President.
Head of Government: Prime minister.
Legislature: People's Assembly: one legislative house of 448 members elected to 5-year terms and 10 appointed by the president.
Voting Qualification: Age 18 with identification card.
Political Divisions: 26 governorates.
Flag: Three equal horizontal stripes of red, white, and black, with the gold Sakr (Hawk) of Koraich on the white stripe (*see* Flags of the World).

ECONOMY

Chief Agricultural Products: *Crops*—sugarcane, tomatoes, corn (maize), wheat, rice, vegetables. *Livestock*—buffalo, cattle, goats, sheep.
Chief Mined Products: Coal, iron ore, salt, natural gas, petroleum, phosphates.
Chief Manufactured Products: Iron and steel, petroleum, prepared foods, textiles.
Chief Exports: Cotton and cotton products, fruits, petroleum, rice, vegetables.
Chief Imports: Cement, chemicals, iron and steel, machinery and transportation equipment, wheat and flour.
Monetary Unit: 1 Egyptian pound = 1,000 millièmes = 100 piastres.

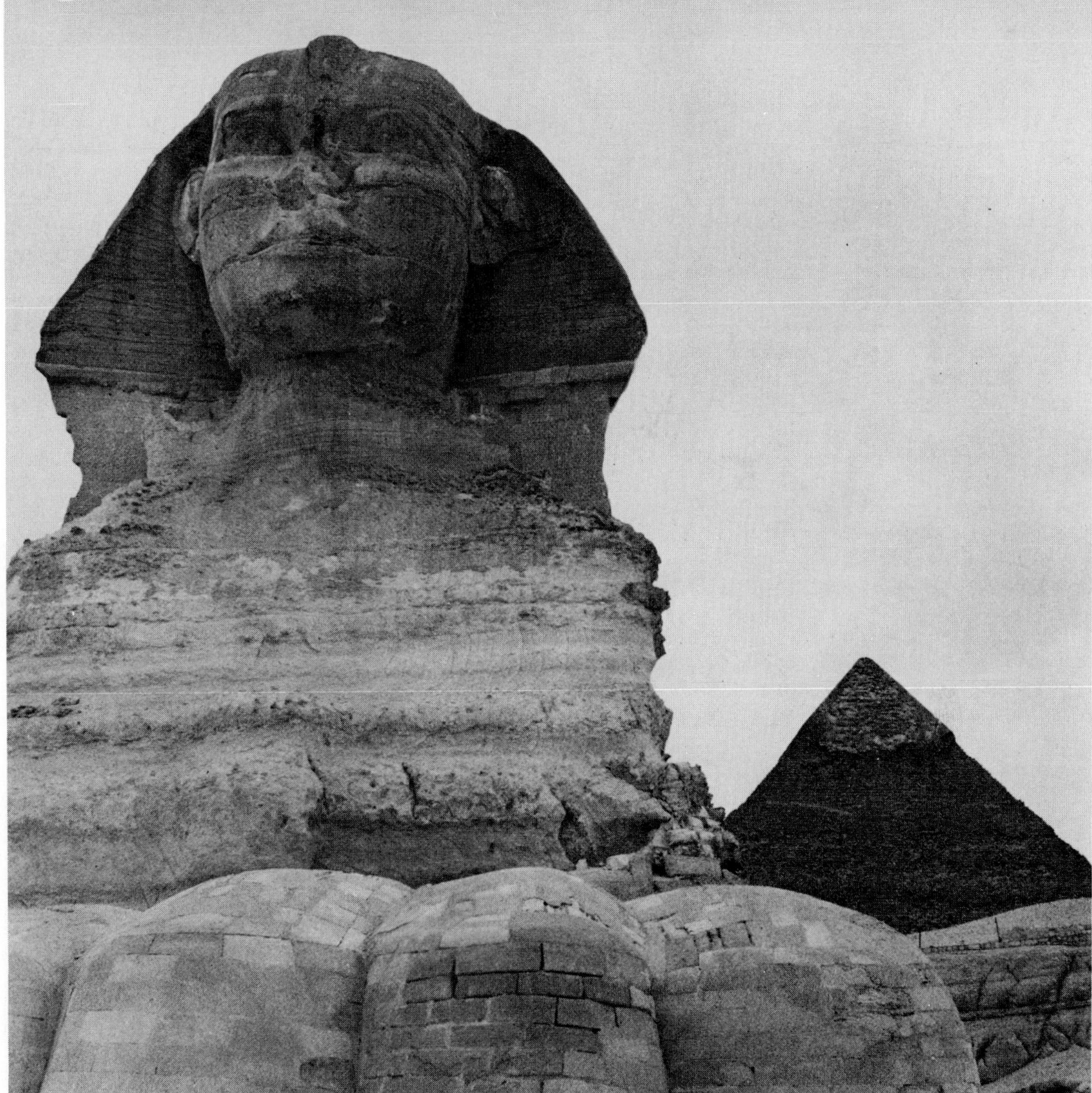

For 45 centuries the Great Sphinx and the pyramids at Giza (Gizeh) have symbolized the wealth and power of ancient Egypt, where the seeds of Western civilization were planted. Egypt has had a longer continuous history than any other country.

EGYPT, ANCIENT. No other country—not even China or India—has such a long unbroken history as Egypt. Nearly 3,000 years before the birth of Christ, the Egyptians had reached a high stage of civilization. They lived under an orderly government; they carried on commerce in ships; they built great stone structures; and, most important of all, they had acquired the art of writing.

Because they lived so long ago, the Egyptian people had to find out for themselves how to do many things that are easily done today. They adopted some inventions of the Sumerians but made more extensive use of them. In the Nile Valley the early development of the arts and crafts that formed the foundation of Western civilization can be traced. (*See also* Babylonia and Assyria.)

The traveler along the Nile sees many majestic monuments that reveal the achievements of ancient Egypt. Most of these monuments are tombs and temples. The ancient Egyptians were very religious. They believed in a life after death—at first only for kings and nobles—if the body could be preserved. So they carefully embalmed the body and walled it up in a massive tomb (*see* Mummy). On the walls of the tomb they carved pictures and inscriptions. Some private tombs were decorated with paintings. They put into the tomb the man's statue and any objects they thought he would want when his soul returned to the body. The hot sand and dry air of Egypt preserved many of these objects through the centuries. Thousands of them are now in museums all over the world. Together with written documents, they show how people lived in Egypt thousands of years ago.

The desert sands have also preserved the remains of prehistoric people. By their sides, in the burial pits, lie stone tools and weapons, carved figures, and decorated pottery. These artifacts help archaeologists and historians piece together the story of life in the Nile Valley centuries before the beginning of the historical period. (*See also* Archaeology.)

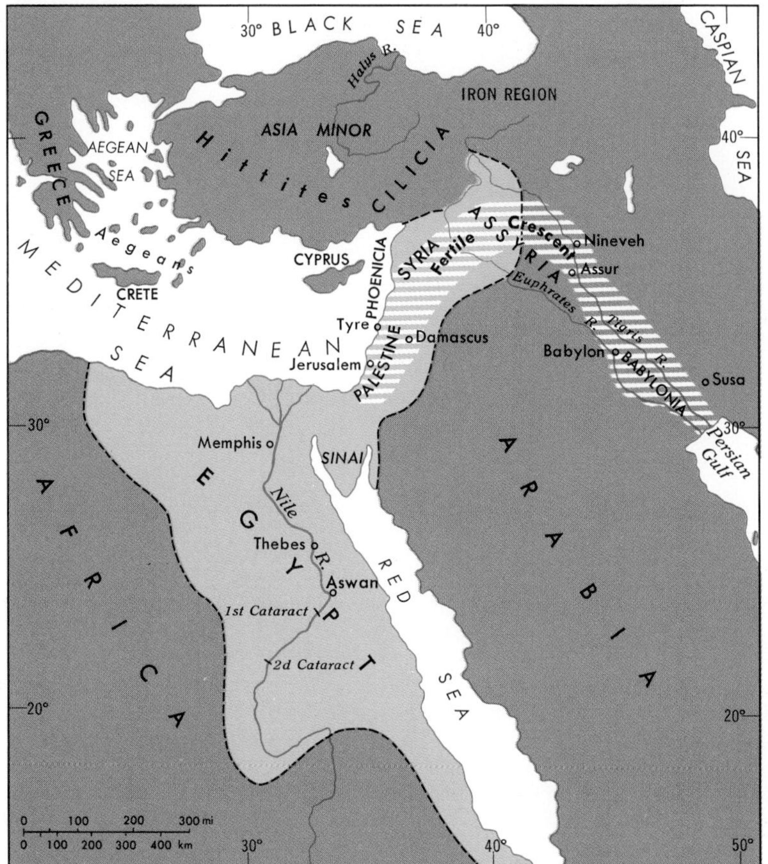

During the New Kingdom period Egypt became a Mediterranean empire. Around 1479 B.C. Thutmose III, riding "in a chariot of fine gold," led his armies out of Egypt into Phoenicia, Palestine, and Syria. In later campaigns he extended the empire to the Euphrates Valley in Mesopotamia. Earlier rulers had already pushed the frontiers south into Nubia, beyond the First Cataract of the Nile.

Prehistoric Era

Ages ago the land of Egypt was very different from what it is today. There was rain. There was no delta, and the sea extended far up the Nile Valley. The plateau on each side of the water was grassland. The people wandered over the plateau in search of game and fresh pastures and had no permanent home. They hunted with a crude stone hand ax and with a bow and arrow. Their arrows were made of chipped flint. (*See also* Egypt; Stone Age.)

Very gradually the rains decreased and the grasslands dried up. The Nile began to deposit silt in the valley and to build up the delta. The animals went down to the valley. The hunters followed them and settled at the edge of the jungle that lined the river.

In the Nile Valley the people's way of life underwent a great change. They settled down in more or less permanent homes and progressed from food gathering to food producing. They still hunted the elephant and hippopotamus and wild fowl, and they fished in the river. More and more, however, they relied for meat on the animals they bred—long-horned cattle, sheep, goats, and geese.

The early Egyptians learned that the vegetables and wild grain they gathered grew from seeds. When the Nile floodwater drained away, they dug up the ground with a wooden hoe, scattered seeds over the wet soil, and waited for the harvest. They cut the grain with a sharp-toothed flint sickle set in a straight wooden holder and then ground it between two flat millstones. The people raised emmer (wheat), barley, a few vegetables, and flax. From the grain they made bread and beer, and they spun and wove the flax for linen garments.

The first houses were round or oval, built over a hole in the ground. The walls were lumps of mud, and the roofs were matting. Later houses were rectangular, made of shaped bricks, with wooden frames for doors and windows—much like the houses the Egyptian farmers live in today. To work the lumber, the people used ground stone axheads and flint saws. Beautiful clay pottery was created, without the wheel, to hold food and drink. They fashioned ornaments of ivory, made beads and baskets, and carved in stone the figures of people and animals. They built ships that had oars, and they carried on trade with nearby countries. Instead of names, the ships had simple signs, probably indicating the home port. These signs were an early step in the invention of writing.

Good farmland was scarce. The desert came down close to the marshes that edged the river. To gain more land, the people rooted out the jungle, filled in marshes, and built mud walls to keep out floodwater. In time they engaged in large-scale irrigation work, digging canals that cut across miles of land. This required the cooperation of many people living in different places. Leaders became necessary to plan the work and direct the workers. Because of this need, orderly government arose.

Population and wealth grew with the increase in farmland. There was food enough to support a professional class, who worked at crafts instead of farming. Villages grew into towns. Large towns spread their rule over nearby villages and became states. At the end of the prehistoric period, there were only two political units—Lower Egypt (the delta) and Upper Egypt (the valley). Later, when Egypt was united, the people still called it the Two Lands, and the king of all Egypt wore a double crown combining the white crown of the south with the red crown of the north.

Before the prehistoric period ended, the Egyptians were stimulated by their contact with people who lived in a Mesopotamian river valley in Asia. These people were more advanced than the Egyptians in working metal, and they also had writing. Although this was probably the inspiration for Egyptian writing, the Egyptians did not take over the Mesopotamian script but developed a script of their own. This great invention brought Egypt abruptly to the threshold of history, for history begins with written records. (*See also* Mesopotamia.)

DYNASTIES OF EGYPT

The beginnings of writing in Egypt go back to about 3100 B.C., when the Two Lands became united in a single kingdom. According to tradition, it was Menes, a king of Upper Egypt, who brought about the union. He stands first in the long line of kings who ruled Egypt for about 3,000 years. Egyptian priests made lists of their kings, or pharaohs, and noted the most important events of their reigns. About 280 B.C. one of these priests, Manetho, grouped the pharaohs into 30 dynasties. (A dynasty is a succession of rulers of the same line of descent.)

Modern historians group the dynasties into periods. The periods when Egyptian civilization flourished are the Old Kingdom, the Middle Kingdom, and the New Kingdom. These are separated by periods of decline called the First Intermediate Period and the Second Intermediate Period. The final period of decline is called the Late Period.

The Old Kingdom

Little is known of Menes' successors until the reign of King Zoser, or Djoser, at the end of the 3d dynasty. Zoser's capital was located at Memphis, on the Nile's west bank near the point where the Two Lands met. Imhotep, a master builder, erected Zoser's tomb, the step pyramid of Saqqara, on high ground overlooking the city. This monument—the first great building in the country made entirely of stone—marked the beginning of Egypt's most creative period, the Pyramid Age.

Later kings built their tombs in true pyramidal form. Each pyramid guarded the body of one king, housed in a chamber deep within the pile. The climax of pyramid building was reached in the three gigantic tombs erected for Kings Khufu (Cheops), Khafre, and Menkure at Giza (Gizeh). Near them in the sand lies the Great Sphinx, a stone lion with the head of King Khafre. (*See also* Pyramids; Sphinx.)

The Old Kingdom lasted about 500 years. It was an active, optimistic age, an age of peace and splendor. Art reached a brilliant flowering. Sculpture achieved a grandeur never later attained. The pharaoh kept a splendid court. The people worshiped him as a god on earth, for they believed him to be the son of Ra, or Re, the great sun-god. They called him *pr-'o* (in the Bible, *pharaoh*), meaning "great house."

About 2200 B.C. the Old Kingdom came to an end. Nobles became independent and ruled as if they were kings. The country was split up into small warring states. Irrigation systems fell into disrepair. According to writers of the time: "The desert is spread throughout the land. The robbers are now in the possession of riches. Men sit in the bushes until the benighted traveler comes to . . . steal what is upon him." Thieves broke into the pyramids and robbed them of their treasures.

The Middle Kingdom

The Middle Kingdom period began about 2050 B.C. After a long struggle, the rulers of Thebes won out over their enemies and once again united Egypt into a single state. Thebes was then a little town on the Nile in Upper Egypt. In the New Kingdom it became one of the ancient world's greatest capitals.

The pharaohs of the Middle Kingdom constructed enormous irrigation works in the Faiyûm. Noting the annual heights of the Nile flood at Aswân, they laid plans to use the Nile water wisely. They sent trading ships up the Nile to Nubia and across the sea to Mediterranean lands. They got gold from Nubia and copper from the mines in Sinai. Construction of the most colossal temple of all time, the Temple of Amen (Amon) at El Karnak, was begun.

After two centuries of peace and prosperity, Egypt entered another dark age. About 1800 B.C. it fell for the first time to foreign invaders. Down from the north came the Hyksos, a barbarian people who used horses and chariots in combat and also had superior bows. The Egyptians, fighting on foot, were no match for them. The Hyksos occupied Lower Egypt, living in fortified camps behind great earthen walls. They failed to conquer Upper Egypt, and the pharaohs stayed on at Thebes. When the Egyptians had learned the new methods of warfare, the ruler Kamose began a successful war of liberation.

PERIODS IN EARLY EGYPTIAN HISTORY*

Prehistoric Period	Before 3100 B.C.
Archaic Period	
Dynasties I–II	3100–2700 B.C.
Old Kingdom	
Dynasties III–VI	2700–2200 B.C.
First Intermediate Period	
Dynasties VII–X	2200–2050 B.C.
Middle Kingdom	
Dynasties XI–XII	2050–1800 B.C.
Second Intermediate Period	
Dynasties XIII–XVII	1800–1570 B.C.
New Kingdom	
Dynasties XVIII–XX	1570–1090 B.C.
Late Period	
Dynasties XXI–XXX	1090–332 B.C.
Ptolemaic Period	332–30 B.C.
Roman Period	30 B.C.–A.D. 395
Byzantine Period	A.D. 395–640

*Dates are approximate until about 500 B.C. For the earliest period, about 3000 B.C., historians estimate the margin of error may be up to 100 years. At about 1000 B.C. the margin narrows to 10 to 15 years.

The colossal statues of King Amenhotep III—all that remains of his temple near Thebes—once weighed more than 700 tons each and were nearly 70 feet high. The Romans thought they depicted Memnon, a Trojan hero.

The New Kingdom

A new era dawned for Egypt after the Hyksos had been expelled. This period, the New Kingdom, was the age of empire. The once-peaceful Egyptians, having learned new techniques of warfare, embarked on foreign conquest on a large scale. The empire reached its peak under Thutmose III, one of the first great generals in history. He fought many campaigns in Asia and extended Egypt's rule to the Euphrates.

Slaves and tribute poured into Egypt from the conquered nations. The tribute was paid in goods, for the ancient world still did not have money. Wall paintings show people from Nubia, Babylonia, Syria, and Palestine bearing presents on their backs and bowing humbly before the pharaoh.

The Egyptian rulers used their new wealth and slaves to repair the old temples and build new ones. Hatshepsut, Egypt's first great queen, enlarged the great Temple of Amen at El Karnak. She also built her own beautiful temple at Deir el Bahri.

Amenhotep III built the wonderful temple at Luxor and put up the famous pair of colossal seated statues called the Colossi of Memnon (*see* Memnon). In the Middle Kingdom period, the pharaohs of Thebes had built modest brick pyramids for their tombs. In the New Kingdom period they broke with this tradition and began to hew tombs deep in the cliffs of an isolated valley west of Thebes. About 40 kings were buried in this "Valley of the Tombs of the Kings."

In the last years of his reign Amenhotep III paid little attention to the empire. It was already decaying when his son Amenhotep IV came to the throne. This king was more interested in religion than in warfare. Even before his father's death, he began to promote a new religious doctrine. He wanted the people to give up all their old gods and worship only the radiant sun, which was then called Aten. He changed his name from Amenhotep ("Amen is satisfied") to Ikhnaton (Akhenaton) ("It is well with Aten"). He left Thebes and built a splendid new capital sacred to Aten at El Amarna in middle Egypt. Throughout the land he had the word "gods" and the name "Amen" removed from tombs and monuments.

Ikhnaton's idea of a single god gained no hold on the Egyptian people. His successor, Tutankhamen, moved the capital back to Thebes and restored the name of Amen on monuments. Tutankhamen is famous chiefly for his lavishly furnished tomb, discovered in 1922. Its treasures reveal the luxury of the most magnificent period of Egyptian history.

Half a century later Ramses II completed the gigantic hall at El Karnak and set up many statues of himself. He also had his name carved on monuments built by earlier rulers, so that he became better known than any other king. He regained part of Egypt's Asian empire. But the kings who followed him had to use the army to defend Egypt against invaders.

The Late Period

In the Late Period, the final decline of Egypt's power set in. The treasury had been drained by extensive building projects and by the army. Hungry workers had to resort to strikes to get their wages in grain. The central government weakened, and the country split up once more into small states.

About 730 B.C., Ethiopian invaders entered Egypt and established a strong, new dynasty. However, they were unable to withstand an invasion from the north by the Assyrians. When Assyria's power waned, a new Egyptian dynasty reorganized the country. Persia conquered Egypt in 525 B.C. and held it until 404 B.C. Three brief Egyptian dynasties followed, ending with the 30th, which fell to a second Persian conquest in 341 B.C.

Postdynastic Periods

Persian rule lasted until Alexander the Great invaded Egypt in 332 B.C. After Alexander's death, Ptolemy, one of his generals, seized the throne. The Ptolemys introduced Greek manners and ideas into Egypt. The city of Alexandria, founded by Alexander, became the center of Greek civilization in the Near East (*see* Alexandria).

The rule of Egypt by the Ptolemaic line ended with the beautiful Queen Cleopatra, who reigned first with her brother Ptolemy XIII, then with her brother Ptolemy XIV, and finally with Caesarion, her son by Julius Caesar (*see* Cleopatra). In 30 B.C. Egypt was proclaimed a province of Rome.

After the Roman Empire was divided in half in the 4th century A.D., Egypt was ruled from Constantinople by the Byzantine emperors (*see* Byzantine Empire). During this period most Egyptians were converted to Christianity. In the 7th century, Egypt fell to the Arabs. (For later Egyptian history, *see* Egypt, subhead "Moslem, Turkish, and British Control.")

Everyday Life in Ancient Egypt

PEOPLE TODAY live in an age when every year brings forth new inventions and discoveries, new fads and fashions that affect everyday life. Through communications, migration, and travel, foreign cultures merge into new life-styles. The Egyptians had their greatest creative period at the very beginning of their long history. After that, their way of living changed very little. It is therefore possible to describe their homelife and their art without reference to the historical periods of Egyptian history.

Upper-Class Homelife and Dress

Of all the early peoples, the Egyptians were the least warlike. Their country was protected by the sea on the north and by deserts to the east and west. For many centuries they could develop their own way of life without fear of invasion by foreign armies. Their interests were centered in their homes and families and in their work. Their stone tombs were a kind of insurance against death. They loved life and wanted it to go on forever.

Villages and towns were situated near the Nile because it was the chief highway as well as the only source of water. Even the rich lived in houses of mud brick. The walls were richly colored. Windows were small, high openings covered with loosely woven matting to keep out the heat and glare of the sun. The most fashionable district was near the king's palace. Even here, houses were crowded close together to leave more space for farmland. Some dwellings were two stories high. Usually houses were built back to back to save space. Some opened onto a narrow street; others faced a small walled garden.

The walls were decorated with bright frescoes. Straw matting and rugs covered the floors. Lamps were saucers of oil with a floating wick. Rich people had beds, chairs, and stools but no real dining tables (*see* Furniture, "Ancient Egypt, Greece, and Rome"). They kept their clothes and linen sheets in box chests or in baskets. The linen was sent to professional laundrymen to be washed in the river.

The ancient Egyptians stored their water and food in huge pottery jars. The cook used pottery bowls, placing them directly on the fire or in a clay oven. She baked bread and cake and roasted beef, mutton, goose, or wildfowl. The common drinks were beer, wine, and milk. Honey and dates were the only sweets. Almost everything the family needed was grown or made by workers belonging to the estate.

The members of Egypt's upper classes spent much of their time tending to their appearance. They bathed with soda instead of soap and then rubbed perfumed oil into the skin. Men shaved with a bronze razor. They cut their hair short and wore wigs. Women also wore wigs or added false braids to their own hair. They had combs and hairpins and mirrors of polished bronze or silver. Both men and women darkened their eyelids with black or green paint. Women rouged their cheeks and lips and stained their nails with henna. They kept their cosmetics in beautiful box chests. (*See also* Cosmetics.)

Because of the hot climate, both men and women wore white linen clothes. Men usually wore only a skirt. In the early centuries the skirts were short and narrow; later they were long and full. Women wore low-cut white dresses with bands over the shoulders. Young children wore nothing at all. Both men and women wore jewelry—collars and necklaces, strings of beads, bracelets, anklets, earrings, and finger rings. Silver was more precious than gold.

Peasants and Craftsmen

The luxurious life of the pharaoh and the nobles was made possible by the continual labor of the peas-

In contrast to the bare home of the peasant, that of the noble was well furnished. He used vessels of pottery, glass, and faience (upper left and far right); a bed with a raised headrest (bottom left); and chairs with seats of hide or rope (bottom right). His children played with "paddle dolls" with hair of clay beads (top center) and with shell beads (top right).

ants who tilled the soil. After the crops were harvested, the pharaoh could call on them to leave their village huts and go off to labor on irrigation works, to quarry stone with primitive tools, or to build tombs and temples. Their only pay was grain from the state granaries, oil, fish, vegetables, and clothing.

The craftsmen and artists had an easier life. They worked in shops close to the palace of the pharaoh or on the estates of priests and nobles. Their professions were hereditary, passed down from father to son. An artist was never hurried. If he could produce a masterpiece, it did not matter whether he worked on it for one year or ten.

The smiths forged bronze tools and weapons and made fine copper and bronze dishes for the homes of the rich. Goldsmiths and silversmiths also made tableware as well as richly wrought jewelry set with turquoise, carnelian, lapis lazuli, and other semiprecious stones. Craftsmen in stone ground out vases, jars, bowls, and platters in hard diorite and porphyry or in soft, cream-colored alabaster, which could be ground so thin it let the light through.

Potters turned clay vessels on a potter's wheel and then baked them in closed clay furnaces as tall as a man. They covered some of the pottery with a blue glaze. Women wove sheer fabrics of linen for clothing and for tapestries and awnings to decorate the houses of the rich.

Egypt then as now had little timber. Cedar and cypress were imported from Lebanon and tropical woods from Nubia. Cabinetmakers fashioned chairs and couches. Other craftsmen overlaid the furniture with precious metals or inlaid it with ebony or ivory. The leatherworker contributed cushions. Shipbuilders made Nile vessels with curving hulls and tall sails and cargo ships to sail to foreign lands (*see* Ship and Shipping). Paperworkers took the papyrus reeds gathered from the Nile marshes, split them, and pasted them crosswise into double sheets of pale yellow writing paper (*see* Papyrus Plant).

This painting from a tomb of the 18th dynasty shows musicians entertaining at a banquet. The performers are playing (left to right) a harp, a lute, a double-reed pipe, and a lyre. The three girls in the center are also dancing.

Religion and Culture of Ancient Egypt

IN VERY EARLY times each town had its own town-god as well as a number of lesser gods. There were also gods that everybody worshiped. The most important of these were Ra, the sun-god; Horus, the sky-god; and Osiris, the god of the dead.

When a town grew in influence, its town-god became more important too. People worshiped him as part of their allegiance to the town. After Thebes became the capital, the worship of its town-god, Amen, spread throughout Egypt. The people combined his worship with that of Ra, and in this form called him Amen-Ra. Temples were raised to Amen throughout Egypt. The most splendid was the temple at El Karnak, in Thebes.

The Story of Ra and Osiris

The people believed that every day Ra, the sun, sailed across the sky in his boat. Every night he disappeared into the underworld, in the west. In the underworld, they thought, was another Nile River. Osiris, the ruler of the underworld, had the sun's boat pulled along this river until at last it crossed the horizon and the sun rose again.

Osiris had been murdered by his brother Set but lived again in the underworld as king of the dead. The people looked to Osiris to give them, too, a life after death. Osiris was usually shown in human form, tightly swathed in linen like a mummy and wearing a high crown. (*See also* Isis; Mummy.)

Other Gods and Sacred Animals

Other important deities were Nut and Hathor, goddesses of the sky and of joy; Ptah, master artist and craftsman; Thoth, the moon-god, who was also scribe of the gods and the inventor of writing; and Khnemu, who fashioned men and women on a

Oriental Institute, the University of Chicago

Grapes are gathered from the vine (top) and then pressed for juice for wine making (center). In the bottom panel, wine jars are brought into port (left), and rope is made from papyrus reeds (right).

Oriental Institute, the University of Chicago

In this tomb painting, a sportsman aims his serpent-headed throwing stick at fowl hidden among the lotus and papyrus plants in a marsh. The figure clinging to his leg in the skiff is his daughter.

potter's wheel. Some gods, such as Amen and Osiris, were always represented in purely human form. Others were pictured as animals or with human bodies and animal heads. Thus Horus was worshiped in the form of a hawk, or falcon, or of a hawk-headed man. Thoth was an ibis, Khnemu was a ram, and Hathor was a cow. The sun had various symbols—the obelisk, the sacred scarab beetle, the uraeus cobra, and the sun disk.

Certain sacred animals were carefully kept in the temples. When Egyptian civilization decayed in its very late days, the people came to regard every animal of these species as sacred. They embalmed thousands of crocodiles, cats, and ibis and buried them in special cemeteries. Bulls were buried in stone vaults in an underground cemetery called the *Serapeum*, at Memphis. (*See also* Cat.)

Architecture of the Temples

Egyptian architecture was designed to blend into the setting of the Nile Valley, which is as level as a floor and is walled in on both sides by sheer limestone cliffs. The temples erected by the Egyptians are gigantic; their surfaces, flat. The form is rectangular, like that of the flat-topped cliffs. The only decorations are reliefs and inscriptions that do not break the straight lines of the stone surfaces on which they are carved. Private tombs were decorated and inscribed in the same way.

Temples were built on a grand scale. The front wall consisted of two massive sloping towers, together called a pylon, with a door between them. The door gave entrance to a huge unroofed court, bordered on two or three sides by colonnades. Here the public

Oriental Institute, the University of Chicago

In ancient Egypt, even the dead had to make religious pilgrimages, as shown in this depiction of a voyage to a temple of Osiris. In the prow of the boat the captain directs his crew. Overseers with whips, posted atop either end of the cabin, urge the oarsmen on to greater effort. The oars are decorated with painted eyes to help the men find their way through the water.

Queen Hatshepsut, the greatest of Egypt's women rulers, built this temple against the stone cliffs of Deir el Bahri. She ruled during the 18th dynasty in the New Kingdom period.

assembled for worship. Beyond the court rose the hypostyle hall—a forest of huge pillars holding up a roof. Past the hall was the sanctuary of the temple-god. Only priests and the pharaoh were allowed to enter the sanctuary. There were many variations of this plan. Large temples—particularly the great temple at El Karnak—had a series of courts, each faced by a pylon. An avenue of sphinxes led from El Karnak to the temple at Luxor.

Painting and Sculpture

Wall paintings took the place of reliefs in many private tombs of the New Kingdom. Some of the paintings and reliefs of this period rank with the world's finest masterpieces in art. In order to appreciate them, it is necessary to understand the principles upon which Egyptian artists worked.

Like other early peoples, the Egyptians did not use perspective. Figures at different distances from the observer were drawn in the same size. Humble people and servants, however, were pictured smaller than the great lord. Furthermore, the artist did not limit himself to a single point of view. He drew what he knew, not merely what he saw. A fisherman in a boat might be sketched as if the artist were looking at the scene from the shore, but fish would be shown swimming under the water. The same picture might even outline the pond as if seen from above. Nevertheless, Egyptian paintings are beautiful and harmonious, and they reveal more than they would if drawn from a single point of view.

In sketching the human figure, the artist usually followed conventions established in early times. Since he wanted to show all the principal parts of the body, he combined front and side views. The head is always in profile, but the eye is drawn as it appears from the front. The shoulders and skirt are front view, but the legs and feet are side view.

Sculptors carved thousands of statues in all sizes, from colossal figures to miniatures. In addition to gods, kings, and nobles, their works included animals and sphinxes. The pharaoh is always shown in a dignified pose, never in movement. The face is often an expressive portrait. The sculptor painted the bodies of men red and women pale yellow and set in eyeballs of colored stone or crystal.

Three Ways of Writing

The ancient Egyptians had three different ways of writing. They are called hieroglyphic, hieratic, and demotic. Hieroglyphs were chiseled on a stone surface. The word comes from two Greek words—

This temple in honor of the supreme god Amen-Ra was erected at El Karnak by Ramses III, one of the rulers of the 20th dynasty, who reigned during the 12th century B.C. The view here is from the top of a pylon into the main hall of the temple.

hieros, meaning "sacred," and *glyphein,* meaning "to carve." From hieroglyphs the Egyptians developed a cursive writing. Called hieratic, this was written on papyrus with a pen. Out of hieratic a much more rapid script—demotic—developed in the Late Period.

Hieroglyphic writing developed out of picture writing toward the end of the prehistoric period. Until then the only way to record an event had been to draw a picture of it. Picture recording evolved into writing with the realization that pictures of objects could be used to express all kinds of ideas if the words for these ideas had the same sounds as the names of the objects pictured. The picture of a house meant *house;* but it could also stand for the sound of the word for *house, pr.* The Egyptians did not write vowels. Because the word for *to go* also consisted of the consonants *pr* with a different vowel sound, the sign for *house* could be used to write *to go* by adding to it a pair of walking legs. The legs sign—called a determinative—was not pronounced but indicated a verb of motion. Hieroglyphic writing was therefore sound writing. Some of the pictures stood for one consonant and were thus alphabetic, while others were used to represent two or three consonants.

In hieratic and demotic writing, the signs no longer resembled the pictures from which they were developed. Rapid cursive writing with a pen on the soft surface of papyrus led to shortening the signs.

The ability to read hieroglyphics died out with the Egyptian religion. Throughout the Middle Ages people thought the inscriptions on monuments were not writing but symbols with some deep religious meaning.

When Napoleon went to Egypt in 1798, he took with him a large staff of scholars and scientists to study the civilization of ancient Egypt. Near Rashid (Rosetta) one of his officers discovered a stone inscribed with three kinds of writing. Napoleon's scholars recognized the writing as Greek at the bottom, demotic in the middle, and hieroglyphic at the top. They could read the ancient Greek and guessed that the other sections must have the same content.

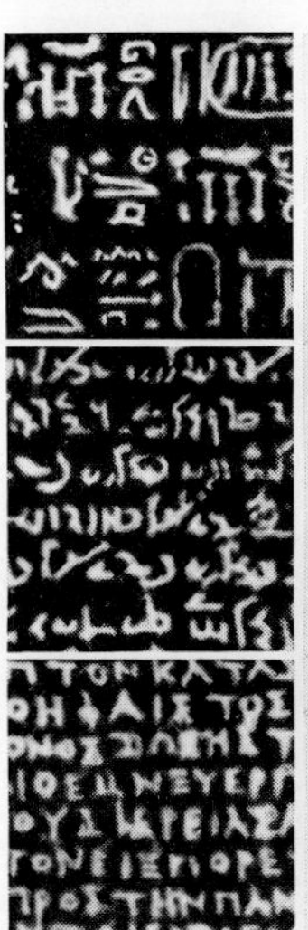

The Rosetta stone's text, which is magnified at left, is written in hieroglyphics at the top, demotic script in the middle, and Greek at the bottom.

Carved on a wall of the Medinet Habu temple at Luxor, a relief portrays King Ramses III reviewing prisoners who were taken in battle.

The stone fell into the hands of the British, who sent copies to scholars throughout the world. In 1822 Jean–François Champollion deciphered the hieroglyphs. Written about 196 B.C., they commemorate the accession of Ptolemy V Epiphanes, about 205 B.C. Champollion's work was the basis of the science of Egyptology. (*See also* Writing.)

The Literature of Ancient Egypt

Ancient Egyptian literature consists of both religious and nonreligious texts. The principal religious texts were designed to guide the dead into the underworld. In the Old Kingdom period such texts were for the use of the king only. They were written on the burial chamber walls in the pyramids of the 5th and 6th dynasties and are called Pyramid Texts. Later, "coffin texts" were written on the coffins of private citizens. Still later, religious texts—now called 'Book of the Dead'—were written on papyrus rolls and buried with the dead. Nonreligious writings relate events in the lives of kings or citizens. (*See also* Ancient Civilization.)

EHRLICH, Paul (1854–1915). "We must learn to shoot microbes with magic bullets," Paul Ehrlich often exclaimed. By "magic bullets" Ehrlich meant chemicals which would kill disease microbes in the body. His most spectacular discovery was the "magic bullet" *Salvarsan,* which was long used to treat syphilis. Equally important was his "side chain" theory, dealing with the way the body fights off certain disease poisons. Ehrlich also discovered a way to standardize the manufacture of antidiphtheria serum, and he made important contributions to the knowledge of cancer. In 1908 Ehrlich was the co-winner of the Nobel prize for medicine.

Ehrlich, the son of Jewish innkeepers, was born in Silesia (now a part of Poland) on March 14, 1854. He received his M.D. degree from the University of Leipzig in 1878. He served as assistant to Robert Koch (*see* Koch). In 1896 he became director of the Institute for Serum Study near Berlin, Germany.

One of Ehrlich's first discoveries was a dye that would move through the body and deposit only at nerve endings. In 1907 he compounded a dye he called trypan red. When injected into mice it destroyed the microbes called trypanosomes.

Trypanosomes are similar to the *Treponema pallidum,* the microbe that causes syphilis. In 1909, after 605 failures, Ehrlich and his assistants found an arsenic compound that acted against syphilis as trypan red did against trypanosomes. They named the compound Salvarsan. The following year Ehrlich announced his "side chain" theory of immunity.

Ehrlich was nervous and energetic but cool and precise when he worked. He often said, "It is because we are not exact that we fail." Ehrlich died at Bad Homburg, Germany, on Aug. 20, 1915.

EIFFEL TOWER. There is no more famous landmark in the world than the Eiffel Tower. It announces to all who see it: This is Paris. Not only does it dominate the skyline of Paris, but it is also a landmark of building construction history. (For a picture, *see* France.)

When the French government was organizing the Centennial Exposition of 1889, a fair to commemorate the 100th anniversary of the French Revolution, the noted bridge engineer Alexandre-Gustave Eiffel was asked to design and build a structure to symbolize the occasion. His finished product aroused both praise and criticism and a good deal of amazement.

Nothing like it had ever been built. It is a 984-foot (300-meter) tower of open-lattice wrought iron. Not until the Chrysler Building was completed in New York City in 1930 was there a taller structure in the world. The base of the tower consists of four semicircular arches, inspired by both artistic design and weight-bearing engineering considerations. Glass-walled elevators, designed by the Otis Elevator Company, ascend on a curve up the legs of the tower to the first and second platforms. Two new pairs of counterbalanced elevators go from the second level to the third platform near the top. From this platform the view extends for 50 miles (80 kilometers) on a clear day.

After the 1889 fair closed, Eiffel realized that the only way to save his monument would be to find new and profitable uses for it. He supervised changes to accommodate a meteorological station in 1890, a military telegraph station in 1903, and a laboratory for studying aerodynamics in 1909. Further modifications were made for the expositions of 1900, 1925, and 1937. Additions made for television transmission added about 66 feet (20 meters) to the height.

For many years the Eiffel Tower was in the hands of a public firm, but in 1981 the government of the city of Paris took over its management. In the years 1981 to 1983 the tower underwent extensive renovation and reconstruction in preparation for its 100th anniversary in 1989. The renovation, costing about $40 million, stripped off the paint down to the girders, removed the excess weight of structures on the upper levels, and built new lighter-weight facilities for visitors.

On the first level are three glass-enclosed structures. One is a museum, the Cinémax, which shows films about the tower. The central structure consists of two levels, each of which has a restaurant: Le Parisien on the lower and La Belle France on the upper. The third facility is the Salle (hall) Gustave Eiffel, which provides space for business conferences, expositions, cultural events, and social gatherings.

On the smaller second level there is a souvenir shop and a snack bar. From this level it is possible to get an excellent view of Paris without the need to ascend to the top.

Glass-enclosed elevators take tourists from the ground to the first and second platforms of the Eiffel Tower.

Derek Lepper—Black Star

EINSTEIN, Albert (1879–1955). Any list of the greatest thinkers in history contains the name of the brilliant physicist Albert Einstein. His theories of relativity led to entirely new ways of thinking about time, space, matter, energy, and gravity. Einstein's work led to such scientific advances as the control of atomic energy and to some of the investigations of space currently being made by astrophysicists.

Einstein was born in Ulm, Germany, on March 14, 1879, of Jewish parents. He was a shy and curious child. He attended a Munich elementary school where he showed an interest in science and mathematics. He finished high school and technical college in Switzerland. At age 22 he became a Swiss citizen. In 1903 he married Mileva Marec. They had two sons but were later divorced. He married his cousin in 1919.

In 1902 Einstein became an examiner in the Swiss patent office at Bern. In 1905, at age 26, he published five major research papers in an important German physics journal. He received a doctorate for the first paper. Publication of the next four papers forever changed mankind's view of the universe. The first one provided a theory explaining Brownian movement, the zigzag motion of microscopic particles in suspension (*see* Colloid). Einstein suggested that the movement was caused by the random motion of molecules of the suspension medium as they bounced against the suspended particles.

A second paper laid the foundation for the photon, or quantum, theory of light. In it he proposed that light is composed of separate packets of energy, called quanta or photons, that have some of the properties of particles and some of the properties of waves. The paper redefined the theory of light. It also explained the photoelectric effect, the emission of electrons from some solids when they are struck by light. Television and other inventions are practical applications of Einstein's discoveries (*see* Energy; Light; Photoelectric Devices).

A third paper, which had its beginnings in an essay at age 16, contained the "special theory of relativity." Einstein showed that time and motion are relative to the observer, if the speed of light is constant and natural laws are the same everywhere in the universe (*see* Relativity). This paper introduced an entirely new concept.

The fourth paper was a mathematical addition to the special theory of relativity. Here Einstein presented his famous formula, $E = mc^2$, known as the energy mass equivalence. What it says is that the energy (E) inherent in a mass (m) equals the mass multiplied by the velocity of light squared (c^2). The formula shows that a small particle of matter is the equivalent of an enormous quantity of energy. These papers won Einstein a place among Europe's most respected physicists.

In 1916 Einstein published his general theory of relativity. In it he proposed that gravity is not a force, a previously accepted theory, but a curved field in the space-time continuum that is created by the presence of mass (*see* Astronomy; Universe).

Courtesy of the Nobelstiftelsen, Stockholm

Albert Einstein

Between 1909 and 1912 Einstein taught theoretical physics in Switzerland and Germany. He returned to Zurich to teach from 1912 to 1914. Worldwide fame came in 1919 when the Royal Society of London announced that predictions made in his general theory of relativity had been confirmed. This happened when a scientific expedition in the Gulf of Guinea photographed the solar eclipse of May 29 of that year. Although he was awarded the 1921 Nobel prize for physics, the prize did not refer to his relativity theories, which were still considered to be controversial.

Einstein spoke out frequently against nationalism, the exalting of one nation above all others. He opposed war and violence and supported Zionism, the movement to establish a Jewish homeland in Palestine. When the Nazis came to power in 1933, they denounced his ideas, seized his property, and burned his books. That year he moved to the United States. In 1940 he became an American citizen.

Beginning in the 1920s Einstein tried to establish a mathematical relationship between electromagnetism and gravitation. He spent the rest of his life on this unsuccessful attempt to explain all of the properties of matter and energy in a single mathematical formula.

In 1939, shortly before the outbreak of World War II in Europe, Einstein learned that two German chemists had split the uranium atom. Enrico Fermi, an Italian physicist who lived in the United States, proposed that a chain-reaction splitting of uranium atoms could release enormous quantities of energy. In 1939 Einstein wrote to President Franklin D. Roosevelt warning him that this scientific knowledge could lead to Germany's developing an atomic bomb. He suggested that the United States prepare for its own atomic bomb research. Out of this effort came the Manhattan Project, in which the first two atomic bombs were developed in 1945 (*see* Nuclear Energy). Einstein died in Princeton, N.J., on April 18, 1955.

EINSTEINIUM *see* CHEMICAL ELEMENTS; PERIODIC TABLE.

DWIGHT D. EISENHOWER

34th President of the United States

EISENHOWER, Dwight D. (1890–1969; president 1953–1961). In World War II Gen. Dwight D. Eisenhower became one of the most successful commanders in history. After the war he added to his military reputation by his work as Army chief of staff. Later he became the first head of the armies of the North Atlantic Treaty Organization (NATO).

Turning to politics in 1952, Eisenhower proved to be a successful commander in that field also. After winning the Republican nomination for president he overwhelmingly defeated the Democratic candidate, Adlai E. Stevenson. He thus became the 34th president of the United States and the first Republican to occupy the White House in 20 years.

During Eisenhower's first term as president, 1953–57, the war in Korea was ended and the United States went on to achieve the greatest prosperity in its history. In 1956 the Republican party unanimously renominated Eisenhower for the presidency.

Campaigning on a platform of "peace and prosperity," President Eisenhower decisively defeated the same Democratic opponent, Stevenson. He polled more than 35 million popular votes and 457 electoral votes. Stevenson received more than 26 million popular votes and 73 electoral votes. Richard Nixon was again elected vice-president. The Democrats, however, won control of both houses of Congress.

Boyhood in Kansas

The name *Eisenhower* comes from German words meaning a kind of ironworker. The president's father, David Eisenhower, was descended from German immigrants who had settled in Pennsylvania during the 1730's. In 1878 the family moved to Abilene, Kan. The president's mother, Ida Elizabeth (Stover) Eisenhower, had moved from Virginia to Kansas in 1883.

Eisenhower's parents met at a United Brethren school in Lecompton, Kan. They were married in 1885. A few years later David Eisenhower moved his family from Abilene to Denison, Tex. There Dwight was born Oct. 14, 1890. Two years later the family returned to Abilene.

The future president, with his brothers Arthur, Edgar, Roy, Earl, and Milton, grew up on the old homestead of his grandfather Jacob Eisenhower. In 1947 this home became a national shrine. Family souvenirs and papers are housed in the Eisenhower Foundation Museum, opened at Abilene in 1954.

During his school days young Dwight was usually called Ike by his friends. The nickname stayed with him throughout his life. Ike's favorite school subjects were English, history, and geometry. In sports he starred in both basketball and football.

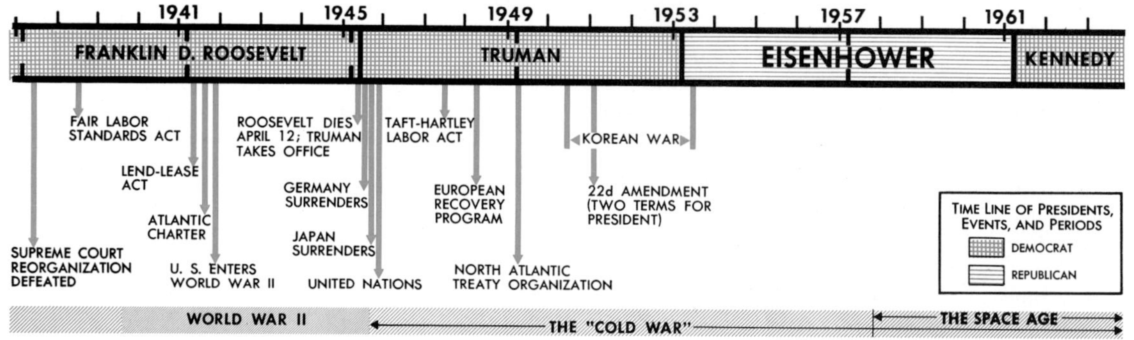

EISENHOWER'S ADMINISTRATIONS

1953–1961

Tenth Cabinet post added—Department of Health, Education, and Welfare (1953)

Armistice halts Korean war (1953)

Supreme Court declares racial segregation in public schools to be unconstitutional (1954)

United States joins Southeast Asia Treaty Organization (SEATO) (1954)

Eisenhower re-elected (1956)

Congress adopts Eisenhower Doctrine to aid Middle East (1957)

United States launches earth satellites (1958)

Alaska and Hawaii become states (1959)

Kennedy elected president (1960)

Early Military Career

Ike was graduated from Abilene High School in 1909. For the next two years he worked in a creamery to help pay Edgar's expenses at law school. In 1911 he took the entrance examination for the Military Academy at West Point. He ranked second in the tests but obtained the appointment when the top candidate failed to pass the physical examination.

The young cadet was a promising halfback on the academy football team but had to give up the game after injuring his knee. Eisenhower was graduated from West Point in 1915 and was commissioned a second lieutenant of infantry. He had ranked 61st in a class of 168 students.

Eisenhower was assigned to the 19th Infantry Regiment at Fort Sam Houston, Tex. In nearby San Antonio he met Mamie Doud of Denver. He married her July 1, 1916, the day he was promoted to first lieutenant. The Eisenhowers reared one son, John, who also became an officer in the Army. (*See also* White House, sections "Hostesses of the White House" and "Children in the White House.")

Soon after the United States entered World War I Eisenhower was promoted to captain. He later received the temporary rank of major and then lieutenant colonel. The war ended one day before he was to sail for France. For his work in organizing a tank corps he was awarded the Distinguished Service Medal, his highest Army decoration. (Two oak leaf clusters were added to this medal in World War II. He received the Navy Distinguished Service Medal in 1947.)

After World War I Eisenhower was returned to the rank of captain but was soon promoted to major. In the years that followed he had assignments in the United States, the Panama Canal Zone, and Europe. His administrative abilities earned him an executive post in Washington, D. C., from 1929 to 1933. When Gen. Douglas MacArthur became military adviser to the Philippines in 1935, Eisenhower became his assistant. Promoted to lieutenant colonel in 1936, he learned to fly and trained Filipino pilots.

Service in World War II

Eisenhower returned to duty in the United States in 1940. World War II brought him quick promotions to colonel and brigadier general in 1941 and to major general and lieutenant general in 1942. In July 1942 Army Chief of Staff Gen. George C. Marshall appointed Eisenhower to take over planning for the proposed invasion of North Africa.

In this position Eisenhower showed great talent for combining officers of different nations into a single team. He also proved he knew how to solve both military and political problems on an international scale. Eisenhower commanded the American forces in the invasion of North Africa Nov. 8, 1942, and soon became commander in chief of the whole operation. In February 1943 he was promoted to four-star general. During the year he launched the successful attacks on Tunisia, Sicily, and Italy.

In December 1943 Eisenhower became Supreme Commander, Allied Expeditionary Forces, in charge of the forthcoming invasion of France. His forces landed in Normandy June 6, 1944, in the greatest am-

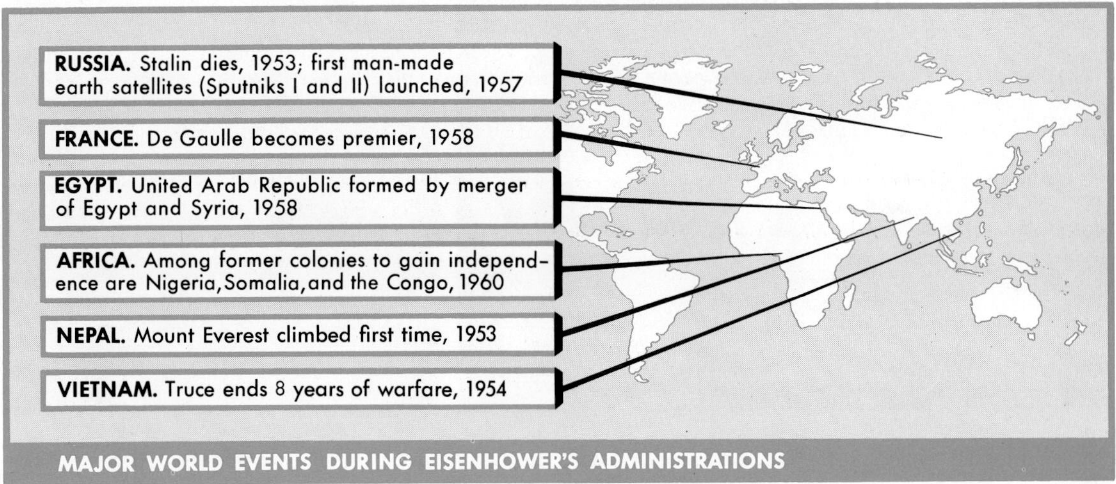
RUSSIA. Stalin dies, 1953; first man-made earth satellites (Sputniks I and II) launched, 1957
FRANCE. De Gaulle becomes premier, 1958
EGYPT. United Arab Republic formed by merger of Egypt and Syria, 1958
AFRICA. Among former colonies to gain independence are Nigeria, Somalia, and the Congo, 1960
NEPAL. Mount Everest climbed first time, 1953
VIETNAM. Truce ends 8 years of warfare, 1954
MAJOR WORLD EVENTS DURING EISENHOWER'S ADMINISTRATIONS

The day this picture was taken, July 1, 1916, Dwight Eisenhower married Mamie Doud and was promoted to first lieutenant.

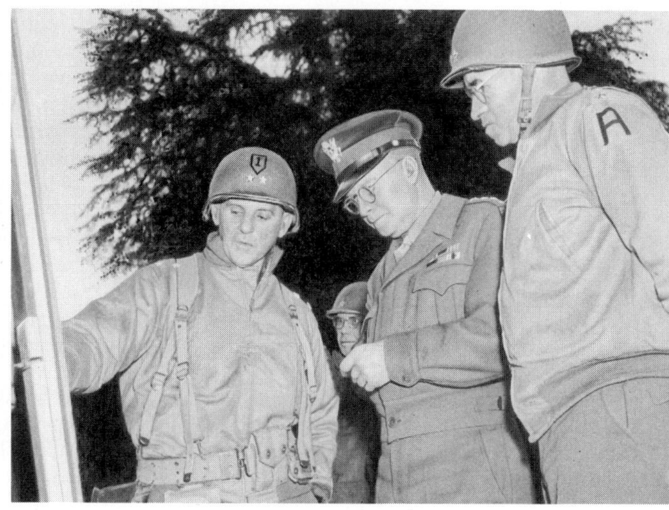

In 1944 Eisenhower, now a four-star general, directed the Allied invasion of France. At his left is Gen. Omar Bradley.

phibious operation in history. By the spring of 1945 the Allies had driven through the heart of Germany. The Nazis surrendered May 8 (*see* World War II). Meanwhile Eisenhower had received the highest American military rank, general of the Army (five stars), on Dec. 20, 1944.

Late in 1945 Eisenhower returned to Washington, D. C., to succeed General Marshall as Army chief of staff. In 1948 he retired from the Army to become president of Columbia University in New York City. The next year he obtained leave from this post to preside over the joint chiefs of staff during the unification of the armed forces. In that year also his report of the European campaign was published in a best-selling book, 'Crusade in Europe'.

Eisenhower returned to Columbia University in 1949. He took leave again late in 1950 to develop the defenses of Western Europe against possible Communist aggression. During the next 18 months he organized the various armed services of the North Atlantic Treaty Organization (NATO) into a unified combat group. This success increased his already high military and political standing throughout the free world.

Nomination and Election

During his army career Eisenhower had taken no part in politics and there was some uncertainty as to which party he favored. Early in 1952, however, he revealed publicly that he had always been a Republican. The general also said that he would run for president if he received a "clear-cut call to political duty." Several Republican leaders then entered his name in various state presidential primaries.

Relaxing from his duties as NATO commander in 1951, Eisenhower talked with his eldest grandchild, Dwight David.

In 1955 President Eisenhower addressed Congress. Vice-President Nixon is at the left; House Speaker Rayburn at right.

Wide World

The official voting residence of President Eisenhower was this farm near Gettysburg, Pa., which he bought in 1954.

In early election contests Eisenhower showed great political strength in New Hampshire, Minnesota, and Nebraska. Recognizing his rising popularity he resigned from the NATO command and retired from active duty with the Army. He then opened a vigorous campaign for the Republican presidential nomination with a speech at Abilene, Kan., June 4.

As a political campaigner Eisenhower was an immediate success. His expressive face and warm sincerity contributed much to his effectiveness as a public speaker. At the Republican convention in Chicago he won the nomination on the first ballot in a close race with Senator Robert Taft of Ohio. Senator Richard Nixon of California was selected as the nominee for vice-president.

Eisenhower's leadership and great personal charm united all factions of the Republican party behind his candidacy. Throughout the campaign he called for a firm, middle-of-the-road policy in both foreign and domestic affairs. In an effort to find a solution to the stalemated Korean war he dramatically promised: "I shall go to Korea."

On Nov. 4, 1952, Dwight Eisenhower was elected president by a landslide. He received almost 34 million popular votes, until that time the greatest number ever given an American candidate for political office. His electoral vote of 442 came from 39 states, including such traditionally Democratic states as Florida, Texas, and Virginia. His opponent, Adlai Stevenson, had a popular vote of about 27 million and an electoral vote of 89.

The general's sweeping victory helped his party to win control of the 83d Congress, although the Republican majority in both houses was small. The Republicans scored gains in most state and local elections.

Four weeks after his election as president, Dwight Eisenhower honored his most colorful campaign promise by making a special trip to Korea. In a closely guarded visit he toured the battlefront studying the possibilities of an honorable peace settlement.

The First Year in Office

Immediately after taking office on Jan. 20, 1953, President Eisenhower made clear his intentions to work for world peace. He pledged the United States to a constant search for an honorable settlement of international problems.

In domestic affairs the president started a policy of "progressive conservatism." He tried to eliminate or reduce many activities previously carried out by the federal government. One of his first acts was to lift the ceiling imposed on wages in 1951. Then price controls were either removed or allowed to expire. To bring the budget near balance Eisenhower helped block some tax cuts and ordered federal spending reduced to about 74 billion dollars a year.

Early in 1953 the 83d Congress extended for two years the president's power to reorganize government agencies in order to secure greater economy and efficiency. Under this act the chief executive transformed the Federal Security Agency into the Department of Health, Education, and Welfare and gave it cabinet rank. The first head of the department was Oveta Culp Hobby, the second woman Cabinet member in United States history. Frances Perkins had served as secretary of labor in 1933–45.

The first sharply partisan issue to confront the new administration was the tidelands oil bill—an act to give coastal states title to their offshore areas out to historic state boundaries. (For most states, this is three miles; for Florida and Texas, it is about ten and a half miles.) Democratic opposition delayed passage of a bill giving title to these oil-rich lands to the states, but the act was finally approved May 22, 1953. The first session of the 83d Congress also voted to admit an additional 214,000 European refugees into the United States.

Late in July the president formally announced the

signing of an armistice in Korea. He warned, however, that the United States must remain on guard against the possibilities of other Communist aggressions. This warning received added emphasis August 8 when Russia revealed that it had developed an H-bomb.

In domestic affairs, Gov. Earl Warren of California became chief justice of the Supreme Court October 5. He succeeded Frederick M. Vinson, who had died the previous month.

Problems and Issues in 1954

An important domestic issue in 1954 was the work of Republican Senator Joseph McCarthy of Wisconsin, chairman of an investigating subcommittee. Many people thought McCarthy's tactics (labeled "McCarthyism") were a necessary part of his anti-Communist investigations. Others charged that McCarthy violated democratic principles. Late in the year the Senate by a vote of 67 to 22 "condemned" McCarthy on two counts for abusing other senators.

The Supreme Court made news May 17 when it ruled unanimously that racial segregation in public schools was unconstitutional. This nullified the doctrine of "separate-but-equal" facilities. The verdict affected 17 states in which segregation was compulsory and 4 states in which segregation was permitted.

Meanwhile the second session of the 83d Congress reduced excise taxes by about one billion dollars a year. Congress also voted the most comprehensive tax revision in 75 years. This measure decreased the national revenue by another 1.3 billion dollars. As a result of these reductions in federal income, Congress was forced to raise the national debt limit from 275 to 281 billion dollars.

In April 1954 President Eisenhower signed a bill establishing an Air Force Academy, similar to the Army's West Point and the Navy's Annapolis. The site chosen for the new school was near Colorado Springs, Colo. Five weeks later Congress authorized the United States to join Canada in constructing the St. Lawrence Seaway, a project recommended by every president since Warren Harding.

In other action the 83d Congress outlawed the Communist party in the United States and tightened several security regulations. Despite Democratic opposition Congress also enacted an Eisenhower-supported bill to provide flexible supports of farm prices (between $82\frac{1}{2}$ and 90 per cent of parity).

The increasing threat of Communist aggression in the Far East led to a meeting of eight nations at Manila. On Sept. 8, 1954, these nations formed the Southeast Asia Treaty Organization (SEATO) for the collective defense of the area. Member nations were the United States, Australia, France, Great Britain, New Zealand, Pakistan, the Philippine Islands, and Thailand.

In November 1954 the voters of the nation went to the polls to elect a new House of Representatives and one third of the Senate. Late in the campaign the president made a vigorous plea for the election of a

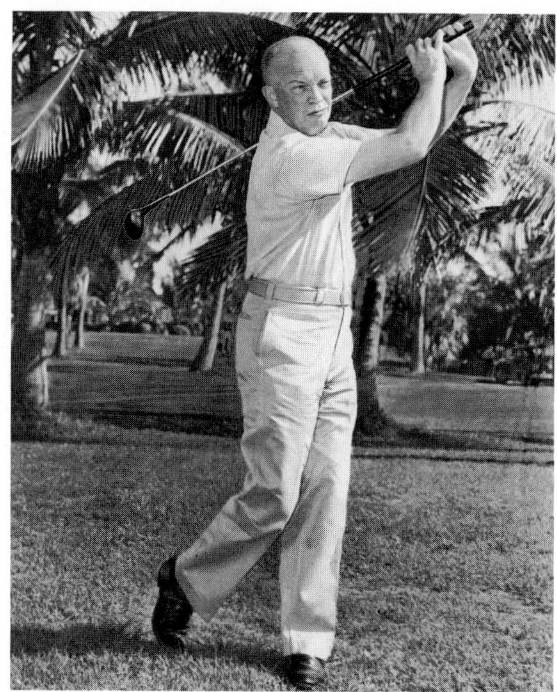

Beginning in his army days Dwight Eisenhower was an enthusiastic golfer. Here he practices his swing at Coral Gables, Fla.

Republican Congress. Despite his efforts, the Democrats won control of both houses of Congress in a close election. They also won 8 new governorships to bring their total to 27.

The election results seemed to indicate a dissatisfaction with the Republican party rather than with the president himself. Many political observers believed that only Eisenhower's campaigning prevented an even larger Democratic victory. In addition, a public opinion poll revealed that more than two thirds of all the voters thought the president was doing a good job.

The Nation in 1955

One of the first acts of the 84th Congress was to increase the salaries of Senate and House members and federal judges (*see* table in United States Government). Congress also increased the minimum wage for workers in interstate commerce from 75 cents to $1.00 an hour and provided pay raises for military personnel. Another successful project of the Eisenhower administration was a three-year extension of the reciprocal trade agreements law. This measure was enacted by Congress in June.

Early in 1955 two important appointments by the President became effective. Judge John Marshall Harlan of New York was named to the Supreme Court to replace Justice Robert H. Jackson, who had died the year before. Harold Stassen was named to the newly created post of special assistant to the president for disarmament. The position was to have the rank of a Cabinet office.

AP/Wide World

In 1956 President Eisenhower and Vice-President Nixon accepted renomination by the Republican party in San Francisco.

A medical breakthrough came on April 12, 1955, when a poliomyelitis vaccine was pronounced a success. The vaccine was discovered by Dr. Jonas E. Salk of Pittsburgh. (*See also* Salk; Vaccines.)

On May 31 the Supreme Court gave its long-awaited ruling on the means of eliminating racial segregation in public schools. The Court voted unanimously that segregation problems should be handled by federal district courts and by local school authorities.

The continuation of the Cold War was a grave problem for the president (*see* Cold War). In an effort to ease world tensions, the heads of the Big Four powers—the United States, Great Britain, France, and the Soviet Union—met at Geneva, Switzerland, in July 1955. (It was the first top-level conference since the 1945 meeting at Potsdam, Germany.) Although the president tried to find peaceful solutions to international problems, hostile feelings continued between West and East.

On Sept. 24, 1955, President Eisenhower suffered a heart attack at the summer White House in Denver, Colo. He made a steady recovery and after seven weeks was released from the hospital. After additional rest he resumed his duties in Washington, D. C.

Events of 1956

After the president's heart attack there was much uncertainty about whether he would seek another term in office. This speculation was ended on Feb. 29, 1956, when President Eisenhower announced his candidacy for re-election. He told the voters that his health was good enough to carry on his duties for an additional four years. He remained determined to run despite an intestinal disorder that necessitated an operation in June 1956.

In its second session the 84th Congress passed a compromise farm bill that had flexible price supports and soil-bank features. Congress also voted a grant of 32.9 billion dollars for improved interstate highways.

In the election campaign Eisenhower stressed his moderate approach to problems. He was re-elected by the largest margin achieved by any Republican president up to that time.

Second Term

In his second administration the president faced serious problems abroad and at home. Abroad, the chief trouble spot was the Suez Canal area (*see* Suez Canal). To guard against Communist aggression in that region, the president proposed military and economic aid to Middle East countries. Congress adopted this plan, called the Eisenhower Doctrine, in March 1957.

At home the administration's proposed 1957–58 budget of more than 71 billion dollars was cut by Congress to about 68 billion dollars. Congress did, however, pass the administration's civil-rights bill. This was the first such bill passed since Reconstruction days. It created a civil-rights commission within the Department of Justice. It also gave the federal government authority to act in support of the Supreme Court's ban on school segregation.

AP/Wide World

Here President and Mrs. Eisenhower are riding in the second inaugural parade in Washington, D. C.

Shown at a reception for Queen Elizabeth II are, left to right, Prince Philip, Mrs. Eisenhower, the British queen, and President Eisenhower.

In September Arkansas's governor, Orval E. Faubus, used the National Guard to prevent the admission of nine black students to a high school in Little Rock. The president tried to settle the problem through negotiation. When this failed, he ordered federal troops into Little Rock and federalized the Arkansas National Guard.

In October and November the Soviet Union launched two artificial Earth satellites, Sputniks I and II. The Soviet Union also said it had successfully developed an intercontinental ballistic missile. President Eisenhower then made a series of talks to reassure the country regarding national security. Eisenhower also appointed James R. Killian, Jr., special assistant for science and technology.

British Visitors; Cabinet Changes

Great Britain's Queen Elizabeth II and her husband, Prince Philip, visited the United States and Canada in October. British Prime Minister Harold Macmillan also came to Washington after the Soviet satellites were launched.

There were major changes in the president's Cabinet in 1957. George M. Humphrey resigned as secretary of the treasury. Appointed in his place was Robert B. Anderson. Charles E. Wilson resigned as secretary of defense. He was succeeded by Neil H. McElroy. Attorney General Herbert Brownell, Jr., resigned and was succeeded by Deputy Attorney General William P. Rogers. Two new Supreme Court justices were appointed. They were William J. Brennan, Jr., who replaced Sherman Minton, and Charles E. Whittaker, who succeeded Stanley F. Reed.

On November 25 the White House announced that Eisenhower had suffered a chill during welcoming ceremonies for King Mohammed V of Morocco. Physicians said the president had suffered a mild stroke.

Once again the president's recovery was rapid. He was able to attend the mid-December meeting of the North Atlantic Treaty Organization in Paris. At this meeting a general agreement was reached to arm Western Europe with United States nuclear missiles.

Events During 1958

President Eisenhower announced that Army scientists had successfully placed an artificial Earth satellite, Explorer I, in orbit on Jan. 31, 1958. On March 17 Navy scientists also launched a satellite, Vanguard I. The Air Force launched an Atlas intercontinental ballistic missile on August 2. More than 200 rockets were also launched during the 18-month International Geophysical year that ended in 1958. (*See also* Space Travel.)

During his second term in office, President Eisenhower suggested a major change in the organization of the Department of Defense. The plan provided for the merging of operational Army, Navy, and Air Force units under unified commands. They would report directly to the secretary of defense. There would be an increase in the defense secretary's control over strategic planning and military operations.

President Eisenhower also asked Congress to create a civilian national aeronautics and space agency to administer the country's nonmilitary space research and exploration projects. The new National Aeronautics and Space Administration (NASA) was established in July.

Recession Problems

The administration faced serious economic recession problems in 1957 and 1958. In October 1957 stock prices on the New York Stock Exchange fell in the sharpest decline since Eisenhower's heart attack in 1955. Industrial production also declined. Unemployment rose to more than 5 million in the spring of 1958. Consumer prices, however, rose to record levels.

Major tax cuts were considered, but Eisenhower refused to present a tax cut proposal to Congress. The government did furnish funds to be made avail-

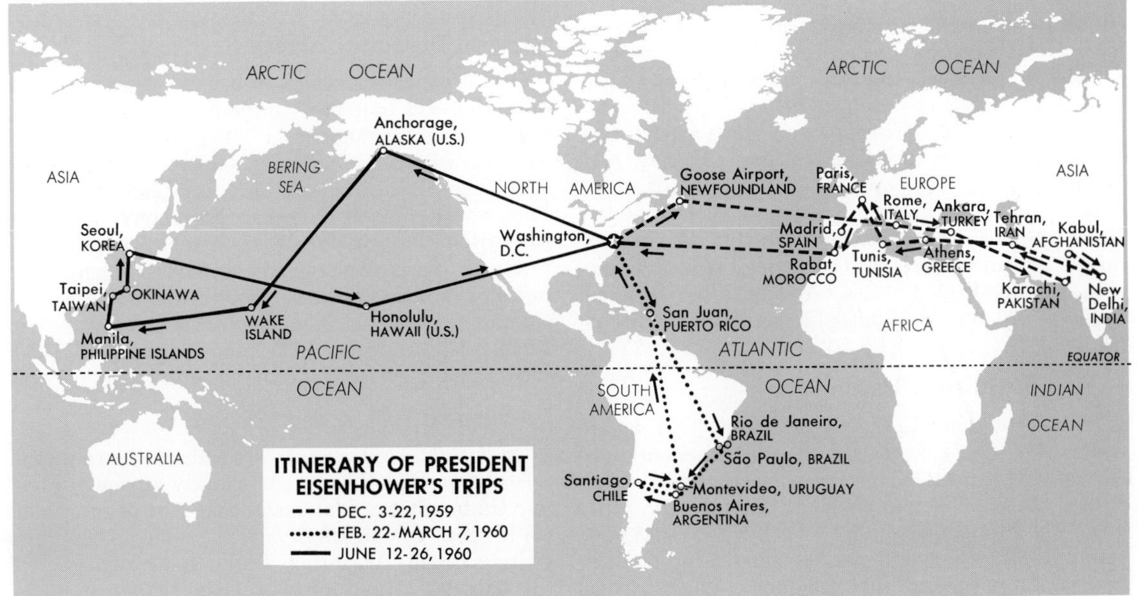

Dwight D. Eisenhower was one of the most widely traveled American presidents. He traveled more than 100,000 miles (160,000 kilometers) overseas during his two terms in office. He delivered goodwill messages to many nations.

able to the states for those whose unemployment compensation had run out. By July 1958 government economists said the nation was recovering from its worst recession since the end of World War II.

Summit Meeting

The Middle East continued to be a trouble spot in 1958. During this difficult period Soviet Premier Nikita S. Khrushchev suggested a high-level East-West meeting.

Eisenhower, however, said that high-level meetings were worthwhile "only if there were reasonable grounds for expecting that they would bring beneficial results." In June the Kremlin-ordered execution of Hungary's former premier, Imre Nagy, further dimmed the prospects of an early summit meeting.

Strauss and Adams Resign

Lewis L. Strauss, an original member of the Atomic Energy Commission in 1946, quit as a member and chairman June 30. To succeed Strauss, Eisenhower named John A. McCone, a shipping executive from California. In 1959 Congress refused to accept the president's appointment of Strauss as secretary of commerce.

A member of the president's official family voluntarily appeared before a Congressional investigating committee in June 1958. He was Sherman Adams, assistant to the president. Adams admitted he had accepted gifts and hospitality from Bernard Goldfine, a textile manufacturer. On September 22 Adams resigned. Major General Wilton B. Persons, former deputy assistant to the president, succeeded Adams.

In October Supreme Court Justice Harold H. Burton retired. Eisenhower appointed Judge Potter Stewart to take his place.

Alaska and Hawaii Statehood

In June final Congressional approval was given to making Alaska the 49th state of the Union. The president, who had urged its passage, signed the Alaska statehood bill on July 7. (*See also* Alaska.)

Also in July President Eisenhower and Secretary of State John Foster Dulles visited Canada. The "good neighbor" visit was made at the invitation of Canadian Prime Minister John Diefenbaker.

A few days after his return to Washington the president ordered the United States Marines to Lebanon at the request of President Camille Chamoun for armed assistance following a revolt in Iraq. (*See also* Iraq; Lebanon.)

In March 1959 Congressional approval was given to Hawaii statehood. The president signed the statehood bill March 18 and Hawaii was admitted to the Union on August 21. Alaska had officially become a state on January 3. (*See also* Hawaii.)

Secretary of State John Foster Dulles, ill with cancer, resigned on April 15. He was succeeded by Christian A. Herter. One of the new secretary's first duties was to attend a United States-sponsored meeting of the Big Four foreign ministers at Geneva, Switzerland. The meeting had been arranged by Dulles and President Eisenhower to study new ways of achieving world peace. It ended in failure.

Emphasis on World Peace Continues

Despite this unsuccessful effort at Geneva, the president continued to emphasize the achievement of world peace as one of the prime objectives of his administration's foreign policy. In order to promote its accomplishment as well as to achieve better understanding between the United States and other countries, the president initiated a program of personal diplomacy. He proceeded to carry it out through a series of good-will tours to different parts of the world.

On Aug. 26, 1959, Eisenhower began a 12-day trip to Europe. He visited Great Britain, France, and West Germany. His purpose was to discuss Western policy with Allied leaders. He assured them that the United States would stanchly support this policy during an anticipated visit of Soviet Premier Khrushchev to the United States. Arranging the visit had been one of Dulles' last official acts. He died on May 24, 1959.

Host to the Russian Premier

From September 15 through September 27 President Eisenhower was official host to the Russian leader, whose visit included a transcontinental tour of the United States. The tour ended at Camp David, Md., where the two men held talks. They agreed that outstanding issues between nations should be handled by peaceful means and that general disarmament was the most important question of the day.

The Soviet premier also agreed to withdraw his previously issued ultimatum demanding that the Western Allies get out of Berlin. Following these discussions it was announced that President Eisenhower had been invited to pay a state visit to the Soviet Union the following year.

Wearing a Hawaiian lei, the president reviews an honor guard of troops during a visit to Honolulu. Eisenhower was en route to the United States following a tour of the Far East in 1960.

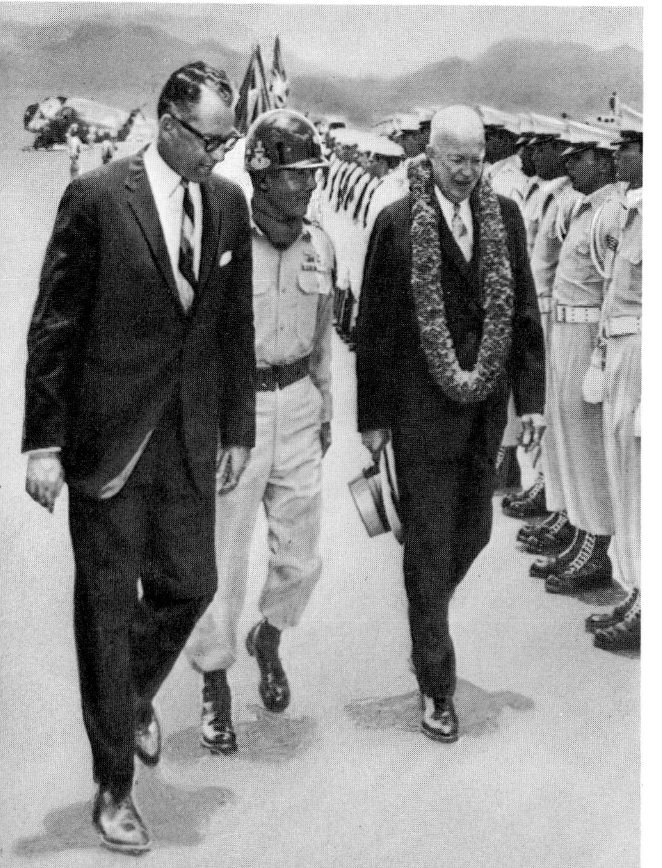

Personal Diplomacy Abroad

On December 3 Eisenhower began a 19-day, 22,000-mile good-will tour of 11 nations in Europe, Africa, the Middle East, and Asia. The countries he visited were Tunisia, Morocco, Italy, Greece, Turkey, Pakistan, India, Iran, Afghanistan, Spain, and France. In Paris on Dec. 19–21 President Eisenhower met with the British, French, and West German leaders.

At the Paris conference Eisenhower suggested a series of summit meetings between the Western powers and the Soviet Union. An invitation was sent to Premier Khrushchev. He accepted, and May 16, 1960, was the date set for the conference to begin in Paris.

Presidential Visit to South America

On Feb. 22, 1960, Eisenhower embarked on a tour of South America. He was particularly anxious to bolster United States relations in that part of the world. On his tour the president covered some 15,000 miles visiting Brazil, Argentina, Chile, and Uruguay. On this trip, during which he also visited Puerto Rico, he delivered six major speeches and was enthusiastically cheered by more than 3 million people. At the conclusion of his tour, on March 7, he renewed the United States pledge contained in the Rio de Janeiro Treaty of 1947, which calls for mutual defense of the Americas.

In the meantime plans for holding the East-West summit conference had been completed. The participants included President Eisenhower, Soviet Premier Khrushchev, British Prime Minister Harold Macmillan, and French President Charles de Gaulle. Among the major issues on the agenda were the problems of Germany and world disarmament. The Western nations had agreed on their policies in a series of meetings in Washington, D. C., April 12–14. The foreign ministers of Great Britain, France, West Germany, Italy, Canada, and the United States had attended.

Cold War Tensions Renewed

On May 1, 1960, however, shortly before the president's departure for Paris, an American U-2 observation plane was brought down deep inside Russia. Its pilot was imprisoned by the Russians, who accused him of being a spy. Khrushchev bitterly attacked the United States and President Eisenhower because of the incident, which he called an "aggressive provocation aimed at wrecking the summit conference."

Khrushchev demanded that Eisenhower apologize for the U-2 flight. He also insisted that the president guarantee all such flights would cease. Eisenhower was also called upon to punish those responsible for the May 1 spy-plane incident.

Eisenhower's announcement that all flights over Russian territory had been canceled failed to appease the Soviet premier. At the opening session of the Paris summit meeting, the belligerent attitude of Khrushchev wrecked any hope of continuing the conference. The Russian leader also withdrew his invitation to President Eisenhower to visit Russia in June.

The President Continues His Peace Efforts

Despite the collapse of the summit meeting, the president continued his policy of personal diplomacy. In June he again went abroad. On this tour he visited Alaska, The Philippines, Taiwan, Okinawa, South Korea, and Hawaii. A scheduled stop in Tokyo, Japan, was canceled, however. The Japanese capital had been the scene of a series of riots protesting the proposed ratification of a new United States-Japan mutual security treaty. The pro-Western government of Japanese Prime Minister Nobusuke Kishi admitted that it was unable to guarantee the president's safety. The treaty, however, was ratified by the Japanese Diet on June 19, 1960. (*See also* Japan, section on History.)

Other Policies of the Administration

Earlier in the year Eisenhower had approved a program to improve United States relations with Panama. It included pay raises for unskilled and semiskilled Canal Zone employees and a plan to place more Panamanians in supervisory positions (*see* Panama; Panama Canal). In July 1960, because of anti-American activities in Cuba, the administration abandoned its position of tolerance toward Premier Fidel Castro's regime. On Jan. 3, 1961, during the last weeks of his presidency, Eisenhower broke off diplomatic relations with Cuba (*see* Cuba).

In domestic affairs Eisenhower sought to hold down inflation in the final months of his administration. He checked spending by Congress and by bureau and department heads in a drive to balance the budget. The Democrats, however, were in firm control of Congress. Eisenhower, though a lame-duck president, was able to win support for much of his program.

Eisenhower in Retirement

John F. Kennedy, a Democrat, was elected Eisenhower's successor. Eisenhower cooperated fully with Kennedy in making smooth the country's transition from one president to another. Kennedy was inaugurated on Jan. 20, 1961, and Eisenhower returned to his farm at Gettysburg, Pa. Eisenhower remained active in politics.

In 1962 he dedicated the 3-million-dollar Eisenhower Presidential Library in Abilene, Kan., which houses the bulk of his personal and state papers. He made a sentimental journey to Europe in 1963.

After a long period of illness and a hospital confinement of almost one year, Eisenhower died of heart failure on March 28, 1969, at the Walter Reed General Hospital in Washington. A three-day state funeral was held in Washington. Eisenhower's body lay in state in the rotunda of the national Capitol, where President Nixon delivered a eulogy. Many high-ranking officers of the World War II Allied forces attended the funeral rites, including Gen. Charles de Gaulle. Eisenhower's body was then moved to Abilene for burial in the chapel at the Eisenhower Center. In 1971 Eisenhower became the first president to be honored by having his image on a dollar coin.

BIBLIOGRAPHY FOR DWIGHT D. EISENHOWER

Ambrose, S.E. Ike: Abilene to Berlin (Harper, 1973).
DeGregorio, W.A. The Complete Book of U.S. Presidents (Dembner, 1984).
Eisenhower, David. Eisenhower at War: 1943–1945 (Random, 1986).
Lee, R.A. Dwight D. Eisenhower (Nelson-Hall, 1981).
Lovelace, D.W. Ike Eisenhower, rev. ed. (Harper, 1969).
Neal, Steve. The Eisenhowers, rev. ed. (Univ. Press of Kan., 1984).
Richardson, Elmo. The Presidency of Dwight D. Eisenhower (Univ. Press of Kan., 1979).

EISENSTEIN, Sergei (1898–1948). He has been called the epic poet of the Soviet cinema, and many consider Sergei Eisenstein to be the finest craftsman ever to direct motion pictures. His films 'Potemkin', released in 1925, 'Alexander Nevsky' (1938), and 'Ivan the Terrible' (Part One, 1944; Part Two, completed 1946, released 1958) are classics of movie art.

Eisenstein was born in Riga, Latvia, on Jan. 23, 1898. Twelve years later the family settled in Saint Petersburg (now Leningrad), where he attended the Institute of Civil Engineering and the School of Fine Arts. During the Russian Revolution he helped organize defense and provided entertainment for the troops. Following the war he became assistant decorator at the Theater of the People. Soon he was chief decorator and then co-director. His first film, 'Strike', was released in 1924. It was about the czar's repression of workers. In this and other movies he proposed a new way of filming—what he called the "montage of attractions"—in which arbitrarily chosen images were presented not in chronological sequence but in whatever way they created the maximum psychological impact.

During his career Eisenstein worked in Paris and Mexico as well as Moscow. Among his other films were 'October', or 'Ten Days That Shook the World' (1928), the story of the 1917 Revolution; 'Old and New' (1929), on Soviet agriculture; and 'Sentimental Melody' (1929). He also wrote several books on directing. Eisenstein died in Moscow on Feb. 11, 1948.

Sergei Eisenstein lounges on the set of 'October' in 1927.

Sovfoto

ELBE RIVER. After the Rhine, the Elbe River is Germany's most significant commercial waterway. It is 724 miles (1,165 kilometers) long, with about 525 miles (845 kilometers) navigable for large ships. More than 350 miles (565 kilometers) of the river are in East Germany. Its drainage basin covers 55,620 square miles (144,055 square kilometers). Located here are Germany's chief sugar beet fields and many grain farms, pasture lands, forests, mines, and factories. Cargoes on the river include coal, lumber, salt, fertilizers (potash), sugar, wheat, rye, cattle food, paper, glass, and machinery. These total millions of tons of shipping each year.

The Elbe rises on the southern side of the Riesengebirge, or Giant Mountains, in Czechoslovakia. It curves westward and northward and then breaks through the Erzgebirge, or Ore Mountains, into Saxony. The river continues northwestward across the German Plain. At Hamburg it flows into the North Sea through a broad fan-shaped mouth, or estuary, 75 miles (120 kilometers) long.

Navigation for large boats begins at Melnik, Czechoslovakia. The chief ports downstream include Aussig, Dresden, Riesa, Wallwitzhaven (the port for the city of Dessau), Schönebeck, Magdeburg, and Hamburg, which is one of Europe's greatest seaports.

A large volume of freight enters the Elbe from its three tributaries—the Moldau, or Vltava, the Saale, and the Havel. At Magdeburg the Mittelland-Kanal (which means Midland Canal) connects the Elbe with the Rhine, the Ems, and the Weser to the west and with the Oder to the east. The Elbe-Trave Canal leads to the Baltic Sea port of Lübeck, and the Kiel Canal links the river to Kiel, Germany's former naval port on the Baltic.

The Elbe-Saale line has played a significant role in the history of the north European lowland. It marked the 8th-century limit of Charlemagne's conquests. At the end of World War II, a point on the river near Torgau was the meetingplace of the United States and Soviet armies. Today it forms part of the boundary between East and West Germany.

ELBURZ MOUNTAINS. A major mountain range in northern Iran, the Elburz Mountains extend from west to east parallel with the south shore of the Caspian Sea in a crescent-shaped arc for 560 miles (900 kilometers). Its steep, rocky slopes divide the coastal plains of the Caspian Sea from the desertlike central Iranian plateau. Many of its peaks rise more than 10,000 feet (3,000 meters); the highest is the volcanic Mount Damavand at 18,934 feet (5,771 meters). (For map, *see* Iran.)

A striking feature of the Elburz range is the contrast between its northern and southern slopes. The northern slopes have heavy snowfall and rainfall—from 40 to 80 inches (100 to 200 centimeters)—resulting in a humid forest that extends the whole length of the chain. In contrast, the southern slopes share the dry character of the Iranian plateau. Annual precipitation varies from 11 to 20 inches (28 to 50 centimeters) and is very irregular.

A major resource of the mountains is the water of its rivers, which is used for irrigation, for generating hydroelectric energy, and for supplying Tehran, Iran's capital city, with water. Major dams include the Safid Rud, Karaj, and Jajrud. The natural forests cover more than 8 million acres (3 million hectares), of which some 3 million can be exploited commercially for timber and other uses.

The Elburz Mountains have played an important part in Iranian history and legend. Alexander the Great crossed the range after defeating the Persian monarch Darius III in the 4th century BC. In medieval times the mountains sheltered the religious sect known as the Assassins. For two centuries the Assassins, under the leadership of their chiefs, each known as the "old man of the mountain," carried out acts of terrorism and murder under the influence of the drug hashish.

ELEANOR OF AQUITAINE (1122?–1204). In an age known largely for the exploits of kings, princes, dukes, and their warriors, Eleanor of Aquitaine stood out as one of the most remarkable of women. She was the wife and mother of kings. Beautiful, strong-willed, tenacious, and powerful, she was a dominant political force in the Europe of her time.

Eleanor was born about 1122. Her father was William X, duke of Aquitaine. When he died in 1137 she inherited his domain, which was larger than that ruled by the king of France. The same year she married the heir to the French throne, who became King Louis VII a month afterward. During their 15-year marriage, she exerted considerable influence upon the running of the country and even accompanied him on the Second Crusade from 1147 to 1149. His jealousy led to separation, and the marriage was annulled; but she regained possession of Aquitaine. In 1152 she married Henry Plantagenet, who became Henry II of England two years later. They had eight children, among whom were Richard I the Lion-Hearted and John, both of whom became kings of England. This union brought together England, Aquitaine, Anjou, and Normandy under one rule. Two centuries later England's French possessions became an underlying cause of the Hundred Years' War.

As in France, Eleanor was active in running the kingdom. But after the revolt of her sons against Henry II, she was kept in semi-confinement from 1174 to 1189, when Henry died. After her release she became active in affairs of state under her son Richard I and, after his death without an heir in 1199, under John. She worked for peace between France and England and helped preserve John's French domains. Eleanor died on April 1, 1204, in the monastery at Fontevrault in Anjou.

AP/Wide World

United States President Ronald W. Reagan waits for the cheering and applause of delegates at the 1984 Republican convention in Dallas to end so he can make his speech accepting his party's nomination for a second four-year term.

ELECTIONS

ELECTIONS. Alternatives are what elections are all about. The word election is derived from the Latin verb *legere,* meaning "to choose." If there is to be a real choice, there must be alternatives. If public officials are being chosen, there must be at least two candidates. If an issue is being decided, there must be the opportunity to vote either yes or no.

Elections and Representative Government

There are two kinds of countries in the world: those made up of people who form governments to run their public affairs, and those in which government runs the affairs of the people without their consent. Both types usually have elections, and both claim that elected officials represent the people.

The difference between the two types of elections is the presence or lack of alternatives. In constitutional democracies—such as Great Britain, Canada, Australia, New Zealand, Japan, India, the United States, and the countries of Western Europe—there are two or more political parties, each of which runs slates of candidates for office. The people are allowed to vote for the candidates of their choice, those who the people believe will do the best job.

In other nations that call themselves republics or democracies—such as the Soviet Union, China, North and South Korea, Chile, Cuba, and the Eastern European communist regimes—opposition parties are either outlawed entirely or are severely limited. In the most extreme example, the Soviet Union, there is only one candidate for each office on the ballot. Such an election cannot therefore be a choice among alternatives. It can only be a seal of approval on choices already made by the government. Those who are elected in this process do not represent the people in the government; they represent the government to the people.

Real Representation

That every citizen of a nation should be allowed to vote for public officials is a fairly modern idea. It dates from the 18th century, when such writers as John Locke, Jean-Jacques Rousseau, and Thomas Jefferson voiced the idea of civil rights for all citizens. The events of the American and French revolutions enabled this idea to be put into practice. (*See also* Constitution; Democracy.)

Originally, from the ancient world until the early modern period, what was represented in government were certain wealthy and powerful vested interests: landowners, nobles, corporations, and churches. The common people did not count for much in the councils of government. They simply did the work and supplied the military manpower.

During the 19th century the suffrage (who is allowed to vote) was gradually extended. It was first extended to the working classes of Europe and the United States—but to males only. Women won the right to vote in many states of the United States but not in presidential elections until 1920. At about the same time they won the vote in Belgium, The Netherlands, Germany, Poland, and Canada. Not until 1928 did women get the right to vote in Great Britain. In France, Italy, Japan, and some other countries this did not happen until after World War II. In the Arab nations women's right to vote is still restricted by

Jean-Claude Francolon—Gamma/Liaison

François Mitterrand, during his victorious 1981 campaign for the presidency of France, visited a small woodworking firm at Autechaux, near Besançon.

law. Communist countries generally have universal suffrage for all adults.

In some countries—the United States and Britain—voting rights have been extended to 18-year olds. It was decided that since so many of them serve in the armed forces and receive higher education, their role in the social order cannot be denied. (*See also* Suffrage; Women's Rights.)

Types of Elections

Elections may be categorized in several ways. They include what is being voted for, the level of government at which the voting takes place, and whether the election is held to select candidates or to elect public officials.

Officeholders and issues. When a voter enters the voting booth, the names of individuals seeking public office are found on the ballot. There may also be a number of public issues to vote for or against: local tax increases for schools are among the most common. (For coverage of issue-oriented elections, *see* Initiative, Referendum, and Recall.)

With regard to officeholders, elections give them the right to make public policy decisions. Voters, therefore, want to know what the candidates think about public issues. Every society is made up of people with a great diversity of interests—farmers, bankers, blue collar workers, teachers, lawyers, corporation managers, small businessmen, to name a few—and each of these groups forms what is called a constituency. Every candidate running for public office must appeal to the constituencies within his district, state, province, or nation. An individual seeking to be president of the United States, for example, must appeal to all of the interests within the country—or at least to a good many of them—in order to win an election. The prime minister of Great Britain and the chancellor of West Germany, however, are elected to their respective legislatures from local constituencies and after election are chosen to head the government if their parties win. Therefore it is the party program that must appeal to the majority of the electorate, or voting public (*see* Cabinet Government).

In many countries the various interests and constituencies are represented by political parties. In the United States there are only two major parties, the Democratic and Republican; but in most countries there are several parties competing for the allegiance of the voters. Political parties provide the pools of talent from which candidates are drawn. Those who belong to a party believe that its candidates can best serve the public interest, if elected. Once elected, of course, an officeholder feels many pressures, some of which may result in broken campaign promises (*see* Political Parties; Lobbying).

Levels of election. In every large democratic nation, elections take place at a variety of levels: local, state, and national. A local election may be a citywide affair, or it may only include part of a city. A special aldermanic election, for instance, takes place only within one ward, or election district, of a city. In some countries there may be an election in one province or state without the rest of the country being affected.

American Elections

In the United States nearly every political unit has elections—from small towns, cities, counties, and states, to the nation itself. There is, however, only one national election every four years, and it is for the offices of president and vice-president. The rest of the general elections, which are held every two years, are really simultaneous state elections. Candidates are elected for all of the House of Representatives, one third of the Senate, and a variety of state and local offices.

Geographical districts. Most candidates for public office run in specific geographical districts. Each member of the House of Representatives, for instance, is elected from a district within a state. The size of the district is based on population. As states gain or lose population, they are redistricted and gain or lose representatives. The same is true of most large cities. They are divided into wards, and each ward is entitled to one representative—usually called an alderman.

At-large elections. Sometimes, however, candidates are elected at-large. In an at-large aldermanic election, the candidate who wins does not represent a ward but all the city residents. A state legislator at-large represents all the people of the state, not just one legislative district. Such elections are not common, but they are occasionally used to avoid district or geographical representation in a legislative body.

Primaries. Those who will become candidates for office can be chosen by political conventions—both state and national; they may be chosen by meetings of party leaders; or they may be elected. Elections to select candidates are called primaries. Primary means "first," or "preliminary." Primaries emerged as a means for allowing the people to choose their own candidates rather than have candidates foisted on them by party bosses.

An election in which all members of a political party are entitled to select candidates is called a direct primary. The first one was held in Crawford County, Pa., in 1842 by the Democratic party. As corruption in government grew toward the end of the 19th century, there were increased demands for primary elections. Under the leadership of Governor Robert M. LaFollette, Wisconsin passed a direct primary law in 1903. In some later cases an indirect primary was preferred. In an indirect primary the voters choose delegates to a state party convention, and the convention chooses the candidates.

States have different ways of running primaries. Some have what are called open primaries, in which voters can ask for a ballot for either political party. They may vote for one party in one primary and for another party in the next. Other states have closed primaries; here the voters can only vote in the primary of the political party of which they are registered members.

To be listed as a candidate on the primary ballot, a person must file a declaration of intent and party affiliation with an official of the city, county, or state government. Usually a filing fee must be paid, and in some cases it is necessary to turn in a petition signed by voters who favor the candidate. The number of signers is fixed by law.

California had an exception to this practice. From 1913 until 1959 it allowed what is called cross-filing. Cross-filing allowed candidates to file for office on the primary ballots of all political parties. If they won in each party, they were automatically elected to office.

Primary elections have come to play a significant role in presidential elections. Potential candidates begin two or three years before a general election to travel the states that have primaries, seeking to persuade the electorate to their views. Some of the primary elections are popularity contests only—no delegates, or people pledged to a candidate, to a national convention are chosen. In others the voters choose a party ballot and, from the names listed, choose the candidate of their choice or convention delegates pledged to their candidate. One of the earliest primaries in election years is New Hampshire's. Potential candidates eagerly await its outcome because—as of 1984—no one who lost the New Hampshire primary had ever won a presidential election.

Election Practices

Since the mid-19th century, election procedures have become fairly standardized and formal in the large democratic nations. Voters are registered according to where they live; they are entitled to vote in secret; use of the ballot makes secret voting possible; and some societies make voting compulsory by law.

Secret voting depends for its success on most people's being able to read and being willing to make their own decisions in private. Those who cannot read must have help in marking a ballot, and the helper might vote for anyone—the illiterate voter would never know the difference. Secret voting also requires that citizens stop taking instructions on voting from social superiors. They must think for themselves how their interests can best be served. Secret voting also

Large crowds wait to vote during a national election. Once in a booth, voters make their selections by pushing down small levers next to the names of candidates. Opening the booth curtain registers the voter's choices.

John Lopinot—Black Star

makes it more difficult for committed party workers to "deliver" the vote, or get large numbers of people to vote for the candidate they are promoting.

Voting is done at polling places. After voters identify themselves, they are given printed ballots with the names of all candidates as well as ballots with the various issues to be decided. Or the individual voter may simply enter a voting booth where all the names and issues are on a voting machine. Whereas ballots have squares next to the names to be filled in with an "X," voting machines have small levers by each name. To vote for a candidate, the voter simply pushes down a lever. After making all selections, the voter opens the typical booth's curtain by pulling a large handle on the front of the machine. This action also registers the choices within the machine.

There is also a system of punch-card voting. In the booth is a book containing the names of the candidates on several pages. A card is inserted in the book, and the voter uses a pin to push through holes next to the names selected. Holes are punched in the card at the proper places, and this becomes the completed ballot.

In Australia, Belgium, and some other nations, voting is compulsory, or required by law, for all citizens of voting age. The purpose of compulsory voting is to ensure the equal voting rights of all.

Election Participation

The rate at which individuals vote depends on a variety of circumstances: the significance of the election, how strongly the voters feel about issues, the social groupings to which voters belong, and the voter's personality and beliefs. Electoral turnout is greater in national elections than in state contests, and usually greater in state elections than in local ones. This is probably because there is more drama connected with larger elections, and the candidates and issues are better known because of television and newspaper coverage.

Levels of education, income, and occupational status also affect voter participation. Groups in society that have more recently received the right to vote tend to participate less. Hence women vote less often than men, blacks less than whites, working-class members less than middle-class citizens, and young people less than older ones. Nonparticipation naturally has an effect on the outcome of elections. If everyone were to vote, the balance of power in a society would shift toward the most recently enfranchised and less privileged citizens.

Participation tends to be higher among voters who are committed to a political party. These individuals usually feel that government policies have a direct influence on their lives.

Independent voters may or may not be poorly informed or relatively uninterested in politics. Although independence is often based on strongly held convictions, sometimes it results from an unwillingness to be committed unless they see that an issue or candidate directly affects them.

ELECTORAL COLLEGE. In the United States presidential election of 1876, the Democratic candidate, Samuel J. Tilden, received 4,284,020 votes; the Republican Rutherford B. Hayes received 4,036,572 votes; but Hayes became president (*see* Hayes, "The Disputed Presidential Election"). Similarly, Benjamin Harrison got fewer popular votes than did Grover Cleveland in the 1888 presidential election but won anyway. How can this be? The answer is that United States presidents are not elected by popular vote but by an institution called the electoral college.

The men who drew up the United States Constitution in 1787 were framing a document for the government of a republic in which power was to be allocated to three branches—executive, legislative, and judicial. This was to prevent the abuse of power by any one branch. But the framers feared more than misuse of power by government. They were also wary of letting the people control the government through direct elections. The one case of direct election of public officials they allowed was for members of the House of Representatives. Senators, though now elected by popular vote, were chosen by the state legislatures until the 17th Amendment was ratified in 1913.

The election of the president and vice-president was taken out of the hands of the population and vested in an electoral college, as stipulated by Article II, Section 1, of the Constitution. Each state is allowed a number of electors equal to the total of its Congressional representation: one for each House member and one for each of its two senators. An elector cannot be any person holding office in the federal government. In some states electors are chosen at political party conventions.

When individuals cast their vote for a candidate in a general election for the presidency, they actually vote for a slate of electors. The party of the candidates who win the most votes in a state thereby elects its slate of electors. Losing candidates win no electors.

The successful slates of electors meet in their respective state capitals on the Monday following the second Wednesday in December to cast their votes for president and vice-president. Although electors have the constitutional right to vote for any person they choose, regardless of the outcome of the general election, they rarely vote for someone other than the person to whom they are pledged. The votes are delivered to Congress, and the candidates are formally elected when Congress counts the electoral votes on January 6 of the next year. The candidates who receive a majority, more than half, of the votes become president and vice-president. Should no candidate receive a majority, the election is thrown into the House of Representatives. (The first time this happened was in the election of 1800.)

By current practice the party that wins the most votes in a state receives all of its electoral college votes. Votes cast for defeated candidates do not count in any way. Hence it is still possible for a candidate to receive less than a majority of the popular vote and win.

ELECTRICITY

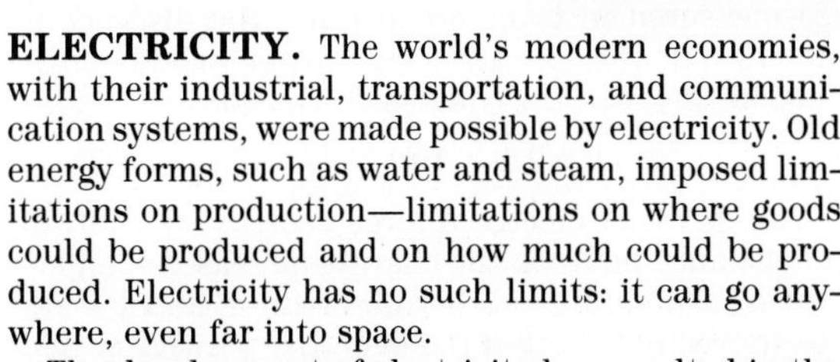

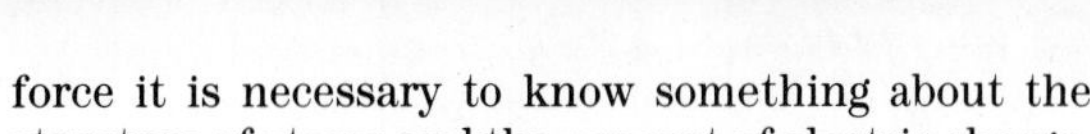

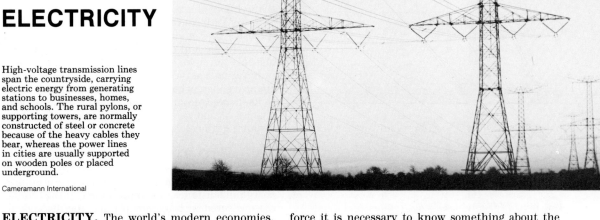

High-voltage transmission lines span the countryside, carrying electric energy from generating stations to businesses, homes, and schools. The rural pylons, or supporting towers, are normally constructed of steel or concrete because of the heavy cables they bear, whereas the power lines in cities are usually supported on wooden poles or placed underground.

Cameramann International

ELECTRICITY. The world's modern economies, with their industrial, transportation, and communication systems, were made possible by electricity. Old energy forms, such as water and steam, imposed limitations on production—limitations on where goods could be produced and on how much could be produced. Electricity has no such limits: it can go anywhere, even far into space.

The development of electricity has resulted in the total transformation of civilization in most countries. It brings power into homes to operate lights, kitchen appliances, television sets, radios, furnaces, computers, garage doors, and more. So common are its uses that one cannot imagine today's world without it. Streets would not be lit. Telephones would not work. Storefronts and factories would be dimmed.

Electrical forces are also responsible for holding together the paper on which these words appear, for bonding these printed words to the page, and for holding body cells together in the shape they have. In fact, electrical forces are fundamental in holding all matter together. As printed words are being read, electric currents speed along nerve cells from eye to brain. The effect of an electric current can be seen in the flash of lightning between thundercloud and Earth as well as in the spark that can be produced when one walks on a carpet in a dry room.

Static Electricity and Electric Charge

Understanding electricity begins with describing its effects. One way to begin is to examine interactions that occur when electricity is at rest, or static electricity. Static electricity can be seen at work when hair is combed on a cold, dry day. As the comb is pulled through the hair, strands of hair stand out stiffly. Some kind of force seems to pull the hair upward toward the comb. To understand the nature of this force it is necessary to know something about the structure of atoms and the concept of electric charge.

If a glass rod is rubbed with silk and touched to a small sphere of aluminum foil suspended by a thread, the sphere is observed to move away from the glass rod. The rod and sphere repel each other. If the process is repeated with a second sphere and the spheres brought near each other, they too repel. If a plastic rod is rubbed with wool and brought near either sphere, the spheres are observed to move toward the plastic rod. These objects attract each other. If two new aluminum foil spheres are touched to the plastic rod, they are repelled by the plastic, as well as by each other. But they are attracted to the glass rod and the spheres touched by the glass rod.

These experiments can be explained by a two-charge model. Rubbing the glass with silk causes the glass to acquire a positive charge. When touched to the spheres it shares some of its positive charge with the spheres and these objects repel. Rubbing the plastic with wool causes the plastic to acquire a negative charge. When touched to the spheres it shares some of its negative charge with the spheres and these objects repel. This interpretation of the experiment leads to the conclusion that like charges repel. When a positively charged sphere is brought near a negatively charged plastic rod or sphere, attraction is observed. When a negatively charged sphere is brought near a positively charged glass rod, attraction is observed. This leads to the conclusion that unlike charges attract. No matter how an object is charged, if it attracts the negatively charged sphere, it will also repel the positively charged sphere, and vice versa. This leads to the belief that there are only two kinds of electric charge.

A model of matter is needed to explain how only two kinds of charged rods can be produced. Atoms contain two kinds of charge, which are arbitrarily called positive and negative. Every atom is composed of a positively charged nucleus around which are distributed negatively charged electrons. Each nucleus

This article was contributed by Robert Applebaum, physics and chemistry teacher at New Trier High School, Winnetka, Ill.

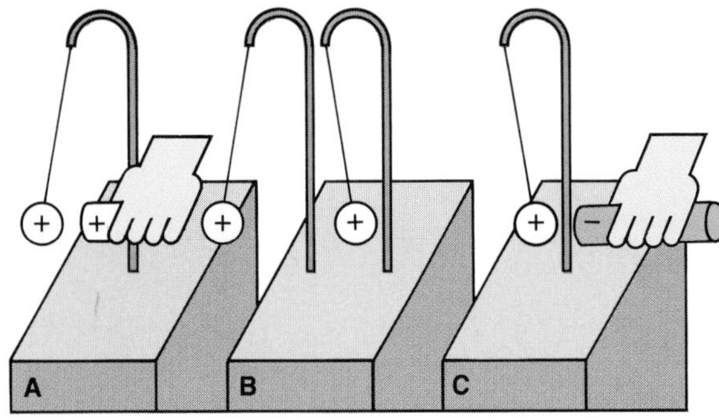

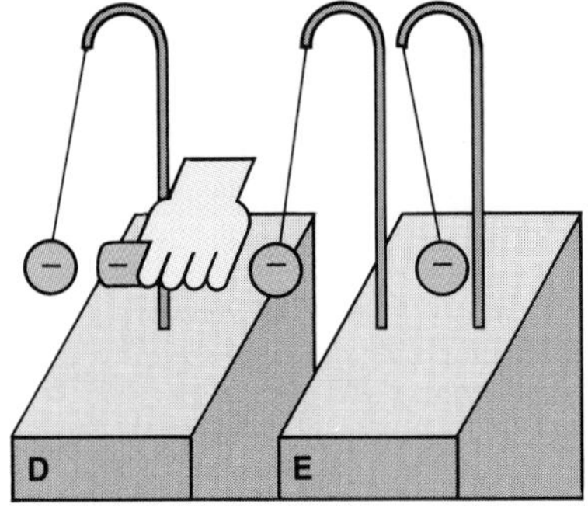

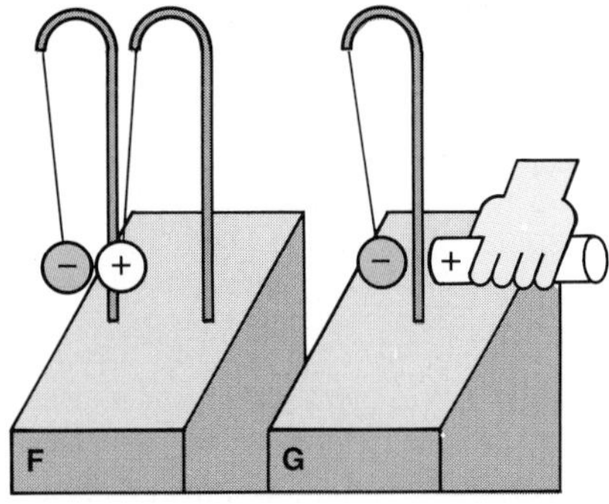

Aluminum foil spheres (white) are touched by a glass rod (white) that has been rubbed with silk. These have positive charges and repel each other. Other aluminum foil spheres (colored) are touched by a plastic rod (colored) that has been rubbed with wool. These have negative charges and repel each other. Oppositely charged spheres and rods, however, attract each other.

contains a specific number of protons—particles that carry the positive charge. (With the exception of the hydrogen atom, nuclei also contain uncharged neutrons.) In an uncharged atom there are equal numbers of protons and electrons, and such an atom is said to be neutral. If a neutral atom loses one or more of its electrons, it has an excess number of protons and it is positively charged. If a neutral atom gains one or more electrons, it has an excess number of electrons and it becomes negatively charged.

How does the simple atomic model relate to the static electricity experiments? Rubbing action creates charged objects because it tears electrons loose from some kinds of atoms and transfers them to others. In the case of plastic rubbed with wool, electrons are taken from the wool and pile up on the plastic, giving the plastic a net negative charge and leaving the wool charged positively. When glass is rubbed with silk, the glass loses electrons and the silk gains, producing glass that is charged positively and silk that is charged negatively.

In the 18th century the French physicist Charles-Augustin de Coulomb showed the relationship between the amount of electric force that two charged objects exert upon each other and the distance separating them. For two point charges (a point charge is a charged sphere whose radius is very small compared to its distance from a second point charge), carrying charges q_1 and q_2, whose centers are separated by distance d, the electric force F is determined by:

$$F = \frac{k\, q_1 q_2}{d^2}$$

In this equation, k is a constant for converting units of charge and distance into units of force. If the charges are measured in coulombs (C) and the distance in meters (m), the electric force can be calculated in newtons (N) with the conversion constant:

$$k = 1.0 \times 10^{-9}\, N\, m^2/C^2$$

The fact that electrical force decreases rapidly as the distance between the charges increases is important in explaining another observation about static electricity. If a charged rod (whether positive or negative) is brought near some uncharged bits of paper, the paper is initially attracted to the rod. How can this happen? When a positively charged rod is brought near a neutral scrap of paper, the electrons in each atom of the paper are drawn somewhat toward the rod and the nuclei, which are positive, are pushed slightly away. This repositioning of the charges in the neutral scrap of paper is called electrostatic induction. Because the electrons on the average will be slightly closer to the positive rod than to the nuclei, the force of attraction will be somewhat larger than the force of repulsion. Thus the paper experiences a net attractive force, and it is drawn toward the rod. A negatively charged rod will also attract uncharged bits of paper, but the repositioning of charges in the paper is reversed. Again, the attractive force will be somewhat larger than the repelling force. Electrostatic air cleaners attract neutral dust particles to a charged screen by induction. The electrostatic scrubbers used to clean the smoke produced by coal-burning power plants use the same principle on a larger scale. Charging by induction also occurs when the lower, negatively

One atom is attracted by a negatively charged rod (left) and by a positively charged rod (right).

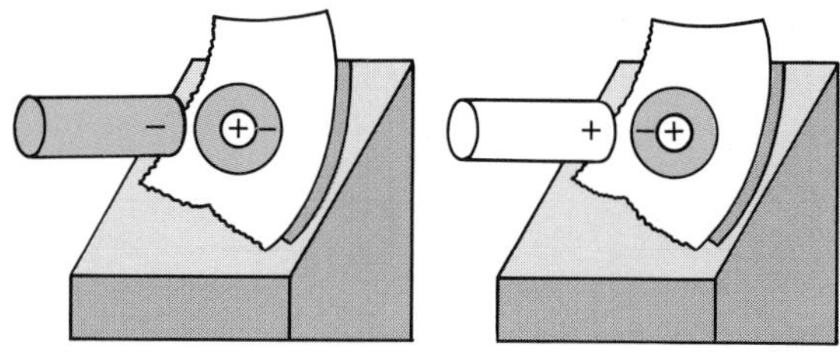

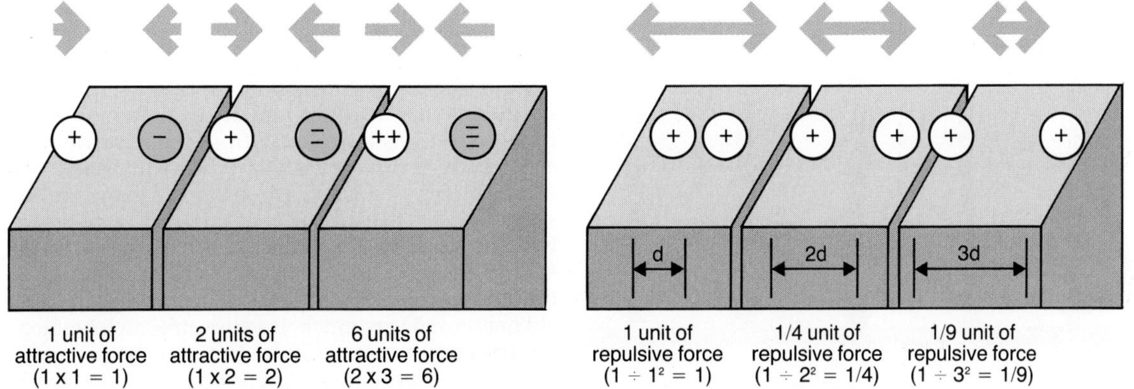

The amount of electrostatic force between two charges is directly proportional to the product of the charges (left) and inversely proportional to the square of the distance between the charges (right).

charged regions of thunderclouds induce a positive charge on the Earth's surface. If the charges become large enough, the resistance of the air is overcome and lightning occurs (*see* Lightning).

Electric Field

Charged objects can exert forces on uncharged objects over a distance. The electric field provides a way to describe possible effects at a point in space about an electric charge. The electric field strength at a point, E, is defined as the ratio of the electric force F on a test charge to the size of the test charge, q_{test}, placed at that point:

$$E = F/q_{test}$$

(A test charge is an infinitesimal charge placed in an electric field to probe the strength of the field.) This formula defines a specific value for E at each point in space. Regardless of the size of the test charge, the ratio of electric force to q_{test} will be a particular value at each position in the field.

The electric field strength is a vector quantity. Vectors have direction as well as magnitude. An arrow can be used to represent the electric field strength: the stronger the field, the longer the arrow. The direction of the electric field vector is taken to be the same as the direction of the electric force on a positive test charge placed in the field. If the separate electric field vectors for many points in space are joined, lines are obtained that give an overview of the electric field. These lines, called lines of force, were conceived by the 19th-century English scientist Michael Faraday. Where these lines are more concentrated, the field is stronger and the electric force on a test charge will be larger. If a positive test charge is placed somewhere in the field, the force on that charge will be directed along a line tangent to the field line. An especially simple electric field occurs in the space between two oppositely charged flat plates. The field lines are equally spaced between the plates, showing that the electric field strength is the same everywhere. Such a field is called a uniform electric

Lines of force between two similarly charged point charges veer away from each other (A). Lines of force between oppositely charged point charges merge toward each other (B).

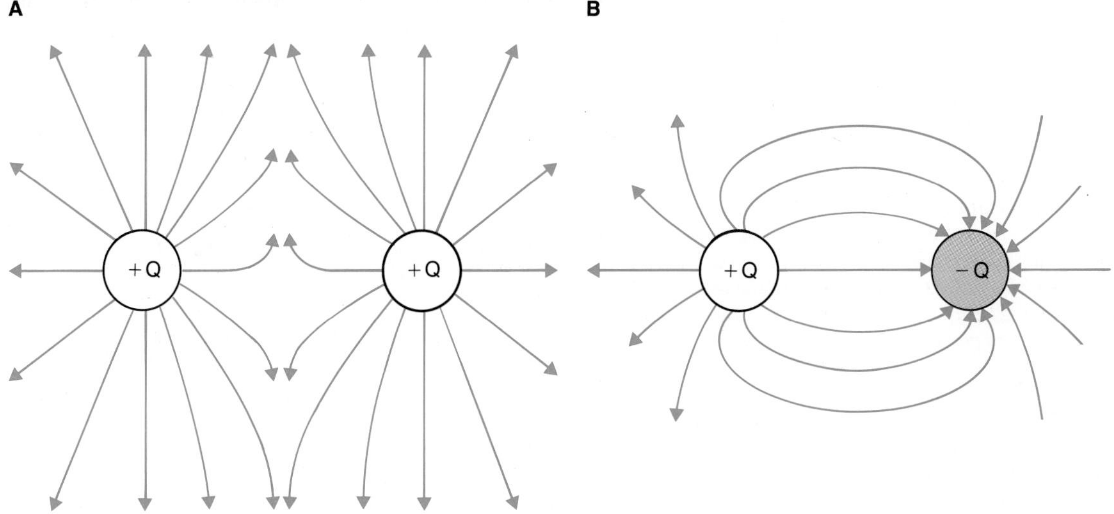

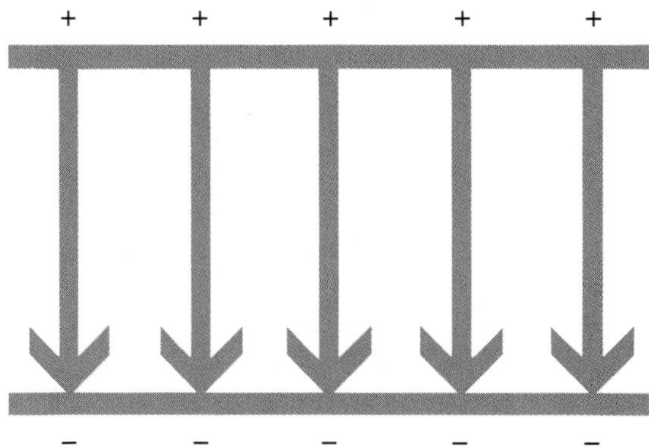

The lines of force, which are represented by arrows here and in the diagram below, are parallel in a uniform electric field between two oppositely charged plates.

field. An electron placed in such a field at any spot in the field will accelerate at a constant rate toward the positive plate because the electrical force on it is constant. (It should be noted that the electron, which is negatively charged, moves in a direction opposite to that of the field lines.) If an electron enters a uniform field parallel to the plates, it will veer toward the positive plate. The stronger the field is, the more the deflection. Fields such as these are used to control the scan of the electron beam in oscilloscope tubes.

Potential Difference

A positive test charge placed near a fixed positive point charge will accelerate away, increasing in velocity and kinetic energy. Conversely, to move this positive test charge back toward the fixed positive charge, work must be done on the test charge. The energy put into this process is stored as electric potential energy by virtue of the new position of the test charge in the field. Electric potential difference is a measure of this change in energy as the charge moves from one place to another in an electric field. Mathematically it is given by:

$$\text{electric potential difference} = \frac{\text{energy change}}{\text{charge moved}}$$

The unit for measuring electric potential difference is the volt. Sometimes the electric potential difference is called voltage. When there is no difference in electrical potential—that is, when there is zero voltage—between points in a field, there is no tendency for electric charge to move between those points. On the other hand, if there is a large potential difference between two points in a field, positive electric charge will tend to move from higher to lower potential; negative charge would move the opposite way.

A dry cell battery rated at 1.5 volts has an electric potential at the positive terminal that is 1.5 volts above the negative. Frequently this potential difference is called the emf, or electromotive force, of the battery, but this name is misleading because the voltage capacity is not really a force; the 1.5-volt rating indicates the energy change per coulomb of electric charge moved between the terminals. Each coulomb of charge moved between the terminals acquires 1.5 joules of energy. When connected by a conductor—a material that does not inhibit the motion of electrons—electrons move away from the negative dry-cell terminal (−) toward the positive terminal (+) through the conductor. The electrons move in response to the electric field set up in the conductor. When the terminals of the battery are connected by an insulator—a material in which electron motion is inhibited—the electrons in the insulating medium are not moved very much. Because air is an insulator, electric charge does not move between the terminals of the dry cell until they are connected by a conductor.

If the potential difference is very high, electric charge may be moved through the field even without a good conductor. In the picture tube of a television set, for example, electrons ejected from a heated electrode, called the cathode, are accelerated by a very high voltage (10,000 to 50,000 volts) and fly through an evacuated tube, crashing into a screen coated with a fluorescent material to produce the bursts of light that are seen as the picture. Such a tube is known as a cathode-ray tube, or CRT. (Electrons at one time were called "cathode rays.") Cathode-ray tubes have many other applications—for example, in the oscilloscopes used by medical personnel for displaying heartbeat and brain-wave data.

Electric Current

Electric current is the rate of charge motion. The moving charges may be electrons, protons, ions, even positive "holes" in semiconductors. When the charge q is measured in coulombs and the time t in seconds, the current I will be expressed in amperes, which is defined as coulombs per second:

$$I = q/t$$

A one-ampere current means that one coulomb of electric charge passes each point in the circuit each second. Because each electron carries only 1.6×10^{-19} (1.6 10-quintillionths, or 1.6/10,000,000,000,-000,000,000) coulomb of charge, the one-ampere current—normally used in the operation of a 120-watt incandescent bulb—implies that in one second about 6×10^{18} (6 quintillion, or 6,000,000,000,000,000,000)

An electron, left, accelerates uniformly toward the positive plate in a uniform electric field. A horizontally moving electron, right, follows a parabolic path in the field.

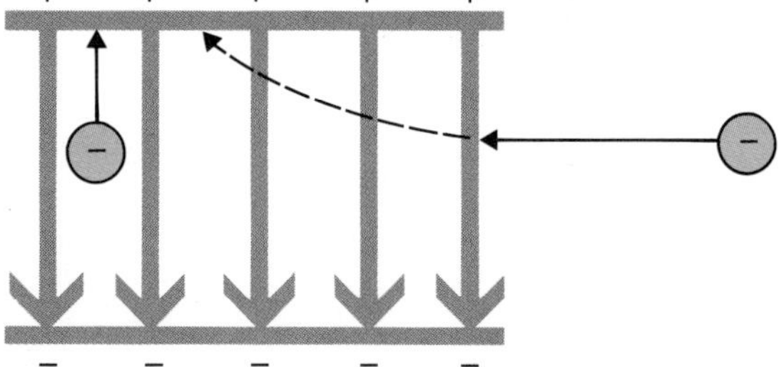

electrons pass each point in the filament of the bulb. Traditionally, the direction of electric current has been described as the direction of positive charge motion (conventional current), even though in most circuits it is the electrons that actually move. Even though electric charge moves through the filament of the bulb, the filament itself is not charged. The amount of positive and negative charge in the filament is equal. The positive and negative charges are simply moving in opposite directions relative to each other.

It is the quantity of electric current, or the amperage—not the potential difference, or voltage—that can produce a lethal shock. Currents of less than 0.005 ampere that pass through the heart are not likely to cause damage. Currents of about 0.1 ampere are usually fatal, even if endured for only one second, but those above 1 ampere are frequently not fatal. The larger currents may stop the heart, but often the heart will resume its normal beating when the current is halted.

Electrochemical Cells

An electrochemical cell, or battery, can be used to provide a flow of electrons. A simple cell can be made from strips of zinc (Zn) and copper (Cu) metal suspended in a salt solution. Prior to connecting the strips by a conductor, a dynamic equilibrium exists at each metal surface. Some zinc atoms lose a pair of electrons, becoming Zn^{2+} ions. The electrons remain on the zinc metal, while the Zn^{2+} moves into the solution. The reverse process occurs at an equal rate: Zn^{2+} ions gain two electrons and adhere to the zinc strip as zinc atoms. A similar equilibrium exists at the copper surface, involving copper metal and Cu^{2+} ions.

When the metals are connected by a conductor, these equilibria are thrown out of balance. Because zinc atoms lose electrons easier than copper atoms do, electrons are forced through the conductor from the zinc strip to the copper strip. As electrons leave the zinc, net formation of Zn^{2+} ions occurs at the zinc strip. At the copper strip, Cu^{2+} ions gain electrons, becoming copper metal. As electrons move in the outer circuit, positive ions in the solution migrate away from the zinc strip, and negative ions move away from the copper strip.

Batteries can be constructed using a variety of chemicals. Any two substances with different affinities for electrons can be suspended in a medium that allows ions to migrate, producing a battery. (*See also* Battery and Fuel Cell.)

Electric Circuits

When the terminals of a battery are connected with a conductor an electric circuit is produced. By means of chemical reactions within the battery, a potential difference is created between the terminals, and electrons flow in the conductor in one direction, away from the negative terminal toward the positive. The 19th-century German physicist Georg Simon Ohm showed that the current in such a circuit was directly related to the voltage of the battery but noted that the

Series circuit　　Parallel circuit

The symbol ‖ indicates a source of potential difference such as a battery. Electrons move in the circuit from the negative terminal (shorter line) toward the positive terminal (longer line). The symbol ⁓ represents a resistor.

amount of current also depended on the nature of the conductor. Different kinds of conductors differed in the degree to which they resisted movement of electrons with a given voltage. He defined the resistance of a conductor as the ratio of the potential difference across the conductor (in volts) to the current (in amperes) through the conductor:

$$\text{resistance} = \frac{\text{potential difference}}{\text{current}} = \frac{\text{volts}}{\text{amperes}}$$

The unit of resistance is now known as the ohm, usually abbreviated as the Greek letter omega—Ω.

The greater the potential difference across a circuit, the more electric current is made to flow through it and the greater the heat effects produced as electrons force their way through the wire. A wire in which a current generates a substantial quantity of heat energy is called a resistor. In a circuit diagram resistors are represented by the symbol ⁓. For example, in the filament of an incandescent light bulb and in the heating element of an electric toaster or clothes dryer, heat energy is generated as electrons are forced through these resistors. If the current is large enough, the heat generated can be used for welding metals or for smelting in electric furnaces. Two or more resistors can be connected in a circuit in series or, more often, in parallel.

Series circuits. When resistors are connected in series, the electric current that flows through one resistor will flow through the next resistor and so on. Everywhere in a series circuit the current is the same. The total resistance in such a circuit is simply the sum of the resistances of the separate resistors—R_1, R_2, and so on:

$$R_{\text{total}} = R_1 + R_2 + \ldots R_n$$

If the total potential difference across these resistors is V_t, then the current in the circuit will be limited by the total resistance:

$$I_{\text{total}} = \frac{V_t}{R_1 + R_2 + \ldots R_n}$$

The voltage drop across any particular resistor is given by:

$$V_n = I\,R_n$$

Wiring in series is satisfactory if the devices need only low amounts of power for operation since each added resistor will cause the current in the circuit to drop. The disadvantage of wiring in series is that if one element of the circuit burns out, the entire circuit is broken.

Parallel circuits. Parallel wiring allows the electric current to move through different pathways. Each branch can be switched on or off independently, allowing some or all of the devices to be used. In general, if the resistance along a given parallel branch is increased, a smaller amount of current will flow through that branch. The more branches that are available in parallel wiring, however, the lower the total resistance in the circuit becomes, and thus the higher the total current. This may seem to be a contradiction, but it is very similar to what happens when people leave a crowded theater that has several exits. Although there is resistance to movement at each exit, there will be a larger overall rate of movement with more exits. The total resistance for resistors connected in parallel is given by the equation:

$$\frac{1}{R_{\text{total}}} = \frac{1}{R_1} + \frac{1}{R_2} + \ldots \frac{1}{R_n}$$

The total current that flows into the branches will equal the sum of the currents in each branch:

$$I_{\text{total}} = I_1 + I_2 + \ldots I_n$$

Regardless of which branch the charges follow, they all move between points of equal potential as they move through the parallel resistors. Thus the voltages across each resistor wired in parallel are equal:

$$V_1 = V_2 = V_n$$

Besides the advantage of being able to use resistors along each branch independently, the parallel scheme of wiring allows the addition of extra branches without changing the current in the branches already in use, thus keeping the energy consumption in each branch unchanged. In the home each additional device that is plugged into a given circuit adds another parallel branch. This may create a problem, however. With each device added, the total resistance drops and the total current increases. If too much current flows through the conducting wires, they may overheat and a fire may occur. A fuse or a circuit breaker can be included in a parallel circuit to prevent overheating. If the current increases to a dangerous point, a filament in the fuse overheats, burns out, and the circuit is broken. In order for the parallel circuit not to be overloaded, it is necessary to remove one or more of the branches to increase the overall resistance and decrease the current.

Switches

If a circuit is complete, electrons will flow as long as the cell acts. Usually it is desirable to be able to turn current on and off. This can be done with switches, which act like a drawbridge.

If the bridge is open, traffic cannot move along the road. When the bridge is closed, traffic can move. If the switch is open, current cannot flow. Closing the switch makes it possible for the current to flow. Circuits are called open or closed according to the position of the switch.

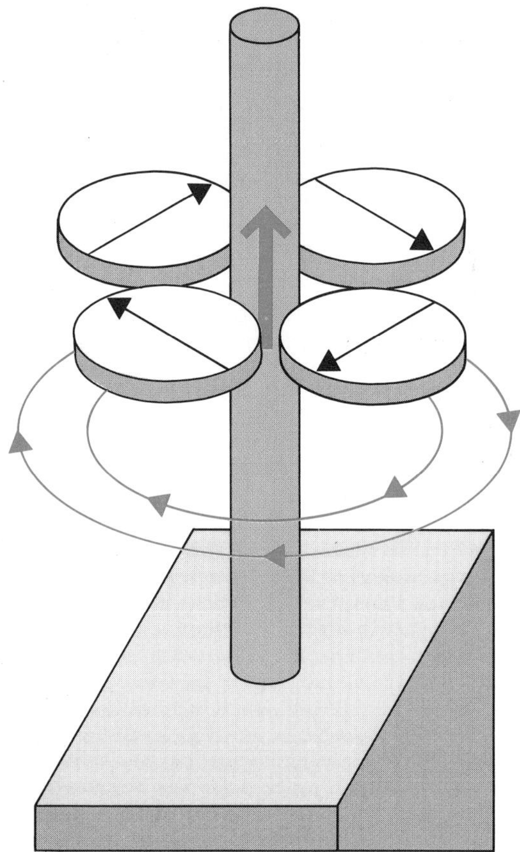

Moving electric charges produce magnetic fields. Magnetic lines of force encircle a conductor (vertical rod) through which electrons are moving. Compass needles placed near the conductor are deflected by the magnetic lines of force.

Resistance in Different-sized Conductors

A thicker wire offers less resistance to current than a thinner one of the same material. This is because current consists of electrons flowing through the metal of the wire.

The electrons jump from atom to atom in the metal in response to the electric field in the circuit. A conductor with a larger cross section allows more electrons to interact with the field. Because there is more current with a given voltage, a conductor with a larger cross section has lower resistance.

Electrons and Heat

Conduction of electrons explains the relation between electricity and heat. When the electric field in a circuit acts on an electron, the field imparts to the electron kinetic energy (energy of motion). When the electron strikes an atom, it transfers most of the energy to the atom. The atom then vibrates faster. Faster vibration means more heat, since heat is energy of motion (*see* Heat).

In turn, heat in metals reduces conductivity, or increases resistance, slightly. More vibration makes atoms "get in the way" of the electrons more often. The electrons then must spend extra time on deflected courses instead of going straight ahead. This cuts down current slightly. In modern theory, the atoms scatter the electron waves carried by the electrons.

Heat can also generate electricity by acting upon the joined ends of two different kinds of metal. The unheated ends must also be joined in order to complete a circuit. Voltage can be increased by joining several junctions in series to make a thermopile. A pile made of antimony and bismuth, for example, with unheated ends kept at a constant temperature, can be used to detect temperature changes of a hundred-millionth of a degree. Thermopiles are also used to measure high temperatures such as those in furnaces (*see* Thermometer).

Magnetic Fields

In 1820 the Danish scientist Hans Christian Oersted found by accident that the magnetized needle of a compass would realign if brought near a current-carrying wire. The diagram on page 154 shows how the needle would point if placed at various positions in a plane perpendicular to a conductor carrying electrons upward. If the direction of the current were reversed, the compass needle would reverse its orientation. Apparently a magnetic field encircles the current-carrying wire. This magnetic field can be represented as a series of concentric field lines in planes perpendicular to the current. A simple rule allows the prediction of the field direction if the direction of electron motion is known: if the wire is encircled by the fingers of one's left hand, with the thumb pointing in the direction of electron motion, the magnetic field lines encircle the wire in the same direction as the fingers, and a compass needle will align itself tangent to these lines. (The direction of a magnetic field is taken as the direction in which the north-seeking pole of a compass needle points.) A magnetic field is produced around any moving electric charge, positive or negative, whether in a conductor or free space. (For a moving positive charge, the right hand is used to predict the magnetic field direction.) It was the German-born theoretical physicist Albert Einstein who showed in his theory of relativity that the magnetic field produced by a moving electric charge is caused by a warping of the charge's electric field; this is caused by its relative motion. An observer moving along with the charge would not detect any magnetic effects. Thus an electric charge at rest relative to an observer does not produce a magnetic field. (*See also* Magnet and Magnetism.)

It is believed that all magnetism arises from moving electric charge. If a current flows in a helical coil, called a solenoid, the magnetic field will be directed through the solenoid and out one end. The field curves around and reenters the other end of the solenoid. This is similar to the shape of the magnetic field around a bar magnet with a south and north pole and led the French physicist André-Marie Ampère to speculate in the early 1820s that the magnetic field of a bar magnet is produced by circulating currents in the magnet. Today it is believed that those circulating currents are caused by the motions of electrons, particularly by their spin within individual atoms. The tiny magnetic fields of the individual atoms align themselves into domains in which the magnetic effects add together. It should be noted that physicists are reluctant to picture electrons as actually spinning because quantum theory indicates that it is impossible to prove such motion by experiment (*see* Quantum Theory). If an unmagnetized iron rod is inserted into a solenoid, the magnetic field inside the solenoid forces the electrons in the iron atoms to align their

The electromagnetism of a current-carrying solenoid, the ferromagnetism of a bar magnet, and the geomagnetism of the Earth all produce similar magnetic fields.

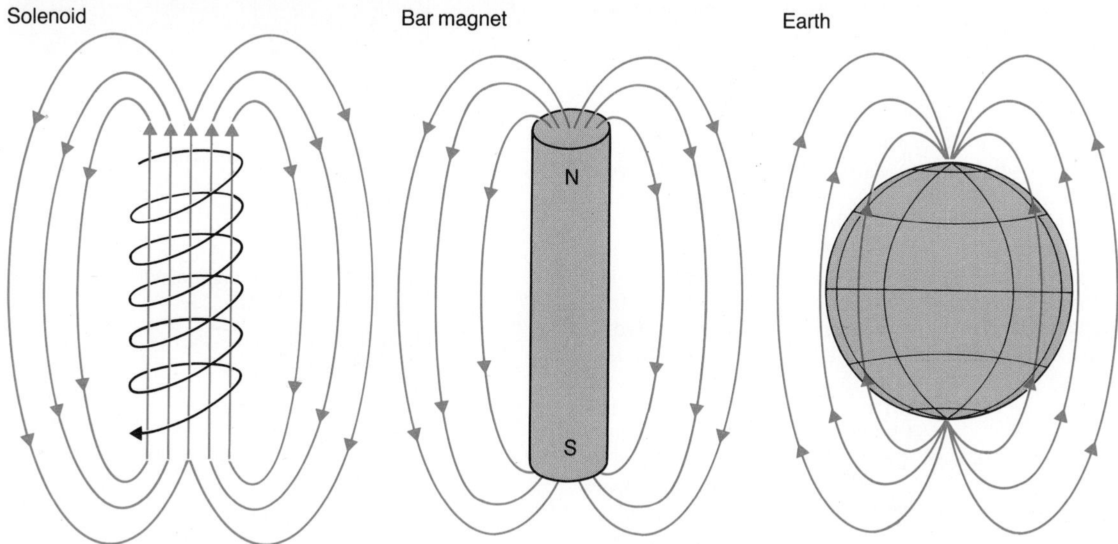

spins, producing domains that reinforce the magnetic field strength. This arrangement of solenoid and iron rod is an electromagnet and gives a magnetic field considerably stronger than that caused by the current in the solenoid alone.

The tape recorder and the video recorder demonstrate practical uses for the magnetic field produced by an electric current. In recording, as current varies in a tape head (itself an electromagnet), the magnetized particles on the tape are realigned to conform to the magnetic field produced by the changing current (*see* Tape Recorder). Magnetically coated disks record computer data in a similar way (*see* Computer). The solenoid is also used in a variety of devices with a cylindrical piece of iron inserted. When a switch is closed, the current in the solenoid produces a magnetic field, which pulls the iron through the solenoid. A device like this is used in doorbells, in the starter motor of automobiles, in the water valves in washing machines, and even in switches for the tape-transport system of some tape recorders.

Moving Charges in Magnetic Fields

Moving electric charges are surrounded by a magnetic field, and magnetic fields interact with magnets. Thus it is not surprising that charges moving through a magnetic field experience a force. What is surprising is the direction of the deflecting force. For deflection to occur, the charge must have some component of its motion perpendicular to the magnetic field. An electric charge—whether positive or negative—that is moving directly along a line of force of the magnetic field will not be acted on by any force from the field (*see* diagram on this page). However, a positive charge that moves across the field shown from left to right will be deflected by an outward force. If the positive charge moves from right to left, it is deflected inward. A negative charge moving across the field will be deflected oppositely. The deflection for positive charges can be predicted by positioning the right hand so that the thumb points in the direction of the moving positive charge and the fingers point in the direction of the magnetic field. (Magnetic fields point away from north poles and toward south poles.) The positive charge will be deflected from its original path in a direction out of the palm of the hand. A similar left-hand rule applies to negative charges moving across magnetic fields.

In television picture tubes, magnetic fields are used to steer the electrons from the cathode. As the magnetic field strength is varied, the electrons are deflected so that they scan across the screen. In a loudspeaker, the current from the amplifier is fed to a coil of wire attached to the speaker cone. The coil is arranged so that it is in line with a permanent magnet. As current in the coil is varied, the moving charges are deflected by the field of the permanent magnet. As the coil moves, the cone of the speaker vibrates, causing sound waves to be produced. Powerful magnetic fields keep charged particles moving in circles in the rings of high-energy accelerators used to investigate the substructure of protons and neutrons. The magnetic field of the Earth deflects and traps charged particles that travel from the sun and other stars toward the Earth. These trapped charged particles have formed two doughnut-shaped regions known as the Van Allen radiation belts. (For illustration, *see* Van Allen.) Some particles not trapped by the Earth's magnetic field are steered by that field into the atmosphere near the poles. It is believed that the aurora borealis, or northern lights, is produced as these deflected charges crash into molecules of gas in the Earth's atmosphere (*see* Aurora).

Measurement

Instruments designed to detect and measure electric current in circuits make use of the deflecting force on charges moving through magnetic fields. The galvanometer and ammeter detect and measure electric current as it flows in a coil pivoted between the poles of a permanent magnet. As the current in the coil increases, the moving charges are increasingly

A positive charge, top, moving through a magnetic field is deflected. The right-hand rule, bottom, predicts the direction of the deflecting force on the positive charge. A similar left-hand rule predicts the deflection of negative charges.

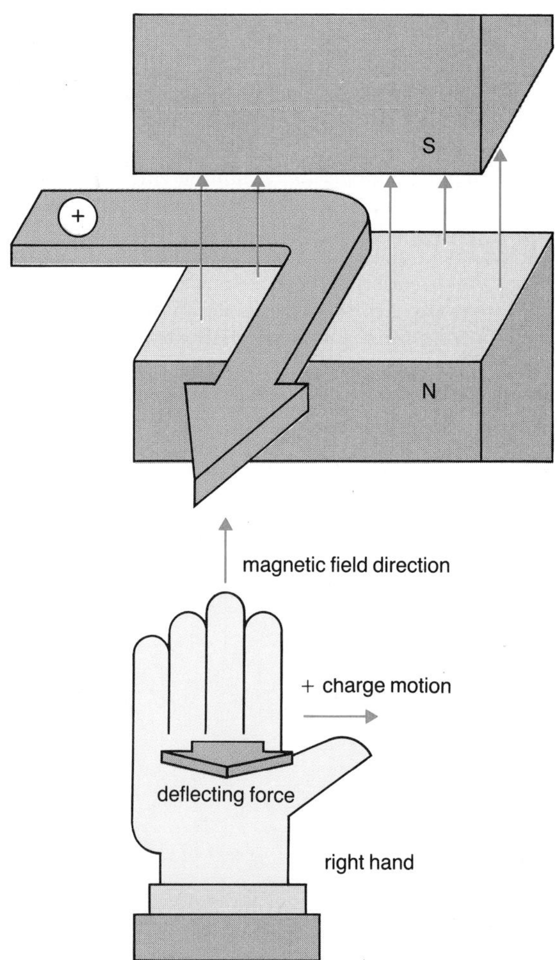

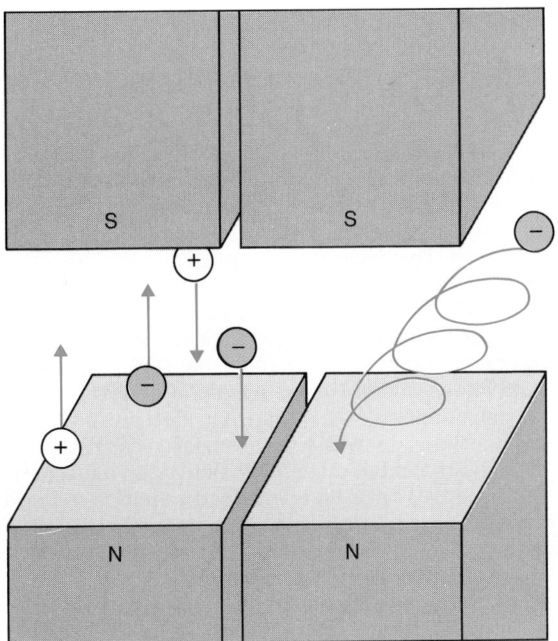

Electric charges, left, that move parallel to magnetic lines of force are not deflected; they continue to move at constant velocity. A charge, right, that moves neither parallel nor perpendicular to the field spirals through the field.

deflected by the magnetic field. By standardizing the scale, the quantity of current in amperes can be determined. In measuring current, the ammeter is connected in series in the circuit. A voltmeter is used to measure the potential difference, or voltage drop, between points in the circuit. Like the ammeter it has a movable coil positioned in a magnetic field. But the voltmeter has an extremely high internal resistance. The trickle of current through the voltmeter depends on the potential difference between the terminals of the meter. The voltmeter is connected in parallel across a resistor to measure the potential difference in volts (*see* Galvanometer).

Motors and Generators

The electric motor demonstrates a common application of the interaction between moving charge and a magnetic field. In a motor, electrical energy is converted into energy of motion. A simple motor can be represented as a loop of wire attached to a source of direct current (DC). The loop is pivoted to rotate in a magnetic field. As electric charge moves along the loop, deflecting forces begin to cause the loop to rotate. To keep the loop rotating, the direction of current in the loop must be reversed every 180 degrees. A device called a split-ring commutator is used for this purpose (*see* Motor and Engine).

Special features of motors. Common commutator motors have generator features in reverse. They can be of the armature-and-fixed-field type, or they can consist of a rotor and a stator.

The field coils of the motor can be series wound, shunt wound, or compound wound. A series winding builds up field strength rapidly when the motor starts under load. In fact, the field may build up too rapidly. This can be avoided by using a starting box to increase the supply of current by steps as the motor gains speed. A shunt winding has advantages once a motor is running at operating speed. A compound winding combines the advantages of both types. The motor uses the series winding at the start, and an automatic control switches to the shunt when heavy pulling is no longer needed to gain operating speed.

In an induction motor, a magnetic field revolves around a piece of metal and creates eddy currents in the metal. These currents produce magnetic fields that interact with the revolving field. This makes the metal rotate if it is pivoted properly. The rotating metal constitutes a motor.

The smallest motors of this type use a rotor made of metal disks notched at the edges to place the eddy currents properly. Larger types may use a squirrel-cage rotor. This is made of metal bars arranged to form a skeleton cylinder. The ends of the bars may be attached to disks, or the bars may be mounted on a cylinder of enameled iron and connected at the ends. The eddy currents flow through the bars and end connections.

The revolving fields are produced by using two-phase or three-phase current to energize the field coils. Because different-phase currents can be used, induction motors are classified as polyphase. The phases of the current amount to different alternating currents (AC) in the same circuit. The currents reach maximum and minimum strengths in each direction of flow at different times. The field coils are connected to place maximums at different points in turn around a circle. This produces the revolving field.

Synchronous motors are like a rotor-stator alternator in reverse. A polyphase current provides revolving

In a DC motor, electrons from the DC power supply cause the wire loop to rotate in a clockwise direction, converting electrical energy into mechanical energy.

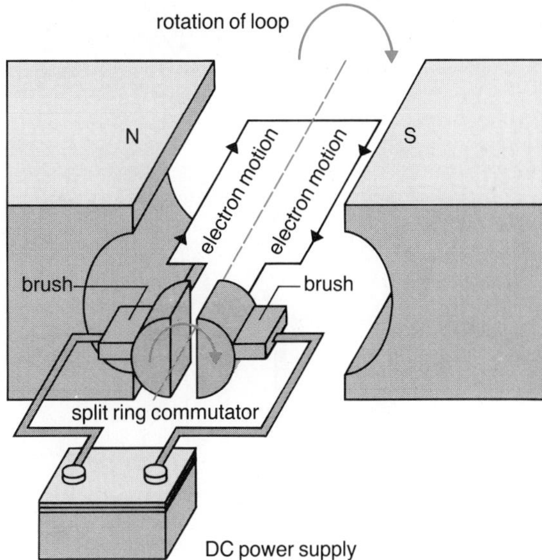

fields in the stator, and other current (sometimes direct) gives the rotor a field that follows the stator fields around. Such motors run at constant speeds, which are related to the frequency of the current supplied to the stator.

Generators. A generator is a motor working in reverse: a motor changes electrical energy into mechanical energy, but a generator produces electrical energy from mechanical energy. Superficially the diagram of a generator appears identical to that of a motor. Each consists of a loop that can rotate in a magnetic field. In a motor, electric current is fed into the loop, resulting in rotation of the loop. In the generator, the loop is rotated, resulting in the production of electric current in the loop. For 180 degrees of the rotation, electron deflection produces an electric current in the loop that moves in one direction; for the next 180 degrees, the electron deflection is reversed. As the current leaves the loop to an external circuit, the current will be observed to move in one direction and then the other. This is called alternating current. For a generator to generate direct current it is necessary to use a split-ring commutator at the point where the generator feeds current to the external circuit. The current in the loop is still alternating, but it is direct in the external circuit.

Electromagnetic induction. Michael Faraday, the English scientist, and Joseph Henry of the United States independently showed in 1831 that moving a magnet through coils of wire would generate a current in the wire. If the magnet was plunged into the coil, current flowed one way. When the magnet was removed, the current direction was reversed. This phenomenon is called electromagnetic induction, and it is the principle underlying the operation of the generator. As long as the magnet and the coil move relative to each other, a potential difference is produced across the coil and current flows in the coil. A potential difference is also produced if the magnetic field through the coil grows stronger or weaker. The greater the rate at which the magnetic flux through the coil changes, the greater the potential difference produced. The key is that the magnetic field through the coil must be changing.

In 1864 the Scottish physicist James Clerk Maxwell suggested what is considered to be the modern explanation for all of these phenomena: (1) If an electric field changes with time, a magnetic field is induced at right angles to the changing electric field. The greater the rate at which the electric field changes, the stronger the induced magnetic field. (2) If a magnetic field changes with time, an electric field is induced at right angles to the changing magnetic field. The greater the rate at which the magnetic field changes, the stronger the induced electric field.

Maxwell calculated that these electric and magnetic fields would propagate each other and travel through space as time-varying fields. The speed of these electromagnetic waves is 3.0×10^8 (300,000,-000) meters per second. That happens to be the same as the speed of light. In fact, visible light is merely a narrow range of frequencies in what is known as the electromagnetic spectrum. As people read a printed page, electromagnetic waves reflected from the page pass into their eyes. As the electric field of that wave reaches the eye's retina, electrons in molecules of the

Electric current in the loop of a DC generator (left) alternates—that is, it changes directions—but in the outer circuit it travels in only one direction, and drops to zero twice with each rotation of the loop. By arranging more loops a steadier direct current can be obtained. In an AC generator (right) the current is alternating in both the loop and in the outer circuit.

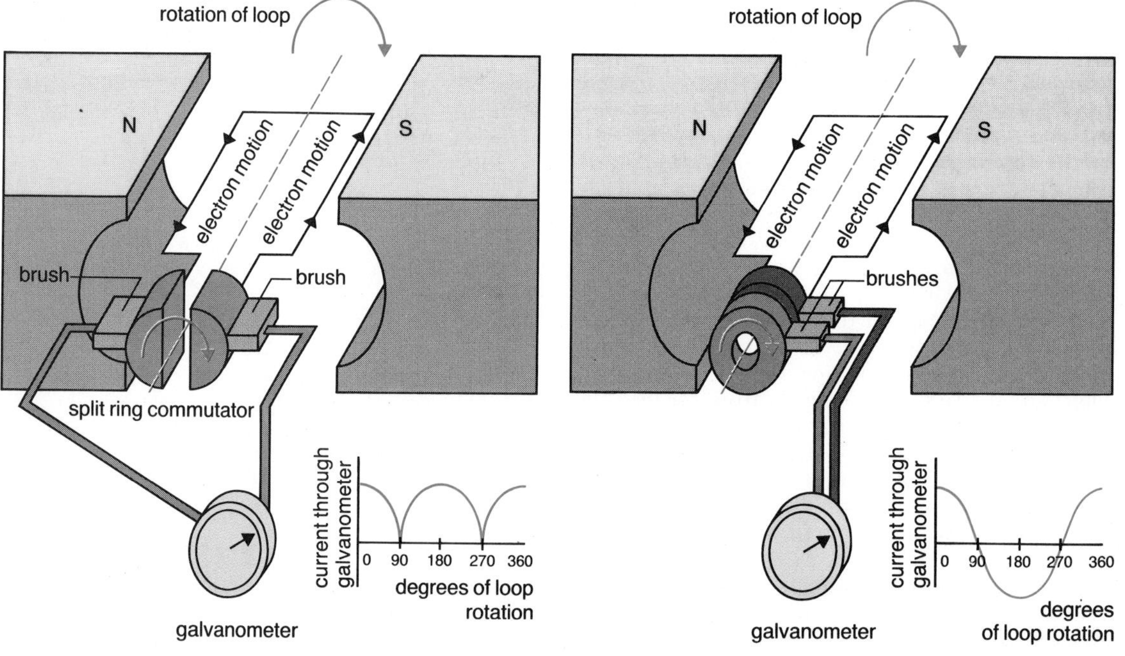

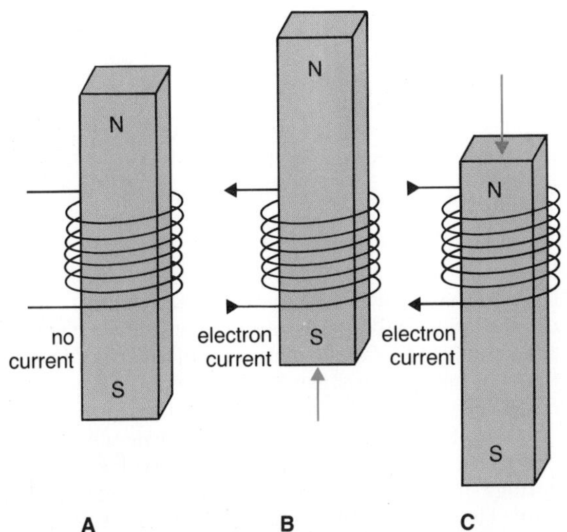

No electric current is induced when magnet A is at rest with respect to the loop. When magnet B is pushed up through the loop, a current is induced. When magnet C is dropped through the loop, current is induced in the opposite direction.

retina interact with the field, change position, and start the message to the brain that eventually allows a person to understand what has been read.

Lenz's law. Whenever a changing magnetic field generates a current in a coil of wires, the current produced will generate a magnetic field. That induced magnetic field will always tend to oppose the original change in the magnetic flux through the coil. This rule was first suggested by Heinrich F.E. Lenz of Germany in 1834. The effects of the induced field can be observed during the operation of a hand-cranked generator. When the generator is cranked slowly, little current is produced and weak electromagnetic forces oppose the rotation. But as the cranking rate is increased and more current is produced, the forces on the rotating loop become stronger, and the loop is correspondingly more difficult to turn.

Lenz's law also applies to motors, where a current-carrying wire moves in a magnetic field. That movement, in turn, produces a current in the wire that opposes the original direction of current in the wire. Because electric current cannot occur without a potential difference, this opposition effect is sometimes called a back-emf. When a motor is started, a large current flows at first, and, as the motor begins to turn rapidly, a large back-emf is induced and the net current in the motor drops. If a large load is suddenly added to the motor, slowing it drastically, the back-emf will drop, and the sudden rise in current may cause overheating and burn out the motor.

Even a simple coil of wire in a DC circuit exhibits the effects of back-emf. As the current in the coil increases, the changing magnetic field produced around the coil will tend to produce a back-emf. This is called self-inductance. Normally the current in a circuit rises rapidly after the switch is closed. But in this circuit, the current rises relatively slowly. On the other hand, when the switch is opened, the current in the circuit normally falls to zero almost instantly. But as the magnetic field around the coil decreases, an emf is generated that tends to keep the current from decaying as rapidly. A coil like this is used in devices designed to prevent damage to electronic equipment caused by voltage spikes—sudden increases in potential difference that would tend to produce rapidly changing currents.

Transmission

Generators do not create energy. To produce electricity either the loop or the magnets must be rotated relative to one another. The energy for this rotation can be provided by a variety of sources. In some sources water is converted to steam, which is used to drive turbines that operate generators. The energy to boil the water and convert it to steam comes from burning coal, oil, or natural gas, or from the heat released by controlled nuclear reactions. The rotation may be driven by the gravitational potential energy stored in water held behind the dam of a hydroelectric plant, by wind in wind turbines, or by the steam produced naturally within the Earth.

In the United States electric power is delivered to homes as alternating current. For example, when an incandescent lamp is switched on, electrons vibrate back and forth within the filament 60 times per second, matching the frequency at which the alternating current is produced by the generators at the power plant. The electrons that move in the filament are not the same electrons that were deflected in the generator loop. When the lamp is turned on, it lights almost instantly because the changing electric field produced in the generator loop travels through the circuit at close to the speed of light. As the field passes along the conductor, electrons in the conductor interact with the field, but they cannot move very far unimpeded because they bump into vibrating atoms in the conductor. Thus the electrons themselves do not fly through the wires at close to the speed of light, nor do they move along by a domino effect. It is the electric energy carried by the field that moves the electrons in the circuit.

It is energy, not charge, that flows from the electrical outlet. The electric charges that move in a lamp are already in the lamp. Thus electric companies bill their customers not for electrons but for electrical energy. The charges on an electric bill are based on kilowatt-hours. A kilowatt is a unit of power, or energy consumed per time unit. When power is multiplied by time, the result is a measure of energy:

$$\text{power} \times \text{time} = \frac{\text{energy}}{\text{time}} \times \text{time} = \text{energy}$$

So the kilowatt-hour is a unit of energy.

The companies that supply electrical power try to deliver that power as efficiently as possible. This necessitates transmitting the energy in a way that minimizes power losses due to heating within the transmission lines from power station to home, school, or workplace. The relationship between power in watts, potential difference in volts, and current in amperes is:

$$\text{power} = \text{voltage} \times \text{current}$$

If the transmission lines obey Ohm's law, resistance × current can be substituted for voltage to obtain:

$$\text{power} = (\text{resistance})(\text{current})^2$$

This relationship is important in considering the power loss during transmission. Lowering the resistance in the power lines would be helpful. Experiments with superconductivity may someday produce low-resistance power lines. When materials become superconductive, all resistance disappears because electrons pair up and do not collide; current flows without losing power. Some conductors must be cooled to temperatures near −273 ° Celsius, or absolute zero, before they become superconductive. Because of the high cost of cooling such superconductors, progress in the commercial application of superconductivity was impeded. In the 1980s, however, a new class of high-temperature superconductor was discovered. In normal power transmission the current is even more critical to the power loss. Doubling the current means four times the power loss. Alternatively, if the currents are too low, they may be insufficient to power appliances like toasters. The problem of having sufficiently high currents at the point of delivery and low currents for efficient transmission is solved by using transformers (*see* Transformer).

A simple transformer consists of a coil of wire fed by a voltage source such as a generator. The coil is wound around one side of an iron frame. This is the primary coil. The other side of the iron frame is wound with another coil, the secondary, that feeds electricity to a separate circuit. As alternating current from the generator flows in the primary coil, the magnetic field in that coil strengthens, weakens, and then reverses direction as the alternating current changes. The iron core intensifies these magnetic-field changes. As the magnetic field in the secondary coil changes with time, electric charges in the secondary are deflected and current is produced. The alternating voltage produced in the secondary depends on the relative number of turns in the secondary compared to the primary coil. If V_1 is the voltage across the primary, V_2 the voltage across the secondary, N_1 the number of turns of coil in the primary, and N_2 the number of turns of coil in the secondary, then

$$\frac{V_1}{V_2} = \frac{N_1}{N_2}$$

If the secondary coil, for example, is wound with 100 times as many turns as the primary, the voltage across the secondary will be 100 times larger than that across the primary. A transformer used in this way is said to be a step-up transformer. If there are fewer turns on the secondary, it is a step-down transformer.

It might seem that a step-up transformer gives more energy than it uses: after all, the larger secondary voltage means a larger energy change per charge moved in the field. But that voltage increase comes at the expense of a reduced current. If the transformer were 100 percent efficient, then

$$\text{power}_{\text{primary}} = \text{power}_{\text{secondary}}$$

If I_1 and I_2 are the currents in the primary and secondary coils, then

$$V_1 I_1 = V_2 I_2$$

So increasing the voltage in the secondary coil by a factor of 100 results in a current reduction by a factor of 100.

By using a step-up transformer between generator and transmission lines, the current can be reduced to a low value, thereby reducing power losses due to heating of the transmission lines. The voltage across these power lines will be correspondingly large. By using a step-down transformer between the transmission lines and the point of delivery, the voltage will be reduced and the current increased to a level allowing effective operation of electrical devices.

Step-up transformers raise voltage prior to transmission. Step-down transformers lower voltage prior to use.

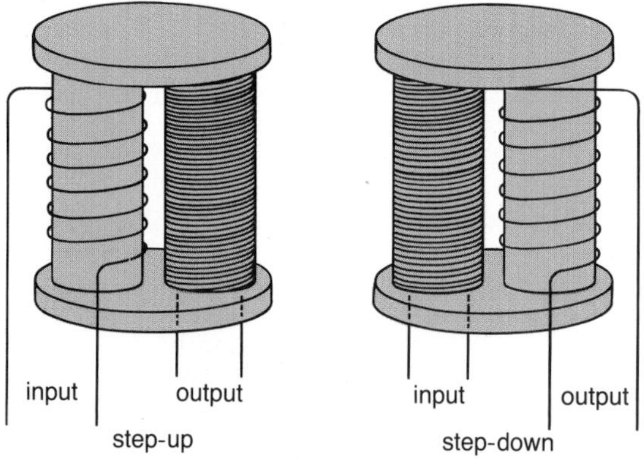

Electrolysis

In a battery-driven circuit, the flow of electric current is produced by spontaneous chemical changes that occur at each battery terminal. In a battery, stored chemical energy is converted to electrical energy (*see* Battery and Fuel Cell).

In electrolysis the process is reversed. By forcing an electric current through some substances, it is possible to change electrical energy into stored chemical energy. The process of electrolysis causes chemical reactions that do not occur spontaneously. For example, when common table salt, or sodium chloride ($NaCl$), is heated to 1,486° F (808° C), the solid turns to a stable melt consisting of sodium ions (Na^+) and chloride ions (Cl^-). If inert electrodes are immersed in the melt and an electric current is forced through the molten salt by a sufficiently high voltage, sodium metal will be produced at one electrode and chlorine gas at the other. A similar electrolytic process is used to obtain pure aluminum from solutions of aluminum oxide.

Electrolysis is important in silverplating. In this process an electric current is passed through an object that is immersed in an appropriate solution of a silver compound. If the voltage is sufficient, silver ions (Ag^+) will accept electrons from the object being plated. The ions thereby change to silver atoms (Ag), which plate the surface. A similar technique is used in electroplating copper, chromium, and gold (*see* Chemistry; Electrochemistry).

History

The earliest recorded observations about electricity date from about 600 BC and are attributed to the Greek philosopher Thales of Miletus. He noted that when amber, a fossil resin, was rubbed it would attract feathers or bits of straw. The Roman author Pliny the Elder wrote about similar experiments in AD 70 in his 'Natural History'. He also mentions shocks given by torpedo fish. In 1600 William Gilbert, an English scientist who was physician to Queen Elizabeth I, published 'De Magnete' (About Magnets). In that book he studied what was already known about amber and lodestone, a mineral that attracts iron. He gave a proof that the attraction exhibited by amber was not magnetic. He also proposed that the Earth behaved as though it were a spherical lodestone. In 1672 the German physicist Otto von Guericke reported the invention of an electric machine: A ball of sulfur on a shaft was rotated; if he touched the rotating sulfur ball with his hand, he noted that sparks were produced. He also proved that electrified objects can transfer some of their ability to attract, called charge, to nonelectrified objects. About 1736 the French chemist Charles-François Du Fay learned that rubbing glass and rubbing resinous substances seemed to produce charges of different kinds. He found that two charges of the same kind repel while unlike charges attract. He suggested that electricity may consist of two kinds of "invisible fluid," which he named "vitreous" and "resinous."

About 1745 a German clergyman, E. Georg von Kleist, and a professor at the University of Leiden (sometimes spelled Leyden), Pieter van Musschenbroek, discovered independently that a glass vessel filled with water and charged by a friction source could store the charge for later use. The device became known as the Leyden jar. Sir William Watson and Dr. John Bevis of England improved the jar by coating the inside and outside with tinfoil. This vessel could store enough charge to make sparks that would explode gunpowder or set alcohol afire. Watson's most important discovery was that electricity traveled almost instantaneously along a wire about 2 miles (3.2 kilometers) in length. In 1746 he suggested that electricity was only one kind of fluid and that an excess or lack of that fluid would account for the two kinds of electricity proposed earlier by Du Fay.

The statesman and inventor Benjamin Franklin of the United States, who is credited with the invention of the lightning rod, was an advocate of Watson's one-fluid model. Apparently the enormous respect commanded by Franklin was significant in the widespread acceptance of Watson's model. It was not until the 1890s, however, that a clear understanding of what electricity is finally emerged, showing that both Du Fay and Watson were correct in some ways.

In 1753 the Englishman John Canton discovered electrostatic induction. Henry Cavendish, another Englishman, found that the force of electric attraction varies inversely with the square of the distance between the charges. He did not publish his findings, and the law is named for Charles-Augustin de Coulomb, who also discovered the relationship.

The study of electricity was greatly aided by the invention of a device for producing a steady current of electricity. In 1780 Luigi Galvani, an Italian anatomist, noted that the legs of a dead frog hung from an iron hook twitched when touched with different kinds of metals. He thought a special "animal electricity" caused this, but an Italian professor of physics, Count Alessandro Volta, suspected a chemical cause. He placed unlike metals in piles between pads moistened with acid or salt solutions. The piles produced a steady electrical current: Volta had invented the battery. In 1807 Sir Humphry Davy of England used current from a powerful battery to obtain pure sodium and potassium from molten soda and potash. The Frenchmen Siméon-Denis Poisson, Joseph-Louis Lagrange, André-Marie Ampère, and Dominique Arago and the Englishman George Green worked out many fundamental laws of electrodynamics. In 1826 the German physicist Georg Simon Ohm announced dis-

Luigi Galvani

The Bettmann Archive

Alessandro Volta

The Bettmann Archive

André-Marie Ampère

The Mansell Collection

Georg Simon Ohm

Historia-Photo

The Bettmann Archive

Hans Christian Oersted

EB Inc.

Michael Faraday

The Bettmann Archive

Heinrich Hertz

Crown Copyright, The Science Museum, London

Nikola Tesla

coveries concerning voltage, current, and resistance in circuits.

In 1820 the Danish physicist Oersted discovered that an electric current caused deflection of a compass needle. This was followed by the invention of the electromagnet by the Englishman William Sturgeon. In the United States Joseph Henry improved this device and made other discoveries. Unfortunately, he lacked contact with European scientists, and his findings remained almost unknown for many years.

In 1821 the English chemist Michael Faraday, who had no formal training in mathematics or science, undertook a survey of the experiments and theories of electromagnetism that had appeared in the previous year. Faraday started by repeating Oersted's experiment. He began to develop his own ideas for describing electric and magnetic fields using lines of force. By 1831 he had discovered the principle of electromagnetic induction and the working basis for motors and generators. In 1873 the Scottish physicist James Clerk Maxwell published a profound mathematical analysis predicting that any changing electric or magnetic field would generate electromagnetic waves that would be propagated through space at the speed of light. In 1888 Heinrich Hertz of Germany produced the predicted waves and confirmed the speed Maxwell had calculated. In 1901 Pyotr N. Lebedev of Russia confirmed the existence of radiation pressure, also predicted by Maxwell.

In 1897 the Englishman Sir Joseph J. Thomson discovered that a negatively charged particle was ejected from the cathode in high-voltage gas discharge tubes. This particle was the electron. Scientists became convinced that electric current in a conductor consisted of electrons flowing from negative to positive. Between 1907 and 1911 Ernest Rutherford, a New Zealander working in Canada, discovered that the positive charges of the atom were clustered in an incredibly tiny space—the nucleus—which occupied only about 10^{-15} (1 quadrillionth, or 1/1,000,000,000,000,000) of the volume of the entire atom. In 1909 Robert Millikan of the United States determined that the basic unit of charge was 1.6×10^{-19} (1.6 10-quintillionths, or 1.6/10,000,000,000,000,000,000) coulomb and that this is the electric charge carried by each proton and electron.

Thomson's discovery of the electron became the working basis for new discoveries and advancements in the United States. Marvelous developments in electronics were opened up in 1907 when Lee De Forest provided the needed technical instrument by developing John A. Fleming's diode tube into a triode. Charles P. Steinmetz developed high-tension transmission of current largely by mathematical studies. Nikola Tesla did much the same for the induction motor. Practical inventors such as Thomas Edison and Alexander Graham Bell applied the principles of electricity and magnetism in a wide variety of devices.

In 1925 the Austrian physicist Erwin Schrödinger combined the theoretical work of Niels Bohr, Louis de Broglie, Max Planck, and Werner Heisenberg to develop quantum mechanics. This theory treats electrons and protons as wavelike particles that can exist only in certain allowable energy states and whose location and momentum are describable in terms of probability and not certainty.

Since 1965, when the American physicist Murray Gell-Mann first proposed that protons and neutrons are actually composed of quarks, physicists have explored high-energy particle collisions to find support for their theories of quantum chromodynamics (*see* Quark). These theories have already pointed to a convincing unity between what once had been thought to be three different forces in nature: electromagnetism, the nuclear strong force, and the nuclear weak force. This work offers the promise of uniting these forces and the force of gravity into a single unified theory: a theory that will account for all physical phenomena. (*See also* Ampère; De Forest; Faraday; Gell-Mann; Hertz; Lagrange; Maxwell; Rutherford; Tesla; Thomson.)

BIBLIOGRAPHY FOR ELECTRICITY

Buban, Peter and others. Understanding Electricity and Electronics, 4th ed. (McGraw, 1981).

Hood, W.E. Beginner's Guide to Electricity and Electrical Phenomena (TAB, 1984).

Lackey, J.E. Fundamentals of Electricity and Electronics (Holt, 1983).

Panofsky, W.K. and Phillips, Melba. Classical Electricity and Magnetism, 2nd ed. (Addison, 1962).

Williams, G.E. The Basic Book of Electricity and Electronics (American Tech. Pub., 1984).

Wilson, J.A. and Kaufman, Milton. Learning Electricity and Electronics Through Experiments (McGraw, 1979).

ELECTRIC LIGHT

Here are a few of the many familiar types of lamps that are made to satisfy different needs for electric light. Many other types are too large or too small to be shown here.

ELECTRIC LIGHT. The light by which we see at night is a great help to modern living. We can light houses as though sunlight were pouring in. Out of doors, we can have well-lighted streets. Business districts can be "bright as day" to attract visitors. We can floodlight airports, outdoor work spaces, and fields for night sports.

All this is done with electricity. There are many other ways of getting light; but none are as powerful, convenient, or flexible. All that is needed to have power is a pair of wires connected to the local supply lines. With electric power, light is produced in two ways. In the common *incandescent* lamp, current is forced through a fine metal filament that has a high resistance. The energy used in overcoming this resistance produces a white heat, and the filament glows brilliantly. In another type of lamp, electronic bombardment excites some material until it glows, or *fluoresces*. Each method is so flexible and free from danger that electric lighting can be used to meet any need.

Beginnings with Arc Lights

Electric lighting began with the carbon-arc lamp. Sir Humphry Davy invented such a lamp in 1801, but it was not practical. In 1878 C. F. Brush produced a lamp that came into wide use for lighting streets. This lamp consists of a pair of carbon rods, or *electrodes,* in contact at pointed ends. Electric current is sent through them, and the electrodes are pulled slightly apart. Instantly a brilliant *arc* appears between the carbon points. The electric current makes the arc glow by vaporizing enough carbon to bridge the gap. Most of the light comes, however, from one of the hot, glowing points.

Arc lamps are still one of the best sources of brilliant artificial light. We use them in searchlights and in the projectors for motion pictures (*see* Motion Pictures). They are too brilliant, cumbersome, and hot, however, to use for lighting the interiors of buildings.

These disadvantages are largely overcome in the Cooper-Hewitt mercury lamp, brought out in 1901. This lamp produces light by ionizing mercury vapor between electrodes in a vacuum tube. The light is blue-green and gives unusual color effects. The lamp is delicate and costly. It is still used for photography and to light factories where "nonglare" light is needed and color effects do not matter. Both carbon-arc and mercury-vapor lamps are good sources of ultraviolet radiation (*see* Ultraviolet Radiation). The tube of the mercury lamp is made of fused quartz because glass absorbs ultraviolet rays.

Development of the Filament Lamp

Between 1878 and 1880 Thomas A. Edison and Joseph W. Swan developed a practical lamp for interior lighting. After many attempts they discovered a filament that glowed satisfactorily in a vacuum (to prevent burning) with a moderate consumption of current. The filament was rugged enough to resist shock and did not melt at the high temperature needed. This filament was a thread of carbon.

Edison and Swan had tried to make filaments by charring cotton thread. Later they used bamboo fiber. They enclosed the filament in a glass bulb and pumped out the air. They sealed the bulb by melting the glass tip that had been left open for the pumping.

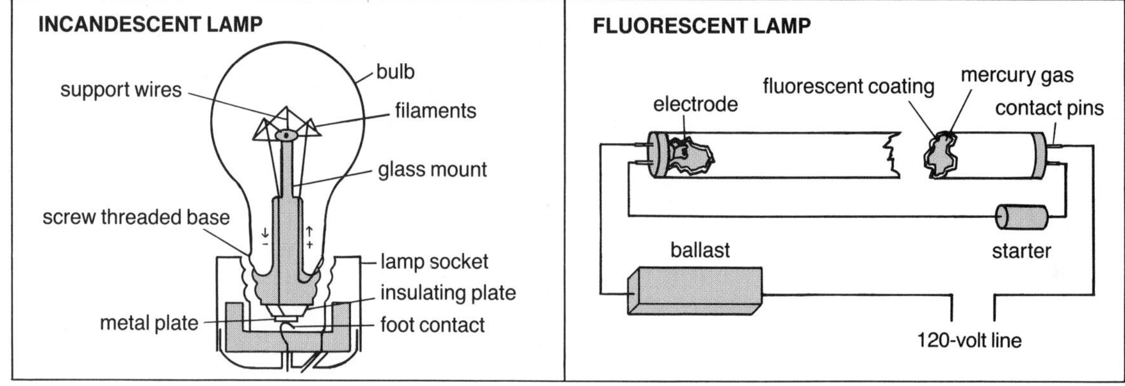

The lead-in wires at the base of the bulb had to be made of a metal that would expand by exactly the same amount as glass when heated. At first costly platinum was thought to be the only suitable metal. Modern lamps use a copper-plated nickel alloy.

The carbon filament burned out rapidly when it was heated enough to give the white glow required for the best lighting. Early lamps therefore could only give a yellowish light. This disadvantage was overcome when the tungsten filament was discovered in 1910 (*see* Tungsten). Beginning in 1925 lamps were given an inside frosting with a fine spray of hydrofluoric acid. This diffuses the light with little loss from internal reflection.

Even a tungsten filament evaporates slowly at high temperatures. It throws off particles and thins until it burns out. The particles blacken the inside of the bulb. This effect is reduced in gas-filled lamps, first introduced in 1913. After the air is pumped out the bulb is filled with argon or nitrogen or a mixture of both. This gas is inert, and it exerts a pressure that resists evaporation of the tungsten particles. Thus a brighter light is produced.

In most lamps the filament is wound into a tight spiral to help maintain heat. Vacuum lamp filaments are supported on tungsten wire. Gas-filled lamps use molybdenum. This metal withstands heat almost as well as tungsten, and it has better mechanical properties.

During the late 19th century an electric discharge tube was developed filled with low-pressure neon gas. When a high voltage was applied to the two electrodes at either end of the tube, it emitted a deep red light. Its value for decorative and advertising purposes was quickly recognized. Other gases give other colors. Mercury vapor produces blue; helium in an amber tube gives a golden glow; green is obtained with a blue glow in a yellow tube. When several gases that produce different colors are used in a tube, the colors combine to give white (*see* Color). Neon signs soon decorated the exteriors of commercial buildings in the cities of the world. The discharge tube, however, had little application in interiors until the development in the 1930s of the fluorescent tube, a long tube with a mercury-vapor filling. The inner wall of the tube was coated with a material that fluoresced white or near white when irradiated by the mercury discharge, multiplying the illumination a hundredfold.

Somewhat before the fluorescent tube came into use, lamps with much shorter arcs, in which the gas or vapor operated at a higher pressure, were introduced, including the high-pressure mercury-vapor-discharge lamp and the sodium-discharge lamp. Neither of these found much use for interior lighting, however, because the light they gave off made people look ghostly. Mercury- and sodium-discharge lamps were acceptable for lighting streets.

New developments in both the mercury- and sodium-discharge lamps overcame to some extent the disadvantages of the parents. Lamp manufacturers continued to experiment with new devices. In this category might be included the xenon-discharge lamp, a high-powered source with color almost identical to natural sunlight.

Great lamps of massive light output have been made using the arc principle, the vapor-discharge principle, and the incandescent-filament principle for lighthouses, searchlights, and the floodlighting of large areas such as airport runways and playing fields. Microscopic filament lamps have been created for insertion in the body to enable the surgeon, aided by suitable optical equipment, to make visual inspection to supplement other methods of diagnosis.

The development of flexible optic fibers, thin wires of transparent plastic that "conduct" light by internal reflection from a suitable lamp at one end to the target at the other, have also been used for medical and other purposes. Other lamps for special uses include lamps for photography, color television, and cinematography; lamps with emission in selected parts of the spectrum for industrial uses; infrared lamps for paint drying; and both infrared and ultraviolet lamps for therapeutic use.

Solid-state light-emitting diodes (LEDs) are replacing incandescent bulbs in many applications because of their small size, low power requirements, durability, and long life. LEDs already provide light for digital clocks, radios, calculators, and some television screens. In an LED an electron releases energy by emitting a photon when it drops into a lower energy state. LEDs have been developed to emit light of virtually any color, even infrared light.

Jerry Kalyniuk

The Braidwood nuclear power plant operated by Commonwealth Edison in rural Illinois has two 20-story containment buildings and a 730-foot- (220-meter-) long turbine building.

ELECTRIC POWER. Most of mankind's energy needs, except transportation, are met by electric power. It is a willing servant in home, office, factory, school, and theater. Electric energy is available almost everywhere and ever ready to be used. Its ease of production, distribution, and utilization—coupled with stable costs—has accounted for the rapid rise of electrical devices during the 20th century.

Most electric power is generated in large plants that use coal, gas, oil, or nuclear energy. These are generally called central stations, and they require only a few workers. Central stations can be located at any convenient site, generally as long as cooling water is available. Sometimes it is convenient to place a plant near the source of fuel and at other times near the majority of users. The only exception is for hydroelectric plants, which must be on a body of water with a large enough water drop, or head, and a steady flow.

Power is brought from the generating plant to the user through a network of wires called transmission and distribution lines. The power can be used as needed simply by turning on a switch.

Electric Utility Industry

The electric utility industry began when Thomas Edison opened the Pearl Street station in New York City on Sept. 4, 1882 (*see* Edison). That station contained six direct current (DC) generators of about 100 kilowatts (KW), each of which could serve an area of about 1 square mile (2.6 square kilometers). Following the development of polyphase alternating current (AC) systems by Nikola Tesla around 1885 and the introduction of the improved transformer by George Westinghouse in 1887, the way was opened for the modern AC power generation and distribution system (*see* Tesla; Westinghouse). Early generators were driven by steam engines. These were replaced by large steam turbines, and the size of power plants grew to the point where the typical modern plant can generate from 500 to 4,000 megawatts (MW), or millions of watts.

There are about 3,500 individual power systems in the United States. They comprise investor-owned public utilities, cooperatives, federal or local government-owned systems, and manufacturing industries that also produce power. The federal government owns about 10 percent of the generating capacity—including such large organizations as the Tennessee Valley Authority (TVA)—but few distribution facilities (*see* Tennessee Valley Authority). Nonfederally-owned systems have few generators but focus on transmission and distribution systems to account for another 10 percent of the total power. About 1,000 cooperatives are usually small distributors of power to rural areas. Industry-owned systems generate power mostly for their own use but may sell surplus power to utilities. Nearly 80 percent of the nation's power generation comes from the approximately 400 investor-owned public utilities.

A utility is a monopoly; that is, the customer has no choice but to buy electricity from the local utility company. To assure that the customer is charged a fair rate for electricity and that the utility has a fair return on its investment, state governments (and sometimes the federal government) determine rates through appropriate regulatory commissions.

Generation, Transmission, and Distribution

Conventional steam power plants. Most modern power plants generate high-pressure (from 2,400 to 4,500 pounds per square inch), high-temperature steam (about 1,000° to 1,200° F, or 540° to 650° C) in boilers up to ten stories high that may be fired by coal, natural gas, or oil. The steam expands through the turbines, which are connected to generators, to do useful work. The steam is then turned back into water

This article was contributed by Harold Boettcher, Professor of Electrical Engineering, University of Wisconsin—Milwaukee.

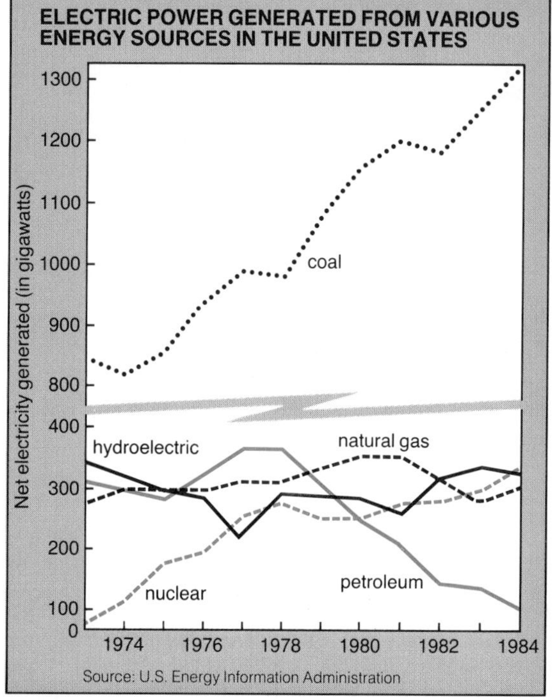

in a condenser and finally is fed back to the boiler. The large amount of water that is needed to condense steam demands access to cooling water either from rivers or from large lakes. If neither is close by, cooling towers must be constructed. Some of the water is evaporated in these while it cools the remainder and also condenses the steam. In desert areas "dry" cooling towers, in which air is passed over the condenser in large towers, may be used. This, however, increases the cost.

In the mid-1980s about 57 percent of electricity in the United States was generated in coal-fired plants, and the percentage was rising. Only 5 percent was generated from oil, about 10 percent from natural gas, and about 12 percent from nuclear power. Some plants are able to switch from gas to oil, depending on the price of the fuel.

Nuclear plants. The energy source in a nuclear reactor is the heat released by the splitting of uranium-235 or plutonium-239 atoms when they are bombarded by neutrons. The heat is transferred to a coolant, which also serves to control the reaction. The coolant then retransfers the heat to water and converts it into steam. This in turn drives a conventional turbine-alternator combination. Most plants in the United States use either pressurized water or boiling water as the coolant. Other systems may use liquid sodium, a pressurized gas (usually carbon dioxide), or heavy water (deuterium oxide) as the coolant. The coolant is kept separate from the steam to minimize radiation dangers.

By the mid-1980s there were nearly 100 operable nuclear reactors with a total capacity of more than 81,800 MW. There were a number of units under construction, but no new orders were placed after 1978 as a result of public concern about reactor safety and the high costs of construction.

Hydroelectric plants. Electric energy may also be obtained from waterpower. About 16 percent of United States generating capacity is in hydroelectric plants. Water passes downward through a hydraulic turbine that is connected to a generator. Large plants, which depend on large volumes of water dammed upstream, can generate more than 2,000 MW. There are many small plants on rivers, some generating only a few hundred kilowatts. Among the largest plants in the United States are Hoover Dam, which forms Lake Mead on the Colorado River at the Arizona-Nevada border, and the Grand Coulee Dam on the Columbia River in eastern Washington state (*see* Dam; Grand Coulee Dam). Hoover Dam has an installed capacity of 1,244 MW. Grand Coulee has an installed capacity of 2,025 MW. It is part of the Columbia River Basin project, which has a planned capacity of 9,770 MW.

Other commercial plants. The inability to store electric energy cheaply and efficiently requires that every utility have the capacity to adjust its power output instantaneously to meet the demand. While there is considerable flexibility in operating large steam-power plants, such a plant might not be able to meet a sudden peak demand. It may take as long as eight hours to start another boiler. Many utilities, therefore, have installed gas-turbine peaking plants to produce additional power within a few seconds. These are only about half as efficient as large plants and are used for peak production only.

Small and remote villages and towns may rely on diesel engine-driven generators. These may not even be connected to larger power systems.

The generator. Steam turbines, diesel engines, and hydraulic turbines are connected to alternators that generate AC electricity. Most generators produce three-phase current at voltages ranging from 2,000 to 4,000 volts. Three separate but connected windings are used within each unit. Alternators are rated by the number of volt-amperes they can supply. This is the sum of the products of the winding voltage multiplied by the full load current for the three windings. Modern units are rated from 1 to 1,300 million volt-amperes (MVA), with a typical rating of 500 to 600 MVA for a large generator. Large units are preferred, as they are more efficient, they initially cost less per MVA, and they have fewer parts to maintain than do several smaller units.

The frequency of the alternating current must be kept constant by assuring that the turbines and the generator turn at an exactly fixed speed. Considerable engineering effort is devoted to the controls on the steam or water flow to bring this about. In the United States the standard frequency is 60 hertz (cycles per second); in parts of Canada it is 50 hertz. Some electric railroads run on 16⅔ hertz. Power systems with different frequencies cannot be interconnected directly.

Constant frequencies make electric AC motors run at essentially constant speeds. If variable speed con-

THERMOELECTRIC GENERATOR

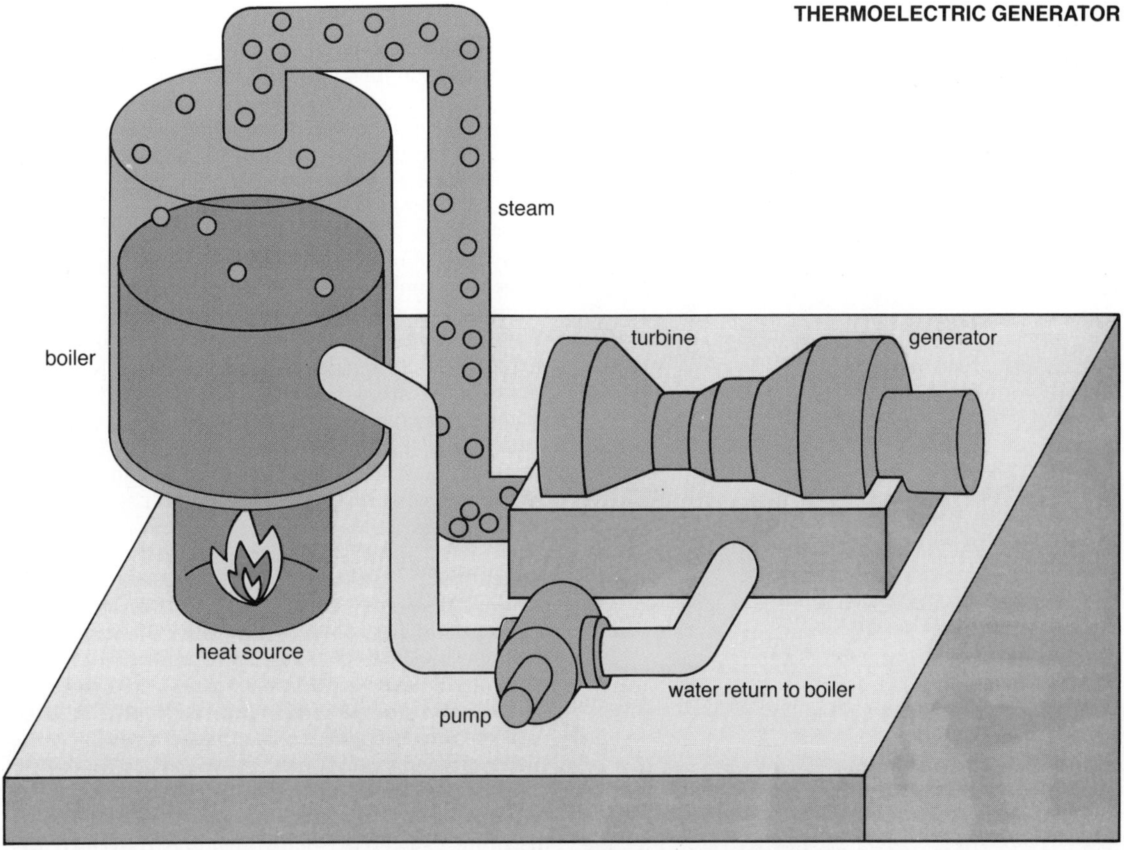

In a thermoelectric generating system a heat source—usually fueled by coal, oil, or gas—is used within a boiler to convert water to high-pressure steam. The steam expands and turns the blades of a turbine, which turns the armature of a generator, producing electric power. A condenser converts any remaining steam to water, and a pump returns the water to the boiler.

trol is desired, it can be achieved by electronically varying the frequency just ahead of the motor.

Load management. Power plants run most economically when each unit operates near its maximum capacity. In this case the cost per kilowatt-hour (KWH) becomes a minimum. Sometimes this is best achieved when the utility either purchases some power from, or sells it to, a neighboring utility. This interchange is usually computer controlled to achieve minimum generating costs. Wilmington, Del., for example, is an industrial center that needs maximum power during the day, while nearby Atlantic City, N.J., is a resort area with its maximum power demand at night. By interchanging power between the two locations, both benefit from lower rates and reduce the need for additional generating units that would not be fully utilized.

Transmission and distribution systems. The electricity generated in the power plant must be transformed to higher voltages for long-distance transmission. It is most efficient to use the maximum voltage, especially for long distances. Modern trans-

Three-phase current gives users a choice of two voltages. The lower voltage is used for lighting and small appliances. Two phases provide nearly double the voltage for high-current appliances.

PRINCIPLE OF THE GENERATOR

TIME RELATION OF PHASES

POWER LINES AND SERVICE CONNECTIONS

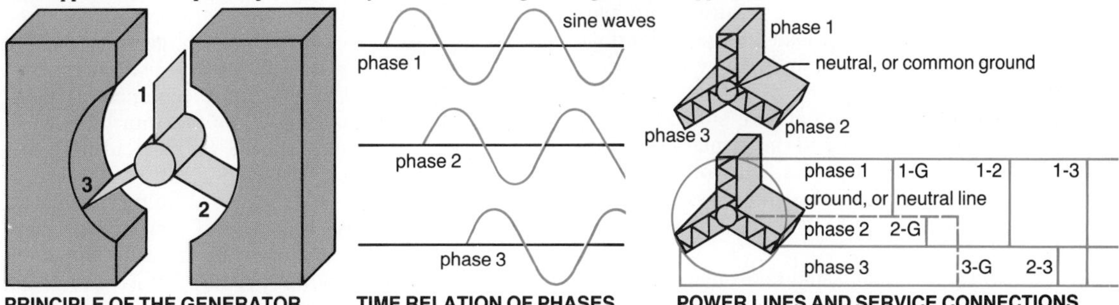

(Top) © Mitch Kezar—Phototake; (center) Cameramann International; (bottom) Jerry Kalyniuk

The output of electricity from a coal-fired power plant is carefully monitored from a control room (top) to assure that power demands are met at all peak periods. Steam turbines are connected to generators (center) to produce electric power. The transformer (bottom) at an electric generating plant increases voltage prior to transmission.

mission systems operate at voltages of from 66,000 to 765,000 volts.

The interconnection of transmission systems forms a so-called power grid, which permits the interchange of electricity between utilities. A failure in one part of the system, however, can lead to a power outage for the whole system unless emergency disconnect devices can be actuated.

Transmission lines terminate at substations in which the voltage is reduced to the primary distribution voltage, usually 23,000 volts. This voltage is then supplied directly to large industrial users or further transformed down to 2,300 or 4,100 volts for local distribution.

To this point all transmission takes place as three-phase power using four wires. Residences usually require only lower voltage single-phase power, or one phase of the three-phase system. Most residential customers are supplied with 220 to 240 volts (nominally 230 volts) using three wires. The secondary winding of the distribution transformer has a center tap that is usually grounded at both the transformer and at the customer's service entrance, resulting in a voltage from the center tap to the end of either winding of 115 volts (*see* Transformer). This is the voltage generally used at outlets for small appliances and lights. Large appliances—such as water heaters, large air conditioners, and ovens—use 230 volts directly.

A different distribution system is sometimes used in high-density residential areas such as New York City, where power is taken directly from a three-phase system. Here the so-called line-to-line voltage is 208 volts, while the line-to-neutral voltage is 120 volts. Although most large appliances are designed for 230 volts, they will work at 208 volts with some loss of performance.

In the Home

Single-phase power is brought to the home either aboveground (aerial) or below the ground (buried) through three wires. Two of these are covered with insulation and carry the power, while the third—often bare—is the ground wire. Before entering the house, the wires go through a watt-hour meter. It measures the power consumed, forming the basis for billing electric charges. On entering the home the wires are fed to a circuit breaker or fuse box. This contains a disconnect switch to isolate the home from the power line, a main fuse or circuit breaker, and breakers for the various circuits in the house. Separate breakers protect the 230-volt lines for large appliances. Modern homes are equipped with three wire connections to each outlet to provide full grounding protection.

Such 115-volt devices as microwave ovens should only be connected to grounded outlets. Other small appliances are only supplied with two-pronged connections and can be safely operated on a two-wire outlet. In most homes the wall outlets in two or more rooms share a common fuse or circuit breaker. The total use of electricity in residences accounts for about 34 percent of the national electric power output.

Industrial and Commercial Uses

The introduction of small electric motors in the 1920s allowed factories to couple a motor to each machine. Before that time all machines were powered from one central steam engine or large motor, which drove a maze of shafts, pulleys, and leather belts to each machine. This resulted in uneconomical, noisy, and unsafe operation. Today motors can be built in a variety of sizes and speeds to meet almost any requirement.

Many industries—notably the aluminum and steel industries—use large amounts of power. Electricity is required to produce aluminum from its ore. Much of the hydroelectric power produced at Niagara Falls, for example, is used by the Aluminum Company of

Courtesy of ARCO Solar, Inc.

Cameramann International

A solar power plant (left) in California's Carrisa Plain generates 6 megawatts of electricity and is connected to the local electric power grid. Wind turbines (right) generate electricity at the west end of the Coachella Valley in California, one of the most consistently windy areas in the United States.

America. Electric arc furnaces are common in steel production. They readily provide the controlled high temperatures needed to produce many special alloys.

The total industrial use of electricity in the United States accounts for about 36 percent of the national output. Stores, businesses, banks, theaters, hospitals, and other nonmanufacturing organizations account for about 25 percent of the national output.

Uses in Agriculture

Initially electric power was limited to high-density areas such as cities, where distribution costs were lower than in rural areas. Small farms especially were generally not served. By 1935 only about 11 percent of United States farms had electricity. In 1935 the Rural Electrification Administration (REA) began to extend long-term loans to utilities for constructing power lines and wiring farms, and, more significantly, to about 1,000 rural cooperatives. These were formed especially to distribute electric energy to rural areas and usually to purchase power from investor-owned or public-owned utilities. Today more than 95 percent of the nation's farms are connected to electric utilities, with only a few isolated farms depending on their own power generation.

Electric motors on the farm grind feed, pump water, and run milking machines. Electric power pasteurizes milk, refrigerates food products, and keeps newborn livestock and chickens warm. Electricity has allowed farmers to increase their output and their productivity just as it has helped industry.

Direct Current

The most common source of DC, which is required in some applications, is the battery, though AC can also be rectified, or made one directional. The voltage per cell is usually low—between 1 and 2 volts—as is the maximum amount of current that can be drawn for any length of time (*see* Battery and Fuel Cell).

Very high-voltage—300,000 to 750,000 volts—DC is sometimes used for very long-distance—more than 500 miles (800 kilometers)—power transmission. Transmission of DC also permits the interconnection of power systems at different frequencies such as those in parts of Canada and the United States. The high-voltage AC is rectified by using thyristers, or silicon-controlled rectifiers, into high-voltage DC, which is then transmitted. At the other end thyristers in an inverter circuit convert the DC back to AC, which can then be at a different frequency.

Additional Developments

Alternative energy sources have recently gained prominence, but their total power output is still small. Photovoltaic research promises to make solar cells eventually competitive with other energy sources. Here the light of the sun is converted directly into low-voltage DC electricity, which is then converted to AC.

The wind has also been used to harness energy and to produce electricity. About 500 MW of generating capacity are available, mostly in California. Few locations, however, have steady winds at appropriate speeds, and costs have been very high.

Steam for conventional power plants can also be produced from geothermal reservoirs. Another source is from the incineration of municipal trash.

Fuel cells use electrochemical reactions—such as between hydrogen and oxygen—to produce power directly. Several are under development in Japan. In the United States fuel cells have been used in a few special-purpose applications.

Cogeneration. An organization that requires low-pressure steam for heating finds that it is not much more expensive to produce high-pressure steam instead. This is then expanded through a turbine to generate some electric power and is subsequently available at low pressure. If this power is not needed by the plant, it can be sold to a utility. Since 1978 federal legislation in the United States requires utilities to buy such excess power that is "cogenerated" by qualified customers. Since this cogeneration usually takes place during periods of high energy demand, it can be an advantage to both the customer and the utility. The customer receives income for the power sold, while the utility finds less need to build additional power plants. (*See also* Electricity.)

ELECTROCHEMISTRY. The use of electric current to produce a chemical change is a powerful aid to science and industry. This is the only way to obtain some metals quickly, cheaply, and free of impurities. Many gases, salts, and other products are also made this way. A current produced in an electrolytic solution can deposit a film of metal on objects with microscopic accuracy. Electrochemical methods are used in chemical analysis and to produce electric current from a cell or battery.

The science that deals with these processes is called *electrochemistry.* Its principal application is to break down a complex compound into simpler ones or to separate a compound into its elements. This is done by *electrolysis.* The name is from Greek words that mean "loosening by electricity."

Electrochemical terms imply the use of current. The substance to be changed is called the *electrolyte.* Current is applied to the electrolyte through *electrodes* (*-ode* means "path"). The electrodes are named from the older theory that current flows from an excess of "electric fluid" (+) to a lack (−). The pole that supposedly led this flow into a solution is called an *anode.* (The *an* means "up" or "excess.") The exit pole is named a *cathode* (from *kata,* meaning "down" or "lack").

Thin, flexible sheets of steel pass through electrochemical baths in the stacks of this machine. In the baths a film of tin is laid on the steel with microscopic accuracy.

Why Solutions Conduct Electrolysis

Some electrochemical processes separate gaseous or molten substances; but most electrolytes are dissolved in water. Water is neutral enough to dissolve acids, bases, or salts; and usually it does not produce great heat or other violent reactions.

Electrolytes dissolve by *dissociation*—that is, the molecules of the substance break down into charged particles called *ions.* An ion with a − charge is called an *anion* (*ăn′ī-ŏn*) because it is drawn through the solution to the + charge on the anode. A particle with a + charge is called a *cation* (*kăt′ī-ŏn*). It moves through the solution to the cathode.

Water has its solvent properties because it is *polar.* The molecule has charged ends (+ and −), as explained in the article Solutions. These charged ends react with charges on other polar substances to dissolve them. They do so by taking hydrogen atoms from the substance to form *hydronium ions* (H_3O), as explained in Chemistry. Sulfuric acid, for example, is dissociated as follows:

$$H_2SO_4 + 2H_2O \longrightarrow 2H_3{}^{+}O + SO_4{}^{=}$$

Sulfuric acid water hydronium ions sulfate ion

The hydronium ion is written accurately as H^+H_2O. The H^+ is often used as a symbol for the entire ion.

Donors and Acceptors

The active process in dissociation is the transfer of an electron or electrons from an atom in one substance (leaving the atom as a + ion) to one or more atoms in another substance (making them − ions). The transfer makes an *electrovalent bond* (*see* Chemistry).

Substances that form ions may be classified in one of two groups, according to the part they play in electron transfer. Cations are called *donors,* because they give up one or more electrons in an electrochemical process and thereby gain a + charge. Anions are called *acceptors,* because they gain one or more electrons and thus have a − charge.

The donor-acceptor classification matches the great division between metallic and nonmetallic elements. This division is shown in the modern Periodic Table (*see* Periodic Table). The metallic elements (grouped toward the left of the table) have one, two, or three electrons in their outer shells. These electrons are lost or displaced readily to fulfill the tendency shown by all atoms to have an outer shell of two or eight electrons. Metallic elements therefore are donors and form cations.

Nonmetallic elements (at the right of the Periodic Table) have from four to eight electrons in the outer shell. This group furnishes the anions. Their outer shells tend to complete the shell by gaining one or more electrons from metallic elements. This gives them added − charges.

Acids, Bases, and Salts

Common *acids* are hydrogen compounds in which the hydrogen can be replaced by other metallic elements. The other part of the acid compound is an *acid radical,* which is negative (−) in charge. H_2SO_4 is sulfuric acid. The radical is SO_4, a sulfate. HNO_3 is nitric acid. The radical is NO_3, a nitrate. HCl is hydrochloric acid. The Cl (chlorine) serves as the acid radical, although it is only one atom.

Bases consist of one or more *hydroxyl* (OH) radicals with a − charge, combined with one or more elements that can form + ions. One common form of base is called an *alkali*. This is a combination of the hydroxyl radical with an alkali metal. After a base dissociates, the hydroxyl ion may combine with a hydrogen ion (H^+) to form a water molecule. *Salts* are compounds which result when the hydrogen of an acid is replaced by a metallic element. Such a compound does not have a hydroxyl radical. (*See also* Acids; Salt.)

The Displacement, or Electromotive, Series

Since atoms differ in structure and properties, some enter into combinations more readily than others. The more active, or stronger, ones enter into combinations more readily than others. They also displace less active, or weaker, ones from compounds in which either could be a part. The following list shows 21 metallic elements and hydrogen, which acts like a metal in electrolytic processes. The elements are listed according to their displacement strength, from the strongest (lithium) to the weakest (gold).

1. Lithium	9. Chromium	16. HYDROGEN
2. Potassium	10. Iron	17. Bismuth
3. Calcium	11. Cadmium	18. Copper
4. Sodium	12. Cobalt	19. Mercury
5. Magnesium	13. Nickel	20. Silver
6. Aluminum	14. Tin	21. Platinum
7. Manganese	15. Lead	22. Gold
8. Zinc		

Elements above hydrogen are more active chemically than those below. Hence these elements are rarely found free in nature. Elements below hydrogen are often found free.

The higher on the list an element stands, the more firmly it is bound to other elements in a solution. Greater voltage is needed accordingly to draw it out of solution as a deposit on an electrode. Because hydrogen is relatively low in the series, it is easily displaced in acids by metallic elements above it. Such a displacement is the acid action that produces salts.

Action at the Electrodes

The electrodes produce continuous electrochemical change by drawing ions in the solution toward themselves. The cathode and the anode maintain their negative or positive charges despite the + ions or − electrons which they collect. This happens because of the chemical nature of the electrodes in relation to the electrolyte, plus the fact that the liberated charges (+ ions and electrons) are moved through the external circuit to be neutralized by the opposite charge. They do not pile up at either electrode and neutralize the electrode.

The transfer starts when − ions reach the anode. The anode takes away the electrons that gave the ions their charges. As the electrons gather, they repel or force some of their number into the external circuit. Meanwhile, the cathode is drawing + ions from the solution and electrons from the external circuit. The electrons neutralize the charges of the + ions, making them normal atoms. The normal atoms formed in these ways from ions may join as molecules, or take part in other reactions.

An example of a reaction ending as gases is the separation of hydrogen and oxygen by electrolysis:

$2H_2O$	$\longrightarrow$	$4H^+ + 2O$	$\longrightarrow$	$2H_2 + O_2$
water molecules	current applied	dissociation by ionization		formation of gases

Solutions may contain ions that attract each other strongly enough to form molecules of an insoluble compound. These molecules settle out (precipitate) from the solution. An example is silver (+ ions) and chlorine (− ions) joining to form a precipitate of silver chloride when electric current passes through a solution of silver nitrate and sodium chloride. The sodium and nitrate ions remain as dissolved sodium nitrate.

Many metals will form a deposit on a suitable cathode. Copper from copper chloride does this in the example shown below. The chlorine ions lose their charges and form molecules of chlorine gas.

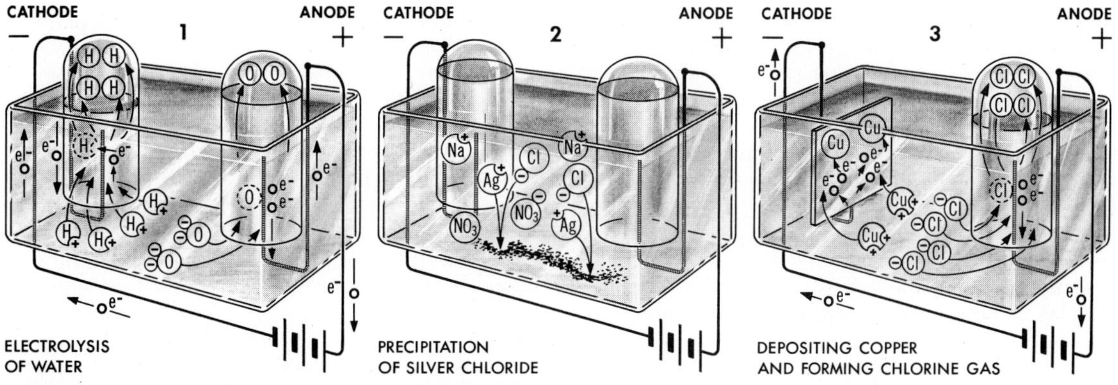

TYPICAL RESULTS FROM ELECTROCHEMISTRY

1. Electric current decomposes water into gaseous hydrogen (H_2) and gaseous oxygen (O_2). 2. Ions in a solution may be strongly attracted to each other, forming an insoluble substance. Silver chloride (AgCl) forms from sodium chloride (NaCl) and silver nitrate ($AgNO_3$). 3. Copper chloride ($CuCl_2$) breaks down into metallic copper (Cu) and gaseous chlorine (Cl_2).

Dan McCoy—Rainbow

The Dream Machine, a video arcade in Massachusetts, is a game emporium where "addicts" and novices alike can test their skill against the machines.

ELECTRONIC GAMES

ELECTRONIC GAMES. It began with a game called Pong in the early 1970s. But the Pong fad only lasted a couple of years because people tired of playing a game that was predictable and that they learned so easily. Then in 1979 came Space Invaders, an electronic game manufactured by the Taito Corporation in Japan. What had at first been a fad turned rapidly into an addiction. Video arcades, already a popular place in which to spend money and time in Japan, appeared all over the United States and in nearly every other country where people had some extra money to spend.

Space Invaders was not alone in the arcades for very long. It was quickly followed by Pac Man, Defender, Centipede, Scramble, Donkey Kong, Star Castle, Asteroids, Missile Command, and an ever increasing variety of electronic versions of sports and card games.

Many of the arcade games also became available for play at home. Some were played on home computers; others used the television screen as a monitor; some were self-contained, hand-held, battery-powered, or table-model games. Pong, manufactured by Atari, was available early as an arcade game and for home television.

The most popular arcade games are played by one person against the machine. The most common of the games, though they may appear complicated, are really a simple matter of attack and defense. A player can pile up a large score, but the fun is in the playing. Some games, such as simulated athletic contests, can be played by two or more people at once. Electronic card games can be played by one or more, depending on the game.

The Technology

Electronic games are a by-product of computer technology. Their operation depends on silicon microchips with so-called read only memory, or ROM, and a vast array of circuitry. Some of the games require as many as six ROM chips, each with 32K memory. This means that each chip can store more than 32,000 bits, or pieces, of information. The microprocessor controls what appears on the screen as well as any sounds the game may make. The player operates the game with a lever called a "joystick" and a combination of buttons. Some advanced games offer the simulation of being inside a flying craft, operating its controls, and firing its weapons.

Social Effects

In 1982 Walt Disney studios released a movie entitled 'Tron'. In it a video game fanatic is taken into the microchip and circuitry world of the game itself. The film is symbolic of the millions of people who became addicted to playing in arcades and at home. At its peak the video game industry took in more than 5 billion dollars a year through the arcades alone. In addition was all the money spent for home equipment.

So great was the fascination with the games that adolescents skipped school and adult workers took long lunch hours in order to pass as much time as possible with Pac Man, Asteroids, and other games. This seeming obsession, of course, led to a reaction. Schools demanded that arcades be moved away from their vicinity, or they refused to allow students outside during lunch hours. Some towns, in a mood reminiscent of the old antipathy toward pool halls and pinball parlors, closed the arcades or limited their number. In the Philippines the reaction was so strong that President Ferdinand Marcos decreed in 1981 that all machines be destroyed.

But nothing so popular as a national fad can be curtailed easily. Video games appeared not only in arcades but in bars, family grocery stores, and other locations where they could make a profit.

The Industry

There was, in fact, no need to try to limit the number of arcades or put them out of business. By 1984 the fad was in decline. In 1982 there were about 10,000 game parlors in the United States. By the beginning of 1984 about 2,000 had closed, and many had cut the cost of playing the machines. The largest maker of arcade machines, Bally Manufacturing Corporation, found its profits down by more than 80 percent in one year, and other manufacturers were in much the same position.

The production and sales of home software showed an even greater decline within a one-year period. Such manufacturers as Atari, Coleco Industries, Inc., Mattel Inc., Milton Bradley Company, Imagic, Avalon Hill, Fox Video Games, and others had so increased their production of game cartridges that there was a tremendous oversupply.

One factor was competition from computer makers. They were selling video-game software that could be played on home computers. As the market for home computers expanded rapidly, the cost of these devices fell because of mass production and rapidly increasing competition. The advantage of the computer is its ability to do so many more things than merely play games. (*See also* Computer.)

Children (below) enjoy a variety of home electronic games, including educational ones. The Exterminator (top right) uses a liquid crystal display. The entire game is only the size of a credit card. Two teenagers (bottom right) play a Super Mario II game made by Nintendo, the Japanese software firm that dominated video game sales in the late 1980s.

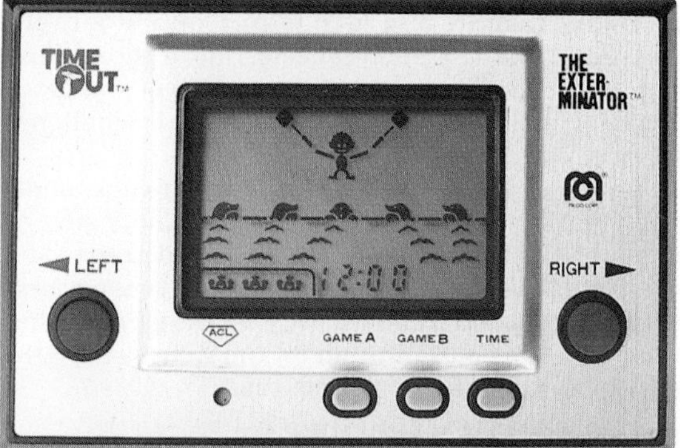

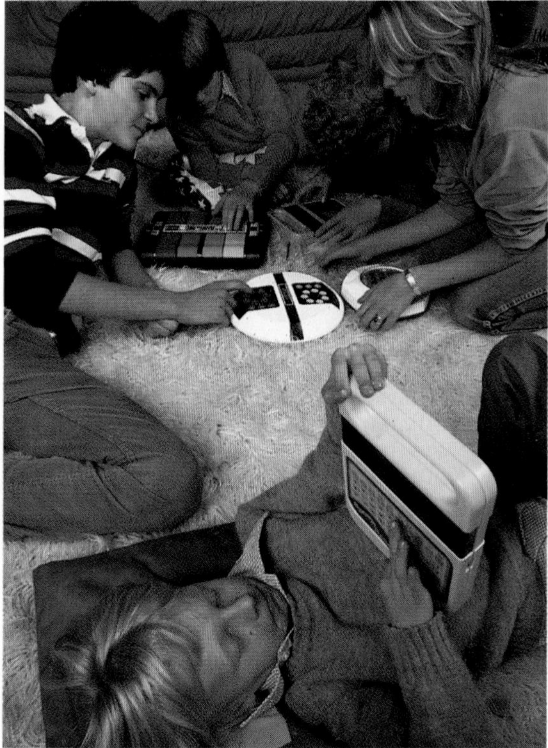

Photos, Dan McCoy—Rainbow

One of the problems with home video games is that, after being played many times, people lose interest in them. To counter this drop in interest, game manufacturers turned to laser-disc technology in the early 1980s. The disc projects an animated cartoon on the screen, and the player is able, by working the controls, to direct the game-movie and put in all the action. The advantage of the laser disc is greatly increased realism for the player, as computer graphics are combined with moving pictures of actual or cartoon-drawn places and characters.

The industry continued to decline, however, until the late 1980s, when it was revived by the success of the Nintendo Entertainment System. A sophisticated machine able to run more interesting graphics, the availability of more than 100 games, and a special computer chip built into the game cartridges so that games without the chip could not be played on Nintendo's machines all combined to make Nintendo extremely popular and profitable.

Educational and Therapeutic Applications

Computer manufacturers and the makers of video games have learned to combine the fascination and excitement of a game with lessons to teach language, mathematics, reading, and science. Computers are used in schools to teach programming and basic computer literacy. With the creation of new software programs, they are also used to introduce even very young children to school subjects. One of the earliest and most popular software programs leads preschool children into the complexities of science by challenging them to unravel simple mysteries.

Video games have also been used to treat a condition called amblyopia, or lazy eye, in which one eye does not function as well as the other and needs to be exercised to correct the fault. The good eye is covered with a patch, so the child must play the games using the weak eye. Concentration on the games strengthens the eye and improves the vision.

A therapist treats a young patient with amblyopia using a video game. The child's right eye is patched to force the left eye to exercise.

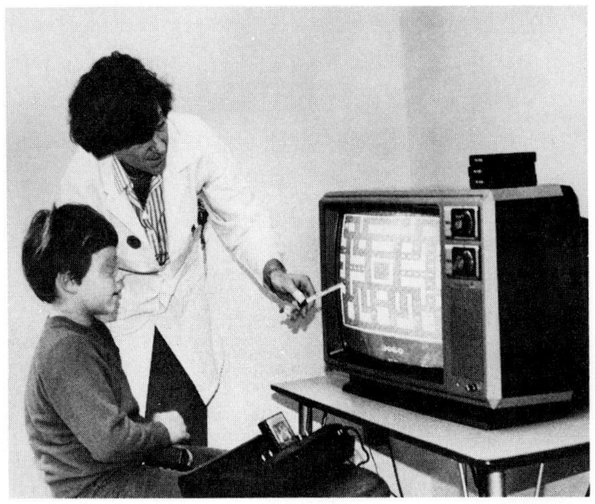

Courtesy of the New York Eye and Ear Infirmary

ELECTRONIC INSTRUMENTS. Although electricity was first applied to the mechanism of a musical instrument in an electric harpsichord in 1761, the first major development began about 1920. The first stage of this development, which lasted until the beginning of World War II, covers two basic types of instruments. The first type includes those whose sound is initiated in such familiar mechanical ways as the striking, plucking, or bowing of strings and the activation of reeds and then amplified and heard through a loudspeaker. The second type includes those that produce sounds as a result of electrical vibrations. These sounds are also amplified and heard through a loudspeaker. Examples of the first type are electric pianos (Superpiano, invented in 1927; Neo-Bechstein-Flügel, 1931; Elektrochord, 1933); electronic organs that have vibrating reeds (Rangertone, 1931; Orgatron, 1934); and electric violins, violas, cellos, basses, guitars, banjos, and mandolins.

The second type can be subdivided into instruments that simulate existing sounds and those designed to produce new sounds. A familiar example of the former is the electronic organ (Hammond, rotating electromagnetic generators, 1935; Electrone, using rotating electrostatic generators, 1938; Organova, a photoelectric cell). Among the latter are the Theremin, 1920; Ondes Martenot, 1928; Trautonium, 1930; and MixturTrautonium, 1952. These instruments have been used in works by such composers as Richard Strauss, Paul Hindemith, Arthur Honegger, Darius Milhaud, Olivier Messiaen, and Edgard Varèse.

The next stage of development began with the discovery of magnetic tape recording and continued with its technical improvement, especially during and after World War II. Since any sound can be recorded on tape and then manipulated in a variety of ways, the tape recorder can be both an instrument for performance and a device used by the composer to create new sounds.

This is also true of the music synthesizer, introduced by the RCA laboratories in 1955 and refined in the 1960s in such models as the Moog, Buchla, and Syn-Ket. Some of these synthesizers have traditional keyboards or some modification of other traditional performing mechanisms.

The computer is still another electronic device used both as an instrument and as a composer. An early result of the latter is 'Illiac Suite' for string quartet, done by the Illiac high-speed digital computer in 1957. The direct synthesis of sound by a computer was first described in 1963 at the Bell Telephone laboratories. The musical score was a deck of punched cards that the computer read.

Such popular music styles as rock and roll, country and western, and rhythm and blues, among others, rely heavily on electronically amplified instruments. Rock and roll in particular has incorporated a wide variety of synthesizers and other electronic apparatus, such as control boards, that combine and vary the electronic outputs from all the instruments in the group. (*See also* Instrumentation; Music, Popular.)

ELECTRONICS

ELECTRONICS. Television, stereophonic recording and playback, the computer, robots, and space probes are all products of a single basic technology: electronics. Electronics is the use of electricity to control, communicate, and process information. Its products have caused greater changes in everyday life than those of any other technology in the second half of the 20th century.

The Electronic Signal

The basis of electronics is the electronic signal, an electric current that represents information. There are two basic types of electrical signals: analog and digital. In analog signals, some continuously variable aspect of the electrical current represents the information. In amplitude modulated (AM) radio transmissions, for example, the amplitude, or strength, of the electromagnetic radio wave is proportional to the amplitude of the signal—the volume of the sound that the radio wave carries. The greater the amplitude of the radio wave, the louder the sound that radiates from the radio speaker.

In contrast, digital signals use standardized pulses to represent numbers. With a digital audio signal, the amplitude of the signal for a set amount of time is converted to a number represented by, for example, 16 pulses of fixed duration and amplitude. The audio signal as a whole is transmitted as a series of such 16-pulse codes.

Most electronic devices deal with digital signals. In these signals the numbers are almost always represented in a binary code; that is, instead of using a number system based on 10, as is used in writing numbers and manual arithmetic, electronic systems use numbers based on 2. There are only two basic numbers in this system: 0 and 1, with 1 being represented by a pulse and 0 by the absence of a pulse, or some similar arrangement.

The number 40 in the base-10 system, for example, would be represented in the base-2 system by 101000, meaning $1 \times 2^5 + 0 \times 2^4 + 1 \times 2^3 + 0 \times 2^2 + 0 \times 2^1$. Letters and words can be encoded in much the same manner, as can be logic codes, such as 0 meaning "no" and 1 meaning "yes."

Semiconducting Devices

Electronic devices that manipulate digital and analog signals are predominantly semiconductors in today's technology. A semiconductor is a material that conducts electricity, but only under certain conditions, in contrast with conductors that always conduct well and insulators that always conduct poorly. Semiconductors are generally made of silicon or silicon

> This article was contributed by Eric J. Lerner, writer on scientific and technical subjects and electronics editor of *Aerospace America*.

TRANSISTOR

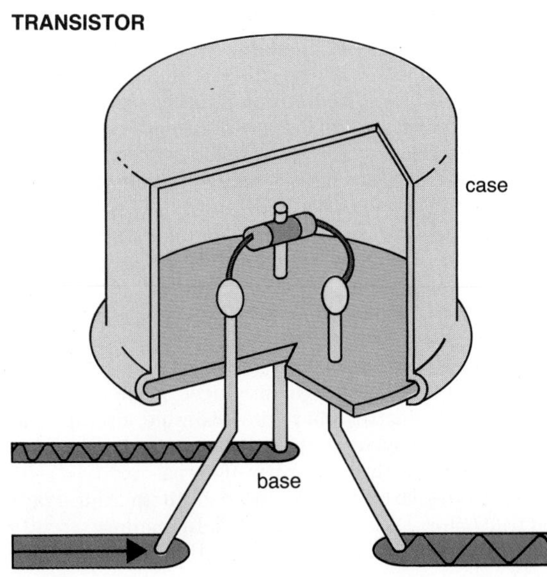

In a transistor the current flowing from emitter to collector varies with and is amplified by the signal flowing in the base.

compounds that are "doped" with certain impurities to alter their electrical properties.

The basic semiconductor device is the transistor, invented in 1947 by American scientists William B. Shockley, Walter H. Brattain, and John Bardeen. The typical transistor consists of three semiconductor materials bonded together. In the so-called n-p-n type, the first part, called the emitter, is doped to give it an excess of negative charges; the second, the base, is doped to give it excess positive charges; and the third, the collector, is doped to give it an excess of negative charges. The voltage applied between the emitter and collector is fixed and relatively high, while the voltage between the emitter and the base is low and variable—it is the incoming signal. When there is no base voltage, the resistance from the emitter to the collector is high, and no current flows. A small voltage across the base to the emitter, however, lowers the resistance and allows a large output current to flow from emitter to collector. The transistor thus acts as a signal amplifier. (*See also* Transistor.)

Electronic Circuits

Transistors and other semiconductor devices come in a wide variety of types capable of performing many different functions when linked together with other elements into electronic circuits. The most important of these other elements are resistors, which impede the flow of electrons and regulate voltages and currents; conductors, which connect different circuits or different circuit elements together; and capacitors, which store electrical charges.

The functions that such circuits perform are generally of two broad types: logic circuits transform or process information carried by electronic signals, while memory circuits and devices store the information. Logic circuits are built up out of identical components that perform elementary manipulations on each piece of information, called a bit. A bit consists of either a 1 or a 0. Sometimes another unit of information, known as a byte, or eight bits, is also used.

There are three basic types of logic circuits: AND, OR, and NOT. NOT circuits are combined with AND and OR circuits to make NAND and NOR circuits. In an AND gate, two inputs produce an output only if both inputs are 1. In other words the output says, "Both A and B are true (or 1)." Similarly the OR gate produces an output 1 if either of its two inputs are 1. The NAND and NOR gates do just the opposite: NAND produces an output of 1 in any case where the AND gate produces 0, and NOR produces 1 whenever OR produces 0. Put together, these simple circuits can perform any logical or arithmetic operation that can be defined in a finite number of steps.

The fastest memory circuits are built up from arrays of transistors, as are logic circuits. In memory circuits a transient impulse—the information to be stored—

All of the amazing feats performed by computers and other sophisticated electronic devices are ultimately made possible by combinations of the basic types of logic circuits.

LOGIC CIRCUITS

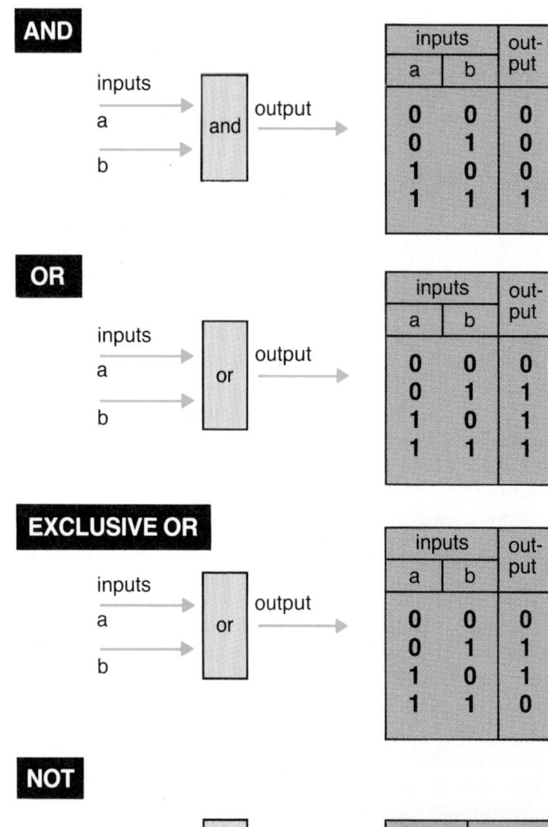

is directed to a particular unit, or address, in the array. This impulse changes the electrical state of a simple circuit in such a way that the change is stable once the impulse has passed. One simple way of making such a flip-flop circuit is to have the output of a given transistor feed back to its base through an OR gate. The other input to the OR gate is the external pulse. A single external pulse will turn on the transistor output current, which will feed back through the gate to maintain itself. An additional external pulse will turn the input off, thus flipping the circuit back.

Information can be obtained from complex arrays of flip-flop circuits by various means in which the transistor signals to external circuits whether it is in a conducting or a nonconducting state. Such arrays are termed random-access memories, or RAMs, because each of the addresses can be accessed in any order. Other types of memory circuits include read-only memories, or ROMs. Here, the data is permanently stored in the array at the time of its manufacture.

Semiconductors may someday be replaced in logic circuits, at least for some applications requiring extreme speed. Researchers are developing new electronic devices based on superconductive materials. (When certain materials are cooled to near absolute zero, their resistance to the flow of electrons disappears entirely, allowing them to become superconductors.) These new devices, called Josephson junctions, are many times faster and smaller than the smallest possible semiconductor. In the late 1980s the discovery of a new class of high-temperature superconductors led to the belief that a low-cost alternative to expensive cooling techniques was within reach.

Storage Devices

Not all electronic devices are based on semiconductors. Many important types of information storage media are based instead on magnetic materials. In computers the most widely used form of storage is the magnetic disk, in which the bits of information are stored in strips of magnetic materials laid in concentric circles around the disk. Each bit of information to be stored is coded as a left-right or right-left magnetic field and impressed onto the disk by a recording head, which is a form of electromagnet. The rapidly spinning disk is read by the head, which moves quickly to the appropriate part of the disk and detects the magnetic fields in a given region. Magnetic tape is also used for storing computer and broadcast information as well, such as in video and audio recording (*see* Tape Recorder).

The most recently developed type of information storage technology is the magneto-optical disk. The disk is made of a special magnetic material that can easily change its magnetic orientation only when heated by a small laser. The laser is focused at the point at which information is recorded, and a magnetic field is impressed. Another laser can read the field by bouncing light off the disk. The polarization of the light (the direction in which the electrical and magnetic fields making up the light vibrate) is changed by the magnetic field, and such changes can be detected by polarized filters and photodetectors. This optical and magnetic technology allows many billions of bytes to be stored on a single disk.

Electronic Tubes

For producing radio and radar signals, electronic tubes are often used, though tube technology is no longer applied to switching circuits as it was in the early days of electronics. Two common types are magnetrons and klystrons. Both are partially evacuated, sealed tubes. A magnetron tube has a cylindrical anode and a single wire filament running along the cylinder axis, which emits the electrons. The tube is mounted inside a magnet whose field runs parallel to the filament. Electrons starting from the filament are bent into curved paths by the magnetic field, and their oscillations emit radio radiation. Magnetrons are capable of generating extremely high frequencies and also short bursts of very high power. They are an important source of power in radar systems and in microwave ovens. A klystron tube contains hollow copper cavities within which the electrons oscillate. Klystrons are used in ultrahigh-frequency circuits, where they can produce oscillations up to 400,000 megahertz (400,000 megacycles per second) in the short microwave range.

Another important type of electronic vacuum device is the cathode-ray tube, which is used in television receivers, among many other applications. The cathode-ray tube is a two-electrode tube in which the electrons are focused by a system of electric lenses into a fine beam. This beam falls on a fluorescent screen at the end of the tube, where it produces a spot of light. If an electric field is applied at right angles to the direction of the beam, the paths of the electrons, which first followed a straight line, are bent. This displacement is a measure of the strength of the applied field. The cathode-ray tube can be used as a voltmeter, a device that measures electric potential difference. If the field applied to the deflecting plates is an alternating field, the light point moves constantly over the screen from right to left and back. This appears as a straight horizontal line. If another alternating field operates at right angles to the first one and to the electron beam, the light point is at the same time pulled up and down, and a more complicated figure is seen on the screen. This permits study in detail of the relation of frequencies, phases, and amplitudes of the two fields.

If, however, one of the fields operates so that the light point is slowly moved over the screen from left to right and returned very fast to the left, the viewer gets a simple picture of the properties of the second field, which moves the spot up and down. A cathode-ray tube of this type is called an oscilloscope.

Integrated Circuits

Despite the importance of these other types of electronic devices, semiconductor-based circuits are the essential feature of modern electronic equipment. These circuits are not made up of individual, separated components as was once the case. Instead, thousands of tiny circuits are embedded in a single complex piece of silicon and other materials called an integrated circuit (IC).

The manufacture of integrated circuits begins with a simple circular wafer of silicon a few inches across. Designers have produced drawings of exactly where each element in the finished circuits is to go. Usually these diagrams are themselves made with the help of computers. Photographs of the diagrams are then reduced in size many times to produce a photolithographic mask. The wafers are first coated with a material called a photoresist that undergoes a chemical change when exposed to light. Light shone through the mask onto the photoresist creates the same pattern on the wafer as that on the mask. Solvents then etch away the parts of the resist exposed to light, leaving the other parts intact.

After this another layer of material—for example, silicon doped with some impurities—is laid down on top of the wafer, and another pattern is etched in by the same technique. The result of several such operations is a multilayered circuit, with thousands of tiny transistors, resistors, and conductors created in the wafer.

The wafer is then broken apart along prestressed lines into dozens of identical square or rectangular chips—the finished integrated circuits.

During the 1970s and 1980s advancing technology reduced the size of individual circuit elements by a factor of two every two years, leading in the same period to a fourfold increase in the number of elements that can fit on a chip. This rapid increase in the power of the chips and the simultaneous rise in their speed allowed the development of microprocessors. Microprocessors, which are at the heart of millions of personal and home computers, pack the same computing power into a tiny chip a fraction of an inch on a side that 20 years earlier would have been provided by a computer that filled a whole room and cost many millions of dollars.

Individual chips are mounted on carriers with several dozen connector leads emerging from them. These, in turn, are soldered together onto printed circuit boards that may contain many dozens of chips. In large computers the boards themselves are mounted into large racks and again connected together.

By the mid-1980s integrated circuits made with the most advanced technology could carry as many as a million individual transistors, each only a few microns on a side. (A micron is a thousandth of a millimeter, or 0.00004 inch.) Many electrical engineers and scientists believe that the ultimate limits of size in these circuits might soon be reached. It was expected that the circuit elements would become too small and contain too few individual atoms to be manufactured reliably. To continue the reduction in size and cost of microcircuits, new principles of operation may be required, perhaps involving specially designed organic molecules.

AN "ELECTRONIC DETECTIVE"—THE OSCILLOSCOPE

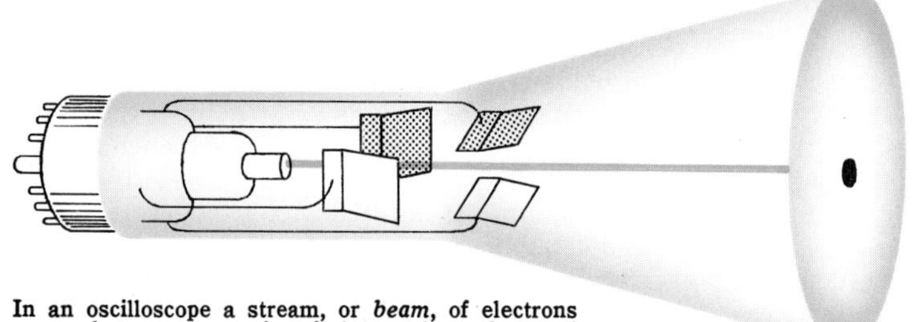

In an oscilloscope a stream, or *beam*, of electrons passes between two pairs of plates (electrodes) and strikes the end of the tube. The end is coated inside with fluorescent material, and the electrons excite a spot of light. The spot moves in response to electric charges placed upon the electrodes.

Hameg Inc.

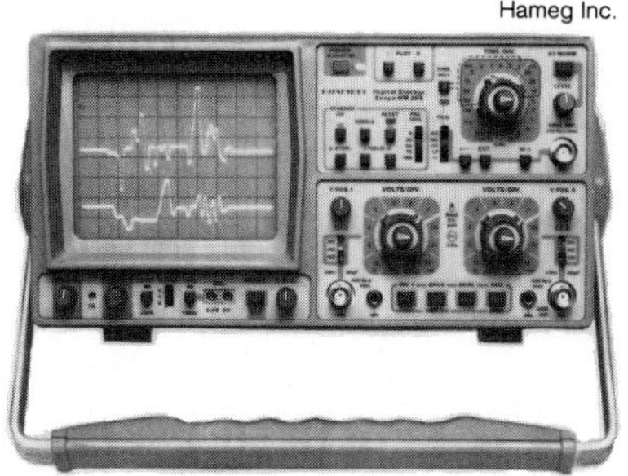

The oscilloscope tube and its controls are assembled in a case.

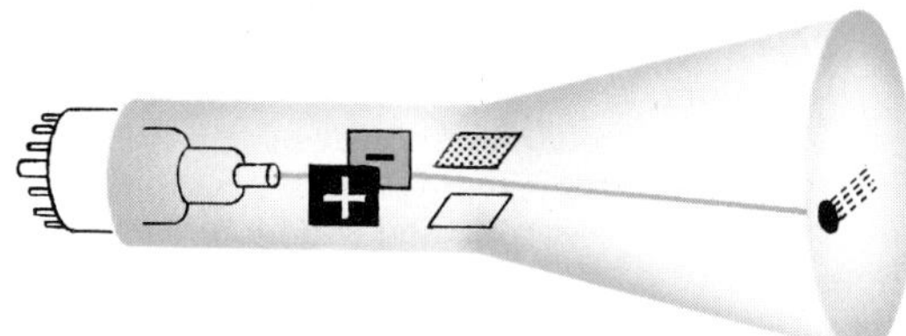

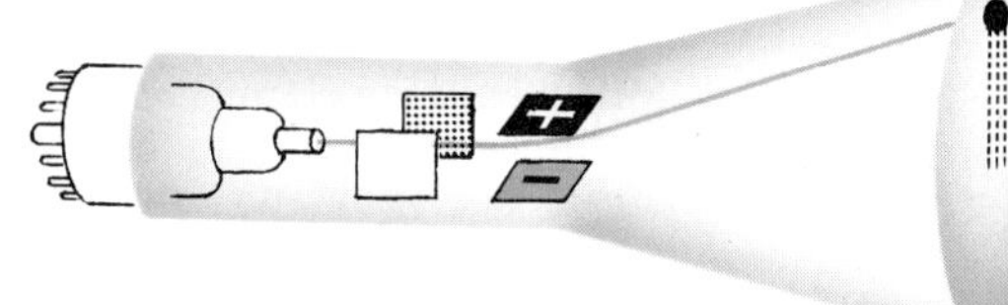

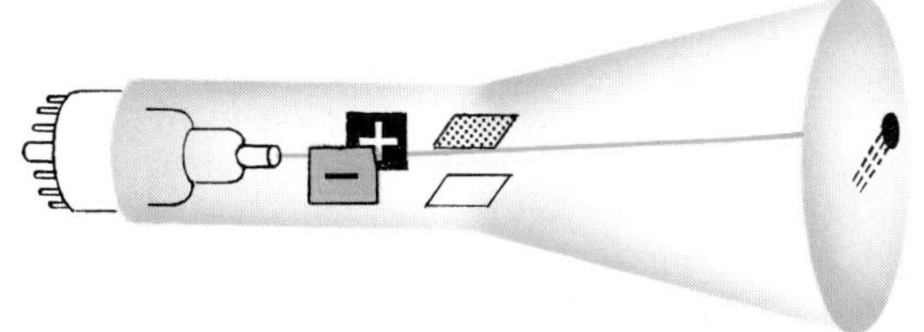

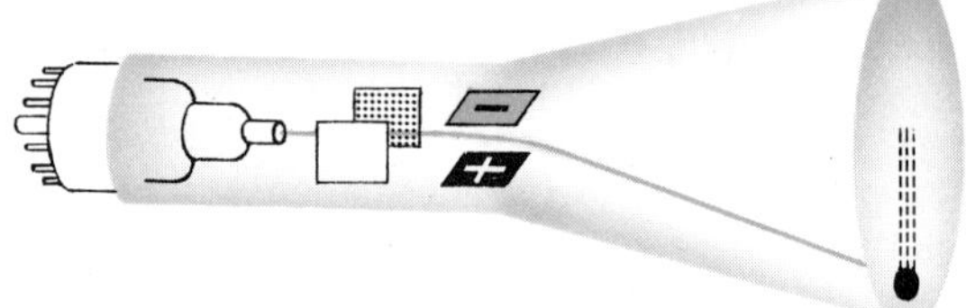

The electrons in the beam have a negative electric charge. Therefore the beam will be deflected toward the plates that have a positive charge (black) and away from the plates that have a negative charge (color). Thus the plates nearer the base of the tube cause a horizontal movement (left). The other pair produces a vertical movement (right). These movements are used to analyze any kind of vibration that can be translated into alternating electric current, as shown below.

1

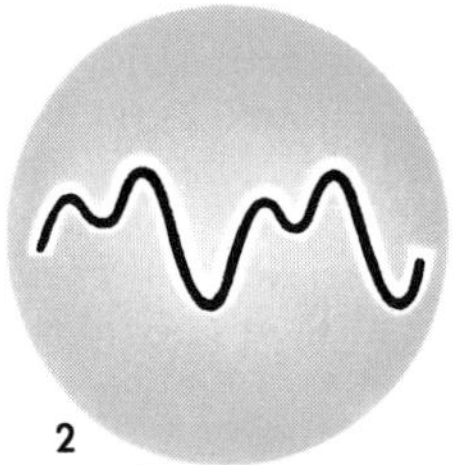

2

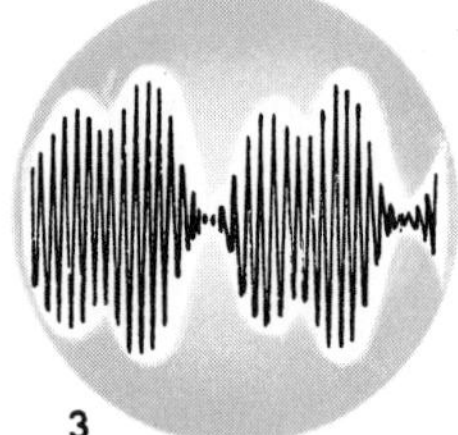

3

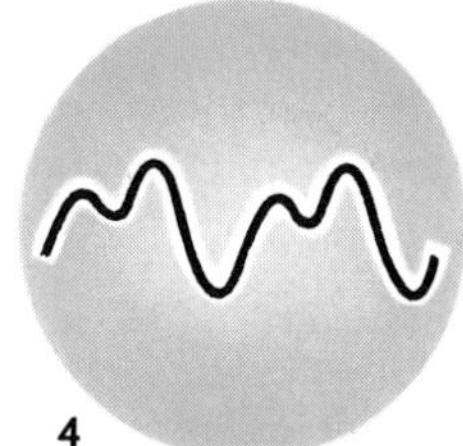

4

Here the oscilloscope analyzes the oscillating electric current that creates a radio wave. The first pair of plates is connected to an automatic control circuit. The second pair is connected to the current which is to be analyzed.

The control circuit is arranged to make the beam sweep from side to side of the tube, then jump back and make another sweep. Each sweep is made by gradually increasing the ratio between the positive and negative charges. The beam is made to jump back by reversing the charges thousands of times a second. Because of the speed, the sweep appears on the screen as a straight, horizontal line.

The radio current being analyzed meanwhile causes vertical movements, as its charges are on the second pair of plates. The combinations of movements caused by the two pairs of plates make wave patterns. These pictures show how the wave patterns on the screen of a tube are used to analyze radio waves.

Picture 1 shows the fast-vibrating *carrier* wave that carries the radio message (*see* Radio). The number of up-and-down zigzags shows the frequency of the wave. Picture 2 shows the electric oscillations created by a musical tone in a microphone. Picture 3 shows the tone "loaded onto" the carrier by amplitude modulation. Picture 4 shows the tone "sorted out" in a receiver.

Applications

Integrated circuits are extremely versatile—a single basic design can be made to perform hundreds of different functions, depending on the wiring of the circuits and the electronic programs or instructions that are fed into them (*see* Computer). Most ICs perform calculations or logic manipulations in devices ranging from hand-held calculators to ultrafast supercomputers performing billions of calculations per second.

There are many other functions, however, that can be done with electronic circuitry. In radio and television receivers a primary function of circuits is the amplification of weak signals received by the antenna. In amplification a small signal is magnified to a large signal that is used to drive other circuits such as the speakers of a radio.

In many cases this amplification is performed with the help of oscillator circuits. Such circuits have a natural period or cycle of electrical current, similar to the natural beat of a pendulum. When driven by external signals of the same period, such as the transmission from a particular radio channel, the oscillator circuit increases its amplitude of oscillation.

To tune out other radio or television stations also received by a single antenna, filter circuits are frequently used. Such filters strongly reduce the signals at all but a single frequency, preventing interference among channels in a receiver.

These and other basic circuit types are used in a vast array of electronic devices. Consumer electronics, a field that was first developed in the 19th century with the invention of the phonograph, now includes radios, television sets, high-fidelity stereo systems, tape recorders, calculators, video games, and personal computers. Most of these devices contain one or more integrated circuits. Electronic controls have also been added to many electrical appliances such as dishwashers, washing machines, ovens, and food processors.

In industry and trade the computer, made up of from one to several thousand integrated circuits, has become an invaluable tool, controlling industrial operations and keeping track of voluminous business records. When connected to mechanical arms and grippers, electronics is the brain of the industrial robot that has come into increasingly widespread use for painting, welding, and assembling products that range from automobiles to watches.

Scientists use electronic computers to perform extremely complex calculations such as determining exactly the course of distant space probes; the probes themselves are packed with electronic instruments and communications equipment. Electronic instruments are used on Earth for scientific measurements and in the electronics industry itself to test equipment as it is manufactured. The oscilloscope, for example, is used to diagnose problems in electronic circuits, through a comparison of expected test patterns with actual results.

In the field of medicine electronic diagnostic instruments have given physicians a much clearer view of the human body than ever before. Computerized axial tomography (CAT) scanners, which are a sophisticated form of X-ray machines, use computers to analyze X rays and produce three-dimensional views of internal organs. Nuclear magnetic resonance (nmr) scanners analyze the response of the body's chemicals to radio waves and magnetic fields, producing maps of the body's biochemistry and clearly highlighting areas of disease.

Virtually all modern communications rely on electronics. Electronic circuits switch telephone calls both on Earth and in communications satellites. Satellite electronics systems amplify and retransmit television and radio communications. Computers are tied together by electronic networks.

Conventional electronics is now supplemented in communications by optoelectronics, the use of laser light carried by optical fibers to transmit information at high speed. Laser pulses are modulated by electronic signals, and the light at the other end of the fiber many kilometers away is converted back into electronic signals by photodetectors.

Electronics has also come to play a central role in transportation. ICs are used in the engines of almost all new cars, acting to control the engine and to

In an amplifier circuit when the current to the transistor's base circuit is large (left), the collector circuit current is larger. When the base current is small (right), the collector current is smaller.

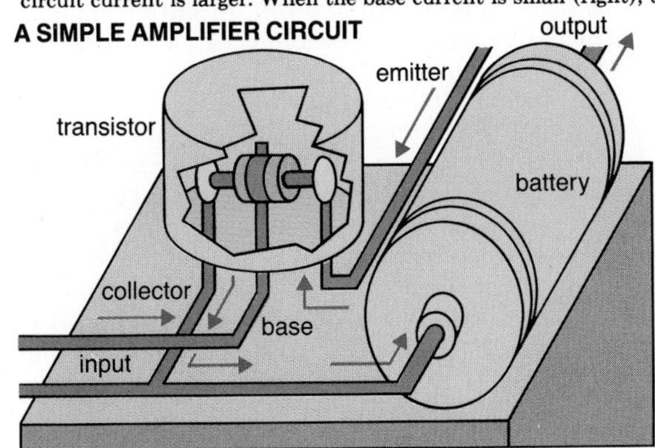

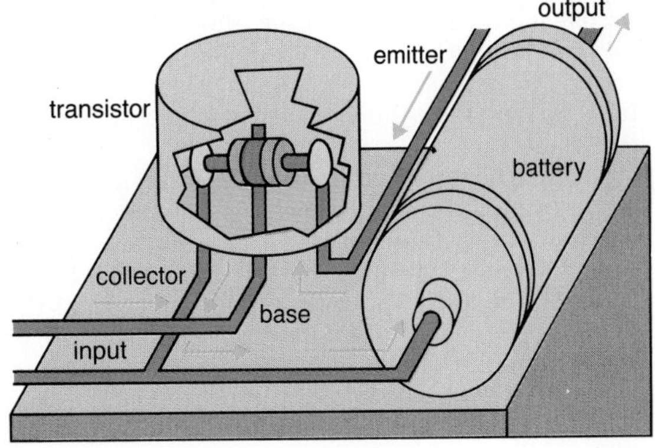

use fuel efficiently. Much more complex circuits and computers greatly assist pilots in flying transport aircraft and are, of course, even more vital when used in space such as on board United States space shuttles.

Finally, electronics has come to be central in modern warfare and preparations for war. Nearly half the cost of advanced United States fighter aircraft is in the sophisticated electronic radar, weapons control, and automated missiles carried by the planes. Electronic computers and navigation equipment guide ballistic nuclear missiles on their paths and control the detonation of nuclear weapons.

History

The working principles of electronics can be demonstrated by tracing the history of radio tubes and photoelectric cells. The history began in 1883, when Thomas Edison found that the heated filament in his incandescent lamp gave off material that blackened the inside of the bulb. This was called the Edison effect, and it led to the development of the modern radio tube. In the Edison effect, also called thermionic emission, heat supplies some electrons in the filament with at least the minimal energy to overcome the attractive forces holding them in the structure of the metal. This discharge of electrons from heated materials is widely used as a source of electrons in conventional electron tubes—for example, in television picture tubes.

In 1887 Heinrich Hertz, while trying to prove the existence of radio waves, discovered the photoelectric effect. If polished metal is given a negative charge and then is flooded with ultraviolet radiation, it steadily loses the charge. Some chemical elements such as cesium and selenium are sensitive to visible light. This discovery led to photoelectric cells.

The development of the radio tube began in 1904, when John A. Fleming of England produced the Fleming valve, which today is called a diode, meaning "two electrodes." He started by heating a filament (also called a cathode) in a vacuum tube with "A-circuit current." The heat drove electrons out of the filament and into surrounding space.

If nothing more happened, the first electrons to escape would soon have formed a negative space charge that would have kept others from being driven out because like charges repel. Fleming avoided this by placing a plate in the tube and connecting the plate and filament through an outside B circuit. The electrons driven from the filament then crossed the tube to the plate and followed the circuit back to the filament.

Fleming next placed a battery in the B circuit. The battery was used to supply electrons—that is, negative charges—to the filament, or cathode, and draw them from the plate, or anode, leaving a positive charge. Electrical heating drove electrons steadily from the filament and sent a strong current through the B, or plate, circuit. The strength of the current depends partly upon the heat and partly upon the voltage from the battery.

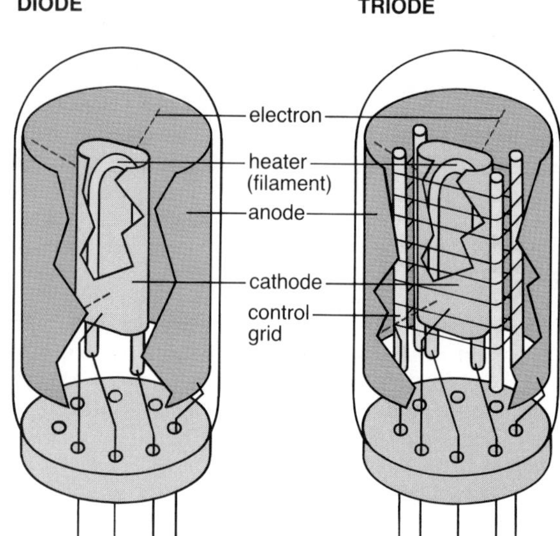

Although important in the history of electronics, the diode and triode have largely been replaced by semiconducting devices.

This device could be used as a radio detector. The changing voltages created by radio signals in an antenna circuit are placed on the filament and plate. The changes produce corresponding changes in the strength of the plate current, which is used to reproduce the signal in the receiving apparatus.

In 1906 the American inventor Lee De Forest transformed the diode into a device that he called an audion, the modern name of which is triode. He did this by inserting a grid of fine wire mesh between the filament and the plate. If variable voltages from an antenna circuit are placed on the filament and the grid, they cause variations in the flow of electrons to the plate. Moreover, the variations in current are much stronger than those caused by the voltage of the incoming signal acting alone. Thus the triode amplifies, or strengthens, the signal.

Because the tube uses free electrons only and has no mechanical moving parts, it responds within a few microseconds, or millionths of a second, to any change placed upon it. It can be made sensitive to changes of less than a millionth of a volt. Resulting changes in the plate current can be amplified by passing the signal through more tubes.

The vacuum tube became the basis of radio, television, and computers, the latter first developed at the end of World War II in 1944 and 1945. The invention of the transistor in 1948 initiated a radical reduction in the size of electronic circuits and in their power requirements. The later development of the integrated circuit set into motion the continuing miniaturization of all electronic devices, which has at the same time greatly increased their speed and computing power.

ELEMENTS *see* CHEMICAL ELEMENTS; PERIODIC TABLE.

Although the Indian elephant (left) and African elephant (right) weigh about the same amount, the African species is a little taller. African elephants also have bigger tusks and larger ears.

ELEPHANT. The largest living land animals are the elephants. Adult Indian male elephants average about four tons in weight and nine feet in height. The tallest reach 11 feet. African males are somewhat taller. They reach 12 feet in rare cases, though they are no heavier than the Indian elephants. The average female of either species is about a foot shorter than the male.

The great size of elephants and the thickness and toughness of their skins protect them from every other wild animal. Since they have no enemies to fear except man, elephants are usually peaceful and easy-going. They show great affection for one another and spend their lives as members of a family herd. This is made up of several generations of blood relatives, with occasional additions by mating from other herds.

Family Life of the Herd

The typical elephant herd contains from 20 to 40 members of all ages. The males (bulls) and females (cows) are about equal in number. The leader is usually an old cow. She is more likely to keep an even temper than is a male. Although the males are generally peaceful they sometimes go mad during their mating periods. When a bull goes *must*, as it is called, he may trample down everything that crosses his path. If he causes too much disturbance, his relatives drive him out of the herd. Usually he recovers and returns. Sometimes, however, he becomes a lone "rogue elephant"—a dangerous outcast that often attacks men or destroys villages.

Except in cool, cloudy weather or when disturbed by hunters, elephants do not travel by daylight. They feed at night. During the hottest hours the members of a family herd huddle together in any shade they can find and sleep standing up. Toward sundown the herd walks to the nearest river, lake, or water hole to drink and bathe. The pace is set so that even the very young and the very old can keep up. If a mother with a baby falls behind, her mate and several other members of the herd will remain to pro-

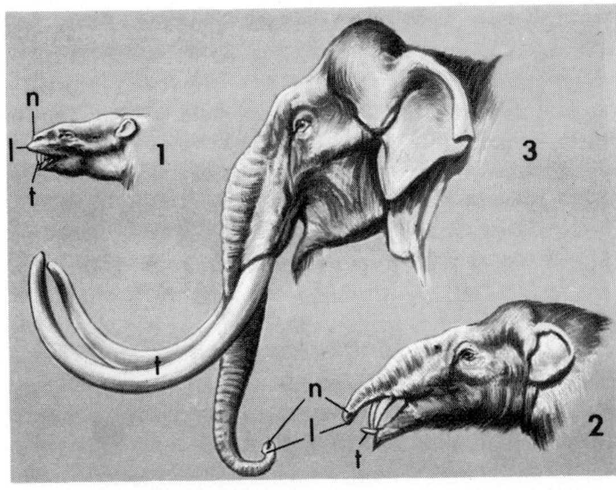

1. Several million years ago the elephant had a tapir-shaped head. 2. This drawing is based on a fossil found in northern Africa. Gradually the upper lip grew longer and drooped, while the "eyeteeth" began to sprout out into tusks. 3. This development reached its height in the mammoth of glacial times. The modern elephant is a smaller variety of the mammoth type. The letters *n*, *l*, and *t* show the position of nostrils, lips, and tusks in each example.

A statue of a group of elephants by Carl Akeley stands in the American Museum of Natural History in New York City. It shows two elephants supporting a wounded comrade between them. Elephants are social animals, and it is their habit to stand by each other in danger.

tect them. A male and female, once mated, will usually continue to travel together. Their attachment, naturalists believe, endures as long as they both live.

As the herd straggles along, the elephants push down young trees with their shoulders and chests or uproot them with their tusks to feed on the tender roots, twigs, and leaves. In the open meadows they gather up tufts of grass with their trunks and stuff them into their mouths. At times a herd will invade the fields of natives to feed on bean plants, millet, banana trees, and other crops, but it will never enter villages or destroy huts. Only the solitary rogue elephants do this.

A herd may range over a 50-mile radius in the course of a single season. Seldom does it sleep in the same place for two days in succession. Bulls of different herds occasionally fight when they meet, but usually herds mingle on friendly terms. Many pictures have been taken from airplanes showing vast elephant armies made up of many family herds traveling over the same route toward new feeding grounds.

At birth the baby elephant is about 3 feet tall and weighs about 200 pounds. It has a sparse coat of woolly hair, which gradually disappears. It takes its mother's milk with its mouth and not, as some people imagine, with its trunk. The young elephant is nursed by its mother for about two years and remains under her protection for two years more. The period between mating and the birth of a young elephant is about 22 months. Thus female elephants as a rule bear young once every four or five years.

Structure of Elephants—The Trunk

Trunk, tusks, and feet are the elephant's most conspicuous features. The trunk is a prolongation of nose and upper lip combined. The two tubes of the nostrils, surrounded by muscle, run the whole length. The trunk is an extraordinarily powerful and yet delicate instrument. With it the elephant can break a large branch from a tree or pick up a peanut. The upper side is tough and is often used for pushing, but the under side is very sensitive.

The elephant guards his trunk carefully and never strikes down with it in fighting. The common idea that he uses his trunk in this way arose from the attitude he takes when he suspects danger. Because his eyesight is poor, he relies for warning on his keen senses of smell and hearing. Hence, when he is suspi-

Most elephants spend their lives as members of herds like this one. The herd is composed of many generations of blood relatives living and traveling together. These African elephants are huddling in the shade to sleep. Except in cool weather or when they are being stalked by hunters, elephants in herds generally sleep by day and travel by night.

cious, he raises his ears to catch the slightest sound and thrusts his trunk outward to probe the air with noisy sniffs. But when charging or defending himself, he curls up his trunk out of harm's way.

The elephant drinks by drawing water half-way up his trunk and then squirting it down his throat. He can draw in corn and other grain and blow it into his mouth in the same way.

The Useful Tusks

The lower jaw has no front teeth, and the upper jaw has only one pair. It is these two teeth, corresponding to incisors, that grow so long and form the tusks. They are "second teeth" which grow out after the baby elephant's tiny milk tusks are shed. The ivory of which they are composed is pure dentine, with a short cap of enamel at the tip which is soon scraped off (*see* Ivory; Teeth).

The tusks keep on growing as long as an elephant lives. If he uses them a great deal, they wear away at the points as they grow at the roots. Because one tusk is likely to be used more than the other in digging up roots, the two are seldom of equal length. The heaviest known single tusk weighs 235 pounds; the longest measures 11 feet, 5 inches. These are freaks. A tusk weighing 100 pounds is well above the average for African elephants; the average for Asiatic elephants is much less. An elephant burdened with very heavy tusks may have to abandon the family herd because their weight prevents him from keeping up.

There are six molar teeth on each side of the upper jaw and six on the lower jaw; but never more than one or two of the six are in use at the same time. As those in front are worn away, the successively larger molars behind come into place. Thus an old elephant may be left with only a single huge molar above and one below on each side.

The Elephant's Padded Feet

An elephant's foot closely resembles the *plantigrade* foot of man (*see* Foot), except that the heelbone rests on a thick pad of flesh. Thus the elephant's hind leg has no conspicuous heel or hock joint as does the hind leg of a horse or dog. The free joint is the knee, and the elephant is one of the few animals that can kneel on its hind legs.

When the elephant walks he sets his hind feet down in the track left by his front feet. Picking his way with amazing silence through a forest, he needs to watch only where he puts his front feet. In deep mud or bog his flanged feet spread out as they go in and contract as they come out, so they do not stick.

Elephants seldom run as fast as 15 miles an hour, or about half the speed of a good running horse. An

To make ready for an elephant roundup in the jungles of Southeast Asia, a *keddah*, or corral, with a long V-shaped approach is built. Then beaters surround a wild herd and with loud shouting drive it toward the pen. Bellowing furiously, the animals charge down the runway into the trap. The men prod the captives with poles to keep them from the walls.

infuriated African elephant, however, has been known to charge 120 yards at a speed of 24.5 miles an hour (*see* Animal). Their running gait is the same as their walk—a shuffling stride. They can neither trot, gallop, nor jump. A deep ditch only 7 feet wide stops them, for this is wider than the longest stride they are able to take. They are, however, at home in deep water and can swim for six hours at a time. They sink almost out of sight, with the trunk held up high for air.

Only the rhinoceros, the hippopotamus, and the tapir have hides as thick as the elephant's. That is why these animals are called *pachyderms*, which means "thick-skinned." The hide on an elephant's shoulder may be an inch and half thick. All over his body it is loose and wrinkled. On the tail grow long coarse hairs larger than the lead in a pencil. These hairs are made into rings and ornaments.

Contrasts in African and Asiatic Species

On the forefoot the African elephant has four nails; the Asian elephant, five. On the hind foot, the African has three nails; the Asian four. The African elephant has two nipple-like "fingers" on the tip of its trunk; the Asian elephant has only one. The surface of the African elephant's trunk is divided crosswise into pronounced ridges and grooves; the trunk of the Asian elephant is smoother. The African elephant has much larger ears and holds its head higher than does the Asian elephant. Virtually all African males and most females have tusks; many Asian males and nearly all females are tuskless.

Before white people began to settle in Africa, the African species ranged over the whole tropical region from sea level to the timberline of such snow-capped peaks as Kilimanjaro and Ruwenzori. Today elephants are plentiful only in the less settled central and eastern sections. The range of the Asian elephants extends through the forested parts of Sri Lanka, India, Burma, Thailand, Vietnam, and the Malay peninsula to the island of Sumatra in Indonesia.

Pygmy Elephants and Albinos

The pygmy elephant is found in the Congo region and west-central Africa. Some biologists regard it as a separate species, others as a subspecies of the African elephant. It differs from the African elephant chiefly in its size and in the rounded shape of its ears. The pygmy elephant reaches a height of 7 feet and weighs more than a ton.

The white elephants, occasionally found in Asia, are not a separate species but merely albino varieties of the common species. Elephant worship plays a part in several Oriental religions. The white elephant, however, is particularly honored in Thailand. For many years it was pictured on Thailand's national flag.

The use of elephants as beasts of burden in peace and war can be traced far back in history. The elephant corps attached to Hannibal's army is famous (*see* Hannibal). How the ancients obtained their elephants is not known. Today the *keddah* system of capture, shown in a picture with this article, is the chief method employed in India and neighboring countries where work elephants are most in demand.

After capture, two tame elephants close in on the wild one and hold it until men can hobble its feet with ropes. The next step is to get it used to the presence of a mahout, or driver. Feeding, friendliness, and firm discipline, plus the example of the tame elephants, soon complete the taming.

Elephants in Captivity

The elephant is a striking exception to the rule that wild animals captured when full grown can rarely be domesticated. Most elephants that are used as beasts of burden, as well as those in zoos and circuses, were born in the wilderness and remained there until they were 10 or 12 years old. There are several reasons for this. Elephants do not breed readily in captivity, and the young are delicate and hard to raise. Furthermore, a baby elephant matures very slowly and meanwhile eats enormous quantities of food. Thus it is cheaper to let it grow to a useful size in its native haunts and then to catch and tame it. The elephant's extraordinary docility makes this possible.

The record made by Karl Hagenbeck, the famous German animal dealer, is an extreme example of this docility. Within two days he trained six African elephants that had never been worked before to carry loads and their drivers. Hagenbeck and many other experienced men say that there is no foundation for the belief that the African elephant is more savage and dangerous, or less easily trained, than the Asian elephant. In recent years many elephants have been trained to work in the Congo River basin.

Many Tasks Performed

In its work an elephant may be called upon to push heavy burdens with its head, to pull with a harness, or to drag logs with a cable that it holds in its teeth. If it has tusks, it may use them in various ways; but it never pulls loads with its trunk.

In India elephants are sometimes used in tiger hunts. The hunter takes his place on a platform saddle, or howdah, strapped to the elephant's back. Beaters range through the jungle to drive out the tigers. When the great cats draw near, the elephant gives warning and so prepares the hunter for his shot. The chief danger to the hunter, it is said, is on the rare occasions when a wounded tiger leaps on an elephant's back and the elephant madly runs under overhanging tree branches to get rid of its attacker.

In captivity as in the wilds, female elephants are the more steady and trustworthy. Males are seldom found in circus herds. An exception to this was Jumbo, the huge African male made famous by P.T. Barnum, the showman.

The elephant's usual willingness to obey commands and perform stunts has given it a reputation for great intelligence. Animal trainers and keepers of zoos, however, question this reputation.

Folklore and Fact

The ancient and fascinating relationship between mankind and the elephant is referred to in various forms of mythology. In India the religion of Hinduism has an elephant-faced god named Ganesha, who is considered to be the remover of obstacles. He is also the patron of literature and learning. His name, traditionally, has been the first to be called out at the start of worship or at the beginning of a new enterprise. There is also a Hindu legend that says that the first elephants created had the power of flight, but they lost it when they landed on a banyan tree and fell through to crush the house of a hermit. The hermit's curse grounded them forever.

Although it has been said that elephants live as long as 150 years, there is no actual record of any such age. Sixty years is believed to be the maximum length of life in captivity. Stories have long been told of elephant graveyards to which all the elephants from the surrounding country go when they feel death approaching. Ivory hunters have searched in vain for these graveyards. Perhaps the legend arose from the fact that Africans sometimes set fire to the grasslands to clear the ground for cultivation and thus may occasionally cause the death of a whole elephant herd by accident. It may also be that such graveyards are really places where groups of elephants drowned at one time, perhaps while crossing a river or trying to get through a bog.

Elephants are not naturally afraid of mice, as legend claims. What they seem to fear is getting some small object or little animal lodged in their trunks.

Elephant Hunting

Elephants are protected by law in most regions of the world where they are found today. Special licenses to hunt them are usually required. Opinions differ about the degree of danger involved in elephant hunting. Usually a herd flees from the hunter. If surprised at close range, however, both males and females are likely to charge. They try to trample the hunter and pin him to the ground with their tusks. A hunter is usually safe if he can get higher than the elephant's line of vision.

Elephants stem from a line of animals that developed in Eocene or Oligocene times, as long ago as 54 million years (*see* Geology). The mammoths were close relatives of elephants, and the mastodons were more distant ones (*see* Mammoth and Mastodon). The elephants' closest living relatives are the water-dwelling sea cows (*see* Manatee).

Elephants belong to the order Proboscidea and to the family Elephantidae. The scientific name of the Asian elephant is *Elephas maximus*. The African elephant and the pygmy elephant both belong to the species *Loxodonta africana*.

ELEVATOR AND ESCALATOR. The movement of people and freight within relatively confined areas—such as office buildings, airport terminals, and large ships—is usually accomplished by means of elevators, escalators, or moving sidewalks. Elevators, or lifts, carry passengers and freight up and down; escalators are moving staircases from one story of a building to the next; and moving sidewalks carry people horizontally or at a slight incline.

Elevators

When it became possible to construct tall, multistoried buildings in the 19th century, the need arose to move people and freight from one level to another by means other than staircases. The mechanism used was the elevator. The invention of the elevator, moreover, made even taller buildings possible.

Lifting loads by mechanical means had been known since at least 236 BC, when Archimedes made a hoist operated by ropes and pulleys (*see* Archimedes). But the first practical elevator was not developed until the early 19th century. It was a hydraulic elevator that operated by means of a vertical plunger traveling up and down a cylinder, pushing and lowering the car above it. The plunger was moved by liquid under pressure (*see* Hydraulics).

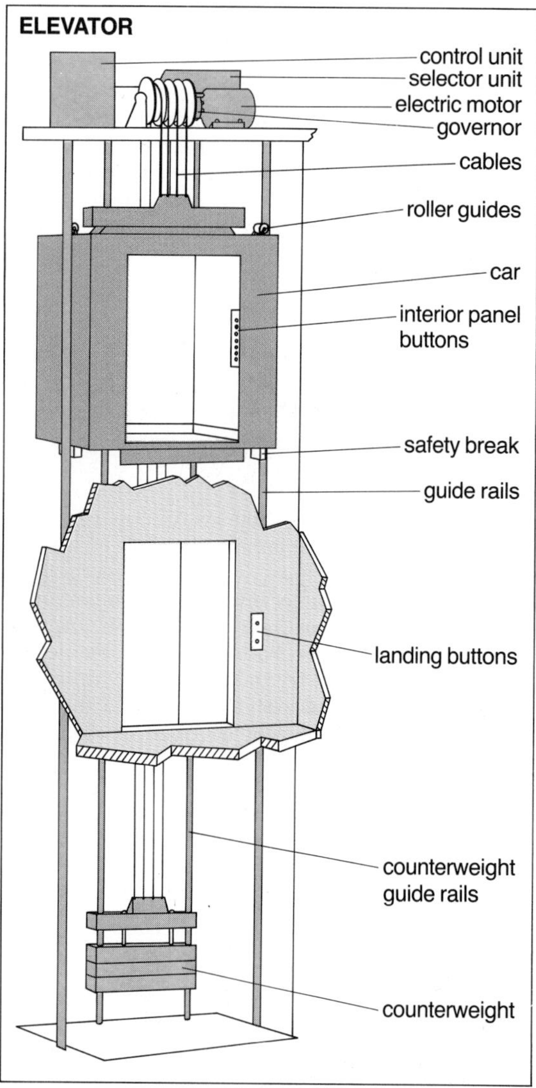

Most modern elevators are pulled from above by steel cables, though hydraulic elevators are still in use in some low-rise buildings and for some heavy-duty freight elevators. A cable-hoisted elevator travels up and down in a shaft, which has doors opening from within at each floor. Above the shaft, in a room of its own, is an electric motor with a governor to control speed and a panel of switches and relays—called a control unit—to control stopping, starting, and reversing. The steel cables that support the cab are looped around a drum attached to the driving motor. The greater the weight in the cab, the tighter the cables grip the drum. From the drive mechanism the cables drop down the depth of the elevator shaft, holding a heavy counterweight.

It was an American, Elisha Graves Otis, who invented the safety brake that made today's passenger elevators practical. His device, first demonstrated at the Crystal Palace Exposition in New York City in 1854, incorporated a clamping arrangement that gripped the guide rails on which the elevator car moved when tension was released from the hoist cable. The first passenger elevator, driven by steam power, was put into service in the five-story Haughwout department store in New York in 1857.

The first commercial installation of an electrically driven passenger elevator was in 1889 in the Demarest Building in New York City. This elevator utilized an electric motor to drive a winding drum in the building's basement. Push-button controls were introduced in 1894, and the next year a hoisting apparatus was demonstrated in England that applied electric power to a pulley at the top of the shaft. The weight of the car and counterweights guaranteed traction. This made it possible to move the cable drum to the top of the shaft, leading to higher shafts in taller buildings.

In 1915 automatic car leveling was introduced. This control took over at each floor to guide the car to a precisely positioned stop. Power control of doors was added shortly thereafter. In an attempt to minimize the space taken by elevator shafts in a building, the double-deck elevator was devised in 1932. But it did not come into significant use until 1971, when it was installed in Chicago's Time-Life Building.

Most modern elevators are completely automatic. The earliest control system was the single push-button panel, allowing riders to control the car. Group-automatic operation of two or more cars keeps them spaced at specific intervals. This type of control is normally used in heavy traffic areas.

Most elevators have inner and outer doors and will not operate unless both sets of doors are closed. There are usually photoelectric devices to keep doors

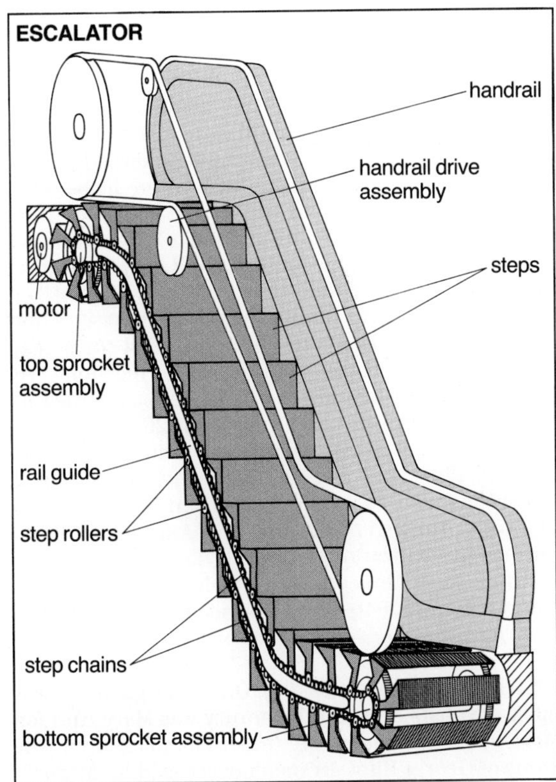

from closing while passengers are entering or leaving. While passenger elevator doors close sideways, freight elevator doors frequently close vertically, with half the door coming down to meet the rising lower half. Most elevators are required to have alarm systems and a telephone that connects them to an outside exchange in case of trouble.

Transparent-walled elevators have become popular in some buildings. They may be used on the outside of a building or in an open court lobby of a hotel. The first such observation elevators were probably those installed in 1899 in the Eiffel Tower in Paris.

Escalators

The escalator is a moving staircase in which the steps move as a unit upward or downward at an incline of about 30 degrees. The advantages of the escalator over the elevator are a greater passenger capacity (as many as 6,000 persons per hour on larger types), continuous availability, comparatively small space requirements, and lower operating cost.

The first escalator was an inclined belt invented in 1891 by Jesse W. Reno in the United States. Passengers rode on cleats, or wedge-shaped supports, attached to the belt, which was at an incline of 25 degrees. In the same year a moving handrail was added. Horizontal steps were added by Charles D. Seeberger later in the 1890s. The Otis Elevator Company acquired both inventions, and the first installations were at the Paris Exposition of 1900 and in the New York City subway system.

The average distance between stories in a building is about 12 feet (3.7 meters). Because of the 30-degree incline, a story-to-story escalator is about 60 feet (18 meters) long. Some, however, are much longer. In some London underground, or subway, stations, there are escalators that rise four stories. The longest escalator in service is located in the Ocean Park area of Hong Kong: it is 740 feet (226 meters) long and rises to a height of 377 feet (115 meters). It can carry 4,000 people an hour in each direction. In some rare cases escalators are attached to the outside of buildings, as at the Pompidou Center in Paris.

Moving sidewalks

Moving sidewalks, or people movers, use the technology originally developed for the escalator to carry people over horizontal levels or at a slight incline. The ramps have either solid or jointed treads or a continuous belt.

Their chief use has been in enclosed areas in which people need to walk moderately long distances in a short time such as airports. A number of the world's largest and busiest airports have installed them in their terminal buildings and in tunnels from one building to another. These include London's Heathrow Airport, the Rhine-Main Airport at Frankfurt, West Germany, the Charles de Gaulle Airport near Paris, Copenhagen's Kastrup Airport, and Peking's international airport.

There are several enclosed moving sidewalks in Terminal No. 1 at the Charles de Gaulle Airport near Paris.

Courtesy of the Paris Airports Authority

ELGAR, Edward (1857–1934). Millions of American high school, college, and university graduates have marched down the aisles of auditoriums to the music of Sir Edward Elgar's 'Pomp and Circumstance'. Elgar actually wrote five 'Pomp and Circumstance' marches, and it is the middle section of the first, set to the words 'Land of Hope and Glory', that has become so popular.

Elgar was born in Broadheath in Worcestershire, England, on June 2, 1857. His father was an organist and music dealer, and the young man himself, without formal training in composition, pursued a musical career. He produced several oratorios, or sacred choral works, including 'Lux Christi' in 1896, 'The Dream of Gerontius' (1900), 'The Apostles' (1903), and 'The Kingdom' (1906). Other vocal works included 'Caractacus' (1898) and 'Sea Pictures' (1900), a song cycle for contralto. One of his most unusual compositions was the 'Enigma Variations' for orchestra, first performed in 1899. Its variations are based on the countermelody to an unheard theme, a supposedly well-known tune that Elgar never identified.

Elgar was knighted in 1904 and in the years 1905 to 1908 was Birmingham University's first professor of music. He was the first English composer of international stature after Henry Purcell in the 17th century. He stimulated a renaissance in English music and aided younger composers. He died at Worcester on Feb. 23, 1934.

ELIOT, Charles W. (1834–1926). When Charles W. Eliot became the president of Harvard University in 1869, higher education emphasized principally mathematics and the classics. Eliot, eager to give every student an opportunity to discover his individual abilities, broke down this traditional system. He brought new subjects into the curriculum, introduced the elective system, abolished compulsory religious worship, made it possible to complete the work for a bachelor's degree in three years, and built up a first-rate graduate school. His writings, speeches, and correspondence were influential in bringing about reforms in the elementary and secondary schools.

Charles W. Eliot

Library of Congress

Charles William Eliot was born in Boston on March 20, 1834, a member of an old New England family. He attended the Boston Latin School and entered Harvard when he was 15. After graduation in 1853 he taught at Harvard and the Massachusetts Institute of Technology. He spent several years abroad studying European educational methods before he became president of Harvard, an office that he held from 1869 until 1909. Eliot wrote and spoke extensively on educational, political, economic, and religious questions. He gained wide fame for his "five-foot shelf" of books, better known as the 'Harvard Classics'. After he suggested that "all the books needed for a real education could be set on a shelf five feet long," a publisher asked him to select such a list. He died in Northeast Harbor, Me., on Aug. 22, 1926.

Eliot was married twice. His first wife, Ellen Peabody Eliot, died in 1869, leaving two young sons. His second wife was Grace Hopkinson Eliot.

Eliot's principal books are: 'Five American Contributions to Civilization, and Other Essays', published in 1898; 'More Money for the Public Schools' (1903); 'John Gilley' (1904); 'Four American Leaders' (1906); and 'The Durable Satisfactions of Life' (1910).

ELIOT, George (1819–80). One of England's foremost novelists of the 19th century was Mary Ann (or Marian) Evans, who wrote under the masculine pen name of George Eliot. In such novels as 'Silas Marner' and 'The Mill on the Floss', George Eliot created realistic pictures of English country and village life. In 'Felix Holt', 'Middlemarch', and 'Daniel Deronda', she worked on a broader theme. In these novels she depicted the effects of the powerful new forces that were reshaping English ideas (*see* English Literature). In 'Romola' she used her vast knowledge of history to portray the life of a young woman living in the world of the Italian Renaissance.

George Eliot was born in Warwickshire, England, on Nov. 22, 1819. Her father, Robert Evans, was agent, or manager, of the Newdigate estate. The family, including Mary Ann's sister, Chrissie, and her brother, Isaac, lived at Griff House on the estate. When she was 7, Mary Ann was sent to boarding school. She spent week-ends and long vacations at home, most of the time in the company of Isaac, whom she adored. The scenes between Maggie Tulliver and her brother Tom in 'The Mill on the Floss' come directly from these childhood days with Isaac.

Mrs. Evans died when Mary Ann was 16. Soon after, Chrissie married, and Mary Ann assumed charge of Griff House. When Isaac married, Robert Evans retired, and father and daughter went to live in nearby Coventry. Here Marian (as she now wrote her name) became a close friend of Charles Bray and his family. Bray, a prosperous manufacturer, had forsaken conventional Christianity for his own system of ethics. Bray's ideas greatly influenced the girl, much to her father's anguish. During these years at home she translated David Friedrich Strauss's 'Life of Jesus' from the German.

George Eliot in a chalk drawing by F.W. Burton of 1865

Courtesy of the National Portrait Gallery, London

London and a New Life

After her father's death, Marian had to find a new life. A London publisher, John Chapman, who had published her translation of Strauss's 'Life of Jesus', offered her a job as assistant editor of the *Westminster Review*. The work completely absorbed her. She often worked 18 hours a day, but she still found time for social life with the leading writers and thinkers of the day. Among them was George Henry Lewes, a fairly well-known but not very successful journalist.

Lewes's wife had deserted him, leaving him their three young sons. In 1854 Marian became his common-law wife in a union that lasted until his death. Marriage was impossible because under English law at the time Lewes could not get a divorce without insurmountable difficulty.

Literary Success

Lewes soon recognized Marian's growing genius and urged her to try fiction. Her first effort was a short story, "The Sad Fortunes of the Reverend Amos Barton." It was accepted by *Blackwood's Magazine* for the January 1857 issue. Marian used her pen name for the first time, and for some years no one but Lewes knew who George Eliot was. *Blackwood's* accepted several more stories and reprinted them in a book, 'Scenes of Clerical Life', published in 1858.

For the next 20 years each new book by George Eliot was acclaimed by the critics and widely read by the public. She published 'Adam Bede' in 1859; 'The Mill on the Floss' (1860); 'Silas Marner' (1861); 'Romola' (1862–63); 'Felix Holt the Radical' (1866); 'The Spanish Gypsy' (1868), a dramatic poem; 'Brother and Sister' (1869), a sonnet sequence; 'Middlemarch' (1871–72); 'Daniel Deronda' (1876); and 'Impressions of Theophrastus Such' (1879). Income from the books enabled George Eliot and Lewes to live fashionably, to entertain, and to travel.

Their happy life together ended with Lewes's death in 1878. George Eliot wrote no more, and for a long time she mourned him deeply. In 1880 she became the wife of John W. Cross, a friend of many years. Only a few months later, on Dec. 22, 1880, she died. Cross arranged her letters and journals into a 'Life', published in 1885. This has been the main source for succeeding biographies.

ELIOT, T.S. (1888–1965). "I am an Anglo-Catholic in religion, a classicist in literature, and a royalist in politics." T.S. Eliot so defined, and even exaggerated, his own conservatism. The ideas of this stimulating writer were perhaps traditional, but the way in which he expressed them was extremely modern. Eliot was one of the first to reject conventional verse forms and language. His experiments with free expression contributed to his reputation as one of the most influential writers of his time.

Thomas Stearns Eliot was born in Saint Louis, Mo., on Sept. 26, 1888. His family had produced distinguished Americans since colonial days. He entered Harvard University in 1906, completed his course in three years, and earned a master's degree the next year. After a year at the Sorbonne in Paris, he returned to Harvard.

Further study led him to Merton College, Oxford, and he decided to stay in England. He worked first as a teacher and then in a bank. Precise and moderate in his habits, he devoted his evenings to study and writing. He liked cats and wrote a book about them—'Old Possum's Book of Practical Cats', published in 1939. It was the basis for 'Cats', a spectacular musical comedy of the 1980s.

In 1915 the verse magazine *Poetry* published Eliot's first notable piece, 'The Love Song of J. Alfred Prufrock'. This was followed by other short poems such as 'Portrait of a Lady'. 'The Waste Land', which appeared in 1922, is considered by many to be his most challenging work (*see* American Literature).

In 1927 Eliot became a British citizen and was confirmed in the Church of England. His essays ('For Lancelot Andrewes', 1928) and his poetry ('Four Quartets', 1943) increasingly reflected this association with a traditional culture.

His first drama was 'The Rock' (1934), a pageant play. This was followed by 'Murder in the Cathedral' (1935), a play dealing with the assassination of Archbishop Thomas à Becket, who was later canonized (*see* Becket). 'The Family Reunion' appeared in 1939.

T.S. Eliot

Angus McBean

'The Cocktail Party', based upon the ancient Greek drama 'Alcestis' by Euripides, came out in 1950 and 'The Confidential Clerk' in 1953. The dialogue in his plays is written in a free, rhythmical verse pattern. Eliot won the Nobel prize for literature in 1948 and other major literary awards. The author was married twice. He died on Jan. 4, 1965, in London.

ELIZABETH I (1533–1603). Popularly known as the Virgin Queen and Good Queen Bess, Elizabeth Tudor was 25 years old when she became queen of England. The golden period of her reign is called the Elizabethan Age.

Elizabeth became queen after the death of her half sister in 1558. She rode at once to London from her country home, traveling in a slow procession to give the people a chance to see her. Guns boomed, bells rang, and the people cheered her and scattered flowers in her path.

At the beginning of her reign England was in despair. The country had been weakened by war and religious strife, and the treasury was empty. Spain and France were powerful, and both wanted to rule England. The people hoped their young queen would soon marry a strong man who would guide her.

But Elizabeth at once took the government into her own hands; and, though she had many suitors and close friendships with several men, she steadfastly refused to marry. When she died at the age of 69, she was still called the Virgin Queen. By then rich and secure, England was enjoying its greatest literary period. English ships were sailing into all seas, and the island kingdom had begun to establish its position as a world leader.

Courtesy of the National Portrait Gallery, London

An oil portrait of Elizabeth I was painted by an unknown artist about 1575. It measures 79 by 113 centimeters.

Elizabeth's Childhood and Youth

Elizabeth was born near London on Sept. 7, 1533. Her father was Henry VIII, "bluff King Hal" (*see* Henry, Kings of England). Her mother was Anne Boleyn, the second of Henry's six wives. Henry's first wife, Catherine of Aragon, had only one surviving child, Mary (*see* Mary, Queens of England). Henry wanted a male heir, so he asked the pope to annul the marriage. Because the pope refused, Henry broke away from the Roman Catholic church and set himself up as head of the church in England. Then he married Anne. He was disappointed that Anne's child also was a girl. Before Elizabeth was 3 years old, he had her mother beheaded.

Henry gave Elizabeth a house of her own in the country. He paid little attention to her, and her governess complained that the princess "hath neither gown, nor kirtle, nor petticoat." Henry provided excellent tutors, however, and Elizabeth showed a love for learning. One of her tutors, Roger Ascham, wrote: "Her perseverance is equal to that of a man, and her memory long keeps what it quickly picks up. She talks French and Italian as well as she does English. When she writes Greek and Latin, nothing is more beautiful than her handwriting. She delights as much in music as she is skillful in it."

Henry's third wife, Jane Seymour, gave birth to a son, Edward. Henry died when Edward was 10 years old, and the boy came to the throne as Edward VI. Elizabeth and Edward were both brought up in Henry's new church. Their half sister Mary was brought up a Roman Catholic. When Edward died in 1553, Mary became queen and at once made Catholicism the state religion. Mary suspected Elizabeth of plotting with the Protestants to gain the throne and had her imprisoned for two months in the Tower of London.

When Mary died, there were two claimants to the throne. If Elizabeth did not succeed, the next heir was Mary Stuart of Scotland, a Catholic. Mary Stuart was about to be married to the dauphin Francis of France. If she won the throne of England, both Scotland and England would be joined to France. Philip II of Spain, though a Catholic, threw his influence on the side of Elizabeth because he was jealous of France's power. Later the Spanish ambassador hinted to Elizabeth that she owed her throne to Philip. Elizabeth replied that she owed it to her people. "She is very much wedded to her people," the ambassador wrote, "and thinks as they do."

Queen Elizabeth at 25

Elizabeth at 25 was tall and slender. Her eyes were bright, and her long, pale face was crowned with a mass of curly reddish hair. Her health was excellent and she loved riding and shooting. She could hunt all day and dance all night. But she would turn from these pleasures to spend long hours with her secretaries, reading dispatches, dictating, and carefully examining the accounts. She spoke in splendid sentences when she addressed Parliament or the people. With her courtiers her speech was elegant and witty—and sometimes coarse, because she liked a resounding oath as well as had her father. She laughed loudly when amused; when angered, she showed furious fits of temper. She was vain of her good looks, especially of her long beautiful hands, and she loved extravagant dress and jewels. She had a genius for diplomacy, being both cautious and wily. She understood finance and was extremely frugal in the expenses of government. She hated war because it was wasteful of both men and money.

The young queen chose as her chief minister Sir William Cecil (Lord Burghley), who was cautious and conservative like herself. For 40 years he was her mainstay in both home and foreign affairs. Her favorite courtier was the charming and handsome Robert Dudley, earl of Leicester.

The Problem of Religion

In religious matters Elizabeth steered a middle course between the extreme Protestants and the Catholics. She restored the Protestant service but retained many features of Catholicism, including bishops and archbishops. She hoped this compromise would produce unity in the state; but the Catholics, who formed a majority of her subjects, were not reconciled. From time to time some of them plotted with Spain or France to put Mary Stuart on the throne in place of Elizabeth. France and Spain were rivals, and Elizabeth was usually able to play one off against the other. She even used courtship as part of her diplomatic game. She refused to marry Philip II of Spain but held out hopes to more than one of his royal relatives when France seemed to threaten. Later, when Philip turned against England, Elizabeth encouraged French princes. To cut Scotland's ties with France, she gave secret help to the Scottish Presbyterians. She also aided the Protestant Netherlands when they revolted against Spain.

Mary Stuart returned to Scotland in 1561 after the death of her husband, Francis, king of France. In 1568 she was compelled to flee across the English border to ask Elizabeth's help. Elizabeth kept her a prisoner for 19 years. Finally Mary was accused of having a part in the so-called Babington plot to assassinate Elizabeth. Parliament demanded her execution. Elizabeth signed the warrant; and Mary Stuart was beheaded in 1587 (*see* Mary, Queen of Scots). In the last years of Elizabeth's reign, Catholics were cruelly persecuted and many were put to death.

Defeat of the Spanish Armada

During the first 30 years of Elizabeth's reign England was at peace. Commerce revived, and English ships were boldly venturing across the seas to the West Indies. There they came into conflict with Spain and Portugal, which owned and ruled the whole New World and claimed a monopoly of trade. English smugglers broke through the blockade and made huge profits by selling, in the West Indies, Negroes they had seized in Africa. John Hawkins, Sir Francis Drake, and other English seamen also waylaid Spanish ships on their way home and seized their gold. Elizabeth aided the English privateers with ships and money and shared in their profits and stolen treasure. Philip II finally decided to put an end to these attacks by invading and conquering England.

After years of preparation, Philip assembled a great fleet of his best and largest warships, called by the Spanish the Armada (that is, fleet). In 1588 the Armada sailed into the English Channel. The English were waiting for them and at once put out to sea. Their ships were of newer design, smaller than the Spanish galleons, but faster and more heavily armed. In a nine-day battle they inflicted terrible losses on the enemy. The ships that escaped ran into bad weather and only a few returned to Spain. (*See also* Armada, Spanish.) English ships then carried the war to Spain. When the struggle ended—after the deaths of both Elizabeth and Philip—no Spanish fleet dared to contest England's command of the seas.

England's "Golden Age"

The most splendid period of English literature, called the Elizabethan Age, began in the later years of Elizabeth's reign. Francis Bacon, writer of the 'Essays', was one of the queen's lawyers. Edmund Spenser wrote 'The Faerie Queene' in her honor. Shakespeare acted before her; but at the time of her death he had not yet written most of his great tragedies. Elizabeth enjoyed plays, but there is no evidence that she appreciated Shakespeare's genius.

Elizabeth was 55 years old when the Spanish Armada was defeated. Her joy in the victory was soon followed by grief, because her great favorite, Leicester, died a few months later. In 1598 her faithful minister Lord Burghley passed away. In her court appeared young men—Sir Walter Raleigh, brilliant and adventurous, and the earl of Essex, a handsome young soldier. Essex fell from favor and Elizabeth had him executed for trying to stir up a rebellion against her. She died two years later, in 1603, at the age of 69, and was buried with great magnificence in Westminster Abbey. Mary Stuart's son, James VI of Scotland, was proclaimed James I of England, thus uniting the crowns of the two kingdoms.

The things we think of chiefly as marking the reign of Elizabeth are the religious question, the defeat of the Spanish Armada, and the flourishing of literature. Also important, however, were hundreds of laws on shipping, commerce, industry, currency reform, roads, poor relief, and agriculture. These laws shaped the policy of England for more than two centuries after Elizabeth's reign had ended. (*See also* English Literature.)

ELIZABETH II

ELIZABETH II (born 1926). Like Elizabeth I of England's Golden Age, Elizabeth II came to the throne when she was 25 years old. "A fair and youthful figure," said Winston Churchill, "princess, wife, and mother, is heir to all our traditions and glories." The young queen had already won the affection of the British people by her charm and thoughtfulness, her modesty and simple dignity. On her 21st birthday she had broadcast from South Africa: "I declare before you all that my whole life, whether it be long or short, shall be devoted to your service and the service of the great imperial family to which we belong."

Karsh—Camera Press/Photo Trends

Elizabeth II in 1985

Elizabeth's father was Albert, Duke of York, second son of George V. Her mother was Lady Elizabeth Bowes-Lyon, a member of the Scottish aristocracy. Princess Elizabeth was born April 21, 1926, at the London home of her mother's parents, Lord and Lady Strathmore. Five weeks later she was baptized at Buckingham Palace and christened Elizabeth Alexandra Mary, after three queens of her country. She was four years old when her sister, Margaret Rose, was born (Aug. 21, 1930). In spite of the difference in their ages, the princesses became close companions. Margaret Rose was lively and mischievous; Elizabeth, rather serious and thoughtful.

Childhood of the Little Princesses

The family's London home was a large Victorian house at 145 Piccadilly. Summer vacations were usually spent in Scotland and week ends at the Duke's country house, Royal Lodge, in Windsor Great Park, 25 miles west of London. Here the children had a playhouse, a gift of the people of Wales. Its name was "Y Bwthyn Bach," or The Little Thatched House. It was complete with small furniture, linens, electric lights, plumbing, and windows that opened and shut. Since only children could stand up in it, the princesses themselves cleaned it and kept it in order.

The little princesses did not go to school but were taught by a governess, Miss Marion Crawford, a young Scottish woman. Their daily routine varied little from day to day. Elizabeth, at the age of five, rose at six o'clock and went out for a riding lesson with a groom. After breakfast she and her sister went to their parents' room. They spent the rest of the morning with their governess. After lunch they had lessons in French, voice, and piano. In the afternoon they played in the garden, usually with their governess. They would become so absorbed in their games of hide-and-seek or "sardines" that they seldom noticed the people who would gather outside the garden fence to watch them. They rarely had the company of other children, but they had many pets, particularly horses and dogs. Occasionally their governess would give them a special treat by taking them for a ride in the Underground (subway) or on top of a bus. They dressed simply, in cotton dresses at home and in tweed coats and berets when they went out. They went to bed early, after a visit with their parents.

Heiress to the Throne at the Age of Ten

Elizabeth's carefree days ended in 1936. George V, her grandfather, died early in that year, and before the year ended her Uncle David (Edward VIII) abdicated. Elizabeth's father then became king, as George VI, and Elizabeth became heiress presumptive to the throne (*see* Edward VIII; George VI). The family moved into Buckingham Palace, the royal residence, which was more like a museum than a house. From the princesses' rooms, in the front, it was a five-minute walk to the garden in the rear.

From this time, Elizabeth began to be trained for her future duties. From her parents and her grandmother, Queen Mary, she learned court etiquette and diplomatic practices. She studied the geography and history of the Commonwealth countries and the United States and was driven to Eton College for private lessons in constitutional law. She disliked arithmetic, and Queen Mary decided she would have little use for it.

Elizabeth was 13 when the second World War broke out (1939). The next year bombs began to fall on London and the princesses were sent for safety to the grim fortress of Windsor Castle. On Oct. 13, 1940, Elizabeth returned to London to make her first broadcast, from a room in Buckingham Palace. In a clear confident voice she told children everywhere that the children of Britain were "full of cheerfulness and courage." Before the war ended, she joined the women's branch of the army and took training as an automobile driver and mechanic.

Elizabeth had the privilege, often denied to royalty, of marrying a man she loved. During the war she met Prince Philip, a blond, handsome officer in the royal navy. Philip was born June 10, 1921, on the Greek island of Corfu. As a son of Prince Andrew of Greece, he was in line for the Greek throne; but he had no Greek blood. Through his mother, Princess Alice, he was descended, like Elizabeth, from Queen Victoria of England. He had been educated in Scotland under the care of his uncle and guardian, Earl Mountbatten.

As soon as the war ended, Philip became a frequent visitor at the palace, coming in, the governess said, "like a refreshing sea breeze." Before the king announced the betrothal of the young couple, Philip dropped his title of prince to become a British citizen and took his mother's family name, Mountbatten. The king then created him duke of Edinburgh. On Nov. 20, 1947, the couple were married at Westminster Abbey. A son, Prince Charles Philip Arthur George, was born on Nov. 14, 1948, and a daughter, Princess Anne Elizabeth Alice Louise, on Aug. 15, 1950. On Feb. 19, 1960, the queen had a third child, Prince Andrew Albert Christian Edward. Her fourth child, Prince Edward Antony Richard Louis, was born on March 10, 1964.

Elizabeth Is Proclaimed Queen

Even before she became queen, Elizabeth served the government as a skilled ambassador. In 1948 she visited Paris and was acclaimed by the French people. In 1951 she and her husband made a six-week tour of all the provinces of Canada and then flew to Washington, D.C., for a brief visit with President and Mrs. Harry S. Truman at Blair House.

The royal couple were in Kenya, on the first stage of a five-month tour to Australia and New Zealand, when George VI died on Feb. 6, 1952. Elizabeth automatically became queen. She and her husband immediately flew to London. On February 8 the queen took the oath of accession before the Privy Council.

The coronation took place on June 2, 1953. Elizabeth was crowned queen of Great Britain, Northern Ireland, Canada, Australia, New Zealand, South Africa, Pakistan, and about 50 other lands.

In 1957 the queen conferred upon her husband the title prince of the United Kingdom. In 1958 she named Prince Charles, her oldest son, prince of Wales. He was invested as the prince of Wales in 1969. He married Lady Diana Spencer on July 29, 1981.

On Feb. 8, 1960, the queen announced that a new surname, Mountbatten-Windsor, would be borne by the third generation of her family. Occupants of the throne and heirs apparent remain Windsors.

ELIZABETH, N.J. Since its settlement in 1664, Elizabeth has grown because of its nearness to New York City and New York Bay. One of Greater New York's residential and industrial centers, it is the southernmost of the closely built cities on the New Jersey shore of New York Harbor. Staten Island is reached by bridge.

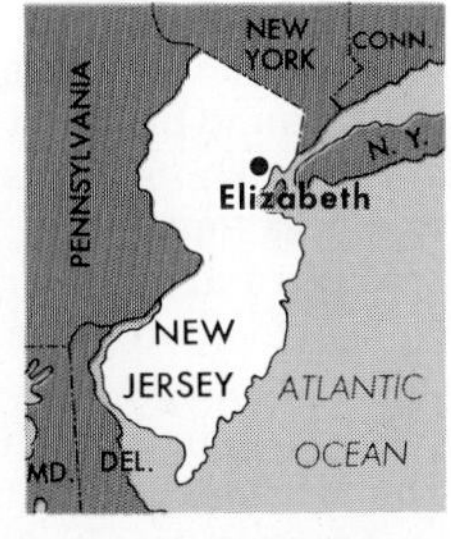

Elizabeth is highly industrialized with major shipping operations that include the Elizabeth-Port Authority Marine Terminal. Manufactured products include sewing machines, textiles, chemicals, automobiles, and machinery. The New Jersey Turnpike passes through the city.

Boxwood Hall, built about 1752, was the home of Elias Boudinot, a president of the Continental Congress. Princeton University, now in Princeton, was chartered as the College of New Jersey in Elizabeth in 1746.

Settlement of the site began in 1664 with the purchase of land from the Delaware Indians. It was named Elizabethtown for the wife of Sir George Carteret of New Jersey. In 1740 King George II chartered Elizabeth as a free borough and town. During the American Revolution, British soldiers from Staten Island often raided the town.

Elizabeth, part of metropolitan Newark, is the seat of Union County. In 1789 the state incorporated Elizabeth as a town and in 1855 granted it a city charter. The city has a mayor-council form of government. Population (1984 estimate), 107,455.

ELK *see* DEER.

ELLINGTON, Duke (1899–1974). The A Train, part of the New York City subway system, ran to north Manhattan's Harlem area. There could be found the Cotton Club, a white-owned nightclub for white audiences but featuring black entertainers. From 1927 to 1932 Duke Ellington was closely associated with the Cotton Club, so there is little wonder that his best-known signature tune became 'Take the A Train', composed by his longtime collaborator, pianist Billy Strayhorn.

Ellington was a composer, pianist, jazz band leader, and one of the most eminent and creative American musicians of the 20th century. The range of his accomplishments was so great over a 55-year career that his impact on music has yet to be assessed adequately.

Edward Kennedy Ellington was born in Washington, D.C., on April 29, 1899. Although he showed considerable artistic talent as a youth, he turned down a scholarship to devote himself to music. He was largely a self-taught pianist. By his teens he was influenced by the ragtime composers of the era. Around 1918 he formed a band to play local engagements. About 1923 he was in New York City leading a small band at the Kentucky Club. From there he went to the Cotton Club, where his band included such jazz greats as Johnny Hodges, Barney Bigard, and Cootie Williams. This period and the years that followed brought him and his band international recognition for such compositions as 'Mood Indigo', 'Sophisticated Lady', 'I Got It Bad', 'Solitude', 'Satin Doll', and 'Black and Tan Fantasy'. Appearances on the Broadway stage and concert tours of the United States and Europe further enhanced their reputation.

In 1943 a longer Ellington piece, 'Black, Brown, and Beige', premiered at Carnegie Hall. He wrote 'Liberian Suite' in 1947 for the centennial of Liberia. He was commisioned by Arturo Toscanini in 1950 to write 'Harlem' for the NBC Symphony Orchestra. A later aspect of his career was religious jazz, compositions to be performed at worship services (*see* Jazz). In 1969 he was awarded the Presidential Medal of Freedom. Ellington died on May 24, 1974, and the band passed to the leadership of his son, Mercer.

ELLIS, Havelock (1859–1939). The first modern student of human sexual behavior was a British physician named Havelock Ellis. Through his writings he helped bring about more open discussion of sexual problems. He also influenced the psychological theories of Sigmund Freud, who consulted him by mail.

Ellis was born at Croydon in Surrey, England, on Feb. 2, 1859. He was educated at private schools in London and spent some years at sea with his father, a sea captain. In his early years he was concerned with what he called "the ugliness and beauty of sex," a problem he believed could only be solved through scientific studies. Ellis enrolled at Saint Thomas's Hospital in London to study medicine in 1881. He finished the course of studies eight years later but never practiced medicine regularly.

For a time he turned his attention to the arts and made the acquaintance of such people as George Bernard Shaw. He translated some of Heinrich Heine's prose, introduced the plays of Henrik Ibsen to England, and wrote books of essays. His first book, published in 1890, was a study entitled 'The Criminal'. In 'The Nationalisation of Health' (1892) he anticipated the much later British national health service.

Ellis' first study on sexuality was 'Man and Woman' (1894) on the psychophysiological differences between the sexes. His major work, 'Studies in the Psychology of Sex', ran to seven volumes and was published from 1897 to 1928. At first it was considered pornographic and released only to physicians. Later works included 'The Task of Social Hygiene' (1912), 'Erotic Rights of Women' (1918), and 'Little Essays of Love and Virtue' (1922)—all of which earned Ellis a reputation as a champion of women's rights. Ellis died in Suffolk, England, on July 8, 1939.

ELM. The stately American elm tree has historically been a familiar sight in many towns and cities of the United States. Some elms are enormous, often reaching a height of about 120 feet (37 meters). The American elm is one of about 18 species of elm native primarily to the North Temperate zone. It grows from Newfoundland to Florida and westward to the Rocky Mountains. The American elm and many other elm species are susceptible to Dutch elm disease, a fungus carried by insects. Even though state and national governments have spent millions of dollars to combat this and other tree diseases, large populations of elms have been killed by Dutch elm disease.

The slippery elm, also called the red elm, is another common American species. The inner bark has a pleasant taste, and it becomes slippery or slimy when it is chewed. At one time it was used as a thirst quencher and for medicinal purposes. It is a medium-size tree, 60 to 70 feet (18 to 21 meters) high, having a broad flat crown and spreading branches.

The rock elm, or cork elm, is found from Canada south to Tennessee and west to Nebraska. It can be identified by the small corky ridges that appear on its twigs. The winged elm, or wahoo elm, is a much smaller species in the southeastern states. It seldom grows higher than 50 feet (15 meters). The cedar elm blossoms in the autumn and grows only in a region from Mississippi to Texas and New Mexico.

The English elm is native to western and southern Europe. Although it is somewhat taller than the American elm, it looks stockier because its upper foliage is compact and oval-shaped. Its leaves stay green longer than those of the American elm.

The bark of the elm is rough and ashy gray. The leaves grow in an alternate pattern on the twigs and branches, and the flowers bloom in drooping clusters. The nutlike fruit, surrounded by a flat, sometimes hairy, winglike structure, is called a samara. The scientific name of the American elm is *Ulmus americana;* slippery elm, *U. rubra;* rock elm, *U. thomasi;* winged elm, *U. alata;* cedar elm, *U. crassifolia;* and English elm, *U. procera.*

EL PASO, Tex. Situated at the far western tip of Texas, El Paso is a main gateway to Mexico. It is the largest of the United States-Mexican border cities. The Mexican city of Ciudad Juárez is just across the Rio Grande.

El Paso's industries include metals, petroleum and gas, food products, and clothing. A smelter and copper refinery refines about 25 percent of the United States' copper. Other economic activities include Fort Bliss, home of the United States Army Air Defense Center, the William Beaumont General Hospital, and the White Sands Missile Range in nearby New Mexico. El Paso is the commercial and financial center for a large trade territory. Livestock ranching, irrigated cotton farming, and mineral production are major economic activities.

The city is a port of entry and a major center for foreign trade. It is also a transportation hub at the crossroads of several major highways. It is served by both United States and Mexican railroads.

El Paso is a modern metropolis, though it still has old adobe buildings that are distinctively Mexican. Many scenic areas are nearby, including the Carlsbad Caverns and Big Bend national parks as well as several old Spanish missions. The University of Texas at El Paso was founded in 1913 as the Texas State School of Mines and Metallurgy. It is the site of the Sun Bowl college football game.

The strategic site of El Paso was recognized in 1598 by Juan de Oñate, the colonizer of New Mexico. The Mission of Guadalupe was established in 1659 by Franciscans. In 1827 a village developed at the present site, and it became a United States territory in 1848 when an army post was built. Four railways arrived in 1881, and the population increased more than ten times—to 10,338 by 1890. There were many border disputes between the United States and Mexico that were finally resolved in 1967. El Paso has a mayor-council form of government. Population (1980 census), city, 425,259; metropolitan area, 479,899.

A. Keler—Sygma

Workers spread coffee beans to dry in the sun at the Aqua Fria Farm, Santa Ana, El Salvador.

EL SALVADOR. One of the smallest, poorest, and most crowded nations in Central America, El Salvador is equal in area and population to the state of Massachusetts. Unlike its neighbors, it does not border on the Caribbean Sea, and it has no empty frontiers into which people may move.

Shaped like a rectangle, it extends 150 miles (241 kilometers) westward from the Gulf of Fonseca to the border with Guatemala. The mountainous Honduran frontier lies 60 miles (97 kilometers) north of El Salvador's southern Pacific shoreline. There are about 8,100 square miles (21,000 square kilometers) within its borders. Because it is such a small nation, El Salvador lacks a wide range of natural resources. Nevertheless, it is strategically located in terms of its easy access to the markets of other nations in Central America.

Land and Climate

Between the southern Pacific shoreline and its northern border with Honduras, four distinct landscapes extend across the east-west breadth of El Salvador. A 10- to 12-mile- (16- to 19-kilometer-) wide coastal plain, interrupted by volcanic hills, parallels the Pacific Ocean. It is separated from a narrow interior valley by a row of recent volcanoes, both active and inactive. Between the interior valley and the Honduran border to the north lies an old and badly eroded volcanic upland. Although two peaks in the volcanic row and several summit areas in the volcanic plateau near the Honduran border reach 7,000 feet (2,134 meters), very little of the land surface in El Salvador lies above 5,000 feet (1,524 meters) in elevation.

The Río Lempa, a major source of hydroelectric power, drains the northwestern part of El Salvador. Taking a course southward midway across the country, the river cuts across the interior valley, the volcanic row, and the coastal plain before emptying into the Pacific.

Because El Salvador is small and without major high mountains, there are fewer variations in rainfall and temperature than elsewhere in Central America. Since El Salvador lies on the drier Pacific side of the isthmus, it receives less rain and only during the summer. Yearly rainfall throughout the country averages between 60 and 85 inches (152 and 216 centimeters). Ninety percent of this falls between the months of May and October.

The average annual temperature in the capital, San Salvador, at an elevation of 2,230 feet (680 meters), is 74° F (23° C). On the coastal plain it is slightly warmer.

El Salvador has suffered repeatedly from natural catastrophes. Earthquakes have badly damaged or destroyed the city of San Salvador on 14 occasions. Major eruptions of the nearby volcano of Boquerón last occurred in 1917. Hurricanes are rare, but severe droughts have caused widespread losses.

People and Culture

When the Spanish entered El Salvador, they encountered a dense population of Indians. Since the countryside was open, Spaniards managed to settle throughout the land. Thus most of the natives came under their direct influence. Because of this, Indians gradually adapted many European customs and came to be classified as Ladinos. Today Indians make up less than 5 percent of the population.

There were 800,000 people in El Salvador in 1900. They increased to 1.6 million by 1940 and now number about 5.5 million. Because of the high rate of population increase, it is predicted that the country will have 8.5 million people by the year 2000. The density of population is 644 persons per square mile (249 per square kilometer). This is three and a half times denser than Guatemala and up to 10 times denser than other Central American nations. Because

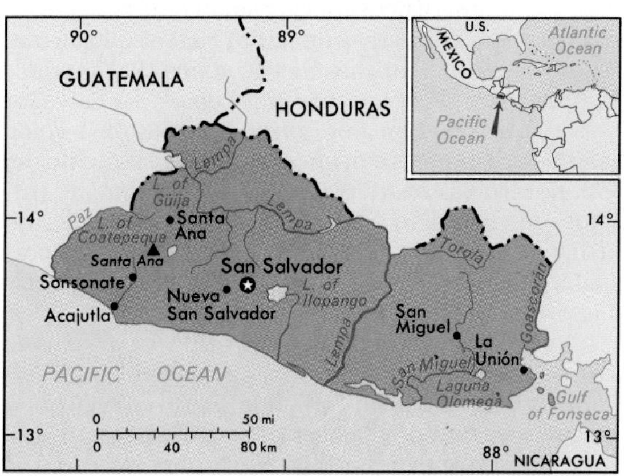

of the high density, many Salvadorans have migrated to less populated areas in surrounding countries.

Urban and rural populations are about equal, and both are concentrated on the inner coastal plain and within the volcanic row and interior valley. The three largest cities—San Salvador, Santa Ana, and San Miguel—lie in basins along the lower flanks of volcanoes.

Economy, Transportation, and Communication

For 100 years coffee has dominated the economy of El Salvador. It has been the major source of employment, has financed the cost of governments, and has paid for the construction of highways, railroads, and ports. Village lands were converted into coffee estates on which peasants labored. The owners became the aristocracy of El Salvador. Present-day culture and politics are products of the coffee economy.

After its introduction in the 1850s, the planting of coffee spread rapidly within the volcanic row. By 1870 it had replaced the dye indigo as the nation's major export. Coffee made up about 90 percent and never less than 75 percent of Salvadoran exports between 1900 and the early 1940s.

After World War II forested areas and natural pastures on the coastal plain were converted into cotton farms. Sugar produced for export increased in the 1960s.

The limited area within El Salvador makes the further expansion of commercial agriculture difficult. There are no empty lands onto which poor subsistence farmers, who make up 40 percent of the population, can move to produce their corn, beans, and sorghum.

A disciplined work force and the favorable location of El Salvador have contributed to the development of manufacturing. Textiles, food processing, and the manufacture of shoes, clothing, and pharmaceuticals are leading industries. Manufacturing increased dramatically during the 1960s after the establishment of the Central American Common Market, which eased the exchange of products between member nations of the region. During the 1970s the growth of manufacturing slowed as a result of a war with Honduras.

Because El Salvador is a small nation restricted to a landscape of volcanic origin, few minerals are available for mining. There is a very small output of silver. There are no domestic supplies of coal or petroleum. Energy requirements are met by dams that produce hydroelectric power on the Río Lempa. El Salvador was the first nation in Central America to develop geothermal energy from underground volcanic steam.

Lumbering is restricted, as few forests remain. Offshore in the Pacific fishermen harvest shrimp and fish, but the industry is not well developed. The port of La Unión on the Gulf of Fonseca is the primary harbor for fishing fleets.

Exports have expanded since World War II from the rise of manufacturing and the expansion of agriculture into cotton and sugar. Coffee, however, continues to make up half of all sales abroad. The agricultural products are sent primarily to western Europe, the United States, and Japan. Manufactured products are exported to neighboring countries of Central America.

Imports come primarily from the United States, Central America, Europe, and Venezuela. They consist of petroleum, textiles, food products, chemicals, machinery, and transport equipment.

Since landforms offer limited obstacles to transportation, it has been possible to build the best system of railroads and highways to be found in Central America. Railroads were constructed after 1880 to carry coffee to the ports of Acajutla and La Unión. A railroad was completed to the Caribbean coast through Guatemala in 1927 that allowed coffee to be shipped more directly to Europe and the United States. The Inter-American Highway passes through the interior valley with links to the coastal highway and to the seaports on the Pacific.

Education

Although education is supposed to be compulsory, many people neither read nor write. Thirty percent of all children do not attend primary schools. While 80 percent of those living in cities can read and write, this is true of only half of those living in rural areas.

History

After defeating Indian armies in Guatemala in 1524, the Spanish conqueror Pedro de Alvarado continued into El Salvador. Here he encountered the armies of the Pipil, a Nahuatl people of Mexican origin. It was not until the following year that the conquest was completed. During Spanish rule El Salvador was a province of the Kingdom of Guatemala.

Facts About El Salvador

Official Name: Republic of El Salvador.

Capital: San Salvador.

Area: 8,124 square miles (21,041 square kilometers).

Population (1983 estimate): 5,235,700; 644 persons per square mile (249 persons per square kilometer); 50 percent urban, 50 percent rural.

Major Language: Spanish (official).

Major Religion: Roman Catholicism.

Literacy: 64.2 percent.

Highest Peak: Santa Ana.

Major River: Lempa.

Form of Government: Republic.

Chief of State and Head of Government: President.

Legislature: Constituent Assembly.

Voting Qualification: 18 years of age.

Political Divisions: 14 departments.

Major Cities (1983 estimate): San Salvador (445,100), Santa Ana (132,200), Mejicanos (86,500), San Miguel (86,500), Delgado (64,600).

Chief Manufactured and Mined Products: Clothing, food products, pharmaceuticals, shoes, silver, textiles.

Chief Agricultural Products: *Crops*—beans, coffee, corn, cotton, rice, sugarcane. *Livestock*—cattle, chickens, pigs.

Flag: *Colors*—blue and white. The white has the arms of the republic at the center (*see* Flags of the World).

Monetary Unit: 1 colón = 100 centavos.

The first revolt in Central America against the Spanish took place in El Salvador in 1811, but it was not until 1821 that independence from Spain was achieved. In 1823 El Salvador joined the United Provinces of Central America. The breakup of the United Provinces led to complete independence for El Salvador in 1840. For nearly a century there was a succession of conservative governments. Several short wars were fought with Guatemala and Honduras. The early 1930s were marked by revolt and violence.

The 1970s were a period of political turmoil, when José Napoleón Duarte failed to be seated as president after an election. The outbreak of civil war between the right-wing military and left-wing guerrilla forces in the late 1970s resulted in the deaths of thousands of civilians. The government was accused of atrocities and ousted in 1979. A new constitution in 1983 paved the way for the election of Duarte in 1984 as president and marked the return to civilian government.

As the civil war entered its tenth year, presidential elections were held on March 19, 1989. Alfredo Cristiani of the ultraconservative Nationalist Republican Alliance was elected. After successful preliminary talks, peace negotiations between the government and the rebels were called off in October. Two weeks later the rebels made their largest offensive of the war. Several hundred people were believed killed. In April 1990 the rebels and the government agreed to United Nations–sponsored peace talks.

ELYTIS, Odysseus (born 1911). The winner of the 1979 Nobel prize for literature, Odysseus Elytis is not well known outside his native Greece. There he is popular for his poetry that expresses the ideals, history, mythology, and hopes of his country.

Elytis was born Odysseus Alepoudhelis on Nov. 2, 1911, to a prosperous family on the island of Crete. He later changed his name to dissociate himself from his family's soap business. He received his education in Athens. His first book of poems, 'Orientations', was published in Greek in 1939. During World War II he published 'Heroic and Elegiac Song for the Lost Second Lieutenant of the Albanian Campaign' (1945) about the death of a young soldier.

Elytis is probably best known for the intricate and abstract 'To Axion Esti' (Worthy It Is), a spiritual autobiography. Sections of the poem were later set to music. Later books of poetry were 'Six and One Remorses for the Sky' (1960) and 'The Stepchildren' (1974). 'Open Book' (1974) is a collection of his essays.

EMANCIPATION PROCLAMATION. On Sept. 22, 1862, United States President Abraham Lincoln issued a proclamation that he later called "the central act of my administration, and the greatest event of the 19th century." The proclamation promised freedom for slaves held in any of the Confederate states that did not return to the Union by the end of the year.

When the American Civil War broke out in 1861, the abolitionists had urged Lincoln to take this step and had criticized him for refusing to do so. He had replied, "My paramount object is to save the Union, and not either to save or destroy slavery." If he had decreed emancipation at the beginning of the war, Missouri, Kentucky, and probably Maryland would have joined the South in secession. After the war had been in progress for more than a year, there was no danger of this, but there was need at that time to enlist the public opinion of the world in behalf of the Union. Freeing the slaves would do this.

Lincoln had drawn up the proclamation in July 1862 and laid it before his Cabinet. All the members approved, but Secretary of State William Henry Seward urged that the proclamation should not be issued at that time. Since the Union armies were being defeated, it might seem as if the North were appealing to the slaves for help instead of aiding them. Lincoln agreed to the postponement, but he vowed to issue the proclamation after the first Union victory.

The occasion came with the battle of Antietam on September 17, and a preliminary proclamation that affected about 3 million slaves was issued on September 22. The Confederate states and their slaveholders paid no attention to its warning, and so on Jan. 1, 1863, Lincoln issued the final proclamation. (*See also* Civil War, American; Lincoln, Abraham.)

The final proclamation did not apply to the border states, which were not in rebellion against the Union, and it could not be enforced in the regions held by Confederate troops. But as soon as the Northern armies captured a region, the slaves there were given their freedom. Many of the freed blacks joined the Union Army. The remaining slaves in the United States were freed by the 13th Amendment to the Constitution (ratified on Dec. 18, 1865), which decreed that "Neither slavery nor involuntary servitude, except as a punishment for crime whereof the party shall have been duly convicted, shall exist within the United States, or any place subject to their jurisdiction."

EMBARGO. Derived from the Spanish word *embargar,* meaning "to restrain," an embargo is the detention, or holding, of ships or other property within a nation to prevent their departure to a foreign territory. A notable embargo occurred after the Soviet Union invaded Afghanistan in December 1979: United States President Jimmy Carter forbade the shipment of grain and high-technology equipment to the Soviet Union. The grain embargo was lifted by President Ronald Reagan 15 months later, but the high-technology embargo was maintained.

To achieve its objective, an embargo should prevent shipment by air and land as well as by sea. In order to get around an embargo, shippers often send goods to an intermediate country from which they are sent on to their final destination. Computers and other sophisticated equipment of American manufacture were sent to the Soviet Union in this way.

An embargo may be either civil or hostile. A civil embargo is the detention of vessels in home port to protect them from foreign plunder or to keep goods from reaching a particular destination. A hostile embargo is the detention of another nation's transport or property.

19th Century

An embargo may be used either as a reprisal for some act or for a political purpose. An example of embargo as reprisal occurred in the United States in 1807 and 1808, when Great Britain and France were engaged in the Napoleonic wars. Britain interfered with neutral vessels going to French ports, and Napoleon ordered that ships that obeyed the English orders be seized. As a result, neutral American shipping suffered severely.

Hoping to bring one or both countries to consider the rights of neutrals, Congress passed a nonimportation act in 1806 forbidding the entrance of British goods. It proved ineffective. Then, upon President Thomas Jefferson's recommendation, an embargo act was passed on Dec. 22, 1807. It forbade American vessels to put to sea, in the hope that the lack of American goods would bring the other nations to terms.

The embargo made little impression on Britain and France, but it almost ruined American commerce. New England was so damaged by the embargo that it considered seceding from the Union. Although the embargo was repealed, its ill effects lasted for years.

20th Century

A political embargo was imposed by the United States against Japan in 1940 to prevent the shipment of petroleum and strategic materials to a nation waging war. Since World War II, embargoes have tended to deal mainly with the export of military materials and high-technology equipment. In the late 1940s the free-world nations agreed to prohibit trade in arms and strategic materials with Communist-bloc countries. In 1951, during the Korean War, the United Nations General Assembly adopted an American recommendation that all members of the UN prohibit shipments of arms and other strategic materials to China and North Korea. From the early 1960s the United States maintained a general trade embargo against the shipment of American goods to Cuba.

In 1963 the UN Security Council voted for an arms embargo against South Africa because of its apartheid policy. In 1966, for similar reasons, it imposed an embargo on Rhodesia (now Zimbabwe). A United States grain embargo against the Soviet Union from 1979 to 1981 hurt American farmers as much or more than it did the Soviets.

In 1989 the European Communities (EC) imposed a ban on all imports of beef from hormone-treated cattle, most of which came from the United States. The United States retaliated by placing high tariffs on imported EC food products.

Lists of embargoed goods change as developments affect strategic values of commodities. Trade with Eastern-bloc nations was increased when Soviet economic control over them was relaxed in the 1960s. The United States prohibition on trade with China was relaxed in the 1970s when relations were normalized.

EMBOSSING.

EMBOSSING. Designs on metal, leather, paper, textiles, cardboard, wood, and similar materials, when raised above the surrounding surface, are the products of embossing. It is one of the oldest of the arts, and beautiful examples are preserved in museums. Embossing is widely used on leather and cloth in the making of fine bookbindings.

Patterns in relief may be hammered from the reverse side of such materials as sheet metals, brass, silver, and gold. This process is called repoussé, a French word meaning "pushed back." Craftsmen of the Old World used this method for ornamentation. Repoussé was chiefly a process performed by hand, but now it is often done by machine. Two dies are used: one has the figure inset, and the other, or the counterdie, has the figure raised. Coins are made by dies that compress the metal disks and leave a raised design on each side. Another process, by which the design is pressed into the material, is called chasing. This technique is often used in metalwork and leatherwork.

Pressed-metal containers, such as teapots and ice pitchers, are embossed by placing them inside metal counterdies that have the figures inset. The object to be embossed is filled with water under great pressure, and the water transmits the pressure to the metal, forcing it into the design in the counterdie.

Embossing in needlework is done by making many stitches over a preformed pad of felt, wool, or other material. Another process is used with wood, with figures pressed into the wood. When the wood is planed and then soaked in water, the depressed parts swell above the surrounding surface.

Designs can be raised mechanically on paper. Decorations or monograms are frequently embossed on quality stationery, greeting cards, business cards, and wedding invitations.

Gray Dove

EMBRYOLOGY

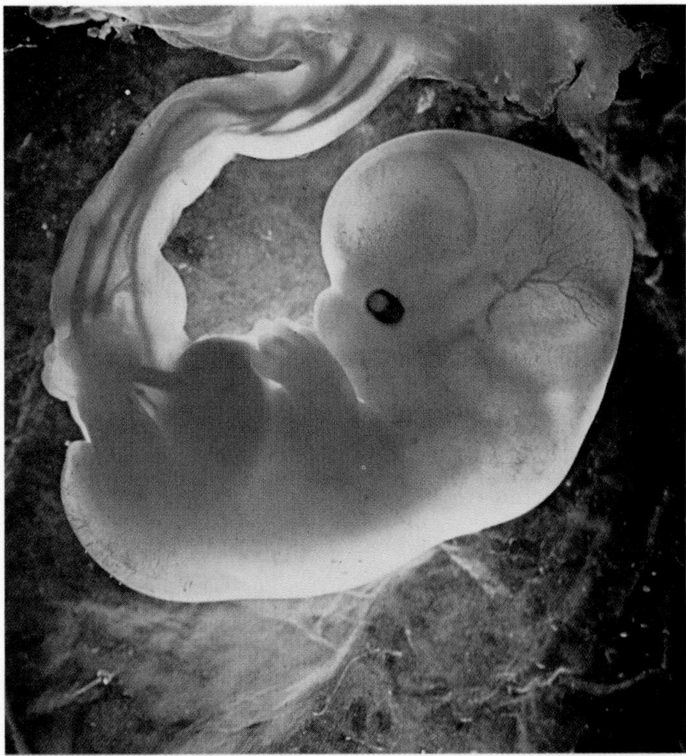

By means of an extraordinary technique, this 6½-week-old human embryo was photographed in the mother's womb. The embryo is linked with the placenta (at the top of the photo) by the umbilical cord, through which food and wastes pass. By the ninth week, the embryo will look distinctively human.

EMBRYOLOGY. One of the marvels of nature is the way in which a complex organism develops from a single cell. The fully formed organism, however, is not produced in an instant. It is the outcome of a number of increasingly intricate changes occurring over a protracted period of time. This sequence takes place in the very young organism —the *embryo*. The study of the embryo's development is a branch of biology called *embryology*.

The term for all the phases of embryonic development is *embryogeny*. During embryogeny, cells divide countless times to form the tissues and organs of the body. A human being, for example, begins as a single cell that could be lost in a pinhole. At birth, however, after a period of development that lasts about nine months, the human body contains some 200 billion cells, is 2 billion times larger, and has all the parts necessary for life.

THE EGG—ORIGIN OF THE EMBRYO

The starting point of all many-celled organisms is the one-celled *ovum*, or *egg* (*see* Egg; Cell). Throughout the animal world there are hundreds of different types of eggs. Some have shells; others do not. There are large eggs and tiny ones. The number of eggs produced varies enormously from species to species. A codfish, for example, may lay up to 6 million eggs in one breeding season. A whale, by contrast, produces only one egg every two years.

Size, Content, and Destiny of the Egg

Egg cells are usually very small. The human ovum is about 1/175 inch in diameter, and frog eggs average about 1/10 inch in diameter. Some species, however, produce comparatively large eggs. Ostrich eggs, for example, are about three inches in diameter.

Large eggs have a great deal of *yolk*, a stored food. Hard or horny shells, protective white, or jelly enables eggs to survive in harsh surroundings. Variations in the amount of yolk and in the number and types of protective structures are associated with the food needs and environment of the embryo. A bird embryo, which completes its development within the confines of a shell, is fed by great amounts of yolk. The frog egg develops in water, and its moderate yolk is sufficient to nourish the embryo until it hatches as a free-swimming tadpole. The egg of a mammal is almost yolkless, and the mammalian embryo, which develops within the body of the female parent, gets the bulk of its food from her.

Human egg cells grow and mature in *follicles*, compartments located in the woman's *ovaries*. About once a month one of these follicles enlarges and ruptures. The egg is then discharged into the *oviduct* and begins its journey to the *uterus*. Embryonic development gets under way in the uterus if the egg is fertilized by a sperm cell. Should the egg remain unfertilized, however, it soon disintegrates.

Fertilization and Cleavage of the Egg

Fertilization takes place when a free-swimming *spermatozoon* (sperm cell) penetrates the ovum's protective outer layer. Once this has happened, no other sperm has an effect on the fertilized egg, or *zygote*.

Prior to their encounter, the egg and sperm undergo *meiosis*, a type of cell division that leaves each cell with only half the usual number of *chromosomes* (hereditary structures) characteristic of the species (*see* Cell). Soon after fertilization, however, the egg and sperm nuclei merge to form a zygote with the proper number of chromosomes. At the same time *cleavage*, a series of consecutive cell divisions (mitoses), is initiated.

Cleavage produces a rapidly increasing number of cells smaller than the zygote. The patterns of cleavage vary, in part because of variations in the amount and distribution of yolk. In reptiles and birds, which have a great deal of yolk in the egg, cleavage leads to the formation of a plate of cells on top of the yolk. In amphibians and mammals, with smaller amounts of yolk, cleavage results in a hollow ball, the *blastula*. As the cells continue to multiply, the various regions of the plate or the ball fold and shift in position. In this manner three distinct layers develop. These are known as the *primary germ layers*.

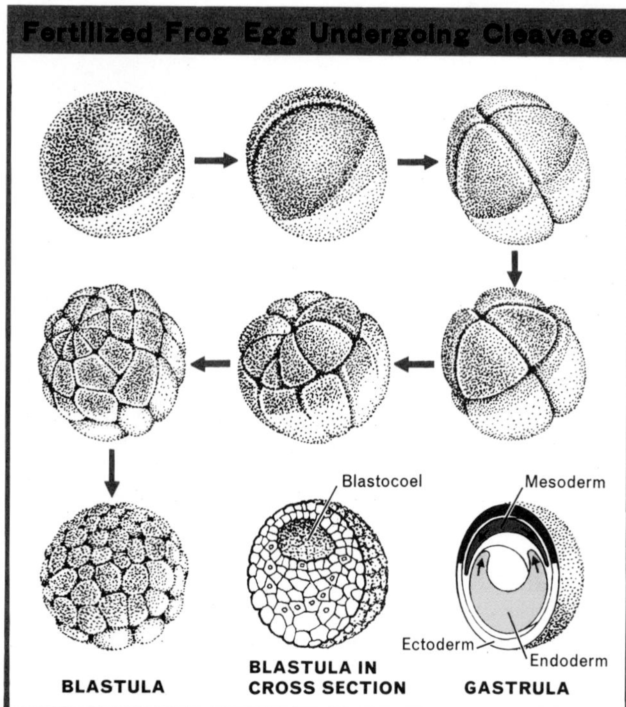

Egg fertilization initiates *cleavage* (progressive splitting of cells). One cell splits into two, two into four, four into eight, and so on. At the 256-cell stage the cell mass shown here has encircled a hollow *blastocoel* to form the *blastula*. Then the primary germ layers—ectoderm, mesoderm, and endoderm—move into their respective positions in the *gastrula* (shown in diagrammatic cross section, bottom right).

VERTEBRATE EMBRYOGENY

The three germ layers develop early in the embryonic life of vertebrates and invertebrates alike, and there are also many similarities in the subsequent development of both vertebrate and invertebrate body structures. However, the following discussion of embryological action applies mainly to *vertebrates*, or animals with backbones.

The Primary Germ Layers—Origin of the Adult Organs

The primary germ layers form quite early in embryogeny. They appear, for example, during the 16th day of human embryonic development. The outermost layer is called the *ectoderm;* the innermost, the *endoderm*. Between these two layers lies the *mesoderm*. At first, the three layers are more or less uniform. Soon, however, they begin to take on different characteristics. In each layer, unique tissues and organs begin to take shape.

Every adult organ is identified with one of the germ layers. The diagram and chart near the end of this article show the germ-layer source of the main parts of the adult vertebrate. However, it should be understood that no structure in the adult body is the exclusive product of a single germ layer. Actually, only the physiologically unique portion of a particular organ can be traced to just one of the layers. Thus, though the intestine is said to originate from the endoderm, this is true only of its secreting and absorbing inner lining. The muscles, connective tissue, blood vessels, and nerves which comprise the bulk of the intestine originate from the mesoderm or the ectoderm.

Structures Arising from the Germ Layers

By the 19th day of human embryonic development, ectoderm along the mid-back portion of the elongated embryo becomes thicker than adjoining ectoderm. Unequal cell growth causes the edges of the thickened plate to roll upward as the center buckles. The *neural tube* forms when the edges meet. A mass of cells called the *neural crest* is pinched off the top of the tube. These cells migrate to other parts of the embryo, where they give rise to neural and other structures. Eventually, the front part of the neural tube bends, thickens, and bulges to form the brain. The rest of the tube becomes the spinal cord.

Meanwhile, cells of the endoderm roll to form the *archenteron*—the primitive digestive tube, or "gut." The archenteron later gives rise to the lungs, the liver, and the lining of the digestive tract.

The mesoderm also begins to spread around the sides of the embryo. As it does, its top portion separates from the lateral segments and rounds into the long, solid *notochord*. The lateral sheets of mesoderm move down each side of the embryo until they meet at mid-bottom. At the same time, they split into two layers separated by a cavity. The inner layer, *splanchnic mesoderm*, lies next to the archenteron; the outer layer, *somatic mesoderm*, next to the ectoderm. Between these layers is the *coelom*, in which the vital organs will lie.

On each side of the embryo the mesoderm becomes organized into three distinct regions. Topmost, flanking the notochord and neural tube, is the *epimere*. At the bottom, next to the archenteron, is the *hypomere*. The narrow *mesomere* lies between them. At this stage, a human embryo is in its fourth week.

The epimere undergoes further differentiation. The lateral wall of each epimere, called the *dermatome*, provides the dermis of the skin (*see* Skin). The upper

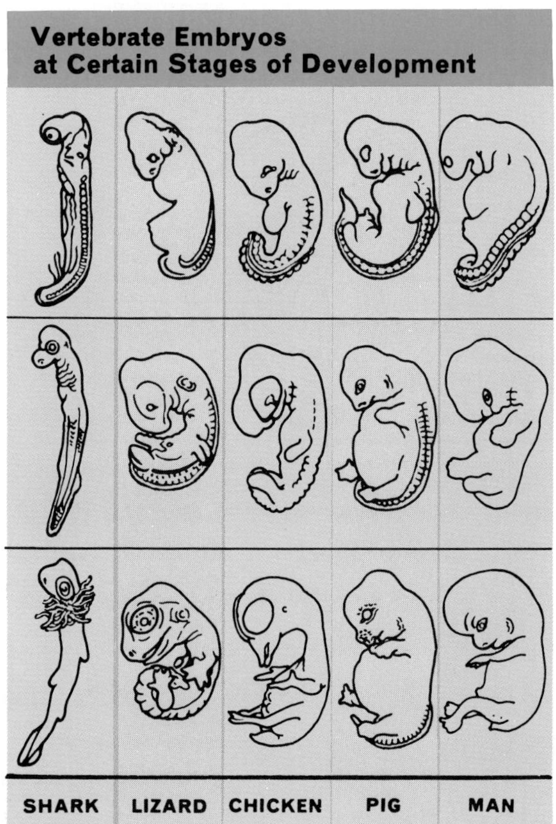

Vertebrate embryos look a great deal alike in the very early stages of development (top row). As time goes on, however, they become more and more dissimilar.

wall, the *sclerotome,* produces the vertebrae (*see* Skeleton). At about the ninth week of human embryogeny, the bony vertebrae begin to form around the notochord, and the skull starts to encase the developing brain. The lower wall, the *myotome,* gives rise to the muscles of the body wall and the appendages (*see* Muscles).

From the fifth through the eighth week of embryogeny, cells derived from the primitive tissues are organized into the organs and body structure that mark an embryo as human. The ears, eyes, and nose can be distinguished. Limbs and other external body parts take form. Beginning with the ninth week, the now recognizable individual is called a *fetus.* From then until birth most of the already well-established body structures continue to grow and develop.

Extraembryonic Membranes

Most reptiles and all birds enclose their eggs in a shell. Within the shell, extraembryonic membranes take form. Two saclike membranes—the inner *amnion* and the outer *chorion*—are produced by the mesoderm of the embryo. From the end of the embryo's digestive tract the *allantois,* an endodermal sac, grows between the amnion and the chorion.

The amnion encloses a fluid-filled chamber within which the embryo grows. The allantois serves as a receptacle for embryonic wastes. Its outer wall fuses with the chorion. The chorion of birds and reptiles, linked with the embryo by blood vessels, lies adjacent to the inner surface of the porous egg shell. Oxygen passing through the shell is picked up by the chorionic blood vessels and carried to the embryo. Carbon dioxide received from the embryo is dissipated through the shell. Vessels in the yolk sac, formed from endoderm and mesoderm, carry digested food to the bird or reptile embryo.

Except for such primitive egg-laying mammals as the platypus and the echidna, mammalian embryos develop within the mother's uterus. The fertilized mammalian egg, like the eggs of reptiles and birds, develops an amnion, a chorion, an allantois, and a yolk sac. (For illustration of the amnion and chorion of the human fetus, *see* Multiple Births.) The embryo floats in the protective amnionic fluid. The chorion, with its many blood vessels, lies close to or fuses with the lining of the mother's uterus to form the *placenta.* The allantois is incorporated into the *umbilical cord* connecting the embryo with the placenta. Only a little food is supplied to the mammalian embryo by the yolk sac. The embryo's principal supply of food, as well as its supply of oxygen, passes from the uterus through the placenta's thin walls to the blood vessels of the chorion.

FACTORS IN EMBRYONIC DEVELOPMENT

A number of forces play a part in the formation of embryonic tissues and organs. These forces include genetic directives, cell interaction, and biochemical controls.

Growth and Differentiation of Tissues

Growth is an increase in mass. It often results from the formation of new *protoplasm,* the jellylike constituent of all life (*see* Living Things). Growth occurs also when water intake is increased and when supportive tissue is deposited between cells.

An increase in mass is usually accompanied by cell multiplication. From the initiation of cleavage, the multiplication of cells continues throughout the life of the organism. The rate of cell division, however, is not uniform in all parts of the embryo. Some tissues and organs build up rapidly, others slowly. Moreover, the growth rate of certain parts is different at different stages. For all these reasons, changes are constantly taking place in the relative size of the various embryonic structures.

As a rule, growth by cell multiplication is rapid during early development, then tapers off until it is confined to only a few sites. Differentiation, the formation of different types of cells and tissues, goes hand in hand with growth.

Morphological differentiation occurs when groups of multiplying cells become structurally different from one another. For example, from a common starting point in generalized ectoderm, nerve cells and outer skin cells acquire distinctive features of size, shape, and internal organization.

Behavioral differentiation is the acquisition of the capacity to perform special tasks. All cells exhibit irritability, contractility, and metabolism, but some develop a particular property to a marked degree. For nerve cells, the property is irritability; for muscle cells, contractility; for gland cells, the ability to secrete.

Chemical differentiation, which underlies morphological and behavioral differentiation, occurs when groups of multiplying cells acquire special biochemical properties (*see* Biochemistry). The chemical qualities acquired by a given area of the embryo dictate the further course of its development—that is, whether it will become, for example, the heart, the kidneys, or the thyroid gland.

The type of differentiation in operation is based on directives from *enzymes,* proteins that control the manufacture of specific organic compounds (*see* Enzymes). What makes a cell unique is its protein "patterns," and these patterns depend, in turn, on the cell's *genes,* its hereditary material (*see* Genetics).

The Genetic Determination of Embryonic Structures

Genetic characteristics are determined by the nucleic acid called *deoxyribonucleic acid* (DNA), a giant molecule in the cell nucleus composed of two long, twisted chains of *nucleotides (see* Biochemistry). Each nucleotide chain is made up of units containing the sugar deoxyribose; phosphoric acid; and a nitrogenous base—adenine (A), thymine (T), cytosine (C), or guanine (G). Only two combinations of these nitrogenous bases can be opposite each other in the nucleotide chains—A with T, C with G. Thus only four kinds of double units can run along the length of a DNA molecule—A-T, T-A, C-G, or G-C. However, the varying sequence of these double units constitutes a "code" that makes possible the transmission of a countless variety of genetic traits.

DNA manufactures the chemically related *ribonucleic acid* (RNA), a messenger that passes on this genetic information. The messenger RNA moves from the cell nucleus to the *ribosomes* of the cytoplasm (*see* Cell). There, it directs the assembly of *amino acids,* the "building blocks" of proteins (*see* Proteins).

The nucleotide code of messenger RNA reflects that of its parental DNA. Consequently, the many amino acids brought to the ribosomes for protein manufacture are pieced together in a sequence determined by the code laid out by DNA and delivered by RNA. (*See also* Genetics.)

The Derivation of Adult Structures from Embryonic Tissue

(For illustrations of some of the adult structures named below, *see* Anatomy.)

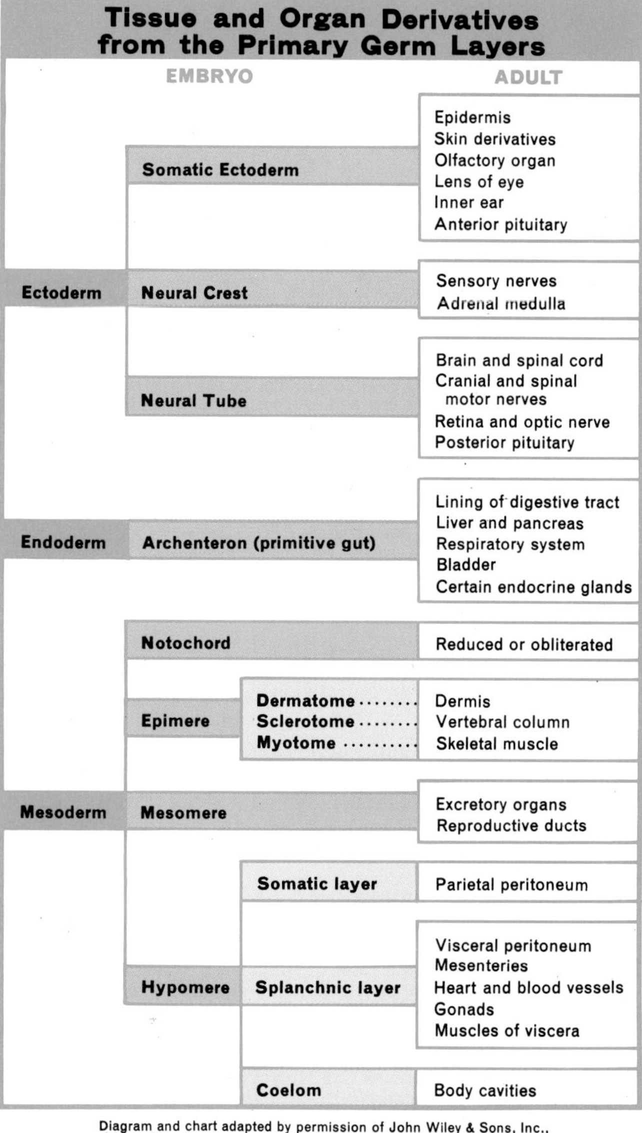

Tissue and Organ Derivatives from the Primary Germ Layers

EMBRYO			ADULT
Ectoderm	Somatic Ectoderm		Epidermis Skin derivatives Olfactory organ Lens of eye Inner ear Anterior pituitary
Ectoderm	Neural Crest		Sensory nerves Adrenal medulla
Ectoderm	Neural Tube		Brain and spinal cord Cranial and spinal motor nerves Retina and optic nerve Posterior pituitary
Endoderm	Archenteron (primitive gut)		Lining of digestive tract Liver and pancreas Respiratory system Bladder Certain endocrine glands
Mesoderm	Notochord		Reduced or obliterated
Mesoderm	Epimere	Dermatome	Dermis
Mesoderm	Epimere	Sclerotome	Vertebral column
Mesoderm	Epimere	Myotome	Skeletal muscle
Mesoderm	Mesomere		Excretory organs Reproductive ducts
Mesoderm	Hypomere	Somatic layer	Parietal peritoneum
Mesoderm	Hypomere	Splanchnic layer	Visceral peritoneum Mesenteries Heart and blood vessels Gonads Muscles of viscera
Mesoderm	Hypomere	Coelom	Body cavities

Diagram and chart adapted by permission of John Wiley & Sons, Inc., from 'Morphogenesis of the Vertebrates', by Theodore W. Torrey

Nongenetic Factors

Initially, the nature of a cell is determined by its DNA code. The interaction of cells and of tissues affects their subsequent development. Thus, differentiation seems to depend in part on critical mass, or the existence of a minimum number of cells. Experiments show that embryonic muscle tissue appears only after such a minimum has been reached. It is known also that the interaction of the neighboring parts of an embryo affects their differentiation. To illustrate, the mesoderm along the top portion of an early embryo is closely associated with the overlying ectoderm, from which the brain and spinal cord are normally produced. If the mesoderm is experimentally prevented from assuming its normal position, these structures fail to appear.

Tissue affinity also plays a part in embryonic development. When the cells of various kinds of tissues are separated and a mixture of these cells is prepared, those of a like kind have the remarkable ability to sort themselves out and to reconstitute the original tissues. This demonstrates that tissue construction is aided by the ability of cells to cohere selectively during normal embryogeny.

Finally, embryonic development is influenced by chemical controls. Hormones secreted by such endocrine glands as the pituitary, thyroid, and sex glands affect structural differentiation (*see* Hormones). A number of vitamins, notably vitamins A and D, also exert developmental control (*see* Vitamins).

HISTORY

During the early 19th century embryologists were concerned mainly with describing and comparing the embryos of various species at different stages in their development. In 1828 the Russian zoologist Karl Ernst von Baer observed that in their earlier phases the embryos of higher species resemble those of lower species but that the embryos of the higher species are never like the adults of the lower species. In 1867 the German biologist Ernst Heinrich Haeckel used Von Baer's findings to formulate his "biogenetic law"—ontogeny recapitulates phylogeny. According to Haeckel, the development of an embryo (ontogeny) retraces the evolution of its species (phylogeny).

Toward the close of the 19th century the German anatomist Wilhelm Roux founded experimental embryology, the study of the causes of embryogeny. In 1924 the German experimental embryologist Hans Spemann discovered "embryonic induction." He found that the mesoderm of an undifferentiated embryo was the "organizer" of brain and spinal cord formation from the overlying ectoderm. In the 1950s the Chinese-born American embryologist Man Chiang Niu discovered that a substance containing a nucleic acid passes from the "organizer" mesoderm to the ectoderm. Later work was aimed at finding the specific ways in which nucleic acids induce differentiation in the early embryo. (*See also* Biology; Biochemistry; Cell; Genetics; Physiology.)

Library of Congress

Ralph Waldo Emerson in 1859

EMERSON, Ralph Waldo (1803–82). The writings of Emerson had a powerful influence on his generation. They have also stood the test of time. Emerson is regarded as the most inspirational writer in American literature.

Ralph Waldo Emerson was born in Boston on May 25, 1803. When he was 8 years old, his father, who was pastor of the First Church in Boston, died. His mother took in boarders to support the family of six children. Young Emerson was frail and undersized.

His education had begun early. Before he was 3, his father had complained that he did not yet read very well. He entered Harvard College when he was 14. He was graduated at 18 but received no honors because he preferred to read what he pleased rather than the lessons assigned to him.

After leaving Harvard, Emerson taught school for three years. This gave him enough money to enter the divinity school at Cambridge. In 1826 he began to preach. In 1829 he was ordained and was appointed minister of a large Unitarian church in Boston. In the same year he married Ellen Louisa Tucker. Emerson at this time was quiet, retiring, and self-contained. He thought much, wrote a little, and said less. He was genial and kind toward the people around him, but he was most difficult to know intimately.

When he was 28, Emerson began to experience his darkest years. His wife died in 1831 at the age of 19. Her death was soon followed by those of Emerson's brilliant brothers, Edward and Charles. Emerson's health broke. He suffered also from doubts about church doctrine and felt that he could no longer administer the Lord's Supper. In 1832 he resigned his pastorate, explaining "It is my desire to do nothing which I cannot do with my whole heart."

He then sailed for Europe. In England he met most of the great men of letters of the day: Landor, Coleridge, John Stuart Mill, and, above all, Carlyle, whom he greatly admired. But travel and even the famous men he met seemed to mean little to Emerson. He said in his essay on 'Nature', published some years later: "The difference between landscape and landscape is small, but there is a great difference in the beholder." As for the men, they seemed to him inferior in intellect, except Carlyle, with whom he corresponded for many years.

Emerson married Lydia Jackson in 1835. Previously he had purchased a house with a garden in Concord, and there, surrounded by his family, he passed the rest of his life except for occasional lecture engagements and two journeys to Europe. When his house burned in 1872, a nationwide popular subscription was taken and the funds used to rebuild it. He died after a short illness on April 27, 1882, and was buried in Sleepy Hollow Cemetery.

To understand Emerson's aloofness from people and events, it is necessary to understand his way of thinking. He believed that great truths come by intuition—that is, that they come unbidden. Furious striving avails nothing; truth comes gently. Most modern philosophers do not agree with Emerson; they think that truth may be reasoned. They are also interested in the working out of truth in relation to life, while Emerson was always on the alert for the first glimmer. He never finished but was always beginning, and his beginnings have been inspirations to the people of two continents.

How are people to arrive at truth? Emerson gives his answer in his essay "Self Reliance." "To believe your own thought, to believe that what is true for you in your private heart is true for all men—that is genius. Speak your latent conviction and it shall be the universal sense; for always the inmost becomes the outmost—and our first thought is rendered back to us by the trumpets of the last judgement." "God is in every man." The last phrase is the keynote of what is called the transcendental movement, or that faith in the inner light of which Emerson was the chief exponent (*see* Transcendentalism).

When Emerson returned to the United States in 1833, he had begun to lecture and to write freely. He helped launch *The Dial,* a paper that spoke truth fearlessly, in 1840 and later edited it for a few years. Harvard asked him to give several addresses, one of which, "The American Scholar," was called by Oliver Wendell Holmes "our intellectual Declaration of Independence." His lecture tours took him everywhere at a time when travel was a series of hardships and inconveniences. Through his lectures Emerson reached a large number of people, though most of them did not understand him.

There was something more than truth that drew the crowds, something that still holds all those who turn to Emerson for enlightenment. In the early days people often came to scoff and remained to listen, much impressed. Emerson the man held them. He was a man of charm and vigor; he had a style almost unequaled. Oliver Wendell Holmes said: "No one who ever heard him speak will forget the play of his features, the lighting up of his eyes with a rapt inner illumination, the emphatic stamp of his foot when some weighty thought required enforcement." In the matter of style he stands supreme for his power of saying much in little, of so phrasing his thoughts that they sparkle and glow. Every sentence seems as good as the one it follows. This is true of his poetry as well as his prose—that is, the power of stating truth in sharp relief. His poems are ranked among the greatest ever written in America.

Emerson has been criticized for the lack of organization or plan in his essays, but he never tried to put plan there. He said what he had to say as it came to him and considered himself as the mouthpiece. Emerson is still read—while many of his critics have long been forgotten.

Emerson's principal works are: 'Essays, First Series', published in 1841; 'Essays, Second Series' (1844); 'Poems' (1847, 1865); 'Representative Men' (1850); 'English Traits' (1856); 'The Conduct of Life' (1860); 'Society and Solitude' (1870).

EMIGRATION *see* MIGRATION OF PEOPLE.

EMOTION. Human beings are very complex psychologically. They have minds with which they are able to reason, remember, learn, and form concepts or ideas. With their minds they are able to direct their actions toward specific goals. In other words, they can be motivated by their reason and intelligence. But people are also subject to passions, desires, and other assorted feelings that can also motivate them strongly—often in a different direction from that which reason directs. These feelings are called emotions, derived from the Latin verb *movere*, which means "to move."

This does not mean that emotions are the only source of motivation. All individuals are impelled to satisfy the basic needs for food, shelter, and warmth. These needs are required for survival. Therefore they are rational needs. It is possible, however, for a person to seek to satisfy needs excessively. Some individuals, for example, are driven beyond reason to accumulate more than they ever need.

The philosopher Aristotle noted that to live a good life an individual had to be able to distinguish between what was really good for him and what was apparently good for him. Making this distinction is a matter of judgment, of clear and rational thinking that has been able successfully to weigh alternatives. It is at this point that emotions may come into play and divert a person from a rational decision to an irrational, or ill-considered, one.

This is not to suggest that all emotions are negative, or contrary to rational thought. Ideally, emotions should complement reason. An individual who has a specific talent but does not care to apply himself will probably accomplish little. Caring and ambition are proper emotions that can help support ability; they can provide the drive toward accomplishment and excellence.

Defining emotions. No one, including the most capable scientist, fully understands how the brain functions, what the mind is, or what the source of the emotions is. The brain, at least, can be identified as a specific physical organ. Mind is a term applied to brain function, and emotion is a name for certain reflexes and expressed feelings. To precisely what extent emotions are brain-produced is unknown. It is also likely that emotions have a great deal to do with chemical balance or imbalance in the body. Emotions are also related to a human characteristic called will power. This may be defined as freedom of choice bolstered by an energetic determination to act on one's own behalf.

Traditional terms associated with emotion are love, hate, fear, happiness, surprise, anger, determination, disgust, and contempt. Another way to describe emotion is to note that there are certain things that a person considers pleasant, while other things are viewed as unpleasant; certain things appeal to an individual, while other things are rejected. The basis for deciding what is pleasant or unpleasant, the appealing or the objectionable, is quite uncertain. Why, for instance, are some people very afraid of snakes and spiders, while others show no fear at all? One answer is that such a fear is a reflex conditioned by an experience early in life. But fear is also expressed at the unknown, without prior conditioning. For example, one may come suddenly upon an animal never before encountered and be instantly afraid of it.

Emotional maturity. There are no firm standards of emotional maturity such as there are for physical development. Nor are there easy rules to follow in attaining it. Individual behavior, derived from a combination of reason and emotions, has a variety of origins. It may originate partly in one's genetic code, partly in learning, partly in the body's chemistry, and partly in the values of the society in which one lives. It is, therefore, quite difficult for any person to sort out all of the motivations that lead to specific behavior patterns. It is also quite likely that anyone will regard himself as emotionally mature regardless of other people's opinions. Perhaps the general guideline used by the ancient Greeks is helpful: nothing too much. This means avoid excess in anything, because excessive attachments tend to be uncontrollable and moderation in all things can lead to a balanced life. There is one incontestable fact about emotional maturity: if it comes at all, it comes with the passage of time and is based on experience and reflection on the past.

EMPLOYMENT AGENCY. To get a job, one can go directly to a company and visit its personnel office, or one may visit an employment agency. Nearly every industrialized nation has agencies, government sponsored or privately operated, that are used to help workers find employment and employers find workers. The services of government agencies are free, but private agencies normally charge a fee to employers, employees, or both.

In the United States, government-sponsored employment services began emerging in the 19th century, when the economy was expanding rapidly and there were often not enough laborers available. The earliest publicly financed agencies were established by cities. The first was in New York City in 1834. Private agencies appeared about the same time. It was not until 1890 that a state (Ohio) established an agency for employment services. Today every state operates an employment department.

The first federal public employment work began in 1907, when the Bureau of Immigration and Naturalization began distributing immigrant labor among the states. A United States Employment Service, used to allocate manpower during World War I, was reestablished in 1933. Its present responsibilities include making labor surveys, certifying training needs, providing testing and counseling, expanding job placement for trainees, and providing guidance on occupational needs.

EMPLOYMENT AND UNEMPLOYMENT. The age of industry and technology has only occupied about one fiftieth of the course of human history, and the period of advanced industrial development only began in the second quarter of the 19th century. Prior to that most people worked at agriculture. As late as 1820 about 73 percent of the population in the United States was in farming. Today this percentage has dropped to less than 3. In underdeveloped and undeveloped nations, a very high proportion of people are still involved in agriculture. In Egypt the percentage is just under 50, while in most of the poor nations of Africa it ranges from 70 to 80 percent. In India the percentage was 72 in 1901, the same in 1971, but down to about 60 today. China, with its enormous population, has between 50 and 60 percent of its people in agriculture.

Kinds of Employment

Work may be categorized in two ways: as productive or nonproductive and by the sectors, or parts, of the economy in which it is involved. These are divided into agricultural, industrial, and service enterprises.

Productive and nonproductive labor. Adam Smith, the classical economist, made the distinction of productive and nonproductive labor in his book 'The Wealth of Nations' in 1776. In doing so he did not mean to say anything negative in using the term nonproductive labor. It is a way of looking at things based on his understanding of wealth. For Smith, as for any economist, money is not wealth. Wealth is the total production of land and industry. Therefore, those who are engaged in producing goods of all kinds are creating the wealth of a nation (productive labor). Money, the means of exchange, is the economic equivalent of wealth in that it may be turned into real wealth by the purchase of products at any time.

Any society, as it develops a strong economy, needs things other than tangible products. It needs services such as those provided by physicians, teachers, government workers, clergymen, lawyers, street sweepers, travel agents, and a military force. None of these produces goods or commodities (nonproductive labor). The existence of these service personnel, however, is dependent on the wealth of the nation—on its production of agricultural and industrial goods.

Rick Browne—Stock, Boston

An electromechanical technician undergoes retraining in the California program called Employment Training Panel (ETP). The program trains experienced workers who are, or soon will be, unemployed. ETP was started in 1983.

Employment sectors. In societies both ancient and modern, where agricultural productivity is low, nearly the whole population must be employed in farming if everyone is to be fed. When productivity increases so that shortage is no longer a problem, a smaller proportion of the population can be engaged in agriculture. The demand for agricultural, or primary, goods drops in relation to the demand for such things as housing and manufactured products, and nonindustrial employment grows.

As the demand for manufactured goods grows and remains high, a third sector of employment develops—the service industries. These include public administration, the military, physicians, teachers, artists, entertainers, professional athletes, scientific researchers, and many others. In nations with a high standard of living—such as the United States, Canada, those of Western Europe, and Japan—demands on the service sector tend to rise dramatically in relation to the agricultural and industrial sectors.

The remarkable shift in employment from the farming sector to the manufacturing and service sectors can be seen from statistics compiled by several countries. France in 1800 had 80 percent of its population in agriculture, 10 percent in manufacturing, and 10 percent in service trades. By 1980 only 9 percent was in agriculture, while the manufacturing sector claimed 35 percent and the service sector 56 percent. In the United States by the early 1980s, the service sector occupied about 68 percent of employment, while manufacturing had 29 percent and agriculture only about 3 percent. In the United Kingdom the proportions were 60.9 percent for service trades, 37.5 for industry, and only 1.6 for farming.

The role of technology. The decrease in the number of people engaged in farming in the advanced nations results largely from improvements in farming technology. At the same time, all of technology is improving, creating jobs for many of those no longer required on the farm. Many improvements in technology of all kinds, of course, appeared in the early stages of the Industrial Revolution. Thus the factory system arose precisely at the time when more laborers, leaving the farms, were available to engage in manufacturing (*see* Industrial Revolution). Conversely, in those countries that have remained underdeveloped industrially but have improved agricultural output, hordes of people have left farming with no place to go. They head for cities seeking opportunity, only to add to already overburdened urban areas and to increase the demand on limited and overworked city services (*see* City).

Hence, if technology is to benefit a nation, the whole economy must develop at once. This is the only way a society can achieve healthy rates of employment.

Economic growth comes about because of two types of technological progress: intensive and extensive. Intensive progress comes about through improved methods of doing one task, whether it is the manufacture of automobiles or the raising of cotton. Extensive progress enlarges the economy through the creation of new kinds of employment. Companies that once manufactured only radios now make television sets, videocassette recorders, and television cameras. The increased complexity of a product—such as the automobile—expands the economy by creating new jobs as well.

Intensive progress allows people to satisfy existing needs with less labor. The use of robots to make automobiles is an example. Extensive progress, on the other hand, creates new wants that soon become needs and by doing so makes new jobs. If it were not for extensive technological progress, demand for farming and manufactured goods would stabilize and the economy would stagnate.

Classification. The 'Standard Industrial Classification Manual', published by the United States government, divides the American economy into ten segments and certain nonclassifiable types. The segments are agriculture, forestry, and fishing; mining; construction; manufacturing; transportation, communication, electric, gas, and sanitary services; wholesale trade; retail trade; finance, insurance, and real estate; services (including hotels, amusements, health, education, and more); and public administration (all government work). These divisions are further broken down into about 1,000 major job groupings containing more than 15,000 different jobs performed daily in the United States. This represents a very complex economy based on both intensive and extensive technological growth and many other factors.

Unemployment

In its most obvious sense, unemployment means being without work. As an economic definition, however, this is inadequate because unemployment refers to the condítion of the labor market at a given time. People are employed in different ways. Homemakers perform work, but they are not paid and therefore are not part of the labor market. The same is true of college students. In some countries graduates of colleges and universities are not able to find work that is up to their abilities and desires. They are considered unemployed if working at something less than they are capable of and desire.

Unemployment figures are published monthly by the United States Bureau of Labor Statistics for every segment of the economy that is readily discernible. Some aspects of unemployment are more difficult to measure: underemployment, part-time work, the so-called underground economy, and structural unemployment.

Underemployment is a category that comprises a large variety of workers, including farmers, construction workers, house painters, and others whose work may be seasonal or sporadic because of weather. It may also refer to employees of a manufacturing industry whose plants run on less than a full schedule because of a decline in demand.

Part-time work. Some people choose not to work at full-time jobs; many housewives fall into this category. Others work part-time because they can find no full-time employment. Some people who hold full-time jobs seek to add to their incomes through a second, part-time job. This is usually called "moonlighting" because it has traditionally been evening part-time work after a day's full-time work.

Underground economy is a category that refers to those who work outside the labor market and are paid in cash to avoid the need to report it on their tax forms. As inflation and taxation increased in the 1950s, many individuals with specific abilities used their talents to earn extra money this way. A full-time plumber, electrician, or carpenter, for example, may do work for friends completely apart from his daily job in a shop or on a work force.

Structural unemployment. The industrial dislocations—inflation combined with recession—that have plagued advanced economies since the late 1960s have produced the phenomenon called structural unemployment. Some industries, such as steel production in the United States, have fallen on hard times and may never recover their former vigor. Thousands of persons have been put out of jobs at which many have spent all of their adult years. They are trained to do nothing else, and in many cases there is nothing else to do nearby. In a fast-growing economy the slack of unemployment is taken up after a recession, but, when whole segments of an economy are threatened with permanent decline, those out of work are forced to find new livelihoods through retraining or by moving to a more prosperous area.

Rates of Unemployment

All economies—even the planned economies of the socialist and communist nations—are in a perpetual state of change. Relative stability is the desired goal, but there are business cycles. During recessions and depressions, unemployment rises dramatically. In the United States about 25 percent of the labor force was out of work in 1933 during the Great Depression. This same percentage was reached in Sweden in 1921 and 1933. From the start of World War II until the early 1970s, unemployment rates were at a much lower level. But declining economic conditions from 1973 pushed them up. (*See also* Business Cycle.)

Dealing with Unemployment

Governments try to soften the impact of unemployment through such programs as unemployment compensation and other social insurance. But the main goal is full employment. Governments use fiscal policy to keep economies functioning at a high level of employment (*see* Business Cycle, "Government Policies"). Some nations use economic planning on a large scale. This is especially true in communist countries, though it has never proved very successful anywhere. Economic planning sets targets for the various sectors of the economy, and these targets are tied to expected manpower needs. Unfortunately, no government has yet found a way to achieve full and stable employment through avoiding economic fluctuations. (*See also* Economics; Labor; Labor Movements; Vocations.)

EMU *see* BIRDS, FLIGHTLESS.

ENAMEL. The delicate pieces of cloisonné ware in the jeweler's window; glazed cups, plates, and vases preserved in museums; many vanity cases; the bright white equipment of bathrooms; and the shining kitchenware that never rusts are all examples of enameling. Enamels are finely powdered glass used to coat a base of metal, pottery, or other mineral substance and then heated until the particles melt and form a glaze.

One of the most beautiful of enamels is cloisonné ware. Thin metal strips are soldered to a base, usually of the same metal, to form a design. The cells thus outlined are then filled with enamel pastes of various colors—bright hues for flowers, green for leaves, black for shadows. The piece is then fired, or baked, several times until the enamel has been built up to a sufficient height. There follow weeks of polishing with pumice stone under running water. During this process the rough surfaces become smooth.

Another form of inlaid enamel is champlevé. This is made by cutting grooves in the metal itself—usually bronze or some other metal less precious than gold—to form the design and then filling these grooves with the enamel. A considerable portion of the metal is left as a background for the enamel design. Many valuable old Chinese enamels are champlevé.

In the later Middle Ages artists began to make painted enamels. A coat of enamel is fused over a metal surface, and a design is painted on this background with colored enamels. Numerous firings are necessary

By courtesy of the trustees of the British Museum

A hanging bowl with millefiori glass and champlevé enamel is an artifact from the Anglo-Saxon burial ship found at Sutton Hoo estate in England in 1939. It dates from the 7th century.

before the work is completed. In the great cathedrals of Europe are some translucent enamel windows. Fine enamels are produced at Limoges, France.

Into the making of enamels go many substances—feldspar, quartz, fluorspar, borax, boric acid, soda, potash, saltpeter, clays, ammonium carbonate, stannic acid, and water. Many coloring agents are employed. If the enamelware is an intense blue, it is probable that cobalt oxide was used to give it this color. The soft grays are generally made with nickel oxide.

After the ingredients are mixed, they are melted to a liquid glassy mass that is poured into cold water. This quenching shatters the whole mass into millions of tiny fragments called frit. The frit is then ground with clay, water, coloring material, and other ingredients. The product is a creamy liquid known as slip. Articles to be enameled are cleaned and dipped into the slip, or the slip may be applied by spraying. After they are dried while supported on metal points, they may be stenciled or colored by other means. Finally the articles are fired in a kiln, or oven. For most enamelware further coats of slip are applied and the piece refired. In a variant of the process, dry-ground frit is applied directly to the piece as it comes from the kiln while the enamel is still hot and plastic. Agateware and graniteware are names for some varieties of enamelware.

Ancient Egyptians and Assyrians used enameled bricks of high luster in the walls of their palaces. They also used enamel in the decoration of jewelry. The Greeks and Romans were masters of the art, employing it in jewelry and as an accessory of sculpture. In Ireland and England numerous ancient enamel ornaments have been found, including shields and helmets studded with enamel. Many old crowns have enamel ornamentations. The art also existed in the Orient. The Japanese are especially famous for enamel work.

Most enameling techniques have been kept alive by goldsmiths. In the 20th century works by Peter Carl Fabergé and René Lalique are outstanding (*see* Fabergé). Painters Georges Braque and Georges Rouault have also contributed to the craft. New processes have been invented that produce enamels of a much greater variety of colors than was formerly known and that are superior in brilliance and durability. The most important industrial use of enamel is giving iron and steel utensils coats of opaque glass.

Distinct from true enamel are the so-called brushing and automobile enamels. The first are glossy pigmented varnishes and the second synthetic lacquers.

The 'Pala d'Oro' altar screen in Saint Mark's Basilica in Venice, Italy, is gold cloisonné enamel. It dates from the 10th to the 12th century but was reassembled with later additions in a Gothic frame between 1342 and 1345.

SCALA—Art Resource/EB Inc.

ENDANGERED SPECIES

ENDANGERED SPECIES. The United States Endangered Species Act of 1973 defines an endangered species as any plant or animal "which is in danger of extinction throughout all or a significant portion of its range." An extinct species is one in which living individuals of its kind no longer exist. The act identifies a threatened species as one "likely to become endangered within the foreseeable future throughout all or a significant portion of its range." A rare species has no legal definition but refers to any kind of plant or animal that occurs in low numbers. Hundreds of species in the world are now recognized as endangered or threatened.

History

Plants and animals have become extinct, and new species have evolved, since life began. Primitive human cultures may have eliminated some species, but the primary causes for species to become extinct have been natural ones. Major environmental changes resulted in the eventual disappearance of species unable to adapt to new conditions. Well-known natural extinctions include dinosaurs and many other species represented in the fossil record.

Natural forces are still at work, but human activities cause most of the rapid and widespread environmental changes that affect plants and animals today. Many species have been unable to make the biological adjustments necessary for survival. Thus more species than ever before are threatened with extinction.

Destruction of forests, draining of wetlands, and pollution are environmental changes that may eliminate species in an area. Some herbicides and pesticides can cause severe effects on certain species. Many species have small geographic ranges, so habitat alteration may eliminate them entirely. The logging of tropical forests, with their tremendous diversity of species having specialized requirements, has caused a steady increase in the extinction rate. Excessive hunting and trapping for commercial purposes also cause major problems. Many crocodile species have been reduced to critically low numbers because of uncontrolled killing for hides. Plants also can be reduced to near extinction levels by extensive collecting. Many cactus species of the arid Southwestern United States are now legally protected by state laws to prevent their removal.

This article was contributed by J. Whitfield Gibbons, Senior Research Ecologist and Adjunct Professor of Zoology, Savannah River Ecology Laboratory, University of Georgia; author of 'Their Blood Runs Cold: Adventures with Reptiles and Amphibians' (1983).

The planned or accidental introduction of exotic species to a region can also lead to extinction. An introduced species often has no natural enemies to control its spread, and native species may have no natural protection against it. The introduction of Dutch elm disease to North America, mongooses to Jamaica, and pigs to Hawaii resulted in the loss of native species with inadequate defenses.

Government Involvement

Only since the 19th century has there been worldwide concern about the plight of species occurring in natural environments. In earlier times, when human population sizes were small and modern technology was developing, the impact of human activities on natural populations seldom seemed significant. Protection of animal species on an international scale was initiated as early as 1916 with the Migratory Bird Treaty between the United States, Great Britain, Canada, and, later, Mexico. A far-reaching wildlife conservation measure came from a United States-hosted conference in 1973 that resulted in an international treaty known as CITES—the Convention on International Trade in Endangered Species of Wild Fauna and Flora. This program involves more than 80 nations working together to protect endangered species through worldwide control of exports and imports. The United States Fish and Wildlife Service (FWS) of the Department of Interior is authorized to assist in the development and management of endangered species programs in foreign countries.

First federal legislation. One of the earliest official recognitions of an endangered species problem in the United States was the Buffalo Protection Act of 1894. The enormous herds of buffalo that roamed through North America had been reduced to just a few individuals by the late 1800s. The law to protect the few remaining in Yellowstone National Park was the first federal legislation that focused on conserving a once vast wildlife resource. Other national laws and regulations followed. In 1900 the Lacey Act made it illegal to import certain birds and mammals that other countries had identified as requiring protection. The National Wildlife Refuge System was started in 1903 to protect habitats that harbored fast-disappearing wildlife species. In 1940 Congress enacted the Bald Eagle Act to protect the national bird.

The Endangered Species Preservation Act of 1966 and Endangered Species Conservation Act of 1969 demonstrated concern for disappearing species on a worldwide scale, but the laws did not directly protect the species themselves. The 1973 Endangered Species Act was the most effective and far-reaching law ever passed in the United States to protect plants and animals in natural ecosystems. The act made it illegal for anyone to injure, molest, kill, capture, or transport species identified as endangered or threatened. Protection was also extended to animals other than vertebrates (animals with backbones) such as insects, mollusks, and crustaceans. The legislation provided habitat protection programs for endangered

Passenger Pigeon
(Ectopistes migratorius)

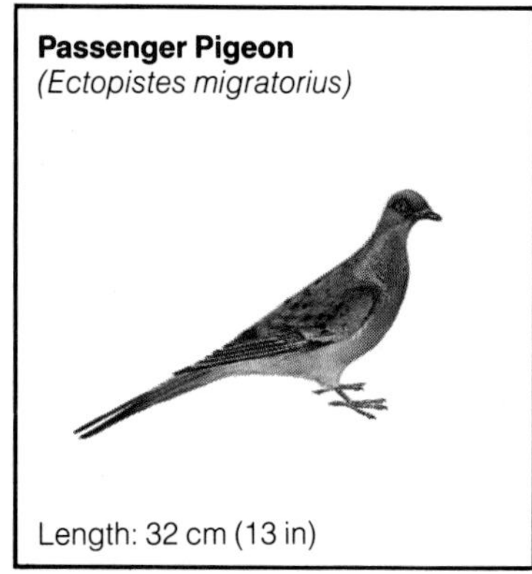

Length: 32 cm (13 in)

Tasmanian Wolf
(Thylacinus cynocephalus)

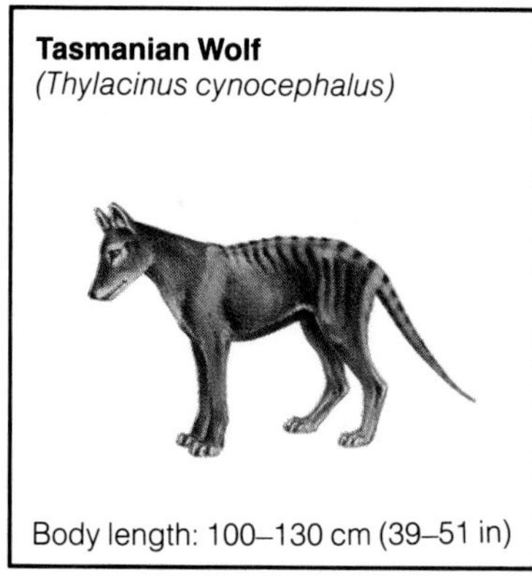

Body length: 100–130 cm (39–51 in)

In this table the two species at left are extinct; the twelve species at right are considered endangered. Heights or lengths are given where appropriate; "body length" includes head to rump but excludes the tail. The table is an attempt to show the range of species that are endangered and is not intended to be inclusive.

plant species and led to the protection of endangered species in other countries through the control of the importing of skins, feathers, shells, and living specimens for commercial purposes.

State programs. Most states and territories of the United States attempt to protect endangered plants and wildlife in cooperation with federal goals. Some states even require permits for collection of nongame species that are not endangered because of the rapid disappearance of natural habitats and the steady decline of many native species. The Heritage Trust Programs of some states are designed to identify and preserve natural areas potentially in danger from habitat destruction. During the early 1980s several states initiated a wildlife check-off system that allows taxpayers to contribute directly to the state's wildlife programs. These place particular emphasis on nongame species, including those that are threatened or endangered.

Private organizations. An additional measure of concern for vanishing species is the upsurge in private organizations involved in educating the public about environmental issues. Many of these give major emphasis to species preservation through national and international magazines, lecture series, and television programs.

Official listing. Species are officially added to the endangered list in the United States through an established administrative process. A proposed listing of a species is published in the 'Federal Register'. Scientists, conservationists, and government officials are asked to provide information about the biological status of the species. The FWS accumulates the data and makes a decision about the species within the guidelines specified in the Endangered Species Act. A species may be listed as endangered or threatened, removed from consideration, or requiring more information. Once a species has been listed, the FWS assesses what must be done to ensure protection.

Once a species is officially listed, any federal agency with a project that might affect an endangered species or its critical habitat must seek FWS consultation. According to the law the foremost consideration must be given to the welfare of the species, and to conform some federal projects must be cancelled or modified. A strength of the act lies in its enforcement capabilities. No one, including federal and state agencies or private citizens, is exempt from activities that might harm an endangered species. Heavy fines and jail sentences can be given for violating the laws.

Major responsibilities of the FWS include programs to protect the remaining members of the species and to develop a recovery program designed to return the species to a point at which it can function in a natural manner. Recovery programs may include direct involvement of biologists in research, management, and habitat manipulation. Programs for raising some species in captivity have been carried out in attempts to restore former population levels.

Examples

The list of plant and animal species recognized as endangered or threatened is too long for discussion of each. Selected examples, however, serve to indicate the problems faced and solutions being applied.

Birds provide several modern examples of how extinction can occur. One of the best known is the passenger pigeon, a species said to have occurred in greater numbers than any other bird or mammal for which there are records. Passenger pigeons looked very similar to mourning doves, a close relative that is still common. One distinction—a requirement for nesting in colonies—ultimately led to the downfall of the passenger pigeon. The birds, concentrated at nesting sites, were slaughtered for food by the millions. The extinction of the passenger pigeon is a commentary on the erroneous belief that if a species occurs in large numbers it is not necessary to be concerned about its welfare. Although John James Audubon reported seeing more than 1 billion of these birds in Kentucky during the 1800s, the last member of the species died in 1914.

In 1918 the last Carolina parakeet died. This colorful green bird with an orange or yellow head was reported throughout much of the Eastern United States in the 1800s. Parakeets were shot for their attractive feathers and because they damaged crops. Little in the written record, however, is available concerning their behavior, so no one knows for sure whether hunting resulted in their extinction. Many other native birds were hunted without restraint but did not become extinct.

Sneed Pincushion Cactus
(Coryphantha sneedii sneedii)

Height: up to 5 cm (2 in)

Mission Blue Butterfly
(Icaricia icarioides missionensis)

Length: 1.9–3.2 cm (0.75–1.25 in)

Snail Darter
(Percina tanasi)

Length: 7.5 cm (3.0 in)

Leatherback Sea Turtle
(Dermochelys coriacea)

Length: 127–213 cm (50–84 in)

American Crocodile
(Crocodylus acutus)

Length: 2.1–4.6 m (6.9–15 ft)

Whooping Crane
(Grus americana)

Height: 114–127 cm (45–50 in)

Spanish Imperial Eagle
(Aquila heliaca adalberti)

Length: 79–84 cm (31–33 in)

West Indian Manatee
(Trichechus manatus)

Length: 2.5–4.0 m (8.2–13.1 ft)

Blue Whale
(Balaenoptera musculus)

Length: 24–27 m (79–89 ft)

Giant Otter
(Pteronura brasiliensis)

Body length: 86–140 cm (34–55 in)

Northern White Rhinoceros
(Ceratotherium simum cottoni)

Body length: 3.6–5.0 m (11.8–16.4 ft)

Jaguar
(Panthera onca)

Body length: 112–185 cm (44–73 in)

The ivory billed woodpecker, the largest woodpecker to inhabit North America, was believed to be extinct in the United States, though occasional reports are made of sightings in remote areas of the South. The cause of its disappearance is presumed to be the major habitat destruction that resulted from logging of large Southern forests. Ivory bills required large tracts of land with old trees and were unable to cope with timbering activities.

As habitat destruction and alteration continue throughout the world, major problems are created for species dependent on large geographic areas. The California condor, North America's largest inland bird, is expected to become extinct within a few years, in part because of the alteration of the large natural areas it relies on for food.

Insects. More than a dozen insects, most of them butterflies, are officially listed. Populations of two butterfly species—the San Bruno elfin and mission blue—have been reduced in size or eliminated because of urban development in the San Francisco area. The FWS recovery plan focuses primarily on conserving the few remaining habitats where the species occur. Threats to the species and their habitats include new urban development, herbicides that destroy plants on which the species depend, insecticides that kill butterflies as well as pests, off-road vehicles that destroy vegetation, and the introduction of nonnative plants that compete with native species required by butterflies. The recovery plan also provides for research programs designed to understand the requirements of each species so that proper habitat management decisions can be made.

Fishes. More than 50 species of United States fishes, most restricted to specific bodies of water, are in danger of extinction. Most live in deserts of the Southwest, where water is scarce. Channelization and draining for agriculture or urbanization can eliminate or alter fragile aquatic ecosystems.

Many species of desert fishes and invertebrates became extinct before protective measures were taken. Despite laws for protection, many of the desert aquatic habitats and their associated species are still in danger. Overgrazing, for example, can result in erosion and runoff that spoils the aquatic habitat. Groundwater depletion that results in the drying of aquatic habitats is a major threat. Numerous conservation groups and concerned individuals are working in cooperation with the FWS to assure more lasting protection for desert fishes through land acquisition and the passage and enforcement of stricter laws.

Reptiles. More than 100 reptiles and amphibians are recognized as being in danger, including crocodiles and sea turtles. Many species have been seriously depleted by international trade. Among the United States amphibian species listed as endangered or threatened by the FWS are the Red Hills salamander, confined to a few streamside habitats in Alabama, and the Houston toad of Texas. Reptile species in the United States include: the American crocodile in Florida, the blunt-nosed leopard lizard in California, the indigo snake in the Southeast, and the San Francisco garter snake. The American alligator is endangered in certain parts of its range but is considered only as threatened in others.

Mammals. More than 300 mammals of the world are recognized as threatened or endangered. These include eight whales, more than two dozen apes and monkeys, and more than 20 deer as well as leopards, tigers, elephants, and other large mammals whose numbers have been severely reduced by overhunting and habitat destruction. Included among United States mammals that are protected to some degree are the gray wolf, Florida panther, and grizzly bear.

Why Preservation?

The 1973 Endangered Species Act officially addressed the issue of why an endangered species of plant or animal should be offered formal protection. As stated in the act, such species "are of esthetic, ecological, educational, historical, recreational, and scientific value to the Nation and its people." This assessment was based on the facts and opinions of numerous individuals from a variety of professions.

Working to preserve a particular species may seem difficult to justify in some instances. The evidence shows, however, that sufficient scientifically accurate information is seldom available on any species to demonstrate a thorough understanding of its role in the natural ecosystem or its potential value to mankind. Numerous species are medically or agriculturally significant because scientists discovered unique properties or traits. It cannot be predicted when a species might be discovered to be of direct value to humans. Once a species becomes extinct, however, the opportunity is lost forever.

As scientists unravel the intricate network of plant-animal relationships in the natural world, more and more species are discovered to have a vital, and often unsuspected, dependence on other species. Obviously, if the extinction of one species is permitted through rapid, human-caused activities that do not permit natural adaptations and evolution to occur, certain other species may also be affected. This can result in a "domino effect" of potential extinctions.

The final consequences could be the loss of species of direct importance to humans because of a lack of concern for seemingly unimportant ones. All species are part of a natural heritage. Many feel that each should be viewed as a significant component with its rightful place in the world's ecosystems and deserving of protection.

BIBLIOGRAPHY FOR ENDANGERED SPECIES

Ehrlich, Paul and Anne. Extinction: the Causes and Consequences of the Disappearance of Species (Random, 1981).

Hoage, R.J., ed. Animal Extinctions: What Everyone Should Know (Smithsonian, 1985).

Stone, L.M. Endangered Animals (Children's, 1984).

U.S. Dept. of the Interior. Endangered and Threatened Wildlife and Plants (U.S. Fish and Wildlife Service, annual).

ENDOCRINE GLAND *see* GLAND.

Joe Benge

ENERGY

As kids leap into the air or splash down into water, the potential energy in their bodies is transformed into kinetic energy.

ENERGY. A rock falling off a cliff is different from the same rock lying on the ground below. The lively child eager to join his playmates after a night's rest and a hearty breakfast is different from the child who can barely keep his eyes open after dinner. A glowing light bulb screwed into an electric socket is different from the same bulb when the electricity is switched off. In each case, the substance itself—matter—has not changed. It is the same rock, the same child, the same light bulb. Yet there is a difference. The difference is one of energy.

Energy is one of the most basic ideas of science. All the observed occurrences in the universe can be explained in terms of energy and matter (*see* Matter). But the definition of energy is not at all simple since energy occurs in many different forms, and it is not always easy to tell how these forms are related to one another and what they have in common. One of the best-known definitions of energy is the classical definition used in physics: Energy is the ability to do work.

Physicists define work in a way that does not always agree with the average person's idea of work. In physics, work is done when a force applied to an object moves it some distance in the direction of the force. Mathematically, $W = Fs$, where W is the work done, F is the force applied, and s is the distance moved. If either F or s is equal to zero, W is also equal to zero.

If a person walks up a flight of stairs he may regard it as work—he exerts effort to move his body to a higher level. In this instance, he also does work according to the definition accepted by physicists, for he exerts a force to lift himself over a distance—the distance from the bottom to the top of the stairs.

However, if a person stands without moving with a 100-pound weight in his outstretched arms, he is not doing any work as physicists define work. He is exerting a force that keeps the 100-pound weight from falling to the floor, but the position of the weight remains unchanged. It is not moved any distance by the force. In other words, $s = 0$, so $W = 0$. The person is, of course, exerting considerable muscular effort to avoid dropping the weight, and the average man would say that he is working very hard indeed. But he is not doing any work according to the definition accepted in physics.

Energy from Gravity

Energy is readily transferred from object to object. For this reason it is often necessary to study an entire group of objects that may be transferring energy back and forth among themselves. Such a group is called a system. The energy of a system is the ability of the entire system to do work. If the parts of a system

This article was contributed by Max Dresden, Professor of Physics, Institute for Theoretical Physics, State University of New York at Stony Brook.

E. F. Hoppe—Alfa Studio

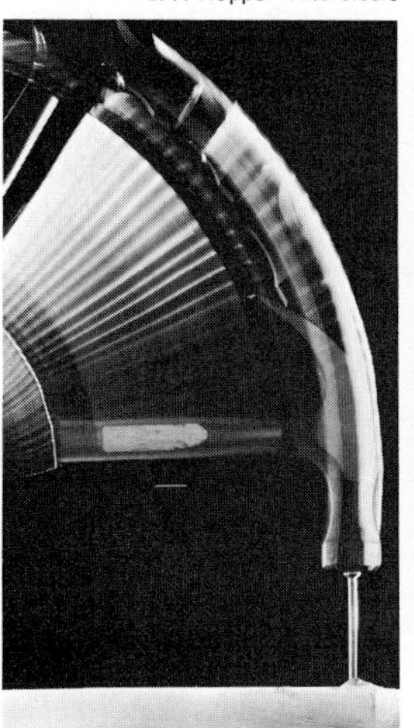

KINETIC ENERGY

E. F. Hoppe—Alfa Studio

CHEMICAL (FOOD) ENERGY

E. F. Hoppe—Alfa Studio

ELECTRICAL ENERGY

California Institute of Technology

RADIANT ENERGY

do work on one another but do not change anything outside the system, then the total amount of energy in the system stays the same. However, the amount of energy in one part of the system may decrease and the amount of energy of another part may increase.

Consider a system consisting of a jungle with many trees, a vine hanging from the central tree, the earth supporting the trees, and a boy standing beneath the tree from which the vine is hanging. The boy, holding the free end of the vine, climbs up the central tree. He then moves several treetops away, maintaining the same altitude. Finally, the boy grasps the vine that is still tied to the central tree and swings down, past the central tree, and up again until he lands in a third tree. An observer watching the boy swinging from one tree to the other will conclude that the system possesses energy and can do work.

The necessary elements in this system are the boy, who provides the initial energy by climbing the trees; the trees, which support him against the force of gravity, which is vertically downward; the earth, whose gravitational attraction is the force that does the work of drawing him downward; and the vine, which supports him so that he remains free to swing upward against the force of gravity when his energy is great enough. When all these elements occur together, the system is capable of doing work; it has energy.

As the boy swings by the vine, he is acting like a pendulum (*see* Pendulum). Like any pendulum, he is exhibiting the difference between two kinds of energy —potential energy and kinetic energy.

As the boy stands at the top of the second tree, he is not moving. But the system has energy because of his location away from the surface of the earth. This energy is called potential energy.

Gravity is pulling at the boy. When the boy jumps off the tree, gravity pulls him down. He travels faster and faster until, as he sweeps by the earth, he is traveling very fast. The system has lost potential energy and gained energy from the speed of his motion. The new energy is called kinetic energy. If the boy were to grab his pet monkey at the bottom of the tree, he would be applying a force to the monkey and the monkey would be moved up into the tree with him. When they landed in the tree, the system would again have potential energy but no kinetic energy.

If a rock rolls down a hill and dislodges another rock which then also rolls down the hill, kinetic energy is at work. A hammer driving a nail into a board is an example of kinetic and potential energies. The hammer applies several forces in succession to the nail, and the nail is moved deeper and deeper into the board.

If a force is applied to compress a spring, the resulting compressed spring possesses energy. It can do work in the process of returning to its natural length. For example, it can lift a weight. Energy of this type is called elastic energy or deformation energy.

Chemical Energy

When several chemicals are mixed together to form gunpowder or dynamite, a violent explosion can occur. An explosion can do work against the force of gravity, for example, by throwing pieces of material into the air. A mixture of chemicals that can do work is said to have chemical energy. Not all chemical systems that can do work are as dramatically energetic as gunpowder or dynamite, and often the amount of energy a chemical system possesses is hard to measure.

To understand chemical energy it is necessary to study what happens during a chemical reaction. All matter is made up of tiny units called atoms. An atom can bond to other atoms to form a group called a molecule. All the substances on earth—rocks, wood, air—are made up of atoms or molecules. For example, one kind of atom is the oxygen atom (O). A molecule of oxygen gas contains two oxygen atoms (O_2). An oxygen atom and two hydrogen atoms combine to form a water molecule (H_2O). One kind of sand molecule—silicon dioxide (SiO_2)—contains one atom of silicon (Si) and two atoms of oxygen. (*See also* Chemistry.)

By courtesy of U. S. Atomic Energy Commission

NUCLEAR ENERGY

E. F. Hoppe—Alfa Studio

HEAT ENERGY

Molecules are formed in chemical reactions. Some molecules give off a great deal of energy when they are formed from individual atoms. Such molecules are very stable because all that energy must be put back into them before they decompose. Other molecules release very little energy when they are formed. Such molecules are very unstable. They react easily to form more stable molecules. During these reactions much energy is given off. Nitroglycerin—a dense, oily liquid—changes readily to water, carbon dioxide, nitrogen, and oxygen. This reaction is explosive because it occurs very rapidly and because the suddenly formed gases take up much more room than did the liquid nitroglycerin. Other chemical reactions can produce energy but not be explosive. They may occur more slowly, and the resulting molecules may take up the same amount of room as the original molecules.

Food energy is a form of chemical energy. Plants absorb energy from sunlight and store it in energy-rich chemicals, such as glucose. This process is called photosynthesis. Animals that eat plants use the chemicals created by photosynthesis to maintain life processes. Other animals may eat plant-eating animals to gain the energy-rich chemicals that the plant-eaters formed from the chemicals of plants. Since food energy is what keeps living things moving, it is clearly able to do work.

Electrical Energy

One of the most important kinds of energy in the modern technological world is electrical energy. Electric currents turn motors and drive machinery. Electric currents provide the energy of laborsaving appliances such as electric mixers, power drills, vacuum cleaners, and automatic dishwashers. Clearly, the currents possess energy.

Electrical energy is linked with the basic structure of the atom. According to modern atomic theory an atom has a heavy, positively charged center called the nucleus. One or more light, negatively charged electrons circulate around the nucleus (*see* Matter). The positive nucleus and the negative electrons attract one another. This attraction keeps most of the electrons circulating near the nucleus. But sometimes a neighboring nucleus will also attract the electrons of the first atom. This is how a chemical bond is formed. So, in a way, all chemical energy is a special, microscopic kind of electrical energy.

Metals are made up of atoms that contain many electrons. Because of the peculiar structure of metal atoms, the atomic nuclei are not strong enough to hold on to all their electrons (*see* Crystals). Some of the electrons more or less float from nucleus to nucleus. These free electrons can take part in an electric current (*see* Solid State Physics).

Work must be done to separate positive and negative charges if one is to produce a surplus of electrons in one place and nuclei that are missing one or more electrons at another place. When this situation occurs, as in a battery, energy is stored. If one end of a metal wire is connected to the place where excess electrons are collected (the negative terminal on a battery) and the other end of the wire is connected to the place where excess nuclei are collected (the positive terminal on a battery), the electrons of the wire flow to join the nuclei. Electrons farther down the wire flow after the first electrons, and the electrons from the battery move into the wire. This total electron flow from the negative terminal of the battery through the wire and into the positive terminal is called an electric current. Since a force is applied that makes the electrons move a certain distance down the wire, work is done. (*See also* Battery; Electricity.)

Magnetic energy is closely related to electrical energy. Magnetic fields are set up whenever electric charges move (*see* Magnets and Magnetism).

Radiant Energy, or Electromagnetic Waves

Some kinds of energy can travel across empty space. Such energy, called radiant energy, can travel through a vacuum. Radiant energy is caused by accelerated electric charges or by electric or magnetic fields that increase or decrease with time. The motion of these charges and fields disturbs space. The disturbance causes a wave to travel away from the site of the original electrical or magnetic motion. The wave consists of growing and collapsing electric and magnetic fields which are oriented at right angles to one another (for diagram, *see* Light). Since waves of radiant energy consist of electrical and magnetic disturbances, they are often called electromagnetic waves.

Light is one form of electromagnetic radiation. Other forms include radio waves, infrared waves, ultraviolet radiation, X rays, and gamma rays. Some of these forms have longer wavelengths than light; others have shorter wavelengths. Human eyes are sensitive to light waves only. For this reason, human eyes can detect light from the sun and the stars as well as from other sources in space. But humans cannot see X rays and radio waves, though stars emit these radiations too.

Special instruments that work somewhat like Geiger counters are used to sense X rays from the sun and the stars. Huge radarlike instruments called radio telescopes are sensitive to radio waves. Using these radio telescopes, scientists have been able to detect waves from many parts of the universe—from the sun and the stars and from the huge clouds that float in outer space.

All of the forms of radiant energy are able to do work, though it is necessary to use special instruments to measure it. These instruments generally change radiant energy to the energy of moving electric currents, as in a radio receiver, for example (*see* Radiation; Light).

Nuclear Energy

Yet another kind of energy is locked in the nuclei of atoms. The nuclei of atoms contain two kinds of particles—protons and neutrons. The nuclear particles can store energy. Some nuclei spontaneously rearrange, or lose some particles, and emit energy. This process is called radioactivity. For example, a radium nucleus can spontaneously eject a cluster of two neutrons and two protons (called an alpha particle) and a gamma ray (electromagnetic radiation). These carry away energy from the nucleus, which changes into a smaller, more stable form.

Two techniques exist by which nuclear energy is released by human intervention. The first makes use of elements with very heavy atoms, such as uranium. More energy is required to hold together the uranium nucleus than to hold together two nuclei that are half the size of a uranium nucleus. In atom bombs and in fission reactors, free neutrons bombard uranium atoms. When a neutron hits a nucleus, the nucleus splits into two smaller nuclei, releasing a great deal of energy. In the reaction, some of the neutrons of the uranium nucleus fly off and hit other nuclei, causing them to split in two and release more energy and more neutrons. The process can continue explosively unless metal rods are inserted in the middle of the uranium to cap-

USING ENERGY TO DO WORK

Hauling the metal ball to one side has created *potential energy* (energy of position). When the ball is released, it will start swinging. As it swings, it transforms potential energy into *kinetic energy* (energy of motion).

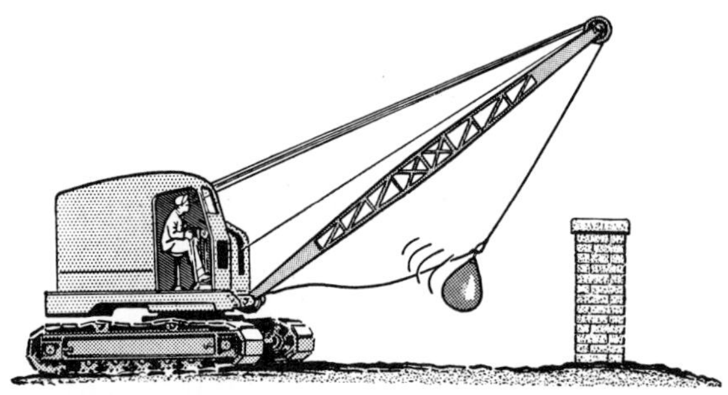

The swinging ball now has all its energy in the kinetic form, but it is not exerting *force* as yet. It is not producing any effect upon matter (except for trifling effects produced upon the air and in the swinging cable).

The ball is exerting *force* against the wall. Kinetic energy is being converted to *work*, moving a weight of material in the portion toppled over and breaking up the chemical bonds which held the bricks and stones of the wall together.

Here is *work done*, shown by the amount of wall broken down and by the effects produced in the material itself. The ball is hanging idle, ready to receive renewed potential energy when it is hauled back to deliver another blow.

ENERGY UNITS AND RELATED CONCEPTS

System	Work (W) and Energy	Force (F)	Distance (s)	Mass (M)	Acceleration (a)	W = Fs = (Ma)s
mks	joule	newton	meter	kilogram	m/sec^2	joule = nt • m = kg • m^2/sec^2
cgs	erg	dyne	centimeter	gram	cm/sec^2	erg = dyne • cm = g • cm^2/sec^2
English	foot-pound	pound	foot	slug	ft/sec^2	ft-lb = slug-ft^2/sec^2

Conversions: 1 joule = 10 million ergs (10^7 ergs) 1 foot-pound = 1.36 joules 1 eV = 1.6×10^{-12} ergs

Energy is the ability to do work. The amount of energy in a system can be precisely measured.

Work equals the force applied multiplied by the distance an object is moved. W = Fs

Force equals the mass of the object to which the force is applied multiplied by the acceleration of the object. F = Ma

Acceleration is a change in speed or direction or both. Thus, an object moving at a constant speed in a circle is always accelerating because it is always changing its direction.

The **speed** of an object is the distance it moves per unit time; the **velocity** of an object is the distance it moves in a certain direction per unit time. Thus, an object that maintains the same speed as it turns a corner is changing its velocity, or accelerating, as it turns the corner.

Power is the work done per unit time. If it takes a given amount of power to pull a 100-pound load in one hour, it takes twice as much power to pull a 200-pound load in one hour or a 100-pound load in half an hour. A familiar unit of power is the watt: 1 watt = 1 joule/sec; 1 kilowatt = 1000 watts.

When units of power are multiplied by units of time, the result is units of energy. A kilowatt-hour is an energy unit.

ture some of the neutrons and slow down the reaction. This sort of reaction is called a *fission* reaction because in it nuclei are broken apart.

The second kind of nuclear reaction is harder to produce and control. It makes use of the fact that very small nuclei, such as hydrogen and its isotopes, require slightly more energy per proton and neutron to exist than do somewhat heavier nuclei. (The situation is exactly opposite to that of the uranium nucleus, where the lighter nuclei require less energy.) If two hydrogen nuclei can be combined to form one heavier nucleus, energy is released. This type of reaction goes on in the sun. By a somewhat complicated series of reactions, four hydrogen nuclei join together to form a new helium nucleus, giving off a great deal of energy in the process. This is the source of all the energy emitted by the sun (*see* Sun).

Temperatures in this kind of reaction must be very high (in the millions of degrees) before the nuclei have enough energy to collide with the force needed for them to join together. The reaction is called a thermonuclear fusion reaction. "Thermonuclear" refers to the heat required for the nuclei to react, and "fusion" means that in the reaction nuclei join together.

A thermonuclear fusion reaction occurs when a hydrogen bomb explodes. Scientists are trying to develop a way of releasing energy by fusion reactions under controlled conditions (*see* Plasma and Plasma Physics).

Heat Energy

One very common form of energy is heat energy. Strictly speaking, this is not an additional type of energy, since heat energy is the kinetic energy of the individual molecules in a system. The faster the average motion of the molecules, the higher the temperature of the system. Heat can do work. When heat is applied to a liquid, the liquid may eventually boil, changing to a gas which takes up more space than does the liquid. And the gas from a boiling liquid can exert great force. It drives the turbines that generate the electricity of large cities.

The great importance of heat energy arises from the fact that most of the times that energy is used to do work, part of the energy is wasted as heat. For example, when a hammer is used to pound a nail into a board, much of the energy of the hammer goes to heating up the nail, the head of the hammer, and the parts of the board that touch the nail. Only a small part of the total energy actually moves the nail into the board.

The same is true of an automobile engine. Such engines would be much more efficient if all of the chemical energy generated by the explosion of gasoline and air changed to the kinetic energy that moves the pistons. Instead, much of the chemical energy changes to heat energy, which is of no help in running the car.

Kinetic and Potential Energy

It is possible to regard all the different forms of energy as being simply the kinetic or potential energy of various atomic or nuclear particles. For example, a stretched spring has energy, which is usually called elastic energy. This is a useful and correct way to look at the energy of a spring.

However, it is also correct to take a smaller view. The spring is made up of atoms which contain nuclei and electrons. The nuclei and electrons exert electrical forces on each other. The work done to stretch the spring is used to overcome the electrical forces that hold the atoms close together. The energy of the stretched spring can, in this view, be considered as electrical rather than elastic in nature. It is potential energy because it exists in the position of the particles relative to one another, rather than in their speeds. As soon as the spring is released, the electrical attraction of the individual atoms for one

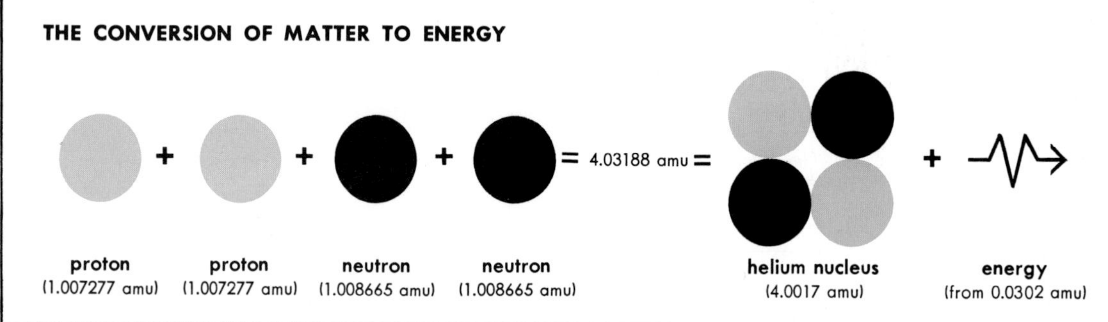

The sum of the masses of two protons and two neutrons is 4.03188 amu. When they are joined in a helium nucleus, their mass is 0.0302 amu smaller. The difference has been converted to energy. The helium nucleus is very stable.

another causes them to draw closer together, with the result that the spring snaps together tightly. The potential energy changes to the kinetic energy of the atoms moving closer together.

The energy in a uranium nucleus is potential energy, too, because it is caused by the conditions in which the nuclear particles exist rather than by the speed of the particles. When a neutron collides with a uranium nucleus, much of the potential energy of the uranium nucleus is changed to the kinetic energy of the newly formed nuclei, of the extra neutrons, and of the radiation that is given off.

Mass Energy

For hundreds of years scientists thought that matter and energy were completely different from each other. But early in the 20th century Albert Einstein concluded that mass and energy were closely related, that mass could change to energy and energy could change to mass. Einstein described the relationship between mass and energy quantitatively in the famous equation, $E = mc^2$. In this equation E stands for energy, m for mass, and c for the speed of light. The change in mass that is given by this equation is $m = E/c^2$. Since c^2 is a very large quantity, E must be very large indeed for m to be observable. This relationship has been experimentally confirmed. (*See also* Einstein, Albert; Relativity.)

Chemical and nuclear reactions both involve a change in energy linked with a change in mass. Both may involve a reaction in which two entities form two new entities. In a chemical reaction the entities are atoms or molecules. In a nuclear reaction they are nuclei. In both cases the reaction may end up with a loss of mass. This loss is converted to energy, usually in the form of the kinetic energy of the two new entities.

In a chemical reaction each particle may gain up to 10 eV (electron volts). This corresponds to a loss of about 10^{-31} grams from each particle, an extremely small amount. If 12 grams (almost half an ounce) of carbon were involved in the reaction, the loss of mass would be only 10^{-8} grams, an amount that is still too tiny to be observed. For this reason the conversion of mass to energy in chemical reactions was not noticed by chemists.

In a nuclear reaction the energy produced per particle is usually more than 1 MeV (million electron volts). The loss in mass is about a million times larger than the loss in chemical reactions and is readily observable. Nuclear physicists routinely take account of the conversion of mass to energy in their study of nuclear reactions. However, the only difference between the loss of mass in chemical and nuclear reactions is a difference of magnitude. The source of both chemical and nuclear reactions is the same: the transformation of a certain amount of mass into energy.

The Changing Forms of Energy

One of the most useful facts about energy is that it can be changed from one form to another. These changes are happening all the time. Most machines have as their purpose the conversion of energy from one form to another. Furthermore, even in ordinary activities energy changes form. A person opening a door uses chemical energy stored in his muscle tissues. This is changed to the elastic energy of the muscle fibers. The elastic energy of the muscle applies a force—a push—to the door and is changed to the mechanical energy of the door as it swings open. If the door bangs against a wall, some of its energy is changed to sound energy.

Over centuries of scientific observation, scientists have noticed that energy seems to act in certain uniform ways. A regularity exists in its behavior to which no exceptions have been observed. This regularity has been expressed in the law of the conservation of energy. The law asserts that the total energy of an isolated system does not change. The energy can be redistributed or can change from one form to another, but the total energy remains the same. When a system is not isolated, however, outside forces are able to act on it. In such instances, any change in the energy of the system must exactly equal the work done on it by the outside forces.

The law of the conservation of energy is remarkable because it states that a certain numerical quantity is unchanged throughout all processes. It does not say why or how this happens. It just says that while the forms of energy are constantly changing, energy itself can neither appear out of nowhere nor

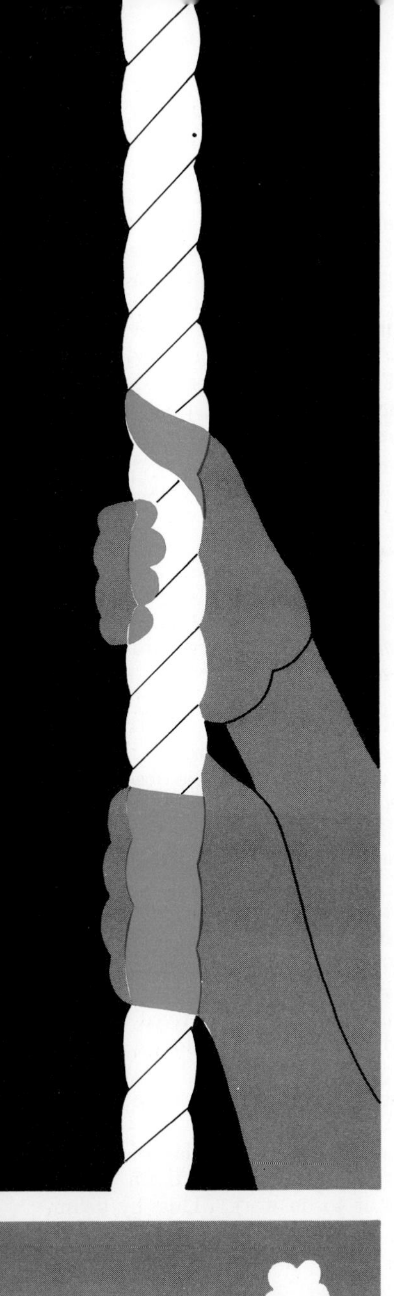

Energy is often changed from one of its forms to another. A person sliding his hands down a rope feels heat because friction has changed mechanical energy to heat energy. Thermonuclear reactions that take place in the sun's core change nuclear energy to radiant energy. An automobile engine changes the chemical energy of gasoline to the mechanical energy of moving wheels. Green plants change light energy to food energy, which is a kind of chemical energy. An electric mixer changes electrical energy to the mechanical energy of its whirling blades. An electric stove changes electrical energy to heat and light energy.

vanish into nowhere. The conservation of energy seems to be one of the truly general laws, for it is followed by all observed examples of living and nonliving things. Somehow, despite the great diversity of energy forms, scientists were able to establish that an amount of one kind of energy had exact equivalents in the other kinds of energy.

What makes the law of the conservation of energy so remarkable is that most of the quantities that physicists measure are not necessarily conserved. Velocities, accelerations, temperatures, and chemical units, such as atoms and molecules, are not always conserved. However, the amount of matter in a system, like the amount of energy, is also conserved unless some of the matter is changed to energy or some of the energy is changed to matter. To take account of such changes, the law of the conservation of energy is combined with the law of the conservation of mass to form an expanded law of the conservation of mass-energy (*see* Matter).

The simplest examples of the conservation of energy are provided by systems in which only mechanical forces are acting. A swinging pendulum, such as the boy swinging by the vine in the jungle, continually interchanges kinetic and potential energy. At the top of the swing, the velocity is zero and the energy is purely potential. At the bottom of the swing, the energy is purely kinetic. In intermediate positions, the energy is partly potential and partly kinetic. The sum of the kinetic and the potential energy, however, is constant throughout.

Actually, very few examples exist of purely mechanical systems. A pendulum does not keep on swinging forever. After a while the swings get smaller, and eventually they stop. This happens because the mechanical energy of the pendulum is changed to heat energy by a force called *friction*. This force changes energy to heat whenever two moving pieces of matter are in relative motion.

The motion of the pendulum is retarded by the frictional forces that it experiences when it moves through the air and rubs against the hook that holds it up. The energy of the pendulum is transferred to the molecules of the air through which it moves and of the hook. Their kinetic or elastic energy is increased. The temperature of the air and the hook rises. Mechanical energy has been changed to heat energy.

Frictional forces play a role in most mechanical situations. They may change some or all of the mechanical energy of the system to heat energy. A considerable amount of heat may be developed. For example, if a nail is driven into a wall, the work done by the hammer goes into energy of deformation (the nail changes the form of the wall as it moves through it) and into a large amount of heat. The nail and the head of the hammer grow hot.

The Laws of Thermodynamics

In the early 19th century the Industrial Revolution was well underway. The many newly invented machines of the time were driven by energy provided by burning fuel. These machines provided scientists with a great deal of information about how heat could be converted to other types of energy, how other types of energy could be converted to heat, and how heat could do work. Some of these observations were condensed into the laws of *thermodynamics*. (Thermodynamics is the branch of physics which studies interconversions between heat and mechanical energy.)

The first law of thermodynamics—a mathematical statement of the conservation of energy—says that the amount of heat added to a system exactly equals any change in energy of the system plus all the work done by the system. The equations derived from the first law of thermodynamics describe three variables: the internal energy of a system, the heat energy added to the system, and the work done by the system on its surroundings.

The practical importance of the first law of thermodynamics is that it shows that the addition of heat to a system enables it to do work. This, by defini-

The entropy, or amount of disorder, in a system tends to a maximum. When two powders of different colors are placed in one system, they tend to mix and become disordered. To bring order into the system, a great deal of work must be expended by forces outside the system.

E. F. Hoppe—Alfa Studio

tion, means that heat is a form of energy. When the first law was proposed, many people found it difficult to accept because they did not believe that heat was a form of energy. They thought of it as a mysterious fluid. But the first law did describe the action of heat engines and of many other kinds of heat interactions, so it came to be accepted as valid.

The first law says that the total energy of the universe remains constant. It does not say what kinds of energy can be changed into what other kinds of energy. After many false starts, a principle—the second law of thermodynamics—was worked out that described the kinds of energy conversions that are possible. This law states that conditions in any system tend to change to a condition of maximum disorder. (The amount of disorder in a system is called *entropy.*) Work must therefore be done from outside the system to impose more order on the system or to decrease its entropy.

The second law of thermodynamics may not seem to make sense, yet it does describe many common experiences. For example, when someone kicks off his shoes, it is far more likely that they will not land in the closet where they belong than that they will land there. To get them where they belong the person must exert work. He must pick them up, carry them to the closet, and place them in their proper location.

Heat is the most disordered form of energy. Therefore, according to the second law only a fraction of the heat available can be converted to useful work. Heat engines can transform some but not all of the heat available to them into mechanical energy. The remainder returns as heat at a lower temperature whether or not it is needed, wanted, or welcome.

Mechanical energy, on the other hand, can be completely converted to heat. This is a significant asymmetry. In both conversions the total amount of energy is conserved. But the second law of thermodynamics describes a restriction in the direction in which the conversions of energy can take place.

An automobile engine changes the chemical energy of gasoline into heat energy. The heat energy causes the gas to expand and push on a piston, thereby changing the heat energy partially to mechanical energy. Much of the heat energy, however, simply heats up the engine. The mechanical energy of the pistons is transferred to the tires, which push against the road's surface and move the car forward. But some of the energy in the tires is changed to heat energy by friction. In this and in all other processes involving conversions of heat energy to mechanical energy, much of the original heat energy remains.

To illustrate the difference between the second law of thermodynamics and the first, consider a pan of water that is heated by a burner. The first law of thermodynamics would perfectly well allow the water to freeze and the flame of the burner to get hotter, just as long as the total amount of energy remained the same. The second law of thermodynamics asserts that this is impossible. The process must proceed in the direction which transfers heat from the hotter to the colder body. The general direction of all processes occurring in the observed universe is that which increases entropy.

The third law of thermodynamics concerns a temperature called absolute zero. Absolute zero occurs at −273° C (−460° F). At absolute zero all substances theoretically would possess the minimum possible amount of energy, and some substances would possess zero entropy (be completely ordered). The third law states that, while absolute zero may be approached more and more closely, it is impossible actually to reach it (*see* Cryogenics).

Energy and Modern Physics

Early in this century the rise of quantum theory completely changed the notion of energy. Quantum theory is as important to 20th-century physics as the theory of relativity. Quantum theory states that energy occurs not over an infinitely divisible range but in certain distinct and specific amounts, called *quanta.* Thus, a given amount of electromagnetic energy cannot be subdivided into smaller and smaller amounts of energy. A smallest amount, or quantum, of energy exists which cannot be subdivided.

This view is illustrated by the respective ways in which classical physics and modern quantum physics treat a light wave. According to classical theory, the energy of a light wave can be made as small as desired by reducing the amplitude of the vibrations. According to modern quantum theory, however, the energy of a light wave of a definite frequency is the combined energy of a number of quanta. The smallest energy the light wave can have occurs when only one quantum is present.

For quantum physics, therefore, a beam of a given color of light consists of a very large number of quanta. However, it is impossible to discern the individual light quanta in a beam just as it is impossible to observe the individual molecules in a liquid. In both cases the very large numbers of very small objects present an unbroken, continuous appearance. (*See also* Light; Matter.)

BIBLIOGRAPHY FOR ENERGY

Books for Children

Adler, David. Wonders of Energy (Troll, 1983).
Asimov, Isaac. How Did We Find Out About Energy? (Avon, 1981).
Diener, C.S. and others. Energy (Humanics Ltd., 1982).
Podendorf, Illa. Energy (Children's, 1982).
Santrey, Lawrence. Energy and Fuels (Troll, 1985).
Satchwell, John. Energy at Work (Lothrop, 1981).

Books for Young Adults and Teachers

Fogel, Barbara. Energy: Choices for the Future (Watts, 1985).
Fowler, J.M. Energy and the Environment, 2nd ed. (McGraw, 1984).
Gates, D.M. Energy and Ecology (Sinauer, 1985).
Gordon, Douglas. Energy (David & Charles, 1984).
Nelson, R.V. Understanding Basic Energy Terms (Ide, 1981).
Radford, Don. Looking at Energy (David & Charles, 1984).
Smith, Howard. Exploring Energy (Goodheart, 1985).
Smith, N.F. Energy Isn't Easy (Putnam, 1984).
Yates, Madeleine. Earth Power: the Story of Geothermal Energy (Abingdon, 1980).

ENGINE *see* MOTOR AND ENGINE.

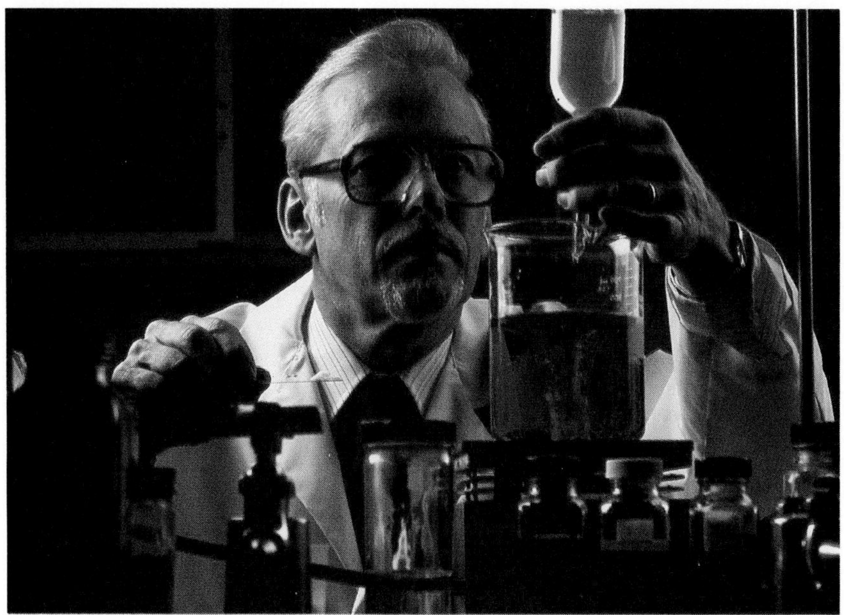

A chemical engineer deals with the production of chemicals for industrial or commercial use.

Courtesy, Servicemaster; photo, Bruce Quist

ENGINEERING

ENGINEERING. Broadly defined, engineering is the science-based profession by which the physical forces of nature and the properties of matter are made useful to mankind in the form of structures, machines, and other products or processes at a reasonable expenditure of time and money. An engineer is a person trained or skilled in designing machines and structures and in supervising their implementation.

The various branches of engineering serve a wide range of industries. Electrical engineers, for example, design communications equipment, electric power plants, and computers. Mechanical engineers deal with machines and engines as well as with manufacturing such equipment. Such major projects as spacecraft or hydroelectric power plants require the talents of many people with different technical backgrounds and experiences. Just as physicians with various specialties, nurses, and medical technicians are needed in medicine, the variety of engineering-related activities demands people with different levels of competence. Engineers deal with the advanced areas in which the latest tools of technology are required. Work that combines established approaches and often considerable practical work may be performed by technologists. Work in the shop or in the laboratory is normally carried out by technicians.

This article was contributed by Fred Landis, Professor of Mechanical Engineering, University of Wisconsin—Milwaukee.

Branches of Engineering

An engineer working in one specialty usually requires some knowledge in allied fields, as most engineering problems are complex and interrelated. A mechanical engineer designing a power plant, for instance, must deal with materials, structures, and electrical equipment in addition to purely mechanical engineering problems.

Aeronautical engineering deals with the design, manufacture, maintenance, testing, and use of aircraft for both civilian and military purposes. The field involves knowledge of aerodynamics, structural design, propulsion equipment, controls, and electronic communications, or avionics. Closely related is aerospace engineering, which deals with the design and operation of spacecraft. Here a background in rocket propulsion and space navigation is also required. (*See also* Airplane; Aerospace Industry; Jet Propulsion.)

Bioengineering combines engineering and medicine. The design and construction of medical instruments and of the advanced equipment used in a modern hospital are the result of the cooperation between engineers and medical personnel. The design of artificial limbs, artificial hearts, and other organ substitutes depends on bioengineers who must have a background in the biological sciences in addition to engineering. (*See also* Bioengineering.)

Chemical engineering deals with the production or conversion of chemicals for industrial use. Because of the variety of chemicals that may be used, problems are usually divided into unit operations or unit processes such as distillation, evaporation, absorption, humidification or drying, adsorption, separation of various constituents, size reduction, mixing, and others. A knowledge of chemical reactions—coupled with the basic laws of conservation of matter and energy as well as those defining chemical equilibrium—is prerequisite to the understanding of most unit processes. The chemical engineer must be able to move from the laboratory to large-scale and economical industrial production by arranging all the unit operations in their proper sequence. Continuous production is utilized in many modern plants for efficiency of operation rather than processing a batch of material at a time. This is possible only when well-designed automatic controls have been incorporated in the plant.

A petroleum refinery is a good example of a chemical engineering achievement. Depending on the crude oil being refined, different processes are employed to produce gasoline, jet engine fuel, and diesel oil.

Civil engineering, after military engineering, is the oldest of the engineering fields. It is one of the broadest with many subspecialties. Structural engineers are concerned with the design and erection of both large and small structures. These can range from small warehouses to skyscrapers, from highway overpasses to large bridges, and include dams of all sizes. Both steel and concrete designs may be called for.

Geotechnical and soil mechanics engineers evaluate the capacity of rocks and soils to bear heavy structures. Water resource engineers deal with water collection and purification: the erection of dams, flood control, irrigation, and water distribution systems. Environmental, or sanitary, engineers are concerned with water and sewage treatment as well as the disposal of residential and industrial wastes. The protection of rivers and lakes is part of their responsibility. Here a knowledge of chemistry and biology must be added to the engineering base. Transportation engineers design highway and public transportation systems to meet the needs of local and intercity traffic.

Electrical engineering began with the production, distribution, and utilization of electric power. The design and manufacture of generators, motors, transmission systems, and their appropriate controls are all part of electric power engineering. With the invention of the vacuum tube at the beginning of the 20th century, electrical engineering branched into communications systems—including radio and television—or electronic engineering. The complex systems required to switch telephone calls are the responsibility of the communications engineer. With the advent of the transistor, the transfer of information—including the large-scale use of the computer—became the responsibility of electrical and computer engineers. A computer engineer deals primarily with the equipment required for computation, or hardware. A computer scientist is more concerned with programs to carry out computations, or software. Electric circuits, electronics, logic and switching, electrical machines, and communications systems are just a few areas with which the electrical engineer must be conversant. (*See also* Computer; Electricity; Radio; Telecommunication; Telegraph; Telemetry; Telephone; Television; Transistor.)

Geological and mining engineering deals with the discovery and exploration of mineral deposits, the various processes to extract these minerals, and their conversion into useful metals or other refined products. Petroleum engineering, a subspecialty of this field, is directed to the discovery of oil and gas sites and the economic recovery of these fuels. Geology, rock mechanics, extraction processes, and an understanding of the behavior of ores and metals are part of the working tools of engineers in these specialties.

Industrial and management engineering. The efficient use of a modern factory—including the layout of machines, the best use of human labor, and the safe operation of the plant—fall into the domain of industrial engineers. They are also involved in quality control and inspection to check that the final product meets specifications. Production techniques, automation, statistics, operations research, and the interaction between human beings and machines (ergonomics) are some of the fields that need to be mastered by the industrial engineer. Management engineering is an extension that adds the role of management to complex technical processes.

Materials and metallurgical engineering. The development of appropriate materials and alloys to meet various industrial needs is involved in materials engineering. If the emphasis is on metals, the term metallurgical engineer is generally applied. Materials engineering also covers the development of plastics and other artificial materials. An understanding of the characteristics and behavior of metals and alloys and of artificial materials must be combined with manufacturing techniques and many aspects of chemical engineering. (*See also* Metal and Metallurgy.)

Mechanical engineering encompasses the design, construction, and utilization of machines. These may be involved in the conversion of energy such as in the production of useful work from fuels. Automotive engines, gas turbines, and steam power plants fall into this category. The conversion of fluid and mechanical power in pumps, fans, propellers, and hydraulic turbines is another aspect.

Mechanical engineers also design machine components. The transmission, steering system, and brakes of a car are examples. Mechanical design can involve large machines, such as presses or forges, or complex equipment such as textile machinery. Frequently it deals with the design of machines that help to make other machines—the so-called machine tools, including computer-controlled lathes and milling machines. Manufacturing engineering, the making of parts and components (sometimes with the help of robots), is usually considered a subspecialty of mechanical engineering. Air conditioning, refrigeration, ventilation, and the control of air pollution also fall into mechanical engineering. The knowledge of thermodynamics, fluid mechanics, heat transfer, machine

Courtesy, Gas Research Institute; photo, George Allen

Electrical technicians (above) carry out final assembly on a 40-kilowatt fuel cell package at an onsite installation. Civil engineers (below) review plans for the construction of a highway in the state of Virginia.

© Joe Viesti

design, vibrations, controls, and robotics are all involved in the background of the mechanical engineer. (*See also* Air Conditioning; Automation; Automobile; Automobile Industry; Diesel Engine; Fan, Electric; Furnace; Heat; Heating and Ventilating; Internal-Combustion Engine; Mechanics; Refrigeration; Steam Engine; Tools; Turbine.)

Naval, or marine, engineering deals with the design and operation of the powerplants and all accessory equipment on ships.

Nuclear engineering deals with the safe design and operation of nuclear power plants for energy generation. Nuclear engineers are concerned with shielding systems to safeguard people from the harmful effects of radiation and with the safe disposal of nuclear wastes. In addition to a knowledge of nuclear physics, the field involves an understanding of materials that can withstand high temperatures and bombardment by nuclear particles as well as many aspects of mechanical engineering.

Functions of the Engineer

Most engineers are employed in industry, working in large manufacturing organizations. Their jobs differ significantly in such areas as design, construction, operations, and maintenance. The many different engineering functions include the following:

Research. The research engineer tries to develop new principles and processes by using mathematics, scientific concepts, and experimentation. For instance, large computer simulations developed by research engineers permit the prediction of the performance of an airplane to the point that wind-tunnel and flight testing have been significantly reduced. Most research engineers hold advanced degrees, usually doctorates.

Development. Complex engineering systems need long periods of time for their development. Involved are the designing of components, often using new materials or new ideas, testing these components, and then improving the original ideas. All of the components must then be put together to build the final engineering system. This often implies that the small-scale experiments performed by the researcher must be scaled upward to the level of industrial practice. The chemical engineer, for instance, must extend the findings of a laboratory experiment to a small pilot plant and, if successful, to full-scale production. Engineers engaged in development usually hold advanced degrees.

Design. Coupled with and following development is design. An engineering project must not only work, but it must be safe, economical, and reliable and must meet the needs of the customer. The specific layout of an engineering product or structure becomes the responsibility of the design engineer.

Testing. Most engineering products must be fully tested before they can be delivered to a customer. Testing may show possible failures. The product then requires redesigning. Development, design, and testing must work closely together.

Manufacturing or construction. The actual making of the parts, whether in a factory or by assembling a structure on site, involves all the tools of production. The manufacturing engineer selects the right tools, schedules the flow of material and parts for the right machines, and supervises assembly.

Quality control and inspection. To check that all parts and assemblies meet their technical and other requirements is the responsibility of the quality engineer.

Sales and marketing. Interaction between the manufacturer and the customer is the responsibility of sales or marketing engineers. They must know all the technical aspects of their products as well as fully understand the needs of their customers. Frequently they may need to educate the customers. These needs may require special features or even major redesign of a product. Thus the sales engineer must be in contact with all parts of the manufacturing organization.

Maintenance. The continued safe and reliable operation of equipment and efficient repairs are the responsibility of the maintenance engineer.

Management. The management of a complex technical venture is different from normal business management. It requires knowledge of both engineering

A mining engineer (left) measures the amount of methane gas in a coal bed. Although methane is a useful gas, it is also highly combustible and therefore a danger to miners. A petroleum engineer (right) takes a core sample from a sand formation to determine the presence and quantity of oil. This testing is performed during the experimental drilling stage.

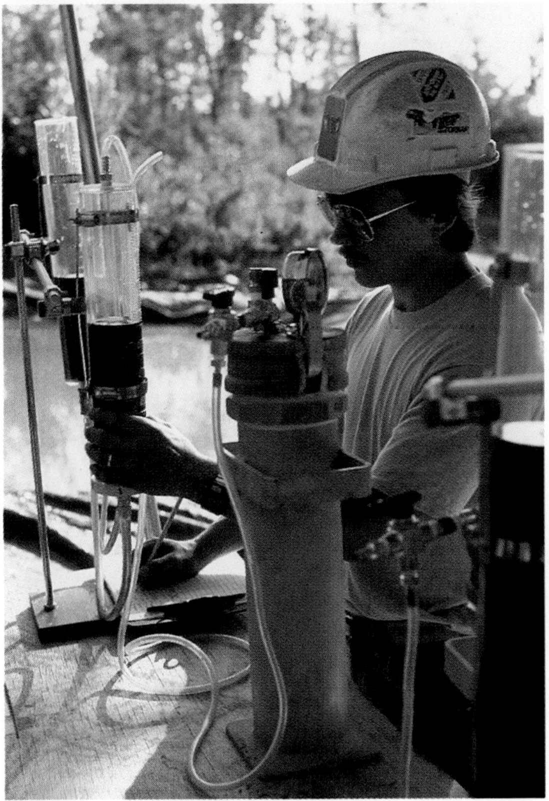

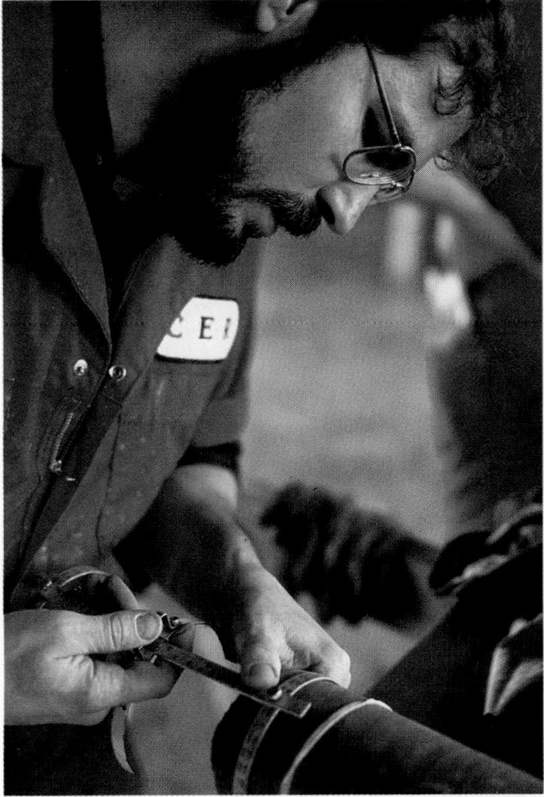

Courtesy, Gas Research Institute; photos, Bruce Quist

The regenerative furnace, originally developed for the metallurgical industry, has greatly speeded the glass-melting process.

Courtesy, Gas Research Institute; photo, Bruce Quist

and of management techniques. Most engineering managers are promoted from the ranks of engineers. Often these engineers take advanced work in business administration.

Employment in the Field

The National Science Foundation estimates that in the early 1980s there were nearly 2 million engineers employed in the United States. Nearly 90 percent of them had bachelor's or advanced degrees. These included about 471,000 electrical or electronic engineers, 372,000 mechanical engineers, 272,000 civil engineers, and 115,000 chemical engineers. The greatest concentration of engineers was in the following industries: electrical machinery 15 percent, transportation equipment 13 percent, nonelectrical machinery 12 percent, communications equipment 8 percent, and aircraft and parts 7 percent. About 76 percent of all engineers were employed in business and industry, about 8 percent by the federal government, nearly 4 percent in educational institutions, and the remaining 12 percent in various areas, including state and local governments. From 1976 to 1983, according to the Bureau of Labor Statistics, engineering employment in the United States grew by about 40 percent. It promises continued growth. The greatest demand is expected to be for computer, electronic, and aeronautical engineers. Engineering in general promises to be one of the few careers with high chances of professional employment.

Development of Engineering

The building of canals, bridges, and roads was carried out by specially trained civil engineers as early as the middle of the 18th century. With the advent of steam power at the beginning of the Industrial Revolution in the last part of the 18th century, mechanical engineers started to develop engines, locomotives, and various other machines. The automatic knitting machine was probably the most advanced. Originally steam was used merely to extend power beyond that of animals. During the 19th century, however, mechanical engineering expanded to include such labor-saving devices as the sewing machine and the mechanical reaper (*see* Industrial Revolution; Technology).

The increasing need for metals furthered mining engineering. With the invention of the Bessemer steel-making process, steel began to replace iron in both machinery and construction. Large bridges and skyscrapers became possible. This led to the development of metallurgical engineering as a separate field.

The invention of electric generators and motors and the development of the electric light bulb led to the growth of electrical engineering. This was originally a subspecialty of mechanical engineering.

Advances in chemistry during the latter half of the 19th century demanded that small-scale laboratories be extended to large-scale production, opening the way for the chemical engineer. By 1900 these various fields of engineering had been established.

Following the introduction of the assembly line by Henry Ford in 1913, the demands of the growing automobile industry led to a specialty in automotive engineering. The rapid spurt of airplane development following World War I led to the new field of aeronautical engineering. The increasing need for petroleum products to provide fuels for transportation, energy generation, and heating fostered petroleum engineering.

With the development of radio just after the turn of the 20th century, electronic engineering—a part of electrical engineering—was born. Radio, television, and almost all modern communications techniques depend on the electronic engineer. Following the invention of the transistor in 1948, new vistas in communications and in computing were opened. The information revolution caused by the computer added computer engineering as a new specialty.

The advent of nuclear power was reflected in the field of nuclear engineering. Combinations of medicine and technology to build artificial limbs or organs and to improve medical instrumentation started the field of bioengineering.

The need to produce goods cheaply and efficiently became a primary responsibility of the industrial engineer. Following the development of space flight, aerospace engineering was added to aeronautical engineering. A number of further specialty areas also came about such as ceramic, safety, agricultural, environmental, and transportation engineering.

The increasing role of computers is significant. Machine parts are designed with the aid of computer graphics. They carry out all the technical computations needed to make a part meet performance requirements. This aspect of computer-aided design (CAD) is frequently coupled with computer-aided manufacture (CAM) to produce parts automatically.

The use of robots is a major factor in the increasing automation of factories. New energy conversion devices—such as direct conversion of the sun's energy and advances in nuclear power—are expected to be significant. The protection of the environment against pollution, including acid rain, remains a challenge. Advances in medical technology and the increased use of artificial materials—such as plastics and ceramics replacing more expensive and heavier metal parts—are additional challenges for engineers.

Engineering Education

Until the 18th century, engineering was essentially a craft in which cumulative experience was considered more important than formal learning. The exception was military engineering in which formal education dates back to the middle of the 17th century. Civil engineering education began in 1747 with the founding in France of the National School of Bridges and Highways. France influenced the United States. The first American school initially devoted to engineering was the United States Military Academy at West Point, N.Y., founded in 1802. Several two-year schools were founded before 1830 that emphasized technical education. Some of these eventually evolved into engineering colleges. The oldest are Norwich University in Vermont, founded in 1819, and the Rensselaer Institute of Technology in Troy, N.Y. (1824). Engineering education did not grow, however, until after the Civil War, when state universities were founded with federal land grants to "teach agriculture and the mechanic arts." By that time mechanical engineering programs were added to those in civil engineering. Electrical engineering followed by the end of the century.

Although mathematics and the physical sciences were incorporated into engineering education early on, the development of scientifically based engineering courses was much slower. Such practical crafts courses as machine shop, surveying, drafting, and welding were offered in almost all schools. The emphasis on the scientific background of engineering began only after 1950.

Undergraduate. Engineering is a challenging course of study that requires a thorough understanding of mathematics and science. These are normally taken in the first two years. English, humanities, and social studies also form a part of every program. Such courses are included because engineers must consider the social effects of the products and processes they

An astronaut (below) conducts an electrophoresis experiment aboard the space shuttle *Columbia*. The test is a forerunner of experiments to purify biological materials in the low-gravity environment of space. A computer engineer (right) uses a microscope to monitor production of computer chips.

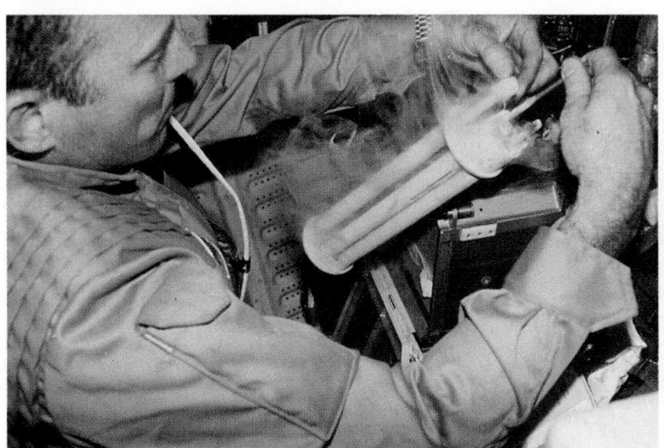

NASA

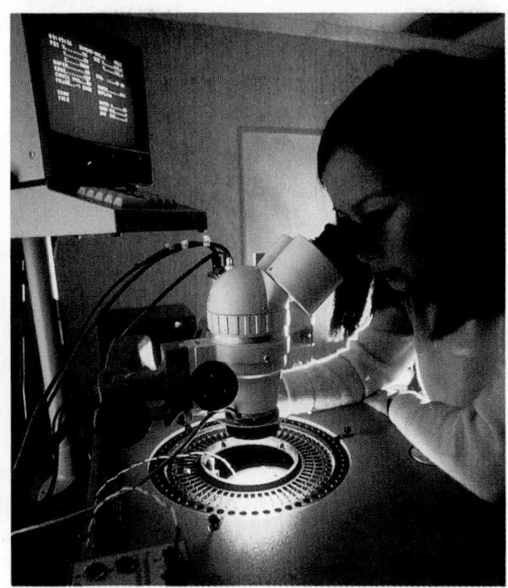

Index Stock Inc.

Courtesy, Gas Research Institute; photo, Bruce Quist

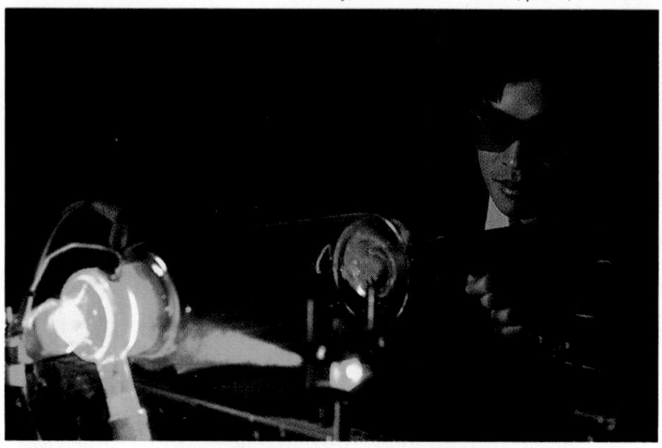

© Joe Viesti

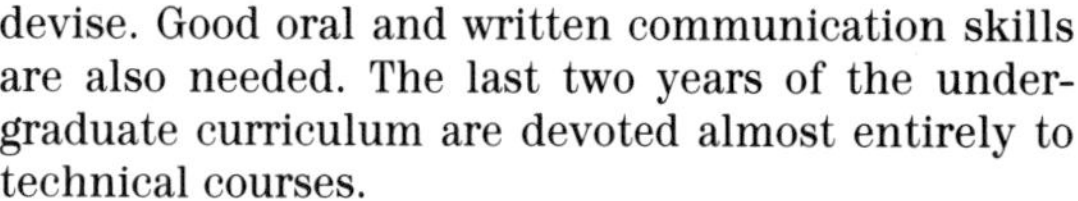

An engineer (above) applies pulse-combustion technology to find more efficient ways of burning natural gas. An engineer (right) at the National Oceanic and Atmospheric Administration works with a trainee, left, on updating a map of the Great Lakes.

devise. Good oral and written communication skills are also needed. The last two years of the undergraduate curriculum are devoted almost entirely to technical courses.

The vast majority of the more than 70,000 engineering students who graduate annually from American engineering schools with a bachelor's degree are hired as engineers by industry. About 15 percent of the total go on to full-time graduate work. Many undertake graduate work part-time while employed as engineers. Others use their engineering education to enter a variety of fields, including business administration, medicine, and law. About 260 colleges in the United States that have one or more engineering programs are accredited by the Accrediting Board for Engineering and Technology (ABET). There are also non-accredited programs, but graduation from a non-accredited program may make the student ineligible for a professional engineering license in some states or bar employment by federal agencies.

Accreditation in Canada is carried out by the Canadian Accrediting Board of the Canadian Council of Professional Engineers. Programs in about 30 colleges and universities are accredited.

The majority of accredited programs are in electrical and electronic, mechanical, civil, chemical, and industrial engineering. Fewer schools offer programs in aeronautical, nuclear, and materials engineering. There are also a few highly specialized programs such as ceramics, environmental engineering, bioengineering, and geologic or petroleum engineering.

Graduate. With the continuing and rapid changes in technology, it is ever more difficult to teach enough engineering in a four-year undergraduate curriculum. Students who wish to stay in the forefront of technology, therefore, find that further study at the graduate level is required. Both master's and doctoral programs stress further technical depth. In the latter an independent research program resulting in a thesis is also required. Engineers planning to enter management also frequently take advanced work in business administration.

Continuing education. Electrical engineers who graduated in the early 1950s would not know about transistors or computers unless they learned about them after leaving college. There is a danger that engineers can become rapidly obsolete unless they recognize the need for lifelong learning in the profession. This is made possible by continuing education courses offered by universities, professional societies, and other groups.

Professional Societies

To remain current in their field, most engineers join one or more professional engineering societies. They publish technical journals, encourage engineering research, provide assistance to various levels of government, hold meetings at which technical advances are presented, offer continuing education courses, and look after the technical welfare of their members.

The major American engineering societies date back to the late 1800s. The American Society of Civil Engineers was founded in 1852; the American Institute of Mining, Metallurgical, and Petroleum Engineers in 1871; the American Society of Mechanical Engineers in 1880; the forerunner of the Institute of Electrical and Electronics Engineers in 1884; and the American Institute of Chemical Engineers in 1908. Most professional societies of other branches of engineering were founded in the 20th century.

BIBLIOGRAPHY FOR ENGINEERING

Crump, D.J. How Things Work (National Geographic, 1980).

Florman, Samuel. The Existential Pleasures of Engineering (St. Martin, 1977).

Florman, Samuel. Engineering and the Liberal Arts: a Technologist's Guide to History, Literature, Philosophy, Art, and Music (Krieger, 1982).

Kerrod, Robin. The Way It Works (Mayflower, 1980).

Kock, W.E. The Creative Engineer: the Art of Inventing (Plenum, 1978).

Parsons, S.A. How to Find Out About Engineering (Pergamon, 1972).

Pawlicki, T. How to Build a Flying Saucer and Other Proposals in Speculative Engineering (Prentice, 1980).

Schaub, J.H. and Dickison, S.K. Engineering and the Humanities (Wiley, 1982).

Weiss, Harvey. Machines and How They Work (Crowell, 1983).

J. Allan Cash Ltd.

The warship *H.M.S. Belfast* is anchored near the Tower Bridge in London as a tourist attraction. The bridge, built in 1886–94, was designed by Horace Jones and John Wolfe Barry. The lower section can be raised to permit vessels to pass.

ENGLAND

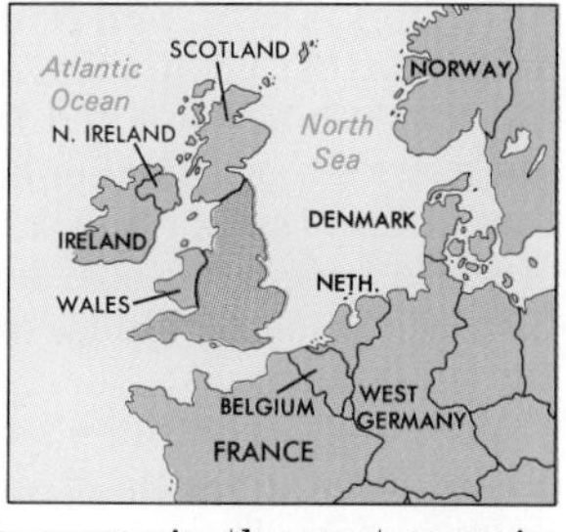

ENGLAND. The largest and most populated country of the United Kingdom of Great Britain and Northern Ireland is England. By world standards, however, it is not large nor is it particularly rich in natural resources; yet its political and economic power in the past was virtually unrivaled. Today England's influence on the international scene is not as great, but it still remains a cultural force in the English-speaking world. (*See also* United Kingdom; Ireland, Northern; Scotland; Wales.)

England is fortunate in being part of an island that has never been occupied or invaded by foreign troops since the Norman Conquest in 1066. Its island location encouraged the use of the surrounding seas by its inhabitants as major routes of travel. These routes led the English to distant parts of the world and resulted in the founding of a vast empire in which its language, its law, and its social institutions were established.

English wealth and inventiveness, combined with those of the other peoples of the British Isles, helped to put England in the forefront of European nations as an industrial power in the 19th century. Weakened by World War II and by political, economic, and social problems, England lost much of its importance as an industrial power in Europe to other countries, while the loss of parts of the British Empire abroad removed some of its previous international political influence.

This article was contributed by Ian M. Matley, Professor of Geography, Michigan State University, East Lansing.

NATURAL ENVIRONMENT

Land

England's total area is about 50,000 square miles (130,000 square kilometers), or 53 percent of the total area of the United Kingdom. It is bounded by Scotland on the north and Wales on the west. From the Scottish border to the south coast is about 360 miles (580 kilometers), and from the western tip of Land's End to North Foreland on the east coast is about 330 miles (530 kilometers). The east coast of England is washed by the North Sea and its northwest coast by the Irish Sea. Its southwestern corner juts into the Atlantic Ocean, while the south coast is separated from France by the English Channel. At its narrowest point, the Strait of Dover, the channel measures only 22 miles (35 kilometers). The estuaries of major rivers penetrate the coast, and no place in England is more than 75 miles (120 kilometers) from the sea.

England is mainly a lowland country. Only in the northwest, in the area known as the Lake District, are there mountains of any height. Here the highest summit is Scafell Pike with a height of 3,210 feet (978 meters). These mountains are of the same geologic age as the mountains of Scotland and northern Wales and were worn down during the Ice Age by the movement of glaciers, which formed valleys now filled by lakes.

A chain of lower mountains and hills extends from east of the Lake District in a southward direction to the center of England. This range is known as the

Pennines and contains Pen-y-ghent and the Peak, both more than 2,000 feet (600 meters) in height. The Pennines, though geologically younger than the mountains of the Lake District, contain softer rocks that have been leveled and rounded by erosion. The southwestern peninsula of England consists mainly of mountains and hills of the same age as the Pennines. They also reach more than 2,000 feet on Dartmoor, one of several moors in the region.

The complex geology of central and southern England gives rise to a number of small ranges of hills of different geologic origins. Many of these are low escarpments, which give some variety to the predominantly plains landscape of the south. The North and South Downs are chalk hills that surround a complex geological area of ridges and valleys known as the Weald. Where the Downs reach the sea at Dover and Beachy Head, there are high chalk cliffs. Farther north the Chiltern Hills are also of chalk origin, while the Cotswolds are formed of limestone.

Preview

The article England is divided into the following sections:

The largest area of plains is found in the Midlands and along the east coast. The area of East Anglia, which bulges into the North Sea, is particularly flat and low and at one time contained large marshes known as the Fens that have now been drained. The relatively flat nature of the east coast has made it an easy route for north-south movement.

There are few islands of any size along the English coast. The exception is the Isle of Wight on the south coast, which is easily reached by ferry across the Solent. To the west of Land's End lie the Scilly Isles.

Because of its relatively small size, England contains few long rivers. The longest are the Severn, which begins in Wales and flows for 210 miles (340 kilometers), the Thames (200 miles, 320 kilometers), and the Trent (175 miles, 280 kilometers). These rivers have a number of tributaries. There are few lakes of any size, the largest being Lake Windermere in the Lake District.

Although inadequate for present industrial requirements, mineral deposits have been of great value to the development of England's economy. In particular, coal enabled England to become the leading industrial nation at the time of the Industrial Revolution. The largest, and at present most productive. coalfield is the York, Derby, and Nottingham coalfield located in the northern Midlands. Another important field is the Northumberland and Durham in the northeast. There are several smaller coalfields in the Midlands, Lancashire, the northwest, and the southeast. Some of these have little coal left, and many coal mines have been closed because of the high costs of getting out what remains.

Most of Great Britain's North Sea petroleum lies off the coast of Scotland, and there is little near the English coast. There are some small onshore oilfields, however, notably in the east Midlands and in Dorset on the south coast. As part of the United Kingdom, England shares in the benefits of Scottish North Sea oil production. Several large natural gas fields are located off the east coast between East Anglia and the mouth of the Humber River.

Another significant mineral resource is iron ore. During the Industrial Revolution local iron ore was of great importance for the development of the English iron and steel industry. Much of this ore came from deposits close to the Midlands and northeastern coalfields, but now most of these deposits are exhausted. Iron ore now comes from the east and south Midlands but supplies less than one quarter of British industrial requirements. Other metallic minerals are of little significance. Some tin ore is mined in Cornwall in the southwest, where such mining has been carried on since ancient times. Small quantities of copper, zinc, tungsten, and silver are found along with the tin, and some lead is mined in the northern Pennines. Nonmetallic minerals include salt, gypsum, china clay, chalk for cement production, and limestone and dolomite for iron smelting and chemical production.

(Below) J. Allan Cash Ltd.; (right) Lorraine Wilson—Robert Harding Picture Library; (bottom right) Thomas B. Hollyman—Photo Researchers

Wicken Fen (above) is part of a 1,400-square-mile area called the Fens that has been reclaimed for agriculture. The summits of the Pikes in the Lake District (top right) can be seen from Loughrigg Tarn, a small lake. Land's End, Cornwall (right), is the westernmost point of England.

Climate

The climate is dominated by the influence of the sea. England's location on the western edge of the European continent and within the westerly wind belt ensures that its climate is rainy and temperate. Winters are mild, summers cool, and rain falls in all seasons. Winter temperatures are modified by the influence of the warm current of the north Atlantic Drift, which moves along the west coast of the British Isles. Summer temperatures are influenced by the country's location in northern latitudes. Most of England has summer temperatures of 60 to 62° F (16 to 17° C) and winter temperatures of 40 to 42° F (4 to 6° C), with somewhat warmer temperatures in the southwest. The amount of rain and snow varies greatly with location. It is about 20 inches (50 centimeters) on the average per year in parts of the east and more than 45 inches (115 centimeters) in the southwest. Cornwall in the southwest is one of the warmest and rainiest parts of England. The mountains of the Lake District, however, receive the most precipitation, with more than 80 inches (200 centimeters) on the average in a year. Because of the mild winter temperatures, snow does not lie for long even on the mountains. The sunniest region is the southeastern coast, where many vacation resorts are located.

Plants and Animals

The original vegetation—before human action greatly changed it—was deciduous forest consisting mainly of oaks, beeches, ashes, and elms. Clearance of forests for farmland began in the Middle Ages, and now less than 7 percent of the area is covered by forests and woods. Recent replanting of forests has been carried out—mainly with coniferous trees such as spruces, larches, and pines, which grow rapidly. Moorlands occur in the Lake District, the Pennines, and the southwest. Many of these moors are covered by heather, cotton grass, and other varieties of moor grasses. They are often used for sheep grazing.

The most common soils of England are brown forest soils. There is, however, a large variety of other soil types. The nature of local soils and climate has a great influence on the type of farming found in a particular region. For example, loam soils (a mixture of sand and clay) are good for cultivation, while areas of poor, thin soils are often used for grazing lands.

The animals of England are similar to those of the rest of northwestern Europe. Wolves, bears, and elks, though, have become extinct. The largest animal is the red deer, found mainly in the southwest. Roe and fallow deer also exist in wooded areas and parks. Badgers, foxes, and otters are found in most rural areas. Small animals include squirrels, hedgehogs, hares, rabbits, rats, and mice. The most numerous birds are blackbirds, thrushes, starlings, chaffinches, and sparrows. Ducks, geese, and other water birds are found near marshes, lakes, and ponds. Gulls and other seabirds nest in coastal areas.

PEOPLE

There are nearly 47 million people living in England, of which almost 80 percent live in cities. The density of population is 929 persons per square mile (359 persons per square kilometer), one of the highest in Western Europe. The greatest concentrations of population are in the London area, the Midlands

(Left) Christina Gascoigne—Robert Harding Picture Library; (top right) Susan McCartney—Photo Researchers; (bottom right) Lawrence Migdale—Photo Researchers

York Minster (left), the largest medieval church in England, dates from the 13th to the 15th century. The Royal Shakespeare Theatre at Stratford-upon-Avon (top right), built from 1920 to 1932, was designed by Elizabeth Scott. The Egyptian Collections of the British Museum in London (bottom right) are among the institution's many fascinating exhibits.

area around Birmingham, West Yorkshire, and Lancashire—including Manchester—and the northeast around Newcastle. There are also many people living along the southern coast. Greater London has a population of nearly 7 million and Birmingham more than 1 million. Leeds, Sheffield, and Liverpool each have populations of more than 500,000. Birmingham has grown the most rapidly of all cities since 1900—apart from London—and has overtaken Manchester and Liverpool to become England's second city.

Origins

Although the original English-speaking people came from northern Germany, the present-day English are a mixture of racial types. The original Celtic inhabitants either intermarried with the Anglo-Saxon invaders or sought refuge in the mountains of Wales or in Cornwall. Even today some Cornish people do not consider themselves English. Further invasions by the Norse and the Danes, and later by the Normans, added to the north European racial characteristics of the English, and there are many living in the east and north of the country in particular who have fair hair and blue or gray eyes. Darker types are also found, the result of Celtic or other earlier racial influences.

The existence of several minority groups adds to the mixed racial composition. The Irish are the largest group, but there are also communities of such European peoples as Italians, Poles, and Greek and Turkish Cypriots. The most recent addition to the population has been the immigrants from the ex-colonies of the British Empire—including blacks (mainly West Indians), Pakistanis, and Indians—who now total some 2.2 million, or about 4 percent of the total British population. About 40 percent of these were born in Great Britain. The majority of the nonwhite population lives in London and the industrial cities of the Midlands—such as Birmingham, Liverpool, and Manchester—often in poor conditions in inner-city areas.

Language

Apart from languages spoken by some immigrants, the native language is English. Although standard English is taught in the schools, there are many local dialects and accents. People from different regions sometimes have difficulty understanding one another. The influence of television and radio, however, has spread standard English words and pronunciation around the country. In some cities, particularly London, there are groups of Welsh people who maintain the use of the Welsh language. In Cornwall the old Cornish language—a Celtic language similar to Welsh—has been revived after about 200 years of virtual extinction and is taught in some schools. But the language is rarely used in everyday life.

Religion

The majority of the people of England belong to the Church of England, sometimes known as the Anglican church. It is the established state church with the reigning king or queen as its head. The Church of England is governed by bishops. There are two archbishoprics with seats at Canterbury and York. The archbishoprics are divided into bishoprics, each with its own bishop. These are in turn divided into parishes under the control of a vicar and sometimes an assistant curate. The two archbishops and 24 bishops sit in Parliament in the House of Lords. Although a state church, the Church of England receives no direct financial contributions from the state.

Other churches in England are known as nonconformist. The largest of these is the Methodist Church. Methodism is particularly strong in the north of England. Other churches are the Baptist, United Reformed church (formed by a merger of Congregationalists and Presbyterians), Unitarian, Quaker, and Salvation Army. The Roman Catholic church has a considerable following, especially around Liverpool, where many people of Irish origin live.

The Jewish community is one of the largest in Europe. The biggest non-Christian group, however, is the Muslims, who number about 1.5 million. Most are Pakistanis in origin, but there is also a sizable Arab community in London. There are also many Hindus and Sikhs living in London and the industrial cities of the Midlands.

Institutions

Many Englishmen are particularly proud of their country's history as a major world power with a large empire. This attitude can be seen in the regard shown for the institution of royalty and the members of the royal family, who act as a link with the past. The role of the monarchy, however, has gradually changed from one of authority to one of symbolism.

The English are proud of their cultural heritage. They have a rich literary and artistic tradition, which has influenced the development of English-speaking cultures around the world. London is a world center for the theater, music, and opera, and many English actors, playwrights, composers, performing musicians, dancers, writers, sculptors, and painters are internationally famous. Annual festivals of the arts are held in several English towns and cities. For coverage of English contributions in these areas, *see* Acting; Drama; Motion Pictures; Theater; Music; Opera; Ballet; Dance; Folk Dance; English Literature; Sculpture; and Painting.

Sports

In spite of the great attachment of many of the English to their culture, their love of sports is probably even more significant in their everyday lives. Many sports now played internationally were invented in England. Of these, the most important is soccer, or association football. There are more than 40,000 clubs, some of which are professional. It is the most popular sport in England. (*See also* Soccer.)

Rugby football is also played. It has two forms—Rugby Union, played by amateurs with a largely middle-class following, and Rugby League, played partly by professionals. It is found mainly in the north of England with a largely working-class following.

Cricket is the most popular summer sport. It is more than 300 years old. It is played at all levels—from professional national and county teams to amateur college, school, town, and village teams. It is not very popular in the parts of the British Isles outside England and thus can be regarded as the English national sport. But the game spread to many parts of the British Empire, and today test matches—as international games are called—are played with Australia, New Zealand, India, Pakistan, and a team representing the West Indies. (*See also* Cricket.)

The English have done fairly well in international track and field athletics, which attract a small but enthusiastic following. Middle-distance runners have been most successful. Perhaps most notable is Roger Bannister, who became the first person to run the mile in under four minutes in 1954. Others of note in the 1980s include Sebastian Coe, Steve Ovett, and David Moorcroft, all of whom set world records.

Among American sports, basketball is popular and is played in many schools and amateur clubs. Horse racing is an important spectator sport, and many people with little knowledge of horses still bet on the results of such major national events as the Derby and the Grand National. People also bet on the results of soccer games by filling out weekly "football pools" coupons.

Education

Education in England has a long and distinguished history. Some of its most famous schools and universities were founded in the Middle Ages and are among the oldest in Europe. Education remained for long the privilege of a small elite group, and education for everyone did not appear until the beginning of the 20th century.

Everyone between the ages of 5 and 16 must now go to school. Children generally first attend primary schools, though many under-5-year-olds attend nursery schools or "playgrounds." They generally transfer to secondary school at the age of 11. Most attend comprehensive schools, which accept pupils without reference to ability and offer a variety of subjects. Others go to grammar and secondary modern schools, which they enter after taking a special examination at age 11.

A small number enroll in private schools, which are not part of the government system but are subject to government inspection. Some of these are known as "public" schools, which are generally attended by the children of the well-to-do, though some pupils receive government scholarships. Most public school pupils live in residential houses attached to the school. Considerable emphasis is placed on sports, especially cricket and rugby. Among the most famous public schools for boys are Eton (founded in 1440), Winchester (1380), and Harrow (1611). Many of those in the higher levels of government or public life attended a public school.

The oldest universities are Oxford and Cambridge, founded in the 12th and 13th centuries, respectively. These universities have remained the most prestigious in England, and their alumni have formed the core of the educated elite for many years. In the 19th century new city universities were established. Known as "redbrick" universities, they included London, Birmingham, Manchester, and Newcastle. In the early 20th century universities were opened in Liverpool, Leeds, and Reading. But the greatest expansion came in the 1950s and 1960s, when many new universities were opened. Among these were Exeter, Sussex, York, and Kent. There are now 35 universities in England.

ECONOMY

During the 19th century England emerged as one of the most important manufacturing and trading nations in the world. There are few other countries where foreign trade has been so important to their economies. Exports have been mainly manufactured goods such as machinery, electrical equipment, and textiles, while imports have consisted primarily of farm products and raw materials.

Energy

The most significant economic development in recent years has been the elimination of the reliance on petroleum supplies from abroad. As a result of the North Sea petroleum fields, Britain is now self-sufficient in oil and produces more than 75 percent of its natural gas requirements. The increased use of oil and natural gas has reduced reliance on coal, once by far the most important source of energy and a major export.

Although coal still provides for about one third of England's total energy requirements, including use in about three quarters of its electric power generating stations, coal production has been falling since the 1960s. The coal industry has been weakened by labor unrest in recent years, culminating in the massive coal strike of 1984 and 1985, which was caused by the decision by the government to close several uneconomical coal mines.

Mining is becoming increasingly concentrated in the more economical coalfields such as Yorkshire, where new mines have been opened. These decisions are made by the National Coal Board, a government corporation that controls this nationalized industry. In spite of these problems, the English coal mining industry is the largest in Western Europe, and coal is still exported.

The development of nuclear power has increased the production of electricity. The first major nuclear station in the world began operation in 1956 in England at Calder Hall in the northwest. There are now 10 nuclear power stations. The government has announced plans for further stations, but there is considerable public opposition.

Hydroelectric power is of no importance in England because the rivers are unsuitable for the construction of dams. There are three small hydroelectric plants in Dartmoor in the southwest.

Industry

England's energy supplies are used in a variety of industries. Of these, the most important historically has been the iron and steel industry. This industry formed the basis for England's rise as a major manufacturing nation in the 19th century. Based on the coalfields of the Midlands and the northeast, it used local supplies of iron ore. The main centers were the Middlesbrough district in the northeast, Scunthorpe (east), and Sheffield (Midlands). More recently Corby in the south Midlands grew rapidly as a steel town. The major markets for iron and steel were the shipbuilding, automobile, machine-building and other branches of the engineering industry. With shrinking demand for steel from these industries, along with worldwide overproduction, several steel centers—such as Corby—have been closed. The production of such others as Sheffield and Scunthorpe has been reduced. In the last few years the labor force of this industry has been reduced by one third.

The decline in steel making is tied to the problems that also face other traditional English manufacturing industries. The shipbuilding industry is located mainly on the estuaries of rivers—such as the Tyne and Wear (northeast), the Mersey (west Midlands), and in the town of Barrow in Furness (west Midlands). Competition from Japan, West Germany, and other countries—along with a demand for large tankers and other ships that cannot be built in the small English shipyards—has led to the decline of this industry.

The automobile industry, located mainly in the Midlands between Birmingham and Liverpool and in the area northwest of London, also faces problems of competition from European and Japanese manufacturers. The largest company is the British Leyland Corporation, which has been plagued by strikes, as have Ford and other, smaller car companies. Companies producing luxury automobiles—such as Rolls-Royce and Jaguar—have been most successful in maintaining their competitive position because of worldwide demand.

The aerospace industry has been more successful than some other modern English industries. England's aerospace industry is the largest in Western Europe and produces military and civil aircraft, engines, helicopters, missiles, hovercraft, and equipment used in space exploration. Several companies joined together forming a British Aerospace Corporation for the manufacture of airframes. Engines are built mainly by the Rolls-Royce company.

The chemicals industry is one of the largest in Europe. It manufactures a wide variety of products, using mainly imported raw materials and petroleum from the North Sea.

The nonferrous metals industry is also of major importance. Most of the smelting and refining industries use imported ores and produce mainly aluminum, copper, lead, zinc, tin, and titanium. The industry is located mainly in the Midlands. Major markets are the United States and Western Europe. A drop in demand for some nonferrous metals on the world markets has affected the industry in recent years.

One of the great traditional English industries is the manufacture of textiles. This industry, however, is a shadow of its former self. During the 19th century cotton textiles and clothing were England's chief export. The industry was located in Lancashire, near coal for power and the port of Liverpool for imported American cotton. By the 1930s competition from Japan, China, and India created problems. Since World War II—and ever-increasing competition from countries with cheap labor—the industry has declined rapidly and many mills have closed.

The wool textile industry has been more fortunate. It is located partly in West Yorkshire, where wool, coal, and the required suitable soft water are available. Most woolen and worsted cloths—as well as carpets—are made in this area. Knitwear is made largely in the east Midlands. Relatively low prices and good quality have helped to maintain international demand for English woolen goods.

Another English product with a worldwide reputation is china. The china and pottery industry is located mainly in the district of Staffordshire—known as the Potteries—though other factories are found at Derby, Worcester, and elsewhere. The most famous companies are Wedgwood and Royal Doulton, which export their products all around the world.

Since World War II when socialist governments were in power, many of England's basic industries—such as coal mining, iron and steel, the British Leyland automobile company, and others—have been nationalized and run by the state. Later the Conservative government returned many of these state-run companies to private ownership, including British Aerospace, Britoil, and Jaguar automobiles.

Agriculture

Although England is predominantly an industrial country, agriculture still plays an important role in the economy. In spite of a decline in the number of farm workers to about one third of the number employed in the 1930s, English agriculture now feeds about two thirds of the population, compared with less than one half of a smaller population 50 years ago. English farming is efficient, with a high degree of mechanization.

Environmental factors influence the types of crops grown in different parts of the country. The major grain crop is barley, which can be grown in areas with relatively cool summers and poor soil conditions. Wheat, the second crop in terms of area and production, requires hot, dry, sunny weather for ripening and is thus grown mainly in eastern England. English wheat is too soft for bread making without mixing with imported wheat. About half the barley crop is used for animal food, and part of the remainder is used to brew beer. Potatoes are an important crop and are grown in a number of areas. Sugar beets are grown in the drier east and supply almost 50 percent of the country's sugar requirements. Hops for beer brewing and rapeseed for vegetable oil are also significant crops.

Fresh vegetables are grown in market gardens near major urban centers and also in those areas with relatively warm climates such as Cornwall and the Scilly Islands. Fruits are grown in several farming areas, and the southeast, the west Midlands, and the southwest

The sculptor (below) shaping a small statue of seals works at the Royal Doulton, Ltd., china factory. The Selby Coalfield's Stillingfleet mine (right) in North Yorkshire still produces a valuable resource. Sheep near Bratton, Wiltshire (bottom right), provide wool for textile mills in England and abroad.

(Below) Ronny Jaques—Photo Researchers; (right) J. Allan Cash Ltd.; (bottom right) James P. Rowan—CLICK/CHICAGO

are noted for their apples, pears, and plums. Apples from Devon and Somerset are used for making cider, which in England is an alcoholic drink. Strawberries and raspberries are grown mainly in the southeast and in the Fens.

The raising of livestock is a major activity on the majority of English farms. Dairy farming is found mainly in areas with mild winters and considerable rainfall, where rich grass grows. Such areas are the southwest and the west, especially Cheshire. Beef cattle are raised mainly in the lowlands of the east. Sheep are kept mainly on areas of poorer soils and grass, such as the Pennines, the southwest, and the Lake District. Some sheep are also raised in the south, mainly on the Downs and adjacent lowland areas. Pig and poultry raising are also important. England's farms produce enough poultry, meat, and eggs to meet the country's needs.

The development and patterns of English farming have been greatly influenced by British membership in the European Economic Community since 1972. The community has a common agricultural policy to which member countries must adhere. Types and quantities of crops grown and their prices are strongly affected by these rules. Certain crops and farming activities are encouraged by subsidies and price supports.

England's location encouraged the development of the fishing industry, now one of the most important in Europe. The principal English fishing ports are Grimsby, North Shields, Fleetwood, Hull, and Lowestoft. Some of England's fishing fleets operate in distant waters off Newfoundland, Greenland, and northern Norway.

Tourism

Tourism is an important branch of the economy. More than 12 million foreign tourists arrive annually in Great Britain. The majority comes to England, though some tourists may only pass through on their way to Scotland or Wales. About two thirds of the visitors come from Western European countries and about 20 percent from North America. London is by far the most visited city. The English Tourist Board is a government-supported agency that promotes tourism by advertising, publishing promotional literature, and encouraging the improvement of tourist accommodations, restaurants, and other amenities.

The English themselves are great travelers, and there are many travel agencies. The biggest of these is Thomas Cook, founded in the 1850s as the first travel agency in the world. In recent years more than 20 million British people have made trips abroad annually. Most travel in Europe, with France as the popular destination in summer and Spain in winter.

In the past most English travelers vacationed in the British Isles. A number of seaside resorts arose that catered to visitors from nearby urban areas. The major resorts for London were Brighton, Hastings, and others on the southern coast. Blackpool served the industrial northwest and Hartlepool the north.

Transportation

England has a dense transportation network consisting of railroads, highways, canals, pipelines, and airways. The railroad as a form of transportation had its birth in England with the opening in 1830 of the first passenger line from Manchester to Liverpool. By World War I the railroad network covered most of the country. The railroad dominated transportation until World War II, but in the 1950s motor transportation became a serious competitor. In 1963 the government began to close many uneconomical rail lines. At present the total length of the rail system is 10,540 miles (16,960 kilometers) compared with 19,690 miles (31,690 kilometers) in 1950. About 2,330 miles (3,750 kilometers) of this network are electrified, but most trains are pulled by diesel locomotives. The railroads are state-owned and are run by British Rail.

More than 80 percent of freight is moved by highway, about 15 percent by rail. Almost 85 percent of passenger traffic also moves by road. The biggest increase in highway traffic took place after the construction of the first motorway, or four-lane highway, in 1958. Motorways now total about 1,726 miles (2,778 kilometers) of the total highway network of 227,760 miles (366,534 kilometers). The motorways have improved links between major cities and have improved access to more remote parts of the country. Because of high costs, there has been little major road construction since the 1970s. In recent years several road tunnels and bridges have been built, including a bridge over the Humber River that opened in 1981.

Most motor freight is carried by small private truck operators. Most passengers who travel by road go by private automobile, but those who go by bus are usually carried by the state-owned National Bus Company and its subsidiaries. These companies operate both local buses and long-distance coaches, as they are known in England.

During the Industrial Revolution a number of canals were dug to provide a system of low-cost transportation. This system is now hardly used except for recreation. The only waterways still used to any extent for commercial purposes are the River Thames and associated waterways and the Manchester Ship Canal.

England depends on overseas trade and has a large merchant marine. The British merchant fleet is the sixth largest in the world. About half of the fleet by weight consists of oil tankers. In common with other developed countries, England has been affected by the recent decrease in demand for shipping, and many ships have been scrapped or sold. The tonnage of the fleet has dropped by about one third since 1975.

The most important English port in terms of tonnage handled is London, followed closely by Tees and Harlepool in the northeast and Grimsby and Immingham on the Humber River. Other ports of note are Southampton, Manchester (with its ship canal), and Liverpool. The leading ports that handle passenger traffic are Dover, Folkestone, Southampton, and Newhaven. These south coast ports are well located for cross-channel ferry traffic to France and Belgium. Harwich on the east coast is the main port for ferry services to The Netherlands.

The English were among the pioneers in the development of aviation. To serve a widely dispersed empire, Imperial Airways was founded in 1924. The main airline today is British Airways, formerly state-owned but now a private company. Its network is one of the largest in the world. British Airways uses, among other planes, the supersonic Concorde aircraft, developed in cooperation with France and first operational in 1976. The Concorde flies from London to New York City and to Washington, D.C. Other airlines include British Caledonian, British Midland, Air UK, and Dan-Air Services, which is mainly a charter company.

London's Heathrow Airport is the world's busiest for international flights and is used by British Airways. The other British airlines mainly use Gatwick Airport to the south of London, which is the world's fifth busiest airport. Other important airports are Manchester, Birmingham, and Luton (north of London).

Because of its relatively small size, internal air travel in England is rather limited. Trains compete effectively with air travel in terms of both fares and time. This makes it possible for businessmen and other travelers to commute from city to city easily.

Communication

Radio and television broadcasting in Great Britain is controlled by two public organizations—the British Broadcasting Corporation (BBC) and the Independent Broadcasting Authority (IBA). These bodies must adhere to guidelines set down by Parliament, but they are independent from government control in their daily operations. Domestic services of the BBC are paid for by the people, when they buy a required annual license for the ownership of a television set. The IBA contracts with a number of companies to offer television programs in different regions of the country. These companies get most of their money from commercial advertising. The BBC does not carry advertising.

The English are great newspaper readers: there are more than 100 daily papers and a large number of weekly ones. The quality of reporting and coverage of the news varies greatly. The most popular newspapers—*The Sun*, *Daily Mirror*, *Daily Express*, and *Daily Mail*—often offer a somewhat sensational view of the news. The *Daily Telegraph*, *The Times*, and *The Guardian*, on the other hand, are noted for their high standards of reporting and their accuracy. Most newspapers have special Sunday editions. Several support political parties and reflect their views.

Until 1981 the Post Office ran the telephone and telegraph services as well as a savings bank. Since then the telephone and telegraph services have come under the control of British Telecommunications (British Telecom), which is now a private corporation. The Post Office handles the mail, acts as the agent for the National Savings Bank, and provides a number of other services for the public.

J. Allan Cash Ltd.

Stonehenge, the prehistoric monument on the Salisbury Plain, dates from between 1850 and 1400 BC.

HISTORY

Long ages ago the British Isles formed a peninsula of continental Europe, and the English Channel was a broad plain. People and animals from southern Europe traveled across this plain and made their home in the dense forests that then covered Britain. The people belonged to the earliest stage of civilization, the Old Stone Age. They moved over the damp green woodland, stone ax in hand, hunting mammoths, horses, and reindeer. They lived in caves, had no domestic animals, and took no care of their dead.

Over an immense stretch of time the land subsided, and Ireland was separated from Britain. Later the sea flowed into the narrow Strait of Dover and made Britain also an island. New waves of colonists crossed over from the east. The people advanced slowly to the New Stone Age. In this period they mined flints for their weapons and polished them to give a sharp cutting edge. They laid away their dead in long or round chambers called barrows and heaped over them mounds of earth and stone. The remains found in these barrows reveal that these people tamed horses, sheep, goats, cattle, dogs, and pigs and grew wheat and barley and, later, flax to make linen.

Later, sea merchants from countries bordering the Mediterranean discovered the islands in the northern seas. The Phoenicians, who traded with many lands, came again and again to buy tin, which lay close to the surface in Cornwall. The native people learned how to smelt tin with copper to make bronze tools and weapons. With this knowledge the long Stone Age ended and the Age of Bronze began. The people of Britain erected avenues and circles of huge granite slabs, like those at Stonehenge. These were probably temples.

Celtic Domination

Some five or six centuries before the birth of Christ, a tall fair people called Celts came across the channel in small boats. The Goidels, or Gaels (who are still found in Ireland and in the Highlands of Scotland), formed the first great migration. Then came the Brythons, or Britons (still found in Wales and Cornwall), who gave their name to the island of Britain. The Celts knew how to smelt iron and were skilled in arts and crafts. They became the ruling class, and the native folk adopted the Celtic language and the Celts' Druid religion. (*See also* Celts.)

Roman Rule

Julius Caesar raided Britain in 55 BC and again in 54 BC. Nearly 90 years later Rome undertook the conquest of the island in earnest. In AD 43 Emperor Claudius gathered a force of about 40,000 to invade the island. All the area that is now England was soon subdued and added to the Roman Empire as the province Britannia.

A widowed Celtic queen, golden-haired Boadicea, led a great uprising against the Romans in AD 61, but her barbarian horde was no match for the Roman soldiers. The people of Scotland were harder to subdue. Emperor Hadrian decided conquering them was not worth the trouble, so he had a wall built 100 miles (160 kilometers) long across the narrow neck of the island to keep them out. South of this wall the Romans built more than 50 cities and connected them with military roads. Some of these roads, such as the famous Watling Street, still serve as the foundations for modern highways.

The cities contained Roman baths and open-air theaters; temples to Jupiter, Mars, and Minerva; and houses with colonnaded terraces, mosaic floors, and hot-air furnaces. Upper-class Britons in the towns spoke Latin and wore the Roman toga. Commerce and industry prospered, protected by Roman law. Later, when Rome became Christian, Roman missionaries spread Christian teachings in Britain.

In AD 410 the Goths swept down on Rome, and no more Roman legions came to protect Britannia. The Britons, left to themselves, were unable to form a government. Local chieftains warred with one another. Barbarians from Scotland and pirates from Ireland ravaged the land. In vain a Briton wrote for aid to a Roman consul, saying: "The barbarians drive us to the sea; the sea throws us back on the barbarians."

Anglo-Saxon Invasions

Soon a more dangerous enemy appeared. Across the North Sea came bands of pirates in long black ships. They were of Teuton (German) stock—Angles, Saxons, and Jutes—from the region of modern Denmark. They found the island easy to invade. In the south and west a low coast thrusts out toward the continent. From the coast navigable rivers lead inland across a rolling plain. The land itself, covered with green the year round, seemed miraculous. Centuries later people learned that the British Isles, so far north, owe their mild climate to the warm Gulf Stream.

The invaders plundered city after city and drove the Britons ever farther westward. Farmers and herdsmen followed in the wake of the warriors. The newcomers were pagans, worshipers of Odin and Thor, and had no use for Roman cities or Roman law (*see* Mythology). They cleared the forests to make farmland and built longhouses grouped around the large log hall of their chief, which was decorated with carving and paint and hung with shining armor.

By the year 600 the ruin of Rome's Britannia was complete. The original Celtic stock survived only in the mountains of Wales and in Cornwall. Except in these areas Christianity and the Celtic language died. Britain came to be called Angle-land (later England) after the Angles, and the people spoke Anglo-Saxon (*see* English Language).

The small Anglo-Saxon tribes gradually merged into seven or eight little kingdoms. The Jutes, a small tribe, held the Isle of Wight and land to the north. The Saxons established themselves in Wessex on the south coast. The Angles ruled Mercia in the Midlands, East Anglia on the east coast, and Northumbria in the northeast. When a king died an assembly called the Witan, meaning "wise men," chose a new king from the royal family.

Mission of Augustine

In the year 597 Augustine, an Italian monk, landed with 40 followers on the coast of Kent. He had been sent by Pope Gregory I to win the Angles to the Christian faith. He baptized Ethelbert, king of Kent, repaired the old Roman church at Canterbury, and founded a Benedictine abbey there. The pope made him archbishop for his services. From that time on, the archbishop of Canterbury has been primate of the church in England (*see* Canterbury).

Christianity spread rapidly. Learned monks brought to England a knowledge of architecture, law, philosophy, and Latin. A new civilization began to take shape, but it was checked by another invasion.

Danes Invade England

The new invaders were Scandinavians from Norway and Denmark (*see* Vikings). The English called them Danes. Summer after summer these bold pirates rowed up the rivers in their longboats, plundered the rich monasteries, and went home with the gold and gems. Soon after 850 a great force remained in England, bent on conquest. Then permanent settlers poured in. The Danes were farmers and traders as well as warriors. When they founded a town—usually a port—they fortified it and opened a market. All of eastern England north of the Thames passed under the rule of the Danish jarls, or earls, and came to be known as the Danelaw, the part under Danish law.

The Danes would probably have wiped out Christianity in England if it had not been for Alfred the Great, king of Wessex. Alfred defeated the Danes' great army at Chippenham in 878 and forced the Danish leader to sign a treaty agreeing to leave Wessex free. The Danes promised also to be baptized, and many did become Christians. Alfred began English prose literature by translating Latin books into Anglo-Saxon. He also built schools and ordered the 'Anglo-Saxon Chronicle', the first historical record of England, to be begun. (*See also* Alfred the Great.)

A century after Alfred's time the Danes started once more to raid England's shores. In 991 the incompetent Ethelred the Unready tried to buy them off by paying them yearly a large sum in silver, called the Danegeld, or Dane tax, which was raised by a heavy tax on the people. Nevertheless the Danes came again, and in 1016 Canute, the king of Norway and Denmark, made himself king of England also. He proved to be a wise and strong ruler, but after his death his empire fell apart, and in 1042 the Danish dynasty in England ended. (*See also* Canute the Great.)

The English line then returned to the throne with Edward, son of Ethelred. He had been reared by French monks and was called The Confessor.

Norman Conquest (1066)

While the Danes were invading England, other Norsemen raided the coast of France. On the southern shore of the English Channel they established the Duchy of Normandy. These Norsemen, or Normans, became French in language and culture. In the 11th century Normandy was rich, populous, and powerful.

When Edward the Confessor died childless, William, duke of Normandy, claimed the English crown. He was a second cousin of Edward, and he had exacted an oath from Harold, earl of Wessex, to support his claim. The English Witan nevertheless elected Harold king. William appealed to the pope. The pope supported William and declared Harold guilty of perjury.

William gathered together a "host of horsemen, slingers, and archers" and set sail for England. Harold met him with foot soldiers armed with battle-axes. The two armies clashed in the famous battle of Hastings on Oct. 14, 1066. Harold was killed on the battlefield. The victorious William went up to London and was crowned king of England in Westminster Abbey on Christmas Day. (*See also* Harold, Kings of England; William, Kings of England; Hastings, Battle of.)

Feudal System Under William I

For five years William I was busy putting down revolts in his new kingdom. He seized the land of all Saxons who fought against him and distributed it among his Norman followers—except for vast tracts that he kept for himself as crown lands. On his own estates and on those of favored barons he ordered strong fortified castles built.

In return for the grant of land—called a fief—each lord had to swear loyalty to the king, furnish

The finest group of Roman ruins in England are these baths built in about AD 54, using waters from a hot spring. Victorian columns and parapets were added in the 18th century, when Bath reached its zenith as England's fashionable watering place.

BBC Hulton Picture Library

Every town had to be a fortress in the Middle Ages. Within the thick walls the houses were crowded close together. This is a typical 11th-century English town.

knights for the king's army, attend the king's court, and aid the king with money on certain occasions. Farmers were reduced to the class of serfs, or *villeins*, as the Normans called them. A villein could not leave the manor on which he was born. This system of land tenure was the basis of *feudalism*, which held sway all over Europe in the Middle Ages. (*See also* Feudalism; Knighthood; Middle Ages.)

The efficiency of William's rule is shown by the survey he had made of all the property in England. His agents visited every manor, found out who owned it, how many people lived there, and reported what the feudal lord ought to pay the king in taxes and feudal service. The findings were recorded in the famous Domesday Book. It was called Domesday (day of doom) because no one could escape its judgment.

The date of the Norman Conquest—1066—is one of the most important dates in English history. The Conquest cut England's ties with Scandinavia and connected England with France. French, the language of the Norman rulers, became blended with the Anglo-Saxon speech of the common people, enriching the native language with many new words and ideas. Wooden churches and abbeys were replaced with beautiful stone buildings in the Norman style. Foreign monks and bishops, brought in by the Normans, made the monasteries centers of learning. Anyone who wanted to study went into the church as a matter of course. The king's secretaries, judges, and most of his civil servants were churchmen, because only churchmen had the necessary education.

When he was crowned, William I, the Conqueror, promised to govern according to the laws of Edward the Confessor. The Witan survived in his great council of advisers, the *curia regis*, which was attended by earls, barons, bishops, and abbots; but the council no longer had the power to choose the king. As feudal overlord of the whole country, William bequeathed England to his second son, William II. He left Normandy to his eldest son, Robert.

William II, Henry I, and Stephen

William II (called William Rufus, the "Red King") came to the throne in 1087. He was a harsh ruler and few mourned him when he was killed by an arrow—shot by an unknown hand—while he was hunting (*see* William II). Robert had gone off on the First Crusade, to recover the Holy Land from the Turks. A

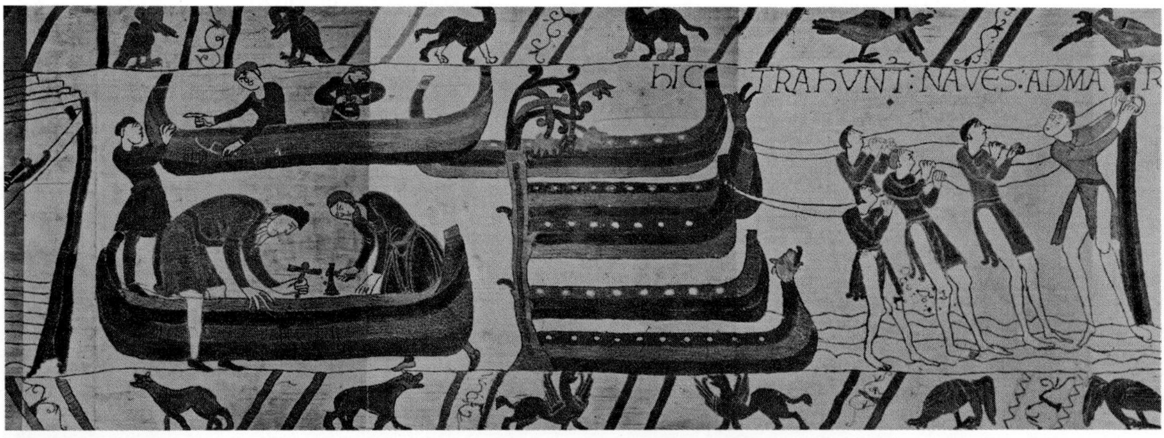

The Bayeux tapestry is not a woven tapestry, but a strip of linen 230 feet long and 20 inches wide on which many scenes are embroidered. One tradition holds that the embroidery was stitched by Queen Matilda, wife of William the Conqueror. An-

third son, Henry I, was therefore able to become king without a struggle, in 1100. When Robert returned, Henry crossed the Channel, defeated him, and gained Normandy also. He gave both England and western France a peaceful, orderly rule (*see* Henry I).

Henry I exacted a promise from the barons to recognize his daughter Matilda as their ruler. However, when he died, some of the barons broke their promise and chose instead Stephen, a grandson of William the Conqueror. Stephen was a gallant knight but a weak king. Throughout his reign lawless barons fought private wars, each seeking to increase his power. When Stephen died (1154), the people were ready to welcome a strong ruler who would restore order.

Henry II Restores the Royal Power

The strong ruler was found in Henry Plantagenet, count of Anjou. His mother was Matilda (or Maud), daughter of Henry I of England; his father was Geoffrey of Anjou. He came to the throne of England as Henry II, first of the Plantagenet line of kings, who were to rule England for 245 years. By marriage and inheritance, he came into possession of all western France. He spent most of his long reign, 1154–89, in his French possessions; yet he became one of England's great rulers.

Henry II sent out trained justices (judges) *on circuit* to different towns in England to sit in the county courts. The judges kept records of their cases. When one judge had decided a case, other judges trying the same kind of case were likely to adopt the decision that had been recorded. In the course of years, legal principles came to be based on these decisions. Because this "case law" applied to all Englishmen equally, it came to be called the *common law*. The circuit justices also made more extensive use of juries and started the grand jury system in criminal law. (*See also* Jury; Law.)

Henry carried on a long and bitter struggle with Thomas Becket, archbishop of Canterbury, who asserted the independence of the church courts against the king's authority. The church triumphed when Becket was murdered. After making peace with the pope, Henry did penance at Becket's tomb. Becket became a sainted martyr, and for centuries people made pilgrimages to his shrine at Canterbury. (*See also* Henry II; Becket.)

Richard the Lion-Hearted, the brave and reckless son of Henry II, succeeded his father in 1189. After a few months he left England and went off on his long crusade. The country suffered little in his absence because Hubert Walter governed it better than Richard himself would have. (*See also* Richard I; Crusades.)

King John and Magna Carta

In 1199 Richard I was succeeded by his brother John, the most despicable of English kings. By a series of blunders John lost almost all his French possessions except the southwest corner. The English barons refused to help him regain his territory. Angered by his tyrannical rule, they drew up a list of things that even a king might not do. On June 15, 1215, they forced him to set his seal to this Great Charter (in Latin, Magna Carta) of English liberties.

Magna Carta is regarded as one of the most notable documents in history. The rights it listed were, in the main, feudal rights of justice and property that had been recognized by previous kings; but now for the first time these rights were insisted upon against the king's will. Thus an important principle was established—that the king himself must govern according to law. In later years, whenever a king overextended his powers, the people could remind him of Magna Carta. (*See also* John; Magna Carta.)

The Rise of Parliament

Henry III, John's eldest son, was crowned at the age of nine and ruled 56 years, 1216–72. He was pious and well meaning but incompetent and extravagant. The barons took a strong stand against him in Parliament. (The term *parliament* was gradually coming into

other says the work was commissioned by William's half brother, Bishop Odo. These pictures show Norman workmen building and loading Viking ships for the channel crossing. Animals in the borders are mythical and real.

use for the Great Council.) In 1264 the barons, led by Simon de Montfort, rose against the king and brought on the Barons' Wars. These wars ended when Earl Simon was killed in battle. (*See also* Henry III; Montfort.)

Henry III's son, Edward I, who ruled from 1272 to 1307, wisely accepted the limitations on the king's authority. His parliament of 1295 is called the Model Parliament because it included representatives of both shires and towns as well as the Great Council. Many of the laws passed in Edward's reign exist in modified form today.

Edward I conquered Wales and joined it to England but failed in his effort to subdue Scotland. He died on his way north to put down an uprising led by the Scottish hero Robert Bruce. His incompetent son, Edward II, then took up the task and was decisively defeated by Bruce at Bannockburn. In 1327 Parliament used its new power to depose Edward II and place his son, Edward III, on the throne. (*See also* Edward, Kings of England.)

Flowering of English Medieval Life

The 13th century was a time of great enthusiasm for art and learning. In architecture the low square towers and round arches of the Norman period gave place to the delicate spires and pointed arches of the Early English, or Gothic, style. New learning was brought into England by friars and other scholars from the Continent. Oxford University won renown all over Europe. One of its teachers, Roger Bacon, a friar, urged the study of nature and the experimental method in seeking knowledge, but the world was not yet ready for science. The Crusades opened commerce with the Orient and brought in new ideas.

Towns became noted for particular manufactures. Craft guilds held a monopoly of manufacture, and merchant guilds controlled local markets. Foreign merchants were allowed to sell their wares only at certain annual fairs. (For information on the growth of towns, crafts, and guilds, *see* Middle Ages. *See also* Architecture; Bacon, Roger; Guild.)

The Hundred Years' War and the Black Death

Knighthood was still in flower while Edward III was on the English throne from 1327 to 1377. The king himself excelled in "beautiful feats of arms." He soon had a chance to prove his skill. During his reign began the long struggle with France called the Hundred Years' War. In 1346 Edward's army won a brilliant victory at Crécy with a new English weapon, the longbow. The next year Edward took Calais, a French seaport. In 1356 his son, the Black Prince, won the famous battle of Poitiers. (*See also* Knighthood; Hundred Years' War.)

The war was brought to a temporary halt when the Black Death swept over Western Europe in 1348–49. When the great plague had spent its fury, more than a fourth of England's population had perished. Whole villages were wiped out, and great areas of farmland went to weeds. The serfs who survived demanded high money wages. If their lord refused, they moved to another manor. The government tried to halt the rise in wages and bind the laborers to their manors

Two serfs and four oxen were needed to operate the clumsy plow in the top picture. Oxen were lightweight animals in medieval times. Workhorses were rare. In the lower illustration a horse is pulling a harrow. The harrow is shown as if it were standing on its side. The pictures are from a 14th-century illuminated manuscript, the Luttrell Psalter.

once more, but it could not enforce its Statute of Laborers. The landlords sought labor at any price, and the laborers formed combinations (what would now be called unions) to resist the law. John Wycliffe's "poor priests" (Lollards) and other traveling preachers increased the discontent by denouncing the landlords. (*See also* Wycliffe.)

Richard II, grandson of Edward III, was 14 years old when a great band of peasants, headed by Wat Tyler and John Ball, marched on London (1381) from Kent. The boy king went out boldly to meet them. "I am your king," he said, "I will be your leader." "We will that you make us free forever," the peasants asked. Richard promised to help them, and they returned peaceably to their homes. The king did not keep his promise. Within a week the judges hanged 1,500 ringleaders of the revolt (*see* Tyler, Wat). The feudal system of villenage, however, could not be revived. The serfs were gradually giving place to a new class of farmers—free yeomen.

Built by William I, Windsor Castle was extended by Henry III and Edward III. Its present appearance dates from restorations under George IV.

Richard II thirsted for absolute rule and came into conflict with the powerful barons. His cousin Henry, duke of Lancaster, led a revolt against him in 1399, imprisoned him in the Tower of London, and compelled him to abdicate. Parliament then placed Henry on the throne of England as Henry IV. (*See also* Richard II.)

The House of Lancaster ruled England only 62 years, 1399–1461. During this period three Henrys—father, son, and grandson—wore the crown. Their reigns were filled with plots and rebellions, murders and executions. Parliament had made them kings, and they needed its support to keep the throne. They therefore consulted it on all affairs. (*See also* Henry IV; Henry V; Henry VI.)

The End of the Middle Ages in England

In 1455, two years after the Hundred Years' War ended, the House of York and the House of Lancaster plunged into a long and bloody struggle for the crown called the Wars of the Roses. Henry VI, of the House of Lancaster, was captured and murdered. Edward IV, of the House of York, spent most of his reign fighting to keep his crown. The last Yorkist king, Richard III, gained the throne when Edward's sons were declared not to be the rightful heirs. Peace came with Richard's death in the battle of Bosworth Field. The date of Richard's death—1485—may well be used to mark the close of the Middle Ages in English history. (*See also* Roses, Wars of the; Edward IV; Edward V; Richard III.)

The Wars of the Roses were the death throes of the feudal system. Battles and executions thinned the ranks of the nobles, and their fortified castles were no longer impregnable after the invention of gunpowder. A new aristocracy was pushing up through the broken crust of feudal society. In the towns a rich capitalist class appeared. Country squires—the landed "gentry"—also grew wealthy. The new aristocracy began to seek political power.

England was now the chief cloth-exporting country in the world. Enterprising employers, tired of the restrictions of the guild system, supplied wool to farmers and villagers to be spun and made up into cloth. This method of manufacture was called the "domestic system." It grew steadily and caused the breakup of the guild system. Serfdom also gradually died out. The gentry leased their land to yeomen who paid money wages to their free laborers.

French, the speech of the governing classes, had become blended with Anglo-Saxon into an English speech somewhat similar to the language used today. The great poet Geoffrey Chaucer wrote in this English and the Bible was translated into it (*see* Chaucer). These works were among the first printed by William Caxton, who brought a printing press to England from Belgium in 1476. Printing made it possible for many more people to have books and helped spread the New Learning of the Renaissance (*see* Renaissance). Before the 15th century ended, Spanish and Portuguese explorers had opened up new continents across the Atlantic Ocean.

Henry VII, First of the Tudors

After a century of wars, England now enjoyed a century of almost unbroken peace under the Tudors (*see* Tudor). When this strong dynasty ended, Eng-

HAMPTON COURT PALACE AND CHESTER'S "ROWS"

This magnificent palace was built by Cardinal Wolsey and presented to his sovereign, Henry VIII. It attracts throngs of visitors daily.

These fine old Tudor buildings are in Chester. Open galleries form a continuous passage, called a "row," above the ground-floor shops.

land was a modern nation and had taken the first steps on the road to empire.

Henry VII, first of the Tudor line, became king by defeating and slaying Richard III in the battle of Bosworth Field (1485). He crushed the barons and made Parliament once more obedient to the king's will. Only the medieval church, still wealthy and powerful, remained an obstacle to his authority. He was popular with the "commons"—the middle classes in town and country—because he built up an orderly government, aided commerce and industry, and kept the country at peace and out of debt. With his encouragement, John Cabot in 1497 piloted an English ship across the Atlantic Ocean to Newfoundland, five years after Columbus discovered the New World. (*See also* Henry VII; Cabot.)

The English Reformation

Henry VIII, ruled 1509–47, is famous as the king who had six wives in succession. When he put aside his first wife, Catherine of Aragon, the pope excommunicated him. Henry, enraged, had Parliament cut the ties that bound the English church to the papacy (1534) and forced the English clergy to acknowledge the king rather than the pope as the "only supreme head of the Church of England."

Henry's quarrel with the pope was made easier by the Protestant Reformation, then sweeping over Europe (*see* Reformation). Yet Henry all his life claimed to be a devout Roman Catholic. He burned Protestants at the stake almost as readily as he hanged and beheaded the "traitors" who upheld the pope. His attack on the papacy was prompted in part by greed. By dissolving the monasteries he was able to seize their immense wealth in lands and buildings and the costly ornaments of the shrines. He used some of his new riches to fortify the coasts and build England's first real navy. At his death the royal fleet numbered 71 vessels, some of which were fitted out with cannon. (*See also* Henry VIII.)

Henry VIII's only son, Edward VI, was ten years old when he came to the throne (1547), and he died at the age of 16 (*see* Edward VI). The Lord Protectors who ruled in his stead favored the Protestant cause. They forbade the Catholics to hold Mass and required Thomas Cranmer's English Prayer Book to be read instead of the Latin Mass.

These laws were speedily repealed when Mary, daughter of Henry VIII and Catherine of Aragon, ascended the throne (*see* Mary I). Mary had been brought up in the Catholic faith and she held resolutely to it.

Elizabeth I and England's Golden Age

Elizabeth I, Mary's half sister, in turn repealed Mary's laws. In her reign the Church of England took the form it has today. It kept the

Catholic governmental organization of archbishops, bishops, and deans, but it rejected the headship of the pope. It permitted the clergy to marry, and it again ordered the reading of the English Prayer Book. Many people accepted this "middle way." But it was bitterly opposed by the Roman Catholics ("Papists"), and also by the extreme Protestants ("Puritans"), who insisted on a simpler, "purer" form of service with no "Popish rites."

The long reign of Elizabeth I, 1558–1603, was England's Golden Age. The Renaissance, which began in Italy in the 14th century, at last reached the northern island. "Merry England," in love with life, expressed itself in music and literature, in architecture, and in adventurous seafaring. William Shakespeare, poet and dramatist, mirrored the age in verse that lifted the English language to its fullest beauty. (*See also* Elizabeth I; English Literature; Shakespeare.)

Throughout the land could be heard the sound of hammers and saws of builders—a sure sign of prosperity. Elizabethan manor houses, usually built around an open court, blended the English style with the new Italian. English glassworks supplied small clear panes for lattice windows. The increasing use of brick made it easier to build chimneys and fireplaces even for common houses.

Exploration; Defeat of the Spanish Armada

English seamanship and shipbuilding reached the highest point they had yet attained. Francis Drake sailed around the world. Walter Raleigh made the first attempt to found an English colony in America. These and other courageous "privateers" reaped rich rewards—chiefly at the expense of Spain—from plundering, piracy, smuggling, and the slave trade. Elizabeth encouraged them on the ground that they protected Protestant England against Catholic Spain. (*See also* America; Drake; Raleigh.)

The defeat of the Spanish Armada (1588) established the superiority of English ships and sailors and made the English conscious of their ocean destiny (*see* Armada). English merchants began to seek distant markets for their goods. In 1600 the now old queen chartered the famous East India Company, giving it a monopoly of trade with the Far East. From this small start Britain's Indian Empire was to grow.

Unemployment and Poor Relief

Not all classes shared in the increasing prosperity. The population had doubled since the Black Death and now numbered about 4 million. There was land hunger again. The growth of the cloth industry increased the demand for wool and made it profitable for the landowners to turn farmlands into pasture. They fenced in ("enclosed") the pastures with hedgerows. "Where 40 persons had their livings," the laborers complained, "now one man and his shepherd hath all." Men thrown out of work by the enclosures became vagabonds and terrorized the townfolk. Whipping the "sturdy beggars" failed to solve the problem.

Throughout the Middle Ages the monasteries had given alms to the poor. Now that the monasteries were no more, the government took over the task. Elizabeth's famous statute of 1601, an Act for the Relief of the Poor, required every parish to levy *rates* (local taxes) for poor relief. Children were to be put out as apprentices if their parents could not support them. Wages of artisans and farm laborers were fixed by law. All able-bodied men were compelled to work. They could no longer move freely from place to place. They were practically serfs again, except that they had no rights in the land.

Birth of the British Empire

The Tudor dynasty came to an end when Elizabeth I died in 1603. The crown of England then passed to the Stuart line of Scotland (*see* Stuart). The new king was called James VI in Scotland and James I in England. The two countries, having the same ruler, were now bound together in a personal union, but for another century they had separate parliaments.

James boldly announced that he would rule as an absolute monarch, responsible to God alone. This view of monarchy was called the *divine right of kings*. It was generally accepted on the continent of Europe, but it ran counter to the nature of the English people. Parliament resisted James at every point. By insisting that all people conform to the Church of

Edward V and his younger brother Richard were murdered in the Tower of London. This painting is by Sir J. E. Millais.

England, he won the enmity of the Puritans and the Catholics. A small band of Catholic extremists, including Guy Fawkes, formed the Gunpowder Plot to blow up king and parliament together (*see* Fawkes).

James allowed the navy to decay and suppressed privateering. Yet it was in his reign that colonial expansion began and the British Empire was born. The colony of Jamestown, Virginia, was started in 1607. In 1620 the Pilgrims landed on the rocky shore of New England. Other colonists swiftly followed. Some went to escape religious persecution and some to find free land. They spread English civilization into the wilderness. (*See also* America, Discovery and Colonization of.)

Under Charles I, who ruled 1625–49, active colonization continued. Charles was glad to have the troublesome Puritans leave England. Great wealth flowed into London from American tobacco, the African slave traffic, and the silks and spices of India.

England's Civil War

Charles was as obstinate a despot as his father. In 1629 he dissolved Parliament, determined to rule by himself alone. Eleven years later he became involved in a war with Scotland and was obliged to summon Parliament to raise money for his armies. When Parliament refused to vote the money, Charles dissolved it. Before the year ended he summoned it again. This time Parliament forced the king to agree not to dissolve it without its consent. It lasted, with some interruptions, from 1640 to 1659 and is known as the Long Parliament.

Puritans dominated the House of Commons. Instead of aiding the king, they passed laws to curb his power. The king went in person to the House, determined to arrest five of its leaders, but "the birds had flown." Parliament issued a call to arms, a revolutionary act. The powerful new middle class put its great resources behind the Puritans. The king rallied the royalist aristocracy, High Church Anglicans, and the Catholics to his standard.

The Parliamentary army went into battle singing psalms. In 1644 the Puritans defeated Charles's "Cavaliers" at Marston Moor. In this battle Oliver Cromwell, the Puritan leader, won the name "Ironsides." The next year he gained a decisive victory at Naseby.

In 1648 Colonel Pride, a Puritan, stood at the entrance to the Commons with a force of soldiers and allowed only "Roundheads" to enter. (The Puritans were called Roundheads because they cut their hair short. The Cavaliers wore long flowing locks.) The group that remained after "Pride's Purge" was called the "Rump Parliament."

The Rump sentenced Charles to execution, and he was beheaded on Jan. 30, 1649 (*see* Charles I). The Rump then declared England a Commonwealth (that is, a republic), without a king or a house of lords.

The Commonwealth and the Protectorate

The Rump Parliament governed England while Cromwell put down revolts in Ireland and Scotland with great cruelty. In 1653 he came back from the wars, dismissed Parliament, and "nominated" a Parliament of his own (called "Barebone's Parliament" after one of its members, Praisegod Barebone). The Commonwealth then took the name of Protectorate, with Cromwell as Lord Protector (*see* Cromwell).

The Puritans closed the theaters, suppressed horse racing, cockfighting, and bearbaiting, and made Sunday strictly a day of worship. Cromwell's rule was more despotic than the king's. Yet the revolution accomplished its purpose. When the monarchy was revived it became a limited monarchy. The Church of England never again tried to include all Englishmen.

When Cromwell died in 1658 his eldest son, Richard Cromwell, became Lord Protector. Too weak to control the army, "Tumbledown Dick" resigned the next year. In 1660 George Monk, one of Cromwell's generals, brought an army from Scotland and had the Rump of the Long Parliament recalled to dissolve itself. A new Parliament was elected and at once offered the crown to the exiled son of Charles I.

England Under the Restoration

The people of London joyously welcomed Charles II when he arrived from France with the gay court of Cavaliers that had been exiled with him (*see* Charles II). The bleak Puritan age was suddenly ended. Theaters opened again. Footlights, curtains, and

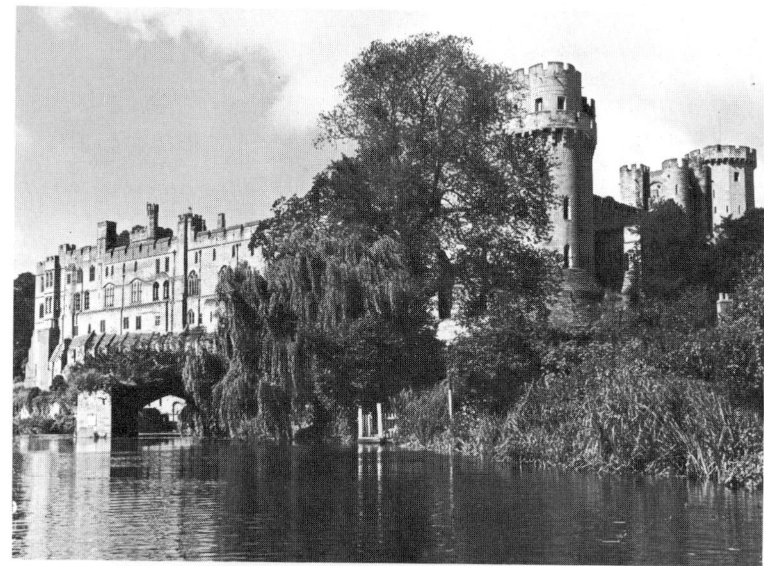

Warwick Castle, overlooking the Avon River, was last used for defense in the Civil War. The castle's exterior is an example of 14th-century fortifications. Inside the castle is a luxurious 17th-century mansion.

painted scenery were introduced. For the first time women appeared on the stage. Restoration dramatists delighted Londoners with sparkling comedies that laughed at Puritan virtues. John Dryden best represented the Restoration period. Its greatest poet, however, was still the Puritan John Milton, who had faithfully served Cromwell. Now blind, he retired from public life to write the greatest epic in the English language, 'Paradise Lost'. (*See also* Dryden; Milton; Drama; English Literature.)

These charming half-timber houses in London are typical of the Elizabethan period. The street ends at Blackfriars' Stairs, from which a ferryboat carried passengers across the Thames River. In the background is old Saint Paul's Cathedral, which was destroyed in the Great Fire of 1666.

England's greatest architect, Sir Christopher Wren, rebuilt St. Paul's Cathedral, following London's Great Fire of 1666 (*see* Wren, Christopher). Science flourished along with the arts. Isaac Newton formulated laws of the universe (*see* Newton). An observatory was established at Greenwich.

Catholics fared somewhat better than Puritans under Charles II. His "Cavalier Parliament" in 1662 passed an Act of Uniformity depriving of their offices all clergymen who did not accept everything in the Anglican Prayer Book. This act tended to throw all nonconformists (Independents, Presbyterians, Baptists, and the new Quaker sect) into a single class, called "dissenters." To make things easier for Catholics, Charles issued a "Declaration of Indulgence" in 1672. Parliament forced him to retract this and passed a Test Act (1673), which made it impossible for Catholics to hold public office.

The Birth of Political Parties

Charles II leaned toward Catholicism. His brother James, heir to the throne, was an avowed Catholic. In 1679 an "Exclusion Bill" was presented in Parliament to bar James from the kingship. Charles prevented its passage by dissolving Parliament. The governing classes at once split into bitter factions—the Tories, who opposed the bill, and the Whigs, who favored it. Thus were born the first great political parties in history.

The names *Whig* and *Tory* were both terms of derision. Tory was Irish slang for a "popish" outlaw. Whig was a term of contempt in Scotland for a fanatic Presbyterian. The Tories, descended from the Cavaliers, represented the landed aristocracy. They upheld the divine right of kings and the Anglican church. The Whigs, descended from the Roundheads, represented the commercial classes of the cities. They championed Parliament against the king and urged toleration for nonconformists.

Following the decline of Spanish and Portuguese sea power, the Dutch Netherlands became a serious rival of England in the Far East, in Africa, and in America. In the 17th century England fought three commercial wars against the Dutch (1652–54, 1665–67, and 1672–74). The Netherlands then dropped out of the race for world commerce and American dominions. In the third war the English joined forces with the French—not yet aware that France was to be the next rival England had to face.

The "Glorious Revolution" of 1688

Charles II died in 1685, and his brother, James II, stepped quietly to the throne. However, when a male heir to James was born, in 1688, Tory and Whig leaders joined together and decided to set aside the Catholic line of kings. They invited Mary, a daughter of James, and her Dutch husband, William of Orange, to occupy the throne as joint sovereigns. When William arrived from Holland, James fled to the continent. (*See also* James II; William III; Mary II.)

Parliament was careful to lay down conditions for the new sovereigns. William and Mary accepted its Declaration of Rights, and Parliament speedily enacted it into law as the famous Bill of Rights (*see* Bill of Rights). The act made the king responsible to Parliament and subject to the laws and provided that henceforth no Roman Catholic could wear England's crown. Parliament, and not inheritance or divine right, would determine the succession to the throne. This was the fruit of the so-called "Glorious Revolution"—a revolution without bloodshed. John Locke published a defense of the Revolution in which he proclaimed the supremacy of the legislative assembly as the voice of the people (*see* Locke, John).

The Struggle with France

While England was in the throes of revolution, France, under Louis XIV, was achieving a dominant

During England's Civil War, the Puritan Parliament brought Charles I to trial and convicted him of treason. He wears the ornate dress of a Cavalier as he walks to Whitehall, where he was beheaded in 1649. A Puritan marches ahead.

position in Europe. With internal conflict ended, England turned its attention abroad. In 1689 it joined with Holland and several German states in the War of the Grand Alliance against France. The war spread to America, where it was called King William's War. It marked the beginning of a long struggle to decide whether France or England was to control India and North America (*see* King William's War).

When William died, in 1702, Louis XIV proclaimed James Stuart, son of James II, king of England, Scotland, and Ireland. Parliament, however, had provided that if William and Mary had no children, the crown should pass to Anne, a Protestant, daughter of James II by his first wife. James Stuart kept up his claim to the throne for 65 years and became known as the Old Pretender. His son, Bonnie Prince Charlie, known as the Young Pretender, made an unsuccessful attempt to obtain the throne in 1745 (*see* Pretender).

Queen Anne's Reign

As soon as Anne came to the throne in 1702, England entered upon another war with France to break up a threatened combination of France and Spain. This was called in Europe the War of the Spanish Succession. In America it was known as Queen Anne's War. The Duke of Marlborough led the English, Dutch, and Germans to brilliant victories, and the Treaty of Utrecht (1713) gave England important territories (all Nova Scotia and Newfoundland) in the New World. (*See also* Queen Anne's War; Marlborough.)

Birth of the Kingdom of Great Britain

THE MOST notable event in Anne's reign was the union of England with Scotland. Since 1603 the two nations had been loosely associated under the same king. The Act of Union (1707) united them in a single kingdom, called Great Britain, and joined their parliaments. Thereafter the government and parliament in London were called British rather than English. (*See also* Scotland; United Kingdom.)

Walpole, Britain's First Prime Minister

The Stuart line came to an end when Anne died, since none of her 17 children survived her. She was succeeded in 1714 by the nearest Protestant heir, George I, a prince of the House of Hanover, a small state in Germany (*see* Hanover; George I). George did not speak English, and he was so wrapped up in his beloved Hanover that he took little interest in British affairs. He soon began to stay away from meetings of his inner council, or cabinet, and left the government in the hands of Sir Robert Walpole, the able Whig leader. George II, who ruled 1727–60, also stayed away from meetings of his ministers. Walpole made himself supreme in the government, selected his colleagues, and insisted they work with him or leave the cabinet. He thus became the first prime minister. (*See also* George II; Cabinet.)

Walpole promoted trade and commerce and strove to avoid war. But in 1739 the British people became aroused over the story of Robert Jenkins, a sea captain, who claimed the Spaniards had boarded his ship and cut off his ear. Walpole was persuaded to declare war against Spain in 1739—the War of Jenkins' Ear. He resigned when this war merged into another continental war, the War of the Austrian Succession, in America called King George's War (*see* King George's War; Austria-Hungary). When peace was made, in 1748, the real issue—whether France or Britain was to prevail in India and North America—was still unsettled.

Britain Wins French Territory

The struggle with France was renewed in the Seven Years' War, which broke out in 1756. This war brought to the fore a leader of genius, William Pitt, earl of Chatham. He carried on the struggle against France in America, Africa, and India, as well as in Europe and on the sea. The war cost France almost all its territory in North America and India and vastly extended Britain's empire. Horace Walpole wrote to Sir Horace Mann, in Italy: "You would not know your country again. You left it a private little island living upon its means. You will find it the capital of the world." (*See also* Seven Years' War; French and Indian War.)

The American Revolution

Before the Seven Years' War ended, George III began his 60-year reign, 1760–1820. Determined to "be a king" and quite unfit to be one, he got rid of Pitt and put his own Tory friends in power.

The Tory government imposed new taxes on the American Colonies. The colonists insisted the British Parliament had no right to tax them without their consent. Pitt and Edmund Burke counseled compromise (*see* Burke), but George III and his ministers obstinately insisted on their course. Troops were sent to enforce the decrees, and the colonists met force with force. On July 4, 1776, the Continental Congress adopted a Declaration of Independence. Two years later France entered the war on the side of the colonists. The Americans won their independence, and Britain lost the most valuable part of its colonial empire. (*See also* Revolution, American; Declaration of Independence; Stamp Act.)

George III's attempt at personal rule was now completely discredited. Parliament regained its leadership. William Pitt, second son of the earl of Chatham, became prime minister in 1783 and held the position for 17 years. (*See also* George III; Pitt.)

Britain's "Classical Age"

The numerous wars of the 18th century were fought with small professional armies and hardly disturbed the even tenor of life in the "fortunate isle." Even the loss of the American Colonies was little felt. Britain was still mistress of the seas, and its mariners and traders soon built a second empire greater than the old. Before the century ended, the French Revolution and the Industrial Revolution were to produce tremendous upheavals. Until the storm broke, Britain was quiet and settled.

The years 1740–80 were Britain's "classical age"—an age of art and elegance, of enlightenment and religious tolerance. Wealth and leisure became more widely diffused. In town and country the middle class put up comfortable, dignified homes in the Queen Anne and Georgian styles. Into them went furniture designed by Thomas Chippendale, Thomas Sheraton, and the Adam brothers, and beautiful china, glass, and silver plate made by skilled English handicraftsmen. The dress of the age was extravagant. Men wore bright-colored silk coats, waistcoats, and breeches; women appeared in hoopskirts and elaborate headdresses or high pompadours. The three great portrait painters of the age—Joshua Reynolds, Thomas Gainsborough, and George Romney—pictured the fashionable aristocrats, while William Hogarth caricatured both the fashionable and the common people.

Alexander Pope, a bitter satirist, was the leading poet of the age; but the most characteristic literary figure was Samuel Johnson, who gathered with other writers in London's coffeehouses to discuss and debate. (*See also* Adam; Chippendale; English Literature; Furniture; Gainsborough; Hogarth; Interior Design; Johnson, Samuel; Painting; Pope, Alexander; Reynolds.)

The government was little concerned with reform. Individuals, however, were showing a growing sensitivity to the wretched condition of the poor. Hundreds of charity schools, Sunday schools, and hospitals

Courtesy of the trustees of the British Museum

Hundreds of coffeehouses sprang up in London in the 18th century to serve the new drink brought in by ships of the East India Company. Every well-to-do Londoner had his favorite house. In some, writers and critics gathered; in others, politicians or businessmen. Ladies were not invited.

were founded, all at private expense. John Howard made prison reform his life's work (*see* Prisons). William Wilberforce set in motion a campaign that was to free the slaves in all the British colonies by 1833 (*see* Slavery). The new humanitarian spirit was quickened by the Methodist movement, a tremendous religious revival led by John Wesley (*see* Wesley).

The Industrial Revolution

Britain now entered upon the greatest revolution in all history—a revolution that was to spread over all the world. It began with inventions in the textile industry—John Kay's flying shuttle, to speed up weaving, and James Hargreave's spinning jenny, for making yarn. These inventions transformed the textile industry, which had seen almost no change for thousands of years. By 1781 James Watt had developed a steam engine to run these and other machines. During the next 15 years cotton manufactures trebled. The great Industrial Revolution was under way. (*See also* Industrial Revolution; Hargreaves; Watt.)

The revolution in agriculture also began in the 18th century. In the time of Queen Anne, British landowners began to devote their wealth and personal attention to improving methods of cultivation. On their enclosed fields they practiced scientific rotation of crops and pasture and new methods of draining, drilling, sowing, and fertilizing. They began to grow root crops (turnips and potatoes) in fields instead of in small gardens. By selective breeding and proper winter feeding of stock they doubled the average weight of cattle and sheep.

Improved Nutrition and Transportation

Fresh beef and mutton replaced salt meat in the winter diet. Scurvy and other skin diseases, prevalent in earlier centuries, grew rare even among the poor. The increasing knowledge of medicine combined with better nutrition to bring about a sharp drop in the death rate—from 33 in a thousand in 1830 to 23 at the end of the century. As a consequence population increased enormously.

Great improvements in inland transport accompanied the revolutions in industry and agriculture. In Queen Anne's reign coal was still carried on packhorses. Roads were so poor that wheels stuck in the mud or broke on hard, dry ruts and huge stones. The government still took little interest in road building. Private initiative supplied the need. Turnpike companies laced the land with roads and made their profit by collecting fees at tollgates. Heavy wagons lumbered over the new turnpikes, and light stagecoaches sped along them at ten miles an hour, stopping at coaching inns for new relays of fast horses. In 1750 a great era of canal building began. Before the end of the century the land was interlaced with a network of waterways. Like the roads, the canals were built for profit by private companies.

Britain's threefold revolution was accomplished by private initiative. Individualism, the spirit of the age, freed men's minds and energies. Yet many government restrictions still shackled industry and commerce. Adam Smith, creator of the science of political economy, called attention to their harmful effect. Complete freedom of industry and trade, he said, would unleash even greater productive energy. His ideas, published in 'Wealth of Nations' (1776), gave direction to the new industrial age.

Challenge of Napoleon

The outbreak of the French Revolution ended the harmony of 18th-century Britain. Class faced class in bitter controversy. Thomas Paine upheld the revolutionists in a stirring appeal to the masses, 'The Rights of Man'. Edmund Burke eloquently voiced the attitude of conservative Englishmen: "The French," he declared, "have shown themselves the ablest architects of ruin who have hitherto existed in the world." (*See also* Burke; Paine.)

People were horrified when France set up a republic and executed Louis XVI. George III went into mourning and expelled the French envoy. France declared war, and Britain promptly joined the coalition of European monarchs against the new French republic (*see* French Revolution). The war dragged on without much result until the young general Napoleon Bonaparte began to win amazing victories. By 1797 Britain was left to carry on the war alone.

Weaving was still a cottage industry when William Hogarth engraved this picture about 1747. The master, at the door, has his eye on Tim Idle, who is asleep at his loom. Apprentices lived in the master's house while learning a trade.

Britain, weak on land, was supreme on the sea. Admiral Horatio Nelson's victory of the Nile (1798) gave the British navy control of the Mediterranean and secured the route to India. At Trafalgar (1805) Nelson annihilated the French fleet (*see* Nelson). Napoleon, victorious on the Continent, was unable to invade the island kingdom; so he sought to ruin the "race of shopkeepers" by forbidding Europe to trade with Britain. Britain countered by blockading all European ports controlled by Napoleon. The United States, exasperated by Britain's interference with its commerce, declared war on Britain in 1812 (*see* War of 1812).

Britain meanwhile had built up an army, led by the duke of Wellington. Wellington first drove the French out of Spain. In 1815 he commanded the British forces at the battle of Waterloo, which destroyed Napoleon's army. Before the year ended, a British ship carried off Napoleon to an island prison. (*See also* Wellington; Napoleon I; Waterloo.)

In this engraving, Hogarth satirizes 18th-century politics. A candidate's agent offers trinkets to women and asks them to see that their husbands vote the right way.

Effects of the War with France

Triumph over France brought Great Britain national glory and financial profit. The empire expanded and British control over sea routes was made secure. The increased demand for British goods stimulated commerce and quickened the pace of the Industrial Revolution. British blast furnaces and textile mills supplied munitions and clothes not only for the armies of Great Britain but for its allies as well.

English poetry reached the highest point it had touched since the age of Shakespeare. The ideas of the French Revolution ended the Classical Age on the continent as well as in Britain and gave birth to a new "back-to-nature" movement in art and literature called the Romantic Movement. The Romanticists extolled emotion as the Classicists had reason. They sought the beautiful in nature or in medieval art rather than in classical models. (*See also* English Literature; Painting.)

Changes appeared also in dress and morals. Women ceased to powder their hair. Men discarded wigs and cut their hair short. Wool and cotton began to replace silks, satins, and velvets for both men and women. The reformers of the age sent missionaries into foreign lands, but they took little interest in the increasing wretchedness of Britain's poor.

The war swelled the fortunes of landlords, merchants, and manufacturers. To the poor it brought misery. Men and women toiled 12 to 18 hours a day in mines and factories. Wages were at starvation levels. Child labor was widespread. *Laissez faire* ("let it alone") was becoming the order of the day in industry. The new freedom, unfortunately, did not extend to the working classes. They were forbidden to hold meetings, to organize unions, even to publish pamphlets. When workers rioted and smashed the new machines, the government made machine breaking a capital crime. Fourteen "Luddites" (so called after a feebleminded youth who destroyed two stocking frames) were put to death in Yorkshire in 1811.

Inspired by the revolt of the French peasants, the Irish rose against English rule in 1798. In 1800 Pitt succeeded in bringing Ireland into a union with Great Britain similar to that between England and Scotland. The Act of Union went into force Jan. 1, 1801, creating the United Kingdom of Great Britain and Ireland (*see* United Kingdom). The mass of the Irish, however, being Catholics, were still excluded from the government. George III allowed only Church-of-England Irish to sit in Parliament.

The Coming of Democracy

The factory system made tremendous changes in the social structure. Two new classes had appeared—the capitalists, or *entrepreneurs,* who owned the factories and machines, and the mass of the workers, who were dependent upon the capitalists for employment. Large manufacturing cities had risen in the north, close to the coalfields. Many of these cities had no representation in Parliament because no new "boroughs" had been created to send up members since the time of Charles II. In the south of England Tory proprietors of boroughs with few or no inhabitants (called "pocket boroughs" or "rotten boroughs") continued to send representatives. Cornwall sent as many members to the House of Commons as all Scotland.

The spirit of reform was gradually making itself felt. Jeremy Bentham, called the *utilitarian*, made "utility" the test of law and said government should promote "the greatest happiness of the greatest number" by scientific legislation. Philosophic radicals such as James Mill advocated a *laissez-faire* individualism. Robert Owen showed in his New Lanark mills in Scotland that good hours, good wages, and healthy factory conditions could be made to pay.

William Cobbett, a radical journalist, led a campaign for universal suffrage because he believed workmen could improve their condition only by achieving the right to vote. The great industrial city of Manchester had no parliamentary representation. In 1819 a crowd of 60,000 assembled on St. Peter's Field to choose a "legislative representative." Mounted soldiers charged into the crowd, killed 11 persons, and wounded many. This "Peterloo Massacre" aroused great indignation and gave the deathblow to the old Toryism.

The Regency and the Trend to Reform

George III became insane in his later years and blind as well. For nine years before his death his incompetent eldest son governed as prince regent. (This period, 1811–20, is therefore known as the Regency.) On his father's death, the prince regent became King George IV (*see* George IV).

The more progressive Tories now began a series of reforms that opened a new era. Trade unions were partially legalized in 1825. Catholics were admitted to Parliament—after a struggle of many years—by the Catholic Emancipation Act of 1829. Harsh criminal laws were reformed, reducing capital offenses to about a dozen. (In 1800, 200 offenses had been punishable by death.) In 1829 Robert Peel set up, for the first time in history, a civilian police force. Started in London, it spread quickly to other cities. The people called the police by either of Peel's names—"bobbies" or "peelers" (*see* Peel).

William IV, brother of George IV, began his short reign in 1830 (*see* William IV). The "reform" of Parliament had by now become the burning issue. Extreme Tories, led by the duke of Wellington, stood fast against it. Reform groups in Parliament, including the moderate Tories, drew together and supported Earl Grey, the Whig leader. Wellington's government fell and the Whigs came into power. Lord John Russell introduced a strong reform bill. In the face of tremendous opposition in the House of Lords, the Great Reform Act was passed in 1832. (*See also* Wellington; Russell.)

Parliamentary Reform

The Reform Act created 43 new boroughs and deprived the "rotten boroughs" of their representatives in Parliament. The battle for universal suffrage, however, was still to be fought. The Reform Act slightly increased the number of voters by lowering the property qualifications; but the mass of the working people were still too poor to vote.

During the 1830's the Tories dropped their some-

At left is exquisite Wells Cathedral in Wells, Somerset. Lincoln Cathedral, right, rises on Castle Hill in the city of Lincoln. Both of these structures were begun in the 12th century and both are of the Early English Gothic style of architecture.

Victoria was a girl of 18 when she came to the throne in 1837. Before her 64-year reign ended, Britain had become the workshop of the world as well as its banking house, and she had been crowned empress of India.

what discredited name and became known as the Conservative party. The free-trade Conservatives (Peelites) gradually merged with the Whigs, who were to become the new Liberal party. Liberalism in the 19th century meant individualism. The true Liberal of that day championed freedom of thought and religion, freedom of trade, freedom of contract between the individual employer and the individual workman, and unrestricted competition. The party was made up chiefly of the industrial middle class.

The Victorian Age

William IV died in 1837, in the seventh year of his reign, and Victoria, his 18-year-old niece, became queen of Great Britain. Three years later she married her cousin Albert, a German prince. As prince consort, Albert gave valuable aid to the queen until his death in 1861 (*see* Victoria).

The young girl entered eagerly upon her new duties. Her long reign, 1837–1901, was to be immensely creative in literature and science, and before its close Britain reached the first place among nations in wealth and power. In the first years of her rule, however, the country seemed to be almost on the verge of revolution.

A series of bad harvests, beginning in 1837, continued into the "Hungry Forties." England suffered a wheat famine, Ireland a potato famine. A high tariff on grain (called "corn" in England) kept out foreign wheat. The price of bread soared. A new Poor Law (1834) had ended the outdoor relief for paupers that had been begun in the time of Queen Elizabeth I. The workhouses that took its place (described in Dickens' novel 'Oliver Twist') were more dreaded than jails. Wages were miserably low. A tremendous migration began from the British Isles to Canada, Australia, New Zealand, and the United States.

A group of reformers called *Chartists* drafted in 1838 a bill called the People's Charter, calling for universal manhood suffrage. Meanwhile an Anti-Corn Law League had been formed in 1836, to campaign for the free entry of foreign wheat to feed the hungry poor. Sir Robert Peel, the Conservative prime minister, was finally converted to their view; and in 1846 he put through Parliament the famous bill repealing the Corn Laws. Wheat at once poured in from overseas. Prosperity returned, even for the farmers. The working people now began to turn their attention to the new trade unions and to the cooperative movement, started in 1844 by the Rochdale Pioneers. (*See also* Peel; Cooperatives.)

Free Trade and Prosperity

The success of the Corn Law repeal encouraged the government to remove the tariff on other foods and on the raw materials needed by manufacturers. With free trade, Britain entered upon its period of greatest prosperity. Iron and steel output expanded greatly.

Steam and machinery came to be used increasingly in every kind of manufacturing process. A tremendous boom in railway building caused many old posting inns to fall into disuse. By 1848 a large part of the new trackage was paralleled by telegraph wires. "Penny postage," introduced throughout the British Isles in 1840, provided a cheap and uniform postage rate prepaid with an adhesive stamp (*see* Postal Service, Worldwide). Commerce was set free in 1849 by the repeal of the old Navigation Laws, which had permitted only British ships to carry goods between different parts of the empire. The application of steam power to oceangoing vessels stimulated the growth of the merchant marine and the navy. Commerce expanded enormously. In 1851 the country celebrated its industrial progress in the first great international fair, called the Great Exhibition (*see* Fairs and Expositions). The government began to take more interest in the empire, which provided the manufacturers with both markets and raw materials. The Crimean War (1854–56) was fought to protect British and French imperial interests against Russia's threatened advance toward the Mediterranean and India (*see* Crimean War). After helping the British East India Company put down the Sepoy Rebellion in India (1857), Parliament deprived the company of its political powers and transferred the government of India to the British crown (*see* India).

Wider Suffrage and Imperialism

The Reform Act of 1832 had benefited only the middle class. In 1867 Parliament took another long step in the direction of democracy by putting through the second Reform Act. This gave the vote to almost all adult males in the towns. The bill had been introduced by Benjamin Disraeli, a Conservative. Nevertheless the new voters, many of them workingmen, supported William Gladstone, Liberal leader. With Gladstone's first and greatest ministry, 1868–74, an era of reform set in. (*See also* Gladstone.)

The Suez Canal was a vital link in an empire on which "the sun never set." Britain bought controlling interest from Egypt.

The Education Act of 1870 set up elementary schools financed in part by the government. In the same year competitive examinations were introduced for employment in the civil service. The Trade Union Act of 1871 gave full legal recognition to trade unions. In 1872 the secret ballot was introduced in parliamentary elections.

Imperialism came into the ascendancy in 1874 with Benjamin Disraeli's Conservative ministry (*see* Disraeli). Disraeli obtained for Britain financial control of the Suez Canal, key to Britain's eastern empire (*see* Suez Canal). In 1876 he had Queen Victoria declared empress of India. When Russia defeated Turkey and advanced close to Constantinople, he called the Congress of Berlin (1878), which checked Russian ambitions (*see* Berlin, Congress of).

During Gladstone's second ministry, 1880–85, a third Reform Bill was enacted, in 1884. This gave rural voters the same voting privileges as the townspeople. The "Grand Old Man" went down to defeat because he championed Home Rule for Ireland. The Irish question split the Liberal party into Home Rulers and Unionists. The Liberal Unionists, led by Joseph Chamberlain, gave their support to the Conservative party because they wanted no separate parliament for Ireland (*see* Chamberlain, Joseph). A coalition of Conservatives and Liberal Unionists took office.

During the three ministries of Robert Salisbury, the government brought the navy to a high state of efficiency and secured for Britain the lion's share in the partition of Africa. To stimulate interest in the empire, it celebrated the 50th and 60th years of Victoria's rule (1887 and 1897) with magnificent "jubilees" attended by Indian princes and representatives of all the far-flung dominions and colonies. Before the century ended, the British were engaged in the Boer War (1899–1902) against the Dutch farmers (Boers) in South Africa. After some humiliating defeats, Britain won the war and annexed the two Boer republics, the Transvaal and the Orange Free State. Following annexation, Britain granted self-government to South Africa under the leadership of Jan Smuts, a Boer. Before the war was over, Queen Victoria died (1901), ending the longest reign in British history. Edward VII, her son, succeeded her. (*See also* Boer War; Smuts.)

An Age of Peace and Progress

The Victorians called their age "modern" and thought it superior to all past centuries. It was an age of progress with peace and plenty. Wages and working conditions steadily improved. Dividends from British industry and from foreign investments supported a leisure class. The population of the United Kingdom increased in the last half of the century from 28 million to nearly 42 million people.

Eton students in their school uniforms drill for World War I duty. The outbreak of the war found England's youth eager to serve but unprepared.

The age was extraordinarily creative in literature and science. The poets Alfred Tennyson and Robert Browning expressed the Victorians' optimism and religious feeling. But it was chiefly an age of the novel, represented by William Thackeray and Charles Dickens, and the essay (*see* Novel; English Literature). In pure science, Charles Darwin's theory of evolution had worldwide influence (*see* Darwin).

The Victorians did not excel in music or in painting. Architecture actually deteriorated, owing in part to the progress in technology that caused a breakdown of craftsmanship and tradition. Cheap manufactured knickknacks cluttered Victorian parlors.

The Labor Party and the New Liberalism

When Edward VII came to the throne, in 1901, Britain was no longer the only "workshop of the world." The Industrial Revolution was now in full swing in other countries. Germany, the United States, and Japan competed strongly with Britain in foreign markets. Unemployment soon became chronic. Serious unrest stirred the working classes.

Germany not only competed with British industry but had become the greatest military power on the Continent; and in 1900 it began to expand its navy, challenging British control of the seas. To meet this threat, Britain abandoned its "splendid isolation" and entered into an alliance with Japan in 1902. In 1904 it concluded the *Entente Cordiale* with France, and in 1907 it reached a similar agreement with Russia. (*See also* Edward VII.)

In 1900 the British Trades Union Congress held a conference to form a new political party. Delegates were invited from various socialist organizations. Chief among these was the Fabian Society. The Fabians were middle-class intellectuals who had been advocating national ownership of land and industry since 1883 (*see* Socialism). The new party became known at once as the Labor party.

Fabian teachings had been spreading also in the Liberal party. The "new" Liberals of the 20th century no longer advocated a policy of *laissez faire* in government. They had turned against individualism and "classical" economics and favored extending the powers of the state to abolish poverty. They still held to the 19th-century Liberal doctrine of free trade. On this issue they won the election of 1906. Labor party representatives supported the Liberal program of social legislation.

Lloyd George's Social Legislation

The driving power of the new government was David Lloyd George, chancellor of the exchequer under Herbert Asquith from 1908 to 1916 (*see* Lloyd George). In 1908 he put through Parliament an Old Age Pensions Act granting pensions to all old people with a small income. On Jan. 1, 1909, over half a million men and women drew their first pensions.

Pensions and the constantly expanding navy vastly increased the expenses of government. In 1909 Lloyd George proposed heavy taxes on the wealthy and a new tax on land. The House of Lords rejected his budget. A constitutional struggle took place that ended in the Parliament Act of 1911, which stripped the House of Lords of much of its power (*see* Parliament, British). The way was now open for the passage of a National Insurance Act (1912) to pay wage earners unemployment and sickness benefits.

In the midst of the parliamentary struggle Edward VII died (1910). He was succeeded by his only surviving son, George V (*see* George V).

World War I and Its Aftermath

On the eve of World War I the people of Great Britain were concerned with militant suffragettes, workingmen's strikes, and an Irish crisis (*see* Ireland). War broke out with startling suddenness on Aug. 1, 1914. Britain declared war three days later, and the British dominions and colonies were automatically drawn in. British and empire troops fought in France and Belgium, at Gallipoli, and in Palestine, while the navy held the seas and prevented food and supplies from reaching Germany.

Lloyd George became the war leader in 1916 when he succeeded Asquith as head of the Nationalist government, a coalition of Liberal and Conservative parties. The peace treaties, which he negotiated, added more territory to the vast British Empire in Asia, Africa, and the Pacific (*see* World War I, section "The Peace and Its Results"). The United Kingdom itself, however, was made smaller by an act of Parliament granting self-government to southern Ireland as a dominion of the British Commonwealth.

In 1918 Lloyd George's government passed an Education Act abolishing all fees in state-supported ele-

Air-raid wardens search the ruins for victims after a Luftwaffe bomb hit a London street in World War II. A bus has been thrown against a building by the force of the explosion.

mentary schools. The same year it extended manhood suffrage and granted the right to vote to single women over 30 and married women over 35 who met certain property qualifications. In 1919 women became eligible for Parliament. Universal adult suffrage was not achieved until 1928.

The war had vastly increased the national debt. By imposing heavy income taxes, the government managed to balance the budget while increasing payments to the unemployed. Industrial peace, however, did not return. After a few years of prosperity, exports declined and unemployment rose. A wave of strikes engulfed the country.

More than 100,000 London schoolchildren were sent from their homes to rural areas for safety during World War II. Some children living in air-raid zones were evacuated overseas.

The Conservatives deserted the Nationalist coalition and defeated the Liberals in 1922. The Labor party (which had come out openly for socialism in 1918) voted with the Liberals to turn out the Conservatives, and in 1924 Ramsay MacDonald was chosen to head Britain's first Labor government. He remained in office only nine months, going down to defeat partly because he advocated closer relations with Russia.

Under Stanley Baldwin as prime minister, the Conservatives returned to power for almost five years (1924–29). Again unemployment relief was increased. The cause of unemployment was the shrinking world market for British coal, textiles, and steel. The Labor party believed full employment could be attained by government ownership of basic industries. The unions called a general strike in 1926 to force through their demands. The strike was quickly ended except for the coal miners, the most distressed of the workers.

The regular election of 1929 favored the Labor party, and MacDonald formed a cabinet. The world depression dislocated international trade and currencies and plunged Britain into a financial crisis. The number of unemployed mounted to nearly 3 million. The leaders of the three parties then formed a coalition cabinet called the National government. MacDonald retained the premiership, but he now owed his support chiefly to the Conservatives. The Labor party had expelled him when his government introduced drastic economies. He resigned in 1935 and Baldwin again became prime minister.

Three Kings in One Year

George V died in January 1936, and his eldest son, Edward, the popular prince of Wales, came to the throne as Edward VIII. Before his coronation, the king announced his intention of marrying an American, Mrs. Wallis Warfield Simpson, as soon as her second divorce became absolute. Parliament and the dominions' governments disapproved. Edward abdicated on Dec. 11, 1936, and his brother, the duke of York, was proclaimed king as George VI. (*See also* Edward VIII; George VI.)

Britain Abandons Free Trade

Since the repeal of the Corn Laws in 1846, Britain had been practically a free-trade country. Almost all other nations had put up tariffs that handicapped British exporters. When the world depression caused a slump in trade, the dominions asked Britain to import more raw materials from them. In return, they would favor British manufactures. In 1932 Parliament passed the Import Duties Act. The act imposed a basic tariff of 10 percent on all goods not specifically exempted. This paved the way for the Ottawa imperial conference in the same year, which worked out "preferential" tariffs within the empire.

The Statute of Westminster (1931) had recognized the complete control by the dominions of their foreign as well as domestic affairs. The Ottawa conference strengthened the ties of the Commonwealth of Nations by binding its members into a closer economic union. This, however, did not check the growth of nationalism, particularly in India and other Asian dependencies.

Outbreak of World War II

In 1933 Adolf Hitler came to power in Germany and soon began to rearm the country. Britain, absorbed in domestic troubles, was unprepared for war. Hitler seized Austria in March 1938, then made demands on Czechoslovakia. Britain, along with France, adopted a policy of "appeasement," hoping Hitler's demands could be satisfied short of war. Neville Chamberlain, who had become prime minister in 1937, believed he had achieved "peace in our time" when Hitler pledged at Munich (Sept. 30, 1938) that he had "no further territorial claims in Europe." Six months later Hitler broke the pact and took over most of Czechoslovakia. (*See also* Chamberlain, Neville.)

Britain joined with France in guaranteeing Poland's independence. Hitler took no action until after Russia signed a peace pact with Germany (Aug. 24, 1939). Eight days later (September 1) his army marched into Poland. Britain and France declared war two days later. Within a week all the members of the Commonwealth (except Eire) also declared war.

The Battle of Britain

On May 10, 1940, Germany invaded Belgium and the Netherlands. On the same day Winston Churchill succeeded Chamberlain as prime minister (*see* Churchill). Britain lost most of its armament in the famed retreat from the Dunkirk beaches (*see* Dunkirk). When France fell in June the British began their "year alone" and suffered the furious onslaught of German bombers. "Let us therefore brace ourselves to our duty," said Churchill, "and so bear ourselves that if the British Commonwealth and Empire last for a thousand years, men will say, 'This was their finest hour'."

The battle of Britain was a victory that ranked in importance with the defeat of the Spanish Armada. Britain was saved from invasion by its navy and its air force. British and Commonwealth troops fought on the far-flung battlefields of this war, and British leaders played a strong role in the formation of the United Nations. (For British military and naval action in the war, *see* World War II.)

Six years of war cost the United Kingdom 397,762 in dead and missing and thousands of civilian casualties. Millions of properties were damaged or destroyed. Britain received extensive United States Lend-Lease aid but met most of the huge war expenditures by selling overseas investments, by large overseas borrowing, by domestic loans, and by a tremendous increase in taxation.

Britain's Socialist Revolution

In 1945 Britain held its first general election in ten years. The Labor party received an overwhelming majority. Clement Attlee, its leader, succeeded Churchill as prime minister. The party was elected on a socialist platform and at once embarked on a nationalization program. The state bought out shareholders in the Bank of England, the coal mines, all inland transport, aviation, gas, and electricity. It subsidized housing and food. It put through the "cradle-to-grave" social insurance plan drawn up under Churchill's ministry. It also set up a National Health Service to provide free medical care.

The postwar government faced grave financial difficulties. It cut imports to bare necessities and ruled that almost the entire output of Britain's factories must be sold abroad instead of in the home market.

The *Ark Royal* shown at top was the flagship of the English fleet that defeated the Spanish Armada in 1588, proving the superiority of English ships and sailors. Its modern namesake, the *Ark Royal*, shown at bottom, is a 43,000-ton aircraft carrier.

It fixed prices, rationed scarce goods, limited wages, and called on people to practice "austerity."

To offset the loss of income from foreign investments, Britain needed to double its exports above the prewar level. In 1949 the postwar "sellers' market" ended, and the high prices of British products caused a swift drop in exports. The government scaled down the value of the British pound from $4.03 to $2.80. This made it possible for British manufacturers to sell their goods in dollar markets but increased the price of necessary imports from dollar countries. Foreign loans and credits, especially Marshall Plan aid from the United States, helped in financial crises and in the task of rehabilitating overage and war-damaged industrial plants.

Decline in World Power

The British Empire suffered severe losses in territory and world influence in the years 1947–49. India, Pakistan, and Ceylon (now Sri Lanka) became self-governing nations within the Commonwealth, and Burma gained complete independence. Eire (southern Ireland) cut all ties with Britain and took the name of the Republic of Ireland.

On the continent of Europe, Britain no longer held its historic balance of power. For centuries it had helped prevent a strong nation from dominating the continent by throwing its weight toward that nation's rivals. Now Russia controlled all Eastern Europe. The only other world power was the United States. It used its influence to organize the nations of Western Europe for cooperation in defense and economic progress. Britain was not ready to share in a united Europe. It joined the North Atlantic Treaty Organization (NATO), formed in 1949 to meet the threat of Russian aggression, and expanded its armament production. British land, sea, and air forces shared in the United Nations action in South Korea in 1950–53. Later, Britain joined the Central Treaty Organization (CENTO) of the Middle East and the Southeast Asia Treaty Organization (SEATO).

In the 1950's many of Britain's postwar problems remained unsolved, but its economy rode on a wave of prosperity. Manufacturing output exceeded prewar production early in the decade. In 1959 the output of steel had risen 55 percent above that of 1938. Between 1949 and 1959 domestic production increased every year but two, and exports rose by 40 percent. Most Britons in the early 1960's were earning twice as much as they had been in 1949.

In 1951 the Conservatives returned to power. Winston Churchill, then 76, again became premier. On Feb. 6, 1952, George VI died. His elder daughter succeeded him as Elizabeth II (*see* Elizabeth II).

The Conservatives lifted certain controls set by the Socialist government. In 1953 they denationalized iron and steel and trucking. Food rationing ended in 1954. Churchill resigned as premier in 1955 and was succeeded by Sir Anthony Eden.

Great Britain withdrew its last troops from the Suez Canal zone in June 1956, according to an earlier agreement. In July Egypt nationalized the Suez Canal. Britain and France protested vigorously. In October Israeli forces invaded Egypt. After demanding a cease-fire between them, Britain and France sent forces into the canal zone. They were branded as aggressors in the United Nations. The Anglo-French troops withdrew as a United Nations task force moved in. In January 1957 Eden resigned as prime minister and was succeeded by Harold Macmillan. (*See also* Suez Canal; Egypt; Macmillan.)

Independence for Colonies

The death knell of colonialism sounded in the 1950's and 1960's as most of the foreign territories of the European powers won independence. The British had trained their colonies for self-government, so they usually parted with Britain as friends and the

When the heart of Coventry was destroyed by bombing in 1940, only the steeple and walls of its cathedral remained. In 1962 a new cathedral of striking design was dedicated. The shell of the old one adjoins it—a symbol of war's tragedy.

new nations remained in the Commonwealth. A notable exception was South Africa, which became a republic and left the Commonwealth in 1961.

Between 1956 and 1966 independence was achieved by more than 20 British colonies and trusteeships in Africa, Asia, South America, and the West Indies. In 1965 Rhodesia (now Zimbabwe) declared itself independent unilaterally; that is, its independence was not granted or recognized by Britain. By 1969 several of the few remaining possessions were independent—what is now the People's Democratic Republic of Yemen (formerly Aden), Mauritius, and Swaziland.

In the 1970's independence came to many of the Pacific and West Indies island units—Fiji, Tonga, the Bahamas, Grenada, the Solomon Islands, Dominica, Saint Lucia, Saint Vincent and the Grenadines, and the former Gilbert and Ellice Islands colony, which was divided into the new nations of Kiribati and Tuvalu. Seychelles, located in the Indian Ocean, also became independent. The secessionist state of Rhodesia, which had declared itself a republic in 1970, reverted to colonial status in 1979 before finally achieving independence as Zimbabwe in 1980. (*See also* Commonwealth, The; articles on individual nations.)

Membership in EC

In 1959 Great Britain helped found the European Free Trade Association (EFTA). The commerce of the member nations benefited from the lowering of tariff barriers among them, but the more tightly knit European Economic Community (EEC; from 1967, the European Communities, or EC), or Common Market, made greater economic gains than EFTA (*see* European Communities). In 1961 the Macmillan government decided that entry into the thriving EEC would stimulate Britain's trade. Since the tariff agreements between Commonwealth countries conflicted with EEC regulations, long negotiations and compromises were necessary. In 1963 France vetoed Britain's bid for EEC membership. Although supported by the other EEC members, Britain was again barred by a French veto in 1967. Britain signed and ratified a treaty of accession in 1972 and joined the EC on Jan. 1, 1973. In 1988 Prime Minister Margaret Thatcher attacked a concept to establish a European federal economic and political "state" that would also create a central bank and a single EC currency.

In 1963 Macmillan resigned. He was succeeded by Conservative Sir Alexander Frederick Douglas-Home. In 1964 Laborite Harold Wilson became prime minister. After a Conservative victory in 1970, Edward Heath became prime minister. A pay strike by coal miners, in the wake of a worldwide energy crisis, led Heath to call a new election in February 1974, and Wilson returned as prime minister. A general strike in Northern Ireland in May led to the collapse of its five-month-old coalition government and forced Britain to resume direct rule over the province. (*See also* Douglas-Home; Heath; Wilson, Harold.)

Wilson resigned in March 1976 and was succeeded by another Laborite, James Callaghan. In 1979 Callaghan, who had headed a minority government for two years, became the second British prime minister to lose office after a no-confidence motion. Thatcher, Conservative party leader since 1975, became Britain's first woman prime minister. (*See also* Callaghan; Thatcher.)

War with Argentina

In 1982 Britain went to war with Argentina over a colony in the South Atlantic. Known as the Islas Malvinas in Argentina and the Falkland Islands in Britain, the two countries had been discussing the future of the islands for some years, but Argentina's invasion of the Falklands came as a complete surprise. Britain's recapture of the islands ten weeks later restored Conservative popularity to a remarkable degree. The so-called Falklands factor encouraged Thatcher to call a general election in 1983, a year earlier than required. The Conservatives won an overwhelming victory. In 1987 Thatcher became the first British prime minister in more than 150 years to win a third consecutive election. In 1990 the Conservative government abolished the local property tax and established a flat-rate community charge. (*See also* Falkland Islands.)

A bitter coal miners' strike dominated 1984. The government was determined to close 20 uneconomical mines and to exercise its constitutional and political authority. Although the year was marked by violence and much political wrangling, the striking miners marched back to work almost exactly a year later. The victory had tilted the balance of power against the trade union movement.

Northern Ireland

An accord was signed with the Republic of Ireland in 1985 giving it a role as consultant in the governing of Northern Ireland. This was the latest attempt by Britain to help stabilize the long-standing dispute between Northern Ireland's Protestant majority and its Roman Catholic minority. The years of terrorism continued, with a bombing in November 1987 in Enniskillen, Northern Ireland, that killed 11 people, and the shooting deaths of three IRA terrorists in March 1988. (*See also* Ireland, Northern.)

Violence was not confined to the problems in Northern Ireland. Riots in Birmingham and two London neighborhoods in 1985 were related to economic and racial problems in the inner city. Violence by Liverpool soccer fans in Brussels, Belgium, resulted in 39 deaths and was defined as hooliganism. Increasing fear of violence and terrorism caused English police to begin carrying guns openly, breaking a long-standing tradition.

BIBLIOGRAPHY FOR ENGLAND

Briggs, Asa. A Social History of England (Penguin, 1986).
Burke, John. Roman England (Norton, 1984).
Ferguson, Sheila. Village and Town Life (Batsford, 1983).
Laing, Lloyd and Jennifer. Anglo-Saxon England (Scribner, 1987).
Rossiter, Stuart, ed. Blue Guide: England (Norton, annual).
Trevelyn, G.M. English Social History: a Survey of Six Centuries from Chaucer to Queen Victoria, new ed. (Longman, 1978).

ENGLISH LANGUAGE. Geographically the most widespread language on Earth is English, and it is second only to Mandarin Chinese in the number of people who speak it. English is the national language of the United Kingdom, the United States, Australia, and New Zealand. It is one of the two national languages of Canada. It is an official or semiofficial language in many former and present British possessions such as South Africa, India, and Hong Kong.

Members of the diplomatic corps in most lands have some knowledge of English. English has long been the language of commerce, and it is becoming the language of international relations as well.

CHARACTERISTICS

English belongs to the Indo-European family of languages. It is, therefore, related to most of the languages spoken in an area stretching from Iceland across Europe to India (*see* Language, "Indo-European"). The language most closely resembling Modern English is Frisian, which is spoken in the Dutch province of Friesland. Icelandic, on the other hand, has changed little in more than 1,000 years. It is the living language most closely resembling Old English.

Inflection

German, Latin, Russian, Greek, and French are inflected languages. This means that many words undergo changes of spelling—and often of pronunciation—to mark changes in tense of verbs, gender of nouns, case or plurality of nouns, mood of verbs, agreement of adjectives, and other distinctions. For example, the French word for "beautiful" or "fine" is *beau*. When used to modify the plural noun *arts*, it becomes *beaux*, as in the expression *beaux-arts*, meaning "fine arts." When used before a vowel, it becomes *bel*, as in *le bel âge*, an idiom for "youth." When used to modify a noun of the feminine gender, it becomes *belle*, as in *la belle dame*, or "beautiful lady."

English, on the other hand, is relatively uninflected. Adverbs, adjectives, prepositions, conjunctions, and interjections are invariable. They are spelled the same way no matter how they are used. Nouns, pronouns, and verbs, however, are inflected. Most English nouns show a plural by adding an *s* or an *es*: cow, cows; box, boxes. Some nouns have what are called mutated, or changed, plurals: man, men; woman, women; foot, feet; tooth, teeth; goose, geese; mouse, mice; louse, lice. A very few nouns—for example, ox, oxen—have plurals ending in *en*. A few nouns remain unchanged in the plural: deer, sheep, moose, and grouse.

Five of the seven personal pronouns have distinctive forms for subject or object use: I, me; he, him; she, her; we, us; and they, them. And there are also distinctive possessive pronouns: mine, his, hers, ours, theirs.

Verb forms, while inflected, are not nearly as complicated as they are in Latin, Greek, or German. The one English verb with the most forms is "to be" (be, am, is, are, was, were, been, and being). Weak, or regular, verbs have only four forms: talk, talks, talked, and talking, for example. Strong, or irregular, verbs have five forms: sing, sings, sang, sung, and singing. A few verbs that end in a *t* or *d* have only three forms: cut, cuts, cutting. These verb inflections are in marked contrast to Old English, in which *ridan*, or "ride," had 13 forms, and to Modern German, in which *reiten* has 16.

Flexibility

Along with a loss of inflection came a flexibility of use. Words that were once distinguished as nouns or verbs by their inflections are now used both ways. It is possible to "run a race" (noun usage) or "race someone to the corner" (verb usage).

It is also possible in English to use nouns as adjectives: automobile show, state fair, hot dog stand. Pronouns, adjectives, and adverbs can also function as nouns. English adopts or adapts any word as needed to name a new object or describe a new process.

Word Formation

New words have been frequently formed by adding a prefix or suffix, by combining words, or by blending words. A prefix is attached to the front of a word: way, subway; do, overdo. Sometimes a foreign prefix is added such as the Greek *macro* or *micro*: macroeconomics, microbiology. One of the most common suffixes is *er*, which usually means someone who engages in the act that the verb suggests: singer, player, seeker, writer. Other suffixes also denote activity: act*or*, hat*maker*, merch*ant*, scient*ist*.

Combining words to form new ones is common: cloverleaf, gentleman, dateline. Some words in combination alter their meanings slightly: already is not

The charter issued to the City of London by William the Conqueror in 1066 was printed in Saxon, a forerunner of English. The opening lines read: "William, King, greets William, Bishop, and Geoffrey, Portreeve, and all the Burghers within London, French and English, friendly. And I make known unto you that I will that ye be worthy all those laws the which ye were in King Edward's day . . . ."

Historical Pictures service

quite the same as all ready, and a gentleman is not quite the same as a gentle man. Blackbird is a specific kind of fowl, but black bird suggests a bird of a particular color.

Blends of words fall into two categories—a coalescence or a telescoped word. One of the most commonly used coalescent forms is smog, a blend of the words smoke and fog. A telescoped form is motorcade, made by combining motor with a remnant of cavalcade. In the same way a travel monologue becomes a travelogue, and a cable telegram a cablegram.

Vocabulary

There are an estimated 750,000 words in the English language. Nearly half of these are of Germanic (or Teutonic) origin, and nearly half from the Romance languages (languages of Latin origin—such as French, Spanish, and Italian—or Latin itself). There also have been generous borrowings from other languages, including Greek, Dutch, Modern German, and Arabic. A good etymological dictionary serves as a guide to the origins of English words (*see* Etymology).

Among the many words that come from the Germanic are the nouns father, mother, brother, man, wife, ground, land, tree, grass, summer, and winter. Germanic-based verbs include bring, come, get, hear, meet, see, sit, stand, and think.

From French have come such political terms as constitution, president, parliament, congress, and representative. Also borrowed from French are city, place, village, court, palace, manor, mansion, residence, domicile, cuisine, diner, café, liberty, veracity, carpenter, draper, haberdasher, mason, painter, plumber, and tailor. Many terms relating to cooking, fashion, drama, winemaking, literature, art, diplomacy, and ballet also come from France.

English has acquired many words from Spanish. Some of these have been borrowed directly: cigar, armada, guerrilla, matador, mosquito, and tornado. Others have come to Spanish from one of the Indian languages of the Americas: potato and tomato, for example. Many Spanish words have come directly into the United States from Latin America: canyon, lasso, mustang, pueblo, and rodeo.

Borrowings from Latin have been especially numerous. Many of these represent combinations of Latin words: malnutrition, transfer, circumference, supernatural, submarine, suburb, substantial, contemporary, multilingual, conjunction, compassion, and hundreds more.

Borrowings from Greek are heavy in the sciences and technology. In addition to *macro* and *micro*, often-used prefixes include *poly* and *tele*. Among the well-known English words from Greek are alphabet, geometry, geology, photography, psychology, psychiatry, pathology, biology, philosophy, telephone, logistics, and metamorphosis.

Arabic words have usually come into English by way of another European language, especially Spanish. Arabic was spoken in Spain during the period of the Muslim domination (*see* Caliphate). Among the

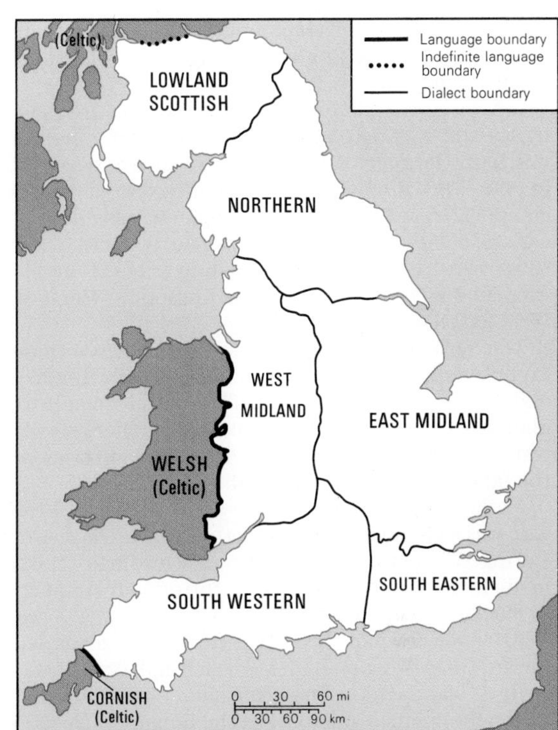

Middle English dialects of England

common English words that have come from Arabic are: alcohol, alchemy, algebra, alkali, almanac, arsenal, assassin, cipher, elixir, mosque, naphtha, sugar, syrup, zenith, and zero.

Common words borrowed from other languages are: coffee (Turkish); gull (Cornish); flannel (Welsh); brogue, blarney, shamrock, clan, and plaid (Gaelic and Irish); mammoth, soviet, and vodka (Russian); robot (Czech); paprika (Hungarian); jungle, thug, shampoo, dungarees, loot, pajamas, and polo (Hindi); paradise, lilac, bazaar, caravan, chess, shawl, and khaki (Persian); marmalade, flamingo, and veranda (Portuguese); ketchup, bamboo, and orangutan (Malay); taboo and tattoo (Polynesian); and ukulele (Hawaiian). Other words from native languages include hammock, hurricane, tobacco, and maize (Caribbean) and voodoo and chimpanzee (African).

HISTORY

Forging the English language into its present form was dependent on the bringing together of several early linguistic traditions over many centuries, dating from pre-Roman times in the British Isles. To this process was added a measure of standardization at a much later date.

The language of the ancient Britons was Celtic, and it survives in Modern Welsh, which is still the language of Wales. When the Romans conquered England, they introduced a number of Latin words. After the Romans withdrew, the conquest lost impact, and Latin had to be reintroduced when the islands were converted to Christianity in the 6th and 7th centuries.

The periods of development of the English language are called Old English (or Anglo-Saxon), Middle English, and Modern English. Old English was spoken from about AD 449 to 1100. The first invasion by the Jutes, Angles, and Saxons from the area of northern Germany and southern Denmark occurred in 449. Old English was very inflected: it had a complicated system of grammatical changes to indicate case, number, person, and tense. Because of the settlement patterns of the invading tribes, four Old English dialects developed: Northumbrian, Mercian, West Saxon, and Kentish.

The Norman Conquest of 1066 brought in Norman French and eventually placed the four Old English dialects on an even footing. The center of culture gradually shifted to London, and usages there slowly came to dominate. Latin persisted for centuries as the language of the church and of learning.

Middle English lasted from about 1100 to 1450 and was less highly inflected than its predecessor. During this period the Statute of Pleadings (1362) made English instead of French the official language of Parliament and the courts.

After the dawn of the 16th century the movement toward the development of Modern English prose was swift. It was aided by the printing of certain literary works that helped standardize the language. In 1525 William Tyndale published his translation of the New Testament. The next 90 years were the golden age of English literature, culminating in the plays of Shakespeare and in publication of the King James Version of the Bible in 1611.

Apart from printing literary works, another means of standardization was the dictionary. The first significant dictionary was compiled and published by Samuel Johnson in 1755 (*see* Johnson, Samuel; Reference Books, "Dictionaries"). Further aids to standardization were Lindley Murray's 'English Grammar' (1795) and 'English Spelling Book' (1804).

VARIETIES OF ENGLISH

The British writer George Bernard Shaw once remarked that "England and America are two countries separated by the same language." This humorous statement is a simple way of noting that the English language is not the same everywhere it is spoken. It is a living, evolving language that attains distinctive qualities in different environments. An American tourist in London, in search of public transportation, takes the underground rather than a subway. In a hotel the tourist takes the lift up to his room, not an elevator.

British English. What might be called the standard English of Britain is the speech of the educated people who live in London and the southeastern part of England. But this is only one of the regional dialects that has, over the centuries, achieved more extensive use than others. Other dialects include the class dialect London Cockney and Northern dialects, Midland dialects, South Western dialects, Welsh dialects, Lowland and Highland Scottish, Cornish, and Irish.

American English. In spite of the standardizing effects of radio and television, there are still a number of dialect regions across the United States. Significant contributions have been made to the creation of new dialects by black Americans and Hispanics. Neither of these groups, however, has a uniform dialect. Each has its regional variations.

The influence of the United States on Canadian English has been strong because there is no natural boundary between the two countries. Most Americans would be hard pressed to distinguish the English used in the western provinces from that spoken in the United States.

Australia and New Zealand. Both Australia and New Zealand were settled by the British, and the English language taken there came from a variety of British dialects. New terms were coined to describe the unusual plants and animals, and some words were picked up from the speech of the native aborigines in Australia and Maoris in New Zealand. There is little regional variation in Australia, but there is significant social variation, as in Britain. The language of New Zealand is quite similar to that of Australia.

South Asia is made up of the countries of India, Pakistan, Bangladesh, Sri Lanka, Nepal, and Bhutan. The area is a vast complex of ethnic and linguistic differences; there are more than 1,600 dialects and languages in India alone. English, brought by a colonizing nation, became a second language. Today it exhibits wide diversity, depending on the background of those who adopt it and the native vocabularies they bring to it.

South Africa, the oldest British settlement in Africa, has two accepted European languages—English and Afrikaans, or Cape Dutch. Although the English spoken in South Africa differs somewhat from standard British English, its speakers do not regard it as a separate dialect. Residents have added many Afrikanerisms to the language to denote features of the landscape.

Elsewhere in Africa—the most multilingual area of the world—English helps answer the needs of wider communication. It functions as an official language in Botswana, Lesotho, Swaziland, Zimbabwe, Zambia, Malawi, Uganda, and Kenya. The West African states of The Gambia, Sierra Leone, Nigeria, Ghana, and Liberia have English as the official language. (*See also* African languages.)

BIBLIOGRAPHY FOR ENGLISH LANGUAGE

Bailey, R.W., and Gorlach, Manfred. English as a World Language (Univ. of Mich. Press, 1982).

Branford, Jean. Dictionary of South African English, 2nd ed. (Oxford, 1980).

Bolton, W.F. Living Language: the History and Structure of English (Random, 1982).

Clairborne, Robert. Our Marvelous Native Tongue: the Life and Times of the English Language (Times Books, 1983).

Holm, J.A. and Shilling, A.W. Dictionary of Bahamian English (Lexik House, 1982).

Mencken, H.L. American Language (Knopf, 1977).

Wilkes, G.A. Dictionary of Australian Colloquialisms (Sydney Univ. Press, 1978).

James Press

ENGLISH LITERATURE

This picture for 'Paradise Lost', a great English classic, is by Gustave Doré. Beelzebub is in the lake of fire, and Satan is rising above it.

ENGLISH LITERATURE. The literature of England is one of the highest achievements of a great nation. It should not, however, be read simply as a national expression. It is a body of significant statements about the abiding concerns of man everywhere and in all times.

The literature of England is a vital, growing force. The language in which it is written has evolved over hundreds of years and is still changing. Several nations are indebted to England for a literary heritage (*see* American Literature; Australia, section on literature; Canadian Literature).

Old English Literature

THE BEGINNINGS of English literature appeared in the 7th or 8th century A.D. After the Romans withdrew their troops from Britain in 410, the Britons were forced to defend themselves alone against Picts and Scots from Scotland. Then the Angles, Saxons, and Jutes came from the European continent. They plundered city after city. By the middle of the 6th century the Britons had been pushed to the western borders of England, where they set up small tribal governments. When this society became established, English literature began.

In 597 Pope Gregory I sent Augustine to convert the British to Christianity. He established a Benedictine abbey at Canterbury as the seat of his diocese. This became the center of learning and scholarship of all Western Europe.

The Venerable Bede (673?–735), a monk, was the greatest Anglo-Saxon scholar. His beautifully written 'Ecclesiastical History of the English Nation' is a monumental account of his times.

Another monk, Alcuin (735–804), was probably the most learned man in Western civilization and was largely responsible for the revival of Latin scripts under Charlemagne. Alfred the Great (848?–899) made contributions to this already rich literature by writing in the native tongue and encouraging scholarly translations from Latin into Old English (Anglo-Saxon).

Alfred translated some Latin texts himself into the tongue of the West Saxons; and it was under him, probably, that the 'Anglo-Saxon Chronicle' was begun. This history of the chief events of each year is of prime importance to historians. Under Alfred, Bede's 'Ecclesiastical History' also was

The conquering hero of the Old English epic poem 'Beowulf' is shown here engaged in a fierce fight to save his people from destruction.

translated from the Latin, so that the people could study their past. (*See also* Alfred the Great.)

Old English Poetry

'Beowulf', the most notable example of the earliest English poetry, is an odd blend of Christianity and paganism. Old English, the language of 'Beowulf', is the source of modern English. Although Old English differed greatly from the language of today, much of the vigor and precision of modern English comes from the many Anglo-Saxon forms still used. The older language was a highly inflectional one; that is, it had many case endings for the nouns, pronouns, and adjectives and a complex system of verbs. It resembled modern German in grammar and in much of its vocabulary.

The story of 'Beowulf' takes place in lands other than England; but the customs and manners described were those of the Anglo-Saxon people. This epic poem describes their heroic past. It tells of Beowulf's three fierce fights—with the monster Grendel, the equally ferocious mother of Grendel, and the fiery dragon. By conquering them, Beowulf saves his people from destruction. (*See also* Beowulf.)

The versification of 'Beowulf' is highly stressed, with the strong beats falling upon syllables which alliterate—(that is, which repeat the same sound). These lines illustrate this forceful technique:

> Lonely and waste is the land they inhabit,
> Wolf-cliffs wild and windy headlands.

Much of Old English poetry, such as 'The Battle of Brunanburg' and 'The Battle of Maldon', is heroic and martial. 'The Wanderer' and 'The Sea-Farer' have a sad and pleasing lyric quality.

Only two Old English poets are known by name. Caedmon (7th century) was an unlearned cowherd (*see* Caedmon). According to legend, he was inspired by a vision and miraculously acquired the gift of poetic song. Unfortunately, only nine lines by this first known poet survive. The second known poet was Cynewulf (8th century). Little is known of him except that he signed his poems in a kind of cypher, or anagram, made up of ancient figures called *runes* (an alphabet used by early Germanic tribes preceding the use of the Roman alphabet in England). His poems, such as 'Christ', deal with religious subjects.

Middle English Literature

IN THE battle of Hastings, fought on Oct. 14, 1066, Harold II, last of the Anglo-Saxon kings, was killed (*see* Hastings, Battle of). William the Conqueror then assumed the kingship. After subduing vicious resistance, he established a rule that was almost entirely Norman-French. The Norman conquest greatly changed English life. All positions of power were filled by Frenchmen. Over all the old English vigor was imposed this foreign culture.

The Old English language went untaught and was spoken only by "unlettered" people. The language of the nobility and of the lawcourts was Norman-French; the language of the scholars was Latin. This situation lasted for nearly 300 years. During this period the Old English language changed. Its old case endings broke down, and the grammar became quite simple. Anglo-Saxon words were lost, and French words were added. The strong, crude iron of the Old English language was being slowly shaped into the flexible steel of present-day English.

The cult of chivalry came into being, fed by the great Crusades. The tales of King Arthur and his Round Table were a result of this movement. Education flourished; and the first universities, Oxford and Cambridge, were founded in the 12th century.

During these 300 years there was little literature in the changing English language. The few lyrics ('Sumer is icumen in', 'Alysoun', 1300?) and other works ('Ormulum', 1200?; Layamon's 'Brut', 1205?) have a small interest.

The Middle English period also marked the beginning of a native English drama, which was at first closely associated with the church. About 900 the antiphonal chant "Quem quaeritis in sepulchre, o Christocolae?" was first used preceding the Introit of the Mass. Other dramatic additions were made to the sacred offices, and soon dialogue between individual members of the choir was added in celebrations of certain feast days. Finally, what might be regarded as miniature dramas developed. In time these little plays (or *tropes*), becoming more secular, were moved out doors. (*See also* Drama.)

The early cycles of *miracle* and *mystery* plays possibly began as celebrations of traditional religious feasts and fasts. In any case, by the end of the 14th century the observances of certain festivals, for example, Corpus Christi, regularly involved pageants. These plays were staged in larger towns, such as York, Wakefield, and Chester, on wagons which were moved from place to place in a procession, perhaps chronological, of events. (*See also* Miracle Plays.)

In addition to mystery and miracle plays, *morality* plays were also popular at the end of the Middle English period. They usually personified such abstractions as Health, Death, or the Seven Deadly Sins and offered practical instruction in morality.

Chaucer Heralds a New Literature

By the end of the 14th century the language (in its altered form called Middle English) was being used by nobles as well as commoners. In 1362 it became the language of lawcourt pleadings, and by 1385 it was widely taught in place of French.

Most of the great literature of the time was written from 1360 to 1400, a good part of it by one man, Geoffrey Chaucer (1340?–1400). Chaucer was one of the world's greatest storytellers. His 'Canterbury Tales' is a masterpiece, with characters who remain eternally alive—the Wife of Bath, with her memories of five husbands; the noble Knight, returned from heroic deeds; his gay young son, the Squire ("He was as fressh as is the month of May"); the delightful Prioress ("At mete [meat] well ytaught was she with alle/ She let no morsel from her lippes falle."); and entertaining scoundrels, such as the Friar, Summoner, and Pardoner. (*See also* Chaucer.)

At the same time as Chaucer, another man was writing in the northern part of England. He is known as the Pearl Poet (14th century), from the name of one of his four poems in an old manuscript. Generally he is remembered for his narrative poem 'Sir Gawain and the Green Knight'. There are a number of poems about Sir Gawain (just as there are about Sir Lancelot, Sir Perceval, and King Arthur); but this is the best. Unfortunately, it is written in the Lancashire dialect and is almost as difficult to read as Old English. Chaucer may be read with a little study because the Midland dialect in which he wrote became the standard one for English writing. Even in translation, however, 'Sir Gawain and the Green Knight' is fascinating.

Another poet contemporary with Chaucer was William Langland (1330?–1400?), a figure almost as shadowy as the Pearl Poet. His masterpiece, also in a somewhat difficult dialect, is 'The Vision of William Concerning Piers the Plowman'. It consists of a series of dream-visions in which human life passes in review. Langland wrote with power and sincerity. He attacked the social ills of his time, rebuked evildoers, and urged men to "learn to love."

For nearly 200 years after the death of Chaucer there were almost no great literary works produced in England. One noteworthy exception is 'Morte d'Arthur', by Sir Thomas Malory (died 1470?). Malory made up this great collection of stories about King Arthur and his knights of the Round Table from the Arthurian legends circulating in French plus the English romances about the knights. 'Morte d'Arthur' was the main source for later retellings of the stories.

The other outstanding literary achievement of the times was the creation of the great English and Scottish ballads. These were probably sung by people at social gatherings. The ballads preserved the local events and beliefs and characters in an easily remembered form. It was not until several hundred years later that people began to write down these ballads. They are immensely vivid stories that modern readers find especially attractive. Three familiar ballads are 'The Wife of Usher's Well', about her three ghost sons; 'Sir Patrick Spens', concerning his death by drowning; and 'Edward', about his murderous revenge.

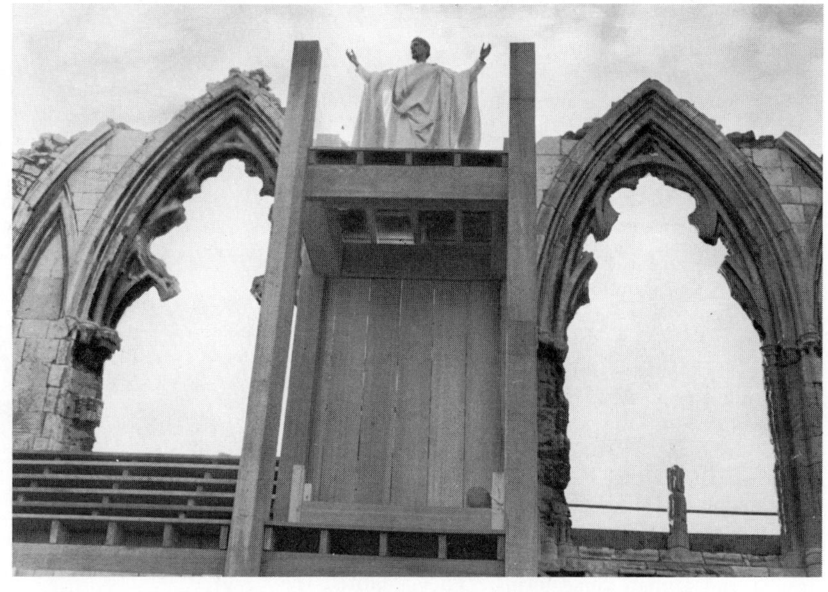

In this revived version of a famous mystery play, from the most complete cycle, the creation of the world is portrayed. God is seen coming out of the upper-level stage.

The Renaissance in English Literature

DURING THE 15th century an intellectual movement called the Renaissance swept Western Europe. The word means "rebirth" and refers especially to the revival of ancient Greek learning. For centuries scholars in Italy, Spain, and elsewhere had been translating the ancient works into Latin. Printing from movable type, invented about 1450, provided the means for circulating the books widely. This spread of ancient learning kindled a new spirit of inquiry and hastened the overthrow of feudal institutions. (*See also* Renaissance.)

Some modern scholars have questioned whether a total rebirth of learning actually took place. There had been, for example, Latin scholars in the earlier medieval period. It is certain, however, that something did happen in the course of the 15th century which changed the history of Western civilization and the set of men's minds. For England, the year 1485 is a convenient date for marking this change from medievalism. In that year two significant events took place: the Wars of the Roses ended on Bosworth Field and William Caxton printed Malory's 'Morte d'Arthur'.

The printing of 'Morte d'Arthur' was a radical departure from the past. Before Caxton established his first press in England, Johann Gutenberg and his partners had printed the Bible, in about 1455, in Germany; and printers were at work in several other European countries before the end of the 15th century. Caxton, however, turned to his native language rather than to Latin for his text. His first printed book was 'The Recuyell of the Historyes of Troye' (1475), which he translated.

Before the end of the century he printed several more books in English, including Chaucer's 'Canterbury Tales' (1478). The number of presses quickly increased in England, and with them, of course, the number of printed books.

In England the Renaissance coincided roughly with the reigns of the Tudor rulers Henry VIII, Edward VI, Mary I, and Elizabeth I. Under Elizabeth's brilliant rule England became a world power.

English Renaissance Poets

The three great poetic geniuses of Elizabethan times were Christopher Marlowe, Edmund Spenser, and William Shakespeare. All were typical Renaissance men, trained in the classics, fond of fine living, full of restless energy and a zest for ideas.

Writing was a social fashion of this time, a pastime enjoyed by the nobles as well as by men of lower stations. Henry Howard, earl of Surrey (1518?–47), and Sir Thomas Wyatt (1503–42) are two striking instances of a talent for poetry existing in men of affairs. Though active in England's service, in their short lives the two became familiar with French and Italian verse forms. They adapted the Italian sonnet for English use, and Surrey introduced blank verse in his translation of the 'Aeneid'.

A third nobleman with a talent for writing was Sir Philip Sidney (1554–86). He wrote a beautiful sonnet series, 'Astrophel and Stella' (1591), and produced a tremendously long and somewhat tedious novel called 'Arcadia' (1590). These men wrote only for amusement, but they also gave money and encouragement to poor, struggling writers.

Spenser and Marlowe

Edmund Spenser (1552?–99), also active in public service, was much more the professional man of letters than Wyatt or Sidney. His 'Shepheardes Calender' (1579) is made up of 12 poems, one for each month of the year. These poems were more charming than any England had seen for 200 years. Spenser wrote many other poems, including a sonnet series called 'Amoretti' (1595).

'The Faerie Queene' (1589–96), Spenser's masterpiece, was left unfinished; but the 6 books written, out of 12 planned, are of great length. 'The Faerie Queene' is an elaborate allegory built on the story of a 12-day feast honoring the Queen of Fairyland (Elizabeth I). Spenser worked out a poetic stanza well adapted to telling a story, a special form which is now known as the Spenserian stanza. (*See also* Spenser.)

Christopher Marlowe (1564–93) promised more greatness than he achieved. He died at 29, stabbed in a tavern brawl. A line from his own 'Doctor Faustus' is his best epitaph: "Cut is the branch that might have grown full straight." His plays, such as 'Tamburlaine' (1587?) and 'Doctor Faustus'

Sir Philip Sidney, an Elizabethan nobleman, was considered an ideal gentleman in his day. He is known for his sonnet series 'Astrophel and Stella'.

Shakespeare wrote more than 35 plays. The most powerful of these probably is the one about King Lear, who is portrayed here mad with grief.

(1588?), bring passion and tragedy onto the stage in lines of great force.

Thomas Kyd (1558–94) is known for his very successful play 'The Spanish Tragedy' (1587?). To a modern audience it is an overwhelming story of carnage. It is exciting drama, however. Some critics believe that Kyd also wrote a tragedy of Hamlet which became the source for Shakespeare's great play.

Shakespeare—Genius of Drama

The great genius of the Elizabethan Age was William Shakespeare (1564–1616). He wrote more than 35 plays as well as 154 sonnets and 2 narrative poems ('Venus and Adonis', 1593; 'The Rape of Lucrece', 1594).

Like Chaucer, Shakespeare had a genius for telling a story. Although he generally took over stories already told by others, his adaptations of these narratives made them into something new and wonderful. Shakespeare surpassed even Chaucer in creating character. Noble and disturbed Hamlet, pathetic Ophelia, wise Portia, ambitious Macbeth, witty Rosalind, villainous Iago, dainty Ariel—these are a few of the characters Shakespeare made immortal.

In addition to his ability to tell a story and to create character, Shakespeare was able to use words brilliantly. Phrases and whole lines from his works have become part of daily speech—for example, "the milk of human kindness" or "the play's the thing." Entire speeches are universally familiar—"To be or not to be," from 'Hamlet'; "All the world's a stage," from 'As You Like It'; "The quality of mercy is not strained," from 'The Merchant of Venice'. No one in all history has had a greater command of the right word, the unforgettable phrase, or the sentence that strikes straight to the heart of the truth. (*See also* Shakespeare.)

Jonson and His 'Volpone'

Contemporary with Shakespeare was Ben Jonson (1573?–1637). Many people once thought him to be a greater playwright than Shakespeare because his plays ('Every Man in His Humor', 1598; 'The Alchemist', 1610) are more "correct"—that is, they are more carefully patterned after the drama scheme of the ancient Greek and Roman writers. Only later did critics begin to prefer the deeper genius of Shakespeare and to realize that mechanical "correctness" is not the highest aim of a play or poem. Jonson's comedy 'Volpone' (1606?) is a comical and sarcastic portrait of a wealthy but selfish old man who keeps his greedy would-be heirs hanging on his wishes, each thinking that *he* will inherit Volpone's wealth. (*See also* Jonson.)

After the greatest days of Shakespeare and Jonson, the English drama declined in excellence. A taste for melodrama and sensationalism hurt much of the excellent writing done by such dramatists as John Webster (1580?–1625?), Thomas Middleton (1570?–1627), and John Ford (1586–1640?). These playwrights took such liberties with their subjects and with the language that in 1642 the Puritan reformers controlling London ordered that the theaters be closed. They did not reopen officially until the Restoration of 1660. Then a new sort of drama arose, one much influenced by French dramatic styles and methods.

The King James Bible

One of the supreme achievements of the English Renaissance came at its close, in the King James Bible. This translation was ordered by James I and made by 47 scholars working in cooperation. It was published in 1611 and is known as the Authorized Version. It is rightly regarded as the most influential book in the history of English civilization.

There had been translations of the Bible before 1611. William Tyndale (1492?–1536) first translated the New Testament from the Greek into English (1525). Miles Coverdale (1488?–1569) made the first complete translation of the Bible into English using Tyndale's version (1535). There had also been other translations; but the King James Version combined homely, dignified phrases into a style of great richness and loveliness. It has been a model of writing for generations of English-speaking people.

Changing Mood in the 17th Century

THE 17th century has sometimes been called an age of transition; sometimes an age of revolution. It was both, though much of the revolution of thought had actually been accomplished by the end of the 16th century.

The difficulties which brought about such fierce political and social struggles as resulted in the civil war and the government under Oliver Cromwell are mirrored in the writings of the 17th century (*see* England, History). The old unity of Elizabethan life was gone. The national pride of Englishmen lessened as the Crown lost dignity through the behavior of James I, Charles I, and Charles II. A new middle class began to show its power.

The glowing enthusiasm of such men as Marlowe and Spenser gave way to a cool, scientific attitude, to a spirit that studied small details rather than large generalizations and looked to the world of fact more than to that of the imagination. Late in the 16th century Sir Francis Bacon (1561–1626) had taken "all knowledge for his province"—a typical Renaissance ambition. Later, scientists would stake out much smaller and more workable claims. Exploration on the grand scale gave way to exploitation of the discoveries and to colonization and trade, activities which helped the mercantile class to wealth and power late in the century.

17th-Century Prose

The 17th century was an age of prose. Interest in scientific detail and leisurely observation marked the prose of the time. This new writing style emphasized clarity, directness, and economy of expression. It first appeared just before 1600 in the 'Essays' of Bacon (*see* Bacon, Lord Francis). The physician Sir Thomas Browne (1605–82) wrote with dry precision in 'Pseudodoxia Epidemica' (1646), as he amusingly and gravely discussed such beliefs as "an elephant hath no joints" or "hares are both male and female."

Robert Burton (1577–1640) was one of the "originals" of his age. His 'Anatomy of Melancholy' (1621) is important not only as a document of 17th-century thought but also as one of the first attempts to explain human behavior in materialistic terms. This rambling and much-revised book is a storehouse of medical lore and fact, moral observation, and anecdote. In recent times scholars have recognized that Burton's observations were deeply perceptive.

Jeremy Taylor (1613–67), a brilliant student and preacher, wrote 'Holy Living' (1650) and 'Holy Dying' (1651). He was one of the great prose writers of the period. Izaak Walton (1593–1683) is famous for his biographies and 'The Compleat Angler' (1653). The former began when he was asked to write a brief life of John Donne. 'The Compleat Angler' delights readers whether they are fishermen themselves or are only slightly interested in what Walton called the "contemplative man's recreation."

Bunyan and Pepys

The prose masterpiece of the century was 'The Pilgrim's Progress' (1678). John Bunyan (1628–88) had studied the King James Version of the Bible; and with it as a style model, he wrote a study of a Christian's journey through life and the difficulties that beset him as he tries to reach the Celestial City. 'The Pilgrim's Progress' was, for more than 200 years, second only to the Bible in popularity. Even today it is much read for its vigorous scenes of English country life. (*See also* Bunyan, John.)

Izaak Walton and a student relax on a riverbank. The London shopkeeper's discourse on the delights and the finer points of fishing, 'The Compleat Angler', is a classic.

The religious zeal of Bunyan contrasts with the cavalier spirit of Samuel Pepys (1633–1703). As secretary to the Admiralty, Pepys was a career man. He loved London and its life, and he recorded his daily experiences in shorthand and cipher in a diary (published in 1825). It is a splendid book of gossip, a record both of trivial matters, such as the behavior at court, and of major events, such as the Great Plague (1664–65), and the Great Fire (1666). Pepys's

'Diary' is a window on the last part of the 17th century in England. (*See also* Pepys.)

Milton—Puritan Poet

The sober, scientific spirit of the 17th century did not destroy poetry. The great poet of the first half of the century was John Milton (1608–74), a Puritan who served Cromwell as Latin secretary. He first wrote some short poems, the best known being 'L'Allegro' (1645) and 'Il Penseroso' (1645). The first tells of the day's activities of a cheerful man; and the second, of the night's activities of a thoughtful scholar. A music-play (or masque) known as 'Comus' was produced in 1634, with music composed by Henry Lawes. Milton's greatest early poem is 'Lycidas' (1638), a lament on the death of a college friend.

Milton's service under Cromwell brought on blindness. This did not stop his writing poetry. He dictated his masterpiece, 'Paradise Lost' (1667), to his daughters. This is an epic poem telling of the fall of the angels and of the creation of Adam and Eve and their temptation by Satan in the Garden of Eden ("Of Man's first disobedience, and the fruit/ Of that forbidden tree . . ."). It is written in blank verse of great solemnity.

'Paradise Regained' (1671) is Milton's sequel to 'Paradise Lost'. He considered the later work his masterpiece, but most readers have not agreed with him. Milton's last work is a blank-verse tragedy in the ancient Greek manner. It deals with the story of Samson and Delilah. 'Samson Agonistes' (1671) is in many ways Milton's allegorical description of himself as a Samson bound in chains by his enemies, the followers of King Charles II. (*See also* Milton.)

The Metaphysical and the Cavalier Poets

An important group of 17th-century writers were the metaphysical poets. Metaphysical poetry makes use of *conceits*—that is, of farfetched similes and metaphors intended to startle the reader into an awareness of the relationships among things ordinarily not associated.

John Donne (1573–1631) was the greatest of the metaphysical poets. His chief subject was love as it perfects man. He never treated the subject profanely. He was occasionally earthy, but only because he recognized that man is a creature who must love in a natural way. His poem 'The Extasy' is a celebration of sacramental love. His prose is as rich as his poetry; but nothing can match the mastery of such poetry as his 'Hymne to God My God, in My Sicknesse'.

George Herbert (1593–1633), like Donne, was both a metaphysical poet and an Anglican priest. Some of Herbert's most effective poetry deals with man's thirst for God and with God's abounding love. Herbert's collection, 'The Temple' (1633), was published posthumously (he probably did not intend his poetry to be published). Andrew Marvell (1621–78), Richard Crashaw (1612?–49), and Henry Vaughan (1622–95) were other metaphysical poets of merit. Most easily understood, perhaps, is Marvell, at least in the well-loved lyric 'To His Coy Mistress'.

John Donne was the outstanding metaphysical poet. The clergyman's poems, many of them deeply religious, are remarkable for their intricate imagery and striking phrases.

The Cavalier poets were followers and supporters of Charles I. They wrote with a sense of elegance and in a style which emphasized wit and charm and the delicate play of words and ideas. Chief among the Cavalier group were Thomas Carew (1595?–1639), Richard Lovelace (1618–58), Sir John Suckling (1609–42), and Robert Herrick (1591–1674). Herrick was a clergyman in the Church of England; but his ministerial duties did not prevent him from admiring a pretty face or the loveliness of the English landscape. His poems deal with familiar subjects.

Dryden—Giant of the Late 1600's

The major literary figure of the last quarter of the century was John Dryden (1631–1700). Such poems as 'Absalom and Achitophel' (1681–82) and 'Alexander's Feast' (1697) establish his superiority in both satire and lyric. He was also the leading dramatist, writing both comedy ('Marriage-à-la-Mode', 1673; 'The Kind Keeper', 1680) and tragedy ('Aureng-Zebe', 1676) of great popularity. In addition, he was the leading critic. His prose, best seen in the prefaces of his plays, has the flexible, modern style to be found in good writing of the 20th century.

Much of what Dryden wrote, however, is so closely connected with political and social events of his day that to read it requires a scholar's knowledge of the period. The virtues of his best writing—clarity, good sense, and intellectual vigor—became the dominant virtues of the writing of the 18th century. (*See also* Dryden.)

The 18th Century—Age of Reason

With Joseph Addison, Steele created the modern essay in *The Tatler* and *The Spectator.*

THE MOST striking quality of the 18th century was its optimism. Even the descriptive historical titles of the period express the spirit of improvement and progress. Many people of the time thought they were passing through a golden period similar to that of the Roman emperor Augustus. For this reason the name "Augustan" was given to the early 18th century. The century has also been called the Age of Enlightenment. Many writers of the era used ancient Greek and Roman authors as models of style. Hence the period in literature is often described as neoclassic.

Merchants and tradesmen achieved tremendous economic power at this time. Scientific discoveries were encouraged. Many important inventions—for example, the spinning jenny, the power loom, and the steam engine—brought about an industrial society. Cities grew in size, and London began to assume its present position as a great industrial and commercial center.

In addition to a comfortable life, the members of the middle class demanded a respectable, moralistic art that was controlled by common sense. They reacted in protest to the aristocratic immoralities in much of the Restoration literature.

Addison, Steele, and Defoe

The modern essay began in two periodicals, *The Tatler* (1709–11), founded by Sir Richard Steele (1672–1729), and *The Spectator* (1711–12), founded by Steele and Joseph Addison (1672–1719). The kindly and witty essays by these men appealed to the middle class in the coffeehouses rather than to the nobility in their palaces. The aim of *The Spectator,* Addison said, was ". . . to enliven morality with wit, and to temper wit with morality." Steele and Addison's essays are still models of clear, informal writing. (*See also* Addison.)

Most people think of Daniel Defoe (1661?–1731) only as the author of 'Robinson Crusoe' (1719); but when Defoe wrote that novel, he had already lived a life full enough for three ordinary mortals. Defoe was first of all a journalist, with an eye for a news story. Single-handedly he produced a newspaper, *The Review* (1704–13), which was an important ancestor of modern newspapers. The list of Defoe's writings runs to more than 400 titles. In all of them, articles and books, is the kind of writing that Defoe recommended to others—a "plain and homely style." Even the great novels of his last years, 'Moll Flanders' (1722) and 'Robinson Crusoe', read like a modern reporter's account of events. (*See also* Defoe.)

Swift—Scornful Prose Genius

Jonathan Swift (1667–1745) is one of the great prose writers of all time. Although born in Ireland, Swift always said that he was an Englishman. His defense of the Irish people against the tyranny of the English government, however, was whole-hearted. As much as he may have disliked Ireland, he disliked injustice and tyranny more. In a bitter pamphlet, 'A Modest Proposal' (1729), he ironically suggested that the Irish babies be specially fattened for profitable sale as meat, since the English were eating the Irish people anyhow, by heavy taxation.

Swift's masterpiece is 'Gulliver's Travels' (1726). It is a satire on human folly and stupidity. Swift said that he wrote it to vex the world rather than to divert it. Most people, however, are so delightfully entertained by the tiny Lilliputians and by the huge Brobdingnagians that they do not bother much with Swift's bitter satire on human pettiness or crudity. No one has ever written English prose with greater

This picture was the frontispiece for the first edition of Defoe's famous story of a man stranded on a desert island.

The poet Alexander Pope, one of the most famous writers of his day, was probably the first English author to live by writing alone.

Thomas Gray was a noted scholar, letter writer, and critic as well as a poet. He is best known for 'Elegy Written in a Country Churchyard'.

sharpness and economy than Swift. His literary style has all the 18th-century virtues at their best. (*See also* Swift.)

Satire in Pope's Poetry

The genius of Alexander Pope (1688–1744) lay in satirical poetry. He said that he wanted to "shoot folly as it flies,/And catch the manners living as they rise." 'The Dunciad' (1728) lists the stupid writers and men of England by name as dunces. These "dunces" proceeded to attack Pope in kind.

Pope excelled in his ability to coin unforgettable phrases. Such lines as "fools rush in where angels fear to tread" or "damn with faint praise" illustrate why Pope is the most quoted poet in English literature except for Shakespeare.

One of his lighter, though still satirical, poems is 'The Rape of the Lock' (1712). It mockingly describes a furious fight between two families when a young man snips off a lock of the beautiful Belinda's hair. Pope wrote in heroic couplets, a technique in which he has been unsurpassed. In thought and form he carried 18th-century reason and order to its highest peak. (*See also* Pope, Alexander.)

New Voices in Poetry

James Thomson (1700–48) was another major poet of the period. In his simplicity and love of nature he foreshadowed Romanticism. Edward Young (1683–1765) wrote 'The Complaint: or, Night Thoughts on Life, Death, and Immortality' (1742–45), which put in practice his ideas about the personal quality of poetry. Robert Blair (1699–1746) wrote one important poem, 'The Grave' (1743), which advanced the "graveyard school" of poetry. William Collins (1721–59) was not a popular success in his lifetime, but his 'Ode on the Popular Superstitions of the Highlands of Scotland' (published posthumously, in 1788) clearly marked a turn to the wild and irregular as proper subjects for poetry.

Thomas Gray (1716–71) was probably the most typical man of letters of the period. He was a scholar of ancient languages, a letter writer, and a critic as well as a poet. His 'Elegy Written in a Country Churchyard' (1751) is a collection of 18th-century commonplaces expressing concern for lowly folk.

George Crabbe (1754–1832) was the last poet of the century who used the couplet in didactic poetry. His political and social satire 'The Village' (1783) is a realistic appraisal of country life in his times. William Cowper (1731–1800) exemplifies the strange decay of the spirit in the 18th century. He was given to extreme, morbid sensibilities. 'The Task' (1785) is a falsely cheerful poem of a man who feels himself to be condemned. (*See also* Cowper.)

Start of the Modern Novel

The 20th century can be grateful to the 18th for developing the novel (*see* Novel). Samuel Richardson (1689–1761) wrote the first modern novel—that is, one with a fairly well-planned plot, with suspense and climax, and with some attempt to understand the minds and hearts of the characters. This important novel, 'Pamela' (1740), is made up of letters from Pamela Andrews. She tells of her unhappy attempts to get a husband, but the book ends happily.

Henry Fielding (1707–54) was amused by 'Pamela' and tried to parody it in 'Joseph Andrews' (1742), which purports to be the story of Pamela's brother. Seven years later he wrote 'Tom Jones' (1749), in many ways one of the greatest novels in English literature. It tells the story of a young foundling who is driven from his adopted home, wanders to London, and eventually, for all his suffering, wins his lady. The picture of English life, both in the country and in the city, is brilliantly drawn. The humor of the book is delightful.

The first novel by Tobias Smollett (1721–71) was 'Roderick Random' (1748). Although it is a striking collection of adventures, it lacks the good plot of 'Tom Jones'. Smollett's best work is 'Humphry Clinker' (1771). It tells, by means of letters, the story of a trip by the Bramble family across England, from Bath to London, and up into Scotland. The eccentric characters have many comic experiences.

Laurence Sterne (1713–68) wrote 'A Sentimental Journey' (1768) partly in answer to a travel book written in ill temper by Smollett. Sterne's greatest book is 'Tristram Shandy' (1760–67), a topsy-turvy collection of episodes with little organization but a wealth of 18th-century humor.

Johnson and His Circle

If the 18th century made much of elegance and good manners, it also made much of honesty and common sense. These useful virtues were personified by Dr. Samuel Johnson (1709–84), the leading literary figure of the century. He wrote some sensible but uninspired poetry ('The Vanity of Human Wishes', 1749). His novel, 'Rasselas' (1759), is equally sensible and equally dull. His masterpiece is 'A Dictionary of the English Language' (1755). Johnson's common sense is shown in the clear definitions of words. He made some mistakes, however. A woman asked him why he defined "pastern" as "the knee of a horse." Johnson answered, "Ignorance, Madam, pure ignorance."

Johnson is immortal not only for what he wrote but also for his forceful personality and his wonderful conversation. This has been recorded by James Boswell (1740–95) in 'The Life of Samuel Johnson, LL.D.' (1791), the greatest of English biographies. Boswell had a keen eye for significant detail and a proper reverence for his subject. He noted all of Johnson's peculiarities—his rolling walk, his twitching face, his horrible table manners, his rudeness to stupid people—but he also saw his subject's sturdy common sense and his honesty. (*See also* Johnson, Samuel.)

Johnson and others organized the Literary Club in 1764. The club gathered together the most celebrated artists of the time. The great orator Edmund Burke (1729–97) and the great historian Edward Gibbon (1737–94) were members. Another member was Oliver Goldsmith (1728–74). He wrote one of the best plays ('She Stoops to Conquer', 1773), one of the best poems ('The Deserted Village', 1770), and one of the best novels ('The Vicar of Wakefield', 1766) of the latter half of the 18th century. Johnson said of his versatile friend: "[He] touched nothing that he did not adorn." (*See also* Goldsmith.)

Richard Brinsley Sheridan (1751–1816), orator and political figure, was also a writer of comedies of

A lawyer who began novel writing to make fun of Richardson, Fielding became famous as the greatest early novelist.

Sterne, an Irish clergyman, skillfully combined humor and pathos. His best novel is 'Tristram Shandy'.

manners which lampooned social affectations and pretentiousness. His masterpiece, 'The School for Scandal' (1777), features malicious gossips with such revealing names as Sir Benjamin Backbite, Lady Sneerwell, and Mrs. Candour.

For another of his clever plays, 'The Rivals' (1775), Sheridan invented the unforgettable Mrs. Malaprop, whose name remains the designation for a person who misuses words. In one memorable speech she says, "if I reprehend anything in this world, it is the use of my oracular tongue and a nice derangement of epitaphs."

A lively scene from Goldsmith's novel 'The Vicar of Wakefield' was drawn by Thomas Rowlandson, a well-known 18th-century caricaturist. (From Garnett and Gosse, 'English Literature', Macmillan.)

The Romantic Movement in England

AT THE END of the 18th century a new literature arose in England. It was called *Romanticism,* and it opposed most of the ideas held earlier in the century. Romanticism had its roots in a changed attitude toward mankind. The forerunners of the Romanticists argued that men are naturally good; society makes them bad. If the social world could be changed, all men might be happier. Many reforms were suggested: better treatment of people in prisons and almshouses; fewer death penalties for minor crimes; and an increase in charitable institutions.

The Romanticists believed that all men are brothers and deserve the treatment to which human beings are by nature entitled. Every man has a right to life, liberty, and equal opportunity. These ideas had been well stated in the American Declaration of Independence. In France a revolution of the common people began in 1789. Many Englishmen hoped that the new democracies—France and the United States—would show the way for the rest of the world to follow. Along with democracy and individualism came other ideas. One was that the simple, humble life is best. Another was that people should live close to nature.

Because of this concern for nature and the simple folk, authors began to take an interest in old legends, folk ballads, antiquities, ruins, "noble savages," and rustic characters. Many writers started to give more play to their senses and to their imagination. Their pictures of nature became livelier and more realistic. They loved to describe rural scenes, graveyards, majestic mountains, and roaring waterfalls. They also liked to write poems and stories of such eerie or supernatural things as ghosts, haunted castles, fairies, and mad folk.

Thus Romanticism grew. The movement cannot be precisely defined. It was a group of ideas, a web of beliefs. No one Romantic writer expressed all these ideas, but each believed enough of them to set him apart from earlier writers. The Romanticist was emotional and imaginative. He acted through inspiration and intuition. He believed in democracy, humanity, and the possibility of achieving a better world.

Pre-Romantic Writers

Before the Romantic movement burst into full expression there were beginners, or experimenters. Some of them are great names in English literature. Robert Burns (1759–96), a Scot whose love of nature and of freedom has seldom been surpassed, scorned the false pretensions of wealth and birth ("A man's a man for a' that."). His nature lyrics are tenderly beautiful ('To a Mountain Daisy'); his sentimental songs are sung wherever young or old folks gather ('Auld Lang Syne', 'Flow Gently Sweet Afton'). His rich humor can still be felt in 'Tam o' Shanter', 'To a Louse', and 'The Cotter's Saturday Night'. (*See also* Burns.)

Cowper had cried out against the inhumanity of slavery and political oppression. William Godwin (1756–1836) and his wife, Mary Wollstonecraft Godwin (1759–97), were also intense social critics. Mary Godwin's 'Vindication of the Rights of Women' (1792) was one of the first feminist books in all literature. Godwin's 'Political Justice' (1793) had a great influence on the Romantic poets Wordsworth, Coleridge, and Shelley.

James Macpherson (1736–96), a Scotsman, composed an elaborate epic poem which, he claimed, he had translated from the work of the ancient Gaelic bard called Ossian. Thomas Percy (1729–1811) collected old English songs and ballads. His 'Reliques of Ancient English Poetry' (1765) is the best source for the ballads of medieval England.

Another group of forerunners of Romanticism included the writers of stories of terror and imagination—the Gothic school of "spine chillers." Representative novels are 'The Castle of Otranto' (1764), by Horace Walpole (1717–97); 'The Mysteries of Udolpho' (1794), by Ann Radcliffe (1764–1823); and 'The Monk' (1796), by Matthew Gregory Lewis (1775–1818). All these novels are filled with the machinery of sensationalism—unreal characters, supernatural events, and overripe imagination. These qualities reached a fever pitch in 'Frankenstein' (1818), by Mary Wollstonecraft Shelley (1797–1851).

The First Great Romanticists

William Blake (1757–1827) was both poet and artist (*see* Blake, William). He not only wrote books, but he also illustrated and printed them. Many of his conservative contemporaries thought him insane because his ideas were so unusual. Chief among these "insane" ideas was his devotion to freedom and universal love. He was interested in children and animals—the most innocent of God's creatures. As he wrote in 'Songs of Innocence' (1789):

When the voices of children are heard on the green,
  And laughing is heard on the hill,
My heart is at rest within my breast,
  And everything else is still.

Certainly no one has put more wonder and mystery into beautiful melodic verse than did Samuel Taylor Coleridge (1772–1834). The strange, haunting supernaturalism of 'The Rime of the Ancient Mariner' (1798) and 'Christabel' (1816) have universal and irresistible appeal. (*See also* Coleridge.)

A close friend of Coleridge's for many years was William Wordsworth (1770–1850). Together they brought out a volume of verse, 'Lyrical Ballads' (1798), which sounded the new note in poetry. Coleridge found beauty in the unreal, Wordsworth found it in the realities of nature. From nature Wordsworth learned that life may be a continuous development toward goodness. He believed that if man heeds the lessons of nature he will grow in character and moral worth. (*See also* Wordsworth.)

Charles Lamb (1775–1834), a schoolmate of Coleridge's, for the most part had little of the serious quality that one sees in the authors of 'Lyrical Ballads'; nor was he an ardent lover of nature. A city man, he showed how a person could live happily among his books by his own fireside. His best-known essay is the playful 'Dissertation on Roast Pig' (1822). In 'Tales from Shakespear' (1807), he and his sister Mary rewrote many of Shakespeare's plays into stories for children. (*See also* Lamb.)

Interest in the past and in people and a love of rugged scenery are found in the works of Sir Walter Scott (1771–1832). 'The Lay of the Last Minstrel' (1805) and 'The Lady of the Lake' (1810) are representative of Scott's poems. Between 1814 and 1832 Scott wrote 32 novels. They include 'Guy Mannering' (1815) and 'Ivanhoe' (1819). (*See also* Scott, Sir Walter.)

Jane Austen (1775–1817), a gifted writer of realistic novels, had difficulty finding a publisher for her skillfully drawn portraits of English middle-class people. 'Pride and Prejudice' (1813) is her best-known work. (*See also* Austen.)

Among the lesser Romantic figures was Robert Southey (1774–1843), who was poet laureate of England and author of 'The Three Bears' and 'The Battle of Blenheim'. An industrious writer, he earned his living solely by his pen. William Hazlitt (1778–1830) earned his way by lecturing and by writing for critical magazines, such as *The Edinburgh Review* (*see* Hazlitt).

Burns is reminded of himself in childhood by this boy. The picture is from 'Burns—by Himself', arranged and illustrated by Keith Henderson (Methuen).

The Younger Romanticists

By 1812 the older Romanticists had become conservative in politics. They no longer supported radical causes or championed the oppressed. The younger Romantic writers, however, quickly and noisily took up the cry for liberty and justice.

George Gordon Byron (1788–1824) was an outspoken critic of the evils of his time. He hoped for human perfection, but his recognition of man's faults led him frequently to despair and disillusionment ('Manfred', 1817; 'Cain', 1821). Much of his work is satire, bitterly contemptuous of human foibles ('Don Juan', 1819–24). His narrative poems ('The Corsair', 1814; 'Mazeppa', 1819), about wild and impetuous persons, brought him success. He was a skilled versifier with a remarkable ear for rhythms. Byron influenced the youth of his day more than any other Romanticist.

"Byronism" was a mood adopted by thousands of young men. (*See also* Byron.)

Percy Bysshe Shelley (1792–1822) was the black sheep of a well-to-do, conservative family. Sonnets, songs, and poetic dramas flowed from his pen in the last four years of his life. Many of these works are profound and meditative ('Prometheus Unbound', 1820). Others are exquisitely lyrical and beautiful ('The Cloud', 'To a Skylark', 'Ode to the West Wind'). 'Adonais' (1821), his tribute to Keats, ranks among the greatest elegies. (*See also* Shelley).

John Keats (1795–1821) was a greater poet than either Byron or Shelley (*see* Keats). He believed that true happiness was to be found in art and natural beauty ('Ode on a Grecian Urn', 1819; 'Ode to a Nightingale', 1819). His verses are lively testimony to the truth of his words in 'Endymion' (1818):

> A thing of beauty is a joy forever:
> Its loveliness increases; it will never
> Pass into nothingness;

Other Romanticists that deserve mention are Leigh Hunt (1784–1859), whose 'Abou Ben Adhem' continues to be a favorite; Thomas Moore (1779–1852), whose 'Believe Me, If All Those Endearing Young Charms' is still a favorite of vocal groups; and Thomas De Quincey (1785–1859), known best for his 'Confessions of an English Opium Eater' (1822). De Quincey, however, ought to be better known for his useful distinction between the "literature of knowledge" and the "literature of power."

An impractical dreamer, Shelley wanted to be a political reformer; instead he became one of England's great lyric poets.

English Literature of the Victorian Age

THE LITERATURE written during Queen Victoria's reign (1837–1901) has been given the name Victorian. The basic characteristics of the period, however, would have been the same with or without Queen Victoria. Many great changes took place in the first half of the 19th century. Intellectual rebellions, such as those of Byron and Shelley, gave place to balance and adjustment. Individualism began to be replaced by social and governmental restraints. More and more people were gaining comfort and prosperity. Great Britain changed from a provincial nation to a worldwide empire. This progress brought its problems. Often men had to choose between ideals and material gain.

Science made rapid strides in the 19th century. The theory of evolution gave new insight into the biological sciences. Technical progress transformed Britain into a land of mechanical and industrial activity, but science created doubts as well as materialistic optimism. Old ideas of faith and religion were put to serious tests by the new attitudes brought about by scientific progress. There was a reemphasis—oftentimes stuffy and pompous—of moral and religious beliefs. Literature, said some, should show people how to be good.

Nevertheless, many people in England were still poor—badly housed, undernourished, and sick. Progress, obviously, would not come by itself—it had to be earned. Freedom had to be guarded zealously. Would the spirit of man be destroyed by the machine? Would people become slaves to industry and the pursuit of wealth? Would art be replaced by skills and crafts? These were the questions that troubled Englishmen in the age of Queen Victoria.

The transition from the late Romantic to the Victorian period is best understood in the figure of Thomas Carlyle (1795–1881). His life spanned the years of Romantic excitement and Victorian achievement. Carlyle thoroughly repudiated the Romanticists. To him the universe seemed the "living garment of God." In 'Sartor Resartus' (1833–34) he counseled that the way out of the "Everlasting Nay," or negative denial, was first to find what one could do; then to give all one's energies to it. The effort of the moral will, he said, would bring freedom from despair. (*See also* Carlyle.)

Major Victorian Poets

Poets shifted from the extremely personal expression (or *subjectivism*) of the Romantic writers to an objective surveying of the problems of human life. The poems of Tennyson, Browning, and Arnold especially reflect this change. Much Victorian poetry was put to the service of society.

Alfred Tennyson (1809–92) attempted to give direction to his readers. 'Idylls of the King' (1859) is a dis-

Charlotte Brontë's 'Jane Eyre' is a melodramatic novel about an orphan who eventually marries her moody employer after a youth marked by unhappiness.

guised study of current ethical and social conditions. 'Locksley Hall' (1842), 'In Memoriam' (1850), and 'Maud' (1855) deal with conflicting scientific and social ideas. Much of Tennyson's poetry, however, can be read without worrying about such problems. His narrative skill makes many of his poems interesting just as stories. Each of the Arthurian tales in 'Idylls of the King' brings the reader a wealth of beauty and experience. 'The Lady of Shalott' and 'The Death of Oenone' are pleasing tales to young readers. (*See also* Tennyson.)

For those who have seen Rudolph Besier's modern play 'The Barretts of Wimpole Street', Elizabeth and Robert Browning need no introduction. Elizabeth Barrett Browning (1806–61) wrote the most exquisite love poems of her time in 'Sonnets from the Portuguese' (1850). These lyrics were written secretly while she was being courted by Robert Browning. (*See also* Browning, Elizabeth Barrett.)

Browning (1812–89) is best remembered for his dramatic monologues. 'My Last Duchess' (1842), 'Fra Lippo Lippi' (1855), and 'Andrea del Sarto' (1855) are excellent examples. The stirring rhythm of 'How They Brought the Good News from Ghent to Aix' (1845) and the simple wonder of 'The Pied Piper of Hamelin' (1842) endear Browning to readers. His expressions of personal faith have inspired thousands of readers ('Epilogue to Asolando', 1889; 'Rabbi Ben Ezra', 1864; 'Prospice', 1864). The poetic drama 'Pippa Passes' (1841) is one of his finest efforts. (*See also* Browning, Robert.)

The poetry of Matthew Arnold (1822–88) is marked by an intense seriousness and classic restraint. 'Sohrab and Rustum' (1853) is a fine blank-verse narrative. His elegiac poems on the death of his father, Dr. Thomas Arnold ('Rugby Chapel', 1867), and of his friend Arthur Hugh Clough ('Thyrsis', 1867) are profound and moving. His interest in the problem of making Englishmen aware of higher values of life caused him to quit writing poetry and turn to critical prose. As a critic, he drove his ideas home with clarity and force. (*See also* Arnold, Matthew.)

Arnold's somber and disillusioned poem 'Empedocles on Etna' (1852) was characteristic of the poetry dealing with the conflict between religion and science. A much more popular poem on the same theme was the free translation of the 'Rubáiyát of Omar Khayyám' (1859), by Edward Fitzgerald (1809–83). The poem was originally written by Omar, a Persian astronomer. Fitzgerald claimed that the only course of action left to the man whose religious ideals had been destroyed by science was self-indulgence.

The Pre-Raphaelite Brotherhood

The Pre-Raphaelites, a group of painters and poets, rebelled against the sentimental and the commonplace. They wished to revive the artistic standards of the time before the Italian painter Raphael (1483–1520). Their poems are full of mystery and pictorial language. One member was Dante Gabriel Rossetti (1828–82). His 'Blessed Damozel' (1850) and 'Sister Helen' (1870) are typical of this highly sensuous verse. 'Goblin Market' (1862), by his sister Christina Georgina Rossetti (1830–94), is one of the most fanciful poems in the language. (*See also* Rossetti, Dante Gabriel; Rossetti, Christina Georgina.)

William Morris (1834–96) also was interested in both painting and poetry. His interest in handicrafts grew into a philosophy of art, and he dedicated the rest of his life to the attempt to bring a love of workmanship back into the English workingman's life. This activity took two forms: the promotion of the crafts through such organizations as the Kelmscott Press and the promotion of the worker's happiness through guild socialism. 'The Earthly Paradise' (1868–70) is a series of tales linked by the same device used in 'Canterbury Tales'. In 'The Dream of John Ball' (1888), a prose romance, Morris dealt with one of the leaders of the 14th-century revolt of Wat Tyler. (*See also* Morris, William.)

Another poet closely associated with the Pre-Raphaelites was Algernon Charles Swinburne (1837–1909). Swinburne wrote many verse dramas on classical and historical subjects ('Mary Stuart', 1881). Many of his lyrics were criticized for their eroticism.

All his poetry is filled with rich, melodic effects. Some critics have said that his verse is all "sound and fury signifying nothing." (*See also* Swinburne.)

The direct opposite of Swinburne was Gerard Manley Hopkins (1844–89), a Jesuit priest. His imagery and metrical technique are quite modern, and his subject matter is intensely religious. His poems, written between 1876 and 1889, were not published until 1918 because their unusual rhythm and metaphors were considered too strange to be accepted earlier.

There were other notable poets writing at the end of the century. They included Francis Thompson (1859–1907), author of 'The Hound of Heaven' (1893); Ernest Dowson (1867–1900), who wrote 'Cynara' (1896); and the pessimist John Davidson (1857–1909), author of 'Fleet Street Eclogues' (1893).

Victorian Novelists

The English novel came of age in the Victorian period. There had been a decline in novel writing at the beginning of the century, partly because fiction had turned to horror and crude emotionalism and partly because of religious and moral objections to the reading of novels. Even Sir Walter Scott, at first, considered the craft of the novelist degrading and kept his authorship a secret. In the Victorian period, however, these attitudes toward the novel were to change.

With the rise of the popular magazine, authors began to experiment with serialized fiction. Soon they were writing novels. Such was the beginning of Dickens' 'Sketches by Boz' (1836) and of Thackeray's 'The Yellowplush Correspondence' (1837–38).

Charles Dickens (1812–70) became a master of local color, as in 'The Pickwick Papers' (1836–37). Few of his novels have convincing plots; accident and coincidence govern the action. In characterization and in the creation of moods, however, he was outstanding. By 1850 Dickens had become England's best-loved novelist. (*See also* Dickens.)

The talents of William Makepeace Thackeray (1811–63) produced a different type of novel. He was not a reformer, as Dickens was, and he was not moved to tearful sentiments by the world's unfortunates. Instead, he attempted to see the whole of life, detached and critically. He disliked sham, hypocrisy, stupidity, false optimism, and self-seeking. The result was satire on manners. Literature would be the poorer without 'Vanity Fair' (1847–48) and its heroine, Becky Sharp. (*See also* Thackeray.)

The Brontë sisters (Charlotte, 1816–55; Emily, 1818–48; Anne, 1820–49) wrote strange, tortured novels as an escape from their own drab lives. Charlotte's 'Jane Eyre' (1847) is wildly melodramatic, as is Emily's 'Wuthering Heights' (1847). The latter is redeemed by its ventures beyond reality into the world of mad genius. (*See also* Brontë Family.)

English novelists turned to the logical plot and the concept of a central theme. Anthony Trollope (1815–82) dealt with middle- and upper-class people interestingly, naturally, and wittily ('Orley Farm', 1862). George Eliot (1819–80) was one of England's greatest women novelists. In 'Silas Marner' (1861) and 'Middlemarch' (1871–72) she used the novel to interpret life. (*See also* Trollope; Eliot, George.)

Wilkie Collins (1824–89) was one of the earliest writers to build a novel wholly around an ingenious plot—the formula that is used in the modern mystery story. 'The Moonstone' (1868) is his best.

Birth of the Psychological Novel

As biology and psychology advanced, it became clear that human beings could no longer be shown simply as heroes and villains. The study of human character demanded the examination of motives and causes rather than the making of moral judgments. To find the cause of action meant probing into the secrets of individual psychology.

George Meredith (1828–1909) was one of the first to apply psychological methods to the analysis of his characters. For the average reader the brilliance of such novels as 'The Ordeal of Richard Feverel' (1859) and 'The Egoist' (1879) is obscured by the absence of plot and the subtleties of the language. Meredith was also a poet of merit, and his essay on comedy and the comic spirit is a masterly interpretation of the function of comedy in literature.

Thomas Hardy (1840–1928) brought to fiction a philosophical attitude that resulted from the new science. He believed that the more science studies the universe the less evidence is found for an intelligent guiding force behind it. If there is just

Charles Dickens' 'Oliver Twist' begs for food in a drawing by the famous English illustrator George Cruikshank. The novel was published in 1838.

chance—meaningless blind force—in the universe, what hope is there for mankind? In a series of great novels, from 'The Return of the Native' (1878) to 'Jude the Obscure' (1895), Hardy sought to show how futile and senseless is man's struggle against the forces of natural environment, social convention, and biological heritage. (*See also* Hardy.)

Samuel Butler (1835–1902) entered into the scientific controversies of his day. Holding that evolution is the result of the creative will rather than of chance selection, Butler wrote a novel about the relations of parents to children—'The Way of All Flesh' (1903). The point of the story, made with irony, is that the family restrains the free development of the child.

Charles Reade (1814–84) was, like Dickens, an ardent critic of the social abuses of his day. His most famous novel, 'The Cloister and the Hearth' (1861), however, is a historical romance with a 15th-century setting. Filled with exciting incidents, intrigue, and witchcraft, it is based on the birth and boyhood of the Dutch scholar Erasmus.

George Gissing (1857–1903) was greatly influenced by Dickens. His hatred of the degrading effects of poverty is reflected in many of his novels. Gissing's most successful book was 'The Private Papers of Henry Ryecroft' (1903), the imaginary journal of a retired writer who lives in happy solitude in the country amid his beloved books (as Gissing always wished that he could do).

Forces of the houses of York and Lancaster battle in the snow in a picture by N.C. Wyeth in Robert Louis Stevenson's 'Black Arrow' (Scribner).

Romance and Adventure

Not all fiction of the late 19th century falls into the intellectual or scientific classification. Robert Louis Stevenson (1850–94) wrote stories in a light mood. His novels of adventure are exciting and delightful: 'Treasure Island' (1883), 'Kidnapped' (1886), 'The Master of Ballantrae' (1889). Stevenson also wrote for adults. 'David Balfour' (1893) and 'The Strange Case of Dr. Jekyll and Mr. Hyde' (1886) are quite suited to adult tastes. As a short-story writer Stevenson ranks high. In light verse and in the informal essay Stevenson was unusually successful. (*See also* Stevenson.)

One of England's most popular writers was Rudyard Kipling (1865–1936). He glamorized the foreign service and satirized the English military and administrative classes in India. He stirred the emotions of the empire lovers. Kipling also wrote delightful children's tales. He was, however, neither a cheap versifier nor a vulgar imperialist. Whoever has not read 'Barrack Room Ballads' (1892), 'Soldiers Three' (1888), 'The Jungle Books' (1894, 1895), and 'Captains Courageous' (1897) has a treat in store for him. (*See also* Kipling.)

Lewis Carroll (Charles Lutwidge Dodgson) (1832–98) belongs in a category by himself. 'Alice's Adventures in Wonderland' (1865) combines fantasy and satire in an inimitable way to the immense satisfaction of old and young. (*See also* Carroll.)

19th-Century Drama

Drama did not flourish early in the 19th century. Romantic poetry had its dramatic phases, and Shelley and Byron both wrote verse dramas. These were *closet dramas*, intended for reading rather than for staging. Several of Tennyson's plays were produced. The stage, however, was primarily interested in low melodrama and sentimental farce-comedy. Musical comedy achieved respectability when librettist William Gilbert (1836–1911) teamed up with composer Arthur Sullivan (1842–1900) in 'Trial by Jury' (1875). Many successful collaborations by these two followed. (*See also* Gilbert and Sullivan.)

As was the case among readers of fiction, some theatergoers matured. They were ready for satire, for serious treatment of social problems, and for drama that was well constructed. From the Continent came realistic, intellectual, and socially significant works.

The first English dramatists to attempt the "new drama" were Henry Arthur Jones (1851–1929) and Sir Arthur Wing Pinero (1855–1934). Neither, however, could compare in wit and brilliance with two young contemporaries—Wilde and Shaw. Oscar Wilde (1854–1900), also a poet and novelist, wrote several fine plays. His 'Importance of Being Earnest' (1895) is brittle in its humor and clever in its dialogue and is probably the best of his dramas.

The plays of George Bernard Shaw (1856–1950) read even better than they act. They are important for their prefaces, sizzling attacks on Victorian prejudices and attitudes. Shaw began to write drama as a protest against existing conditions—slums, sex hypocrisy, censorship, war. Because his plays were not well received (often they were not even allowed to be presented), Shaw wrote their now-famous prefaces. Not until after 1900 did the Shavian wit achieve acceptance on the stage. Controversial ideas and Shaw productions came to be synonymous. Shaw had the longest career of any writer who ever lived. He began in the Victorian Age and wrote until 1950. (*See also* Shaw.)

Alice visits the Mad Hatter and the March Hare in Lewis Carroll's 'Alice's Adventures in Wonderland'. The picture is by Sir John Tenniel, famous illustrator of 'Alice' and 'Through the Looking Glass'.

Essayists and Historians

There are other great names in Victorian literature, chiefly in criticism and history. Thomas Babington Macaulay (1800–59) is known for his 'History of England' (1848–61). Although it is often inaccurate, it represented a new concept of historical writing: history must be detailed, vivid, and pictorial. (*See also* Macaulay.)

Social, religious, and educational criticism was the field of John Henry Cardinal Newman (1801–90). His essays on liberal education are especially important, and his 'Apologia pro Vita Sua' (1864) is a fine autobiography. (*See also* Newman.)

John Stuart Mill (1806–73) dealt with political and economic problems. His essay 'On Liberty' (1859) was the most important discussion of that subject since Milton's time.

Of those who wrote about aesthetic matters, Ruskin and Pater are best remembered. John Ruskin (1819–1900) made his first bid for fame in 'Modern Painters' (1843–60). He studied architecture and wrote 'The Seven Lamps of Architecture' (1849). Ruskin's ideas on art were at odds with social conditions. He became a reformer, devoting his writing to social and economic problems. (*See also* Ruskin.)

Walter Pater (1839–94), in 'Marius the Epicurean' (1885), developed a theory of beauty which ignored the social situation. It held that art could have no ethical content, that it must be a matter of personal ecstasy.

Modern English Literature

THE GROWTH of science and technology in the 19th century had held forth the promise of a new and richer life. It became clear, however, that what man did with his discoveries and his newly found mechanical power would depend upon his ability to master himself. With new inventions upsetting old ways, it became increasingly difficult to find order or pattern in life. People began to talk of the "machine age" and to ask whether it was wholly good. Could man trust science to bring about a better life?

Other developments began to influence man's thought. Psychologists explored the mind and advanced varied and conflicting theories about it. Human behavior was no longer easily explainable. The new sciences of anthropology and sociology contributed to the upheaval of ideas. Religious controls and social conventions again were challenged. Naturally, there were changes in literary taste and forms. Old values were replaced by new values or were lost. Literature became pessimistic and experimental.

Early 20th-Century Prose

Before 1914 the post-Victorian writers were in the unhappy position of looking back at a well-marked literary road and looking ahead at a pathless jungle. They had to grapple with new forces—sociological, psychological, and scientific—because these forces were a part of their lives. They were writers in transition.

John Galsworthy (1867–1933) turned to the social life of an upper-class English family in 'The Forsyte Saga' (1922), a series of novels which records the changing values of such a family. Galsworthy also wrote serious social plays, including 'Strife' (1909) and 'Justice' (1910). (*See also* Galsworthy.)

The first works of H. G. Wells (1866–1946) were science fiction—'The Time Machine' (1895), 'The Island of Dr. Moreau' (1896), 'The War of the Worlds' (1898). Then he turned to social and political subjects. Of his many books criticizing the middle-class life of England, 'Tono-Bungay' (1909), a satire on commercial advertising, is probably the most entertaining. (*See also* Wells.)

Arnold Bennett (1867–1931) was a literary experimenter who was drawn chiefly to realism, the slice-of-life approach to fiction. 'The Old Wives' Tale' (1908) and 'Clayhanger' (1910) are novels of people in drab surroundings. (*See also* Bennett.)

Lillian Gish, center, stars in a scene from a stage production of E.M. Forster's 'A Passage to India', a novel about Englishmen in India. The book was published in 1924.

Out of his years as a merchant-marine officer Joseph Conrad (1857–1924) wrote such remarkable novels as 'The Nigger of the Narcissus' (1898) and 'Lord Jim' (1900). The scenes, chiefly of a wild and turbulent sea, are exotic and exciting. The characters are strange people beset by obsessions of cowardice, egoism, or vanity. (*See also* Conrad.)

A master of the traditional plot was E. M. Forster (1879–1970). His characters are ordinary persons out of middle-class life. They are moved by accident because they do not know how to choose a course of action. 'A Passage to India' (1924) is a splendid novel of Englishmen in India.

The naturalist W. H. Hudson (1841–1922) will long be remembered for 'Green Mansions' (1904), a fanciful romance of the South American jungles. Hudson's skill as a nature writer, however, surpassed his skill as a novelist.

John Buchan (1875–1940), who served as governor-general of Canada, wrote exciting novels of adventure and mystery. 'The Thirty-Nine Steps' (1915) is perhaps his best-known work.

Early 20th-Century Poetry

The poetry of the Edwardian and Georgian periods (Edward VII, 1901–10; George V, 1910–36) showed many new and unusual characteristics. Robert Bridges (1844–1930) experimented in verse forms. He employed the usual subjects of the poet but brought strange rhythms and unusual music to his verse. The poet A. E. Housman (1859–1936) was an anti-Victorian who echoed the pessimism found in Hardy. In his 'Shropshire Lad' (1896) nature is unkind; people struggle without hope or purpose; boys and girls laugh, love, and are untrue (*see* Housman).

John Masefield (1878–1967) stressed the bold, the rugged, the violent in his poetry. 'The Everlasting Mercy' (1911), a poem containing a Homeric prizefight, and 'Dauber' (1912), the story of a painter among unsympathetic seamen, will please the most masculine mind. His descriptions of sea and land and of brutal people are powerfully realistic. (*See also* Masefield.)

A different sort of poet from his contemporaries was Walter de la Mare (1873–1956). The wonder and fancy of the child's world and the fantasy of the world of the supernatural were his to command. 'Peacock Pie' (1913) is representative of his verse. As a novelist and teller of tales, De la Mare was a supernaturalist who believed in the reality of evil as well as of good. (*See also* De la Mare.)

Sir James M. Barrie (1860–1937) was probably the greatest master of the romantic-fantasy drama of the period. Beginning with 'The Admirable Crichton' (1903), in which a butler becomes a Swiss Family Robinson character, and continuing through 'Peter Pan' (1904) and 'Dear Brutus' (1917), Barrie wrote of life as seen by children, for an audience that was tired of adult viewpoints. (*See also* Barrie.)

Intensely nationalistic, the Irish writers were looking to their own country for literary inspiration. William Butler Yeats (1865–1939), John Millington Synge (1871–1909), and Lord Dunsany (1878–1957) worked vigorously for the Irish cause. All were dramatists and all helped found the famous Abbey Theatre. (*See also* Yeats; Irish Literature.)

Impact of World War I

World War I cut forever the ties with the past. It brought discontent and disillusionment. Men were plunged into gloom at the knowledge that "progress" had not saved the world from war.

World War I left its record in literature. Rupert Brooke (1887–1915), who died during the war, has been idealized for what is actually a rather thin performance in poetry. Wilfred Owen (1893–1918), also a war casualty, was far more realistic about the heroism and idealism of the soldier. Siegfried Sassoon (1886–1967) and Edmund Blunden (1896–1974), both survivors of the carnage, left violent accounts of the horrors and terror of war.

In fiction there was a shift from novels of the human comedy to novels of characters. Fiction ceased to be concerned with a plot or a forward-moving narrative. Instead it followed the twisted, contorted development of a single character or a group of related characters.

Of these writers W. Somerset Maugham (1874–1965) achieved the greatest popular success. 'Of Human Bondage' (1915) portrays a character who drifts. 'The Moon and Sixpence' (1919), based on the life of the artist Paul Gauguin, continues the examination of the character without roots. 'Cakes and Ale' (1930) shows how the real self is lost between the two masks—public and private—that every man wears. (*See also* Maugham.)

The writer D. H. Lawrence (1885–1930) was a man trying to find himself, trying to be reborn. This tragic, heroic search is reflected in his curious novels about the secret sources of human life. The records of his search and torment are his great novels 'Sons and Lovers' (1913) and 'Women in Love' (1920).

James Joyce (1882–1941) was searching for the secret places in which the real self is hidden. He believed he had found the way to it through human vocal language. To him language was the means by which the inner, or subconscious, feelings gained expression. Civilized man tries to control his spoken language; natural man would let his language flow freely. If one could capture this free flow of language in writing, he would have the secret of man's nature. Thus was born *stream of consciousness*, a technique that has been employed in much contemporary literature. 'Ulysses' (1922), a vast, rambling account of 24 hours in the lives of Leopold Bloom and Stephen Dedalus, has greatly influenced modern fiction. (*See also* Joyce.)

The Bettmann Archive

James Joyce is shown here with Sylvia Beach, the first publisher of 'Ulysses'. Joyce's influential novel stirred a great literary controversy.

Joyce's stream-of-consciousness technique was refined by Virginia Woolf (1882–1941). For her, reality, or consciousness, is a stream. Life, for both reader and characters, is immersion in the flow of that stream. 'Mrs. Dalloway' (1925) and 'To the Lighthouse' (1927) are among her best works. Katherine Mansfield (1888–1923), Dorothy M. Richardson (1882–1957), and Elizabeth Bowen (1899–1973) also wrote fiction of this type (*see* Mansfield).

While these writers were concerned with the realities of the mind, Aldous Huxley (1894–1963) worked with the external world. He found it false, brutal, and inhuman. In 'Point Counter Point' (1928), 'Brave New World' (1932), and 'After Many a Summer Dies the Swan' (1939), his cynicism reached its peak.

British Poetry After World War I

Poetry, like fiction, shifted from traditional forms and moral pronouncements to experimental verse and new techniques. The leader of the new school was T. S. Eliot, an American who became a British citizen (*see* Eliot, Thomas Stearns; American Literature).

In the 1930's one group of young poets arose who viewed the world with clearer eyes. They were, in Carlyle's phrase, "yea-sayers" rather than cursers and complainers of life. They had hope but little optimism. Of this group Stephen Spender (born 1909), C. Day-Lewis (1904–72), Louis MacNeice (1907–63), and W. H. Auden (1907–73) were the most effective. Each of them experimented with rhyme, rhythm, imagery, language, symbolism, and allusion. The result was an uneven poetry that more nearly represented the unevenness of life.

Although Eliot was an American who became a British citizen and Auden an Englishman who became an American, their earliest literary influences came to them in the countries of their birth. Hence Auden is usually considered an English poet and Eliot an American.

Another group of poets, like the stream-of-consciousness novelists, sought to escape from the world of ideas and problems. William Empson (1906–84) and Dylan Thomas (1914–53), for example, found their inner chaos best expressed in ambiguity (*see* Thomas, Dylan). To them, precision represented a departed world and today's chaos is better portrayed

Three Lions

Essayist and literary critic Virginia Woolf gained her greatest fame for her stream-of-consciousness novels.

(Left) UPI; (center and right) Brown Brothers

MAUGHAM

GRAVES

SNOW

through the confused, the irrelevant, and the inexact. Theirs was a literature filled with vivid imagery.

As poet and critic, Robert Graves (1895–1985) advocated "pure" impersonal poetry. He is perhaps better known for his novels and studies of myths.

Literature After World War II

World War II had an even more profound impact than World War I on people's ideas about themselves and their place in the universe. The terrible fact of the atom bomb's existence shook their sense of stability. The postwar threat of the spread of communism brought to attention the dangers to individual freedoms in a totalitarian state.

William Golding (born 1911) was one of the most significant postwar novelists. His first novel, and the one for which he will probably be best remembered, was 'Lord of the Flies' (1954). This story of a group of schoolboys isolated on an island who revert to savagery is an imaginative interpretation of the religious theme of original sin. It was made into a successful movie in 1963. Among Golding's later books are 'Pincher Martin' (1956), 'Rites of Passage' (1980), and 'The Paper Men' (1983). Golding was awarded the Nobel prize for literature in 1983.

George Orwell (1903–50) published several books before the war, including 'The Road to Wigan Pier' (1937) and 'Homage to Catalonia' (1938). His greatest renown, however, came after the war, with the powerful anticommunist satire 'Animal Farm' (1945). This was followed in 1949 with his attack on totalitarianism entitled 'Nineteen Eighty-Four'.

C.P. Snow (1905–80) was both a scientist and a novelist. His best-known nonfiction work is 'The Two Cultures and the Scientific Revolution' (1959) in which he argues that people working in the arts and the sciences know very little of each other's work; therefore communication between them is almost impossible. As a novelist he will be best remembered for his series entitled collectively 'Strangers and Brothers'. Published from 1940 to 1970, the novels are about the public and private life of a man named Lewis Eliot. The books are noted for their careful analysis of bureaucracy and the corrupting influences of power.

The turbulent 1930s, ending in World War II, turned many of the already established writers toward traditional values. T.S. Eliot (1888–1965), Edith Sitwell (1887–1964), Evelyn Waugh (1903–66), and Graham Greene (born 1904) turned increasingly to Christianity. Of these, only Greene lived to have a career that endured into the 1980s. Among his better-known later novels are 'The Quiet American' (1955), 'Our Man in Havana' (1958), 'A Burnt-Out Case' (1961), 'The Human Factor' (1978), and 'Monsignor Quixote' (1982). (*See also* Greene, Graham.)

Malcolm Lowry (1909–57), another of the older generation of writers, published his finest work, 'Under the Volcano', in 1947. Now considered one of the major English novels of the latter half of the 20th century, the story depicts the nightmarish world of an alcoholic Englishman living in Mexico.

Anthony Powell (born 1905) published five novels prior to the war, but none was as interesting or well done as his 12-novel series, 'A Dance to the Music of Time' (1951–75). These novels are a satiric survey of British society from the 1920s through the 1960s as portrayed in the lives of a group of young men.

The literature of the 1950s was as varied as at any time, but much of it was made notable by the appearance of a new breed of writers called the Angry Young Men. Most of these were of lower middle-class or working-class backgrounds. Although not all personally known to one another, they had in common an outspoken irreverence for the British class system and the pretensions of the aristocracy. They strongly disapproved of the elitist universities, the Church of England, and the drabness of working-class life.

The trend of the period was crystallized in John Osborne's play 'Look Back in Anger' (1956). But it had been evident earlier in the writings of John Wain (born 1925), author of 'Hurry on Down' (1953), and in 'Lucky Jim' (1953) by Kingsley Amis (born 1922). Other writers of the generation included John Braine (born 1922), author of 'Room at the Top' (1957; later

(Left) Lutfi Özkök; (center and right) Mark Gerson

GOLDING

LESSING

AMIS

a successful motion picture); Alan Sillitoe, author of 'Saturday Night and Sunday Morning' (1958); and the playwrights Bernard Kops and Arnold Wesker.

Amis is considered by many to be the best of the writers to emerge from the 1950s. The social discontent he expressed made 'Lucky Jim' a household name in England. It is the story of Jim Dixon, who rises from a lower-class background only to find all the positions at the top of the social ladder filled. Later novels include 'That Uncertain Feeling' (1955), 'Take a Girl Like You' (1960), and 'Girl, 20' (1971). His 1984 novel 'Stanley and the Women' was considered so antifeminist that it was difficult getting it published in the United States. His son Martin Amis won notoriety in 1984 with his novel 'Money'.

While Amis was a realist, he also stood well within the humanist tradition, which attempts to put the writer's talent in the service of society. Other novelists in this tradition are Iris Murdoch (born 1919), Angus Wilson (born 1913), Anthony Burgess (born 1917), Doris Lessing (born 1919), and Muriel Spark (born 1918).

By the late 1950s Murdoch had gained recognition as one of the foremost novelists of the generation. Her books include 'Under the Net' (1954), 'The Red and the Green' (1965), 'The Sea, the Sea' (1978), and 'Nuns and Soldiers' (1980).

Wilson took as his subject the crisis of the educated British middle class after World War I. His collection of short stories 'The Wrong Set' (1949) portrays the emotional crisis of World War II. His first novel, 'Hemlock and After' (1952), is considered among his best.

Burgess was a novelist whose fictional exploration of modern dilemmas combines wit, moral earnestness, and touches of the bizarre. 'A Clockwork Orange' (1962), made into a film in 1971, was both comic and violent. His other novels include 'Enderby Outside' (1968), 'Earthly Powers' (1980), 'The End of the World News' (1983), and 'The Kingdom of the Wicked' (1985).

The novels of Doris Lessing are largely concerned with people involved in the social and political upheavals of the 20th century. Her 'Children of Violence', a series of five novels, begins with 'Martha Quest' (1952) and ends with a vision of the world after nuclear disaster in 'The Four-Gated City' (1969). In 1979 she began publication of a science-fiction sequence entitled 'Canopus in Argos: Archives'.

Muriel Spark's early novels were characterized by a humorous fantasy: 'The Ballad of Peckham Rye' (1960) and 'The Girls of Slender Means' (1963). Her later books were of a definitely sinister nature, including 'The Mandelbaum Gate' (1965), 'The Driver's Seat' (1970), and 'Not to Disturb' (1971). Her best-known works are 'Memento Mori' (1959) and 'The Prime of Miss Jean Brodie' (1961). Her 'The Only Problem' (1984) is a remarkable blend of religious thought and sexual comedy.

After 1975 there were several intentionally experimental novels such as 'The White Hotel' (1981) by D.M. Thomas (born 1935) and 'Midnight's Children' (1981) by Salman Rushdie (born 1947). Rushdie's later novel 'The Satanic Verses' (1988) sparked an international uproar. The book was considered blasphemous by Muslims throughout the world, and it prompted Iran's Ayatollah Khomeini to issue a death threat against the author.

But the more traditional literature persisted in popularity. Anita Brookner (born 1928) wrote carefully crafted and unpretentious fiction in 'A Start in Life' (1981) and 'Hotel du Lac' (1984).

British poetry was as diverse as the rest of the literature in the postwar era. The poets who made the greatest impression were those firmly rooted in Western values who preferred clarity to clever obscurity. The outstanding ones were Thom Gunn (born 1929), Ted Hughes (born 1930), Donald Davie (born 1922), and Philip Larkin (1922–85).

Other significant poets include Jon Silkin (born 1930), Elaine Feinstein (born 1930), Charles Tomlinson (born 1927), Elizabeth Jennings (born 1926), Geoffrey Hill (born 1932), and R.S. Thomas (born 1913). The novelist Kingsley Amis belongs to the group of better poets, as does the Irish-born Seamus Heaney (born 1939).

Representative British Authors

OLD ENGLISH PERIOD

Aelfric (955?–1020?), ecclesiastical biographer—'Lives of the Saints'.

Alfred the Great (848?–899), translator—Boethius' 'Consolation of Philosophy'.

Bede (673?–735), historian—'Ecclesiastical History of the English Nation'.

Caedmon (7th century), poet—'Paraphrases'.

Cynewulf (8th century), poet—'Christ'; 'Juliana'.

MIDDLE ENGLISH PERIOD

Chaucer, Geoffrey (1340?–1400), poet—'Canterbury Tales'.

Geoffrey of Monmouth (1100?–54), historian—'Historia Regum Britanniae'.

Langland, William (1330?–1400?), poet—'The Vision of William Concerning Piers the Plowman'.

Layamon (about 1200), metrical historian—'Brut'.

Lydgate, John (1370?–1451?), poet—'Troy Book'.

Malory, Sir Thomas (died 1470?), translator—'Morte d'Arthur'.

"Pearl Poet" (14th century), poet—'Sir Gawain and the Green Knight'.

THE RENAISSANCE

Bacon, Sir Francis (1561–1626), philosopher, essayist—'New Atlantis'; 'The Advancement of Learning'; 'Essays'.

Beaumont, Francis (1584–1616), dramatist—with John Fletcher, 'The Knight of the Burning Pestle'.

Chapman, George (1559?–1634), poet, dramatist, translator—Homer's 'Iliad' and 'Odyssey' (*trans.*).

Coverdale, Miles (1488?–1569), translator—Bible.

Daniel, Samuel (1562–1619), poet—'Defence of Ryme'.

Dekker, Thomas (1570?–1641), dramatist—'The Shoemaker's Holiday'.

Fletcher, John (1579–1625), dramatist—with Francis Beaumont, 'The Maid's Tragedy'.

Ford, John (1586–1640?), dramatist—'The Broken Heart'; 'Perkin Warbeck'.

Heywood, Thomas (died 1641?), dramatist—'A Woman Killed with Kindness'.

Jonson, Ben (1573?–1637), poet, dramatist—'Song to Celia'; 'Volpone'.

Kyd, Thomas (1558–94), dramatist—'The Spanish Tragedy'.

Lodge, Thomas (1558?–1625), poet—'Rosalynde'.

Lyly, John (1554?–1606), novelist, dramatist—'Euphues: the Anatomy of Wit'; 'Euphues and His England'.

Marlowe, Christopher (1564–93), dramatist—'Doctor Faustus'; 'The Jew of Malta'; 'Tamburlaine'.

Massinger, Philip (1583–1640), dramatist—'A New Way to Pay Old Debts'.

Middleton, Thomas (1570?–1627), dramatist—'Michaelmas Terne'.

More, Sir Thomas (1478–1535), prose writer—'Utopia'.

Shakespeare, William (1564–1616), dramatist, poet—'Hamlet'; 'Macbeth'; 'King Lear'; 'Sonnets'.

Sidney, Sir Philip (1554–86), poet, novelist—'Astrophel and Stella'; 'Arcadia'.

Skelton, John (1460?–1529), poet—'Colyn Clout'.

Spenser, Edmund (1552?–99), poet—'The Faerie Queene'.

Tyndale, William (1492?–1536), translator, tract writer—New Testament (*trans.*).

Webster, John (1580?–1625?), dramatist—'The Duchess of Malfi'.

Wyatt, Sir Thomas (1503–42), poet—'Certayne Psalmes'.

THE 17TH CENTURY

Browne, Sir Thomas (1605–82), prose writer—'Religio Medici'; 'Pseudodoxia Epidemica'.

Bunyan, John (1628–88), prose writer—'The Pilgrim's Progress'.

Burton, Robert (1577–1640), prose writer—'The Anatomy of Melancholy'.

Butler, Samuel (1612–80), satirist, poet—'Hudibras'.

Carew, Thomas (1595?–1639), poet—'Poems'.

Donne, John (1573–1631), poet, preacher—'Poems'.

Dryden, John (1631–1700), poet, dramatist—'All for Love'; 'Alexander's Feast'; 'The Hind and the Panther'.

Herbert, George (1593–1633), poet—'The Temple'.

Herrick, Robert (1591–1674), poet—'Hesperides'.

Hobbes, Thomas (1588–1679), philosopher—'Leviathan'.

Locke, John (1632–1704), philosopher—'An Essay Concerning Human Understanding'.

Lovelace, Richard (1618–58), poet—'To Althea'.

Marvell, Andrew (1621–78), poet—'To His Coy Mistress'.

Milton, John (1608–74), poet—'Paradise Lost'; 'L'Allegro'; 'Il Penseroso'; 'Lycidas'; 'Samson Agonistes'.

Pepys, Samuel (1633–1703), diarist—'Diary'.

Suckling, Sir John (1609–42), poet—'Ballad upon a Wedding'.

Taylor, Jeremy (1613–67), theological writer—'Holy Living'; 'Holy Dying'.

Vaughan, Henry (1622–95), poet—'The Retreat'.

Walton, Izaak (1593–1683), essayist, biographer—'The Compleat Angler'.

THE 18TH CENTURY

Addison, Joseph (1672–1719), poet, essayist—Sir Roger de Coverley papers in *The Spectator*.

Blair, Robert (1699–1746), poet—'The Grave'.

Boswell, James (1740–95), biographer—'The Life of Samuel Johnson, LL.D.'.

Collins, William (1721–59), poet—'The Passions'; 'Ode to Liberty'; 'Ode to Evening'.

Cowper, William (1731–1800), poet—'The Task'.

Crabbe, George (1754–1832), poet—'The Village'.

Defoe, Daniel (1661?–1731), novelist, journalist—'Robinson Crusoe'; 'Moll Flanders'.

Fielding, Henry (1707–54), novelist—'Tom Jones'.

Gay, John (1685–1732), poet, dramatist—'The Shepherd's Week'; 'Fables'; 'The Beggar's Opera'.

Gibbon, Edward (1737–94), historian—'The Decline and Fall of the Roman Empire'.

Goldsmith, Oliver (1728–74), novelist, poet, dramatist—'The Vicar of Wakefield'; 'The Deserted Village'; 'She Stoops to Conquer'.

Gray, Thomas (1716–71), poet, critic—'Elegy Written in a Country Churchyard'; 'The Progress of Poesy'.

Hume, David (1711–76), philosopher, historian—'An Enquiry Concerning Human Understanding'.

Johnson, Samuel (1709–84), lexicographer, novelist—'A Dictionary of the English Language'; 'Rasselas'.

Pope, Alexander (1688–1744), poet, critic—'The Rape of the Lock'; 'Essay on Criticism'; 'Essay on Man'.

Richardson, Samuel (1689–1761), novelist—'Pamela'; 'Clarissa'.

Sheridan, Richard Brinsley (1751–1816), dramatist—'The School for Scandal'; 'The Rivals'.

Smollett, Tobias (1721–71), novelist—'Roderick Random'; 'Humphry Clinker'.

Steele, Sir Richard (1672–1729), essayist, dramatist—essays in *The Spectator* and *The Tatler*.

Sterne, Laurence (1713–68), novelist—'Tristram Shandy'; 'A Sentimental Journey'.

Swift, Jonathan (1667–1745), satirist—'Gulliver's Travels'; 'A Tale of a Tub'; 'Journal to Stella'.

Thomson, James (1700–48), poet—'The Seasons'.

Young, Edward (1683–1765), poet—'The Complaint: or, Night Thoughts on Life, Death, and Immortality'.

THE ROMANTIC MOVEMENT

Austen, Jane (1775–1817), novelist—'Pride and Prejudice'; 'Mansfield Park'; 'Sense and Sensibility'.

Blake, William (1757–1827), poet—'Songs of Innocence'; 'Songs of Experience'.

Burns, Robert (1759–96), poet—'The Cotter's Saturday Night'; 'Tam o' Shanter'.

Byron, George Gordon (1788–1824), poet—'Childe Harold's Pilgrimage'; 'Don Juan'; 'Manfred'.

Coleridge, Samuel Taylor (1772–1834), poet, critic—'The Rime of the Ancient Mariner'; 'Kubla Khan'.

De Quincey, Thomas (1785–1859), essayist—'Confessions of an English Opium Eater'.

Godwin, Mary Wollstonecraft (1759–97), essayist—'Vindication of the Rights of Women'.

Godwin, William (1756–1836), political writer, novelist—'Political Justice'.

Hazlitt, William (1778–1830), essayist, critic—'Table Talk'; 'Characters of Shakespeare's Plays'.

Hunt, Leigh (1784–1859), essayist, poet—'Abou Ben Adhem'; 'The Story of Rimini'; 'Autobiography'.

Keats, John (1795–1821), poet—'The Eve of St. Agnes'; 'Ode on a Grecian Urn'; 'Endymion'.

Lamb, Charles (1775–1834), poet, essayist—'Essays of Elia'; 'Tales from Shakespear' (with Mary Lamb).

Landor, Walter Savage (1775–1864), poet, prose writer—'Imaginary Conversations'; 'Hellenics'.

Lewis, Matthew Gregory (1775–1818), novelist, dramatist, poet—'The Monk'; 'Romantic Tales'.

Macpherson, James (1736–96), poet—'Temora'.

Moore, Thomas (1779–1852), poet, novelist, historian, biographer—'Irish Melodies'.

Percy, Thomas (1729–1811), anthologist—'Reliques of Ancient English Poetry'.

Radcliffe, Ann (1764–1823), novelist—'The Romance of the Forest'; 'The Mysteries of Udolpho'.

Scott, Sir Walter (1771–1832), poet, novelist—'The Lady of the Lake'; 'Waverley'; 'Ivanhoe'; 'Kenilworth'.

Shelley, Mary Wollstonecraft (1797–1851), novelist—'Frankenstein'.

Shelley, Percy Bysshe (1792–1822), poet—'Ode to the West Wind'; 'Prometheus Unbound'; 'To a Skylark'; 'Adonais'.

Southey, Robert (1774–1843), poet, historian—'The Battle of Blenheim'; 'Life of Nelson'.

Walpole, Horace (1717–97), novelist, letter writer—'The Castle of Otranto'; 'Letters'; 'Memoirs'.

Wordsworth, William (1770–1850), poet—'Tintern Abbey'; 'Intimations of Immortality'; 'The Prelude'.

THE VICTORIAN AGE

Arnold, Matthew (1822–88), poet, essayist—'The Scholar-Gypsy'; 'Sohrab and Rustum'; 'Essays in Criticism'.

Brontë, Anne (1820–49), novelist—'Agnes Grey'.

Brontë, Charlotte (1816–55), novelist—'Jane Eyre'.

Brontë, Emily (1818–48), novelist—'Wuthering Heights'.

Browning, Elizabeth Barrett (1806–61), poet—'Sonnets from the Portuguese'; 'Aurora Leigh'.

Browning, Robert (1812–89), poet—'The Ring and the Book'; 'Pippa Passes'; 'Rabbi Ben Ezra'; 'My Last Duchess'.

Bulwer-Lytton, Edward (1803–73), novelist—'The Last Days of Pompeii'; 'Harold'.

Butler, Samuel (1835–1902), novelist, critic—'The Way of All Flesh'; 'Erewhon'; 'Notebooks'.

Carlyle, Thomas (1795–1881), historian, essayist—'Sartor Resartus'; 'French Revolution'; 'On Heroes, Hero-Worship, and the Heroic in History'.

Carroll, Lewis (Charles Lutwidge Dodgson) (1832–98), children's writer—'Alice's Adventures in Wonderland'; 'Through the Looking Glass'.

Collins, Wilkie (1824–89), novelist—'The Woman in White'; 'The Moonstone'.

Davidson, John (1857–1909), poet—'Fleet Street Eclogues'.

Dickens, Charles (1812–70), novelist—'David Copperfield'; 'The Pickwick Papers'; 'Oliver Twist'.

Disraeli, Benjamin (1804–81), novelist, statesman—'Vivian Grey'; 'Coningsby'.

Dowson, Ernest (1867–1900), poet—'Cynara'.

Doyle, Sir Arthur Conan (1859–1930), novelist—'The Adventures of Sherlock Holmes'; 'Sir Nigel'; 'A Study in Scarlet'.

Eliot, George (Mary Ann Evans) (1819–80), novelist—'Adam Bede'; 'The Mill on the Floss'; 'Silas Marner'.

Fitzgerald, Edward (1809–83), poet—'Rubáiyát of Omar Khayyám'.

Gilbert, Sir William (1836–1911), librettist—'The Mikado'; 'The Yeoman of the Guard'.

Gissing, George (1857–1903), novelist—'The Private Papers of Henry Ryecroft'; 'The Whirlpool'; 'New Grub Street'.

Hardy, Thomas (1840–1928), novelist, poet—'Far from the Madding Crowd'; 'The Return of the Native'; 'Tess of the D'Urbervilles'; 'The Mayor of Casterbridge'; 'Jude the Obscure'; 'Wessex Poems'; 'The Dynasts'.

Henley, William Ernest (1849–1903), poet, critic, dramatist—'London Voluntaries'; 'Invictus'.

Hopkins, Gerard Manley (1844–89), poet—'Wreck of the Deutschland'; 'Pied Beauty'.

Jones, Henry Arthur (1851–1929), dramatist—'Michael and His Lost Angel'; 'Mrs. Dane's Defence'.

Kingsley, Charles (1819–75), novelist—'Westward Ho!'; 'Alton Locke'; 'Hereward the Wake'.

Kipling, Rudyard (1865–1936), novelist, poet, short-story writer—'Kim'; 'Barrack Room Ballads'; 'Plain Tales from the Hills'; 'Just So Stories'; 'The Jungle Books'.

Macaulay, Thomas Babington (1800–59), historian, poet—'History of England'; 'Lays of Ancient Rome'.

Meredith, George (1828–1909), novelist, poet—'The Egoist'; 'The Ordeal of Richard Feverel'; 'Diana of the Crossways'; 'Evan Harrington'; 'Modern Love'.

Mill, John Stuart (1806–73), philosopher, economist—'Principles of Political Economy'; 'Autobiography'; 'Representative Government'; 'On the Subjugation of Women'.

Moore, George (1852–1933), novelist—'Esther Waters'; 'Héloïse and Abélard'; 'Confessions of a Young Man'.

Morris, William (1834–96), poet—'The Defence of Guenevere'; 'The Earthly Paradise'.

Newman, John Henry (1801–90), theologian, essayist—'Idea of a University'; 'Apologia pro Vita Sua'.

Pater, Walter (1839–94), essayist, novelist—'Imaginary Portraits'; 'Studies in the History of the Renaissance'; 'Marius the Epicurean'.

Pinero, Sir Arthur Wing (1855–1934), dramatist—'The Second Mrs. Tanqueray'; 'Mid-Channel'.

Quiller-Couch, Sir Arthur Thomas ("Q") (1863–1944), poet, critic, novelist—'On the Art of Reading'; 'On the Art of Writing'.

Reade, Charles (1814–84), novelist—'The Cloister and the Hearth'; 'It Is Never Too Late to Mend'.

Rossetti, Christina Georgina (1830–94), poet—'Sing-Song'; 'Goblin Market'.

Rossetti, Dante Gabriel (1828–82), poet—'The Blessed Damozel'; 'The House of Life'.

Ruskin, John (1819–1900), art critic, essayist—'Modern Painters'; 'The Seven Lamps of Architecture'; 'Sesame and Lilies'.

"Saki" (Hector Hugh Munro) (1870–1916), novelist, short-story writer—'Reginald'; 'The Unbearable Basington'.

Shaw, George Bernard (1856–1950), dramatist, essayist—'Saint Joan'; 'Pygmalion'; 'Major Barbara'; 'Man and Superman'; 'The Devil's Disciple'; 'The Intelligent Woman's Guide to Socialism and Capitalism'.

Stevenson, Robert Louis (1850–94), novelist, essayist, poet—'Treasure Island'; 'Kidnapped'; 'The Strange Case of Dr. Jekyll and Mr. Hyde'; 'Travels with a Donkey'; 'A Child's Garden of Verses'.

Swinburne, Algernon Charles (1837–1909), poet—'Atalanta in Calydon'; 'Songs Before Sunrise'; 'Poems and Ballads'.

Tennyson, Alfred, Lord (1809–92), poet—'Idylls of the King'; 'In Memoriam'; 'Locksley Hall'; 'The Death of Oenone'; 'The Lotos-Eaters'.

Thackeray, William Makepeace (1811–63), novelist—'Vanity Fair'; 'Henry Esmond'; 'The Newcomes'.

Thompson, Francis (1859–1907), poet—'The Hound of Heaven'.

Trollope, Anthony (1815–82), novelist—'Barchester Towers'; 'Framley Parsonage'; 'Doctor Thorne'.

Wilde, Oscar (1854–1900), poet, novelist, dramatist—'The Ballad of Reading Gaol'; 'The Picture of Dorian Gray'; 'Lady Windermere's Fan'; 'The Importance of Being Earnest'.

MODERN ENGLISH LITERATURE

Amis, Kingsley (born 1922), novelist, poet—'Lucky Jim'; 'That Uncertain Feeling'; 'Girl, 20'; 'Stanley and the Women'.

Amis, Martin (born 1949), novelist—'Success'; 'Other People'; 'Money'.

Auden, W(ystan) H(ugh) (1907–73), poet—'The Age of Anxiety'; 'Nones'; 'The Shield of Achilles'.

Barrie, Sir James M(atthew) (1860–1937), novelist, dramatist—'The Little Minister'; 'Peter Pan'.

Beckett, Samuel (born 1906), dramatist—'Waiting for Godot'.

Beerbohm, Sir Max (1872–1956), essayist, novelist—'More'; 'Zuleika Dobson'; 'A Christmas Garland'.

Belloc, Hilaire (1870–1953), essayist, historian, biographer—'On Nothing'; 'Danton'; 'Richelieu'; 'Towns of Destiny'.

Bennett, Arnold (1867–1931), novelist, dramatist—'The Old Wives' Tale'; 'Clayhanger'; 'Riceyman Steps'; 'Imperial Palace'.

Bowen, Elizabeth (1899–1973), novelist, short-story writer—'The House in Paris'; 'The Death of the Heart'.

Braine, John (born 1922), novelist—'Room at the Top'; 'Life at the Top'; 'The Queen of a Distant Country'.

Brooke, Rupert (1887–1915), poet—'Collected Poems'.

Brookner, Anita (born 1928), novelist—'A Start in Life'; 'Hotel du Lac'.

Buchan, John (1875–1940), novelist—'The Thirty-Nine Steps'.

Burgess, Anthony (born 1917), novelist, critic—'The Wanting Seed'; 'A Clockwork Orange'; 'Earthly Powers'; 'Kingdom of the Wicked'.

Cary, Joyce (1888–1957), novelist, poet—'Herself Surprised'; 'To Be a Pilgrim'; 'The Horse's Mouth'.

Chesterton, G(ilbert) K(eith) (1874–1936), poet, essayist, novelist, critic—'The Man Who Was Thursday'; 'Heretics'; 'The Everlasting Man'.

Colum, Padraic (1881–1972), poet, writer of children's stories—'Wild Earth'; 'The Adventures of Odysseus and the Tale of Troy'.

Compton-Burnett, Ivy (1892–1969), novelist—'The Present and the Past'; 'Mother and Son'.

Conrad, Joseph (1857–1924), novelist, short-story writer—'The Nigger of the Narcissus'; 'Lord Jim'; 'Youth'; 'Victory'; 'Heart of Darkness'.

Coward, Noel (1899–1973), dramatist—'Private Lives'; 'Blithe Spirit'.

Cronin, A(rchibald) J(oseph) (1896–1981), novelist—'The Green Years'; 'The Citadel'; 'The Keys of the Kingdom'; 'A Thing of Beauty'.

Davie, Donald (born 1922), poet, critic—'Brides of Reason'; 'A Winter Talent and Other Poems'; 'In the Stopping Train'.

Day-Lewis, C(ecil) (1904–72), poet—'Short Is the Time'.

De la Mare, Walter (1873–1956), poet, novelist—'Memoirs of a Midget'; 'The Listeners'; 'Peacock Pie'.

Drinkwater, John (1882–1937), poet, dramatist, critic, biographer—'Collected Poems'; 'The Lyric'; 'Pepys'.

Durrell, Lawrence (born 1912), poet, novelist—'Justine'; 'Balthazar'; 'Mountolive'; 'Clea'.

Empson, William (1906–84), poet, critic—'Collected Poems'; 'Some Versions of Pastoral'.

Feinstein, Elaine (born 1930), poet, novelist—'In a Green Eye'; 'The Circle'; 'Some Unease and Angels'.

Ford, Ford Madox (1873–1939), novelist, critic—'Some Do Not'; 'No More Parades'; 'Return to Yesterday'.

Forster, E(dward) M(organ) (1879–1970), novelist—'Howards End'; 'A Passage to India'.

Fry, Christopher (born 1907), dramatist—'A Phoenix Too Frequent'; 'The Lady's Not for Burning'; 'Venus Observed'; 'The Dark Is Light Enough'.

Galsworthy, John (1867–1933), novelist, short-story writer, dramatist—'The Forsyte Saga'; 'Caravan'; 'Justice'; 'Strife'; 'The Skin Game'; 'Loyalties'.

Godden, Rumer (born 1907), novelist, dramatist, poet—'Black Narcissus'; 'An Episode of Sparrows'; 'The River'.

Golding, William (born 1911), novelist—'Lord of the Flies'; 'Pincher Martin'.

Grahame, Kenneth (1859–1932), children's writer—'The Golden Age'; 'The Wind in the Willows'.

Graves, Robert (1895–1985), novelist, poet, critic—'Goodbye to All That'; 'Fairies and Fusiliers'; 'I, Claudius'; 'Claudius the God'.

Greene, Graham (born 1904), novelist, dramatist—'The Power and the Glory'; 'The Quiet American'; 'The Heart of the Matter'; 'The End of the Affair'; 'A Burnt-Out Case'; 'The Potting Shed'; 'The Human Factor'; 'Travels with My Aunt'; 'The Honorary Consul'.

Gunn, Thom (born 1929), poet—'Sense of Movement'; 'Garden of the Gods'; 'Passages of Joy'.

Heaney, Seamus (born 1939), poet—'Room to Rhyme'; 'Night Drive'; 'Selected Poems'.

Hilton, James (1900–54), novelist—'Good-bye, Mr. Chips'; 'Lost Horizon'; 'Random Harvest'.

Holden, Molly (born 1927), poet—'Bright Cloud'; 'Air and Chill Earth'; 'The Country Over'.

Housman, A(lfred) E(dward) (1859–1936), poet—'A Shropshire Lad'; 'Last Poems'; 'More Poems'.

Hudson, W(illiam) H(enry) (1841–1922), novelist, essayist—'The Purple Land'; 'Green Mansions'; 'Far Away and Long Ago'.

Hughes, Richard (1900–76), novelist—'A High Wind in Jamaica'; 'The Fox in the Attic'.

Hughes, Ted (born 1930), poet—'Hawk in the Rain'; 'Burning of the Brothel'; 'Crow Wakes: Poems'.

Huxley, Aldous (1894–1963), poet, novelist—'Antic Hay'; 'Point Counter Point'; 'Brave New World'.

Isherwood, Christopher (1904–86), novelist, dramatist—'Prater Violet'; 'The Dog Beneath the Skin' (with W.H. Auden); 'The World in the Evening'.

Joyce, James (1882–1941), poet, novelist—'A Portrait of the Artist as a Young Man'; 'Dubliners'; 'Ulysses'; 'Finnegans Wake'.

Kennedy, Margaret (1896–1967), novelist—'The Constant Nymph'; The Ladies of Lyndon'; 'Return I Dare Not'.

Kops, Bernard (born 1926), novelist, poet—'The Hamlet of Stepney Green'; 'Yes from No Man's Land'; 'On Margate Sands'.

Larkin, Philip (1922–85), novelist, poet—'The North Ship: Poems'; 'The Whitsun Weddings'; 'The Explosion'.

Lawrence, D(avid) H(erbert) (1885–1930), poet, novelist, essayist—'Sons and Lovers'; 'Sea and Sardinia'; 'The Plumed Serpent'; 'Birds, Beasts and Flowers'.

Lawrence, T(homas) E(dward) (1888–1935), travel writer—'Seven Pillars of Wisdom'.

Lessing, Doris (born 1919), novelist, poet—'A Proper Marriage'; 'Fourteen Poems'; 'The Golden Notebook'; 'Canopus in Argos: Archives' series.

Lewis, C(live) S(taples) (1898–1963), essayist, novelist—'The Screwtape Letters'; 'That Hideous Strength'; 'Chronicles of Narnia'; 'Mere Christianity'; 'Allegory of Love'.

Llewellyn, Richard (1907?–83), novelist—'How Green Was My Valley'; 'None but the Lonely Heart'.

Lowry, Malcolm (1909–57), novelist—'Under the Volcano'; 'Dark as the Grave Wherein My Friend Is Laid'.

MacNeice, Louis (1907–63), poet—'Springboard'; 'Holes in the Sky'.

Mansfield, Katherine (1888–1923), short-story writer—'The Garden Party'; 'Bliss'; 'The Doves' Nest'.

Masefield, John (1878–1967), poet, novelist, dramatist—'Salt-Water Ballads'; 'The Daffodil Fields'; 'Sard Harker'; 'Reynard the Fox'; 'So Long to Learn'.

Maugham, W(illiam) Somerset (1874–1965), novelist, short-story writer, dramatist—'Of Human Bondage'; 'The Moon and Sixpence'; 'Cakes and Ale'; 'Our Betters'; 'The Constant Wife'; 'The Razor's Edge'.

Milne, A(lan) A(lexander) (1882–1956), essayist, children's writer—'When We Were Very Young'.

Muir, Edwin (1887–1959), poet—'The Voyage'; 'One Foot in Eden'; 'The Labyrinth'.

Murdoch, Iris (born 1919), novelist—'Under the Net'; 'The Red and the Green'; 'The Sea, the Sea'; 'Nuns and Soldiers'.

Noyes, Alfred (1880–1958), poet—'Tales of the Mermaid Tavern'; 'The Wine-Press'; 'Drake: an English Epic'.

O'Casey, Sean (1880–1964), dramatist—'Juno and the Paycock'; 'The Plough and the Stars'.

O'Flaherty, Liam (1896–1984), novelist, short-story writer—'The Informer'; 'Two Lovely Beasts'.

Orwell, George (Eric Hugh Blair) (1903–50), novelist, essayist—'Nineteen Eighty-Four'; 'Animal Farm'.

Osborne, John (born 1929), dramatist—'Look Back in Anger'; 'Luther'; 'Epitaph for George Dillon'.

Plath, Sylvia (1932–63), poet—'The Colossus'; 'The Bell Jar'; 'Ariel'; 'Crossing the Water'.

Powell, Anthony (born 1905), novelist—'A Dance to the Music of Time' series.

Powys, John Cowper (1872–1963), poet, novelist, critic—'Visions and Revisions'; 'The Meaning of Culture'; 'Wolf Solent'.

Priestley, J(ohn) B(oynton) (1894–1984), novelist, dramatist—'The Good Companions'; 'Dangerous Corner'.

Rattigan, Terence (1911–77), dramatist—'O Mistress Mine'; 'The Winslow Boy'; 'Separate Tables'.

Richardson, Dorothy M. (1882–1957), novelist—'Pilgrimage' (12 novels).

Rushdie, Salman (born 1947), novelist—'Grimus'; 'Midnight's Children'.

Russell, Bertrand (1872–1970), mathematician, philosopher—'Human Knowledge'; 'New Hopes for a Changing World'; 'Satan in the Suburbs'.

Russell, George William (Æ) (1867–1935), poet, essayist—'Gods of War'; 'The Interpreters'.

Sansom, William (1912–76), novelist, short-story writer—'A Bed of Roses'; 'Something Terrible, Something Lovely'.

Sassoon, Siegfried (1886–1967), poet, novelist—'Counter-Attack'; 'Memoirs of a Fox-Hunting Man'.

Silkin, Jon (born 1930), poet—'The Peaceable Kingdom'; 'Flower Poems'; 'The Lapidary Poems'.

Sillitoe, Alan (born 1928), novelist, poet—'Without Beer or Bread'; 'Loneliness of the Long Distance Runner'; 'A Tree on Fire'; 'Travels in Nihilon'; 'The Victory'.

Sitwell, Dame Edith (1887–1964), poet, critic—'The Mother'; 'Street Songs'; 'Green Song'; 'Façade'; 'Victoria of England'; 'Poetry and Criticism'.

Sitwell, Sir Osbert (1892–1969), poet, critic—'The Winstonburg Line'; 'Left Hand, Right Hand'.

Snow, C(harles) P(ercy) (1905–80), novelist—'Strangers and Brothers'; 'The Masters'.

Spark, Muriel (born 1918), novelist—'The Ballad of Peckham Rye'; 'The Girls of Slender Means'; 'Memento Mori'; 'The Prime of Miss Jean Brodie'; 'The Only Problem'.

Spender, Stephen (born 1909), poet, critic—'Ruins and Visions'; 'The Destructive Element'.

Strachey, Lytton (1880–1932), biographer—'Eminent Victorians'; 'Queen Victoria'; 'Elizabeth and Essex'.

Synge, John Millington (1871–1909), dramatist—'Riders to the Sea'; 'The Playboy of the Western World'.

Thomas, D.M. (born 1935), novelist, poet—'The Granite Kingdom'; 'Love and Other Deaths'; 'Birthstone'; 'Dreaming in Bronze'.

Thomas, Dylan (1914–53), poet—'Collected Poems'; 'Under Milk Wood' (radio play).

Thomas, R.S. (born 1913), poet—'Stones of the Field'; 'Frequencies'; 'Between Here and Now'.

Tolkien, J.R.R. (1892–1973), novelist—'Lord of the Rings' trilogy.

Tomlinson, Charles (born 1927), poet—'A Peopled Landscape'; 'Written on Water'; 'The Flood'.

Toynbee, Arnold (1889–1975), historian—'A Study of History'; 'Civilization on Trial'.

Wain, John (born 1925), novelist—'Living in the Present'; 'The Smaller Sky'; 'Young Shoulders'.

Walpole, Sir Hugh (1884–1941), novelist—'Fortitude'; 'Jeremy'; 'The Cathedral'; 'Rogue Herries'.

Waugh, Evelyn (1903–66), novelist—'Decline and Fall'; 'A Handful of Dust'; 'Vile Bodies'; 'Brideshead Revisited'; 'The Loved One'.

Wells, H(erbert) G(eorge) (1866–1946), novelist, historian—'Tono-Bungay'; 'The Time Machine'; 'The War of the Worlds'; 'The Outline of History'.

Wesker, Arnold (born 1932), dramatist—'Chicken Soup with Barley'; 'Their Very Own Golden City'; 'The Old Ones'; 'The Journalists'.

West, Dame Rebecca (Cicily Fairfield) (1892–1983), novelist—'The Judge'; 'Harriet Hume'; 'The Return of the Soldier'.

Wilson, Angus (born 1913), novelist—'Hemlock and After'; 'The Old Men at the Zoo'; 'Late Call'; 'No Laughing Matter'; 'Setting the World on Fire'.

Woolf, Virginia (1882–1941), novelist, critic—'Mrs. Dalloway'; 'The Voyage Out'; 'Night and Day'; 'To the Lighthouse'; 'The Waves'; 'The Common Reader'.

Yeats, William Butler (1865–1939), poet, essayist, dramatist—'The Wild Swans at Coole'; 'Ideas of Good and Evil'; 'Cathleen ni Houlihan'; 'Deirdre'.

BIBLIOGRAPHY FOR ENGLISH LITERATURE

History and Criticism

Adams, R.M. The Land and Literature of England (W.W. Norton, 1983).

Blamires, Harry. Twentieth Century English Literature (Schocken, 1982).

Bowen, Elizabeth and Burgess, Anthony. The Heritage of British Literature (Hudson, 1983).

Evans, B.I. A Short History of English Literature, 4th ed. (Penguin, 1976).

Hawthorn, J. British Working Class Novel in the 20th Century (Arnold, 1984).

Sampson, George. The Concise Cambridge History of English Literature, 3rd ed. (Cambridge Univ. Press, 1970).

Stapleton, Michael, ed. Cambridge Guide to English Literature (Cambridge Univ. Press, 1983).

Anthologies

Abrams, M.H., ed. Norton Anthology of English Literature, 4th ed. (W.W. Norton, 1979).

Amis, Kingsley, ed. The New Oxford Book of English Light Verse (Oxford, 1978).

Cruse, Amy. English Literature Through the Ages (Folcroft, 1973).

Dobson, Austin. A Handbook of English Literature (Arden, 1981).

Gardner, Helen, ed. The New Oxford Book of English Verse, 1250–1950 (Oxford, 1972).

Lowry, H.F. and Thorp, W., eds. Oxford Anthology of English Poetry, 2 vols. (Granger, 1979).

Noyes, Russell, ed. English Romantic Poetry and Prose (Oxford, 1956).

ENGRAVING *see* GRAPHIC ARTS.

ENLIGHTENMENT. To understand the natural world and mankind's place in it solely on the basis of reason and without turning to religious belief—this was the goal of the wide-ranging intellectual movement called the Enlightenment. The movement claimed the allegiance of a majority of thinkers during the 17th and 18th centuries, a period that Thomas Paine called the Age of Reason. At its heart it became a conflict between religion and the inquiring mind that wanted to know and understand through reason based on evidence and proof.

Like all historical trends and movements, the Enlightenment had its roots in the past. Three of the chief sources for Enlightenment thought were the ideas of the ancient Greek philosophers, the Renaissance, and the scientific revolution of the late Middle Ages.

The ancient philosophers had noticed the regularity in the operation of the natural world and concluded that the reasoning mind could see and explain this regularity. Among these philosophers Aristotle was preeminent in discovering and explaining the natural world (*see* Aristotle).

The birth of Christianity interrupted philosophical attempts to analyze and explain purely on the basis of reason. Christianity built a complicated world view that relied on both faith and reason to explain all reality. (*See also* Christianity.)

The Renaissance, with its revival of classical learning, and the Reformation of the 16th century, which broke up the Christian church, ended the world view that the church had presented for a thousand years (*see* Reformation; Renaissance). Coupled with these events was the scientific revolution, a modern discipline that soon lost patience with religious quibbling and what was seen as the attempts of churches to hamper progress in thought. Among the leaders of this revolution were Francis Bacon, René Descartes, Copernicus, Galileo, Gottfried Leibniz, and—most significant of all—Sir Isaac Newton. It was Newton who explained the universe and who justified the rationality of nature.

Religious Issue

The response of organized religion to the avalanche of new ideas and facts was far from friendly. A perfect example of this is that Galileo was called before the Inquisition in Rome and forced to take back his statements that the sun, not the Earth, is the center of the solar system.

But religion in the 17th and 18th centuries was on the defensive, and the great number of new denominations after the Reformation made a united front impossible. While most early supporters of rationalism and new scientific methods did not deny either God or religion, they brought both under the microscope of reason. They were negative about biblical religion and Christianity while expressing a belief in a God who was the author of nature's wonders, a God who had set the world in motion and formulated the laws by which it operated. This religious view—called deism—found many followers during the Enlightenment, but it was never an organized religion like Christianity.

Eventually both Christianity and its deistic opponents were faced with an extreme rejection of religion in an upsurge of atheism, the denial of God's existence. This reaction had its roots in the ancient philosophy of materialism that had been set forth by Epicurus and his followers—a world of atoms and empty space and nothing more. If reason could not discover God, said the atheists, there was no purpose served by deciding there was one.

Positive Aspects

Very little escaped examination by Enlightenment thinkers. Besides criticizing religion and broadening the range of scientific effort, they provided new points of view on society, politics, law, economics, and the course of history.

Society. The deist search for a natural religion led to an investigation of peoples in all parts of the world. The conclusion was, according to philosopher David Hume, that "there is a great uniformity among the acts of men in all nations and ages." This led to a sense that all people are linked together in a universal brotherhood. The Swiss lawyer Emmerich von Vattel urged the creation of a society of states living together in peace under the binding rules of natural law. Toward the end of the 18th century, Immanuel Kant wrote 'Toward Perpetual Peace', but by that time Europe was embroiled in the wars of the French Revolution and of Napoleon, wars that lasted until 1815.

The optimistic view of a universal brotherhood was reinforced by John Locke's notion that people are the result of their environment. This led to the idea that the existing social, economic, and political abuses should be corrected. The brutality of law enforcement and the institution of slavery were both attacked by those who believed in the moral improvement of society through reason.

Politics. Nowhere was the turmoil of Enlightenment thought more evident than in discussions about government. On the continent of Europe reason and natural law seemed to dictate that powerful monarchs should rule society. In France, Voltaire poured much of his energy into supporting the powers of the crown against the legislatures and the nobility. In England, by contrast, a constitutional democracy was in the process of being born. But all across Europe—even in England—it was thought that the best hopes for positive change lay with a vigorous monarchy.

Two thinkers undercut this—John Locke in England and Jean-Jacques Rousseau in France. Locke, in his 'Second Treatise of Government', proposed a regime of people of good will and a society in which natural law guaranteed men the rights to life, liberty, and property. Rousseau, in his 'Social Contract', claimed that under government people had substituted civic freedom for natural freedom. His book was an emotionally charged work calling for political democracy. (*See also* Locke; Rousseau.)

Before the 18th century was over, the ideas of these two men won significant victories. In what became the new United States, Thomas Jefferson wove the principles of Lockean rights into the 'Declaration of Independence', and in France, following the Revolution of 1789, the thought of Rousseau could be seen behind the 'Declaration of the Rights of Man'. (*See also* Bill of Rights.)

Law. The men of the Enlightenment realized that for all of history the hand of law had been turned against the masses of people and in favor of the few. Law was therefore criticized on the ground that it was invalid unless it conformed to the natural law. Law was not simply made by rules but was discovered by right reason.

Economics. Against the background of long, extensive involvement of government in economic affairs, Enlightenment thinkers proposed changes. In both France and England early classical economists—among whom the most famous was Adam Smith—claimed that individuals freed from government interference would serve their own economic interest, and by so doing they would serve the general good of society as well. (*See also* Capitalism; Economics.)

Meaning of history. The ancient Greeks and Romans felt that the history of mankind moved in cycles—from growth and prosperity to decay and death—much like the seasons of the year. The church looked forward to the kingdom inaugurated by God. Thinkers like Francis Bacon, however, criticized these views. He believed that by the proper methods of inquiry mankind could move to greater benefits through the conquest of nature. By the end of the 18th century, the idea of scientific and intellectual progress turned into a general belief in the progress of mankind, a progress that was both moral and material but that would depend on the rule of sound reason.

End of the Enlightenment

Many of the effects of the Age of Reason persist today, particularly in the respect given to science and in the growth of democracy. Enlightenment thought, however, failed in many respects. It tried to replace a religious world view with one erected by human reason. It failed in this because it found reason so often accompanied by will power, emotions, passions, appetites, and desires that reason can neither explain nor control. In the end, the adequacy of reason itself was attacked, first by David Hume in his 'Enquiry Concerning Human Understanding', and later by Immanuel Kant in the 'Critique of Pure Reason'. Most thinkers came to realize that cool and calculating reason is insufficient to explain the variety of human nature and the puzzling flow of history.

Late in the 18th century there was already under way a sweeping revolt against the claims of reason, a revolt called Romanticism. This was a conscious rebellion against science, authority, tradition, order, and discipline. Romanticism manifested itself primarily in the arts. It emphasized individuality, subjectivity, the goodness of the natural world, and the irrational.

ENZYMES. Substances in plants and animals that speed biochemical reactions are called enzymes. Enzymes can build up or break down other molecules. The molecules they act on are called substrates.

Enzymes are catalysts—chemicals that hasten a chemical reaction without undergoing any change. An enzyme can engage with the substrate, perform its catalytic action, and break off unchanged.

Enzymes are huge protein molecules (*see* Proteins). Highly specific, each usually catalyzes only one type of chemical reaction. Some enzymes consist of a protein and a helpful nonprotein component called a prosthetic group. When the prosthetic group is loosely linked to the protein, it is called a coenzyme. Vitamins are important parts of these coenzymes (*see* Vitamins). However, whatever its composition, each enzyme works on a specific substrate.

How Enzymes Work

Some enzymes help plants and animals digest food. Animals use enzymes in their digestive systems to break down foods into their simpler components so that the body can readily absorb them. Plants use enzymes in photosynthesis, the process by which plants obtain their food. Enzymes also help plants and animals get energy from food. Energy is freed from digested food by oxidation in the individual cells of a plant or animal. In this process, oxygen, usually obtained from air, receives electrons from the breakdown products of sugars, fats, or proteins to liberate the energy they contain. In living things, oxidation must take place slowly to minimize destructive heat. It does so through a series of enzyme-controlled reactions that release heat and energy step by step in small amounts. These reactions occur best in the temperature range between 68°F and 104°F.

Since enzyme molecules are far larger than those of their substrates, chemists believe that their catalytic action occurs only at a small active site on the enzyme. The substrate and probably the enzyme fit together at the active site like a lock and a key. This would account for an enzyme's specificity for a particular substrate. Then the chemical bond holding the substrate together is weakened in the enzyme-substrate activated complex, and the substrate molecule is broken down into smaller products. After disengagement, the enzyme is free to perform its catalytic action again and again. If a coenzyme is needed to reduce a substrate it probably floats to the basic enzyme molecule when a reaction is about to take place, links with the enzyme and substrate, and then disengages itself from the enzyme when the biochemical task is finished.

Many enzymes are catalysts in reactions that build molecules. In a similar lock-and-key fashion, they probably fasten smaller molecules together to make longer, larger ones.

How Enzymes Are Made

Enzymes are formed at cell sites called ribosomes. Amino acids, the building blocks of proteins, are brought to the ribosomes and strung together in a precise manner to form the enzymes. These then float free within the cell or into nearby body areas where they are needed.

The genetic code that determines protein structure also directs the amino-acid sequence of enzymes. The genes of a species control the kinds of enzymes its members make. (*See also* Genetics.)

How Enzymes Are Named

The more than a thousand enzymes that exist in nature are usually named for their substrates, with *ase* as a suffix. The enzyme *lipase*, for example, acts on fatty lipids. However, some of the first enzymes discovered were not named in this way. Among them was the enzyme *pepsin*, which breaks down proteins.

Enzymes are divided into six categories based on their function. The *hydrolases* usually split their substrates with the aid of water. The *lyases* split their substrates without aid. The *transferases* transfer chemical groups between different molecules. The *isomerases* rearrange the molecules of their substrates. The *oxidoreductases* transfer hydrogen ions. The *ligases* help release energy. (*See also* Biochemistry; Organic Chemistry; Fermentation.)

SOME ENZYMES AND THEIR ACTIONS

Enzyme	Action	Source
Hydrolases		
Acetylcholine esterase	Inhibits signals between nerve cells	Nerve tissues, muscles
Lipase	Splits fats	Stomach, pancreas
Lysozyme	Splits bacterial carbohydrates	Spleen, egg white
Maltase	Splits maltose	Intestine
Pepsin	Splits proteins	Stomach
Rennin	Curdles milk	Stomach
Ribonuclease	Splits compounds in food for inclusion in ribonucleic acid chains	Pancreas
Trypsin	Splits proteins	Pancreas
Lyases		
Adenosine deaminase	Breaks down amino acid adenine	Kidney, liver, muscles
Transferases		
Glutamine transaminase	Transfers part of glutamic acid to another amino acid	Liver, kidney
Phosphoglucomutase	Exchanges phosphates between carbohydrates	All tissues
Isomerases		
Aconitase	Rearranges citric acid	All tissues
Phosphomannose isomerase	Rearranges a carbohydrate	Muscles
Oxidoreductases		
Cytochromes	Transfer electrons in cell respiration	Cell mitochondria
Ligases		
Glutamine synthetase	Helps build amino acid glutamine	Brain

EPIC. The nature of the literary form known as epic can be summed up by the title of James Agee's book 'Let Us Now Praise Famous Men'. Most epics are legendary tales about the glorious deeds of a nation's past heroes. The term originally referred to long narrative poems of heroic deeds among ancient peoples. Today the word epic is often more loosely applied to a book or motion picture that deals in a grand way with significant historical events. Leo Tolstoy's 'War and Peace' about Napoleon's invasion of Russia and Margaret Mitchell's 'Gone with the Wind' are examples.

Epic poetry has been used by peoples in all parts of the world to transmit their traditions from one generation to another. The poems may deal with such topics as heroic legends, histories, religious tales, animal stories, or moral theories. The most ancient of these stories were passed from one generation to the next by storytellers long before they were written. The oral epic tradition continued for as long as the people of a nation were largely unable to read and write.

The purpose of the epic was to educate and inspire one generation of people to value and follow the deeds of their larger-than-life predecessors. It was hoped thereby that the present generation would live up to the best of its traditions.

The earliest epic in Western civilization comes from the ancient Sumerians of Mesopotamia before 3000 BC. It is the 'Epic of Gilgamesh', the story of King Gilgamesh, who is part human and part divine. The quest of his life, at which he fails, is to find a way to achieve immortality.

Best known to modern readers are the great Greek epics by Homer—the 'Iliad' and the 'Odyssey'. The 'Iliad' is the story of the Trojan War, and the 'Odyssey' deals with the 10-year voyage of Odysseus to his home after the war. Less well known are a pair of epic poems by the Greek Hesiod—'Theogony' and 'Works and Days'. The 'Theogony' is about the formation of the world from chaos, the emergence of the gods, and the several ages of mankind. The 'Works and Days' explains, through a series of myths, why it is the fate of mankind to endure daily toil in order to become rich.

The Bible, though primarily a religious work, contains several epic sections: the story of Moses, the greatest hero of ancient Israel; the story of Israel's conquest of Palestine, beginning with the book of Joshua; and the highly philosophical and moral exposition in the book of Job.

Most famous of the Latin epics is the 1st-century BC 'Aeneid' of Virgil about the founding of Rome. The 1st-century AD 'Pharsalia' of Lucan is also considered a Roman epic because it deals in a heroic way with the lives of Caesar, Pompey, and Cato.

Other notable epics include the 'Ramayana' and 'Mahabharata' of India (*see* Indian Literature); 'Beowulf', a Germanic epic (*see* English Literature); 'Chanson de Roland' from medieval France (*see* French Literature; Roland); 'Heike monogatari' of Japan (*see* Japanese Literature); and 'Kalevala' of Finland (*see* Finland; Lönnrot, Elias).

EPICTETUS. In his youth the Greek Stoic philosopher Epictetus was a slave. His real name is unknown; Epictetus means "acquired." He was born in Phrygia about AD 60, and when he was a boy he became the property of (was acquired by) a Roman. In Rome the slave managed to attend lectures on philosophy. After he won freedom, he became a teacher.

About AD 90 Emperor Domitian forced all philosophers out of Italy. Epictetus went to Nicopolis, in Epirus, where he taught the doctrines of Stoicism. His teachings were based on freedom of the will, trust in Providence, and obedience to conscience. His philosophy was preserved by Arrian, one of his pupils, in 'Discourses' and 'Handbook'.

EPICUREANISM. Freedom from pain in the body and from trouble in the mind is the goal of a happy life. This was the teaching of the Greek philosopher Epicurus, who lived from 341 to 270 BC. To many people Epicureanism has often meant a simple devotion to pleasure, comfort, and high living with little thought for the consequences. But the ideas of Epicurus were far more complex. In his lifetime, and for centuries afterward, he was considered a moral reformer.

The ideas of Epicurus on how a person should live were based on his understanding of the natural world and on his beliefs about the human body-soul relationship. Like Democritus before him, Epicurus believed that the universe is made up of material bodies and space, or the void. Bodies are composed of individual elements called atoms. The universe is unlimited, and so is the number of atoms. Atoms are of different shapes, and the number of atoms of each shape is infinite.

Both the human body and soul are composed of atoms. The atoms of the soul are thin and distributed throughout the body. It is the soul that is responsible for all sense perception. Sensation is the sole source of knowledge, as all sense perceptions are true—whether of seeing, hearing, touching, smelling, or tasting. Error may arise, however, if the mind forms a wrong opinion about what the senses perceive. As long as the soul is protected by the body, it is capable of communicating sensations to it. When it leaves the body it is scattered and lost, and the body is no longer able to feel anything.

If sensations are the basis of knowledge, the purpose of knowledge is to avoid those sensations that cause pain and to seek out those that give pleasure both to body and mind. While every pleasure is in itself good, not every pleasure is to be pursued because some pleasures may entail painful consequences or annoyances that outweigh the pleasures themselves. This means that the individual must learn to discriminate between pleasures that are really good and those that only seem to be good.

To live well requires the exercise of practical wisdom—moderation, justice, and courage—to balance pleasures against pains and to accept when necessary those pains that lead to greater pleasures. Thus Epicureanism is not just a self-serving attitude. It may be necessary, for example, to engage in battle in order to achieve the greater goal of peace. It is necessary to treat other people with justice because it is painful to be treated unjustly. Epicurus recommended the cultivation of friendship as both useful and desirable. He also claimed that the pleasures of the mind are more enduring than those of the body.

EPIDEMIOLOGY. The branch of medical science that studies the spread of disease in human populations and the factors influencing that spread is termed epidemiology. Unlike other medical disciplines, epidemiology concerns itself with groups of people rather than individuals. It developed in the 19th century out of the search for causes of human disease—especially of epidemics—and one of its chief functions remains the identification of populations at high risk for a given disease so that the cause may be identified and preventive measures begun (*see* Disease).

Epidemic

When a disease occurs in a high number of people in a population, an epidemic is said to exist. An epidemic occurring over a wide area is called a pandemic. For an infectious disease, its prevalence—that is, the number of cases existing at a certain time—depends upon the transfer of an effective dose of the infectious agent from an infected individual to a susceptible one. After an epidemic has subsided, the affected host population contains a sufficiently small proportion of susceptible individuals that reintroduction of the infection will not result in a new epidemic. Since the parasite population cannot reproduce itself in such a host population, the host population as a whole is immune to the epidemic disease, a circumstance termed herd immunity.

Following an epidemic, however, the host population tends to revert to a condition of susceptibility because the immunity of individuals deteriorates and susceptible persons are added to the population by birth. In time the population as a whole again becomes susceptible. The time that elapses between successive epidemics is variable and differs from one disease to another.

The modern definition of epidemic has been enlarged to include outbreaks of any chronic disease—as, for example, heart disease or cancer—influenced by the environment. The term epidemic is sometimes reserved for disease among human beings. In such instances the term used for epidemics among animals other than man is epizootic.

In addition to providing clues to the causes of various diseases, epidemiologic studies are used to plan new health services, determine the incidence of various illnesses in the population to be served, and to evaluate the overall health of a given population. (The incidence of a disease is the number of new cases that occur during a certain period.) In most countries of the world, public-health authorities regularly gather epidemiologic data on specific diseases and death rates in their populaces.

Descriptive Epidemiology

Epidemiologic studies may be classified as descriptive or analytic. In descriptive epidemiology, surveys are used to find out the nature of the population affected by a particular disease, noting such factors as age, sex, ethnic group, and occupation among those afflicted. Other descriptive studies may examine the occurrence of a disease over several years to determine changes or variations in incidence or death rates; geographic variations may also be noted. Descriptive studies also help to identify new disease syndromes or suggest previously unrecognized associations between risk factors and disease.

To use the example of typhoid, a disease spread through contaminated food and water, it first becomes important to discover if the disease observed is truly caused by *Salmonella typhosa,* the typhoid organism. Once the diagnosis is established it is important to know the number of cases, whether the cases were scattered over the course of a year or occurred within a short period, and what the geographic distribution is. It is critically important that the precise addresses and activities of the patients be established. Two widely separated locations within a city might be found to have clusters of cases of typhoid all arising at nearly the same time. It might be found that each of these clusters revolved about a family unit including cousins, nephews, and other friends, suggesting that in some way personal relationships might be important. Further investigation might show that all of the infected persons had dined at one time or at short intervals in a specific home. It might further be found that the person who had prepared the meal had recently visited some rural area and had suffered a mild attack of the disease and was now spreading it to family and friends by unknowing contamination of food. This fictional case suggests the importance of studying the causes as well as the spread of disease.

Analytic Epidemiology

Analytic studies are carried out to test the conclusions made from descriptive surveys or laboratory observations. These studies divide a sample population into two or more groups selected on the basis of suspected cause of the disease—for example, cigarette smoking—and then monitor differences in incidence, death rates, or other variables. In one form of analytic study called the prospective-cohort study, members of a population are examined over time to observe differences in disease incidence.

Statistics are used to analyze the incidence of diseases and their prevalence. If, for example, a disease has an incidence rate of 100 cases per year in a given region, and, on the average, the affected persons live three years with the disease, the prevalence of the disease is 300. Statistical classification is another important tool in the study of possible causes of disease. These studies—as well as epidemiologic, nutritional, and other analyses—have made it clear, for example, that diet is an important consideration in the causes of atherosclerosis—the buildup of fatty deposits on the walls of arteries. The statistical analyses drew attention to the role of high levels of animal fats and carbohydrates in the diet as the possible causes of atherosclerosis. The analysis further drew attention to the fact that certain populations that do not eat large quantities of animal fats but instead live largely on vegetable oils and fish have a much lower incidence of atherosclerosis. Thus statistical surveys are of great importance in the study of human disease. (*See also* Health; Health Education and Physical Education; Medicine.)

EPILEPSY *see* DISEASE.

EB Inc.

Jacob Epstein in 1949

EPSTEIN, Jacob (1880–1959). In his long career as a sculptor, Jacob Epstein drew storms of criticism. Each new carving in stone or marble was greeted with cries of "ugly!" or "deformed!" Gradually many people would learn to appreciate the rugged strength of the new work, but the same argument began again when Epstein showed his next statue.

Epstein also made many portrait busts of well-known people. These were modeled in clay, then cast in bronze. The busts have been accepted with less argument because Epstein worked to achieve realistic likenesses. Among his famous subjects were George Bernard Shaw, Albert Einstein, and Winston Churchill. He also did many charming portrait busts of children. (*See also* Sculpture.)

The sculptor was born on Nov. 10, 1880, on New York City's East Side, where he spent his teenage years sketching the teeming ghetto life of the city. At 20 he entered the Art Students' League to study drawing and painting. Soon he turned to sculpture. He worked days in a foundry that made bronze casts and studied sculptural modeling at night. Epstein also studied in London and Paris and in 1905 settled in London. He married Margaret Dunlop, a Scot, in 1906 and became a British subject. They had two children.

Epstein's early portrait busts won recognition. His sculpture for a public building, however, aroused protests. He did not yield to criticism and continued to carve massive and often grotesque figures. In them he expressed what he called the "problems of man." Occasionally Epstein painted and drew illustrations for books. In contrast to his sculpture, his pictures are delicate and appealing. In 1954 he was knighted. His wife died in 1947. He remarried in 1955. Epstein died on Aug. 19, 1959, in London.

EQUATOR. The imaginary east-west line encircling the Earth midway between the North and South poles is called the equator. The circumference, or distance around, the equator is about 24,900 miles (40,000 kilometers). The equator divides the Earth into two equal parts, the Northern and Southern hemispheres. The latitude of the equator is defined as zero degrees. Latitude is a system of imaginary east-west lines, called parallels, that encircle the Earth parallel to the equator. Parallels are used to measure distances in degrees north or south of the equator. Latitude increases northward and southward from the equator, reaching 90 degrees at the North and South poles (*see* Navigation).

Longitude lines, known as meridians, are the other measurement needed to locate points precisely on the Earth's surface. Longitude is measured in degrees eastward and westward from a line known as the prime meridian. The prime meridian, or zero longitude, is

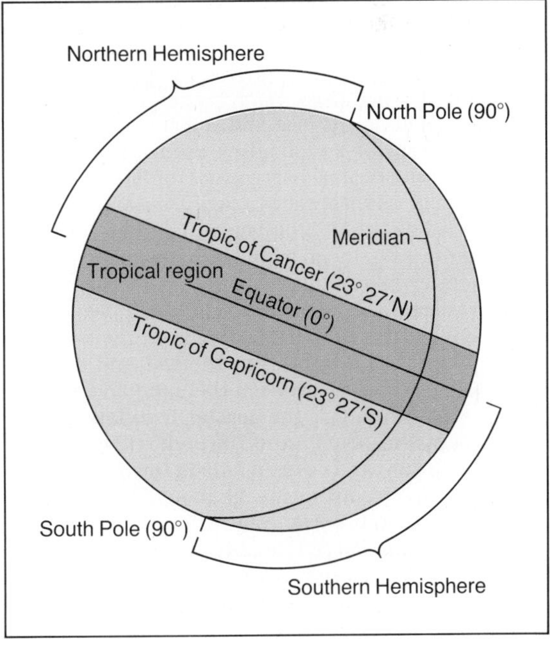

drawn between both poles and passes through the former site of the Royal Greenwich Observatory in Greenwich, England. Longitude increases eastward and westward from the prime meridian, reaching 180 degrees. Parallels and meridians are usually drawn on maps and globes and are used to locate any place on the Earth. (*See also* Latitude and Longitude.)

Two especially significant parallels are known as the Tropic of Cancer and the Tropic of Capricorn. They encircle the Earth at about 23 degrees, 27 minutes north and south of the equator. The region between these parallels is called the tropics, or the torrid zone. The Tropic of Cancer marks the northern boundary of the tropics; the Tropic of Capricorn, the southern boundary. Altitude and distance from the sea determine the climate in this region, which varies considerably. Some areas have heavy rainfall, and others are hot and dry with little rain.

There is also an imaginary line on the Earth called the magnetic equator, or the aclinic line. The term aclinic comes from the Greek word meaning "bending to neither side." At the magnetic equator the magnetic attraction of the North and South poles is equal. The needle of a compass lying on this east-west line will point neither north nor south. The magnetic equator does not follow the geographic equator precisely because the North and South magnetic poles do not coincide with the North and South geographic poles.

EQUATORIAL GUINEA. A republic on the west coast of Africa, Equatorial Guinea includes an area on mainland Africa and the island of Bioko. Its total land area is 10,831 square miles (28,052 square kilometers). The mainland region is bordered on the north by Cameroon and on the east and south by Gabon. It is separated from Bioko Island by the Gulf of Guinea.

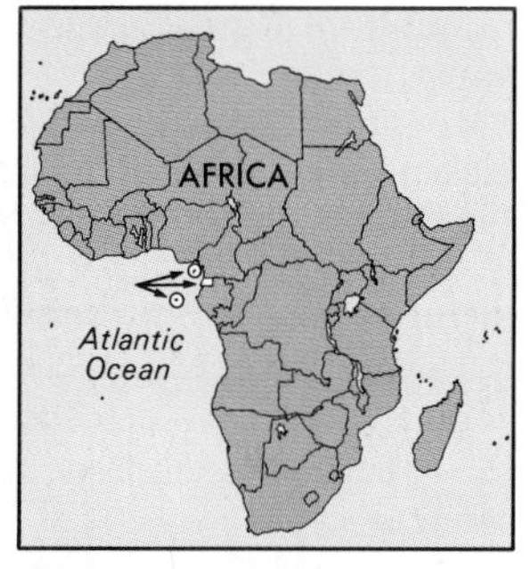

The mainland area has coastal hills and inland plateaus that rise eastward toward the Gabon border. It is divided by the Mbini River, which runs generally from east to west. Bioko Island is made up of volcanic cones, crater lakes, and rich lava soils. There is an extinct volcano in the north that is 9,868 feet (3,008 meters) high. The capital, Malabo, is on the island.

The climate is tropical, but the wet and dry seasons differ somewhat between the mainland and the island. The rainfall of the coastal mainland region ranges between about 95 and 180 inches (240 and 457 centimeters) a year. Less rain falls in the interior. The average yearly temperature is about 79° F (26° C). Thick tropical rain-forest vegetation dominates the mainland region. More than 140 species of wood are found, including *okume*, African walnut, and various mahoganies. Animal life—including the gorilla, monkey, leopard, elephant, and crocodile—has been hurt by overhunting. Bioko Island has mangrove swamps along the coast and no big game.

Equatorial Guinea has a mixed, developing economy based largely on agriculture. Cacao, coffee, and lumber are the only exports. Cacao accounts for more than 95 percent. Coffee is grown mainly along the Cameroon border. Other crops are bananas, grown on Bioko, and palm oil and cassavas on the mainland. Petroleum was discovered off the north coast of Bioko in 1981, and testing continues. A fishing industry is developing.

The country depends heavily on international aid, mostly from the International Monetary Fund and from Spain. The country's economic progress depends mainly on its good relations with Spain.

Industry is limited to the processing of agricultural products. Electrical shortages are a continuing problem. The country has a fairly extensive road system, though it is in urgent need of repair. The main harbor, Malabo, is being updated by a French firm and has regular services to Europe. There is an international airport.

Traditional customs have a large influence. Witchcraft, traditional music, gorilla and elephant hunting, and storytelling are important to the Fang people, who form the majority of the population on the mainland. Spanish is the official language, though each ethnic group also speaks its own. About four fifths of the population is Roman Catholic, but the Bubi people on Bioko Island retain their traditional forms of worship.

Five years of primary education are required. In the late 1970s it was estimated that more than 70 percent of school-age children were attending primary school. Only a small percentage goes on to secondary school. There is no higher education, so students must go abroad for further study. Most go to Spain.

Health conditions are generally poor. The average life expectancy is 45 years with an infant mortality rate of almost 150 per 1,000 live births. Malnutrition is common, and more than four fifths of the people suffer from malaria at some point in their lives. Health problems are worsened by poor sanitation and a shortage of physicians. In the early 1980s major steps toward preventive health care were begun.

The first inhabitants of the mainland appear to have been Pygmies. The Fang and Bubi, who form the majority of the modern-day population, reached the mainland region and Bioko, respectively, in the 17th and 19th centuries. Equatorial Guinea was part of the large area that went from Portuguese to Spanish domination in the late 18th century. It was a stopping point for slave traders and British, German, Dutch, and French merchants. Bioko Island, known as Fernando Po until 1973, was administered by the British from 1827 to 1858.

Through the early and mid-20th century, the site was called Spanish Guinea. Independence was declared in 1968 and was followed by a reign of terror and economic troubles brought on by the dictatorial president, Francisco Macías Nguema. He was overthrown by a coup in 1979 and was later executed. Equatorial Guinea has since been governed by a Supreme Military Council and is attempting to develop democratic social and political norms and its economy. A new constitution was approved in 1982, and on Aug. 28, 1983, a 41-member National Assembly was elected. Population (1984 estimate), 325,000.

EQUESTRIAN SPORTS. The Latin word for horse is *equus*. Equestrian sports are certain riding events held at horse shows and most specifically competitive horse and rider events held at the summer Olympic Games. The three events that comprise equestrian sports are dressage, show jumping, and hunter trails. The term excludes horse racing, rodeos, and polo. (*See also* Horse; Polo; Rodeo.)

Dressage. The French word *dressage* means "training." Dressage is the systematic and progressive training of riding horses to execute a wide range of maneuvers precisely. The elementary kind of training, called *campagne*, teaches a young horse obedience, balance, and relaxation. The horse is taught first on a training rope, then under the saddle, a variety of gaits, full and half halts, backing, and turning. Beyond learning these basic movements, a capable horse is then taught diagonal movements, basic figures, and canter variations.

The advanced dressage is called *haute école* (high school), a level of training that is best displayed by the Lipizzans at the Imperial Spanish Riding School in Vienna. (For a picture *see* Horse, "The Lipizzan.") Some circus riding is also of haute école caliber. There are two kinds of movements taught in haute école: those that the horse does with feet on the ground and jumps from a stationary position. The on-the-ground moves are pirouettes, the *piaffe*, the *passage*, and the *levade*. A pirouette is a turn on the haunches in four or five strides at a collected canter. ("Collected" refers to the location of the center of gravity toward the rear of the horse.) The *piaffe* is a trot in place. A *passage* is a cadenced, high-stepping trot. In the *levade* the horse rises to stand on its hind legs, with its forelegs drawn in. Off-the-ground movements are the *courbette, ballotade,* and *capriole.* A *courbette* is a jump forward while the horse is at the *levade* position. A *capriole* and a *ballotade* are both jumps from a four-legged standing position, but in a *capriole* the horse extends its hind legs to a nearly horizontal position. All of the haute école dressage movements can be performed with or without a rider on the horse. Competition in dressage has been part of the Olympics since 1912.

Jumping. Training is begun by walking a horse over bars or poles laid flat on the ground. When the horse is used to these, its speed is increased and the obstacles systematically raised and spaced irregularly. The purpose of this training is to teach the horse to keep its head down, to approach obstacles at a quiet and energetic pace, to decide how and where to take off, and to land in such a way as to proceed to the next obstacle without difficulty.

In the Olympics the Prix des Nations jumping event is a competition that involves 13 or 14 obstacles varying in height from 51 to 63 inches (1.3 to 1.6 meters). There is also a water jump that is 13 feet (4 meters) across. The course has 200 feet (60 meters) between obstacles. Penalties are meted out for knocking down

Torrance W. Fleischmann puts her horse through its paces (top) at the Chesterland, Pa., competition. Horse and rider went on to the 1984 Summer Olympics. Michael Matz and his horse Sandor (center) ride in the Olympics trials. A horse and rider (bottom) run the hunter trails course at the 25th annual Los Altos Hunt Race at Pebble Beach, Calif., in 1983.

(Top) Burk Uzzle—Woodfin Camp & Associates; (center) Allsport/West Light (bottom) Craig Aurness—West Light

or touching an obstacle, disobedience, and falls. Riders with the lowest penalty scores win.

Hunter trails. This event is based on the traditional cross-country gallop, as if one were fox hunting or riding in a cavalry charge. In the Olympics, on the second day of what is called the three-day event, it is an endurance test over a course 16 to 22 miles (25 to 35 kilometers) in length covering swamp roads, tracks, obstacles, and cross-country sections. It is the most grueling of the riding events for both horse and rider.

History. Although there have been organized mounted games since the 7th century BC, modern riding competitions originated in the 16th century during the Renaissance. Horse riding, long a necessity for military men, became of interest to the wealthy in their leisure. Riding schools were established in several European countries to teach riding skills. Dressage was probably started in Italy by a trainer named Frederiga Grisone about 1550.

Show jumping started in 1869, when the first such competition was held at the Agricultural Hall Society horse show in London. Today most horse shows and competitions are under the auspices of such organizations as the British Horse Society, the American Horse Shows Association, the Italian Federation of Equestrian Sports, and the French Federation of Equestrian Sports. These and other similar societies are affiliated with the International Equestrian Federation founded in 1921 and based in Brussels, Belgium.

ERASMUS, Desiderius (1466–1536). Often called simply Erasmus of Rotterdam, he was the leading scholar of the northern Renaissance. While the Renaissance in Italy was chiefly concerned with the revival of the ancient Greek and Roman classics, that of northern Europe was centered on reforming and revitalizing Christianity by going back to its sources in the New Testament and the church fathers.

Desiderius Erasmus was born on Oct. 27, 1466, in either Rotterdam or Gouda in The Netherlands. After his early schooling he had a religious education and became a priest in the Augustinian order. But he found no satisfaction in his duties. He won a release in 1494, and from that time he was a traveling scholar. He made several trips to England; lived in various cities in Belgium, France, and Italy; and finally settled in Basel, Switzerland, where he stayed from 1521 to 1529. He then left for Freiburg and remained there until 1535 before returning to Basel, where he died on July 12, 1536.

Desiderius Erasmus in an oil painting by Hans Holbein the Younger in 1523

Giraudon—Art Resource/ EB Inc.

His greatest influence resulted from his writings and other scholarly efforts. He wrote on theology, religious issues, education, and philosophy. He published editions of the works of the church fathers, including Jerome, Augustine of Hippo, Cyprian, Irenaeus, and Origen. His publication of the Greek New Testament was a landmark achievement for its time, enabling scholars to examine a more accurate text than had been available for centuries. Among his own books the most popular and enduring are 'Enchiridion', on Christianity, published in 1503, and 'The Praise of Folly'(1509), his best-known book.

In one respect Erasmus differed from the spirit of his time. He wanted a reformed Christianity, but he was opposed to a divided church. Thus he opposed the Reformation, though he praised many of its goals.

ERBIUM *see* CHEMICAL ELEMENTS; PERIODIC TABLE.

ERHARD, Ludwig (1897–1977). For his role in restoring to prosperity the ruined economy of West Germany after World War II, Ludwig Erhard has been called the "father of the economic miracle." He became the chancellor of his country in 1963.

Ludwig Erhard was born on Feb. 4, 1897, at Fürth, near Nuremberg, in Bavaria. He was a commercial apprentice until he was drafted into the German army during World War I. In 1917 he was wounded and while convalescing took up the study of economics. He received his doctor's degree at the University of Frankfurt. In 1923 he married Luise Lotter.

Erhard became the director of a government-supported market research institute in Nuremberg. In 1942 the Nazis forced his dismissal because he repeatedly refused to join the Third Reich Labor Front.

Foreseeing Germany's defeat in World War II, Erhard in 1944 conceived a program of German economic recovery based on free-trade principles. In May 1945 the Allied authorities appointed him to reorganize industry in the Nuremberg area; in October he became minister of economics in the first postwar government of Bavaria.

When the first postwar national election was held in West Germany in 1949, Erhard was elected to the Bundestag as a member of the Christian Democratic Union party from Ulm. He was appointed minister of economic affairs in the cabinet of Chancellor Konrad Adenauer, a post he held for 14 years. Under his broad policy of free trade, the West German economy prospered. He became vice-chancellor in 1957.

In 1963 the Bundestag elected Erhard to succeed Adenauer as chancellor. Erhard resigned on Nov. 30, 1966, in the aftermath of an economic decline. He died in Bonn on May 5, 1977.

ERICSON, Leif. The first European to land on the North American continent was a Viking seaman, Leif Ericson. A son of the explorer Eric the Red, he was born in Iceland about AD 980. When Leif was about 2 years old, Eric took his family to Greenland. The boy grew up in Brattahlid, now the Eskimo village of Kagsiarsuk, on Eric's Fjord, on the southwest coast.

At 19 Leif voyaged to Norway, where he spent a winter at the court of Norway's Christian king, Olaf Tryggvessön. When he returned home, he converted his mother to Christianity. She built the first church in Greenland; its foundations and those of other old Viking buildings may be seen in Kagsiarsuk.

There are different versions of how Leif discovered America. According to the 'Saga of Eric the Red', he was blown off his course on his return from Norway and was carried westward to the continent.

Another saga, the 'Flatey Book', says that in 985 Biarni Heriulfsson saw land—probably the coast of North America—but did not go ashore. Years later in Greenland Leif bought a ship from Biarni, gathered a crew of 35, and set off for the unknown land. They put ashore at a place described as a barren tableland of flat rocks backed by great ice mountains.

Going to sea again, they dropped anchor off a level wooded land with broad stretches of white sand; they called it Markland (Forest Land). Once again they sailed southward. This time they went ashore where the land was green with "fields of self-sown wheat," trees, and sweet "grapes." They named it Vinland (Wineland) the Good, and here they built shelters and spent the winter. The "grapes" they saw were squashberries, used to make wine.

The Newfoundland historian W.A. Munn believed that Leif landed somewhere on the northernmost tip of Newfoundland on the Strait of Belle Isle, probably at Lancey Meadows (L'Anse aux Meadows). His analysis of old records was confirmed in 1963, after a Norwegian expedition uncovered the remains of a Viking settlement near the fishing village. Radiocarbon dating of charcoal found in hearths shows the site was used about AD 1000.

Further evidence that Leif's Vinland was a part of the North American continent was claimed in 1965 when Yale University acquired the so-called Vinland Map. Although its 1440 date was at first authenticated, it was branded a forgery in 1974. Two early 15th-century books that were also donated to Yale, however, confirm the Vikings' settlement.

Leif earned his nickname "Leif the Lucky" on his trip home to Greenland, when he rescued a shipwrecked party of 15. Later his brother Thorvald was killed by Eskimo on a trip to Vinland.

Thorfinn Karlsefni, an Icelander who married the widow of Leif's other brother, Thorstein, established a colony in Vinland. This colony of 160 men and 5 women spent three years at Leif's wintering place. Karlsefni's son Snorri was the first white child born in North America. The colony was abandoned because of the hostility of the Eskimo. The remains found by the expedition may be those of Karlsefni's colony.

ERICSSON, JOHN (1803–89). The Swedish-American inventor John Ericsson became famous for his construction of the ironclad ship *Monitor*, which fought in the most important naval battle of the Civil War (*see* Civil War). As a boy in Sweden he had shown early mechanical talent.

When he was 12 years old he began to learn to be a draftsman. From 1820 to 1827 he was in the Swedish army, where his excellent military maps won him a captaincy. Then he obtained leave to go to London.

After losing a prize competition for a steam locomotive, Ericsson turned to other experiments and completed a number of marine inventions. He built a new kind of naval engine that was to be placed below the waterline and received a prize of $20,000 from the British admiralty for the invention of a screw propeller. In 1838 he designed the engines and propeller used by the first vessels to cross the Atlantic in regular steamship service.

The United States government ordered an iron vessel at a British shipyard to be fitted with his screw and engines. Ericsson followed the ship across the Atlantic and established himself in New York in 1839 as a shipbuilder. His design for the *Monitor*, which was at first called a "cheesebox on a raft," revolutionized naval construction. Later he worked on the development of torpedoes and solar-heat motors.

Ericsson became an American citizen in 1848. After he died in New York City on March 8, 1889, a United States warship took his body to Sweden for burial.

ERIC THE RED. About AD 982 a brawny, red-bearded Norseman named Eric set sail from the northwest coast of Iceland. After killing a neighbor in a quarrel, he had been banished from Iceland for three years. He intended to sail his Viking ship west to a land he had heard of but never seen.

About 100 years before, a mariner named Gunnbjörn had been blown off his course from Norway to Iceland. Sailing back, he had sighted a bleak, snow-covered land. Men told tales of his discovery, but no one ventured to explore the unknown country.

Into an open boat Eric loaded his family, servants and slaves, and friends. After sailing for days in the North Atlantic, they reached the coast of a huge island, which he named Greenland (*see* Greenland).

Eric and his people found country much like their own Iceland. They fished and lived as they had at home. At the end of his exile, Eric returned to Iceland to persuade others to live with him in Greenland. In 986 he returned with about 500 new settlers. They built two colonies.

Eric had three sons—Thorvald, Thorstein, and Leif. Leif was the first European who touched the North American continent (*see* Ericson).

ERIE, LAKE. So many ships have been wrecked on Lake Erie that it has been called "the marine graveyard of the inland seas." The shallowest and stormiest of the Great Lakes of North America, it has a maximum depth of only 210 feet (64 meters). It is fourth in size among the five Great Lakes with a length of 241 miles (388 kilometers) and an area of about 9,910 square miles (25,667 square kilometers). (*See also* Great Lakes.)

Despite its relatively small size, Erie has four major lake ports. Detroit stands at the west end where the Detroit River, Lake Saint Clair, and the St. Clair River enter from Lake Huron. Buffalo is at the east end where Lake Erie empties over Niagara Falls into Lake Ontario. Other important Lake Erie ports are Cleveland and Toledo on the Ohio shore. Ships can pass between Lake Erie and Lake Ontario through the Welland Ship Canal.

The industrial economy of the lakeshore area depends heavily upon water transportation. The steel industry, especially south of Pittsburgh, depends on the movement of iron ore and limestone across the Great Lakes to Lake Erie ports. The port at Toledo handles soft coal shipments, and Buffalo is a grain port. Pollution of the lake resulted in the closing of many beaches and resorts in the 1960s, but by the late 1970s the environmental damage had begun to slow.

The first European to see Lake Erie was probably the French-Canadian explorer Louis Jolliet in 1669. Iroquois Indians lived in the region at that time. Lake Erie was the scene of an important naval battle in the War of 1812. United States Commodore Oliver H. Perry defeated the British in a battle at Put-in-Bay, Ohio, and secured the Northwest for the United States (*see* Perry). The lake was named after the Erie Indians who once inhabited the shores.

ERIE, Pa. Modeled on the plan of Washington, D.C., Erie has a spaciousness about it unusual in an industrial center. A port of entry on Lake Erie, the city is a strategic shipping point for lumber, coal, petroleum, grain, chemicals, and iron. It is also Pennsylvania's only port on the Saint Lawrence Seaway.

Erie's industry includes the manufacture of electrical equipment, construction machinery, ships, paper, railroad equipment, aluminum forgings, clothing, chemicals, plastics, and rubber products. Early industries were largely related to agriculture. The city's economic development began with the opening of the Erie and Pittsburgh Canal in 1844 and railway construction in the 1850s.

Erie's colleges include Gannon, Mercyhurst, Villa Maria, and the Behrend College campus of Pennsylvania State University. An art gallery and a planetarium are associated with the public museum, and there is an orchestra. Sports events are held in Memorial Stadium. The Northwestern Pennsylvania Winter Carnival is held each February.

Points of historic interest include the Old Customs House, built in 1839 and now the county historical society headquarters; Wayne Blockhouse, a replica of the one in which General Anthony Wayne died in 1796; the Perry Memorial House and Dickson Tavern, which was a station on the Underground Railroad for runaway slaves; and the *Niagara*, Oliver Hazard Perry's flagship, a memorial of the battle of Lake Erie in the War of 1812 (*see* Perry). Fort-Le-Boeuf, the last French outpost in the French and Indian Wars, is 16 miles (26 kilometers) south. The curving, 7-mile (11-kilometer) Presque Isle Peninsula shelters Erie's harbor.

Named for the Erie Indians, Erie was the site of the Fort-Presque-Isle, built by the French in 1753 and now a state park. Given up to the British in 1759, the fort was destroyed by Indians in 1763. The area remained a wilderness until after the American Revolution. The town was laid out in 1795. In 1803 it became the seat of the newly formed Erie County; in 1805 it was incorporated as a borough and as a city in 1851. It has a mayor-council form of government. Population (1984 estimate), 117,461.

ERVING, Julius (born 1950). Basketball great Julius Erving, better known as Doctor J., once said of his amazing airborne moves: "It's easy once you learn how to fly." His flights quickly made him one of basketball's all-time top scorers.

Julius Winfield Erving was born in Hempstead, N.Y., on Feb. 22, 1950. He started playing basketball in local parks and with a nearby Salvation Army team. In his first year at the University of Massachusetts, he broke records for scoring and rebounding. He left the university in 1971 to sign a contract as a forward with the Virginia Squires of the American Basketball Association (ABA).

Erving, who is 6 feet 6 inches tall, changed the idea of the way the game should be played. His great skill and remarkably large hands worked together to make his ball handling an awesome art. His airborne feats popularized the slam dunk, the hanging rebound, and the finger roll. His ability to block shots and rebound, as well as pass and handle the ball skillfully, encouraged faster and flashier playing.

In 1973 Erving moved to the New York Nets and, with an average of 27.4 points and 10.7 rebounds per game, led them to the ABA title. Sports enthusiasts believe that, when the NBA (National Basketball Association) absorbed the ABA in 1976, it was primarily to get Erving, who joined the Philadelphia 76ers. His first years in Philadelphia were frustrating because the 76er style of play and tendinitis in his knees limited him. But by the 1979–80 season conditions had changed, and Erving was averaging 26.9 points a game.

Erving's honors included ABA Most Valuable Player in 1974, 1975, and 1976, NBA Most Valuable Player in 1981, and numerous elections to ABA and NBA all-star teams. He was praised for his team spirit, his work for charities, and his success in business. Erving claimed he chose the Doctor J. nickname to replace one reporters had adopted in reference to his large hands—The Claw.

ESCALATOR *see* ELEVATOR AND ESCALATOR.

An Eskimo in his kayak near Disko Bay, Greenland, uses modern weapons for hunting in his traditional environment of ice and snow. The white rectangle in the kayak is a hunting blind to prevent game from seeing him against the snow. Behind it sits a stand for his gun.

Wedigo Ferchland

ESKIMO. The name they use for themselves is Inuit, which means simply "the people." It was apparently the Cree Indians of Canada who gave the Inuit the name Eskimo, which means "eaters of raw meat." If so, it was a misnomer, because the Inuit care no more for meat that has not been cured or otherwise prepared than does anyone else. But popular terminology catches on, so these people of the far north shall probably always be called Eskimo. There are about 100,000 Eskimo living in the Arctic region—in a belt stretching from Greenland in the east, across northern Canada and Alaska, to eastern Siberia.

Although they have long lived near some of the northern Indian tribes, the Eskimo do not seem to be related to Indians. They can be distinguished by their more Mongoloid features. A high percentage of Eskimo also have type B blood, a characteristic that seems to be completely absent from their Indian neighbors. The origins of the Eskimo are uncertain. They probably came from the Far East, but they have lived in the Arctic for more than 2,000 years.

Their language is called Inuktitut, and it is one of the more complex languages of the world. Because of the wide geographical area in which the Eskimo live, there are many dialects, or local forms, of Inuktitut.

Since the end of the 19th century, their contacts with people in North America and from Europe have resulted in the creation of a special limited jargon, or mixed language, of from 300 to 600 words. Most of these words were derived from Inuktitut, but some came from English, Hawaiian, and other tongues. It was this jargon that some visitors to the Arctic mistook for the Eskimo language.

Traditional Life and Customs

The common image of Eskimo sitting around an igloo eating whale meat is only partially accurate. For all the centuries that they lived without much contact with outsiders, they developed a fairly static way of life that suited their environment. Now the traditional life is fading as more and more Eskimo become integrated into the economic and political structures of the countries in which they live. Only a people of great ingenuity and endurance could have survived in a region that is frozen under ice and snow for six to nine months a year, an area in which most vegetable foods were unobtainable and where trees exist in only a few marginal districts.

The Eskimo relied for their food supply on fishes, sea mammals, and the few land animals of the Arctic. In the winter a dozen or more families congregated in a small community, and each morning the men would set out to harpoon any seals that appeared coming up for air in the few open lanes of water. But in the spring the communities would break up. Some families pursued seals over the open water in kayaks, skin-covered, one-man boats much like canoes (*see* Canoeing). Other families hunted whale or fished. In the summer most families hunted caribou and other land animals. Then, as winter drew on, the families would congregate together again, and the cycle of the year was finished. It was never a completely uniform cycle, for it varied from region to region in accordance with conditions.

Against land animals the Eskimo used the bow and arrow—replaced later by the rifle. Against sea mammals the weapon was the harpoon. Some groups of Eskimo used rawhide nets to capture seals, but for some reason the nets were never adapted for fishing.

Water transport was provided by the kayak for hunting the smaller mammals, but for whaling the Eskimo used a larger boat called the umiak. It was also skin-covered, and it resembled the traditional European whaling boat. On land, transportation was provided by dogsled, which may have been an adaptation of the Siberian reindeer sled.

In such a severe climate only fur clothing offered sufficient protection. Among the available animal

Dr. A. Farquhar—Image Finders

Eskimo hunters in Repulse Bay, Canada, prepare to go hunting. Snowmobiles, not dogs, will pull their provisions.

furs, the Eskimo preferred caribou, though they sometimes used furs of such other animals as seals, polar bears, mountain sheep, and hares. Clothing consisted of coat, trousers, stockings, and shoes or boots. In very cold weather two of each garment were worn. The inner one had the fur against the skin and the outer one had the fur outside. Boots were normally made from sealskin because it is particularly resistant to damage and does not spoil with dampness. One Eskimo garment, the hooded coat called the parka, has been adopted by ski enthusiasts and others who spend time in cold climates.

Dwellings. That well-known word igloo actually means any type of dwelling. The snow block house that is usually pictured as the typical Eskimo home was used primarily in the region stretching from Labrador west to north central Canada. It was unknown in Alaska and very little used in Greenland. To make this structure, hard-packed snow was cut into blocks with a long knife made of bone, ivory, or metal. It was usually possible for a man to put up this kind of igloo in an hour. In the igloo, Eskimo slept on a low snow platform covered with twigs and caribou furs. Each igloo had a skylight made of freshwater ice. When summer arrived the igloo melted, and the family had to move into tents made of animal skins.

In the western Arctic and Greenland, the Eskimo lived in log cabins made from driftwood and insulated on the outside with turf. Skylights were made from thin, translucent animal gut. These cabins were entered by way of a semi-underground passage that led to a trapdoor in the floor. When summer arrived and the passageways flooded, it was necessary to move into tents of seal or caribou skin.

Animal fat burned in shallow, saucer-shaped lamps of pottery or stone provided some heat. Fish and meat could be cooked over these lamps.

In such severe circumstances people had few possessions. There was no money economy as known today. Eskimo family members had their dogs, their dwelling, and the few things they made for themselves: tools, sled, weapons, and kayak. There were occasionally some pieces of folk art, such as whale bone carvings, but not much else. Even the house ceased to belong to a family once it was deserted. Someone else might come along and take it over. The land was considered to belong to all, and food was shared in common. Fishing and hunting were such hazardous and uncertain pursuits that no one dared let anyone else do without food, for fear that he might be the one to do without the next time.

Family and work. There was a fairly sharp division of labor between men and women. Men were the hunters and home builders, while women prepared the food, worked on skins, and made the clothing. Men and women, therefore, were so dependent on each other that all Eskimo married. Some men occasionally married a second or even a third wife, especially if the first had no children. Some women occasionally had two husbands. Eskimo were fond of children, and orphans normally found homes with relatives and were well treated. In a land where there were no vegetable foods or roads, a mother nursed her children and carried them everywhere on her back until they were about 3 years old.

Religion. Traditional Eskimo religion was quite similar to animism. Eskimo saw a spiritual force in every natural phenomenon: in beast, bird, and fish; in wind and snow; in stones and sticks. Each of these was viewed as having human characteristics. These spiritual forces were neither friendly nor hostile, but they could become dangerous if they were not respected. (*See also* Animism.)

The souls of the Eskimo dead went to join this world of spirits, and they could become hostile to their surviving relatives or to other Eskimo. It was especially necessary never to offend the spirits of game animals, since they could bring on sickness or famine. There arose, therefore, complicated systems of regulations concerning the preparation of food, all

An Eskimo near Perry River in Canada's Northwest Territories builds an igloo from cut slabs of snow.

Richard Harrington—Miller Services

Photos (left and right) Bryan & Cherry Alexander; (center) Steve McCutcheon

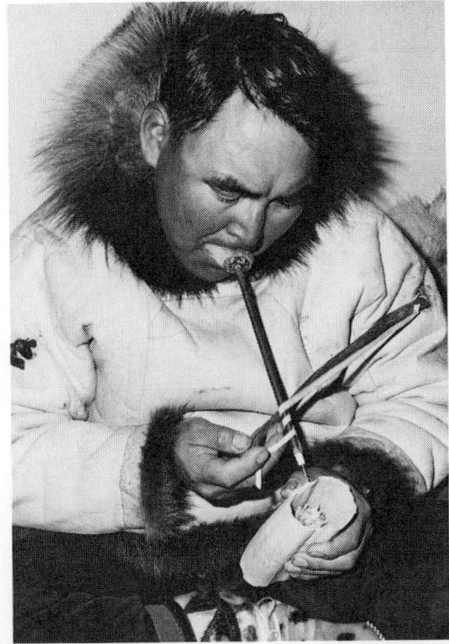

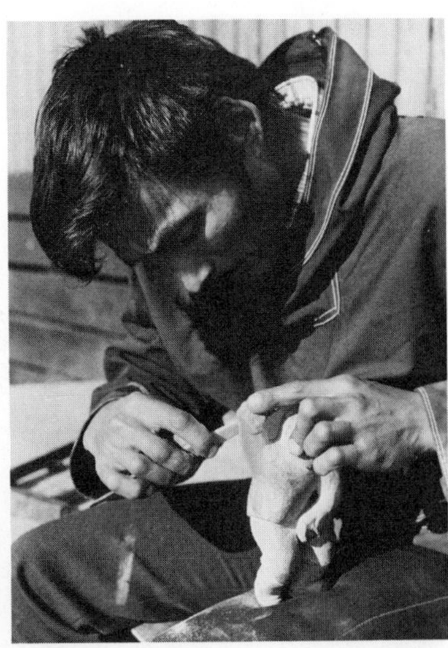

An Eskimo woman (left) uses an ulu, a semicircular knife, to clean a polar bear skin stretched over a wooden frame. The ivory carver (center) uses a traditional rather than modern means of drilling because it gives him better control of his work. An Eskimo sculptor (right) in Greenland carves a stone figurine.

with the avowed purpose of keeping harmony between the Eskimo and the environment.

The Eskimo Today

Snowmobiles are replacing dogsleds. This is only a small example of the extent to which Eskimo life has been adapting to the cultures that made contact with it over the centuries.

Culture change has been going on slowly for a long time. The Vikings settled in Greenland from the 11th to the 14th century, and they traded with the "Skraelings," as they called the Eskimo. In the 17th century the Danes colonized Greenland and brought the Eskimo within the political and religious orbit of Denmark.

The Eskimo of Alaska were also reached fairly early by white men, mostly Russians moving across the chain of Aleutian Islands to the mainland. More contacts were made after the United States purchased Alaska in 1867.

As with the Indians of North and South America, the first contacts were not always beneficial. Thousands of Eskimo died of diseases new to them: small pox, the common cold, measles, tuberculosis, and influenza.

The early establishment of trade centers, later followed by industrialization and mining, have influenced life among the natives of the Arctic. The petroleum discoveries in Alaska and northern Canada have brought many new jobs, not only in the fields themselves but on the pipelines. In Greenland many Eskimo have learned to grow vegetable crops during the short summer. Many work in the cryolite mines, and others have become traders and shopkeepers.

These economic changes have led many Eskimo to leave their usual Arctic habitats and move into towns and cities. Money has become a necessity, as has the purchase of guns, ammunition, whaling bombs, outboard motors, yard goods for clothing, and numerous other industrial items. Eating habits have also been influenced by these changes, as more types of food are brought from the warmer regions of Canada and the United States.

By the mid-20th century, most Eskimo were Christian, though traditional religion was certainly not forgotten. In areas governed by Canada and the United States, education is now required for Eskimo children. After primary schooling they normally must leave their home communities to attend high schools or trade schools elsewhere. In Canada schooling is now being more and more conducted in the Inuktitut language in the early grades. Adult education centers have also been founded to help qualify older Eskimo for better employment in industry and government.

In Canada the Eskimo economy has been improved by the starting of cooperatives. Instead of marketing their goods as families or individuals, they have formed cooperatives to obtain a better return from their handicrafts, fishing, clothing production, and tourism ventures. The cooperatives are the largest employers of native labor in the Arctic region. (*See also* Cooperatives.)

An acknowledgement that the Eskimo no longer live in isolation from other peoples or governments came in 1977 with the meeting of the first international Eskimo organization. Delegates representing United States, Canadian, and Greenland Eskimo met at a conference to plan and undertake joint economic, social, and cultural programs. Through the conference the Eskimo sought to participate in the policymaking of the various governments under which they live.

ESP *see* EXTRASENSORY PERCEPTION.

ESPERANTO *see* LANGUAGE.

AP/Wide World

The Soviet embassy building in Washington, D.C., has antennas and other electronic gadgetry on the roof. The building, to be replaced by a new structure in the 1980s, serves as a base for Soviet espionage.

ESPIONAGE

ESPIONAGE. Anyone walking past the Soviet embassy in Washington, D.C., would probably pay little attention to the television antennas and other electronic gadgets on the roof. But these fairly nondescript items are a reminder that the embassy is the command center for a vast network of Soviet spies working in the United States to funnel information and arrange for the transfer of technology to the Soviet Union.

The Soviet Union is not alone in the field of intelligence gathering. Espionage is a major enterprise for all of the industrialized nations, and the cold war has made it a vital undertaking in order to protect national security and to help prevent a major war (*see* Cold War). The embassies and consulates of the United States are also used as headquarters for the gathering of military and industrial secrets of other nations, particularly the Soviet Union and its allies.

Espionage may be defined as the secret gathering of information about a rival, but very often the spying is done on friendly or neutral countries as well. There is also a type of intelligence gathering called industrial espionage: the stealing of trade secrets from one company by another in order to profit by the information.

The Spy Business

Not all espionage is a secret, furtive activity with the romance and thrills of a "James Bond" novel. Much intelligence work is slow, painstaking, and tedious effort engaged in by the employees of national intelligence agencies such as the Central Intelligence Agency (CIA) of the United States or the Soviet KGB (*see* Intelligence Agencies). The agencies receive masses of information about a given country from fairly accessible sources such as publications, scientific and business conferences, public meetings, and industrial expositions.

To get less accessible information requires a variety of techniques. In part it is the work of professional spies who, by various means, steal government and industrial secrets and arrange for illegal purchases of sophisticated technology. Some of these spies are citizens of the nations on which they spy.

Modern technology is itself a significant aid in intelligence gathering. Computers are used to sift and evaluate information. Spy satellites and high-flying aircraft relay data back to Earth by electronic signals and advanced aerial photography. Seismographs can record underground nuclear testing. Eavesdropping devices can listen to private telephone conversations, and miniature cameras can photograph data, meetings, conferences, or private personal encounters.

Open and Closed Societies

It is easier for spies from the Soviet Union and its allies to work in the United States, Western Europe, and Japan than it is for American or other Western spies to gather information in the Soviet Union, China, and the Eastern-bloc nations. The Soviet Union is a closed society, and its Eastern European satellites are nearly so. Every area of public life is under government control, and private lives are always subject to government surveillance. All publications are monitored, and there is little access to information that the government does not want released. For any nation to set up an elaborate spy network within the Soviet Union is virtually impossible (*see* Totalitarianism).

The United States, Canada, the nations of Western Europe, Japan, Australia, and New Zealand are open societies. Nearly all of their political, social, and economic activities are carried out under the glare of public scrutiny and media reporting. Open societies have few secrets except for those they find necessary to classify for security reasons.

Under these conditions agents from hostile nations find it relatively easy to establish spy networks. Foreign spies operate out of embassies, consulates, business headquarters, and the United Nations. Spies working in an open society have access to all government and private publications. They are able to attend industrial expositions, business conferences, and meetings of scientific groups. They may even get jobs working for the government or in highly sensitive industries that do business with the Department of Defense. Many industries have poor internal control, or security, procedures, thus enabling spies or their collaborators to steal blueprints, design plans, or pieces of equipment.

Stealing technology and getting it to the end user is a task that frequently calls for collaboration. Advanced technology that can have military applications is a prime target. One means of getting computers or other sophisticated machinery to the desired destination is to send it by way of a neutral country and then have it shipped on to its real destination. This often takes the assistance of an intermediary to make the actual purchase and to arrange for shipment. The intermediary can be a member of the firm that manufactures the technology, or it may be a middleman who deals with a number of firms.

In southern California in the late 1970s, an American named Christopher John Boyce stole satellite technology from the TRW Corporation and sold it to the Soviets. He was caught and imprisoned only after the Soviets had the information. (A feature film entitled 'The Falcon and the Snowman' was made about Boyce's exploits.) Another collaborator, William H. Bell, took designs in 1981 for fighter plane radar from Hughes Aircraft in California and gave them to an intelligence officer from Poland who then relayed them to the KGB.

It is impossible to estimate the number of collaborators working for foreign governments. In 1985 alone a sizable number were caught. Of particular interest was a spy ring that included three members of one family: John Walker, Jr., a retired navy war-

SOME NOTABLE SPIES

Some prominent persons are not included below because they are covered in the main text of this article or in other articles in Compton's Encyclopedia (see Fact-Index).

Abel, Rudolf (1902–72). Headed Soviet spy network in United States in 1950s. Worked for Soviet intelligence from 1930s. Arrived in United States, via Canada, with forged passport 1948. Arrested 1957 and convicted. Exchanged for American pilot Francis Gary Powers, captured U-2 spy-plane pilot, 1962.

Blunt, Anthony (1907–83). British art historian who served as double agent for Soviet Union. Became communist while at Cambridge University in England in 1930s. Associate of Guy Burgess, Kim Philby, Donald Maclean. Early in World War II joined British intelligence (MI5). Helped Burgess and Maclean flee to Moscow 1951. Confessed 1964, made public 1979.

Boyce, Christopher John (born 1953). Collaborated with Soviets to steal military secrets from TRW Corporation. He and friend Daulton Lee were unhappy about American involvement in Vietnam and from 1975 spied for Soviets. Both arrested 1977, convicted, imprisoned. Film about their exploits released 1985: 'The Falcon and the Snowman'.

Culper Ring. Group that spied for George Washington during American Revolution, including Benjamin Tallmadge, Abraham Woodhull, and Robert Townsend. Worked throughout war, mainly in New York-New England area. British never learned of network, and few Americans knew of it.

Fouché, Joseph (1759–1820). Radical anti-loyalist early in French Revolution. Became supporter of Napoleon, who made him minister of police. Operated efficient network of spies and double agents until Napoleon's fall 1815. Temporarily minister of police again under Louis XVIII.

Gehlen, Reinhard (1902–79). Spied on Soviets for Nazi Germany. Collected extensive files, which, after war, showed to Americans. Worked for United States until director of intelligence for West Germany 1955–68. Gathered masses of intelligence on East Germany and Soviet activities in Europe.

Greenhow, Rose O'Neal (1817–64). Lived in Washington, D.C., and spied for South during Civil War. Used couriers to send messages to Confederate government regarding Northern troop movements and battle plans during early part of war. Arrested and deported to South 1862.

Mata Hari (1876–1917). One of most famous persons in espionage; real name Margaretha Zelle. Lived in Dutch East Indies with husband 1895–1902. Returned to Europe, left husband, became exotic "Indian" dancer Mata Hari. Spied for Germans against France in World War I. Eventually arrested by French and executed 1917.

Philby, Kim (1912–88). Real name Harold Adrian Russell Philby. Most famous British double agent for Soviet Union. Born in India and educated in England at Cambridge, where acquainted with Guy Burgess, Donald Maclean, and Anthony Blunt. Became communist. Recruited by Burgess, went to work for British military intelligence (MI6) 1940. Suspected of being Soviet spy but remained with MI6 until 1963, when defected and fled to Moscow.

Sorge, Richard (1895–1944). German national who spied for Soviet Union in China and Japan. Born in Baku, Russia; educated in Germany; and served in World War I. Joined German Communist party 1918 and by 1930 worked for Soviet intelligence. Served as spy in China and, after 1933, Japan. Reported on Japanese and German war preparations to Moscow. Predicted Japanese attack on United States 1941. Arrested by Japanese 1943, executed 1944.

Walsingham, Francis (1532?–90). English lawyer and diplomat in reign of Elizabeth I. Secretary of state 1573–90. Knighted 1577. Given responsibility of uncovering Catholic plots against queen. Established extensive spy network in Europe, putting agents in high places in Spain, France, and Italy. Through agents received full data on Spanish Armada before it sailed, thus enabling British to prepare to meet it.

Webster, Timothy (1821–62). Spied on Confederacy for North during early Civil War. Born in England, raised in New Jersey. Worked for Allan Pinkerton Detective Agency. Passed as Northerner with Southern sympathies. Caught by Confederates in 1862 and executed as spy.

Whitworth, Jerry A. (born 1939). Member of the United States Navy spy ring headed by John A. Walker, Jr., that also included Walker's son Michael and brother Arthur. Sold information on Navy codes, coding machines, and satellite communications to the Soviets from the early 1970s. Joined Navy in 1962. Retired from service in 1983. Arrested June 3, 1985. Convicted July 24, 1986, of spying and failure to pay taxes on money received. Sentenced to 365 years and fined $410,000.

(Left) AP/Wide World; (center and right) UPI/Bettmann Newsphotos

German-born Richard Sorge (left) was a Soviet spy in Japan from 1933 to 1943. The exotic Mata Hari (center), a German spy in France in World War I, was executed by the French in 1917. Kim Philby (right) was the most notorious Soviet mole in British intelligence.

rant officer; his son Michael, a navy yeoman; and his brother Arthur Walker, a retired navy lieutenant commander. Other arrested spies included Sharon Scranage, a clerk in the CIA office in Ghana; Edward Howard, a former CIA officer; Jonathan Jay Pollard, an employee of the Naval Intelligence Service who was charged with spying for Israel; and Larry Wu-tai Chin, a retired CIA analyst who was accused of spying for China for 30 years.

Industrial Espionage

On June 22, 1982, the United States Justice Department charged 18 Japanese executives with conspiring to steal computer secrets from the International Business Machines (IBM) Corporation. The executives were employees of Hitachi, Ltd., and of the Mitsubishi Electric Corporation. The operation was uncovered through a Federal Bureau of Investigation (FBI) "sting" operation. An FBI agent posed as a seller of the information. When the executives tried to pay for the data, they were apprehended. A year later the affair was settled out of court by an apology from the offenders and a substantial payment to IBM, a payment estimated to be $300 million.

Industrial espionage is a by-product of the technological revolution, which has made possible the introduction of more than a half million new products into the world market every year. When a new product is introduced by a company, competitors are immediately at a disadvantage and want to market something similar. Competitors are willing by fair means—and sometimes by foul—to obtain trade secrets. Such espionage is not confined to new technology. The highly competitive fashion industry, toy companies, and drug firms frequently participate in industrial espionage.

As with international espionage, the sources of information are often quite routine: trade journals, business meetings, data from the Patent Office, or trade shows. Analysis of a competitor's products is another way to learn about them.

Trade secrets, however, can find their way to a competitor through a less savory means. A disgruntled employee may sell a company's secrets, or employees may be hired away in order to find out what they know. Sometimes employees leave a corporation and form a new company, using the information they learned while with their former employer. This has frequently happened in the computer industry, where technological change is very swift.

An apparently legal way of stealing company secrets is by using the Freedom of Information Act, passed by the United States Congress in 1966 to help people and the press get information for the public good. The law has often been used instead by companies for private gain. Thousands of documents of government agencies such as the Food and Drug Administration and the Federal Trade Commission have been made available upon request. This has led to the loss of corporate information. In 1982, for example, a competitor of the Monsanto Chemical Company obtained data on one of Monsanto's new herbicides. The use of the formula could have cost Monsanto millions of dollars had the release of the information not been discovered. Monsanto sued and retrieved the information.

What makes industrial espionage so advantageous is weak enforcement of the laws that exist against it. If a company is convicted, there is normally only a small fine. The profits a company can make with a stolen design or formula may far outweigh the minor inconvenience of a fine.

To combat theft of trade secrets, companies use counterespionage. Several organizations in the United States and Europe specialize in this work. Some companies retain counterspies on their payrolls as a precaution against leakage of information. In West Germany there is an institution called the School for Economic and Industrial Security, a privately funded organization for training industrial counterspies. It was founded in 1979 because of the great amount of espionage committed there by East Germans.

(Left) Sven Simon—Katherine Young Agency; (Center left) AP/Wide World; (others) UPI/Bettmann Newsphotos

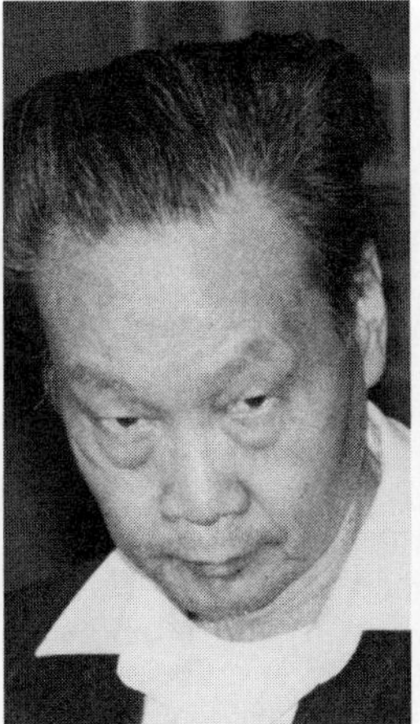

From left: In 1985 Hans Tiedge was found to be an East German mole in West Germany's government; John Walker, Jr., was arrested for espionage; Larry Wu-tai killed himself after his arrest; and Soviet spy Vitaly Yurchenko defected to the United States, then returned to Moscow.

The Spy in History

Espionage is an ancient craft. In the Bible's book of Joshua, when the Israelites were about to conquer Palestine, their leader Joshua sent two spies out "secretly with orders to reconnoiter the country." This happened earlier than 1200 BC.

During the Middle Ages and the Renaissance, diplomacy and intelligence were so closely bound together that ambassadors were normally regarded as little more than spies. By the time of Elizabeth I in England, spying was well on its way to becoming a necessary practice for national security. Under Elizabeth an elaborate intelligence system was organized by Sir Francis Walsingham in order to obtain information about Spain, England's leading enemy.

Military espionage played a role in all major modern wars: the American Revolution, the Napoleonic Wars, the American Civil War, and the Franco-Prussian War, for example. And it made great strides during World War I, when the general conditions favored intelligence activities in neutral countries such as Switzerland and Belgium. British intelligence proved especially effective during the war, and Britain's MI5 organization became legendary. Among the best-known World War I spies were Mata Hari, Franz von Rintelen, and Wilhelm Canaris. Canaris later became head of military intelligence for Adolf Hitler.

By World War II intelligence gathering had become a major government undertaking, and many countries set up organizations to do the work. The means of espionage were greatly enhanced by technological developments. The United States broke the Japanese cipher before the attack on Pearl Harbor in 1941, and the British deciphered the German code. The British were thereby able to remain aware of most happenings in Germany and German-occupied nations. Soviet intelligence—through its chief agent in Japan, Richard Sorge—was kept fully informed of German moves both before and after the attack on the Soviet Union.

After World War II much of the world's map was redrawn: Eastern European nations became Soviet satellites, and former colonies in Asia and Africa became independent. Millions of persons became displaced from their homelands. These conditions made infiltration by spies relatively easy. East Germans, for example, could get into West Germany and work their way into government service or into sensitive positions in the private sector.

The division of the world into two camps—communist and non-communist—produced subversive elements of a new type. During the 1930s and 1940s, educated men and women who held responsible positions in the West joined the Communist party—mostly for idealistic reasons—and took on a loyalty to the Soviet Union. This loyalty was bolstered by the Western alliance with the Soviet Union during World War II. Many of these individuals worked avidly for the Soviet cause in the early years of the cold war. Conversely, there were many from communist lands who defected to the West.

The cold war period became the era of the double agent, or mole. The British secret service agencies were especially afflicted with this problem: high-level agents for the British government who were secretly working for the Soviet KGB. The most notorious was Kim Philby, who fled to Moscow in 1963. Others were George Blake and Anthony Blunt.

Many individuals who became famous for other reasons have often assisted their governments by temporarily serving as spies. One of the best known was T.E. Lawrence, more commonly known as Lawrence of Arabia. He served Britain in the Middle East during World War I. Other famous persons who worked briefly as spies were Daniel Defoe, author of 'Robinson Crusoe'; the entertainer Josephine Baker; the Italian writer-adventurer Giovanni Giacomo Casanova; the British explorer Richard Burton; the spy novelists Ian Fleming and John Le Carré; the French art historian and novelist André Malraux; and the English novelist and short-story writer Somerset Maugham.

ESSAY. In 1588 the French writer Michel de Montaigne published the completed version of his 'Essais'. In so doing he gave a name to a type of literature that has become enormously popular in the English-speaking world as well as in other societies. The word essay is related to the French verb *essayer*, meaning "to attempt."

An essay is a composition of moderate length that reveals in an easy and general way the writer's views on a chosen subject. Montaigne said, "It is myself I portray." It is indeed mainly the author's personality as revealed in it that makes a good essay. Unlike the novel, short story, or drama, the essay does not aim primarily to create characters and to tell a story through them. It speaks directly to the reader, giving the author's views on customs, events, people, art, literature, or life in general. It may teach, argue, persuade, arouse emotion, or simply amuse. Its subjects may be almost anything—from the effects of rock music to the need to limit immigration.

Montaigne was not the first essayist, though he coined the term. The ancient Greek writer Plutarch, famous for his 'Lives', wrote 'Moralia', a series of more than 60 essays on ethical, literary, religious, physical, and political topics. The Roman dramatist and philosopher Seneca also wrote essays, published under the title 'Epistles'.

Since Montaigne, a great number of writers have used the essay form to express their opinions. The father of the English essay was Abraham Cowley, who wrote in the 17th century. His 'Essays in Prose and Verse' closely resembles Montaigne's style. The first outstanding English essayist, however, was Francis Bacon. He published 58 essays on serious matters such as 'Of Adversity', 'Of Beauty', and 'Of Riches'. Two notable essayists of the early 18th century were Joseph Addison and Richard Steele, whose writings appeared in the *Tatler*, a journal founded by Steele, and, later, the *Spectator*. Other outstanding English essayists of the 18th century were Henry Fielding, Samuel Johnson, and Oliver Goldsmith, though their literary fame rests on works other than essays.

In the 19th century one of the greatest of all essayists appeared—Charles Lamb, famous for his 'The Essays of Elia'. They were written with a keen insight into human nature and with a combination of humor and pathos (*see* Lamb). Among other popular English essay writers were Thomas de Quincey, Thomas Babington Macaulay, Matthew Arnold, Robert Louis Stevenson, Samuel Taylor Coleridge, John Ruskin, Thomas Carlyle, Max Beerbohm, Hilaire Belloc, G.K. Chesterton, Virginia Woolf, and J.B. Priestly.

In the United States the use of the essay has generally followed the English pattern, though it has frequently been developed as the tool for literary criticism. The best of the 19th-century essayists were Ralph Waldo Emerson and Henry Thoreau. Emerson's essays on nature, self-reliance, and other subjects are still widely read. Thoreau's 'Walden' is a masterpiece of narrative essay. The 'Autocrat of the Breakfast Table' by New England writer Oliver Wendell Holmes delighted generations of readers. Other 19th-century essayists were Edgar Allan Poe, Washington Irving, and James Russell Lowell.

Several European countries have produced outstanding essayists in the 20th century. Among them are Johan Huizinga of The Netherlands; Hermann Keyserling in Germany; Jean Paul Sartre and Albert Camus in France; and Salvador de Madriaga, José Ortega y Gasset, and Miguel de Unamuno y Jugo in Spain.

Other twentieth-century writers who deserve mention are Clarence Day, James Thurber, philosopher George Santayana, and Christopher Morley. One of the most noted essayists of recent times was E.B. White, who for years wrote the "Notes and Comment" column for *The New Yorker* magazine.

ESSEN, West Germany. Situated in the Ruhr valley, West Germany's mighty industrial and mining region, Essen became the area's chief city in the 19th century. The development of ironworks, steelworks, and coal mines during the 19th century stimulated rapid growth, making a once small town the largest industrial city in the Ruhr coalfield.

As the industrial hub of the Ruhr, Essen is also a retail trade center and a rail junction. In addition to coal and steel, the city has diversified heavy, medium, and light industries, including construction, chemical- and glassworks, and factories for textiles and precision instruments.

The coal mines and most industry are located in the north toward the Rhine-Herne Canal, while the south has woods and parks. There are large, modern administrative and office buildings, concert halls, and an economic research institute.

The city's museums include the German poster museum, which has an international collection of poster art dating from the 19th century. The Minster treasury is one of the world's richest church collections, and the Folkwang Museum features 19th- and 20th-century art. There is also a botanic garden with an aquarium, terrarium, and park.

Essen was originally the seat of an aristocratic convent founded in 852. It is still represented by a cathedral completed in the 15th century. In the suburb of Werden, the abbey church was founded in 796 as part of a monastery. The convent and the abbey exercised local sovereignty as imperial states until they were dissolved in 1802 at the time Essen passed to Prussia. Essen was occupied by the French from 1923 to 1925. During World War II it suffered heavy destruction as a center of German war industry. The Ruhr River is dammed in Essen to form the Baldeney-See, a lake. Nearby is the Villa Hügel, originally the home of the Krupps, a family of noted German industrialists (*see* Krupp Family). Since 1953 it has been used for meetings and cultural events. Population (1984 estimate), 628,800.

ESTATE AND INHERITANCE LAW. In most societies property rights do not end with the death of the property owner. Therefore, means have been found to pass property on to survivors—especially to a husband or wife, descendants, or ascendants (parents, grandparents) if there are no other survivors. In many places even distant relatives are allowed to inherit a deceased's property.

In British and American law it is customary to distinguish between real estate holdings (land and buildings) and personal property such as the contents of a home, an automobile, stocks and bonds, savings accounts, and other material goods. Business enterprises may also be part of an estate if they are privately owned or part of a partnership. Public corporations cannot be subject to inheritance laws, but closely held (privately owned) corporations can be (*see* Corporation).

In the Soviet Union and other communist nations, personal property such as consumer goods or savings accounts can be passed on by inheritance. The form of property known as the means of production—agricultural land, factories, or stores—cannot be, as they are the property of the state. This rule has exceptions, however, in some communist societies that allow some forms of private ownership in the economic sector, especially in farmland.

Many people decide before they die who shall inherit their property and how it will be divided. To do this, they make a will, a legal document whose provisions must be carried out. This is called testate succession. An individual who dies without leaving a will is called intestate. (*See also* Will.)

Testate succession. In societies that allow inheritance, two significant issues arise concerning the distribution of wealth: the extent to which an owner of property has the power to determine the course of inheritance by his own free decision, and whether estates are allowed or even required to pass undivided to a single heir. Freedom of testation developed slowly over the centuries, and nowhere does it exist without limits. The extent to which an owner of property is allowed to disinherit family members or have power to tie up property beyond the grave are issues that have been dealt with in a variety of ways.

In the United States the surviving spouse is protected against disinheritance in every state, no matter what the provisions of the will. But surviving spouses (husbands or wives) are not protected in all places against the other spouse's giving away property before death. In states that have community property laws, a definite share in family wealth is assured the surviving spouse, who is entitled to one half of the community property. This is generally considered to be property acquired during the marriage. Descendants are not protected against disinheritance in the United States, except for Louisiana.

Laws about the division of property have not been a significant issue in the United States, but they have played a major role in the distribution of wealth in Europe and other areas. In Great Britain and on the Continent the undivided descent of land to one heir was long the rule. Primogeniture—descent to the first-born son—was used to keep an estate from being broken up or alienated from the family. In Europe this system collapsed during the French Revolution and was never re-established. Equal division among descendants became the general rule during the 19th century. Some nations enacted special laws on farm inheritance in order to keep land from being divided into plots too small to support a family and to keep people on the land.

Intestate succession. The legal systems of the world have a great variety of laws on intestate inheritance, but the laws have one feature in common: those who receive the estate are necessarily persons having a kinship relation to the deceased. Ancient and medieval laws were concerned to keep the estate within the family—the bloodline—of the deceased. This issue is much less significant in modern law. There is a widespread trend to favor the rights of the surviving spouse along with, or even above, the deceased's blood relatives. In many places community property laws assure this right. Illegitimate children now have a more sure claim on an inheritance than was true in the past. Of practical importance are the rights to pensions, social security benefits, and other claims, which are now available to a surviving spouse.

ESTATES-GENERAL. When Philip IV of France needed help in his struggle with the pope in 1302, he called together representatives of the nobles, of the clergy, and of the townspeople of France—the three estates, or classes—in order to gain their aid. Although there had been meetings of similar groups in the preceding ten years, this date may be taken as the first meeting of the Estates-General of France. In the beginning it corresponded roughly to the Parliament of England, which was then less than 50 years old.

The French monarchy was more firmly fixed in power by the unfailing succession of the Capetian line, and the Estates-General never gained the right to make laws as the English Parliament did. During the Hundred Years' War, from 1337 to 1453, the Estates-General could frequently force the king to do as it wished by refusing him money to carry on the struggle, but it sometimes lost public respect by favoring civil strife or by allying itself with the English invaders. In 1439, near the close of the war, it granted a land tax, the *taille,* from which the nobles were exempted. Since there was no opposition when the king chose to consider such grants to be permanent, the king became independent. He had plenty of revenue, he had a standing army, he dominated the clergy and dispensed favors to the nobles, and so had little need of the Estates-General.

For 174 years, beginning in 1614, the representatives of the three estates were not summoned to consider the affairs of the kingdom. In 1788, however, the treasury was empty, and Louis XVI was forced to call this almost forgotten body together again. When it met on May 5, 1789, the representatives of the third estate, equal in numbers to the other two, refused to vote according to the old method by which each estate cast one vote. They insisted on voting as individuals and declared themselves the National Assembly. On June 20, 1789, they took the famous "Tennis Court" oath not to disperse until they had given France a constitution. This bold attitude showed clearly that a revolution was at hand (*see* French Revolution).

The name estates-general was not uncommon in medieval Europe. In Spain there were four estates, or classes, in the assembly. In The Netherlands the name States-General is still applied to the legislative body of that kingdom. It is composed of two houses—the upper, elected by the provincial assemblies, and the lower, chosen by the people.

ESTONIAN SOVIET SOCIALIST REPUBLIC. Three small republics of the Soviet Union—the Estonian, Latvian, and Lithuanian Soviet Socialist Republics—face the Baltic Sea. The smallest and northernmost of these Baltic States is the Estonian Soviet Socialist Republic, often called by its former name, Estonia. Its area of 17,400 square miles (45,100 square kilometers) includes about 800 islands off the coast. These control the traffic lanes from the Baltic Sea to Leningrad, the chief Soviet port. Tallinn, the capital and largest city, is a picturesque seaport with a railway connecting it with Leningrad.

Except in the southeast, where the land is hilly, the ground is flat with many lakes, streams, and marshes. Dairying is a major industry. The chief crops are rye, wheat, oats, and barley. Forests are abundant and furnish wood for match, furniture, and paper industries as well as for fuel.

The most significant mineral is oil shale, from which petroleum and fuel gas are obtained. Estonia accounts for about 80 percent of the Soviet Union's output, and one fifth of its industrial workers are employed in its production. The shale-processing industry is also responsible for 75 percent of the Soviet Union's synthetic gas, and it contributes to the production of thermal electric power for its own industry as well as that of the other Baltic states. A chemical industry that relies on shale manufactures benzine, adhesives, tanning agents, resins, formaldehyde, and detergents. The chief manufacturing centers are Tallinn, Tartu, and Parnu.

Woodworking has long been a traditional industry in Estonia, but exploitation of the forests threatened the enterprise until extensive reforestation policies were implemented in the 20th century. Estonia is also noted for its textiles, especially cotton cloth. It produces wool, linen, silk, knitted and woven garments, and shoes.

Agriculture was collectivized at the end of World War II. About 120,000 small, private farms were converted into about 450 collectives and state farms, employing about one fourth of the labor force.

The Esths, or Estonians, are a blond people related to the Finns. Their language is much like Finnish, which is Mongolian and not European in its origins. Most of the people are Lutheran in religion.

History

Little is known of the early history of Estonia. The Danes held the north from 1219. In 1346 they sold it to German landholders—the so-called Balts, or Baltic barons—who held the south. Later the land was divided between Sweden and Poland. Sweden ruled all of Estonia for about 100 years until 1721, when Charles XII lost it to Peter the Great of Russia.

The oldest section of Tallinn, the capital of Estonia, contains a small town square, narrow streets, and historic churches and public buildings.

Anatoly Rukhadze—Tass/Sovfoto

Estonia won its freedom after the Bolshevik Revolution of 1917, becoming an independent republic. Estonia's later destiny was decided by a nonaggression pact signed by Germany and the Soviet Union in August 1939. A secret protocol assigned Estonia and other Eastern European nations to the Soviets. In 1940 during World War II, Soviet forces occupied the Baltic States, and Estonia became the Estonian Soviet Socialist Republic. The next year the Germans drove out the Soviets. With the return of the Red Army in 1944, about 30,000 Estonians escaped to Sweden and 33,000 to Germany. Peasant farms were brought into collectives, and industries were nationalized.

In 1988 Estonia's constitution was amended to give the republic the right to veto Soviet laws, and Estonian was made the official language. As Eastern Europe abandoned Communism in 1989, efforts continued to secure political and economic independence from Moscow. An Estonian congress completely outside the official Soviet structure—Estonian voters had to establish that they or their ancestors lived in the republic before it was annexed—called on the Soviet parliament and the United Nations to restore the "free and independent republic of Estonia." Estonia's Communist party voted to split with Moscow but agreed to a six-month transition to wait for a party congress. On March 30, 1990, the Estonian parliament approved a declaration of a gradual transition to independence. By April, however, it ended compulsory service in the Soviet Army and declared Soviet rule over its territory to be illegal. Population (1989 preliminary census), 1,573,000.

ETHICS AND MORALITY. How to behave toward oneself and toward other individuals is a matter of making choices: whether to be friendly or unfriendly; whether to tell the truth or lie; whether to be generous or greedy; whether to study in order to pass an exam or to spend valuable study time watching television and cheat to pass it. These, and all other questions about how people act toward themselves and one another are dealt with in a field of study called ethics. Another name for ethics is morality. One word is derived from the Greek *ethos,* meaning "character," and the other from the Latin *mores,* meaning "custom."

Because both words suggest customary ways of behavior, they are somewhat misleading. The Greek philosopher Aristotle had a better term—practical wisdom. It was called practical because it was concerned with action, both on the part of the individual and on the part of society. It had to do with what should or should not be done. Aristotle divided practical wisdom into two parts: moral philosophy and political philosophy. He defined them together as a "true and reasoned state of capacity to act with regard to the things that are good or bad for a man."

Branches of Moral Philosophy

The field of ethics has several subdivisions. Descriptive ethics, as its name suggests, examines and evaluates ethical behavior of different peoples or social groups. Normative, or prescriptive, ethics is concerned with examining and applying the judgments of what is morally right or wrong, good or bad. It examines the question of whether there are standards for ethical conduct and, if so, what those standards are. Comparative ethics is the study of differing ethical systems to learn what their similarities and contrasts are. The history of ethics studies the many schools of thought that have contributed to the growth of ethics as a discipline.

In modern developed societies the systems of law and public justice are closely related to ethics in that they determine and enforce definite rights and duties. They also attempt to repress and punish deviations from these standards. This has to some extent been true in most societies. They have set standards, whether by custom or by law, to enable those in a society to live together without undue disruption.

It is possible for law to be neutral in moral issues, or it can be used to enforce morality. The prologue to the United States Constitution says that insuring domestic tranquility is an object of government. This statement is morally neutral. Such laws as those passed to enforce civil rights, however, promote a moral as well as legal commitment.

Bases of Behavior

So much human activity is simply a matter of custom or habit that little thought may be given to many actions. When an individual in Western society gets up in the morning, it is normal to get dressed and to put on shoes before going out. But in doing so, one does not usually bother thinking "This is a good and necessary thing that I'm doing." There is a great deal of behavior, however, in which people are conscious of why they act in a certain way. They are confronted with the need to make choices. At the basis of choice two questions arise: "What good do I seek?" and "What is my obligation in this circumstance?"

Ethics is primarily concerned with attempting to define what is good for the individual and for society. It also tries to establish the nature of obligations, or duties, that people owe themselves and each other.

Philosophers have said for thousands of years that people do not willingly do what is bad for themselves but may do what is bad for others if it appears that good for themselves will result. It has always been difficult to define what is good and how one should act to achieve it. Some teachers have said that pleasure is the greatest good (*see* Epicureanism). Others have pointed to knowledge, personal virtue, or service to one's fellow human being. Individuals, and whole societies, have performed outrageous criminal acts on people, and they have found ways to justify doing so on the basis of some greater "good."

The difficulty in deciding what good and obligation are has led moral philosophers to divide into two camps. One says that there are no definite, objective standards that apply to everyone. People must decide what is good and what their duties are in each new situation. Others have said that there are standards that apply to everyone, that what is good can generally be known. If the good is known, the obligation to pursue it becomes clear. The position that insists there are ethical standards is called ethical absolutism, and the one that insists there are no such norms is called ethical relativity.

Aristotle's solution. One of the clearest and most useful statements of ethical absolutism came from Aristotle in his 'Nichomachean Ethics'. He realized that what people desire they regard as good. But to say no more than this means that all desires are good no matter how much they conflict with one another. Consequently, there can be no standards at all.

Aristotle solved this problem by delineating between two types of desire—natural and acquired. Natural desires are those needs that are common to all human beings such as food and shelter. Beyond these, people also have a desire for health, knowledge, and a measure of prosperity. By being natural, these desires, or needs, are good for everyone. Since there can be no wrong basic needs, there can be no wrong desire for these needs.

But there are other desires as well. These are not needs but wants. It is at the level of wants that the nature of good becomes clouded. Individuals may want something they desire as a good, but it may be bad for them. People with sound judgment should be able to decide what is good for them, in contrast to what is only an apparent good. This sound judgment comes with experience. Young children have little experience of what is good or bad for them, so they must be guided by parents and other adults. Mature adults, however, should be able to decide what is good for them, though history demonstrates that this is not always the case.

People must decide what is good for others as well as for themselves. That is, they expect that goods for them apply equally to other people. To be able to treat others in the same way one treats oneself, Aristotle said it is necessary to have the three virtues of practical wisdom: temperance, courage, and justice.

The relativist solution. Relativists do not believe that there are self-evident moral principles that are true for everyone. They say that people's moral judgments are determined by the customs and traditions of the society in which they live. These may have been handed down for centuries, but their age does not mean they are true standards. They are simply norms that a certain society has developed for itself. What is right is what society says is right, and whatever is considered good for society must be right.

Another relativist approach was taken by the school of philosophy called pragmatism. One of the leading pragmatists, John Dewey, claimed that moral problems arise out of a conflict of impulses or desires, and the goal of moral deliberation is to find a course of action that will turn this conflict into harmony. Each individual problem must be viewed in the light of the actions necessary to solve it, with some understanding of the consequences that follow the actions. A choice is right if it leads to a solution of the specific conflict, but there is no absolute right or good, as every successful solution gives rise to new problems that must be evaluated on their own terms. Moral rules are only hypotheses, or tentative assumptions, that have been found to work in certain circumstances.

The school of existentialism also proclaims moral relativism. All individuals, it says, have their own life situations. No two are identical, for everyone else is part of the environment in which decisions must be made. All choices involve risk. There are no principles or standards that are right for all people at all times. New situations demand new approaches. What was once valid may be inappropriate now. In the world of the 20th century—with its rapid changes, endless wars, and moral upheaval—the ideas of existentialism have seemed correct to many people in the world. (*See also* Existentialism.)

Some existentialists base their position on religion. Even here they say it is impossible to fall back on moral laws or principles in making decisions. Choices must be made on faith, often in conflict with traditional moral guidelines. Individuals trust that what they are doing is right, but they can be entirely wrong. They commit themselves to the unknown, and the decision can often be an agonizing problem.

Common Moral Elements

Students of comparative ethics have found that most societies—from the ancient to the modern period—share certain features in their ethical codes. Some of these have applied only within a society, while others have been more universal.

Most societies have had customs or laws forbidding murder, bodily injury, or attacks on personal honor and reputation. Property rights also exist in some form almost everywhere.

Societies rely on rules that define elementary duties of doing good and furthering the welfare of the group. Within the family, mothers look after their children, and men support and protect their dependents. In turn, grown-up children are expected to provide care for their aging parents. Helping more distant relatives is also considered a duty in some places, depending on the extent of kinship ties.

In societies where the major religions—Judaism, Christianity, Islam, and Buddhism—are predominant, the duty of helping the needy and the distressed has been implanted. These obligations extend beyond family to acquaintances and even strangers. Telling the truth and keeping promises are also widely regarded as duties, though they are sometimes withheld from strangers.

In the last 200 years, modern nations have evolved a kind of universal ethic that originated with ideas about human rights to life, liberty, and property that developed during the period of the Enlightenment. Whether honored in practice or not, there is at least an acceptance of the notion that the lives of human beings are meant to be improved by abolishing disease, poverty, and ignorance. (*See also* Enlightenment.)

The Simen Mountains rise above the Ethiopian Plateau in northern Ethiopia. They contain the country's highest peak, Ras Dashan.

Photo Almasy

ETHIOPIA. Located in northeastern Africa, an area known as the Horn, Ethiopia is the tenth largest and third most populous country in Africa. It is bordered by the Red Sea and Djibouti on the north, Somalia on the east, Kenya on the south, and Sudan on the west. Ethiopia's landscape varies from lowlands to high plateaus and its climate from very dry to seasonally very wet. The Ethiopian population is also very mixed, with broad differences in cultural background and traits, methods of gaining a livelihood, languages, and religions.

Ethiopia's history of independence dates to pre-Christian times. While influenced and even occasionally occupied by other nations, Ethiopia is one of the few countries in Africa or Asia never truly colonized. Since World War II Ethiopia has often been economically, politically, or militarily dependent on the major world powers—on the United States until the mid-1970s and on the Soviet Union since then.

Land and Climate

The landscape of Ethiopia is dominated by central highlands of plateaus and mountains that rise to 6,000 feet (2,000 meters) and higher above sea level. Surrounding these highlands are hot, usually arid, lowlands. The highlands are cut by deeply entrenched river valleys.

Situated in the tropics, Ethiopia has a climate that varies with height. Ethiopians describe their landscape by altitude zones: the hot and arid lowlands called *bereha* and *qolla* (both describing desertlike conditions) at elevations from below sea level to about 5,000 feet (1,500 meters); the densely inhabited uplands *weyna dega* and *dega,* which are warmer and cooler uplands at about 5,000 to 7,500 feet (1,500 to 2,300 meters) and 7,500 to 10,000 feet (2,300 to 3,000 meters) elevation, respectively; and alpine regions called *wirch* above 10,000 feet (3,000 meters). Daily temperatures range seasonally from well above 100° F (40° C) in the lowlands to below freezing in the *dega* elevations and above.

Moisture is also unevenly distributed. Most areas have regular wet and dry periods in the year. The amount of rainfall often depends on altitude—higher areas are wetter, lowlands drier. There is also a fairly predictable annual amount of rainfall from the drier northeast to the wetter southwest. Drier areas occasionally receive much less moisture than even their already low average. Rains may start later or end earlier than usual, or storms may be separated by a few weeks, allowing the soil to dry out. Such drought is most common in the northern and eastern highlands and in lowland areas. When this happens farming and herding suffer, causing local hunger and famine.

Environment and Resources

Under natural conditions the nondesert parts of Ethiopia are grasslands or forests. After many thousands of years of farming and herding, much of this natural landscape is altered. At least 85 percent of

This article was contributed by Robert W. Roundy, Assistant Professor of Human Ecology, Rutgers University, New Brunswick, N.J.

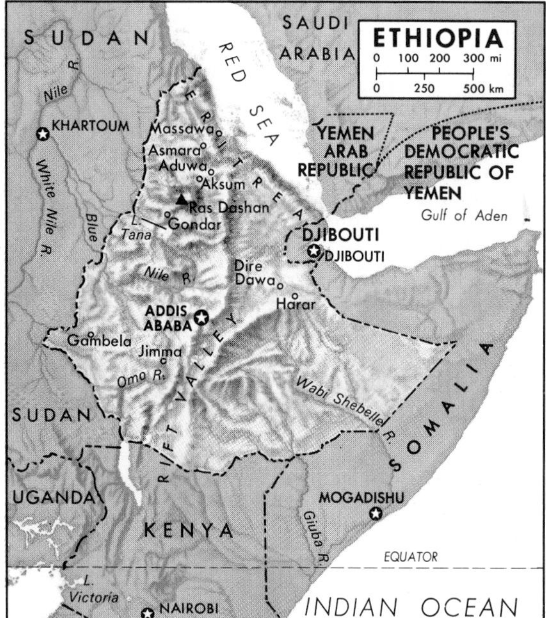

the natural forest has been cleared, especially in the northern half of the country, usually to create fields. From the 1960s onward local and government efforts at environmental rehabilitation have led to the replanting of trees in some deforested areas.

The most valuable natural resource is the soil. It is potentially highly productive for traditional and modern agriculture, but this potential is largely unmet. In parts of Ethiopia soil resources suffer from declining fertility and erosion. The decline results from the continuous inefficient use of the soil, including the cultivating of land that is better for grazing or that should be left fallow, or unplanted, for awhile. Partly this is the result of a socioeconomic system that does not reward investment in soil protection and partly of the increasing demands of a rapidly growing population. As a consequence, agricultural production per person is down since the 1960s. This decline in agriculture is common not only in Ethiopia but also in much of the rest of Africa.

Little has been done to find possible mineral resources in Ethiopia. Those known and exploited include gold, platinum, manganese, and salt. There is little extraction of either metallic ores or mineral fuels such as coal or petroleum.

People and Culture

Ethiopia has historically been an empire, expanding in area and incorporating new groups into the population. A major expansion of the empire in the latter half of the 19th century incorporated new peoples in the west, south, and east. The result is a population of great diversity.

Many languages and dialects are spoken. The greatest numbers of people speak either Semitic or Cushitic languages and their dialects. Semitic includes Amharic, the official national language, Tigrigna, Tigre, and Guragingna. Cushitic includes Oromigna, Somali, Sidama, and Afar. In the west and southwest some people speak Nilotic languages. Some of the Semitic languages have been written since before European influences.

Various religions are represented, with numerous people following Christianity, Islam, and traditional sects. Most Christians are Coptic, or Ethiopian Orthodox, Christians who follow rites similar to those of Eastern Christianity. Christianity was introduced into Ethiopia in the 4th century and was the official state religion until 1974. Although there is often a great mix of religions in any given place, Christians tend to be the most numerous in highland areas, Muslims in the lowlands, and traditional religious groups in the south and west. There is also a small Jewish religious group known as Falasha in the northwest.

The diversity in people has always played a significant role in Ethiopia. Disagreements and problems between groups are often tied to differences in language, religion, and other cultural lines.

According to a preliminary report from the 1984 census, the national population is about 42 million. It is most densely concentrated in the highland areas of the *weyna dega* and *dega*. More than 80 percent of the population live outside cities. About 43 percent of the people are 15 years of age and younger. Both birth and death rates are high, with a natural growth estimated at from 2.4 to 2.7 percent per year. The average life expectancy at birth is about 40 years, among the world's lowest.

Economy

The Ethiopian economy is one of poverty. Average annual incomes are estimated at between $100 and $150 per person in United States dollars. Little is produced that is not needed within the country. Most people work as farmers or as herdsmen. Traditionally farmers have worked small, scattered plots and have low harvests per cultivated area. Until 1974 most Ethiopians worked the land either as tenants, as members of a community or a lineage, or as private owners. Since the government officially took ownership of all land in 1975, the country's rural land is public. All farming families now have possession of up to a maximum of 25 acres (10 hectares). They can use the land, but they do not own it nor can they sell it. No one but the very old or households without adult males may hire others to work land for them.

Throughout most of Ethiopia there is mixed farming, the raising of both plants and animals. In most areas the major crops include grains such as *teff* (a grain native to and commonly grown only in Ethiopia), wheat, barley, sorghum, millet, and corn. In the southern half of the country, an additional main crop is *enset,* a bananalike plant whose starchy stem is eaten rather than the fruit.

Other crops include oilseeds like *nugg* (another crop common only to Ethiopia), linseed, and sesame. Pulses—especially beans, peas, and lentils—are important protein sources in the diet. Regionally, fiber crops such as cotton and stimulants such as coffee and *chat* (grown for a leaf that is chewed for its mild narcotic effect) are important to subsistence and cash economies. Animals raised include cattle, sheep, goats, donkeys, mules, horses, camels, and chickens.

There are some areas with large commercial farms. Their products go largely to Ethiopian urban markets or international trade. When the government took the land, these farms were converted to collective, or state, farms. Their significant crops include sugarcane, cotton, and fruits from the Awash Valley, sesame and sorghum from the Humera area, and grains from the Rift Valley.

Manufacturing forms only a small part of the Ethiopian economy. Factories are concentrated in and around the two largest cities, Addis Ababa and Asmara. Processed foods, textiles, and beverages are the major products, mostly for local consumption.

Ethiopia's main exports are agricultural products. Coffee makes up about two thirds of exports by value. Other significant exports are hides and skins, edible seeds, and oilseeds. The major imports are machinery and manufactured goods.

Transportation, Communication, and Education

Until the 20th century transportation in Ethiopia was on foot or on pack or riding animals. Even with the development of mechanized transport, a high proportion of people and goods move on foot or on the backs of animals.

Central Ethiopia was connected to the Red Sea coast in 1917, when the railway from Djibouti reached

A cross is carried in procession (top left) at a Coptic Easter service. Monks and soldiers participate in the spring Maskal festival at Addis Ababa (top right). Hot peppers are sold at an outdoor market in Gondar (bottom left). Shepherds tend cattle and goats (bottom right) in a field near Gondar.

Photos, Brian Seed—CLICK/Chicago

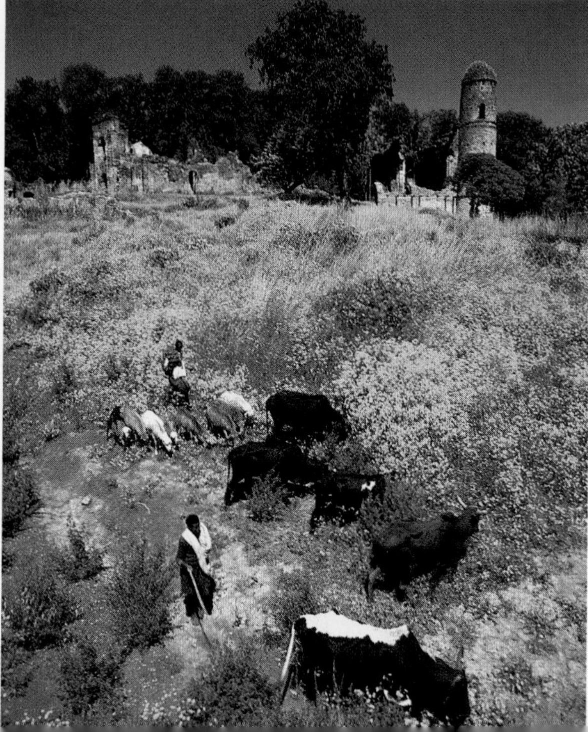

Addis Ababa. This line still functions as a major mover of goods between the highlands and the rest of the world.

A highway network for motor vehicles was built by the Italians during their occupation from 1935 to 1941. Since 1951 the Ethiopian government has received periodic loans for highway construction and maintenance, resulting in all-weather roads that connect most of the larger cities and towns. There are few feeder roads connecting the countryside to this network. People and goods still move from the countryside to the roads or towns on foot or on animal backs.

Ethiopia has telegraph, telephone, and postal services between the larger towns. With the availability of inexpensive battery-operated radios since the middle 1960s, radio broadcasts are received everywhere. Television reception is still confined to a few of the largest cities.

There is a long history of church-based education in Ethiopia, but modern education dates only from the early 20th century. There was limited access to classroom education until the 1960s, with no high school, or secondary, level until the 1950s. Elementary schools have been built in market towns since the 1960s, making formal education more accessible to children in the countryside. But until the 1980s only a limited number of school-age children actually entered school. Now more than 40 percent of the appropriate age group is enrolled in elementary schools and approximately 11 percent in secondary schools.

University education began in Addis Ababa in 1950, and by the late 1950s specialized colleges of agriculture and public health opened in the provinces. Education development has often been with international aid and dependent upon teachers from other countries. It is estimated that only 15 to 17 percent of Ethiopian adults can read and write. Most of these live in towns and cities and are men. This picture has been steadily improving with more children attending school and with the influence of national literacy campaigns that began in the late 1960s.

While there has been much expansion of the education system since the 1950s, opportunities remain concentrated in the major cities and towns. This is also true for many other services, including health care, piped sanitary water, electricity, telecommunications, and banking.

History and Government

Ethiopia's history is virtually that of a continuous feudal monarchy. Originally centered in the north of modern Ethiopia, the monarchy predates the Christian Era and continued under various guises to 1974. Over the last 2,000 years Ethiopia and its center of power have moved southward. The greatest expansion was in the conquests of Emperor Menelik II in the late 19th century, when the current national boundaries were drawn.

The Ethiopian monarchy was a Solomonic dynasty, claiming descent from the Biblical joining of Solomon and Sheba. Anyone accepted as possessing Solomonic descent could claim monarchical rights. This caused frequent internal strife, civil wars, and wars of succession.

Ethiopian history also includes wars with neighbors and colonial nations. The 16th-century war with forces from the eastern lowlands of the Horn of Africa nearly succeeded in conquering Ethiopia. Italian colonial influences expanded into Ethiopia in the last two decades of the 19th century, but the Italian armies were defeated in 1896 at the Battle of Aduwa. This preserved Ethiopia as one of the few non-colonized nations of Africa, but in 1935 Ethiopia was once again attacked by Italy—this time successfully.

Much of Ethiopia's 20th-century history is dominated by Emperor Haile Selassie. He was named regent in 1916 and crowned emperor in 1930. His regency

Brian Seed—CLICK/Chicago

Guards in ceremonial dress (left) still stand guard at the Royal Palace in Addis Ababa, though the monarchy has been abolished. The stone lion represents the former emperor, the "Lion of Judah." A Coptic priest (below) uses an ancient, hand-printed, illuminated copy of the Bible to teach young people about Christianity.

Lawrence Manning—CLICK/Chicago

Ethiopia Fact Summary

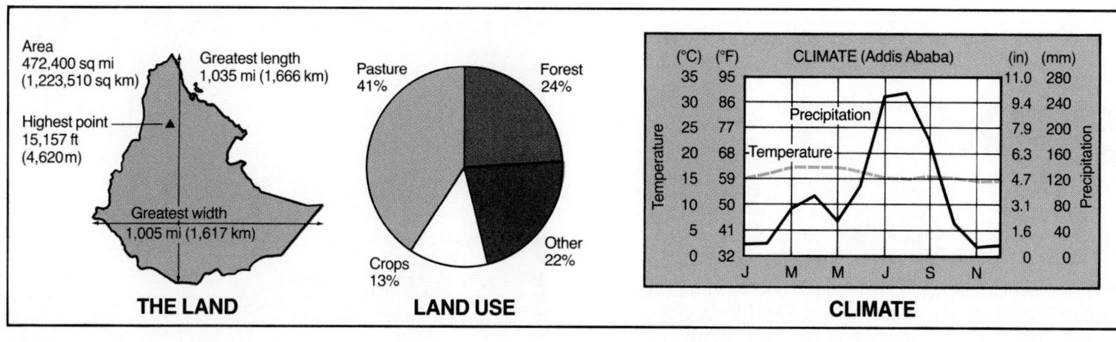

Official Name: People's Democratic Republic of Ethiopia.
Capital: Addis Ababa.

NATURAL FEATURES

Highest Peak: Ras Dashan, 15,157 feet (4,620 meters).
Major Rivers: Abay (Blue Nile), Awash, Baro, Dawa, Ganale Dorya, Omo, Tekeze, Wabi Shebelle.
Mountain Range: Simen.
Largest Lakes: Abaya, Chamo, Tana, Zwai.

PEOPLE

Population (1989 estimate): 48,898,000; 103.5 persons per square mile (40.0 persons per square kilometer); 10.8 percent urban; 89.2 percent rural.
Major Cities (1985 estimate): Addis Ababa (1,495,300), Asmara (295,-700), Dire Dawa (107,300).
Major Religions: Ethiopian Orthodox, Islam.
Major Language: Amharic (official).
Literacy: 5 percent.
Leading Universities: Addis Ababa University, Asmara University.

GOVERNMENT

Form of Government: People's republic.
Head of State and Government: President; chosen by the Shengo for 5-year term.
Legislature: Shengo (National Assembly); one legislative house of 835 members, popularly elected for 5-year terms.
Voting Qualification: Age 18.
Political Divisions: 24 administrative regions, 5 autonomous regions.
Flag: Three horizontal stripes of green, yellow, and red (*see* Flags of the World).

ECONOMY

Chief Agricultural Products: *Crops*—barley, coffee, corn, cotton, millet, sorghum, sugarcane, teff, wheat. *Livestock*—camels, cattle, chickens, donkeys, goats, horses, mules, sheep.
Chief Mined Products: Gold, manganese, platinum, salt.
Chief Manufactured Products: Beverages, processed foods, textiles.
Chief Exports: Coffee, edible seeds, hides and skins, oilseeds.
Chief Imports: Machinery and manufactured goods.
Monetary Unit: 1 Ethiopian birr = 100 cents.

and rule were characterized by the breaking of regional feudal powers. He encouraged some movement toward becoming a modern nation and ruled until 1974, when he was deposed. His power had been weakened by his advancing age, his inability to do anything about the country's famine, corruption within his government, and the growing strength of the military and conflicting urban interests (*see* Haile Selassie).

After the revolution in 1974 Ethiopia had a Marxist military government run by the Provisional Military Administrative Council (PMAC). The head of state was Mengistu Haile Mariam. Separatist movements arose in attempts to break away from Ethiopia or to change the people or the pattern of government. The most active of these movements were in the north, in Eritrea, where there have been active movements to break away from Ethiopia since 1961, and in Tigrai.

There has also been warfare with the Somalia-backed Western Somali Liberation Front, beginning in 1977. During this war Ethiopia shifted its international ties with the United States and Western Europe to an alignment with the Soviet Union and Eastern Europe. In 1987 a new constitution was approved to make the country the People's Democratic Republic of Ethiopia. This constitution established a Soviet-style, civilian Communist government. On September 5 the PMAC was dissolved. On September 9 members of the Shengo, the new assembly, were installed. The next day Mengistu became the first president of the republic. Following the Soviet Union's lead in economic restructuring, in 1990 Mengistu proposed scrapping Ethiopia's rigid economic system for a mixed market economy.

Ethiopia was struck by major famines from 1973 to 1975 and from 1983 to 1986. More than 200,000 people may have died in the first of these. In both famines Ethiopia has been heavily dependent upon international donations to overcome starvation in famine areas. Poor weather conditions and the worst locust infestation since 1958 occurred in 1987 and created a massive food shortage. The army and air force made an unsuccessful attempt to overthrow the government in May 1989.

Conflict between Eritrean and Tigrean rebel groups and the government continued in 1989. Former United States president Jimmy Carter held peace talks between the Eritrean People's Liberation Front and the government in Atlanta, Ga., in September.

BIBLIOGRAPHY FOR ETHIOPIA

Fradin, D.B. Ethiopia (Children's, 1988).
Kleeberg, I.C. Ethiopia (Watts, 1986).
Levine, D.N. Wax and Gold: Tradition and Innovation in Ethiopian Culture (Univ. of Chicago Press, 1986).
Ottaway, Marina and Ottaway, David. Ethiopia: Empire in Revolution (Holmes & Meier, 1978).
Pankhurst, Richard. Ethiopia (Chelsea House, 1988).

ETHNOLOGY *see* ANTHROPOLOGY.

ETHOLOGY *see* ANIMAL BEHAVIOR.

ETIQUETTE

Jules Bucher—Photo Researchers

Many regions of the world have traditional forms of greeting. In Thailand, a person places his hands together as in prayer and lifts them to his face, bowing the head slightly.

ETIQUETTE. "You're so nice to be with!" These words are a fine compliment for anyone to receive. Good manners, those that help people become "nice to be with," are what etiquette is all about.

Etiquette is a French word that first meant a "label" or "ticket." Later a new meaning was added. *Etiquettes*, printed lists of rules for proper behavior, were given to persons being presented at court to prevent them from making embarrassing blunders before the king. The word *etiquette* came to mean a code of good manners, and in that sense it was adopted into the English language in the 18th century.

Modern etiquette books serve much the same purpose as the *etiquettes* of the old French court. They explain the rules of good behavior that have developed through the years to help people feel sure of themselves in every social situation. Some of these books are listed and described in the bibliography at the end of this article.

Manners and Etiquette in Everyday Life

Good manners and etiquette are not complicated. Anyone can demonstrate courtesy and consideration for others—the stuff of which good manners are made—without knowing the specific rules of etiquette.

And no one is born knowing those rules. They are learned gradually—at home, in school, at work, and in everyday contacts with both friends and strangers. To expand their knowledge of good conduct, many people continue to read etiquette books as adults.

There are a number of reasons why people want to learn good manners and the rules of etiquette. Good manners help win friends. People who treat others with kindness and sympathy are most likely to become popular because they are good companions.

Good manners also help please members of the family, "special" girl friends or boyfriends, teachers, employers, and strangers like salespeople and law officers. Good manners help put people at ease, make them cooperative and just plain happy.

People who practice good manners and understand the rules of etiquette also make themselves happy. Knowing how to behave properly, in familiar as well as in strange situations, builds self-confidence. Meeting new people and visiting new places become pleasurable instead of frightening experiences.

Good manners begin at home. Even the youngest children quickly learn to say "please" and "thank you" when their parents, brothers, and sisters are courteous toward each other. Respect for family members can be demonstrated in many ways. Being on time for meals, showing responsibility in handling an allowance, and taking care of belongings are all part of manners at home. So are respecting privacy, sharing household chores, and taking turns using the telephone, television set, or family car.

Good manners are equally important at school. Paying attention in class and handing in neatly prepared homework are ways to show respect for teachers. Classmates can show mutual consideration by respecting each other's property, by not "showing off" superior knowledge or possessions, and by making new students feel welcome.

On the job, good manners mean arriving on time, being reliable, and caring about neatness in both work and personal grooming. Thoughtfulness toward other employees helps improve the working atmosphere. Employers appreciate willingness to work and accept criticism and an ability to keep confidences.

Any number of situations in social life call for a knowledge of etiquette. For instance, knowing how to make proper introductions helps avoid confusion and embarrassment at parties. Knowing how to order from a menu and whom and how much to tip, can help make a date go smoothly. Today, when foreign travel is so popular, the person who learns in advance the customs of a country he intends to visit will increase his enjoyment of the trip as well as leave a good impression in the host country.

Sometimes the rules of etiquette one has learned may not seem to fit a particular situation. Then it is up to the individual to use his own common sense and good judgment in deciding what sort of behavior

This article was reviewed by Joan Beck, Syndicated Editorial Page Columnist, *Chicago Tribune*.

ADDRESSING OFFICIALS

Air Force, U.S. Same as Army officers. *See* Army, U.S., in this table.

Ambassador, American. "The Honorable — —, American Ambassador." Begin letter: "Dear Ambassador — —."

Ambassador, Foreign. "His/Her Excellency — — (name and title if known), Ambassador of — —" or "The — — Ambassador" (British, French, etc.). Begin letter: "Dear Ambassador — —" or "Your Excellency."

Archbishop, Roman Catholic. "His Excellency (or Grace), the Archbishop of — —" or "The Most Reverend — —, Archbishop of — —." Begin letter: "Your Excellency," "Most Reverend Archbishop," or "Dear Archbishop of — —."

Archimandrite, Eastern Orthodox. "The Very Reverend — —." Begin letter: "Reverend Sir."

Army, U.S. Officers and enlisted personnel should be addressed by their titles, as "General — —," "Colonel — —," "Corporal — —" (titles may be abbreviated). Business salutation for all ranks and grades is "Dear General (etc.) — —." In informal letters, the titles may be used in the salutations, as "My dear General," "My dear Lieutenant," "My dear Corporal." For all ranks and grades below second lieutenant, the title "Mr." or "Ms." may be used in the salutation.

Associate Justice of the Supreme Court. "The Honorable Justice — —, The Supreme Court." Begin letter: "Dear Justice — —."

Attorney General. "The Honorable — —, Attorney General" or "The Attorney General." Begin letter: "Dear Attorney General — —."

Bishop, Methodist. "The Reverend — —, Methodist Bishop." Begin letter: "Dear Bishop — —."

Bishop, Protestant. "The Right Reverend — —." Begin letter: "Dear Bishop — —."

Bishop, Roman Catholic. "The Most (or Right) Reverend — —, Bishop of — —." Begin letter: "Most (or Right) Reverend Sir," "Your Excellency," or "Dear Bishop — —."

Cabinet member. "The Honorable, The Secretary of — —" or "The Honorable — —, The Secretary of — —." Begin letter: "My dear Mr. Secretary (or Madam Secretary)" or "Dear Secretary of — —."

Canon. "The Reverend — —, Canon of —." Begin letter: "Dear Cannon — —."

Cantor. "Cantor — —." Begin letter: "Dear Cantor — —."

Cardinal. "His Eminence — Cardinal —." Begin letter: "Your Eminence" or "Dear Cardinal — —."

Chief Justice of the Supreme Court. "The Chief Justice of the United States," "The Chief Justice," or "The Right Honorable — —." Begin letter: "Dear Chief Justice."

Clergyman, Protestant. "The Reverend — —," or if a doctorate was earned, "The Reverend Dr. — —." Begin letter: "Dear Dr. — —" or "Dear Reverend — —."

Dean, Protestant. "The Very Reverend — —" or "The Very Reverend — —, Dean of —." Begin letter: "Dear Dean — —."

Director of Central Intelligence. "The Honorable — —, Director of Central Intelligence." Begin letter: "Dear Director."

Governor. "The Honorable Governor of — —" or "The Honorable — —, Governor of — —." Begin letter: "Dear Governor — —."

House of Representatives, Member of. "The Honorable — —, House of Representatives." Begin letter: "Dear — —."

Judge. "The Honorable — —, Judge, Appellate Division" or "The Honorable — —, Supreme Court." Begin letter: "Dear Judge — —."

King. "His Majesty the King." Begin letter: "Sir" or "Your Majesty."

Librarian of Congress. "The Honorable — —, Library of Congress." Begin letter: "Dear Dr., Mr., or Ms."

Marine Corps, U.S. Same as Army officers. *See* Army, U.S., in this table.

Mayor. "The Honorable — —, Mayor of — —" or "The Mayor of the City of — —." Begin letter: "Dear Mayor — —."

Member of Parliament. "The Honorable — —, M.P." Begin letter: "Dear Sir" or "Dear Madam."

Monsignor. "The Right Reverend Monsignor — —" or "The Very Reverend Monsignor — —." Begin letter: "Right Reverend Monsignor" or "Dear Monsignor — —."

Navy, U.S. Officers and enlisted personnel should be addressed by their titles, as "Admiral — —," "Commander — —," "Ensign — —" (titles may be abbreviated). For petty officers the title is written after the name, as "— —, Gunner's Mate 1." Business salutation for all ranks, rates, and grades is "Dear Admiral (etc.) — —." For officers of high rank the titles may be used in the salutation, as "My dear Admiral," "My dear Captain." For all ranks, rates, and grades below commander, "Mr." or "Ms."should be used in the salutation.

Patriarch, Eastern Orthodox. "His Holiness, the Ecumenical Patriarch of Constantinople." Begin letter: "Your Holiness."

Pope. "His Holiness, Pope — —" or "His Holiness the Pope." Begin letter: "Your Holiness" or "Most Holy Father."

President. "The President, The White House, Washington, D.C." Begin letter: "Dear President," "Mr. President," or "Madam President."

Priest, Roman Catholic. "The Reverend Father — —" or "The Reverend — —." Begin letter: "Dear Reverend Father," "Dear Father — —," or "Dear Reverend — —."

Queen. "Her Majesty the Queen." Begin letter: "Your Majesty."

Rabbi. "Rabbi — —." Begin letter: "Dear Rabbi — —" or "My dear Rabbi (or Doctor, if rabbi has such a degree)."

Secretary General of the United Nations. "His or Her Excellency — —, Secretary General of the United Nations." Begin letter: "Dear Mr. or Madam Secretary General of the United Nations."

Senator. "The Honorable — —, The United States Senate." Begin letter: "Dear Senator — —."

Speaker of the House of Representatives. "The Honorable — —, The Speaker of the House of Representatives" or "The Speaker of the House of Representatives." Begin letter: "Dear Mr. Speaker" or "Dear Madam Speaker."

Treasurer, Comptroller, or Auditor of a State. "The Honorable — —, Treasurer (Comptroller, Auditor) of (city, state)." Begin letter: "Dear Mr. or Ms. — —."

Vice-President. "The Vice-President" or "The Honorable — —, The Vice-President of the United States." Begin letter: "Dear Vice-President," "Dear Mr. Vice-President," or "Dear Madam Vice-President."

Forms of address used in speaking and writing are commonly included in modern etiquette books. The table above gives forms used in letter writing. It tells how to address an envelope to an important official and how to begin the letter itself.

is appropriate. Naturalness and sincerity can help him master even the most complicated situations.

Courtesy, Caste, and Law

In most societies, general forms of courtesy were developed to enable people to get along together pleasantly. Most people will conform to the accepted rules of behavior in their community because violations of the rules might be ridiculed.

In some societies, however, rules of behavior have gone beyond simple courtesy to establish divisions between higher and lower classes of society. In India, for instance, the division of classes known as the caste system rigidly governs everyday manners. The higher castes are allowed to wear fine clothes and ornaments, which are forbidden to the lower castes. Higher castes may not accept cooked food or water from lower castes. Persons from the highest and the lowest castes may even be required to walk a certain distance away from each other in the streets. In modern cities, however, where people of all castes live and work closely together, many of these rules have been relaxed.

Sometimes matters of courtesy can become part of written law. In driving, for example, spattering mud on pedestrians standing at the curb is simply bad manners. Blocking a driveway, however, or tailgating (following too closely behind the car ahead) are not only discourteous but may also be against the law and punishable by a fine.

Origin of Modern Courtesies

Most forms of etiquette used today evolved from ancient beginnings. The courtesies used when people greet each other are one example. The handshake probably originated when early man began to hold out his right hand—the weapon hand—as a sign of friendliness and peace. The handshake has taken different forms. In the United States during the late 1800's, it was fashionable for a time to give a high handshake at about the level of the nose.

Table manners differ throughout the world. These Arabs share a meal in which the courses are served in single bowls. Each man dips his fingers into the part of the bowl nearest him.

Gianni Tortoli—Photo Researchers

The gesture of lifting the hat as a sign of respect is another old custom that was already established by the Middle Ages. It was probably made even more fashionable by the armored knights, who lifted their helmet visors when meeting as a signal of recognition. When a knight joined a gathering of friends, he removed his helmet entirely to show that he felt safe among them.

The titles of respect used today also have distant origins. *Mister* (*Mr.*), a form of *master*, came from the Latin term *magister*, meaning a ruler and lawmaker. During the 18th century in the United States, many women customarily addressed their husbands as "Mr. Jones," or whatever, instead of using first names. Today *Mr.* is a common courtesy title given to virtually all men. *Sir*, another courtesy title in general use, evolved from *seigneur*, the medieval French title for the lord of a feudal manor. The woman's courtesy title *Madam* comes from an old French term meaning "my lady," which was used by the lower classes to address noblewomen at court.

Etiquette Around the World

Rules of etiquette have varied all over the world at different times in history. The customs dealing with hospitality furnish good examples of this.

The sending of invitations has long played a significant role in the etiquette of hospitality. Among the first people to use invitations were the North American Indians. One of their methods was to burn messages in buckskin, which were then carried by runners to all the intended guests. In Shakespeare's time invitations in England were written on large sheets of white paper and colorfully decorated. Pages or messengers carried them to the prospective guests, from whom answers were usually required. It was considered insulting to issue invitations any other way. But today, mailing or telephoning invitations are acceptable ways of getting guests together.

To early man, hospitality meant sharing food and shelter with friends or strangers. This has remained one of the chief ways of expressing friendship. Among the Bedouin Arabs, for example, it is considered ill-mannered and insulting to ride up to a man's tent without stopping to eat with him. A ceremony of hospitality among the Bedouin is the coffee-brewing ritual. The host always makes a fresh pot, using elaborate utensils which are handed down from father to son. Another such ritual is the *chanoyu*, or tea ceremony, of Japan (*see* Tea).

A guest in Japan is given small candies and cakes, which are served on pieces of paper. To be polite, he must wrap the food he cannot finish in the paper and carry it away with him. In the United States too, hostesses often give their guests food to take home, such as a piece of cake from a birthday party.

Many other rituals have been used to make guests feel welcome. Early Greeks gave salt to a guest as a symbol of hospitality. Arabs poured melted butter on the hands of their guests to refresh them. In Arab lands today, a guest must be careful not to admire his host's possessions, because if he does the host will offer them to him. Among the North American Indians, smoking a tobacco pipe, the calumet, was the chief ritual of hospitality. Passing around the calumet became a feature of tribal gatherings for making peace or forging alliances.

Table manners evolved along with the development of hospitality. The ancient Greeks did not use knives, forks, or spoons for eating. They used their fingers to eat solid foods, which were cut into small pieces before being served. They drank liquids directly from vessels or sopped them up with bread. The Romans did not use individual plates but took food with their fingers directly from the platters. The Egyptians also shared a common dish.

The Chinese traditionally use chopsticks to eat solid foods, which are prepared in small pieces. Chopsticks may be used to send a signal to the host. Placing them across the top of a bowl is a sign that the guest wishes to leave the table.

Table knives and forks were uncommon in Europe as late as the 17th century. People carried their own knives, which they took out and used whenever large portions of food were served. Today the use of the knife and fork varies in different countries. In the United States, the knife is held in the right hand and the fork in the left. After the food is cut, the knife is put down and the fork is transferred to the right hand. In most European countries the fork remains in the left hand.

Just as the rules of etiquette vary around the world, they also vary with time in any given area. Some customs disappear through disuse. Others are added as new situations arise. The development of the automobile, for instance, made it necessary to develop rules of courtesy for both drivers and passengers. Customs can also be changed by political means. In 1925 the president of Turkey, Kemal Atatürk, attempted to abolish the traditional veiling of women. Most women in the cities discarded the veil, but it is still worn by many women in rural areas.

Nations as well as individuals follow rules of etiquette. In their dealings with each other, the nations of the world developed a system of international courtesy known as protocol. The establishment of an order of precedence among diplomatic representatives is one of the most important matters of protocol. Today, for instance, diplomats rank one another according to their length of service in a nation's capital. In the United Nations, however, the delegates of each country are regarded as equals and are seated according to the alphabetical order of the countries they represent. Since diplomats symbolize their countries, any discourtesy shown to them is considered a discourtesy to their countries. Thus, a violation of diplomatic courtesy might endanger international relations and even become a cause for declaring war.

Early Etiquette Codes

Since ancient times, people have developed formal rules of ideal behavior. These rules, written or unwritten, are known as codes of etiquette.

One of the first rules established to help people get along well became known as the Golden Rule: "Do unto others as you would have them do unto you." It is derived from the Old Testament injunction to "love thy neighbor as thyself" (Lev. xix, 18). Various forms of the Golden Rule appear in the New Testament and in the writings of such early philosophers as Confucius and Plato.

In ancient China, proper conduct for the upper classes was described in documents like the 'I-Li' (Book of Etiquette and Ceremonial), which instructed government officials how to behave at various ceremonies. Its rules covered such matters as proper dress and hair style, which direction to face, and how many bows to make. To the Chinese, ceremonious behavior was a way to achieve orderliness and self-control.

The medieval warriors of Japan—the *samurai*—were governed by an unwritten code of conduct known as *Bushido*. Dignity, honesty, and courage were stressed along with absolute loyalty to one's lord or master. A samurai was expected to show affection, but it was considered undignified to express his devotion to his family outside the privacy of his home. To achieve fame and honor, a samurai would undergo great suffering and even willingly lose his life. If dishonored, he could redeem himself by committing the form of ritual suicide known as *hara-kiri*.

The ideal man of ancient Athens was the *kalos kagathos* (the beautiful and the good). He was supposed to be wise, just, and courageous as well as generous, truthful, and amiable. Modesty was not required, however, and consideration for others was not regarded as important. The kalos kagathos also had to be especially handsome, since a person thought ugly was not considered ideal.

Roman citizens were expected to conduct themselves according to *gravitas*, a traditional rule of dignity. Vulgarity and boasting were considered ill-mannered. Romans were to show respect to all men, particularly officials and the aged, and even to the poor and to slaves. Personal appearance was less important to the Romans than to the Athenians.

Etiquette Codes in Europe

During the 11th century chivalry arose in France. Later it spread to the other countries of Europe. Young boys of noble birth were trained in the manners they would need to know as knights. They were taught to honor the Christian church, to respect women, and to devote their lives to the service of a lady. Such service was supposed to increase their abilities as warriors. Often a knight would worship his lady at a distance, never speaking to her and perhaps never even seeing her. This medieval knightly conduct is called courtly love. (*See also* Knighthood.)

Rogers, Lunt & Bowlen

The procedures for setting a formal dinner table and a buffet table are a part of etiquette at home. The elements of a formal table setting (left) are a service plate with folded napkin, forks and knives (not more than three of each), soup spoon, salt and pepper containers, and goblets for water and wines. Bread and butter plates are not used at a strictly formal dinner. The table must be evenly set, with the places at equal distances. The proper utensils for each course are arranged in the order in which they will be used, with the first to be used on the outside. The beginning seafood and soup courses are usually served on plates and bowls which are put on top of the service plate. After the soup course the service plate is removed, and subsequent courses are served on their own plates. The table is cleared before dessert plates and utensils are set out. A buffet table (right) is more casual. The setting and decorations may vary according to the time of day and the mood of the meal. For instance, a breakfast, a picnic lunch, or a candlelight dinner may all be served buffet style.

The etiquette of courtly love was included in manuals of conduct even during the Renaissance. These manuals, now called courtesy books, discussed the training and duties of men and women who lived at court. One of the most influential courtesy books, 'Il Cortegiano' (The Courtier), was published in Italy in 1528 and was later translated into English. The first English courtesy book, the 'Book of the Governour', appeared in 1531.

Etiquette books were also available for the ordinary citizen. William Caxton, the first English printer, published the 'Book of Courtesy' about 1479. The Italian clergyman Giovanni della Casa wrote 'Galateo', probably around the middle of the 16th century. In it he criticized the rude habits and offensive speech of the period. In 1526, the great scholar Erasmus published 'De Civilitate', a book on polite manners for young people. In this work he advised that good manners should be based on consideration for others, not on the desire to make an impression.

Many 15th- and 16th-century etiquette books were devoted to the training of children and of servants. One of the most popular works was 'The Babees Book', which appeared around 1475. Young boys being brought up in a courtier's home were instructed not to fidget when being spoken to, not to spill food, and not to fall asleep over their meals. They were expected to help their lords bathe and to hold candles for them while they ate. Girls were taught how to behave modestly and how to treat their future husbands. Servants had to learn the proper way to set a table and to seat guests at dinner.

In the 17th century in France, social life centered upon the court of Louis XIV at Versailles. The king himself wrote a book of rules for court ceremonies which all his attendants were expected to obey. Ordinary citizens attempted as well as they could to imitate courtly manners. During this period the ability to converse sensibly and brilliantly was considered the finest social accomplishment.

In England during the 17th and 18th centuries, courtly manners fell out of favor somewhat. Besides being merely polite, English gentlemen were expected to be modest, pious, and compassionate and to devote more time to their country homes than to life at court. New in this period was the advice that gentlemen should never be idle and that they should do some kind of work for a living.

One famous English etiquette manual, however, still advocated the more elaborate courtly manners of France over those of the English country gentleman. The letters of Philip Dormer Stanhope, the 4th earl of Chesterfield, to his son Philip Stanhope, were published in 1774. Lord Chesterfield indicated repeatedly that polite behavior could help win favors from influential people. Although many readers were critical of this selfish attitude, the work was popular, and by 1800 it had gone through 11 editions.

By courtesy of Lenox, Inc.

The Industrial Revolution in England caused the middle class to expand rapidly in numbers and importance. Soon they, rather than the aristocracy, began to have the greatest influence on manners. During the Victorian Age, the ideal of every person was respectability. Families were expected to say grace at meals and to hold daily prayer meetings with their servants. Modesty in dress and behavior was demanded. Women had to wear simple clothes, shun cosmetics, and avoid loud and excessive talking. They had to be particularly careful not to read any literature that might be considered immoral. The ideal young lady ate very little, fainted easily and often, and blushed whenever she was looked at.

Etiquette Codes in the United States

When the English first settled in America, they were met by Indian tribes that had a tradition of generous hospitality. Often the Indians would share their last bit of food with the early colonists.

The Puritan settlers of New England had a rigid standard of conduct. They enacted laws against drinking toasts, bowling, and dancing. They frowned upon many forms of simple recreation because these diverted attention from religious matters. They believed that the frivolous persons who indulged in such recreations might be tempted by the Devil.

The first American etiquette book, the 'School of Good Manners', appeared in 1715. Its author was probably Eleazar Moody, a Boston writing master. Many 18th-century schoolmasters taught manners and encouraged their students to copy advice on proper behavior from the books they read. In 1747, at the age of 15, George Washington put together from his school notes a series of maxims which became the book 'Rules of Civility and Decent Behaviour in Company and Conversation'. Included were "Give not Advice without being Ask'd & when desired do it briefly" and "In visiting the Sick, do not Presently play the physician if you be not Knowing therein."

By the end of the 18th century, Lord Chesterfield's 'Letters' had become popular in the United States. As in England, however, many Americans were disturbed that Lord Chesterfield seemed to separate good manners from good morals. After the Revolutionary War, many patriots wished to break away from English manners as they had done with English rule. But English etiquette manuals continued to be influential until the 19th century.

During the first half of the 19th century, the custom of dueling to defend one's honor was frequently practiced. The usual reason for a duel was some personally offensive remark. In 1804 Aaron Burr killed Alexander Hamilton in a duel which was ostensibly fought because Hamilton had called Burr "dangerous." Before the Civil War many duels were fought over disagreements about the extension of slavery. The etiquette of dueling included rules on

By courtesy of Northwestern University

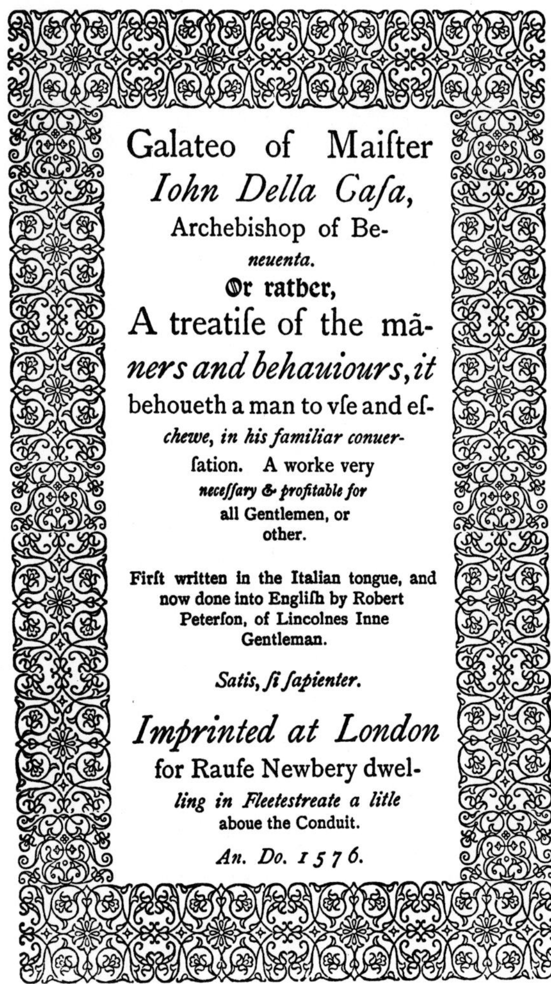

Galateo of Maiſter
Iohn Della Caſa,
Archebishop of Be-
neuenta.
Or rather,
A treatiſe of the mã-
ners and behauiours, it
behoueth a man to vſe and eſ-
chewe, in his familiar conuer-
ſation. A worke very
neceſſary & profitable for
all Gentlemen, or
other.

Firſt written in the Italian tongue, and
now done into Engliſh by Robert
Peterſon, of Lincolnes Inne
Gentleman.

Satis, ſi ſapienter.

Imprinted at London
for Raufe Newbery dwel-
ling in Fleetestreate a litle
aboue the Conduit.
An. Do. 1576.

By courtesy of the Newberry Library, Chicago

LETTERS
WRITTEN BY
THE LATE RIGHT HONOURABLE
PHILIP DORMER STANHOPE,
EARL OF CHESTERFIELD,
TO
HIS SON,
PHILIP STANHOPE, Eſq;
LATE ENVOY EXTRAORDINARY AT THE COURT OF DRESDEN:
TOGETHER WITH
SEVERAL OTHER PIECES
ON VARIOUS SUBJECTS.
PUBLISHED BY
Mrs. EUGENIA STANHOPE,
FROM THE ORIGINALS NOW IN HER POSSESSION.
IN TWO VOLUMES.
VOL. II.
LONDON:
Printed for J. DODSLEY in PALL-MALL.
M.DCC.LXXIV.

The 'Galateo' by Giovanni della Casa, an influential 16th-century Italian etiquette book, has been translated into several European languages. It was first published in England in 1576 and was paraphrased in many later English etiquette books. The letters of the 4th earl of Chesterfield to his son, first published in England in 1774, became a well-known guide to polite behavior in both Great Britain and the United States. It remained popular well into the 19th century.

how to handle an insult and how to shoot a gun with courtesy. After the Civil War era, dueling was no longer considered necessary, but etiquette books suggested that boxing might be a useful replacement.

Victorian manners spread from England to the United States. Particularly strict was the emphasis on modesty. It was considered poor taste for men and women to sit together on the grass. Sometimes men and women would be separated before being allowed to view nude sculptures in an art museum.

After the Civil War a prosperous industrial middle class arose. Many people who had grown up in unsettled areas needed guides to polite conduct to polish their rough manners. Hundreds of etiquette manuals were written in the United States, and many magazines, such as *Godey's Lady's Book,* included articles on proper behavior. The manuals dealt with such varied topics as conduct at funerals, regular bathing, entertaining, and kitchen management.

Nineteenth-century standards for behavior were influential up to World War I. In the postwar era, manners and morals relaxed. Women began to smoke in public. Motion pictures made free behavior seem glamorous. Hoping to recapture some of the elegance that had characterized the Victorian Age, Emily Post wrote 'Etiquette in Society, in Business, in Politics, and at Home', which appeared in 1922. The book was directed to the wealthy and included advice on managing servants and joining exclusive clubs. Subsequent revisions gave more attention to the needs of people with modest incomes. In 1931 the title was changed to 'Etiquette: the Blue Book of Social Usage'. It is still considered a standard guide to good manners.

Etiquette Today

The rules of etiquette are always alive and changing. They are modified somewhat by each new generation. Young people are usually more interested in knowing what behavior their friends will approve than the kind that has been accepted traditionally.

But even today, when young people are questioning whether there is any *right* way to behave, the basis of good manners remains unchanged. Consideration for others, understanding, loyalty, and a sense of justice are the qualities that have helped make life pleasant and rewarding in every age.

BIBLIOGRAPHY FOR ETIQUETTE

Books for Children

Adachi, Kelly. The Kids' Handbook (Lyle Stuart, 1984).
Allison, Alida. The Children's Manners Book (Price Stern, 1981).
Baker, E.H. Your Manners Are Showing (Child's World, 1980).
Brown, Marc and Krensky, Stephen. Perfect Pigs: an Introduction to Manners (Atlantic, 1983).
Jefferds, Vincent. Disney's Elegant Book of Manners (Simon & Schuster, n.d.).
Joslin, Sesyle. What Do You Do, Dear? (Addison, 1961).
Joslin, Sesyle. What Do You Say, Dear? (Addison, 1958).

Books for Young Adults and Teachers

Drobot, Eva. Class Acts: Etiquette for Today (Avon, 1984).
Free, A.R. Social Usage, 2nd ed. (Prentice, 1969).
Landers, Ann. The Ann Landers Encyclopedia A to Z (Ballantine, 1979).
McCall, Andrew. The Ghastly Guest Book (St. Martin, 1982).
Martin, Judith. Miss Manners' Guide to Excruciatingly Correct Behavior (Warner, 1983).
Martin, Judith. Miss Manners' Guide to Rearing Perfect Children (Atheneum, 1984).
Nelson, J.H. Handy Etiquette Manual (Branden, n.d.).
Post, E.L., ed. The Emily Post Book of Etiquette for Young People (Funk & Wagnalls, 1967).
Schlesinger, A.M. Learning How to Behave: a Historical Study of American Etiquette Books (Cooper Sq., 1968).
Stewart, M.Y. and Buchwald, Ann. What to Do—When and Why (McKay, 1975).
Thiry, Joan. How to Cope with an Artichoke and other Mannerly Mishaps (Chateau Thierry, 1982).
Van Buren, Abigail. The Best of Dear Abby (G.K. Hall, 1982).
Vanderbilt, Amy. The Amy Vanderbilt Complete Book of Etiquette (Bantam, 1981).

Books for Special Situations

Bride's Magazine Editors. Bride's Book of Etiquette (Putnam, 1985).
Brett, Gerard. Dinner Is Served: a Study in Manners (Shoe String, 1968).
Cahn, Julie. The Dating Book (Messner, 1983).
Fruehling, R.T. and Bouchard, Sharon. The Art of Writing Effective Letters (McGraw, 1972).
Gunn, M.K. A Guide to Academic Protocol (Columbia Univ. Press, 1969).
Robert, H.M. Robert's Rules of Order Revised (Morrow, 1971).

ETNA, MOUNT. The highest active volcano in Europe is Mount Etna. It rises on the east coast of the island of Sicily. The name comes from the Greek word Aitne, which is from *aithō*, meaning "I burn." Its topmost elevation is more than 10,000 feet (3,000 meters). Like other active volcanoes, its height varies. More than 135 eruptions have been recorded since ancient writers mentioned outbreaks 800 years before the Christian era. In AD 1169, 15,000 people lost their lives in the town of Catania at the volcano's base. In 1669 some 20,000 were killed.

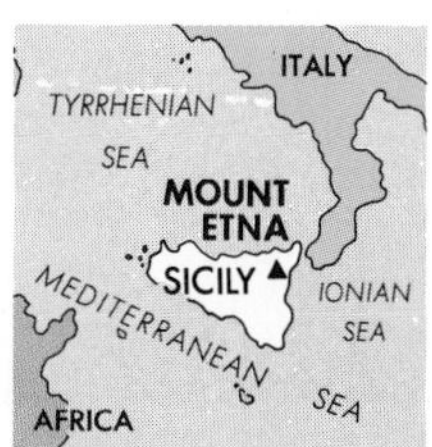

The base of Mount Etna is thickly populated. The rich soil formed from old lava has attracted farmers despite the danger. The mountain rises through three zones: first the cultivated and populous zone, rising to about 3,000 feet (914 meters), where vegetables, olives, grapevines, and fruits are grown; next the wooded region, with forests of chestnut, oak, beech, and pine; and at about 6,500 feet (1,980 meters) a dreary waste of black lava and ash, which is covered with snow during the winter. Geologic characteristics show that Etna has been active for more than 2.5 million years. It has had at least two main active centers.

The Greeks created many legends about the volcano. Some said it was the workshop of Hephaestus, the god of fire, and of the Cyclopes. Others said that underneath the volcano the giant Typhon lay, making the Earth shake when he turned. The ancient poet Hesiod spoke of Etna's eruptions. Seventy-one eruptions were recorded from 1500 BC to AD 1669.

The eruption in 1669 lasted from March 11 through July 15. The lava flow destroyed a dozen villages and submerged the western part of Catania. Workers attempted to turn the lava stream away from

Mount Etna, the highest volcano in Europe, covers about 500 square miles (1,300 square kilometers). Much of the land below the snowline is farmed.

Elmar Schneiwind—Rapho/Photo Researchers

Catania by digging a trench above the village. This attempt is recognized as the first in history to divert a lava stream. In 1983 an eruption lasted almost four months. Authorities exploded dynamite in an attempt to divert lava flow.

ETRUSCANS. Long before the days of Rome's greatness, Italy was the home of a people far advanced in civilization—the Etruscans, or Tyrrhenians. These people rose to prosperity and power, then almost vanished from recorded history, leaving unsolved many questions about their origin and culture.

Some scholars think that the Etruscans were a seafaring people who came from Asia Minor. As early as 1000 BC they were living in Italy in an area that was roughly equivalent to modern Tuscany, from the Tiber River north almost to the Arno River. Later their rule embraced a large part of western Italy, including Rome. When the Tarquin Dynasty was expelled from Rome about 500 BC, Lars Porsena, king of Etruria and Clusium, sought to reestablish his influence over Rome but without success.

The Etruscans already controlled the commerce of the Tyrrhenian Sea on their western border. After losing control of Rome, they strengthened their naval power through an alliance with Carthage against Greece. In 474 BC their fleet was destroyed by the Greeks of Syracuse. From that time their power rapidly declined. The Gauls overran the country from the north, and the Etruscans' strong southern fortress of Veii fell to Rome after a ten-year seige (396 BC). The Etruscans were absorbed by the Romans, who adopted many of their advanced arts, their customs, and their institutions.

Because little Etruscan literature remains and the language of inscriptions on their monuments has been only partially deciphered, scholars have gained most of their knowledge of the Etruscans from studying the remains of their city walls, houses, monuments, and tombs. Weapons and other implements, exquisite jewelry, coins, statues of stone, bronze, and terra-cotta, and black pottery (called bucchero) have been found. Grecian and Oriental influences are seen in the art of this trading folk.

ETYMOLOGY. Chemistry students learn that water is made up of hydrogen and oxygen. They do not always learn that the word hydrogen comes from Greek words meaning "water-producing," or that oxygen is from Greek words meaning "acid-producing." The study of the origin of words is fascinating and useful. It is a help in thinking clearly and expressing oneself accurately. This study is called etymology, the branch of linguistics that is concerned with finding the origin and derivation of words. The word etymology comes from Greek words meaning "true" and "account."

Much can be learned about the Etruscans from their painting, sculpture, and crafts. The gold ear stud with colored glass (left) is from the 6th century BC. The terra-cotta coffin (bottom left) from the 5th century BC is from Caere. The fresco of musicians (below) is in the Tomb of the Leopards, Tarquinia, Italy.

(Left) By courtesy of the Trustees of the British Museum, London; (bottom left and below) SCALA—Art Resource

Scientific etymology did not appear until the 19th century, when the groundwork of modern linguistics was laid (*see* Linguistics). The general principles involved in present-day etymology are: (1) The earliest form of a word and its related forms must be determined. (2) Every sound of a modern word must be compared to the form from which the word is derived. (3) Any deviation in sound correspondence must be adequately explained—deviations such as changes in or loss of letters from the ancient to the modern. (4) Any shift in meaning between the original and the modern derivative must be explained. (5) Words that contain sounds not native to a given language are probably borrowed, and the language of origin must be determined. (For more information on word origins, *see* Language; Name.)

Courtesy of the Australian Tourist Commission

The ghost gum eucalyptus of Australia is distinguished by the smooth white bark from which it derives its name.

EUCALYPTUS. Next to the Douglas fir and the giant redwoods of the American West, the tallest tree in the world is *Eucalyptus regnans* of Australia. The tallest ones measured have been more than 300 feet (90 meters) high.

The eucalyptus is native to Australia, New Zealand, Tasmania, and nearby islands. There are about 500 species in Australia. It has been planted in other warm parts of the world, notably California, South America, southern Europe, and northern Africa.

Most species have long, slender, leathery evergreen leaves that turn edgewise to the sun, thus retarding evaporation. The name eucalyptus comes from two Greek words meaning "well-covered," which probably refers to the tight-fitting cap that covers the flower until it is ready to bloom. Flowers differ in color in the various species. They range from creamy white to yellow and many shades of pink and red. The trees grow rapidly. This is one reason why they have been so widely planted. They are used for timber and fuel, as windbreaks and avenue trees, and for such conservation purposes as slowing erosion and reclaiming swamps.

The wood is tough and durable. It is used for wharves, piles, poles, railway ties, and other outdoor construction because it resists decay in water or moist ground. It takes a high polish and is valuable for interior finishing and furniture. The wood is also turned into paper pulp. The leaves of some species secrete an oil that is extracted by steam distillation to furnish the eucalyptus oil used in medicine. Certain trees yield a gummy sap from which tannin is obtained.

The eucalyptus belongs to the myrtle family (Myrtaceae). Among the most common species are the blue gum, *Eucalyptus globulus*; jarrah, *E. marginata*; Sydney peppermint, *E. piperita*; red gum, *E. camaldulensis;* salmon gum, *E. salmonophloia*; swamp mahogany, *E. robusta*; and giant gum, *E. regnans.*

EUCLID. It has been said that, next to the Bible, the 'Elements' of Euclid is the most translated, published, and studied book in the Western world. Of the man himself almost nothing is known. It is recorded that he founded and taught at a school of mathematics in Alexandria, Egypt, during the reign of Ptolemy I Soter, who ruled from 323 to about 283 BC. It is assumed from his books that he was not a first-class mathematician, but he was a first-rate teacher of geometry and arithmetic. The 'Elements' remained unchallenged for more than 2,000 years. Not until the mid-19th century was a non-Euclidean geometry devised. (*See also* Geometry, "Euclid" and "Other Kinds of Geometry.")

To compile his 'Elements' Euclid relied on the work of several predecessors, so the book is of uneven quality. Once it was published, the 'Elements' superseded all previous mathematical treatises and became the standard text. During the Middle Ages three Arabic translations were made of the book, and it was through these that it became known in Europe. The English traveler and philosopher Adelard of Bath went to Spain disguised as a Muslim student and obtained an Arabic copy, from which he made a Latin translation in 1120. The first Latin translation of the Greek without an Arabic intermediary was made by Bartolomeo Zamberti and published in Venice in 1505. There have been several more recent translations into other languages.

Among Euclid's other works on geometry were 'Data' and 'On Divisions'. He also wrote 'Optics' and 'Elements of Music'. Some of his writings have been lost, while other works are wrongly credited to him.

EUGENICS. Can people control their own evolution in order to achieve a population free of physical and mental defects? For more than 100 years, individuals who support eugenics, the study of human change by genetic means, have answered "yes."

The word eugenics comes from a Greek word that means "well-born." Supporters of eugenics seek to change the human race through artificial selection, the controlled breeding of people who have certain physical characteristics or mental abilities. Eugenics is based on the science of genetics, the science that studies how genes are structured and passed on through generations (*see* Genetics; Heredity). Eugenics also involves use of information obtained from other areas of knowledge. Psychology, the study of personality; medicine, as it relates to the genetic factors of certain diseases and conditions; sociology, the study of group interaction; and demography, the statistical study of human populations, are some of the disciplines on which eugenic theories are based.

History of Eugenics

Ideas about improving animal and plant stocks have existed since ancient times. Many animals, especially dogs and horses, have been bred to improve specific characteristics. Plants and trees have also been bred to obtain hardier and more productive strains (*see* Plants, Improvement of). Thoughts about improving human beings by such means existed in ancient times. These ideas can be found in the Old Testament. The famous Greek philosopher Plato discussed such possibilities in his 'Republic'.

It was not until 1883, however, that the British scientist Francis Galton coined the word eugenics. Galton was a cousin of Charles Darwin, the leading supporter of evolutionary theory. Darwin's work influenced Galton, who began to write about the possibilities for humans to direct their own evolution. In a book written in 1869, Galton had used studies of the families of important men to show that "it would be quite practical to produce a highly gifted race of men by judicious marriages during several successive generations."

Galton was not alone in his search for human improvement. During the 17th and 18th centuries an intellectual movement called the Enlightenment developed. The Enlightenment was based on the idea that man could improve his condition through the celebration and use of reason. In the late 1800s an American feminist leader named Victoria Woodhull stated that: "If superior people are desired, they must be bred; and if imbeciles, criminals, paupers, and [the] otherwise unfit are undesirable citizens, they must not be bred." In 1872 Woodhall became the first woman to be nominated for president by a political party.

From the late 19th century through the end of World War II in 1945, eugenics became a part of a broad, and often destructive, social movement to "improve" the human race. This was particularly evident in Germany beginning in the 1920s and throughout World War II. Actions taken by Adolf Hitler and the Nazi Party, which he controlled, were stimulated by eugenic theories. About 12 million people, about half of them Jews, were murdered in death camps because of the Nazi belief that "inferior" people should be controlled by the German master race.

During those same years in the United States, many eugenicists supported the sterilization of people considered to be defective. Sterilization is a medical procedure that can prevent men or women from producing children. By 1931 sterilization laws had been enacted by 27 states in the United States. And by 1935, five other countries had passed similar laws.

Most of the people who supported eugenics were not scientists. But some, like Karl Pearson, a British mathematician and follower of Galton, were prominent. In the early 1900s, Pearson, who was a controversial public figure, emphasized the belief that certain social classes and races were superior to others. This theory greatly influenced Nazi doctrine (*see* Genocide; Hitler; World War II). He and his supporters generally ignored the possibility that a poor social environment could have an adverse effect on human behavior. Pearson was part of the reason that eugenics, as a scientific discipline, was later discredited in the United States.

The work of anthropologists, people who study the diverse peoples of the world, and other scientists changed the emphasis of eugenics. In the United States during the early 1900s, Franz Boas, a German-born anthropologist, made important contributions to the understanding of race (*see* Boas). Researchers began to concentrate more on such factors as social and economic conditions to explain human behavior. But if eugenics has been restored to scientific respectability, it was through continued studies of cell structure and the nature of heredity (*see* Cell).

Current Issues

Current interest in eugenics involves studying the nature and causes of genetic defects, the ways in which psychological traits are determined, and the relationship between environmental factors and heredity (*see* Genetic Engineering; Genetic Disorders).

Scientists believe that today the number of people who are carrying defective genes is increasing. Part of the explanation for this is that more people are being exposed to damaging radiation, chemicals, and other environmental hazards. Another reason may lie in generations of poor nutrition. Medical advances, however, have made it possible for those people with inherited diseases and other deficiencies to live longer, marry, and to produce children.

Each year increasing numbers of genetic defects are being defined, the ways in which they are transmitted are better understood, and methods for identifying carriers of such defects are being improved. Part of the current solution to the problem of genetic defects is to educate people who have these serious genetic defects and diseases about the risks in the bearing of children. In many industrialized countries genetic counseling informs such individuals and couples about the human tragedy that may occur if they choose to have children.

EULER, Leonhard (1707–83). The Swiss mathematician and physicist Leonhard Euler not only made important contributions to the subjects of geometry, calculus, mechanics, and number theory but also developed methods for solving problems in observational astronomy. A founder of pure mathematics, he also demonstrated useful applications of mathematics in technology and public affairs.

Euler was born in Basel, Switzerland, on April 15, 1707. In 1727 he became, upon the invitation of Catherine I of Russia, an associate of the Academy of Sciences at Saint Petersburg. In 1730 he became professor of physics. The author of innumerable papers, Euler overtaxed himself and in 1735 lost the sight of one eye. Invited by Frederick the Great, Euler in 1741 became a member of the Academy of Sciences at Berlin, where for 25 years he poured forth a steady stream of publications. When Frederick became less cordial, Euler in 1766 returned to Russia. Soon after his arrival in St. Petersburg, a cataract formed in the other eye, and Euler spent the last years of his life in total blindness. Despite this and other misfortunes, his productivity continued undiminished, sustained by an uncommon memory and a remarkable ability to compute mentally.

The mathematician J.L. Lagrange, rather than Euler, is often regarded as the greatest mathematician of the 18th century. But Euler never has been excelled either in productivity or in the skillful and imaginative use of computational devices for solving problems.

EUPHRATES RIVER. The longest river of western Asia is the 1,700-mile (2,700-kilometer) Euphrates. It begins in the high mountains of eastern Turkey, crosses eastern Syria, and then flows southeastward through the length of Iraq. Because of Iraq's hot, dry climate much of the river's water is lost through evaporation and use for irrigation. The river receives most of its water from winter rains and snowfall. It is navigable only by flat-bottomed riverboats. The Tigris, its twin river to the east, runs almost parallel with it. The two merge in a swamp to form the Shatt Al 'Arab, which flows into the Persian Gulf about 100 miles (160 kilometers) to the southeast. There are two flood periods each year. The rivers carry a heavy load of silt and have deposited much of it, forming a great, agriculturally productive alluvial plain. The major tributaries of the Euphrates are the Balikh, Al Khabur, and Gharraf Channel.

The land between the two rivers was an early center of civilization called Mesopotamia (*see* Babylon; Babylonia and Assyria). In the 13th century its irrigation system was destroyed by the Mongols, and the rich plain again became desert and marsh. In spite of some modern irrigation, its ancient fertility is not yet entirely recovered. With hot summer temperatures and little rainfall, large areas of the plain must be irrigated with waters from the Euphrates and Tigris to support crops of wheat, barley, millet, rice, and dates. (*See also* Iraq; Tigris River.)

EURIPIDES (484?–406 BC). In 405 BC the comic dramatist Aristophanes staged his play 'The Frogs'. It was based on the idea that Athens no longer had a great tragic poet. It was true. Euripides had died in 406. Along with Aeschylus and Sophocles, Euripides was one of the three great tragic poets of ancient Greece. Of his life very little is known. He was born about 484. Later in life he married a woman named Melito, and they had three sons. In 408 he left Athens for Macedonia, probably because of disgust with the seemingly endless Peloponnesian War with Sparta.

Euripides is believed to have written 92 dramas, but only 19 of them are now known. They show him to have been a tragedian of incomparable merit. He saw the world as a place where chance, order, and reason were constantly thwarted by unreason and passion. He was aware of so much meaningless suffering and tragedy that his view of life verged on despair. He was especially troubled by the ferocity and folly of the Peloponnesian War, which broke out in 431 BC and outlasted his life.

As with those of the other tragedians, the plays of Euripides deal with legendary and mythological events of a time far removed from 5th-century Athens. But the points he made were applicable to the time in which he wrote, especially to the cruelties of the war.

During the last 20 years of his life, Euripides wrote a number of plays that might be called romantic tragicomedies. They were unusual in that they had happy endings. Among these were 'Ion', 'Iphigenia in Tauris', and 'Helen'. In them he turned his back on the tragic real world and dealt purely in dramatic form. It is for his tragedies, however, that he is best remembered: 'Medea', first performed in 431 BC; 'Hippolytus' (428); 'Andromache', 'The Suppliants', 'Children of Heracles', and 'Hecuba' (all before 423); 'Electra' and 'The Trojan Women' (415); 'Helen' (412); 'Phoenician Women' (411–409); and 'Heracles' (408) are among the best. (*See also* Drama; Theater.)

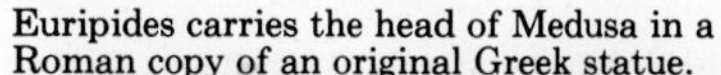

Euripides carries the head of Medusa in a Roman copy of an original Greek statue.

E. Streichan—Shostal Associates

Glaciers in the Bernina Alps contribute to the magnificent scenery that is abundant in eastern Switzerland along the Italian border.

EUROPE

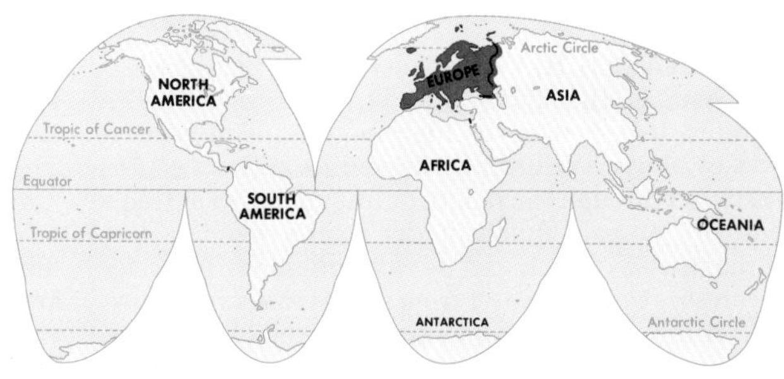

EUROPE. Despite its relatively small size, the continent of Europe has been a dominant force in world development. This next-to-smallest continent possesses a large, ethnically diverse, and highly productive population. A united Europe would rank as a third superpower along with the United States and the Soviet Union. The continent, however, consists of 25 independent countries plus eight small constitutional monarchies, principalities, duchies, and republics. Normally the most populated western part of the Soviet Union is also included in Europe as is European Turkey.

Europeans and their ideas have penetrated into every corner of the Earth. This influence has been expressed through the development of empires, the widespread distribution of European peoples and their cultures, and the adoption and adaptation of European political, economic, and social innovations throughout the world. The democratic form of government and modern, technological, industrial development both originated in Western Europe and have had a major influence on the rest of the world.

This article was contributed by Lawrence M. Sommers, Professor of Geography, Michigan State University, East Lansing.

NATURAL ENVIRONMENT

Europe is a peninsula of the much larger Eurasian landmass. The traditional boundary of the continent follows roughly the crest of the Ural Mountains, the Ural River, the Caspian Sea, the crest of the Caucasus Mountains, the Black Sea, Bosporus, Sea of Marmara, Dardanelles, Aegean Sea, Mediterranean Sea, and the Strait of Gibraltar. This definition includes the European part of the Soviet Union. Other significant boundary lines are the line separating the European countries from the Soviet Union and the ideological boundary between Eastern, communist Europe and Western Europe that follows the eastern boundaries of Finland, West Germany, Austria, and Italy.

Land

The continent of Europe totals more than 4 million square miles (10.5 million square kilometers), or 7 percent of the world's land area. It spreads from 35° to 71° N latitude and from 60° E to about 10° W longitude. Norway's Svalbard (Spitzbergen) extends European islands to more than 80° N, and Iceland extends to nearly 25° W. Europe is centrally located among the world's landmasses. Fortunately, its location in the westerly wind belt brings to the land the marine influences of the nearby oceans, seas, and bays. The peninsular shape of the continent and its numerous islands and indentations along the coasts facilitate the influence of the marine winds. The result is a moderate climate with a long growing season over much of Western Europe. This is quite in contrast to the severe cold conditions of comparable northerly latitudes along the east coast of North America for much of the year.

The highly disrupted coastline brings the advantages of a saltwater location to much of the continent. The Scandinavian, Iberian, Italian, and Balkan peninsulas—plus the major islands of Crete, Sardinia, Corsica, and Sicily in the Mediterranean Sea and Ireland, Great Britain, Iceland, Greenland, and Svalbard off northwestern Europe—are features of the irregular, disrupted coastline. The Mediterranean and Black seas on the south and the North, Baltic, and Barents seas on the north give many countries and many peoples easy access to ocean transportation. No one in Western Europe is more than 450 miles (725 kilometers) from salt water, and even in the European Soviet Union the maximum distance is 800 miles (1,300 kilometers).

Europe has a complex geologic structure. The highlands in the north contain some of the oldest known rock formations, and the Alps in the south are a geologically young mountain system. East of the Carpathian Mountains and the Vistula River is a low, stable, geologic platform. West of this platform repeated uplift, folding, and erosion have left mountains, plateaus, hills, and plains close to one another. The Caucasus, the Pyrenees, and the Alpine system are young mountains in Southern Europe that result from plates, or large portions of the Earth's crustal rock structure, pushing northward from Africa. Mount El'brus in the Caucasus rises 18,481 feet (5,633 meters). The highest peak in the Pyrenees is 11,168

Preview

The article Europe is divided into the following sections:

For a brief review of essential information about Europe, *see* EUROPE FACT SUMMARY.

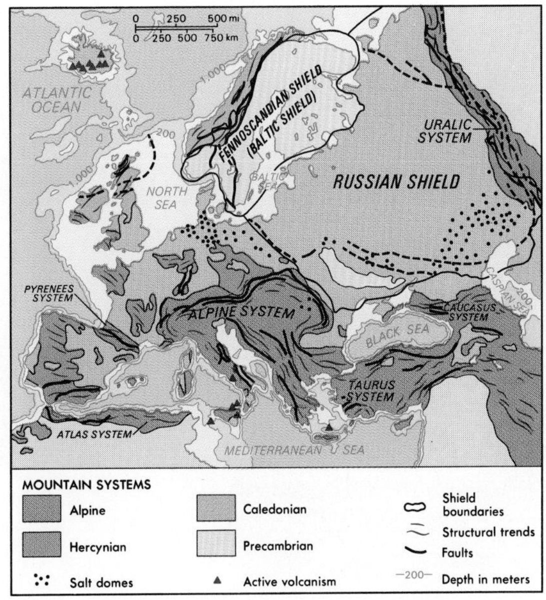

Tectonic map of Europe

feet (3,404 meters), and Mt. Blanc in the French Alps is 15,771 feet (4,807 meters). The highlands in Norway, Sweden, and Finland are part of the old Fennoscandian Shield. This is a rock base composed of crystalline, resistant rocks that have been uplifted and eroded many times over geologic history. The Kjölen Mountains are on the border between Norway and Sweden and occupy most of southern Norway. They have peaks averaging from 6,000 to 8,000 feet (1,800 to 2,400 meters). The highest point of 8,104 feet (2,470 meters) is Glittertinden in Norway.

The most recent event that affected much of Europe was the Pleistocene Ice Age. The huge ice sheets sculptured, scoured, and smoothed the highland topography of Northern Europe and deposited sands, silts, and clays over lowland Europe to the south.

The mountains and plateaus of Central and Western Europe are middle in geologic age between the Alps and the Scandinavian highlands. The long erosion periods have resulted in rounded landforms that extend from the Bohemian, or western portion, of Czechoslovakia through the highlands of southern West Germany, the Vosges Mountains and Central Plateau of France, and the upland Meseta, or plateau, of Spain. These highlands are broken up by frequent river valleys and lowlands.

The Alpine system, a complex system of young folded mountains with associated forelands and basins and plains between the mountain systems, dominates Southern Europe. The Alps average 12,000 feet (3,700 meters) in height, with higher, individual, sharp peaks such as Mt. Blanc. The river valleys are narrow, steep, and rocky with fertile, water-deposited soil normally found in narrow valley bottoms. The southern slope of the Alps is steep and abrupt. The northern slope is a gradual decline to the plateaus of

(Top left) H. Fristedt—Ostman Agency; (top right) Bob and Ira Spring; (bottom left) J. Allan Cash Ltd.; (bottom right) D.C. Williamson

The landforms on the continent of Europe are as varied as any in the world. Finland has extensive evergreen forests (top left) in the Fennoscandian Shield region. The west coast of Norway (top right) is indented with numerous, deep-penetrating fjords. The Greek island of Crete in the Mediterranean (left) has rugged coastlines and a mountainous interior that are much like the mainland. Farmland in Poland (bottom right) is part of the East European Plain.

southern Germany. Despite the high altitude of the Alps, numerous passes and tunnels allow easy north-south communication. The Pyrenees and Caucasus are much more formidable transportation barriers than the Alps. The highlands of Italy and Balkan Europe are unstable and subject to devastating earthquakes and periodic eruptions from such volcanoes as Mt. Etna and Mt. Vesuvius.

Most of the rivers of Central and Western Europe have their sources in the Alps and associated mountains. Large northward-flowing rivers—such as the Vistula and the Oder—drain into the Baltic, and the Elbe and the Rhine flow into the North Sea. They have swift currents and are valuable for waterpower near their source, but they become broad and sluggish streams when crossing the European Plain. France has three major rivers flowing to the west—the Seine, Loire, and Garonne—and the Saône-Rhône flowing to the south. The Po in Italy, the Tagus, Ebro, and Guadalquivir in the Iberian Peninsula, the Thames in England, and the Shannon in Ireland are also major waterways. In Eastern Europe the Danube and Don, which flow into the Black Sea, and the Volga, which empties into the Caspian Sea, are the principal rivers.

Climate

The moderate climates of Europe result from the peninsular, marine, and mid-latitude location in the path of the prevailing westerlies. These winds bring the warmth and moisture of the North Atlantic to Western Europe. The almost daily changes in weather conditions result from the passing of large low- and high-pressure systems. These have cold and warm fronts that cause temperature changes and frequent but normally slow precipitation. The lack of blocking mountains allows air and moisture to flow into the plains of Central and Eastern Europe, though the amounts of precipitation decrease toward the east. Temperature ranges—both daily and seasonal—are narrow in Western Europe and wide in Eastern

Europe. The Alps and the high-pressure system of the Azores help prevent moisture from entering the Mediterranean region during the summer. As the Azores high moves southward in winter, the cyclonic storm systems penetrate from the north and west into the Mediterranean and give Southern Europe a cool and rainy winter season.

Reliability is the keynote of Western European climate. The decreasing precipitation toward the east reaches drought conditions north of the Caspian and Black seas as well as in eastern Greece and eastern Spain. Summer droughts are common throughout the Mediterranean lowlands. The heaviest precipitation occurs in the mountains and coastal regions of Western Europe and reaches 200 inches (500 centimeters) per year in the high peaks of Wales and Scotland. The average precipitation ranges from 20 to 30 inches (50 to 75 centimeters) in the Western European lowlands and from 30 to 80 inches (75 to 200 centimeters) in higher areas, and it decreases eastward to less than 10 inches (25 centimeters) north of the Caspian Sea.

The water-moderated climate of Western Europe is called west coast marine; the warm to hot summer and cold winter conditions of Eastern Europe make a continental climate; and the dry, hot summer and cool, rainy winter in the south form a Mediterranean climate. Central Europe has a frequently changing climate as the area shifts from marine to continental influences. The highland climates change in temperature and precipitation characteristics from the lower slopes to the higher peaks, depending on orientation and elevation. Parts of the higher Alps are permanently covered with snow and glaciers.

Vegetation and Soils

The natural vegetation and soils of Europe relate closely to the varied climate, relief, subsurface rock structure, and drainage conditions. The intensive use of the land by a dense population has greatly changed the original natural patterns of Europe, especially the vegetation. The Ice Age glaciation scoured some areas bare of soil and deposited sandy, gravelly, and stony soils in others. In general the glacier left behind soils highly varied in both composition and fertility.

Broad associations of climate, vegetation, and soil can be better defined in Eastern than in Western Europe. The north to south zones begin with the acid, poor, swampy tundra soils in the far north that have mosses, lichens, and shrub vegetation. To the south of this zone, evergreen trees are found in the taiga zone, which has a gray, acid, infertile soil low in the vegetable matter called humus. Agriculture is more widespread in the next zone south, which has deciduous, or broadleaf, trees that lose their leaves each year. This adds vegetable matter, which results in a brown-colored soil. To the south of the tree zone in Eastern Europe—as precipitation becomes less and less reliable—natural grass replaces trees. The first zone has tall-grass prairies, changing to short-grass prairies, then semiarid shrubs, and finally desert vegetation. In the Mediterranean lowlands the natural vegetation consists of drought-resistant species such as olive, cypress, and scrub trees and maquis shrubs that have leaf adaptations to prevent water loss. Mediterranean soils are often red from the high iron content and are frequently of volcanic origin.

Average annual precipitation for Europe

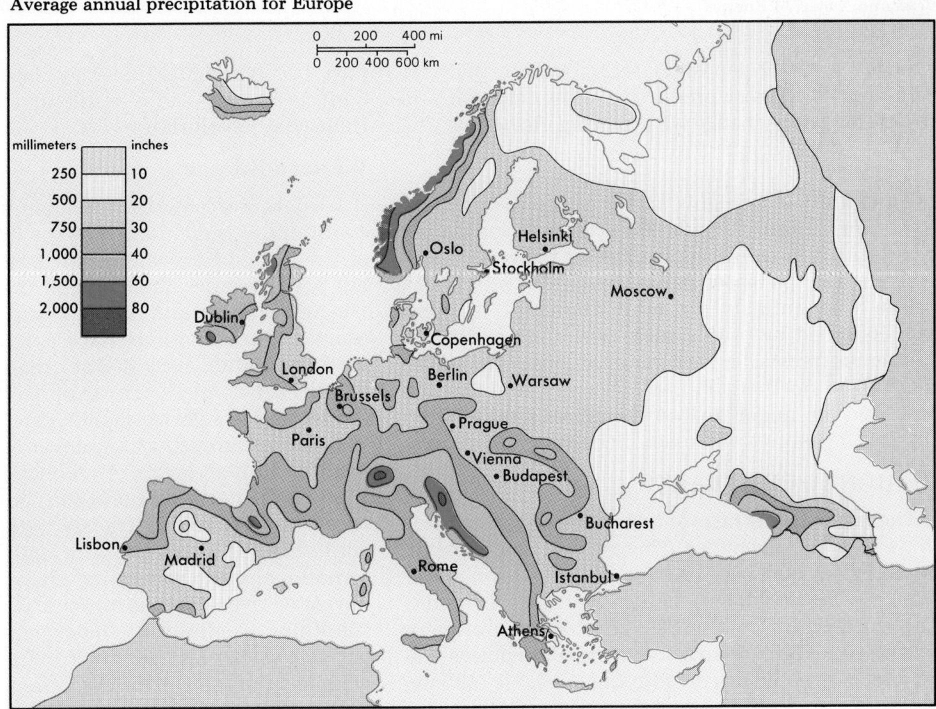

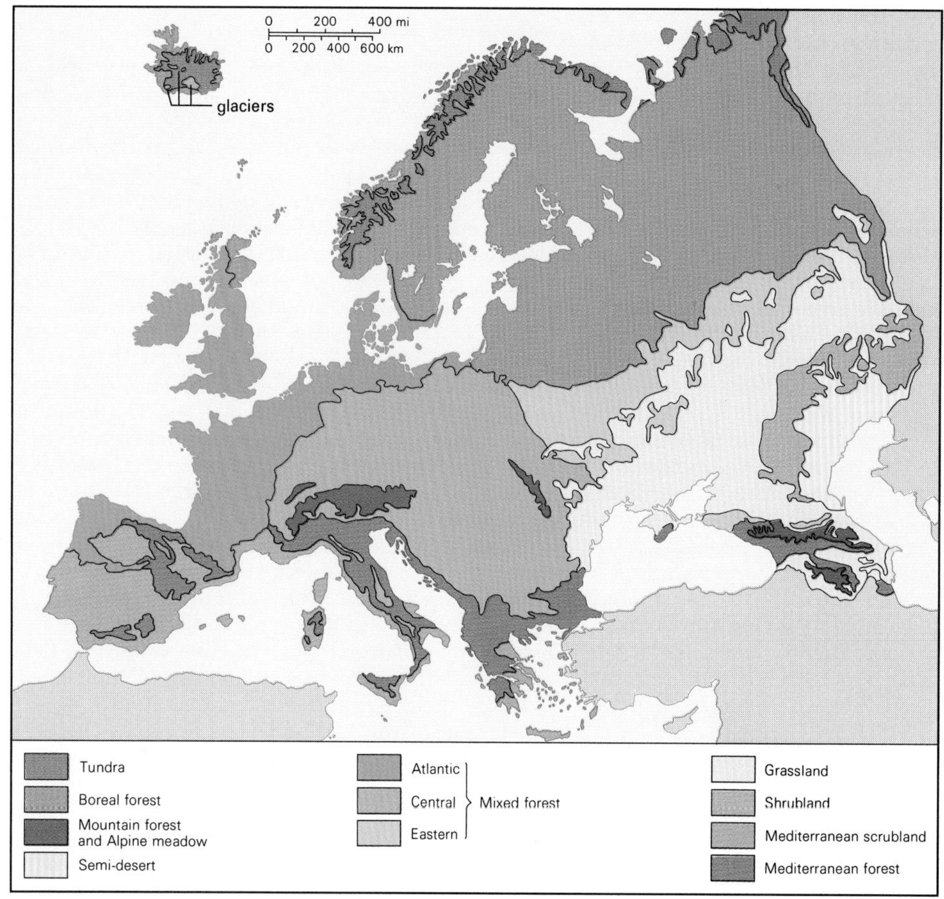

Vegetation zones of Europe

Alluvial, or water-deposited, soils found in the river valleys are the most productive. Mountain soil and vegetation types change with varying elevations.

Animal Life

Animal life is as highly varied as are the physical conditions. Intense population pressure over history has resulted in the disappearance of many wild animals such as the bison, European ox, and wild horse. Native wild animals are most abundant in areas less disturbed by people such as the far north, the coniferous forests, and the mountainous regions. The reindeer in northern Finland, Norway, and Sweden have become major domestic animals that feed on the Arctic pastures of mosses, lichens, and shrubs.

REGIONAL CONTRASTS

The regional contrasts of Europe are related closely to its physical diversities. The geologic and environmental variations have been modified by people over history, which results in marked political, economic, and cultural differences. The physical environment sets the stage for human activity and often places limits on what people can do with the available climate, landforms, and natural resources. Urban landscapes have become dominant—especially in Western and Central Europe—as a result of the impact of the Industrial Revolution.

Western Europe

Western Europe is the urban, industrial core of the continent. It is dominated by the three major powers of the United Kingdom, West Germany, and France but also includes the Benelux countries (Belgium, The Netherlands, and Luxembourg), Switzerland, and Austria. These nations have a large percentage of their population classified as urban. Economic activity has been dominated by manufacturing, but service industries have grown rapidly since 1960.

Western Europe has a number of assets that have resulted in high levels of productivity. With the exception of Austria, all European countries have direct access to world ocean transportation. The countries bordering the North Sea form one of the major international trade generating areas of the world. The navigable rivers flowing into the North Sea, especially the Rhine, facilitate the movement of goods in and out of Western Europe. The level land aided the development of rail and highway transportation and the building of canals. The region has abundant coal and iron ore, the basic raw materials for the Industrial Revolution, but petroleum had to be largely imported until 1970. Streams flowing out of the Alps provide waterpower. The highlands are also sources of forest products. The marine conditions provide a reliable climate with a long growing season for crop and livestock production. These advantages are capped by the skills, education levels, and abilities of the people. The result is the most productive region in Europe and one of the most productive in the world.

Eastern Europe

The countries in the corridor of land between the Baltic Sea on the north and the Adriatic and Black seas on the south make up Eastern Europe. East Germany and Poland largely occupy part of the glaciated plains. Czechoslovakia, Hungary, Romania, Yugoslavia, Albania, and Bulgaria are split between the mountains and highlands associated with the Alpine system and the river valleys and structural basins between the highlands. The two major rivers of the region are the Vistula in Poland and the Danube in the south.

Six of the countries for some 40 years after World War II were in the Soviet realm as satellites. Yugoslavia and Albania stayed relatively independent of the Soviet Union. Albania was aligned with China from 1961 to 1978, and Yugoslavia was governed by an independent form of Communism developed under the leadership of Marshal Tito.

The major mineral resources in Eastern Europe are coal and iron ore on the border between Poland and Czechoslovakia, petroleum in Romania, and bauxite in Yugoslavia. East Germany is the leading industrial nation of the area. Manufacturing industries are growing throughout Eastern Europe with the exception of Albania. Wheat and corn are major products of the Danube Valley countries. Poland and East Germany have an agricultural system based largely on rye, potatoes, and livestock.

Northern Europe, or Norden

Northern Europe is often referred to as Scandinavia, but this term technically covers only the Scandinavian peninsula countries of Norway and Sweden. The Fennoscandian Shield is a geologic term that refers to the old, resistant, crystalline basement rock of the area that extends from the Kola Peninsula of the Soviet Union westward through Finland, Sweden, and Norway to the northern portion of Scotland. The people of Northern Europe have adopted Norden, which simply means the "north," as the preferred term for their area. Norden includes Denmark, Finland, Norway, Sweden, and Iceland.

The Norden countries have much in common physically and culturally, but there are also major differences. Norway, Sweden, and Finland are part of the geologically old Northwest Highlands. The river valleys draining into the Baltic Sea and into Skagerrak

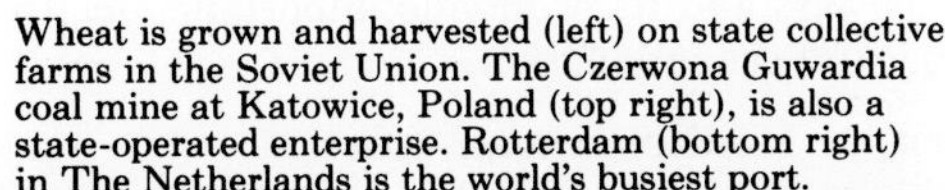

Wheat is grown and harvested (left) on state collective farms in the Soviet Union. The Czerwona Guwardia coal mine at Katowice, Poland (top right), is also a state-operated enterprise. Rotterdam (bottom right) in The Netherlands is the world's busiest port.

TASS—Sovfoto; (top right) Cameramann International;
m right) Eric Carle—Shostal Associates

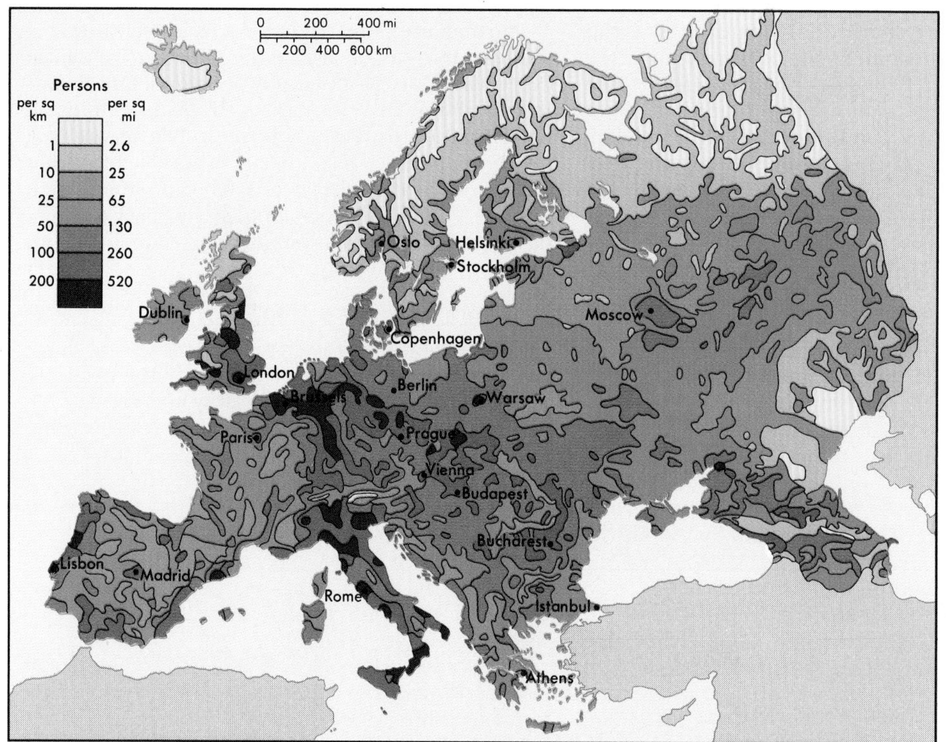

Population density of Europe

between the Baltic and North seas are gentle and produce much hydroelectric power. The streams to the west are short and swift with frequent falls. The west coast of Norway has many beautiful fjords with sheer cliffs and narrow, deep, drowned valley bottoms. The result of severe continental glaciation in Norden is a rocky, often barren, inhospitable, unproductive, and lake-dotted landscape.

The area is sparsely populated compared to the rest of Europe. Most people live along the coast or in the river valleys. Agriculture, fishing, forestry, and mining are the major occupations. Manufacturing has developed rapidly since 1900 based on available hydroelectric power.

Denmark and the southern tip of Sweden are part of the European Lowlands. Glacial hills provide the only relief in these areas. Dairying and crop agriculture are intense on the fertile soil of the eastern islands of Denmark. The western part of the Jutland peninsula of Denmark is sandy, infertile, and less productive. Copenhagen is the major Danish industrial and commercial center. Iceland, a largely volcanic island in the North Atlantic, has fishing, sheep grazing, and food processing as the major economic activities.

Culturally the Norden countries have strong historical ties. The languages and racial characteristics are Germanic except for the Finns and Lapps, who originated in Central Asia. The Lutheran state religion dominates, and the governments are socialist democracies with figurehead monarchies in Norway, Sweden, and Denmark. The region is a strategic area both in terms of its geopolitical location on air and sea polar routes between the Soviet Union and the Western powers and its economic importance in its oil and natural gas production.

Southern, or Mediterranean, Europe

The countries that occupy the three peninsulas—Iberian, Italian, and Balkan—jutting into the Mediterranean Sea make up Southern Europe. They are separated from the rest of Europe by the Pyrenees, Alps, Pindus, and Rhodope mountains. Italy, Greece, and European Turkey are in an unstable geological area with frequent volcanic eruptions and earthquakes. Spain and Portugal occupy a large, high, dry plateau that is separated from areas of similar geologic age in France by the Pyrenees. Until the 1600s, when Western civilization shifted to Western Europe, the centers of Europe and the world were the Mediterranean countries. Political and economic power shifted from Mesopotamia to Greece, to Rome, and lastly to Spain and Portugal. After 1600 Southern Europe did not possess the physical and economic resources for leadership in a world that was becoming increasingly industrialized. The Industrial Revolution largely passed by these countries until the second half of the 20th century, when they broadened and strengthened their economies. Agriculture remains a major occupation throughout the area.

The area has many problems. The excessive slopes and poor soil of the predominantly hilly and mountainous topography limit agricultural productivity.

The lack of water, especially during the dry summer, is a problem throughout Mediterranean Europe. Agricultural techniques and mechanization lag behind those of Western Europe. Raw materials for industry are limited, especially the basics of coal, iron ore, and petroleum. Greece, Italy, Spain, and Portugal have been subject to political instability throughout much of their history. Economic development is spotty. Certain areas are highly developed such as northern Italy, the Costa del Sol of Spain, and the major cities of Lisbon, Madrid, Barcelona, Rome, Naples, and Athens. Rural, southern Italy, northern Portugal, and mountainous Greece typify very poor areas.

Soviet Europe

Soviet Europe consists of a large, relatively flat, stable, geologic plateau. It is bordered on the south by the Black Sea, Caucasus Mountains, and Caspian Sea; on the east by the Ural Mountains; and on the north by the Barents and Baltic seas. Continental glaciation has left its imprint of frequent lakes, glacial ridges, and disrupted drainage systems on the northern half of the region. The area north of the Caspian Sea is among the driest, most unproductive areas in Europe. The area north of the Black Sea, the Ukraine, is the most important wheat growing area of the Soviet Union and also produces sugar beets, potatoes, and livestock. The growing season shortens to the north, making crop agriculture more and more difficult. There are, however, excellent commercial forests. The state collective farm system dominates throughout.

Mass is celebrated behind the main altar at Saint Peter's Basilica in Rome.

J. Ehlers—Bruce Coleman Inc.

Cameramann International

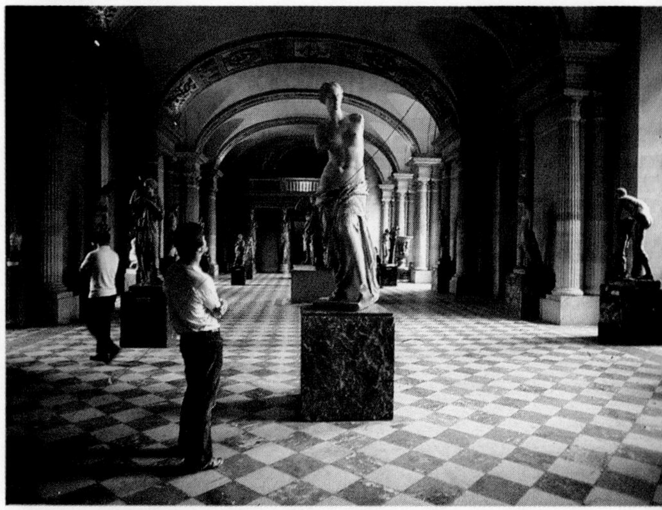

The Venus de Milo is one of the many great works of art on display at the Louvre in Paris.

Soviet Europe contains nine of the 15 union republics and part of a tenth—the large Russian Soviet Federated Socialist Republic that also covers much of Siberia. Soviet Europe is rich in coal, iron ore, petroleum, and natural gas. The major urban-industrial regions are in the Ukraine, the Moscow region, the Ural Mountains, and along the Volga River. Perhaps as much as 75 percent of the Soviet population of nearly 275 million lives in Soviet Europe. The region has a great variety of climatic, geologic, soil, mineral, and vegetation conditions on which the diverse economy is based. The economic and political power of the Soviet Union, much of which is located in Soviet Europe, derives from this great diversity of resources. The use of the resources, the nature of the economy, and the lives of the people are strictly controlled by the strong, central communist government.

PEOPLES AND CULTURES

The continent of Europe had nearly 700 million people in the mid-1980s, or about 15 percent of the world's population. Excluding the Soviet Union, the annual population growth rate is 0.4 percent, with many countries in Western and Northern Europe at or near zero population growth. Today the average birthrate is 14 and the death rate 9 per thousand. Europe's population is expected to grow at 0.3 percent per year for the rest of the 20th century. The average population density for the continent is 168 per square mile (65 per square kilometer). Comparable figures for Norden are 129 (50), Western Europe 396 (153), Southern Europe 277 (107), and Eastern Europe 293 (113). This compares to an average of 88 people per square mile (34 per square kilometer) for the world and 65 (25) for the United States.

Moscow State University (far left), founded in 1755, is the largest institution of higher learning in the Soviet Union. Oxford University's Christ Church College (left) in England was founded in 1546. The university itself dates from the 12th century.

(Far left) Sovfoto; (left) Rod Williams—Bruce Coleman Inc.

Over the thousands of years of settlement in Europe the peoples have been so mixed that it is virtually impossible to find pure racial types. Most of Europe's peoples, however, are fair skinned, or Caucasoid.

Racial and Ethnic Types

There are only small differences in shape of head, stature, and color of skin, hair, and eyes as compared to the peoples of other continents such as Africa and Asia. Some major characteristics and geographic distributions of racial and ethnic types can be identified, however. Fair-skinned people of the Nordic subrace predominate around the Baltic and North seas—in Norden countries, northern Germany and Poland, the Soviet republics on the Baltic Sea, The Netherlands, the east coast of Great Britain, Iceland, eastern Ireland, and portions of the northern European Soviet Union. The largest number of fair-skinned people are found in Denmark, Norway, and Sweden. The people of these areas are also generally tall, averaging more than 5 feet 10 inches (178 centimeters), and have a narrow or oblong head.

Members of the Mediterranean subrace—located in the Iberian Peninsula, southern Italy, the Balkan Peninsula, southern France, and Wales—generally have darker skin color and brown to dark brown hair and eyes. They are also short in stature and tend to have broader head shapes.

Central Europe is a transition zone between the predominantly darker-skinned people to the south and the lighter types to the north. The stature, size, complexion, and head characteristics are a blend of the Nordic and Mediterranean subraces. Exceptions may be found to these broad generalizations. The Lapps in Northern Europe are darker skinned, shorter in stature, and have a broader head shape than their Scandinavian neighbors. Many individuals throughout Europe do not fit the racial generalizations of their region.

Language

The 50 to 60 languages spoken in Europe fall into the two classifications of Indo-European and Ural-Altaic. Germanic, Slavic, and Romance are the three major linguistic groups within Indo-European, but Greek, Albanian, Celtic, and Baltic are also included. The Germanic group includes German, English, Norwegian, Swedish, Danish, Icelandic, Dutch, and Flemish. The Slavic languages include Russian, Ukrainian, Polish, Czech, Slovak, Serbo-Croatian, Bulgarian, and Macedonian. The Romance group, which descended from Latin, is made up of Italian, French, Portuguese, Spanish, Walloon, Romanian, Romansch, and Provençal. Celtic remains as a language in the Breton peninsula (Brittany) of France as well as in Wales, western Ireland, and northwestern Scotland.

Ural-Altaic languages are principally used by the Lapps, Finns, Karelians, Estonians, and Hungarians, or Magyars. Turkic, another Ural-Altaic language found mainly in Asia, is spoken by scattered groups in Balkan Europe. Maltese on the island of Malta and Basque on the French-Spanish border are two other languages used by small groups of people in distinct regions.

During the nationalistic period in the 1800s, attempts were made to adjust political boundaries to include a distinct language and culture within a given country. This has not been successful. Belgium, for example, is nearly equally divided between the Walloons and the Flemish. The large postwar movement of people into Western Europe introduced new languages such as Turkish in West Germany. Many

Europeans are fluent in more than one language, especially those in the small countries in which English, French, German, or Spanish is normally a must in daily activities in addition to their native tongue.

Religion

Three great religions believing in only one god spread from Southwest Asia to Europe in early historical times—Islam, Judaism, and Christianity. Islam, which was introduced temporarily by the Moors into the Iberian Peninsula, is now found only in Balkan Europe—particularly Albania, southern Yugoslavia, Bulgaria, and European Turkey. The Jewish religion is scattered throughout Europe—particularly in the larger cities of Central and Eastern Europe, including the Soviet Union. Jews were greatly decreased in numbers by the genocidal policy of Germany during World War II. Those remaining in communist Eastern Europe and the Soviet Union have experienced postwar difficulties in continuing to practice their religion. Only New York City, however, contains more Jews than the city of Moscow.

Most Europeans are influenced by one of the three major divisions of Christianity—Roman Catholicism, Eastern Orthodoxy, and Protestantism. Roman Catholics are greatest in number and geographic spread. They are dominant in the Iberian Peninsula, Italy, France, southern Belgium, Ireland, southern West Germany, and from Lithuania and Poland to northern Yugoslavia. Eastern Orthodox Christianity follows the leadership of the ecumenical patriarch of Constantinople (Istanbul). The split into two separate churches in 1054 has been a factor separating the peoples of Eastern and Western Europe since that date. The Eastern Orthodox church is not as highly organized as the Roman church, and the influence of the patriarchate is not as effective as that of the Vatican. The communist governments of Eastern Europe do not encourage or support religious activities.

Protestantism is the dominant religion in Northern Europe—northern East and West Germany, Scandinavia, The Netherlands, and the United Kingdom. Protestant churches grew in the 1500s and 1600s as a protest against Roman Catholicism. Martin Luther in Germany was a major contributor to the split of Protestants from Rome. Lutheranism in Scandinavia and Germany, Presbyterianism in Scotland, Anglicanism in England, and the Dutch Reformed church in The Netherlands are major Protestant subgroups.

Religious movements in Europe have been significant in preserving and spreading alphabets, culture, agricultural technologies, and political, economic, and social ideas throughout the continent. Europe's history is very much tied to the religious character of various time periods and of different parts of the continent. The traditional role of religion has been weakened by government actions such as the communist-controlled nations discouraging religion and governments assuming financial support for churches as in Scandinavia. The rise of affluence in Europe also seems to have lessened interest in religion.

Art and Literature

The artistic and literary heritage of Europe is extremely rich and has had a major impact on the rest of the world. Prehistoric art has been found well preserved in caves of southern France and northern Spain. In early historical times the Greeks developed systems of philosophy, the beginnings of science, various kinds of literary expression such as the poems of Homer, and new architectural types. The Romans provided the Latin language, Roman law, an architectural vocabulary, and the art and architecture of Rome and cities throughout the empire.

As the center of civilization shifted to Western Europe in the 1600s, the influence of this region in art and literature grew rapidly. The printing press developed in Europe in the 15th century, aiding greatly the spread of literature and culture. The concentration of more and more people in cities as a result of the Industrial Revolution, the advance of educational systems, and the ability of more Europeans to read and write increased the market for books.

Almost every region in Europe is known for its writers, musicians, actors, and artists. The schools of literature, drama, and art that developed are major influences throughout the world. The opera, symphony, and ballet had their origins in Europe. The Dutch, French, Italians, Spanish, Flemish, and others have all had periods that produced such painters as Rembrandt and Van Gogh. Such composers in Germany as Bach, Beethoven, and Brahms and Austrians Haydn and Mozart had monumental importance in the music world. European literary contributions are too numerous to summarize adequately. Such names as Homer, Dante, Goethe, Shakespeare, Shaw, and Tolstoi stand out.

The innovative abilities of Europeans in the arts and in literature continue and are greatly affected by the free flow of people and ideas. The mixture and movement of people and ideas have been accelerated by wars, changing economic and political conditions, and the voluntary movement of large numbers in search of better employment opportunities and improved lives. Thus new artistic and literary thrusts are constantly evolving. The great works of the past are well preserved in the countless museums, cathedrals, palaces, private homes, and libraries of Europe as well as in private and public collections elsewhere throughout the world.

Health and Education

Europe is a world leader in high standards of health and education. The standards are somewhat lower in Southern and Eastern Europe than in the Western and Northern parts of the continent. The ability to read and write is virtually universal among the population of Northern and Western Europe. Life expectancy at birth in the mid-1980s ranged from 69 to 79 years for the total European population and reached a high of 81 for females in Switzerland. The daily caloric intake is among the highest in the world—with an average of 3,500 calories per day per person—as is the number of physicians and nurses per population. Most European countries have national health insurance plans that provide health care for all residents.

The primary, secondary, and higher education systems are well developed. The proportion of children between the ages of 6 and 11 enrolled in primary school is nearly 100 percent in all countries. Enrollment of those eligible for secondary and higher education varies considerably within Europe but was generally low until after World War II. As countries began to subsidize secondary school and university education, the numbers greatly increased. In the 1980s Sweden had 38 percent of its population of ages 20 to 24 enrolled in institutions of higher education; East and West Germany, 30 percent each; the United Kingdom, 19; Poland, 18; and Albania, 6. Comparable figures for the Soviet Union were 21 and for the United States, 58. In almost all countries increases from 1965 to 1982 were significant.

Education in the Soviet Union and Eastern Europe was designed to promote the virtues of Communism until the Communist parties lost their constitutionally guaranteed controls. The governments in Eastern Europe pay the costs of primary education as well as education at secondary and higher levels.

Universities were first begun in Europe during the Middle Ages by groups of students who had similar interests. Examples of well-known institutions of higher learning are in Cambridge, Oxford, London, Edinburgh, Paris, Leipzig, Vienna, Heidelberg, Moscow, Warsaw, and Leiden.

ECONOMY

The Industrial Revolution, which began in England and spread to Western Europe, changed the leading economic activity from agriculture to manufacturing. Fortunately the continent possessed large amounts of coal and iron ore, which were necessary for the basic metal and chemical industries that dominated early manufacturing in Western Europe. Waterpower was available in addition to coal as an energy source. Europe was poor in petroleum, but its location made importing from the Middle East and other producing areas relatively easy. Raw materials not available in Europe were obtained from other countries and from colonial territories scattered throughout the world.

The highest per capita gross national product (GNP) in the late 1980s was in Switzerland, with $21,250. The lowest GNP was in Albania, with $880. Western Europe's lowest GNP was $2,890, in Portugal; the highest in Eastern Europe was $12,430 in East Germany.

Post–World War II economic development in Europe was facilitated by regional economic and political organizations. These integrating organizations helped offset the small size of countries that resulted from the nationalistic movements of the 19th century. In Western Europe the union that became the Benelux Economic Union was formed during the war to integrate the economies of three small political units—Belgium, The Netherlands, and Luxembourg. This idea was enlarged upon in 1952 when the European Coal and Steel Community (ECSC) was established. France was the major promoter, but it also included Belgium, The Netherlands, Luxembourg, West Germany, and Italy. In 1957 the European Economic Community (EEC), or Common Market, was established, with the same ECSC members agreeing to the terms of the Treaty of Rome. The European Atomic Energy Community (Euratom) was also formed in 1957.

The three communities merged in 1967 as the European Communities (EC), which from 1986 included Belgium, The Netherlands, Luxembourg, the United Kingdom, West Germany, France, Italy, Denmark, Ireland, Greece, Spain, and Portugal (*see* European Communities). The EC agreement promotes "harmonious development of economic policies" by eliminating trade barriers, allowing free flow of labor, and developing other measures to facilitate economic cooperation among the 12 member countries. A single European market with open borders is expected by 1992. Plans for economic and monetary union, a single European currency, and a central bank are being laid for the future.

The remaining Western European countries are members of the European Free Trade Association (EFTA)—Austria, Finland, Iceland, Norway, Sweden, and Switzerland. These countries follow neutrality policies that prevent their joining the EC or have decided not to join, such as Norway and Iceland.

In Eastern Europe, under pressure from the Soviet Union, the Council for Mutual Economic Assistance (CMEA), known unofficially as Comecon, was set up in 1949 to facilitate trade agreements and economic cooperation between the Soviet Union and its satellite countries. Yugoslavia is an observer nation, and Finland has a cooperation agreement with the CMEA. Albania has been inactive since 1961. The organization has closely integrated the economies of Eastern Europe with that of the Soviet Union. With the upheaval in Eastern Europe and the breakup of the Soviet bloc, the CMEA was faced with the prospect of eventual disbandment. The EC was also confronted with the question of the possible membership of some Eastern European nations in the EC and the creation of a united Europe.

Urban-Industrial Dominance

The village and the city are the dominant settlement types in Europe. Scattered or isolated farmsteads are found only in Northern Europe, parts of the British Isles, The Netherlands, and some mountainous areas. Urban development grew rapidly during the Roman period. Ancient Rome was estimated to have reached a population of 1 million people with well-developed water distribution, sewers, roads, and other facilities.

Urban growth declined in the Dark Ages but was begun again by the traders of the Middle Ages. The Industrial Revolution was the major stimulus to urban growth after 1800. Manufacturing became the major economic activity in most cities. The great need for labor drew many people from rural areas to the city.

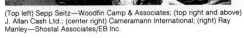

(Top left) Sepp Seitz—Woodfin Camp & Associates; (top right and above) J. Allan Cash Ltd.; (center right) Cameramann International; (right) Ray Manley—Shostal Associates/EB Inc.

The modern Pompidou Center in Paris (top left) contrasts dramatically with its surroundings. The quiet Greek fishing village of Anoja on Crete (top right) has picturesque whitewashed buildings. The city of Rothenburg, West Germany (center right), is a living museum. The walled city of Dubrovnik, Yugoslavia (bottom right), is both a port and seaside resort. The outdoor market (above) is at Cluj, Romania.

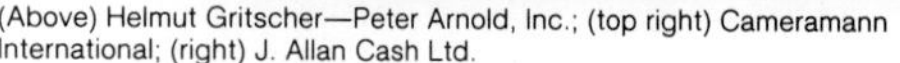

(Above) Helmut Gritscher—Peter Arnold, Inc.; (top right) Cameramann International; (right) J. Allan Cash Ltd.

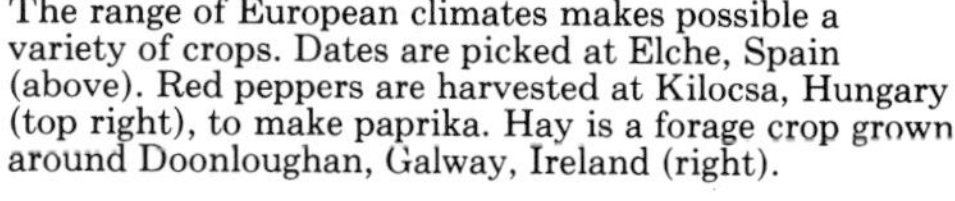

The range of European climates makes possible a variety of crops. Dates are picked at Elche, Spain (above). Red peppers are harvested at Kilocsa, Hungary (top right), to make paprika. Hay is a forage crop grown around Doonloughan, Galway, Ireland (right).

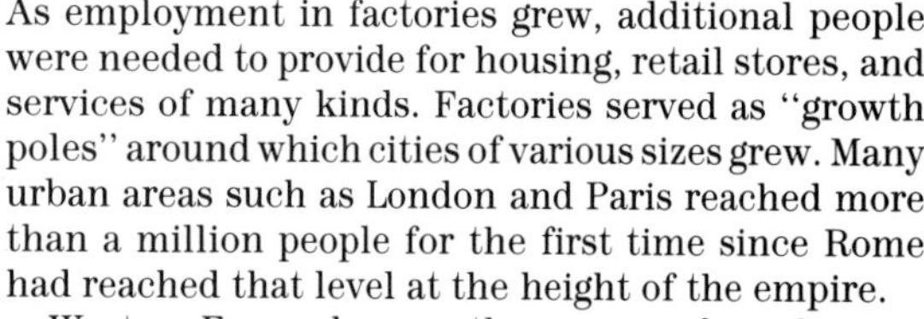

As employment in factories grew, additional people were needed to provide for housing, retail stores, and services of many kinds. Factories served as "growth poles" around which cities of various sizes grew. Many urban areas such as London and Paris reached more than a million people for the first time since Rome had reached that level at the height of the empire.

Western Europe became the core area for industrial Europe based on the rich coal mines of the United Kingdom, the Ruhr area of Germany, northern France, and southern Belgium. Abundant iron ore was also available in the Lorraine area of northeastern France. Labor, capital, raw materials, food, a central location, and both water and land transportation facilitated the rapid industrial growth. The outer, or peripheral, regions of Europe provided raw materials such as minerals, fish, food, and forest products for the factories and urban population of the core region. These peripheral areas were also markets for the manufactured products of Western Europe.

Russia and Eastern Europe followed with urban-industrial developments in the 1900s, utilizing the abundant coal, iron ore, and petroleum that were locally available. Cities such as Moscow, Saint Petersburg (now Leningrad), Kiev, Khar'kov, and Yekaterinburg (now Sverdlovsk) grew to be major industrial, commercial, and government centers. Urban centers in Eastern Europe grew more rapidly after World War II under communist economic planning.

The cities of Europe are different from those in the United States primarily because they are much older. They were built before the railroad and the automobile. The major characteristics of the European city are: a low profile with buildings of three to six stories except for recent tall buildings in large cities; compact form so that they could be more easily defended; the dominance of multiple family, or apartment, residences; many people living and working downtown; frequent outdoor markets; city centers dominated by public squares with churches and government buildings; many downtown public parks; lack of wood as a building material; few areas of slums; large use of public transportation; and narrow, winding side streets.

Most countries in Europe classify more than 50 percent of their populations as urban. In the mid-1980s there were only two exceptions—Portugal with 30 percent and Albania with 38 percent. The United Kingdom with 91 percent and East Germany with 77 percent are the most urban in West and East, respectively. The percentage of urban population is closely related to the degree of industrialization.

Agriculture

As manufacturing and industry increased during the Industrial Revolution, the percentage of the labor force employed in agriculture markedly decreased, especially in Western Europe. Rural manpower was drawn to higher-paying occupations in urban areas, and mechanization and scientific methods developed that required less labor for greater agricultural productivity. Agriculture also changed to meet the food needs of the densely populated cities by placing more emphasis on horticulture, market gardening, and cash crops and less on subsistence-type agriculture that produced food primarily for large farm families.

The percentage of the labor force employed in agriculture in the 1980s ranged from 2 to 18 percent in Western Europe, with the United Kingdom lowest and Ireland highest. In Southern Europe percentages were higher, with 37 percent in Greece, 28 in Portugal, 14 in Spain, and 11 in Italy. Albania was the most rural in Eastern Europe with 61 percent. East Germany was lowest with 10 percent. The Soviet Union had 14 percent, and most of the rest of Eastern Europe averaged in the 30s and 40s.

Despite decreases in the number of farmers, agricultural productivity has been maintained or even increased. In part this results from subsidies provided by governments that artificially support prices for such products as milk, wheat, and potatoes. The price support goal is to assure the availability of certain kinds of farm products and to increase income in the agricultural sector, thus helping assure the continuance of the family farm.

The structure of farm holdings also changed. Farms increased in size to facilitate the use of machinery. Farm holdings were consolidated by government programs in such places as West Germany, France, and the Benelux countries. Inheritance systems over the years had split fields into smaller and smaller plots, which were often not contiguous and were difficult to farm and to utilize machinery. Large state farms and collective farms dominate Soviet and Eastern Europe with the exception of Yugoslavia and Poland.

The degree of farming success is closely related to the nature of climate, soil, and topography. The best yields, often the highest in the world, are found in Western Europe, where moderate temperatures, adequate moisture, and a long growing season combine with high levels of scientific agriculture. The extensive lowland areas generally have productive soils, though sandy, unproductive soils exist in many places. The emphasis in Western Europe is on livestock and dairying, as growing conditions are favorable for pasture and fodder crops. The needs of a large urban market caused a considerable change from livestock to cash crops such as wheat, horticultural crops, and vegetables.

Eastern Europe and the European Soviet Union have much less reliable precipitation, but the higher summer temperatures allow the successful growth of corn (maize) and spring wheat. Average yields are lower than in Western Europe from less scientific agriculture and less reliable natural conditions. The system of state farms and collective farms also lessens private initiative and results in lower productivity.

Southern Europe specializes in fruits and vegetables, often irrigated, as a result of the dry, subtropical, Mediterranean climate. Dry summers make irrigation necessary in the lowlands for successful crop farming. Sheep and goats are common animals in the hilly topography with marginal conditions for crop agriculture. Many farms are small, which makes successful farming difficult. Much land held in large estates by wealthy landowners is often not managed well.

Fishing is one of Europe's major industries. Women of Póvoa de Varzim, Portugal, examine the day's catch (below) at an open market. Caviar is canned on a floating cannery (right) on the Volga River in the Soviet Union.

J. Allan Cash Ltd.

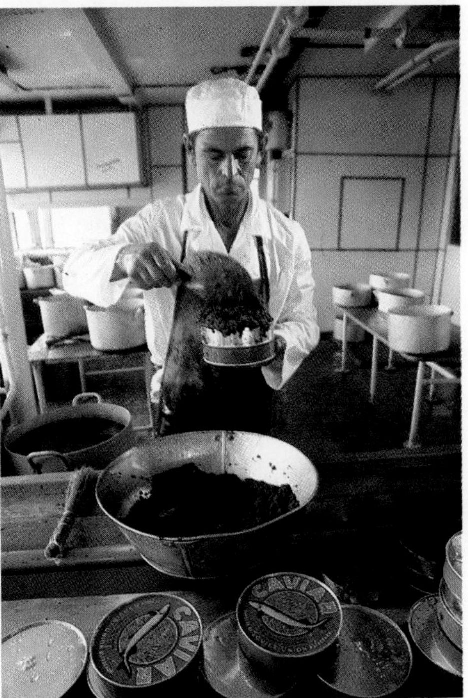

Jonathan T. Wright—Bruce Coleman Inc.

(Left) Hubertus Kanus—Shostal Associates; (right) TASS—Sovfoto

Europe is rich in mineral resources. Kiruna, Sweden (left), is between two mountains of iron ore. Manganese ore is delivered to a concentrating mill (right) in the Chiatura fields of the Georgian Soviet Socialist Republic.

The problems of consolidation of fields and small farms, the production based on subsidy rather than market demand, the continuing movement of farm labor to the cities, the increased cooperative development of agriculture both in Western and Eastern Europe, and the agricultural role of regional organizations such as the EC and CMEA are still in the process of solution. Throughout Europe agriculture remains important for food and employment as well as in the use of land. More than 90 percent of the total area in West Germany, Benelux, and the United Kingdom is in agricultural land.

Fishing

The disrupted, peninsular nature of Europe provides many nations with easy access to nearby bodies of water. Thus it is natural that fishing became a major occupation. About 30 percent of the world's fish catch in the mid-1980s came from nations bordering the Mediterranean, North, Baltic, Norwegian, and Barents seas.

The fishing fleets of these nations have become increasingly efficient in catching and processing their catch. The Soviet Union, Poland, and East Germany have developed a worldwide fishing industry with the aid of specialized equipment, including trawlers and fish processing factories on vessels at sea. The Soviet Union is the leading fishing nation of the world, followed by the United States, Chile, Peru, and Norway. Cod and herring are caught in the largest quantities by European fishermen. Fish products are the principal exports from Iceland.

The significance of fishing to Norway has dropped greatly with the development of petroleum and gas in the North Sea. The fishing industry not only feels the economic competition of offshore oil and gas production but also faces pollution threats that may affect fish reproduction. The extension of territorial waters to 200 miles aids in the control of coastal fishing grounds by such countries as Norway, Iceland, and the United Kingdom, but the legality of this zone is still controversial.

Forestry

Throughout history forests have given way to agriculture, cities, and other needs of increasing populations. It is estimated that four fifths of Europe was once forest covered, of which two thirds has been removed during the long settlement process. Forest destruction is especially severe in the Mediterranean region and the intense urban-industrial core of Western Europe. The best commercial forests are found in the taiga, or coniferous forest zone, of Northern Europe and on the flanks of the mountains, especially the Alps. Reforestation is being promoted in certain poor, sandy soil areas such as the Jutland peninsula of Denmark and the sand dune coast of southwestern France. The leading producers of forest products are Soviet Europe, Sweden, France, West Germany, Finland, and Norway.

Minerals

The variety of mineral resources has been a key to Europe's successful economic development. Abundant coal and iron ore contributed to the Industrial Revolution. Soviet Europe, Poland, the United Kingdom, West Germany, Czechoslovakia, France, and Spain are the leading European coal producers. Soviet Europe, Sweden, France, Spain, and Norway provide iron ore. Copper, zinc, lead, bauxite, potash, sulfur, silver, and gold are also mined in a number of European countries. The Soviet Union is the leading world producer of manganese, an alloy used in hardening steel. European mining activities are increasingly faced with the difficulties of depth, heat, flooding, poisonous gases, and antiquated equipment.

Energy Resources

Until the petroleum and natural gas developments in the North Sea, industrial Western Europe imported most of its petroleum needs from other continents. Prior to 1970 the Soviet Union and Romania were the only European countries producing enough oil and natural gas to supply their needs and have surpluses to export to others. The recent finds in the North Sea have added Norway and the United Kingdom to the surplus producers. The natural-gas field in the northern Netherlands has supplied both local needs and surpluses to neighboring countries since 1950. Italy is also a major producer of natural gas.

The discovery of petroleum and gas in the North Sea is one of the most significant finds in the world since the discoveries in the Middle East. The development of these resources may be able to supply as much as three fourths of Western Europe's needs.

The North Sea bottom was divided into sectors for exploration by international agreements reached from 1958 to 1972. The agreements were based on median lines between countries and resulted in the United Kingdom's and Norway's receiving the largest and most productive areas. Norway has additional offshore continental shelf along its west coast in the Barents Sea and around the Svalbard island group that may supply future riches.

The North Sea and other offshore areas, however, face many problems such as increasing costs in deeper waters, the high winds and cold of a rigorous climate, sufficient and safe offshore living space for labor, transportation costs, and increasing costs for exploration and production platforms and other equipment. But the North Sea energy source is ideally located to help supply the needs of the densely populated and heavily industrial Western Europe.

Soviet Europe also has major petroleum and natural-gas producing regions. These include the Baku field on the flanks of the Caucasus Mountains, the Caspian Sea borderlands, and central and northern Soviet Europe. The Soviet Union produces 22 percent of the world's crude oil, much of which comes from the European part of the country. Pipelines supply oil and gas to Eastern Europe, and Soviet natural gas now reaches West Germany by pipeline. Oil and natural gas have replaced coal as a major energy source.

The mountainous topography and the damming of rivers made possible considerable amounts of hydroelectric energy. Almost all of Norway's electric energy is generated from waterpower. Hydroelectric power is produced from dams in rivers originating in the mountains of France, Switzerland, Austria, Italy, Sweden, Finland, Yugoslavia, Spain, and Portugal. In the European Soviet Union, waterpower is created by huge dams on the major rivers flowing southward into the Black and Caspian seas such as at Dnepropetrovsk on the Dnepr River. Most European countries obtain some electric energy from nuclear plants. More than half of France's electricity comes from nuclear production.

Manufacturing and Services

As the modern industrial economy becomes more complex, increasing numbers of people are required in the service industries such as banking and financial services, personal professional services, the repair of mechanical equipment, and government services. When services in a nation become greater than manufacturing in terms of employment and value produced, a postindustrial economy is reached (*see* Industry). Much of Europe has become postindustrial since 1965, particularly Western Europe. Sweden had the highest percentage, with 61 percent of its labor force employed in services in the early 1980s compared to 34 percent in industry and only 5 in agriculture. Most Western European countries average from 45 to 60 percent of their labor force in services and 35 to 45 percent in industry and manufacturing. In Southern and Eastern Europe, both services and manufacturing are relatively less important and agriculture is more important. The Soviet Union, East Germany, and Czechoslovakia all have a larger percentage of their labor force in manufacturing as compared to services.

Industry and services are the leading contributors to the Gross National Product (GNP) per capita in most European nations. The average for Western Europe was $11,992 GNP per capita in the mid-1980s; for Eastern Europe, including the Soviet Union, $3,654; in Northern Europe, $13,048; and in Southern Europe, $4,797. Using the measure of value added by manufacturing as an indicator of economic development, West Germany ranks fourth in the world behind the United States, the Soviet Union, and Japan.

The Western European manufacturing belt extends from the Scottish Lowlands and England across the English Channel to the Benelux countries, the Rhine and Ruhr valleys of West Germany, northern France, Switzerland, and northern Italy. These areas have changed from basic iron and steel and other so-called

An offshore oil rig in the North Sea off the coast of Eskovic, Norway, is one of many that help lessen Europe's dependence on Middle East petroleum.

D'Arazien—Shostal Associates

Cameramann International

A technician corrects a problem on a wool loom at the Crombie textiles plant in Scotland.

heavy industry to high-quality machine and metal products, textiles based mostly on artificial fibers, chemicals, appliances, and materials needed by the increasingly demanding population of Europe and the world. High-technology production is increasingly significant. The location of this kind of industry can be scattered, as it is dependent on the skill of workers rather than on heavy materials such as coal and iron ore. The overall emphasis is more on quality in order to make products that are competitive in world trade. The manufacturing of Northern Europe also emphasizes quality in processing the raw materials of the region, using cheap hydroelectric power. Major electrometallurgical and electrochemical industries have been developed.

Changes in industrial locations in Western Europe have resulted from the need to import large quantities of raw materials from the rest of the world, the removal of tariffs on goods flowing between EC countries, the large use of petroleum rather than coal as an energy source, and the attempts of governments to decentralize industry to less developed areas of countries. New steel mills and oil refineries, for instance, have been located along the coasts of Western Europe to take advantage of bringing in bulky raw materials by cheap and efficient ocean transportation. Electrical engineering and chemical manufacturing are examples of growth industries that depend primarily on electric power. This source of power allows dispersal of industry throughout Europe rather than concentrated locations when coal is used.

Eastern Europe is in earlier stages of industrialization. Here the more traditional industries are found such as food processing, textiles and clothing, basic iron and steel and metals industries, and those industries that satisfy local needs or that can find a market in the Soviet Union. Manufacturing in Eastern Europe is highly dependent on raw materials, equipment, energy, and capital as supplied by the Soviets. East Germany, Czechoslovakia, and Poland have emerged as industrial leaders in communist Eastern Europe, but manufacturing is increasing in other nations as well. In Soviet Europe the major industrial zones are: Donbas in the southern Ukraine, based originally on abundant local coal and iron ore; the central region focusing on Moscow, with diverse industries; the Ural Mountains, with an abundance of metal manufacturing; and the banks of the Volga River, based on water and land transport and local oil and gas resources for energy. The industrial emphasis in each of these regions changes as the Soviet Union develops resources and population concentrations in other parts of its vast empire. Also the needs of the people and the plans of the communist regime cause shifts in industrial locations.

In Southern Europe manufacturing is very spotty. The major cities stand out, along with northern Italy's Po Valley and northern Spain. The Mediterranean countries do not have the raw materials, energy resources, capital, and skilled labor to compete yet with Western Europe. Manufacturing is increasing in all countries, however, especially in Italy. Greece and Portugal have the lowest proportion of their labor forces in industry.

Tourism

Income from European and international tourists offsets unfavorable balances of trade in most European countries. The attractive scenery, combined with a long and fascinating historical heritage, provides numerous tourist attractions throughout the continent. An example is Switzerland, with its unsurpassed Alpine landscape combined with lakes, picturesque cities, historical buildings, and charming farming scenes on the populated central plateau. The Swiss have developed hotel, restaurant, and recreation site management to become a model for the world.

Europe has varied environments from subtropical to polar, each with its attraction for the tourist. Major cities—such as London, Paris, Copenhagen, Amsterdam, Vienna, Madrid, Rome, Athens, Budapest, and Moscow—attract millions of visitors and billions of dollars each year. In the EC countries about 9 percent

of the labor force, or 10 million people, are involved in tourism. There are some negative effects of rapid tourism growth. These include such things as pollution of lakes and rivers, overcrowding of beach areas, and misuse of rural, mountainous, and scenic land by increasing numbers of recreational visitors. Large numbers of foreigners also tend to change the culture of an area, often in an undesirable direction as far as local inhabitants are concerned.

Transportation and Communication

The dense population and high economic productivity created an early demand for a good transportation network, especially in industrial Western Europe. The small size of most European countries required a transport system to connect bordering and nearby countries. Individual governments provided financial support, and the short distances and relatively flat topography lessened costs of construction. Small-scale systems developed in each country or in regions rather than a single large, internationally integrated system. Europe's oceangoing vessels and a well-developed system of interconnected rivers and canals led to the best water transport system in the world. The railway mileage in Europe represents about one third of the world's total.

Automobiles on the roads of Western Europe in the early 1980s totaled 119 million. The tremendous rise in numbers of private automobiles, trucks, and buses has put great pressure on increasing the effectiveness of the highway system. The Germans had an excellent autobahn network built for military purposes in the 1930s. Most of the remainder of Europe's expressways were built after 1950. Roads in Western Europe now account for more than three quarters of the freight carried in that area and for more than 85 percent in Norden.

The number of automobiles has begun to increase in Eastern Europe, especially in Soviet Europe, East Germany, Czechoslovakia, and Poland. Trucks and buses are still more important than private cars in transporting people and goods in this part of Europe.

As automobiles, trucks, and buses increased, the role of railways decreased. Railroads are used to carry heavy commodities such as coal, iron ore, and bulky manufactured products throughout Europe. The mileage of rail lines has decreased, especially in Western Europe. Some high-speed express trains have been added such as those from Paris to Nice and the Trans-European Express from England to Italy. These fast trains, as well as commuter trains serving cities, have helped maintain railway passenger service.

Water transportation has also suffered in competition with highways and pipelines. The Rhine River system from Basel, Switzerland, to the North Sea is the major European waterway in terms of volume of traffic. It serves as a major artery for goods flowing into and out of the EC countries.

Air transport and pipelines are significant forms of transportation in Europe. Major airports in each country serve primarily passenger traffic but also mail and high-value, low-bulk products. Europe has become a focus for air traffic because of its large population, and it attracts business and tourist traffic from all over the world. The largest generators of air traffic are Soviet Europe, the United Kingdom, France, and West Germany, with their dominant airports at Moscow, London, Paris, and Frankfurt.

Pipelines have grown rapidly as the chief way of transporting oil and natural gas. Pipelines connect coastal refineries with inland consumer cities as well as coastal crude oil terminals to inland refineries. With the oil and gas developments in the North Sea after 1970, pipelines were built to bring these products ashore in Scotland, England, West Germany, and Norway. They are then distributed farther by pipeline to the consuming areas of Western Europe or by tanker to world destinations.

Both winter and summer resorts in Europe are popular. Skiers (left) glide along a glacier in the Stubai Alps of Austria, near Innsbruck. The beach at Messonghi, Corfu (right), is one of many in the Greek islands to which vacationers come to enjoy the Mediterranean climate.

(Left) Cameramann International; (right) Justin B. Ingram—Bruce Coleman Inc.

Thomas Hopker—Woodfin Camp and Associates

Barge traffic moves in both directions on the Rhine River in West Germany, while trains run along the shore.

In both Eastern and Western Europe, regional integration is an important consideration to more effective water, rail, highway, air, and pipeline transportation. The EC has as a major goal the development of a unified, effective, and viable transportation system within its member countries. The CMEA had the same objective in Eastern Europe.

Telephone, telegraph, radio, television, and newspaper communications are well developed throughout the continent. Newspaper circulation is high in all of Western Europe. In Eastern Europe Communist dailies are run by the party and speak for government policy. Independent opposition newspapers—permitted for the first time in the late 1980s as changes swept Eastern Europe—compete with the official party newspapers, outselling them in many cases.

INTERNATIONAL RELATIONS

European countries are major forces in world international relations. Europe is more politically fragmented than any other continent and therefore has many foreign policy systems in a small geographic area. This results from the nationalistic movements of the 1800s and the revising of national boundaries after World Wars I and II.

The political control that European countries once had over the rest of the world through colonies and empires is now virtually gone. There still exist, however, political and economic links that were established through colonialism. Regional economic and defense organizations have developed in both Western and Eastern European countries to offset the reduced size that resulted from political fragmentation. Much difference of opinion and many political policies exist throughout the continent. For 40 years the Soviet Union and the Communist party forced commonality in economic and defense policy in Eastern Europe, but this was not the case in the rest of the continent.

Europe is in an ideal central location for world trade. The excellent land and water transportation network also facilitates intra-European trade. Europe, including the Soviet Union, accounts for almost half of world exports and imports. European countries are major trading partners with almost every part of the world. The needs of Europe's dense population are far more than can be supplied by domestic production. Raw materials are imported, and Europe supplies finished manufactured products in return. Some of the major imports are petroleum from the Middle East, North Africa, and Nigeria; wool and cotton from Egypt, India, Australia, and the United States; wheat, corn (maize), meat, butter, and tea from Argentina, Canada, Australia, New Zealand, and India; and oils and other products from tropical Africa and Asia.

These trading patterns evolved from the former colonial relations of the British, French, Portuguese, Dutch, Spanish, and Belgians. Even after the end of colonialism, the countries that achieved self-government continued to trade with the European powers that had controlled them. Economic colonialism replaced political colonialism. Western Europe is a major supplier of manufactured products to the developing parts of the world. Europe also has major trading relations with the developed world. For example, in 1988 the United States sent 29 percent in dollar value of its exports to Europe, and 23 percent of its imports came from Europe.

Western Europe accounts for most of all European exports and imports. Eastern Europe and the Soviet Union provide only a small portion of Europe's exports and imports.

Intra-European trade is facilitated by the economic organizations created since World War II. The member countries of the EC have dominated the internal trade of Europe since the organization was formed (*see* European Communities). The EC has as its major objective free trade within a common market. Customs duties between nations have been eliminated or equalized. People, capital, and goods flow freely between countries in order to increase trade, improve employment opportunities, and raise standards of living. The EC countries' trading patterns are primarily with one another; secondarily with other industrial market economy countries, including the United States, New Zealand, Australia, Japan, and Canada; and finally with the developing countries of the world that supply raw materials and import manufactured products.

In the years between World War II and 1990, the Soviet Union dominated the trade of Eastern European countries through the CMEA. The Soviet Union provided petroleum and natural gas, iron and steel and other metal products, industrial equipment and machinery of all kinds, lumber, cotton, and arms. It received in turn wheat, corn (maize), and other raw materials as well as some manufactured products. The realignment of many Eastern European countries toward more market oriented economies in 1989 and 1990 ended the postwar methods of doing business based on their relationship with the Soviet Union. The changes brought up the possibility of their membership in an expanded EC.

HISTORY

Prehistoric people lived on the European continent as long ago as the Ice Age. With inconceivable slowness and pain they rose from savagery to barbarism. Civilization began to come from Egypt and Asia by way of the islands of the Aegean Sea in about 2000 BC. In time this flowered into the splendors of Greek and Roman culture. Europe's recorded history begins with these cultures. (*See also* Aegean Civilization; Civilization; Greece, Ancient; Man; Roman Empire.)

After centuries of progress and power, the Roman Empire was divided into two parts at the death of Theodosius the Great in AD 395. The Western Empire had Rome as its capital; the Byzantine, or Eastern, Empire had its capital at Constantinople, now called Istanbul (*see* Byzantine Empire). Beyond the boundaries of the Roman world were numerous barbaric peoples, divided into three main groups: remnants of the Celtic peoples in outlying parts of the British Isles; Germanic, or Teutonic, folk living along the Rhine and Danube rivers and in the Scandinavian peninsula; and the great mass of the Slavs, ancestors of the modern Poles, Russians, Czechs, Serbians, and others, whose tribes even then lived east of the Teutons.

Germanic Invasions of the Roman Empire

The Germanic barbarians were divided chiefly into Goths, Burgundians, Vandals, Alemanni, Bavarians, Langobards (Lombards), Franks, Angles, Saxons, and Frisians. The Gothic tribes (Visigoths and Ostrogoths) had been established along the shores of the lower Danube and the Black Sea for nearly 200 years. This region was invaded by the Huns from central Asia. Its inhabitants pushed westward, causing the great Gothic invasion of AD 375. Gaul was overrun chiefly by Visigoths, Burgundians, and Franks; Spain by Vandals, Suevi, and Visigoths; Africa by Vandals, crossing from Spain. Italy suffered a number of invasions, especially those of the Visigoths, Ostrogoths, and Lombards; Britain, after being abandoned by its Roman garrison in AD 410, became prey to Angles and Saxons sailing in their pirate vessels from their homes about the mouth of the Elbe River. The influence of Rome—its language, law, and government—left a stamp that has not yet been wholly effaced. (*See also* Goths; Huns; Lombards; Vandals.)

By 800 Charlemagne had consolidated the Germanic conquests into an empire that stretched from the Ebro River in Spain to beyond the Elbe and from the North Sea to a little south of Rome (*see* Charlemagne). The decline of classical civilization was checked. Something of the Roman tradition of unity, order, and centralization was preserved in the face of advancing feudalism. Christianity was spread through most of Western Europe. Islam was established in Spain after 711 and lingered there until the Moors were conquered in 1492 (*see* Moors).

Publix Pictorial Service Corp.

The ruins of the Colosseum, which was completed in AD 82, are a reminder of the "grandeur that was Rome." It was originally known as the Flavian Amphitheater.

Rise of Modern States

The division of the Frankish empire between Charlemagne's grandsons in the Treaty of Verdun (843) was the starting point of the kingdoms and nations of France and Germany. In 962, under Otto I, king of Germany, the empire in the West was revived with the title Holy Roman Empire. It included only Germany and Italy. Its power declined until its extinction in 1806. The Byzantine Empire fulfilled its function as a bulwark against Asian conquest and Islam until it was overwhelmed by the Ottoman Turks in the fall of Constantinople in 1453. On the lands of present-day Hungary lived the Asian Avars, whose place was taken in the 10th century by their kindred, the Magyars. Nothing but the little Kingdom of Asturias was left of the Gothic power in Spain. From this seed grew the Christian realms of Castile, León, and Aragon. They were consolidated in the 15th century into the kingdom of the Catholic sovereigns of Spain.

After raiding the coasts of all Western Europe in the 9th century, the Vikings established settlements in western France in 850. As Normans they gave a new dynasty to England (1066) and conquered Naples and Sicily. (*See also* Holy Roman Empire; Norman Conquest; Ottoman Empire; Vikings.)

Gradually the Capetian kings of France were able to reconstitute the unity of their kingdom and set it on a path of internal growth. In the 15th century, under Louis XI, it was the first strong monarchical state of modern times. The States of the Church were set up in Italy as the temporal dominion of the pope. Poland and Russia became settled Christian lands, and the heathen Prussians were Christianized and Germanized by the Teutonic Knights. Feudalism, Christianity, monasticism, and medieval art and learning spread. The Crusades, the growth of town life, and revived commerce helped prepare the way for that rebirth of the human spirit called the Renaissance. (*See also* Crusades; Feudalism; Middle Ages; Renaissance.)

The Castel Sant' Angelo in Rome was originally designed by Emperor Hadrian, who lived from AD 76 to 138, as his tomb. He also designed the bridge across the Tiber River leading to it. In the Middle Ages the tomb was rebuilt as a fortress and used by the popes in times of battle.

Wars of Religion and Conquest

The expedition of Charles VIII of France, in 1494, to assert his claim to inherit Naples and Sicily started a series of wars over Italy which embroiled France and Spain for a half century. The close of the conflict left Charles V, emperor of the Holy Roman Empire, ruler of united Spain and Germany and of Sardinia, Sicily and Naples, Milan, the Netherlands, the county of Burgundy (Franche-Comté), and a great part of the New World. His brother Ferdinand I, archduke of Austria and emperor and head of the German branch of the Hapsburgs, obtained by marriage Silesia, Bohemia, and that part of Hungary which had not fallen to the victorious Turks. The power of the Spanish Hapsburgs, under Charles's son, Philip II, and his successors, steadily declined. During these wars the Protestant Reformation, begun by Martin Luther, got such a strong start that it could not be stamped out by the Catholic rulers (*see* Reformation).

The Thirty Years' War (1618–48) between Catholic and Protestant rulers left the Holy Roman Empire greatly weakened and practically confined to Germany and Austria (*see* Thirty Years' War). France became again the first power of Europe. It had obtained much of the Burgundian lands (including Franche-Comté, conquered by Louis XIV). Savoy, straddling the French Alps, was becoming an Italian power. Spain still held the Spanish Netherlands (Belgium) and a great part of Italy. The Protestant Netherlands (Holland) and Switzerland had freed themselves by successful revolt from the empire. Sweden, independent of Denmark since 1523, was one of the great powers. It had conquered territories from Germany, Poland, and Russia. Denmark still ruled Norway. The Duchy of Prussia, united to the mark of Brandenburg in 1618, was soon (1701) to give its name to a new German kingdom erected by the military power of the Hohenzollerns.

Shifting Fortunes of the Nations

In the 16th century Poland (in union with Lithuania since 1569) was one of the most powerful states of Europe, stretching from the Baltic almost to the Black Sea. The 18th century saw its steady decline. Russia, under Peter the Great and Catherine II, became a formidable and disquieting power in the 18th century. Turkey, though decreased since its high-water mark of conquest in the 17th century, still retained the greater part of the former Eastern Empire. Venice held an extensive sway in the Adriatic and the eastern Mediterranean; and Genoa held Corsica until it passed to France in 1768.

Soon after the outbreak of the French Revolution in 1789, Poland ceased to exist, through partition by its greedy neighbors. Prussia had risen to the rank of a great power following the wars of Frederick the Great. Sweden had lost the leadership of northern Europe. The Spanish Netherlands had passed to Austria in 1713, at the close of the War of the Spanish Succession; and branches of the French House of Bourbon ruled the parts of Italy that had been Spanish, as well as Spain itself. England had become the head of a British Empire. Its people had originated the inventions which led to the Industrial Revolution. The "Mother of Parliaments" was the model to the world of constitutional government and political liberty during the first half of the 19th century.

French Revolution and Napoleonic Wars

The French Revolution and the wars of Napoleon I brought widespread changes in Europe (*see* French Revolution; Napoleon I). Napoleon's direct empire extended over Germany west of the Rhine, the Netherlands, northwestern Germany, and a great part of Italy and Dalmatia. In addition, his brother Joseph was king of Spain, his brother-in-law Joachim Murat sat on the throne of Naples, and the Grand Duchy of Warsaw and the Confederation of the Rhine were under rulers he chose.

After the fall of Napoleon at Waterloo in 1815, the Congress of Vienna forced France to retire within its old limits and in large part restored the old government. Russia was allowed to annex Finland from Sweden and to increase its Polish territories by absorbing the Grand Duchy of Warsaw. Prussia was enlarged. Austria was given northern Italy in exchange for Belgium, which was united with Holland. Norway was taken from Denmark and given to Sweden, with which it remained united until 1905. The German states (reduced from several hundred to 38, including Austria and Prussia) were organized into a loose union called the German Confederation.

The Holy Alliance and the Grand Alliance

In 1815 Czar Alexander I of Russia drafted a vague treaty, called the Holy Alliance, pledging the monarchs of Europe to take for their rule of conduct "only the Christian religion." More effective was the Grand, or Quadruple, Alliance, formed in the same year by Austria, Prussia, Russia, and Great Britain. (France was later admitted.) This had the purpose of preserving legitimate (meaning hereditary) government and the terms of the Vienna settlement.

This group of states dominated the Concert of Europe, the system whereby no important change might take place without the consent of these Great Powers. An accompanying principle, the *balance of power*, required that no one of the Great Powers should become strong enough to dominate the others.

Industrial Revolution and Growing Nationalism

No pressure of the Great Powers could permanently block change. The intense nationalism and hatred of absolute monarchs developed in France by the Revolution had spread. The Industrial Revolution inventions made factories and railroads possible. Wealth increased and the new industrial rich resented control by the landed nobility and demanded government protection of manufacturing and trade.

Yet for 30 years, under the leadership of Prince Metternich of Austria, the Great Powers preserved much of the Vienna settlement. In 1830 Belgium broke away from the Netherlands. France replaced its absolutist Bourbon king by a monarchy more favorable to business. The Concert broke a democratic revolt in Spain, and Russia put down a nationalist revolt in Poland. In 1848 a temporary republic was set up in France. In 1849 the king of Prussia and the Austrian emperor were forced to grant constitutions.

Again reaction triumphed. France submitted to the dictatorship of Napoleon III. The Frankfurt Assembly failed to prepare an acceptable German constitution. Austria suppressed a Hungarian rebellion and reconquered its Italian provinces.

New States and Limited Monarchies

For a half century nationalism developed—the political union of people with common racial, territorial, or emotional attachments (*see* Nation). France helped the Kingdom of Sardinia free the rest of Italy, which was then united into one kingdom. Otto von Bismarck, prime minister of Prussia, undertook three wars which drove Austria out of the German Confederation. He united the rest of the Germans in the German Empire under the rule of the king of Prussia.

The Turkish Empire in Europe gradually fell apart, and the Concert supervised the establishment of the small nations as they broke away—the Christian Balkan states of Greece, Serbia, Bulgaria, and Rumania. When Russia attempted to intervene in Turkey in 1853, the ensuing Crimean War (1854–56) forced Russia to submit to a settlement by the Concert.

Saint Mark's Basilica was first built in Venice, Italy, to shelter the saint's remains brought from Alexandria in 829. It was later reconstructed in the Byzantine style and lavishly decorated with colored marble sculptures, mosaics, precious metals, and inlaid gems. It is surmounted by five domes.

The principle of nationalism was sometimes violated. Bismarck, after the Franco-Prussian War (1870–71), annexed Alsace-Lorraine, with a largely French population, because German industry needed the region's iron and potash. In 1867, after its defeat by Prussia, Austria formed the dual monarchy of Austria-Hungary, making the people of a number of nationalities subject to these two.

Meanwhile, though the poorer classes were becoming more dependent economically on factory owners, they were gaining political freedom. In 1815 Great

Britain was still largely controlled by a few landowning families. Beginning in 1837 the right to vote was given to progressively larger groups of citizens, until by the time of World War I it was possessed by nearly all adult males. In 1911 the House of Lords lost its power to veto laws voted by the more democratic House of Commons. In 1870 Napoleon III was driven from the French throne, and a republic was set up. In Spain a revolt in 1868 against the despotic Queen Isabella succeeded, but the new democratic government failed to find another sovereign. Italy in the process of unification drove out the absolute monarchs formerly in control, substituting the democratic monarchs of the House of Savoy. The Scandinavian countries, The Netherlands, and Belgium lived under monarchs with strictly limited powers.

Ávila, a medieval walled city, was known to the Romans as Ávela. This ancient town lies on a hill above the Adaja River in the Castile-León region of Central Spain. It was often a battleground in the wars between Spaniards and Moors. Its walls, the best preserved of any city in Spain, were reconstructed from 1088 to 1091.

Colonies and Alliances

In the latter part of the 19th century the industrialists of the Great Powers were able to produce more than they could sell at home, and they also needed raw materials produced elsewhere. So they pushed their governments to seek colonies abroad rather than fight one another for European markets. Great Britain, France, and Germany conquered great colonial empires in Asia and Africa. Russia spread all the way across northern Asia. These empires came into contact, and friction developed.

From this situation developed an armaments race and systems of alliances that eventually broke up the Concert. Germany and Austria-Hungary, fearing Russia, formed an alliance. France and Russia, fearing Germany, did likewise. Italy, piqued at France, which blocked its African expansion, joined Germany and Austria in the Triple Alliance but wavered when France made concessions. Great Britain, though preferring to avoid continental alliances, feared Germany's growing navy and entered into the Triple Entente with France and Russia.

World War I

In 1912, against the wishes of the Concert, the Balkan States went to war to capture the Turkish territory inhabited by their nationals (*see* Balkans). Serbia, exulting in the ensuing victory, started propaganda for annexing Bosnia and Herzegovina, part of Austria-Hungary inhabited by Serbs.

The assassination of Francis Ferdinand, Austria's crown prince, in the Bosnian capital of Sarajevo, on June 28, 1914, was a result of this propaganda. Austria's determination to crush Serbia brought Russia, as protector of the Slavic states, to Serbia's side. The two systems of alliances then engulfed all Europe in World War I (*see* World War I).

The changes in Europe that resulted from the war were far-reaching. Old boundaries and political institutions disappeared, social classes rose and fell, and perplexing new economic problems appeared. The czar of Russia was killed and was replaced by a proletarian soviet system under the dictator Lenin. The emperors of Germany and Austria were dethroned, and republics were established. The sultan of Turkey was replaced by Atatürk, who was an army-supported dictator. Revolts of farmers in Eastern Europe broke up

Bruges, Belgium, is noted for its picturesque buildings, which reflect the era when it was a rich Hanseatic port and a wool manufacturing city. The canals that thread the town give it the nickname "Venice of the North."

Rothenburg, a 1,000-year-old city in Bavaria, is one of the most beautiful and best preserved of the medieval towns along West Germany's "romantic road" from the Main River to the Alps. The half-timber houses and the artistic ironwork signs are characteristic of the area.

the great estates into small farms and reduced the old agricultural nobility. Labor received new rights. England, Germany, Russia, and Poland gave women the vote. Subject peoples broke Austria-Hungary apart and tore pieces from western Russia.

Every government was deeply in debt. War taxes, property destruction estimated at 90 billion dollars, and the death of family wage earners had impoverished the people. Insolvent governments issued paper money, which in Germany and elsewhere lost all value and ruined those living on savings.

The Peace Treaties

The Paris Peace Conference attempted the task of reconstruction through a series of separate treaties with the defeated states. It was hoped that the Concert of Europe might be replaced by a democratic League of Nations, in which all states would be represented.

Otherwise the treaties embodied all the war's fears and hatreds. The Treaty of Versailles with Germany returned Alsace-Lorraine to France, took away Germany's colonies, disarmed Germany on land and sea and in the air, and forced it to make undetermined reparations payments for war damages.

The other defeated states were also disarmed. The treaties of Saint-Germain with Austria and Trianon with Hungary were based on the principle of nationalism. Poland achieved independence; Czechoslovakia and Yugoslavia were created; and Rumania and Italy received parts of the old Austro-Hungarian Empire. Bulgaria lost much territory through the Neuilly Treaty. The Ottoman Empire was almost completely dismembered by the Treaty of Sèvres, but Mustapha Kemal revolted and forced more favorable terms in the Treaty of Lausanne in 1923.

The Great Powers recognized by treaties the independence of the Baltic nations carved from Russia—Finland, Latvia, Lithuania, and Estonia—and of Poland, which was restored from fragments of Germany, Austria, and Russia.

Measures to Promote Peace

It was expected that the new League system would later remedy the injustices of the peace settlement and meet new political problems as they arose. In 1920 the Permanent Court of International Justice was set up at The Hague to settle legal disputes and to give opinions at the League's request. The League itself brought about peaceful arbitration of several quarrels between nations. In 1925 the major powers signed the Locarno Treaties, agreeing to maintain their existing frontiers and reaffirming their willingness to submit all disputes to the League. In the Kellogg-Briand Pact of 1928 they further agreed to renounce war "as an instrument of national policy." Along with these pledges to maintain peace came widespread reduction in armaments. Conferences to limit naval construction were held in 1921–22 and in 1930. In 1932 a general disarmament conference, attended by delegates of 59 nations, was held in Geneva.

With such promise of lasting peace, Europe began to rebuild. From 1924 to 1929 business improved, and paper money was again given definite value. Citizens of the United States lent billions to Europe's countries and cities for reconstruction.

Alliances and Treaties of the 1920's

France, always fearful of Germany, helped organize the Little Entente—Czechoslovakia, Rumania, and Yugoslavia, which also were bent on maintaining the Paris peace settlement. France formed alliances with these countries and with Poland, which had equal cause to fear Germany. With the German default on reparations payments in 1922, however, France felt strong enough to act alone. It seized the important Ruhr Valley but then agreed to a reparations settlement, the Dawes Plan, which in turn was replaced by the Young Plan in 1929, granting easier terms.

In 1925 Aristide Briand of France and Gustav Stresemann of Germany agreed on behalf of their states to respect their common frontiers and to maintain the demilitarized zone in the Rhineland. They secured a guarantee from Great Britain and Italy of this settlement (the Locarno Treaties), and Germany was then admitted to the League of Nations. France insisted on keeping Germany disarmed, and the Little Entente applied similar pressure to Austria, Hungary, and Bulgaria.

Rise of Mussolini and Hitler

In the economic crises that rocked the nations after the war, those that had long enjoyed democratic government weathered these storms without changing their political systems. Other countries fell under arbitrary one-man rule. The first to be brought under a dictator was Russia, where Communists seized power in 1917. In 1922 Benito Mussolini made himself master of Italy, and in 1933 Adolf Hitler became the "leader" of the German people. Poland, Austria, Spain, and some of the Balkans also abandoned parliamentary government. In most of these countries free enterprise was supplanted by socialistic government control, free speech by propaganda. Mussolini and Hitler diverted the resources of their nations to building up military power and flouted international law. (*See also* Communism; Fascism.)

After Hitler's rise to power in 1933, Germany and Italy, at first individually and then together, began to upset the political structure that had grown out of World War I. The two dictators regarded their nations as the "have nots," wronged by the Versailles Treaty. France and England were the "haves," interested in maintaining the *status quo*.

So Hitler in 1933 announced Germany's withdrawal from the League. He then threw off the restrictions of the peace treaty by rebuilding Germany's army, navy, and air force. Italy followed the German lead by invading Ethiopia. As Mussolini's forces, despite League sanctions, neared victory, Hitler in March 1936 sent troops into the Rhineland.

Rome-Berlin Axis Defies the Democracies

In October 1936 Italy and Germany announced an agreement to support their "parallel interests." This accord, known as the Rome-Berlin Axis, was later widened by the inclusion of Japan in an "anti-Comintern" pact. Although ostensibly directed against Soviet Russia and communism everywhere in the world, the pact was employed against the democracies.

With Italy checking France, Japan menacing Russia, and Germany forcing concessions from the nations of central Europe, the strong strategic position of the alliance was evident. France was divided by internal strife. England was unprepared to defend itself at home, in the Mediterranean, and in the Far East at the same time. In 1937 the two announced a willingness to satisfy the "legitimate grievances" of Germany and Italy.

Hitler Takes Austria and Czechoslovakia

Hitler then began his conquests. In March 1938 he occupied Austria and annexed it to Germany. Next he demanded the German-speaking Sudetenland from Czechoslovakia. By threatening war, he forced England and France, in an agreement at Munich in September 1938 (the Munich Pact), to permit him to seize the Sudetenland. Russia then asserted that its offer to aid Czechoslovakia had been refused by France and England. Hitler, in March 1939, took

In Florence, Italy, tourists on the Piazzale Michelangelo look across the Arno River to such famous medieval and Renaissance buildings as the cathedral of Santa Maria del Fiore with Filippo Brunelleschi's dome, Giotto's campanile, and the Palazzo Vecchio.

Parisian monuments and palaces reflect French history. At the right is a corner of the Louvre, the world's largest art museum. It was built by French kings as a magnificent palace set in the Tuileries Gardens. Ahead stands the Arc de Triomphe du Carrousel, erected by Napoleon I in 1805.

more of Czechoslovakia. Hungary, now in the anti-Comintern pact, and Poland took the rest.

Armed intervention by Germany and Italy in the Spanish civil war helped the rebels defeat the loyalists. General Francisco Franco seized Madrid on March 28, 1939. Franco then established a Fascist dictatorship and joined the anti-Comintern pact. In March 1939 England and France promised to defend the independence of Poland. After Italy seized Albania in April, England and France extended their pledge to Rumania, Greece, and Turkey.

World War II and Its Aftermath

The new system of guarantees divided Europe into armed factions of Axis and anti-Axis nations, with Russia standing aloof. Defying France and England, Hitler demanded Danzig from Poland. When Poland refused, Hitler invaded Poland on Sept. 1, 1939. Two days later England and France declared war on Germany. Russia entered the war on the Allied side after Hitler invaded it on June 22, 1941. The United States came in after Japan attacked Pearl Harbor on Dec. 7, 1941. (*See also* World War II.)

The war in Europe ended when Germany's surrender was announced on May 8, 1945, which came to be called V-E Day (Victory in Europe Day). V-E Day found all Europe in need of help. Scores of cities lay in ruins. Villages were wiped out. Railways, highways, ports, and canals had been destroyed. Farmers needed seed, draft animals, and machinery.

Dispirited people of most countries tended to shift the burden to their governments. Socialists and Communists vied for political power. The Socialists advocated only moderate control over business and social institutions, while the Communists aimed at total control. Unwilling to sacrifice all self-government, Western Europe inclined to moderate socialism. Eastern Europe, long used to dictatorial rule, leaned to Communism. In all nations except Russia, Communists were a political minority. However, the parties were well organized and firmly directed by Russia.

The Struggle for Peace and Power

A new struggle for power began. For centuries Austrian or German strength had served as a buffer between Western Europe and the Slavic East. The war destroyed this pattern. Russia emerged as the strongest nation on the continent. Britain's power was at an ebb. France and others suffered political strife. The conflict between democratic Western Europe and totalitarian Red Russia obstructed efforts to reconstruct Europe and establish world peace.

Just before the war ended in August 1945 the anti-Axis countries had formed the United Nations (UN). Its purpose was to keep the peace. In the UN Security Council, however, Russia used its veto to block actions unfavorable to its policies. (*See also* International Relations; United Nations.)

Russia set up puppet regimes in nations occupied by its troops—Poland, Hungary, and all the Balkans except Greece, where Britain had a foothold. Soviet troops also held eastern Austria and eastern Germany. Seizing more than reparations, Russia virtually stripped these nations.

Treaties and New Boundaries

In October 1946 delegates from 21 UN nations agreed on peace terms for all Axis nations except

Austria, Germany, and Japan. On Feb. 10, 1947, in Paris, the Allies signed peace treaties with Italy, Romania, Bulgaria, Hungary, and Finland. The Soviet Union made territorial gains from Romania, Finland, Czechoslovakia, Poland, and East Prussia and absorbed the Baltic States. It added some 260,000 square miles (670,000 square kilometers) to its European area. (*See also* World War II, "The Peace Treaties.")

Communism Divides Europe

When the war against the Fascist dictators was won, Communism began to spread throughout Europe. The Soviet Union trained leaders from other countries, who then returned to their homelands to build Communist parties. Behind the Iron Curtain—the term coined by former British Prime Minister Winston Churchill to describe the division of Eastern from Western Europe—the Communists gained control of nearly all the central and eastern parts of Europe. The Soviet Union worked to strengthen the emerging Communist elements in other countries.

A move to prevent rehabilitation in war-torn Europe was to thwart the drawing up of peace treaties for Austria and Germany. The Soviet Union then sapped Britain's aid to Greece by supporting the guerrilla warfare of the Greek Communists.

The Truman Doctrine and the Marshall Plan

After the Soviet Union refused to cooperate with other nations in Europe and in the UN, the United States abandoned its historic isolation. In 1947 it proclaimed the Truman Doctrine, aimed at "containing" Soviet expansion. Financial aid was given to Greece and Turkey. Greece received military aid in the fight against the guerrillas.

The United States then proposed a bold, basic idea for the economic recovery of Europe, the European Recovery Plan, popularly known as the Marshall Plan, named for United States Secretary of State George C. Marshall. Under the plan economic aid was offered to all European nations that worked out a program for rehabilitation. The war and its aftermath had drained Europe's economy. Italy, Britain, France, and The Netherlands had lost valuable colonies. Various trade barriers hindered commerce. Outdated machinery and industrial methods kept European products at high prices in world markets.

The Western European nations voted to accept the Marshall Plan. The Organization for European Economic Cooperation (OEEC) was founded in 1948 to collaborate with the United States in the program. It set up a monetary clearinghouse—the European Payments Union.

The Soviet Union forbade its satellites to take part in the program. It "persuaded" Czechoslovakia to withdraw its original intention to accept. In 1948 Czechoslovak Communists seized control of the country in a political coup.

The Soviet Union continued to block a German peace treaty. Because Germany's economic recovery was hampered by its division into occupation zones, the United States and Great Britain merged their zones in 1947. The French added their area in 1948.

The Cold War

The Soviet Union launched a Cold War—a series of obstructionist acts designed to make the Allies quit Germany (*see* Cold War). The Soviet Union set up a land blockade of the Allied sector of Berlin from mid-1948 to mid-1949 to keep food and supplies from the city. The Allies overcame the blockade of their land routes with a huge airlift in which planes brought even such cargoes as coal and machinery. In 1949 the Allied zones of Germany were united in the Federal Republic of Germany, or West Germany, and the Communists set up the German Democratic Republic, or East Germany.

Mutual Defense Organizations

The North Atlantic Treaty Organization (NATO) was formed in 1949 to protect Western Europe (*see* North Atlantic Treaty Organization). It included most Western European countries as well as the United States and Canada. The objective of NATO was to join the forces of all members in the defense of any member nation that might be attacked. Such neutral nations as Switzerland and Sweden did not join, and such countries as Austria and Finland were excluded by stipulations of the peace treaties drawn up at the end of World War II. France was an original member of NATO but withdrew from the integrated military command in 1966. France's decision to resign from NATO led to the formation in 1955 of the Western European Union (WEU), whose other members are Belgium, Luxembourg, The Netherlands, Italy, West Germany, the United Kingdom, and France.

After West Germany was admitted into NATO the Soviet Union forced the signing of the Warsaw Pact, a treaty establishing the mutual defense organization known as the Warsaw Treaty Organization (WTO) (*see* Warsaw Pact). Members are East Germany, Poland, Czechoslovakia, Hungary, Romania, Bulgaria, and the Soviet Union. Albania, an original signer of the treaty, withdrew in 1968; Yugoslavia, with its independent views on Communism, remained outside.

The Soviet Union meanwhile continued to alternate attack and conciliation in the Cold War. In 1955 the Soviet Union agreed to a peace treaty with Austria. In 1956 some concessions were made to Poland, but, when Hungary's resistance fighters revolted, the Soviets brutally crushed the uprising.

Communists tightened their control over East Germany after an unsuccessful revolt in 1953. Each year thousands of East Germans fled to West Berlin. In 1961 the Communist government closed the border, building a wall to prevent the further escape of East Germans. The Soviet Union demanded that the Allies withdraw from West Berlin. Soviet agreement with the United States and Great Britain to a limited test-ban treaty in 1963 lessened fears of a Soviet nuclear attack (*see* Disarmament). Peace was again threatened in 1968 by the Soviet-led invasion of Czechoslovakia.

Peter Turnley—Black Star

A prodemocracy protester stands atop a building in Bucharest, Romania, in December 1989. He holds a Romanian flag, from which the Communist symbol has been cut out.

In 1989 and 1990, as most of the governments of Eastern Europe relaxed or abandoned Communism for freer economies and greater democracy, the future of the Warsaw Pact appeared in doubt. While the World War II Allies discussed the position of a reunified Germany in Europe, the Soviet Union balked at the idea of Germany as a member of NATO.

Eurocommunism and the Reform of Communism

The invasion of Czechoslovakia in 1968 stimulated a movement that had begun shortly before World War II—a growing independence from Soviet domination of Communists outside the Soviet bloc. The movement became known as Eurocommunism and was especially strong in Italy, Spain, and France as well as in Japan, Australia, and Venezuela. Eurocommunists shared several common principles: rejection of the subordination of all Communist parties to Soviet monolithic world Communism; support of the establishment of socialism through legitimate political means and free elections; backing of alliances with other parties that support similar objectives; and rejection of atheism as an essential ingredient of Communism. The Soviet invasion of Afghanistan in 1979 further strained the ties of Eurocommunists with Moscow.

In the late 1980s and early 1990s Soviet leader Mikhail Gorbachev's policies of *glasnost* (openness) and *perestroika* (restructuring) brought electoral, Communist party, and economic reform to the Soviet Union and to the Soviet bloc (*see* Glasnost and Perestroika). The policies and reforms also brought protests and greater demands for change as people began to vent long-suppressed frustrations and feelings of dissent. In a dramatic event on Nov. 9, 1989, East and West Berliners swarmed through holes in the Berlin Wall when travel restrictions were relaxed in East Germany.

The Soviet-oriented governments of Poland, Hungary, Czechoslovakia, East Germany, Romania, and Bulgaria began to relax the Communist party's monopoly on power or to abandon Communism for democratically elected governments and expanded market economies. Even hard-line Albania liberalized some of its travel and communications restrictions and permitted the practice of religion. The Soviet Baltic states made radical proposals for autonomy and then declared their independence in 1990, though the Soviet Union refused to recognize their declarations and cracked down on the wayward republics. Ethnic violence erupted in several Soviet republics, most notably Armenia and Azerbaijan.

Terrorism

Beginning in the late 1960s, European cities were often the scene of terrorist attacks—sometimes by dissident groups within a country, but often by Palestinian groups that were attacking Israelis. Among the more notorious events of the 1970s and 1980s were the attack in 1972 on Israeli athletes in the Olympic village in Munich, West Germany, by the Palestinian organization known as Black September; the assassination in Madrid in 1973 of Spain's Premier Luis Carrero Blanco by Basque militants, who wanted Basque independence from Spain and France; the kidnapping in Rome and later murder in 1978 of Italy's five-time premier, Aldo Moro, by the Red Brigades; the assassination in 1979 of the English statesman and last viceroy of India, Lord Louis Mountbatten, by a bomb placed in his fishing boat in Ireland by the Provisional Irish Republican Army; the attempted assassination in 1981 of Pope John Paul II in the Vatican by a member of the Turkish nationalist Grey Wolves; the assassination in 1986 of Sweden's Prime Minister Olof Palme in Stockholm; and the bombing of Pan American Airlines flight 103 over Lockerbie, Scotland, in 1988. Attacks on embassies, the hijacking of airplanes and luxury ocean liners, and bombings at airports, railroad stations, stores, and nuclear plants—all in the name of extremist causes—became increasingly frequent. (*See also* articles on European countries and geographic features; Terrorism.)

BIBLIOGRAPHY FOR EUROPE

Barzini, Luigi. The Europeans (Simon & Schuster, 1983).

Gay, Peter and Webb, Robert. Modern Europe, 2 vols. (Harper, 1973).

Holmes, George, ed. The Oxford Illustrated History of Medieval Europe (Oxford, 1988).

Jordan, Terry. The European Culture Area (Harper, 1987).

Périn, Patrick and Forni, Pierre. The Barbarian Invasions of Europe (Silver, 1987).

Pimlott, John. The Cold War (Watts, 1987).

Riordan, James. Eastern Europe: The Lands and Their Peoples, rev. ed. (Silver, 1987).

Sabbagh, Antoine. Europe in the Middle Ages (Silver, 1988).

Taylor, A.J.P. The Struggle for Mastery in Europe, 1894–1918 (Oxford, 1954).

Thompson, W.C. Western Europe (Stryker, annual).

Tuchman, Barbara. The Proud Tower: A Portrait of the World Before the War (Macmillan, 1966).

Tusa, Ann and Tusa, John. The Berlin Airlift (Atheneum, 1988).

Wiskemann, Elizabeth. Europe of the Dictators, 1919–1945 (Cornell Univ. Press, 1966).

POLITICAL UNITS OF EUROPE

Political Unit	Status	Area (sq mi)	Area (sq km)	Population (1989 est.)	Capital
Albania	People's Republic	11,100	28,748	3,197,000	Tiranë
Andorra	Coprincipality	179	464	50,000	Andorra la Vella
Austria	Federal Republic	32,374	83,853	7,603,000	Vienna
Belgium	Constitutional Monarchy	11,784	30,521	9,878,000	Brussels
Bulgaria	People's Republic	42,823	110,912	8,987,000	Sofia
Czechoslovakia	Federal Republic	49,382	127,899	15,636,000	Prague
Denmark	Constitutional Monarchy	16,629	43,069	5,135,000	Copenhagen
Finland	Republic	130,129	337,033	4,960,000	Helsinki
France	Republic	210,026	543,965	56,107,000	Paris
Germany, East	Republic	41,766	108,173	16,613,000	Berlin
Germany, West	Federal Republic	95,963	248,543	61,131,000	Bonn
Gibraltar	Colony (United Kingdom)	2.25	5.8	30,200	Gibraltar
Greece	Republic	50,949	131,957	10,096,000	Athens
Hungary	Republic	35,921	93,036	10,580,000	Budapest
Iceland	Republic	39,769	103,000	252,000	Reykjavík
Ireland	Republic	27,137	70,285	3,515,000	Dublin
Italy	Republic	116,318	301,262	57,436,000	Rome
Liechtenstein	Constitutional Monarchy	62	160	28,300	Vaduz
Luxembourg	Constitutional Monarchy	998	2,586	377,000	Luxembourg
Malta	Republic	124	321	349,000	Valletta
Monaco	Constitutional Monarchy	0.73	1.9	29,100	Monaco
Netherlands, The	Constitutional Monarchy	16,042	41,548	14,846,000	Amsterdam
Norway	Constitutional Monarchy	125,057	323,895	4,228,000	Oslo
Poland	Republic	120,728	312,683	37,875,000	Warsaw
Portugal	Republic	35,516	91,985	10,372,000	Lisbon
Romania	Republic	91,699	237,500	23,168,000	Bucharest
San Marino	Republic	24	61	22,860	San Marino
Spain	Constitutional Monarchy	194,898	504,783	39,159,000	Madrid
Sweden	Constitutional Monarchy	173,732	449,964	8,498,100	Stockholm
Switzerland	Federal State	15,943	41,293	6,689,000	Bern
Union of Soviet Socialist Republics	Federal Socialist Republic	8,649,534*	22,402,200*	287,800,000*	Moscow
United Kingdom	Constitutional Monarchy	94,248	244,100	57,218,000	London
Vatican City	Ecclesiastical and Civil Monarchy	0.17	0.44	750	Vatican City
Yugoslavia	Federal Socialist Republic	98,766	255,804	23,710,000	Belgrade

*Figures include the entire Soviet Union.

THE CONTINENTS COMPARED

Region	Area sq mi	Area sq km	Population	GNP per Capita (U.S. $)	Literacy %	Life Expectancy Male	Life Expectancy Female
World	57,976,000*†	150,157,000*†	5,234,000,000*	3,600	71.5	59.7	64.0
Africa	11,667,000	30,218,000	642,100,000	710	26.3	49.8	52.9
Antarctica	5,500,000	14,245,000	—	—	—	—	—
Asia	17,236,000‡	44,642,000‡	3,048,400,000§	970♦¶	53.2	60.3	62.0
Australia	2,966,200	7,682,400	16,804,000	10,900	99.5	73.0	79.5
Europe	4,056,000 ‖	10,505,000 ‖	498,000,000§	7,280¶**	96.9	70.7	77.4
North America	9,355,000	24,230,000	420,100,000	16,150††	87.3	71.4	78.8
South America	6,878,000	17,814,000	487,500,000	‡‡	87.3	64.7	70.6

*Details do not add to total given because of rounding.
†Includes 3,478,000 sq mi (9,009,000 sq km) of area for Oceania not listed separately.
‡Includes Asian portion of the Soviet Union.
§Figures exclude the Soviet Union, which has a population of 287,800,000.
♦Excludes Afghanistan, Iran, Iraq, Kampuchea, North Korea, Laos, Lebanon, Macao, Mongolia, Taiwan, and Vietnam.
¶Excludes the Soviet Union, which had a GNP per capita of U.S. $8,160.
‖ Includes European portion of the Soviet Union.
**Excludes Albania, Bulgaria, Czechoslovakia, East Germany, and Romania.
††Excludes Latin America, which had a GNP per capita of U.S. $1,700; also excludes Cuba, Guadeloupe, and Martinique.
‡‡Included with Latin America, which had a GNP per capita of U.S. $1,700.

Europe Fact Summary

NATURAL FEATURES

Area: 4,056,000 square miles (10,505,000 square kilometers).

Mountain Ranges: Alps, Apennines, Balkans, Carpathians, Caucasus, Erzgebirge, Kjölen, Pyrenees, Rhodope, Sudetic, Transylvanian Alps, Ural.

Highest Peaks: El'brus (18,481 feet; 5,633 meters); Dykh-Tau (17,070 feet; 5,203 meters); Koshtan-Tau (16,899 feet; 5,151 meters); Shkhara (16,627 feet; 5,068 meters); Dzhangi-Tau (16,565 feet; 5,049 meters); Kazbek (16,512 feet; 5,033 meters).

Largest Lakes: Ladoga (6,826 square miles; 17,678 square kilometers); Onega (3,753 square miles; 9,720 square kilometers); Vänern (2,156 square miles; 5,584 square kilometers).

Major Rivers: Danube, Dnepr, Don, Elbe, Loire, Oder, Po, Rhine, Rhône, Seine, Tagus, Thames, Tiber, Ural, Vistula, Volga.

Climate: Regions—tundra, subarctic, marine, Mediterranean, humid subtropical, undifferentiated highlands, humid continental, semiarid, and arid.

Total annual precipitation and average annual temperature at selected stations:

Station	Precipitation		Temperature	
	in	*mm*	*°F*	*°C*
Athens	16	406	64	18
Helsinki	27	686	41	5
Kuybyshev	14	356	30	−1
Paris	25	635	53	12

Extremes in temperature and precipitation:

Seville, Spain, with the highest recorded temperature, 122° F (50° C). Ust'-Shchugor, U.S.S.R., with the lowest recorded temperature, −67° F (−55° C). Crkvice, Yugoslavia, with the highest annual average precipitation, 183.0 in (4,648.2 mm). Astrakhan', U.S.S.R., with the lowest annual average precipitation, 6.4 in (162.6 mm).

PEOPLE

Population (1987 estimate): 685,000,000.

Density: 167.6 persons per square mile (64.7 persons per square kilometer).

Vital Statistics (per 1,000 population): Birthrate, 14; death rate, 9; annual growth rate, 0.3 percent.

Main Language Groups: Russian (200,000,000); German (78,700,000); Italian (63,000,000); English (57,800,000); French (56,000,000); Ukrainian (42,000,000); Polish (38,000,000); Spanish (38,800,000); Romanian (22,900,000); Dutch (14,600,000); Serbo-Croatian (18,200,000). (Russian and Ukrainian include entire Soviet Union.)

Principal Religions: Roman Catholicism (262,267,000); Protestantism (85,456,000); Eastern Orthodoxy (125,048,000); Islam (40,709,000); Judaism (4,606,000).

Literacy: 96.9 percent.

Largest Cities: Moscow, U.S.S.R. (8,614,000); London, England (6,678,000); Istanbul, Turkey (5,480,000); Leningrad, U.S.S.R. (4,393,000); Madrid, Spain (3,053,000); Rome, Italy (2,815,000); Kiev, U.S.S.R. (2,544,000); Paris, France (2,166,000); Budapest, Hungary (2,104,000); West Berlin, West Germany (1,879,000); Bucharest, Romania (1,991,000); Barcelona, Spain (1,700,000); Warsaw, Poland (1,645,000); Hamburg, West Germany (1,571,000); Milan, Italy (1,495,000); Khar'kov, U.S.S.R. (1,587,000); Vienna, Austria (1,531,000).

Agricultural and Food Products: *Crops*—apples, barley, citrus fruits, corn (maize), flax, grapes, hemp, melons, oats, olives, potatoes, rice, rye, sugar beets, sugarcane, sunflower seeds, tobacco, tomatoes, wheat. *Livestock and fish*—cattle, freshwater fish and seafood, goats, pigs, poultry, sheep.

Manufactured Products: Appliances, bicycles, cheese, chemicals, chocolate, dairy goods, food products, forest products, glass, high-tech products, machinery, perfumes and fashion goods, pharmaceuticals, steel, synthetic fibers, textiles and clothing.

Mined Products: Apatites, bauxite, china clay, coal, copper, gold, iron ore, lead, lignite, manganese, natural gas, petroleum, potash, silver, sulfur, zinc.

Total Foreign Trade (1983): $1,618,000,000,000; imports, 51.1 percent; exports, 48.9 percent.

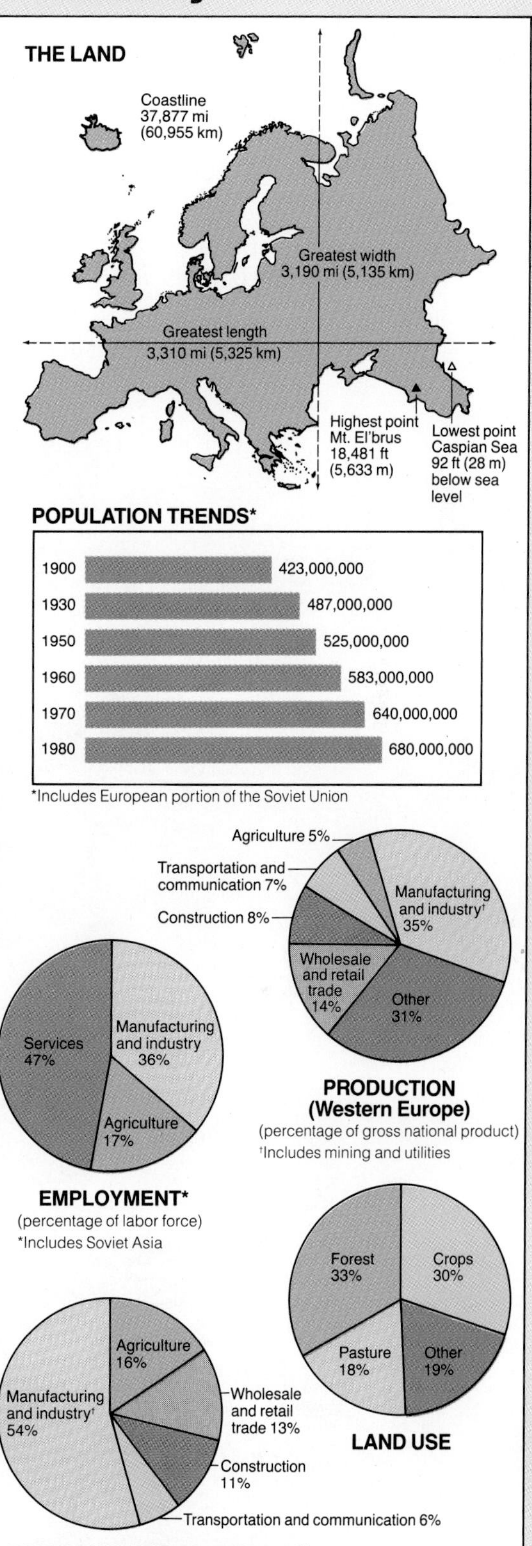

The government of the United States has not recognized the incorporation of Estonia Latvia and Lithuania into the Soviet Union, nor does it recognize as final the de facto western limit of Polish administration in Germany (the Oder-Neisse line).
HIGHWAYS
Important Roads ....
Other Roads ....
40° A 30° B 20° C 10° D 0° E 10° F
60°
50°
40°
1
2
3
4
5
70°
Jan Mayen (Nor.)
NORWEGIAN SEA
Arctic Circle
ATLANTIC OCEAN
ICELAND
Reykjavik
Akureyri
Húnaflói
Breidhafjördhur
Horn
Fontur
Seydhisfjördhur
Hornafjördhur
Hekla
Faeroe Is. (Den.)
Tórshavn
Shetland Is.
Lerwick
Rockall
Orkney Is.
Pentland Firth
Kirkwall
Hebrides
The Minch
Moray Firth
Inverness
Aberdeen
SCOTLAND
Glasgow
Edinburgh
Dundee
BRITISH ISLES
UNITED KINGDOM
NO. IRELAND
Donegal Bay
North Chan.
Belfast
IRELAND
Dundalk
Galway
Dublin
Limerick (Luimneach)
Waterford
Cork
Cobh
C. Clear
I. of Man
IRISH SEA
Carlisle
Newcastle-on-Tyne
Leeds
Manchester
Liverpool
Hull
Sheffield
The Wash
WALES
St. George's Chan.
Swansea
Birmingham
ENGLAND
Cardiff
LONDON
Bristol
Plymouth
Southampton
Portsmouth
Land's End
NORTH SEA
Senja
Vesterålen
Lofoten Is.
Narvik
Vestfjorden
Mo
Trondheimsfjorden
Namsos
Kristiansund
Ålesund
Trondheim
Östersund
Sundsvall
Sognefjord
Lillehammer
Bergen
Hardangerfjord
Haugesund
Stavanger
Oslo
Drammen
Fredrikstad
Larvik
Arendal
Lindesnes
Kristiansand
Skagerrak
Halden
Karlstad
Vänern
Västerås
Uppsala
Stock
Söderhamn
Falun
Gävle
Örebro
Eskilstuna
Norrköping
Linköping
Göteborg
Vättern
Borås
Jönköping
Visby
Gotland
Öland
Kattegat
Aalborg
DENMARK
Aarhus
Esbjerg
Copenhagen
Odense
Hälsingborg
Lund
Malmö
Karlskrona
BALTIC
Bornholm
Gulf
Flensburg
Helgoland
Kiel
Lübeck
Stralsund
Rostock
Słupsk
Kołobrzeg
Gdynia
Gdańsk
Frisian Is.
Amsterdam
The Hague
NETHERLANDS
Utrecht
Rotterdam
Antwerp
Bremen
Hamburg
Elbe
Hanover
Münster
Essen
EAST BERLIN
Szczecin (Stettin)
Bydgoszcz
Poznań
Brunswick
Magdeburg
GERMANY
Oder
Warta
Dortmund
Düsseldorf
Kassel
Halle
Leipzig
Dresden
Wrocław (Breslau)
Łódź
English Channel
Boulogne
Calais
Ghent
Brussels
BELGIUM
Liège
Cologne
Aachen
Bonn
Wiesbaden
Erfurt
Plauen
Karl-Marx-Stadt
Częstochowa
Zabrze
Katowice
Cherbourg
Le Havre
Channel Is. (Br.)
Lille
Amiens
Rouen
LUX.
Mainz
Frankfurt
Prague (Praha)
Ostrava
Ushant I.
Brest
Rennes
Seine
Marne
Versailles
PARIS
Reims
Saarbrücken
Mannheim
Nuremberg
Pilsen
Olomouc
Belle Isle
St-Nazaire
Angers
Loire
Orléans
Nancy
Rhine
Karlsruhe
Regensburg
Brno
Nantes
Tours
Strasbourg
Stuttgart
Danube
Augsburg
VIENNA (Wien)
Bratislava
La Rochelle
I. d'Oléron
Bay of Biscay
Dijon
Mulhouse
Freiburg
Munich
Linz
Salzburg
FRANCE
Limoges
Vichy
Basel
Zürich
L. of Constance
LIECHTENSTEIN
Innsbruck
AUSTRIA
Győr
Sopron
HUNG
Bordeaux
Clermont-Ferrand
Lyon
Lausanne
Bern
SWITZERLAND
Geneva
L. Geneva
Mt. Blanc
Alps
Graz
Maribor
Balaton
Pécs
Dordogne
St-Étienne
Grenoble
Trento
Bolzano
Venice (Venezia)
Ljubljana
Zagreb
Drava
Subotica
Garonne
Montauban
Rhône
Turin (Torino)
Milan
Brescia
Verona
Po
Padua
Trieste
Rijeka (Fiume)
Novi Sad
Sava
Biarritz
Bayonne
Pyrénées
Toulouse
Nîmes
Genoa
Parma
Ferrara
Modena
Bologna
Banja Luka
El Ferrol
La Coruña
C. Finisterre
Gijón
Santander
San Sebastián
Oviedo
Bilbao
Vigo
Miño
León
Burgos
Ebro
ANDORRA
Montpellier
G. of Lions
Nice
MONACO
Marseilles
Toulon
La Spezia
Florence (Firenze)
SAN MARINO
Ancona
Zadar
Sarajevo
Oporto (Pôrto)
Braga
Valladolid
Douro
Coimbra
Salamanca
Duero
Saragossa
Sa. de Guadarrama
MADRID
Leghorn (Livorno)
Siena
Perugia
ADRIATIC SEA
Split
Mostar
Dubrovnik (Ragusa)
Cetinje
Shkodër
Lisbon (Lisboa)
Tejo
Tagus
Tajo
PORTUGAL
SPAIN
Toledo
Tarragona
Barcelona
Corsica (Corse)
Ajaccio
Elba
Tiber
ITALY
ROME
VATICAN CITY
Setúbal
Guadiana
Évora
Badajoz
Sierra Morena
Albacete
Valencia
Balearic Is.
Minorca
Palma
Majorca (Mallorca)
Iviza
Sassari
Olbia
Sardinia (Sardegna)
Foggia
Vesuvius
Naples (Napoli)
Bari
Taranto
Brindisi
Durrës
Tirana
C. St. Vincent
Córdoba
Guadalquivir
Murcia
Lorca
Seville
Alicante
Iglesias
Cagliari
TYRRHENIAN SEA
G. of Taranto
Corfu
G. of Cádiz
Cádiz
Jerez
Granada
Sa. Nevada
Str. of Gibraltar
Málaga
Almería
Cartagena
GIBRALTAR (Br.)
Ceuta (Sp.)
Tangier
MEDITERRANEAN
Catanzaro
IONIAN SEA
Kénitra
Rabat
Casablanca
Melilla (Sp.)
Oran
Algiers (Alger)
Skikda
Bizerte
Palermo
Messina
Reggio
Etna
Sicily (Sicilia)
Catania
Syracuse
Fez
Meknès
Constantine
Annaba (Bône)
C. Bon
Tunis
TUNISIA
Pantelleria
MOROCCO
ALGERIA
Marrakech
Biskra
Sousse
MALTA
Valletta
Longitude West D of Greenwich
0°
Longitude East E of Greenwich
10°
F

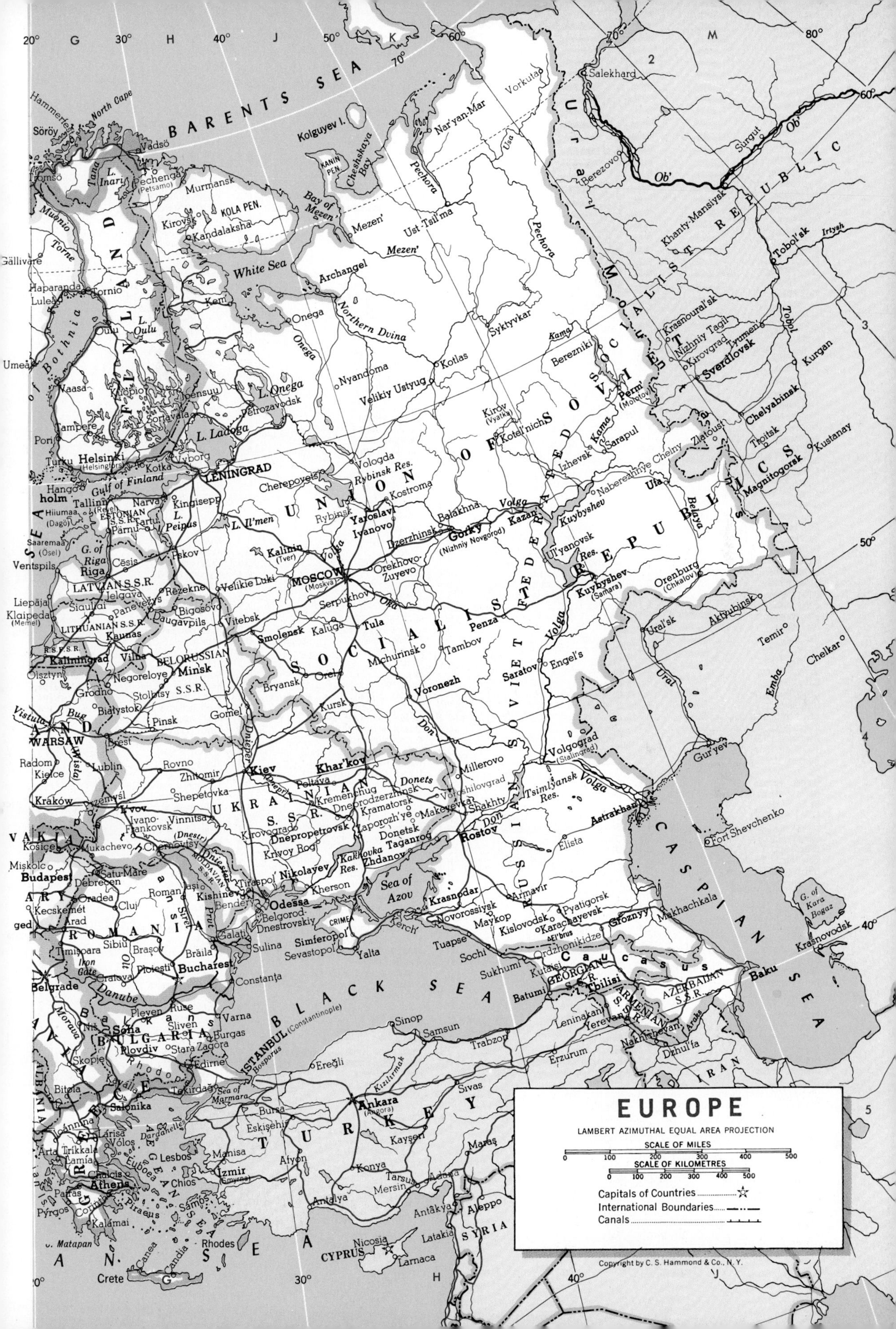
EUROPE
LAMBERT AZIMUTHAL EQUAL AREA PROJECTION
SCALE OF MILES
0 100 200 300 400 500
SCALE OF KILOMETRES
0 100 200 300 400 500
Capitals of Countries
International Boundaries
Canals
Copyright by C. S. Hammond & Co., N. Y.
BARENTS SEA
White Sea
BLACK SEA
CASPIAN SEA
Sea of Azov
Sea of Marmara
UNION OF SOVIET SOCIALIST REPUBLICS
RUSSIAN SOVIET FEDERATED SOCIALIST REPUBLIC
FINLAND
ROMANIA
BULGARIA
TURKEY
SYRIA
IRAN
CYPRUS
UKRAINIAN S.S.R.
BELORUSSIAN S.S.R.
LATVIAN S.S.R.
LITHUANIAN S.S.R.
ESTONIAN S.S.R.
MOLDAVIAN S.S.R.
GEORGIAN S.S.R.
ARMENIAN S.S.R.
AZERBAIJAN S.S.R.
MOSCOW (Moskva)
LENINGRAD
WARSAW
Helsinki (Helsingfors)
Riga
Tallinn (Revel)
Kaunas
Minsk
Kiev
Khar'kov
Odessa
Bucharest
Budapest
Belgrade
Sofia
Athens
ISTANBUL (Constantinople)
Ankara (Angora)
Izmir (Smyrna)
Gorky (Nizhniy Novgorod)
Kuybyshev (Samara)
Volgograd (Stalingrad)
Rostov
Astrakhan
Baku
Tbilisi
Sverdlovsk
Chelyabinsk
Magnitogorsk
Perm' (Molotov)
Kazan
Saratov
Voronezh
Archangel
Murmansk
Kolguyev I.
KOLA PEN.
KANIN PEN.
L. Ladoga
L. Onega
L. Peipus
L. Il'men
Gulf of Finland
G. of Riga
Gulf of Bothnia
Volga
Don
Dnepr
Danube
Ural
Ob'
Pechora
Northern Dvina
Kama
Caucasus
Crete
Rhodes
20° 30° 40° 50° 60° 70° 80°
G H J K L M

EUROPE

EUROPE—*Continued*

Loire (river), France E 4
London (cap.), England D 3
Lorca, Spain D 5
Lübeck, W. Ger. E 3
Lublin, Poland G 3
Luimneach (Limerick), Ireland C 3
Luleå, Sweden G 2
Lund, Sweden F 3
Luxembourg E 4
L'vov, U.S.S.R. G 4
Lyon, France E 4
Madrid (cap.), Spain D 4
Magdeburg, E. Ger. F 3
Mainz, W. Ger. E 4
Majorca (Mallorca) (isl.), Spain E 5
Makeyevka, U.S.S.R. H 4
Makhachkala, U.S.S.R. J 4
Málaga, Spain D 5
Mallorca (Majorca) (isl.), Spain E 5
Malmö, Sweden F 3
Malta F 5
Man, Isle of (isl.), Gr. Brit. D 3
Manchester, Eng. D 3
Mannheim, W. Ger. E 4
Maribor, Yugo. F 4
Marmara (sea), Turkey G 4
Marne (river), France E 4
Marseilles, France E 4
Matapan (cape), Greece G 5
Maykop, U.S.S.R. H 4
Mediterranean (sea) E 5
Melilla, Spain D 5
Memel (Klaipėda), U.S.S.R. F 3
Messina, Italy F 5
Mezen', U.S.S.R. J 2
Mezen' (bay), U.S.S.R. J 2
Mezen' (river), U.S.S.R. J 2
Michurinsk, U.S.S.R. H 3
Milan, Italy E 4
Millerovo, U.S.S.R. J 4
Minch, The (strait), Scot. D 3
Miño (river) D 4
Minorca (isl.), Spain E 5
Minsk, U.S.S.R. G 3
Miskolc, Hungary F 4
Mo, Norway F 2
Modena, Italy E 4
Moldavian S.S.R., U.S.S.R. H 4
Molotov (Perm'), U.S.S.R. K 3
Monaco E 4
Montauban, France E 4
Montpellier, France E 4
Morava (river), Yugo. G 4
Moray (firth), Scot. D 3
Morena (mt. range), Spain D 5
Moscow (Moskva) (cap.), U.S.S.R. H 3
Mostar, Yugo. F 4
Mukachevo, U.S.S.R. G 4
Mulhouse, France E 4
Munich, W. Ger. F 4
Münster, W. Ger. E 3
Muonio (river) G 2
Murcia, Spain D 5
Murmansk, U.S.S.R. H 2
Naberezhnye Chelny, U.S.S.R. K 3
Nakhichevan', U.S.S.R. J 5
Namsos, Norway F 2
Nancy, France E 4
Nantes, France E 4
Naples (Napoli), Italy F 4
Narva, U.S.S.R. G 3
Narvik, Norway F 2
Nar'yan-Mar, U.S.S.R. K 2
Netherlands E 3
Nevada (mt. range), Spain A 5
Newcastle-on-Tyne, England D 3
Nice, France E 4
Nikolayev, U.S.S.R. H 4
Nîmes, France C 4
Niš, Yugo. G 4
Nizhni Novgorod (Gor'kiy), U.S.S.R. J 3
Norrköping, Sweden F 3
North (Horn) (cape), Iceland B 2
North (cape), Norway G 1
North (channel), Gr. Brit. D 3
North (sea) E 3
Northern Dvina (river), U.S.S.R. J 2
Northern Ireland, Gr. Brit. D 3
Norway E 2
Norwegian (sea) D 2
Novi Sad, Yugo. F 4
Novorossiysk, U.S.S.R. H 4
Nuremberg, W. Ger. F 4
Nyandoma, U.S.S.R. J 2

Odense, Denmark E 3
Oder (river) F 3
Odessa, U.S.S.R. H 4
Oka (river), U.S.S.R. H 3
Öland (isl.), Sweden F 3
Olbia, Italy E 4
Oléron (isl.), France D 4
Olomouc, Czech. F 4
Olsztyn, Poland G 3
Olt (river), Romania G 4
Onega, U.S.S.R. H 2
Onega (lake), U.S.S.R. H 2
Onega (river), U.S.S.R. H 2
Oporto (Pôrto), Portugal D 4
Oradea, Romania G 4
Ordzhonikidze, U.S.S.R. J 4
Örebro, Sweden F 3
Orekhovo-Zuyevo, U.S.S.R. H 3
Orel, U.S.S.R. H 3
Orenburg, U.S.S.R. K 3
Orkney (isls.), Scot. D 3
Orléans, France E 4
Ösel (Saaremaa) (isl.), U.S.S.R. G 3
Oslo (cap.), Nor. E 2
Östersund, Sweden F 2
Ostrava, Czech. F 4
Oulu, Finland G 2
Oulu (lake), Finland G 2
Oviedo, Spain D 4
Padua, Italy F 4
Palermo, Italy F 5
Palma, Spain E 5
Panevezys, U.S.S.R. G 3
Pantelleria (isl.), Italy F 5
Paris (cap.), France E 4
Paris, France E 4
Parma, Italy E 4
Pärnu, U.S.S.R. G 3
Patras, Greece G 5
Pechenga, U.S.S.R. H 2
Pechora (river), U.S.S.R. K 2
Pécs, Hungary F 4
Peipus (lake), U.S.S.R. G 3
Pentland (firth), Scot. D 3
Penza, U.S.S.R. J 3
Perm', U.S.S.R. K 3
Perugia, Italy F 4
Petrozavodsk, U.S.S.R. H 2
Petsamo (Pechenga), U.S.S.R. H 2
Pinsk, U.S.S.R. G 3
Piraeus, Greece G 5
Plauen, E. Ger. F 3
Pleven, Bulg. G 4
Ploieşti, Romania G 4
Plovdiv, Bulg. G 4
Plymouth, Eng. D 3
Plzeň, Czech. F 4
Po (river), Italy F 4
Poland F 3
Poltava, U.S.S.R. H 4
Pori, Finland G 2
Pôrto (Oporto), Portugal D 4
Portsmouth, Eng. D 3
Portugal A 5
Poznań, Poland F 3
Prague (Praha) (cap.), Czech. F 3
Prut (river) G 4
Przemyśl, Poland G 3
Pskov, U.S.S.R. G 3
Pyatigorsk, U.S.S.R. J 4
Pyrénées (mt. range) E 4
Pyrgos, Greece G 5
Radom, Poland G 3
Ragusa (Dubrovnik), Yugo. F 4
Regensburg, W. Ger. F 4
Reggio di Calabria, Italy F 5
Reims, France E 4
Rennes, France D 4
Revel (Tallinn), U.S.S.R. G 3
Reykjavik (cap.), Iceland B 2
Rēzekne, U.S.S.R. G 3
Rhine (river) E 4
Rhodes (isl.), Greece G 5
Rhodope (mts.) G 4
Rhône (river) E 4
Riga, U.S.S.R. G 3
Riga (gulf), U.S.S.R. G 3
Rijeka, Yugo. F 4
Rockall (isl.), Scotland C 3
Roman, Romania G 4
Romania G 4
Rome (cap.), Italy F 4
Rostock, E. Ger. F 3
Rostov, U.S.S.R. J 4

Rotterdam, Neth. E 3
Rouen, France E 4
Rovno, U.S.S.R. G 3
Ruse, Bulg. G 4
Russian S.F.S.R., U.S.S.R. J 4
Rybinsk, U.S.S.R. H 3
Rybinsk (res.), U.S.S.R. J 3
Saarbrücken, W. Ger. D 4
Saaremaa (isl.), U.S.S.R. G 3
Saint-Étienne, France E 4
Saint George's (channel) D 3
Saint-Nazaire, France D 4
Saint Vincent (cape), Portugal D 5
Salamanca, Spain D 4
Salonika, Greece G 4
Salzburg, Austria F 4
Samara (Kuybyshev), U.S.S.R. J 3
Sámos (isl.), Greece G 5
San Marino F 4
San Sebastián, Spain D 4
Santander, Spain D 4
Saragossa, Spain D 4
Sarajevo, Yugo. F 4
Sarapul, U.S.S.R. K 3
Saratov, U.S.S.R. J 3
Sardinia (Sardegna) (isl.), Italy E 4
Sassari, Italy E 4
Satu-Mare, Romania G 4
Sava (river), Yugo. F 4
Scotland, Gr. Brit. D 3
Seine (river), France E 4
Serpukhov, U.S.S.R. H 3
Setúbal, Portugal D 5
Sevastopol', U.S.S.R. H 4
Seville, Spain D 5
Seydhisfjördhur, Iceland C 2
Shakhty, U.S.S.R. J 4
Sheffield, England D 3
Shepetovka, U.S.S.R. G 3
Shetland (isls.), Scotland D 2
Shkodër, Albania F 4
Siauliai, U.S.S.R. G 3
Sibiu, Romania G 4
Sicily (Sicilia) (isl.), Italy F 5
Siena, Italy F 4
Simferopol', U.S.S.R. H 4
Siret (river), Romania G 4
Skagerrak (strait) E 3
Skopje, Yugo. G 4
Sliven, Bulg. G 4
Slupsk, Poland F 3
Smolensk, U.S.S.R. H 3
Sochi, U.S.S.R. H 4
Söderhamn, Sweden F 2
Sofia (cap.), Bulg. G 4
Sogne (fjord), Norway E 2
Sopron, Hungary F 4
Sortavala, U.S.S.R. G 2
Southampton, England D 3
Spain D 4
Split, Yugo. F 4
Stalingrad (Volgograd), U.S.S.R. J 4
Stara Zagora, Bulg. G 4
Stavanger, Norway E 3
Stettin (Szczecin), Poland F 3
Stockholm (cap.), Sweden F 3
Stolbtsy, U.S.S.R. G 3
Stralsund, E. Ger. F 3
Strasbourg, France E 4
Stuttgart, W. Ger. E 4
Subotica, Yugo. F 4
Sukhumi, U.S.S.R. L 4
Sulina, Romania H 4
Sundsvall, Sweden F 2
Swansea, Wales D 3
Sweden F 2
Switzerland E 4
Syktyvkar, U.S.S.R. K 2
Syracuse, Italy F 5
Szczecin, Poland F 3
Szeged, Hungary F 4
Taganrog, U.S.S.R. H 4
Tagus (river), Portugal D 5
Tajo (Tagus) (river), Spain D 5
Tallinn, U.S.S.R. G 3
Tambov, U.S.S.R. J 3
Tampere, Finland G 2
Tana (river) G 2
Taranto, Italy F 4
Taranto (gulf), Italy F 5
Tarragona, Spain E 4
Tartu, U.S.S.R. G 3
Tbilisi, U.S.S.R. J 4
Tejo (Tagus) (river), Port. D 5

Tekirdag, Turkey G 4
The Hague (cap.), Neth. E 3
Tiber (river), Italy F 4
Timişoara, Romania G 4
Tiranë (cap.), Albania F 4
Tiraspol', U.S.S.R. G 4
Toledo, Spain D 5
Torino (Turin), Italy E 4
Tornio, Finland G 2
Tórshavn (cap.), Faeroe Isls., Denmark D 2
Toulon, France E 4
Toulouse, France E 4
Tours, France E 4
Trento, Italy F 4
Trieste, Italy F 4
Tríkkala, Greece G 5
Tromsö, Norway G 2
Trondheim, Norway F 2
Tsimlyansk (res.), U.S.S.R. J 4
Tuapse, U.S.S.R. H 4
Tula, U.S.S.R. H 3
Turin, Italy E 4
Turkey H 4
Turku, Finland G 2
Tyrrhenian (sea) F 5
Ufa, U.S.S.R. K 3
Ukrainian S.S.R., U.S.S.R. H 4
Ul'yanovsk, U.S.S.R. J 3
Umeå, Sweden F 2
Union of Soviet Socialist Republics H 3
United Kingdom E 3
Uppsala, Sweden F 3
Ural (mts.), U.S.S.R. L 2
Usa (river), U.S.S.R. K 2
Utrecht, Neth. E 3
Vassa, Finland G 2
Vadsö, Norway H 1
Valencia, Spain E 5
Valladolid, Spain D 4
Valletta (cap.), Malta F 5
Vänern (lake), Sweden F 3
Varna, Bulg. G 4
Västerås, Sweden F 3
Vatican City F 4
Vättern (lake), Sweden F 3
Velikie Luki, U.S.S.R. H 3
Velikiy Ustyug, U.S.S.R. J 2
Venice (Venezia), Italy F 4
Ventspils, U.S.S.R. G 3
Verona, Italy F 4
Versailles, France E 4
Vesterålen (isls.), Norway F 2
Vesuvius (vol.), Italy F 4
Vichy, France E 4
Vienna (cap.), Austria F 4
Vigo, Spain D 4
Vilna, U.S.S.R. G 3
Vinnitsa, U.S.S.R. G 4
Visby, Sweden F 3
Vistula (river), Poland F 3
Vitebsk, U.S.S.R. H 3
Volga (river), U.S.S.R. J 4
Volgograd, U.S.S.R. L 4
Vologda, U.S.S.R. J 3
Vólos, Greece G 5
Vorkuta, U.S.S.R. L 2
Voronezh, U.S.S.R. J 3
Voroshilovgrad, U.S.S.R. H 4
Vyborg, U.S.S.R. G 2
Wales, Gr. Brit. D 3
Warsaw (cap.), Poland G 3
Warta (river), Poland G 3
Wash, The (est.), Eng. E 3
Waterford, Ireland D 3
Weser (river), Germany E 3
White (sea), U.S.S.R. H 2
Wien (Vienna) (cap.), Austria F 4
Wiesbaden, W. Ger. E 3
Wisla (Vistula) (river), Poland G 3
Wroclaw, Poland F 3
Yalta, U.S.S.R. H 4
Yaroslavl', U.S.S.R. H 3
Yerevan, U.S.S.R. J 4
Yugoslavia F 4
Zabrze, Poland F 3
Zadar, Yugo. F 4
Zagreb, Yugo. F 4
Zaporozh'ye, U.S.S.R. H 4
Zara (Zadar), Yugo. F 4
Zhdanov, U.S.S.R. H 4
Zhitomir, U.S.S.R. G 3
Zürich, Switz. E 4

EUROPEAN COMMUNITIES. World War II all but destroyed the European economy and seriously endangered the stability of existing social and political institutions. To the statesmen who were forced to rebuild from the ruins, it was essential that new forms of economic and political cooperation be forged in order to reestablish prosperity and peace. At first the concept of mutual support in trade relations among longtime competitors seemed impossibly idealistic. Nevertheless, the European Communities (EC) that grew out of this ideal attained enviable success.

The mutually cooperative agencies that were created in the 1950s protected the basic interests of Belgium, France, West Germany, Italy, Luxembourg, and The Netherlands—called the Six. A further step in cooperation was taken on July 1, 1967, when the original three economic communities were merged into a single organization—the EC. Other nations later joined the organization. Denmark, the United Kingdom, and Ireland became full members in 1973; Greece, in 1981; and Spain and Portugal, in 1986. Turkey's bid for membership, launched in 1987, was rejected in late 1989 because of human rights violations. Austria applied for membership in 1989.

In April 1990 the economic bloc vowed a "commitment to political union"—including a common foreign and defense policy—by Dec. 31, 1992. Previously the EC had pledged a true common market through the enactment of about 300 initiatives to eliminate internal trade barriers and tariffs, also to be achieved by the end of 1992. A proposed monetary union, with the introduction of a single European currency, has proved a controversial issue.

The overthrow of Communism in Eastern Europe in 1989 and the movement toward reunification of the two Germanys complicated the EC's goal of allowing free movement of people and capital among the 12 member nations. In 1990 the members agreed to grant East Germany membership as soon as it reunited with West Germany. They also considered associate memberships for former Eastern-bloc states that adopt democratic policies, as well as the establishment of a special development bank for the reforming nations.

ECSC. Paul-Henri Spaak of Belgium and Robert Schuman and Jean Monnet of France were among the political leaders who helped guide the first of the three institutions that became the EC (*see* Spaak). The initial step toward the European Coal and Steel Community (ECSC) was a proposal by Schuman in 1950 that an independent agency be established by those nations willing to delegate authority over their coal and steel industries. The Six negotiated the Schuman Plan, drawn up by Monnet, in the Treaty of Paris (1951), and the ECSC became effective on July 25, 1952.

EEC. The success of the ECSC prompted the Six to move toward greater political unity with the creation of two more communities under the Treaty of Rome (1957). The European Economic Community (EEC), an association—popularly called the Common Market—for the removal of trade barriers among member nations, was established on Jan. 1, 1958. The first 10 percent reduction in internal tariffs took place in 1959 (*see* Tariff). A Customs Union was achieved in mid-1968 when all internal tariffs had been discarded. The transitional phase of the EEC ended on Dec. 31, 1969, with full economic union.

Euratom. The European Atomic Energy Community (Euratom) came into existence on Jan. 1, 1958. Its purpose was to form a common market for the development of nuclear energy for peaceful purposes.

EC institutions. Before the 1967 merger of the ECSC, the EEC, and Euratom, each had its own commission and council. Today the EC's single Commission is made up of 17 members appointed for four-year terms by the various governments but not answerable to them. It prepares proposals submitted to the Council of Ministers for action and can take other institutions (or countries) before the Court of Justice. The Council of Ministers, which has one representative from each member nation, has the real power of decision for the EC. It determines how the treaties are to be carried out and how the separate economic policies of the member nations are coordinated.

Policy making on the highest level is the responsibility of the European Council, which is composed of the heads of state or government of each member country. It has met regularly since 1974. Other EC institutions are the Court of Justice, the Court of Auditors, the Economic and Social Committee, and the European Investment Bank.

The Court of Justice, founded in 1958, reviews the legality of the acts of the Commission and the Council of Ministers. It may also hear cases involving disputes between member states. There are 13 judges and six advocates-general. The Court of Auditors, in effect since 1977 when it replaced the Audit Board, is responsible for the external audit of expenditures and revenues of the EC. It has 12 members.

Since 1958 the Economic and Social Committee has advised the Commission and the Council of Ministers on general economic policy. The 189 members of the consultative body represent employers, organizations, labor unions, professions, farmers, consumers, and small businesses. The European Investment Bank was founded in 1958 as an independent public institution for long-term finance. Under the bank the European Monetary System, which began operating in March 1979, aims at regulating currency-exchange rates among most member states.

The European Parliament was inaugurated in 1958 as an assembly of members appointed by the national legislatures of the EC. In 1979 it became a 434-member legislature whose numbers were apportioned among member countries. Members are elected by the direct vote of citizens and have party affiliations much the same as those held by other European legislators. In 1986 the Parliament was enlarged to 518. It is primarily a public forum for the discussion of issues that are significant for the EC as a whole.

EUROPIUM *see* CHEMICAL ELEMENTS; PERIODIC TABLE.

EVANSVILLE, Ind. Located in southwestern Indiana on a horseshoe bend of the Ohio River, the port of Evansville is a busy trade and manufacturing center. It serves a tri-state trading area in Indiana, Kentucky, and Illinois of about 1 million people.

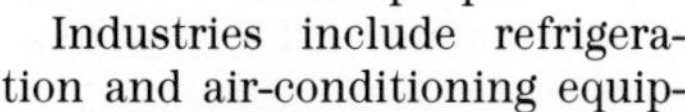

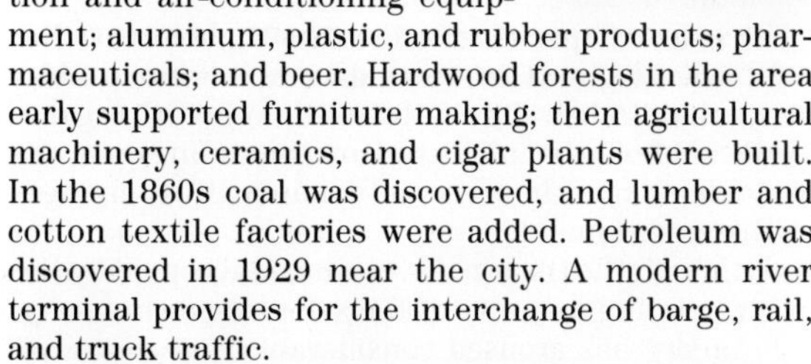

Industries include refrigeration and air-conditioning equipment; aluminum, plastic, and rubber products; pharmaceuticals; and beer. Hardwood forests in the area early supported furniture making; then agricultural machinery, ceramics, and cigar plants were built. In the 1860s coal was discovered, and lumber and cotton textile factories were added. Petroleum was discovered in 1929 near the city. A modern river terminal provides for the interchange of barge, rail, and truck traffic.

Cultural and recreational facilities include the Museum of Arts and Sciences, Koch Planetarium, and Mesker Park Zoo; the Roberts Municipal Stadium hosts circus, rodeo, music, and ice shows as well as trade shows and sports events. The Audubon Raceway has harness racing and Ellis Park thoroughbred races. A branch of Indiana State University is in the city as is the University of Evansville. About 7 miles east of the city is Angel Mounds State Memorial, an Indian town and burial site.

The original site of Evansville was a trading post, founded in 1812 by Colonel Hugh McGary, Jr. In 1817 he laid out the town with James W. Jones and Col. Robert M. Evans, for whom it was named. When Vanderburgh County was formed in 1818, Evansville became the county seat. Incorporated in 1819, it was chartered as a city in 1847. In 1853 the Wabash and Erie Canal was completed to Evansville, connecting Lake Erie with the Ohio River, and a railway to Terre Haute began operations.

The city government is the mayor-council form. Population (1980 census), city, 130,496; metropolitan area, 309,408.

EVEREST, MOUNT. Known in Tibet as Chomolungma, or "goddess mother of the world," Mount Everest is the highest point on Earth but was not recognized as such until 1852 when a government survey by India established the fact. On the crest of the Himalayan range on the border of Nepal and the Chinese autonomous region of Tibet, Everest reaches a height of 29,028 feet (8,848 meters). This peak can be seen directly only from its northeastern side. Four lesser peaks that rise around Everest's base hide the summit from Nepal. (*See also* Himalayas.)

Hy Simon—Photo Trends

The peak of Mount Everest, located on the Nepal-Tibet border, can be seen directly only from its northeastern side.

The summit reaches two thirds of the way through the Earth's atmosphere to heights where oxygen is thin. The lack of oxygen, powerful winds, and extremely cold temperatures prevent any animal or plant life on the upper slopes. Precipitation falls as snow only during the summer monsoon season and lies as powdery drifts. Everest has seven individual glaciers. These ice sheets are fed by frequent avalanches and cover the slopes down to the base. However, they are slowly melting away at the bottom as a result of climate changes. The top of the mountain is blown relatively free of snow cover during the winter by powerful northwest gale winds.

Known in English at one time as Peak XV, it was renamed Everest after Sir George Everest, the British surveyor general of India from 1830 to 1843. Attempts to climb the mountain began with the opening of the Tibetan route in 1920. Ten tries from 1921 to 1952 failed because of the cold dry air, fierce winds, difficult terrain, and high altitude. The peak was finally conquered in 1953 by an expedition sponsored by the Royal Geographical Society and the Joint Himalayan Committee of the Alpine Club. Edmund Hillary of New Zealand and Tenzing Norgay of Nepal climbed the southeastern ridge to the summit. Numerous expeditions sponsored by various countries have since been undertaken, many of them successful.

EVERGLADES. A vast area of land and water in southern Florida, the Everglades cover about 4,000 square miles (10,000 square kilometers). Through this marshy region water moves slowly from the lip of Lake Okeechobee southward and westward to mangrove swamps bordering the Gulf of Mexico and Florida Bay. On the east the marsh reaches near the Greater Miami metropolitan area.

Much of the Everglades is covered with saw grass, which grows 10 to 15 feet (3 to 5 meters) tall. There are many hammocks—or small, fertile, raised areas—on which palms, pines, live oaks, cypresses, saw palmettos, and other trees and shrubs grow. The mild, subtropical to tropical climate and usually large water supply provide an ideal environment for such wading birds as herons, egrets, and ibis as well as for many species of snakes, turtles, and alligators. The hammocks are shelter for deer, wildcats, panthers, bears, smaller mammals, and numerous reptiles. (*See also* Florida, "Recreation and Places of Interest.")

EVERT, Chris (born 1954). American tennis star Chris Evert was a trendsetter. When at age 15 Evert beat the reigning champion, she set a precedent for a phenomenal string of teenagers to follow. Her mental discipline brought the game a new intensity that boosted women's professional tennis.

Christine Marie Evert was born in Fort Lauderdale, Fla., on Dec. 21, 1954. Her father, a tennis instructor, began to teach her the game when she was about 6 years old, and from the age of 10 she was always the champion in her amateur age group.

She entered the limelight in 1970 when she beat the top-ranked player, Margaret Court, in a minor event. In 1971, at the age of 16, she became the youngest player to reach the semifinals of the United States Open. By 1972, when she turned professional, she had already been forced to turn down more than 50,000 dollars in prize money. She became the first woman player to win a million dollars. By the late 1980s she had accumulated on-court earnings of nearly 10 million dollars. Her off-court endorsements, for general products, as well as for tennis equipment, were estimated at twice that amount.

As a professional, Evert was the first woman since the 1930s to hold the number-one ranking for five consecutive years (1974 to 1978). Of her nearly 160 tournament wins, 18 were in Grand Slam events. She won the United States Open women's singles from 1975 to 1978 and again in 1980 and 1982. She emerged victorious at Wimbledon in 1974, 1976, and 1981. Her 1986 win in the French Open marked the 13th consecutive year in which she won at least one Grand Slam title.

Her favorite playing surface was clay; between 1973 and 1979 she won 125 consecutive clay-court matches. Her trademark was a two-handed backhand. Although a few fans disliked her unshakable "ice maiden" image, her strongest attribute was her mental toughness.

Evert's accomplishments include winning the women's singles title in the United States Clay Court Championship from 1972 through 1975 and in 1979 and 1980. She won the French Open in 1974, 1975, 1979, 1980, 1983, 1985, and 1986—the only seven-time winner. She won the Australian Open in 1982 and 1984. She was married to English tennis professional John Lloyd from 1979 until 1987. She married American skier and cable commentator Andy Mill in 1988.

EVOLUTION. People have always wondered how life originated and how so many different kinds of plants and animals arose. Stories of a supernatural creation of life developed among many peoples. The Bible, for example, tells of God's creation of man and the higher animals at a given time. Many people also believed that insects, worms, and other lower creatures spontaneously generated in mud and decay. Long after these stories became rooted in tradition, scientists began to question them.

Theories of special creation usually hold that life retains its original God-created form. It is immutable, or unchangeable. By contrast, theories of organic evolution hold that all organisms, including man, are mutable; that is, they respond dynamically to changes in the environment.

Although the theory of evolution is accepted by the overwhelming majority of the scientific community, this theory has aroused considerable and continual controversy since the 1840s. Most objections have come from religious groups that support what they term the theory of creationism. This concept defends the belief that all beings were created by God. Fundamentalists and others feel that the premise that species are continually changing conflicts with literal interpretations of the Bible. The Roman Catholic church leaves open the question of the evolution of man's body, provided that specific beliefs, including that about man's descent from Adam and Eve, are accepted. Political obstacles to the scientific acceptance of evolution have existed in some countries.

THE ORIGIN OF LIFE

The first serious attack on the idea of spontaneous generation of life began in the 1600s. In 1668 Francesco Redi, an Italian biologist, proved that maggots did not arise spontaneously in decaying matter, as commonly believed, but from eggs deposited by flies. The next hundred years found many scientists beginning to believe that all the larger kinds of life came from similar ancestors, too.

Proof that microorganisms are not generated spontaneously came in 1862, when Louis Pasteur, a French scientist, showed that they, too, develop from preexisting life (*see* Pasteur). But if all living things, large and small, arise from preexisting organisms of the same species, or kind, how did the first life originate on Earth?

Perhaps microorganisms reached Earth from another planet. Most scientists discount this idea, called panspermia, because the radiation in space would kill cells or spores before they reached Earth. They believe that terrestrial life evolved from nonliving matter on the primitive Earth (*see* Extraterrestrial Life). The way in which life first formed may always remain a mystery, but the following explanation is likely.

This article was contributed by Clark Hubbs, Professor of Zoology, the University of Texas at Austin, and Leslie E. Orgel, Senior Fellow, the Salk Institute, San Diego, Calif.

Organic Molecules on the Primitive Earth

Scientists recently discovered fossil remains of microorganisms resembling blue-green algae in rocks that were about 3 billion years old. Since Earth is thought to be about 4.5 billion years old, the first living things probably evolved within a billion years after its formation. In 1924 Aleksandr Oparin, a Russian biochemist, pointed out that the atmosphere of the primitive Earth was probably very different from today's. A so-called reducing atmosphere with much more hydrogen than oxygen probably existed then. It also probably contained methane, other hydrocarbons, and ammonia. Oparin suggested that the organic compounds in the first organisms could have been formed by the action of sunlight and the heat from volcanoes or lightning on the reducing atmosphere of the primitive Earth.

All living things are alike in some respects. For example, they all consist of cells that must have protein enzymes to catalyze, or speed up, the biochemical reactions of life (*see* Cell; Enzymes). Enzymes consist of 20 kinds of amino acids, which are found in the proteins of all organisms. Also, all cells transmit heredity through nucleic acids (*see* Genetics). In all species nucleic acids consist of the same two sugars and the same four or five bases. But were all of these organic molecules available on the primitive Earth? According to the latest studies, they probably were.

In 1953 Stanley Miller, then a young graduate student working with the Nobel-prizewinning United States chemist Harold Urey, passed an electric spark through an experimental atmosphere containing the chemicals suggested by Oparin. A mixture of organic chemicals resulted, including several of the vital amino acids. Since Miller's pioneering work, considerable research has been done in prebiotic chemistry, the study of primitive Earth's chemistry before life took hold. Many of the amino acids and nucleic acid components found in nature have been made in the laboratory under prebiotic conditions. Radio astronomers have also discovered that many related molecules are abundant in dust clouds far from our solar system. The Murchison meteorite that fell on Australia in 1969 contained several amino acids common on Earth. Those organic substances must have originated elsewhere.

From Organic Chemicals to Cells

Scientists think that the simple prebiotic organic chemicals concentrated in lakes and tidal pools, forming a rich prebiotic "soup." Influenced by ultraviolet light and mild heating, the simple molecules then condensed into more complex ones resembling proteins and nucleic acids. This might have taken place on the surface of minerals or in oily colloidal droplets called coacervates floating in the prebiotic soup (*see* Colloid).

The next stage in the formation of life is the vaguest. For life to persist after becoming established there must have been polymer (long-stranded) molecules capable of replicating, or making copies of, themselves. Presumably, these first self-replicating polymers were like nucleic acids.

Once polymers could replicate, those best able to cope with their surroundings survived. The fastest-replicating polymers lasted, while their slower competitors were eliminated. Gradually, the self-replicators used the chemical environment to their advantage. In time they were able to produce enzymes for their vital needs. In addition, they developed membranes to isolate themselves from the environment (*see* Biochemistry). Once these adaptations were achieved, the most primitive cells arose. From then on, only natural selection was needed to give rise to the many species that would inhabit Earth.

THE MUTABILITY OF LIVING THINGS

Fossils show clearly that various living things have existed which no longer do. Did entire groups become extinct only to be replaced by freshly created ones? Or were some of those groups the ancestors from which modern groups evolved? Changes can be demonstrated in living things today, which prompts scientists to believe that evolution through change is the answer. Mosquitoes, for example, can adapt to the insecticide DDT. After a mosquito population has been exposed to DDT repeatedly, it

Lightning and radiation acting on Earth's primitive atmosphere could have produced some substances needed for life.

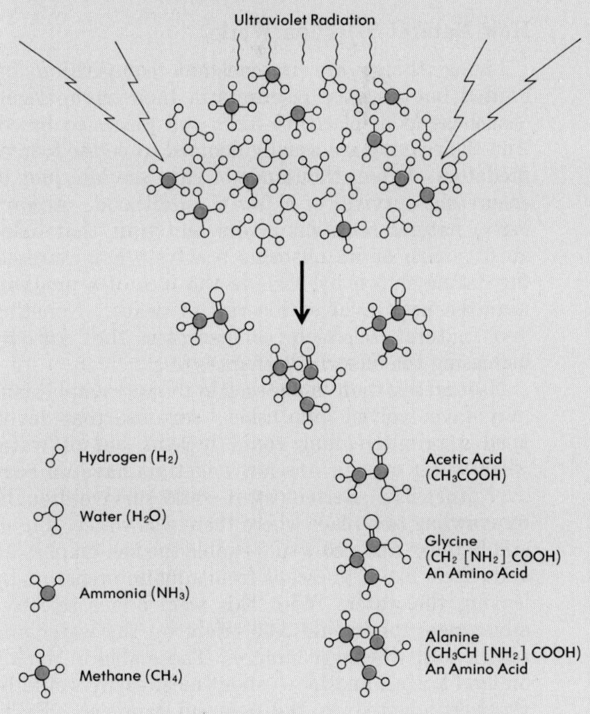

may take a dose a thousand times stronger than the original to kill the surviving population.

Natural Selection Directs Evolution

Acquisition of DDT resistance hints at but does not show how evolution takes place. In 1801 Jean Baptiste Lamarck, a French naturalist, suggested that evolution resulted from the use or nonuse of body structures. Lamarck knew that a structure grows through use, just as the muscles of a weight lifter grow large. He assumed that the enlarged structures of a parent would be inherited by the offspring, and that nonuse, too, would result in a smaller structure capable of being inherited. In this way, an almost infinite number of structural developments or losses would lead to evolutionary change. Several decades ago, Trofim Lysenko, a Russian agronomist, unsuccessfully applied Lamarckian ideas to agriculture.

Charles Darwin, a 19-century English naturalist, argued that natural selection guides evolutionary change (*see* Darwin). Alfred Russel Wallace, another English naturalist, also thought animals and plants could change with time, and in 1858 he and Darwin presented preliminary accounts of the theory of natural selection. In 1859 Darwin published his views in the 'Origin of Species', and a major controversy was immediately sparked between theologians and scientists. Even scientists argued with each other over how the traits Darwin thought were subject to natural selection could be inherited. Ironically, an Austrian priest, Gregor Mendel, published genetic principles in 1866 that could have settled the problem. But Mendel's work was not appreciated until 1900. (*See also* Genetics.)

How Natural Selection Works

Living things are in constant competition for limited but essential resources in their environment—such as food, places to hide, and places to breed. And their young are usually doomed to be the food of predators. Often, thousands of eggs are laid just to ensure the survival of a few to adulthood. Accordingly, natural selection favors any trait that helps an organism or its offspring survive. For example, the daring shown by birds in the face of a predator near the nest involves the risk of death. Nonetheless, natural selection compensates the risk by increasing the offspring's chances of survival.

Natural selection can be seen in the way amphibians may have evolved from fishes. Any fish that developed a primitive lung could breathe out of water when water oxygen was low and thus have an edge over other fish. Better yet, it could survive drought by crawling to a place where there was water. Lungs and limblike fins also would enable the fish-amphibian and others like it to escape from aquatic predators by leaving the water. With this tremendous selective advantage, they could rest safely by the water and return to it whenever hungry. Those able to remain on land longest and move about most easily would be the best-adapted to the new environment. Eventually, predators able to chase the fish-amphibians would evolve. Then any trait that improved agility on land, such as stronger limbs, would increase the survival potential of predator or prey, and the newly emerging amphibians could become firmly established.

Fossils Leave a Record of Evolution

Fossils of animals that no longer exist puzzled the early 19th-century naturalists. Georges Cuvier, a French scientist, believed that the fossil sequence resulted from a series of recurring catastrophes, followed by creation of new plants and animals. Charles Lyell, a British geologist and a friend of Darwin, saw instead that the fossil sequences in progressively younger rock layers agreed with the notion that living things experience gradual body changes over the years.

A complete fossil record for every form of life is nearly impossible. To become fossilized, an animal or plant must die and somehow become buried before it decomposes. The best fossils often occur in soils where minerals replace original tissues and leave a rock replica of the organism. Exposed but undiscovered fossils are usually destroyed by erosion or other geological processes. A fossil deposited 300 million years ago, for example, stood a greater chance of being destroyed than of becoming part of the fossil record.

Hard-shelled marine animals and fairly recent species have the best fossil records. One of the most complete series traces the evolution of the horse (*see* Horse). The fossil record of human evolution is expanding considerably as anthropologists uncover more and more traces of early man. (For a more extensive discussion of human evolution, *see* Man.)

The Role of Species in Evolution

Most living things fall into more than one category. Cats, for instance, can be subdivided into lions, tigers, leopards, house cats, and such. The last handy breakdown of any living group is a species. Racial variants, called subspecies, are only matters of degree. Populations of the same species can interbreed, exchange genes, and pass on traits to their offspring. Amoebas and some other species do not reproduce sexually, but they still resemble their fellow species members, with few intermediate types.

Extinct and recent species in an evolutionary line share structural similarities as a result of natural selection. The ancestors of all living species were the best-adapted individuals of their day, just as future beings will evolve from the best-adapted individuals of today, if natural selection is allowed to run its course. Body makeup or behavioral patterns gave them some survival benefit, and the ability to develop key structures or behave in the selectively valuable way was passed on to their descendants. However, changes in those inherited traits might be valuable, too, if the environment changed. A muscular fin, for example, would be of great value in enabling a lunged fish to crawl out of a drying pond. After generations, the selectively valuable structure might no longer look like the original. Nonetheless, the underlying "raw material" could be recognized. The main limbs of whales, mice, bats, and humans have similar components. Regardless of their function, they are homologous structures. By contrast, structures with the same function but different evolutionary origin, such as the wings of insects and of birds, are analogous structures. Scientists can trace homologies in the embryological development of certain organisms (*see* Embryology).

While the fossil record shows that most evolutionary modifications stem from a gradual accumulation of body changes, scientists sometimes find it hard to classify individual fossils. Remains of the "earliest" modern horse, for example, look almost like those of the "latest" ancestral type that preceded it. Similar classification problems occur in tracing the split of daughter species from a common one. The two daughter species are very much alike during the initial stages of evolution. They are merely different species in a genus. Later descendants diverge more, first forming different genera in a family and then different families in an order. In this manner, a species that existed millions of years ago could have radiated into other groups that successively radiated in turn until, in time, a modern species evolved. But so many changes occurred in the course of evolution that the modern species bears no resemblance to the ancient groups.

Evolution Is a Continuing Process

Natural selection favors inheritable traits that are not too extreme. A highly aggressive animal, for instance, might occupy a food-rich territory; but because of its fierceness it might attack a hungry, more powerful predator and be killed. On the other hand, an extremely docile animal might so avoid predators that it occupies a scanty feeding territory and thus might starve. In certain cases selection could favor either animal. If the number of predators dropped, the aggressive animal would have the advantage. If the number of predators grew, the docile animal would have the advantage.

Geographic barriers are the best stimulants of evolution. Without them, strong selective forces are needed for speciation. Formation of a mountain range, for example, can divide a species into isolated units and thus block gene exchange. Also, a few members of a species might wander across a mountain chain and establish an isolated population. Eventually, the mountains might erode enough for descendants of the isolates to regain contact with descendants of the parent group. If they diverged too much genetically but still interbred, most of their offspring would be infertile hybrids.

A change in the range of a parent species can separate and isolate its populations. If they are separated long enough for genetic changes to accumulate, new species incapable of interbreeding can evolve. Read the diagram from bottom to top.

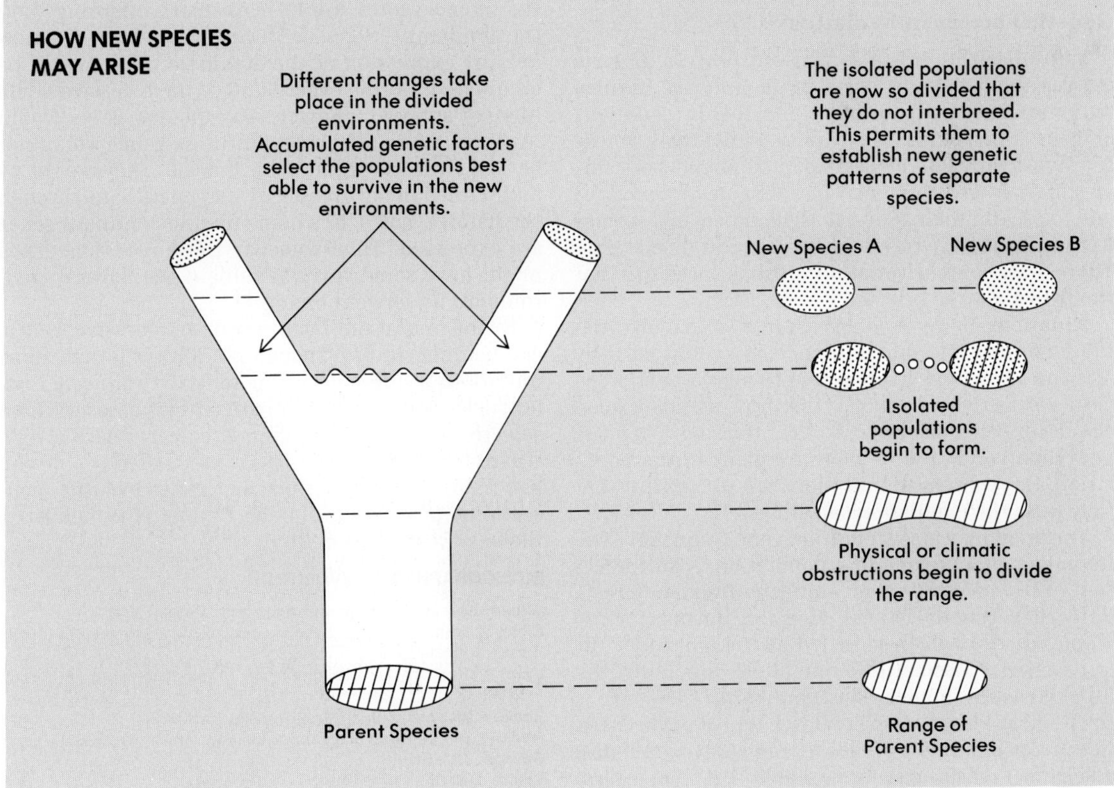
HOW NEW SPECIES MAY ARISE
Different changes take place in the divided environments. Accumulated genetic factors select the populations best able to survive in the new environments.
The isolated populations are now so divided that they do not interbreed. This permits them to establish new genetic patterns of separate species.
New Species A
New Species B
Isolated populations begin to form.
Physical or climatic obstructions begin to divide the range.
Parent Species
Range of Parent Species

Photos, from the experiments of Dr. H.B.D. Kettlewell, Oxford University

The peppered moth shows natural selection in action. The once-dominant grayish variety (encircled, left) blended well against trees. As industrial pollution increased, the darker variety (lower on the tree bark, right), stemming from a gene mutation in the 1880s, began to prevail.

Genetic Factors in Evolution

Natural selection is a sorting-out process. It sorts out variations in body forms, or phenotypes. In turn, an individual's body form is controlled by genotype, or genetic makeup. Thus, those individuals whose genotypes produce the best-adapted phenotypes survive in their environment. They are able to reproduce and to pass on their genes. If all members of a species were identical, there would be no natural selection. There must be some variation within a species so that the fittest may be selected.

Mutations, or gene changes, are a source of variation and have a strong influence on evolution. If by altering a genotype a mutation provides a phenotype with a selective advantage, this trait stands a good chance of being passed on to the offspring. Then the new genotype would be more frequent in the population. However, most mutations are so harmful that they raise the population's death rate.

Variation may also stem from gene frequency. The frequency of any gene in a population is an indication of its selective value, and gene frequency rests on certain genetic factors. Most organisms, for example, carry two genes, called alleles, for any trait (*see* Genetics). Sometimes one allele dominates the other. It is the homozygous dominant. The other is the homozygous recessive. A hidden pool of variation lies in a population's alleles. If a recessive allele has a selective advantage, for example, then the recessive homozygotes would leave more offspring than the dominants. Soon, according to the laws of genetics, any expression of the dominant allele would be eliminated. On the other hand, if the recessive allele hinders survival, the recessive homozygotes would leave few or no offspring. But these genes would not be lost from the gene pool. Instead, they would be maintained in low frequency for generations through the heterozygotes, in whom only the dominant genes are expressed. Then someday those recessive genes might have some survival value if the natural environment underwent changes.

Rising mutation rates, even in recessive genes, can be undesirable. Though not always lethal, some mutations reduce survival potential. Ordinarily, natural selection would eliminate mutant genes with no selective value. Among human cultures with a high regard for life, however, less well-adapted people can live a full life and pass on their genes to future generations. (*See also* Animals, Extinct; Biochemistry; Biology; Ecology; Heredity.)

BIBLIOGRAPHY FOR EVOLUTION

Althea. How Life Began (Cambridge Univ. Press, 1983).

Eisely, Loren. Darwin and the Mysterious Mr. X: New Light on the Evolutionists (Harcourt, 1981).

Karp, Walter. Charles Darwin and the Origin of the Species (Harper, 1968).

Leakey, Richard. Human Origins (Lodestar, 1982).

Radley, Gail. Nothing Stays the Same Forever (Crown, 1981).

Savage, J.M. Evolution, 3rd ed. (Holt, 1977).

Taylor, L.B. Story of Evolution (Watts, 1981).

EXERCISE

Doing sit-ups to strengthen leg, back, and stomach muscles is a common form of aerobic exercise.

Tom Petrillo

EXERCISE. The physical training of the body to improve the way it functions is known as exercise. Exercise can be categorized as active or passive. Exercise involving voluntary physical effort such as walking, swimming, bicycling, and jogging is known as active exercise. Passive exercise involves a machine or the action of another person. It includes many physical therapy techniques.

Physical Fitness

The body's capacity to perform work and defend itself against disease, infection, and the effects of physical stresses such as heat or cold is a measure of physical fitness. The degree of fitness required is related to the degree of stress the body must overcome.

Specific types of physical fitness are required for each person's body to meet special demands. For example, if a job requires that unusually heavy loads be moved, additional strength in certain muscles must be developed. Through exercise or work, muscles develop strength. Nerve-muscle coordination is also improved. A body's ability to change posture suddenly requires orthostatic fitness. Orthostatic fitness can be determined by measuring how well the blood circulation can adjust to a quick change of posture, such as standing up after lying down.

Bursts of physical activity of maximum effort lasting less than 10 seconds require anaerobic fitness. This is the ability of cells to work without oxygen. Anaerobic activity involves sudden rigorous movements such as sprinting to catch a bus or an extra burst of speed needed to make a touchdown. During anaerobic exercise, intense muscle activity is required. This activity exceeds the capacity of the heart and lungs to supply oxygen to the cells.

When anaerobic activity ends, the individual is left gasping for breath while heart and lungs are hard at work supplying oxygen to reverse this oxygen debt condition. Any sport or activity that occasionally requires short bursts of energy followed by long pauses is considered an anaerobic activity.

Exhaustive efforts of longer duration require aerobic fitness. This is distinguished by the body's ability to transport and consume oxygen efficiently. Running, swimming, bicycling, and cross-country skiing are examples of aerobic exercise. Aerobic exercise is characterized by the continuous, moderately strenuous effort that occurs at a pace enabling the heart and lungs to supply the oxygen needed by the muscles.

Health, Fitness, and Skill

In describing the effects of exercise and physical conditioning, it is necessary to differentiate between health and fitness, and between fitness and skill. Health is thought by some to be the absence of disease. More specifically, it is the capacity of all body organs and systems to function at high levels. Fitness relates to performance and survival.

Usually, but not always, good fitness requires good health. Many exceptions are seen in sports competition. Intensely motivated and competitive athletes, even when ill or injured, have won contests and broken world records. During past Olympic contests athletes suffering from such physical disorders as infections, dysentery, flu, and broken bones have performed with superior skill. In contrast, there are perfectly healthy individuals who are unable to perform strenuous work because their bodies are poorly conditioned. Generally, however, a skilled performance is a good indication that the person is physically fit and in good health.

The Need for Exercise

Exercise and physical fitness are obviously necessary for athletes, soldiers, firemen, and all those whose jobs require high levels of physical performance. Then why should a sedentary person living in a comfortable, industrialized society exercise?

Medical and health professionals have determined that everyone, depending on the individual's metabolism, has a minimum level of physical activity that must be maintained to prevent serious physical deterioration. The human body and all of its parts, like any living organism, must be used or they atrophy. The loss of structure and function that occurs when a broken arm is immobilized in a cast clearly

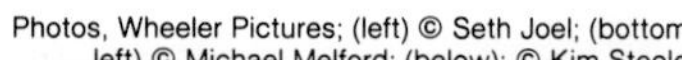

Photos, Wheeler Pictures; (left) © Seth Joel; (bottom left) © Michael Melford; (below); © Kim Steele

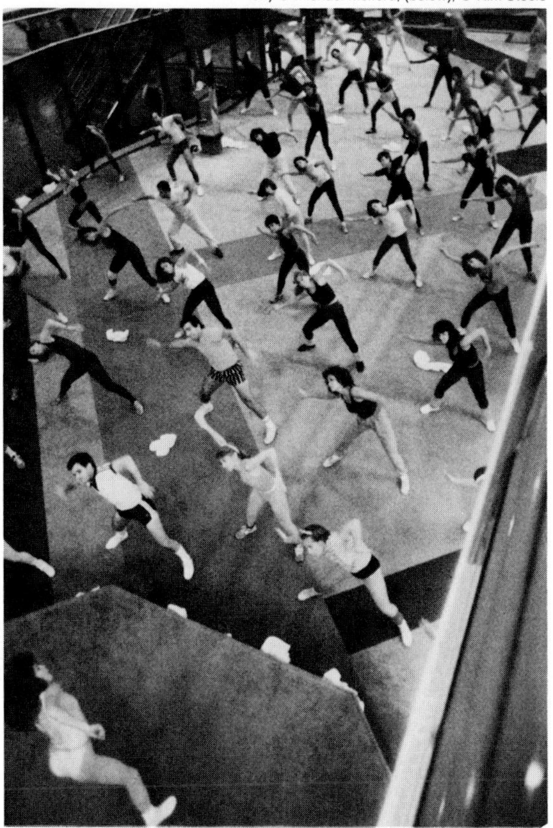

Health clubs (top), with their great array of exercise equipment, have become very popular since the late 1970s. A class of arthritis sufferers (above) exercises in a swimming pool. Aerobic exercise classes (right) attempt to increase the efficiency of the body's oxygen intake.

demonstrates what happens when body parts are not exercised and used.

Basic survival once required the output of enormous physical energy by people on many levels of society. Modern technology has simplified life's physical demands in various ways. Machines—from washing machines to automobiles and elaborate industrial equipment—have reduced the amount of labor required of people.

In more primitive times most individuals burned up the calories gained from the food they consumed through the rigors of their daily activities. This is no longer true for most people, particularly those living in industrialized nations.

Many people have retained their capacity for physical work. Even those who have been physically inactive for a long time can restore lost physical capability with just a month or two of daily physical training. People who exercise and reach their near-maximum physical capability can maintain it by exercising vigorously on alternate days.

Physical fitness and exercise are important for good physical and mental health, including weight control. Exercise helps the individual develop and maintain a strong self-image and a sense of emotional balance. As a person gets older, exercise becomes more important because after age 30 the heart's blood pumping capacity declines at a rate of about 8 percent each decade.

Exercise is also important for children. Vigorous physical activity aids in a child's overall development so he or she reaches optimal size and functional capacities in adulthood. Current research shows that exercise can reduce the accumulation of low density lipoprotein (LDL) and cholesterol on artery walls of children and adults. Excess cholesterol can increase the risk of heart disease. There is, however, no evidence that exercise prolongs life. Former athletes do not live longer than nonathletes, nor are they saved from heart disease. The benefits of exercise cannot be sustained for more than a few months or years without continued exercise. Even Olympic-level athletes will regress rapidly to pre-training levels once they stop exercising. The amount of activity necessary for fitness varies from person to person. Age, physical structure, health, and gender are contributing factors.

Most common forms of exercise, such as bicycling and swimming, rarely cause serious injury. But contact sports, such as football and judo, can cause wear on the joints that can lead to articular disease, or joint problems. The problem for most beginners is overexercise. Many people experience stiffness after the first day of exercise, but this is harmless and does not last long. People who are overweight, past middle age, or who suffer from heart disease should consult a physician before starting any exercise program. Sometimes children who are involved in competitive sports suffer from muscle and joint problems.

Benefits

Today's sedentary man who is past age 30 begins to think about fitness for his survival as he sees his older friends, who are in their 40s, die of heart attacks. Some researchers estimate that people who maintain a moderately high level of physical activity can reduce the risk of coronary heart disease by about a third. Exercise also aids in eliminating such other conditions as obesity and high blood pressure, which are among the causes of heart disease.

To achieve maximum cardiovascular benefits from aerobic exercise, exercise professionals recommend elevating the heartbeat to approximately 70 percent of the individual's maximum heart rate. Once that elevated rate is achieved during exercise, continue exercising to maintain that rate for 30 minutes. This regime should be repeated three times each week.

To calculate the maximum heart rate, an individual should subtract his or her age from 220. Multiply the remainder by 70 percent. For example, a 40-year-old woman subtracts 40 from 220 for a maximum heartbeat rate of 180. Multiplying 180 by 0.7 tells her that she should exercise to elevate her heartbeat to 126 beats per minute and maintain that rate of 126 beats per minute for 30 minutes three times a week. The 70 percent figure is an average. The range is 60 to 80 percent. Older people, or those just starting an exercise program will aim for the 60 percent level, while more active individuals who are more physically fit will strive to reach 80.

The person who has been idle for years does not benefit from a crash attempt to make up for lost years of exercise by an exhaustive regimen. This can do more harm than good. Exercise can be harmful in various circumstances, particularly if people overexert themselves or do not perform the exercises correctly. (*See also* Disease; Health.)

EXISTENTIALISM. The life of a flower is predictable—the seed is planted and the flower grows, flourishes, and dies. Much the same can be said of a fish, a cat, or a dog. The lives of these animals depend a great deal on the circumstances into which they are put, but what they do is done instinctively, seemingly predetermined by their natures. With human beings, however, the situation is different. They can make choices, they can think about their lives and decide what direction they want them to take. And they realize they are in a world that does not always make sense, a world that may be filled with uncertainty—where actions based upon the best-laid plans of individuals and societies often have an unintended effect.

The collection of philosophical attitudes that present this kind of view of human life and the world is called existentialism. It is not a philosophical school; it may more accurately be called a philosophical tendency that has a number of significant themes. These themes have been dealt with by a great variety of writers in conflicting and frequently contradictory ways. The fact that these themes are consistently addressed in a significant way makes it possible to include a great diversity of thought under the term existentialism.

Among the first and most significant of authors writing on existentialist themes was the Dane Søren Kierkegaard, who wrote from a Christian perspective (*see* Kierkegaard). Others include Albert Camus and Jean-Paul Sartre, who were atheists (*see* Camus; Sartre), and the German Martin Heidegger, author of a very complex philosophical explanation. Some 20th-century theologians influenced by existentialism were Karl Barth, Paul Tillich, and Rudolph Bultmann. The psychologist Karl Jaspers used existentialist ideas to explain the self and freedom of choice.

Existence. The chief theme of existentialism, of course, is existence itself. Flowers, animals, and stones all exist. But people exist in a different way. Individuals are unique—able to think about themselves and the world in which they find themselves and to make choices. They can choose because they are free, and the choices they make establish the future into which they project themselves.

Limits. Another theme is that of limits. Individuals are thrust into existence for a short time only. They are caught in what existentialist theologian Karl Barth called "the boundary situation." They come into the world at a specific time, and they leave it at another specific time. About this there is no choice. Because the time is limited, there are urgent decisions to be made. People are free to make them on the basis of whatever facts they have available. But the facts themselves are a matter of choice. Individuals select the criteria by which they decide the course of their lives or particular undertakings.

The world. Another major theme is the world itself—specifically what can be known about it. A pre-existentialist writer, the novelist Dostoevski, said that the universe does not make sense. There are no underlying patterns that can be perceived by everyone, on the basis of which everyone agrees: "This is what the world is all about." Life, and the world itself, are often unpredictable and capricious. All attempts to find or impose an order on the world must fail because no single human mind—nor all human minds together—can adequately perceive all possible facts, make sense of them, and put them into an ordered scheme. If there were such an order or scheme, it would mean that everything is determined as it is for the flower and the fish. Humans would not have free choice but would be fated to whatever course their lives take.

This inability to comprehend the world is compounded by individuals' inability to gain a thorough understanding of other people or even of themselves. The meanings of their own mental processes, emotions, and motivations are never entirely clear to them as they try to make sense of themselves and the larger and smaller worlds in which they live. If there is a standard of truth outside themselves, they must select it and commit themselves to it, though they are unable to prove the certainty of such a truth.

EXPLORATION

A Navy explorer looks back along the trail he has blazed in Antarctica during the International Geophysical Year. His tractor pushes a crevasse detector.

EXPLORATION. When most of the earth was still unexplored, many men made long journeys over uncharted seas and unmapped territories. Some of them were looking for new trade routes. Some were seeking wealth and fame. Others wanted to claim new lands for their rulers. Finally there were explorers who struck out into the unknown simply for the personal thrill of discovery. They wanted to be the first persons to set foot on strange territory.

Today few places in the world remain undiscovered. Most modern explorers are scientific investigators rather than adventurers. Their visits are no longer limited to the land surfaces of the earth. Man has begun the exploration of the oceans, venturing thousands of feet below sea level. When two astronauts walked on the surface of the moon in 1969, man had reached the first destination of his journey into space. Despite the development of testing devices that conduct experiments under remote control, exploration is still the most direct way of answering questions about unknown places.

The Earliest Explorer

The first explorer of whom there is any knowledge was Hannu, an Egyptian. In 2750 B.C. he made an expedition to the limits of the known world.

Hannu traveled to the land of Punt. This was the name for the region at the southeastern end of the Red Sea, including a part of modern Ethiopia and of Somalia. He returned home with great riches in precious metals, myrrh, and wood. Hannu left an account of his adventures carved in rock. In the 15th century B.C. Queen Hatshepsut, eager for wealth to enrich her kingdom, also sent an expedition to Punt.

Phoenician Adventurers

The Phoenicians were the first people to communicate to the inhabitants of other countries a knowledge of distant lands. They explored the Atlantic coast of Europe. According to the Greek historian Herodotus, Phoenician sailors went entirely around Africa about 600 B.C. The expedition was financed by King Necho II of Egypt. From 1000 to 800 B.C., Carthage, which had been founded by Phoenicians from Tyre, was the starting point for many explorers and colonists. (*See also* Phoenicians; Carthage.)

Hanno, a Carthaginian, was one of the greatest of the ancient explorers. He was the first man to visit and describe western Africa. About 500 B.C. he set out at the head of a vast expedition to colonize Africa and to found cities. It is said that he had 60 vessels, each driven by 50 oars, and that he started with 30,000 men and women. He left some people at each place he stopped to begin new settlements.

Greek and Roman Colonizers

Herodotus, the historian who described the Phoenician exploits in his writings, was an explorer in his own right. He wrote descriptions of the lands he visited in the 5th century B.C. (*See also* Herodotus.)

About 400 B.C. an important exploration by ancient Greeks was brought about by a military disaster. Some 13,000 Greek soldiers, in retreat from Sardis, were forced to fight their way over some 1,500 miles of unknown territory in order to reach home. They brought back accounts of the land through which they had traveled. The Greek historian Xenophon led and recorded this adventure (*see* Xenophon).

The expeditions in the 4th century B.C. of Alexander the Great carried the influence of Mediterranean culture to the East and brought the influence of Eastern culture into the Mediterranean area (*see* Alexander the Great). At the same time Pytheas, a navigator from Massalia (modern Marseilles), explored in the north. He probably traveled as far as Iceland.

From 58 to 52 B.C. Julius Caesar conquered great areas of France, Germany, and Britain. He combined exploration with conquest on his military expeditions. (*See also* Caesar.)

The Death and Rebirth of Exploration

For the next thousand years there was little travel or exploration. In the 10th century A.D., however, the Northmen pushed far out on the Atlantic Ocean (*see* Northmen). In the 13th century Marco Polo journeyed overland to China (*see* Polo, Marco).

It was not until the days of Prince Henry of Portugal that the Age of Discovery actually began (*see* Henry the Navigator). Within about 30 years of his death, in 1460, the coast of the Americas, from Greenland to Cape Horn, was explored. The coasts of eastern Africa, Arabia, Persia, and India also were visited. Numerous islands in the Indian Ocean too were discovered.

Columbus found the New World near the end of the 15th century. Later, Vasco da Gama sailed around Africa. (*See* Columbus, Christopher; Gama.) Bartholomew Diaz rounded the Cape of Good Hope in 1488 (*see* Diaz, Bartholomew).

John and Sebastian Cabot reached the north coast of North America in 1497 (*see* Cabot). In 1500 Vicente Pinzón, a Spanish explorer, landed in Brazil. In the same year Pedro Alvarez Cabral, a Portuguese navigator, also landed there.

16th-Century Discoveries

The great explorations during the 16th century were among the world's most important. Vasco Nuñez de Balboa crossed the Isthmus of Panama and discovered the Pacific Ocean in 1513. Shortly thereafter Hernando Cortez conquered and explored Mexico, and Ferdinand Magellan's expedition from 1519 to 1522 was the first to go around the world. (*See also* Balboa; Cortez; Magellan.)

In the 1530's Francisco Pizarro conquered and explored Peru (*see* Pizarro). In 1535 the St. Lawrence River was discovered by Jacques Cartier (*see* Cartier). In 1542 Juan Cabrillo explored the California coast. Also during the first half of the 16th century Francisco Coronado and Hernando de Soto, seeking for gold in North America, covered great stretches of unknown land (*see* Coronado; De Soto).

English exploration flowered under Queen Elizabeth I during the late 1500's. Sir Francis Drake and Sir Walter Raleigh were two of the great sailors who explored the New World in the service of the queen. (*See also* Elizabeth I; Drake; Raleigh, Sir Walter; England.)

Expeditions in Canada

In 1576 Sir Martin Frobisher, seeking the Northwest Passage, traveled the Canadian Arctic. Henry Hudson failed to find the Northeast or Northwest Passage but added to the knowledge of the Arctic and North America. He discovered Hudson Bay in 1610. Samuel de Champlain, in the early 1600's, was the first to systematically investigate the New England coast. (*See also* Hudson, Henry; Champlain.)

Sir Alexander Mackenzie, from 1789 to 1793, explored the Mackenzie River and was the first white man to cross Canada to the Pacific. Captain James Cook, in his three long voyages during the second half of the 18th century, completed the world's knowledge of most of the lands in the southern and eastern Pacific. (*See also* Cook.)

This picture shows Thor Heyerdahl's balsa raft, *Kon-Tiki*, at sea during his 1947 voyage. Heyerdahl wanted to prove the origin of the Polynesian people.

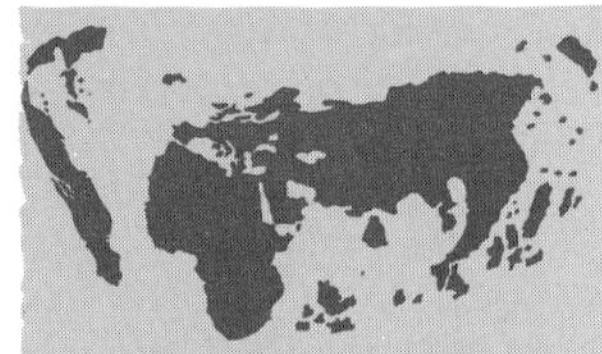
WORLD MAP-1507

PIZARRO-1532-33

COOK-1769-70

LEWIS AND CLARK-1804-5

Many Ventures Into the Unknown

Ancient Explorations

2750 B.C. Hannu explores the limits of the known world; travels to the land of Punt.

1480 B.C. Queen Hatshepsut sends an expedition from Egypt to Punt.

814 B.C. Carthage founded by Phoenicians from Tyre; thereafter becomes the embarkation point for many explorers.

600 B.C. Phoenician seamen sail around Africa.

500 B.C. Hanno becomes the first man to explore and describe western Africa.

401 B.C. Xenophon leads Greek soldiers on a retreat from Persia; brings back an account of his travels.

400–300 B.C. Alexander the Great enters India in 327 B.C. Pytheas explores the north-eastern Atlantic; visits England in 310 B.C.

58–52 B.C. Julius Caesar combines conquest and exploration on his expeditions to France, Germany, and Britain.

83 A.D. Gnaeus Julius Agricola discovers the Scottish Highlands.

159 A.D. Ptolemy draws maps of the known world.

432–461 A.D. St. Patrick explores Ireland.

Medieval Explorations

861. The Vikings are the first to visit Iceland.

874. The Norse colonize Iceland.

986. Eric the Red brings settlers to Greenland.

1000. Leif Ericson discovers North America.

1096–1270. The Crusades bring Europe into contact with the culture of Asia.

1260–69. Maffeo and Nicolo Polo journey from Venice to China and back.

1271–95. Marco Polo travels to China, Southeast Asia, and eastern Africa.

15th-Century Explorations

1418. Prince Henry of Portugal starts a new era of exploration.

1488. Bartholomew Diaz is the first European to round the Cape of Good Hope.

1492. Christopher Columbus sails west and discovers the West Indies.

1497. John and Sebastian Cabot reach the north coast of North America.

1497–98. Vasco da Gama sails around Africa to India.

1498. Christopher Columbus discovers the mainland of South America.

16th-Century Explorations

1500. Vicente Pinzón lands in Brazil; later in 1500 Pedro Alvarez Cabral visits another part of the Brazilian coast.

1501. Gaspar Corte-Real reaches Newfoundland from Portugal.

1502. Christopher Columbus discovers Central America.

1502–7. Lodovico di Varthema visits China, the Malay Peninsula, and the East Indies.

1513. Vasco Nuñez de Balboa crosses the Isthmus of Panama (Darien) and discovers the Pacific Ocean.

1513. Juan Ponce de León discovers Florida.

1519–21. Hernando Cortez conquers and explores Mexico.

1519–22. Ferdinand Magellan's expedition makes the first circumnavigation of the world; party discovers Patagonia in 1520.

1524. Giovanni da Verrazzano reaches present North Carolina; sails north to Newfoundland; describes northeastern North America.

1524–25. Estevan Gómez explores the North American coast from present Maine to New Jersey.

1532–33. Francisco Pizarro conquers and explores Peru.

1535. Jacques Cartier discovers the St. Lawrence River.

1539–42. Hernando de Soto crosses the southeastern section of the present United States.

1540–41. Francisco Coronado explores the southwestern section of the present United States; discovers the Grand Canyon.

1541. Francisco de Orellana crosses the Andes; follows the Amazon River to the Atlantic.

1542. Juan Cabrillo explores the California coast.

1565. Andres de Urdaneta makes the first crossing of the Pacific Ocean from west to east.

1575–89. Martin Frobisher and John Davis explore the straits north of the St. Lawrence River.

1577–80. Francis Drake circumnavigates the earth.

1595. Walter Raleigh explores Guiana and the Orinoco.

17th-Century Explorations

1602. Bartholomew Gosnold visits the New England coast.

1608–16. Samuel de Champlain explores the St. Lawrence River system; discovers Lake Huron in 1615.

1610. Henry Hudson discovers Hudson Strait and Hudson Bay.

1616. Willem Schouten discovers and names Cape Horn, the southernmost tip of South America.

1626. Stephen Cacella and John Cabral explore the eastern Himalayas and visit Tibet.

1634. Jean Nicolet crosses Lake Michigan to the Fox River.

1642. Abel Tasman discovers New Zealand and Tasmania.

1673. Louis Joliet and Jacques Marquette descend the Mississippi River.

1681–82. La Salle sails down the Mississippi to the Gulf of Mexico.

18th-Century Explorations

1768. Louis Antoine de Bougainville explores the New Hebrides.

1769–70. James Cook explores New Zealand and the coast of Australia.

1778. James Cook rediscovers the Hawaiian Islands.

1789. Alexander Mackenzie follows the Mackenzie River from its source to the Arctic Ocean.

1792. George Vancouver explores Puget Sound.

1793. Alexander Mackenzie becomes the first white man to cross Canada to the Pacific.

1795–97. Mungo Park probes the interior of western Africa.

1799–1800. Alexander von Humboldt explores Venezuela.

19th-Century Explorations

1804–5. Meriwether Lewis and William Clark cross North America west to the Pacific.

1805–6. Zebulon Pike explores the Mississippi and Arkansas rivers; discovers Pikes Peak.

1828. René Caillié reaches Timbuktu.

1830. Richard and John Lander determine the course of the Niger.

1831–36. Charles Darwin conducts studies in South America, in the South Pacific, and on islands of the Atlantic.

1842–47. John Charles Frémont explores the Far West.

1849–55. Heinrich Barth makes the first scientific investigation of Africa.

1849–56. David Livingstone makes important finds in Africa, including Victoria Falls.

1858. Richard Burton and John H. Speke discover Lake Tanganyika.

1858–64. David Livingstone continues his travels in Africa; finds Lake Nyasa.

1860. John McDouall Stuart explores central Australia.

1860–61. Robert O'Hara Burke and William John Wills are first to cross Australia south to north.

1866. Nain Singh reaches the Forbidden City of Lhasa, Tibet.

1868. David Livingstone discovers Lake Bangweulu.

1868–72. Ferdinand von Richthofen traces a network of routes over southern and central China.

1870. Georg Schweinfurth discovers the Uele River during his travels through Africa.

1874–77. Henry Morton Stanley follows the course of the Congo River from its source to its mouth.

1887. Francis Younghusband discovers the Muztagh Pass in the Kunlun Mountains of China.

1893–1908. Sven Hedin explores central Asia.

20th-Century Explorations

1907–25. A. Hamilton Rice surveys the South American continent.

1913–14. Gertrude Bell explores the Arabian desert.

1916. Aurel Stein travels throughout central Asia.

1917. Harry St. John Bridger Philby explores unknown parts of Arabia.

1920. Rosita Forbes and Hassanein Bey make studies of the Sahara.

1923. Hassanein Bey travels across the Libyan Desert.

1923–34. Michael Terry leads 12 expeditions into interior Australia.

1927–28. Roy Chapman Andrews conducts an exploration of The Gobi.

1927–31. Bertram Thomas explores Arabia and is the first man to cross the Rub' al Khali Desert.

1929. Charles Lindbergh photographs Mayan ruins in Yucatán.

1930–34. Michael Leahy explores unknown regions of New Guinea.

1953. Edmund Hillary reaches the summit of Mount Everest.

1957. David G. Simons rises over 19 miles in a balloon.

1960. Jacques Piccard and Donald Walsh dive almost seven miles to the bottom of the Pacific Ocean in a bathyscaphe.

1961. Yuri Gagarin becomes first man to orbit the earth.

1969. Neil Armstrong, Edwin Aldrin, and Michael Collins achieve first lunar landing; Armstrong and Aldrin are first men to walk on the moon.

See also Frontier. For Arctic and Antarctic explorations, *see* Polar Exploration. For explorations of America, *see* America. For events in ocean exploration, *see* Ocean; Oceanography. For the history of space exploration, *see* Space Travel. For archaeological discoveries, *see* Archaeology. *See also* in the Fact-Index individual explorers by name.

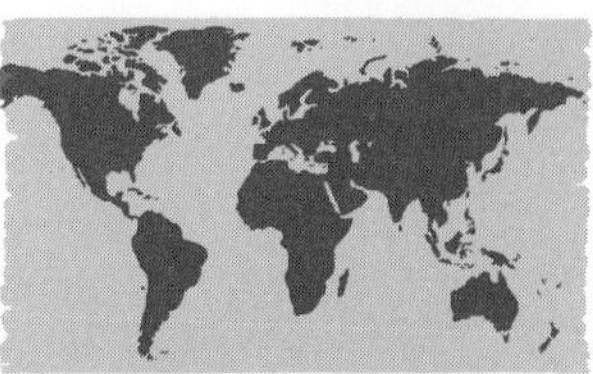

WORLD MAP TODAY

STANLEY- 1874-77

SIMONS-1957

PICCARD AND WALSH-1960

Edmund Hillary (left) and Tensing Norkay (right) look up toward the summit that they were the first to reach. John Hunt (center) led the expedition that was the first to conquer Mount Everest, the world's highest peak.

Scientists Explore South America

In 1799 the naturalist Baron Alexander von Humboldt arrived at Cumaná, Venezuela. He led the best-equipped expedition that had ever gone exploring. Humboldt was looking for new species of plants and animals. In 1800 he traveled in a great arc through Venezuelan territory. He made the first surveys and scientific observations in the region.

The naturalist Charles Darwin traveled around the world from 1831 to 1836. He spent much of the time in South America. He made many observations of plants and animals on his trip and began to formulate his ideas about evolution. (*See also* Darwin.)

Pioneers in Exploring the United States

In 1804–5 President Thomas Jefferson sent an expedition, led by Meriwether Lewis and William Clark, to explore the North American continent west to the Pacific Ocean. They traveled more than 6,000 miles through wild country and made important geographical and scientific discoveries. (*See also* Lewis and Clark Expedition.)

Zebulon Pike surveyed the upper Mississippi in 1805. In 1806 he explored the Arkansas River and first saw the mountain, Pikes Peak, which is named for him.

John Charles Frémont made three major expeditions to the Far West—in 1842, 1843–44, and 1845–47 (*see* Frémont). (For map showing routes of early explorers, *see* United States History, section "The Nation's Westward Advance.")

The Great 19th-Century Achievements

At the beginning of the 19th century four fifths of the land area in the world was still practically unknown. There was only the scantiest knowledge of central and eastern Asia and of the interior of the Americas. Africa was still truly the Dark Continent. Most of the polar lands were still undiscovered, and the existence of Antarctica was laughed at as a fable.

By the end of the century, however, most of these gaps in knowledge had been closed. The polar regions had been explored and mapped in part (*see* Polar Exploration). Africa had been investigated by such men as David Livingstone, Sir Henry Stanley, John Speke, and Georg Schweinfurth (*see* Livingstone; Stanley). Sir Francis Younghusband and Sven Hedin had explored large parts of Asia.

The ruins of the ancient Mayan city of Chichén Itzá are in what is now south central Yucatán state, Mexico. This picture was taken on a flight in October 1929 by the aviation pioneer Charles A. Lindbergh and his wife, Anne Lindbergh.

The Effect of Inventions on Exploration

Modern technology has made an incalculable contribution to the ability to explore the Earth, space, and oceans. Through a wide array of inventions it has been possible to see more of the Earth quickly, to get manned and unmanned vehicles into space, and to venture farther beneath the seas than ever before. Among the many inventions are photography, radio, telephone, recording devices, radar, sonar, television, the gyroscope, computers, ocean-diving gear, the bathyscaphe and bathysphere, robotics, the carbon dating process, lasers, and jet propulsion.

The aviation pioneer Charles A. Lindbergh located important ancient ruins of Mayan civilization in southern Mexico (*see* Lindbergh). In Peru, Bolivia, and elsewhere the airplane was indispensable in surveying and mapping the Andes region and in locating and photographing Inca and pre-Inca ruins.

With the aid of motor-driven boats, scientists penetrated hitherto unexplored swamps and jungles bordering tropical streams. Automobiles and motor trucks made possible the American Museum of Natural History expeditions of 1927 and 1928 into the Gobi, a desert in Mongolia. This adventure was led by the naturalist and explorer Roy Chapman Andrews. By radio, explorers in the most remote regions are able to keep in touch with the outside world.

20th-Century Triumphs

Not until the 20th century were the North Pole and the South Pole reached by human beings. Both the Arctic regions and Antarctica have since claimed much attention from explorers (*see* Antarctica; Arctic Regions; Polar Exploration).

An interesting ocean journey was the 4,300-mile (6,900-kilometer) trip made in 1947 aboard the primitive raft *Kon-Tiki* by Thor Heyerdahl, a Norwegian ethnologist, and five companions. In 101 days their raft sailed from Peru to the Tuamotu Archipelago, thus proving possible Heyerdahl's theory that the Polynesians originally came from South America. In 1957 he led an exploration party to Easter Island (*see* Easter Island).

From 1921 through 1952, 11 unsuccessful attempts were made to reach "the roof of the world"—the top of Mount Everest, 29,028 feet (8,848 meters) above sea level. Finally, in May 1953, two men reached the summit. They were a New Zealander, Edmund P. Hillary, and a Nepalese-Indian guide, Tensing Norkay. Later other climbers also reached the top. (*See also* Everest, Mount.)

The exploration of space began in 1957, led by the Soviet Union and the United States. The first flights were unmanned vehicles. Manned flight began in 1961. The United States goal of putting astronauts on the moon was achieved with the Apollo project. On July 20, 1969, Apollo 11's command pilot, Neil Armstrong, followed by the lunar module pilot, Edwin E. Aldrin, Jr., stepped onto the surface of Earth's closest neighbor in space (*see* Space Travel).

JPL

Previously unknown rings of Uranus were photographed by the unmanned space probe, Voyager 2, in a single 96-second exposure as it flew past the planet in January 1986.

Equally valuable for the knowledge that has been obtained were the unmanned vehicles sent to explore the solar system. The Soviet Union and the United States have both sent several probes to other planets. Soviet probes have landed on, or gone into orbit around, Mars and Venus. The American Voyager craft have sent back data on Jupiter, Saturn, and Uranus.

Exploring the Ocean Depths

Not all explorers have been driven to reach the highest points. Some have preferred to go as deep into the ocean as possible.

The naturalist-explorer Charles William Beebe, with Otis Barton, developed diving devices that could withstand water pressures at 3,000 to 4,000 feet (900 to 1,200 meters) deep. This enabled them to study undersea life as never before (*see* Beebe).

A 1952 expedition found a canyon in the Atlantic Ocean the size of the Mississippi River and its tributaries. Another used scuba gear to enable the explorers to swim as deep as 300 feet (90 meters) below the ocean surface (*see* Diving, Underwater).

The development of deep-diving undersea craft was accelerated from the 1950s through the 1980s as exploration of the world's oceans became a matter not only of research but of seeking out mineral wealth and potential food supplies. In January 1960 "the bottom of the world" was reached when United States Navy Lieutenant Donald Walsh and Jacques Piccard dived 35,800 feet (10,900 meters) to the bottom of the Mariana Trench southwest of Guam in the Pacific Ocean. Their descent was made in a bathyscaphe (*see* Ocean; Oceanography; Submarine). In 1968 the United States National Science Foundation began the Deep Sea Drilling Project, using the *Glomar Challenger,* a drilling ship, to remove cylinders of ocean floor to depths of more than 20,000 feet (6,000 meters). This and other drilling projects are now probing the Earth above and below the sea to incredible depths. In the 1980s deep-sea robots were in use to collect samples from ocean floors, inspect oil rigs, and do underwater photography. These robots are less expensive to operate than manned submersibles, and they have similar abilities. (*See also* Frontier.)

Defense Nuclear Agency

On June 27, 1985, at White Sands Missile Range in New Mexico, technicians detonated 4,740 tons of high explosive, equal to an eight-kiloton atomic bomb, to test the survivability of nearby missile silos.

EXPLOSIVE. The destructive effects of explosives are much more spectacular than their peaceful uses. This is likely to make people forget that explosives are the basis for many of mankind's most constructive efforts. Explosives blast rocks and ores loose in mines and quarries. They also move great masses of earth and break coal into small pieces.

There are three basic types of explosive: mechanical, nuclear, and chemical. A mechanical explosive depends on a physical reaction such as overloading a container with compressed air. Such a device has some application in mining, in which the release of gas from chemical explosives may be undesirable, but otherwise is very little used. A nuclear explosive is one in which a sustained nuclear reaction can be made to take place with almost instant rapidity, releasing large amounts of energy (*see* Bomb; Nuclear Energy). Chemical explosives account for virtually all explosive applications in engineering.

An Explosion Is a Chemical Reaction

When an explosion occurs, a solid material of relatively small bulk is transformed into a large volume of hot gases in a fraction of a second. The explosive breaks down chemically, and a great quantity of heat is released. In an instant, oxygen reacts with other elements such as carbon and hydrogen. The lightning-like expansion of gases produces a shock wave that slams against surrounding surfaces and blasts objects from its path.

Explosions are usually classified as combustion, or burning, type or detonation type. In the first, burning begins at one end of the charge and travels with blinding speed through the entire charge. Complete combustion of a reasonably large charge takes only a few thousandths of a second. Gunpowder explodes in this way. A detonation explosion occurs when the material receives a sudden shock or jar. A shock wave passes through the material. All particles break down together, and the explosion is complete in a few millionths of a second.

Detonating explosives are usually subdivided into two categories, primary and secondary. Primary explosives detonate by ignition from some source such as flame, spark, impact, or other means that will produce heat of sufficient magnitude. Secondary explosives require a detonator and, in some cases, a supplementary booster. A few explosives can be both primary and secondary depending on application.

Dynamite explodes by detonation. Smokeless powder set off by a flame burns rapidly but not violently. If, however, a cap, or primer, or a fuse of some detonating substance such as mercury fulminate is set off in contact with the guncotton, the latter will be detonated. A stick of dynamite can be set on fire with a match without great danger but will explode with shattering force in response to a fulminate cap.

Since the first form of explosion is extremely rapid burning, it follows that any flammable substance can become explosive to some degree if it can be made to burn rapidly enough. Since all ordinary fire or combustion is caused by the combination of the burning substance with the gas oxygen (*see* Oxygen), it follows also that the more oxygen present the faster the blaze will be. For example, coal gas, hydrogen, and the vapors of gasoline, alcohol, ether, and turpentine are themselves nonexplosive, but they become explosive if they are mixed in the right proportions with the oxygen of the air. This principle of explosive mixture of gases and vapors with air is used in all gasoline engines (*see* Internal-Combustion Engine).

Many serious accidents have arisen from so-called dust explosions. When the air is filled with finely powdered charcoal, coal, flour, soap, wood, sugar, starch, or any other combustible substance, a flame or a spark may start a blaze that will travel through the dust cloud so rapidly that it creates a violent and destructive blast.

Explosives that are to be used for practical purposes, however, cannot depend on the air for their supply of oxygen. It must be provided in concentrated form so as to be available even when the explosive is excluded from contact with the air. In black gunpowder, which is a mixture of charcoal, saltpeter, and sulfur, the saltpeter (potassium nitrate) provides the necessary oxygen. In most explosives, however, each molecule of the compound contains all the oxygen needed. Liquid oxygen itself can be used as an explosive. A porous cartridge of wood pulp, powdered aluminum, or other combustible material is soaked in liquid oxygen and fired with a detonator before the oxygen evaporates. Instantaneous combustion produces terrific explosive force. A few detonating explosives, such as nitrogen iodide, have no oxygen. They act when the compound splits, and the parts expand because of heat generated by the break.

Some compound of nitrogen is used in most explosives because this element is extremely "unsocial" and ready to break away from the others in the compounds (*see* Nitrogen). It is usually introduced through the action of nitric acid, which as a rule is mixed with sulfuric acid. With cotton, nitric acid forms guncotton and nitrocellulose; with glycerin, nitroglycerin; and with ammonia, ammonium nitrate. With phenol (carbolic acid) it produces picric acid, the base of such explosives as lyddite and melinite. Nitration of toluene obtained from coal tar or by catalysis of gasoline yields trinitrotoluol or trinitrotoluene (TNT), a common military high explosive. Dynamite is nitroglycerin mixed with some absorbent substance to reduce danger of explosion from shock. Amatol is a mixture of TNT and ammonium nitrate; ammonal contains powdered aluminum, TNT, charcoal, and ammonium nitrate. In World War II scientists developed RDX (hexamine and TNT) and pentolite (pentaerythritol tetranitrate and TNT). Each one is more powerful than TNT.

Gunpowder

It may never be known with certainty who invented black powder, the first explosive. The mixture is thought to have originated in China in the 10th century, but its use there was almost exclusively in fireworks and signals. It is possible that the Chinese also used black powder in bombs for military purposes, and there is written record that in the mid-13th century they put it in bamboo tubes to propel stone projectiles.

There is some evidence, however, that the Arabs invented black powder. By about 1300, certainly, they had developed the first real gun, a bamboo tube reinforced with iron, which used a charge of black powder to fire an arrow.

A strong case can also be made that black powder was discovered by the English medieval scholar Roger Bacon, who wrote explicit instructions for its preparation in 1242 in the strange form of a Latin anagram that is difficult to decipher. But Bacon read Arabic, and it is possible that he got his knowledge from Arabic sources.

Some scholars attribute the invention of firearms to the early 14th-century German monk Berthold Schwarz. In any case firearms are frequently mentioned in 14th-century manuscripts from many countries, and there is a record of the shipment of guns and powder from Ghent to England in 1314.

Not until the 17th century was black powder used in Europe for peaceful purposes. There is a doubtful claim that it was used in mining operations in Germany in 1613 and fairly authentic evidence that it was employed in the mines of Schemnitz, Hungary, in 1627. For various reasons—such as high cost, lack of suitable boring implements, and fear of roof collapse—the use of black powder in mining did not spread rapidly, though it was widely accepted by 1700. The first application in civil engineering was in the Malpas Tunnel of the Canal du Midi in France in 1679.

For 300 years the unvarying composition of black powder has been approximately 75 percent saltpeter (potassium nitrate), 15 percent charcoal, and 10 percent sulfur. The saltpeter was originally extracted from compost piles and animal wastes. Deposits found in India provided a source for many years. During the 1850s tremendous quantities of sodium nitrate were discovered in Chile, and saltpeter was formed by reaction with potassium chloride, of which there was a plentiful supply.

Chilean nitrate was not at first considered satisfactory for the manufacture of black powder because it too readily absorbed moisture. Lammot du Pont, an American industrialist, solved this problem and started making sodium nitrate powder in 1858. It became popular in a short time because, though it did not produce as high a quality explosive as potassium nitrate, it was suitable for most mining and construction applications and was much less expensive. To distinguish between them, the potassium nitrate and sodium nitrate versions came to be known as A and B blasting powder respectively. The A powder continued in use for special purposes that required its higher quality, principally for firearms, military devices, and safety fuses.

Manufacture of Black Powder

In the modern process, charcoal and sulfur are placed in a hollow drum along with heavy steel balls. As the drum rotates, the steel balls pulverize the contents; this device is called a ball mill. The saltpeter is crushed separately by heavy steel rollers. Next, a mixture of several hundred pounds of saltpeter, charcoal, and sulfur is placed in a heavy iron device shaped like a cooking pan. There it is continuously turned by devices called plows, then ground and mixed by two rotating iron wheels, which weigh from 10 to 12 tons each. The process takes several hours; water is added periodically to keep the mixture moist.

The product of the mills is next put through wooden rolls to break up the larger lumps and is then formed into cakes under high pressure. Coarse-toothed rolls crack the cakes into manageable pieces, and the corning mill, which contains rolls of several different dimensions, reduces them to the sizes desired.

Glazing, the next operation, consists of tumbling the grains for several hours in large wooden cylinders, during which friction rounds the corners and, aided by forced air circulation, brings the powder to a specified moisture content. The term glazing derives from the fact that graphite is added during this process, forming a thin film over the individual powder grains. Glazed powder flows more readily than unglazed powder and is more moisture resistant. After glazing the powder is graded by sieves into different sizes and is packaged, usually in kegs.

Because the burning of black powder is a surface phenomenon, a fine granulation burns faster than a coarse one. Grain sizes are designated as F, 2F, and so on, up to 7F, which is the finest, and from C up (C, 2C, and so on) as the grains become larger. For the A powder the letter indicating the fineness becomes 3FA, and, if the powder is glazed, this is followed by the letter g; for example, 3FAg. Pelleted powder was used almost entirely in underground coal mines, but now regulations generally prohibit both it and the granular type.

Except for blasting work and for special military purposes, the old-style gunpowders have been almost entirely replaced by smokeless powders and such high explosives as guncotton, mercury fulminate, nitroglycerin, and dynamite. Smokeless powders, products of guncotton and nitroglycerin, were perfected in 1884 and first put to military use by the French.

Dynamite and Nitroglycerin

Nitroglycerin, the most powerful explosive in common use, was discovered in 1846 by the Italian scientist Ascanio Sobrero. It is made by treating glycerin with a mixture of concentrated nitric and sulfuric acids. Although used as a headache remedy under the name glonoin, it proved too difficult and dangerous for practical blasting purposes until Alfred Nobel of Sweden began his experiments in 1862. Nobel's brother died in an explosion during the tests, and Nobel was forced to move his laboratory to a barge anchored out in the middle of a lake. Then a ship loaded with nitroglycerin blew up off Colón, Panama, and most of the nations of the world forbade their vessels to carry it. Nobel refused to abandon his labors, however, and in 1866 he was rewarded by the invention of dynamite. This is today the commonest and safest of the high explosives, for the first time enabling man to blast away great masses of rock and other obstacles with comparative safety.

Dynamite consists of a mixture of the liquid nitroglycerin with some absorbent substance, or "dope," giving it a solid form. The absorbent used by Nobel was kieselguhr, or diatomite, a kind of earth formed by countless millions of tiny fossil plants known as diatoms. Later, wood pulp, sawdust, charcoal, plaster of Paris, and many other substances came to be used. Perhaps the most powerful form of dynamite is the blasting gelatin devised by Nobel in 1875. This contains nitrocotton colloidally dissolved in nitroglycerin and is waterproof. In many dynamites the nitroglycerin is diluted with ammonium nitrate. This cools the flame and makes the dynamite safer for use in mines. Most dynamites have the nitroglycerin diluted with another explosive to modify the effect in some way. The use of so-called straight dynamite (nitroglycerin alone) is uncommon.

Ordinary dynamite is usually made in sticks from 1 to 2 inches (2.5 to 5 centimeters) in diameter and about 8 inches (20 centimeters) long. These consist of brown paper wrappers coated with paraffin to keep out moisture. If a small quantity is set on fire free from pressure or vibration of any kind, it will burn; but, if the least blow strikes it while burning, it will explode with great violence. Dynamite is usually set off with a detonator, or blasting cap.

Getting "Smooth" Explosives in Firearms

High explosives are used as bursting charges in shells and bombs, but they cannot be used as propelling charges to drive projectiles from guns because they act too violently. Modern propelling charges are made from slower-burning nitrocellulose formed into grains, flakes, or cylinders. Cordite and ballistite contain some nitroglycerin as well.

When a propelling charge is fired, it burns slowly at first and starts the bullet or shell smoothly on its way. The rate of burning increases as the projectile nears the muzzle, and maximum pressure is provided at the instant of discharge. In this way the projectile is given an amount of driving force that would burst the gun if applied earlier.

This action can be obtained by coating the grains with a slow-burning compound. The compound retards emission of gas until it is gone. For bigger guns the United States military services use a powder made into cylindrical grains. Inside each grain are lengthwise perforations. As the grain burns, these perforations become larger and give off more gas.

Shells and bombs are exploded at the target by detonators. These are small charges of a sensitive explosive such as mercury fulminate. They explode

Photos, courtesy of E.I. du Pont de Nemours & Company

A coal miner (left) loads a drill hole with Tovex®, a water-gel explosive that is safer to use than dynamite. Explosives are used to alter the Earth's surface to build a road through hilly terrain (right).

at a blow from a firearm hammer. A detonator is also used as a primer to fire the propelling charge.

Blasting Caps

Also called detonators, blasting caps are devices that initiate the detonation of a charge of a high explosive by subjecting it to a shock wave. Strictly speaking, the term detonator refers to an easily ignited low explosive that produces the shock wave, and the term primer, or priming composition, denotes a substance that produces a sudden burst of flame to ignite the detonator. The primer may be set off by the brief application of heat, as from a burning fuse or an electrically heated wire; by friction; or by mechanical shock, as from the impact of the firing pin of a gun. Depending on the preferred method of initiating the explosion, the blasting cap may contain a primer alone or both a primer and a detonator.

Peaceful Uses of Explosives

Explosives are of immense value in many peaceful pursuits—in mining, quarrying, and engineering enterprises and in making fireworks, signal lights, and rockets. They are used to project lifelines to ships in distress off storm-beaten shores or to the roofs of burning buildings; to cast oil upon rough seas; and to break up ice jams. When pile drivers are not available, their work can be done by exploding dynamite on an iron plate placed on top of the piles. Farmers find explosives useful for breaking up boulders, blowing out stumps, felling trees, and loosening the soil for deep cultivation.

Blind rivets are needed when space limitations make conventional rivets impractical. One type is explosive; it has a hollow space in the shank containing a small charge of heat-sensitive chemicals. When a suitable amount of heat is applied to the head, an explosion takes place and expands the rivet shank tightly into the hole. The shank is normally open but can be sealed to eliminate noise and the ejection of metal fragments. Most explosive rivets are aluminum, but they can be obtained in stainless steel and certain other metals. Their use is mainly in aircraft.

Explosives are sometimes used to bond various metals to each other. For example, when silver was removed from United States coinage, much of the so-called sandwich metal that replaced it was obtained by the explosive bonding of large slabs, which were then rolled down to the required thickness. These slabs are placed parallel to each other and approximately 0.25 inch (6.4 millimeters) apart. An explosive developed especially for the purpose is placed on the top slab, and its detonation slams the slabs together with such force that they become welded. Stainless steel is often joined to ordinary steel in this manner. One especially valuable feature of explosion cladding is that it can frequently be applied to metallurgically incompatible metals such as aluminum and steel or titanium and steel.

Finally, the very fine industrial-type diamonds used for grinding and polishing are produced by the carefully controlled action of explosives on carbon.

EXPOSITION *see* FAIR AND EXPOSITION.

EXPRESS

"Faster and still faster" was the motto of the Pony Express riders. The clothes and equipment shown in this photograph are authentic.

EXPRESS. "If Mr. Wells wants to run an express to the Rocky Mountains, he can for all of me. Personally, I think it would be foolish to try it."

That statement was made in 1840 by William F. Harnden. He was trying to discourage one of his young employees, Henry Wells, who had suggested their express company extend its business westward.

Wells was not discouraged. In a few years he and William Fargo, cofounders of the famous Wells Fargo express company, were able to say, "The Rocky Mountains are only a way station on our line."

Express messengers were known even in ancient times. Perhaps the first ones were the Persian couriers who carried mail to the king. The runners who delivered fresh fish daily to Roman housewives were, in a sense, expressmen. Early stagecoach drivers who carried packages for delivery along their routes were more like our modern expressmen.

How Express Originated in America

Express as it is known today—a company in business to carry goods, valuables, and money safely and quickly to their destinations—originated in America. Some authorities say L. B. Earle and his brother B. D. Earle originated the idea; they carried express messages under their beaver hats between Boston and New York in 1835. Others credit Silas Tyler with its invention. In 1835 Tyler ran an express car on a Massachusetts railroad between Boston and Lowell.

William F. Harnden, however, who later discouraged Henry Wells from looking westward, is generally considered to be the "father of express." He put an advertisement in the *Boston Transcript* on Feb. 13, 1839, offering his services as an express messenger to New York City once a week by boat and train. Harnden had been a conductor on the Boston and Worcester railroad. The railroad officials refused to allow him to be both an express messenger and their employee, so he quit his job and put all his efforts into the express business.

Henry Wells and William Fargo began their partnership in 1844. Starting in 1845, their Western Express operated by stagecoach, steamboat, and wagon train from Buffalo to Chicago, Cincinnati, and St. Louis. Competing with them was the Adams Express Company, founded by Alvin Adams in 1840, with a route from New York City to St. Louis by way of Baltimore, Washington, Pittsburgh, Cincinnati, and Louisville.

Also competing with these companies were the Butterfield and Wasson Express Company, and the firm of Pomeroy and Company, which Henry Wells had helped found when he first left Harnden's employ. All these firms competed fiercely with one another and also with the United States government for the mail-carrying business. For many years express companies, particularly Wells Fargo in the Far West, had better reputations for the successful carrying of letters than did the federal post office.

In 1845 the postage rate for a letter between Buffalo and New York City was 25 cents. Pomeroy and Company offered to carry letters for 6 cents. Out of this controversy grew the uniform postal rate of 3 cents, which the government adopted in 1848.

Invention of C.O.D. and Money Order

The American Express Company invented the C.O.D. (cash on delivery) system. This enabled

The Concord stagecoach, product of Yankee ingenuity and craftsmanship, helped in the winning of the West. At the left is one of these stages, now in the Smithsonian Institution in Washington, D. C. Behind a six-horse team, the Concord stage rolled through the wilderness, carrying passengers, mail, and express. At the right is a stage on the California-Oregon run.

merchants shipping goods to have the express company collect the money from the customer. The government postal service then also adopted the C.O.D. system (*see* Postal Service).

In 1864 the United States Post Office Department started a postal money-order form. This is a written form directing a post office to pay a specific sum of money to a designated person. The money order is bought and cashed at a post office. The American Express Company countered with a money-order form of its own, which for a time proved more popular than postal money orders because it could be bought and cashed almost anywhere.

In 1891 the American Express introduced the traveler's check, which is a form of letter of credit (*see* Credit). A buyer writes his name at the top of a traveler's check. In order to cash it he again signs his name, this time at the bottom. The second signature can then be compared with the original identification. Traveler's checks are accepted across the world. They are now also issued by banks and by other travel companies.

American Express Company Founded

The American Express Company was formed on March 18, 1850. To get business, the rival express companies had cut the price of their service so much that they were all losing money. As a defensive measure, many agreed to sell their express lines to the newly formed American Express Company. Most owners of rival lines became directors in the new company.

Wells and Fargo were the leading figures in this new organization. In 1852 they suggested that American Express extend its operations to California. Here the Adams Express Company had exclusive rights to the business of transporting gold from California mines. The American Express directors would not approve the venture. Wells and Fargo then formed Wells, Fargo & Company, with offices in San Francisco and later in Sacramento.

Wells Fargo and Western Expansion

Wells Fargo played an important and dramatic part in the expansion of the American frontier. In 1859 an enormous silver deposit that has been called the greatest bonanza in the history of the world was discovered at Virginia City, Nev. Miners at the Comstock Lode literally shoveled silver out of the ground in the form of "blue dirt." Wells Fargo, which had taken over the Pioneer Stage Line established in 1851 by Frank S. Stevens, had the monopoly

This is a photograph of an early Wells Fargo "treasure wagon" carrying $350,000 in gold bullion from Deadwood, S. D. Guards were called "the men who rode shotgun."

on carrying the silver from the Comstock and later banking the receipts in San Francisco at its offices on Montgomery Street. In addition, it had the monopoly on carrying goods and passengers to and from the Comstock Lode, from which business alone it made more than a million dollars a year.

Express in the West was carried in Concord coaches, which were built in New England. They were handmade and cost $1,500 each. So well were they built that many of the original coaches are still used in making Western motion pictures in Hollywood. The Concords were drawn by three spans of horses, which cost $3,000 a span. A harness for the six horses cost $1,500. To defend their valuable cargoes, guards, called "the men who rode shotgun," carried either shotguns or the Henry repeating rifle, which could be "loaded on Sunday and fired all week."

The Overland Mail and the Pony Express

The Southern Overland Mail, in which Wells Fargo came to own a controlling interest, was founded on Sept. 15, 1858, by John Butterfield, one of the American Express Company directors. The Overland Mail stagecoaches ran from St. Louis to San Francisco in 24 days through desert, mountains, and bands of hostile Indians. Freight on the Southern Overland was limited; the greatest load, including mail, was no more than 750 pounds. Establishing the Overland Mail, however, meant that mail and express no longer had to go by sea to Panama, across the Isthmus by land, and then by sea again to San Francisco. Wells Fargo shipped express via the Overland right up to the time of the Civil War.

There were minor Pony Expresses before 1860, but the Pony Express that rode its way into American legend was started by Russell, Majors, and Waddell, a firm of Kansas freight masters, on April 3, 1860. It was officially discontinued on Oct. 26, 1861, though it operated until November 20.

Russell, Majors, and Waddell proposed to have its Pony Express riders travel over a central route the 2,000 miles between St. Joseph, Mo., and Sacramento, Calif., in ten days on a regular schedule. If it could do so, it would beat the time taken by Butterfield's Southern Overland to cross the continent. The government would also award it valuable mail contracts.

A number of companies operate money delivery services in the United States. The money is carried in armored trucks equipped with bulletproof glass and is protected by armed guards.

The Pony Express was successful from a time standpoint, but it was a financial failure, losing its owners more than $200,000 in the 18 months of its existence. Nevertheless, it played a major role in establishing rapid communication between the loyal North and the West coast during the Civil War. The Pony Express helped keep California in the Union.

The completion of the transcontinental telegraph ended the Pony Express. At the beginning of the Civil War the Southern Overland Express was moved to the Central Express route, where it continued to operate until a railroad spanned the continent. (*See also* Telegraph; Railroads; Transportation.)

The American "Camel Express"

A curiosity during the mid-19th century was the arrival on the Western scene of what has been called the "American Camel Express." About 1850, Bactrian camels were imported to haul salt between several California and Nevada towns. On Feb. 1, 1856, 33 dromedary camels were landed at Indianola, Tex. Later 41 more camels were added to this group.

The camels had been imported by the United States Army as an experiment in freighting and communication in the arid Southwest. On an expedition to open a wagon road across Arizona from Fort Defiance to California the camels were said to have proved their worth. The Army later abandoned its experiment, however, and the camels were left to shift for themselves on the desert. They caused complaints by stagecoach drivers whose teams upon seeing the beasts would frequently bolt in panic. The camels were seen haunting the Western desert as late as 1912.

Express During the Civil War

During the Civil War express companies performed notable services. They were hired by the federal government to deliver goods to its supply depots. In the national election of 1864 an express company was given the responsibility of taking the vote of the soldiers at the front. Another wartime welfare effort was performed shortly before and during World War I. When the war began, the American Express Company succeeded in getting 150,000 panicky American travelers out of Europe. The American Express also undertook the first delivery of parcels to prisoners of war before the American Red Cross took over this job.

After the Civil War rivalry once again became keen among the express companies. The competition, which grew in intensity for more than a half century, was based on efforts to secure exclusive express delivery contracts with the railroads. Without these contracts the express companies could not deliver their goods. The United States Express, for

Thousands of packages await sorting at the Federal Express Superhub in Memphis, Tenn.

example, had an exclusive contract with the Erie Railroad. Adams and Southern had a contract with the Pennsylvania Railroad, and American Express had its contract with the New York Central. Other leading express companies at this time included the Merchants Union and Wells Fargo.

Wells Fargo did not regard the railroads as a serious threat to its business. This was a mistake. In 1872 the Pacific Union Express Company, an agency of the Central Pacific Railroad, announced it had most of the passengers, merchandise, and express business of the railroad and its connections. Wells Fargo was forced into a complete reorganization, with the Central Pacific owners gaining control.

In 1910 the Mann-Elkins Act declared that the express companies were common carriers subject to the regulations and rate making of the Interstate Commerce Commission. On Jan. 1, 1913, the United States government started its own parcel post service. These two events cut seriously into the profits of the competing express companies.

By 1917 the four leading express companies were Southern, Adams, Wells Fargo, and American Express. On July 1, 1918, these companies merged to form the American Railway Express Company, Inc. Three of the companies—Adams, American Express, and Wells Fargo—maintained their names after the merger. Adams became an investment trust, and American Express concentrated on the expansion of its travel department. Wells Fargo is now a separate, California-based corporation of its own with several subsidiaries, including banking and real estate services.

The American Railway Express Company was renamed the Railway Express Agency (REA) in 1929. The company survived, providing domestic and international service by ground and air transportation, until 1975, when it filed for bankruptcy.

The biggest development in express services since the early 1970s has been the growth of air express delivery. Express took wings for the first time on Nov. 7, 1910, when a merchant in Dayton, Ohio, shipped a bolt of silk by air to Columbus. The 60 miles (100 kilometers) was covered in 56 minutes, and the cost of the shipment was $71.42 per pound.

Air express was slow to develop. Less than 4,000 pounds of air freight was shipped in 1926. By 1960 more than 5 million shipments were made annually by air. Most of these were by regular airline service, but one independent company emerged shortly after World War II to specialize in air freight. This was Flying Tigers. This company had its origin during World War II in the American Volunteer Group—civilian volunteer pilots recruited for combat and transportation in the Far East against Japan. After the war some of the Flying Tigers, as they were usually called, formed the company as an air freight hauler. They have since expanded into the air express business.

Air express, exclusive of normal freight hauling, started in 1973 with the founding of the Federal Express Corporation in Memphis, Tenn. Its business is primarily the delivery of overnight letters and packages. A few other companies that soon joined what has become a highly competitive business include: Emery Air Freight Corporation, Airborne Freight Corporation, and DHL Worldwide Courier Express.

Two other national package delivery services—United Parcel Service, Inc. (UPS) and Purolator Courier Corporation—had been operating with fleets of trucks. They, too, soon became involved in the express delivery service with the use of airplanes. The United States Postal Service also began an express mail service for next-day delivery.

In 1984 Federal Express began a new venture called ZapMail, which provides for the electronic transmission of high-quality copies of documents. Companies can install their own transmission equipment, however, and send documents from one location to another without the use of outside services.

EXTRASENSORY PERCEPTION (ESP). An awareness that some people claim to experience independently of, and beyond, their usual sensory abilities is termed extrasensory perception (ESP). Seeing, hearing, smelling, touching, and tasting are the known and common sensory processes. Believers in ESP claim that it is one of several kinds of psychic phenomena for which there is no obvious explanation. The field of study called parapsychology includes the investigation of extrasensory perception and psychokinesis, a phenomenon similar to ESP. An example of psychokinesis is the falling of dice in a particular way, supposedly influenced by an individual's power of concentration.

Three main types of ESP are generally described. They are clairvoyance, telepathy, and precognition. Clairvoyance, which means "clear seeing" in French, is said to be a supernormal awareness of events, objects, or people obtained without the use of the known senses and not necessarily known to any other person. Telepathy is said to be the direct transference of thoughts or mental states from one person to another, also without use of the usual sensory channels. Precognition is said to be the perception of some future event.

Questions about whether or not ESP really exists have been debated by scientists since the late 19th century. Most experiments that offer supporting evidence involve card guessing. But setting up experiments to test for it is difficult. One of the best-known investigators of such phenomena was the psychologist Joseph Banks Rhine of the United States. One of the tests he used involved the Zener cards. These cards bear five different symbols: a cross, a star, a circle, a wave, and a rectangle. A pack consists of 25 cards. The subject of the experiment tries to name cards laid face down on a table. Results of this and other experiments have proved inconclusive. Most scientists vigorously dispute the existence of ESP.

EXTRATERRESTRIAL LIFE. The search for life away from planet Earth has been called a science without a subject matter. Despite the countless hours that dedicated scientists and amateurs alike have spent searching the skies, there is no evidence that life exists anywhere in the universe except on Earth. Exobiology is a branch of biology that deals with the search for extraterrestrial life, especially intelligent life, outside our solar system. Exobiology is sometimes called xenobiology or astrobiology.

Urey and Miller experiment. One approach to investigating the existence of extraterrestrial life is to discover the conditions necessary to replicate the earliest forms of life on Earth. The first experimental simulation of primitive conditions believed to duplicate Earth's atmosphere before life existed was carried out in 1953 by an American graduate student S.L. Miller under the guidance of chemist Harold C. Urey.

In the experiment a mixture of methane, ammonia, water vapor, and hydrogen was circulated through a liquid water solution and continuously subjected to an electric spark to simulate lightning. After several days amino acids had been produced. These amino acids are building blocks in contemporary life forms. Most, if not all, of the essential building blocks of proteins, carbohydrates, and nucleic acids can be readily produced under similar primitive conditions.

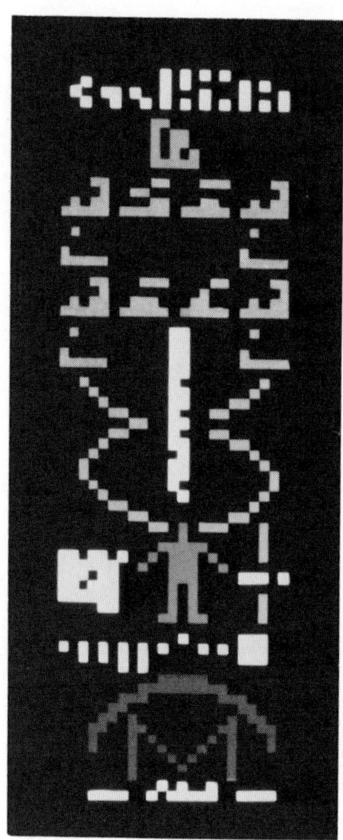

The Arecibo Interstellar Message was transmitted as a radio signal in binary code on Nov. 16, 1974, from Arecibo Observatory in Puerto Rico to the globular cluster M13, about 25,000 light years away. The signal contained 1,679 bits of information about Earth.

The Arecibo Message of November 1974 was prepared by the staff of the National Astronomy and Ionosphere Center, which is operated by Cornell University under contract with the National Science Foundation

Green Bank equation. The Green Bank equation, devised by United States astrophysicist F.D. Drake, represents an attempt to estimate the number of technically advanced civilizations in the Milky Way galaxy. It expresses mathematically the relationship of the number of stars, the number of stars with planetary systems, the number of planets in each system having conditions suitable for the origin of life, the number of planets on which life could actually develop, the number of those planets on which intelligent life could evolve, the number of intelligent populations that could develop civilizations capable of interstellar communications, and, finally, the average lifespan of technical civilizations. Depending on how estimates for various terms in the equation are made, the number of advanced civilizations in the Milky Way is estimated at from 1 to 1,000,000.

Interplanetary exploration. The most elaborate use of an unmanned space probe to investigate a neighboring planet involved the United States Viking 1 and 2 probes that were launched in 1975. These twin spacecraft each consisted of an orbiter and lander. The landers were equipped with cameras, seismometers, soil-sampling scoops, and biological experiments specially designed to search for traces of bacterial life on Mars. Both probes continued to relay detailed close-up pictures and data from Mars. The results of the biological tests proved inconclusive.

EYE

EYE. The human eye is a complex part of the body that is used for seeing. Eyes enable people to perform daily tasks and to learn about the world that surrounds them. Sight, or vision, is a rapidly occurring process that involves continuous interaction between the eye, the nervous system, and the brain. When someone looks at an object, what he really sees is the light reflected from the object. This reflected light passes through the lens and falls on the retina of the eye. Here the light induces nerve impulses that travel through the optic nerve to the brain and then over other nerves to muscles and glands.

The eye is similar to a television camera. Both the eye and the television camera convert light energy to electrical energy. The eye converts light to nerve impulses that are interpreted by the brain as the sense perception called sight. A television camera converts light to electronic signals that are broadcast and transformed into light images in a television receiver.

The eye is well protected. It lies within a bony socket of the skull. The eyelids guard it in front. They blink an average of once every six seconds. This washes the eye with the salty secretion from the tear, or lachrymal, glands. Each tear gland is about the size and shape of an almond. These glands are situated behind the upper eyelid at the outer corner of the eye. After passing over the eye, the liquid from the gland is drained into the nose through the tear duct at the inner corner of the eye. Hearty laughter or weeping causes muscles in the upper eyelid to squeeze the lachrymal gland. This produces tears that flow too fast to be drained away. The eyelashes catch many flying particles that otherwise would enter the eye. As a further protection, the eyelids automatically close when any object suddenly moves close to the eye.

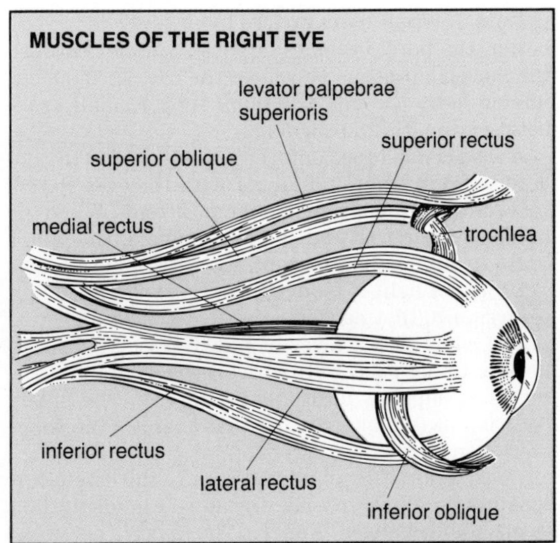

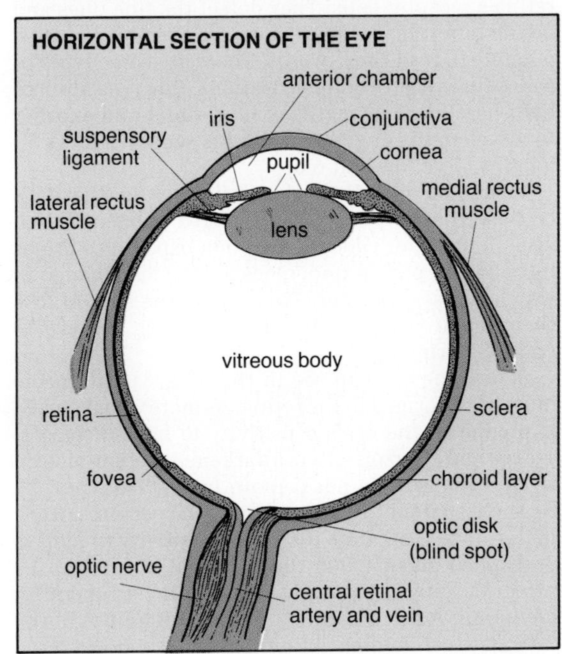

Structure

The eye is shaped like a ball, with a slight bulge at the front. It is this bulge that a person sees when looking at the eyes of someone else. When the eyelids are closed, the bulge is covered. The rest of the eye is protected by the bones of the skull. Each part of the human eye has a special function. (For descriptions of some animals' eyes, *see* Birds; Fish; Insect; Invertebrate.)

Cornea and sclera. The eye is made of three coats, or tunics. The outermost coat consists of the cornea and the sclera; the middle coat contains the main blood supply to the eye and consists of the choroid, the ciliary body, and the iris. The innermost layer is the retina. The sclera, or the white of the eye, is composed of tough fibrous tissue. On the exposed area of the eye the scleral surface is covered with a mucous membrane called the conjunctiva. This protects the eye from becoming dry. The cornea, a part of the sclera, is the transparent window of the eye through which light passes. The focusing of light begins in the cornea.

Behind the cornea is a watery fluid called the aqueous humor. This fluid fills a curved, crescent-shaped space, thick in the center and thinner toward the edges. The cornea and the aqueous humor together make an outer lens that refracts, or bends, light and directs it toward the center of the eye.

Iris. Behind the aqueous humor is a colored ring called the iris. The color of the iris is inherited and does not affect vision. The iris is like a muscular curtain that opens and closes. It controls the amount of light entering the eye through the pupil, an opening in the iris. The pupil looks like a black spot. Light from everything a person sees must go through the pupil. When more or less light is needed to see better, the pupil becomes larger or smaller through the movement of the muscle in the iris. The aqueous humor flows through the pupil into a small space between the iris and the lens.

A simple way to see how the pupils respond to light is to stand in front of a mirror with the eyes closed, covered by the hands for about ten seconds. When the hands are removed and the eyes opened, the pupils begin to get smaller, or contract, in response to the light. When light is reduced, pupils expand; when it is increased, they contract.

The choroid is a layer of blood vessels and connective tissue squeezed between the sclera and the retina. It supplies nutrients to the eye. The ciliary body is a muscular structure that changes the shape of the lens.

Lens. Behind the pupil and iris are the crystalline lens and the ciliary muscle. The muscle holds the lens in place and changes its shape. The lens is a colorless, nearly transparent double convex structure, similar to an ordinary magnifying glass. Its only function is to focus light rays onto the retina. The lens is made of elongated cells that have no blood supply. These cells obtain nutrients from the surrounding fluids—the aqueous humor in front and the vitreous body, a clear jelly, behind.

The shape of the lens—essentially that of a flattened globe—can be changed by the movement of the ciliary muscles surrounding it. Hence, the eye can focus clearly on objects at widely varying distances. The ability of the lens to adjust from a distant to a near focus is called accommodation. By contracting, the ciliary muscle pushes the lens to make it thicker in the middle. By relaxing, the muscle pulls the lens and flattens it. To see objects clearly when they are close to the eyes the lens is squeezed together and thickened. To see distant objects clearly it is flattened.

STRUCTURE OF THE RETINA

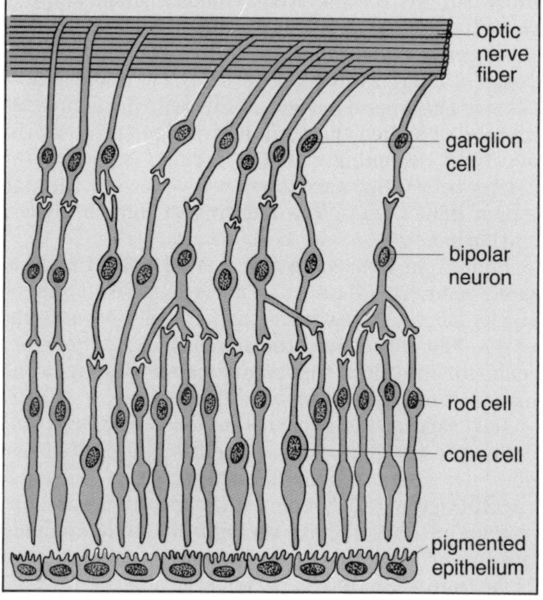

For people with normal vision, the relaxed ciliary muscle flattens the lens enough to bring objects into sharp focus if they are 20 feet (6 meters) or more from the eye. To see closer objects clearly, the ciliary muscle must contract in order to thicken the lens. Young children can see objects clearly at distances as close as $2\frac{1}{2}$ inches (6.4 centimeters). After about age 45 most people must have objects farther and farther away in order to see them clearly. The lens becomes less elastic as a person grows older.

Retina. The retina is a soft, transparent layer of nervous tissue made up of millions of light receptors. The retina is connected to the brain by the optic nerve. All of the structures needed to focus light onto the retina and to nourish it are housed in the eye, which is primarily a supporting shell for the retina.

When light enters the eye it passes through the lens and focuses an image onto the retina. The retina has several layers, one of which contains special cells named for their shapes—rods and cones. Light-sensitive chemicals in the rods and cones react to specific wavelengths of light and trigger nerve impulses. These impulses are carried through the optic nerve to the visual center in the brain. Here they are interpreted, and sight occurs.

Light must pass through the covering layers of the retina to reach the layer of rods and cones. There are about 75 to 150 million rods and about 7 million cones in the human retina. Rods do not detect lines, points, or color. They perceive only light and dark tones in an image. The sensitive rods can distinguish outlines or silhouettes of objects in almost complete darkness. They make it possible for people to see in darkness or at night. Cones are the keenest of the retina's receptor cells. They detect the fine lines and points of an image. The cones, for example, make it possible to read these words. There are three types of cones that receive color sensations. One type absorbs light best in wavelengths of blue-violet and another in wavelengths of green; a third is sensitive to wavelengths of yellow and red.

Visual purple. Rods detect images in the dark because the cells contain a rose-red pigment called visual purple, or rhodopsin. When exposed to bright light, visual purple undergoes a chemical change in which it loses its color. This causes the rods to lose their sensitivity to light, thus enabling the eye to endure glaring light.

Before the eye can see in the dark, visual purple must be re-formed in the retina. As more visual purple is produced, the eye's sensitivity to light increases. Thus when a person enters a darkened motion-picture theater his eyes do not contain much visual purple. As the visual purple is re-formed, the person can see better. In a short time his eyes' sensitivity to light is multiplied about 2,000 times. Visual purple can be produced only if the body has a sufficient quantity of vitamin A (*see* Vitamins). Lack of vitamin A in the diet may lead to night blindness, or nyctalopia.

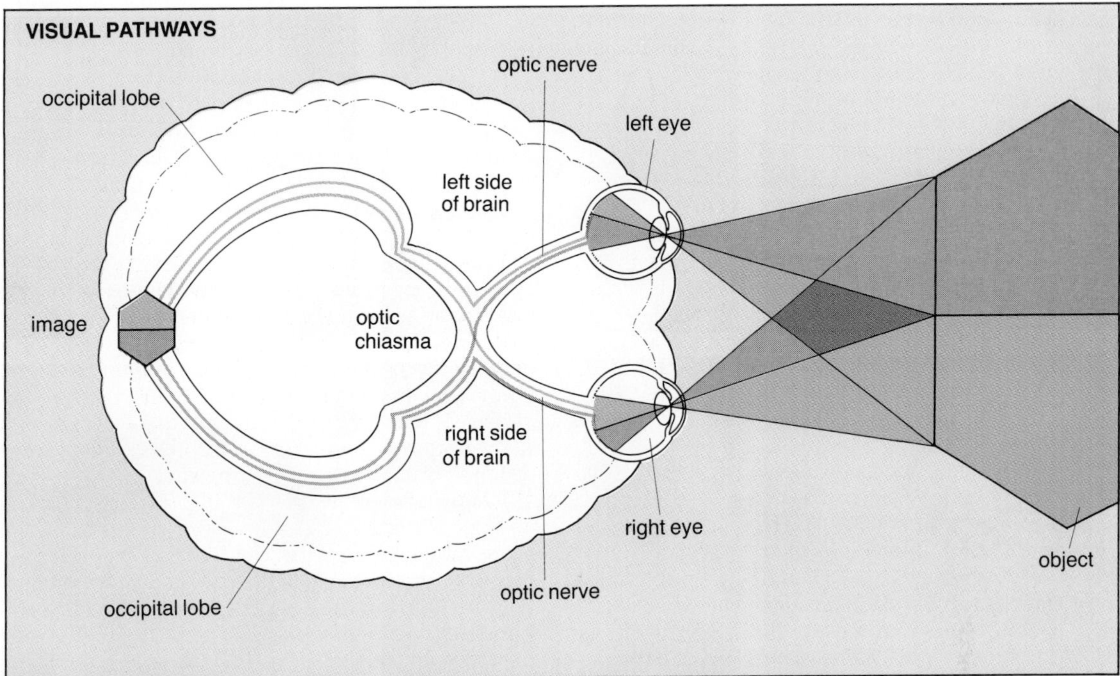

Vision

The optic nerve delivers its impulses to a special area of the brain called the visual center (*see* Brain). This is where people "see" objects in the sense of recognizing and reacting to what their eyes look at. In other words, seeing always involves the brain's visual center. Here sensation turns into perception.

The brain must learn by experience to analyze correctly the impulses it receives from the eyes. For instance, the lens system of the eye, like that of a camera, transmits its light pattern upside down. The brain has to learn that the impulses received from the upper part of the retina represent the lower part of the object sighted and vice versa.

In the brain also are located the centers that control all the eye's muscular movements, such as the opening and closing of the iris, the focusing of the main lens, and the movement of the eyeball. The eyeball's movement is voluntary. Other eye adjustments are reflexes (*see* Reflexes).

How two eyes work together. Most individuals use both eyes to see an object. This type of sensory perception is known as binocular vision. Thus two images of the object are formed—one on the retina of each eye. Impulses from both images are sent to the brain. Through experience these impulses are interpreted as two views of the same object. Because the eyes are about $2\frac{1}{2}$ inches (6.4 centimeters) apart from pupil to pupil and therefore are looking at the object from different angles, the two views are not exactly alike. This is known as the stereoscopic effect. If the object is far away, the difference between the images is slight. If the object is only a few inches away, the difference is very great.

The brain makes good use of this phenomenon. It learns to judge the distance of an object by the degree of difference between the images it receives from the two eyes. In the same way the brain perceives what is called perspective. It estimates differences in distance between two different objects or between two parts of the same object (*see* Stereoscope).

The eyes are turned up, down, and sideways by long muscles. At one end these muscles are attached to the top, bottom, and sides of the eyeball. At the other end, these muscles are attached to the bony walls of the eye socket. They are regulated with the most delicate precision so that normally they turn both eyes toward the same object at exactly the same time.

Persistence of vision. While the eyes are in motion they cannot see an object clearly. The image on the retina must come to rest, if only for a fraction of a second. That is why, when the eyes scan a broad landscape, they move across it in a series of quick jerks. The same thing happens when a line of type is read.

On the other hand, when the image has registered on the retinas, the vision of it persists from $1/50$ to $1/25$ of a second. That is how the eyes receive the impression of motion pictures. A movie consists of a rapid series of still pictures that are flashed on a screen, with about $1/60$ of a second of complete darkness after each image. But persistence of vision fills in the dark moment. It blends each picture perfectly with the one that went before to create the same impression that true motion produces.

Organic Disorders

The conjunctiva, the membrane lining the inner surface of the eyelids and the exposed surface of the sclera, can become irritated and inflamed. This is

(Top left) National Eye Institute, NIH; (top center, top right, bottom center) © Kenn Kostuk—Peter Arnold, Inc.; (bottom left) Scheie Eye Institute—Photo Researchers; (bottom right) © Biophoto Associates—Science Source/Photo Researchers

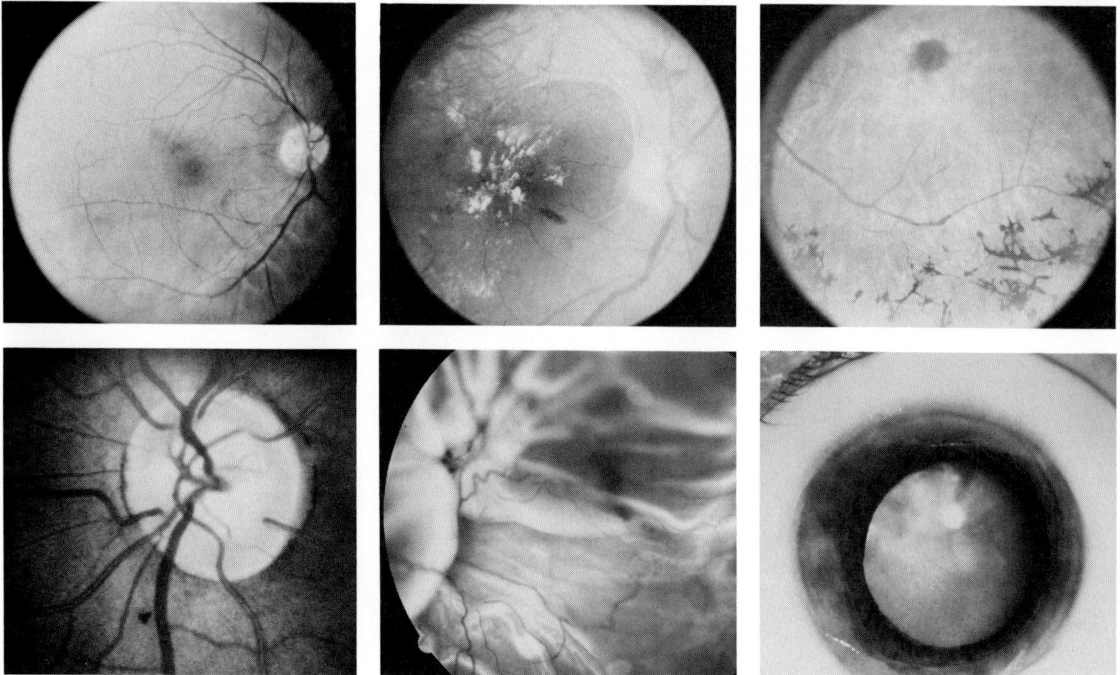

The fundus, or back portion of the retina, can be viewed with an ophthalmoscope. A normal, healthy retina (top left) shows well-defined blood vessels and a bright, clearly defined optic disk, right. In proliferative diabetic retinopathy (top center), fragile blood vessels form, and some bleed into the retina. In retinitis pigmentosa (top right), dark pigments form in the retina. In glaucoma (bottom left), the optic disk has a characteristic appearance. A detached retina (bottom center) displays a crescent-shaped tear. An opaque lens, or cataract (bottom right), fills the pupil, blocking the light.

called conjunctivitis, and is caused by viral infections or by exposure to smoke, dust, or similar irritants.

A common disorder of the eyelid, particularly in children, is a sty—an infection in the small glands of the eyelash. It is caused by the growth of bacteria and results in reddening and swelling of the entire eyelid.

A cataract is a cloudy or opaque discoloration in the lens of the eye. It can develop until the entire lens is covered with a thin, milky film. Treatment for cataract usually involves surgery, after which the patient is fitted with special glasses. Glaucoma is a fairly common disorder caused by an increase in pressure within the eyeball. It can result from heredity, tumors, and other causes. Headache, blurred vision, and eye pain are symptoms of glaucoma. Many treatments are used, and it is sometimes necessary to perform surgery to relieve the pressure.

Retinitis pigmentosa is an inherited eye disease in which the retinal pigments degenerate. In the course of the disease the rods are destroyed early, causing night blindness in youth. Deterioration of the retina is progressive. Eventually the affected person sees objects as if looking through a narrow pipe. This stage is followed by complete blindness, usually by the age of 50.

Diabetes, treated or untreated, may cause serious eye complications. The most common condition occurs in people who have had the disease for a long time. The blood vessels of the retina expand and hemorrhage, or bleed, into the retina. In later stages the hemorrhages become more extensive and eventually the retina becomes detached. These changes invariably lead to blindness. The actual cause of the changes in the vessels of the retina is still unknown.

A large variety of tumors, both benign and malignant, can develop in the eye. Such tumors are extremely serious, not only because they damage the eye but also because they can invade the brain.

There is a wide variation in the causes of blindness through the world. Geographic location and climate are contributing factors. Standards of hygiene, however, and the availability of medical care seem to account for the variations in percentages of blindness worldwide. Blindness in many countries, for example, is caused by cataract. This is tragic because the condition is easily cured by surgery (*see* Blindness).

Optical Defects

Some eyes are abnormally long from front to back. The lens, even when stretched to the utmost, cannot bring distant objects to a focus on the retina. Nearsightedness, or myopia, is the result. This defect is corrected by wearing a concave, or negative, spectacle lens. This lens, together with the convex lens of the eye, makes an optical system of longer focus.

When the distance between the front and the back of the eye is too short, the lens cannot bring near objects to a focus. This is a form of farsightedness called hypermetropia. The condition is corrected by shortening the focus with a convex, or positive, lens.

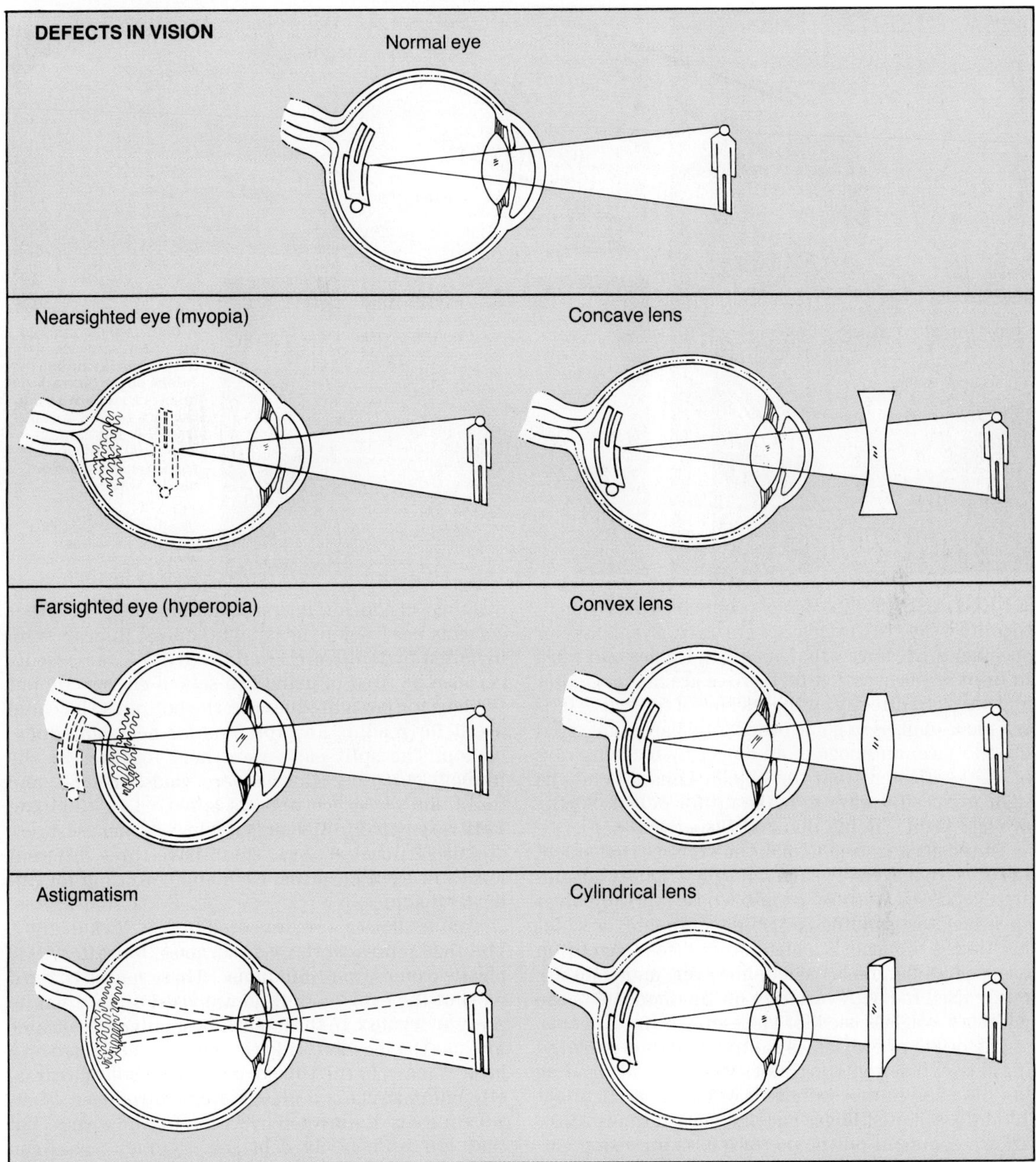

In many eyes the cornea is deformed so that its surface is oval instead of spherical. As a result, light rays are distorted at the entrance of the eye. This produces a blurred image and is known as astigmatism. To correct astigmatism, glasses are given a nonspherical or cylindrical curvature.

Cross-eyes and walleyes are produced when both eyes do not work together because of weakness of the eye muscles. The images formed on the two retinas are so unlike that they cannot be blended in the brain. Thus a double image is perceived. The condition is known as diplopia, or double vision. Prismatic lenses are prescribed to correct this defect.

Imperfections in the cones of the retina, resulting from heredity or disease, cause defective color vision. This is known as color blindness, or Daltonism. In total color blindness, everything appears in shades of gray as in an ordinary black-and-white photograph. In its more common form, color blindness is the inability to distinguish between reds and greens.

Persistent headaches, blurred vision, and painful inflammation of the eyelids are symptoms that may indicate serious eye disorders. Particles lodged in the eye should be removed without delay. Glasses are prescribed to strengthen vision and to reduce strain and fatigue. (*See also* Eyeglasses.)

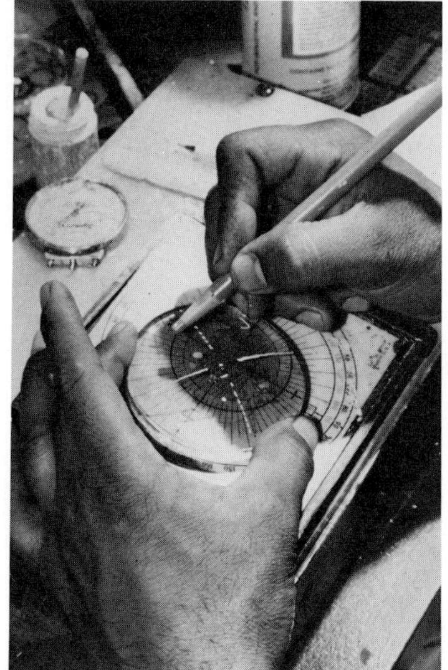

A blank lens is marked on a protractor (far left) before grinding. A lens edger (above) follows a pattern to cut the lens to fit a specific frame. A soft contact lens (left) is filled with transparent fluid, mostly water.

(Left) © Dick Luria—Medichrome/The Stock Shop; (far left) © Jim Markham; (above) Central States Optical Co.; photo, Brian Bosen

EYEGLASSES. To correct problems with vision or to protect the eyes, eyeglasses are worn. Eyeglasses, or spectacles, are lenses that are set in frames and worn in front of the eyes. Contact lenses are much smaller and are worn directly on the surface of the eye. A lens is a piece of glass or some other transparent material used to form an image of an object by focusing rays of light reflected from the object. Lenses bend the light in specific ways to make up for defects in the eye (*see* Light, "Refraction and Dispersion").

Tinted glass is used to make sunglasses that shield the eyes from excessive light and glare. Safety goggles are eyeglasses worn by people whose work involves such tasks as grinding, polishing, chipping, or sandblasting. A monocle is a one-lens eyepiece that often has a small handle attached; however, monocles are rarely used today. A variation on the monocle is the jeweler's eyeglass used for close-up viewing of gems.

The origin of eyeglasses is unknown, but magnifying glasses inserted into frames were used for reading in China and Europe hundreds of years ago. In about 1268 the scientist Roger Bacon recorded the earliest-known comment on the use of lenses for vision correction. Eyeglasses first made their appearance in Europe in 13th-century Italy. The first painting to show eyeglasses was painted by Tommaso di Modena in 1352.

Lenses were originally made of transparent quartz or beryl, but the increased demand for eyeglasses led to the adoption of glass. Venice, Italy, and Nuremburg, Germany, were the chief centers for grinding lenses made of high-quality glass. The availability of ground lenses eventually led to the invention of the compound microscope in the late 16th century and the telescope in about 1608.

Bifocals are eyeglasses made by joining two different lenses within one frame. One lens corrects distance vision, or nearsightedness, and the other corrects near vision, or farsightedness. Bifocals were invented by Benjamin Franklin in 1784, supposedly because he tired of using two sets of glasses. He put the lens for farsightedness on the bottom so he could use it for reading and the lens for nearsightedness on top. The split parts were held together by the frame. Cemented bifocals were made in 1884, and fused and one-piece bifocals appeared in 1908 and 1910 respectively. Although not in common use, there are also trifocal glasses. These have three different lenses in each eyepiece, each compensating for different distances.

Contact lenses were invented by A.E. Fick in 1887. The first lenses were made of glass, but after 1938 plastic came into common use. These lenses covered most of the eye, and a fluid was used under them to prevent dryness. In the late 1940s smaller lenses came into use that covered only the cornea and floated on a layer of tears. In the 1970s soft lenses made of hydroxethylmethacrylate, a plastic, were introduced. Their advantage is diminished irritation for the wearer, but they are more easily damaged. Contact lenses can correct all of the same defects of vision correctable by regular eyeglasses as well as some conditions that are not fully correctable by eyeglasses. It is even possible to make bifocal contacts.

The common types of faulty vision corrected by eyeglasses or contact lenses are nearsightedness, or myopia; farsightedness, or hyperopia; and astigmatism, a defect of the cornea resulting in blurred vision. Cataracts, a clouding of the lens of the eye that may lead to blindness, is corrected by surgery of various types. In some cases the lens is removed, and the individual wears glasses that take the place of the eye's own lens. In other cases the lens is removed and replaced by an inserted artificial lens.

INDEX

The letter E

may have started as a picture sign of a man with arms upraised, as in Egyptian hieroglyphic writing (1) and in a very early Semitic writing used about 1500 B.C. on the Sinai Peninsula (2). The sign meant "joy" or "rejoice" to the Egyptians. About 1000 B.C., in Byblos and in other Phoenician and Canaanite centers, the sign was given a linear form (3), the source of all later forms. The sign was called *he* in the Semitic languages and stood for the sound "h" in English.

The Greeks reversed the sign for greater ease in writing from left to right (4). They rejected the Semitic value "h" and gave it the value of the vowel "e." They called the sign *epsilon,* which means "short e."

The Romans adopted this sign for the Latin capital E. From Latin this form came unchanged into English. The handwriting of Graeco-Roman times changed the letter to a more quickly written form (5). From this is derived the English handwritten and printed small "e."

E. *see in index* Eccentricity

E-3A Sentry, airplane, *picture* **1**:178

Ea, Sumerian deity **3**:7

Eads, James B. (1820–87), U.S. engineer and inventor **7**:2
  Hall of Fame, *table* **10**:16
  St. Louis bridge **3**:446

Eads Bridge, in St. Louis, Mo. **3**:446

Eagle, bird **7**:2
  flight speed **3**:252, *picture* **3**:246
  length of life, *chart* **2**:423

Eagle, in golf **9**:190

Eagle, U.S. gold coin worth $10, first minted 1795; also, double eagle worth $20, first minted 1849; half eagle worth $5, first minted 1795; quarter eagle worth $2.50, first minted 1796; coinage of eagle, double eagle, and half eagle ceased in 1934 and quarter eagle in 1929.

Eagle Mountain, in Misquah Hills, n.e. Minnesota; highest point in state 2,301 ft (701 m); part of extension of Laurentian Hills **15**:440, *maps* **15**:441, 458

Eagle Pass, Tex., city on Rio Grande, opposite Piedras Negras, Mexico; agricultural center; mineral processing; apparel; pop. 21,407, *map* **23**:136

Eagle ray, a fish of the suborder Myliobatoidei **21**:306

Eagles, Fraternal Order of, founded in Seattle, Wash., 1898; pays sick and funeral benefits; has sponsored workmen's compensation, mothers' and old-age pensions, Mother's Day; subordinate bodies called Aeries **8**:387

Eaker, Ira Clarence (1896–1987), U.S. Army officer, born in Field Creek, Tex.; commander 8th U.S. bomber command in Britain 1942 and 8th U.S. Air Force there 1943; Allied air commander in Mediterranean theater 1943–45; deputy commander of Army Air Forces and chief of Air Staff 1945–47; retired 1947.

Eakins, Thomas (1844–1916), U.S. painter and sculptor **7**:2
  'Between Rounds' **18**:54, *picture* **18**:55
  Whitman, *picture* **25**:200

Ealing, England, borough in w. Greater London; interesting tombs in churches; birthplace of Thomas Huxley; pop. 297,910, *maps* **13**:287, **24**:75

Eames, Charles (1907–78), U.S. architect, industrial designer, and toy designer, born in St. Louis, Mo.; worked with Eliel Saarinen at Cranbrook Academy of Art, Bloomfield Hills, Mich.
  furniture **6**:122, **8**:462
  industrial design **11**:170, 174

Eames, Emma (1865–1952), U.S. opera soprano, *list* **17**:570

Eanes, António Ramalho (born 1935), president of Portugal, born in Alcains, Portugal.

Ear 7:3. *see also in index* Deafness; Hearing
  animal **2**:430
    bird **3**:246
    fish **8**:127
    frog **8**:407
    insect **11**:219
  bionics **3**:236
  electromagnetic radiation **3**:238
  health care **10**:88
  human **21**:176
  sound. *see in index* Sound

Ear canal (or external auditory meatus) **7**:3

Eardrum (or tympanic membrane) **7**:3

Eared seal, type of seal **21**:155

Earhart, Amelia (1897–1937), U.S. aviator **7**:5
  aviation **1**:205

Earl, title of nobility **23**:195, 196, *picture* **23**:195

Earle, Ralph (1751–1801), U.S. painter, born in Shrewsbury, Mass.; paintings of battles at Lexington and Concord said to be first historical paintings done in North America.

Earless seal. *see in index* True seal

Earley versus DiCenso, U.S. law case
  education, *list* **7**:104

Earlham College, in Richmond, Ind.; founded 1847 by Religious Society of Friends; became college 1859; arts and sciences, education, religion; biological field station on Dewart Lake; foreign study in Europe, Latin America, Japan; graduate school.

Early, Jubal Anderson (1816–94), Confederate general, born in Franklin County, Va.; opposed secession of Virginia but accepted Confederate States of America commission; won fame at Antietam, Fredericksburg, Chancellorsville; commanded division at Gettysburg
  Civil War **5**:476, 482
  Sheridan **21**:236

Early American style, style of furniture, architecture, or fabric. *see in index* Colonial architecture

Early Bird, a communications satellite **1**:72

Early chrysanthemum, a perennial flower **9**:25

'Early Mace', sculpture, *picture* **2**:743

Early summer phlox, a perennial plant
  flowering time **9**:25

Early-warning aircraft 1:158, *picture* **1**:163

Earp, Wyatt (1848–1929), U.S. frontiersman, well-known gunman **7**:5
  frontier **8**:424
  jail, *picture* **12**:181
  outlaws **17**:619

Earth 7:6. *see also in index* Continent; Geology; World
  ancient element **1**:273
  astronomy **2**:717, 722, *diagram* **2**:725, *picture* **2**:718
  atmosphere **2**:748
  earth sciences **7**:41
  equator **7**:293
  gravitation **9**:238, **14**:266
  greenhouse effect **9**:281
  heat **10**:101
  hemisphere **10**:126
  magnetism **5**:621, **14**:42. *see also in index* Magnetosphere
  matter, *picture* **14**:223
  planets **19**:408, *table* **19**:413
  plate tectonics **19**:456
  solar system **21**:375, *picture* **21**:377
  surveying **22**:720
  water. *see in index* Lake; Ocean; River; Water cycle

Earth almond (or chufa), plant **21**:165

Earth dam 6:15, *picture* **6**:13

Earthenware, pottery **19**:564

'Earthly Paradise, The', work by Morris **7**:276

Earth-moving equipment, machinery
  dredge and power shovel **6**:258

Earthnut. *see in index* Peanut

Earth pig. *see in index* Aardvark

Earthquake (also called temblor) **7**:37
  Armenian S.S.R. **2**:628
  continental structure **5**:688
  Earth **7**:33
  Europe **7**:330
    Bucharest **3**:477
    Greece **9**:255
    Italy **11**:398
    Yugoslavia **25**:434
  flood cause **8**:182, *table* **8**:181
  Japan **12**:60
  Latin America **13**:60
    Central America **4**:253
      El Salvador **7**:195, **21**:50
      Guatemala **9**:297, **9**:300
    Mexico **15**:322
      Mexico City **15**:347
  Oceania **17**:465
  oceanography **17**:485
  Pacific Ocean **18**:5
  plate tectonics **19**:456, **21**:112
  Turkey **2**:492, **23**:318
  United States
    Alaska **1**:246
    Los Angeles **13**:303
    San Francisco **21**:47
  waves **17**:487

Earth satellites. *see in index* Satellites, artificial

Earth sciences (or geosciences) **7**:41. *see also in index* Earth; Geology; Meteorology; Oceanography
  science **21**:121

Earthshine, sunlight reflected to the moon from the daylight region of the Earth **15**:579

Earthstar, fungus-like organism **8**:449

Earthworm (or angleworm), animal of the phylum Annelida, *picture* **2**:433
  digestive system **1**:389
  hibernation, *picture* **10**:148
  phylogenetic tree, *diagram* **25**:468

Earwax. *see in index* Cerumen

Earwig, insect of the order Dermaptera, with pair of movable pincers at end of abdomen; named from erroneous notion that it creeps into ears of sleeping persons, *picture* **11**:213

Easement, in law
  definition, *table* **13**:92
  property ownership **19**:612

Easley, S.C., city 13 mi (21 km) s.w. of Greenville, in agricultural area; clothing, textiles; pop. 14,264, *map* **22**:437

East, Edward Murray (1879–1938), U.S. biologist, born in Du Quoin, Ill.; professor Harvard University 1914–26 ('Heredity and Human Affairs').

East, direction **6**:157

East African Rift Valley. *see in index* Great Rift Valley

East Anglia, early kingdom in e. of Anglo-Saxon Britain, comprising present Norfolk and Suffolk **7**:230

East Aurora, N.Y., village 15 mi (25 km) s.e. of Buffalo; electronics; toys, wood products; pop. 6,803, *map* **16**:268. *see also in index* Roycroft Shop

East Australian Current, oceanography **18**:9

East Bengal. *see in index* Bangladesh

East Berlin, East Germany, capital; pop. 1,185,533 **3**:168. *see also in index* Berlin
  Berlin, *map* **3**:170
  Europe, *map* **7**:360

Eastbourne, England, s. coast resort, between Brighton and Hastings; traces of Roman occupation exist; pop. 69,290, *map* **24**:75

East Cape, at e. tip of North Island, New Zealand, *map* **16**:299

East Carolina University, in Greenville, N.C.; state control; opened in 1909; arts and sciences, art, business, education, health and medicine, home economics, music, nursing; Air Force ROTC; graduate school.

East Central Oklahoma State University (formerly East Central State College), in Ada, Okla.; established 1909; liberal arts and sciences, and education; graduate school in education.

East Chicago, Ind., port city on Lake Michigan, 18 mi (29 km) s.e. of Chicago; extensive rail and lake shipping; petroleum refining; iron and steel products, railroad equipment, chemicals, building materials; port area named Indiana Harbor; pop. 39,786 **11**:91, *map* **11**:102, *picture* **11**:98

East China Sea, part of Pacific Ocean bounded by China, Korea, Japan, Ryukyu Islands, and Taiwan; includes Yellow Sea, *map* **12**:78. *see also in index* Ocean, *table*
  Asia, *map* **2**:697
  China, *map* **5**:384
  Shanghai **21**:214
  world, *map* **25**:297

East Cleveland, Ohio, residential city 5 mi (8 km) e. of Cleveland; electrical research laboratory; incorporated as a city 1911; pop. 36,957, *map* **17**:516

East Detroit, Mich., city 10 mi (16 km) n.e. of Detroit; residential suburb; settled 1827, incorporated 1928; pop. 38,280, *map* **15**:372

East End, region of London, England **13**:294

Easter, Christian festival **7**:41
  calendar **4**:29
  Hungary, *picture* **10**:275
  opera **17**:560

Easter eggs
  Faberge eggs **8**:2
  folk art symbol **8**:251

Easter Island, in s. Pacific; 46 sq mi (119 sq km); belongs to Chile; pop. 2,000 **7**:42
  national park status **16**:27
  Oceania **17**:467, *table* **17**:472
  world, *map* **25**:297

Easter Island, engraved glass sculpture, *picture* **9**:157

Eastern Airlines, U.S. airline **1**:172

Eastern American chipmunk, animal (*Tamias striatus*) **22**:558, 561, *pictures* **22**:557, 559

Eastern American mole, mammal (*Scalopus aquaticus*) **15**:521

Eastern arborvitae. *see in index* Northern white cedar

Eastern Australian native cat, marsupial (*Dasyurus viverrinus*), *picture* **14**:155

Eastern Bay, inlet of Chesapeake Bay, e. Maryland, *maps* **14**:169, 183

Eastern Carpathians, mountain range in Romania **20**:276

Eastern Catholics. *see in index* Eastern rite churches

Eastern Coal Field. *see in index* Appalachian Plateau

Eastern College (formerly Eastern Baptist College), in St. Davids, Pa.; affiliated with the American Baptist Convention; incorporated 1952; liberal arts and sciences.

Eastern Colorado River. *see in index* Colorado River

Eastern Conference, in college football **8**:290

Eastern Connecticut State College, in Willimantic, Conn.; established in 1889; arts and sciences, teacher education; graduate program.

Eastern cottontail rabbit, rodent (*Sylvilagus floridanus*) of the family Leporiade, *picture* **20**:29

Eastern cottonwood, tree (*Populus deltoides*) of the family Salicaceae **19:**537, *picture* **23:**281

Eastern Empire. *see in index* Byzantine Empire

Eastern Front, World War I **25:**304

Eastern garter snake, reptile (*Thamnophis sirtalis sirtalis*), *picture* **21:**335

Eastern glossy ibis, bird **11:**4

Eastern gray squirrel, animal (*Sciurus carolinesis*), *picture* **22:**559

Eastern hare wallaby, animal **2:**779

Eastern hemisphere 10:126

Eastern hemlock, tree
wood, *table* **25:**282

Eastern Highlands, in Australia. *see in index* Great Dividing Range

Eastern Highlands, geographic region in U.S.
Connecticut **5:**650, *map* **5:**651

Eastern hognose snake, reptile (*Heterodon platyrhinos*), *picture* **21:**334

Eastern Ice Yachting Association 11:11

Eastern Illinois University, in Charleston, Ill.; state control; opened 1899; letters and sciences, business, education, health and physical education, music; graduate study.

Eastern Kentucky University, in Richmond, Ky.; state control; founded 1906; arts and technology, business, and education; graduate study.

Eastern kingbird, bird **8:**244

Eastern Mennonite College, in Harrisonburg, Va.; established in 1917; liberal arts and teacher education; seminary.

Eastern Michigan University, in Ypsilanti, Mich.; state control; founded 1849; arts and sciences, business administration, education, and international studies; graduate study.

Eastern Montana College, in Billings, Mont.; state control; founded 1925; arts and sciences, teacher education; graduate study.

Eastern Nazarene College, in Quincy, Mass.; affiliated with Church of the Nazarene; chartered 1918; arts and sciences, education, and theology; graduate studies.

Eastern New Mexico University, in Portales, N.M.; state control; opened 1934 as junior college, senior college 1940; general studies, liberal arts and sciences, business administration, education and psycholcgy, music, speech and drama, technology; graduate school; branches at Clovis and Roswell.

Eastern Oregon State College (formerly Eastern Oregon College), in La Grande, Ore.; state control; established in 1929; teacher education; graduate study.

Eastern Orthodox Churches (also called Eastern Orthodoxy, or Orthodox Catholic church) **7:**42
Balkan conflict **3:**31
birth control **3:**283
Byzantine period conflicts **3:**533, 536
calendar **4:**28
canon law **4:**142
ecumenism **7:**69
Europe **7:**337
Fathers of the Church **8:**45
Leo IX **13:**130
monks and monasticism **15:**539, 543
Paul VI **18:**156
Roman Catholicism **20:**265
U.S.S.R. **24:**32

Eastern Question, in European politics, the complicated problems arising out of European interference in affairs of Turkey and Balkan States formerly under Turkish rule.

Eastern red cedar, tree **12:**157

Eastern rite churches 7:44

Eastern Roman Empire. *see in index* Byzantine Empire

Eastern Rumelia, Bulgaria. *see in index* Rumelia

Eastern Solomons, battle of, World War II **25:**345

Eastern spruce, a common name for red spruce, white spruce, and black spruce
wood, *table* **25:**282

Eastern Star, secret female order founded by Masons **8:**386

Eastern starfish, echinoderm, *picture* **11:**285

Eastern State Hospital, in Williamsburg, Va. **25:**209

Eastern States, India, formerly an agency comprising 42 states in e. and n.e. Indian Empire; now part of Madhya Pradesh and Orissa states.

Eastern Townships, section of Appalachian Region in s. Quebec **20:**11

Eastern Washington University (formerly Eastern Washington State College), in Cheney, Wash.; established in 1890; arts and sciences, teacher education; graduate study.

Eastern white pine, evergreen tree (*Pinus strobus*), of pine family; leaves to 5 in. (13 cm) long, grow in clusters of 5, blue green with white tinge; cones to 8 in. (20 cm) long, *table* **25:**282
pine **19:**387

Eastern yellow-shafted flicker (also called golden-winged woodpecker, or wake-up, or yellowhammer), bird **8:**178, *picture* **8:**179

Easter Revolt, abortive attempt of Irish to throw off British rule; much of Dublin seized Easter Monday (1916)
De Valera **6:**124

East European Plain, in Belorussia **3:**159
Russian Soviet Federated Socialist Republic **20:**356

East Florida, name given by English in 1763 to a part of Florida; n. boundary was from mouth of St. Mary's River to junction of Chattahoochee and Flint rivers, w. boundary Apalachicola River, and e. the Atlantic Ocean.

East Germany. *see in index* Germany, East

East Goths. *see in index* Ostrogoths

East Grand Rapids, Mich., residential city just s.e. of Grand Rapids in Kent County; first settled 1835, incorporated as city 1926; pop. 12,565, *map* **15:**372

East Greenland Current, cold ocean current of the Atlantic, along e. coast of Greenland; carries many icebergs.

East Gulf Coastal Plain, geographic region in U.S.
Louisiana **13:**309, *map* **13:**310

East Haddam, Conn., on Connecticut River, 13 mi (21 km) s.e. of Middletown; pop. of township 5,621, *map* **5:**664

Easthampton, Mass., just s. of Northampton and about 12 mi (19 km) n.w. of Springfield; textile industries; elastic webbing, metal products; pop. of township 15,580, *map* **14:**206

East Harlem (or Spanish Harlem), a neighborhood in Manhattan, New York, N.Y. **16:**273
Puerto Ricans **10:**165, *picture* **10:**166

East Hartford, Conn., urban town on Connecticut River, opposite Hartford; tobacco; aircraft engines, brushes, paper products, metal products; pop. 52,563, *map* **5:**664

East Haven, Conn., urban town just e. of New Haven; street lighting equipment; pop. 25,028, *map* **5:**664

East India companies, formed in 17th century for trade with East Indies; known as British, Dutch, French, Danish, Spanish, Portuguese, Swedish, Scottish, Austrian. *see in index* Dutch East India Company; East India Company (English)

East India Company, English **7:**44
America **1:**332
American Revolution **20:**184
England **7:**245, 254
India **11:**77
Bombay **3:**340
Clive **5:**504
Hastings **10:**52
Lucknow revolt **13:**328
international trade **11:**271
tea **23:**47

East Indians, people
Guyana **9:**321
Mauritius **14:**233
South Africa **22:**396
West Indies **25:**157

East Indies (or Malay Archipelago) **7:**45. *see also in index* Borneo; Celebes; Indonesia; Java; Malaysia; New Guinea; Philippines; Sumatra
history
East India Company **7:**44
The Netherlands **16:**130
reptiles **6:**238
spices **22:**533

East Islip, N.Y., residential village on Long Island, near s. shore; Heckscher State Park nearby; pop. 6,861.

East Kildonan, Man., residential city, part of metropolitan Winnipeg; in an area of small farms; supports light industry; pop. 30,152.

Eastlake, Charles Lock (1793–1865), English painter and art critic, born in Plymouth, England; elected president of Royal Academy 1850 ('Pilgrims in Sight of Rome'; 'Christ Blessing Little Children').

Eastlake, Ohio, city 7 mi (11 km) n.e. of Euclid, in Lake County; near Lake Erie; s.w. of Headland Beach State Park; pop. 22,104, *map* **17:**516

East Lansing, Mich., city just e. of Lansing; residential suburb; Michigan State University; settled 1850, incorporated as city 1907; pop. 48,309, *map* **15:**372
Lansing **13:**45

East Latvian Plains, geographic area in U.S.S.R. **13:**83

East Liverpool, Ohio, city on Ohio River, in e. part of state, 18 mi (29 km) n. of Steubenville; ceramics center; brick, tile, steel products; pop. 16,687, *map* **17:**516

East Locris, district of ancient Greece. *see in index* Locris

East London, South Africa, seaport of Cape of Good Hope Province, on Indian Ocean; many industries; exports corn, wool, fruit, meat, dairy products; pop. 116,056, with suburbs, *map* **1:**115

East Longmeadow, Mass., 4 mi (6 km) s.e. of Springfield; games, school equipment; incorporated 1894; pop. of township 12,905, *map* **14:**206

East Los Angeles, Calif., residential city just e. of Los Angeles; part of Los Angeles metropolitan area, in which major industries include aircraft, electronics, and petroleum refining; pop. 105,033, *map* **4:**52

Eastman, Charles Alexander (also called Ohiyesa) (1858–1939), U.S. physician and writer, born in Redwood Falls, Minn.; son of Santee Sioux father and Anglo-Sioux mother; held U.S. government offices among Indians; authority on Indian life ('Indian Boyhood'; 'The Indian Today').

Eastman, Crystal (1881–1928), U.S. social worker, feminist, and pacifist, born in Marlborough, Mass., sister of Max Eastman; her treatise 'Work Accidents and the Law', 1910, did much to promote progress of workmen's compensation laws; active in Woman's Peace party; helped found London branch of National Woman's party
women's rights movement **25:**278

Eastman, George (1854–1932), U.S. pioneer in photographic industry **7:**47
motion pictures **15:**616
photography **19:**351

Eastman, Max Forrester (1883–1969), U.S. poet, essayist, born in Canandaigua, N.Y.; taught philosophy at Columbia University; editor *The Masses*, a socialistic periodical ('The Enjoyment of Poetry'; 'The Colors of Life', poems; 'The Enjoyment of Laughter').

Eastman Kodak Company (originally Eastman Dry Plate and Film Company), founded by George Eastman **7:**47
headquarters, *picture* **16:**250

East Massapequa, N.Y., community 30 mi (50 km) s.e. of New York, N.Y., on Long Island; pop. 15,926.

East Meadow, N.Y., residential community 23 mi (37 km) e. of New York, N.Y., in Nassau County, on Long Island; location of Nassau County Historical Museum; pop. 46,290, *map* **16:**268

East Moline, Ill., city in n.w. part of state, on Mississippi River, adjoining Moline (these two cities, with neighboring Rock Island, Ill., and Davenport, Iowa, known as the Quad Cities); farm equipment, scales, machinery; state hospital; pop. 20,907, *map* **11:**52

East North Central States, name used by the U.S. government for the geographic division including the states of Ohio, Indiana, Illinois, Michigan, and Wisconsin.

'East of the Sun and West of the Moon: Twenty-One Norwegian Folk Tales', work by Parin d'Aulaire **22:**658

Easton, Mass., 8 mi (13 km) s. of Stockton; carbonated beverages; Stonehill College; incorporated 1725; pop. of township 16,623.

Easton, Pa., city on Delaware River, at mouth of Lehigh, opposite Phillipsburg, N.J.; steel and cement products, machinery; slate quarries nearby; Lafayette College; pop. 26,027, *map* **18:**204

East Orange, N.J., residential city n.w. of Newark and 12 mi (19 km) w. of New York, N.Y.; waterworks supplies; insurance center; Upsala College; pop. 77,878 **16:**206, *map* **16:**210

East Pacific Rise, underwater mountain range **17:**461
Pacific Ocean **18:**4

East Pakistan. *see in index* Bangladesh

East Pass, jetty in Destin, Fla., *picture* **12:**111

East Paterson, N.J. *see in index* Elmwood Park

East Peoria, Ill., city opposite Peoria, on Illinois River; farm machinery, engines; incorporated 1919; pop. 22,385, *map* **11:**52

East Point, Ga., city 6 mi (10 km) s.w. of Atlanta; textiles, fertilizers, chemicals, machinery, auto batteries, paint; pop. 37,486, *map* **9:**100

Eastport, Me., easternmost city of the U.S.; pop. 1,982, *maps* **14:**53, 66

East Providence, R.I., city on Seekonk River, opposite Providence; petroleum products, machinery, chemicals; pop. 50,980, *map* **20:**210

East Prussia, formerly the easternmost province of Prussia, on Baltic Sea; 14,401 sq mi (37,298 sq km); cap. Königsberg; in 1945 n. part of East Prussia was included in U.S.S.R., s. part in Poland **19:**628

East Ridge, Tenn., residential town just s. of Chattanooga; food products, iron and steel, and textiles manufacturing; incorporated 1921; pop. 21,236, *map* **23:**98

East Riding, administrative district in York County, England.

East River, N.Y., strait separating Long Island from Manhattan Island; 15 mi (25 km) long, *map* **16:**269

East Rockaway, N.Y., residential village on Long Island, 20 mi (30 km) s.e. of New York, N.Y.; instrument parts; pop. 10,917, *map* **16:**268

East Room, largest room in the White House where state receptions and balls are held **25:**199

East Saint Louis, Ill., city on Mississippi River, opposite St. Louis, Mo.; railroad center; meat products, chemicals, alumina, metal products; pop. 55,200 **11:**36, *maps* **11:**35, 52

East South Central States, name used by the U.S. government for the geographic division including the states of Kentucky, Tennessee, Alabama, and Mississippi.

East Stroudsburg State College, in East Stroudsburg, Pa.; established in 1893; formerly a teachers' college; arts and sciences, education; graduate study.

East Tennessee State University, in Johnson City, Tenn.; opened 1911; arts and sciences, business administration and economics, education, health, nursing; graduate studies; centers at Bristol, Greenville, and Kingsport.

East Texas Baptist College, in Marshall, Tex.; affiliated with Southern Baptist convention; chartered 1912; liberal arts, humanities, natural sciences, social sciences, and teacher education.

East Texas State University, in Commerce, Tex.; founded 1889 as private school; arts and sciences, business administration, and education; graduate study.

East Tirol, region in Austria **23:**192

East-West Center, in Honolulu, Hawaii **10:**63

East Windsor (formerly Ford City), Ont., former municipality, now part of city of Windsor, on Detroit River, opposite Detroit, Mich.; automobiles.

Eastwood, Clint (born 1931), U.S. motion-picture actor and politician, born in San Francisco; ranked No. 1 international box office attraction since 1970; appeared in U.S. television series Rawhide in 1959–65; became famous as the "Man with No Name" in spaghetti Westerns ('A Fistful of Dollars', 'The Good, the Bad, and the Ugly'); known for tough guy roles ('Dirty Harry', 'Sudden Impact'); also stylish director ('Play Misty for Me', 'Bronco Billy'); mayor of Carmel, Calif., 1986–88, *picture* **5:**769

'Easy Rider' (1969), motion picture by Hopper, *picture* **15:**626

Eating customs. *see in index* Food and nutrition, *subhead* eating customs

Eaton, Anne Thaxter (1881–1971), U.S. author, book reviewer, and school librarian, born in Palmer, Mass.; librarian at Lincoln School, Teachers' College, Columbia University, 1917–47; author of 'Reading with Children' and 'Treasure for the Taking: a Book List for Boys and Girls'; compiler of anthologies for children: 'The Animals' Christmas', poems, carols, and stories, and 'Welcome Christmas!', poems.

Eaton, Cyrus Stephen (1883–1979), U.S. industrialist and financier **11:**195

Eaton, Dorman Bridgman (1823–99), U.S. lawyer and civic leader, born in Hardwick, Vt.; wrote Pendleton Act for Civil Service reform; chairman Civil Service Commission 1873–75, 1883–86.

Eaton, Jeanette (1886–1968), U.S. author of children's books, born in Columbus, Ohio (biographies: 'David Livingstone, Foe of Darkness', 'That Lively Man, Ben Franklin', 'Gandhi, Fighter Without a Sword', 'The Story of Eleanor Roosevelt', 'America's Own Mark Twain').

Eaton, Theophilus (1590–1658), one of organizers of New England Confederation (1643), born in Stony Stratford, England; drew up code called "Connecticut Blue Laws"; early settler of New Haven.

Eaton, Walter Prichard (1878–1957), U.S. author, drama critic, and lecturer, born in Malden, Mass.; professor of drama Yale University; outdoor enthusiast ('Boy Scouts of Berkshire'; 'The Bird House Man'; 'Echoes and Realities', verse; 'The Actor's Heritage'; 'Theatre Guild: the First Ten Years').

Eatontown, N.J., borough 3 mi (5 km) s. of Red Bank; hydraulic jacks, precision instruments; Fort Monmouth nearby; pop. 12,703, *map* **16:**210

Eau Claire, Wis., chief city in n.w. of state, 75 mi (120 km) e. of St. Paul, Minn., on Chippewa and Eau Claire rivers; dairying and stock-raising area; packed meat; tires and tubes, paper, machinery, pressure cookers, sewer pipe; Wisconsin State University-Eau Claire; pop. 51,509 **25:**250, 260, *map* **25:**264

Eau de Cologne. *see in index* Cologne, perfume

Eave swallow. *see in index* Cliff swallow

Ebbinghaus, Hermann (1850–1909), German psychologist **7:**47

Ebenezer (Stone of Help), place in Judea where Samuel defeated Philistines (Bible, I Sam. vii, 10–12).

Eberhart, Richard (born 1904), U.S. poet and educator, born in Austin, Minn.; professor Dartmouth College 1956– ; won 1962 Bollingen Prize in Poetry ('Burr Oaks'; 'Brotherhood of Men'; 'Selected Poems, 1930–1965', awarded 1966 Pulitzer prize).

Eberle, Abastenia St. Leger (1878–1942), U.S. sculptor, born in Webster City, Iowa; studies of children and old women especially notable.

Eberle, Irmengarde (pen name Phyllis Ann Carter) (1898–1979), U.S. author, born in San Antonio, Tex.; writer of both fiction and factual books for children ('Very Good Neighbors'; 'Grasses'; 'Evie').

Ebers, Georg Moritz (1837–98), German Egyptologist and novelist, born in Berlin; professor at Jena and Leipzig; wrote historical romances with Egyptian settings ('An Egyptian Princess'; 'Uarda'; 'Homo Sum').

Ebers Papyrus, ancient treatise on pharmacology **18:**274

Ebert, Friedrich (1871–1925), German statesman, born in Heidelberg; leader Social Democrats and first president of the German Republic 1919–25 **9:**123

Ebla, ancient Mesopotamian civilization
  Syria **22:**751

EBM (electron-beam machining), a metalworking operation **23:**226

Ebony, tropical tree **7:**48
  forest fires **8:**94

'Ebony', magazine **14:**34

Ebright Road, highest point in Delaware, 442 ft (134 m) high, *map* **6:**72

Ebro River, n.e. Spain; flows s.e. 465 mi (750 km) from Cantabrian Mts. to Mediterranean, *map* **7:**360
  Iberian peninsula **11:**2
  Spain **22:**487

EBV. *see in index* Epstein-Barr virus

EC. *see in index* European Communities

ECA (Economic Commission for Africa), United Nations **24:**86

ECAFE (Economic Commission for Asia and the Far East), United Nations **24:**86

Ecbatana, Persia, ancient capital of Media; summer residence, successively, of Median, Persian, and Parthian kings by whom it was captured and pillaged; archaeological excavations. *see also in index* Hamadan

'Ecce Ancilla Domini', work by Rossetti **20:**328

Eccentricity (*e*), in mathematics, measure of elongation of an ellipse; ratio of distance between foci to major axis; used in astronomy **9:**76, *diagrams* **9:**77

Ecclefechan, Scotland, village 14 mi (22 km) e. of Dumfries; birthplace of Thomas Carlyle.

Eccles, John Carew (born 1903), Australian physiologist, born in Melbourne; on medical school faculty University of New York, Buffalo. *see also in index* Nobel Prizewinners, *table*

Eccles, England, city on the Manchester Ship Canal, 4 mi (6 km) w. of Manchester; cotton fabrics; engine works; famous for Eccles cakes; pop. 39,830, *map* **24:**75

Ecclesia cathedralis. *see in index* Cathedral

Ecclesiastes (the preacher), a book of the Bible attributed by Jewish tradition to Solomon.

'Ecclesiastical History of the English Nation', work by Bede **7:**263
  Caedmon's poetry **4:**13

Ecdysome, insect hormone **10:**240

ECE (Economic Commission for Europe), United Nations **24:**86

Ecevit, Bülent (born 1925), Turkish poet, journalist, and politician, born in Constantinople (now Istanbul), prime minister of Turkey in 1974, 1977, and 1978–80 **23:**325

ECG. *see in index* Electrocardiogram

Ecgberht. *see in index* Egbert

Echegaray, José (1832–1916), Spanish mathematician, statesman, and dramatist, born in Madrid, Spain ('Mariana'; 'The Great Galeoto'; 'The Son of Don Juan'; 'The World and His Wife'). *see also in index* Nobel Prizewinners, *table*
  Spanish literature **22:**506, *picture* **22:**504

Echelon, in aviation, formation in which planes fly; each plane is at a certain altitude above or below the others and left or right of the one ahead
  warfare innovations **2:**641

Echeveria, a genus of perennial plants of the orpine family, native chiefly to Mexico; the fleshy, often hairy, many-colored leaves covered by white powdery material; used as foliage plants.

Echeverría Alvarez, Luis (born 1922), Mexican lawyer and government official, born in Mexico City; undersecretary of interior 1958–63, secretary 1963–70; president of Mexico 1970–76 **15:**338

Echidna (or spiny anteater), Australian mammal related to the duckbill **2:**435, *picture* **2:**434
  Australia **2:**780
  mammal **14:**81
  reproductive system **20:**168

Echinacea (also called purple coneflower), a genus of perennial plants of composite family, similar to the rudbeckias; tall; leaves rough; flowers daisylike, pink, rose, purple; native to North America; roots source of an oleoresin.

Echinoderm, marine invertebrates that include the starfish, sea urchins, and sea cucumbers
  invertebrates' classification **11:**284
  prehistoric animals **2:**459, *picture* **2:**460

Echinodermata, phylum of marine invertebrates
  phylogenetic tree, *diagram* **25:**468
  starfish and sea urchins **22:**593

Echinoid, an echinoderm
  animal life record, *table* **7:**24

Echinops. *see in index* Globe thistle

Echium. *see in index* Viper's bugloss

Echiura. *see in index* Spoon worm

Echmiadzin, Armenian Soviet Socialist Republic, city 12 mi (19 km) w. of Erivan; famous for monastery, seat of Armenian church.

Echo, figure in Greek mythology **7:**48
  Narcissus **16:**18

Echo, a reflected sound **7:**48
  petroleum exploration **18:**255
  radar **20:**37
  sound **21:**391

Echolocation, process for locating distant or invisible objects by means of sound waves reflected back to the emitter by the objects **21:**176
  bat **3:**104
  dolphin and porpoise **6:**224

'Echo of a Scream', painting by Siqueiros
  painting **18:**71, *picture* **18:**70

Echo I, communications satellite **3:**45

Echo sounder, instrument for measuring ocean depths **17:**464
  oceanography **17:**482

Eck, John (or Johann Maier von Eck) (1486–1543), German theologian, born at Eck, Swabia; opponent of Luther and the Reformation; defeated Luther in debate at Leipzig 1519; in 1520 obtained from Rome bull of excommunication against Luther; at Diet of Augsburg (1530) among those selected to refute Luther's theory of confession.

Eckener, Hugo (1868–1954), German airship builder, born in Flensburg; president of Zeppelin Construction Works; associate and successor of Count Zeppelin; built *Graf Zeppelin* and in 1929 commanded it on three-week world flight.

Eckerd College (formerly Florida Presbyterian College), in St. Petersburg, Fla.; chartered 1958; opened 1960; present name adopted 1972; liberal arts, teacher education.

Eckert, J. Presper, Jr. (born 1919), U.S. engineer **5:**633, 635

Eckert, William Dole (1909–71), U.S. Air Force officer, born in Freeport, Ill.; in Air Force 1931–61, retired as lieutenant general; commissioner of baseball 1965–69.

Eckhart, Johannes (also called Meister Eckhart) (1260?–1327?), German Dominican monk, father of German mysticism.

Eckman, F.R. *see in index* Hartog, Jan de

ECLA (Economic Commission for Latin America), United Nations **24:**86

Eclipse, in astronomy **7:**48
  amateur astronomy **2:**736
  astronomy **2:**719
  moon **15:**577
  observatory **17:**458
  speed of light experiments **13:**198

Eclipsing binary star (or variable star) **22:**580, 582

Ecliptic, in astronomy **2:**725
  constellations **5:**683, **22:**586
  moon **15:**577
  Uranus **19:**413

'Eclogues', work by Virgil **24:**358

ECM (electrochemical machining), a metalworking operation **23:**226

École de Musique Ancienne, French conservatory
  Landowska **13:**27

École des Beaux-Arts (full name, École Nationale Supérieure des Beaux-Arts), French government's school of fine arts at Paris; founded 1648 by Cardinal Mazarin; abolished as independent college 1968; noted for department of architecture; gave competitive examinations for Prix de Rome **1:**14. *see also in index* Prix de Rome

École Polytechnique, in Paris, France; founded in 1794; once primarily a military school; now also provides civil service and business training **15:**411

École Spéciale Militaire, in Coëtquidan, France; founded by Napoleon in 1802; trains military officers **15:**411

Ecology 7:50. *see also in index* Adaptation; Animal migration; Balance of nature; Conservation; Environment; Habitat; Struggle for existence; Symbiosis
  Arctic **2:**570
  biology **3:**208, **3:**232
  birds of prey **3:**281
  botany **3:**381, **19:**433
  communities of animals and plants. *see in index* Biogeography
  Earth **7:**7
  fire fighting **8:**108
  grasslands **9:**237
  hobby **10:**183
  microbiology **15:**374
  pest control **18:**245
  pollution **19:**523
  sociology **21:**360
  world **25:**301
  zoology **25:**469

Econometrics, special application of mathematics to describe, analyze, and predict economic activity; may include mathematical models, some containing many equations **7:**65

Economic Achievements, Exhibition of, in Moscow, U.S.S.R. **15:**592

Economic and Social Commission for Asia and the Pacific (ESCAP), United Nations **24:**86

Economic and Social Committee, an institution of the European Communities **7:**362

Economic and Social Council (ECOSOC), United Nations **24:**81, 86

Economic botany, field of botany that deals with plants and plant products in relation to human's needs **3:**381. *see also in index*Forest management

Economic colonialism 7:346

Economic Commission for Africa, (ECA), United Nations **24:**86

Economic Commission for Asia and the Far East (ECAFE), United Nations **24:**86
Economic Commission for Europe (ECE), United Nations **24:**86
Economic Commission for Latin America (ECLA), United Nations **24:**86
Economic Commission for Western Asia (ECWA), United Nations **24:**86
Economic Community of West African States (ECOWAS) **1:**109
'Economic Consequences of the Peace, The', work by Keynes **12:**230
Economic democracy 6:93
Economic Development Administration, United States
  American Indians **11:**154
Economic Development Institute, United Nations **25:**301
Economic geography 9:68
Economic geology 9:72
Economic mineralogy 9:71
Economic Opportunity, Office of, United States, created 1964; programs transferred 1973 to Departments of Health, Education, and Welfare, and Housing and Urban Development and to Community Services Administration.
Economic Opportunity Act (1964), United States
  education, *list* **7:**104
Economic Recovery Tax Act (1981), United States **23:**38
Economics, science of the production, distribution, and consumption of wealth **7:**60. *see also in index* Bank and banking; Capitalism; Communism; Labor; Money; Panics and depressions; Socialism; *also* chief topics below
  Asia **2:**686
  black Americans **3:**301
  business cycle **3:**517
  census **4:**249
  central bank **4:**260
  city **5:**448
  civilization **5:**465
  colonialism and imperialism **5:**556
  commodity exchange **5:**597
  employment and unemployment **7:**205
  Enlightenment **7:**289
  franchise **8:**373
  government **9:**199, **24:**209
  gross national product **9:**290
  India **11:**73
  Industrial Revolution **11:**178
  industry **11:**184
  inflation **11:**198
  international relations **11:**259
  labor law **13:**5
  literacy and illiteracy **13:**239
  marketing **14:**140
  migration of people **15:**400
  monopolies **15:**543
  national debt **16:**24
  Nobel prize **17:**330
  revolution **20:**181
  saving and investment **21:**81
  science **21:**122
  South America **22:**410
  subsidy **22:**687
  tariff **23:**30
  taxation **23:**34
  theories
    Galbraith **9:**5
    Smith **21:**325
  Third World **23:**169
  vocation **24:**391, 394, 399
  warfare **25:**18
  world **25:**301
  World Bank **25:**301
  World War I **25:**314
Economic Stabilization, Office of (OES), United States, established 1942, terminated 1946 **20:**310
Economic Stabilization Act Amendments of 1971, in U.S. law **24:**221
Economic zoology (or applied zoology) **25:**470
'Economist, The', news magazine **14:**31
Economy, Pa., former communal village; pop. 9,538 **5:**605, *map* **18:**204
'Economy of Cities, The', work by Jacobs **19:**576
Ecorse, Mich., city situated on Detroit River, 8 mi (13 km) s.w. of Detroit; steel; pop. 14,447, *map* **15:**372
ECOSOC. *see in index* Economic and Social Council
Ecosystem, a community and its environment **7:**54, *diagram* **7:**57
  jungle **12:**157
  plant **19:**417, 433
  pollution **19:**523
  world **25:**296
Ecotone, a transition area between two adjacent ecological communities; usually exhibits competition between the various organisms.
ECOWAS (Economic Community of West African States) **1:**109
ECSC (European Coal and Steel Community), founded on Aug. 10, 1952 **7:**338. *see also in index* European Communities
ECT. *see in index* Shock therapy
Ectoderm, embryonic germ layer
  coelenterate **2:**433
  vertebrate **7:**200, *chart* **7:**202
Ectoparasite, a variety of parasite **18:**123
Ectopic pregnancy (or tubal pregnancy) **19:**581
Ectoplasm, in spiritualism **22:**544
Ecuador, South American republic, on Pacific coast; area estimated at 104,500 sq mi (270,600 sq km); cap. Quito; pop. 8,604,000 **7:**66
  cities. *see also in index* cities listed below and other cities by name
    Guayaquil **9:**300
    Quito **20:**26
  flag, *picture* **8:**164
  Galápagos Islands. *see in index* Galápagos Islands
  literature **13:**73
  national anthem, *table* **16:**64
  Organization of Petroleum Exporting Countries **17:**606
  South America **22:**401, *map* **22:**418, *table* **22:**414
  United Nations, *table* **24:**84
  world, *map* **25:**297
Ecumene, fertile region in U.S.S.R. **24:**21
Ecumenical council, in Christianity **5:**410, **7:**69
  Roman Catholicism **20:**264
Ecumenism (or ecumenical movement), movement toward worldwide Christian unity **7:**69
  Methodism **15:**318
  Mott **15:**632
  Protestantism **19:**625
  Söderblom **21:**363
ECWA (Economic Commission for Western Asia), United Nations **24:**86
Eczema (or dermatitis), superficial inflammation of the skin **6:**178
'Edad de Oro, La', Cuban children's magazine **13:**251
Edam, The Netherlands, town in n., 12 mi (19 km) n.e. of Amsterdam; cheese; ships, rope, leather; pop. 3,928.
Edaphology, study of soil **21:**372
EDC. *see in index* European Defense Community
Ed Debevic's Restaurant, restaurant in Chicago, Ill., *picture* **20:**177
Eddington, Arthur Stanley (1882–1944), British astronomer, born in Kendal; director observatory Cambridge ('The Mathematical Theory of Relativity'; 'Stars and Atoms'; 'The Nature of the Physical World').
Eddy, Mary Baker (1821–1910), U.S. religious leader **7:**70
  Christian Science **5:**402
Eddy, Nelson (1901–67), U.S. baritone, born in Providence, R.I.; debut, Philadelphia, 1922; popular in opera, musical films, radio, concert.
Eddy, circulation of water in whirlpool fashion
  fishing, *list* **8:**146
  ship **21:**246
Eddy-current speedometer 22:525
Eddy kite (or bow kite) **12:**252
Eddystone lighthouse 13:204
Edelinck, Gérard (1640–1707), Flemish engraver, born in Antwerp; with French school of portrait engraving.
Edelman, Gerald Maurice (born 1929), U.S. molecular biologist, born in New York, N.Y.; professor Rockefeller University. *see also in index* Nobel Prizewinners, *table*
Edelweiss, a small white velvety flower of the composite family, found in Alps.
Edema, an abnormal accumulation of fluid **1:**272
  lymphatic system **13:**343
Eden, Anthony (1897–1977), British statesman **7:**70
  United Kingdom **7:**258
Eden, N.C., town 9 mi (15 km) n. of Reidsville; corn, wheat, tobacco; blankets, linens; pop. 15,672, *map* **17:**370
Eden, in Bible, garden of paradise
  Mesopotamia **14:**305
Edens Expressway, expressway in Chicago, Ill., *picture* **20:**230
Edentata, an order of mammals comprising the sloths, armadillos, and anteaters; so called because members have few or no teeth, *table* **14:**80
Ederle, Gertrude (born 1906), U.S. swimmer **7:**70
Edessa. *see in index* Urfa
Edfu (or Idfu), **Egypt,** ancient town on Nile, 54 mi (87 km) s.e. of Thebes; favored by the falcon-headed god Horus.
Edgar (944–975), king of England; called the peaceful because of his quiet reign; supported monasteries, improved courts of law, and encouraged commerce.
Edgar Allen Poe National Historic Site, site in Philadelphia, Pa. **16:**46
Edge, Walter Evans (1873–1956), U.S. journalist and diplomat, born in Philadelphia, Pa.; proprietor *Atlantic Daily Press,* also *Evening Union;* governor New Jersey 1917–19, 1944–47; U.S. senator 1919–29; ambassador to France 1929–33; prominent Republican.
Edgecliff College, in Cincinnati, Ohio; Roman Catholic; established 1935; arts and sciences and education **5:**415
Edge dislocation, in crystals **5:**799
Edged-weapon warfare 25:19
Edgehill, England, ridge 12 mi (19 km) s. of Warwick; first battle of Civil War, Oct. 1642, between Parliament forces under the earl of Essex and Royalists under Charles I.
Edgerton, Harold Eugene (1903–90), U.S. electrical engineer, born in Fremont, Neb.; professor Massachusetts Institute of Technology after 1932; invented stroboscopic high-speed photography apparatus.
Edgewood College, in Madison, Wis.; Roman Catholic; established in 1927; arts and sciences, medical technology, and teacher education.
Edgeworth, Maria (1767–1849), British novelist, born in Oxfordshire; influenced Thackeray and Turgenev; her 'Belinda' introduced natural heroine, who failed to faint and blush constantly; work colored by life in Ireland, where she moved in 1782 with Irish father **11:**326
Edging, in skiing, *table* **21:**311
Edible snail, a mollusk (*Helix pomatia*) of the class Gastropoda, *picture* **21:**327
Edict of Restitution, act by Ferdinand II in Thirty Years' War **23:**169
'Edifying Monthly Discussions', magazine **14:**32
Edina, Minn., village 10 mi (16 km) s.w. of Minneapolis; home of several publications for banking, printing, and agricultural industries; pop. 46,073 **15:**442, *map* **15:**456
Edinboro State College, in Edinboro, Pa.; founded 1857; liberal arts, teacher education; graduate study; formerly a teachers' college; off-campus centers at Farrell and Warren.
Edinburg, Tex., city 50 mi (80 km) n.w. of Brownsville; natural gas and oil; citrus-fruit and vegetable processing, cotton ginning; Pan American University; pop. 24,075, *map* **23:**136
Edinburgh, duke of. *see in index* Philip, Prince, duke of Edinburgh
Edinburgh, Scotland, cap., divided into Old Town and New Town; pop. 419,187 **7:**71
  Royal Botanic Garden, *table* **3:**370
  Scotland **21:**125, 127
  United Kingdom, *maps* **7:**360, **24:**79
Edinburgh, University of, in Edinburgh, Scotland; arts, medicine, law, theology, music **7:**71, **24:**225
Edinburgh Castle, in Edinburgh, Scotland **7:**71, *pictures* **21:**128, **24:**72
'Edinburgh Review', critical journal **14:**33
  Macaulay **14:**3
Edinburghshire, county of s.e. Scotland. *see in index* Midlothian
Edirne, Turkey. *see in index* Adrianople
Edison, Charles (1890–1969), U.S. political leader, born in West Orange, N.J.; son of Thomas A. Edison; secretary of Navy 1939–40; governor of New Jersey 1941–44 **7:**74
Edison, Thomas Alva (1847–1931), U.S. inventor and manufacturer **7:**72
  audio recording **2:**760
  Edison N.H.S. **16:**46
  electricity **7:**162
  electric power **7:**165
  electronics **7:**180
  Hall of Fame, *table* **10:**16
  inventions **11:**274, *table* **11:**273
    lighting contributions **13:**205
    motion pictures **15:**616
    phonograph **18:**325
    storage battery **3:**109
    telegraph **23:**58
  laboratory, *picture* **15:**366
  New Jersey **16:**203
  Ohio **17:**506, *picture* **17:**510
  radio **20:**67
  Roosevelt, *picture* **20:**297
  Swan **22:**724
  Tesla **23:**114
Edison, N.J., urban township 3 mi (5 km) n.e. of New Brunswick; building materials, chemical, electrical, and electronic equipment; pop. 70,193 **16:**206, *map* **16:**210
Edison cell (or nickel-iron cell), electricity **3:**109
Edison effect, electronic emission from hot filaments; discovered by Edison **7:**180
Edison Institute, in Dearborn, Mich.; consists of Greenfield Village, Edison Institute Museum, and Edison Institute schools
  Ford **8:**306
Edison National Historic Site, site in West Orange, N.J. **16:**46
Edison Tower, memorial tower in New Jersey **16:**203
Edisto Memorial Gardens, gardens near Orangeburg, South Carolina, *picture* **22:**431
Edisto River, s. and s.w. South Carolina; 150 mi (240 km) long, *map* **22:**437
Edith Cavell, Mount, in Jasper National Park, Alberta, height, 11,033 ft (3,363 m).
Edith Ronne Land, in Antarctica, extends s.e. from base of Antarctic Peninsula to Coats Land; discovered by Finn Ronne 1947–48 and named for his wife, who recorded expedition.
Editing (or cutting), in motion pictures **15:**612, *picture* **15:**611
  audio recording **2:**761
  directing **6:**154
Editing, in publishing
  book publishing **3:**363
Editor 16:239, 242
Editorial, an article in a newspaper or magazine with opinions of the editor or publisher; also a similar expression on radio or TV.
EDM (electric-discharge machining), a metalworking operation **23:**226
Edman, Irwin (1896–1954), U.S. philosopher, born in New York, N.Y.; taught philosophy at Columbia University after 1918 (essays: "Philosopher's Holiday," "Philosopher's Quest," and "Under Whatever Sky").
Edmond, Okla., city 12 mi (19 km) n. of Oklahoma City; hosiery, furniture; Central State University; incorporated 1890; pop. 34,637, *map* **17:**536
Edmonds, Walter Dumaux (born 1903), U.S. novelist, born in Boonville, N.Y.; author of historical fiction ('Wedding Journey'; 'In the Hands of the Senecas'; 'The Boyds of Black River') and children's books ('The Matchlock Gun', awarded Newbery medal 1942; 'Tom Whipple'; 'Two Logs Crossing').

) How were the lives of Native Americans changed by the arrival of European settlers. (Provide 3 examples)

1.) the European encroachment of land caused natives to migrate.

2.) Introduced new diseases trigering epidemics wich led to wide spred natie fatalities.

3.) native wars common before colonization. violence and warfare escalated as natives confronted their European rivals.

4.) Europeans forced natives to adapt to christianity, European customs, and farming techniques.

) What were the consequences of contact between North American Natives and European settlers during the Age of Discovering

· Economic change:

1.) formal and informal trades of goods including: citrus, bananas, veggies, grains, livestock, & fur

· Exchange of Ideas:

1.) religous beliefs, economic Ideas and practices, technology.

· Natives Resistance to chang:

1.) created farming alliances

2.) open hostility including violent attacks on settlers.

3.) migration to new lands.

4.) King Phillips War, Opechancanough wars

	Belief System	Poli-
Native Americans	Spiritual relationship with the earth and nature. Incas, Aztec, Maya believed in sacrafice to gods Women after giving birth would go outside and anything that happened outside is what they would name their child.	Wom when or lea ranked unit t empir
Europeans	based on Christianity and missionary spirit.	mona limited →king →king w/ Ch evolvin John L politica democ individ libritie

...al ...ructure	Economic System	Technology
...nad power ...osin chief ... ...n simple tribal ...nfederations &	grew crops. agriculture. traded with groups or tribes close by. Communial land- didn't believe in ownership of land. loved nature used land to substain life, not create wealth. roles of men and women were well defined.	bows and arrows tomahawk Spear Subsistant farming hunting tools & weapons
...ies and ...narchies. ...ost powerful ...nbo, shares power ...n. ...gal system. ...e - philosopher, ...ncepts of ... and respect for ... rights and	belief of private property and ownership. combine labor & property to create wealth. roles of men and women, well difined.	advanced weaponry guns cannons armor. *navigational abilities*

Angela Camacho

2.) Why & how did Europeans explore and settle North Americ
(Provide info. about Motives & Strategies.)

1. gold
2.) glory
3.) god
4.) political expantion of new teritorries for emerging nations.
5.) expansions of markets to acumulate wealth.
6.) spread of christianity.
☆ 7.) Many sought better economic opportunities and religons freedoms.

1.) government sponsers explorations colonizations.
2.) joint stock companies - ex. charters of VA company
3.) establish trading posts.
4.) roles of church convert natives, establish missions. (churches)
☆ 5.)

education; University Center at Harrisburg.

Elizabeth Tudor. *see in index* Elizabeth I

Elizabeth Woodville (1437?–92), queen of Edward IV of England, mother of Edward V and Elizabeth, queen of Henry VII
Edward IV **7**:107

El Jadida (or Mazagan), **Morocco,** seaport 55 mi (90 km) s.w. of Casablanca; farm products; pop. 102,000, *map* **1**:115

'El Jarabe Tapatío', Mexican hat dance **8**:256

Elk, name given in North America to the wapiti and in Europe to the moose
deer **6**:62, *picture* **6**:61
mutualism, *picture* **22**:749

El Karnak, Egypt. *see in index* Karnak, El

Elkhart, Ind., city on St. Joseph and Elkhart rivers, about 15 mi (25 km) e. of South Bend; railway division point; musical instruments, pharmaceuticals, mobile homes and recreational vehicles, radio and television parts, metal products, paper products; pop. 41,305, *maps* **11**:94, 102

Elkhorn River, river in n.e. Nebraska, flows s.e. into Platte River, 333 mi (536 km) long.

Elkins Act, U.S. legislation **20**:318

Elk Island National Park, Alberta **16**:29
Alberta **1**:263, *map* **4**:109

Elk Mountains, range of the Rocky Mountains in w. Colorado, just w. of Sawatch Range; several summits reach over 14,000 ft (4,270 m), including Snowmass Peak, Capitol Peak, Maroon Peak, and Mt. Carbon.

Elko, Nev., city in n.e., on Humboldt River, about 90 mi (140 km) from Utah border; ranching and mining; incorporated 1917; annual Silver State Stampede; pop. 8,758 **16**:134, 137, *maps* **16**:148, **17**:350

Elk River, river in Maryland, 40 mi (64 km) long; flows s. and s.e. into Chesapeake Bay, *map* **14**:169

Elks, Benevolent and Protective Order of, a fraternal society, organized in New York, N.Y., in 1868 from an older society known as the Jolly Corks, and now having branches in practically all large cities of U.S. and its dependencies; in addition to assistance to members, known for response to outside requests.

Ell, obsolete measure of length, varies from 27 to 48 in. (68 to 102 cm) in different countries; English ell, 1¼ yards (1.1 meters), used primarily for measuring fabrics, *table* **25**:140

Ellensburg, Wash., city 27 mi (43 km) n. of Yakima; farm and timber region; Central Washington University; incorporated 1867; pop. 11,752, *map* **25**:64

Ellery, William (1727–1820), signer of Declaration of Independence, born Newport, R.I.; member of Continental Congress 1776–81, 1783–85; state chief justice 1785.

Ellesmere Island, Canada, n.w. of Greenland, from which it is separated by Smith Sound and Kennedy Channel; 82,119 sq mi (212,687 sq km); mountainous, almost covered by glacial ice caps; vegetation in ice-free areas, *map* **17**:350
Arctic regions **2**:571
size, comparative. *see in index* Island, *table*
world, *map* **25**:297

Ellesmere Island National Park, park in Northwest Territories, Canada **16**:29

Ellice Islands. *see in index* Tuvalu

Ellington, Duke (1899–1974), U.S. pianist, conductor, and composer **7**:193
jazz **12**:85
popular music **15**:682

Elliot, Robert Brown (1842–84), U.S. public official and lawyer, born in Boston, Mass.; South Carolina House of Representatives 1868–70, speaker 1874–76; U.S. House of Representatives 1871–74
political movement **3**:292

Elliot Bay, Seattle, Wash. **21**:159, *picture* **25**:57

Elliot family
heraldic shield, *picture* **10**:136

Elliotson, John (1791–1868), English physician, born in London; one of the first to urge clinical lectures as method of teaching medicine; physician to both Dickens and Thackeray; 'Pendennis' dedicated to him.

Ellipse, a closed curve, generated from two points called foci; the sum of the distances from any point on the curve to each of the foci is always the same for any given ellipse; can be drawn by placing a loop of string loosely over two pins stuck in a drawing board and passing a pencil around inside the loop; character of the ellipse will be determined by the length of the loop and the distance between the pins. *see also in index* Conic sections
Apollonius of Perga **2**:506
geometry **9**:76, *diagram* **9**:77
Kepler **21**:106
mathematics **14**:214
moon **15**:577
planet orbits **19**:414

Ellipsis point, punctuation mark **19**:661

Ellipsoidal mirror 15:464

Elliptical bowl, in stadium design **22**:566

Elliptical galaxy (or globular galaxy) **2**:730, *pictures* **2**:731, **22**:580

Ellis, Havelock (1859–1939), English psychologist and philosopher **7**:194

Ellis, Henry (1721–1806), English hydrographer and colonial official; elected fellow of Royal Society for book about voyage to Hudson Bay in search of northwest passage; as governor of Georgia (1757–60), provided for guarantee of titles to land; protected coast during French and Indian War.

Ellis, James (born 1940), U.S. boxer, born in Louisville, Ky. **3**:392

Ellis, Perry (1940–86), U.S. fashion designer, noted for sportswear **6**:271

Ellis Island, island in New York, N.Y. **16**:261, **16**:275
Statue of Liberty National Monument **16**:59

Ellison, Harlan (born 1934), U.S. writer, born in Cleveland, Ohio
science fiction **21**:118

Ellison, Ralph Waldo (born 1914), U.S. writer, born in Oklahoma City, Okla. (novel: 'Invisible Man'; essays: 'Shadow and Act') **3**:300, *list* **3**:302
American literature **1**:362

Ellmann, Richard (1918–87), U.S. writer and educator, born in Highland Park, Mich.; professor of English Northwestern University 1951–68, Yale 1968–70, Oxford 1970–84; books on famous writers; 1960 National Book Award for 'James Joyce', a biography.

Ellora, India, town in Maharashtra State; famous Buddhist, Hindu, and Jain rock-cut temples; one, the Kailasa temple, was cut downward from top of hill.

Ellsworth, Elmer Ephraim (1837–61), U.S. soldier, colonel of Ellsworth's Zouaves, born near Saratoga Springs, N.Y.; shot at Alexandria, Va.; regarded in his day as first martyr to Union cause.

Ellsworth, Lincoln (1880–1951), U.S. explorer, born in Chicago, Ill.; with Amundsen in Arctic flights 1925, 1926; in 1935 raised U.S. flag over 300,000 sq mi (777,000 sq km) of unclaimed land in Antarctica; explorations in interior of Antarctica 1936, 1938, 1939 ("My Four Antarctic Expeditions", a magazine article; 'Exploring Today', a book)
polar exploration **19**:501, *list* **19**:502

Ellsworth, Oliver (1745–1807), U.S. statesman and jurist, born in Windsor, Conn.; U.S. senator from Connecticut 1789–96; drafted bill organizing federal courts; introduced Connecticut Compromise; chief justice of the U.S. 1796–99
U.S. Constitution **24**:195

Ellsworth Highland, Antarctica; region extending s.w. from base of Antarctic Peninsula; discovered 1935 by Lincoln Ellsworth **2**:473

Ellwood City, Pa., borough 33 mi (53 km) n.w. of Pittsburgh, in coal and limestone district; metal products, machinery, textiles; pop. 9,998, *map* **18**:204

Elm, tree **7**:194. *see also in index* Elm bark beetle
fungi **8**:450
plant **19**:423
wood, *table* **25**:283

Elman, Mischa (1891–1967), U.S. violinist, born in Russia, became citizen of U.S. 1923; pupil of Leopold Auer; made debut at age of 13; won international fame.

El Mansura, Egypt. *see in index* Mansura

Elm bark beetle, an insect of engraver beetle group (family Scolytidae); two species carry fungus of Dutch elm disease, the native *Hylurgopinus rufipes* and the European *Scolytus multistriatus,* which is more prevalent; adults feed in twig crotches of healthy trees, then fly to recently cut, dead, or dying elms, tunnel under bark and lay eggs; larvae tunnel as they feed; fungus grows in tunnels; adults emerging from tunnels carry fungus spores on their bodies and thus transfer spores to healthy trees. *see also in index* Dutch elm disease; Elm-leaf beetle.

Elmendorf, Theresa Hubbell West (1855–1932), U.S. librarian, born in Pardeeville, Wis.; became deputy librarian 1880, librarian 1892–96, Milwaukee (Wis.) Public Library; first woman president American Library Association 1911–12.

'Elmer Gantry', work by Lewis **13**:142

Elm family (or Ulmaceae), a family of shrubs and trees including the American elm, hackberry, sugarberry, English elm, Chinese elm, slippery elm, sawleaf zelkova, and the water elm.

Elmhurst, Ill., residential city about 15 mi (25 km) w. of Chicago; limestone quarry; Elmhurst College; settled in 1843; pop. 44,251, *map* **11**:52

Elmhurst College, Elmhurst, Ill.; founded 1871 by Evangelical and Reformed church, which became United Church of Christ; arts and sciences, teacher education.

Elmira, N.Y., manufacturing city on Chemung River, 7 mi (11 km) n. of Pennsylvania boundary; metal, glass, and electrical products, fire-fighting equipment; food products; prefabricated homes; electronic tubes; Elmira College; pop. 39,945
New York, *map* **16**:268
reformatory **19**:605

Elmira College, Elmira, N.Y.; private control; chartered 1855 as the first college for women in the United States but now coeducational; arts and sciences, nursing and teacher education, secretarial studies; graduate study **16**:255

Elmira Reformatory, reformatory in United States **20**:141

El Misti, dormant volcano in southern Peru, *picture* **18**:238

Elm-leaf beetle, a coleopterous insect *(Galerucella luteola),* accidentally introduced into the U.S.; larvae feed on the lower side of elm leaves. *see also in index* Elm bark beetle

Elmont, N.Y., residential community just e. of Queens, New York, N.Y., on Long Island; apparel; Belmont Park racetrack nearby; pop. 29,363, *map* **16**:268

El Monte, Calif., city 12 mi (19 km) e. of Los Angeles; electronics, aircraft, mobile homes; dairy products, poultry; truck farms; pop. 79,494, *map* **4**:52

El Morro National Monument, monument in New Mexico **16**:47, *maps* **16**:40, **16**:229
Inscription Rock, *picture* **1**:332

Elmwood Park, Ill., residential village adjacent to n.w. section of Chicago; metal products; incorporated 1914; pop. 26,160, *map* **11**:52

Elmwood Park (formerly East Paterson until 1973), **N.J.,** borough on Passaic River, opposite Paterson; paper products, television sets; electronics; pop. 18,377.

El Niño, ocean current **18**:9. *see also in index* La Niña

Elodea (also called water weed, or ditch moss, or choke pondweed), a water plant *(Elodea canadensis),* loosely rooted or floating free entirely under water; solid beds of it fill many ponds and slow streams; branches crowded with dark green leaves arranged in circles of 3 or more leaves around the stem; flowers very small; snails feed on its leaves.

Elohim (often called El), name for God used in some Hebrew Scriptures; used in Old Testament for heathen gods also.

Elon College, Elon College, N.C.; affiliated with United Church of Christ; chartered 1889, opened 1890; arts and sciences, teacher education.

Elongation of a planet, in astronomy, the angular distance between a planet and the sun, as seen from the Earth.

El Paso, Tex., city on Rio Grande, in extreme w. part of state; pop. 425,259 **7**:194
Ciudad Juárez **5**:462
Mexico **15**:338
North America, *map* **17**:350
Texas **23**:119, *map* **23**:136
world, *map* **25**:297

El Qahira, Egypt. *see in index* Cairo

El Qantara (or Kantara), Egypt, town on Suez Canal; Allied military base in World War I.

El Reno, Okla., city near North Canadian River, 25 mi (40 km) w. of Oklahoma City; wheat, livestock center; railroad shops; grain elevators; historic Fort Reno nearby; pop. 15,486, *map* **17**:536

El Salvador, smallest of Central American republics; 8,124 sq mi (21,041 sq km); cap. San Salvador; pop. 5,083,000 **7**:195
Central America **4**:253, 257
flag, *picture* **8**:164
gross national product, *table* **19**:576
Latin American conflicts **13**:66
literature **13**:73
national anthem, *table* **16**:64
North America, *map* **17**:350, *table* **17**:346
San Salvador **21**:50
United Nations, *table* **24**:84
world, *map* **25**:297
World War II **25**:328

El Segundo, Calif., city 14 mi (22 km) s.w. of Los Angeles; oil refining; aircraft, electronic components; pop. 13,752, *map* **4**:52

Elsinore, Denmark. *see in index* Helsingör

Essler, Fanny (1810–84), Austrian dancer, born in Vienna; debut at age of 6; U.S. debut 1840; remarkable for beauty and skill; most successful in ballet and in dances of Spain; often danced with sister Therese (1808–78) **3**:33, 36, **6**:27

Elster (or White Elster), river of central Germany; rises on the East German-Czechoslovak border; flows n. and empties into Saale, 3 mi (5 km) s. of Halle; 115 mi (185 km) long, *map* **9**:131

Elston, Dorothy Andrews (1917–71), U.S. public official, born in Wilkes-Barre, Pa.; president National Federation of Republican Women 1963–68; treasurer of the United States 1969–71.

Eltville (formerly Elfeld), **West Germany,** town on Rhine River, 6 mi (10 km) s.w. of Wiesbaden; printing press set up by Gutenberg in 1465; pop. 6,875.

Eltz Castle, castle in West Germany, *picture* **20**:176

Éluard, Paul (1895–1952), French poet, born in Saint-Denis; identified first with Dadaists, later with surrealist movement.

Elvehjem, Conrad Arnold (1901–62), U.S. biochemist, born in McFarland, Wis.; on faculty University of Wisconsin after 1925, became professor 1936, dean of graduate school

1946–58, president 1958–62; noted for researches on vitamin B complex.

Elver, stage in development of an eel **7:**109

Elves. *see in index* Elf

Elwood, Ind., city about 40 mi (60 km) n.e. of Indianapolis; tomato and other fruit and vegetable canning; metal products, hand-blown glass; annual glass festival; home of Wendell L. Willkie; pop. 10,867, *map* **11:**102

Ely, Richard Theodore (1854–1943), U.S. political economist, born in Ripley, N.Y.; professor University of Wisconsin 1892–1925, Northwestern University 1925–33 ('Outlines of Economics'; 'Studies in the Evolution of Industrial Society'; 'Hard Times—the Way In and the Way Out').

Ely, England, city 15 mi (25 km) n.e. of Cambridge, on Ouse River; beet-sugar refinery; leather products; cathedral part of 10th-century Benedictine monastery; pop. 10,020, *map* **24:**75

Ely, Minn., city in n.e. part of state, in Superior National Forest, about 20 mi (30 km) s. of Canadian border; hunting, fishing; starting point for wilderness canoe trips; iron ore mining; pop. 4,904, *map* **15:**456

Ely, Nev., city in e. of state; copper mining and smelting center; farming, ranching; tourist area; pop. 4,882, *maps* **16:**134, 148

Elyot, Thomas (1490?–1546), English diplomat and scholar; friend of Sir Thomas More; remembered for his books 'The Castle of Health', a popular treatise on medicine, and 'Book Named the Governor', a moral philosophy.

Elyria, Ohio, city on Black River, 24 mi (37 km) s.w. of Cleveland; auto accessories, electric motors, heating and air-conditioning equipment, metal products, chemicals, plastics, pipe tools, air brakes, golf balls; incorporated 1833; pop. 53,427
  Ohio, *map* **17:**516

'Élysée Montmartre Bal Masque', lithograph by Chéret, *picture* **9:**234

Élysée Palace, Paris, official residence of French presidents 1848–52, 1871–1940, and again since 1945; built in 1728 for a French count but made residence of Madame de Pompadour by Louis XV.

Elysium (or Elysian Fields), in Greek and Roman mythology **10:**124
  mythology **15:**702

Elytis, Odysseus (born 1911), Greek poet and essayist **7:**197. *see also in index* Nobel Prizewinners, *table*

Elzevir, family of 17th-century Dutch printers famous for beautiful types and choice grade of paper; **Louis** (1540–1617) began printing in 1583; his five sons carried on the work
  type and typography **23:**337

EM. *see in index* Electromagnetism

Em, a type measure **23:**336

Emakimono, Japanese hand scroll **12:**50

Emanation. *see in index* Radon

Emancipation Proclamation (1863), statement by President Lincoln **7:**197
  black Americans **3:**291
  Civil War **5:**475, 481
  Confederate States of America **5:**643
  Douglass **6:**236
  Lincoln **13:**222
  United States **24:**167, 181

Emancipists, in Australia
  Maquarie **14:**22

Emanuel I, the Happy (1469–1521), king of Portugal in whose reign, called Portugal's golden age, Vasco da Gama opened sea route to India, Cabral took possession of Brazil, and Albuquerque established Portuguese rule in East Indies.

Emba, river in Kazakh Soviet Socialist Republic; flows s.w. 385 mi (620 km) to Caspian Sea; rich petroleum fields located along lower course, *map* **24:**59

Embalming, a procedure of using preservatives to keep a dead body intact for as long as possible **6:**50, *picture* **15:**651

Embankment, an artificial bank or dike to resist the encroachment of water. *see also in index* Breakwater; Dike; Jetty; Levee

Embarcadero Center, building complex in San Francisco, Calif. **21:**43

Embargo, the holding, or detention, of ships or other property within a nation to prevent their departure to a foreign territory **7:**197

Embargo Act (1807), United States **7:**198
  Jefferson's administration **12:**94
  Massachusetts **14:**195
  War of 1812 **25:**30

Embarras River, rises in e.-central Illinois and flows in a generally southerly direction, 185 mi (300 km) long; enters Wabash River 7 mi (11 km) w. of Vincennes, *map* **11:**53

Embassy 6:150, **8:**339a

Embattled line (or crenellé), in heraldry **10:**136

Ember Days, fast days (12 in all) observed by Roman Catholic and Anglican churches at four seasons of the year; the Wednesday, Friday, and Saturday after December 13, after the first Sunday of Lent, after Whitsunday, and after September 14. On February 17, 1966, Pope Paul VI excluded the Ember Days as days of fast and abstinence for Roman Catholics.

Emberley, Edward Randolph (born 1931), U.S. illustrator and children's author, born in Malden, Mass.; illustrated books by himself ('The Wing on the Flea'; 'Punch and Judy'; series on drawing for children), by his wife, **Barbara Emberley** ('Paul Bunyan'; 'One Wide River to Cross'; 'Drummer Hoff', awarded 1968 Caldecott Medal), and by other authors.

Embezzlement, the fraudulent appropriation of money, cargo, or other personal property by one entrusted with it; considered a felony **5:**771

Embioptera, an order of tiny silk-producing insects that inhabit silk-lined underground tunnels; found mostly in the tropics.

Emblems. *see also in index* Flags; Flags of the United States; Flags of the world
  uniform and insignia **24:**16

Embossing, producing raised figures upon various materials **7:**198
  metalworking **14:**310

Embouchure, mouthpiece **25:**228

Embroidery
  antiques **2:**494
  needlework **16:**110

Embryo, animal **7:**199, *picture* **7:**201
  birth defects **3:**284
  egg **7:**110
  pregnancy and birth **19:**580

Embryo, plant **19:**427
  nut **17:**448
  seed **21:**165
  wheat **25:**192

Embryogeny, all phases of embryonic development **7:**199

Embryology 7:199. *see also in index* Cell; Embryo, animal; Embryo, plant; Fertilization; Metamorphosis; Ovum; Pregnancy; Protoplasm; Reproductive system; Sperm cell
  biological fields **3:**231
  evolution **7:**367
  Fabricius **8:**5
  zoology **25:**469

Embryo transfer, fertilization technique **4:**231

EMCAT (Emergency Management Computer Aided Training), fire fighting **22:**483

Em dash, punctuation mark **19:**661

Emden, West Germany, seaport in n.w., at mouth of Ems River; handles ore, grain, and wood imports; exports include coal, fish, and agricultural machinery; pop. 48,525, *map* **9:**131

Emek. *see in index* Esdraelon, Plain of

Emerald, precious stone
  jewelry **12:**115, *picture* **12:**113
  minerals **15:**436

Emerald cut, gem cutting
  diamond, *picture* **12:**116

Emergency Broadcast System, radio information system used for civil defense; superseding Control for Electromagnetic Radiation in 1963 **20:**61

Emergency Fleet Corporation, in U.S. shipping history **21:**252

Emergency Home Finance Act (1970), United States, *list* **10:**304

Emergency Management Computer Aided Training (EMCAT), fire fighting **22:**483

Emergency medicine, medical specialty **14:**280, *table* **14:**277
  ambulance **1:**326
  first aid procedures **8:**115
  hospital **10:**282

Emergency Relief Act (1932), United States **10:**235

Emeritus, term applied to an official who has resigned or been honorably retired from active duty because of long service, age, or illness (emeritus professor, emeritus pastor); originally applied to Roman soldier or official who received compensation and special privileges after honorable dismissal from service.

Emerson, Peter Henry, British photographer **19:**352

Emerson, Ralph Waldo (1803–82), U.S. philosopher, essayist, and poet **7:**203
  American literature **1:**347
  Concord, Mass. **5:**639
  essays **7:**306
  Hall of Fame, *table* **10:**16
  transcendentalism **23:**248
  Whitman **25:**200

Emerson, Roy (born 1936), Australian tennis player, *list* **23:**107

Emerson, William (1906–84), British poet and critic ('Collected Poems'; 'Some Versions of Pastoral').

Emerson College, Boston, Mass.; private control; founded 1880; liberal arts with specialization in broadcasting, drama, speech, and speech pathology and audiology; graduate study.

Emery, powdered corundum **15:**435
  abrasives **1:**13

Emesa, Syria. *see in index* Homs

Emett, Rowland (born 1906), British cartoonist, born near London; creator of famous character, Nellie, an old railroad engine; visited U.S. 1952 (author and illustrator of 'New World for Nellie'; collection of his cartoons from *Punch,* 'Emett's Domain').

Emf (electromotive force), in physics **20:**68

EMG. *see in index* Electromyogram

'Emigrants, The', work by Moberg **21:**88

Emigration, departure from one country to settle in another. *see also in index* Immigration
  Asia **2:**703
  Cuba **5:**804
  Mexico **15:**326, 338
  migration of people **15:**399
  population biology **19:**541

Emigrés, peoples in French Revolution **8:**402

Emi Koussi, volcano 11,204 ft (3,415 m), highest elevation in the Sahara **21:**15

'Émile', novel by Rousseau **13:**246, **20:**332

Emilia (formerly called *Cacalia*), genus of annual and perennial plants of the composite family; the tassel flower *(E. sagittata),* native to the tropics, has small heads of red or gold flowers and is also called Flora's paintbrush.

'Emilia Galotti', drama by Lessing **13:**138

Emilia-Romagna, region of northern Italy, s. of the Po River and n. of Tuscany; 8,542 sq mi (22,124 sq km); cap. Bologna; pop. 3,666,680, *map* **11:**401

Eminent domain, property ownership **19:**614

Eminescu, Michael (1849–89), Romanian poet; work marked by melancholy mysticism.

Emin Pasha (or Eduard Schnitzer) (1840–92), German explorer and administrator in Africa, born in Oppeln, near Breslau
  Stanley's expeditions **22:**579

Emir. *see in index* Amir

Emission, of radioactive particles **20:**73

Emission spectra 22:520

Emma (1858–1934), queen of William III of The Netherlands, mother of Queen Wilhelmina, for whom she was regent 1890–98.

'Emma', work by Austen **2:**767

Emmanuel. *see in index* Immanuel

Emmanuel College, Boston, Mass.; Roman Catholic; for women; founded 1919; arts and sciences, teacher education; graduate study.

Emmanuel Holiness church 10:202

Emmaus, Pa., borough 4 mi (6 km) s. of Allentown; electrical products and acid-proof castings, textiles, foundry products; pop. 11,511, *map* **18:**204

Emma Willard School (formerly Middlebury Female Seminary), Troy, N.Y.; founded in 1814 **25:**204

Emmental, fertile valley in canton of Bern, Switzerland; 25 mi (40 km) long, 11 mi (18 km) wide.

Emmer wheat, plant *(Triticum dicoccon)* **25:**188

Emmet, Robert (1778–1803), Irish rebel, born in Dublin; led unsuccessful revolt against Dublin Castle; escaped but returned to his betrothed, Sarah Curran; was caught and hanged.

Emmett, Daniel Decatur (1815–1904), U.S. actor and songwriter, born in Mount Vernon, Ohio; composed 'Old Dan Tucker' at age of 16; originator of Negro minstrel performances
  patriotic song **16:**65

Emmons, Mount, Uinta Range, Utah; 13,428 ft (4,093 m).

Emmy, statuette presented annually by Academy of Television Arts and Sciences, Hollywood, Calif.; designed and sculptured by Louis McManus; first awarded 1949; name suggested by Harry R. Lubcke, Academy president 1949, from Immy, engineering term referring to Image Orthicon camera. *see also in index* Academy of Television Arts and Sciences

Emory and Henry College, Emory, Va.; affiliated with United Methodist church; established 1836, opened 1838; arts and sciences, teacher education.

Emory University, Atlanta, Ga.; Methodist; founded 1836; arts and sciences, business administration, dentistry, education, law, medicine, nursing, theology; graduate school; junior college at Oxford, Ga.

Emotion 7:204
  adolescence **1:**48
  arts **2:**667
  automobile driving **2:**864
  child
    child abuse **4:**319
    development and training **4:**323
    play **19:**460
  communication **5:**609
  fatigue **8:**46
  memory **14:**294
  pregnancy **19:**581
  psychosomatic disorder **10:**81, **19:**640
  Romanticism **20:**281
  suicide **22:**699

Empathy, ability to see the world from another's point of view
  communication **5:**610

Empedocles (490?–430 BC), great Greek philosopher, poet, statesman, superhuman character in legend; said to have cast self into crater of Mt. Etna (Matthew Arnold's 'Empedocles on Etna')
  philosophy **18:**315
  physics **19:**363

'Empedocles on Etna', work by Arnold **7:**276

Empennage, in airplane **1:**184

Emperor (derived from Latin *imperium,* power of a general to enforce his commands), head of empire; wife of emperor or woman ruling empire in own right is empress. *see also in index* individual emperors by name
  abdications. *see in index* Abdications, *table*

ENGLAND'S KINGS AND QUEENS

Saxon	
802–839	Egbert
839–858	Ethelwulf
858–860	Ethelbald
860–865	Ethelbert
865–871	Ethelred
871–899	Alfred the Great
901–924	Edward the Elder
924–939	Athelstan
939–946	Edmund I
946–955	Edred
955–959	Edwy
959–975	Edgar
975–978	Edward the Martyr
978–1016	Ethelred "the Unready"
1016	Edmund II, Ironside
Danish	
1016–1035	Canute (Cnut)
1035–1040	Harold I
1040–1042	Harthacanute
Saxon	
1042–1066	Edward the Confessor
1066	Harold II
Norman	
1066–1087	William I, the Conqueror
1087–1100	William II
1100–1135	Henry I
1135–1154	Stephen
Plantagenet	
1154–1189	Henry II
1189–1199	Richard I
1199–1216	John
1216–1272	Henry III
1272–1307	Edward I
1307–1327	Edward II
1327–1377	Edward III
1377–1399	Richard II
Lancaster	
1399–1413	Henry IV
1413–1422	Henry V
1422–1461	Henry VI
York	
1461–1483	Edward IV
1483	Edward V
1483–1485	Richard III
Tudor	
1485–1509	Henry VII
1509–1547	Henry VIII
1547–1553	Edward VI
1553–1558	Mary I
1558–1603	Elizabeth I
Stuart	
1603–1625	James I
1625–1649	Charles I
[1649–1660	Commonwealth]
1660–1685	Charles II
1685–1688	James II
1689–1702	William III and Mary II (until her death in 1694)
1702–1714	Anne
Hanover	
1714–1727	George I
1727–1760	George II
1760–1820	George III
1820–1830	George IV
1830–1837	William IV
1837–1901	Victoria
Saxe-Coburg-Gotha (Windsor)	
1901–1910	Edward VII
1910–1936	George V
1936	Edward VIII
1936–1952	George VI
1952–	Elizabeth II

Engle, Paul Hamilton (born 1908), U.S. writer, born in Cedar Rapids, Iowa; professor of English University of Iowa 1937– (poetry: 'Corn', 'West of Midnight', 'American Child'; essays: 'Prairie Christmas'; poetry and essays: 'An Old Fashioned Christmas').

Englewood, Colo., city, suburb s. of Denver; farm region; carnation center; machinery; electronics; pop. 30,021
Colorado, *map* **5**:582

Englewood, N.J., residential city on w. slope of Hudson Palisades, 13 mi (21 km) n. of Jersey City; manufactures include metal goods, electrical fixtures, and leather products; pop. 23,701
New Jersey, *map* **16**:210

English, a category of chickens **19**:572

English (or spin), in billiards **3**:192

English Channel, separates England from France; breadth 20 to 100 mi (30 to 160 km), length 350 mi (560 km); mean depth 175 ft (50 m) long; favored by endurance swimmers, *map* **8**:372. *see also in index* Ocean, *table*
Dover **6**:236
England **7**:229
Europe, *map* **7**:360
United Kingdom, *map* **24**:75
world, *map* **25**:297

English Classical School (or English High School), school founded in the United States
establishment **7**:90

English cocker spaniel, dog, *picture* **6**:198

English composition. *see in index* Writing, Communication by; Writing, Creative

English cottage garden, *picture* **8**:221

English daisy, flower (*Bellis perennis*) of the Compositae family **6**:8, **9**:25

English Dresden, diamond, *picture* **6**:129

English elm, tree (*Ulmus procera*) **7**:194

'English Fables and Fairy Stories', work by Reeves **22**:658

'English Fairy Tales', work by Steel **22**:658

'English Folk and Fairy Tales', work by Jacobs **22**:658

English foxhound, dog, *picture* **6**:200

English High School (or English Classical School), school founded in the United States
establishment **7**:90

English holly (or European holly), plant (*Ilex aquifolium*) **10**:204

English horn (or cor anglais), wind instrument **25**:227

English ivy, plant (*Hedera helix*) of the family Araliaceae **11**:406, *picture* **11**:407
growing conditions **9**:27

English Justinian. *see in index* Edward I

English language **7**:260. *see also in index* Grammar; Rhetoric; Spelling; Writing, Communication by; Writing, Creative
alphabet development **1**:315
Asian language patterns **2**:683
Australian heritage **2**:785
dictionaries. *see in index* Dictionary
encyclopedias **20**:130
England **7**:232, **7**:264
Germanic languages **9**:103
India **11**:72
language construction **13**:31, *diagrams* **13**:32
lingua franca **1**:119
linguistics **13**:229
phonics **18**:322
poetry **19**:483
slang **21**:316
United States **24**:150
Webster **25**:130

English literature **7**:263
Arthurian legends **2**:655. *see also in index* Arthurian legends
Australian heritage **2**:785
children's literature **13**:246, *list* **13**:254
drama **6**:243, **23**:159
Elizabethan Age **1**:26
folklore **8**:261
poetry **19**:483
Romanticism **20**:283
short story **21**:274
storytelling **22**:649, 658

English lute song, in vocal music **24**:387

English Merchantman, ship, *picture* **21**:241

English oak, tree (*Quercus robur*) **17**:452

English primrose (or common primrose), plant (*Primula vulgaris*) **19**:586

English saddle (or flat saddle) **10**:264, *diagram* **10**:265

English setter, dog, *picture* **6**:198

English sonnet (or Shakespearean sonnet), type of sonnet **19**:484

English sparrow (or house sparrow) **22**:510
birdhouse **3**:262

English springer spaniel, dog, *picture* **6**:198

English toy spaniel, dog, *picture* **6**:205

English walnut (or Persian walnut), tree (*Juglans regia*) known for the wood and the nuts that it produces **25**:10

English yew, tree (*Taxus baccala*) of the Taxaceae family **25**:416

Engrailed line, in heraldry **10**:136

Engraver beetle, any of numerous beetles of family Scolytidae; most live under bark of trees and engrave the wood by burrowing **3**:141. *see also in index* Elm bark beetle

Engraving and etching,
glass, *pictures* **9**:157, 161
graphic arts **9**:231
maps **14**:128
postage stamp **22**:574
printing **19**:597
sulfuric acid **22**:702
wood. *see in index* Wood engraving

Engraving and Printing, Bureau of, United States
postage stamps **22**:574

Enhanced oil recovery, *list* **18**:254

ENI (National Hydrocarbons Agency), Italian government agency **11**:388

ENIAC (Electronic Numerical Integrator and Calculator), first general-purpose electronic computer **5**:635, *picture* **5**:634

Enid, Okla., city about 65 mi (105 km) n.w. of Oklahoma City; wheat, livestock, oil center; grain elevators, oil products, Phillips University; Vance Air Force Base; pop. 50,363 **17**:524, *maps* **17**:523, 536

'Enigma Variations', music by Elgar **7**:188

Eniwetok, Pacific Ocean, atoll at extreme w. end of Marshall Islands; measures 21 by 17 mi (34 by 27 km); air and sea base.

Enkephalin, natural chemical produced by the body **1**:387
drug addiction **10**:3

Enki, Sumerian god of the waters **15**:698

Enlargement, process of plant growth and development **19**:432

Enlarger, in photography **19**:348, *picture* **19**:346

Enlightenment (or Age of Reason), European intellectual movement **7**:288
abolitionist movement **1**:10
civilization **5**:467
English literature **7**:270
Gothic fiction **9**:196
eugenics **7**:326
history writing **10**:172
human rights **10**:320
Judaism **10**:113, **12**:150
labor law development **13**:4
philosophy **18**:318
Protestantism **19**:624
revolution **20**:181
Romanticism **20**:280
Rousseau **20**:332
universities **24**:226

Enlil, Sumerian god, creator of the universe **3**:6

Enlisted personnel, in armed forces
United States navy **16**:80

'Enneads', work by Plotinus **23**:163

Enneagon (sometimes called nonagon), in mathematics
geometry **9**:76, *diagram* **9**:75

Ennis, Tex., city 35 mi (55 km) s. of Dallas; cotton-growing area; business forms; incorporated 1872; pop. 12,110, *map* **23**:136

Enniskillen (or Inniskilling), **Northern Ireland,** market town; defeated James II's forces at battle of Crom 1689; famous cavalry regiment Inniskilling Dragoons formed by defenders; pop. 7,020, *map* **24**:78

Ennius, Quintus (239–169 BC), Latin epic poet, called father of Roman poetry; introduced the hexameter **13**:76

Enoch, Hebrew patriarch who "walked with God" and after 365 years "was not, for God took him" (Bible, Gen. v. 18–24).

'Enoch Arden', poem by Tennyson about Enoch Arden, a shipwrecked sailor who, returning years later, finds wife married again, leaves her untroubled, and conceals his identity until death.

'Enola Gay', United States' bomber from which atomic bomb was dropped on Japan in World War II **25**:349

Enology. *see in index* Winemaking

'Enquiry Concerning the Principles of Natural Knowledge', work by Whitehead **25**:195

'Enrico di Borgogna', opera by Donizetti **6**:229

Enrico Fermi award, cash award and medal presented by the Atomic Energy Commission for achievements in atomic energy; authorized by Congress 1954.

Enright, Elizabeth (1909–68), U.S. illustrator and author of children's books, born in Chicago, Ill. ('Kintu'; 'Thimble Summer', winner of 1939 Newbery medal; 'The Saturdays'; 'A Spiderweb for Two'; 'Gone-Away Lake'; 'Tatsinda'; 'Zeee'); writer of adult stories.

Enrober, machine that coats candy **4**:138

Enschede, The Netherlands, city near e. border, on Twente Canal; cotton textiles; printing; rebuilt after being destroyed by fire in 1862; pop. 10,548.

'Enseigne de Gersaint', work by Watteau **25**:109

Ensemble, music for two or more parts **17**:576

Ensenada, Mexico, seaport in n. Lower California, 65 mi (105 km) s.e. of San Diego; tuna and shellfish; wheat and beans; iron ore nearby; pop. 45,561, *map* **15**:341

Ensi, ruler of a city-state **3**:4

Ensign, United States Navy officer **16**:80

Ensign, national flag flown by ships **8**:161, *list* **8**:149

Ensign wasp, insect (*Evania appendigaster*) **25**:74

Ensilage. *see in index* Silage

Ensor, James, Baron (1860–1949), Belgian painter of realistic interiors, panoramic scenes, mystical fantasies, burlesques, born in Ostend; called a father of expressionism and a presurrealist.

Entail, law restricting inheritance to a particular heir or class of heirs; an interference with the usual dispersal of inheritance
Jefferson **12**:91
Virginia **24**:366

Entamoeba, unicellular organism **1**:375

Entamoeba histolytica, parasite, *picture* **6**:170

Entasis, in architecture
illusions **11**:54

Entebbe, Uganda, former capital, situated on n.w. shore of Lake Victoria; extensive botanical gardens; famous for tropical plants; pop. 21,096, *map* **1**:115
Israeli hostage rescue **11**:373

Entente cordiale, French for "cordial understanding"; in international politics, friendliness between nations
Balfour **3**:24
United Kingdom **7**:255

Enteritis, disease that causes inflammation of the bowel
sulfa drug treatment **22**:700

Enterprise, Ala., city in s.e., 28 mi (45 km) n.w. of Dothan; peanut butter, oil; electronics; food processing; textiles; pop. 18,033, *map* **1**:236

Enterprise, deep-sea mining of International Seabed Authority **11**:258

'Enterprise', U.S. Navy aircraft carrier **16**:88, *picture* **16**:89

Enters, Angna (born 1907), U.S. dancer, born in New York, N.Y.; famous for cleverly patterned pantomime; also writer, painter, and sculptor; 'Artist's Life'.

'Entertaining Nights, The' (in Italian, Le Piacevoli Notti), Italian folktales **22**:650

Entertainment center, home appliance **10**:213

Entisol, classification of soil **21**:372

Entomology, the scientific study of insects. *see in index* Insect

Entomophily, insect pollination **8**:218

Entr'acte, in music. *see in index* Music, *table*

Entrance jetty (or training jetty) **12**:111

Entrecolles, Père d', Jesuit missionary
porcelain description **19**:567

Entrenchment, military science **2**:643

Entrepreneur, in economics **4**:152

Entropy
cryogenics **5**:794
mathematical calculation and communications **11**:202, 204
physical chemistry **19**:355
thermodynamics **7**:221, *picture* **7**:220

Entry, mining tunnel or shaft
coal mining **5**:521

Enver Pasha (1881–1922), Turkish soldier; leader in Young Turk Movement; after Balkan War, 1912–13, shot Nazim Pasha and took his position as war minister; at outbreak of World War I took over government, making alliance with Germany; on collapse of Turkey fled to Germany, then U.S.S.R.; killed by Bolsheviks while leading revolt in Soviet Turkestan.

Environment. *see also in index* Ecology
acid rain **1**:19
biogeography **3**:220
cities **5**:456
conservation. *see in index* Conservation
endangered species **7**:209
environmental geology **9**:72
eugenics **7**:326
evolution **7**:366
growth **9**:293
health hazards **10**:87
intelligence and intelligence tests **11**:238
pest control **18**:245
plant **19**:432
plastics **19**:453
pollution **19**:523. *see also in index* Pollution, environmental
prehistoric changes **2**:459
public health **19**:641
reclamation **20**:118
safety **21**:6
science **21**:101
transportation **20**:231, **23**:265
West German Greens political party **9**:126
work place **11**:175

Environmental geology **9**:72

Environmental pollution. *see in index* Pollution, environmental

Environmental Protection, Department of, agency, New Jersey **16**:196

Environmental Protection Agency (EPA), United States
archaeology **2**:537
Bush **3**:516
establishment **5**:678
garbage and refuse disposal **9**:18
pest control **18**:245
pollution **19**:529
polychlorinated biphenyl **19**:532
safety **21**:13

Enzymes **7**:290
bacteria **3**:13
biochemistry **3**:198, 202
bioengineering **3**:207
bionic research **3**:234
catalyst **4**:219
cheese **4**:287
digestion **6**:144
disease prevention **6**:167
embryology **7**:202
evolution **7**:365
fermentation **8**:55
genetic engineering **9**:49
genetics **9**:54
membrane enzymes **3**:199, *diagram* **3**:203
metabolism **14**:306
mold **15**:519
molecule **15**:522
pancreas **18**:106
plant **19**:431
protein **19**:623
spider **22**:535
starch **22**:592
vitamins **24**:381

Eocene epoch, in geological time
earth, *map* **7**:25, *table* **7**:24
elephant **7**:185
horse evolution **10**:268

Eohippus, ancestor of the horse **10**:268

EPA. *see in index* Environmental Protection Agency

Epaminondas (418?–362 BC), Theban general and statesman; in 371 BC defeated superior Spartan force; supported Theban democracy **9**:267, **23**:163

Epaphus, in Greek mythology, son of Zeus and Io; king of Egypt and founder of Memphis; Libya is said to be named for his daughter, Libya.

Epcot Center (Experimental Prototype Community of Tomorrow), amusement park, Lake Buena Vista, Fla., near Orlando; opened 1982 **1**:386, **6**:185
Orlando **17**:607

Epée, Charles Michel, Abbé de l' (1712–89), French priest noted for pioneer work in communication for deaf, born in Versailles; founded school for deaf-mutes, later taken over by government; developed finger alphabet to help his two deaf sisters.

Épée, type of sword
fencing **8**:52

Ephedra, plant classification, *list* **19**:420

Ephedrine, an alkaloid drug frequently used as a nasal decongestant to alleviate hay fever and asthma and as a stimulant for the central nervous system.

Ephemera. *see in index* Mayfly

Ephemeris time (ET) **23**:188

Ephesians, Epistle to the, 10th book of the Bible's New Testament; written by the Apostle Paul to the church at Ephesus about AD 61.

Ephesus, ancient Greek city, greatest of 12 on coast of Asia Minor; famous for Temple of Artemis (Diana); also seat of two notable church councils in 5th century; St. Paul labored there three years (Bible, Epistle to the Ephesians) **5**:461
Temple of Artemis **21**:183

Ephialtes, traitor at battle of Thermopylae **23**:168

Ephraim, Hebrew patriarch, younger son of Joseph; ancestor to tribe of Ephraim (Bible, Josh. xvi).

Ephraim, Mount, in Israeli-occupied territory, 25 mi (40 km) n. of Jerusalem; one of the many low peaks in the ridge extending s. from Lebanon Mountains.

Ephrata, communal colony in Pennsylvania; founded by Johann Conrad Beissel **5**:604
Cloisters, *picture* **18**:193

Ephthalites, a people of central Asia. *see in index* White Huns

Epic **7**:291
folk music **8**:273
Homeric legend **10**:220
novel **17**:414
poetry **19**:485
'Beowulf' **3**:165
Greek literature **9**:272, **9**:274
Indian literature **11**:105
Islamic literature **11**:364
'Kalevala' **8**:89
'Orlando Furioso' **2**:588
'Song of the Nibelungs' **16**:302

Epicenter, point on earth's surface above origin of earthquake **7**:37

'Epic of Gilgamesh', tale of great flood in Mesopotamia **7**:291
flood legends **8**:185
storytelling **22**:636, 645

Epicotyl, part of a seed **21**:167, *picture* **21**:165
plant **19**:429

Epictetus (AD 60?–130?), Greek philosopher **7**:291
Greek literature **9**:279
Stoicism **18**:316, **22**:628

Epicureanism, philosophy **7**:291

Epicurus (341–270 BC), Greek philosopher who thought that the chief good of life is pleasure but that true pleasure comes from the practice of virtue **7**:291
philosophy **18**:315

Epicycle, planetary motion
Kepler's observations **21**:106

Epidaurus, seaport city of ancient Greece, in n.e. Peloponnesus, s.w. across Saronic Gulf from Piraeus, port of Athens
theater **23**:158, *picture* **23**:156

Epidemic disease control, service performed by health agencies **10**:89
public health **19**:641

Epidemics. *see in index* Plagues and epidemics

Epidemiology, study of the spread of disease **7**:292
plagues and epidemics **19**:402
Snow **21**:338

Epidermis, a layer of skin **21**:314, *picture* **21**:315
burn classification, *picture* **3**:511

Epidermis, outermost layer of plant cells **19**:422

Epididymis, male reproductive structure **20**:166

Epiglottis, lidlike structure of cartilage that covers the entrance to the windpipe during the act of swallowing
digestive system **6**:144, *diagram* **6**:143
throat **23**:176
voice **24**:401

Epigram, from the Greek words "on" and "to write"; originally applied to an inscription on a tomb or monument, next used for short pithy verse, and now used also for a concise pointed saying, as: "The greatest of faults, I should say, is to be conscious of none"—Carlyle
La Rochefoucauld **13**:51
Martial **14**:158

Epigyny, in botany **8**:218

Epilepsy, disease of the nervous system, frequently from subtle brain damage, less often from injury; characterized by sudden, recurrent seizures with loss of consciousness and severe convulsions (grand mal), or in mild form by brief blackouts and fainting spells (petit mal) **6**:179
brain disorder **3**:402
first aid **8**:119
nervous system **16**:123
special education **22**:513

Epimenides (fl. 6th or 7th century BC), poet and prophet of Greece, born in Crete; purified Athens from a pestilence; said to have slept 57 years and to have lived almost 300 years; among works attributed to him are an epic poem on Argonautic expedition, and a work on purifications and sacrifices.

Epimere, dorsal part of a mesodermic segment **7**:200, *chart* **7**:202

Epimetheus, character in Greek mythology, brother of Prometheus
Pandora **18**:107

Epinephrine. *see in index* Adrenaline

Epiphany, festival of Christian church (Jan. 6) commemorating showing of Jesus to the Magi
Christmas **5**:403

Epiphyte (or air plant), plant **19**:434, *picture* **19**:432
fern **8**:56
orchid **17**:580
rain forest **12**:155

Epirus, region of n. Greece, on Ionian Sea
Greece **9**:254, 260
Pyrrhus **19**:672

Episcopal church, Protestant. *see in index* Protestant Episcopal church

Episcopal college (college of bishops), in Roman Catholicism **20**:264

Episcopal miter (or Bishop's miter), mollusk shell (*Mitra episcopalis*); characterized by folds on inner lip of opening of shell, which is usually turreted, *picture* **21**:225

'Episodios nacionales', work by Pérez Galdós **18**:218

Epistemology, branch of philosophy **18**:312

Epistle, a written communication, more formal than a letter, that has literary merit, such as the epistles in the Bible and those of Plutarch and Seneca **3**:183, **13**:139. *see also in index* epistles by name, *e.g.,* Romans, Epistle to

'Epistle of Pardon', work by al-Ma'arri
Islamic literature **11**:366

'Epistle to the Romans', work by Barth **3**:85
Protestantism **19**:625

'Epistola', work by Saint Patrick **18**:153

Epistolary novel, novel that is written as an exchange of letters **17**:411

Epitaph, an inscription on a tomb or anything written for that use.

Epitaxy machine, electronics, *picture* **14**:11

'Epithalamion', work by Spenser **19**:530

Epithelium, the layer of essentially protective tissue that forms the outer body surface (epidermis) and lines body cavities; sometimes modified for a secretory role, as in intestinal epithelium
cancer **4**:133
pancreatic secretions **18**:106

Epizootic, animal epidemic **7**:292

Epler, Stephen (born 1909), U.S. educator, born in Brooklyn, Iowa; originated six-man football in 1934 to make the sport as active but less injurious for younger players.

E Pluribus Unum (one out of many), Latin motto suggested by Franklin, Adams, and Jefferson, members of committee of Continental Congress appointed to design seal of U.S.
Great Seal **8**:156, *picture* **8**:157

Epoxy, a thermosetting plastic with high resistance to heat and chemicals; used as protective coating on casting tools and dies
insulating materials **11**:232
plastics, *list* **19**:448
synthetic adhesives **1**:43

EPR (or engine-pressure-ratio), indicator
airplane **1**:196

Epsilon Argus, fixed star, *chart* **22**:583

Epsom and Ewell, England, municipal borough 15 mi (25 km) s.w. of London; the name Epsom salts comes from its mineral springs; famous horse races at Epsom Downs; pop. 72,190, *map* **24**:75

Epsom salts (or magnesium sulfate), occurs naturally as the mineral epsomite **14**:41
minerals **15**:436

EPSPs (excitatory postsynaptic potentials), positive voltage changes in nerve cells **16**:122

Epstein, Jacob (1880–1959), British sculptor **7**:293

Epstein-Barr virus (EBV), a type of herpes
cancer **4**:132
fatigue **8**:46

Epworth, England, small town located in Lincolnshire, notable as the birthplace of John Wesley, the founder of Methodism.

Epworth League. *see in index* Methodist Youth Fellowship

Equal-arm balance, weighing machine **25**:134

Equal Employment Opportunity Act (1964), United States legislation
labor movements **13**:10

Equality, condition necessary for people to have civil and human rights **5**:468
democracy **6**:92, 94
women's rights **25**:272

Equality State. *see in index* Wyoming

Equal Pay Act (1963), United States
labor movements **13**:10
women's rights **25**:272

Equal Rights Amendment (ERA), proposed 27th Amendment to the U.S. Constitution, stated that "Equality of rights under the law shall not be denied or abridged by the United States or by any state on account of sex."

Equation, in algebra **1**:285

Equation of time
watch and clock **25**:83

Equator, in geography **7**:293
direction **6**:158
earth **7**:10
geography **9**:62
hemisphere **10**:126
Latin America **13**:60
latitude and longitude **13**:79, *picture* **13**:81
navigation **16**:71
Pacific Ocean **18**:8
weather **25**:117

Equatorial air (E), air mass **25**:118

Equatorial currents, warm surface ocean drift currents moving westward near the equator; North and South Equatorial currents separated by Equatorial Counter Current, which flows eastward **18**:9

Equatorial Guinea (formerly Spanish Guinea), republic in w. Africa, including Bioko Island; 10,831 sq mi (28,052 sq km); cap. Malabo; pop. 328,000 **7**:294
Africa, *map* **1**:115, *table* **1**:112
flag, *picture* **8**:164
Malabo **14**:68
United Nations, *table* **24**:84
world, *map* **25**:297

Equatorial mount, a type of telescope mounting **23**:67

Equatorial rain forest. *see in index* Rain forest

Equator system, in astronomy **2**:725, *diagram* **2**:727

Equestrian sports **7**:295

Equidae. *see in index* Horse family

Equilateral triangle, in mathematics
geometry **9**:74

Equilibrium, a state of balance
inner ear **7**:3
mechanics **14**:264
physical chemistry **19**:355
sensory hairs **21**:176

Equilibrium constant, physical chemistry **19**:355

Equinoctial. *see in index* Celestial equator

Equinox, time of year when the sun is equidistant from both of Earths' poles
folk art traditions **8**:252
hemisphere **10**:126
seasons **21**:158

Equinoxes, precession of, slow shift in time of year when poles are equidistant from the sun
gyroscope **9**:327

Equipment trust certificates, bonds **22**:627

Equisetophyta, division of plants **19**:419, *list* **19**:420

Equites, knights of ancient Rome; a privileged order of society; at first restricted to patricians serving as cavalry; later open to any favored person of wealth whether or not in military service.

Equity, in law, *table* **13**:92
housing, *list* **10**:305
women's rights **25**:272

Equity capital, in banking
banks and banking **3**:64

Equity jurisprudence, in American law **22**:635

Equuleus, constellation, *chart* **5**:681

Equus, animal genus including the ass, horse, zebra. *see in index* Ass; Horse; Zebra

Er, a rare chemical element. *see in index* Erbium

ERA. *see in index* Equal Rights Amendment

Eradication, a form of disease control **19**:438

Era of Good Feeling, in U.S. history
Madison **14**:25, 28
Monroe **15**:548

Era of Reptiles. *see in index* Mesozoic era

Érard, Sébastien (1752–1831), French maker of musical instruments, born in Strasbourg; most famous instrument was a double-action harp
stringed instruments **22**:673

Erasable pen, a writing instrument **18**:178

Erasistratus (3rd century BC), ancient Greek physician and anatomist; first to classify nerves into motor and sensory
autopsy procedure **2**:875

Erasmo da Narni. *see in index* Gattamelata

Erasmus, Desiderius (1466–1536), Dutch scholar and theologian **7**:296
etiquette **7**:320
Holbein **10**:201
humanism **10**:319
Latin literature **13**:78
More **15**:582
Netherlands **16**:127
Reformation **20**:140
Renaissance **20**:160
satire **21**:73
'The Cloister and the Hearth' **7**:278

Erato, in Greek mythology, one of the nine Muses **15**:701

Eratosthenes, of Alexandria (276?–194 BC), Greek scientist, chief librarian of Alexandrian Library **9**:268, **9**:278
earth science **7**:35
Homeric legend **10**:224
scientific breakthroughs, *list* **21**:114

Erbil, Iraq. *see in index* Arbela

Erbium, grayish-silver rare-earth metal found in rare-earth minerals euxenite and xenotime. Because many of erbium's compounds are beautifully pastel-colored, it is used to make infrared-absorbing glass and as an activator in phosphorescent materials. There are 9 known isotopes. It was discovered in 1843 by Carl Gustav Mosander, who originally called it terbia. Name became interchanged with terbium in 1860s due to similarity in properties.

Symbol	Er
Atomic number	68
Atomic weight	167.26
Group in periodic table	IIIb
Boiling point	5,185° F (2,863° C)
Melting point	2,727° F (1,497° C)
Specific gravity	9.066

periodic table, *list* **18**:226, *table* **18**:225

Ercilla y Zuñiga, Alonso de (1533–94), Chilean poet **13**:68

Erckmann-Chatrian, signature of French literary collaborators **Émile Erckmann** (1822–99) and **Louis Gratien Charles Alexandre Chatrian** (1826–90); writers of novels, short stories, dramas ('Madame Thérèse'; 'L'Ami Fritz').

Erebus, a place of utter darkness between the Earth and Hades; in Greek mythology, the son of Chaos and the brother of Nyx, with whom he ruled the gloomy regions.

Erebus, Mount, active volcano, highest point about 12,280 ft (3,930 m) on Ross Island, in Ross Sea, off Antarctica.

Erech, Iraq. *see in index* Uruk

Erechtheum, temple on Acropolis **1**:23, **2**:742, *map* **2**:741

'Erechtheus', work by Swinburne **22**:737

Eregli (or Bender Eregli, ancient Heraclea), Asiatic Turkey, town on Black Sea 130 mi (210 km) e. of Istanbul; coal mines **19**:672

E region (or Kennelly-Heaviside layer), in upper atmosphere; suggested by Oliver Heaviside and A.E. Kennelly **2**:750

Eremitic monasticism 15:540

Eremurus (also called desert candle, or foxtail lily), a genus of perennial plants of the lily family native to Asia; these desert plants grow to 8 ft (2.4 m); have long, narrow leaves and a long spike of rose, yellow, or white star-shaped flowers.

Erevan, Armenian Soviet Socialist Republic. *see in index* Yerevan

'Erewhon', novel by Butler **3**:519

Erfurt, East Germany, city 70 mi (110 km) s.w. of Leipzig; flowers, vegetables, seeds; had famous university; pop. 195,994, *maps* **7**:360, **9**:131

Erfurt, University of, Erfurt, Germany **24**:225

Erg, desert formation **6**:105
Sahara **21**:15

Erg, in physics, work done when a force of one dyne acts through one centimeter of distance
quantum theory **20**:5

Ergonomics 7:223
machine **14**:9

Ergosterol, a substance isolated from vegetable fats (and also found in the body) from which vitamin D can be produced by irradiation with ultraviolet light.

Ergot, rye fungus **8**:450
hallucinogen **10**:18
rye **20**:360

Erhard, Ludwig (1897–1977), German economist and political leader, chancellor of West Germany **7**:296
Germany **9**:126
Kiesinger **12**:236

Erhard Seminar Training (EST), a self-help psychotherapy **19**:632

'Erh ya', one of the Confucian Classics **5**:387

Ericaceae. *see in index* Heath

Erickson, Arthur C. (born 1924), Canadian architect **2**:566

Ericson, Leif (11th century), Norse mariner and adventurer **7**:297
America **1**:328, *picture* **1**:328
Scandinavia **21**:88
Vikings **24**:352
Vinland **1**:328, **4**:89

Ericsson, John (1803–89), U.S. inventor and engineer **7**:297
Monitor **5**:480
navy **16**:83
Nobel **17**:329
ship **21**:243

Eric the Red (10th century), Norse navigator **7**:297
Greenland **9**:282
polar exploration, *list* **19**:502
Vikings **24**:351

Eridanus, constellation, *charts* **5**:682, **22**:587, 591

Eridu, ancient city of Mesopotamia (Iraq); originally built on Persian Gulf but now 120 mi (190 km) s.w. of Ur; famous archaeological excavations 1855 and 1918; most important finding, a brick stamp of 8th king of Larsa, Nur-Adab, which aided historical identification of city.

Erie, an Indian tribe of North America who formerly lived in New York, Pennsylvania, and Ohio; in war with the Iroquois, 1654–56, most of those not killed were absorbed by the Six Nations and the rest dispersed, *map* **11**:136, *table* **11**:138

Erie, Pa., lake port in extreme n.w.; pop. 119,123 **7**:298
North America, *map* **17**:350
Pennsylvania **18**:188, *maps* **18**:185, 204

Erie, Lake, shallowest and stormiest of the Great Lakes; area 9,910 sq mi (25,670 sq km) **7**:297
Detroit **6**:120
Great Lakes **9**:243, *maps* **9**:245, **17**:350
Michigan **15**:358, *maps* **15**:356, 373
New York **16**:248
Ohio, *maps* **17**:499, 518
Pennsylvania, *map* **18**:206
United States, *map* **24**:193
War of 1812 **21**:260
Welland Ship Canal. *see in index* Welland Ship Canal

Erie Canal, N.Y., now included in New York State Barge Canal system **9**:247
Albany **1**:259
canals **4**:128, *map* **4**:126
Cleveland **5**:495
Detroit **6**:123
Michigan **15**:357, 361
New York **16**:245, 255, *picture* **16**:255
roads and trails, *map* **20**:234
transportation **23**:253, 261
United States **24**:106, 161

Erie Railroad Company, United States
Gould **9**:197

Erie Triangle, section of Pennsylvania claimed by New York and Massachusetts **18**:192

Erigena, Johannes Scotus (800?–877?), medieval Irish philosopher and theologian (later branded as heretic); under Charles the Bald, head of the palace school founded by Charlemagne **13**:78

Erigeron, plant genus. *see in index* Fleabane

Eriha, Jordan. *see in index* Jericho

Erik VII (1381?–1459?), king of Denmark, Norway, and Sweden **22**:730

Erikson, Erik (born 1902), U.S. psychoanalyst and educator, born in Frankfurt, Germany; applied Freudian theory to child behavior; professor University of California 1939–51, Harvard University 1960–70 ('Childhood and Society'; 'Young Man Luther'; 'Identity: Youth and Crisis'; 'Life History and the Historical Moment')
psychoanalysis **19**:634

Erin, ancient name for Ireland, now used poetically. *see in index* Ireland

Erinus, a perennial plant (*Erinus alpinus*) of figwort family, native to mountainous regions of Europe; grows 3 to 4 in. (8 to 10 cm) high; leaves spoon-shaped; flowers purple; used in rock gardens.

ERISA. *see in index* Employment Retirement Income Security Act

Eri silkworm 21:295

Eritrea, province of Ethiopia; 48,000 sq mi (124,000 sq km); former Italian colony, lost by Paris treaty 1947; pop. 1,889,700 **7**:315, *map* **1**:115

Erivan. *see in index* Yerevan

Erlanger, Joseph (1874–1965), U.S. physiologist and author, born in San Francisco, Calif.; taught at Johns Hopkins University 1900–06, University of Wisconsin 1906–10, Washington University, St. Louis, 1910–46. *see also in index* Nobel Prizewinners, *table*

Erlanger, Ky., city 7 mi (11 km) s.w. of Covington, in n. of state; industrial controls, fabricated metal products; dairy products; pop. 14,433.

Erl-king (or Erlkönig), in Teutonic folklore, the king of the elves who was said to haunt the Black Forest and prepare mischief for children; subject of a poem by Goethe (set to music by Franz Schubert and translated by Sir Walter Scott).

Ermine (or stoat), carnivorous mammal (*Mustela erminea*); valued for winter fur; found in Europe, Asia, North America **25**:114, *picture* **25**:115
fur, *table* **8**:464

Ermine, heraldic fur, *picture* **10**:136

'Ernani', opera by Verdi. *see in index* 'Hernani'

Erne, name of river in Ireland and Northern Ireland; also name of two lakes (Upper Lough Erne and Lower Lough Erne) that are connected by the river, *map* **24**:78

Ernest Augustus (1771–1851), king of Hanover, duke of Cumberland, 5th son of George III of England, born in Kew, England; succeeded to Hanoverian throne 1837 instead of Queen Victoria (males alone being eligible), thus separating English and Hanoverian crowns after personal union of over 100 years; abolished Hanoverian constitution; unpopular in both countries.

Ernestine line, in German history **21**:86

Ernst, Max (1891–1976), French painter, illustrator, and sculptor, born in Brühl, near Cologne, Germany; active in Dadaist movement; in Paris after 1922, where he was member of surrealist group; in U.S. 1941, became citizen 1948; citizen of France from 1958.

'Eroica', work by Beethoven
classical music **15**:670

Eros, Greek name for Cupid. *see in index* Cupid

Eros, asteroid **2**:714, *diagram* **2**:722

Erosion, gradual wearing away of land surfaces
agriculture
conservation techniques **5**:673
pollution **19**:527
beach and coast **3**:112
canyon. *see in index* Canyon
climate **5**:503
earth **7**:13, 31
ecology, *picture* **7**:53
food supply **8**:285
forests **8**:315
glacier **9**:151
Niagara Falls **16**:302
oceanography **17**:486
plateaus **19**:456
soil **21**:368
Greece **9**:258
land reclamation **20**:119
willow **25**:211
wind **25**:220

ERP. *see in index* European Recovery Program

Errol, Leon (1881–1951), U.S. comedian, *picture* **8**:80

Ersatz materials, substitutes for natural raw materials; term applied to many synthetic products, including foods, fuels, and textiles.

Erse (corruption of word Irish), name given to Scottish Highlanders and their language, also to Irish Gaelic.

Ershad, Hussain Mohammed, Bangladeshi official **3**:63

Erskine, John (1879–1951), U.S. author, pianist, educator, born in New York, N.Y.; taught English literature at Amherst College and Columbia University; at Columbia established honors course that grew into Great Books program; later director Juilliard School of Music; satiric novels ('The Private Life of Helen of Troy'; 'Adam and Eve'); also poetry, essays, literary criticism, autobiography.

Erskine College, Due West, S.C.; affiliated with Associate Reformed Presbyterian church; established in 1839; arts and sciences; seminary for men only.

Erubescite. *see in index* Bornite

Eruptions, volcanic. *see in index* Volcano

Ervin, Samuel James, Jr. (1896–1985), U.S. political leader, born in Morganton, N.C.; member North Carolina General Assembly 1923–27, 1931–33; judge Burke County Criminal Court 1935–37, North Carolina Superior Court 1937–43; U.S. representative 1946–47; associate justice North Carolina Supreme Court 1948–54; U.S. senator 1954–75; chairman Select Committee to Investigate 1972 Presidential Campaign Activities (Watergate case) 1973.

Ervine, Saint John Greer (1883–1971), Irish writer, born in Belfast; manager of Abbey Theatre, Dublin, 1915 (plays: 'John Ferguson', 'The First Mrs. Fraser'; novels: 'Mrs. Martin's Man', 'The Wayward Man'; biographies: 'Parnell', 'Bernard Shaw').

Erving, Julius (born 1950), U.S. basketball player **7**:298

Erymanthian boar, mythological creature **10**:138

Eryngium, plant genus. *see in index* Sea holly

Erysimum (or blistercress), genus of annual and perennial plants of the mustard family, native to the north temperate zone; related to wallflowers and stocks; small orange, yellow, or purple fragrant flowers; coast wallflower (*E. capitatum*); fairy wallflower (*E. perofskianum*).

Erysipelas, streptococcal infection of the skin often characterized by red swellings on face and scalp; treated with antibiotics.

Erytheia, in Greek mythology, island beyond the Strait of Gibraltar; home of the monster Geryon **10**:138

Erythrina (or coral tree), genus of plants, shrubs, and trees of the pea family, native to tropics; all are thorny, with showy red or yellow flowers in clusters; seeds in twisted pods; cockspur coral tree (*E. christa-galli*); bucare (*E. poeppigiana*), which grows to 60 ft (18 m), used for shading coffee and cacao plantings; seeds of some used as medicines and poisons; flowers cooked and eaten.

Erythrocytes. *see in index* Red cells

Erythropoietin, drug
blood disorders **3**:317

Erzberger, Matthias (1875–1921), German political leader, born in Buttenhausen, s.w. Germany; leader of Democratic Catholic party in Reichstag; secretary of state without portfolio 1918; negotiated armistice and peace terms World War I; finance minister 1919; assassinated.

Erzerum. *see in index* Erzurum

Erzgebirge (or Ore Mountains), on border of East Germany and n.w. Czechoslovakia; range about 100 mi (160 km) long; heavily mined **9**:111, *map* **9**:131

Erzurum (or Erzerum), **Turkey,** ancient city in Armenia; trade in barley, wheat, potatoes; capture by Russians in World War I (Feb. 1916) ended projected Turkish invasion of Egypt; pop. 90,069.

Es, chemical element. *see in index* Einsteinium

ESA (European Space Agency) **22**:480

Esaki, Leo (born 1925), Japanese physicist, born in Osaka; while working for Sony Corporation developed tunnel diode that enables electric current to pass through electronic barriers; consultant to IBM's Thomas

J. Watson Research Center in U.S. *see also in index* Nobel Prizewinners, *table*

Esarhaddon (died 668 BC), king of Assyria; son of Sennacherib and father of Assurbanipal; brought Egypt under Assyrian rule, rebuilt Babylon **3:9**

Esau, son of Isaac and Rebekah and elder twin brother of Jacob; sold his birthright to his brother for a mess of pottage and was cheated by Jacob (Bible, Gen. xxv, xxvii).

Esbjerg, Denmark, seaport on w. coast of Jutland; submarine cable connects with Calais; pop. 55,171 **6:**97, *maps* **6:**100, **7:**360

Escalante, Silvestre Vélez de (fl. 1768–79), Spanish Franciscan missionary and explorer; dispatched (1775) by governor of New Mexico to investigate Moqui (Hopi) tribes; traveled from Zuni to Grand Canyon; next year undertook to survey route between Santa Fe and Monterey, Calif.; went n.w. to Utah Lake, thence 200 mi (320 km) w. across desert; winter forced return by way of Zuni; diary and reports valued by historians
  explorations **5:**586

Escalator 7:186

Escalibur (or Excalibur), King Arthur's sword **2:**655

Escanaba, Mich., city on Upper Peninsula, on inlet of Green Bay; lumber, veneers, paper, machinery, metal products; summer resort; good harbor; pop. 14,355, *map* **15:**372, *picture* **15:**357

Escanaba River, Michigan, rises in n.w. part of Upper Peninsula and flows s.e. about 100 mi (160 km), emptying into Green Bay at Escanaba, Mich. **15:**355, *map* **15:**373

ESCAP (Economic and Social Commission for Asia and the Pacific), United Nations **24:**86

'Escape from Freedom', book by Fromm **8:**417
  psychoanalysis **19:**634

Escapement, watches and clocks **25:**78, *picture* **25:**81

Escape velocity (or parabolic velocity), spacecraft **22:**465

Escape wheel, watches and clocks **25:**78

Escarpment, in geology, steep face of cliff, usually caused by erosion or by prehistoric changes in the water line
  Great Rift Valley **9:**250
  waterfall **25:**96

Escaut. *see in index* Scheldt

Eschenbach, Wolfram von. *see in index* Wolfram von Eschenbach

Escher, M.C. (1898–1971), Dutch artist known for his lithographs and woodcuts that use realistic details to create bizarre conceptual and optical effects, born in Leeuwarden; studied at Haarlem's School of Architecture and Decorative Arts; achieved technical virtuosity in prints that attracted the general public, mathematicians, and psychologists with their unusual perspective of everyday objects, *picture* **14:**216

Esch-sur-Alzette, Luxembourg **13:**340

Escoffier, Auguste (1846–1935), French chef and culinary artist
  restaurant **20:**176

Escondido, Calif., city 28 mi (45 km) n.e. of San Diego; located in a farming valley; vineyards; produce includes avocados and citrus fruit; electronic equipment, chemicals; pop. 62,480, *map* **4:**52

Escorial, formerly the residence of Spanish kings; now has an art collection and tombs of the Spanish monarchs, *picture* **22:**498

Escrow, in law
  definition, *table* **13:**92
  housing, *list* **10:**305

Escrow agent, in housing **10:**295

Escudo, monetary unit of Guinea-Bissau, Mozambique, and Portugal, historic value of Portuguese escudo $1.08.

Escutcheon, in heraldry **10:**135

Esdraelon, Plain of (also called Emek), Israel, the greatest plain in the country; fertile, level, bounded by Mt. Carmel on w., Mt. Gilboa on s.e., highlands of Galilee on n.; battlefield in all ages.

Esenin, Sergei Aleksandrovich (1895–1925), Soviet poet, born near Moscow; considered poet laureate of the Russian Revolution
  Russian literature **20:**350, 352

Esfahan (or Isfahan, or Gabae), **Iran;** a major textile center; modern industries include steelmaking and petroleum refining; pop. 661,510 **11:**306, *map* **11:**312
  Persia **18:**231

Eshkol, Levi (originally Levi Shkolnik) (1895–1969), Israeli political leader, born in Oratova, Ukraine; settled in Palestine 1914; active in Zionist movement; minister of finance 1952–63; minister of defense 1963–67; prime minister 1963–69.

Esker, glacial mound **11:**6

Eskimo (or Inuit), people of the Arctic regions **7:**299
  Alaska **2:**572
  American Indians **11:**116, 137, 156, *map* **11:**136, *table* **11:**138
  appearance, *pictures* **15:**628, **20:**32
  Canada **4:**76
    Newfoundland **16:**167
    Northwest Territories **17:**388
  clothing **5:**506, *picture* **5:**505
  dogsled racing **21:**322
  Greenland **9:**282
  North America **17:**337, 344
  shelter **21:**232, *picture* **21:**231
  shoes **21:**263
  storytelling **22:**661, *picture* **22:**655

Eskimo curlew. *see in index* Curlew

Esmeralda, character in Victor Hugo's 'Notre Dame de Paris', a beautiful street dancer of Paris (supposedly a Gypsy) who is accused of witchcraft, is hidden from her accusers in the belfry of Notre Dame Cathedral by the hunchback bell ringer Quasimodo, but is finally executed, *picture* **17:**410

Esophageal speech 24:401

Esophagus (or gullet), muscular tube from mouth to stomach
  human digestive system **6:**144, *diagram* **6:**143
  stomach **22:**629
  throat **23:**176

ESP. *see in index* Extrasensory perception

Espartero, Baldomero (1792–1879), Spanish soldier and statesman, born in Granátula, near Ciudad Real; conspicuous for successes against Carlists 1836–40; then for three years regent for Isabella, child queen; retired from public life 1856; modest man of strongly liberal tendencies.

Esparto grass (or alfa plant), a fibrous grass, native to n. Africa and s. Spain; used for mats, baskets, rope, sandals, and in papermaking.

Espejo, Antonio de, 16th-century Spanish merchant-explorer; his journeys in n. Arizona (1582) and discovery of rich mines while searching for a lake of gold spurred prospectors and inspired Oñate's trip 20 years later.

Esperanto, international language **13:**39
  spelling **22:**528

Esperey, Louis Franchet d'. *see in index* Franchet d' Esperey

Espina de Serna, Concha (1877–1955), Spanish novelist, born in Santander ('Mariflor'; 'Altar Mayor'; 'The Woman and the Sea').

Espinel, Vicente (1550?–1624), Spanish writer and musician **22:**676

Espionage, the secret gathering of information about a rival **7:**302. *see also in index* Spy
  East Germany **9:**127
  Hitler **10:**175
  labor movements **13:**8
  satellites **21:**73
  West Germany **9:**126

Espírito Santo, small state of Brazil, on s.e. coast; 15,281 sq mi (39,577 sq km); cap. Vitória; pop. 2,063,679, *map* **3:**425

'Espolio', painting by El Greco **9:**253

Esposito, Phil (Philip Anthony Esposito) (born 1942), Canadian ice-hockey player, born in Sault Ste. Marie, Ont.; center with Chicago Black Hawks 1963–67, Boston Bruins 1967–76, New York Rangers 1976–81; set scoring records; brother of Tony Esposito.

Esposito, Tony (Anthony James Esposito) (born 1943), Canadian ice-hockey player, born in Sault Ste. Marie, Ont.; goalie with Montreal Canadiens 1968–69, Chicago Black Hawks 1969–84; trophy winner; brother of Phil Esposito.

Espresso, coffee **5:**537

'Esprit des lois, L' ', work by Montesquieu. *see in index* 'Spirit of Laws, The'

Espronceda, José de (1808–42), Spanish poet **22:**506

Espy, James Pollard (1785–1860), U.S. meteorologist, born in Westmoreland County, Pennsylvania; instituted telegraphic weather bulletins; appointed meteorologist to U.S. War Department 1842, later to Navy Department; laid foundation of present U.S. Weather Bureau; published 'Philosophy of Storms'.

Espy, Michael (born 1953), U.S. politician, born in Yazoo City, Miss.; graduated from Howard University 1975, University of Santa Clara Law School 1978; attorney with Central Mississippi Legal Services 1978–80; Public Lands Division assistant secretary 1880–84; assistant state attorney general 1984–85; U.S. Representative (Democrat) 1987– .

Esquire. *see in index* Squire

ESRO 2B, European Space Research Organization satellite, *table* **22:**468

Essad Pasha (1863–1920), Turkish soldier, bandit, and provisional president of Albania (1914); killed in Paris.

'Essais', work by Montaigne **7:**306

Essaouira (or Mogador), **Morocco,** seaport on Atlantic; fish processing, tanning, palm-fiber working; pop. 30,061, *map* **1:**115

Essay, form of writing **7:**306
  American **1:**345
  Lamb **13:**26
  Montaigne **8:**395, **15:**549

'Essay and General Literature Index' 20:135

'Essay Concerning Human Understanding', work by Locke **13:**278

'Essay on Man, An', work by Pope **19:**481, 483, **19:**536

'Essay on Projects', work by Defoe **6:**64

'Essay on the Principle of Population, An', work by Malthus **14:**79
  Darwin **6:**38
  food supply **8:**286

'Essays, Moral and Political', work by Hume **10:**321

'Essays of Elia, The', collection of works by Lamb
  essay **7:**306
  Lamb **13:**26

Essen, West Germany, industrial center in Ruhr valley; pop. 628,800 **7:**306
  Germany, *maps* **7:**360, **9:**131

'Essence of the Novel, The' (in Japanese, Shosetsu shinzui), work by Shoyo Tsubouchi **12:**82

Essenes, Judaic religious sect **6:**46
  nonviolence **18:**160

Essential amino acid, natural occurring amino acid **19:**623

Essentialist. *see in index* Conservative

Essential oils, volatile, odoriferous oils **8:**48
  perfume **18:**221

'Essentials of the Three Treatises', work by Kobo Daishi **12:**266

Essequibo, largest river of Guyana, South America; about 600 mi (970 km) long; flows into Atlantic by estuary 20 mi (30 km) wide South America, *map* **22:**418

Essex, Robert Devereux, 2nd **earl of** (1566?–1601), English soldier and courtier, born in Netherwood, Herefordshire; favorite of Queen Elizabeth I; won distinction in war with Spain; later fell into disfavor, tried to incite insurrection, was executed for treason
  Elizabeth I **7:**191

Essex, Robert Devereux, 3rd **earl of** (1591–1646), English general, born in London; son of 2nd earl; commander of Parliamentary forces 1642–45 in Civil War.

Essex, ancient kingdom of the East Saxons, in England; conquered by Egbert, king of Wessex, and became part of Wessex.

Essex, maritime county in s.e. England; 1,528 sq mi (3,958 sq km); cap. Chelmsford; grazing, wheat, and barley; extensive manufactures; included in kingdom of East Saxons; pop. 2,288,058.

Essex, Md., community 7 mi (11 km) n.e. of Baltimore; clothing, tractors; pop. 39,614, *map* **14:**182

Essex, Vt., town 7 mi (11 km) n.e. of Winooski, includes industrial village of Essex Junction; town chartered 1763; pop. of township 14,392
  Vermont, *map* **24:**318

'Essex', U.S. frigate **8:**37
  famous ships **21:**260

Essex Junction, Vt., village on Winooski River, e. of Burlington; railroad center; pop. 6,511
  Vermont, *map* **24:**318

Essex Junto, U.S. group of Federalist leaders, including Timothy Pickering, Fisher Ames, George Cabot, and some of the Lowell family, living in Essex County, Mass.; accused by John Adams of being a British faction; opposed war with England in 1812.

Essling, Austria, former village on Danube River, 7 mi (11 km) e. of central Vienna; now part of Vienna.

EST (Erhard Seminar Training), a self-help psychotherapy **19:**632

Estaing, Jean-Baptiste-Charles-Henri-Hector, comte d' (1729–94), French admiral, born in Auvergne; served first in army, later in navy; aided U.S. against England in Revolutionary War; active in French Revolution; executed because of sympathy with Marie Antoinette.

Estancia, Spanish-American term for a cattle ranch
  Argentina **2:**582

Estate, in law, a person's entire property, more particularly property left at death; an estate is said to be closed when the decedent's will has been carried out, or when, if no will was left, the estate has been divided in accordance with state laws **7:**307
  definition, *table* **13:**92
  property **19:**615
  taxation **23:**38

Estate agent (or real estate agent, or broker) **20:**115

Estate law 7:307

Estates-General, former representative assembly of France **7:**307
  French revolt **8:**401
  Louis XVI **13:**306

Este, House of, old and illustrious family of Italy, capital at Ferrara; famous for political importance and splendid court; encouraged poets, painters, and scholars; **Alberto Azzo II** (11th century) was common ancestor both of House of Este and of House of Guelf, to which the British royal House of Hanover belonged; **Alfonso d'Este** (1476–1534), duke of Ferrara, husband of Lucretia Borgia, was patron of Tasso **2:**588
  Tasso **23:**33

Ester, one of a large group of liquid and solid compounds formed by reaction of an acid and an alcohol with elimination of water; for example, acetic acid (CH_2COOH) plus methyl alcohol (CH_3OH) gives the ester, methyl acetate ($CH_3CO_2CH_3$) plus water(H_2O); most oils, fats, and waxes are esters; so are many plastics **8:**47
  fibers **8:**72
  organic chemistry **17:**604, *diagram* **17:**603
  wax **25:**110

Esterházy, noble Hungarian family of ancient origin, members of which have held prominent places in Hungarian

history down to recent times; **Prince Nicholas Esterházy** (1765–1833), patron of the arts, friend of Haydn, refused Napoleon's offer of crown of Hungary
classical music **15**:669
Haydn **10**:75
Liszt **13**:239

Esterhazy, Ferdinand Walsin, (1847–1923), French army officer who was chief figure in the Dreyfus Case **6**:272

Esterhazy, Sask., town 42 mi (68 km) s.e. of Yorkton; established by Hungarians 1886; pop. 3,065
Saskatchewan **21**:67

Esterházy Palace, in Fertod, Hungary, *picture* **10**:328

Estes, Eleanor (1906–88), U.S. writer of children's books, born in West Haven, Conn. ('The Moffats'; 'The Middle Moffat'; 'Rufus M'; 'The Hundred Dresses'; 'Ginger Pye', winner of Newbery Medal 1952; 'A Little Oven'; 'Pinky Pye'; 'The Witch Family'; 'The Alley'; 'Miranda the Great'; 'The Tunnel of Hugsy Goode').

Estes Park, Colo., town located in valley at e. entrance to Rocky Mountain National Park; tourist center and summer resort; pop. 2,703
Colorado, *map* **5**:582

Estevan (also called Estevanico, or Little Steven) (died 1539), African explorer with ill-fated Narváez expedition reaching Florida 1528; worked way to n. Mexico by 1536; discovered Zuñi pueblo in New Mexico 1539 **2**:601, **3**:289

Estevan, Sask., city in s.e., near North Dakota border; petroleum and coal-mining center; meat and dairy products; pop. 9,523, *map* **4**:112

Estevan Point, on Vancouver Island, British Columbia; situated in the Canadian Rockies; wettest point of Canada with more than 120 in (300 cm) of precipitation each year **4**:74

Estey, Willard Z. (born 1919), Canadian jurist, born in Saskatoon, Sask.; private law practice 1947–72; judge of court of appeals, and of high court of Ontario 1973–76; chief justice of Ontario 1976; judge of the Supreme Court of Canada 1977–

Esther, heroine of the Bible's book of this name
folklore **8**:263
Purim **12**:150

'Esther', work by Handel **10**:28

Esthetics, branch of philosophy. *see in index* Aesthetics

Estienne, Henri (or Henri Étienne, or Henri Stephanus) (1460?–1520), French printer, founder of the family that was supreme in printing for three generations; after his death his foreman, Simon de Colines, married his widow and continued the business **23**:337

Estienne, Henri (1528–98), French author, editor, and printer, son of Robert; compiled great Greek thesaurus, still used; wrote 'An Apology for Herodotus', bitter satire on contemporary life; his writings important in standardizing literary French.

Estienne, Robert (1503–59), French printer and scholar, son of the first Henri; noted for editions of Greek classics and for magnificent Greek New Testaments (1546 in 16mo, 1550 in folio) that remained the accepted text for three centuries.

Estigarribia, José Félix (1888–1940), Paraguayan general and statesman, born in Caraguatay; leader and hero of the Chaco War; minister to U.S. 1938–39; president of Paraguay 1939–40; self-proclaimed dictator 1940 **4**:263

Estivation. *see in index* Aestivation

Estonian Soviet Socialist Republic (also called Estonia), **U.S.S.R.,** on Baltic Sea; area 17,370 sq mi (44,990 sq km); cap. Tallinn; pop. 1,556,000 **7**:308
Europe, *map* **7**:360
storytelling **22**:657
U.S.S.R. **24**:54, *maps* **24**:59, 63

Estoque, sword used in bullfighting **3**:499

Estournelles de Constant de Rebecque, Paul-Henri-Benjamin Balluat, baron d' (1852–1924), French diplomat, born in La Flèche; founded French parliamentary group for voluntary arbitration. *see also in index* Nobel Prizewinners, *table*

E Street Band, band formed by Bruce Springsteen **22**:554

Estremadura, province, located on the coast of central Portugal; 2,062 sq mi (5,341 sq km); Lisbon capital of both province and nation; pop. 1,806,383.

Estremadura, region in w.-central Spain; about 16,000 sq mi (41,400 sq km); agriculture (livestock, olives, grapes, wheat, barley) and mining (phosphate, lead, iron, zinc, tin, copper).

Estrogen, hormone group that causes menstruation and controls development of secondary female characteristics; secreted primarily by ovaries; also made synthetically; used in treatment of prostate cancer and disorders of menstruation and menopause; ingredient in birth control pills; produces estrus in animals
adolescence growth rate **1**:47
bone injuries **3**:343
hormones **10**:243, *diagram* **10**:242, *table* **10**:241
menstruation **14**:300
reproductive system **20**:166

Estrus (or heat), period when a female mammal is receptive to mating; prior changes in sex hormone concentration trigger growth of the egg-bearing follicles in the ovaries; during estrus, sexual intercourse ensues and eggs are released for fertilization **20**:167

Estuary, widened mouth of a river where it joins the sea; may be caused by the current of the stream and tidal action or may be a submerged section of a river valley
delta **6**:90
river **20**:228

ET (ephemeris time) **23**:188

ETA (Euzkadi ta Azkatasuna), Basque separatist organization in Spain seeking autonomy for their homeland **22**:499

Eta Argus, fixed star, *chart* **22**:583

Etah, Eskimo (Inuit) settlement on n.w. coast of Greenland, n. of Thule Air Base; known as base for Arctic expeditions.

Etchemin. *see in index* Malecite

Etching. *see in index* Engraving and etching

Eternal City. *see in index* Rome

Eternal fires of Persia, underground petroleum fields in Soviet Union **18**:263

Eternal Light, peace memorial at Gettysburg, Pa. **9**:137

Etesian wind (or meltemi), *list* **25**:225
Greece **9**:255

'Ethan Allen', U.S. Navy submarine, *picture* **22**:684

Ethane, colorless and odorless gaseous compound of hydrogen and carbon (C_2H_6); forms ethyl radical in chemical combinations. *see also in index* Paraffin series
alcohol **1**:275
natural gas **9**:38, **18**:261
organic chemistry, *diagrams* **17**:602, 603

'Ethan Frome', work by Wharton **25**:186

Ethanol. *see in index* Ethyl alcohol

Ethchlorvynol (or Placidyl), a sedative **16**:19

Ethelbald (or Aethelbald) (died 860), king of Wessex 858–60; eldest brother of Alfred the Great.

Ethelbert (or Aethelberht) (552?–616), king of Kent 560–616, bretwalda or overlord over all the English s. of the Humber, and author of the first written English laws
Augustine of Canterbury **2**:763
England **7**:238

Ethelbert (or Aethelberht) (died AD 866), king of Wessex 860–65; son of Ethelwulf and brother of Alfred the Great.

Etheldreda (or Aethelthryth, known as Saint Awdrey), daughter of king of East Anglia and wife of king of Northumbria; founded religious house at Ely AD 673; her festival became occasion for annual large fair at which cheap, trifling objects were sold, whence came the word tawdry, a contraction of St. Awdrey; festival observed in Roman Catholicism June 23, in Anglican Church Oct. 17.

Ethelfleda (or Aethelflaed) (died 917?), eldest daughter of Alfred the Great, wife of the earl of Mercia.

Ethelred (or Aethelred), king of Wessex and Kent 865–71, brother of Alfred the Great **1**:282

Ethelred the Unready (968?–1016), king of the English 978–1016; his marriage with Norman princess Emma opened distinct policy that led to the Norman conquest of England
England **7**:239

'Ethel Scull Thirty-six Times', painting by Warhol **18**:66, *picture* **18**:67

Ethelwulf (or Aethelwulf) (died 858), king of the West Saxons 839–58, father of Alfred the Great; successfully repulsed a Danish invasion.

Ether, any of the light, volatile, highly flammable liquids made by action of sulfuric acid on alcohol; used in industry as solvent for fats and oils
anesthetic **1**:413
hospital **10**:280
Long **13**:295
Snow **21**:338
organic chemistry **17**:604, *diagram* **17**:603

Ether, in physics
Michelson–Morley experiment **15**:353

Etherege, George (1635?–91), English dramatist, first important figure in Restoration comedy; originated comedy of intrigue ('The Comical Revenge: or, Love in a Tub'; 'She Wou'd, if She Cou'd'; 'The Man of Mode: or, Sir Fopling Flutter').

Ethical absolutism **7**:310

Ethical culture, movement inaugurated by the founding of New York Society for Ethical Culture by Felix Adler in 1876; two federations have been formed, the American Ethical Union, organized in 1886, composed of ethical societies in seven U.S. cities, and the International Ethical Union, organized in 1896; affirming the supremacy of moral law and seeking social reforms, the societies have pioneered in areas such as progressive education, settlement work, housing.

Ethical relativity **7**:310

Ethics and morality **7**:309
philosophy **18**:313
public speaking **19**:647
Socrates **21**:362
Stoicism **22**:628
storytelling **22**:643, 650
Zoroastrianism and Parsiism **25**:471

Ethiopia, nation in n.e. Africa, formerly an empire; 472,400 sq mi (1,223,510 sq km); cap. Addis Ababa; pop. 48,898,000 **7**:311
Africa **1**:110, 111, *map* **1**:115, *table* **1**:112
camel caravan, *picture* **23**:262
cities. *see in index* cities by name
Communist world, *map* **5**:619
flag, *picture* **8**:164
food supply **8**:285
fossil findings **8**:326
Lucy **2**:538, *picture* **2**:538
genealogy **9**:47
history
ancient Egypt **7**:126
Italy **11**:395
Mussolini **25**:321
Korean War losses, *table* **12**:296
Menelik II **14**:298
Somalia **21**:387
national anthem, *table* **16**:64
Red Cross **20**:124
storytelling **22**:654
United Nations, *table* **24**:84
world, *map* **25**:297

Ethiopian Orthodox Church. *see in index* Coptic Church

Ethiopic, dialect of Arabic language **21**:171

Ethmoid bone, sievelike bone at the base of the skull, behind the root of the nose **21**:310

Ethnic group. *see in index* Race and ethnicity

Ethnicity. *see in index* Race and ethnicity

Ethnology, science that deals with the groups and classifications of people. *see also in index* Anthropology; Evolution; Man; Race and ethnicity
American Indians **11**:137, 142

Ethology, observational study of animal behavior **2**:438
zoology **25**:469

Ethos, in public speaking and philosophy **19**:647

Ethyl (C_2H_5), chemical radical made up of 2 carbon and 5 hydrogen atoms; formed by removing 1 hydrogen atom from ethane; a part of many organic molecules
organic chemistry **17**:603, *diagram* **17**:602

Ethyl acetate, hobby **10**:186

Ethyl alcohol (or grain alcohol, or ethanol) **1**:275
alcohol **1**:275
automobile fuel **2**:861
drugs **6**:276
methanol **15**:317
organic chemistry **17**:603

Ethylene, gaseous hydrocarbon (C_2H_4) of high fuel value
citrus fruits' ripening **5**:446
organic chemistry, *diagram* **17**:603
petrochemicals **18**:250
synthetic fibers **8**:74

Ethylene glycol, thick, sweet, colorless liquid, the simplest type of dihydric alcohol **1**:275, *table* **1**:274
alcohol **1**:275
organic chemistry **17**:603
synthetic fibers **8**:73
wax **25**:110

Ethyl formate, organic chemistry, *diagram* **17**:603

Ethyl gasoline, antiknock motor fuel containing tetraethyl lead **9**:42

Étienne, Henri. *see in index* Estienne, Henri

Etiolation, blanching or whitening of plants by excluding the sunlight.

Etiquette **7**:316
Louis XIV **13**:306
U.S. flag code **8**:151

Etna, Mount, volcano 10,705 ft (3,263 m) on e. coast of Sicily **7**:323, *maps* **7**:360, **11**:404
lava flow diverted **11**:388
Sicily **21**:284

Etolia. *see in index* Aetolia

Eton College, famous English public school at Eton, on Thames River, opposite Windsor **7**:234
school systems **21**:96, *picture* **21**:95

Etruria, ancient country n.w. of Rome, situated between Arno and Tiber rivers; inhabited by Etruscans; modern Tuscany.

Etruria, Wedgwood's factory in England **25**:131

Etruscans (or Tyrrhenians) **7**:324
gladiators **9**:152
Italy **11**:391, **20**:269
Roman art **9**:273

Etruscan Sea, ancient name of Tyrrhenian Sea. *see in index* Tyrrhenian Sea

Etruscan ware, pottery **19**:566

Ets, Marie Hall (born 1895), U.S. author and illustrator, born in present Milwaukee, Wis.; best known for animal stories for children ('Mr. T.W. Anthony Woo'; 'Play with Me'; 'Penny's Race Horse'; 'Nine Days to Christmas', awarded Caldecott medal 1960; 'Gilberto and the Wind').

'E.T. The Extraterrestrial', motion picture by Spielberg, *picture* **15**:627

Ettrick Shepherd, the. *see in index* Hogg, James

Étude, in music. *see in index* Music, *table*

ETV Network, educational television system in South Carolina **22**:425

Etymology **7**:324
American Indian languages **11**:140
language development **13**:36, *diagram* **13**:37

Eu, chemical element. *see in index* Europium

Euboea, island of Greece. *see in index* Évvoia

Eucalyptus, gum tree of the family Myrtaceae; native to Australia **7**:325
Addis Ababa **1**:41

MEMBERSHIP IN PRINCIPAL EUROPEAN ORGANIZATIONS*

Austria	CE			EFTA			OECD	
Belgium	CE		EEC		NATO		OECD	
Bulgaria		CMEA						WTO
Cyprus	CE		EEC†					
Czechoslovakia		CMEA						WTO
Denmark	CE		EEC		NATO	NC	OECD	
Finland				EFTA†		NC	OECD	
France	CE		EEC		NATO		OECD	
Germany, East		CMEA						WTO
Germany, West	CE		EEC		NATO		OECD	
Greece	CE		EEC		NATO		OECD	
Hungary		CMEA						
Iceland	CE			EFTA	NATO	NC	OECD	
Ireland	CE		EEC				OECD	
Italy	CE		EEC		NATO		OECD	
Liechtenstein	CE			EFTA‡				
Luxembourg	CE		EEC		NATO		OECD	
Malta	CE		EEC†					
Netherlands	CE		EEC		NATO		OECD	
Norway	CE			EFTA	NATO	NC	OECD	
Poland		CMEA						WTO
Portugal	CE		EEC		NATO		OECD	
Romania		CMEA						WTO
Soviet Union		CMEA						WTO
Spain	CE		EEC		NATO		OECD	
Sweden	CE			EFTA		NC	OECD	
Switzerland	CE			EFTA			OECD	
Turkey	CE		EEC†		NATO		OECD	
United Kingdom	CE		EEC		NATO		OECD	
Yugoslavia							OECD‡	

Key to Organizations

CE—Council of Europe
CMEA—Council for Mutual Economic Assistance (Comecon)
EEC—European Economic Community (Common Market)
EFTA—European Free Trade Association
NATO—North Atlantic Treaty Organization
NC—Nordic Council
OECD—Organization for Economic Cooperation and Development
WTO—Warsaw Treaty Organization

*As of mid-1990. Only European members are listed. †Associate member. ‡Special status.

and the subsequent prospect of a reunified Germany in 1990. The new Germany would be the wealthiest and most productive nation in Europe. *see also in index* European Communities; European Economic Community

Europium, silvery-white rare-earth metal found in small amounts in monazite and other minerals. It has been detected by spectroscope in certain stars, including the sun. Used as activator in color television tubes and as an agent in the manufacture of fluorescent glass, it is also a good absorber of thermal neutrons, making it valuable in electric atomic power-station construction. It was discovered in 1896 by Eugène-Anatole Demarçay, who named it after Europe.

Symbol	Eu
Atomic number	63
Atomic weight	151.96
Group in periodic table	IIIb
Boiling point	2,907° F (1,597° C)
Melting point	1,519° F (826° C)
Specific gravity	5.243

periodic table, *list* **18**:226, *table* **18**:225

Europoort, The Netherlands, shipping and industrial complex at Rotterdam
harbor and port **10**:36

Eurospace, international organization involved in space research and technology.

Eurus, in Greek mythology, the east wind; the Romans sometimes called it Vulturnus.

Eurydice, in Greek mythology, wife of Orpheus; killed by serpent's bite, rescued from the underworld by Orpheus, but lost again.

Eurypterids (also called sea scorpions), class of extinct arthropods, related to the scorpions; abundant during the Silurian period **7**:23

Eurystheus, mythological figure; cousin of Hercules who made him perform the famed 12 labors **10**:138

Eusden, Laurence (1688–1730), English poet, born in Spofforth, near Leeds; chiefly remembered for Alexander Pope's satirical allusions to him; poet laureate 1718–30.

Eusebius of Caesarea (also called Pamphili) (260?–340?), Christian theologian, most learned man of his age; 'History of the Christian Church', most important ancient record of church; called Father of Church History; chief figure at Council of Nicaea
Byzantine literature **9**:279
history writing **10**:172
New Testament canon **3**:185

Eusebius of Nicomedia (called the Great) (died AD 341?), leading defender of Arius, and after death of Arius leader of his party; a politician rather than a theologian; banished from his see; pardoned through sister of Constantine; promoted to bishop of Nicomedia and later of Constantinople.

Euskara, language spoken by the Basques in Spain **22**:490

Eustachi, Bartolomeo (died 1574), Italian anatomist, born near Ancona; described various structures in human body, including Eustachian tube, which was named for him.

Eustachian tube, connection between throat and middle ear **7**:4, **23**:176

Eutaw Springs, battle in Revolutionary War 1781, led British to abandon South Carolina; near Santee River, 60 mi (100 km) n.w. of Charleston; Americans led by Greene and Marion, British by Stuart
flag **8**:154, *picture* **8**:155

Euterpe, in Greek mythology, one of the nine Muses **15**:701

Euthanasia (or mercy killing), painless death, also painless killing, especially of a person or animal suffering from an incurable disease
bioethics **3**:215

Eutrophication, process of aging and eventual drying up of a lake
water pollution **19**:527

Euzkadi ta Azkatasuna (ETA), Basque separatist organization in Spain seeking autonomy for their homeland **22**:499

Eva, character in 'Uncle Tom's Cabin' by Harriet Beecher Stowe, beautiful, affectionate, and exceedingly good child, daughter of Uncle Tom's master, Augustin St. Clare.

Evangel College, Springfield, Mo.; affiliated with Assemblies of God; opened 1955; arts and sciences, education, music.

Evangelical Adventists, a Christian religious body **1**:53

Evangelical Alliance, association of members of Protestant churches organized in London 1846; extended to many other countries; U.S. branch organized 1867; purpose to strengthen Protestantism and to promote religious interest.

Evangelical and Reformed church, established 1934; formed by union of Evangelical Synod of North America (which originated with a synod organized at Gravois Settlement, Mo., 1840) and the Reformed church in the United States (established 1725 near Philadelphia, Pa.); accepts Bible as ultimate rule of life and faith; in 1957 united with the General Council of the Congregational and Christian churches to form the United Church of Christ.

Evangelical church, Christian religious body, formerly the Evangelical Association, founded among German-speaking people in Pennsylvania about 1800 by Jacob Albright, former Methodist; in 1946 united with United Brethren in Christ to become the Evangelical United Brethren church; in 1968 merged with Methodist church to form United Methodist church; until 1894 included Evangelical Congregational church, formerly United Evangelical church
Methodism **15**:319

Evangelical United Brethren church. *see in index* Evangelical church; United Brethren in Christ

Evangeline, heroine of Longfellow's poem of that name
American verse **1**:348
deportation of Acadians **1**:14
Longfellow **13**:296
Nova Scotia **17**:397
poetry **19**:483

Evangelists, writers of the Bible's New Testament Gospels of Matthew, Mark, Luke, and John.

Evans, Arthur John (1851–1941), English archaeologist, born in Nash Mills, Hertfordshire; knighted 1911; noted for excavations on Aegean civilization ('Palace of Minos'; 'Scripta Minoa')
Aegean civilization **1**:61
Cretan excavations **2**:536, **5**:763
linear script's discovery **1**:62

Evans, Bergen Baldwin (1904–78), U.S. educator and author, born in Franklin, Ohio; on faculty at Northwestern University 1932–75, professor 1942–75; moderator of TV programs Down You Go and The Last Word ('The Natural History of Nonsense'; collected and arranged 'Dictionary of Quotations').

Evans, Chick (Charles Evans, Jr.) (1890–1979), U.S. golfer, born in Indianapolis, Ind.; founder of Evans Scholars Foundation 1930 **9**:189

Evans, Dale, U.S. actress and singer. *see in index* Rogers, Roy

Evans, Edgar, British explorer
Scott **21**:130

Evans, Edward Ratcliffe Garth Russell, first **Baron Mountevans** (1881–1957), British naval officer and explorer, born in London; member of British Antarctic Expedition, assumed command after Robert Falcon Scott's death; served in World War I; author 'Keeping the Seas', 'South with Scott', and 'Man of the White South'.

Evans, Gil (originally Ian Ernest Gilmore Green) (1912–88), U.S. jazz musician, born in Toronto, Ont.; superb improviser, collaborated with Miles Davis (singles 'Moondreams', 'Boplicity'), ushering in "cool" jazz in 1950s; arrangements for Davis albums *Miles Ahead, Porgy and Bess, Sketches of Spain;* later incorporated rock, electric sounds for own bands.

Evans, Herbert McLean (1882–1971), U.S. anatomist and embryologist, born in Modesto, Calif.; discovered vitamin E; research in reproduction and in endocrinology.

Evans, James (1801–46), Canadian Methodist missionary, born in Kingston-upon-Hull, England; went to Canada in 1823; served among American Indians on St. Clair River and Lake Superior; became general superintendent of Northwest Indian Missions 1840; invented syllabic character still used by Crees.

Evans, Mary Ann (or Marian Evans). *see in index* Eliot, George

Evans, Maurice (1901–89), U.S. actor, manager, born in Dorset, England; first appeared in U.S. 1935, became citizen 1941; best known for Shakespearean acting; won 1961 Emmy for 'Macbeth', *picture* **21**:212

Evans, Oliver (1755–1819), U.S. inventor, born in Newport, Del.; invented machine for making teeth for carding machines, machinery for flour mills, the first high-pressure steam engine, and a steam dredge **11**:182
railroads **20**:85
steam engines **22**:611

Evans, Robley Dunglison (Fighting Bob Evans) (1846–1912), U.S. Navy officer, born in Floyd Court House, Va.; ordered to Chile 1891, and with gunboat *Yorktown* defied Chilean navy; in 1898, at Santiago, his ship *Iowa* fired first gun at Cervera's fleet; rear admiral 1901; chosen commander in chief U.S. fleet 1907.

Evans, Ronald E. (born 1933), U.S. astronaut, born in St. Francis, Kan.; U.S. Navy officer chosen for NASA program 1966.

Evans, William George (1884–1956), U.S. baseball umpire and executive, born in Chicago, Ill.; umpire, A.L., 1906–27; general manager Cleveland, A.L., 1927–35; farm director Boston, A.L., 1936–40; president Southern Association 1942–46; vice-president and general manager Detroit, A.L., 1946–51; baseball columnist.

Evanston, Ill., residential city just n. of Chicago; electronic and photocopy equipment, hospital supplies; Northwestern University; National College of Education; world headquarters Rotary International; national headquarters Woman's Christian Temperance Union; pop. 73,706, *map* **11**:52, *picture* **13**:176

Evanston, Wyo., town near s.w. corner of state; railroad center in farm area; Wyoming State Mental Institution; pop. 6,421, *map* **25**:400

Evansville, Ind., city on Ohio River, in s.w. corner; pop. 130,496 **7**:363
Indiana **11**:91, *maps* **11**:89, 102, **17**:350, *picture* **11**:90

Evansville, University of, Evansville, Ind.; Methodist; founded 1854 at Moores Hill, Ind.; moved to Evansville 1919; arts and sciences, business administration, education, engineering, fine arts, and nursing; graduate studies.

Evaporated milk 15:415, *list* **6**:6

Evaporation
air conditioner **1**:150
conservation **5**:672
flood control **8**:184
ink **11**:207
refrigeration **20**:144
solvent **21**:385
water **25**:86, 89, *picture* **25**:88

Evaporator fan, of a refrigerator **10**:210

Evarts, William Maxwell (1818–1901), U.S. lawyer and statesman, born in Boston, Mass.; chief counsel for President Andrew Johnson in impeachment trial; U.S. attorney general 1868–69; U.S. senator from New York 1885–91.

Evatt, Herbert Vere (1894–1965), Australian government official, born in East Maitland, New South Wales; leader Labor party 1951–60; chief justice New South Wales 1960–62.

Eve. *see in index* Adam and Eve

Eve, Nicolas, and his son **Clovis** (16th and 17th centuries), French bookbinders, important in history of binding design; introduced fanfare style; patterns were originally geometrical but later filled in with decorations.

'Evelina', Fanny Burney's first and best novel; told in form of letters; early example (1778) of novel of domestic manners.

Evelyn, John (1620–1706), English diarist of the Commonwealth and Restoration, born in Wotton, near Dorking.

Evening grosbeak, bird (*Coccothraustes vespertinus*) of the family Fringillidae **9**:290

Evening primrose, flowering plant of genus *Oenothera*; flowers commonly yellow, *picture* **8**:234

'Evening's Love, An', work by Dryden **19**:483

Event, in dance **6**:24

'Eve of Saint Agnes, The', poem by Keats; Madeline, the heroine, believing in an old superstition, goes to bed supperless on St. Agnes' Eve that she may dream of her future husband; Porphyro, her lover, who has hidden in her bedchamber, arouses her with music and persuades her to flee with him **25**:379

Everest, George (1790–1866), English surveyor and geographer, born in Wales; superintended first survey of India 1823–43; first fixed position and altitude of Mount Everest; height corrected to 29,028 ft (8,848 m) by survey of India 1952–54
Mount Everest **7**:363

Everest, Mount (or Chomolungma, or Sagarmatha formerly known as Peak XV), in Himalayas 29,028 ft (8,848 m); loftiest mountain on earth **7**:363
Asia **2**:674, *map* **2**:697
China, *map* **5**:384
earth **7**:10, 14
exploration **7**:377
Hillary **10**:152
mountain climbing **15**:637
height, comparative. *see in index* Mountain, *table*
Himalayas **10**:152
mountain **15**:633
Tibet **23**:180

Everett, Edward (1794–1865), U.S. statesman, clergyman, and orator, born in Dorchester, Mass.; Unitarian minister at 20; professor of Greek at Harvard at 21; member of House of Representatives 1825–35; governor of Massachusetts 1836–40; minister to England 1841–45; president of Harvard 1846–49; secretary of state 1852–53; U.S. senator 1853–54; fine example of the scholar in politics **13**:222

Everett, Mass., city 3 mi (5 km) n. of Boston; transportation equipment, chemicals, metal and leather products; pop. 37,195, *map* **14**:206

Everett, Wash., industrial city on Puget Sound, 27 mi (43 km) n. of Seattle, in rich agricultural and timber district; lumber; pulp and paper mills; dairying, food processing; steel products, machinery; pop. 54,413 **25**:50, 60, *map* **25**:64

Everglade kite, bird
predatory feeding behavior **3**:278

Everglades, vast area of land and slowly moving river in s. Florida **7**:363
ecology **7**:57, *picture* **7**:55
Florida, *maps* **8**:195, 211
land reclamation **20**:119
swamp, marsh, and bog **22**:723
United States, *map* **24**:193

Everglades National Park, park in Florida **16**:47, *map* **16**:40
Florida **8**:198, *map* **8**:211
hobby, *picture* **10**:185

Evergreen, tree or plant that retains its foliage all year or for several years, such as the pine, fir, laurel, and hemlock, in contrast to deciduous trees. *see also in index* Conifers
Christmas custom **5**:405
forests **8**:309